Handbook of Research
on Educational Administration

Handbook of Research on Educational Administration

A Project of the American Educational Research Association

Norman J. Boyan, Editor
University of California, Santa Barbara

Longman
New York & London

Longman Inc., 95 Church Street, White Plains, N. Y. 10601

Associated companies:
Longman Group Ltd., London
Longman Cheshire Pty., Melbourne
Longman Paul Pty., Auckland
Copp Clark Pitman, Toronto
Pitman Publishing Inc., New York

Executive editor: Raymond T. O'Connell
Production editor: Elsa van Bergen
Text design: Dee Josephson
Cover design: Steven August Krastin
Production supervisor: Judith Stern

Library of Congress Cataloging-in-Publication Data

Handbook of research on educational administration.

Includes bibliographies and index.
1. School management and organization—United States.
I. Boyan, Norman J.   II. American Educational Research
Association.
LB2805.H2864 1988   371.2   87-3663
ISBN 0-582-28517-8
Compositor: Best-set Typesetter Limited
Printer: R.R. Donnelley & Sons Company

88 89 90 91 9 8 7 6 5 4 3 2 1

Editorial Advisory Board

To **Alfred Dexter Simpson**, 1891–1955
Pathbreaker, mentor, friend, and more

Contents

The Contributors

Max G. Abbott is professor emeritus of educational administration at the University of Oregon in Eugene. He was previously on the faculties in educational administration at the University of Rochester and Auburn University. He received his Ph.D. in educational administration from the University of Chicago. He served for 8 years as director of the federally funded Center for the Advanced Study of Educational Administration at the University of Oregon and also was a member of the editorial board of the *Educational Administration Quarterly*.

Charles S. Benson is professor and associate dean at the Graduate School of Education, University of California, Berkeley. A graduate of Princeton, he later received his Ph.D in economics from Columbia. Prior to joining the faculty at Berkeley, he taught at Bowdoin College and Harvard University. His research interests include evaluation of alternative patterns of resource distributions for public education, cost benefit analysis, and exploration of the relationship between education and economic development in Third World countries. He is a past president of the American Education Finance Association.

Kathryn M. Borman is associate professor in the Department of Educational Foundations at the University of Cincinnati. She did her advanced studies at Mills College and the University of Minnesota. Her current interests include the transition from school to work and dilemmas facing urban schools. She is the author with Joel Spring of *Schools in Central Cities* (Longman, 1984).

Steven T. Bossert is professor and chairman of the Department of Educational Administration at the University of Utah. He has contributed to the understanding of the effects of schooling and instruction through publication of *Tasks and Social Relationships in Classrooms* (1979) and articles about the effects of activity structures on teacher-pupil and peer relationships. His recent studies focus on instruc-

tional management, organizational effectiveness, and school climate. Currently senior associate editor for the *Educational Administration Quarterly*, Dr. Bossert received his Ph.D from the University of Chicago and served as assistant professor of sociology at the University of Michigan and as director of Research and Development at Far West Laboratory in San Francisco.

Norman J. Boyan is professor of education at the University of California at Santa Barbara, where he also served as dean of the Graduate School of Education for 11 years. He previously held positions in the Bureau of Research, U.S. Office of Education, as division director and associate commissioner, and at the University of Wisconsin-Madison and Stanford University. He received his advanced degrees at Harvard University. His current research interests are administrator behavior and administrator effects.

William Lowe Boyd is professor of education in the Division of Education Policy Studies of the College of Education at Pennsylvania State University, University Park, PA. He received his doctorate from the University of Chicago. He specializes in educational policy and politics and is co-editor of the volumes *Problem-Finding in Educational Administration*; *Educational Policy in Australia and America*; and *The Politics of Excellence and Choice in Education*.

Paul T. Brinkman is a senior associate at the National Center for Higher Education Management Systems in Boulder, Colorado. He received his Ph.D. in higher education administration from the University of Arizona and is currently pursuing research interests in higher education microeconomics and finance.

Frank Brown is dean and professor of educational administration, the University of North Carolina at Chapel Hill. He received his Ph.D. in policy, planning, and administration from the University of California at Berkeley. His research specialties are educational leadership, organizational analysis, school law, and minority education. He has published extensively in the areas of educational leadership and policy.

Martin Burlingame is University Professor of Educational Leadership, School of Educational Administration and Research, the University of Tulsa. He received his Ph.D. from the University of Chicago. He has served as senior associate, National Institute of Education, and on the faculties of the University of New Mexico and the University of Illinois. His research and teaching interests are in the politics of education and power in organizations.

Francisco Caracheo is professor/investigator at the Centro Interdisciplinario de Investigación y Docencia en Educación Tecnica, Querétaro, Qro., Mexico. He received his Ph.D. in curriculum and instruction from the University of Oregon. His major interests are research design and instructional program planning.

Grace Butler Chisolm is professor of educational administration at Texas A&M University. She received her Ph.D. in educational administration from New York University and has served as associate director of the University Council for Educational Administration (UCEA) and as assistant to the president at TA&MU. Her research interests include organizational behavior, organizational change and development, academic governance, student recruitment and retention, institutional responsiveness to legislative mandates, and women's educational equity.

H. Dickson Corbett is director of Improvement Studies at Research for Better Schools, Philadelphia, PA. He received his Ph.D. in social foundations of education from the University of North Carolina at Chapel Hill. His major interest is district- and school-level implementation of programs and policies, and he has published widely on the topic. His books include *School Context and School Change* (1984), written with Judith Dawson and William Firestone.

Ronald G. Corwin is professor of sociology at The Ohio State University. He has taught at Teachers College, Columbia University, and has served in the Research Section of the U.S. Office of Education. He received his Ph.D. from the University of Minnesota. He has also served as associate editor of *Sociology of Education*, chair of the sociology of education section of the American Sociological Association, and vice president of the American Educational Research Association. He has published extensively in the sociology of education and has a forthcoming book entitled *The Organization-Society Nexus*. He is currently editor of the annual series, *Research in Sociology of Education and Socialization*. In 1976 fellow specialists ranked him among individuals who have made "the greatest contributions to the growth and development of *Sociology of Education* over the past 25 years."

Jack A. Culbertson is an adjunct professor at The Ohio State University. He received his M.A. from Duke University and his Ph.D. in educational administration from the University of California at Berkeley. Executive director of the University Council for Educational Administration from 1959 to 1981, he has since concentrated largely upon the study and the teaching of education administration at The Ohio State University.

Suzanne E. Estler is associate professor of educational administration and director of equal opportunity at the University of Maine, Orono. She received her Ph.D. in educational administration and policy analysis from Stanford University. Dr. Estler's recent research focuses on leadership and effective schooling, administrative competencies in public education, and gender analysis of administrative role demands.

Robert B. Everhart is professor of education and sociology and dean, School of Education, Portland State University. After receiving his doctorate from the University of Oregon, he was a research associate with the Northwest Regional Educational Laboratory and was a member of the faculty at the University of California–Santa Barbara. His research interests are the sociology of education, with a specific focus on qualitative methodologies.

William A. Firestone is on the faculty of the Graduate School of Education and is a member of Center for Policy Research in Education, Rutgers, the State University of New Jersey. He was formerly director of the Applied Research Project at Research for Better Schools in Philadelphia. He received his Ph.D. in sociology and education from the University of Chicago and has done studies of planned change in a variety of urban and rural situations. His interests include the study of organizational behavior in schools, school cultures, and the application of qualitative and quantitative research methods.

Daniel E. Griffiths is dean emeritus of the School of Education, Health, Nursing and Arts Professions at New York University. He received the Ph.D. in educational administration from Yale University. He has published widely in educational administration, specializing in administrative theory.

James W. Guthrie is professor, Graduate School of Education at the University of California–Berkeley and directs, with Michael W. Kirst of Stanford University, Project PACE (Policy Analysis for California Education). Having received a Ph.D. from Stanford, he was also awarded an Alfred North Whitehead Postdoctoral Fellowship to study the economics of education at Harvard University. He has worked as special assistant to the Secretary of Department of Health, Education, and Welfare and as the Education Specialist for the U.S. Senate. He has written extensively on educational policy, school finance, the governance of education, and the reform of educational systems, and has written textbooks in school finance and educational administration.

Meredydd G. Hughes is professor and head of the Department of Educational Studies at the University of Birmingham, England. Following practitioner experience as secondary school teacher and headmaster, Professor Hughes received his Ph.D. from the University of Wales for a sociological study of the school principalship. He was founding editor of the British Educational Management and Administration journal, *Educational Management and Administration*, and has researched extensively on administrator preparation and professional leadership in educational administration. Currently president of the Commonwealth Council for Educational Administration, Professor Hughes is also Standing Committee Chairman for the International Intervisitation Programs (IIPs) in Educational Administration.

Glenn L. Immegart is professor of education at the University of Rochester. He received his Ph.D. from The Ohio State University. He has served on the staff of the University Council for Educational Administration, as editor of the *Educational Administration Quarterly*, and as a departmental chair at the University of Rochester. His research interests include problem finding, leadership, and organizational decision making.

Susan Moore Johnson is an assistant professor of educational administration and social policy at the Harvard Graduate School of Education where she received her doctorate. She has studied the institution of collective bargaining in education and is the author of *Teacher Unions in Schools*. Her current research areas are teacher policy and the school as a workplace.

Richard K. Jung is a member of the Special Studies Staff within the U.S. Department of Education's Office of Educational Research and Improvement. He received his doctorate in educational administration and policy analysis from Stanford University. He has served as the director of the Department of Education's Analysis Center for State and Local Grants and as the research director for the National Advisory Council on the Education of Disadvantaged Children. His special interests are compensatory education and public support of private schools.

James M. Lipham (deceased 1986) was professor of educational administration at the University of Wisconsin-Madison for over 25 years before his untimely death in 1986. He earned his advanced degrees from The Ohio State University and the University of Chicago. Prior to his graduate study he had served as a teacher and administrator in the public schools. At the University of Wisconsin Professor Lipham was a central figure and participant in its original federally supported Center for Research and Development in Education and in its recently established Center for Research on Secondary Schools. Professor Lipham was a diligent and meticulous scholar and prodigious publisher, whose work has appeared in monographs, textbooks, book chapters, journal articles, and technical reports. His best known publications include *The Principalship: Foundations and Functions* (written with two of his students, James A. Hoeh, Jr. and Robb E. Rankin) and *Educational Administration as a Social Process* (written with two of his mentors, Roald F. Campbell and Jacob W. Getzels).

Larry L. Leslie is director of the Center for the Study of Higher Education at the University of Arizona. He received his Ed.D. in higher education from the University of California, Berkeley. He serves on numerous editorial boards and is co-author, with Paul T. Brinkman, of *The Economic Value of Higher Education*. His specialty is the financing of colleges and universities.

Catherine Marshall is associate professor of Educational Leadership and Policy at Vanderbilt University, senior research associate at the Vanderbilt Institute of Public Policy, and editor of the *Peabody Journal of Education*. Her research has focused on administrator socialization, particularly gender issues and the assistant principalship. Another major focus in her work is state education policy formulation. She also has written extensively about qualitative research methodology.

James F. McNamara is a professor of educational psychology and educational administration at Texas A & M University. He received his Ph.D. in educational administration from The Pennsylvania State University. In 1980 he was an Advanced Study Center Fellow at Ohio State University. His research interests are decision sciences, research strategies in the behaviorial sciences, and educational policy studies.

Erwin Miklos is a professor of educational administration at the University of Alberta. He has served as editor of *The Alberta Journal of Educational Research* and of *The Canadian Administrator*. His current interests relate to emerging developments in administrative and organizational theory. Those interests find expression through his activities as director of the UCEA Program Center on the Practice and Study of Educational Administration.

Cecil G. Miskel is dean of the Graduate School of Education and professor of educational administration at the University of Utah. He received his doctorate from Oklahoma State University. He has published extensively in the areas of organizational administrative theory. He is editor of the *Educational Administration Quarterly*.

Douglas E. Mitchell is professor of education, University of California–Riverside, where he teaches educational policy and politics. During 1985–1986, he served as director of Policy Support Services at the Far West Laboratory for Educational Research and Development in San Francisco. Recent policy research studies include *Work Orientations and Job Performance: The Cultural Basis of Teaching Rewards and Incentives* (with Flora Ida Ortiz and Tedi K. Mitchell, 1987) and *The Idea of a Teachers Union* (with Charles T. Kerchner, forthcoming). He has just completed work with a team of scholars funded by the Department of Education to study "Alternative State Policy Mechanisms for Pursuing Educational Quality Efficiency and Equity Goals."

Rodney T. Ogawa is an associate professor of educational administration at the University of Utah. He received his doctorate from The Ohio State University and completed a postdoctoral traineeship in the Organizations Research Training Program at Stanford University. His research interests are leadership and sensemaking in educational organizations.

Flora Ida Ortiz is an associate professor of education at the University of California–Riverside. She received her Ph.D. in educational administration from the University of New Mexico at Albuquerque. She has written works on women and minorities and instructional processes. Her research interests are socialization processes, organizational structures and decision-making processes, the superintendency, and the education of Hispanics.

John S. Packard is associate professor of nursing and science technology and society at The Pennsylvania State University, from which he received a Ph.D. in educational administration. He has instructed and done research also at the Universities of Utah and Oregon. His current inquiries concern stress and work performance and moral reasoning in professionals and preprofessional students.

Paul E. Peterson is Benjamin H. Griswold III Professor of Public Policy, Johns Hopkins University. After receiving his Ph.D. from the University of Chicago, he served as chairman of Public Policy Studies and as professor of political science and education there and was director of the Governmental Studies Program of The Brookings Institution. He received the Woodrow Wilson Foundation Award for his book *City Limits* (1981), the Gladys Kammerer Award for the best book published in 1976 on U.S. national policy (*School Politics, Chicago Style*), and John Simon Guggenheim and Woodrow Wilson Fellowships. Author of seven other books, his chief fields of research are federalism, urban policy, education, race relations, and deficit politics.

Nancy J. Pitner, now a consultant in Eugene, OR, was previously assistant professor of educational administration at the University of Oregon and the University of Southern California. She received her Ph.D. degree from The Ohio State University in organizational studies and anthropology. Her research interests center around administrator work and its effects, with particular attention to contextual variables, and the training of school administrators.

Barry G. Rabe is an assistant professor in the Department of Public Health Policy and Administration in the School of Public Health at the University of Michigan. He received his Ph.D. in political science at the University of Chicago and has served as a research fellow at The Brookings Institution and the Conservation Foundation. He is the author of *Fragmentation and Integration in State Environmental Management* (Conservation Foundation, 1986) and co-author, with Paul E. Peterson and Kenneth K. Wong, of *When Federalism Works* (Brookings Institution, 1986).

Craig Richards is an assistant professor in the Graduate School of Education at Rutgers University, where he teaches in the Department of Educational Theory, Policy and Administration. He is currently a Research Fellow at the Center for Policy Research in Education, funded by the U.S. Department of Education, also at Rutgers University.

Paula Silver was an associate professor of administration, higher, and continuing education at the University of Illinois at Urbana-Champaign, and had been named president-elect of the University Council for Educational Administration just prior to her untimely death in March 1987. She had previously served UCEA as an Associate Director and had been on the faculty in educational administration at the University of Tulsa. She received her Ph.D. from New York University and specialized in organizational behavior and administrative theory. She was the author of the book *Educational Administration: Theoretical Perspectives on Practice and Research*.

Daniel L. Stufflebeam is professor of education and director of The Evaluation Center at Western Michigan University. He received his Ph.D. from Purdue University and previously served on the faculty at The Ohio State University. He has co-authored eight books and is a co-editor of the Kluwer-Nijhoff series on evaluation in education and human services. He is chairman of the Joint Committee on Standards for Educational Evaluation and was the 1985 recipient of the American Evaluation Association's Lazersfeld Prize for his contributions to evaluation theory and standards.

Maurice M. Tatsuoka is a professor of educational psychology and of psychology at the University of Illinois at Urbana-Champaign. After receiving his doctorate from Harvard University, Dr. Tatsuoka taught mathematics and statistics at the University of Hawaii, Hilo Campus. He is the author of *Multivariate Analysis: Techniques for Educational and Psychological Research* and of many articles on educational statistics and measurement. He is co-principal investigator, with his wife Kikumi, of an on-going project on computerized diagnostic adaptive testing, sponsored by the Office of Naval Research since 1978.

Leonard A. Valverde is chairman and professor of the Department of Educational Administration at the University of Texas–Austin. He also serves as the director of the Office for Advanced Research in Hispanic Education. He received his Ph.D. in education from the Claremont Graduate School in California. Dr. Valverde has published extensively and is the recipient of various research grants. He is a national W. K. Kellogg Fellow and is a member of a number of editorial boards of national education journals.

Tyll van Geel is professor of education and political science at the University of Rochester at Rochester, New York. He received his J.D. from Northwestern University School of Law and his Ed.D. from the Harvard Graduate School of Education. He is the author of *The Courts and American Education Law*. His research interests are in the law and educational policy.

William J. Webster is special assistant to the superintendent in charge of the Dallas Independent School District's Department of Research, Evaluation, and Audit. He received his Ph.D. from Michigan State University. He has served on the editorial boards of the *American Educational Research Journal* and *Educational Evaluation and Policy Analysis* as well as being a past vice-president for Division H, American Educational Research Association. He has published extensively in the areas of educational evaluation and methodology.

Donald J. Willower is professor of education and chairman of the graduate program in educational administration at The Pennsylvania State University. He is author of more than 120 publications on schools as organizations and on philosophical aspects of educational administration. He was a W.K. Kellogg Fellow at the University of Oregon, a member of the National Commission on the Preparation of School Administrators of the American Association of School Administrators, president of the University Council for Educational Administration, and distinguished visiting professor of the University of Alberta. He received the Ed.D. in general administration from the University of Buffalo.

Preface

Norman J. Boyan

The idea for a handbook of research on educational administration occurred to me during the Business Meeting of Division A (Administration) of the American Educational Research Association in 1974 in Chicago. Although Joseph Cronin, then Vice President for Division A, and the members present supported the idea enthusiastically, the meeting adjourned without our having clarified responsibility for shepherding the project. There seemed to be an implicit agreement that I would push the project ahead, a responsibility that I discharged only sporadically, for various reasons, over the next 8 years.

During that time I consulted ad hoc advisory groups at several AERA meetings and on two other occasions. Participants included W. W. (Sandy) Charters, Donald A. Erickson, Wayne K. Hoy, Laurence Iannaccone, the late James M. Lipham, Henry Levin, Frank Lutz, William J. Russell, and William G. Spady. Each of these individuals helped to shape the mission and the content of what has become the first *Handbook of Research on Educational Administration*.

We quickly agreed that the audience for the volume was the community of research scholars in educational administration and that the handbook would report the output of established lines of inquiry. Thus, the archival function of the proposed handbook moved rapidly to center stage. The delay in launching the handbook project has fortuitously added almost a decade of research and thinking about educational administration to report. There is no question that a handbook of research on educational administration in the mid-1970s would have looked different from the book that has appeared. And as Donald Willower observes in the final chapter, the volume that may appear two decades from now will look different still.

At the 1982 meeting of AERA in New York City, Peter Cistone, newly elected Vice President for Division A, asked me straightaway to assume responsibility for moving the project ahead. I accepted his invitation with enthusiasm, prepared the presentation that sought Association sponsorship to the AERA Council in 1983, and received a formal invitation from Richard C. Anderson, President of AERA for 1983–1984, to serve as editor.

Meanwhile, the project had gathered momentum. I opened conversation with an interim editorial advisory board, later added to and approved by AERA, in search of agreement on mission and audience, on the definition of an outline and constituent chapters, and on the nomination of authors. The interim board quickly agreed that the volume should stress inquiry *qua* inquiry and that the audience was to be the scholarly community in educational administration.

My initial ideas about scope and content of the *Handbook* had taken shape during the previous 8 years, and I was also influenced by my involvement in the fifth edition of *The Encyclopedia of Educational Research*, both as Consulting Editor for the Educational Administration section and as author of the entry on "Administration of Educational Institutions." I believed that the tripartite rubric of personal, intra-organizational, and extraorganizational variables that Andrew Halpin presented in 1957 in his paradigm for research on administrator behavior offered a reasonable set of categories for organizing the *Handbook*. Accordingly, I proposed and the board accepted, a three-way design for reporting research on (a) The Administrator, (b) Organizations, and (c) Environments, supplemented by sections on Methodologies and Special Topics that would attend to comparative educational administration, the administration of higher education, developments in educational policy making, and the pursuit of equity. The board accepted my proposal but recommended reducing the number of proposed chapters, advice that I accepted quickly and gratefully.

I had also presented along with my initial proposal of sections and chapter titles a list of suggested authors, and invited the board to make its own nominations. By late winter of 1983, after some three iterations of proposals on and reactions to both a table of contents and participating authors, consensus was reached at just about the time of the 1983 AERA meeting in Montreal. The proposal was presented to several potential publishers and also to the AERA Publications Committee and Council. Two publishers responded with particular enthusiasm. After several months the proposal was approved by the Council, confirming the *Handbook* as an official publication of the Association.

The interim board, and later the formally appointed Editorial Advisory Board, and I had agreed that the author roster should include a mix of well-established and up-and-coming scholars. We met that objective. We also wanted to respect the international condition and state of educational administration. That objective was less well met, particularly with respect to representation of scholars from the Commonwealth nations. So the *Handbook* is guilty of the "narcissism and the tyranny of isolation" that William Walker (1984) attributes to scholarship in educational administration in the United States in the period from 1954 to 1984. Invitations went to two more Commonwealth authors than appear here. One declined; the other was unable to meet his original commitment. If the invitation had been accepted and the commitment met, there would have been two chapters by British scholars and two chapters by Canadians. Even that would have hardly represented adequately sources that have produced such zesty scholarship for so long. By early 1986, however, it was no longer possible to change the highly ethnocentric distribution of authorship. I do recognize it, wish it were otherwise, and hope that the editor of the second *Handbook of Research on Educational Administration* will repair this oversight by including not only more Commonwealth scholars but also researchers from other parts of the world.

Comments are also in order about chapters that do not appear. A chapter on "Personal Variables" became a casualty of unfilled commitment. We had also hoped to include chapters on "The Economics of Education: The International Experience" and "Research on the Administration of Higher Education." However, after three different potential authors declined invitations to prepare the economics chapter, Board members whom I consulted agreed that we should drop it. As for "Research on the Administration of Higher Education," the author who agreed to pinch-hit late in the game for a scholar who found it necessary to withdraw fashioned an excellent chapter *for* administrators rather than *about* administrators and administration. Unfortunately, the chapter did not fit the mission of the *Handbook*, so an important area of research on educational administration is missing. Readers interested in the area will find "The Nature of Administrative Behavior in Higher Education" by David D. Dill (1984) a review worth consulting. I hope that these areas will be treated in future editions of the *Handbook*.

Between the spring of 1983 when the first commissions for chapter preparation were accepted and the summer of 1986 when the last of the completed manuscripts arrived, five other changes of authorship took place. Each required adding to the roster replacements who began their work up to a year and more after the first set of authors had started theirs. These shifts account in part for a delay in delivering final copy to the publisher, but the colleagues who jumped so willingly and effectively into the breach deserve commendation as well as special thanks.

Given the commissions accepted by the authors, the *Handbook* presents the output of the "normal science" that has prevailed in driving inquiry in educational administration over the past 30 and more years. Each author's task was to report and critically comment on the output of inquiry that had already been conducted, with appropriate suggestions for future work. In my judgment, the contributors have set in place a bench mark that deserves respect, one that tells travelers what research on educational administration has sought to accomplish circa 1986 and that points to further heights to scale.

Some may look at the bench mark and say that the *Handbook* is already out of date, but setting bench marks in place requires a look around, not just ahead. The straightforward archival function of the *Handbook* has required telling where scholarship in educational administration has been as well as where it might be going. Ideology or belief about where a field ought to go cannot change the history of where the field has been and where it came from. So, if what have been the subjects and modes of inquiry over the past 30 years do not fit readers' tastes, they will not be able to erase by dialectic, no matter how persuasive, what happened over the course of one-third of a century. It is not necessary that readers agree that what transpired was good (or bad), but there is no way that readers can expunge the record of the past. The volume will not serve well the purposes of those combatants who strain to enter the lists as champions of one ideological preference or another in search of redefining how and what to study in educational administration, but it may provide perspective for all who believe that today is prologue to tomorrow, just as yesterday was prologue to today.

One of the more fascinating things I have learned from editing a handbook is the need for accommodating and redirecting the uninhibited expression of scholars who want to say what they want to say rather than to fit themselves neatly and primly into the management scheme of the editor and editorial advisory board. The most extreme case involved an exchange among author, two consultant/reviewers, and editor that produced three preliminary and eventually a fourth and final draft. No less than six other chapters required three drafts. Every chapter incorporates the recommendations for revision of the consultant/reviewers and the editor.

This is the place, then, to thank the 59 consultant/reviewers. They rendered critical assistance in reading, reacting to, and helping to improve every chapter in the volume. No single scholar in educational administration could have reacted knowledgeably to all of the material prepared for the *Handbook*. Without the dedicated participation of the consultant/reviewers, the volume would not have reached completion. My reliance on specialists in some fields was complete; in others, substantial. Still, the responsibility for the product rests solely with the several authors and the editor.

The final presentation reflects my decision to move a number of chapters from their originally planned locations. For example, the chapter on "The Technical Tools of Decision Making" was originally intended as a companion piece to the "Decision Making" chapter in the section on Organizations. "Evaluation as an Administrative Function" also seemed at first to belong in the Organizations section. However, when these chapters appeared in finished form, they clearly belonged more properly in the section on Special Topics. The same applied to the chapters on "Unionism and Collective Bargaining in the Public Schools" and on "The Law and the Courts," originally placed in a section entitled Environments. The upshot of shifts led to deletion of the section on Environments in favor of separate sections on Economics and Finance and on Politics and Policy, with a new array of chapters under Special Topics.

A comment is also in order about the chapter on "Evaluation as an Administrative Function" and two chapters in the section on Politics and Policy. Although the evaluation chapter departs from the organizing scheme for the *Handbook* in the proportion of descriptive to normative material included, the relative distribution accurately represents the state of this comparatively new specialization. As for Politics and Policy, there are two chapters on federal politics and policy where only one was intended, but the original research by Rabe and Peterson was so valuable that I decided to include it and to commission a second chapter, by Jung, to fulfill the archival function.

Every review of a handbook of research observes, in one way or another, that "as might be expected in an edited volume," the chapters are not uniform in quality and there is an inevitable disconnectedness about the entire enterprise. The *Handbook of Research on Educational Administration* is no exception. So be it. Unevenness and disconnectedness are not the significant criteria of assessment. Of more moment is whether collectively the chapters have enlightened yesterday's investigations and tomorrow's path. Readers must answer that question for themselves.

I have already formally thanked the consultant/reviewers for their immeasurable help in bringing the project to completion. But it is the 44 authors who deserve special thanks for their dedication to the task and their high scholarship. Some of them discharged their commissions with incredible dispatch; others took longer. But all of them have paid serious attention to their respective commissions and have advanced the field a notch. Unhappily, with the deepest regret and sorrow I must note here the untimely deaths of James M. Lipham and Paula Silver, friends and esteemed colleagues, who not only contributed so much to the *Handbook* as authors but also as members of the editorial advisory board. Our profession and all of us personally are the losers.

I cannot leave this Preface without expressing my very special affection and gratitude to my dear wife, Priscilla, whose support over the past three years, and especially the summer months of 1986, made all the difference in the world in producing this volume. For more than 40 years, she has been a woman for all seasons and this last one was no exception.

I also wish to express my heartfelt appreciation for the loyalty and devotion to task of Hildegard Lagerquist, the project secretary. May it be the good fortune of every editor to enlist the assistance of such a delightful and hardworking colleague. Equally deserving of thanks is Pat Kelly for her sharp editorial eye and never-failing good humor.

My colleagues, Laurence Iannaccone nearby and

Donald Willower across the continent, deserve special recognition for wise counsel and unstinting support. Also meriting particular thanks is the editorial staff at Longman Inc., especially Elsa van Bergen, for patience and encouragement even under the most trying of circumstances.

PART
I

The Administrator

CHAPTER 1

A Century's Quest for a Knowledge Base

Jack A. Culbertson

While serving as Superintendent of Schools in Adrian, Michigan, William Harold Payne wrote the first book on school administration (1875). In its preface, he deplored the fact that "up to this time, no work, not even the most elementary, has been published on an art whose importance can scarcely be over-estimated" (p. vi). Payne surmised that individuals did not comprehend the art of school "superintendence" because they could not easily acquire "sense impressions" of it. Nevertheless, he was highly optimistic that a science of education could be developed to advance understanding of the "high" art. In outlining his hopes for an educational science, Payne expressed aspirations that were to persist in the thoughts and actions of educational leaders and scholars for at least a century.

One hundred years after Payne's book appeared, Thomas Greenfield, in a searching critique of inquiry in educational administration (1975), concluded that investigators using quantitatively oriented science to study educational organizations were traveling on a deadend highway. He argued that educational organizations are not "objective" phenomena regulated by general laws; rather, they are mental constructs that reflect the perceptions and interpretations of their members. Students of organizations should turn their backs, then, upon logical positivistic science and adopt interpretive modes of inquiry.

Like Greenfield, William Harris, Superintendent of Schools in St. Louis from 1868 to 1880 and author of the introduction to Payne's book, argued for a phenomenological approach to inquiry. Both Harris and Greenfield stressed that physical and social phenomena differ and that human constructs are more important than sense data. In contrast to Greenfield, however, Harris, contended that a science of education and management was needed and could be achieved. He contended that many fields, including "phenomenology," would have to be used to build the needed science (1879). The fact that both Greenfield and Harris could support similar research approaches and yet differ on the role of science in inquiry is explained by their contrasting concepts of science, concepts linked to the respective intellectual and social contexts of their times.

Payne's call (1875) for a science to buttress school superintendence and Greenfield's and Harris's compatible views on phenomenology set this essay's mission: namely, to examine the changing meanings of science from 1875 to 1985 and to explore their impact on the study of educational administration. The origins, the advocates, the key presuppositions of the dominant concepts of science in different time periods will be delineated. How prevailing scientific concepts in given time periods were related to the research strategies used, the boundaries between educational administration and other fields of study, and the research exemplars produced will be explored. Finally, some observations that cut across the different eras examined will be set forth.

Consultant/reviewers: H. Warren Button, State University of New York–Buffalo; and Roald F. Campbell, University of Utah

A SCIENCE OF EDUCATION AND MANAGEMENT AS ENVISAGED BY PRACTITIONERS: 1875–1900

The conditions that nurtured the scientific study of superintendence predated Payne's pioneering book (1875). They emerged as simple agrarian communities served by rural schools ineluctably gave way to complex industrial cities served by urban school systems. As leading urban school board members faced increasingly complex management problems, they decided, after decades of debate, that school superintendents with special "expertise" should lead in the management of urban school systems (e.g., see Callahan, 1966; Reller, 1935).

Two penetrating practitioner-scholars, William Harold Payne and William Torrey Harris, led in formulating the elements of the new science needed for the new management. Born in the mid-1830s, each, after serving as a teacher and principal, accepted a superintendency at the age of 33, Harris in St. Louis in 1868 and Payne a year later in Adrian, Michigan. After superintending for a decade, Payne moved to the University of Michigan, where he headed the first department of education in the United States (Poret, 1930). In 1880 Harris assumed a leadership role in the Concord (Massachusetts) School of Philosophy, where he worked with transcendentalists Ralph Waldo Emerson and Bronson Alcott, among others (Leidecker, 1946). In 1887 Payne accepted the chancellorship of the University of Nashville and the presidency of the Peabody Normal School, where he served for 14 years. Harris became United States Commissioner of Education in 1889 and remained in the post until 1907.

Harris's and Payne's capacities to conceptualize a science of education and school management were undoubtedly buttressed by their scholarly accomplishments. Editor of *The Michigan Teacher*, and author of numerous works, Payne concentrated on educational subjects. He designed and implemented the first teacher training program in a U.S. university. He wrote textbooks and translated French treatises for use in teacher training programs, and he launched in 1881–1882 the *first* course designed to train principals and superintendents.

Harris, on the other hand, addressed many social and human questions beyond those in schools. While serving as a school principal, he launched the first U.S. journal on philosophy (*The Journal of Speculative Philosophy*) and edited it for a quarter of a century. Head of the education department of the American Social Science Association (ASSA), Harris published more articles in its *Journal of Social Science* than any other contributor but one. He wrote on such varied

subjects as unemployment, socialism, and peace for publication in such journals as *The Forum* and *Atlantic Monthly*. Initiator of the International Education Series, Harris edited and wrote prefaces to 58 of its volumes. An active long-time member and president in 1875 of the National Education Association (NEA), he spoke frequently at its meetings and wrote often for its journal.

In the mid-1880s the National Council on Education—a new policy study arm of the NEA—established a five-member committee to address the issue of the "Science of Pedagogics" (National Education Association [NEA], 1885). Harris and Payne were influential members of that committee. Defining science as "maxims or ethical axioms" and "data arranged systematically and causally or logically connected," the committee declared that the purpose of a science of pedagogics was to provide educators "laws" of the "mind and body." Stressing the danger inherent in narrow scientific specialization, the committee warned that "ethics" could easily be removed from education's "center of gravity."

The concepts that shaped the 28 propositions of the NEA report (1885) had their origins in "speculative" philosophy. In defining "speculative," Harris (1867) drew upon the ideas of Plato and emphasized that reason arrives at conclusions "without the aid of [sensuous] images, but solely through ideas themselves" (p. 2). As the foremost U.S. interpreter of Hegelian thought, Harris also emphasized that reason, through the logical analysis of opposing or contradictory ideas, must produce higher-order generalizations directed at wholes and not, as in the case of narrowly defined science, at parts.

Since Harris and Payne, as self-educated superintendents, were committed to concepts of speculative philosophy, their views of science were inevitably shaped by this philosophy. What vision did they offer, then, to guide the development of a science of education and management? Payne (1886) began delineating his views by distinguishing between theory and art with a homely example drawn implicitly from Aristotle:

> The baker's knowledge of his own art is practical; he can perform all of its processes, but explain none of them. On the other hand, the chemist's knowledge of the baker's art is speculative; he can explain all of its processes, but perform none of them. (p. 2)

Payne believed that educators were like bakers—they had empirical information but not scientific knowledge or theory. Highly critical of the "the errors and vagaries of empirics" (1886, p. 11) in the field, he envisaged a science of education and organization that would displace "the stronghold of empiricism" (1886, p. 158) with theory. For Payne the disciplines of physiology, psychology, and ethics, respectively, were the sources from which scientific principles for guiding the physical, mental, and moral growth in students could be derived. Logic's capacity to help teachers achieve lucid communication, a critical characteristic of instruction, comprised another notable source of science.

At one point Payne (1886) observed, "In passing from the single child to aggregates of children, there arises the need of the organization of schools and school systems" (p. 4). Scholars building a science of organization, Payne (1886) contended, had to borrow "material" from "history, sociology, political science and legislation" (p. 4). He recommended that scholars take into account national differences in educational organization and use principles of sociology to explain variations in diverse systems of education.

Educational science for Payne was largely deductive. The scholar's task was to evolve laws from the "various disciplines and to deduce from these laws generalizations that educators could use in practice. For example, from his study of psychology Payne (1886) formulated the following "law": "The most instructive of the general characteristics of mind is its self-activity in the line of growth" (p. 69). He then deduced 17 applied generalizations from the law.

Keenly aware that these crucial generalizations about educational purpose could not be derived from the established sciences, Payne proposed that a special science be created. Such a science would gather and analyze facts and inductively arrive at generalizations about education's ideals.

The ASSA, whose education department Harris headed, "struggled valiantly to accommodate social theory and social practice to the emerging realities of an urbanizing and industrializing society" (Haskell, 1977, p. vi). Since academic social science did not exist in 1865 when ASSA was founded, its activities were organized around problems of health, education, jurisprudence, and social economy. In the mid-1880s Harris served as a member of an ASSA committee whose mission was to study social science instruction in higher education (Harris, 1886b). In developing a model social science curriculum, the committee elaborated its views on what divisions comprised the social sciences. Of the ten departments of social science identified by the committee, two were in education: theory of public elementary education and higher education.

Harris believed that the social science designated as public elementary education consisted of four major domains: course of study, method, discipline, and plan

of organization or management. These domains offered marked challenges to scholars (Harris, 1886a):

> Here are four great provinces of pedagogical inquiry, each capable of endless subdivision and specialization, and requiring such division of labor and such concentration and observation upon details as may absorb the attention of a whole generation of teachers and educational specialists. (p. 494)

These provinces, however, were limited parts of the science of education. To determine the school's mission, scholars had to define clearly the educational functions of society's four "cardinal institutions": family, state, civil society, and church. The school, as a "special institution," supplemented the work of the cardinal institutions. The science of education, then, was necessarily linked to the broader problems of social science.

In Harris's view (1886a), to study education as only a school phenomenon was a grievous error—one which would "develop false and injurious tendencies" (p. 492). Constant inquiry into education as a whole and comparative study of the "ideals" of civilizations were needed to counteract narrower views:

> ...only such comparative studies could throw light on the relative proportions of the entire function of education which particular civilizations have assigned respectively to the cardinal institutions...; only such study will explain the origin of the school, or define its proper functions. (pp. 492–493)

Given the role Harris assigned to speculative reason in inquiry, he sharply opposed the positivistic view of Auguste Comte expressed in the 1830s that social science knowledge could best be advanced through the use of natural science modes of inquiry. Humans, as reasoning beings pursuing ideals not fully realizable, differ markedly from objects, Harris stressed. He did not reject narrowly defined natural science methods in the study of objects, including the human body; rather, he assigned to speculative reason a higher role in the study of human institutions and processes than he did to predictive science. As a deep believer in creative "self-activity," Harris concluded that Comte's view was hostile to human freedom and education.

Harris also rejected Herbert Spencer's positivistic view, which Comte earlier had formulated in somewhat different terms, that science should limit its inquiry to "knowable" objects about which facts could be acquired. As a believer in "pure thought," "self-consciousness," "mind," and other unobservables, Harris could not accept Spencer's increasingly influential view, a view that simply nullified reason's role, as Harris conceived it. While serving as a school principal, he wrote (1867) about the harmful effects on science's mission that result from banishing "unknowables" from science's purview:

> Some wish to use it as a lubricating fluid upon certain religious dogmas that cannot otherwise be swallowed. Others wish to save themselves the trouble of thinking out the solutions to the Problem of Life. But the Sphinx devours him who does not faithfully grapple with and solve her enigmas. (p. 12)

Although Payne and Harris differed on particulars, their "scientific" tent rested largely on shared foundations: inquiry should encompass both ideals and facts; use induction and deduction; employ social science and philosophy; value ideas more than data; use concepts in existing disciplines; probe relationships between the missions of cardinal institutions and those of schools; and develop generalizations that educators and managers could apply in practice. The two scholars recognized that school management was unique; however, they did not clearly distinguish it from teaching. They stressed that superintendents needed deeper understandings of educational science than did teachers.

Harris and Payne, then, elaborated clear views about the scope of the science of education and management, its major components, its relationship to other disciplines, and its general modes of inquiry. Harris was keenly aware of the difficulties scholars would confront in pursuing this science. He emphasized (1879) that education's boundaries are so expansive and its presuppositions so vast that inquiry can easily suffer from a "lack of logical sequence [and from] mere collections of unjustified and unexplained assumptions, dogmatically set forth" (p. 206).

Payne's and Harris's own exemplars of inquiry reflected their concepts of science. Notable in this regard were Payne's *Outlines of Educational Doctrine* (1882) and Harris's *Psychologic Foundations of Education* (1898). More influential than these were the uses the two scholars made of their scientific concepts in their leadership initiatives. For example, when Harris launched the first public school kindergarten in the United States and a pioneering science curriculum for Grades 1 to 8, he articulated explicit rationales for the proposed changes. When Kasson (1888) was asked what individual had exerted the "the most profound influences on teachers and school systems" (p. 620), he placed Harris and Payne on his small list of leading influencers, with the former at the top. The distinguished historian Curti, although labeling Harris a "conservator," still observed: "While it was Barnard and Mann who laid the foundations of the American public school system, it was William T. Harris who presided over the rearing of the structure" (Curti, 1974, p. 310). The edifice Harris built reflected his philosophical concepts of science.

Various factors, however, constrained the influence of Payne's and Harris's philosophical science. One was the trend toward academic social science. The ASSA, for example, between 1884 and 1905 created four new organizations to serve historians, economists, political scientists, and sociologists, respectively. In 1909 (the year of Harris's death and two years after Payne's) ASSA succumbed. However, the symptoms of its fatal illness had already appeared in the 1880s, when its younger members expressed aspirations for specialized social science and argued that ASSA's members should produce empirical generalizations, not "speculative" abstractions. Having heard the calls for positivistic science from Comte and Spencer, they were moving in new directions—often from the vantage point of newly created university posts and with advanced training from German universities. Such developments foreshadowed an inductive science directed at concrete societal problems.

Payne and Harris won almost reverential respect from their peers. However, their long-range influence upon the science of education and management was limited. Harris's 1898 book, *Psychologic Foundations of Education*, a monumental intellectual achievement that brought him a Doctor of Philosophy *causa honoris* from the University of Jena in Germany, came at the end of an era as did Payne's "scientific" abstractions. Their work predated the existence of full-time professors of educational administration. When New York City's school superintendent, William Maxwell (1891), highlighted the status of "educational literature" by discussing Aristotle's *Ethics*, Dante's *Divine Comedy*, Spencer's *Education*, and the Gospels, he implicitly revealed the primitive state of educational inquiry. To be sure, writers did produce some books and articles in the 1880s and 1890s related to school management. For example, as the 19th-century hourglass emptied, Lucy Salmon (1896) of Vassar College used political science concepts to study education. However, the scientific study of educational administration had not yet gained a significant foothold by 1900. Nor had scholars of educational administration, in contrast to social scientists, acquired a university home. That attainment had to await the 20th century.

THE SCIENCE OF SCHOOL MANAGEMENT FINDS A HOME AND A NEW VIEW: 1901–1925

As early as the 1860s, 19th-century leaders criticized universities for ignoring the study of education. Payne, for example, in an address to the Michigan State Teachers Association in 1869 attacked the University of Michigan for its negligence in the training of teachers (Poret, 1930, p. 19). Later he noted (1886) the "charming" naiveté of those who were skeptical about the study of education when its ever-present problems were continually "discussed and settled by boards of trustees, teachers' associations, and institutes, by newspapers, by everybody in fact; and still the wonder is what a professor of education can do" (p. 264).

Charles Adams, grandson and son of U.S. presidents, sent a harsher message (1880). The immediate difficulty in achieving a new "scientific phase" in the superintendency, Adams asserted, was "in the universities" (p. 72). While universities supported the study of law, agriculture, mining, and technology, they ignored the study of education and the improvement of instruction in school. Adams, who was converted to the positivistic thinking of Comte in 1865 (Adams, 1916, p. 179), asserted (1880) that universities "grade the child's mind as lower than its teeth.... We thus have to turn over our children to those whom we would never dream of entrusting with our potato patch" (p. 71).

However, university presidents such as James Angell at Michigan, Daniel Gilman at Johns Hopkins, Frederick Barnard at Columbia, and Andrew White at Cornell—leaders who were seeking to incorporate the new "sciences" into higher education—did not find the task easy. For example, in 1874, three years after Payne's criticism, Angell recommended to the University of Michigan's Board of Regents that a department of education be established, but the board rejected the proposal, which was not reactivated until 1878.

Still, developments in human thought and inquiry were beginning to create conditions favoring an academic home for students of educational administration. The scientific concepts elaborated by Comte and Spencer were helping to stimulate new research initiatives in higher education, as were such dramatic examples of inquiry as Charles Darwin's.

Comte, after conducting extensive historical research, defined three stages in the evolution of science: the theological or supernatural, the metaphysical, and the positive (Lenzer, 1975). In the theological stage of scientific evolution, individuals and groups associate the causes of given events with the pleasure or displeasure of deities. Those praying for rain, for example, presume that cause resides in divine will rather than in invariable laws. In the metaphysical stage, invisible forces or entities are presumed to regulate events. Thus, Aristotle believed that "animating principles" control plant and animal behavior. In the positive stage, those who seek causes through theological and metaphysical thinking learn that they

are engaged in useless digressions. Positive thinkers limit their study to phenomena that can yield factual or sensory data needed to classify phenomena and to arrive at laws. Reason's role in this stage is limited to data analysis and to the discovery of laws (Comte, 1974).

Comte stressed that every developed science has evolved from earlier stages of thinking. Physics, he concluded, was already in the positive stage, biology in the metaphysical stage, and sociology in the theological stage. For Comte, mathematics was the queen of the sciences. According to Lewes (1890), Comte was the first to argue that the social sciences could best be advanced by using such methods from the natural sciences as observation, experiment, and comparison.

Spencer (1910), although arguing that he was not influenced by Comte, defined his concept of "unknowable" in terms of "ultimate" scientific ideas (e.g., force) or religious ideas (e.g., God)—ideas that were closely linked to Comte's concepts of the metaphysical and theological. For Comte the "knowable" was that which could be investigated through empirical or positive inquiry.

During the last half of the 19th century, Comte's and Spencer's concepts of science became increasingly influential. Even before Harris became a superintendent, he recognized that a "revolution" was developing and "spreading into all departments of mental activity" (1867, p. 6). He identified 18 active scientists and philosophers who, in his view, were inspired by the new revolutionary "spirit."

Late 19th- and early 20th-century scientific norms, then, were very different from those propounded by Harris and Payne. The new norms moved away from deriving laws from moral disciplines and toward discovering laws in the real world; away from speculative abstractions and toward fact-based generalizations; away from the probing of ultimate reality and toward the investigation of immediate reality; away from predominantly deductive and toward more inductive thought; and away from philosophizing about the "essences" of phenomena and toward studying the observable characteristics of phenomena.

As Cremin, Shannon, and Townsend make clear in *A History of Teacher's College* (1954), the founding in New York City of the Kitchen Garden Association to teach industrial arts to lower-class children proved to be an important step toward the development of an academic home for educational management. This event in 1880, and others later, led to the incorporation in 1889 of Teachers College (of Columbia University). Leapfrogging the departmental unit implemented by Payne and others, Grace Dodge, Nicholas Murray Butler, and their colleagues created a new organization for advancing the study of education: the college.

The 1880 philanthropic initiative, led principally by Dodge, experienced immediate success as the demands for courses and effective teachers ballooned. In 1887 when Butler, a young professor at Columbia, assumed the presidency of the Industrial Education Association (the successor to the Kitchen Garden Assocation), Dodge gained a helpful ally. Having earlier outlined his vision for the study of education in a series of popular lectures, Butler understandably moved the Association toward the functions of teacher training and educational inquiry. The new college, then, was a response to human problems created by the developing industrial society, to the demand for greater numbers of trained teachers, and to the growing pressures for more enlightened educational inquiry.

In 1897 James Russell, Dean of Teachers College, established what was apparently the second course (after Payne's) for school administrators. He asked Superintendent Gilbert of the nearby Newark (New Jersey) schools, author of a small volume on school management, to teach a two-hour weekly course for a year. Gilbert replied that he could teach all he knew in six weeks. Russell then suggested to Gilbert that students in the course could investigate "what the schools are doing" and "how school systems are being managed"—ideas reflecting the real-world orientation, the emphasis on fact gathering, and the inductive approaches to inquiry inherent in the new perspectives on science. Gilbert's pointed response (Russell, 1937) sheds light on the state of knowledge and the barriers to inquiry in 1897:

> Do you propose to have these students visit schools, pry into their methods, and quiz the superintendent about how he conducts his business? If so you are barking up the wrong tree. All that the superintendent wants the public to know can be found in his reports...Snooping around just can't be done; it isn't ethical. (p. 35)

By 1905, the barriers notwithstanding, Teachers College had made a great leap forward. In that year it awarded eight doctorates in educational administration (Sears & Henderson, 1957). Although most recipients chose administrative careers, Ellwood Cubberley and George Strayer became leading professors at Stanford University and Teachers College, respectively.

J. M. Rice served as a bridge between the old and the new as well as an effective diffuser of the Comtean concepts of science into education. During seven years of medical practice, his interests turned increasingly toward the education of children (Travers, 1983). After leaving medicine, Rice advocated the use of positivistic science; more important, he produced a research

exemplar that he called the "first of its kind that has ever appeared in print" (Rice, 1912, p. vi).

As early as the 1890s, Rice (1896) succinctly telegraphed his awareness of the old and the new concepts: "Everything is *speculative*; nothing is *positive* [italics added] (p. 387). "Definite knowledge" could only be obtained through positive science. The question of what the schools should teach, he noted, was philosophical, not scientific. Science had to pursue questions for which data existed, such as what educational means are actually used, what results do the means achieve, and how are the results related to school standards? As editor of the widely read *Forum*, he described its scholarly mission in positive terms (Rice, 1902): "It will endeavor to limit its duties to the publication of facts, the analysis of facts, suggestive opinions based on facts, and suggestions of new ways of getting facts" (p. 117). He emphasized, however, that facts should help establish "laws" to support school superintendence. Superintendents, he argued, should be more loyal to the laws of science than to school boards.

Rice's own inquiry began with a general question: Could the new learning activities, which progressives were advocating, be encompassed in the school curriculum without detriment to the three *R*s? In pursuing this question, Rice visited 36 school systems and obtained usable data on 50,000 students. He found little correlation between time spent on the teaching of given subjects and the learning acquired. Thus, when he set forth some of his negative findings in "Futility of the Spelling Grind" (1897), he not only created a great stir but he also moved research into a realm not occupied by his predecessors. After having clearly described the essential tenets of Comtean science, he had *used* them successfully in inquiry.

Cubberley and Strayer, pioneering scholars of educational administration, did not escape from the influence of the newer concepts of science. Cubberley studied mathematics and science and majored in physics at Indiana University. Upon graduation, he accepted a so-called science professorship at Vincennes University, where he taught seven courses in various sciences. For a time he planned to specialize in geology, his favorite subject, but in 1896 he became superintendent of schools in San Diego. He called on his background in the sciences again when he moved in 1898 from San Diego to Stanford University.

Strayer did his undergraduate work at Johns Hopkins. While studying there, he also taught mathematics and accounting at a neighboring business school. As a student he considered a career in physical science. However, by the time he graduated, Phi Beta Kappa, he had turned his back on physics and had chosen a career in educational administration. His later work on measures of school building needs, educational accounting systems, enrollment projections, and student test data all reflected the new quantitative bent in inquiry.

Strayer was well known for his many "scientific" surveys—the last one conducted in 1958 at the age of 81—and for the long list of scholars and leaders he taught. As a skilled spanner of school and academic settings, he served as president of the NEA and the National Society for the Study of Education in 1918–1919. Cubberley is perhaps best remembered for his abundant scholarship. Known as the Stanford Wizard, he wrote an average of a book a year between 1905 and 1919 (Cremin, 1965). His strong bent toward fact gathering surfaced early. In accepting the Stanford appointment, he announced his intent to collect from educational institutions "half a ton of material...from all parts of the United States" (Sears & Henderson, 1957, p. 59). He first used these materials in the courses he taught in 1898–1899, including one on school administration.

In the 1901–1925 period, science was much more than a mode of inquiry. Wiebe (1967) has called it "the basic word that every school of thought claimed and worshiped" (p. 147). Among those whom science awed were social scientists, social workers, educators, other "new" professionals, and also political progressives seeking "scientific" government. Science was also rooted firmly in the industrial world. A groundbreaking article on the piece-rate system written by the intense Frederick W. Taylor (1895) at century's end foreshadowed the "scientific management" movement with its promised efficiencies.

The worshipers of science highly valued its role. Its inventions, as Cubberley (1909) stressed, had helped create an astounding new society: "Science has been freed and made the common possession of all, and its wonders have become so common that discoveries and inventions have almost ceased to awaken a feeling of wonder" (p. 19). Even though industrialization, at least partially a product of science, had created bewildering and troublesome social problems, leaders in the late 19th century still looked hopefully toward science for solutions.

In a sense Strayer and Cubberley faced a more difficult challenge than did Rice. What methods could they use to build a science whose boundaries extended far beyond the classroom? What would best advance inquiry when, in Cubberley's words (1924), there were "practically no tools with which to work" (p. 180)? One such research strategy was the survey method, which, in Strayer's words (1925), facilitated the "analysis of a total situation into the many problems which demand solution" (p. 822). Cubberley also valued the historical method. Both research means were consonant with the prevailing emphases of science on fact gathering, inductive reasoning, and empirical generalizations.

According to Cubberley (1924, pp. 189–190), the early surveyors developed specific techniques, which later surveyors used in combination. Among the techniques were the comparative study of school data, descriptive statistics, analysis of test data, depth studies of particular functions, mapping, charting, and joint evaluation of findings by survey staffs. Cubberley (1924) saw in the survey a "most important means for educational administrative diagnosis" (p. 189) and a source for developing suggestions for improving education. Jesse Sears (1922), Cubberley's colleague at Stanford, stressed that the survey method was "a technique for the scientific study of educational problems" (p. 281) and, further, that it had two major contributions to make to a science of education: "the extensive and clear analysis [of] facts and situations [and] additions [to] actual methods and techniques of educational investigation" (pp. 281–282). The school survey provided a roof under which all available means for studying education and its policies could be assembled.

Cubberley (1909) stressed the unique value of history: "The proper means for reconstructing our social institutions are best suggested by a careful accumulation and analysis of our institutional experience," and "wider accumulation and saner interpretation of the facts of our educational history" can point the way to the needed reconstruction of schools (p. v). He used history in dual ways: "As administrator, he turned to history for explanation of problems; as historian, he sought especially for threads of meaning that reach out toward issues of the present and future" (Sears & Henderson, 1957, p. 127).

Both Cubberley and Strayer advocated the use of social science but did not delineate its potential. Other leaders did probe its utility at a meeting of the National Society of College Teachers of Education (Spaulding, Burris, & Elliott, 1910). There, Frank Spaulding, Superintendent of Schools in Newton, Massachusetts, and possessor of a German doctorate, projected that future school staffs would include psychologists, political economists, and anthropometrists, among others. His projections implied that school staff members, not academicians, should produce social science findings. Professor Edward Elliott of the University of Wisconsin emphasized the need to use economics, statistics, and public administration in training and inquiry. He assigned political science a more important role than "specialized educational technique" because school systems could not "be regarded in isolation from the intimately related political institutions" (Elliott, 1910, p. 90).

Paul Hanus (1910), Head of the Department of Education at Harvard University and a member of the audience at that meeting, later wrote an editorial for the *School Review* on the presentations made by Spaulding and Elliott. Noting that the discussion was the first of its kind ever held before a group of assembled professors, Hanus expressed skepticism about the results: "A cynic, listening to the discussion at the meeting, might have said that most of us were not yet ready to study school administration, much less to give a university course in that subject" (p. 426). He was also skeptical about looking for principles in other disciplines: "For on further reflection it seems clearer than ever that the way to study school administration is to study school administration and not to study the social and philosophical sciences..." (p. 426). Hanus's words offered another witness to the shift away from late 19th-century views about the most fruitful sources of the science of education and management.

Academic social scientists were pressed during the first quarter of the 20th century to resolve issues internal to their disciplines. Professors of educational administration, in their new academic home, had to demonstrate to skeptical classicists and others that they could develop a knowledge base. Internal pressures tended, then, to separate the two groups of scholars; in addition, neither had as yet realized large bodies of scientific knowledge to share.

Of the ideas that guided educational science in the 1901–1925 period, none was more influential than the view that fact gathering and analysis are central to inquiry. This view, which implied close linkages between research and practice, encouraged varied developments beyond the conduct of specific studies. Through newly established bureaus of educational research, researchers in school systems, for example, began to gather facts on such topics as the school census, staff, testing results, and experiments in instruction.

Research directors elaborated persuasive rationales for the new bureaus. S. A. Courtis and P. C. Packer (1920), in the Detroit research bureau, began with the proposition that "education is conceived as a war waged by society to gain control of its own evolution" and concluded that the role of research bureaus was to gather the intelligence needed by educational leaders to remain in "constant touch with what happens on every front" and to appraise actions taken in the field (p. 5). Significantly, the University of Illinois and The Ohio State University, following the lead of practitioners, established campus bureaus of educational research in 1918 and 1920, respectively.

Soon after school bureaus were founded, their directors saw the need to exchange research findings and to improve inquiry. Toward these ends, six leaders, five of whom were directors of research bureaus, decided, at an informal dinner meeting in 1915, to establish the National Association of Directors of Research (now the American Educational Research Association). Five years later the Association launched the *Journal of Educational Research*. B. R. Buckingham (1920), former director of research in Cincinnati and head of the new research bureau at the University of Illinois, became the journal's first editor. In announcing the journal, he stressed that it would "emphasize applications, and practice rather than theory" (p. 1). David Hill (1916), in an article written four years earlier for the relatively new journal *Educational Administration and Supervision*, repeated Rice's dicta when he called for the gathering of facts, the careful consideration of facts by boards and superintendents, the publication of facts for the benefit of the people and follow-up action based on facts (p. 577).

Textbooks that moved beyond classroom management and described general functions and units of administration also appeared. For example, the best general text of the period (Dutton & Snedden, 1908) offered chapters on functions titled "Financing of Education" and "The Teaching Staff." It also provided chapters on administering subunits of school systems as, for example, the high school, the normal school, and the evening and continuation school. In contrast to the Latin phrases, quotations from poets, and legal references found in Payne's book (1875), the Dutton-Snedden text contained extensive bibliographies, but their inductively oriented text, and more specialized ones written by Cubberley and Strayer, largely ignored the concept of scientific law. Normative "principles," with their mixtures of facts and values and their delineation of "what ought to be done and why," dominated the literature. Nor did scholars of the period resolve the problem Payne identified; namely, how to distinguish educational administration from teaching. Relationships between education and administration remained fuzzy.

Cubberley, writing in 1924, described the previous quarter of a century as a "great creative period" in education (p. 179). The subject pedagogy, he noted, had given way to "the rapidly expanding professional subject, education" which was grounded in "scientific methods" (p. 179). Cubberley likely exaggerated the period's progress; nevertheless, there was change during the 1901–1925 period. Although reflective essays reminiscent of 19th-century writings still abounded, works based on facts grew rapidly in number.

In sum, then, concepts of science in the 1901–1925

period differed markedly from those of the previous century. Rooted in the thinking of Comte and Spencer, these concepts were positive rather than speculative. Diffused into education by Rice through a sensational research exemplar, the scientific view emphasized fact gathering and downplayed the Comptean desideratum to discover scientific laws. The factual emphasis appeared and reappeared in surveys, historical studies, articles in new practice-oriented journals, textbooks, and publications of school and university research bureaus.

Strayer and Cubberley, as the leading professors of educational administration in their time, used the concept of "science" more as a rhetorical expression than as a well-defined mode of inquiry. As energetic activists, they were more interested in clarifying educational policies than in discovering laws or defining the deeper meanings of educational science. In contrast to Payne and Harris, who strove to make explicit the presuppositions which shaped their inquiry, Cubberley and Strayer left theirs largely implicit. Their stance reflected that of professors of educational administration generally. The 1901–1925 period did not produce a critical and systematic analysis of the underpinnings of the science of education and management. Such an analysis awaited the work of John Dewey in the post-1925 period.

THE STREAM OF EDUCATIONAL AND MANAGEMENT SCIENCE WIDENS AND DEEPENS: 1926–1950

About the time Payne and Harris ended their superintendencies, John Dewey was studying at the University of Vermont for a career in philosophy. When he sent a manuscript to the *Journal of Speculative Philosophy*, Harris encouraged Dewey to hold to his bold career goal. At Vermont he was influenced by such disparate thinkers as Plato, Comte, and especially Hegel. Although he gradually moved away from Hegel's philosophy, Dewey was permanently influenced by the idealist's concept of the dialectic, his view that reason is located in life's struggles, and the idea that social and moral processes have no fixed ends (Curti, 1974, p. 502). During his graduate study at Johns Hopkins, Dewey's interest in science deepened. A decade later, as a professor of philosophy and education at the University of Chicago, he began to test "scientifically" his educational ideas in the Laboratory School there.

Dewey's philosophy of pragmatism was rooted in scientific concepts. While he accepted the positivist view that science is centered in experience rather than in metaphysical speculation, he rejected the idea that the study of ideals falls outside scientific inquiry. For Dewey, "the scientific method functioned...even in value determination" (Bowyer, 1970, p. 83). Rather than emphasizing science's role in establishing general laws, as had Comte and Spencer, Dewey stressed science's capacities for expanding intelligence and enlarging experience. Sensitive to the contextual constraints of inquiry, he believed firmly in the relativity of knowledge. In rejecting the view that scientific disciplines have identifiable and standard features, he opted for a "looseness" of definition in science (Dewey, 1929, p. 8). He described science in terms of method, which, when "brought to bear upon a range of facts, could enable us to understand them better and to control them more intelligently, less haphazardly and with less routine" (1929, pp. 8–9). As had Comte, Dewey (1910) stressed the methods of comparison and experiment (p. 195ff). However, he assigned greater significance to problem-defining than did Comte. If an idea or solution, when tested, solved a defined problem, it was valid.

Although Dewey affirmed early his belief in a science of education (1885), he was slow to publish his thoughts on the subject. Decades passed, following his book *The School and Society* (1899/1980), before he unveiled, in his Phi Delta Kappa lecture, detailed views on educational science (1929). Reflected in the lecture were Dewey's democratic temperament and his anti-authoritarian attitude. Rejecting worshipful attitudes toward science, he was critical of those who saw in it "a guarantee that goes with the sale of the goods" (1929, p. 15). His view that no discipline, no method of inquiry, no scholar, and no practitioner should be left out of efforts to build knowledge in education reflected his democratic temperament.

Administrators, Dewey asserted, could not use scientific findings or even systematized science slavishly; practice was simply too complicated, given the countless variables that influenced it. To be sure, many practitioners yearned for rules; however, science could not supply rules. For Dewey (1929), educational science could only develop within practice contexts: "The final reality of educational science is not found in books, nor in experimental laboratories, nor in the class-rooms where it is taught but in the minds of those engaged in directing educational activities" (p. 32).

Dewey believed the sources of the problems of educational science always resided in practice, whereas the intellectual means for studying problems resided in disciplines. Problem-defining could not be achieved by "armchair thinking" only; there had to be "some kind of vital current flowing between the field worker and the research worker" (1929, p. 44). Theory could provide an antidote to the ever-present pressures for practical results; however, it had to fit the actualities of schools. According to Dewey (1929) an independent science of education could not exist; it had to draw materials from varied sciences: "Any methods and any facts and principles...that enable the problems of administration...to be dealt with in a bettered way are pertinent" (pp. 48–49). The isolation of social scientists from educational practice, Dewey affirmed (1929), tended to make disciplines "barren and susceptible to loose speculation" (p. 41). However, educators, in order to overcome their erroneous views of education as a "segregated" science, needed better understandings of the ways of science.

Dewey's *Sources of a Science of Education* (1929) still stands as a searching critique of science and educational inquiry. The critique serves as a danger sign for those who would separate scientific activities from educational practices. However, given his view that the "final reality" of educational science is in the "minds" of practitioners and given his loosely defined concepts of science, it is not easy to trace the actual impact of his ideas on inquiry.

During the decade of Dewey's famed lecture, a second generation of professors came to the fore. Among these were Arthur Moehlman, recipient of a University of Michigan doctorate in 1923 from the department Payne founded; Paul Mort, a student of Strayer's who received his doctorate at Teacher's College in 1924; and Jesse Sears, Cubberley's long-time associate at Stanford, who was awarded his doctorate by Teachers College in 1920. These leading professors adhered to a number of Deweyan dicta: The sources of research problems are in practice; the researcher and the practitioner need to be in close contact in inquiry; scientific study is a method for generating "intelligence"; and loose definitions of science are preferable to rigorous ones. However, they did not acquire in their training the discipline-based methods that, from Dewey's perspective, were needed to study problems; in fact Sears (1959) declared that his "training for research...was not of the best" (p. 54). Thus, this second generation used mainly the methods their mentors had employed; Sears in fact wrote a major textbook (1925) on the school survey.

Of the three professors, Sears had the deepest interest in epistemology. As a Stanford undergraduate, he expressed his wonderment about knowledge of education (1959):

> The field of education seemed a bit vague to me as I tried to think of the subject matter it might represent. The thing that puzzled me the most was that I could not seem to think of education as I had thought of geometry, biology, Latin, or ancient history. I could see botany as a field of study, as a definite body of knowledge to be

mastered, but how to get a similar notion of education I could not see. I recall remarking to a group of fellow students that I wished someone would take me by the hand and lead me up on a hill and show me the field of education. No one volunteered.... (p. 39)

Although Sears did not take lightly the severe criticisms of educational inquiry by university professors, he concluded that such criticisms were warranted. Mort (1935) shared Sear's stance: "Viewed from the accepted set methods of the sciences, or even of the older social studies, much of the research in education seems unworthy of the name." (p. 542). However, the two scholars were not deterred by the low state of inquiry. Sears (1959) firmly believed that in time a science of education and school management could be realized. Mort (1935) stressed that those in the youthful field of education could "bear with equanimity [criticisms from] the older sciences" and could be satisfied, even after 30 years of study, with "two or three techniques for reliably approaching knowledge" (p. 542).

Early in their careers Moehlman, Mort, and Sears gave a boost to the specialized study of administrative functions. While serving as Director of Statistics, Reference and Administrative Research in the Detroit Public Schools, Moehlman developed a strong interest in public relations. His *Social Interpretation* (1938) provided a penetrating and comprehensive view of the subject. Mort (1924) developed precise measures of educational need and more equitable formulas for distributing financial aid. By studying school finance throughout his career, he advanced the specialization significantly. A special topic that caught Sears's attention, in addition to the school survey, was city school administration (1938).

The three professors also broke new ground in the use of the social sciences. In delineating education's close relationship to culture, Moehlman drew upon the ideas of Franz Boas, who earlier in the century had set the directions for anthropological inquiry at Columbia University, and the works of Ruth Benedict and Leslie White (e.g., 1951, Chapters 1 & 2). In his study of school system adaptability (Mort & Cornell, 1938), Mort used sociological studies and, as a specialist in school finance, looked to public administration and political science for insights into municipal government, taxes, and revenues. Sears (1950), on the other hand, in developing his theory of administrative process, borrowed content from a half-dozen law reviews, from extensive readings in political science, from references on business and public administration, from the writings of selected anthropologists, and from such classic works as *Papers on A Science of Administration* (Gulick & Urwick, 1937).

Others also built bridges between the social sciences and educational administration. Jesse Newlon (1934), after sharply criticizing the narrowness of studies in the field, argued that educational administration should become an applied social science. In the 1940s professors of educational administration drew increasingly upon the acclaimed Western Electric studies (Roethlisberger & Dickson, 1939), which had dramatized the importance of human factors in administration. When "human relations" and "democratic school administration" became buzzwords some melded the meanings of the two concepts (e.g., see Yauch, 1949).

Mort, Moehlman, and Sears also addressed emergent needs of their time. A major problem resided in the relationships among the concepts of education in a democracy, democracy in education, and school administration. The stress of the Great Depression and the authoritarian threat of World War II threw this problem into bold relief. Of the three professors, Moehlman analyzed the ideas most thoroughly. In a book he facetiously called his Bible, Moehlman (1951) stressed that public education is "not a protected academic island in a windless civic sea" (p. 57). In turbulent civic seas, democratic ideals can serve both as ballasts and compasses to decision makers. He elaborated democratic and educational ideals and set forth the implications for "executive activity." Beginning with the "principles" that education (a) "is an essential and integral part of the total culture" and that (b) its "purposes...should be in harmony with the developing cultural pattern," he deduced 13 generalizations that pinpointed what educational policy makers "ought" to do (Moehlman, 1951, p. 57ff).

Mort led in vigorously criticizing the research of his day and in pursuing diverse strategies to improve it. Contending that inquiry needed the "severest of analyses," he charged that professors were "too uncritical, too kind for the cause" (Mort, 1935, p. 550). A believer in close connections between researchers and practitioners, he created in 1942 the Metropolitan Schools Study Council in the New York City area, the forerunner of dozens of such councils that still function. A proponent of programmatic and cooperative research, he also founded the Associated Public Schools Systems. Finally, he pioneered what he called basic research in his probes of school system "adaptability" (e.g., see Mort & Cornell, 1938). Mort's research experience may have enabled him to foresee impending changes (1935):

Between survey techniques on the one hand and historical techniques on the other, there will probably fall other set of validated techniques for use in research.... Experimental techniques based on the rapid advance in the field of statistics have already gained validity. (p. 542)

Fifteen years in the making, Sears's book *The Nature of the Administrative Process* (1950) also represented a pioneering effort. While writing the book he felt "alone and unsupported by anything...in the literature" (Sears, 1959, p. 111). An important thesis of the book was that the "types of activities covered by the term administration" in education are "similar" or at least "parallel" to "those covered by it in government, in industry and commerce, in institutions of religion, and in social clubs" (Sears, 1950, p. 4). His generic concept of administration foreshadowed developments ahead.

Mort, Moehlman, and Sears, then, advanced the science of school management through specialized studies; they expanded the range of inquiry by drawing on content from the social sciences and other fields of administration. In addition, they responded to needs of their time: Mort through his adaptability studies and newly created research organizations; Sears through his generic definition of administration; and Moehlman through his analyses of democracy and educational administration.

By 1940 the school survey, as a "stimulative force," was losing its influence (Sears, 1959, p. 71), and the use of the historical method was declining. Questionnaire studies were in the ascendancy, as were uses of simple statistics and the search for effective research designs. However, since advocacy "principles" still substituted for theory, concepts to guide research were missing. Although Mort's deep dissatisfaction with inquiry reflected a more general malaise, the 1926–1950 period did not produce major breakthroughs. Published books, surveys, monographs, and articles, although more copious than in previous periods, were filled with prescriptive generalizations. Scholars used science more as a rhetorical tool than as a set of well-defined procedures, as had scholars in previous periods.

During the 1926–1950 period, Mort, Sears, and Moehlmann used simplified versions of both Deweyan and Comtean concepts of science. In addition, the three leading scholars joined values with facts in their inquiry, as Dewey had recommended and as their distinguished mentors had done. Since Mort's study of adaptability (Mort & Cornell, 1938) reflected Deweyan views of science, it likely constitutes the best research exemplar of the period.

The National Conference of Professors of Educational Administration (NCPEA) came into being in 1947, with a mission to "improve educational leadership." In 1950 a cooperative initiative, which was to involve eight universities, was poised for liftoff. This and related endeavors would bring a new set of scientific concepts into the field—concepts that would depart markedly from those of past periods and that would effect a radical turn in the quest for knowledge. As had the decade of the 1890s, the decade of the 1940s marked the end of an era. Mort, Moehlman, and Sears followed largely in the footsteps of Strayer and Cubberley; however, in their struggle to go beyond traditional modes of inquiry, they produced some significant portents of the future.

THE LEAP TOWARD AN ADMINISTRATIVE SCIENCE: 1951–1966

In 1923, about the time Mort, Moehlman, and Sears published their first works, the philosopher Moritz Schlick began a seminar in the great cultural center of Vienna. From this seminar sprang a new philosophy of science. Soon transformed into the famous Vienna Circle of scholars, the seminar generated a powerful intellectual movement which Toulmin (1969) a half-century later described as "radical, . . . apocalyptic [and an] international Liberation Front" (p. 51). Known as "logical positivism," the movement's ideas about theory and science differed sharply from those of the past.

The Vienna scholars combined two very disparate streams of thought to arrive at their views: the older positivism of Auguste Comte and the symbolic logic of Bertrand Russell and Alfred North Whitehead. They found especially meaningful Comte's concepts of theological, metaphysical, and positive thinking and the view that the two former types of thinking make for useless digressions in science (see Kraft, 1953, pp. 16–17) They were also attracted to Comte's thesis that physics was already in a positive stage of science; further, that social scientists, who were still mired in prescientific thinking, could best advance their disciplines by employing natural science modes of inquiry.

Symbolic logic provided the second foundation of logical positivism; the Vienna visionaries saw in the new logic a tool that could give philosophy the "same degree of logical rigor, cogent argument and precise clarity" found in mathematical and scientific statements (Culbertson, 1981, p. 32). However, since logico-mathematical statements admittedly dealt with symbolic, not real, objects, they were faced with a challenge. How could the new logic be joined with positive thinking to shape effective inquiry? Their answer: the creation of "hypothetico-deductive systems"—sets of postulates, stated in logico-mathematical terms, from

which hypotheses could be derived and tested in the real world.

Although the ideas of Comte, the "father of positivism," influenced logical positivism, it departed from his views in significant ways: logical positivism was much more deductive in character, placed higher importance on theory, strongly emphasized the quantitative, and was more structured and standardized in its conceptions. Logical positivism was also created more by a group than by an individual.

In 1930 when Schlick addressed the Seventh International Congress of Philosophy at Oxford University, he naively asserted that the new philosophy of science "provided a means of settling all so-called philosophical disputes in an absolutely final and ultimate manner" (cited in Joergensen, 1951, p. 40). His remarks created no great stir. However, as logical positivists launched new publications, especially the journal *Knowledge* (*Erkenntnis*), interest in the Vienna thinking sharply increased (Joergensen, 1951, pp. 41–42). When the Circle, on the eve of World War II, broke and most of its members moved to the United States, its influence grew even more.

Scriven (1969) has written that the impact of the new philosophy on the behavioral sciences was enormous (p. 197). The discipline most sharply and quickly changed was psychology. Thus, Clark Hull and his colleagues pursued the ideals of logical positivism by setting forth an elegant system of "mathematico-deductive" learning theorems (Hull, Ross, Hall, Perkins, & Fitch, 1940). Kurt Lewin (1938), who described psychological forces in logical and mathematical terms, observed that "more important for psychology today. . .is the development of a type of 'Theoretical Psychology' which has the same relation to 'Experimental Psychology' as Theoretical Physics has to Experimental Physics" (p. 4).

Richard Bernstein (1976), in his searching study of social and political theory, concluded that Robert Merton played a very crucial role in bringing the thinking of the Vienna Circle into sociology. While warning his colleagues in sociology that they should not develop unrealistic hopes, Merton argued for adaptive uses of the new science. He opted for middle-range theories or "logically interconnected conceptions which are limited and modest in scope, rather than all embracing and grandiose" (Merton, 1949, p. 6).

Perhaps the most influential of all the social science books of the 1940s was Herbert Simon's *Administrative Behavior* (1945). Innovative in its design, the book influenced administration in far-reaching ways. Early in the book Simon noted he had not elaborated "first principles" but had used the tenets of logical positivism "as a starting point" for his decision-making theory (pp. 45–46). His work provided the most direct conduit in the 1940s for the flow of "administrative science" into educational administration.

In 1947, shortly after Simon's influential book appeared, leading U.S. educators began discussions with officers in the W. K. Kellogg Foundation. These discussions led to an auspicious development—the Cooperative Program in Educational Administration (CPEA). CPEA, which was directed at improving preparatory programs for educational administrators, was launched in 1950–1951 at five universities: Chicago; George Peabody College for Teachers; Harvard; Teachers College, Columbia; and Texas. The next year three additional universities joined the group: Ohio State, Oregon, and Stanford. CPEA professors played leading roles in transmitting simplified versions of logical positivism to the field and in the process activated the "theory movement," whose goal was to build an "administrative science."

CPEA leaders agreed that they should make greater use of the social sciences in training and inquiry. This strategy brought professors of educational administration and their students into contact with social scientists, thereby facilitating the exchange of ideas and stimulating leading professors in the field to read more widely in the literature of the social and natural sciences. The ideas they acquired helped create a climate for the new science and for its uses in educational administration.

Among those who led in nurturing the new inquiry were Jacob Getzels of the University of Chicago; Daniel Griffiths of Teachers College; and Andrew Halpin, initially at The Ohio State University and later at the Chicago CPEA Center. Halpin (1958), a skillful writer and long-time student of science, led in communicating the new norms into the field of educational administration; Getzels (1958), by offering a well-conceived research exemplar, gave professors and students needed insights into the meaning of theory; and Griffiths (1959), with his marked dissatisfaction with existing inquiry, led in disseminating ideas about theory and administrative science within the field.

Getzels, a psychologist, was the first to utilize the new norms in a theory. His renowned "social process" theory (1952) was strongly influenced by the "grand theorist" Talcott Parsons, with whom Getzels studied during his doctoral work in the Department of Social Relations at Harvard. The exemplar Getzel created began, in one sense, with an invitation he received to speak to a seminar on school administration during his first year at the University of Chicago. In preparing his presentation he sought information about educational administration (personal correspondence, February 11, 1980):

> I tried to find out from the students of the seminar what conceptual stance they took; they did not seem to know what I was talking about. I tried a couple of texts in educational administration but I couldn't figure out what *they* were talking about; they seemed more like training manuals than conceptual or research treatises. So I gave a...discourse on conceptual frameworks and systematic research.

The lecture brought puzzlement to the "immobile" students and frustration to Getzels. Immediately after the lecture he hurried to his office, sat down at his desk and wrote on a piece of paper "A Psycho-Sociological Framework for the Study of Educational Administration." Before evening's end he had outlined the "framework" and in an early paragraph had observed (1952):

> Systematic research requires the mediation of theory—theory that will give meaning and order to observations already made and that will specify areas where observations still need to be made. It is here that we would place the root of the difficulty in administration: there is a dearth of theory-making. (p. 235)

The immediate outcome of his writing was catharsis. However, some months later the theory, with its new research norms, was published in the *Harvard Educational Review* (Getzels, 1952). The field apparently was ready for it (personal correspondence, February 11, 1980): "The response was immediate and exhilarating; it has been unmatched in the two-hundred articles, chapters, and books since." Offering a set of logically related concepts featuring, for example, "institution," "role," "individual," and "personality," the article went beyond abstract descriptions of theory to a needed example. Later refined by Getzels with the aid of Egon Guba, the theory stimulated much inquiry as it made its way into classrooms, conferences, textbooks, and dissertations.

As a senior at Columbia University (the first U.S. institution to have a professor who participated in Vienna Circle discussions), Halpin in 1930–1931 first learned about the new concepts. He was especially stimulated by Matthew Chapple, a neurophysiologist, who was intrigued with the new directions in inquiry. As a graduate student at Cornell, Halpin was strongly influenced by Professor Karl Dallenbach, whom he later described as a "strict scientist type." In 1980 he assessed the impact of his earlier study of logical positivism as follows (personal correspondence, March 1980): "The imprint was strong enough to have stayed with me for half a century." Halpin's unique experience

and skills enabled him to communicate clearly and
vividly the new concepts to the field.

After receiving his doctorate in 1949 at Cornell in
educational psychology, Halpin served two years at the
University of Tennessee and then joined the Personnel
Research Board at Ohio State. The Board was then
responsible for guiding the study of leadership in
industrial, military, educational, and other organizations. Active in the Ohio State CPEA Center, Halpin
(1955) provided an example of the new research
through a comparative study of the leadership behaviors of superintendents and aircraft commanders.
Later he helped shape the new movement as a member
of the University of Chicago CPEA Center.

Griffiths received his doctorate in educational
administration from Yale in 1952. He immediately
became involved in the Middle Atlantic CPEA Center
activities—first at the New York State College for
Teachers in Albany and later at Teachers College. He
welcomed and found appealing the new concepts of
science (Griffiths, 1982):

> I taught physical science from a historical case ap-
> proach at Colgate, was thoroughly disgusted with what
> passed for research and serious thought in educa-
> tional administration, and was influenced by a number
> of social scientists trained in the logical positivist
> mode...It seemed to me that the logical positivist
> approach was the proper antidote for self-serving testi-
> monials, the pseudotheories..., and the plain nonsense
> that constituted the field of educational administration.
> (pp. 3–4)

A skilled writer, Griffiths disseminated ideas about
theory and its new norms via monographs, books,
articles, and many conference presentations. At mid-
decade, for example, he offered a synthesis of social
science concepts for use in training (Griffiths, 1956).
His widely read *Administrative Theory* (1959) helped
many professors understand theory and its logical
positivistic underpinnings.

The NCPEA helped nurture the new movement
by providing forums where scholars could challenge
existing research and advocate theory-based norms to
professors in attendance from across the nation. Of
special significance was a forum, held in Denver in
1954, which Halpin (1970) has described as follows:

> At that meeting the first "real" confrontation be-
> tween behavioral scientists and professors of educational
> administration took place. Coladarci (of Stanford),
> Getzels (of Chicago), and Halpin (then of The Ohio
> State University) pointed out to the group—and not
> gently—that what the CPEA Centers and members
> of NCPEA were doing in the name of research was dis-

tinctly a-theoretical in character and sloppy in quality.
The reception that these three behavioral scientists
received at that meeting can scarcely be described as
cordial. (p. 161)

At the 1954 meeting the NCPEA Committee
approved a plan for a book titled *Administrative
Behavior in Education*. The volume, edited by Roald
Campbell and Russell Gregg, appeared three years
later (1957). An admixture of the old and the new, it
did provide clues about the new directions in inquiry.
In his chapter, Griffiths (1957) discussed the nature,
development, and uses of theory and set forth some
elements of a theory; and Halpin (1957) elaborated a
well-conceived "paradigm" for guiding research on
administrator behavior.

Shortly after the NCPEA book appeared in 1957, a
national seminar for professors of educational administration took place in Chicago. Sponsored by the
University of Chicago and the newly formed University
Council for Educational Administration—a mediator
of the "theory movement"—the seminar's message was
clear: namely, that high priority should be placed on
theory development and on the building of a "science
of administration."

Early in the seminar, Halpin and James Thompson, editor of the one-year-old *Administrative Science
Quarterly*, articulated six ideas that were at the heart of
the theory movement (Culbertson, 1983, p. 15).

1. Statements about what organizations and admin-
    istrators ought to do cannot be encompassed in
    theory or science. In discussing this idea Halpin
    (1958) quoted Neal Gross as follows: "Theory must
    be concerned with how the superintendent *does*
    behave, not with someone's opinion of how he
    ought to behave" (p. 3).
2. Scientific theories treat phenomena as they are.
    Theories describe, explain, and predict, but do *not*
    prescribe. Radically departing from the past, the
    Chicago scholars, by separating the "is" from the
    "ought," closed the door, in theory at least, upon a
    75-year history of advocacy practiced by Payne,
    Harris, Cubberley, Strayer, Moehlman, and many
    others.
3. Effective research has its origins in theory and is
    guided by theory. Halpin wrote about the "poverty
    of theory" in the field and expressed his dismay that
    research was "anchored" to "naked empiricism."
    Only by developing and using theory in research
    could the field move beyond its state of poverty.
4. Hypothetico-deductive systems are the best exem-
    plars of theory. Halpin argued, as had Vienna Circle
    scholars before him, that theory, given its diffuse
    meanings, should be defined as "hypothetico-

deductive systems." He quoted Feigl's widely used definition—"a set of assumptions from which can be derived by purely logico-mathematico procedures, a larger set of empirical laws" (Halpin, 1958, p. 6)—and suggested that Getzels's "social process" theory had some of the features of a hypothetico-deductive system.

5. The social sciences are essential to theory development and training. Since social science theories and modes of inquiry are already available, starting from scratch in theory-building would be a very unwise policy for the field; further, social science theories can and should be used to develop in administrators needed understandings of organizations and society.

6. For the purposes of theory development, administration is best conceived as a general phenomenon found in all organizations. "Adjectival" definitions of administration had to be jettisoned. The proposed new theories, which would apply to all organizations, would provide the field very powerful tools for inquiry and understanding.

Especially significant in the proposed shift in directions were the moves from loosely defined to precisely defined concepts of science, from qualitative to quantitative emphases, and from a factual to a theoretical orientation. The sharp rejection of advocacy and the desire for "value-free" inquiry reflected an even more marked turn in the quest for knowledge. By allying educational administration conceptually with other fields of administration, scholars at last had clearly differentiated administration from teaching.

Understandably, the new norms were not easily translated into actual inquiry. The old "principles of administration" were much too strong to give ground immediately. Consequently, "nakedly" empirical and prescriptive generalizations prevailed widely in the literature of the 1951–1966 period. The novel concepts, nevertheless, did help to establish new beachheads.

Each of the six ideas noted above brought changes to the field. The concept of administration *qua* administration, for example, provided the rationale for the influential *Administrative Science Quarterly*; for graduate schools designed to prepare administrators for diverse organizations; and for the Administrative Science Center at the University of Pittsburgh (see, e.g., Thompson, Hammond, Hawkes, Junker, & Tuden, 1959). Theories of organization informed new courses and guided some dissertations. One text contained a 27-page chapter devoted entirely to Getzels's "social process" theory (Campbell, Corbally, & Ramseyer, 1962). By the 1970s textbooks devoted entirely to theory appeared.

Psychology and sociology—disciplines that had privileged relationships to education, according to Dewey (1929)—were at first prominent. However, some economists and political scientists became active and, as the 1960s unfolded, began to build such subdisciplines as the economics of education and the politics of education. Some newly trained professors of educational administration began to specialize in these areas.

To facilitate the exchange of the new ideas, the *Journal of Educational Administration* and *The Educational Administration Quarterly* were founded in the mid-1960s, followed by the establishment of *Educational Administration Abstracts*, the last designed to provide summaries of relevant content from social science and educational journals. Among other things, these journals facilitated the flow and use of information about social science theories and methods.

The University of Chicago, in the last half of the 1950s, developed a doctoral program to provide the skills and concepts needed to advance the new inquiry. In the program prospective professors worked closely with social scientists and gained experience in conducting theory-based research. By the early 1960s the University of Chicago was the leading supplier of professors of educational administration (Shaplin, 1964, pp. 2–4).

In sum, then, the scholars of the Vienna Circle formulated a philosophy of science that departed radically from the systems of thought offered by Comte and Dewey. Called logical positivism, the philosophy had far-reaching impacts on social science inquiry. Diffused in simplified form into educational administration in the 1950s by such leading scholars as Simon, Getzels, Griffiths, and Halpin, the ideas heightened hopes for a science of administration. Research became more theory-based; leading scholars moved away from "ought" generalizations to descriptive and explanatory generalizations; changed relationships between scholars in educational administration and the social sciences brought new inquiry; more conceptual content buttressed training programs; and new journals for disseminating the products of the theory movement were launched.

New developments, however, were constrained by deeply established and long-held inductive norms in inquiry, by loose definitions of science, and by a tradition of professorial advocacy. In addition, the new scientific norms encountered resistance in the social ferment of the 1960s. A century's worship of science suddenly gave way in some quarters to highly negative attitudes toward its technologies. In the new climate, concepts of logical positivism came under increasing criticism, as did the presuppositions of the theory movement.

ADMINISTRATIVE SCIENCE AS AN EMBATTLED
CONCEPT: 1967–1985

Among those in the 1960s who proclaimed the demise of the proud Vienna Circle was Karl Popper: "Everybody knows nowadays that logical positivism is dead" (cited in Schilpp, 1967, p. 69). Certainly, the first Vienna formulations, which Hanson (1969) called "the strident, stentorian and sinewy sallies of the twenties and early thirties," (p. 84) succumbed. Change in Vienna Circle thinking was one indicator of its demise. However, there was a more fundamental reason for its passing: Work on the "icy slopes of logic," to use Otto Neurath's phrase (1973, p. 306), was too far removed from research activity. Rudolph Carnap's brilliant formulations about syntax and semantics could not cope with the cavernous gap between mathematized systems and real-world events, much less ensure final tests of hypothetico-deductive systems. Logic could not be the single progenitor of propositions for inquiry; real-world problems also had to have their influence.

In another sense Popper's proclamation of logical positivism's death was erroneous because the movement's early conceptions produced many offspring. At one level, the Vienna Circle scholars, reacting to criticism, reformulated many of their earliest ideas. For example, the concept of verification gave way over time to disconfirmation. At another level simplified versions of the concepts became embedded in the behavioral sciences and in such fields as educational administration, where they continued to have effects long after Popper's proclamation. At still another level, some scholars, after rejecting the logical positivists' highly formalized and mathematical conceptions of science, set forth their own "post-positivist" views (e.g., see Popper, 1959). Finally, negative reactions to logical positivism stimulated new theories of knowledge. Notable in this regard was the "critical theory" of the Frankfurt School (e.g., see O'Neil, 1976), whose scholars argued that logical positivism had made trenchant critiques of practice impossible.

Logical positivism also engendered a deep malaise among many scholars (McCall & Lombardo, 1978):

> It is no secret that the dissatisfaction with results is rampant among social scientists, across a wide spectrum of content areas...there is a feeling of disillusionment and an urge to throw the captain overboard. No captains can be found...only a yellow document, spelling out the canons of experimental science. (p. xi)

Some contended that a crisis in organization science prevailed—a crisis that was rooted in inadequate epistemological concepts (Susman & Evered,

1978, p. 34). Griffiths (1979) asserted, in less dramatic terms, that educational administration was in a state of "intellectual turmoil" (p. 43).

Diverse and powerful influences helped to create that turmoil, including new theories of science, critiques of logical positivism (and the theory movement), pressures for policy research, and altered relations between social science and educational administration. More fundamentally, new epistemological tenets are in the ascendancy. The field, fraught with contradiction, has lost its sense of cohesion; pluralistic perspectives prevail circa 1985.

First, new theories of science have challenged the tenets of logical positivism. At the heart of the most highly influential challenge is the concept of "paradigm" (Kuhn, 1962). In the 1970s this concept became a buzzword in different scholarly communities and found its way into the literature of educational administration. While some took comfort in the theory movement's paradigmatic qualities and its significant accomplishments, others argued that the movement was passé and needed to be replaced by a new paradigm (see Erickson, 1977; Lincoln, 1985).

Kuhn's theory of science differed significantly from that of the Vienna Circle. Instead of using mathematical concepts to formulate his theory, as had the scholars of the Vienna Circle, Kuhn drew upon historical data. He also attended less to the technical aspects and more to the social aspects of inquiry. He rejected the view that science is a "cumulative enterprise" produced by "methodological directives" (Kuhn, 1962, p. 3). Scholars, through "paradigm-shattering" research, can undermine scholarly views, thus paving the way for new belief systems, new paradigms, and scientific revolutions. Such a perspective could not have resided on the procrustean beds of Vienna. Nor would Vienna scholars have probed the meaning of science by studying how Newton's beliefs, for instance, related to those of his contemporaries.

While the Vienna Circle philosophy was slowly shifting from an influential force to a historical phenomenon, leaders of theory movement were encountering strong headwinds. In the mid-1960s, after the "is-ought" dichotomy helped shape the theory movement, far-reaching questions about educational value moved onto federal, state, and local agendas. Education became a weapon in the war on poverty, a medium for breaking down the walls of segregation, a ladder for the culturally deprived to climb to opportunity, and an engine for propelling a technologically advanced economy. Inherent in these expansive expectations were far-reaching "ought," or policy, questions. However, since policy alternatives could not be deduced from scientific theories, the theory movement's capacities for policy analysis, scholars came to see, were limited.

University centers, often with external support, began to address issues such as desegregation. In the 1970s scholars turned to the study of educational inequities, especially those affecting women, racial minorities, and the handicapped. To probe the problems generated by long histories of discrimination, leaders of the University Council for Educational Administration founded the *Journal of Educational Equity*. When Payne (1875) devoted six pages of his book (pp. 47–53) to why women lacked "fitness" to manage schools, he communicated the conventional view of his time. The inequities suffered by blacks and the handicapped in the period were even more marked. Although the 20th century brought some changes in attitude, only a very small number of women and minority professors were contributing to the study of educational policy at the beginning of the 1967–1985 period.

As policy research grew, more scholars left the "is-ought" dichotomy on the sidelines. Some concentrated on studying the effectiveness of innovative programs in education, especially those supported by federal agencies—a kind of inquiry called evaluation. Evaluators, even though they used very different strategies, shared a common purpose: namely, that of shedding light on which educational or management "innovations" were most effective and fruitful.

Early in the 1970s, James Coleman (1972) contrasted theory-based and policy-oriented research. In defining policy research he emphasized its "world-of-action" properties; it originates, he argued, in action and is fed back into action. Theory-based research, on the other hand, originates in disciplines and is fed back into disciplines. The findings of policy research tend to add to the power of certain groups while diminishing the power of others—a feature not inherent in basic research. Given the special character of policy research, Coleman concluded that it could best be conducted in non-university agencies (e.g., non-profit organizations). In fact, university policy centers proved to be unstable.

Given the special pressures on education and the changing views about inquiry, the roles among disciplines changed. Research on the politics of education expanded, while psychological and sociological inquiry, which had helped spawn the theory movement, declined. The increased study of the politics of education matched the growing political pressures on education. Not unrelated was the fact that economics attained a new subdiscipline—the economics of education. Anthropology, responding to changing research norms, became an ascendant discipline. The work on the

school principal by the anthropologist Harry Wolcott (1973) provided a notable exemplar. A number of ethnographic studies of school principals followed, some of which were supported by the National Institute of Education. These studies reflected once more the declining influence of the theory movement. Anthropological methods were more qualitative than quantitative and more inductive than deductive.

Growing disenchantment with the precepts of the theory movement also surfaced in sharp criticism from practitioners who charged that university research and training content were irrelevant to the needs of practice (Morrow, Foster, & Estes, 1974):

> ...the content and form of the learning experience ought to be defined by what superintendents need and want to know and what they can assimilate. Their on-the-job experiences have to feed into the learning process, and the learning structure ought to be an extension of the superintendents' reality. (pp. 16–17).

Still, the most penetrating criticisms of the theory movement came not from practitioners but from professors (for details, see Culbertson, 1983). Significantly, Halpin was one of the first scholars to recognize the limited fit between theories and the larger realities of educational administration. As the 1960s dawned, he offered a discerning observation: "There is indeed something missing. The fault is that the scientist's theoretical models of administration are too rational, too tidy, too aseptic...we had better examine afresh our current perspectives..." (Halpin, 1960, p. 284).

Joseph Schwab (1964) pointedly argued that the theory movement reflected a false model both for inquiry and training (pp. 47–70). Leaders, in pursuing the "shapely and will-of-the-wisp" theory for which physics and only physics was famous, Schwab contended, had chosen a false objective. Hypothetico-deductive systems were "visciously abstract"; a more immediate "bread-and-butter" approach was required. Needed was a "master" practitioner model, such as existed in medicine, to replace the false one from physics. Medicine's "theory of practice," he observed, entailed the study of biological science *and* medicine proper: "what diseases and pathologies there are—their symptoms, etiology, causes and treatment." The equivalent in educational administration, Schwab (1964) suggested, would be the study of the school: "the missions it has undertaken—with their failures and successes; the varied structures and patterns it has used, their strengths and weaknesses; the needs and problems of the schools—so far as they are known..." (p. 65).

While most professors in the 1970s adjusted in incremental ways to criticism, Greenfield argued for a more radical reorientation. Speaking to those attending the Third International Intervisitation Programme in Bristol, England, in 1974, he fired a shot at the theory movement that was heard around the world (Greenfield, 1975). Striking hard at the key presuppositions of the theory movement, he precipitated controversy which is not yet ended. In the process he reexpressed in somewhat different terms Harris's 19th-century arguments against positivistic science.

Both Greenfield and Harris stressed that organizations cannot be equated with such objective phenomena as planets and stars. Rather, organizations are social inventions, which humans construe in diverse ways. Organizations do not think, choose, or act as theories claim; rather, individuals do. Nor are organizations regulated by scientific laws; rather, they are guided by human intentions and decisions. Greenfield (1975) stressed that academicians, who assume that "social-scientific secrets" can explain "how organizations work or how policy should be made," indulge "at best in a premature hope and at worst in a delusion" (p. 76). He vehemently rejected the thesis that natural science modes of inquiry can advance the study of human phenomena. As he saw it, mathematized and hypothetico-deductive edifices of theory are futile guides for research in educational administration; inquirers must discover, through qualitative analyses of meaning, how diverse people interpret the organizations in which they live and how these interpretations affect action.

As the 1980s began, Foster (1980) mounted yet another attack on the legitimacy of the theory movement by borrowing and using presuppositions from critical theory. Richard Bates, an Australian professor of educational administration, speaking on "critical theory" at a symposium of the American Educational Research Association in 1982, asserted that "the misconceived and misdirected quest for a behavioral science of educational administration continues" (1982, p. 1). Labeling a popular U.S. textbook on theory as "conservative and anachronistic," Bates declared that its authors remained "blissfully unaware of the widely acknowledged revolutions in science, philosophy and social theory" (p. 1). He proposed that the book's "most remarkable characteristic" was its "total absence of any awareness or discussion of contemporary *educational* issues" (p. 1). It offered a "perfect contemporary illustration" of how theory movement followers tend to "separate administrative issues from educational issues and to ignore the latter" (p. 1). Opponents of the "is-ought" dichotomy, critical theorists see theory and practice as closely related. By demystifying the ideol-

ogies of schooling, these theorists hope to help free individuals from coercive conditions.

Since the mid-1960s, then, diverse forces have eroded the strength of the theory movement. Some school administrators have contended that administrative science is irrelevant to practice; some professors have argued that the theory movement reflects a misguided quest; some researchers, pressed to do policy studies, have rejected logical positivistic theory. A politicized and turbulent environment has enhanced the need for studies on the politics and economics of education; changed research norms have brought anthropological inquiry to the fore. Finally, proponents of phenomenology, led by Greenfield, and of critical theory, led by Foster and Bates, have attacked the root assumptions of the theory movement. Today critical theorists, logical positivists, and phenomenologists all vie for center stage.

As proponents of diverse perspectives compete for the allegiance of scholars, the theory movement in its current embattled state has lost its earlier vitality. At the same time its life does not seem dangerously threatened. Conceptual frameworks and theories are dispersed throughout much of the literature. The author of the most recent text on theory (Silver, 1983), in summarizing more than 200 studies that 12 theories have stimulated and guided, underscored the theory movement's impact. However, the field, as Griffiths (1982) has observed, "has not yet entered the period of post-positivism" (p. 2). The same can be said for the field of organizational inquiry and theory generally (Burrell & Morgan, 1979).

Opponents of the theory movement, through trenchant critiques, have stimulated new thought in the field. However, actual studies that imaginatively make use of the proposed new tenets of inquiry are not yet highly visible. Neither the critical theorists nor the phenomenologists have produced an exemplar comparable to the social-process model developed by the theory movement leader, Jacob Getzels. If the challenge of creating visible and compelling research exemplars is not met, the fruitfulness of the proposed new perspectives on inquiry will remain embedded in abstract concepts. On the other hand, if the adherents of the theory movement continue to ignore post-positivistic concepts of science in rationalizing their inquiry, the downward trend in their influence will persist.

SUMMARY AND CONCLUSIONS

During a century's quest for knowledge, leading scholars of educational administration have constantly worn cloaks of science. However, the fabrics from which the cloaks were cut, the patterns that shaped them, the distinctive styles they reflected, and the societal climate in which they were worn have changed as one era gave way to another. By donning scientific cloaks, scholars have made their inquiry more legitimate and have acquired norms, concepts, and methods to guide their research activities.

What can be said summarily about the shifting meanings of science since 1875? Table 1.1 provides selected information related to this question. During the first period (1875–1900), concepts of speculative science were dominant, but in the next period (1901–1925) positivism prevailed. In the 1967–1985 period, humanistic perspectives came to the fore while scientific views declined; some scholars during the period carefully scrutinized the scientific tenets of logical positivism and turned their backs on it. Since the time when Harris had vehemently rejected the tenets of positivism a century earlier, the field had come full circle.

Views about inquiry have shifted as scientific concepts and societal values have changed (see Table 1.2). For Harris the scope of inquiry in the 1875–1900 period was as broad as civilizations, past and present. On the other hand, logical positivists in the 1951–1966 period addressed more narrowly defined subjects (e.g., conflict). In the 1967–1985 period, reformers, rejecting reductionism, opted for holistic perspectives. As scientific tenets have changed, so have approaches to inquiry. Note in Table 1.2, for example, the periodic moves from deductive to inductive and from inductive to deductive reasoning. Views of "is-ought" relationships in inquiry have also undergone cyclical shifts. In speculative philosophy the "is" and the "ought" were closely connected; thereafter, positivism separated them; pragmatism in turn put them back together; logical positivism subsequently rent them asunder; recently, critical theories have sought once more to reunite them.

While supporting the idea of scientific objectivity, scholars in fact have continually prescribed what organizations and administrators ought to do. Strayer and Cubberley, for example, used the banner of science not only to indicate what expanding school systems ought to do but also to reinforce such values as

Table 1.1   Originators and Diffusers of "Scientific" Perspectives: 1875–1985

PERIOD	ORIGINS OF CONCEPTS	PERSPECTIVES ON SCIENCE	ADAPTERS AND DIFFUSERS
1875–1900	Hegel, Plato, Aristotle	Speculative	Payne, Harris
1901–1925	Comte, Spencer	Positivistic	Rice
1926–1950	Dewey	Pragmatic, Positivistic	Dewey
1951–1966	Vienna Circle scholars	Logical Positivistic	Halpin, Getzels, Griffiths
1967–1985	Kuhn, Husserl, Frankfurt scholars	Post-positivistic, Phenomenological, Critical	Griffiths, Greenfield, Bates, Foster

Table 1.2   The Changing Concepts of Science: Some Distinguishing Characteristics

PERIOD	SCOPE OF INQUIRY	RESEARCH EXEMPLARS	REASONING STRATEGIES
1875–1900	Extremely broad; from the school to the nation and to the comparative study of civilizations	Payne's *Doctrine of Education*; Harris's *Psychologic Foundations of Education*	Deductive, dialectical
1901–1925	Emphasis upon local and state school systems	Rice's time-on-task studies	Inductive
1926–1950	Administrative functions within democratic-human contexts	Mort's study of school system adaptability	Inductive
1951–1966	Administrative and organizational behavior	Getzels's social-process theory and the studies it generated	Deductive
1967–1985	Policy and organizations within social, economic, and political contexts	Reformers have concentrated largely on critique; compelling exemplars not realized	Inductive, dialectic

secularization, social-class "harmony," and efficiency. When logical positivism held sway, some professors did successfully banish most "ought" generalizations from their scholarship; at the same time, however, they prescribed what professors, as inquirers, ought to do. More recently, critical theorists have openly directed their efforts at emancipating "alienated" human beings in "coercive" bureaucracies. As scholars have worn cloaks of science, then, they have sought to advance valued ends and practices.

Scholars have continually looked to the social sciences for means to advance inquiry. Actual use, however, has grown slowly. Although amateur social science was giving way to academic social science at the end of the 19th century, the latter contributed little to the study of school management from 1901 to 1925. In the 1926–1950 period, leading professors used the social sciences both in their research and textbooks. In the next period (1951–1966), social science use flourished. Although critics more recently have sharply rejected social science as defined by the logical positivists, they still support its interpretive and critical use. For a century, then, students of educational administration have viewed the social sciences as helpful allies.

As the concepts of social science have changed, so have the general outcomes of inquiry and the modes for validating knowledge (see Table 1.3). It is also true that definitions of administration have changed in each of the periods studied. Classroom management was highlighted in the 1875–1900 period. From 1901 to 1925,

the concept of administration as a general function came to the fore. In the second quarter of the 20th century, specialized functions of administration became focuses for inquiry. In the 1951–1966 era, the concept of administration *qua* administration guided inquiry and theory development. More recently, diverse definitions of administration have prevailed as scholars have pursued pluralistic approaches to inquiry.

The ever-present but changing concepts of science pose a significant question: Why have scholars for a hundred years continuously reformulated its meanings? Even though Kuhn's theory was directed at science per se and, therefore, cannot be applied wholesale to the professional field of educational administration, his thesis that the belief systems of scholarly communities play a critical role in the changing of paradigms has import for the question's answer. However, a more precise answer is dependent upon a delineation of the differences which distinguish a scientist (e.g., a professor of physics or chemistry) from a professor of educational administration.

Scientists, as scholars, work in very different environments than do professors of educational administration. The latter, in contrast to the former, need to maintain links with many knowledge communities; in addition, they must connect with practitioners and with societal developments if they are to avoid the "grievous errors," to use Harris's phrase (1886a, p. 492) of viewing administration too narrowly. Thus, they are susceptible to many influences that emanate from many interconnected communities—communities

Table 1.3   Social Science, Professional Knowledge, and Modes of Validation

PERIOD	SOCIAL SCIENCE ROLES	GOALS OF KNOWLEDGE	MODES OF VALIDATION
1875–1900	Amateur social science used; education viewed as the major domain of social science	Generalizations emanating from speculative philosophy	Generalizations validated by processes of "pure reason"
1901–1925	Use of academic social science proposed; (actual use limited; closest links with psychology)	Laws establishing relationships; ("principles" that combined facts and value judgments actually realized)	Scientific methods used to analyze sense data concerning objects, properties, and relationships in the real world
1926–1950	Professors used concepts from social psychology, sociology, anthropology, and political science in their scholarship	Generalizations to make practice less routine and more rational; ("principles" still prevailed)	Well-conceived hypotheses that have met the test of effective problem-solving
1951–1966	Social science professors played leading roles in the study of administration and organization	Scientifically confirmed empirical laws; (goal not usually realized)	Hypotheses derived from theory and operationally tested to confirm or disconfirm them
1967–1984	Reformers rejected positivistic social science but accepted "critical" and "interpretive" social science	Interpretive generalizations and those denoting critique compete with scientific ones	Coherence of interpretive generalizations and of reasoned critiques

from which scientists are largely isolated. This means that scholars of natural science can concentrate on studying reality as it is. However, professors of educational administration, as events of the previous century have demonstrated, cannot escape the demands for detached scholarship on the actualities of administration *and* for the advocacy of desired policy.

Why then have scientific conceptions affecting scholarship during the last century undergone periodic change? In brief, scholarship has incessantly responded to the shifting norms of the diverse communities to which professors of educational administration are linked. Since knowledge is infused with the norms of the society to which it is connected, it has a distinctively social character. An analysis, for example, of the norms that reinforced the extensive use of the survey method in the 1900–1925 period or the enhanced use of ethnographic methods in the 1970s would reveal that they and the findings they produced were consonant with values shared by practitioners, societal leaders, and other groups in the respective periods. Shifting and diverse values help shape both the questions posed and the methods used in inquiry. Conceptions of science are also consonant with the prevailing *Zeitgeists* of given eras.

Given the social character of knowledge in the field, another significant question arises: Namely, what knowledge, if any, survives a given era and finds use in successive periods? First, it is worth noting that in the mid-1980s, in contrast to 1875, there is an extensive body of knowledge available for use. Inquiry now, in contrast to 1875, is supported by an enormous infrastructure of journals, books, publishing houses, university departments with full-time professors, doctoral programs, certification standards, and professional associations. In the last century's quest for knowledge, many trends can be discerned, including the following: a move from administration as an art toward the concept of administration as a science; a move from the time when scholar-practitioners were the dominant researchers to today, when hundreds of professors are the major inquirers; a move from stylishly written essays to more technically written articles and books; a move from the first books whose references were limited largely to Latin phrases and poetic quotes to today's books, which include extensive bibliographies; a move from general to more specialized knowledge; a move from descriptions of experience to theories of administration; and a move from the time when the school survey was the dominant means of inquiry to today, when diverse means are available.

The flow of knowledge from one period to another is affected by both positive and negative influences. Those creating new norms tend to sharply criticize, downgrade, and reject previous ones and, thereby, negatively influence idea flow. Leaders of the theory movement, for instance, denounced the dominant role of "naked empiricism" in research. Or, while Payne could enthusiastically endorse the use of Compayre's history of education in the 1880s, Cubberley, early in the 20th century, found the work lacking. Or, while Harris effectively applied Hegelian philosophy to many educational problems in the final quarter of the 19th century, Dewey, in formulating a philosophy for the 20th century, found Harris's views conservative if not anachronistic. Scholars, by rejecting the norms they are seeking to replace, brake the flow of ideas from one era to another.

Paradoxically, however, individuals who shape scientific norms for a given period are dependent upon ideas developed previously. Greenfield drew upon the long tradition of idealistic thought, as did Harris. Theory movement leaders drew upon logical positivistic ideas articulated earlier by Vienna Circle scholars, who in turn were dependent upon their predecessors. Since scholars who create new norms of inquiry inevitably use ideas from the past, they also enhance the flow of ideas from one historical context to another.

In examining the issue of the survival of knowledge, it is useful to distinguish between and among the norms that guide inquiry, the research modes used, and the content produced. As already noted, the norms of science are fickle. The survival rate of modes of research, however, is relatively high. Even today some investigators use the survey method to study problems in school districts; further, adapted uses of surveys can be found even in dissertations. To be sure, many reject the survey, especially its sloppy use; however, it still survives.

In the third quarter of the 20th century, scholars developed statistical methods that went far beyond those used by Strayer; both types are still in use. Professors of educational administration acquired from the social sciences sociometric methods, Q-sort techniques, ecco analysis, reputational techniques, projective methods, participant observation, simulation models, and other means of inquiry. In the 1970s they acquired techniques related to organizational development, knowledge utilization, ethnographic inquiry, futures study, evaluation, and policy research. Since all these means (and others) can in theory be used, they constitute a part of the field's accumulated knowledge. The high survival rate of research methods and techniques is supported in part by a diverse and specialized professoriate and by the fact that new norms of inquiry tend to affect research at the growing edge of the field while even the most obsolescent techniques (by modern standards) persist.

The survival rate of knowledge as content is higher than that of the norms that influence it; however, the research methods and techniques, which help produce it, survive much more easily. Thus, the dialectical method Harris employed is still used 100 years later; however, his ideas on the science of management have had limited influence on 20th-century thinking. Although the survey method survives, survey studies on state and city school systems, used in the training programs of the 1901–1925 period, are now of value only to historians. The same is true for the "ought" principles: those deduced from philosophy à la Harris; early 20th-century ones that loosely linked facts and values; or later ones deduced from normative theory or found in the "human relations" literature. "Nakedly empirical" generalizations of the past, based upon questionnaire findings or case studies, have also faded into history.

What about the flow of knowledge across national boundaries? Theories of organization are diffused more easily transnationally than are more specific types of content (e.g., school law). Since theories, by definition, do not explicitly confront national "oughts," they meet international tests of use better than do more specific types of knowledge. International interest in developing and sharing ideas on epistemology also prevails.

To what degree are general theories of organization time-bound? Even though critics have attacked current theories and their uses, not only have those theories survived but they are in widespread use. However, developments over the last 100 years should raise cautions about forecasting their long-range survival. Such caution is reinforced by the fact that extant theories are much more the products of the scholarly imagination than they are the tested products of science. Empirical work has lagged far behind theory formulation.

During the last century, then, even in the face of the shifting norms of science, scholars have accumulated many methods and much content. Throughout a century's quest for knowledge, the high aspirations expressed by Superintendent Payne in 1875 for a science to guide educational administration remain. To be sure, today's critics actively denounce the concepts of science that reigned during the 1951–1966 period. At the same time, however, phenomenologists argue for "interpretive" uses of social science; and critical theorists, in calling themselves "critical scientists," maintain rhetorical links with science. Thus, even the opponents of modern science cannot escape entirely from its deep and continuing influence on scholarship. After a century's pursuit of knowledge, scholars of educational administration still look to science, with its multifaceted and changing definitions, for a legitimizing

cloak, facilitator of inquiry, and a tool to be used in the *continuing* quest for knowledge about the ends, means, and settings of a very complex social process.

REFERENCES

Adams, C. F., Jr. (1880). The development of the superintendency. *Addresses and Proceedings of the National Educational Association.* 61–76.
Adams, C. F., Jr. (1916). *Charles Francis Adams: 1835–1915.* Boston: Houghton Mifflin.
Bates, R. J. (1982). *Toward a critical practice of educational administration.* Paper presented at a meeting of the American Educational Research Association, New York.
Bernstein, R. J. (1976). *The restructuring of social and political theory.* New York: Harcourt, Brace.
Buckingham, B. R. (1920). Announcement. *Journal of Educational Research, I*(1), 1–4.
Bowyer, C. H. (1970). *Philosophical perspectives for education.* New York: Scott Foresman.
Burrell, G., & Morgan, G. (1979). *Sociological paradigms and sociological analysis.* London: Heinemann.
Callahan, R. E. (1966). *The superintendent of schools: A historical analysis.* St. Louis: Graduate Institute of Education, Washington University.
Campbell, R. F., Corbally, J. E., Jr., & Ramseyer, J. A. (1962). *Introduction to educational administration.* Boston: Allyn and Bacon.
Campbell, R. F., & Gregg, R. (Eds.). (1957). *Administrative behavior in education.* New York: Harper.
Coleman, J. S. (1972). *Policy research in the social sciences.* Morristown, NJ: General Learning Press.
Comte, A. (1974). *Discours sur l'esprit positif.* Paris: Librairie Philosophique, J. Vrin, Classic Edition.
Courtis, S. A., & Packer, P. C. (1920). Educational research. *Journal of Educational Research, I*(1), 5–19.
Cremin, L. A. (1965). *The wonderful world of Ellwood Patterson Cubberley.* New York: Bureau of Publications, Teachers College, Columbia University.
Cremin, L. A., Shannon, D. A., & Townsend, M. E. (1954). *A history of Teachers College.* New York: Columbia University Press.
Cubberley, E. P. (1909). *Changing conceptions of education.* New York: Houghton Mifflin.
Cubberley, E. P. (1924). Public school administration. In I. L. Kandel (Ed.), *Twenty-five years of American education.* New York: Macmillan.
Culbertson, J. A. (1981). Antecedents of the theory movement. *Educational Administration Quarterly, 15*(1), 25–47.
Culbertson, J. A. (1983). Theory in educational administration: Echoes from critical thinkers. *Educational Researcher, 34*(10), 15–22.
Curti, M. (1974). *The social ideas of American educators.* Totowa, NJ: Littlefield Adams.
Dewey, J. (1885). Education and the health of women. *Science, 6*(41), 341–342.
Dewey, J. (1980). *The school and society.* Carbondale and Edwardsville, IL: Southern Illinois Press. (Original work published 1899).
Dewey, J. (1910). *How we think.* New York: Heath.
Dewey, J. (1929). *The sources of a science of education.* New York: Liveright.
Dutton, S. T., & Snedden, D. (1908). *The administration of public education in the United States.* New York: Macmillan.
Elliott, C. E. (1910). University Courses in Educational Administration. In F. E. Spaulding, W. P. Burris, & C. E. Elliott, *The Aims, Scope, and Methods of a University Course in Public School Administration.* Indianapolis, IN: National Society for

College Teachers of Education.

Erickson, D. A. (1977). An overdue paradigm shift in educational administration, or how can we get that idiot off the freeway? In L. L. Cunningham, W. G. Hack, & R. O. Nystrand (Eds.), *Educational administration: The developing decades.* Berkeley, CA: McCutchan.

Foster, W. P. (1980). Administration and the crisis in legitimacy: A review of Habermasian thought. *Harvard Educational Review, 50*(6), 496–505.

Getzels, J. W. (1952). A psycho-sociological framework for the study of educational administration. *Harvard Educational Review, 22*(4), 235–246.

Getzels, J. W. (1958). Administration as a social process. In A. W. Halpin (Ed.), *Administrative theory in education.* Chicago: The Midwest Center, University of Chicago.

Greenfield, T. B. (1975). Theory about organization: A new perspective and its implications for schools. In M. Hughes (Ed.), *Administering education: International challenge.* London: Athlone.

Griffiths, D. E. (1956). *Human relations in school administration.* New York: Appleton-Century-Crofts.

Griffiths, D. E. (1957). Toward a theory of administrative behavior. In R. F. Campbell & R. Gregg (Eds.), *Administrative behavior in education.* New York: Harper.

Griffiths, D. E. (1959). *Administrative theory.* New York: Appleton-Century-Crofts.

Griffiths, D. E. (1979). Intellectual turmoil in educational administration. *Educational Administration Quarterly, 13*(3), 43–65.

Griffiths, D. E. (1982). *Theories: Past, present and future.* Paper presented at the Fifth International Intervisitation Program, Lagos, Nigeria.

Gulick, L., & Urwick, L. (Eds.). (1937). *Papers on the science of administration.* New York: Institute of Public Administration, Columbia University.

Halpin, A. W. (1955). The leader behavior and leadership ideology of educational administrators and aircraft commanders. *Harvard Educational Review, 25,* 18–32.

Halpin, A. W. (1957). A paradigm for research on administrator behavior. In R. F. Campbell & R. Gregg (Eds.), *Administrative behavior in education.* New York: Harper.

Halpin, A. W. (1958). The development of theory in educational administration. In A. W. Halpin (Ed.), *Administrative theory in education.* Chicago: The Midwest Center, University of Chicago.

Halpin, A. W. (1960). Ways of knowing. In R. F. Campbell & J. M. Lipham (Eds.), *Administrative theory as a guide to action.* Chicago: The Midwest Center, University of Chicago.

Halpin, A. W. (1970). The fumbled torch. In A. Kroll (Ed.), *Issues in American education.* New York: Oxford.

Hanson, N. R. (1969). Positivism and the logic of scientific theories. In P. Achenstein & S. F. Barker (Eds.), *The legacy of logical positivism.* Baltimore: Johns Hopkins University Press.

Hanus, P. (1910). Editorial notes. *School Review, 18,* 426–427.

Harris, W. T. (1867). Herbert Spencer. *Journal of Speculative Philosophy, 1,* 6–21.

Harris, W. T. (1879). The science of education. *Journal of Speculative Philosophy, 8*(2), 205–214.

Harris, W. T. (1886a). Method of pedagogical inquiry. *The Journal of Proceedings and Addresses of the National Education Association,* 493–503.

Harris, W. T. (1886b). Methodical education in the social sciences. *Journal of Social Sciences,* 13–24.

Harris, W. T. (1898). *Psychologic foundations of education: An attempt to show the genesis of the higher faculties of the mind.* New York: Appleton.

Haskell, T. L. (1977). *The emergence of professional social science.* Urbana, IL: University of Illinois Press.

Hill, D. S. (1916). Meeting the demands for the practical in educational research. *Educational Administration and Supervision, 2,* 572–578.

Hull, C. L., Ross, C. I., Hall, R. T., Perkins, D. T., & Fitch, F. B. (1940). *Mathematico-deductive theory of rote learning.* New Haven: Yale University Press.

Joergensen, J. (1951). The development of logical empiricism. *International Encyclopedia of Unified Science, 2*(9), 1–100.

Kasson, F. H. (1888). William Torrey Harris, L.L.D.: His intellectual growth and his educational and philosophic work. *Education, 8*(10), 619–630.

Kraft, V. (1953). *The Vienna circle.* New York: Philosophical Library.

Kuhn, T. S. (1962). The structure of scientific revolutions. *International Encyclopedia of Unified Science* (1st ed.), *2*(2), 1–210.

Leidecker, K. F. (1946). *Yankee teacher: The life of William Torrey Harris.* New York: Philosophical Library.

Lenzer, G. (1975). *Auguste Comte and positivism.* New York: Harper Torchbooks.

Lewes, G. H. (1890). *Comte's philosophy of sciences.* London: George Ball.

Lewin, K. (1938). The conceptual representation and the measurement of psychological forces. *Contributions to psychological theory.* Durham, NC: Duke University Press.

Lincoln, Y. S. (1985). *Organization theory and inquiry: The paradigm revolution.* Beverly Hills: Sage.

Maxwell, W. H. (1891). The literature of education. *Education Review, 2,* 322–334.

McCall, M. W., Jr., & Lombardo, M.M. (Eds.). (1978). *Leadership: Where else can we go?* Durham, NC: Duke University Press.

Merton, R. K. (1949). *Social theory and social structure.* Glencoe, IL: Free Press.

Moehlman, A. B. (1938). *Social interpretation.* New York: Appleton.

Moehlman, A.B. (1951). *School administration* (2nd ed.). Cambridge, MA: Riverside.

Morrow, J., Foster, R., & Estes, N. (1974). *The urban school superintendent of the future.* Durant, OK: Southeastern Foundation.

Mort, P. R. (1924). *The measurement of educational aid: Basis for distribution of state aid.* New York: Teachers College, Columbia University.

Mort, P. R. (1935). Organization for effective educational research in colleges and universities. *Teachers College Record, 36*(7), 541– 558.

Mort, P. R., & Cornell, F. G. (1938). *Adaptability of public school systems.* New York: Bureau of Publications, Teachers College, Columbia University.

National Education Association. (1885). Report on pedagogics. *The Journal of Proceedings and Addresses of the National Educational Association,* 42–57.

Neurath, O. (1973). Wissenschaftliche Weltauffassung: Der Wiener Kreis. In M. Neurath & R. S. Cohen, *Empiricism and sociology.* Dordrecht, Holland: Reidel.

Newlon, J. H. (1934). George Drayton Strayer: An appreciation. *School Executive Magazine, 49,* 451–453.

O'Neil, J. (Ed.). (1976). *On critical theory.* New York: Seabury.

Payne, W. H. (1875). *Chapters on school supervision.* New York: Wilson, Hinkle.

Payne, W. H. (1882). *Outlines of educational doctrine.* New York: Harper.

Payne, W. H. (1886). *Contributions to the science of education.* New York: Harper.

Popper, K. R. (1959). *Objective knowledge: An evolutionary approach.* Oxford: Oxford University Press.

Poret, G. C. (1930). *The contributions of William Harold Payne to public education.* Nashville, TN: George Peabody College for Teachers, 81.

Reller, T. L. (1935). *The development of the city superintendency of schools in the United States.* Philadelphia: Published by the author.

Rice, J. M. (1896). Obstacles to rational educational reform. *The Forum, 22,* 385–395.

Rice, J. M. (1897). The futility of the spelling grind. *The Forum, 23,* 162–172.

Rice, J. M. (1902). Educational research. *The Forum, 34,* 117–130.

Rice, J. M. (1912). *Scientific management in education.* New York: Publishing Printing Company.

Roethlisberger, F. J., & Dickson, W. J. (1939). *Management and the worker.* Cambridge, MA: Harvard University Press.

Russell, J. E. (1937). *Founding Teachers College: Reminiscences of the dean emeritus.* New York: Bureau of Publications, Teachers College, Columbia University.

Salmon, L. M. (1896). Some political principles applied to education. *Educational Review, 11,* 220–232.

Schilpp, P. A. (Ed.). (1967). *The philosophy of Karl Popper.* La Salle, IL: The Library of Living Philosophers, *14*(1).

Schwab, J. J. (1964). The professorship in educational administration: Theory-art-practice. In D. J. Willower & J. A. Culbertson (Eds.), *The professorship in educational administration.* Columbus, OH: University Council for Educational Administration.

Scriven, M. (1969). Logical positivism and the behavioral sciences. In P. Achenstein & S. F. Barker (Eds.), *The legacy of logical positivism.* Baltimore: Johns Hopkins University Press.

Sears, J. B. (1922). Techniques of the public school survey. *Journal of Educational Research, 6,* 281–299.

Sears, J. B. (1925). *The school survey.* Boston: Houghton Mifflin.

Sears, J. B. (1938). *City school administrative controls.* New York: McGraw-Hill.

Sears, J. B. (1950). *The nature of the administrative process.* New York: McGraw-Hill.

Sears, J. B. (1959). *Jesse Brundage Sears: An autobiography.* Palo Alto, CA: Published by the author.

Sears, J. B., & Henderson, A. D. (1957). *Cubberley of Stanford and his contributions to American education.* Stanford, CA: Stanford University Press.

Shaplin, J. T. (1964). The professorship in educational administration: Attracting talented personnel. In D. J. Willower & J. A. Culbertson (Eds.), *The professorship in educational administration.* Columbus, OH: University Council for Educational Administration.

Silver, P. F. (1983). *Educational administration: Theoretical perspectives on practice and research.* New York: Harper & Row.

Simon, H. A. (1945). *Administrative behavior.* New York: Macmillan.

Spaulding, F. E., Burris, W. P., & Elliot, E. C. (1910). *The aims, scope and methods of a university course in public school administration.* Indianapolis, IN: National Society for College Teachers of Education.

Spencer, H. (1910). *Essays: Scientific, political, and speculative* (Vol. II). New York: Appleton.

Strayer, G. D. (1925). Professional training for superintendents of schools. *Teachers College Record, 26*(10), 815–826.

Susman, G. I., & Evered, R. D. (1978). An assessment of the scientific merits of action research. *Administrative Science Quarterly, 23,* 582–603.

Taylor, F. W. (1895). A piece-rate system, being a step toward a partial solution of the labor problem. *Transactions of the American Society of Mechanical Engineers, 16,* 856–892.

Thompson, J. D., Hammond, P. B., Hawkes, R. W., Junker, B. H., & Tuden, A. (1959). *Comparative studies in administration.* Pittsburgh: University of Pittsburgh Press.

Toulmin, S. E. (1969). From logical analysis to conceptual history. In P. Achenstein & S. F. Barker (Eds.), *The legacy of logical positivism.* Baltimore: Johns Hopkins University Press.

Travers, R. M. W. (1983). *How research has changed America's schools.* Kalamazoo, MI: Mythos.

Wiebe, R. H. (1967). *The search for order: 1877–1920.* New York: Hill and Wang.

Wolcott, H. (1973). *The man in the principal's office.* New York: Holt, Rinehart, Winston.

Yauch, W. A. (1949). *Human relations in school administration.* New York: Harper.

CHAPTER 2
Administrative Theory

Daniel E. Griffiths

The study of administrative theory in education is of relatively recent origin. Although Cubberley (1916) is sometimes considered to be the first to try his hand, it is generally acknowledged that the first major treatise was that of Mort (1946). He undertook to develop a system of principles based upon common-sense value judgments. The result was not a system but rather a collection of principles, several of which were contradictory. Mort introduced a concept of "balanced judgment" as an aid to mediating the contradictions.

The first effort to relate the classical writers in administration—Fayol, Gulick, Taylor, and Urwick—to educational administration was by Sears (1950). His view was that administration derives its nature from the essence of the services it directs. Sears should be considered as an advocate of adjectival administration rather than of administration as a general concept.

During this time period (1946–1950) there were three developments that were organizational in nature but that had a powerful impact on the development of administrative theory. These developments, in fact, gave form to what was later called "the theory movement."

THE ADMINISTRATIVE THEORY MOVEMENT: HISTORY AND ANALYSIS

In 1946 members of an advisory committee on education projects (Paul Hanna, Ralph Tyler, and Maurice

Consultant/reviewers: Bryce Fogarty (deceased) and Donald J. Willower, Pennsylvania State University

Seay) successfully recommended to the W. K. Kellogg Foundation that it support projects in educational administration as a major way of improving community life. In 1947 the American Association of School Administrators (AASA) accepted a recommendation from its Planning Committee "to influence the training of superintendents on university campuses and in other areas by taking an active part in standardizing preparatory courses for school administration" (Moore, 1957, p. 2). The third development was the formation in 1947 of the National Conference of Professors of Educational Administration (NCPEA). Moore (1957) summarized these developments as follows:

> These were the three most important ingredients in the movement which was to follow: a foundation interested in community uplift and aware of the key role of the school administrator in the process; a profession of practicing administrators speaking through their national association in vague, yet sincere, terms about their hopes for "future professionalism"; and a rapidly developing unity and purpose among professors and researchers in the field of school administration. The three forces came together in point of time, and the result was rapid acceleration in building a profession of lofty stature. (p. 3)

While Moore's chronology and correlations were correct, and the institutional structure to undergird the theory movement was in place, his prophecy has yet to come to pass.

At the time there was also a considerable amount of related activity in disciplines other than education. Among the universities and research centers engaged in inquiry into administration were the Graduate School of Business Administration at Harvard, the Yale Labor and Management Center, the Research Center for Group Dynamics at the University of Michigan, and the Personnel Research Board at The Ohio State University. These centers were making contributions to research and theory that changed the nature of the literature of administration. The early 1950s became a period in which the context of administration was one of excitement, of new ideas, and of support on the greatest scale ever.

The Kellogg Foundation and the AASA joined forces and created the Cooperative Program in Educational Administration (CPEA), which operated through eight university centers. Several of the CPEA centers brought in social scientists, generally as consultants, to advise on theory, research, and, in some cases, training. Several social scientists were sent by these centers to Denver for the 1954 NCPEA meeting. They were highly articulate and, in many cases, charismatic individuals who had a message to give:

1. Better research into educational administration was needed.
2. The research must be theory based.
3. Social science was the source of the theories.
4. The social scientists were the ones who could guide the professors of educational administration.

They were also deeply critical of the substance of educational administration, particularly its lack of a theoretical base. Most prominent among these social scientists were Jacob Getzels (University of Chicago), Andrew Halpin (The Ohio State University), and Arthur Coladarci (Stanford University). They were extremely effective in spreading "the word," converting virtually everyone in attendance.

Coladarci and Getzels, largely as an outgrowth of the 1954 NCPEA meeting, wrote *The Use of Theory in Educational Administration* (1955), a devastatingly critical analysis of educational administration as a field of study. It was, however, John Walton (1955), a former superintendent of schools and a professor of educational administration, who wrote the most critical and accurate analysis of the current state of affairs in educational administration:

> The subject matter of educational administration is not a thing of intellectual beauty. Borrowing fragments from several diverse disciplines—law, political science, social psychology, sociology, economics, business, education, engineering, architecture, and statistics—it lacks a well-defined, highly organized body of subject matter; it has no elegant and simple theoretical structure; and as literature it is singularly devoid of aesthetic qualities. In

addition to the fragments appropriated from other disciplines, the content of the courses in administration has consisted of a description of practices, the cautious recommendation of promising techniques, personal success stories, and lively anecdotes, all surrounded with the aura of common sense, and often purveyed by a more or less successful administrator. However helpful this approach has been to the prospective administrator, it has not done much for the development of the subject.

> The mounting interest in the theoretical aspects of educational administration indicates a dissatisfaction with the traditional study of the subject and a desire to formulate a rubric of administrative doctrine, if not a scientific theory. (p. 169)

The criticisms were followed in remarkably short time by substantive theoretical articles and books. Griffiths's *Human Relations in School Administration*, an application of social science research to school administration, appeared in 1956. The NCPEA-sponsored *Administrative Behavior in Education* (Campbell & Gregg) was published in 1957. This volume, a compilation of research and theory, as well as chapters on issues in educational administration, clearly marked a movement away from traditional literature in school administration.

Halpin edited (1958) a collection of papers given at the first University Council for Educational Administration (UCEA) career seminar held at the University of Chicago in 1957. Four of the chapters could be termed "announcements" to professors of educational administration of lines of inquiry. Getzels (in Halpin, 1958) described administration as a social process in which behavior was conceived as a function of both the nomothetic and the idiographic dimensions of a social system and reported on two studies that employed his model. Hemphill (in Halpin, 1958) described administration as a process of solving mutual problems. He introduced the concept of a leader as one who initiates structure-in-interaction in a group, a concept he had developed earlier. Griffiths (in Halpin, 1958) developed the idea that decision making is the central function of the administrator. Parsons (in Halpin, 1958) presented some ideas relevant to a theory of formal organizations. The four lines of inquiry, which had been begun prior to the publication of Halpin's book, were to be the major focuses of research attention in subsequent years. Halpin laid out the ground rules for acceptable theory. He advocated the use of Feigl's definition which, while rather narrow, is relatively clear and concise: "a set of assumptions from which can be derived by purely logico-mathematical procedures, a larger set of empirical laws" (in Halpin, 1958, p. 8).

The only major report of theoretically based

research to appear at this time was by Gross, Mason, and McEachern (1958). They conducted a field test of hypotheses derived from role theory, and found the theory to be somewhat less than fruitful. Griffiths's (1959) small volume *Administrative Theory* was an enlarged presentation of his decision-based thesis presented at the UCEA seminar.

The last volume to appear that can properly be considered a major work in the theory movement was Part II of The 63rd Yearbook of the National Society for the Study of Education(NSSE), entitled *Behavioral Science and Educational Administration* (Griffiths, 1964). The book was an attempt to describe new developments in educational administration and interpret them to workers in the field of education. It can be considered a summary of the theory movement.

The core ideas of the theory movement have been identified by Culbertson (1983, p. 15):

1. Statements about what administrators and organizations ought to do cannot be encompassed in science or theory.
2. Scientific theories treat phenomena as they are.
3. Effective research has its origins in theory and is guided by theory.
4. Hypothetic-deductive systems are the best exemplars of theory.
5. The use of the social sciences is essential in theory development and training.
6. Administration is best viewed as a generic concept applicable to all types of organizations.

These ideas, according to Culbertson, were best presented in Halpin (1958), and he credited the first five to positivism, contending that they came into the literature of administration by way of Simon's *Administrative Behavior* (1945).

To the above list should be added the concept of operationalism. Halpin, in particular, made a great deal of Bridgman's (1927) concept of operationalism, contending that it was the antidote to fuzzy concepts, one of the generally accepted weaknesses in the literature of educational administration.

The question of why the theory movement developed in educational administration is, and was, rarely asked. It was raised, however, by McClellan (1960), whose interest in the question was roused during a visit to Europe and the Soviet Union. As he stated: "During my travels I came to dread the inevitable question: 'What are the most exciting developments in educational theory?'" (p. 210). A professor of philosophy of education, he appeared embarrassed to have to reply that educational administration had the most sophisticated body of literature that was clearly theoretical. McClellan summarized his answer to why the theory movement developed:

I have argued that three conditions must be understood if we are to account for the rapid rise of interest in basic research and, more particularly, theory construction in educational administration. First is the unique place of the administrator in developing a national system of education in this country and the identification with the role of administrator by those who occupy positions of authority and responsibility in our schools. Second is the fact that the professional training of administrators occurs in an academic environment where able and ambitious men are forced to come to terms with academic standards of validity and elegance in what they teach and write, this condition being true not only of education but of all fields of administration. Third is the appearance of powerful theoretical models in other disciplines that can be applied, at least in principle, to various aspects of administration. (p. 217)

One more development must be added to McClellan's list: the introduction of different kinds of people into educational administration. The simplest way to illustrate this is to compare two NSSE yearbooks: the 1946 volume, *Changing Conceptions in Educational Administration* (Grace, 1946), and the 1964 book, *Behavioral Science and Educational Administration* (Griffiths, 1964). The 1946 tome can best be typified as the high-water mark of insularity in educational administration. The authors were all educationists, men who had spent their lives as professional educators. They gave no evidence of being influenced by the work of scholars in philosophy, history, and the behavioral sciences. References to theory are completely missing, references to research nearly so. In contrast the 1964 book was authored by a variety of scholars: professors of educational administration, sociology, psychology, business administration, political science, history, and administration. The volume is replete with references to theory and reports of research. It is hard to imagine how two books written on the same subject over a span of 18 years could be so different. The differences can largely be accounted for by the fact that the people involved in each were so different.

Between 1964 and 1974, which, it will be argued, was the effective terminal point of the theory movement, there were contradictory developments. On the one hand, there were positive results of the theory movement, while on the other there was a mounting volume of criticism of the basic premises and practices of the movement.

The *Administrators' Notebook*, published in 1952 by the Midwest Administration Center at the University of Chicago, was the first of several publications devoted to reports of theory-based research. It anticipated the theory movement and, in part, laid some of the groundwork. Its advent was followed, in 1964, by the appearance of the *Educational Administration*

Quarterly (EAQ), published by the UCEA and devoted to scholarly inquiry into administrator behavior in complex organizations.

A marked change in the content of textbooks was readily apparent:

1. *Organizing Schools for Effective Education* (Griffiths, Clark, Wynn, & Iannaccone, 1962) was a report of field research based on a number of theories of formal and informal organizations.

2. An outstanding example of the change in content was found in Getzels, Lipham, and Campbell (1968) in which the authors presented a social process model of administration and brought together all the published and unpublished research deriving from this model. In this instance, an entire book was written using research and theory derived from a specific model.

3. Many textbooks gave theory token acknowledgment, generally by having a single chapter devoted to the subject. No textbook, however, was without at least a reference to the theory movement.

While no one could say that the theory movement produced a flood of theory-based research, there was enough to sustain the *EAQ*, to warrant lengthy reviews in the *Encyclopedia of Educational Research* (Boyan, 1982; Griffiths, 1969), and others such as Hughes (1985) and Ribbins (1985), to produce more than 200 proposals for presentation annually at the American Educational Research Association (AERA). It is also clear that doctoral dissertations in educational administration were influenced by the central ideas of the theory movement, almost to the complete exclusion of other approaches. As Culbertson (1983) has said of the achievements of the theory movement, it produced "a range of theories, developed largely by social scientists [that] are now widely used in preparatory programs in new types of textbooks, and these theories have met the pragmatic tests of producing inquiry and learning" (p. 21).

The productive part of the theory movement was accompanied, almost from the beginning, by sharp and pointed criticism. Selecting critiques by Graff, Street, Kimborough, & Dykes (1966), Greenfield (1975), Halpin (1970), Halpin and Hayes (1977), Harlow (1962), Hills (1965), Schwab (1964), Trow (1959), Culbertson (1983) summarized these criticisms in this way:

> Critics who have addressed the theory movement as a general phenomenon have produced negative conclusions about the movement's goals, the models it implied for research and training, and the effectiveness of its implementation. Scholars have directed trenchant criticisms at all six of the movement's core ideas, whereas the most prominent criticism of the presuppositions underlying them has come from a phenomenological perspective. Specific theories, although not addressed in this paper, have also attracted critical reactions. (p. 21)

In addition, even operationalism was found wanting (Scriven, 1969).

While the theory movement had been in decline for a number of years (see especially Halpin, 1970), the demise came at the 1974 meeting of the International Intervisitation Programme (IIP) in Bristol, England. The coup de grace was delivered by Greenfield (1975) who made an across-the-board denunciation of every aspect of the theory movement. He followed this with a number of papers that refined and changed his arguments, the most important of which was published in the *International Encyclopedia of Educational Administration* (Greenfield, 1984). Although the first paper was largely an exposition of a phenomenological approach to organizations, the second mentions the word phenomenology only once (Greenfield, 1984, p. 16).

Greenfield hit hard at the theorists—largely Halpin, Griffiths, Getzels, Simon, and March—because they split values off from facts. He contended that this resulted in descriptions of organizations that were lifeless, and that theory based only on facts devoid of values was of no use to administrators. This led, in part, to Greenfield's contention that the theory movement had produced little of consequence to practitioners. He also attacked the Getzels-Guba social system model on the ground that goals and roles were taken as given and were never questioned. He focused on system theory as an object of severe criticism on several scores: systems as "natural" phenomena and, therefore, seen to be "real"; social scientists anthropomorphizing organizations through the system metaphor; systems imposing themselves on the people in them; and the notion that "system" can be equated with "organization."

The major thrust of Greenfield's critique is, however, none of the above; rather, it is epistemological. The first sentence of the published version of Greenfield's Bristol speech (Greenfield, 1975) is the basic theme of his critique: "In common parlance we speak of organizations as if they were real" (p. 71). He then attempts to demonstrate that such is not the case and contends that organizations are "invented social reality" (p. 81). He thus argues that there are two schools of thought—one that views social reality as a natural system and the other that regards it as a human invention—and that the two views have significant and far-reaching consequences for researchers and practitioners.

The Greenfield critique has been hailed in the British Commonwealth countries and largely ignored in the United States. Probably the major reason why Greenfield did not catch on in the United States is that his arguments are too extreme and too inclusive. Further, there is no consistent line of argument in his papers except an attack on the theory movement. In addition, his work has resulted in little, if any, empirical research. Ignoring the critique is unfortunate because what Greenfield did was to tell professors of educational administration that the social sciences are undergoing tremendous changes and that the philosophical and methodological bases on which the theory movement was founded (logical positivism) are now considered by most philosophers of science, and many social scientists, to be outmoded (Griffiths, 1979). (For a chronological listing of statements and/or events that contributed to the theory movement, see Table 2.1.)

Summary

What, in retrospect, did the theory movement accomplish? Even a perfunctory comparison of the literature prior to 1954 with that which followed reveals a great difference in vocabulary. The language of administration has changed. More people from disciplines other than administration, or from professions other than education, are writing and talking about educational administration. For better or worse, depending upon the protagonist, the nature of doctoral dissertations has changed: They are almost exclusively in the mode of Culbertson's core ideas undergirding the theory movement plus extensive use of operationalism. Participants in the National Graduate Student Seminars sponsored

Table 2.1 Major Developments in the Theory Movement

Kellogg Foundation (1946)

AASA Action (1947)

NCPEA (1947)

CPEA (1950)

Denver Meeting NCPEA (1954)

Walton (1955)

Coladarci & Getzels (1955)

Griffiths (1956)

Campbell & Gregg (1957)

Chicago Theory Seminar (1957)

Halpin (1958)

Gross (1958)

Griffiths (1959)

Griffiths (1964)

Educational Administration Quarterly (1964)

Getzels, Lipham, & Campbell (1968)

IIP (1974)

by the National Institute of Education and AREA in the 1980s have noted that the students have exhibited increasing interest in qualitative research, with some also showing interest in phenomenological methods. It appears that the tide is turning and doctoral research will reflect less and less the influence of the theory movement.

Although the quantity of research and theoretical articles has increased tremendously since the early 1950s, it is still small when compared to similar production in business administration. The topics discussed in textbooks and the nature of research have become more theoretical and oriented to the social sciences. The four theories developed during the theory movement—social systems, decision making, role, and mutual problem solving—have survived, although their popularity has diminished considerably.

The theory movement moved educational administration from the status of a practical art toward, if not altogether to, the status of an academic discipline. It developed in a context of excitement and production in business, industrial, public, military, and governmental administration. Although production of theoretical and research articles has increased in all areas, the original excitement has ebbed simultaneously with the ebbing of the theory movement itself.

The passing of the theory movement does not mean that it has been replaced by something else. Rather, the period from 1974 to the present can best be described as a period of transition, not only in theory but also in the society, in people's values and behavior, and in organizations (Griffiths, 1985). How society has changed, what change has meant to organizations, how administration has changed, and what theorists are saying about these changes are examined in the sections that follow.

ADMINISTRATIVE THEORY AND THE NATURE OF THE SOCIAL SCENE AND ITS ORGANIZATIONS IN THE WESTERN WORLD

The function of administrative theorists is to make intellectual sense out of the society, organizations, and administrators they study. Recognizing that we are now in a transitional period in administrative theory, it is important to examine where we are in our understanding of the relationships among the environment, organization, administration, and theory.

The necessity to understand the context in which organizations function in order to comprehend their operations and to develop adequate theory is widely accepted. The significance of the context in which organizations exist has not always been understood nor appreciated. Indeed, although the importance of the context is generally acknowledged in present theoretical literature, many researchers still proceed as if organizations exist *in vacuo* (Griffiths, 1983). The context includes the environment or society and the organizational setting, as well as scientists who bring biases and predispositions to their study. Fraassen (1980) has summarized the current view of context in scientific theory:

> The discussion of explanation went wrong at the very beginning when explanation was conceived of as a relationship-like description: a relation between theory and fact. Really it is a three-term relation, between theory, fact, and context. (p. 156)

> ...in the analysis of the appraisal of scientific theories, it would be a mistake to overlook the ways in which that appraisal is coloured by contextual factors. These factors are brought to the situation by the scientist from his own personal, social, and cultural situation. It is a mistake to think that the terms in which a scientific theory is appraised are purely hygienic, and have nothing to do with any other sort of appraisal, or with the persons and circumstances involved. (p. 87)

Thus, it is pertinent to analyze the social, organizational, university, and public school settings in the United States. Similar trends, however, are apparent in Western Europe, Canada, and Australia, or throughout what is sometimes called the Western world. Settings elsewhere differ in significant ways. Japan, for example, with industrial organizations often compared to those of the United States, presents a different culture and a very different context.

Social Setting

Social scientists and humanists have examined repeatedly the causes of the collapse of consensus in the Western world in the context of societal changes since World War II. Where Americans once held to the ideal of the country as a melting pot, it is now more commonly believed that ethnic identification provides the basic reference group for most minorities. But that is not all. It is estimated that there are at least 200 crusading minorities in the country centering on such diverse topics as abortion, arms control, sexual freedom, environmental pollution, and women's rights. There is also evidence of growing loyalty to one's neighborhood. In large American cities, this is apparent in the decentralization of school systems and in the formation of neighborhood associations.

In a related development, it is said that there are now reportedly more than 2,500 U.S. communes that are characterized by a withdrawal from political society.

And there is the rediscovery of religion, often of a fundamentalist or mystical character, that leads patrons to singular, private views. Perhaps at the base of these inward-seeking trends are what futurologists call "increasingly sensate cultures" expressing protest or revolt, and what they describe with terms such as "overripe," "extreme," "sensation-seeking," "violently novel," "exhibitionistic," and "nihilistic" (Kahn & Weiner, 1967). Also contributing to the collapse of consensus in the United States is the explosion of many assumptions that were once firmly believed by the people. Goldman (cited in Nordheimer, 1976, p. 18) lists them as follows:

- The United States can continue shaping its destiny independently of foreign interference.
- The American political system is basically sound.
- Lower economic groups in the country can look forward to a better life for their children.
- The United States can absorb any diverse group into its mainstream.
- Developing nations desire peace and a form of middle-class democracy much like that of the United States.

Admittedly, these assumptions have lost their validity.

Further, the unmeltable ethnics, the crusaders, the locals, the members of communes, the "new religious efflorescences" (Nisbet, 1974, p. 26), along with a great many other people, have seemingly adopted views that fit the philosophy of phenomenology, which holds that all individuals perceive, experience, and, indeed, create their own reality. They believe there are no objective criteria. Each person is the center of the universe. There are no organizational goals, nor should there be; individuals within the organization have goals and these differ person by person. What is created, then, are organizations populated by people who do not acknowledge institutional goals and who live only for their personal aims and desires. It is the culture of self.

The 1984 presidential election highlighted other causes of divisiveness in the United States. It was thought by many that the country was ready to coalesce on a number of issues, but as James Reston (1984) stated, "instead it has put the factions, the races and the regions against one another and ignored the fundamental problem of correcting the structural flaws in our political system" (p. A−27).

A number of other major changes in society have occurred (Kanter, 1983, p. 43):

- The widespread use of birth control through the pill and abortion has decreased the number of children and changed the proportions of age groups in the society.

- The women's movement has sharply reduced education's best source of able teachers and has placed women in positions of leadership in government, business, and the professions.
- Political parties have been weakened through splintering and the multiplication of special interest groups so that it is difficult, if not impossible, to govern, giving rise to a view best expressed by former Governor Edmund G. Brown, Jr., of California, who remarked during his gubernatorial campaign, "I take a somewhat jaundiced view of the ability of government to perform" ("Campaign '74," 1974), whereupon he was overwhelmingly elected.
- More than half of all wives work.
- Over half of all families have two wage earners.
- The median amount of schooling for all wage earners has moved past one year of college.
- Unions are bargaining for flexible hours of work.

In analyzing the same period of time from the perspective of a political scientist studying education, Boyd (1984) finds that "educators now are confronted simultaneously with four kinds of decline: declining enrollments; declining economic-budgetary circumstances; declining public confidence in schooling; and a declining legitimacy of administrative authority" (p. 303). It should be noted, though, that the 1984 Gallup Poll (Gallup, 1984) indicated a resurgence of public confidence in the public schools, so it may be that the era of at least one kind of decline is over.

All these factors contribute to a society that emphasizes increasingly individual and personal goals, desires, and expectations. The emergent condition was summarized best by Lord Morris of Grasmere (Morris, 1975) in a speech at the 1974 IIP. He described the then current social climate succinctly:

> The people do not want to be governed, and clearly they do not believe there is any real and final necessity to be governed. Their political posture is no longer very far removed from that of the hippies, and the signs are that it is getting not further away but nearer to it. (p. 14)

Organizational Settings

Organizations are a significant part of society and, being more or less open, over time they become quite similar to the societies in which they exist. When societal changes occur, corporate organizations, institutions of higher education, and public schools undergo change in response.

Corporate Settings

More and more U.S. companies are being populated by people whose organizational behavior is in accordance with the values and ideals of the society in which they live. Since society, culture, and people's behavior are changing, organizations are changing also. Douglas

Soutar (1982), a leading American management specialist, characterized the change in this manner:

> The employee mix of the '80s, of course, looks quite different to those of us who have survived recent decades of corporate employment. We now face an "individualized" generation which has "rights," and believes fully in its entitlement to a host of the refinements of life which older employees only aspired to. The new generation is, on the whole, better educated, more inquiring, and not only expects but usually demands greater participation in conduct of the enterprise. (pp. 2–3)

Strange as it seems, a book on management has been at or near the top of the bestseller list in the United States. *In Search of Excellence* by Peters and Waterman (1982) is a study of 62 U.S. companies considered to be excellent—that is, continuously innovative—big corporations. The authors conducted interviews and observations in the 62 companies, contrasted the successful organizations with less successful ones, and compared their findings with the results of a review of 25 years of organizational literature. As a summary, Peters and Waterman list eight characteristics of a successful corporation. It is interesting that they do not include technology, location, or finance. They focus on people and their organizational treatment. The characteristics are as follows:

1. A bias for action: a preference for doing something—anything—rather than sending a question through cycles and cycles of analyses and committee reports.
2. Staying close to the customer; learning his preferences and catering to them.
3. Autonomy and entrepreneurship—breaking the corporation into small companies and encouraging them to think independently and competitively.
4. Productivity through people—creating in *all* employees the awareness that their best efforts are essential and that they will share in the rewards of the company's success.
5. Hands on, value driven—insisting that executives keep in touch with the firm's essential business.
6. Simple form, lean staff—having few administrative layers, few people at the upper levels.
7. Stick to the knitting—remaining with the business the company knows best.
8. Simultaneous loose-tight properties—fostering a climate where there is dedication to the central values of the company, combined with tolerance for all employees who accept those values.

What Peters and Waterman are saying is that successful companies today, in both the United States and Japan, are consciously or unconsciously utilizing the theory and research of the old human relations movement. As Van de Ven (1983) has pointed out, however, they have done more than that. In his review of the book, Van de Ven stresses the numerous paradoxes discussed by Peters and Waterman. Some are within the individual, such as, "For all the focus on self-interest rationality in management theory, organizational participants spend a majority of their time doing things not in their self-interest" (Van de Ven, p. 623). But there are also organizational paradoxes evident in the successful companies that were studied (Van de Ven, p. 623):

1. Small is beautiful in order to get or stay big.
2. Organizations hire a heterogeneous work force, but want homogeneous values.
3. Organizations must develop tight values and beliefs in order to have loose structures and systems. The soft "touchy-feely" human component of the enterprise has become hard.

As Van de Ven notes, modern organization theory cannot account for these paradoxes, yet the managers of successful companies take them in their stride. Traditional theories are apparently incompatible with what underlies the specific findings of Peters and Waterman (1982). They refer constantly to the culture of an organization and try to get at feelings and attitudes of employees. Their comment "The rationalist approach takes the living element out of situations that should, above all, be alive" (p. 46) is a clue to one reason why the organizational theorists are unable to describe modern organizations adequately.

Rosabeth Moss Kanter (1983) has published a volume similar to *In Search of Excellence*, a book entitled *The Change Masters*. In it she reports on a series of systematic research studies and change projects (p. 43). One of the studies investigated 47 "progressive" companies noted for their innovative, overall human resources system. (Twenty-one of these were the same ones studied by Peters and Waterman.) Kanter (1983) found that *the companies with reputations for progressive human resources practices were significantly higher in long-term profitability and financial growth than their counterparts* [italics in original] (p. 19).

Kanter's conclusions are much like those of Peters and Waterman in that she refers constantly to the company "culture." She identifies a "shared philosophy" and a "family feeling" in the successful corporations. Just as Peters and Waterman found a lot of what they call "matrix management," Kanter (1983) found that, "the work is done in an environment of mutual respect, participating teams, multiple ties, and relationships that crisscross the organizational chart" (pp. 32–33). They all agree that traditionalist-rationalist bureaucratic theory is not descriptive of

what is going on in successful modern corporations.

It is interesting and probably quite significant to note that, while Peters and Waterman (1982) are aware of the work of Lawrence and Lorsch (1967), they prefer to quote Pfeffer and Salancik (1978). They accept Scott's (1981) designation of the period from 1970 to the present as the time of the organization as an open system (p. 128), but they pay little attention to the influence of the environment on the organization. Kanter (1983) takes quite the opposite view. She devotes an early, lengthy chapter to transformations in the American corporate environment in the period 1960–1980 (pp. 37–65). Her contention is that the social forces she discusses (very similar to what has been called the social setting) have resulted in a marked change in what she calls assumptions of organization.

Kanter (1983, p. 398) contends that virtually all assumptions regarding organizations have undergone major changes, illustrated by the following: Whereas organizations were conceptualized as closed systems, they should now be thought of as open systems. In like manner organizations having limited purposes now have multiple activities and uses. The key management problems of the past were control, coordination of isolated segments, and reductions of friction around the work process; these have been replaced with problems of strategic decisions, issue management, and external political relations. Organizational effectiveness, once conceived as a technical matter, has become largely a political matter.

Kanter (1983) argues that the old assumptions undergirded a mechanistic structure while the new assumptions result in an organic structure (p. 396). As a consequence, when these assumptions are implemented, the people in the resulting organizations work in markedly different ways. One major difference appears to be that employees understand the organization as a whole rather than seeing their work as segmented and isolated. Interaction is lateral rather than vertical, and employees function in a far less structured way than previously.

The combination of new model assumptions and the new work patterns produces new organizational design factors (Kanter, 1983, pp. 42–43). The resulting organizations require educated, sophisticated career employees who perform complex and intellectual tasks often using electronic and biological technologies in an environment where there is considerable overlap between workers and managers.

Of course the continuum of U.S. corporations ranges from Neanderthal to Space Age in the way in which human resources are managed. Kanter's emerging organizational design factors, however, appear to be descriptive of the successful companies.

University Settings

The emerging design factors are even more descriptive of the leading U.S. universities. Professors are highly educated, sophisticated career employees to a greater degree than the employees of the most successful companies in the country. In their teaching, research, and consulting, they perform complex, intellectual tasks. Most are acquainted with electronic technologies through their use of computers. Certainly in their own disciplines they hold organic views and realize that events have multiple causes and effects. The fluid markets and supply factors are probably not applicable. However, it is in the last factor, overlap between workers and managers, that the universities have reached an extreme point. Most university presidents, virtually all deans, and all department chairs hold tenured professorships. In the case of chairpersons, they hold office while they continue to teach and do research; at the end of their terms, they move back to the professorship. This is often true of deans (more so in liberal arts than in professional schools) and less true of presidents. The overlap among professors, deans, and presidents is almost complete. The emerging design factors are, indeed, descriptive of the leading universities. These factors are found in lesser universities and colleges, but not to the same degree. Nowhere, however, would one find an institution of higher education that could be adequately described by all of Kanter's (1983) traditional organizational design factors. There are some proprietary, religious, and state colleges where there is a sharp distinction between professors and "managers." Some might hold "mechanistic views," but one would not find the other factors present.

Public School Settings

The public schools appear to be in the middle of the continuum from "traditional" to "emerging." Certainly teachers cannot be described as uneducated, unskilled temporary workers, even though many remain in teaching only briefly. On the other hand, many teachers can be described as educated, sophisticated career workers but not in the same proportion found in university professorships and high-technology industries. Nor does the level of education or sophistication equal that of the university academic staff. Public school teachers do perform complex and intellectual tasks but, again, not at the highest level. The same is true of the use of electronic and biological technologies and organic views, multiple causes and effects. It seems that while all six of Kanter's (1983) emerging design factors are significant, the one that most influences the structure of an organization is "overlap between workers and managers" (p. 43). This factor appears to distinguish public schools from universities as far as organizational structure is concerned. The school principal and superintendent of schools perform roles in which there is little or no overlap with teachers, quite in contrast to deans and university presidents with professors. This is probably due to the higher level of education and specialization of professors in universities as well as to the necessity that they perform more complex and intellectual tasks. The distinction, however, is not so great as it once was, as illustrated by the case of Frank Spalding (1955). As a superintendent of schools, Spalding was the only university graduate in the school system; he wrote the curriculum, taught it to the teachers, and then supervised their teaching. With today's faculty educated at levels that at times exceed those achieved by principals and superintendents and with union contracts diminishing the authority of school administrators, the differences between teachers and administrators are growing smaller.

Summary

Recognizing the importance of context, this section has included a description of salient elements of the society that apparently have influenced the nature of its organizations. As a result it appears that a continuum of organizations ranging from "traditional" to "emerging" can be established by using Kanter's (1983) design factors. Many organizations, educational and otherwise, exist at or near the "traditional" end; the majority (including the public schools) are probably in the middle; and a substantial number (including universities) are at the "emerging" end of the continuum. How the society and the resultant organizations influence administrator behavior is examined in the next section.

ADMINISTRATIVE BEHAVIOR IN MODERN ORGANIZATIONS

It is appropriate now to analyze administrative behavior in the modern organizational settings discussed earlier: corporate, university, and public school.

Corporate Administration

In studying the administration of the great U.S. corporations, changes are observable, based largely on social and organizational factors. Among these major changes and developments are the following (Organization Resources Counselors, Inc., 1982, pp. 50–54.):

1. Exploration of the use of "quality circles"—an approach in which workers voluntarily meet with a discussion leader, usually their supervisor, to identify, analyze, resolve and prevent work-related

problems. This Japanese import has yet to prove its success in the United States. Many supervisors and managers are unwilling to accept advice from their subordinates. Moreover, it is not clear just what the quality circles are supposed to accomplish (pp. 51–52).

2. With the increasing complexity of business organization and management systems, the concept of matrix management has been adopted in many places. In matrix management, the individual employee may be a member of several project teams simultaneously, have varied responsibilities, and report to different people on different tasks. Matrix management has been most successful in high-technology industries and in research and development departments (pp. 53–54).

3. There is growing recognition of the importance of external factors in internal human resource management. This recognition has contributed to the use of environmental scanning, in which information is gathered about social, political, economic, and technological developments and their likely impact on the people within the organization (p. 54).

4. There is also increasing acknowledgement that managers should not adopt a single managerial style; rather, they should adopt those styles appropriate to particular situations as they develop. A manager might consider Theory X on Monday, Theory Y on Tuesday, and Theory Z on Wednesday. The idea here is that a manager should be able to respond to internal and external forces in a variety of diverse but equally effective models (pp. 50–51).

John Kenneth Galbraith (1984) has made some penetrating observations on the behavior of top business executives in an article entitled "Corporate Man." He summarizes how societal and organizational forces have shaped the behavior of heads of corporations. The description probably applies, as well, to university presidents and school superintendents. The following is illustrative:

> The modern business executive is...a well-spoken man, disposed always to negotiate—for that is how he spends his time—and otherwise given to persuasion rather than command. In all respects, he is a far more agreeable figure than his predecessor, the great captain of industry, the prototypical entrepreneur (p. 39).

Because of the previously documented changes in the social system and in the nature of organizations, top executives are concerned with external matters. For them, as Kanter (1983) points out: "Management of critical boundary-spanning issues is the task of the top: developing strategies, tactics, and structural mechanisms for functioning and triumphing in a turbulent and highly politicized environment" (p. 49). As a result top executives have to spend more and more time outside their organizations developing relationships

and alliances. In commenting about one group of chief executive officers (CEOs), Kanter (1983) writes: "These CEOs were spending virtually no time inside their organizations; they were spending time allying themselves and bargaining outside" (p. 50). Top executives are also giving increasing numbers of speeches: Kanter notes that Thomas Murphy, Chairman of General Motors, made over 90 speeches in one year.

University Administration

Lewis Thomas (1983), formerly dean of two medical schools and an internationally known researcher, is one of the few to have the courage to tell it as it is. In an essay entitled "The Governance of the University," he asks and then answers his own questions: "How should a university be run? Who is really in charge, holding the power? The proper answer to the latter is, of course, nobody." Thomas modifies this assertion only slightly when he adds, "In normal times, with institutions that are relatively stable in their endowments and incomes, nobody is really in charge" (pp. 168–169). He continues:

> A university, as has been said so many times that there is risk of losing the meaning, is a community of scholars. When its affairs are going well, when its students are acquiring some comprehension of the culture, and its faculty are contributing new knowledge to their special fields, and when visiting scholars are streaming in and out of its gates, it runs itself, rather like a large organism. The function of administration is solely to see that funds are adequate for its purposes and not overspent, that the air is right, that the grounds are tidy—and then stay out of the way. (p. 169)

This idea, well-expressed and only slightly exaggerated by Thomas, has been voiced by others. John Rehfuss (1984), writing in *The Chronicle of Higher Education*, had this to say:

> University presidents have both a difficult and thankless job. They are charged by the trustees to head a balky organization and to correct all previous wrongs. They face a faculty convinced that a president should provide academic leadership (whatever that is) and yet leave well enough alone (not get in the way of the faculty). (p. 64)

D. Dill (1984) cites March (1980, cited in Dill, 1984), who argues that great leadership is unlikely in organizations of higher education. Dill (1984) concludes that this is because "academic administration is an act of small adjustments in which larger and, by inference, slow-moving forces determine the evolution of events" (p. 93).

There is a serious question as to whether the term

"management" or even "administration" should be used when discussing the academic aspects of universities. The two terms have meaning when discussing the business and financial aspects but not the academic component of the university. In most universities virtually all the vital processes are under faculty control: the curriculum; faculty selection, promotion, appointment to tenure, and often salaries of professors; and academic governance. The major goal of faculty governance, it would seem, is to render administration impotent—and generally that goal is successfully met. University faculties have systematically made it impossible (or nearly so) for deans and presidents to lead or to administer, and the better the university, the less it is led.

There are, indeed, no "strong" leaders in higher education today (Berte & Morse, 1985, p. 51). It is doubtful that the general public could name a single university president. Even university professors can name few other than their own.

There have been few syntheses of the literature on the behavior of administrators in higher education, so Dill's (1984) article "The Nature of Administrative Behavior in Higher Education" fills a large void. He studied some 425 publications and, with appropriate caveats, assumes that his review is representative of the accrued knowledge in the field; indeed, it appears to be. Dill's conclusions regarding use of time, types of skills, and networks of people within which the higher education administrator works are similar to those found for business and public school administrators. Deans and presidents work from 55 to 60 hours per week, presidents are out of town about 22 percent of this time, and they spend more time with other administrators than with any other single group (Dill, 1984, p. 75). Dill further concludes that "academic administrators lead a busy, reactive life in which they heavily utilize their verbal skills, particularly in meetings" (p. 76). Dill's final conclusion, however, epitomizes academic administration in higher education:

First, it is apparent that informal influence, negotiations, and networks of contacts are important aspects of academic administration. Second, the results of research on information-related behavior, decision-making, and resource allocation provide some indication that academic management is still highly intuitive, tends to avoid the use of quantitative data or available management technology, and is subject to the political influence of powerful groups and interests. Third, the traditions, beliefs, and values of individuals, disciplines, and institutions appear to play a more substantial role than is generally acknowledged in the extant prescriptive literature on management. In short, the garbage-can model of decision-making and the institutional context of organized anarchy as articulated by March and his colleagues receives much support from the available literature on administrative behavior. (p. 92)

A recent study of university presidents confirms much of what Dill (1984) reports, but, in addition, the increase in external pressures and external involvement is stressed. Evangelauf (1984) surveyed 216 presidents of four-year institutions and reported that "the presidents said the state legislature, the governor, the state board of education, the state budget office, and professional and regional accrediting agencies have the most influence on their decision-making" (p 15).

With reference to deans' activities, Griffiths (1980) concluded that, in his deanship, he was usually the chairperson of group meetings, worked long hours (often 13 hours a day), protected the "turf" of the school, was involved with external forces, helped prepare academic policy papers for the approval of the faculty, "showed the flag," and attempted to resolve problems in a number of nonacademic areas.

Public School Administration

Superintendents

Turning now to the public schools, one finds an organization that is somewhere between the traditional and the emerging nontraditional. Superintendents interviewed by Griffiths in 1983 had this to report about changes then affecting public school administration:

1. There is far more criticism of administrators now than ever before.

2. Few people—if any—are happy with, or even tolerant of, administrators.

3. Problems and issues are becoming increasingly complex. More people are involved, there are more facets to be considered, and everything seems to be interconnected.

4. The composition of school boards appears to be changing. There are more people, mostly women, who have little or no experience in organizations outside the home, and fewer executives and high-level professionals on boards. The quality of board membership is seen as declining.

5. There is less money available to administrators, yet they are expected to do more with less.

6. During this period of intense criticism of U.S. public schools, internal affairs have become easier to manage. It seems that faculty and administration coalesce against the outside world.

7. There is little interest on the part of teachers in becoming administrators. If administration has not totally lost its appeal, it is on the way to doing so.

8. There is more involvement with groups and organizations outside the school system. Superintendents work 50 to 60 hours per week and, in addition, spend time preparing speeches, and attending frequent meetings and other functions.

One of the most insightful discussions of the evolution of the superintendency is that by Fritz Hess (1983), Superintendent of Schools in East Syracuse, New York, who has said that:

> In the last analysis, the evolution of the practice of educational administration during the period 1959–1981 has been an evolution of roles. Sweeping alterations in American society, in student enrollments, in personnel, in regulation, in finance, and in technology have changed school executives from the leaders of an unquestioned institution to conflict managers and advocates in an intensely competitive environment. The transformation has been a dramatic one. It has been accompanied by considerable stress and dislocation. It continues to unfold in many areas; yet it has already encompassed trends that have totally reshaped the assumptions on which administrative practice in 1959 was based. (p. 245)

From the observations of these superintendents, we can see that their job is becoming, in many ways, more like that of the university president and the modern corporate president. A major difference is that superintendents and principals have more authority over all aspects of the school district than do university presidents over their domain. Still, school executives spend more time outside the school and, as stated, their problems have become more complex. In particular, a lack of public confidence and interest in schools appears to have affected the behavior of superintendents.

Principals

Case studies (Jackson, 1981a, 1981b; Lightfoot, 1981a, 1981b; Smith, Prunty, & Dwyer, 1983) have been written about three public schools in districts that range from suburban to urban to rural: Highland Park High School in Highland Park, Illinois; George Washington Carver Comprehensive High School in Atlanta, Georgia; and the Kensington School in Milford, Missouri. Descriptions of the administration of these schools leave the reader with the impression of the principalship as a powerful role. On occasion, an incumbent might not fill the role in such a way as to use all its power (Smith et al., 1983, Vol. 4), but the power resides in the role all the same.

The principals in the case descriptions approach their jobs in singular ways. They have different styles and emphasize different aspects of the role. Lightfoot (1981b) describes the principal at Highland Park as "the smooth, urbane leader who establishes school policies, directs curricular decision-making, deals with the superintendent, and makes public statements" (p. 61). He is able to function in this manner because he

has an excellent assistant who handles the day-to-day operations of the school. He encourages creativity and autonomy among the teachers, and they agree they have "autonomy, support, and comfort in the school" (p. 62). The principal says of himself, "I am long on people skills" (p. 61).

The principal at George Washington Carver projects quite a different image (Lightfoot, 1981a): "A former football player, Hogans is powerful in stature and character. He dominates the school. . . . Everyone agrees Hogans is powerful" (p. 20).

One of the descriptions of Carver High raises the question of just how important a principal is to a school Jackson, 1981b). The answer: "By watching Carver's principal at work, by talking to the people around him, it becomes clear that the principal's role is crucial, his importance inestimable. All those who have anything to say about the school's recent past echo the same conclusion: before Hogans came—near disaster; since he has arrived—unheralded praise" (p. 44). Hogans's personality, drive, and ambition are all part of his success, but added to these characteristics is the fact that he has a set of clear goals that are clearly communicated. Similar to the Highland Park principal, Hogans has an assistant described as "the tall, slender, and impeccable vice-principal [who] takes care of the mundane, everyday, nitty-gritty details" (Lightfoot, 1981a, p. 21). And lastly: "The school is merely the hub of Carver's fast-spinning wheel. The spokes that whirl around the center are attached to businesses, universities, churches, health facilities, and community agencies" (Lightfoot, 1981a, p. 37). Hogans devotes a major part of his time to negotiating with these agencies.

Smith et al. (1983) wrote a lengthy case that includes a detailed analysis of the work of Wales, principal of the Kensington School, summarized in the paper's abstract:

> Wales hailed from the rural South, and was strong on family, church, and discipline. His professional and academic experiences were stronger preparation for secondary than elementary school leadership. His rise through the ranks seems to have resulted from his close relationship with Milford administrators and from his ability to get "the job done in the way they wanted it done." Dr. Wales defined the "way" as traditionalism—maintaining tight discipline and freeing teachers to teach. This one-day view of Wales's professional life demonstrates the easy-going style with which he typically handled most situations at Kensington. True to his word, we saw him disciplining students, buffering teachers from parents, checking on building maintenance, book orders, and insurance programs. Further, in his jovial way, he moved about the building talking with teachers and, sometimes less jovially, conversing with students. In short, Wales freed his teachers to teach. He

did his best to maintain an orderly school environment at Kensington. (Vol. 6, pp. 84–85)

Descriptions of all three schools repeatedly referred to the climate, the "feel," as some would call it, or the culture of the schools. The cultures were different. Observers attributed the differences largely to the principals, but it seems naive not to attribute them at least equally to the socioeconomic levels of the communities, the times (early 1980s), the federal government, and numerous other factors.

Gronn's (1982) analysis of eight researchers purporting to study what principals do is very revealing. Although all the studies used observational techniques, they did not identify what was actually done by the principals. As Gronn (1982) writes:

> Never at any stage was it established what principals, superintendents, or program managers do. Invariably, the researchers suggested that such persons sit at their desks, go on tours, walk up and down corridors, write, attend meetings, talk, and so on.... The question still remains: What do the administrators *do* at their desks, *do* with their talk, *do* in the corridor, *do* on tours, and *do* with their writing? (italics in original) (p. 24)

While highly critical of the Taylorlike techniques used, Gronn (1982) responds well to the fact that six of the eight studies report that the principals talk from two-thirds to three-fourths of the working day. He concludes that "administrative work is largely linguistic work" (p. 30). It follows that the way to study what administrators do is to study their talk.

Willis (1984), in an observational study of three school principals in Australia, confirms the conclusions reported above and adds that the study of managers' work reveals the following:

1. It is susceptible to interruption, superficiality of treatment and shifts of location—all of which contribute to the general discontinuity of the work.
2. Much of it may be "invisible" to others in the organization and lacking in personal feedback. (p. 42)

Summary

As we view the top executives of corporations, the universities, and the public schools, we see, of course, differences, but there is one changing aspects of the job common to all: the growing trend toward working outside the organization. This has come about largely because of increasing demands from the environment. The fact that the sharp distinction between manager and worker no longer holds means that workers have less supervision as the manager interacts more with the environment and less with the internal organization. Special-interest groups, clients, workers, and governmental officials all believe they have legitimate roles in the management of universities, schools, and corporations. As a result, top executives are not so much managers as they are politicians attempting to resolve conflicting demands on the organization. They use negotiation and persuasion as their major tools.

Top executives of corporations, universities, and public schools are, in their internal responsibilities, very concerned with people's goals and values. Another observation of current executive behavior is that a majority of the working time is spent in talking. As President Richard Cyert of Carnegie-Mellon University quipped at a New York University conference, "Generally speaking, college presidents are generally speaking."

While it appears that corporate executives use modern technology, such as computers, to gain information to be used in decision-making, there is little evidence to suggest that this is true of university and public school administrators. And while there are many studies of executives in action, there are few, if any, studies that get at what executives actually do. What, for instance, are principals doing when they walk the halls? What are superintendents doing when they put in an hour of desk time? One concludes that the studies of the behavior of administrators must be carried beyond mere observations of actions.

RESPONSES OF ADMINISTRATIVE THEORISTS TO THE CHANGING SOCIAL SCENE, THE DEVELOPING ORGANIZATIONS, AND THE NEW ADMINISTRATION

The theory movement of the 1950s and 1960s has been discussed and analyzed, and the social scene, the emerging organizations, and the behavior of administrators have been examined. The examination supports the underlying assumption that the past and present decades represent a transitional period in the evolution of administrative theory (Griffiths, 1985). This final section addresses the current status of theory in administration.

Epistemological Issues

It is clear that administrators and researchers (at least those examined in this chapter) have little or no problem with epistemological issues. They seem to be realists of the first order: They have seen organizations function and they know what they have seen. They are unequivocal in their reports. But the world of theory is quite different: There are all sorts of problems and issues being discussed and new directions being followed, of which many practitioners are quite unaware (Lotto, 1984).

It is essential to note that there is great diversity among theoreticians. Functionalism is widespread in the United States, and, therefore, virtually all the theory taught and used in educational administration is functionalist organizational theory (broadly defined). On the other hand, vocal and influential groups in Great Britain, Canada, Australia, and a small but increasing number in the United States are energetic critics of functionalism and advocates of a number of contrary views. The most popular school of criticism in organization theory, generally, is probably Marxist; the most popular in educational administration is critical theory. A growing number of studies employ ethnography, and, occasionally, one is done in the phenomenological mode.

Two sets of events stimulated the attacks on functionalism and the emergence of new approaches: (1) the demise of positivism, which forms the epistemological basis for functionalism; and (2) the realization by many that functionalist theories cannot adequately describe modern organizations.

The logical positivists believed that something had meaning only if it could be verified by direct or indirect observation. More formally, a statement containing theoretical terms should be tested by a statement containing observational (nontheoretical) terms; logical validity is present if a logical or mathematical tautology exists. Because logical positivists were not realists, they regarded theories as neither true nor false but as useful conceptual tools. What died, in most people's view, was the verification principle. The difficulty was with the observation statement, for it is virtually impossible to construct an observation statement that does not include theoretical concepts (Fraassen, 1980, pp. 13–14). Rather than theoretical statements being verified by observation statements, theoretical propositions were actually tested by other theoretical statements, and the verification sought by the logical positivists was never achieved. Howe (1985) sums up the present-day position of virtually all philosophers of science by concluding, "Ultimate, theory-free, factual knowledge cannot exist, and positivism's corollary fact-value distinction is untenable" (p. 11). However, as Phillips (1983) noted, "The principle was eventually discredited among philosophers, but it lingered on in the social science research community" (p. 5). This is particularly true in psychology and educational administration.

The present chaotic situation in organizational studies has come about partly because of the inability of present theories to account for what is observed in organizations. In a paper entitled "Intellectual Turmoil in Educational Administration," Griffiths (1979) attempted to catalogue and analyze the criticisms of organizational theory. These criticisms include charges that organizational theories ignore the presence of unions, fail to account for the scarcity of women and minorities in top administrative positions, and do not account for the degree of external control that is exercised over practically all organizations. Also, while organizational theories strive to be universal, they usually have only limited applicability. Then there is Perrow's (1978) criticism, now accepted by many, that questions the long-held assumption that organizations "are, or can be rational instruments of announced goals" (p. 247). The rejection of this assumption is central to what Perrow terms "demystifying organizations." In a similar vein, Conway (1984) considered a dozen reviews of about 60 studies of participation in decision making (PDM) and concluded that most of the values ascribed to PDM are myths. The rise of ideologically based theories such as Marxism, the introduction of research methodologies such as ethnography, and the popularity of the idea of phenomenology all add up to a confusing picture. C. P. Snow (1971) has said, "The scientific process has two motives: one is to understand the natural world, the other is to control it" (p. 56). This statement is as true for the administrative theorist as it is for the physical scientist, but administrative theorists cannot describe organizations nor can administrators control them, and this is the basis for the present turmoil.

The turmoil so apparent in administrative theory is present also in the social and physical sciences. Confusion has extended to questions concerning the nature of science and the meaning of theory. Frederick Suppe (1977) has summarized the situation as it exists in philosophy of science:

> During the last five or six decades there have been important shifts in philosophical thinking about scientific discovery and the growth of scientific knowledge. The positivists distinguished the context of discovery and the context of justification, dismissing the former as the subject matter of history of psychology. The only aspects of the growth of scientific knowledge relevant to philosophy were the inductive justification or confirmation of knowledge claims and the incorporation of older theories into more comprehensive theories via intertheoretic reduction. The resulting view of scientific knowledge was a static one which, ignoring the dynamics of scientific progress and being tied to an untenable observational/theoretical distinction and associated epistemology, led to a highly distorted portrait of science and the knowledge it provided, which had little to do with the epistemic activities science actually was engaged in. Rejecting such a view, a group of "young Turks"—including Hanson, Feyerabend, and Kuhn— started examining scientific practice and the history of

science and developed *Weltanschauungen* views that, unfortunately, made scientific knowledge a social phenomenon in which science became a subjective and, to varying degrees, an irrational enterprise.

More recently, philosophers such as Lakatos, Toulmin, and Shapere have attempted to steer a middle course between these two extremes wherein science is a rational enterprise concerned with obtaining objective knowledge of the real world. (pp. 704–705)

Educational administrative theorists as a whole, however, have not accepted Suppe's conclusion, and, in fact, some elements of the field might well be considered to be moving away from it. Other elements, as will be seen, have accepted the approach described by Suppe. As the split between the two has widened, basic concepts, once apparently defined to suit everyone, have lost their meanings. Take the term "scientific theory" for instance. Shapere (1969) sums up the present by saying, "There is today no completely—one is almost tempted to say remotely—satisfactory analysis of the notion of a scientific theory" (p. 125). In part, this is true because of what has happened to the concept of science as it is practiced.

When Putnam was asked what a science is, he gave some interesting answers, as quoted from his dialogue with Magee (1978):

> MAGEE: But now that our whole conception of science has altered, it is not so much that some different method has come to be regarded as "the" method, but rather that there is no longer thought of as being only one single valid approach to all scientific problems.
> PUTNAM: There is a sort of paradigm of "the scientific method" (a paradigm which itself is pretty vague, as I just remarked) which one occasionally finds pretty well exemplified, especially in physics. But even in physics there is a great deal of knowledge which doesn't, and shouldn't, fit the paradigm. I don't believe that there is really an agreement in our culture as to what is a "science" and what isn't. Any university catalogue claims that there are subjects called "Social Sciences," and that Sociology and Economics are sciences. But I would bet that if we asked anyone in the Physics Department whether Sociology is a science he would say "No."
> MAGEE: Yes, but what grounds would he have for saying no?
> PUTNAM: I think the real reason is not that the sociologists don't use the inductive method—they probably use it more conscientiously, poor things, than the physicists do. I think it's because they're not as successful.
> MAGEE: So you think "science" is now simply a term for the successful pursuit of knowledge?
> PUTNAM: That's right. (pp. 233–234)

In 1983, a study was published of the work of prominent researchers in educational administration (Griffiths, 1983). Even without making explicit their concept of science, they were working within the meaning given by Putnam (Magee, 1978). These researchers were far more concerned with whether useful knowledge was being generated than with following a particular form of inquiry. The trends have been reported earlier: the Morris (1975) statement "The people do not want to be governed" (p. 14) carries over into science, and researchers do not want to be governed by a set of rigid rules. Just as the society emphasizes individual and personal goals, so too is science moving in this direction. What is valued in the society affects the way science functions.

Current efforts in research and theory in educational administration are now examined against the changing conception of science.

Categorizations of Theory and Research

The wide, albeit uneven, variety of studies and theories, the criticism, and the arguments over epistemology and methodology give the impression that chaos reigns. This is really not the case since it is possible to group present efforts in systematic ways. Three efforts to categorize research and theory are discussed below.

Hage

Hage's *Theories of Organizations: Form, Process, and Transformation* (1980) is an elaborate framework through which he attempted a great synthesis. Benson (1982) evaluated the effort in this way:

> The difficulty is that the current state of the field does not make it susceptible to a great synthesis. Because the differences in the field are rooted in opposing methodological stances and paradigms, Hage's prodigious effort is unlikely to do very much to reconcile them. (p. 166)

Scott

Scott (1981), in a much more modest effort, analyzed developments in organizational theory in terms of closed and open systems and rational and natural models (p. 129). This analysis is depicted in Table 2.1. Scott's set of categories encompasses virtually all the theories used in empirical research on organizations. The time boundaries should be considered as approximating modal practice, although in educational administration one can, at present, observe research underway in all four categories. The overwhelming bulk of the research is, however, Type III.

According to Scott the new and emerging theories are in Type IV: open system, natural models. The theory of this type most familiar to educational administration theorists is that of Cohen, March, and Olson (1972), which is built around the garbage-can concept of decision making.

Table 2.2   Dominant Theoretical Models and Representative Theorists for Four Time Periods

CLOSED-SYSTEM MODELS		OPEN-SYSTEM MODELS	
1900–1930 RATIONAL MODELS TYPE I	1930–1960 NATURAL MODELS TYPE II	1960–1970 RATIONAL MODELS TYPE III	1970– NATURAL MODELS TYPE IV
Taylor (1911) Weber (1947 [translated])	Roethlesberger & Dickson (1939) Mayo (1945) Katz et al. (1951)	Udy (1959) Woodward (1965)	Hickson et al. (1971) March & Olson (1976)
Fayol (1949 [translated]) Gulick & Urwick (1937)	Roy (1952) Dalton (1959) McGregor (1960)	Thompson (1967) Perrow (1967) Pugh et al. (1969) Blau (1970) Galbraith (1973)	Meyer & Rowen (1977) Pfeffer & Salancik (1978)

NOTE. From *Organizations* (p. 128) by W. R. Scott, 1981, Englewood Cliffs, NJ: Prentice-Hall. Copyright 1981 by Prentice-Hall. Reprinted by permission.

Burrell and Morgan

Although Scott's (1981) classification is very useful, it does not include all the work now underway. In a recent book by Burrell and Morgan (1980), more inclusive than that of Scott, the authors take the view that "all theories of organization are based upon a philosophy of science and a theory of society" (p. x). They direct themselves to clarifying the confusion that now exists in social theory, including administrative theory. They have devised four paradigms based upon two dimensions: the nature of social science and the nature of society. Burrell and Morgan contend that each paradigm generates theories that are in fundamental opposition to those generated in other paradigms.

The first strand used by Burrell and Morgan (1980) is called either "subject-objective" or "German idealism-social positivism." The authors raise basic questions relating to ontology, epistemology, human nature, and method. The answers lie on continuums. With regard to the ontological question, there are those who believe that people create their own world. At the other end of the continuum are those realists who believe in an objective world, the same for all, a "social world that exists independently of an individual's appreciation of it" (p. iv). When epistemology is considered, one finds the positivist, who seeks regularities and causal relations, as contrasted with the anti-positivists, who believe that social science is essentially subjective, with no laws or underlying regularities in the social world. In the matter of human nature, the continuum ranges from those who believe in free will to those who believe people are controlled by their environment. The methodological continuum ranges from the idiographic view of social science (only first-hand knowledge counts) to the conduct of research through the use of systematic protocols and other techniques.

The second strand is not quite so clear as the first. It deals with viewing society from the standpoint of regulation or integration on the one hand to viewing society in reference to radical change on the other. In the first case, an effort is made to understand what holds a society together, why it is stable, and what social forces prevent it from exploding. Rather than inquiring as to the stability of society, many sociologists question why societies change. These social theorists identify radical changes in society and attempt to explain them. They see domination and structural contradiction as characterizing modern societies and fashion a sociology based on such observations.

Taken together, the two strands form four paradigms: radical humanist, radical structuralist, functionalist, and interpretive. Burrell and Morgan (1980) include two chapters on each paradigm, the first within sociology and the second within organizational science. The names of some of the paradigms have been changed to reflect the organizational subject matter, so "radical humanist" becomes "antiorganization" theory, and "functionalist" becomes "functional administrative" theory.

The *functionalist paradigm* contains virtually all theory taught and used in educational administration. There are three sources of theories in this cell: practicing administrators (e.g., Barnard), sociologists of organizations (e.g., Weber), and behavior in organizations (e.g., Simon). Cell characteristics are regulation, objectivity, status quo, consensus, social integration, solidarity, need satisfaction, and actuality. Theories tend to be realistic, positivistic, deterministic, and nomothetic. Some examples of theories that fit the functionalist cell and are used in educational administration are the Getzels-Guba social system theory, Griffiths decision-making theory, Immegart systems theory, Barnard-Simon equilibrium theory, and Fielder's contingency theory. In the field of general administrative theory, the most popular books fit the functionalist requirements: Kanter (1983) and Peters and Waterman (1982).

The dominance in educational administration of

what Burrell and Morgan (1980) define as the functionalist paradigm is well documented by Boyan (1982) in an exhaustive analysis of research and theory in educational administration. He first presents an overview of the setting in which educational administration takes place, and he then explores "the research productivity generated by the 'traditional paradigm,' which has guided research in educational administration; the emergence of challenges to the older paradigm; and new ways of looking at administrators' work, as well as conflicting views about the effects of administrator activity" (p. 24). With the exception of seven articles by Greenfield that fall within the radical humanist paradigm, all other studies Boyan (1982) discusses fit the functional paradigm. Even though the older theories—social systems, decision, role—are challenged, they are challenged by people working within the bounds of functionalism as defined by Burrell and Morgan (1980).

One of the criticisms of Burrell and Morgan (1980) is that people are classified together in a paradigm when they should not be (D. H. J. Morgan, 1980, p. 332). The functionalist cell, for instance, includes all theories in Scott's (1981) classification, lumping together open and closed, rational and natural. Similar criticisms can be made of the radical humanist and radical structuralist cells.

The interpretive paradigm is based on the belief that people build the social world in which they live. This paradigm is in the tradition of German idealism and has its roots in the work of Immanuel Kant. There are very few studies of organizations done in the interpretive mode, and Burrell and Morgan (1980) only discuss efforts utilizing ethnomethodological approaches and phenomenological interaction. They use terms in a particular way to describe methodologies that are based on the assumption that reality is a social creation: that individuals create the world in which they live. To them, ethnography is an approach that seeks to determine the way in which individuals make sense of their world, while phenomenology focuses on social context. There is, however, no agreement with this posture in the literature, particularly the literature of educational administration. For instance Smith et al. (1983), in an ethnographic study, devote considerable time and space to the context of the school they researched (Vol. 4, pp. 84–85), while Montalto (1983), in one of the very few studies in education that employed phenomenological analysis, is concerned with individuals and their work and values, all within the context of university schools of art.

There is also some confusion between the use of the terms "case study" and "ethnography." It is often contended that ethnography is a "thick" description, while the case study is a "thin" description (Lutz, 1984, p. 654). Since some case studies are "thick" (e.g., Griffiths, Clark, Wynn, & Iannaccone, 1962) and some ethnographies are "thin" (e.g., Pettigrew, 1979), it would seem that this is not a distinguishing characteristic. Even though Burrell and Morgan (1980) are of the view that ethnography must have roots in the interpretive paradigm, it would seem that actual practice is not in accord. It appears that ethnographies are being done using traditional methodologies, and only the name "ethnography" differs from the old name, "case studies." Even Gronn's (1984) "'I have a solution...': Administrative Power in a School Meeting" appears to be a case study done in the traditional mode. From Gronn's earlier writings (1982, 1983), one would expect him to have written in the interpretive mode, yet he did not. The conclusions (a) that ethnography and case studies are terms used interchangeably and (b) that ethnography, as it is practiced, does not have an interpretive epistemological base seem to be borne out by a well-known study. *The Man in the Principal's Office: An Ethnography* is described by its author as "this case study" (Wolcott, 1973). Willower (1986) comes to the same conclusion when he notes, "Even ethnomethodology...has been described as adhering to a 'concrete, positivistic conception of adequacy.'"

The antiorganization theory paradigm is based on radical humanism, with roots in the French existentialist movement (Sartre) and German idealism (Kant, Fichte, Hegel). Burrell and Morgan (1980) point out that both the interpretive and the antiorganization paradigms are based on the notion that individuals create the world in which they live—the radical humanists are essentially critics. The authors observe that no one appeared to be studying organizations in the radical humanist mode as of 1979, but if anyone were, the result would be antiorganization theory (p. 310). The only person who claims to be studying organizations from a radical humanist perspective is Linda Smircich of the University of Massachusetts ("About the Authors," 1983). What her end product will be is a matter of speculation. Burrell and Morgan's inclusion of the antiorganization theory paradigm is questionable because only criticisms, not theory development or research, are being undertaken in this mode. It seems to be included because of arithmetic; two dimensions normally make four cells. In reality, there are only three cells resulting from two dimensions.

Greenfield appears to be the sole critic in the antiorganizational or radical humanist mode writing in the field of educational administration. It is quite clear that he is completely opposed to positivism, to rationalism, and to all aspects of functional structuralism, but it is very difficult to determine what he would substitute. To paraphrase Burrell and Morgan, what might emerge from Greenfield's thinking would, indeed, be anti-organizational organizational theory (Greenfield, 1975, 1979, 1980; Gronn, 1983).

The radical structuralist paradigm has provided the framework for a vigorous critique of functionalism and, therefore, of most of present-day organizational theory. There are two strands to radical organizational theory, Marxist and Weberian, with the Marxist approach the far more popular. The Marxist critique of traditional organizational theory includes a number of variations such as neo-Marxism, ethno-Marxism, and the Marxist dialectic. In these variations of the Marxist approach, organizational life is interpreted in terms of power, conflict, contradictions, crises, dialectics, and class.

Clegg (1977), for instance, contends that "Much of...organizational theory has been developed at the interface of capitalist theory and capitalist practice in the academic institutions of business" (p. 22). Heydebrand (1977) argues that "organizational theory, like other theories in the social sciences, has been dominated by powerful ideological forces which, taken together, have more or less successfully reproduced and legitimized the structure of capitalist society" (p. 85). In contrast, Perrow (1978) observes that "the ethno-Marxist approach challenges conventional organization theory on almost every score" (p. 247). However, the Marxian dialectical approach is presented most clearly by J. K. Benson (1977), who sees the organization as a concrete, multilevel phenomenon beset by contradictions that continually undermine its existing features (p. 3). He contends that "there are four principles of dialectical analysis—social construction/production, totality, contradiction, praxis" (p. 3).

The central idea of social construction/production is that people are continually constructing the social world, which is Greenfield's (1975) major thesis. The concept of totality means that any particular structure must always be seen as part of a larger, concrete whole, and not as an isolated, abstract phenomenon. The process of social construction contains contradictions, and it is contradiction as seen by writers such as Heydebrand (1977) that is the central principle of the Marxist critique. Heydebrand (1977) illustrates the concept of contradiction with a study of the organizational contradictions within judicial systems. In an effort to introduce efficiency and increase productivity, both administrative and judiciary reforms have been made. On the one hand, this has meant the introduction of administrators into the courts and, on the other, more judges and court personnel. These two developments tend to contradict each other, with the result that "adjudication and the adversary process are increasingly replaced by negotiation, arbitration, and ultimately administration" (Heydebrand, 1977, pp. 99–100).

The fourth principle is praxis, meaning action or activity or practice. Benson (1977) defines praxis as "the free and creative reconstruction of social arrangements on the basis of a reasoned analysis of both the limits and the potentials of present social forms" (p. 5). Theories, for example, reflect the social context in which they are created and the practical concerns of their creators. Theories also are deeply involved in the creation of organizations, and they guide actors in their organizational behavior. From this tautology Benson (1977) concludes: "There is, then, a dialectical relation between organizational arrangements and organizational theories" (p. 16).

There are obvious problems within the Marxist critique, illustrated by frequent inconsistencies. The principle that people create their own world, "social construction/production," is contradicted by the concept of totality, which indicates *how* people should construct their world. Then there is Heydebrand's (1977) contention that ethno-Marxist theory is applicable to all organizations. This seems to be an example of the overenthusiasm that characterizes the traditional theorists, and Heydebrand (1977) is probably in error, too.

Ethno-Marxism is interesting because it raises questions that must be rethought concerning traditional theory. In every aspect of organization, the Marxist finds a meaning significantly different from that seen by the organizational theorist working in the traditional modes. For the Marxist, rules are not so much ways of achieving the stated goals of an organization as they are means to controlling people and exercising power. The hierarchy does not represent levels of ability so much as it does the maintenance of class structure. These are but two examples of how the schools of thought differ. It will be very interesting to see in what form administrative theory emerges from the Marxist challenge.

Marxist Theory in Educational Administration

Relatively little radical structuralist theory has been developed and no empirical research conducted that is based on radical structure in educational administration. There is, however, a growing body of Marxist-based criticism of functionalist organizational science. Bates (1978, 1980, 1982, 1983) is the most prolific of the Marxist writers in this vein. His critique centers on a contention that organizations built on the premises of traditional organizational theory are contradictory to the purpose of providing appropriate education. He sees (1983) four problems with traditional administrative theory:

> Firstly, the dominant traditions of theory and practice in educational administration serve to justify uncritically patterns of organization and control in schools and school systems that both mirror and reinforce the dominant patterns of inequality in the wider society.
>
> Secondly, the preceding analysis has led to certain questions about the way in which knowledge is structured and represented in schools and school systems. It has been my argument that the selection, organisation, transmission, and evaluation of knowledge in bureaucratised schools can be seen as resulting, not from any justifiable epistemological or social basis, but from the demands of bureaucratic convenience. Moreover, as the bureaucratic structures of schools imitate the patterns of dominance and submission of the corporate order, knowledge itself becomes structured in ways that imitate various hierarchies of status. In particular, technical knowledge displaces cultural (i.e., historical, aesthetic, and ethical) knowledge from its position of central importance in the curriculum.
>
> Thirdly, my analysis has suggested that the bureaucratic hierarchy of dominance and submission employed by the school so structures communication and discourse as to produce a didactic pedagogy that is unidirectional and acausal. The effect of such a structure of communication is to replace rational discourse with a form of behavioural management that prevents the development of rationality and the equal consideration of interests.
>
> Fourthly, I have argued that the acceptance of bureaucratic, or systems, models as appropriate patterns for school management involves conceptions of epistemology and collective action that lack a fundamental commitment to the ideas of community and to the mutuality of social concerns. (p. 39)

Bates's solution to the four problems is the creation of an educational theory of administration from which would come an appropriate institutional structure for the management of knowledge. In order to accomplish this theory and structure, four issues must be taken into account: "These are the democratisation of social relations, the democratisation of knowledge, the democratisation of communication, and the democratisation of cultural concerns" (1983, p. 39). Both the analysis and resolution are strictly within the Marxist dialectic and exhibit both the strengths and weaknesses discussed earlier.

Although not in educational administration, Apple (1979) and Giroux (1981, 1983b) appear to have influenced those of Marxist bent who are in the field. In essence, they apply the critical theory of the Frankfurt School to school practice. As Giroux (1983a) states, "I have focused on their [Adorno, Horkheimer, and Marcuse] critique of positivist rationality, their views of theory, their critical reconstruction of a theory of culture, and finally, their analysis of depth psychology" (p. 33).

The influence of Apple and Giroux, among others, is clearly seen in P. E. Watkins's (1983b) analysis of scientific management. Watkins concludes that "the ideology underpinning Taylorism still is *the* dominant force in administration today" (p. 133). This conclusion can be arrived at *only* if one starts from the tenets of Marxist ideology. Once these assumptions are accepted, it is an inevitable conclusion.

Watkins (1983a) also uses critical theory to analyze the importance of class in understanding school organizations. He contends that critical theory "may open up a clearer perspective regarding how and why schools are organized in particular ways and how they might and should be changed" (p. 27). Foster (1983) has used critical theory to analyze loose coupling. He found Weick (1976) to be working within the functionalist paradigm and concluded that there are more radical ways of viewing school organizations. Since it is rather doubtful that Weick was seeking to develop the most radical way possible of looking at schools, Foster's conclusion doesn't seem all that relevant.

There is, then, a growing literature in the radical structuralist mode. In educational administration, this literature has been restricted to analysis rather than to empirical research and is generally discussed under the rubric of critical theory. Considering the success of such Marxists as Heydebrand in their research, it is unfortunate that similar studies have not been undertaken in educational administration.

Emerging Developments

In addition to previously cited developments, there are several in administrative theory and research that do not fit any of Scott's (1981) or Burrell and Morgan's (1980) categories. These are discussed separately since they reflect probable future directions of organizational science.

Paradigm Diversity

The idea is emerging that research on organizations should not be restricted to a single paradigm; rather, research should proceed in all four (more or less) paradigms. Morgan (1981), in particular, makes the point that the paradigms he and Burrell have advanced constitute four world views. Questions raised in the context of each such view add information and understanding about organizations that cannot be gained through other paradigms. Morgan (1981) illustrates this point in a paper in which each paradigm is identified and its unique contributions are enumerated; for example, radical humanism advocates an ideology that places people first (p. 17). Suppose that in studying an organization the researcher looked first at the people and not at organizational goals and structures. What would the resulting theory be like? Viewing organizations through the assumptions of four different paradigms will produce far more and different questions than we have dealt with heretofore.

One of the major values of paradigm diversity is its contribution to the resolution of the methodological squabbles in which the field is now engaged. Each paradigm is based upon different assumptions that, therefore, research methodologies should reflect. As Morgan (1981) states, "Such an approach offers the possibility of replacing debates about the merits of competing methodologies with a consideration of the merits of rival logics of research" (p. 23).

Howe (1985) goes further than Morgan when he says, "The consequence is that quantitative and qualitative methods are not incompatible. On the contrary, they are inextricably interwoven, and all researchers who advocate quantitative and qualitative methods are thus on solid epistemological grounds" (p. 16).

Writing on much the same subject as Morgan (1981), Lincoln (1984) has come to similar conclusions, although rather than merely advocating movement toward what amounts to paradigm diversity, she contends that paradigm diversity is already with us. Her appraisal of the present follows:

> First, researchers are concluding that they cannot engage in research without coming to grips with the epistemological assumptions undergirding that research.
>   Second,...inquirers know they will have to make paradigmatic choices and defend them.
>   Third,...the virtual explosion of qualitatively-oriented journal articles devoted to qualitative methods in research is testimony to this acceptability of non-quantitative methods and provides encouragement to those willing to explore alternate approaches to their craft.
>   Fourth, researchers are increasingly aware that epistemological choices lead inexorably to methodological choices. (p. 15)

There is evidence to support Lincoln's four points in the overall field of organizational science and in education generally; there is, however, little evidence to support such a set of conclusions regarding educational administration. Articles concerned with qualitative methods in educational administration are rare, and if proposals for papers and symposia accompanying the 1985 American Educational Research Association annual meeting in Chicago constitute a valid criterion, Lincoln's conclusion is not true for educational administration. Of 230 proposals, only 3 dealt with qualitative research and 10 (4 percent) utilized research paradigms other than functionalism (as defined by Burrell and

Morgan, 1980). Although paradigm diversity is catching on in many parts of the social sciences, to date there is little interest on the part of researchers in educational administration.

Metaphors

Writers and researchers in educational administration have long been interested in metaphors. The metaphor with the longest history and the greatest impact has been that of the school as a factory. A version generally credited to Bobbitt is best known (cited in Watkins, 1983a):

> If the school were a factory, the child the raw material, the ideal adult the finished product, the teacher an operative, the principal a foreman, then the curriculum could be thought of as whatever processing the raw material needs to change him into the finished product. (p. 125)

When one has in mind the image of school as factory, both practice and theory are very different from what one were to think, for example, of the school as hospital. With the hospital model, rather than assuming that they all need the same curriculum, children would be tested and then sent to parts of the school where particular weaknesses could be treated. As Bates (1982) has pointed out: "Shifts in fundamental metaphors which we use to explore and interpret the world of nature and the nature of society have far-reaching repercussions" (p. 7). He illustrates the significance of a change in metaphor by recalling that "the shift from an animistic view of the universe to a mechanistic one brought about by Newton and his philosophical colleagues Bacon and Locke involved a major shift in attitude towards nature, which became for the first time, viewed as accessible, knowable, and *controllable* [italics in the original]" (p. 7).

Hanson (1984), analyzing the work of five prominent researchers in educational administration, reported that there is a pervasive structural and mechanistic view of schools: "Such a view represents organizations as systems within which people are portrayed as cogs in the machinery" (p. 180). She implies that metaphors used by educational researchers are not the ones used by administrators and the public (p. 182).

The present interest in metaphors springs from a dissatisfaction with the older metaphors, the introduction of paradigms such as the interpretive and radical structuralist into organizational science, and changes in assumptions underlying functionalism, that so far has had the greatest impact on educational administration. When Weick (1976) changed his assumptions about organizations, the metaphor of "loose coupling" emerged as a useful way of viewing relationships among components of a school district. If he had viewed the school as a factory, the idea of loose coupling would never have occurred to him. Much the same can be said for the garbage-can metaphor concocted by Cohen, March, and Olson (1972). At present, organizations are being viewed through many different glasses, and, as a result, new metaphors are being developed. The new metaphors, in turn, change the way people think about organizations. G. Morgan (1980) urges us to continue in this direction:

> Viewing organizations systematically as cybernetic systems, loosely coupled systems, ecological systems, theatres, cultures, political systems, language games, texts, accomplishments, enactments, psychic prisons, instruments of domination, schismatic systems, catastrophes, etc., it is possible to add rich and creative dimensions to organization theory. (p. 615)

Culture

Culture has assumed a position of extreme importance in current writing about organizations. Consider, for instance, the work of Peters and Waterman (1982) and Kanter (1983). Both books make innumerable references to the "culture" of organizations. The entire September 1983 issue of the *Administrative Science Quarterly* was devoted to the topic of culture. Special attention should be given to the lead article by Smircich, in which culture is discussed both as an internal variable and as a root metaphor. There are at least two seminal ideas here (Smircich, 1983), the first dealing with culture as a root metaphor:

> Some theorists advance the view that organizations be understood as cultures. They leave behind the view that a culture is something an organization *has*, in favor of the view that a culture is something an organization *is*.... Culture as a root metaphor for organizations goes beyond the instrumental view of organizations derived from the machine metaphor and beyond the adaptive view derived from the organismic metaphor. Culture as a root metaphor promotes a view of organizations as expressive forms, manifestations of human consciousness [italics added]. (p. 347)

The second seminal idea advanced by Smircich (1983) is to encourage consideration of Pondy and Mitroff's (1979) notion that the culture metaphor replace the open systems metaphor as an analytical framework in organizational studies. Smircich concludes, "Much of the research summarized in this paper and in this special issue stands as evidence that there is a trend in that direction" (p. 354).

The significance of the interest in the study of culture is well put by Smircich (1983):

> Despite the very real differences in research interest and purpose represented here, whether one treats culture as a background factor, an organizational variable, or as a metaphor for conceptualizing organization, the idea of culture focuses attention on the expressive, nonrational qualities of the experience of organization. It legitimates attention to the subjective, interpretive aspects of organizational life. (p. 355)

Feminist Literature

There is a growing body of literature in educational administration written by women. Taken as a whole, there appear to be no theoretical or methodological differences from the literature written by men, and many of the topics are the same as those their male counterparts use. As illustrations we find Silver's (1983) book *Educational Administration: Theoretical Perspectives on Practice and Research*, and Johnston, Yeakey, and Winter's (1981) article "A Study of the Relationship Between the Job Satisfaction of Principals and the Perceived Level of Teacher Militancy." Although these and many other articles and books written by women do not differ from what men have written or would write if so inclined, there is also a more distinctly feminist literature being written by women. The essential characteristic of feminist literature in educational administration lies in a subject matter of deep and personal concern to women. See, for example, Adkison (1981); Adkison and Bailey (1980); Andruskiw and Howes (1980); Elshof and Tomlinson (1981; Johnston, Yeakey, and Moore (1980); Lyman and Speizer (1980); Moore and Sagaria (1981); Ortiz (1979); Pancrazio and Gray (1982); Stent (1978); Stockard (1979); Villadsen and Tack (1981).

The development of a feminist critique of administrative theory and research is in its early stages. Shakeshaft and Nowell (1984) pointed to the exclusion of females and female experience in the Getzels-Guba model, to Fiedler's disregard of the importance of gender to his theory, and to the Leader Behavior Description Questionnaire (LBDQ), conceptualized using a male world and validated using predominantly male samples. Actually, the LBDQ items came from Helen Jenning's (1950) study of delinquent girls in a New York State institution. The article, in general, is a correct analysis of the ignoring of gender by administrative theorists. (See Chapter 6.)

Negotiation

As noted earlier Kanter (1983) has observed that one of the emerging design factors affecting organizational structure is an increasing overlap between workers and managers. This was illustrated in the Yeshiva University case and again in a ruling by an administrative law judge of the National Labor Relations Board, whereby it was determined that professors are managers and supervisors and therefore have no right to bargain under federal law (Watkins, 1984). The reason for the decision is that faculty control the academic program and most of the personnel functions. In situations where faculty members, deans, and presidents are all considered to be managers, how can one administer? It would seem that negotiating is the only activity open to the dean or president.

William Dill (1980), former Dean of the Faculties of Business at New York University and now President of Babson College, has described the use of the Barnard-Simon model as applied to universities:

> They (Barnard and Simon) would see the college or university as, in fact, they saw even the more tightly structured, hierarchically defined institutions of business and government: as assemblages of constituencies, some like faculty inside the boundaries of the institutions and others like alumni or charitable foundations outside these boundaries, drawn by various kinds of inducements to affiliate with the organization. Deans, like presidents, help orchestrate the actions which attract the various constituents, hold them together, and draw from them contributions which in totality yield the output of services and products that characterize a university or school. (pp. 265–266)

Putting the matter more simply, the administrator must have inducements to generate contributions. If a dean wants a professor to head a project that will lead to institutional improvement but entails more work for that person, the dean must have answers for the professor's question "What's in it for me?" The dean must have some control over the reward system (promotion, tenure, salary increments) or must be able to offer released time or some other inducement. In addition, that dean needs to know what the professor wants; sometimes it's merely recognition, and that then becomes the inducement.

Because of changes in society, organizations, and the behavior of organization members, most of the theories developed in the past 30 years have lost their usefulness. However, it seems that the directions indicated by the Barnard-Simon theory will be the ones to follow in the coming years.

RESEARCH, THEORY, AND EDUCATIONAL ADMINISTRATION

When the view of research and theory is restricted to educational administration, one finds the same kind of theory being espoused as 25 years ago—positivism, but the research being done is now somewhat less in the positivist mode. As was pointed out in "Evolution in Research and Theory: A Study of Prominent Researchers" (Griffiths, 1983), present-day researchers in educational administration do not start with clean theory: They have amalgams of assumptions, concepts, ideas, and the like, which "suggest" hypotheses to be verified. These "theoretical" statements are tested against observational statements, which themselves contain theoretical statements. So we can say that the "theories" really aren't theories; they are, as Miller (1983) has said of many theories in the social sciences, more like clotheslines on which the researchers hang their intellectual laundry (p. 5), and the method of research is a type of pseudopositivism. Willower quotes Merton's view of a large amount of sociological theory, which "consists of general orientations toward data, suggesting types of variables which theory must somehow take into account rather than clearly formulated, verifiable statements of relationships between specified variables" (Merton, 1968, cited in Willower, 1975). Willower's (1975) position is that the notion of orientations toward data is sufficient to accommodate much of the theoretical work in educational administration.

It is clear that more informal approaches to theory are increasingly being used. There is also less emphasis on the form of the theory and of the resultant research. The focus is on whether the theory stimulates research that is successful (i.e., research that produces useful knowledge). In this sense researchers in educational administration are in tune with other scientific researchers.

One of the major issues in administrative theory in education appears now to be resolved: the question of generalizability of theory. In other words, is a theory universal (i.e., applicable to all types of organizations in all cultures) or is it specific to education? Virtually all who participated in the "theory movement" of the 1950s contended that theory was universal. Roald Campbell (1957) was one of those who contended that education was a special case, and over the years he has become even more convinced of his position (Campbell, 1986). In fact, it would seem necessary to have theories specific to particular types of educational institutions. Interestingly, the early administrative theorists Taylor, Fayor, and Gulick were highly specific in their writing (Hughes, 1985, p. 31). In reviewing the literature on this subject, Griffiths concluded that *"theories of educational administration should be limited to specific types of organizations which exist in carefully defined contexts* [italics added]" (Griffiths, 1986). This in spite of the fact that Kanter (1983) isolated a number of characteristics that seemingly hold for all organizations. The problem is that they are highly abstract. It is always possible to generalize from highly abstract concepts, but abstract theories are of little use in concrete situations.

Despite the spirited criticism of positivist theory in educational administration, the advance of qualitative theories and research in education, and the moves of organizational scientists in at least three of the four paradigms of Burrell and Morgan (1980), the dominant posture of educational administration in the United States is best expressed by the English social scientist Pugh (1983):

> I eventually came to the conclusion that whatever view I took on the philosophical issues as such, the fact was that in order to pursue any substantive study I would need to assume a realist, determinist, positivist approach. Otherwise I would be condemned to spend my time on the metaphysics, without getting around to the physics, or, in my case, to the social psychology. This is still my view.... I do not see how one can study organizational behavior without making the ontological assumption that people and organizations exist as relatively concrete entities.... I regard the openness of the functionalist paradigm, and the willingness of its practitioners to draw on (steal?) concepts from other approaches, as a strength. (pp. 45–46)

NOTES

[1] I acknowledge with gratitude the help of Professor Donald Willower and the late Professor Bryce Fogarty in thinking through and clarifying the content of this paper. I wish especially to recognize the great skill of Professor Fogarty in detailed editing and analysis. He constantly raised questions that required rethinking and clarification. His passing has been a great loss to those of us who study educational administration.

Joyce McGuinness of New York University worked as an editor and helped greatly with suggestions for reorganizing the paper. Many thanks are due to Jerrilynn Burrowes for her bibliographic work and typing.

REFERENCES

"About the Authors." (1983). *Administrative Science Quarterly*, *28*(3), 499.

Adkison, J. A. (1981). Women in school administration: A review of the research. *Review of Educational Research*, *51*(3), 311–343.

Adkison, J. A., & Bailey, J. E. (1980). The Ices model: Increasing women's participation in educational administration. *Planning and Changing*, *11*(3), 141–149.

Administrator's Notebook (1952–). Chicago: The Midwest Center, University of Chicago.

Andruskiw, O., & Howes, N. J. (1980). Dispelling a myth: That stereotypic attitudes influence evaluations of women as administrators in higher education. *Journal of Higher Education*, *51*(5), 475–496.

Apple, M. (1979). *Ideology and curriculum*. Boston: Routledge & Kegan Paul.

Bates, R. J. (1978). Politics, ideology & education: The possibilities of the new sociology of education. *International Journal of Political Education*, *1*, 315–324.

Bates, R. J. (1980). Perspective: Educational administration, the sociology of science, and the management of knowledge.

Educational Administration Quarterly, *16*(2), 1–20.

Bates, R. J. (1982). Towards a critical practice of educational administration. *Studies in Educational Administration*, (27), 1–15.

Bates, R. J. (1983). *Educational administration and the management of knowledge*. Geelong, Australia: Deakin University.

Benson, J. K. (1977). Organizations: A dialectical view. *Administrative Science Quarterly*, *22*(1), 1–16.

Benson, K. (1982). [Review of *Theories of organizations: Form, process and transformation*. *Administrative Science Quarterly*, *27*(1), 166.

Berte, N. R., & Morse, S. W. (1985). Toward a "proactional" presidency. *Educational Record*, *66*(2), 51–54.

Boyan, N. J. (1982). Administration of educational organizations. In H. E. Mitzel, J. H. Best, & W. Rabinowitz (Eds.), *Encyclopedia of Educational Research* (5th ed., Vol. 1), (pp. 22–49). New York: Macmillan.

Boyd, W. L. (1983). Rethinking educational policy and management: Political science and educational administration in the 1980s. *American Journal of Education*, *92*(1), 1–29. (From *Educational Administration Abstracts*, 1984, *19*(3), 302–303.)

Bridgman, P. W. (1927). *The logic of modern physics*. New York: Macmillan.

Burrell, G., & Morgan, G. (1980). *Sociological paradigms and organizational analysis*. London: Heinemann.

Campaign '74: Now the candid sell. (1974, October 21). *Time*, p. 27.

Campbell, R. F. (1957). Situational factors in educational administration. In R. F. Campbell & R. T. Gregg (Eds.), *Administrative behavior in education* (pp. 228–268). New York: Harper.

Campbell, R. F. (1986). Is educational administration a special case: The question revisited. In G. S. Johnston (Ed.), *Research and thought in administrative theory: Developments in the field of educational administration*. Lanham, MD: University Press of America.

Campbell, R. F., & Gregg, R. T. (Eds.). (1957). *Administrative behavior in education*. New York: Harper.

Clark, D. L., Lotto, L. S., & Astuto, T. A. (1984) Effective schools and school improvement: A comparative analysis of two lines of inquiry. *Educational Administrative Quarterly*, *20*(3), 64–65.

Clegg, S. (1977). Power, organizational theory, Marx & critique. In S. Clegg & R. Dunkerly (Eds.), *Critical issues in organizations* (p. 22). London: Routledge & Kegan Paul.

Cohen, M. D., March, J. G., & Olson, J. P. (1972). A garbage can model of organizational choice. *Administrative Science Quarterly*, *17*(1), 1–25.

Coladarci, A., & Getzels, J. W. (1955). *The use of theory in educational administration*. Palo Alto: Stanford University Press.

Conway, J. A. (1984). The myth, mystery and mastery of participative decision making in education. *Educational Administration Quarterly*, *20*(3), 11–40.

Cubberley, E. P. (1916). *Public school administration*. New York: Houghton Mifflin.

Culbertson, J. (1983). Theory in educational administration: Echoes from critical thinkers. *Educational Researcher*, *12*(10), 15–22.

Dill, D. D. (1984). The nature of administrative behavior in higher education. *Educational Administration Quarterly*, *20*(3), 69–99.

Dill, W. (1980). The deanship: An unstable craft. In D. E. Griffiths & D. J. McCarty (Eds.), *The dilemma of the deanship* (pp. 261–284). Danville, IL: Interstate.

Elshof, A. T. & Tomlinson, E. (1981). Eliminating stress for women administrators. *Journal of the National Association for Women Deans, Administrators and Counselors*, *44*(2), 37–41.

Evangelauf, J. (1984, November 21). Presidents say they're spending more time away from campuses. *Chronicle of Higher Education*, pp. 1, 15.

Foster, W. (1983). *Loose coupling revisited: A critical view of Weick's contribution to educational administration*. Geelong, Australia: Deakin University.

Fraassen, B. van. (1980). *The scientific image*. Oxford: Clarendon.

Galbraith, J. K. (1984, January 22). Corporate man. *The New York Times*, p. 39.

Gallup, A. (1984). The Gallup poll of teachers' attitudes toward the public schools. *Phi Delta Kappan*, 66(2), 97–107.

Getzels, J. W., Lipham, J. M., & Campbell, R. F. (1968). *Educational administration as a social process*. New York: Harper & Row.

Giroux, H. A. (1981). *Theory and resistance in eduation*. Philadelphia: Temple University Press.

Giroux, H. A. (1983a). *Critical theory and practice*. Geelong, Australia: Deakin University.

Giroux, H. A. (1983b). Theories of reproduction and resistance in the new society of education: A critical analysis. *Harvard Education Review*, 53(3), 257–293.

Grace, A. G. (Ed.). (1946). *Changing conceptions in educational administration*. The Forty-fifth Yearbook of the National Society for the Study of Education.

Greenfield, T. B. (1975). Theory about organization: A new perspective and its implications for schools. In M. G. Hughes (Ed.), *Administering education: International challenge* (pp. 71–99). London: Athlone.

Greenfield, T. B. (1979). Organizational theory as ideology. *Curriculum Inquiry*, 9(2), 97–112.

Greenfield, T. B. (1980). The man who comes back through the door in the wall: Discovering truth, discovering self, discovering organizations. *Educational Administration Quarterly*, 16(3), 25–59.

Greenfield, T. B. (1984). Theories of educational organization: A critical perspective. *International encyclopedia of education: Research and studies*. Oxford: Pergamon.

Griffiths, D. E. (1956). *Human relations in school administration*. New York: Appleton-Century-Crofts.

Griffiths, D. E. (1959). *Administrative theory*. New York: Appleton-Century-Crofts.

Griffiths, D. E. (Ed.). (1964). *Behavioral science and educational administration*. The 63rd Yearbook of the National Society for the Study of Education. Chicago: University of Chicago Press.

Griffiths, D. E. (1969). Administrative theory. In R. L. Ebel (Ed.), *Encyclopedia of Educational Research* (4th ed.). New York: Macmillan.

Griffiths, D. E. (1979). Intellectual turmoil in educational administration. *Educational Administration Quarterly*, 15(3), 43–65.

Griffiths, D. E. (1980). Research and theory in the administration of higher education. In D. E. Griffiths & D. J. McCarty (Eds.), *The dilemma of the deanship* (pp. 21–44). Danville, IL: Interstate.

Griffiths, D. E. (1983). Evolution in research and theory: A study of prominent researchers. *Educational Administration Quarterly*, 19(3), 201–221.

Griffiths, D. E. (1985). *Administrative theory in transition*. Geelong, Australia: Deakin University.

Griffiths, D. E. (1986). Can there be a science of organizations? In G. S. Johnston (Ed.), *Research and thought in educational administration: The state of the art*. Lanham, MD: University Press of America.

Griffiths, D. E., Clark, D. L., Wynn, D. R., & Iannaccone, L. (1962). *Organizing schools for effective education* (pp. 225–293). Danville, IL: Interstate.

Gronn, P. C. (1982). Neo-Taylorism in educational administration. *Educational Administration Quarterly*, 18(4), 17–35.

Gronn, P. C. (1983). *Rethinking educational administration: T. B. Greenfield and his critics*. Geelong, Australia: Deakin University.

Gronn, P. C. (1984). I have a solution...: Administrative power in a school meeting. *Educational Administration Quarterly*, 20(2), 65–92.

Gross, N., Mason, W. S., & McEachern, A. (1958). *Explorations in role analysis: Studies in the school superintendency role*. New York: John Wiley.

Hage, J. (1980). *Theories of organization: Form, process, and transformation*. New York: John Wiley.

Halpin, A. W. (Ed.). (1958). *Administrative theory in education*. Chicago: The Midwest Center, University of Chicago.

Halpin, A. W. (1970). Administrative theory: The fumbled torch. In

A. Kroll (Ed.), *Issues in American education*. New York: Oxford University Press.

Halpin A. W., & Hayes, A. E. (1977). The broken ikon, or, whatever happened to theory? In L. L. Cunningham, H. G. Hack, & R. O. Nystrand (Eds.), *Educational administration: The developing decades*. Berkeley, CA: McCutchan.

Hanson, M. (1984). Exploration of mixed metaphors in educational administration research. *Issues in Education*, 2(3), 167–185.

Harlow, J. G. (1962). Purpose-defining: The central function of the school administrator. In J. Culbertson & S. P. Hencley (Eds.), *Preparing administrators: New perspectives*. Columbus, OH: Council for Educational Administration.

Hess, F. (1983). Evolution in practice. *Educational Administration Quarterly*, 19(3), 245.

Heydebrand, W. (1977). Organizational contradictions in public bureaucracies: Toward a Marxian theory of organizations. In K. Benson (Ed.), *Organizational analysis*. Beverly Hills: Sage.

Hills, J. (1965). Educational administration: A field in transition. *Educational Administration Quarterly*, 1(1), 58–66.

Howe, K. (1985). Two dogmas of educational research. *Educational Research*, 14(8), 10–18.

Hughes, M. (1985). Theory and practice in educational management. In M. Hughes, P. Ribbins, & H. Thomas (Eds.), *Managing education*. London: Holt, Rinehart, & Winston.

Jackson, P. (1981a). Comprehending a well-run comprehensive: A report on a visit to a large suburban high school. In *Daedalus, America's schools: Portraits and perspectives*, 110(4), 81–96.

Jackson, P. (1981b). Secondary schooling for children of the poor. In *Daedalus, America's schools: Portraits and perspectives*, 110(4), 39–58.

Jennings, H. R. (1950). *Leadership and isolation*. New York: Longmans, Green.

Johnston, G. S., Yeakey, C. C., & Moore, S. E. (1980). An analysis of the employment of women in professional administrative positions in public education. *Planning and Changing*, 11(3), 115–132.

Johnston, G. S., Yeakey, C. C., & Winter, R. A. (1981). A study of the relationship between the job satisfaction of principals and the perceived level of teacher militancy. *Alberta Journal of Educational Research*, 27(4), 352–365.

Kahn, H., & Weiner, A. J. (1967). The next thirty-three years: A framework for speculation. *Daedalus*, 96(3), 707–708.

Kanter, R. M. (1983). *The change masters*. New York: Simon & Schuster.

Lawrence, P. R., & Lorsch, J. W. (1967). *Organization and environment*. Boston: Harvard University Press.

Lightfoot, S. L. (1981a). Portraits of exemplary secondary schools: George Washington Carver Comprehensive High School. In *Daedalus, America's schools: Portraits and perspectives*, 110(4), 17–38.

Lightfoot, S. L. (1981b). Portraits of exemplary secondary schools: Highland Park. In *Daedalus, America's schools: Portraits and perspectives*, 110(4), 59–80.

Lincoln, Y. S. (1984). Of wakes, monarchies and positivists: The emergent paradigm debate. *Organizational Theory Dialogue*, 4(2), 13–16.

Lotto, L. (1984, April). *Solutions in search of problems: The experiential validity of new views on educational administration*. Paper presented at the meeting of the American Educational Research Association, New Orleans, LA.

Lutz, F. (1984). Tightening up loose coupling in organizations of higher education. *Administrative Science Quarterly*, 27(4), 654.

Lyman, K. D., & Speizer, J. J. (1980). Advancing in school administration: A pilot project for women. *Harvard Educational Review*, 50(1), 25–35.

Magee, B. (1978). The philosophy of science: Dialogue with Hilary Putnam. In B. Magee, *Men of ideas* (pp. 233–234). New York: Viking.

McClellan, J. E. (1960). Theory in educational administration. *School Review*, 68, 210–227.

Miller, G. A. (1983, December 25). Frames of mind. *The New York Times Book Review*, p. 5.

Montalto, L. (1983). A phenomenological examination of dominant painting styles and the effect of ideology on M.F.A. candidates in selected departments of art (Doctoral dissertation, New York University, 1983). *Dissertations Abstracts International, 44*(12–A), 3579.

Moore, H. (1957). *Studies in school administration.* Washington, DC: American Association of School Administrators.

Moore, K. M. & Sagaria, M. D. (1981). Women administrators and mobility: The second struggle. *Journal of the National Association for Women Deans, Administrators, and Counselors, 44*(2), 21–28.

Morgan, D. H. J. (1980). [Review of *Sociological paradigms and organizational analysis.*] *Journal of the British Sociological Association, 14*(2), 332–333.

Morgan, G. (1980). Paradigms, metaphors, and puzzle solving. *Administrative Science Quarterly, 25*(4), 605–622.

Morgan, G. (1981). *Paradigm diversity in organizational research: Threat or opportunity.* Unpublished manuscript.

Morris, L. (1975). Acceptability: The new emphasis in educational administration. In M. G. Hughes (Ed.), *Administering education: International challenge* (p. 14). London: Athlone.

Mort, P. (1946). *Principles of school administration.* New York: McGraw-Hill.

Nisbet, R. (1974, Summer). The decline of academic nationalism. *Change,* p. 26.

Nordheimer, J. (1976, July 5). Americans finding new course is vital. *The New York Times,* p. 18.

Organization Resources Counselors, Inc. (1982, February). *A time for initiative: A review and a forecast of employee relations.* New York: Author.

Ortiz, F. I. (1979). Scaling the hierarchical system in school administration: A case analysis of a female administrator. *Urban Review, 11*(3), 111–125.

Pancrazio, S. B., & Gray, R. G. (1982). Networking for professional women: A collegial model. *Journal of the National Association for Women Deans, Administrators, and Counselors, 45*(3), 16–19.

Perrow, C. (1978). Demystifying organizations. In Y. Hasenfeld & R. Saari (Eds.), *The management of human services* (p. 247). New York: Columbia University Press.

Peters, T. J. & Waterman, R. H., Jr. (1982). *In search of excellence.* New York: Harper & Row.

Pettigrew, A. M. (1979). On studying organizational cultures. *Administrative Science Quarterly, 24*(4), 570–581.

Pfeffer, J., & Salancik, G. R. (1978). *The external control of organizations.* New York: Harper & Row.

Phillips, D. C. (1983). After the wake: Postpositivistic educational thought. *Educational Researcher, 12*(5), 4–12.

Pondy, L. R., & Mitroff, I. I. (1979). Beyond open systems models of organizations. In L. L. Cummings & B. M. Staw (Eds.), *Research in organizational behavior* (pp. 3–39). Greenwich, CT: JAI.

Pugh, D. S. (1983). Studying organizational structure and process. In G. Morgan (Ed.), *Beyond method* (pp. 45–46). Beverly Hills: Sage.

Rehfuss, J. (1984, June 27). What goes wrong (and sometimes right) with presidential searches. *Chronicle of Higher Education,* p. 64.

Reston, J. (1984, October 31). The rise of factionalism. *The New York Times,* p. A–27.

Ribbins, P. (1985). Organization theory and the study of educational institutions. In M. Hughes, P. Ribbins, & H. Thomas (Eds.), *Managing education.* London: Holt, Rinehart & Winston.

Schwab, J. J. (1964). The professorship in educational administration: Theory-art-practice. In D. J. Willower, & J. Culbertson (Eds.). *The professorship in educational administration.* Columbus, OH: University Council for Educational Administration.

Scott, W. R. (1981). *Organizations.* Englewood Cliffs, NJ: Prentice-Hall.

Scriven, M. (1969). Logical positivism and the behavioral sciences.

In P. Achinstein & S. F. Barker (Eds.). *The legacy of logical positivism: Studies in the philosophy of science.* Baltimore: Johns Hopkins Press.

Sears, J. B. (1950). *The nature of the administrative process.* New York: McGraw-Hill.

Shakeshaft, C., & Nowell, I. (1984). Research on theories, concepts, and models of organizational behavior: The influence of gender. *Issues in Education, 2*(3), 186–203.

Shapere, D. (1969). Notes toward a post-positivistic interpretation of science. In P. Achinstein & S. F., Barker (Eds.), *The legacy of logical positivism* (p. 125). Baltimore: Johns Hopkins Press.

Silver, P. (1983). *Educational administration: Theoretical perspectives on practice and research.* New York: Harper & Row.

Simon, H. (1945). *Administrative behavior.* New York: Macmillan.

Smircich, L. (1983). Concepts of culture and organizational analysis. *Administrative Science Quarterly, 28*(3), 339–358.

Smith, L. M., Prunty, J. J., & Dwyer, D. C. (1983). *Innovation and change in American education. Kensington revisited: A fifteen year follow-up of an innovative elementary school and its faculty* (Vols. 1–6). St. Louis: Washington University.

Snow, C. P. (1971). The two cultures: A second look. *Public Affairs* (p. 56). New York: Charles Scribner.

Soutar, D. H. (1982, February 15). *An overview of management development in mining and other industries.* Paper presented at the American Institute of Mining, Metallurgical, and Petroleum Engineers, Dallas, TX.

Spalding, F. E. (1955). *School superintendent in action in five cities.* Rindge, NH: Richard R. Smith.

Stent, A. (1978). Academe's new girl network. *Change, 10*(6), 18–21.

Stockard, J. (1979). Public prejudice against women school administrators: The possibility of change. *Educational Administration Quarterly, 15*(3), 83–96.

Suppe, F. (1977). *The structure of scientific theories* (pp. 704–705). Urbana, IL: University of Illinois.

Thomas, L. (1983). The governance of a university. In L. Thomas, *The youngest science* (pp. 168–169). New York: Viking.

Trow, M. (1959). Administrative theory in educational administration. *Administrative Science Quarterly, 4,* 122–126.

Van de Ven, A. H. (1983). Lessons from America's best-run companies [Review of *In search of excellence*]. *Administrative Science Quarterly, 28*(4), 623.

Villadsen, A. W., & Tack, M. W. (1981). Combining home and career responsibilities: The methods used by women executives in higher education. *Journal of the National Association of Women Deans, Administrators, and Counselors, 45*(1), 20–25.

Walton, J. (1955). The theoretical study of educational administration. *Harvard Educational Review, 25*(3), 169–178.

Watkins, B. T. (1984, July 11). Bargaining rights denied professors at Boston U. *The Chronicle of Higher Education,* p. 1.

Watkins, P. E. (1983a). *Class, control and contestation in educational organisations.* Geelong, Australia: Deakin University.

Watkins, P. E. (1983b). Scientific management and critical theory in educational administration. In R. Bates (Ed.), *Educational administration and the management of knowledge.* Geelong, Australia: Deakin University.

Weick, K. E. (1976). Educational organizations as loosely coupled systems. *Administrative Science Quarterly, 21*(1), 1–19.

Willis, Q. (1984). Studying managers at work. *Practising Manager, 4*(2), 35–42.

Willower, D. J. (1975). Theory in educational administration. *Journal of Educational Administration, 13*(1), 77–91.

Willower, D. J. (1986). Mystifications and mysteries in thought and research in educational administration. In G. S. Johnston & C. C. Yeakey (Eds.), *Research and thought in administrative theory: Developments in the field of educational administration.* Lanham, MD: University Press of America.

Wolcott, H. F. (1973). *The man in the principal's office: An ethnography.* New York: Holt Rinehart, & Winston.

CHAPTER 3

Administrator Selection, Career Patterns, Succession, and Socialization

Erwin Miklos

The major theme of the research reviewed in this chapter encompasses the processes through which members of educational organizations become administrators: the formalized procedures by which people enter administrative positions through recruitment and selection, enroll in programs of study, and follow the career paths that link administrative positions. However, becoming an administrator also involves the more subtle processes of being socialized into thinking and behaving in particular ways in an organizational context. Socialization is a process that begins before recruitment and extends through various stages of formal preparation and employment. Indeed, for those who stay in the field, the socialization continues through a substantial proportion of their adult lives.

The discussion is divided into four major sections: (a) recruitment and selection, (b) career patterns, (c) succession, and (d) socialization. Results of the research reviewed confirm that there are differences in these processes between levels of the educational structure, between types of positions, and between individual administrators. In a number of areas, there are important differences in the experiences of men and women as well as among members of different cultural groups. (See Chapters 6 through 8). Some aspects of becoming an administrator have been researched to a

greater extent for men than for women; for other aspects, the reverse holds. A similar condition exists for research on cultural groups and types of positions.

Although the tone of the review may appear to imply that the generalizability of research results has been assumed, this is not the case. Most summary statements contain highly speculative overtones and are offered as hypotheses for further testing rather than as conclusions firmly grounded in empirical research. These qualifications notwithstanding, there has been a deliberate attempt to ground the discussion in the results of empirical research. As a consequence, critical examination of the theoretical literature which undergirds the empirical inquiry has been defined as beyond the scope of the review.[1]

RECRUITMENT AND SELECTION

Research into recruitment and selection rests on beliefs about the significance of administrative functions in education and about the importance of making sound appointment decisions. Periodic calls for renewed attention to systematic research have been prompted by perceptions of shortcomings in practice as well as in previous inquiry (Fisk, 1953; Grable, 1968; McIntyre, 1966). Studies have been guided by objectives that are more often implicit than explicit. Among these objectives are formulating effective selection policies, identifying valid criteria, reducing the influence of extraneous factors, and developing improved selection

Consultant/reviewers: Richard O. Carlson, Bowling Green State University; and John Hoyle, Texas A & M University

procedures. A substantial body of literature that is based only partially on research has emerged in response to the perceived need to provide practical guides for those who recruit and select administrators.

Selection Policies and Procedures

An area of continuing interest in studies on recruitment and selection is assessment of a school district's policies and procedures for filling administrative vacancies. Typically, researchers make comparisons either with practices advocated in the literature or with a perceived ideal. Despite variations across districts (Boyce, 1961; Bronfield, 1962) and differences between positions such as those of superintendent (Albert, 1968; Curry, 1980; Rodenberger, 1981) and principal (Drake, 1965; Dylewski, 1975; Glover, 1970), the findings tend to fall into two general categories. Some school boards appear to be aware of recommended procedures and are consistent in applying them (Albert, 1968; Schmidt, 1966). In other instances, however, there are noteworthy differences between actual and recommended or ideal practice in selection (Drake, 1965; Holder, 1968; Poteet, 1969).

One of the major discrepancies between ideal and actual practice is the lack of written policy or explicitly stated procedures. Results of surveys have revealed that only a minority of districts have written policies or planned programs for identifying and selecting administrators (DeFrahn, 1974; Glover, 1970; Hamm, 1964; Kelsey & Leullier, 1978; Stapley, 1958). Researchers have also criticized the low priority and limited resources allocated to recruitment and selection, the limited preparation and planning for both activities, the restricted involvement in the process, and the extensive reliance on interviews during the assessment of candidates (Chisholm, 1980; DeFrahn, 1974; Kahl, 1980; Storlein, 1983). Selection of deans (Lutz, 1979) and university presidents (Porter, 1982) has drawn similar criticism.

The focus of research has not been restricted to identifying shortcomings in selection procedures; some efforts have also been directed at identifying possibilities for improvement. A number of studies have provided support for the use of selected instruments and batteries of tests in the initial screening of candidates (Boyce, 1961; Griffin, 1979; Horowitz, 1968; Huffman, 1975; Sharbaugh, 1971). Researchers caution that the use of tests should be regarded as a complementary technique and should not be allowed to obscure other factors that are relevant to the selection decision. The use of tests in conjunction with the judgments of clinicians who are acquainted with candidates has been successful in predicting global

dimensions of administrative behavior (St. Clair, 1962). Assessment of such techniques as tests of interpersonal relations (Thyberg, 1965), role playing (Hartsell, 1960), and a case study (Hoff, 1962) reveal limited potential for aiding the selection process.

Although sociometrics and situational performance tests were once regarded as promising (McIntyre, 1966), there was limited subsequent research. The initial study on simulation of administrator performance by Hemphill, Griffiths, and Frederiksen (1962) appeared to open some avenues for research on administrator selection. However, interest in this area shifted from research to the use of simulation for instructon. There is virtually no trace of research into the validity or usefulness of simulation techniques until they appeared in the use of assessment centers.

Selection Criteria

On the basis of their review of the research on selection, Hemphill et al. (1962) observed a trend toward increased attention to selection criteria. Subsequent research has attended primarily to identifying criteria in use and to issues of the relevance and validity of particular criteria for appointment decisions. The criteria cover a broad range of professional, personal, and functional characteristics, which appear to vary somewhat across positions. Among the general professional criteria are previous preparation, experience, and competence (Briner, 1959; Dylewski, 1975; Schmidt, 1966; Wing, 1975). At a more specific level, studies have confirmed that human relations skills, organizational ability, communication skills, and the ability to elicit cooperation are considered important in the assessment of candidates for administrative positions (Brown, 1977; Hamm, 1964; Powell, 1984; Robertson, 1984).

Personal characteristics that have been viewed as important include judgment, personality, character, openmindedness, physical and mental health, poise, intelligence, sense of humor, voice, and cultural background (e.g., see, DeFrahn, 1974). Studies into criteria considered relevant for the selection of superintendents have examined functions that are closely identified with the position: understanding board operations, board-superintendent relations, fiscal management, and relationships with community-parent groups (Powell, 1984; Robertson, 1984).

On the basis of their study of staff leadership, Gross and Herriott (1965) identified four factors that might have predictive value in selecting principals: academic achievement, interpersonal skills, motive of service, and readiness to commit off-duty time to the job. There is no indication that testing the validity of these or any other factors was actively pursued through subsequent research.

As in the case of policies and procedures, there are areas of correspondence (Justice, 1966) and of discrepancy (Bryan, 1965) between the views of experts and actual practice. The general criteria used may be based on leader stereotypes (Briner, 1959), may be global rather than specific (Bessent, 1962), and may be based on general impressions of superordinates (Baltzell & Dentler, 1983; Bennington, 1966). Even among practitioners agreement on criteria is more likely to be present at the level of principle rather than in specific applications (Marshall, 1959). Obtaining agreement on criteria appears to be more likely for specific situations (Chang, 1964; Stewart, 1963).

Through the use of a projective technique, Brown, Rix, and Chovlat (1983) identified criteria actually used by administrators in making decisions about promoting teachers to vice-principals. Five categories of criteria were derived from the responses of a sample of school administrators: individuality; cognitive skills; rapport with students, teachers, administrators, and community; leadership qualities; and professional qualities. Administrators who responded to the questionnaire also participated in a series of workshops that provided opportunities for reviewing and reflecting on operative criteria (Rix, 1981). The procedures that were tested offer some potential for making implicit criteria explicit and for achieving consensus on the priority that should be attached to different criteria when promotion decisions are made.

Researchers who have looked critically at selection criteria have questioned their empirical justification and trustworthiness (Gross & Herriott, 1965; McIntyre, 1971). With respect to insights gained from research, the situation does not seem to have progressed much beyond the conclusion reached by Hemphill et al. (1962) that the work of administrators is multidimensional and that multiple selection criteria should be used. What those criteria might be has remained elusive.

Selection of Graduate Students

Despite long-standing calls for increased attention to the recruitment and selection of students into graduate programs (American Association of School Administrators [AASA], 1963; Fisk, 1953; Hall & McIntyre, 1957), this issue has received even less research attention than have practices in the field. The results of several surveys (Miklos & Nixon, 1978; Silver & Spuck, 1978) indicate that departments of educational administration do not recruit aggressively or widely.

Students report that self-initiated inquiry, recommendations of friends, and previous contacts are the primary ways in which they become aware of programs. Direct contact between faculty members and prospective degree candidates through such activities as consultation, off-campus teaching, and supervision of internships tends to serve recruiting functions (Meekins, 1974).

The dominant selection criterion at all program levels is grade point average. At the doctoral level, heavy weight may also be assigned to test scores or performance on a departmental interview (Silver & Spuck, 1978). Other factors that enter into admission decisions include letters of recommendation, proof of teaching or administrative experience, and an autobiographical essay or statement of career goals (Miklos & Nixon, 1978). The relative weights assigned to various criteria are seldom made explicit.

Comparisons of candidates who complete doctoral programs with those who become inactive tend to support the use of such criteria for selecting students as academic averages, age at time of admission, and previous professional experience (Bartels, 1963; Franklin, 1971; Snyder, 1972). Although the high completion rate among those who enroll for doctoral studies (McKenzie, 1980) could be taken as indicating support for the selection criteria in use, such findings also prompt questions about program standards and selection procedures.

Factors Influencing Recruitment and Selection

Studies of recruitment practices confirm what critics have mentioned frequently: namely, that administrators come from traditional pools of candidates even when changing conditions support broader recruitment (Socolow, 1978). Members of minority groups and women perceive and encounter barriers that restrict entry into those pools (Fisher, 1979; Hall, 1984; Martin, 1981; Sloan, 1980). Although selection of candidates from outside the traditional pool may be influenced by factors other than administrative competence, such as political pressure (Robinson, 1974), there are indications that members of the public can be objective and relatively free from bias when participating in the selection of administrators (Cogan, 1982).

Political factors may be an inescapable aspect of administrator selection. Success in gaining an administrative appointment may be highly dependent on the judgments of a selection committee (Bennington, 1966; Hopes, 1983). Lack of unanimous support at the time of appointment may be followed by termination of an administrator after short tenure (Reeves, 1971). Characteristics of the selecting committee or board, such as liberal attitudes, may also affect the appointment decision (Morris, 1980).

Particularly at the lower levels of administrative structure, local or internal candidates may have an advantage over those from outside the district (Glover, 1970; Hall, 1984; Justice, 1966; Stapley, 1958). Although there may not be an explicit statement to this effect, the search may be restricted to a particular geographical area.

Certain personality characteristics of candidates may also affect recruitment and selection processes. For example, teachers, vice-principals, and principals who aspire strongly to promotion tend to place significantly higher emphasis on deference than do those who do not desire advancement (Fallinger, 1981; Tronc & Enns, 1969). A relationship between organizational rank and deference suggests that those who defer to superiors may be perceived as loyal and, therefore, more likely to be promoted.

The structure of an educational system also influences recruitment and selection practices. In a centralized (as compared to a decentralized) structure, seniority and longevity are likely to be more important considerations in the selection of principals (Carlson, 1979; Geering, 1980). More generally, the cultural context may be associated with particular practices in the selection of administrators (Hopes, 1983; Olivera, 1979).

Although the reduction of the influence of extraneous factors on determining who becomes an administrator has been defined as a desirable outcome of research (Fisk, 1953; McIntyre, 1966), these factors have not been the subject of extensive study. Only in recent years has there been attention, for example, to gender as a material influence in administrator selection and advancement.

Gender in Recruitment and Selection

Discussions on the question of the number of women in school administration have a long history in the United States. Over the years the proportion of women administrators has actually declined (Hansot & Tyack, 1981). Recently the extent to which gender influences administrative appointments has been examined from a number of different perspectives. Results of the research confirm that women actually encounter, and not just perceive, a variety of barriers that impede access to administrative positions (Covel, 1979).

Women who hold administrative appointments and those who do not report that there is prejudice against women and discrimination in hiring practices (Holtz, 1980; Johnston, Yeakey, & Moore, 1980; Picker, 1979; Piggott, 1980). The perceived discrimination takes the form of restricting information about the availability of opportunities to the "old boys'" network, not encouraging women to compete for administrative positions, expecting women to have higher qualifications, and restricting women primarily to staff positions (Cottrell & Hughes, 1978; Picker, 1979; Sloan, 1980). Studies that have compared the personal and professional characteristics of male and female administrators confirm that women tend to be older and to have had more experience in education than men at the time of first appointment to an administrative position (Johnston et al., 1980; Picker, 1979). Although the proportion of women in administrative positions who were encouraged to apply or who were sponsored is about the same as that for men who received similar encouragement, there is the perception of more frequent sponsorship of men than of women (Ibeawuchi, 1980; Picker, 1979).

Investigations of attitudes toward women administrators and of the possible influence of gender on selection decisions have yielded inconsistent results. Some prevailing beliefs are favorable to the appointment of women, whereas others are unfavorable (Ott, 1983). The perception that women lack skills required for line positions while they do have skills relevant for staff positions might result in discrimination against women who aspire to hold upper-level positions in educational administration. Attitudes toward the appointment of women as administrators may be influenced by percentage of women on school boards (Forlines, 1981), previous experience in working with a female administrator (Mack, 1981), position held (Pawlitschek, 1976), and gender of respondents (Ibeawuchi, 1980).

Several investigators have attempted to assess the effects of gender on selection by asking respondents to make choices among fictional applicants. The outcomes of these studies are difficult to interpret because of variations across different components of the assessment (Couch, 1981; King, 1981). An evaluation of fictional superintendent applicants by graduate students led Frasher and Frasher (1980) to conclude that gender bias operated to the disadvantage of women. In contrast, Bonuso and Shakeshaft (1982) found no difference based on gender in superintendents' ratings of applicants with identical qualifications for the position of secondary school principal. Inconsistent results in such studies may be due, in part, to the effect of the gender of the researchers on responses (Schmeider, 1984).

Several studies yield a general conclusion that gender enters into the recruitment and selection process in complex and undefined ways (Anderson, 1983; Andruskiw & Howes, 1980). Documentation of the low proportion of women who aspire to and who occupy administrative positions is reasonably straightforward, and the findings are fairly consistent. Firm explanations for the imbalance remain elusive. Sloan (1980), for example, concluded that most of the reasons usually given for why women are not, or do not aspire to be, administrators did not hold their explanatory power when considered individually. Explanations must go beyond recruitment and selection practices into the process of socialization within education and to the definitions of roles in the broader culture.

Affirmative Action

Advocates of change in the representation of women and minorities in administration agree that whatever the reason for underrepresentation, affirmative action offers one means of redress. Affirmative action has received endorsement in legislation, administrative regulation, revision of recruitment and selection policies, and the development of special training programs, all intended to reduce the barriers that restrict opportunities for women and minorities to pursue careers in educational administration.

Some studies raise doubts about the extent to which school districts have actually adopted affirmative action policies (Schmuck & Wyant, 1981; Stern, 1976). Questions about the effectiveness of such policies have also been raised (Levandowski, 1977; McCarthy & Zent, 1982). Despite an apparent sense of obligation and sensitivity to the need to implement affirmative action principles in higher education institutions, the actual efforts have been assessed as weak (Bowers, 1981). However, there is some evidence to support the view that affirmative action has had a positive effect on the appointment of women to administrative posts, even though women themselves may not perceive that they have been affected by affirmative action (Tyler, 1980).

Questions have been raised as to whether the returns from affirmative action justify its costs (Bartlett & Barnes, 1978; Dingerson, Rodman, & Wade, 1982). Practices in the appointment of minority-group administrators in higher education would seem to justify raising such questions (van Alstyne, Withers, & Elliott, 1977). Women's colleges and minority institutions tend to employ a disproportionate number of women and minority administrators. Private institutions tend to employ a higher proportion of women but a lower proportion of minority group members than the public institutions.

The pursuit of affirmative action has also led to the development of training programs, such as Project SEEL (Schmuck, 1979), Project DELTA (Konek, 1979), and Project ICES (Adkison & Bailey, 1980), designed to encourage and facilitate the entry of women into administration. Although long-term effects of these efforts have not been assessed, some research results suggest that such programs have potential for helping women and members of minorities to cope with some of the barriers restricting entry to administrative positions (Jones & Montenegro, 1983). The question remains, however, whether the training makes as much difference as does the selection for training.

The emerging evidence that affirmative action policies and procedures can make a difference has reinforced the call for more direct action, particularly assertive hiring policies and specialized training programs (Rudd & Cottrell, 1980), a combination of individual and institutional initiatives (Finlay & Crosson, 1981), and the immediate hiring of large numbers of women (Haven, Adkinson, & Bagley, 1980).

Assessment Centers

The assessment center as a technique for evaluating managerial potential has gained general recognition in organizational psychology and wide use in government and industry. In 1975 the National Association of Secondary School Principals, with the assistance of the American Psychological Association, started using assessment centers in the selection process for assistant principals and principals (Jeswald, 1977). Participants engage in simulation activities representative of the day-to-day administration of a school, including leaderless group activities, fact-finding and stress exercises, paper and pencil in-basket tasks, and a structured personal interview. Typically, six trained assessors observe twelve participants over a 2-day period and prepare for each participant a comprehensive report on his or her strengths, weaknesses, and possibile areas for development. The assessors then discuss the report with each participant.

Schmitt and Noe (1983) described the procedures used to establish the content validity of assessment-center exercises. The specification of major performance domains followed a careful job analysis. Experts then rated the congruence between indicators of effective performance in each domain and the behaviors or skills assessed in the center. Finally, expert judgments were used to confirm that the individual exercises provided information about the behavior/skills rated in the center. On the basis of the ratings of 18 judges, Schmitt and Noe (1983) concluded that all but two of twelve skills (range of interest and personal motivation) were critical to administrator performance. Judges' ratings were also used to establish content validity indexes for individual exercises. The investigators reported that some exercises provided information about a range of skills, that some provided only limited information, and that for some skills additional exercises were needed.

In a 3-year study, Schmitt, Noe, Meritt, and Fitzgerald (1984) addressed the issue of the predictive validity of assessment-center ratings. Although supervisors, teachers, and support staff perceived performance in significantly different ways, the overall assessment-center rating correlated positively and significantly with all but two performance ratings by supervisors and all but three performance ratings by teachers. Less than half the ratings of support staff were significantly related to the placement recommendation. Although most correlations were only in the .20 to .35 range, the consistent presence of a statistically significant relationship was viewed by Schmitt et al. as support for the validity of the overall rating as a predictor of job performance.

Recent studies explore how assessment-center ratings are actually used in selection. Preliminary indications are that the information is used with caution. Center directors' reports may be used more during preliminary screening than in final assessment. The weight assigned to assessment-center reports may also be relatively low (Smith, 1984). No doubt, increased experience with assessment centers and further research will affect the use of these reports.

Participants in assessment centers have generally reacted positively to their experience. They tend to regard the activities as realistic, they are interested in having an opportunity to participate in another center, and they consider the experience to be a source of motivation for making plans about personal and professional development (Kelley, 1984). Assessment-center directors, assessors, and assessees supply further positive anecdotal reports (Hersey, 1980). As experience with assessment centers has grown and as the number of centers has increased, they have received more attention as sites for the professional development of administrators (Hersey, 1982; Kelley, 1982), as instruments for the improvement of preparation programs (Kelley, 1984), and as processes deserving further research (Ogawa, 1984).

The need for more research is not restricted to assessment centers. Calls of several decades ago for increased attention to the importance of recruitment and selection seem to have had limited impact on either practice or research. The current challenge is not only to do more research but also to devise new research strategies for addressing persistent problems.

CAREER PATTERNS

Administrative positions become the focus of career goals for many educators. People prepare themselves to become administrators by acquiring experience and undertaking formal study and, once appointed, they pursue employment opportunities within the context of the administrative structure of education (Covel & Ortiz, 1978). Most of the research on administrative careers has focused on describing the nature of careers and on identifying factors involved in the dynamics of becoming an administrator.

Pathways and Patterns

The concept of career pattern assumes some regularities in the rise of people from position to position in the administrative structure. Research into career paths or patterns has attempted to chart the sequence through which individuals enter administration, move from lower- to higher-rank positions, and exit from administrative work. Regularities and variations have both been identified. For example, the route to the superintendency usually includes stops in the classroom and the principal's office (Cuban, 1976). Within that general route there are variations in rural and urban career patterns (AASA, 1968). Furthermore, the move to the superintendency is easier from a secondary than from an elementary principalship (Cokendolpher, 1959). This difference is evident in contexts other than North America. Bush and Kogan (1982) found that in England and Wales chief education officers tended to have secondary backgrounds and to have served a long apprenticeship as teachers and administrators. Despite such crosscultural similarities, patterns of administrative careers are influenced significantly by situational factors. Consequently, insights into the career dynamics of administrators are probably developed best from research in specific contexts.

An informative analysis of career patterns was reported by Gaertner (1980) based on personnel records of public school administrators in the state of Michigan for the period 1968 to 1973. The number of moves between ten basic positions in the administrative hierarchy as well as exits and entrances revealed two major regularities. The first was that the administrators were relatively immobile over the 5-year period; about 46 percent did not change positions. The second observation was that a high proportion of the moves involved exits and entrances to or from teaching and across school systems. There was limited interposition mobility in the middle of the administrative hierarchy.

According to Gaertner, three patterns of mobility appeared. The first was a path that led to the superintendency from the secondary principal position which, in turn, was fed by the assistant secondary principal position. The source positions for the assistant principal position were the secondary curriculum supervisor and the assistant elementary principal.

The second pattern was also a path to the superintendency and involved the secondary curricular supervisory position leading to administrator of instruction, to assistant superintendent, and then to superintendent. The third pattern led to elementary principal from assistant elementary principal or from teaching. Movements from the elementary principal to other positions in the hierarchy did not occur with sufficient frequency to warrant identifying any connections as a career path.

A number of positions served as entry points to administration from teaching: curricular supervisor, assistant elementary or secondary principal, and elementary principal. The two lower-level positions, elementary and secondary curricular supervisor, were also assessment positions in that they combined administration with teaching and led either to other administrative positions or back to full-time teaching. The assistant superintendency was probably an assessment position for the superintendency. Two demotion moves were also evident: from superintendent to assistant superintendent and from assistant superintendent to administrative specialist. Consequently, the positions of assistant superintendent and administrative specialist may be regarded as plateau positions for some administrators. The two major exit positions from administration were the ceiling positions of superintendent and elementary principal.

The analyses by Gaertner (1978–1979, 1980, 1981) provide a conceptual and methodological base for further research into career patterns. Whether the patterns are generalizable to other educational systems can be established only through comparison with similar studies (see Carlson, 1979). Career patterns are also likely to change over time. McCleary and Thomson (1979) found that in the mid-1960s high school principals tended to have backgrounds as elementary principals or guidance counselors, whereas in the mid-1970s they were more likely to have been middle school administrators or assistant high school principals. In addition, tenure in the initial administrative post and in the principalship increased over the 10-year period.

Changes in career patterns over time are also evident for superintendents. For example, the number of years of professional experience prior to first appointment increased from 1940 to 1960 (Eller, 1963). From 1971 to 1982, the percentage of superintendents who came to their office through the teacher-principal route declined, whereas the percentage of those who followed the route from teacher to principal to the central office increased (Cunningham & Hentges, 1982). During that same period, the tendency to begin administrative careers as assistant principals rather than as principals

increased. Superintendents also tended to have slightly less classroom experience.

Prospects of a lower turnover rate among superintendents (Cunningham & Hentges, 1982) have a parallel in other positions. Trends such as these will reduce opportunities for advancement and, consequently, will affect career patterns (Hentschke & Cline, 1981). Clearly, recognition that research on career patterns must take context into account extends to the time or historical factor and not only to geographical location.

Orderly Career Opportunities

An analysis of the manpower flows through the administrative structures of the educational systems of Oregon and two Australian states (New South Wales and Western Australia) was carried out by Carlson (1979). The comparisons are of interest because of variations in the extent to which movement was regulated by clearly specified criteria for advancement such as education, experience, length of time in a position, and location of present position. In general, the flows of administrators among positions were more highly regulated in New South Wales and Western Australia than in Oregon.

With respect to movement across positions in Oregon, Carlson (1979) noted that there was only a modest probability of changing positions. The highest probabilities of movement were from one superintendency to another or for an assistant superintendent to become a superintendent. Results of the analysis indicated movement both up and down the hierarchy. For example, the probability of movement from a high school principalship to an elementary school principalship was about the same as the probability of movement to an assistant superintendency.

In contrast to the situation in Oregon, there were relatively few moves down the hierarchy in New South Wales. However, primary and central school principalships were ceiling or exit positions because there was only a low probability of moving to the next higher position, namely, that of inspector of schools. Results of the analysis also revealed a clear separation between secondary principalships on the one hand and primary or central principalships on the other hand; there was no movement between the two sets of positions. The pattern of lateral transfers among principals reflected variations in the relative attractiveness of different regions of the state, whereas lateral transfers of primary district inspectors of schools reflected a state policy of transfers every 5 years. Principals in Western Australia were less likely to stay in one position from one year to the next than principals in either of the other two systems. The probabilities were high for both upward and lateral transfers.

The major points of entry from teaching positions into the network in New South Wales and Western Australia were principalships at the lower levels of the hierarchy. By contrast, in Oregon every position could be entered from outside the network. Analysis of movement out of the network shows some variations across positions and systems.

Analyses such as those developed by Gaertner (1980) and Carlson (1979) provide insights into the structure of administrative careers. These studies reveal the presence of considerable horizontal or lateral movement, that is, movements across the same or similar positions in different locations.

Lateral Mobility

Examining the lateral mobility of administrators involves tracing the movement from organization to organization in which an individual holds the same position. In a study of the Wisconsin school superintendency, March and March (1977) raised the question of whether there were any discernible career patterns. Although the researchers found general support for the view that lateral movement was almost random over the period from 1940 to 1972, they also observed patterns in careers, chronologies, and vacancy chains that were not entirely consistent with simple chance models. In part, movement of superintendents was related to variations in the desirability of size and location of districts. Superintendents tended to move toward the "better" districts; however, they did not move very far, confirming a within-state localism to careers.

The analysis of deviance from randomness led March and March (1977) to conclude that if variations due to retirement and localism are ignored, most deviations in careers "seem to reflect either the improvement in mutual compatibility produced by additional perseverance in a match, or the exploitation of chance successes to move to higher status districts" (p. 406). From his analysis of the lateral moves of superintendents in Oregon from 1966 to 1974, Carlson (1979) could not discern any patterns with respect to either size or location of districts. Both the data on size of districts and the geographical character of the moves suggested that they were random.

Although lateral mobility of administrators in a particular position within a specific geographic area may approximate randomness, entry into and progression through a hierarchy of positions is clearly not a random process. A wide range of factors interact to determine who becomes an administrator and

the range of career opportunities available to a particular individual.

Contingencies and Constraints

Among the factors that shape particular careers within the general identified patterns or that cause departures from those patterns are age, socioeconomic background, education, marital status, religion, and political affiliation (Carlson, 1972). The significance of these factors varies, and some of the barriers they present may be more easily surmounted than others. In addition to personal factors, policies of particular education systems also influence entry into and progression through administrative ranks.

Academic Qualifications

Basic academic preparation for administrative posts may be defined by certification requirements. Research has tended to focus on the extent to which holding qualifications beyond those required for certification enhances access to administrative posts or facilitiates upward mobility. Results tend to confirm that holding higher degrees, particularly doctorates, is an important contingency factor for such positions as superintendencies (Craig, 1982; Fuqua, 1983) and college presidencies (Baur, 1976; Kirk, 1971; Mills-Nova, 1980). Not just holding a doctorate but the particular doctoral program may be important for career patterns (Diulio, 1980).

Age

There are indications of age preferences (Carlson, 1972; March & March, 1977; Turner, 1982), which vary with position. The preferred ages appear to be the mid-to-late twenties for entry positions, the early thirties for principalships, and the early forties for superintendencies. The earlier the age at which career goals are formulated and a start is made on an administrative career, the more rapid the rate of upward mobility is likely to be (Fuqua, 1983) and the greater the probability of obtaining a superintendency in a large district (Craig, 1982) and of having an orderly career pattern (Kirk, 1971). Whatever the preferred or optimum age might be, there is a difference between men and women; past practices have resulted in the appointment of women who are from 5 to 10 years older, on average, than men appointed to similar posts (Chamberlain, 1980; Farmer, 1983).

Gender

That males dominate in administrative posts at all levels in education has been well documented in a variety of reports, investigated in numerous specific studies, and examined from a variety of perspectives in books such as *Educational Policy and Management: Sex Differentials* (Schmuck, Charters, & Carlson, 1981) and *Career Patterns in Education: Women, Men and Minorities in Public School Administration* (Ortiz, 1982). Beyond differences in numbers, comparisons of men and women in similar positions reveal fairly consistent differences on a range of personal and professional characteristics. Included among the differences between male and female administrators are years of teaching experience, nature of previous position, tenure, salary, span of control, perceived influence in decision making, opportunities for upward mobility, age at hiring, marital status, and family responsibility (Cryer, 1981; Paul, 1979).

Although specific studies have focused on different factors, the results provide general support for the conclusion that there are substantial differences in the administrative career experiences of men and women. Among these who receive doctoral degrees, women follow more diverse career patterns than men (Hullhorst, 1984). Although women enter teaching at an earlier age than men, they tend to become principals at a later age (Paddock, 1978). In moving into that position, men and women tend to follow different routes (Hall, 1984; Prolman, 1982; Shea, 1984). The most competitive move for women appears to be into the entry position of vice-principal, whereas for men it is from the vice-principalship into the principalship (Rawlins, 1964).

Results of an analysis of the career paths of women public school superintendents by McDade and Drake (1982) tend to support the conclusion that once women are in administrative work, their career patterns are similar to those of their male colleagues. This tendency is regarded by Paddock (1981) as "a testimony to the strength of the educational institutions in forming and reforming careers" (p. 197). An understanding of the ways in which gender influences career patterns requires an understanding of the complex interaction of both institutional and individual contingencies in the evolution of administrative careers.

Minority Status

The underrepresentation of minorities in educational administration has also been documented, as have some distinctive features of their career experiences (Ortiz, 1982). Among these features are the tendency for minority administrators to be placed in schools with high proportions of students of similar ethnic or cultural groups, to hold appointments for particular reasons, and perhaps to have been appointed through application of special criteria. Consequently, the status and career prospects of the minority administrator are likely to be quite different from those of members of the majority. Advancement through an administrative structure is a selective process that may exclude certain groups (Criswell, 1975). In her study of the career patterns of administrators in Michigan, Gaertner (1980) found paths that had a disproportionate number of white males as well as paths with a disproportionate representation of nonwhites. She concluded that the filtering by race, gender, and educational attainment resulted in a stratification process parallel to that in the larger society.

Aspirations and Planning

Much of the research on career aspirations has focused on differences between groups or on aspiration levels of particular groups. The differences between men and women in these studies is particularly marked. In one study of doctoral students (Johnson, 1979), more than twice as many men as women aspired to be superintendents. The largest group of women aspired to central office positions. A study of women principals (Farmer, 1983) revealed that most considered their current position as the final occupational goal. Although some had other aspirations, few were considering a superintendency. These observations have been confirmed in studies at other levels; for example, Shea (1984) found that among male and female aspirants for the principalship, women tended to have lower career aspirations. These differentials become even more significant in light of Fuqua's (1983) finding that aspirations for upward mobility were related to the actual rate of mobility.

But aspirations by themselves are not sufficient to ensure mobility. One of the differences observed by Scally (1982) in a study of women superintendents and aspirants for that position was that the incumbents indicated greater intention and readiness actually to seek the position than did the aspirants. A study of women in administrative posts in home economics (Slimmer, 1984) indicated that these positions were obtained by women who were "in the right place at the right time." However, many who held these posts considered that they had positioned themselves in the "right place."

Somewhat contradictory to the research results that affirm the significance of aspirations and deliberate planning as significant career contingencies are the findings that underline the importance of chance. In a study of women superintendents, Jackson (1981) found that most appointments were acquired without conscious planning. Similarly, a majority of women in higher education in California indicated that they entered administration by "chance" and that an unsolicited job offer was the most facilitating event in their career development (Walsh, 1975). Upward movement in an administrative career seems to be influenced not only by the aspirations and actions under the control of the individual but also by factors that the individual interprets as chance or good fortune (Baltzell & Dentler, 1983).

Attitudes and Skills

The academic qualifications of aspirants to particular administrative positions probably serve to indicate the possession of a broad range of personal and professional characteristics. However, some research has examined skills and attitudes apart from academic qualifications. In a number of these studies, human relations skills and the ability to work with people, in combination with some technical skills, have been identified as relevant career contingencies (Craig, 1982; Jackson, 1981).

Some selected personality characteristics have also been studied. Fuqua (1983) indicated that tolerance for work pressure and deference to paternalism may influence the rate of promotion through a succession of administrative posts. A study of aspirants to superintendency and superintendents revealed differences in personality profiles (Scally, 1982); however, other studies have revealed few differences between administrators and the general population (Goerss, 1975; Jackson, 1981). Career contingencies may be far less subtle and more direct, such as human relations and technical skills or developing a knowledge of the organization as identified by Gordon (1980).

Sponsorship and Support

Sponsorship and support appear to have operated as career contingencies specifically on women and members of minority groups. Sources of support investigated include colleagues and family members as well as superordinates. Even though the major group of administrators, namely, white males, has not been studied specifically, the insights that have been developed seem to have relatively wide application.

Perhaps the reason why these contingencies have not been studied for the majority group of administrators is the belief that their effects are either common knowledge or not an important matter for research. One factor that may be assumed is the importance of support from the vaguely defined "old boys'" network. Male administrators seem to believe that support from the "old boys" is important to their advancement (Fuqua, 1983). Obversely, women administrators and aspirants see the absence of such support as a barrier to advancement (Pacheco, 1982). Encouragement by superordinates is considered to be important to career development by women in higher education and by

women principals (Farmer, 1983; Walsh, 1975). At least one study (Cryer, 1981) has identified colleagues as being influential in career choices; however, the need for support from any source may be recognized less by those who have been successful than by those who have encountered barriers to career advancement (Rowen, 1982).

A number of studies mention the significance of home and family support to careers of women administrators. For example, successful administrators may use their families as a support base, particularly in relation to sharing home and career obligations with husbands and families (Jackson, 1981; Mills-Nova, 1980). McIntosh (1974) reported marked differences in approaches to home life between women teachers who applied for promotion and those who did not apply.

Particularly for women and cultural minorities, the facilitating or supportive structures go beyond those of home and family. External barriers, socialization processes, and cultural expectations do have an impact on the career patterns of individual administrators (Jackson, 1981; Pacheco, 1982).

Visibility and Experience

General understandings about the criteria used in selecting people for administrative posts and previously described career patterns attest to the significance of visibility and relevant experience as career contingencies. Although Griffiths, Goldman, and McFarland (1965) emphasized visibility in their interpretation of "getting attention of superiors [GASing]," the activities associated with GASing also provided experience that was deemed probably important for more senior administrative roles. The chances of attaining a principalship are increased by experience in some types of supervisory roles, such as coaching, lower-level administration, or those associated with extracurricular activities (Turner, 1982).

Particular types of experience are necessary to attain the superintendencies of larger school districts (Craig, 1982), and the upward mobility of women is hampered by lack of line experience (Shea, 1984). The career patterns of female chief student-affairs administrators revealed that a high proportion of those who held acting positions were eventually appointed to the post (Gordon, 1980). In Rowen's (1982) analysis of the career patterns of women administrators in higher education, success included learning to assess situations and to solve problems through experience.

Location

Not only experience but also the circumstances under which the experience is obtained may be relevant. The position occupied and the type and size of district of both first teaching and first administrative appointment appear to be contingencies in relation to desired administrative positions and established career goals (Jackson, 1981; Turner, 1982). Craig (1982) concluded that those who aspire to be superintendents of larger districts should seek initial employment and administrative appointments in such districts. Further support for this contingency comes from Scally's (1982) comparison of women superintendents and aspirants. The two differed in types of initial positions, positions first held after the classroom, and variety of positions. In the same study, geographic location appeared to be a contingency in the appointment of women school superintendents. The largest concentrations of women were in the northern states east of the Mississippi and in California, primarily in small districts (Scally, 1982). Hannah (1980) found that in Michigan women administrators were located mainly in large urban and metropolitan districts, whereas men held administrative posts in all types of districts.

Geographic Mobility

The actual and the perceived significance of geographic mobility appear to be contradictory. Although the analysis of career patterns reveals a strong tendency toward localism (Peterson, 1984; Stanfield, 1982), most administrators seem to believe that geographic mobility enhances career prospects (Fuqua, 1983; Jackson, 1981; Johnson, 1979; Walsh, 1975). The importance of mobility would seem to be confirmed by Scally's (1982) observation that women aspirants to the superintendency were more place-bound than were superintendents in office. Constraints on the mobility of women may explain why they are more likely than men to be promoted from within the district (Hannah, 1980).

The apparent contradiction between perceptions and actual career patterns may be reconciled. Some degree of geographic mobility may indeed be an important contingency in administrative careers. However, the degree or extent of mobility may not be so high as is frequently assumed (AASA, 1968). Readiness to relocate may be important but the distance normally involved may not be very great. Mobility within a limited area would be consistent with the observed localism in the vast majority of administrative careers.

Most of the studies on career contingencies have been restricted to the analysis of specific factors or to a series of factors considered individually. Future research might well be directed more toward examining the complex interaction of various factors and the way in which they influence career patterns.

SUCCESSION

The research on administrative succession in education was stimulated by Carlson's (1961) article in *Administrative Science Quarterly* and the subsequent publication of his *Executive Succession and Organizational Change* (1962). His later publication *School Superintendents: Careers and Performance (1972)* presented an extension of the analysis contained in the earlier reports. For the most part, the concepts and hypotheses introduced in Carlson's studies have served as the conceptual bases for subsequent research.

An assumption underlying the research on administrative succession is that a change of administrators is a significant event in the history of an organization. Furthermore, the characteristics of the successor and the conditions under which succession occurs are significant in determining the impact of the event. The focus of much of the research has been on the origin of the successor, that is, whether the person is appointed from inside or outside the organization. Results of this research offer insights into both the reasons why one or the other type of successor is selected and the consequences of the choice.

Reasons for Succession

Some attention has gone to the reasons for succession, that is, to the basis of administrator turnover. Cokendolpher (1959) found that some superintendents moved because of opportunities for advancement and salary increases. Others moved away from undercurrents of protest or to more desirable communities. Only a small proportion of superintendents who left the position in the late 1940s and early 1950s retired completely; most went to other types of work. Results of a study of succession when enrollments are declining (Berger, 1983) suggested that the relationship of a superintendent with the board as well as high per-pupil expenditures are related to succession. Mobility of principals is affected by both positive and negative factors (Castanga, 1964). Positive factors include prospects for increased leadership opportunities, greater responsibility for the school program, and increased involvement in policy determination. Negative factors include dissatisfaction with present position and conflict within the school system or with the community.

The reasons for succession may have an impact on the predecessor and on the successor as well. One of the propositions in Thiemann's (1968) partial theory of succession states that the degree and level of the predecessor's participation in successor selection varies with the predecessor's success as leader and length of tenure. Whether an insider or an outsider is appointed may be influenced by factors not directly related to the position. For example, in the appointment of super-intendents, outside succession appears to be more likely following the defeat of incumbent school board members (Freeborn, 1967; Iannaccone & Lutz, 1970).

Career-bound and Place-bound Administrators

In his initial publication on succession, Carlson (1961) used the concepts of career-bound and place-bound to differentiate between two types of superintendents. This distinction has served as the basis for examining other characteristics of the two types of administrators, for identifying conditions under which each type obtains an appointment, and for examining the dif-ferential effects on the organization in the two types of succession. Carlson (1962) described the concepts of career-bound and place-bound administrators as de-fining latent social roles in that they reflect orientations or commitments that have the potential for influencing behavior and performance.

The general image that emerges from relevant research (Carlson, 1972) portrays the career-bound superintendent as one who develops an early commit-ment to the superintendency and engages in deliberate career planning to achieve that goal. Place-bound administrators adopt a more passive orientation toward the superintendency and are less favorably inclined toward mobility. Career-bound administrators are much more actively involved in a network of social relations among peers than are place-bound admin-istrators. The former are frequently selected by the latter as friends, hold relatively high status in the social structure of administrators at both local and national levels, and are actively involved in flows of information about educational practices. The meaningfulness of the career-bound and place-bound categories has been explored in and confirmed by a number of specific studies. For example, Hickcox (1967) found that membership in the categories correlated with the social backgrounds, on-the-job behaviors, board relation-ships, and community perceptions of superintendents. Fenske (1971) reported that trends in superintendent mobility were related to local (place-bound)/cosmo-politan (career-bound) orientation.

A major factor in employment of career-bound and place-bound superintendents relates to the expec-tations of those who make the appointment. Outsiders, or career-bound administrators, tend to be appointed when conditions are considered to be unsatisfactory and when there is support for change. Whereas outsiders are expected to demonstrate creative per-formance and are given a mandate to carry out change, insiders, or place-bound administrators, are expected to demonstrate stabilizing performance and are less

likely to receive a clear mandate for introducing change. Both types of administrators are likely to concentrate on rule making during the early part of their terms. Those who are place-bound are more likely to reinforce old rules, whereas the career-bound concentrate on new rules that have potential for changes in goals or procedures. The different condi-tions of appointment suggest that in comparison to the insider the outsider is more likely to gain acceptance for proposals for change. Support of proposals for change offered by the insider will probably be divided.

Succession and Change

One of the most widely discussed differences between place-bound and career-bound administrators relates to the adoption of innovations. Carlson (1972) cited research supporting the conclusion that career-bound superintendents tend to adopt more innovations and to do so at a more rapid rate than do place-bound superintendents. The high level of interest in educa-tional innovation particularly evident during the 1960s and early 1970s stimulated additional research into the relationship of change with various patterns of appoint-ment and succession. For example, principals' patterns of succession were examined at the secondary level by Hoy and Aho (1973) and at the elementary level by Ganz and Hoy (1977). Although there were some differences in the results of the two studies, the observations on change perspectives were consistent. The outsiders at both the elementary and the secondary levels perceived themselves to have a greater degree of influence with superordinates than did the insiders. Furthermore, the outsider principals were more fre-quently described by teachers as change agents. Other characteristics of the outsider elementary principals included a greater commitment to careers, shorter tenure in a position, and a perception that the super-intendent was seeking a change agent. At the second-ary level, the outsiders were characterized by less authoritarianism and greater emotional attachment, greater staff satisfaction and morale, and involvement in leadership roles in professional organizations.

Results of research into the relationship between administrator succession and change are not entirely consistent, but some allowable generalizations do emerge. Administrative turnover by itself does not necessarily influence the rate of diffusion of innovations (Keith, 1975), and mobile principals are not more likely than others to take action in specific areas such as improving staff performance (Manning, 1969). There is some support for the conclusion that differences in the timing, rate, and nature of innovations exist between inside and outside successors. Reynolds (1966) found that outsiders made more changes near the beginning of tenure, whereas for insiders the rate increased over the first few years. Similarly, Deprin (1965) reported that career-bound superintendents initiated more administrative acts in their first few years of incumbency than later and tended to introduce liberalizing rather than restrictive rules. However, even insiders may be more likely to innovate during the first few years than later, but not necessarily during the first year (Fleming, 1967).

Some variations in the level at which succession takes place may also be an important factor. Knedlik (1968) reported that insider-outsider succession of superintendents was related to the adoption of innovations in secondary schools, whereas the pattern of succession of principals did not make a difference. Perhaps one of the problems in studying such variations is that principals tend to be appointed from within the school district and to enjoy relatively long tenure (Fleming, 1967). Comparisons of the results of studies tend to confirm Preising's (1968) conclusion that although the insider-outsider distinction cannot be disregarded, its explanatory power in relation to innovation does not hold for all situations. Even if succession inevitably leads to change, the nature and timing of the change are matters for conscious choice and deliberate strategy (Thomas & Muscio, 1984).

Significance of Succession

Some recent research (Fauske & Ogawa, 1984) prompts questions about the importance of succession to members of an organization. The investigators made a case study of the beliefs shared by the faculty of a public elementary school regarding an impending succession in the principalship. Following announcement of the retirement of the incumbent, researchers in the school observed little discussion about the change. However, interviews revealed that there were some elements of fear about the unknown, as well as certain expectations about what the future principal should be like. About one-third of the teachers held a detached stance that reflected the belief that a change of principal would not be a significant event.

The meaning that organizational members attach to succession merits future study conducted within a broader conceptual framework than that of previous research. Although studies into the origin and orientations of the successor have been fruitful, other dimensions of succession also warrant attention. Miskel and Cosgrove (1985) suggest a framework to guide research that includes prearrival factors, arrival factors, and succession effects. Each of these categories includes specific factors, such as reason for succession and selection process (prearrival factors), school culture and educational programs (arrival factors), and changes in reputations and orientations of leaders (succession effects). The limited extent to which Miskel and Cosgrove (1985) were able to base their review on educational administration research literature adds implicit support to the need for further studies in this area.

SOCIALIZATION

To speak about the socialization or enculturation of administrators is to focus on the ways in which the values, norms, rules, and operating procedures that govern the practice of administration are communicated and learned. Researchers have addressed questions related to the process of administrator socialization and the factors that facilitate or impede that process. Much of the recent interest in researching administrator socialization appears to derive from the issues surrounding the representation of women and minority groups in the administrative structure of education (see, for example, Ortiz, 1982). Studies have focused on three broad areas: socialization prior to appointment as an administrator; the significance of sponsors, mentors and role models; and, socialization following appointment.

Prior Socialization

A number of inquiries that have addressed the possible effects of early socialization on choice of administrative careers have examined specific groups, particularly women and minorities. For example, Duran (1983) concluded that the degree of occupational success of Chicanas (Mexican-American females) was determined by characteristics of the communities in which they found themselves. Chicanas who were appointed to administrative positions had been exposed to positive and supportive female role models during early home life and through their schooling. The possible effects of cultural background on the value orientations of administrators in higher education have also been explored (Matsuo, 1982). On the basis of an investigation into attitudes toward male and female administrators, Beck (1977) concluded that socialization into sex roles contributes to the development of attitudes that favor the movement of men into positions of educational leadership. Women may experience contradictions between feminine and administrator roles during socialization (Marshall, 1981). Other writers support these explanations for the differences in proportions of men and women administrators (e.g., see Lyman & Speizer, 1980).

Socialization of women who do become administrators has been explored, and comparisons have been made between women teachers and women administrators. Pope (1979) indicated that the educational attainments of fathers and husbands may be associated with the career aspirations of women. However, the way these factors impinge on socialization remains somewhat vague. A similar comment can be made about socioeconomic factors. Nixon and Gue (1975) reported that women from high socioeconomic groups tended to be more professionally committed than those from lower groups. In general, however, the socialization of women who aspire to upward mobility contributes to the development of beliefs that they can perform effectively as administrators (Edson, 1981), that they need to demonstrate competence and to establish credibility (Gordon, 1980), and that they should not be constrained by stereotypical views of women (Crochet, 1981). Appropriate female role models during childhood appear to be an important factor in the background of some women administrators (Ocel, 1984).

The socialization that occurs closest to an administrative appointment takes place during service as a teacher. This experience may contribute to administrators' relatively high degree of homogeneity on a number of characteristics. The results of a study of work values of teachers and of administrators revealed few differences between administrators and nonadministrators as well as few differences between parochial and public school administrators (Kelly, 1975; Kelly & Metzcus, 1975). These observations led the researchers to conclude that their respondents had been socialized as educators regardless of their specific roles or types of schools. Cuban (1976) suggests that the experiences of educators as teachers probably lead prospective administrators to value rationality, impartiality, acceptance of authority and hierarchy, and emotional restraint. As administrators move upward in the hierarchy, they may not entirely lose values acquired as teachers but the emphasis may change (Bush & Kogan, 1982). In the course of moving through the hierarchy, different administrative positions may make different contributions to the socialization of an administrator (Ortiz, 1978).

In a comparison of men and women administrators on selected characteristics, Fowler (1984) found that the men tended to major in administration, whereas the women tended to major in counseling or curriculum. Harris (1981) found a strong relationship between social-science backgrounds and careers in school administration. Some support for the possible differential socializing effects of teaching and coaching as preparation for the principalship appears in a study that revealed differences in the leader behavior of coach-principals and teacher-principals (Schmitz,

1972). Other experiences may also have important effects on socialization; for example, Nelson (1982) found that women principals considered membership in professional organizations to be necessary for promotion. Results of a study of doctoral and postdoctoral students revealed that women belonged to more professional organizations than men (Johnson, 1979). A major contrast emerged in the experiences of the two groups within those organizations; women tended to hold office as secretary, whereas men were likely to be vice-presidents or presidents.

During their classroom experiences, prospective administrators seem to develop expertise in teaching and competence in interpersonal skills (Sandorff, 1981). In addition, socialization prior to appointment involves GASing, the behaviors that Griffiths et al. (1965) described as "getting the attention of superiors." Research by Greenfield (1975, 1977a, 1977b) led him to conclude that most of the socialization during the candidacy period is informal and unplanned and that administrative culture is transmitted through interpersonal interaction with the administrator group. Even extensive interaction need not be involved; socialization can occur through observation and casual conversation (Garberina, 1980). Women and ethnic minorities are not likely to have equal access to informal socialization opportunities and, thus, are disadvantaged in competing for administrative positions (Marshall, 1979; Valverde, 1974, 1975, 1980).

In one of the few studies of socialization during preparation, Khleif (1975) concluded that by the end of a 3-year intensive program candidates had abandoned identities as teachers and had been resocialized as administrators. Effects of less intensive programs are not as dramatic. The available evidence suggests that preparation programs have only limited impact on administrator socialization (Greenfield, 1977b) or on initial experiences in an administrative position (Duke, Isaacson, Sagor, & Schmuck, 1984). Since the context of graduate studies is so different from administrative life, there is probably very little direct transfer. If the processes present in educational administration preparation programs are similar to those in other areas of professional study, then the transferable elements may not be favorable to positive socialization. Kjerulff and Blood (1973) found that the communication patterns between graduate psychology students and advisors differed significantly for men and women. For example, women students had fewer discussions about the advisor's interests and interacted with the advisor less frequently outside the office.

On the basis of their investigations, Holmstrom and Holmstrom (1974) concluded that the interaction of students with faculty was biased in favor of men and that faculty attitudes contributed to the emotional stress and self-doubts of women students. Although both graduate students and faculty are aware of the formal aspects of socialization, some students view the acquisition of particular attitudes and behavior more as a strategy for surviving in a program than as learning professional norms (Mix, 1971).

Mentors and Role Models

Although sponsors, role models, and mentors are frequently mentioned in the literature on socialization, the processes involved have not received extensive analysis in educational administration. The relationship of sponsors and mentors to career advancement is fairly direct. Presumably, either the intervention or counsel of influential people can be a significant career contingency. However, sponsorship does not necessarily mean that a sponsor serves as a direct agent in a professional shaping process or in assisting a protégé to understand the culture of a particular group. Without appearing to be directly involved in the process, sponsors in particular and mentors to some extent can take indirect actions that place another in a situation where beneficial socialization occurs. In part, of course, the extent to which influential persons facilitate socialization depends on the expectations of protégés and their readiness to learn.

The movement of an aspirant from candidate to protégé to administrator was described by Valverde (1974, 1975) within the framework of the concept of succession socialization. A major factor in the process appeared to be sponsorship, which involved identifying a protégé and influencing the protégé's attitudes in ways to bring them into conformity with those of the sponsor. The processes associated with sponsorship are selective and may result in filtering out people on the basis of characteristics that are not associated with administrative competence. Some support for Valverde's analysis comes from other studies (e.g., see Acevedo, 1979).

The importance of sponsorship and support for career advancement for various groups and positions has been documented in numerous studies (Dusek, 1983; Esposito, 1983; Farmer, 1983; Fuqua, 1983; Pacheco, 1982; Pope, 1979; Villani, 1983; Walsh, 1975). Somewhat similar importance has been reported for mentors, even though the distinction made between sponsors and mentors is not always clear. Mentoring appears to be pervasive among administrators. Cunningham and Hentges (1982) report that in their study of school superintendents two-thirds of the respondents considered themselves to be mentors, whereas three-quarters reported that others came to

them for career advice. Although 60 percent of respondents felt that they had benefited from the help of a mentor, only a relatively small proportion reported that an "old boy" or "old girl" network had been effective in advancing their careers. The findings tend to confirm Leizear's (1984) conclusion that those who experience successful mentorship may themselves become mentors.

A comparison of the aspirations of men and women teachers for the high school principalship revealed that women had mentors more often than men (Shea, 1984). Similar results were reported by Dickson (1983) in a study of the relationship between mentoring and career development in higher education. The majority of respondents offered the opinion that mentors were influential in accelerating the rate of career advancement. Further support for the influence of mentors on career development is provided by the results of a survey of college faculty and academic administrators (Queralt, 1982). Those who had mentors experienced significantly higher career development as measured by publications, research grants, and professional activities than those who did not have mentors. More generally, mentoring relationships may influence values and personal development as well as career expansion and career advancement (Gilmour, 1984). Mentoring, either by men or women, can be a significant factor in the career development and advancement of women (Leizear, 1984).

Research on the influence of peer groups and role models on socialization of administrators is limited. In a comparison of selected characteristics of central-office administrators Cryer, (1981) found that colleagues were influential in career choice. The socialization of university department heads, although in some respects unique, was still shaped by career experiences and role models (Bragg, 1980). Reference has been made previously to a study indicating that Chicana administrators were influenced by supportive female role models (Duran, 1983). There was some indication in the results of a study of women administrators in higher education that recognition of a female rather than a male role model may be associated with earlier entry into administration (McNutt, 1980). Results of such studies tend to indicate that role models should not be excluded from research on administrator socialization even though the general significance of role models remains uncertain.

Socialization Following Appointment

After completing a review of the literature on the midcareer socialization of administrators, Ortiz (1978) concluded that the perspectives of administrators were altered by the nature of school organization, by the nature of the service functions that schools perform, and by the nature of career options. The continuing process of socialization experienced by one principal was described by Wolcott (1973) in his ethnographic study. Central-office personnel, peers, and general administrative procedures were key others in defining the behavior expected of principals.

Although the socialization of newly appointed administrators may be intensive, the period of induction is probably relatively short, and the process itself is likely to be informal rather than planned (Duke et al., 1984). Many of the surprises—time pressure, loneliness, not being prepared—are likely to cause concern and anxiety. The socialization may not be any easier for insiders than outsiders. Indeed, there is some evidence that outsiders and those with no experience encounter fewer organizational problems than insiders (Alvy, 1984). However, all newcomers to the principalship had to adjust to alienation from the faculty, adjust to constraints, develop patience and flexibility regarding the opinions of others, and develop a broader perspective (Alvy, 1984).

Field notes developed through a participant observation study resulted in the identification of five stages in the process of socialization: absorption of information, emergence of personal concern, establishment of self-assurance, establishment of role, and true contribution (Gussner, 1974). The major dimensions of the socialization process appeared to be learning to carry out tasks and responsibilities and accepting the role internally.

Analysis of the socialization process in terms of stages has also been adopted by other researchers. For example, Mascaro (1974) developed a theoretical model of the perspectives of nonexperienced principals about personal involvement in the classroom. The initial perspective included the components of obtaining first-hand knowledge of what was happening in classrooms and of becoming directly involved. When principals encountered the problem of insufficient time, the perspective shifted to one of emphasizing brief visits to classrooms, relying on secondary sources of information, and effecting change indirectly. In a study of the socialization of school-board members, Stout (1982) identified three stages. The first stage consisted of personalizing the role and discovering the traditions of school-board membership, followed by becoming knowledgeable in areas of school-board operation. Finally, the board member became familiar with various groups and insightful about their actions. Stout's findings, however, do not square with the earlier conclusion reached by Cistone (1977) that school board members come to the role already socialized to a considerable degree.

Although administrative experience itself has served as a variable in numerous studies of administrators, only a few investigations have focused specifically on the socializing effect of experience. Bridges (1965) explored the possibility that the proportions of role and personality factors determining behavior may vary with the amount of experience. Results of his data analysis tend to confirm that with increasing experience behavior is shaped more by role than by personality. A study by Beckner (1981) of risk-taking propensity also provided some support for the hypothesis that socialization occurs over time when tenure in an administrative position is used as an index of socialization. Administrative experience under specified conditions also emerged as a factor in the selection of managerial style categories by superintendents (Tillman, 1974).

Hannah (1980) described the differential socialization experiences of men and women in the informal work systems of school administrators. In activities such as social evenings, attending sporting events, or meeting over lunch, most administrators participate with both male and female colleagues. However, male administrators seldom participated with only female colleagues, whereas female administrators would frequently find themselves only with male colleagues. Stevenson (1974) found that women administrators in universities have difficult social lives due to a demanding job and to a lack of informal interaction, particularly with male colleagues.

The possible socialization effects of both on-the-job and prior experience may be evident in some of the studies on attitudes and values. In a study that involved data on sex-role attitudes, Fowler (1984) found that women administrators perceived themselves as possessing masculine traits to a greater extent than men perceived themselves to possess the same traits. Wood (1980) obtained similar results in a study of managerial models: Scores of women administrators were more congruent with stereotypes of a male managerial model than were the scores of men administrators. The similarities in value patterns of different groups of administrators reported by Kelly (1975) and Rader (1976) are probably explained partly by socialization as educators and partly by continuing socialization following appointment.

Research on the socialization of administrators has confirmed that the process begins in early home life and continues through all levels of schooling. Although administrative socialization is particularly intensive preceding and following appointment to a position, the everyday activities in which administrators engage continue to exert a socializing influence. A broad definition of socialization encompasses facets of the processes associated with recruitment, selection, preparation, and succession. Future research should be guided by an appropriately broad conceptual framework, such as that proposed by Greenfield (1983). Results of such studies might provide new insights into the processes involved in becoming and being an administrator.

CONCLUSION

Perhaps the major contribution of the existing research literature on the processes through which administrative roles are assumed and administrative careers are established lies in sketching out a domain with potential for contributing to qualitative improvement in the practice and performance of administrators. Issues such as who becomes an administrator, through what processes and conditions, and under what circumstances assume a high level of significance if the assumption is made that administrators make a difference in the institution of education. The potential exists for bringing about quantitative and qualitative changes in the differences administrators can make through improved knowledge about the recruitment, selection, preparation, and placement of administrators. In broad perspective, research already completed can help in identifying which problems and questions need further investigation. A more intensive examination of studies in particular areas can significantly assist researchers to define and design specific projects.

To say that an area for research has been sketched out or "mapped" implies that few parts of that domain have been explored intensively. A critical examination of reported research supports such a conclusion. In areas such as the analysis of career patterns, succession, and socialization, particular researchers have made noteworthy contributions. However, few scholars have selected any one of these themes as a major and continuing research interest. Consequently, there is an absence of studies that are comparable in scope and methodological rigor but based on alternative conceptualizations. Most of the research is carried out to meet requirements for a doctoral degree. Results of studies are accessible generally only in *Dissertation Abstracts International* and are seldom reported in journal articles. Although most dissertations make contributions to the development of the field, the constraints under which the research is carried out are not conducive to the systematic development of an area. The elements essential for making significant contributions can be provided only by professorial research.

A second critical comment is directed at the research methodology. Most of the inquiries are small-sample, descriptive studies involving particular categories of positions or administrators with distinc-

tive characteristics. The generalizability of results is problematic. Two other main types of studies are needed: descriptive surveys of wider populations and in-depth case studies. The first of these would yield information on variations in practices and on relationships among variables associated with processes such as recruitment, selection, appointment, and career development of educational administrators. The second would penetrate the depths of how these processes are actually experienced by people who aspire to or actually hold administrative positions. The naturalistic, qualitative, interpretive approaches to research hold potential for yielding insights that would contribute to advancing basic understandings and to developing new conceptualizations of the processes through which people become administrators. The application of critical theory would also seem to be highly relevant to an examination of the ways in which people achieve positions of power, influence, and control in educational organizations. Significant advances in research on the selection, preparation, and socialization of administrators await both the commitment of researchers who recognize the contributions of conducting disciplined inquiry on the processes of becoming and being an administrator and their capability to employ the newer research paradigms.

NOTE

[1] A further consequence of the priority placed on research results is that a section on preparation programs, which was part of the initial draft of this chapter, was removed due to constraints on length. Although much has been written about preparation programs, the literature on the topic lacks an extensive research base. Relevant research must be conducted before the total processes involved in becoming an administrator can be examined.

REFERENCES

Acevedo, B. A. (1979). Socialization: The Mexican-American mid-level administrator in Texas institutions of higher education (Doctoral dissertation, University of Texas at Austin, 1979). *Dissertation Abstracts International, 40,* 3136A.

Adkison, J. A., & Bailey, J. D. (1980). The ICES model: Increasing women's participation in educational administration. *Planning and Changing, 11,* 141–149.

Albert, J. R. (1968). Processes and procedures used in the selection of a superintendent of schools by selected suburban school boards (Doctoral dissertation, University of Nebraska Teachers College, 1967). *Dissertation Abstracts, 28,* 3395A.

Alvy, H. B. (1984). The problems of new principals (Doctoral dissertation, University of Montana, 1983). *Dissertation Abstracts International, 44,* 1979A.

American Association of School Administrators. (1963). *The education of a school superintendent.* Washington, DC: Author.

American Association of School Administrators. (1968) *Selecting a school superintendent.* Washington, DC: Author and National School Boards Association.

Anderson, J. H. (1983). A comparative study of variables that are predictive of hirability and/or promotability of women and men in secondary school administration (Doctoral dissertation, University of Missouri-Kansas City, 1983). *Dissertation Abstracts International*, *44*, 1634A.

Andruskiw, O., & Howes, N. J. (1980). Dispelling a myth: That stereotypic attitudes influence evaluations of women as administrators in higher education. *Journal of Higher Education*, *51*, 475–496.

Baltzell, D. C., & Dentler, R. A. (1983). *Selecting American school principals: A sourcebook for educators.* Washington, DC: U.S. Government Printing Office.

Bartels, G. B. (1963). Criteria relating to the success and failure of candidates at the University of Nebraska in completing Doctor of Education degrees (Doctoral dissertation, University of Nebraska Teachers College, 1963). *Dissertation Abstracts International*, *23*, 3709.

Bartlett, B., & Barnes, E. (1978). *Women's vitae and the problems of perceiving competence.* (ERIC Document Reproduction Service No. ED 192 048)

Baur, B. M. (1976). Admission and employment patterns of women matriculating in educational administration at selected midwestern universities (Doctoral dissertation, Ball State University, 1975). *Dissertation Abstracts International*, *37*, 52A.

Beck, J. A. N. (1977). Sex differences among elementary teachers in attitudes toward pursuing school administration careers (Doctoral dissertation, Northern Illinois University, 1977). *Dissertation Abstracts International*, *38*, 1761A.

Beckner, P. G. (1981). Differences in risk-taking propensity between educational and business administrators: Is socialization the cause? (Doctoral dissertation, University of Kansas, 1980). *Dissertation Abstracts International*, *41*, 4896A.

Bennington, E. J. (1966). An analysis of the criteria used in the selection of principals and assistant principals for the Detroit public secondary schools for the years 1958 through 1962 (Doctoral dissertation, Wayne State University, 1964). *Dissertation Abstracts International* , *26*, 4354.

Berger, M. A. (1983, April). *Predicting succession under conditions of enrolment decline.* Paper presented at the Annual Meeting of the American Educational Research Association, Montreal, Quebec, Canada.

Bessent, E. W. (1962). The predictability of selected elementary school principals' administrative behavior (Doctoral dissertation, University of Texas, 1961). *Dissertation Abstracts International*, *22*, 3479.

Bonuso, C., & Shakeshaft, C. (1982, March). *The influence of gender in the selection of secondary school principals.* Paper presented at the Annual Meeting of the American Educational Research Association, New York.

Bowers, C. H. (1981). California higher education administrative recruitment and selection procedures for minority candidates: Seven case studies (Doctoral dissertation, University of Southern California, 1981). *Dissertation Abstracts International*, *42*, 920A.

Boyce, R. D. (1961). An empirical evaluation of five tests for administration selection: The composite study (Doctoral dissertation, Stanford University, 1960). *Dissertation Abstracts International*, *21*, 2546.

Bragg, A. K. (1980). Relationship between the role definition and socialization of academic department heads (Doctoral dissertation, Pennsylvania State University, 1980). *Dissertation Abstracts International*, *41*, 1966A.

Bridges, E. M. (1965). Bureaucratic role and socialization: The influence of experience on the elementary school principal. *Educational Administration Quarterly*, *1*(2), 19–28.

Briner, C. (1959). Identification and definition of the criteria relevant to the selection of public school administrative personnel (Doctoral dissertation, Stanford University, 1958). *Dissertation Abstracts International* , *19*, 2271.

Bronfield, J. W. (1962). A study to identify criteria utilized in selection and appointment of full-time elementary school principals in the Commonwealth of Pennsylvania (Doctoral dissertation, Pennsylvania State University, 1962). *Dissertation Abstracts International*, *23*, 895.

Brown, A. F., Rix, E. A., & Chovlat, J. (1983). Changing promotion criteria: Cognitive effects on administrators' decisions. *Journal of Experimental Education*, *52*, 4–10.

Brown, E. M. (1977). A Delphi study to determine factors which relate to decisions of women to seek positions in educational administration in selected cities in Texas (Doctoral dissertation, East Texas State University, 1977). *Dissertation Abstracts International*, *38*, 3164A.

Bryan, D. B. (1965). Factors affecting the selection of principals in unified school districts in Southern California (Doctoral dissertation, University of Southern California, 1965). *Dissertation Abstracts International*, *26*, 2003.

Bush, T. & Kogan, M. (1982). *Directors of education.* London: George Allen & Unwin.

Carlson, R. O. (1961). Succession and performance among school superintendents. *Administrative Science Quarterly*, *6*, 210–227.

Carlson, R. O. (1962). *Executive succession and organizational change.* Chicago, IL: The Midwest Center, University of Chicago.

Carlson, R. O. (1972). *School superintendents: Careers and performance.* Columbus, OH: Charles E. Merrill.

Carlson, R. O. (1979) *Orderly career opportunities.* Eugene: University of Oregon, Center for Educational Policy and Management.

Castanga, J. P. (1964). Mobility among public elementary school principals of Connecticut from 1953 through 1961 (Doctoral dissertation, University of Connecticut, 1963). *Dissertation Abstracts International*, *24*, 4497.

Chamberlain, C. M. (1980). The inequity of the sexes in educational administration: A study of the career history, administrative and instructional responsibilities as influenced by the sex of the school principal (Doctoral dissertation, United States International University, 1980). *Dissertation Abstracts International*, *41*, 1994A.

Chang, A. K. (1964). Role norms to guide administrator selection and training in Hawaii (Doctoral dissertation, Stanford University, 1963). *Dissertation Abstracts*, *24*, 3163.

Chisholm, R. B. (1980). The recruitment, selection, and employment of school superintendents in the state of Washington (Doctoral dissertation, Washington State University, 1980). *Dissertation Abstracts International*, *41*, 1856A.

Cistone, P. J. (1977). The socialization of school board members. *Educational Administration Quarterly*, *13*(2), 19–33.

Cogan, S. (1982). The relationship of the social class and personal characteristics of parent association executive board members to the role expectations and personal characteristics which they advocate in the selection of elementary principals in selected American cities (Doctoral dissertation, St. John's University, 1982). *Dissertation Abstracts International*, *43*, 1361A.

Cokendolpher, F. W. (1959). Employment patterns in the school superintendency in Texas (Doctoral dissertation, University of Texas, 1959). *Dissertation Abstracts International*, *20*, 1654.

Cottrell, M. C., & Hughes, D. L. (1978). *Utah women educators in school administration.* (ERIC Document Reproduction Service No. ED 150 744)

Couch, S. (1981, December). *Employer perceptions of male and female applicants for administrative positions in vocational education.* Paper presented at the Annual Meeting of the American Vocational Association, Atlanta, Georgia.

Covel, J. (1979, April). *School administration careers.* Paper presented at the Annual Meeting of the American Educational Research Association, San Francisco, California.

Covel, J., & Ortiz, F. I. (1978). Career patterns among school administrators. *Educational Research Quarterly*, *4*(3), 33–44.

Craig, D. W. (1982). Career patterns of Michigan public school superintendents in districts with an enrollment of 5,000 or more students (Doctoral dissertation, Ball State University, 1982). *Dissertation Abstracts International*, *43*, 316A.

Criswell, L. W. (Ed.). (1975, November). *Socialization and training into the school administrative role.* Papers presented at the Annual Meeting of the California Educational Research Association, San Diego, California.

Crochet, C. M. (1981). An exploratory study of characteristics of women administrators in vocational education in Georgia

(Doctoral dissertation, Florida State University, 1980). *Dissertation Abstracts International, 41,* 4691A.

Cryer, G. C. (1981). A comparative study of the traits, job perceptions, and utilization of male and female central office administrators in selected urban school districts in Tennessee (Doctoral dissertation, Memphis State University, 1980). *Dissertation Abstracts International, 41,* 4901A.

Cuban, L. (1976). *Urban school chiefs under fire.* Chicago: University of Chicago Press.

Cunningham, L. L., & Hentges, J. T. (1982). *The American school superintendency 1982: A summary report.* Arlington, VA: American Association of School Administrators.

Curry, D. L. (1980). Criteria and procedures for the recruitment and selection of superintendents for Class III school districts in Nebraska (Doctoral dissertation, University of Nebraska, 1980). *Dissertation Abstracts International, 41,* 1297A.

DeFrahn, R. G. (1974). A study of recruitment and selection of secondary school principals in New Jersey (Doctoral dissertation, Temple University, 1974). *Dissertation Abstracts International, 35,* 1373A.

Deprin, L. D. (1965). Superintendent succession and administrative patterns (Doctoral dissertation, University of Arizona, 1965). *Dissertation Abstracts, 26,* 1445.

Dickson, A. M. (1983). The relationship between mentorship and other variables and administrators' perceptions of the career development process in higher education (Doctoral dissertation, Boston University School of Education). *Dissertation Abstracts International, 44,* 1263A.

Dingerson, M. R., Rodman, J. A., & Wade, J. F. (1982). Procedures and costs for hiring academic administrators. *Journal of Higher Education, 53,* 63–74.

Diulio, A. J. (1980). Five graduate programs in educational administration: A comparative study (Doctoral dissertation, Stanford University, 1979). *Dissertation Abstracts International, 40,* 3806A.

Drake, J. M. (1965). An analysis of reported criteria and procedures used in the selection of secondary school principals in certain school districts in the state of Illinois (Doctoral dissertation, Columbia University, 1965). *Dissertation Abstracts, 26,* 815.

Duke, D. L., Isaacson, N. S., Sagor, R., & Schmuck, P. A. (1984). *Transition to leadership: An investigation of the first year of the principalship* (A Series of Working Papers). Portland, OR: Lewis and Clark College, Educational Administration Program.

Duran, I. S. (1983). Grounded theory study: Chicana administrators in Colorado and New Mexico (Doctoral dissertation, University of Wyoming, 1982). *Dissertation Abstracts International, 43,* 2841A.

Dusek, C. A. (1983). A reexamination of the differences between career-bound and place-bound school superintendents (Doctoral dissertation, The Ohio State University, 1982). *Dissertation Abstracts International, 43,* 2512A.

Dylewski, R. F. (1975). A study of the procedures and criteria used in the recruitment and selection of public elementary school principals in the State of New York (Doctoral dissertation, Columbia University, 1975). *Dissertation Abstracts International, 36,* 3274A.

Edson, S. K. (1981). Female aspirants in public school administration: Why do they continue to aspire to principalships? (Doctoral dissertation, University of Oregon, 1980). *Dissertation Abstracts International, 41,* 3345A.

Eller, E. B. (1963). An analysis of personal and professional characteristics of Tennessee public school superintendents, 1940–1960 (Doctoral dissertation, University of Tennessee, 1962). *Dissertation Abstracts International, 23,* 3199.

Esposito, D. W. (1983). Selected factors associated with the career paths of female school administrators (Doctoral dissertation, University of Miami, 1983). *Dissertation Abstracts International, 44,* 1263A.

Fallinger, D. L. (1981). Deference to authority as a determinant for the selection of educational administrators (Doctoral dissertation, Pennsylvania State University, 1980). *Dissertation Abstracts International, 41,* 3797A.

Farmer, N. J. (1983). Characteristics of women principals in North Carolina (Doctoral dissertation, University of North Carolina at Chapel Hill, 1982). *Dissertation Abstracts International, 43,* 2513A.

Fauske, J. R., & Ogawa, R. T. (1984, April). *How a faculty made sense of the impending succession of its principal.* Paper presented at the Annual Meeting of the American Educational Research Association, New Orleans, Louisiana.

Fenske, M. R. (1971). Career orientation and career mobility of Oregon school superintendents (Doctoral dissertation, University of Oregon, 1970). *Dissertation Abstracts International, 31,* 3206A.

Finlay, C. S., & Crosson, P. H. (1981). *Women in higher education administration: Status and strategies.* Oneonta, N.Y.: American Association of University Administrators. (ERIC Document Reproduction Service No. ED 200 120)

Fisher, F. P. (1979). A study of the relationship between the scarcity of women in educational administrative positions and the multiple factors which influence the career aspirations of women teachers (Doctoral dissertation, Michigan State University, 1978). *Dissertation Abstracts International, 40,* 574A.

Fisk, R. S. (1953). *CPEA reports to the profession on—Preservice preparation of school administrators.* New York: Teachers College, Columbia University.

Fleming, E. E. (1967). Innovation related to tenure, succession, and orientation of the elementary school principal (Doctoral dissertation, Northwestern University, 1967). *Dissertation Abstracts International, 28,* 2024A.

Forlines, C. L. (1981). Superintendents' perceptions of public opinions toward women administrators and superintendents' opinions toward women administrators (Doctoral dissertation, George Peabody College for Teachers at Vanderbilt University, 1981). *Dissertation Abstracts International, 42,* 1397A.

Fowler, A. H. (1984). Male and female administrators in Washington: A comparison of selected characteristics (Doctoral dissertation, Washington State University, 1983). *Dissertation Abstracts International, 44,* 1988A.

Franklin, J. B. (1971). Attrition and success of doctoral students in the Educational Administration Department at Arizona State University (Doctoral dissertation, Arizona State University, 1970). *Dissertation Abstracts International, 31,* 3810A.

Frasher, J. M., & Frasher, R. S. (1980). Sex bias in the evaluation of administrators. *Journal of Educational Administration, 18,* 245–253.

Freeborn, R. M. (1967). School board change and the succession pattern of superintendents (Doctoral dissertation, Claremont Graduate School and University Center, 1966). *Dissertation Abstracts International, 28,* 424A.

Fuqua, A. B. (1983). Professional attractiveness, inside sponsorship, and perceived paternalism as predictors of upward mobility of public school superintendents (Doctoral dissertation, Virginia Polytechnic Institute and State University, 1983). *Dissertation Abstracts International, 44,* 1640A.

Gaertner, K. N. (1978–79). The structure of careers in public school administration. *Administrator's Notebook, 27,* (6).

Gaertner, K. N. (1980). The structure of organizational careers. *Sociology of Education, 53,* 7–20.

Gaertner, K. N. (1981). Administrative careers in public school organizations. In P. A. Schmuck, W. W. Charters, Jr., & R. O. Carlson (Eds.), *Educational policy and management: Sex differentials* (pp. 199–217). New York: Academic.

Ganz, H. J., & Hoy, W. K. (1977). Patterns of succession of elementary principals and organizational change. *Planning and Changing, 8,* 185–190.

Garberina, M. R. (1980, December). *Rites of passage: Role socialization among novice principals.* Paper presented at the Annual Meeting of the American Anthropological Association, Washington, DC.

Geering, A. D. (1980). *The role of the school principal in comparative perspectives.* (ERIC Document Reproduction Service No. ED 199 930)

Gilmour, S. L. (1984). Toward a model of mentors' influence on the personal and professional development of principals (Doctoral dissertation, Syracuse University, 1983). *Disseration Abstracts International, 45,* 703A.

Glover, G. T. (1970). The selection and retention of elementary school principals in Oklahoma (Doctoral dissertation, University of Oklahoma, 1970). *Dissertation Abstracts International, 31,* 582.

Goerss, K. V. W. (1975). A study of personality factors of selected women administrators in higher education (Doctoral dissertation, University of Southern Mississippi, 1975). *Dissertation Abstracts International, 36,* 1942A.

Gordon, S. E. (1980). Career patterns of female chief student affairs administrators (Doctoral dissertation, Florida State University, 1979). *Dissertation Abstracts International, 40,* 3655A.

Grable, J. R. (1968). An analysis of doctoral programs in educational administration in a five-state region (Doctoral dissertation, University of New Mexico, 1967). *Dissertation Abstracts International, 28,* 3414A.

Greenfield, W. D. (1975, March–April). *Socialization processes among administrative candidates in public schools.* Paper presented at the Annual Meeting of the American Educational Research Association, Washington, DC.

Greenfield, W. D., Jr. (1977a). Administrative candidacy: A process of new role learning—Part I. *The Journal of Educational Administration, 15,* 30–48.

Greenfield, W. D., Jr. (1977b). Administrative candidacy: A process of new role learning—Part 2. *The Journal of Educational Administration, 15,* 170–193.

Greenfield, W. D., Jr. (1983). Career dynamics of educators: Research and policy issues. *Educational Administration Quarterly, 19*(2), 5–26.

Griffin, S. M. P., (1979). An administrator selection procedure (Doctoral dissertation, University of Arkansas, 1979). *Dissertation Abstracts International, 40,* 1781A.

Griffiths, D. E., Goldman, S., & McFarland, W. J. (1965). Teacher mobility in New York City. *Educational Administration Quarterly, 1*(1), 15–31.

Gross, N., & Herriott, R. E. (1965). *Staff leadership in public schools: A sociological inquiry.* New York: John Wiley.

Gussner, W. P. (1974). The socialization of a school administrator (Doctoral dissertation, Washington University, 1974). *Dissertation Abstracts International, 35,* 2081A.

Hall, J. T. (1984). Characteristics of principalship candidates and their relation to selection patterns in eight Illinois communities' public school districts (Doctoral dissertation, University of Illinois at Urbana-Champaign, 1983). *Dissertation Abstracts International, 45,* 33A.

Hall, R. M., & McIntyre, K. E. (1957). The student personnel program. In R. F. Campbell & R. T. Gregg (Eds.), *Administrative behavior in education* (pp. 393–425). New York: Harper.

Hamm, W. C. (1964). Changes in selection and retention of senior high school principals in Oklahoma 1954 to 1964 (Doctoral dissertation, University of Oklahoma, 1964). *Dissertation Abstracts International, 25,* 3353.

Hannah, M. K. (1980). A comparison of demographic characteristics and selected role functions of Michigan public school administrators (Doctoral dissertation, University of Michigan, 1979). *Dissertation Abstracts International, 40,* 579A.

Hansot, E., & Tyack, D. (1981). *The dream deferred: A golden age for women school administrators* (Policy Paper No. 81–CZ). Palo Alto, CA: Stanford University, Institute for Research on Educational Finance and Governance.

Harris, R. (1981). An analysis of Pennsylvania administrators. *Social Studies Journal, 11*(Fall), 58–62.

Hartsell, C. W. (1960). Role playing as a means of selecting administrators (Doctoral dissertation, University of Tennessee, 1959). *Dissertation Abstracts International, 20,* 4319.

Haven, E. W., Adkinson, P. D., & Bagley, M. (1980). *Women in educational administration: The principalship. A literature review.* Annandale, VA: J.W.K. International Corp. (ERIC Document Reproduction Service No. ED 208 486)

Hemphill, J. K. Griffiths, D. E., & Frederiksen, N. (1962). *Admin-istrative performance and personality: A study of the princial in a simulated elementary school.* New York: Columbia University, Teachers College.

Hentschke, G., & Cline, H. (1981, April). *Educational career mobility under organizational growth and contraction.* Paper presented at the Annual Meeting of the American Educational Research Association, Los Angeles, California.

Hersey, P. W. (1980). NASSP's assessment center: Practitioners speak out. *The NASSP Bulletin, 64*(438), 87–106.

Hersey, P. W. (1982). The NASSP assessment center develops leadership talent. *Educational Leadership, 39,* 370–371.

Hickcox, E. S. (1967). Career and place bound orientations of chief school officers in New York state: An exploratory study (Doctoral dissertation, Cornell University, 1966). *Dissertation Abstracts International, 27,* 4073A.

Hoff, F. H. (1962). A case study test and its application to the selection process for high school principals: An exploration of the use of a test dealing with the ability to handle administrative situations as an aid in selecting high school principals (Doctoral dissertation, New York University, 1961). *Dissertation Abstracts International, 23,* 506.

Holder, J. L. (1968). The process of selecting superintendents of schools as viewed by boards of education (Doctoral dissertation, Colorado State College, 1968). *Dissertation Abstracts International, 29,* 1075A.

Holmstrom, E. I., & Holmstrom, R. W. (1974). The plight of the woman doctoral student. *American Educational Research Journal, 11,* 1–17.

Holtz, M. A. P. (1980). A comparison of the personality characteristics and background factors among women administrators in education, business and government (Doctoral dissertation, University of Minnesota, 1979). *Dissertation Abstracts International, 40,* 5669A.

Hopes, C. W. (1983). *Criteria, procedures and methods used in the selection of principals and the relevance of training for the principalship using the example of the State of Hesse in the Federal Republic of Germany* (Author Trans.). Unpublished doctoral dissertation, Johann Wolfgang Goethe University, Frankfurt am Main, Germany.

Horowitz, N. H. (1968). Differences between successful and unsuccessful candidates for the elementary school principalship in the Los Angeles city schools (Doctoral dissertation, University of California, Los Angeles, 1968). *Dissertation Abstracts, 29,* 1715A.

Hoy, W. K., & Aho, F. (1973). Patterns of succession of high school principals and organizational change. *Planning and Changing, 4,* 82–88.

Huffman, L. D. (1975). A comparison of personality traits of doctoral students in higher education and selected chief administrators in Illinois institutions of higher education (Doctoral dissertation, University of Illinois at Urbana-Champaign, 1974). *Dissertation Abstracts International, 35,* 4190A.

Hullhorst, A. J. (1984). A comparative study of the career aspirations, job seeking patterns, and career patterns of male and female doctoral recipients in educational administration (Doctoral dissertation, Western Michigan University, 1984). *Dissertation Abstracts International, 45,* 705A.

Iannaccone, L., & Lutz, F. W. (1970). *Politics, power and policy: The governing of local school districts.* Columbus, OH: Charles E. Merrill.

Ibeawuchi, S. A. (1980). A study of aspects of differences in attitudes of men and women administrators and prospective administrators in Kansas (Doctoral dissertation, University of Kansas, 1980). *Dissertation Abstracts International, 41,* 1867A.

Jackson, C. B. (1981). Career development for women in public school administration: A study of women school superintendents in the United States (Doctoral dissertation, University of Colorado at Boulder, 1980). *Dissertation Abstracts International, 41,* 3353A.

Jeswald, T. A. (1977). A new approach to identifying administrative talent. *NASSP Bulletin, 61*(410), 79–83.

Johnson, J. M. (1979). A comparison of male and female doctoral and postdoctoral students of educational administration at universities in Pennsylvania (Doctoral dissertation, University of Pittsburgh, 1978). *Dissertation Abstracts International, 39,* 4628A.

Johnston, G. S., Yeakey, C. C., & Moore, S. E. (1980). Analysis of the employment of women in professional administrative positions in public education. *Planning and Changing, 11,* 115–132.

Jones, E. H., & Montenegro, X. P. (1983). Factors predicting women's upward career mobility in school administration. *Journal of Educational Equity and Leadership, 3,* 231–241.

Justice, A. E., Jr. (1966). Criteria for the selection of principals of public elementary schools in the state of Georgia (Doctoral dissertation, Duke University, 1965). *Dissertation Abstracts International, 26,* 4378.

Kahl, S. R. (1980). *The selection of teachers and school administrators: A synthesis of the literature.* Denver: Mid-Continent Regional Educational Lab. Inc. (ERIC Document Reproduction Service No. ED. 221 917)

Keith, P. M. (1975). Administrative and faculty turnover and diffusion of an educational innovation. *Urban Education, 10,* 297–304.

Kelley, E. A. (1984, April). *Assessment center technology and the preparation of school administrators.* Paper presented at the Annual Meeting of the American Educational Research Association, New Orleans, Louisiana.

Kelley, M. E. (1982). Same faces, new skills. *Educational Leadership, 39,* 372–373.

Kelly, T. W., & Metzcus, R. H. (1975). Occupational socialization and work values of parochial and public school administrators: A comparative analysis. *Notre Dame Journal of Education, 6,* 36–42

Kelly, T. W. (1975). Occupational socialization and the work value orientation of public and parochial school administrators on the elementary and secondary school levels (Doctoral dissertation, University of Notre Dame, 1975). *Dissertation Abstracts International, 36,* 1213A.

Kelsey, J. G. T., & Leullier, B. (1978). School district policies for the identification, selection and training of principals. *The Canadian Administrator, 27*(5), 1–6.

Khleif, B. B. (1975). Professionalization of school superintendents: A sociocultural study of an elite program. *Human Organization, 34*(3), 301–308.

King, A. L. (1981). The effect of attributive sex of the applicant upon the selection of personnel for community college administration (Doctoral dissertation, University of Washington, 1981). *Dissertation Abstracts International, 42,* 1405A.

Kjerulff, K. H., & Blood, M. R. (1973). A comparison of communication patterns in male and female graduate students. *Journal of Higher Education, 44,* 623–632.

Kirk, R. J. (1971). Orderly and disrupted career patterns in educational administration (Doctoral dissertation, Pennsylvania State University, 1970). *Dissertation Abstracts International, 31,* 4420A.

Knedlik, S. M. (1968). The effect of administrative succession pattern upon educational innovation in selected secondary schools (Doctoral dissertation, New York University, 1967). *Dissertation Abstracts International, 28,* 4415A.

Konek, C. (1979). *Project DELTA, Wichita State University, final report.* Wichita: Wichita State University. (ERIC Document Reproduction Service No. ED 179 153)

Leizear, J. L. (1984). The incidence and influence of mentorship in the career development of upper level women administrators in public school systems in Texas (doctoral dissertation, Texas A & M University, 1984). *Dissertation Abstracts International, 45,* 1256A.

Levandowski, B. S. (1977). Women in educational administration: Where do they stand? *NASSP Bulletin, 61*(410), 101–106.

Lutz, F. W. (1979). The deanship: Search and screening process. *Educational Record, 60,* 261–271.

Lyman, K. D., & Speizer, J. J. (1980). Advancing in school administration: A pilot project for women. *Harvard Educational Review, 50,* 25–35.

Mack, M. H. (1981). A study of attitude toward women as school administrators (Doctoral dissertation, Auburn university, 1981). *Dissertation Abstracts International, 42,* 41A.

Manning, R. F. (1969). The school principalship: A study of mobility and its relationship to educational leadership (Doctoral dissertation, Case Western Reserve University, 1968). *Dissertation Abstracts International, 29,* 4237A.

March, J. C., & March, J. G. (1977). Almost random careers: The Wisconsin school superintendency, 1940–1972. *Administrative Science Quarterly, 22,* 377–409.

Marshall, C. (1979, April). *Career socialization of women in school administration.* Paper presented at the Annual Meeting of the American Educational Research Association, San Francisco, California.

Marshall, C. (1981). Organizational policy and women's socialization in administration. *Urban Education, 16,* 205–231.

Marshall, S. A. (1959). Differential perception of the criteria used for the selection of administrative personnel (Doctoral dissertation, Stanford University, 1959). *Dissertation Abstracts, 20,* 1245A.

Martin, R. V. R. (1981). Minority women administrators' perceptions of barriers in higher education (Doctoral dissertation, University of Connecticut, 1980). *Dissertation Abstracts International, 41,* 3357A.

Mascaro, F. G. (1974). The early on-the-job socialization of first-year elementary school principals (Doctoral dissertation, University of California, Riverside, 1973). *Dissertation Abstracts International, 34,* 7492A.

Matsuo, D. I. N. (1982). A comparative study of value orientations among Japanese American and Caucasian American administrators in higher education (Doctoral dissertation, University of Hawaii, 1982). *Dissertation Abstracts International, 43,* 997A.

McCarthy, M., & Zent, A. (1982). Affirmative action for school administrators: Has it worked, can it survive? *Phi Delta Kappan, 63*(7), 461–463.

McCleary, L. E., & Thomson, S. D. (1979). *The senior high school principalship, Volume III: The summary report.* Reston, VA: National Association of Secondary School Principals.

McDade, T., & Drake, J. M. (1982). Career path models for women superintendents. *Journal of Educational Research, 75,* 210–217.

McIntosh, J. (1974). Differences between women teachers who do and who do not seek promotion. *The Journal of Educational Administration, 12*(2), 28–41.

McIntyre, K. E. (1966). *Selection of educational administrators: A UCEA position paper.* Austin: The University of Texas and the University Council for Educational Administration.

McIntyre, K. E. (1971). Simulating the process for selection of administrators. In D. L. Bolton (Ed.), *The use of simulation in educational administration* (pp. 149–170). Columbus, OH: Charles E. Merrill.

McKenzie, C. M. (1980). Admissions criteria and selection procedures for doctoral study in educational administration in institutions accredited by the National Council for Accreditation of Teacher Education (Doctoral dissertation, Miami University, 1979), *Dissertation Abstracts International, 40,* 3669A.

McNutt, A. S. (1980). A study of the role models of top-echelon women administrators in southern public institutions of higher education (Doctoral dissertation, George Peabody College for Teachers). *Dissertation Abstracts International, 41,* 556A.

Meekins, P. E. (1974). Preparation for educational administrators (Doctoral dissertation, University of Virginia, 1974). *Dissertation Abstracts International, 35,* 2591A.

Miklos, E., & Nixon, M. (1978). *Educational administration programs in Canadian universities.* Edmonton: University of Alberta, Department of Educational Administration.

Mills-Nova, B. A. (1980). A study of variables affecting the career progression of women in higher education administration (Doctoral dissertation, University of Minnesota, 1980). *Dissertation Abstracts International, 41,* 1874A.

Miskel, C., & Cosgrove, D. (1985). Leader succession in school settings. *Review of Educational Research, 55,* 87–105.

Mix, M. C. (1971). Toward a theory of socialization into the academic profession (Doctoral dissertation, State University of

New York at Buffalo, 1971). *Dissertation Abstracts International*, *32*, 1301A.

Morris, M. P. (1980). Critical characteristics of top level women administrators in the overseas American sponsored schools (Doctoral dissertation, University of Denver, 1979). *Dissertation Abstracts International*, *40*, 6094A.

Nelson, C. K. (1982). Factors influencing the promotion of women to the principalship in Arizona (Doctoral dissertation, Northern Arizona University, 1982). *Dissertation Abstracts International*, *43*, 1778A.

Nixon, M., & Gue, L. R. (1975). Professional role orientation of women administrators and women teachers. *The Canadian Administrator*, *15*(2), 1–5.

Ocel, J. M. (1984). The career decision making processes of women elementary school principals (Doctoral dissertation, University of Pittsburgh, 1983). *Dissertation Abstracts International*, *45*, 369A.

Ogawa, R. T. (1984, April). *NASSP assessment centers: Opportunities for research*. Paper presented at the Annual Meeting of the American Educational Research Association, New Orleans, Louisiana.

Olivera, C. E. (1979). *The administration of educational development in Latin America*. Paris, France: United Nations Educational, Scientific, and Cultural Organization, International Institute for Educational Planning. (ERIC Document Reproduction Service No. ED 213 116)

Ortiz, F. I. (1978). Midcareer socialization of educational administrators. *Review of Educational Research*, *48*, 121–132.

Ortiz, F. I. (1982). *Career patterns in education: Women, men and minorities in public school administration*. New York: Praeger.

Ott, M. S. (1983). Expressed attitudes toward women in educational administration (Doctoral dissertation, University of Northern Colorado, 1983). *Dissertation Abstracts International*, *44*, 1653A.

Pacheco, B. A. (1982). Barriers to advancement in educational administration as perceived by women administrators (Doctoral dissertation, University of the Pacific, 1982). *Dissertation Abstracts International*, *43*, 1377A.

Paddock, S. (1978). *Careers in educational administration: Are women the exception?* Eugene: University of Oregon, Center for Educational Policy and Management. (ERIC Document Reproduction Service No. ED 149 468).

Paddock, S. C. (1981). Male and female career paths in school administration. In P. A. Schmuck, W. W. Charters, Jr., & R. O. Carlson (Eds.), *Educational policy and management: Sex differentials* (pp. 187–198). New York: Academic Press.

Paul, C. A. B. (1979). Personal, educational, and career patterns of men and women administrators in the Massachussetts community colleges (Doctoral dissertation, Boston University School of Education, 1978). *Dissertation Abstracts International*, *39*, 5286A.

Pawlitschek, E. A. (1976). *Female administrator acceptance* (Master's thesis, University of Minnesota, 1976). (ERIC Document Reproduction Service No. ED 155 776)

Peterson, K. D. (1984, April). *An organizational perspective on careers*. Paper presented at the Annual Meeting of the American Educational Research Association, New Orleans, Louisiana.

Picker, A. M. (1979). Women educational administrators: Career patterns and perceptions (Doctoral dissertation, University of California, Los Angeles, 1979). *Dissertation Abstracts International*, *40*, 3033A.

Piggott, L. C. J. (1980). The social characteristics and career patterns of women administrators in North Carolina colleges and universities (Doctoral dissertation, University of North Carolina at Greensboro, 1979). *Dissertation Abstracts International*, *40*, 5679A.

Pope, B. W. (1979). Factors influencing career aspirations and development of women holding administrative positions in public schools (Doctoral dissertation, Temple University, 1979). *Dissertation Abstracts International*, *39*, 6449A.

Porter, E. W. (1982). Presidential selection at large state universities. *AGB Reports*, *24*(6), 40–43.

Poteet, R. H. (1969). Criteria for the selection of public elementary school principals in the state of Texas (Doctoral dissertation, East Texas State University, 1968). *Dissertation Abstracts*, *29*, 3395A.

Powell, R. E. (1984). A comparison of selection criteria and performance evaluation criteria for Missouri school superintendents (Doctoral dissertation, University of Missouri-Columbia, 1982). *Dissertation Abstracts International*, *44*, 2000A.

Preising, P. P. (1968). The relationship of staff tenure and administrative succession to structural innovation (Doctoral dissertation, Stanford University, 1968). *Dissertation Abstracts International*, *29*, 447A.

Prolman, S. (1982). Gender, career paths, and administrative perceptions. *Administrators's Notebook*, *30*(5).

Queralt, M. (1982, April). *The role of the mentor in the career development of university faculty members and academic administrators*. Paper presented at the Annual Meeting of the National Association for Women Deans, Administrators, and Counselors, Indianapolis, Indiana.

Rader, R. C. (1976). Superintendent value systems, local-cosmopolitan orientations and patterns of succession (Doctoral dissertation, Rutgers, The State University of New Jersey, 1975). *Dissertation Abstracts International*, *36*, 4179A.

Rawlins, M. D. (1964). A career pattern study of secondary principals in the Los Angles city schools (Doctoral dissertation, University of California, Los Angeles, 1964). *Dissertation Abstracts International*, *25*, 3365.

Reeves, R. L., Jr. (1971). Ten case studies in the selection, evaluation, and termination of California school superintendents (Doctoral dissertation, University of California, Los Angeles, 1970). *Dissertation Abstracts International*, *31*, 3231A.

Reynolds, J. A. (1966). Innovation related to administrative tenure, succession and orientation: A study of the adoption of new perspectives by school systems (Doctoral dissertation, Washington University, 1965). *Dissertation Abstracts International*, *26*, 6482.

Rix, E. A. (1981). Dynamics of promotion decisions. *Comment on Education*, *12*(1), 4–12.

Robertson, M. C. (1984). A survey of the selection of school superintendents in Massachusetts (Doctoral dissertation, Boston University, 1983). *Dissertation Abstracts International*, *44*, 2946A.

Robinson, T. J. (1974). Chief black school administrators: A critical look at the specific factors involved in the selection of chief school administrators who are black (Doctoral dissertation, Michigan State University, 1973). *Dissertation Abstracts International*, *34*, 5548A.

Rodenberger, L. E. (1981). A survey of recruitment and selection of school superintendents in Ohio (Doctoral dissertation, Bowling Green State University, 1980). *Dissertation Abstracts International*, *41*, 2869A.

Rowen, I. B. (1982). Analysis of some elements of career patterns of fifty women administrators in higher education (Doctoral dissertation, Rutgers, The State University of New Jersey, 1981). *Dissertation Abstracts International*, *43*, 1002A.

Rudd, F. G. & Cottrell, M. C. (1980, April). *Women educators in the state of Washington: Status, qualifications and aspirations for educational leadership*. Paper presented at the Annual Meeting of the American Educational Research Association, Los Angeles, California.

Sandorff, P. I. (1981). Women administrators in public elementary education: Factors for successful entry (Doctoral dissertation, Claremont Graduate School, 1980). *Dissertation Abstracts International*, *41*, 3368A.

Scally, Y. H. (1982). A comparison of the personality profiles and other background characteristics of selected female school district superintendents with those selected females aspiring to superintendencies (Doctoral dissertation, Ohio University, 1982). *Dissertation Abstracts International*, *43*, 1003A.

Schmeider, J. H. (1984). Women and the elementary principalship: Does discrimination exist at the pre-interview stage of the employment process? (Doctoral dissertation, Stanford University, 1984). *Dissertation Abstracts International, 45,* 45A.

Schmidt, R. M. (1966). An appraisal of factors relating to the selection of assistant principals and principals for Detroit public elementary schools for the period 1957–1963 (Doctoral dissertation, Wayne State University, 1964). *Dissertation Abstracts International, 26,* 4402.

Schmitt, N., & Noe, R. A. (1983). Demonstration of content validity: Assessment center example. *Journal of Assessment Center Technology, 6*(2), 5–11.

Schmitt, N., Noe, R. A., Meritt, R., & Fitzgerald, M. P. (1984). Validity of assessment center ratings for the prediction of performance ratings and school climate of school administrators. *Journal of Applied Psychology, 69,* 207–213.

Schmitz, D. M. (1972). The function of socialization: Compliance as it affects person and role power in coaching and teaching experience as professional preparation for the principalship (Doctoral dissertation, University of New Mexico, 1971). *Dissertation Abstracts International, 32,* 3575A.

Schmuck, P. A. (1979). *Sex equity in educational leadership in Oregon public schools* (OSSC Bulletin, 23[2]). Eugene, OR: Oregon School Study Council. (ERIC Document Reproduction Service No. ED 177 715)

Schmuck, P. A., Charters, W. W., Jr., & Carlson, R. O. (Eds.). (1981). *Educational policy and management: Sex differentials.* New York: Academic Press.

Schmuck, P. A., & Wyant, S. H. (1981). Clues to sex bias in the selection of school administrators: A report from the Oregon network. In P. A. Schmuck, W. W. Charters, Jr., & R. O. Carlson (Eds.), *Educational policy and management: Sex differentials* (pp. 73–97). New York: Academic Press.

Sharbaugh, W. J., Jr. (1971). Behavioral predictors for the identification of school administrators (Doctoral dissertation, University of Maryland, 1970). *Dissertation Abstracts International, 31,* 5732A.

Shea, L. R. (1984). Women and the high school principalship: A comparison of male and female aspirations and career paths (Doctoral dissertation, Lehigh University, 1983). *Dissertation Abstracts International, 44,* 2647A.

Silver, P. F., & Spuck, D. W. (Eds.). (1978). *Preparatory programs for educational administrators in the United States.* Columbus, OH: The University Council for Educational Administration.

Slimmer, V. M. (1984, April). *Advancement factors of women in administration: Patterns and perspectives.* Paper presented at the Annual Meeting of the American Eductional Research Association, New Orleans, Louisiana.

Sloan, F. W. (1980). A study on the aspirations of women teachers to become school administrators (Doctoral dissertation, North Texas State University, 1979). *Dissertation Abstracts International, 40,* 3686A.

Smith, C. F. (1984, April). *The use of the National Association of Secondary School Principals' (NASSP) Assessment Center reports: A preliminary analysis.* Paper presented at the Annual Meeting of the American Educational Research Association, New Orleans, Louisiana.

Snyder, R. D. (1972). A study of selected characteristics of individuals admitted to doctoral study in the Department of Educational Administration and Supervision in the College of Education at the University of Illinois (Doctoral dissertation, University of Illinois at Urbana-Champaign, 1971). *Dissertation Abstracts International, 32,* 4310A.

Socolow, D. J. (1978). Research: How administrators get their jobs. *Change, 10*(5), 42–43, 54.

Stanfield, R. M. (1982). Career mobility patterns of elementary school principals in the State of Utah (Doctoral dissertation, University of Utah, 1982). *Dissertation Abstracts International, 43,* 1005A.

Stapley, H. A., Jr. (1958). A study of the identification, local pre-service training, selection, and orientation of elementary school principals in selected Indiana schools (Doctoral dissertation, Indiana University, 1958). *Dissertation Abstracts International, 19,* 10006.

St. Clair, J. K. (1962). An evaluation of a clinical procedure for predicting on-the-job administrative behaviors of elementary school principals (Doctoral dissertation, University of Texas, 1962). *Dissertation Abstracts, 23,* 138.

Stern, A. K. (1976). Recommended criteria and reported practices in the recruitment and selection of elementary principals (Doctoral dissertation, University of Oklahoma, 1975). *Dissertation Abstracts International, 36,* 4945A.

Stevenson, F. B. (1974). Women administrators in Big Ten universities (Doctoral dissertation, Michigan State University, 1973). *Dissertation Abstracts International, 34,* 5553A.

Stewart, H. G. (1963). Criteria used by superintendents in the selection of beginning building principals in certain Wisconsin schools (Doctoral dissertation, University of Wisconsin, 1963). *Dissertation Abstracts International, 24,* 1469.

Storlein, H. T. (1983). Recruitment and selection of secondary principals in Alberta: An analysis of procedures, criteria, and identified problems (Doctoral dissertation, University of Montana, 1983). *Dissertation Abstracts International, 44,* 1286A.

Stout, J. G. (1982). The enculturation of new school board members: A longitudinal study in seven school districts (Doctoral dissertation, Arizona State University, 1982). *Dissertation Abstracts International, 43,* 1006A.

Thiemann, F. C. (1968). *A partial theory of executive succession.* Eugene: University of Oregon, Center for the Advanced Study of Educational Admnistration. (ERIC Document Reproduction Service No. ED 024 113)

Thomas, A. R., & Muscio, A. (1984). Credibility, rumour, change: Considerations for the arriving principal. *The Practicing Administrator, 6*(1), 28–30, 31.

Thyberg, C. S. (1965). An exploratory study in the use of interpersonal measures in the selection and evaluation of school administrators (Doctoral dissertation, University of Southern California, 1965). *Dissertation Abstracts International, 26,* 183.

Tillman, F. A., Jr. (1974). The career accomplishments of superintendents in selected school districts in California in relation to management theory, educational background and promotional history (Doctoral dissertation, Brigham Young University, 1974). *Dissertation Abstracts International, 35,* 776A.

Tronc, K., & Enns, F. (1969). Ambition and deference. *The Canadian Administrator, 9*(1), 1–4.

Turner, D. W. (1982). Factors involved in the development of career patterns of Illinois principals (Doctoral dissertation, Illinois State University, 1982). *Dissertation Abstracts International, 43,* 1384A.

Tyler, H. I. (1980). Personal characteristics and career paths of selected women administrators in higher education (Doctoral dissertation, Kent State University, 1979). *Dissertation Abstracts International, 40,* 5685A.

Valverde, L. A. (1974). *Succession socialization: Its influence on school administrative candidates and its implication to the exclusion of minorities from administration. Final report.* (ERIC Document Reproduction Service No. ED 093 052).

Valverde, L. A. (1975). Succession socialization: Its influence on school administrative candidates and its implication to the exclusion of minorities from administration (Doctoral dissertation, Claremont Graduate School, 1974). *Dissertation Abstracts International, 35,* 7586A.

Valverde, L. A. (1980). Promotion socialization: The informal process in large urban districts and its adverse effects on nonwhites and women. *Journal of Educational Equity and Leadership, 1,* 36–46.

van Alstyne, C., Withers, J., & Elliott, S. (1977). Affirmative inaction: The bottom line tells the tale. *Change, 9*(8), 39–41, 60.

Villani, S. (1983). Mentoring and sponsoring as ways for women to overcome internal barriers to heightened career aspirations and achievement (Doctoral dissertation, Northeastern University, 1983). *Dissertation Abstracts International, 44,* 1658A.

Walsh, P. A. (1975). Career patterns of women administrators in higher education institutions in California (Doctoral dissertation, University of California, Los Angeles, 1975). *Dissertation Abstracts International, 36,* 3323A.

Wing, R. N. (1975). Educational administration: The selection process. A comparative study of current procedures correlated with administrative performance and administrative role expectation in metropolitan Detroit (Doctoral dissertation, Wayne State University, 1975). *Dissertation Abstracts International, 36,* 2610A.

Wolcott, H. F. (1973). *The man in the principal's office: An ethno-graphy.* New York: Holt, Rinehart & Winston.

Wood, M. M. (1980). Personality traits of urban female and male administrators and congruence of these traits with the occupational stereotypes of the male managerial model (Doctoral dissertation, University of Oklahoma, 1980). *Dissertation Abstracts International, 41,* 1892A.

CHAPTER 4

Describing and Explaining Administrator Behavior

Norman J. Boyan

Commentaries on the study of administrators and direct examination of the empirical literature reveal that approximately 50 facets of administrator behavior have attracted the attention of investigators. The behaviors investigated include (a) buffering, (b) controlling and coordinating, (c) climate and culture building, (d) communicating, (e) decision making, (f) evaluating, (g) goal setting, (h) handling conflict, (i) instructional leadership, (j) innovating, (k) leading and leader behavior, (l) making meaning, (m) mediating, (n) motivating, (o) political behavior, both macro and micro, (p) problem finding and solving, (q) procuring and allocating resources, (r) rule administration, (s) socializing, (t) supervising, (u) supporting, (v) talking, (w) style and process. (For major reviews and commentaries, see Boyan, 1982; Boyd & Crowson, 1981; Bridges, 1982; Campbell & Gregg, 1957; Erickson, 1967, 1977, 1979; Greenfield, 1982; Griffiths, 1964, 1969, 1979; Halpin, 1966; Immegart, 1977; Lipham, 1964; March, 1978; Moore, 1957. For comprehensive textbook treatments, see Hanson, 1985; Hoy & Miskel, 1987; Silver, 1983.)

Detailed consideration of studies in each of the 23 categories identified above is beyond the scope of this chapter. The intent here is to report specifically on intentional efforts to explain why administrators do what they do. Comment on several general characteristics of the study of administrators at work serves as preamble.

Consultant/reviewers: Edwin M. Bridges, Stanford University; and Donald J. Willower, The Pennsylvania State University.

CHARACTERISTICS OF THE STUDY OF ADMINISTRATORS

Descriptions of what administrators do and why they do so have appeared over 30 years in both thin slices and thick slabs. The thicker descriptions, both monographs and journal articles, say a lot about the administrator life for a few individuals at a time. The thinner descriptions, mostly journal articles, typically provide glimpses into selected segments of the lives of larger samples of school executives. The states of the several arts involved (Boyan, 1981) defy productive meta-analysis.

In addition to its scattered focus, research on school administrators also exhibits distinct shifts over time in activities and behaviors selected for study, lack of cumulativeness, and variable level of interest and associated volume of output. Both shifts in the conceptual schemes that have driven inquiry and changing educational concerns have influenced the choices of behaviors to study (see Boyd & Crowson, 1981; Immegart, 1977). For example, Halpin in 1957 advocated focusing on the administrator as decision maker and group leader in general terms, whereas 25 years later, Bossert, Dwyer, Rowan, and Lee (1982) narrowed attention specifically to the behavior of principals as instructional managers. This shift reflects swings in prevailing concerns and perceived problems in education, particularly the impact in the late 1970s and 1980s of the effective schools and school reform movements.

On the conceptual side, an investigator who found

it intriguing to explore structural effects might, as did Bridges (1965), seek to chart the influence of experience in a presumed bureaucracy on administrator personality. If a scholar tilted toward a human resources orientation, he might focus on participatory decision making and shared governance (e.g., Conway, 1976, 1978, 1984). If a micropolitical view drove the inquiry, the scholar might, as did Baldridge (1971), invoke a political model in interpreting administrator behavior at the university level (see also Pfeffer & Salancik, 1974).

In addition to the impact of different organizational perspectives, the identification of some scholars with the politics of education and some with the economics and public financing of education has also influenced the choices of subject and method (e.g., Boyd, 1974, on the superintendent as educational statesman versus politician; Mann, 1976, and Summerfield, 1971, on the representational behavior of principals; McCarty & Ramsey, 1971, on the mesh of superintendent behavior with community power structure; Thomas, 1963, and Thomas, Kemmerer, & Monk, 1978, on resource allocation behavior).

Fluctuation in the level of interest and volume of inquiry in administrators reflected a shift in focus in the mid-1960s from overwhelming concern with a science of administration to preoccupation with organizational analysis and behavior more broadly conceived. As a result, the study of administrator behavior languished (Griffiths, 1979), to be revivified by the press of learnings from studies of innovation and by the effective schools movement, which identified the site administrator's important role in sponsoring the adoption and implementation of innovation and in enhancing the effects of schools on student outcomes (see Berman & McLaughlin, 1975, 1978; Clark, Lotto, & Astuto, 1984; Rosenblum, Jastrzab, Brigham, & Phillips, 1980).

The prevailing condition of primarily disparate, one-shot, noncumulative inquiry on administrator behavior derives from the relatively small amount of empirical research by professors of educational administrators (see assessments by Bridges, 1982; Campbell & Newell, 1973; Griffiths, 1979; Immegart, 1977). Even into the 1980s, the doctoral dissertation has remained the primary outlet for research in educational administration. Only a few professors have learned how to integrate their own work with their students' into meaningful programmatic lines of inquiry (see, for example, Glasman, 1986, and Griffiths, 1983, on the work of Hoy and Miskel).

How researchers study administrators at work has resurfaced in the 1980s as a contentious issue. Bridges (1982) has crisply summarized study designs and modes of inquiry that prevailed from 1967 to 1980: (a) Survey research design was used in approximately 90 percent of 322 studies examined; (b) the questionnaire was the primary research tool versus interviews, observation, and/or use of documents and records; (c) quantitative methods substantially exceeded qualitative methods; (d) the frames of reference used showed surprisingly little interest in the practical problems of administrators; (e) isolated, unidimensional studies outnumbered both multidimensional and work activities investigations; (f) multidimensional inquiries have relied heavily on the use of the Leader Behavior Description Questionnaire (LBDQ) and the Organizational Climate Description Questionnaire (OCDQ), instruments of somewhat suspect validity; (g) the work activities set, with rare exception, were "simplistic, methodologically and conceptually" (p. 20). This basic pattern did not change materially during the first half of the 1980s, except for increased use of field and qualitative methodologies and arguments over competing conceptual schemes for guiding research.

A slashing attack by Gronn (1982) on a set of eight work activities studies and sharp reaction (Willower, 1983, 1984) to his position illustrate one dimension of the current argument over how to study administrators at work. Gronn accused the eight studies of subjecting educational administration to a dangerous revival of "Taylorism," both conceptually and methodologically. The limited explanatory value of the work activities studies had already been criticized by Willower (Kmetz & Willower, 1981; Martin & Willower, 1981) and Bridges (1982); this type of study subsequently received further, more measured critical review from Pitner and Russell (1985–1986). This kind of identification of the liabilities of the work activities studies, especially their lack of attention to antecedents and consequences and their inability to reveal the full meaning of the nature of managerial work, has well served the field.

Gronn, however, went beyond the application of conventional scholarly tests by introducing an ideological test: Namely, the studies were morally bad because they threatened to revive a reprehensible (to him) managerial ideology. After dismissing the set of eight studies and, by implication, others of the same genre that he did not cite, on the grounds of inappropriate conceptual framework, events to study, and methods of collecting and processing data, Gronn (1982) proposed his own mode of direct observation, "Boswelling." This approach requires lengthy interaction and intimate acquaintance with an administrator. Willower (1983, 1984) and Gronn (1984a) have exchanged critique, rejoinder, and response that locate the issue within the larger debate over the challenge of phenomenological orientation and the radical critique to normal science within educational administration.

At another level, Gronn (1983, 1984b) has also delivered and well illustrated his view that talk is the work of administration and that careful and intensive analysis of talk, especially when interpreted against a background of power, materially enlightens understanding of managerial activity. MacPherson (1984), like Gronn, supports close observation of what he calls "the nature of action at the talk face [treated] as a socio-cultural phenomenon" (p. 72). MacPherson also makes clear his allegiance to the phenomenological orientation advocated by T. Greenfield (1975) in arguing in favor of an approach to the interpretation of action that begins with the existential meaning of being and becoming an administrator. Thomas (1986) has entered the lists of argument about how to study administrators at work with a sharp and full critique of, first, Gronn's out-of-hand dismissal of the value of direct observation in the work activities mode; second, Gronn's zealous advocacy of talk as *the* work of administration based on a remarkably small number of minutes of data collection; and, third, the shortcomings of the conceptual framework for both Gronn's criticism of others and for his own empirical work. The critiques by Willower and Thomas make clear that however persuasive the dialectic supporting existential orientations and radical theory may be in the hearts and minds of their advocates, until those advocates produce more empirical work of quality, they are unlikely to move competing paradigms off the research platform.

Given the experience of the past 30 years, it appears much more likely that the traditional paradigms, along with recent competitors that seek less revolutionary departures from normal science, will continue to drive research on the school administrator. The empirical output and related think pieces demonstrate the ability of scholars of administrator work to accommodate to the inutility of some conceptual frameworks and the utility of newer, competing paradigms. For example, role theory and conceptualization of the school as a formal bureaucracy have been displaced as compelling drivers of inquiry by notions of segmented and negotiated spheres, of variability in the coupling between the managerial and technical levels of organization, of institutional myth and symbol, of organized anarchy and garbage-can modalities of decision making (see Boyan, 1982). The likely scenario for the foreseeable future includes (a) increased interest in the utility of conceptual pluralism rather than unwavering allegiance to a one best way of viewing administrator work or organizations and (b) search for rapprochement between quantitatively oriented and qualitatively oriented approaches to studying both administrators and organizations.

EXPLAINING ADMINISTRATOR BEHAVIOR

The systematic study of administrator behavior in education began with the publication by Getzels (1952) of a "Psycho-Sociological Framework for the Study of Educational Administration." Getzels proposed a model that treated behavior in a social system as the resultant of institutional expectations and individual personality, with provision for the influence of environmental conditions (Getzels & Guba, 1957; for more on the Getzels-Guba model, see Lipham, this volume). Five years later, Halpin (1957) published his "Paradigm for Research on Administrator Behavior," which identified the interaction of the administrator's perception of organizational task with three sets of variables—personal, intraorganizational, and extraorganizational—as crucial for explaining what administrators do.

Twenty-five years after the appearance of Halpin's paradigm, Bossert and his associates published their model for analyzing the instructional management role of the principal (Bossert, et al., 1982). The parallels between the Bossert model and the Halpin paradigm are striking. Where Halpin used the terms *personal*, *intraorganizational*, and *extraorganizational* to identify the sources of influence that shape administrator behavior, Bossert et al. referred to individual, [school] district, and extradistrict. Dwyer (1985) followed with an expanded treatment of contextual antecedents of instructional leadership, which encompass personal, institutional, and community components.

Despite long-standing agreement on where to look for shaping influences and the importance of treating them together conceptually and empirically, few researchers have systematically examined the interaction of personal and situational variables in studying administrators at work. Those efforts will receive attention after examination of the array of studies that have explored the independent association of personal and of situational variables with administrator behavior.

Personal Variables

Administrative Performance and Personality by Hemphill, Griffiths, and Frederiksen (1962) remains after 25 years the most ambitious study of the connection between personal variables and administrator behavior. The project capitalized on Frederiksen's experience with in-basket simulation, on Hemphill's (1958) view of administration as problem solving, and on Griffiths' (1958, 1959) view of administration as the control of the decision-making process. In their search for attributing variability in performance to personal factors, the investigators used a common simulated environment as a vehicle for controlling situational variability.

Decision making and problem solving occupied center stage in construction of protocols, in the exercises for participants (232 elementary school principals), and in the presentation and analyses of findings and the statement of conclusions. The data on personal variables came from a series of psychological tests, 16 ability tests, a personality questionnaire, a long biography, four special tests of general and professional knowledge, and two interest inventories. The investigators also collected ratings on each principal from three "home" supervisors and impressions from teachers in "home" schools on performance as leader and supervisor.

In-basket work in the common simulated situation provided 96 different items for scoring against an initial scoring system of 68 categories. Two "major" and eight "additional" factors emerged from several rounds of data reduction. Major factor X was Preparation for Decision versus Taking Final Action; major factor Y, Amount of Work Done in Handling Items. The eight additional factors, regarded by the investigators as stylistic differences, included (a) Exchanging Information, (b) Discussing before Acting, (c) Complying with Suggestions Made by Others, (d) Analyzing the Situation, (e) Maintaining Organizational Relationships, and (h) Responding to the Work of Others. After settling on the two levels of factors, the researchers crosstabulated the patterns of work identified against the personal variables yielded by the batteries of tests, inventories, and biographical information.

The group of principals who scored high on factor X, Preparation for Decision versus Taking Final Action, (a) received higher ratings from home supervisors, (b) had undertaken more professional preparation, (c) performed better on tests of reasoning, (d) learned new material more quickly, (e) were more fluent linguistically, (f) tended to be strongly concerned with educational programs for children and youth, and (g) generally demonstrated more understanding of administrative complexity. Principals who earned high scores on factor Y, Amount of Work Done in Handling Items, also appeared to be better prepared but did not receive as high ratings from home supervisors as the group who scored high on factor X. Speaking for the research team, Hemphill (1964) reported that principals who scored high on both major factors X and Y, as compared to principals who scored low on both factors, were "more able [as measured by tests] and better prepared [as assessed by records]...[and] most concerned with educational values" (p. 194). Also principals "highly regarded by both superiors and subordinates were those who accomplished a large amount of preparatory work" (p. 194).

Despite the empirical, rather than fully developed conceptual, distinction drawn by the investigators

between the major and additional factors, *Administrator Performance and Personality* presented the first systematic and comprehensive description of administrator decision making in the lower schools. Thus, it is surprising that neither the arrays of factors nor the use of simulated materials significantly shaped further inquiry. Brennan (1973) and Lyons and Achilles (1976) did use simulated materials in subsequent investigations, the first in an exploration of bureaucratic behavior among administrators and the second in an assessment of experimentally created mood states; but for all practical purposes, the original simulation and its sequels developed by the University Council for Educational Administration influenced university training programs rather than research agendas.

Another attempt to test the relationship between personal characteristics of administrators and decision making surfaced in the study by Fogarty and Gregg (1966). They invoked a modified Getzels-Guba model to examine the association between scores on Cattell's 16 Personality Factor Scale and scores on a Decision Point Analysis instrument developed and employed extensively at the University of Wisconsin-Madison for measuring centralization of decision making. Gregg and Fogarty were unable to find any statistically significant relationships between the scores on the two instruments.

Still in the domain of administrator decision making, Glasman and Sell (1972) attempted to calculate the ratio of values to facts in nine administrative decision situations. Their findings provide only proxy data in the search for examining the influence of personal variables but do offer useful insights about the differential effects of "empirical" and "imperative" determinants on administrator choice.

Several students at the University of Chicago in the late 1950s, influenced by the Getzels-Guba model, directed their attention to the association of personal variables with proxies of administrator behavior, specifically, ratings on effectiveness by one or more relevant reference groups. McVey (1957) assessed the association of psychological orientations derived from Fromm with administrator effectiveness ratings and found that the more successful principals exhibited a dominant marketing orientation with a production emphasis. In the same year, Prince (1957) found a direct positive relationship between teacher ratings of principal effectiveness and the extent of agreement between teachers and principals on a Differential Values Inventory (based on the work of Spindler about traditional and emergent values). In 1960, Lipham reported that principals considered effective by central-office superordinates differed consistently from principals considered ineffective on five personal measures.

Composite results of the assessment procedures portrayed the effective principal as inclined to engage in strong and purposeful activity, concerned with achieving success and positions of higher status, able to relate well to others, secure in interpersonal relationships, and stable in the face of highly affective stimuli. The ineffective principal was described as deliberate and preoccupied with speculative reasoning, accepting with a meek and servile attitude his present level of achievement and status, lacking the skills essential for working with adults but anxious to give assistance and consolation to children, highly dependent upon others for support, and likely to exhibit strong emotional reactions in upsetting situations. (pp. 3–4)

Lipham's findings from the late 1950s provide a clue to the interaction of personal with situational variables and appear remarkably timely, given recent commentary on the desirable characteristics of principals. Because neither Lipham nor subsequent investigators systematically probed the provocative clues he offered, his conclusions must remain speculative.

Of somewhat the same genre is the assessment by Croft (1965) of the relationship between principals' dogmatism, measured on the Rokeach scale, and leader behavior, measured by the LBDQ. Croft found no statistically significant relationships on his major variables but did report some evidence of a positive relationship between principals' open-mindedness and their ability to perceive accurately LBDQ ratings by teachers and superintendents. Perceptual accuracy is an ability that has intrigued investigators for more than 30 years, but it still needs full exposition (see Bridges, 1982, p. 25; also see Charters, 1963, for a perceptive critique on the utility and propriety of using perceptual data).

Considerably different is the study by Scott (1978), who investigated the relationship of perceived charismatic authority to tenure in a stratified random sample of superintendents of schools in Kentucky. Scott administered his own Charismatic Authority Scale to establish his independent measure and found that superintendents in the high tenure group were perceived by their staffs as possessing greater charismatic authority than counterparts in the low and medium tenure groups. Silver (1975) also reported that principals who scored high on a test of conceptual complexity were perceived as possessing greater charismatic authority than counterparts in the low and medium tenure groups.

Managerial Ideology

Interest in conceptual pluralism in organizational analysis (Bolman & Deal, 1984) has emerged too recently to have driven inquiry in significant quality and quantity on the association and influence of managerial ideology on administrator behavior. In the mid-1960s,

Gross and Popper (1965) assayed and detected some effects of differences in service versus maintenance orientations of administrators on the activities of junior high schools. Otherwise, only the Pupil Control investigations (see Packard, this volume) and a set of historical accounts have attempted systematic assessment of the association of ideological posture with administrator behavior.

Callahan (1962) really opened the door on historical analysis of the influence of broad social and intellectual movements on thought and action in educational administration. He demonstrated how the doctrines of scientific management and the ideology of professional expertise associated with the municipal reform movement of the early 1900s rapidly infiltrated the writings and speeches of influential public school educators. Callahan's data base did not permit him to describe the actual behavior of superintendents and principals on the job, but he made a persuasive case that the intellectual press of the times did, indeed, create a "cult of efficiency" that dominated thinking about preferred practice in school administration.

Subsequent historical analyses (Button, 1966; Callahan & Button, 1964; Tyack, 1976; Tyack & Hansot, 1982) have examined the changing patterns of managerial ideology that have surfaced, first in the business and industrial world (and sometimes in the larger political community) and later in educational circles. (For an extended treatment of the development of administrative thought and its impact on thinking in educational administration, see Campbell, Fleming, Newell, & Bennion, 1987.)

Each of the historical treatments touches in more or less detail on the influence of managerial ideology on the actions of one or more school administrators, but none offers as full consideration as Cuban (1976), who made an intensive study of three big-city superintendents under fire. Cuban has crafted, from lengthy interviews with former superintendents of schools in Chicago, San Francisco, and Washington, DC, and expert use of documents, an insightful account of the fateful interaction of professional ideologies and environmental conditions and the consequences on the behavior of three chief executives. His analysis will receive further consideration in the section on Extraorganizational Influences.

Summary

Altogether, the exploration of the association of personal variables with administrator behavior must be assessed as disappointing, especially because of the heavy loading over a long time of status studies of administrators' traits and characteristics per se (Bridges, 1982). The descriptive rather than analytic bent of so much of the work on personal variables, combined with lack of cumulativeness, has to date contributed re-markably little that enlightens present understanding and/or directs further study of administrators at work. Greenfield (1982) states that there is real need for and high potential payoff in devoting more systematic at-tention to the personal characteristics of educational administrators. But whether additional inquiry into personal variables as such will add significantly to the storehouse of knowledge about administrator behavior is questionable unless it "employ[s] multiple-factor approaches to data analysis that enable the investigator to rule out plausible rival explanations and to estimate the relative influence of the traits or sentiments being studied" (Bridges, 1982, p. 26). Of equal moment is consideration of personal variables in interaction with situational variables. Meanwhile, the thick descriptions of administrator life and activities that have come from qualitative analysis of field and interview studies convincingly support the position that the person remains important in attempts to explain administrator behavior (Blumberg, 1985; Blumberg & Greenfield, 1980; Cuban, 1976; Dwyer, 1985; Lightfoot, 1983; Metz, 1978; Wolcott, 1973).

Situational Variables

Situational variables cover a vast domain: role-related variables (Bridges, 1982), institutional norms and ex-pectations and cultural values (Getzels & Guba, 1957), district and external conditions (Bossert et al., 1982), and institutional and community factors (Dwyer, 1985). A still-efficient rubric for treating situational variables is Halpin's (1957) parsimonious division into intra-organizational and extraorganizational.

Intraorganizational Variables

Specifically Role-Related Expectations, both of self and others, have figured prominently in studies of role, particularly (a) the discrepancy between expectations and behavior and (b) the degree of consensus between administrators and members of their role sets (Bridges, 1982). (*Explorations in Role Analysis* by Gross, Mason, and McEachern, 1958, remains *the* major study of role in educational administration. Like Cuban's [1976] and Blumberg's [1985] accounts of superintendents, it will be considered under Extraorganizational Influences.)

The "Chicago School" accounted for a substantial number of role-related studies in the late 1950s and early 1960s, once again revealing the influence of Getzels and his associates. Bidwell (1955, 1956, 1957), for example, addressed some of his early work to the study of role conflict. He assessed the sources and extent of conflict and tension between teachers and administrators by asking teachers to identify the

desired and actual behavior of principals. Sometimes describing the same principal, satisfied and dissatisfied teachers reported that their principals exhibited re-markably different behavior. Particularly noteworthy, the dissatisfied teachers said that their principals presented ambiguous and conflicting expectations re-garding preferred teaching behaviors, whereas the satisfied teachers said that their principals presented clear and consistent expectations about preferred teaching behavior. Thirty years later the normative, and some descriptive, literature about effective princi-pal behavior has echoed the major themes of Bidwell's empirical findings. (For a provocative discussion of the extent of variability in teachers' reports of the same principal, see Gross & Herriott, 1965, Appendix D).

Other role-related studies from the Chicago School surfaced in reports by Abbott (1960), Campbell (1959), De Good (1959), Sletten (1958), and Sweitzer (1958). Campbell found support for his hypothesis that principals will rate as more effective those teachers who agree with the principal's expectations regarding the teaching role. Campbell's findings mirror Prince's (1957) earlier findings about extent of agreement between teachers and principals on values.

Sweitzer (1958) discovered not only that super-intendents and school board members viewed instruc-tional leadership quite differently but also that the accuracy of superintendents' perceptions of board members' expectations was low. Sletten (1958) found considerable difference of opinion among board members and between boards and superintendents on the appropriate position to take on major policy questions. Size appeared to operate as a mediating factor in the formal division of administration and policy-making authority. Sletten observed that the superintendent's role is professionally defined outside the culture in which it operates, a condition that readily leads to conflicting expectations between professionals and lay boards. Cuban (1976) picks up this refrain in his in-depth study of three urban superintendents.

De Good (1959) reported that the perceptual accuracy of superintendents about expectations was positively and directly related to judged effectiveness. He concluded that the capacity to perceive accurately the expectations of others appears more important than actually holding similar expectations.

Abbott (1960) collected comparable data from superintendents and board members on their own value positions and their perceptions of the positions of others. He found that (a) values held and perceived do influence interpersonal relations; (b) differences in values, when open and understood, contribute less to difficult relationships than differences that are "underground" and not understood; (c) confidence in leadership was higher when board members and super-intendents held similar values.

Some years later in Oregon, Foskett (1967) and Foskett and Wolcott (1967), from a more anthropological orientation to role than represented in the Chicago School, explored the extent of fit between self-images, central-office images, and community images of the elementary school principal. Considerable ambiguity manifested itself, leading Foskett (1967) to speculate on the implications of the differences in expectations for administrator performance and morale and to opine that differences between principals' perceptions of central-office expectations and actual expectations could blunt the effect of central-office influence. Greenfield's (1982) expression of dismay that Foskett's work has not been updated presents another reminder that lack of cumulativeness has generally characterized research on administrator behavior.

> While there have been hundreds of studies of principals' and others' perceptions of the school principalship, there has not been any major research since 1967 which seeks to refine, clarify, or extend the results of Foskett's study in a systematic and reliable way. Yet, it is clear that the "rules" have changed considerably during the past 15 years. The advent of collective bargaining, legislative mandates in the areas of desegregation and special education, and changing community demographics and student expectations are examples of several of the changes that have occurred which, hypothetically, could be expected to influence norms associated with the principalship. The prescriptive literature has reflected these changing conditions, but the research literature has not. (p. 5)

Several other role-related studies and commentaries reached publication in the 1970s and early 1980s, including two by Israeli scholars. Erez and Goldstein (1981) concluded that role stress derived from conflicting expectations led principals to emphasize their administrative and managerial duties and to neglect their instructional responsibilities. Inbar (1977) found discrepancies across and within the reported perceptions of principals and members of their role-set on issues of authority and responsibility. The Inbar study, like many other role-related studies, reports perceptual data without attempting to relate those data to independently derived measures of either effect or affect.

A set of role-related inquiries that merit mention because they rely less on perceptual data is the treatment by Corwin (1965, 1970) of the conflicts of professionals in public organizations, especially over the control of work. Corwin's findings square with the hypothetical dislocations between organizational levels proposed by Parsons (1958), with reports by Bishop

and George (1973) and Punch (1969, 1970) on differentiation of organizational structure attending to instruction and to management, and with the later findings on negotiated spheres by Hanson (1976).

As a group the role-related studies have confirmed beliefs that (a) perceived expectations do influence the feelings of administrators about what they should do and (b) match of self and others' expectations promotes favorable assessment by the others. Otherwise the role-related studies have contributed little to explaining administrator behavior. The primary short-comings of most of the studies are that they have typically invoked perceptual proxies in lieu of direct observation or even direct reports of administrator behaviors and they have seldom sought data for the proxies from sources independent from the sources of reported perceptions and expectations. The deficiencies in the mine run of role-related studies have contributed to a gradual attrition in the use of role theory in research on administrator behavior (Boyan, 1982, p. 25).

Organizational Socialization The communication of role expectations, reactions thereto, and the exercise of positive or negative sanctions in response to the reactions together comprise organizational socialization, be it in the family, in the school or university, in the military, or on the job. Miklos (this volume) has categorized studies of socialization into three broad areas: socialization before appointment as administrator; the significance of sponsors, mentors, and role models; and socialization after appointment. Other than noting Greenfield's (1977a, 1977b) discovery that for educational administration, as for other professional fields, the process of socialization starts in the period of candidacy, even before formal employment after graduate study, the focus here is on socialization just before and after assumption of an administrative position. One additional point, however, is important: namely, the common socialization as educators experienced by both teachers who remain in teaching and those who later become administrators (Miklos, this volume). Cuban (1976) has stressed this common experience in his analysis of the common professional posture of the three superintendents he studied.

Modeled on earlier work by Merton, Bridges (1965) conducted one of the first inquiries into the influence of organizational work experience on the orientation of school administrators. He assumed the existence of a bureaucratic structure, classified 14 of 28 principals as open-minded and 14 as closed-minded on the basis of scores on the Rokeach Dogmatism Scale, then secured independent measures from teachers of the personal qualities and performances of the principals. Bridges found significant differences in teacher ratings between open- and closed-minded principals with less, rather than more, experience leading him to conclude that,

> Increased experience...has a leveling effect on the personal qualities and performance of elementary principals as perceived by teachers...an upward movement [toward the mean] in the case of the less experienced, closed-minded group, and a downward movement in the case of the less experienced, open-minded group. (p. 23)

Hodgkinson (1970), Ortiz (1982), and Valverde (1974) have also investigated socialization as the vehicle for shaping the beliefs and behaviors of school administrators. Hodgkinson (1970) identified a shift in the value orientation of educators (a particular interest of his) as they moved into and through the administrative hierarchy. Ortiz (1982) added dimension to Hodgkinson's observation by noting the differential contribution of various positions as administrators move up and through the administrative hierarchy.

Sponsorship by graduate advisers, placement officers, and superordinates in the employing organization, both before and after assumption of an administrative position, has revealed itself as an influential factor (Greenfield, 1977; Valverde, 1974). According to Miklos (this volume), the dynamics of sponsorship deserve deeper study; the studies that exist suggest that sponsorship works in subtle and informal ways rather than in just the formal communication of expectations and overt support for some candidates and overt opposition to other candidates.

Licata and Hack (1980) have extended understanding of socialization by noting characteristically different patterns for elementary and secondary (and special) school principals involving distinct "grapevine structures" and informal communication networks. Their interview data revealed a "clanlike" grouping pattern across the elementary set and a "guildlike" grouping across the other set.

Perhaps the most graphic description of the influence of organizational socialization appears in the story of *The Man in the Principal's Office* by Wolcott (1973). In addition to his thick description of what a principal does, Wolcott provides a vivid account of how the activities and communicated expectations of central-office superordinates shaped the life of "Ed Bell," not only after he became principal, but even earlier when he and the district officials were looking each other over. A primary socializing vehicle was the annual evaluation of Ed's performance by the supervisor in charge of his work, but a complementary socializing agency was the group of elementary school principals with whom he regularly associated. His willingness when still a teacher to perform extra services bears a striking resemblance to the GASing (Getting Attention of Superior) observed by Griffiths, Goldman, and McFarland (1965) in New York City.

Central-office Influences   Central-office influences on the behavior of site administrators and members of the central-office hierarchy include but go beyond the boundaries of organizational socialization as such. Analysis of central-office influences calls up the conceptual presentation of school systems and schools as loosely structured (Bidwell, 1965) and as loosely coupled (Weick, 1976). Empirical work in this direction includes studies reported by Cohen, Deal, Meyer, and Scott (1979), Deal and Celotti (1980), and Hannaway and Sproull (1978–1979). These studies portray central offices as exercising loose control and coordination over school sites in instructional matters and somewhat tighter control and coordination on logistical matters and in such areas as school desegregation and affirmative action.

Peterson (1984) offers additional insight on the zoning and differentiation of control. From the theoretical perspective that organizational control systems are many-faceted rather than fundamentally loosely coupled, he examined the patterns of central-office control over principals in a sample of elementary school districts. Peterson identified six different control mechanisms used by central-office administrators to constrain the work of school principals: four hierarchical—supervision, input control, behavior control, and output control; two nonhierarchical—selection-socialization and environmental.

Peterson's focus on the multiplicity of controls that provide a broad-based and pervasive influence enabled him, following Lortie (1969), to confirm that control appears to be zoned—tighter over the administrative domain and looser over the instructional domain—a view strikingly similar to Hanson's (1976) on negotiated spheres. It is the "subtle balancing of control and autonomy" that Peterson sees as particularly, and suitably, characteristic of the relationships between central offices and school sites. His insightful analysis not only reinforces the 1965 report by Griffiths, Goldman, and McFarland, who observed the discretionary latitude exercised by and afforded to principals by the New York City Board of Education, but also supports the report by Morris, Crowson, Porter-Gehrie, and Hurwitz (1984) on principals in Chicago. (See also the earlier versions of this report in Crowson & Porter-Gehrie, 1980, and in Morris, Crowson, Hurwitz, & Porter-Gehrie, 1981).

The Chicago study neatly exposed how school principals not only do, but really must, work their way through the demands placed on them by their communities and their faculties *within* the structures and requirements set in place by the central office. The principals learned, among other things, that the district managers *wanted and needed* the site administrators to exercise considerable discretion in building and maintaining their programs but to cause no trouble for "downtown" in doing so (see Sarason, 1971, for additional commentary on the exercise of discretion by principals). The study by Morris et al. (1984) makes clear that principals varied in their responses to the problems they confronted and the opportunities they perceived, but the data were not really available to assess the effects of the interaction of personal variables with situational conditions.

Hallinger and Murphy (1982) add a properly guarded analysis to the discourse on central-office influence with a crisp report on how a superintendent of schools contributed to the high level of instructional leadership exhibited by elementary school principals, a finding at odds with many reports about the lack of attention by administrators to the technical core. An analogous report by Tronc (1967) describes how the mode of communication used by the Queensland (Australia) State Department of Education to communicate to site administrators was virtually duplicated in their communications to subordinates.

Altogether, the U.S. and Australian studies identify the central office as a strategic source of influence on the behavior of site and program managers, but the reports make it clear that there remains much to be learned about the nature and effects of the structural and dynamic relationships between central offices of school systems and their constituent parts. A simple-minded and simplistic acceptance of the construct of structural looseness/loose coupling will not at all help the expansion of the desired knowledge base about those relationships.

Another feature revealed by examination of studies of central-office influence on schools, and vice versa, is how little the central office itself has served as a site of investigation. Carlson (1961, 1972) has identified several useful leads in his observations of the different patterns of staff expansion initiated by outsiders versus insiders, and McGivney and Haught (1972) have also opened the door to examining the central office as a micropolitical system. Rogers (1968), of course, laid open the New York City Board of Education and its administrative hierarchy in his opus *110 Livingston Street*, but comparable and more recent work has not appeared.

School-level Influences Studies of work activities, in the Mintzberg (1973) mode or via other direct observation approaches, provide clues to pertinent differences in situational conditions in elementary and secondary schools. Kmetz and Willower (1982) summarized as follows the differences they found in their structured observations of five elementary school principals and the five secondary secondary school principals observed earlier by Martin and Willower (1981):

> the elementary principals engaged in fewer activities, had fewer interruptions, and less correspondence. They also had fewer scheduled meetings, but spent more time on planning in such meetings. They had more contacts with superiors and with parents, and spent more time on the schools' instructional programs and less on extracurricular activities. (p. 73)

Morris et al. (1981, 1984), who studied 16 Chicago principals, both elementary and secondary, reported a comparable pattern of differences between the activities of the administrators at the two levels.

Another perspective on the existence of operative situational differences between elementary and secondary schools comes from commentators on the applicability of the OCDQ to the two levels. Watkins (1968) concluded that the instrument just did not fit the secondary school level as well as it had appeared to fit the elementary schools in the original Halpin and Croft (1963) investigation. Carver and Sergiovanni (1969) built on Watkins's observations and estimated that size of school made the difference in the applicability of the OCDQ. Hoy (1972) disagreed with Watkins and with Carver and Sergiovanni on the applicability of the OCDQ to the secondary school on the grounds that secondary schools simply may be more closed in climate. Even if Hoy is correct, his argument explicitly recognizes important structural differences between the two levels.

Firestone and Herriott (1982a, 1982b; see also Herriott & Firestone, 1984) have focused attention directly on the meaning of structural differences between elementary and secondary schools for administrator behavior. A first study assessed the fit of some 50 schools with the competing organizational models of rational bureaucracy and organized anarchy. Firestone and Herriott found more agreement on goal consensus at the elementary school level and more agreement within junior high than senior high schools. They also found, somewhat to their surprise, more centralization of influence at the elementary school level. At both levels, the division between principals and teachers of influence over program and staffing was about the same, but at the secondary school level, teachers had significantly more influence over classroom management than principals.

Their second study convinced the investigators of the soundness of the findings and conclusions of their first study. Of particular relevance to the study of administrator behavior is, as Firestone and Herriott put it, whether structural differences between elementary and secondary schools constrain the type of leadership that is possible at the two levels or whether the nature of the leadership actually offered at the two levels moves schools at those levels closer to one organizational image than the other.

Glatthorn and Newberg (1984), basing their position on ethnographic studies of four junior high school principals, argue persuasively that secondary schools differ so much structurally from elementary schools that it is unrealistic to expect secondary principals to exert their instructional leadership in the same way.

> The [four junior high school] principals in our study were more concerned [than elementary school principals] with classroom discipline, school facilities, office responsibilities, and faculty relations . . . they simply perceived that there were more pressing demands on their time and had delegated responsibility for instructional leadership to trusted subordinates. (pp. 60–62)

Another dimension in which school level appears to make a difference among administrators is felt stress. Koff, Laffey, Olson, and Cichon (1979–1980) explored stress in the lives of elementary and secondary school principals and found that four of the five most stressful events involved conflicts with teachers over forced resignation, unsatisfactory performance, strike preparations, and refusal to follow policies. A factor analysis yielded four factors: 1, Helplessness/Security; 2, Management Tasks/Problem Solving; 3, Teacher Conflict; and 4, Student Conflict. Factors 1 and 2 applied with equal salience to both elementary and secondary schools, with 1 more stressful overall than 2. The stressfulness of student conflict varied directly with school level, secondary more than elementary, but surprisingly teacher conflict varied inversely with level, secondary less than elementary. Koff et al. surmise that the intensity of interpersonal relationships between principal and teacher in the elementary school, compared to a somewhat more buffered state for the secondary school principal, accounts in large measure for the more stressful conditions reported at the elementary level.

Farkas (1983) was particularly interested in assessing "the relative impact of the variables of locus of control and situational powerlessness on . . . levels of stress" (p. 1). He collected data on three demographic characteristics (building level, school setting, and gender) as well as on perceived stress. Farkas found (a) that to his surprise principals reported considerably lower stress than is projected by the popular literature; (b) that female principals perceived less stress than male counterparts; (c) no evidence of stress differentials between principals in urban and nonurban settings; and (d) evidence of more stress among

elementary school principals than among secondary school principals. "It appears . . . that the bureaucratic structure of secondary schools, with assistant principals and department chairs, may actually help to 'buffer' the principal from many possible sources of stress" (p. 4). The agreement between Farkas and Koff et al. (1979–1980) on the differences between the reported stress levels of elementary and secondary schools is convincing, if unexpected.

Although it is intuitively reasonable to expect that structural differences between elementary and secondary schools are important in the playing out of administrator roles and a modest amount of data exist to support that intuition, students of administrator behavior in education have not yet systematically incorporated school-level differences into their conceptual models and research designs. The elementary school, because it is more available and is relatively easy to study, remains the preferred site of investigation.

Succession and Career Patterns   Carlson (1961, 1972, and 1979) has investigated careers and performance at both the superintendent and principal level. His early work brought into the vocabulary of educational administration the notions of insider-outsider and place-bound and career-bound educational executives. On the personal side, Carlson found that outsiders exhibit a higher level of interest in mobility and commitment to career, insiders a lower level of interest in mobility and higher commitment to community; insiders also show a lower commitment to the development and exercise of highly specialized skills.

On the performance side, reflecting the preferred institutional-managerial interface of employing school boards, superintendents from the outside act as innovators, whereas superintendents from the inside act as adapters. When boards employ outsiders, they do so generally because they are dissatisfied with existing conditions and expect outsiders to make changes, and generally the outsiders do. When boards employ insiders, they expect insiders to keep things as they are, and generally the insiders do. Carlson points out that not only do board expectations direct the insider to adopt an adapter position, but also insiders' personal and professional connections to existing internal and external organizational structures make it difficult for them to institute or even want to institute significant change. In brief, the behavioral responses of outsiders and insiders fit both actual and perceived expectations. The administrative activity of the insider is oriented toward organizational maintenance; of the outsider, to change, in the form of new operational rules, increased size of central-office staff, and new programs.

March and March (1977) present quite a different treatment of succession and careers. In their study of the movement of superintendents in Wisconsin over the period from 1940 to 1972, they concluded that the patterns come closer to almost random movement than representing any particular design. In addition, March and March (1977) argue that

> most of the time most superintendents are organizationally nearly indistinguishable in their behaviors, performances, abilities, and values. This is partly a consequence of the filters by which they come to the role, partly as a consequence of the ambiguity of inference in educational settings, partly a consequence of the long-run stability of educational activities and organization, partly a consequence of a lifetime spent in educational institutions. Joint adaptation and other forms of mutual control appear to have run far enough to reduce variation in superintendents to a level that is only slightly outside the noise level of the interpretation and evaluation processes that regulate differential rewards. (pp. 405–406)

The March and March interpretation of superintendents' careers rests on a number of generalizations about socialization that go well beyond their data. Their interpretation does not square with Carlson's either in approach or emphasis. When the two different interpretations are played against Iannaccone and Lutz's (1970) model of school board incumbent defeat and involuntary superintendent turnover and the pattern of career structure identified by Gaertner (1978–1979), the need for rationalization stands in bold relief. Until that rationalization is at hand, the utility of career patterns and succession as explanatory variables in studies of administrator behavior remains highly uncertain.

Subordinate Influences Through expression of his views of the administrator as both pawn and origin, Bridges (1970) set the stage conceptually for systematic consideration of the impact of subordinate preferences and actions on the behavior of administrators. He argued that empirical and theoretical work through the 1960s devoted to decision making had ignored the intrusion and influence of subordinate goals, a refrain adopted later by conceptual pluralists who posited the existence of competing goals within organizations.

Early studies of the influence of informal organizations in the schools (Boyan, 1951; Congreve, 1957; Iannaccone, 1958, 1962, 1964) did not draw specific attention to impact on administrators. Hanson (1972, 1973, 1975, 1976) did so through a series of inquiries that focused on the influence of the "lowerarchy." Hanson contributed particularly to the identification and elaboration of the continuous process of reaching a negotiated order between the administrative and instructional domains. His data and reasoning offer convincing evidence of limitations on the arbitrary exercise

by school managers of positional authority. Lally (1974) found much the same conditions in his study of an Australian high school.

The provocative line of inquiry on loyalty of subordinates undertaken by Hoy and several associates (Hoy, Newland & Blazovsky, 1977; Hoy & Rees, 1974; Hoy, Tarter, & Forsyth, 1978; Hoy & Williams, 1971) unfortunately does not directly test the relationship of subordinate loyalty to principal behavior, because of the lack of independent measures of the variables used. However, the studies collectively suggest that the extent of subordinate loyalty is not trivial in limiting or extending the scope and character of administrator behavior in both elementary and secondary schools. Other reports that shed light on actual and potential subordinate influence include those by Barnett (1984), Clear and Seager (1971), Croft (1968), Glasman and Paulin (1982), Goldman and Gregory (1977), and Kunz and Hoy (1976).

Summary

The studies of intraorganizational variables encompassing role expectations, organizational socialization, central-office influences, school-level influences, succession and career patterns, and subordinate influences together present a disparate and uncoordinated portrait of salient contributors to and shapers of administrator work. Intuitively and empirically, there appear to be grounds for believing that each of these sources contributes something to explaining why administrators do what they do. Assembling the pieces into a clearly coordinated explanatory design remains unfinished business.

Extraorganizational Influences

The third major set of influences, extraorganizational, moves the analyst outside the organization into local, regional, state, and federal communities. Much of the relevant literature pertains to the superintendent of schools and falls primarily into the domain of the politics of education. However, organizational analysts, as well as students of politics, have focused on the superintendent of schools. Analysts of both organizational and political persuasions have also examined extraorganizational impact on other administrators.

Superintendent Studies

Organizational Analysts *Explorations in Role Analysis* by Gross, Mason and McEachern (1958) used long interviews with incumbents and school board members to explore the role performance of 105 superintendents of schools in Massachusetts. The focus of attention was the interaction between superintendent and school board, viewed from the sociological perspective of strategic role set. Gross et al. organized their findings primarily around the issues of role consensus and role conflict, and they developed a three-way typology (moral, expedient, moral-expedient) of superintendents based on response patterns to the nature of perceived role conflicts with board members. In brief, the typology constitutes a category system of superintendent-reported behaviors that seemed appropriate or necessary, either in response to press from board members or in pursuit of a particular objective sought by the superintendent. A different typology, drawn more from the perspective of the politics than the sociology of education, will receive attention below in the discussion of the work of McCarty and Ramsey (1968, 1971).

Approaching the territory from a different perspective, Thomas and Gregg (1962) reported on the patterns of verbal interactions between superintendents and board members at board meetings. Use of a modified Bales system for interaction process analysis generated five classes of behavior, including mediating personality clashes, maintaining group integrity, and task-centered activity. Thomas and Gregg report that boards of education, irrespective of membership, tended to insist that one or more of their members occupy the mediating and maintaining roles and that the superintendent remain in the task-centered domain. Superintendents who lacked the resources to shape board decisions in the task-centered domain could find their prestige in serious jeopardy, suggesting the need for superintendents to stake out their "task-centered" turf.

Erickson (1972) offers another organizational analysis of extraorganizational influences in his treatment of administrator powerlessness. He assembled data on four cases that demonstrate how environmental conditions seriously and severely constrained the freedom of action of Louisiana bishops who were caught in the middle of constitutional pressure for desegregation and communicants highly resistant to desegregation. Erickson thoughtfully extends his discussion to administrators in other organizations, including schools, and closes with a challenging analysis of the moral dilemmas experienced by presumed power holders.

Work activities studies of the superintendent fall within the organizational analysis category, but they unfortunately say little about extraorganizational influences. The investigations do offer clues to the structural conditions within which superintendents work, but they stop short of useful explanation. For example, Duignan (1980), Larson, Bussom, and Vicars (1981), and Pitner and Ogawa (1981) all identify the proportion of time their subjects spent on outside versus inside

work, but none of the investigators really describes the loading of external relationships and the nature or routes of influence from the environment. The three work activities studies as a set leave no doubt that the environment does weigh heavily in shaping executive work, but the patterns and routes of influence remain only partially developed.

Political Analysts In an altogether different kind of study, McCarty and Ramsey (1968, 1971) explored the relationship of community power structures with educational decision making at both the board and superintendent levels. Their observations and interviews led them to infer a typology of communities (dominated, factional, pluralistic, inert), of boards (dominated, factional, status congruent, sanctionary), and of superintendents (functionary, political strategist, professional adviser, decision maker). The extent of congruence across indicators of community power structure, board structure, and superintendent response prompted McCarty and Ramsey to infer that boards of education mediate the direct influence of the power structure of the community on the superintendent. The investigators also speculated that the vulnerability of the superintendents to short-term demands can interfere with desired conditions of complementarity and sharing between boards of education and their professional executives. Earlier, Callahan (1962) had spoken to the vulnerability of superintendents to external influence.

Boyd (1976) has prepared a wide-ranging treatise on the relationships of school boards and superintendents that thoroughly mines the literature on "Who Governs?" through the mid-1970s. His exhaustive review includes insightful critiques of the McCarty-Ramsey analysis and of two other quite different analyses by Iannaccone and Lutz (1970) and by Zeigler and Jennings (1974). While McCarty and Ramsey focused their attention on the influence of community power structure, as mediated by a school board, on the behavior of superintendents, Zeigler and Jennings examined the influence of the professional executives over the operation of lay boards and concluded that boards are much more captives of superintendents than the latter are creatures of boards. Iannaccone and Lutz address themselves systematically to the effects on superintendents of the defeat of school board incumbents, identifying the professional as a casualty of involuntary turnover when rapid social and political changes in a community suddenly overtake a stable board and executive who have reached mutual accommodation.

Boyd (1974) had earlier offered his own thoughts about whether superintendents should opt to act as educational statesmen or political strategists. He observes that sometimes they must adopt the more hazardous role of the *political strategist*, i.e., a leader who, because he cannot generally count on being given support, must instead win support through adroit maneuvering and persuasion based upon careful analysis of existing and potential coalitions on the school board and within the community. (Boyd, 1974, p. 1)

Boyd found that the socioeconomic condition, as well as the power structure, of a community operated as an influential variable in explaining both board and superintendent behavior.

[T]he combined effect of the political culture and management resources in the white collar districts tended to minimize conflict and maximize the effectiveness of the role of the superintendent as an "educational statesman." On the other hand, the reverse was true in the blue collar districts, where the superintendents were generally pressed to adopt the role of a "political strategist." (Boyd, 1974, p. 3).

All in all, Boyd concludes that professionals can become victims of their own professional concepts and precepts, especially by ignoring the preferences of their constituents on what appear to be strictly educational matters but turn out to be distinctly political issues. This is a lesson that Cuban (1976) reinforces. In the same vein are the messages from three of the articles (Culbertson, 1983; Goldhammer, 1983; Hess, 1983) included in a special 1983 issue of the *Educational Administration Quarterly* to the effect that environmental conditions have pressed the superintendent more and more toward adoption of a political role.

Other Perspectives on Superintendents Two qualitative studies of superintendent work and life (Blumberg, 1985; Cuban, 1976) add further dimension to the political analyses. Using in-depth interviews and careful consultation of documentary sources, Cuban studied the experiences of Carl Hansen (Washington, DC, 1958–1967), Harold Spears (San Francisco, 1955–1967), and Benjamin Willis (Chicago, 1953–1966). He traced the successes and failures, the wins and losses, the joys and despairs of their respective careers, which ended in resignation under pressure for two and disillusioned retirement for the third. Each superintendent started his tenure with the full support of his board of education but gradually lost that support as conditions in the environment changed, especially the pressure for desegregation.

Cuban addressed himself centrally to two questions: How did the superintendents respond to outside pressure, and what accounted for the similarities in the patterns of response to critical incidents? He answers both questions in terms of "three integrating contexts,"

identified as (a) the historical residue of beliefs about and practice in the superintendency itself, (b) individual socialization within public education as an institution and as a career, and (c) conflicting organizational demands. On the first, Cuban speaks to the norms that have developed around the superintendency, especially the big-city superintendency, and that contributed to the development of a particular ideology. On socialization within the institution, Cuban identifies the length and nature of previous experience as teacher and principal (Hansen, 20 years; Spears, 17 years; Willis, 12 years) and previous experience as a superintendent as sources that shaped the particular views of each man. "Evidence suggests that rationality, impartiality, acceptance of authority and hierarchy, emotional restraint are but a few of the organizational traits acquired in the process of schooling, teaching and administering" (pp. 166–167).

The three integrating contexts, says Cuban, explain the similarity of response to external pressure, but it was the interaction of a particular larger environment with beliefs and practices developed in and shaped by the contexts that yielded two resignations and one retirement. The larger environment included the prevailing political, socioeconomic, and intellectual climates that came together in Chicago, San Francisco, and Washington, DC, in the late 1950s and early 1960s. Altogether, Cuban's book provides persuasive testimony to the influence of extraorganizational conditions and the routes through which they come to bear on educational administrators whose experiences have contributed to the development of similar professional norms and managerial ideologies.

A decade later, Blumberg (1985) picked up the story line started by Cuban in a report of interviews with 25 school superintendents (24 men, 1 woman) from widely varied districts. The sample was unabashedly one of convenience: "It was simply a matter of getting in touch with a number of superintendents who I knew would be open with me." (p. xiii). The subtitle of the book, *Living with Conflict*, makes clear Blumberg's orientation in carrying out and reporting his study.

He found that only 2 of his 25 informants disagreed that dealing with conflict was the dominant condition of work. One of the 2 attributed absence of continuous conflict to the nature of the peaceful community in which he worked; the other, more to his accommodating style of responding to the differences in opinion others expressed.

For the 23 who did feel that living with conflict was the dominant motif, the words they use to describe sources and routes read almost as if lifted from Cuban's report on urban school chiefs. And Blumberg, as did

Cuban, makes it clear that superintendents do not just wait for conflict to seek them out. The nature of the job is partly to create conflict in the sense of attempting to push people in directions preferred by the superintendents. Very much like Cuban, Blumberg establishes the importance of the interaction of particular environmental conditions surrounding the schools at particular times with professional norms and goals to explain the behavior of superintendents.

Governmental Mandates

Glasman has effectively and persuasively documented the impact of federal and state governmental mandates on and for evaluation in a series of articles published by the *Administrator's Notebook* (1978–1979, 1981, 1982) and in a monograph (1986). Other observers have spoken in general terms of the effects of governmental actions on school operations, but Glasman has collected data from both principals and superintendents that reveal direct influences on their lives. In follow-up studies, Glasman explores further the implications of the "broker" role that he sees as especially relevant for the principal who is to meet both state mandates and intraorganizational requirements of working with teachers. Sproull (1981) also documents the shaping of administrator behavior by external regulations from governments, not only in respect to evaluation requirements but in other dimensions as well.

Other Extraorganizational Influences

Socioeconomic status (SES) of the community served by schools and school districts has also surfaced as a factor that shapes administrator behavior. A decade before Boyd (1974) noted the salience of SES, Feldvebel (1964) reported one of the early attempts to assess the relationship, if any, between social class and organizational climate and the connection between those variables with educational output. He concluded, after seeking valiantly for other statistically significant relationships involving the three variables under study that "social class of the community and certain dimensions of the principal's behavior are related [but that] it is not clear how these relationships should be explained" (p. 3).

Almost 20 years later, Hallinger and Murphy (1983) offered support for Feldvebel's somewhat shaky findings. Hallinger and Murphy found 16 elementary schools, out of a total of 3,100 in California, that had achieved beyond expectations in the California Assessment Program for at least 3 years on reading and mathematics scores, at the third- and sixth-grade levels, with all scores above the 50th percentile. The investigators involved seven of the "effective" schools in their study. The seven schools varied widely in the socioeconomic background of students. In six of the seven schools, principals exercised strong instructional leadership, as assessed by the Instructional Management Rating scale developed by Hallinger; in the seventh school, a head teacher provided the leadership. Hallinger and Murphy (1983) offer a properly circumscribed inference from their data: "The results suggest that school SES is associated with the type of instructional leadership exercised by principals in effective schools, though the research design does not allow us to make causal inferences" (p. 2). Hallinger and Murphy summarize their report as follows:

> The difference between the high and low SES schools was primarily in the extent to which principals influenced or controlled classroom instruction through their direct activity. Principals in the lower SES schools were more forceful in asserting themselves in making instructional decisions and in intervening in classrooms where teachers were not meeting their expectations. In the upper income schools principals tended to orchestrate more from the background, actively coordinating the educational programs of their schools, but not exercising as much control as principals in the lower SES schools. (pp. 3–4)

Several additional reports (e.g., Crespo & Haché, 1982; Firestone, 1975–1976) confirm the salience of environmental influences on administrative and managerial behavior. A type of demurrer on extraorganizational influence comes from Sara (1981), who undertook a study, invoking the Halpin (1957) paradigm and using the LBDQ, of principal behavior in four developing nations. His finding that certain similarities prevail in the way administrators are reported to behave in different cultures led Sara to question the importance of extraorganizational, especially cultural, influences. Sara's position, however, stands on the minority side in a discussion of almost 30 years' duration that has found the environment salient. For example, Dill (1958) reported a study of managers in two Norwegian firms that documented how the structure of the environment influenced the level of autonomy that could be exercised by managerial personnel. It is just possible, of course, that because extraorganizational influences are so pervasive, irrespective of cultural setting, that crosscultural differences may not show up, especially on an instrument like the LBDQ.

Interactive Treatments of Influence

The number of truly interactive treatments of personal and situational variables intended to explain administrator behavior is modest. Cuban (1976) comes close to an interactive treatment through his insightful description of extremely powerful environmental forces operating on the professional ideologies of three urban school chiefs. Cuban's case studies provide what so many case studies say they will offer but never really do: namely, hypotheses to test. Scholars in search of worthy investigations should study Cuban's book carefully for the leads it provides for futher investigation.

An investigation that looks at proxies of administrator behavior from the perspectives of both organizational and personality variables appears in a comparative analysis by Brown (1970) of risk propensity among business administrators and public school administrators. The scores of business administrators on risk taking were significantly higher than the scores of school administrators. "Business administrators had higher scores on all the personal and organizational variables—except the need for security, where they showed a lower need" (p. 476). Unfortunately, Brown did not use a design that permitted him to analyze the interaction of the organizational and personal variables, so he could only speculate about the probable differences of working in schools and in business firms.

Two studies by Miskel (1977a, 1977b) border on interactive treatments. Both explore the interaction of situational variables with perceptions of administrator style or rated effectiveness. However, neither really qualifies as an exemplar of exploring the effects of the interaction of both personal and situational variables on independently assessed measures of administrator behavior.

Another line of inquiry that appears on the surface to be both representative and exemplary of interactive treatments is that associated with the use of Fiedler's Least Preferred Coworker instrument. (See Fiedler, 1967; Fiedler & Chemers, 1974). Hanson (1985) noted, for example, that Fiedler's concepts and the LPC had displaced during the 1970s the use of the LBDQ and the OCDQ in leadership studies in educational administration, a somewhat suspect claim for the latter, if not the former. In any case, as Boyan (1982) reports, the use of LPC did expand significantly during the 1970s (see Badcook, 1980; Dufty & Williams, 1979; Garland & O'Reilly, 1976; Holloway & Niazi, 1978; Martin, Isherwood, & Lavery, 1976; McKague, 1970, who also cites four Canadian studies of the same genre; Williams & Hoy, 1971). The LPC studies in education have helpfully focused attention on the importance of considering the interaction of personal, group, and situational variables, especially by keeping the issue of favorableness or unfavorableness of situation in the foreground as a matter of real consequence.

The study by Williams and Hoy (1971) illustrates

the point. They found that in cases where the faculty supported the principal, a task-oriented style was associated with judged effectiveness; where the principal was less well supported, a relationship style was associated with judged effectiveness. Still, the LPC studies in education collectively just have not persuasively captured the field of interactive treatments, partly because one of the critical features of the Fiedler thesis "is availability of a relatively unequivocal measure of group effectiveness, a requirement that introduces problems for applying the theory to educational organizations" (Boyan, 1982, p. 29).

Salley (1979) and Salley, McPherson, and Baehr (1979) have published two of the most comprehensive surveys on the interaction of personal and organizational characteristics; the first on superintendents ($n = 194$), the second on principals ($n = 619$). The dependent variable was rating of job importance rather than job behavior itself. Findings for superintendents indicated:

1. Organizational structure and size of district accounted for the largest number of differences in ratings of job importance.
2. Size of boards and process of selection and terms of board members did not materially affect rankings of importance.
3. Ethnic characteristics (dominant race of students, teachers, and other professional staff) accounted for the second largest number of differences in rankings.
4. SES appeared inoperative as a distinguishing feature in rankings.
5. Personal characteristics yielded the fewest number of differences, with some indication that gender, immediately prior position, and highest academic degree might be operative and worthy of further study.
6. Age, race, length of tenure in present position, total number of years as superintendent, and major field of academic/professional specialization were inoperative as explanatory variables.

The pattern for principals was quite similar. Size and type of school accounted for the largest number of differentiations in rankings of job importance, with ethnic makeup of staff and student body of material consequence. Again, personal characteristics, especially age and years in present position, yielded no significant differences, although gender and race invited further analysis. A major distinction between the superintendent and principal analyses occurred with SES, which made a difference in rankings of job importance for the latter but not the former. Salley and his associates deserve high marks for their serious attempts to treat both personal and situational variables in interaction. Unfortunately, their respective reporting fails to do justice to the data on the interactive operation of the two sets of variables. Further, the dependent variable of ranking of job importance, although relevant and informative, still stands only as a proxy measure of administrator behavior per se.

The report of an even earlier and more ambitious effort to assess the interaction of personal and situational variables appears in Schutz (1977). About the same time that Hemphill, Griffiths, and Frederiksen (1962) launched the project that culminated in the publication of *Administrative Performance and Personality*, Morphet and Schutz, working out of the University of California at Berkeley, set in motion a project eventually reported as *Procedures for Identifying Persons with Potential for Public School Administrative Positions* (Schutz, 1961). The project team collected "(1) personality data on administrators and their interactors, (2) sociological data on school districts, and (3) criteria for administrator effectiveness" (Schutz, 1977, p. 3).

Schutz's own Fundamental Interpersonal Relations Orientation (FIRO) instruments served as the sources of personal measures. Two-hour-long questionnaires completed by board members, superintendents, principals, administrative staff, teachers, and parents provided data on school district characteristics and operations. More than 5,000 individuals, including 77 superintendents and 147 principals, participated in one or more stages of the project. Effectiveness scores for superintendents came from school board members and administrative staff members; for principals, from teachers.

Of a possible 144 correlations of individual predictors with ratings of effective principals, only 9 (6 percent) were above 0.20, with 1 alone accounting for 4 of the 9. For superintendents, only 23 of 216 possible correlations (11 percent) fell above 0.20. The researchers inferred from the patterns of ratings that different predictors "work" for different rating groups, a finding that squares with later evaluation studies that suggest that visibility of performance makes a difference in level of group agreement. When all three sets of predictors were combined for multiple regression analysis, adjusted for bias in the technique itself, the multiple correlations were substantial, with an average increment of predictability in the order of 0.34. In Schutz's (1977) words: "This is a startlingly large improvement and gives strong support to the hypothesis that different types of districts require different types of administrators" (p. 121).

There are some methodological problems in the investigation reported by Schutz, such as the particular measures used for the personality variables and effectiveness and even the very notion of "predicting" success from the indicators employed in the project. However, this study still represents one of the most carefully constructed attempts to tease out the interaction of personal and situational variables on administrator performance. In that other investigators never followed the lead, it also represents another case of the general condition of noncumulative research in educational administration.

One of the most useful and revealing interactive treatments is by Dwyer (1985), who has summarized a set of field studies undertaken by the staff of the Instructional Management Program of the Far West Laboratory for Research and Development in Education. After the staff set in place the model of instructional management behavior reported in Bossert et al. (1982), along with expositions of several crucial methodological issues (Rowan, Bossert, & Dwyer, 1983), its members went into the field to find out more about the way principals organized their work, how they behaved in doing so, and what meaning they attributed to what they did. The group also attempted to broaden the array of student outcomes used in considering school effectiveness. After a preliminary round of interviews with 32 principals, the investigators employed with five principals a shadow observation technique to identify activities and reflective interviewing to probe for the meaning of the activities. Following the pilot phase, 12 more principals who had been nominated as successful by their superiors joined the project, providing for an even broader array of school types, principals, and instructional practices. (See Dwyer, Lee, Barnett, Filby, & Rowan, 1984, for a full discussion of methodology and procedures used in the study of the 12 principals.)

As they examined the context of instructional management, a first impression that struck the investigators was the sheer uncertainty of the environment experienced by the participating principals, including fluctuations in resources, enrollments, and public confidence; court actions; and changing political climates in their immediate communities and school districts. In addition, the observers confirmed the operative presence of school and central-office structures and processes.

Dwyer (1985) notes that the model set in place by the Far West group (reminiscent as it is of Halpin, 1957) neatly exposes the strategic location of the principal, not only in respect to affecting what happens in the school but also in respect to being affected by what happens in the community and in other places in the school district. He reports, insightfully, that participating principals were not just captives of the external pressures placed on them. Rather, "through their routine activities they attempted to bring to life their over-arching visions, while at the same time monitoring their systems to keep their visions relevant" (p. 6). The reference to "overarching visions" recalls the report by Blumberg and Greenfield (1980) of their interview study of eight "effective" principals and the report by Lightfoot (1983) on the heads of good high schools.

The work of the Far West team led to more complete exposition of the original model identified by Bossert et al. (1982) through elaboration of the original set of antecedent variables and through substitution of nine "routine behaviors" for the domain of activity previously identified globally as Instructional Management Behavior. The thick descriptions of the work of four of the participating principals, including the results of the reflective interviews about the meaning of that work, track about as well as has been done in the literature through the mid-1980s the interaction of personal, institutional, and community variables on administrator behavior. Particularly insightful are the comments on how the nature of schools and of the work of principals set basic parameters that the various work activities studies have identified, but how the personal characteristics of principals and situational characteristics in given schools combine to create idiosyncratic conditions of operation.

Brookover, Beady, Flood, Schweitzer, and Wisenbaker (1979), Lightfoot (1983), and Metz (1978) have also reported richly developed field studies of principals who appear to have made a difference on the job. Together, the Far West reports and the studies of Brookover et al., Lightfoot, and Metz, combined with the inquiries of Blumberg (1985), Blumberg and Greenfield (1980), Cuban (1976), and Wolcott (1973), have set in place strong foundations for inquiry into how personal and situational variables combine to shape administrator behavior.

SUMMARY AND CONCLUSION

The explanatory aspect of the study of administrator behavior in education over 30 years appears to be an incomplete anthology of short stories connected by no particular story line or major themes. With apologies to March and his associates, the condition of inquiry approaches disorganized, rather than organized, anarchy. The goals are, indeed, uncertain; who participates is surely fluid; and the technology is by no means clear.

The attempt to use personal variables alone for explaining significant dimensions of administrator behavior peaked, to use the term loosely, in the 1960s, although the thicker descriptive studies of later years make it eminently clear that the person remains important in the quest for understanding.

Exploration of structural variables at the intra-organizational level has left a disconnected collection of findings, mostly only partly directed at explaining administrator behavior, almost completely driven by shifting conceptual orientations in the so-called "parent disciplines" and/or by rapidly changing conditions in the field of practice. The latter as a force of consequence in direct study of managers in a professional field makes perfectly good sense. The problem is not that rapid changes in the environment change what is important in school but that the study of school managers at different time periods pays so little attention to previous study and the connections of events at a given time. Another problem is that overdependence on conceptual perspectives developed outside the schools underestimates the unique characteristics of educational organizations.

As one moves through studies on socialization, succession, central-office and school-level influences, and the press of subordinates, the anticipation of possible relationships stirs the senses, urging the reviewer to pull the findings together into a meaningful gestalt. But the threads are too scattered to permit even an approximation of a meta-analysis. The separate reports, including as they do small studies of discrete variables, the work activities studies, the other observational and interview inquiries, have generated an as-yet unmanageable number of disconnected findings deeply in need of integration.

Conditions are little better in the extraorganizational domain, even if a scholar like Boyd here and there has attempted to knit together extraorganizational and intraorganizational lines of inquiry. The study of extraorganizational variables has removed all doubt about whether schools are open systems and has identified a number of operative conditions, including SES and governmental mandates. Just how these influences enter the system and exact their respective press still remains uncertain.

As of the mid-1980s, the least amount of systematic study has gone to the interaction of personal and situational variables as a source of explanation, the very area that offers most hope for gaining clearer understanding of why administrators do what they do. It is also, of course, the most difficult condition to investigate. Models for directing inquiry have been in place for 30 years, however. At least one group of scholars (the Far West Laboratory group) has applied an invigorated version of one of the models, the Halpin paradigm, excitingly and productively. While most scholars interested in and concerned about administrators could well direct their attention (as Erickson,

1979, has urged) to assessing administrator effects, a few should remain committed to explaining why school managers do what they do. And, it is to be hoped, those few will employ designs that systematically inquire into the interplay of personal characteristics and situational conditions.

REFERENCES

Abbott, M. G. (1960). Values and value-perceptions in superintendent school board relationships. *Administrator's Notebook*, 9(4).

Badcock, A. M. (1980). Combinations of effective leadership styles in Victorian state high schools. *Journal of Educational Administration*, 18, 55–68.

Baldridge, J. V. (1971). *Power and conflict in the the university*. New York: John Wiley.

Barnett, B. G. (1984). Subordinate teacher power in school organizations. *Sociology of Education*, 57, 43–55.

Berman, P., & McLaughlin, M. W. (1975). *Federal programs supporting educational change. Vol. 4: The findings in review*. Santa Monica: Rand Corporation.

Berman, P., & McLaughlin, M. W. (1978). *Federal programs supporting educational change. Vol. 8: Implementing and sustaining innovation*. Santa Monica: Rand Corporation.

Bidwell, C. E. (1955). Some causes of conflict and tensions among teachers. *Administrator's Notebook*, 4(7).

Bidwell, C. E. (1956). The administrative role and satisfaction in teaching. *Journal of Educational Sociology*, 29, 41–47.

Bidwell, C. E. (1957). Some effects of administrative behavior: A study in role theory. *Administrative Science Quarterly*, 2(2), 163–181.

Bidwell, C. E. (1965). The school as a formal organization. In J. G. March (Ed.), *Handbook of organizations*. Chicago: Rand McNally.

Bishop, L. K., & George, J. R. (1973). Organizational structure: A factor analysis of structural characteristics of public elementary and secondary schools. *Educational Administration Quarterly*, 9(3), 66–80.

Blumberg, A. (1985). *The school superintendent: Living with conflict*. New York: Teachers College Press, Columbia University.

Blumberg, A., & Greenfield, W. (1980). *The effective principal: Perspectives on school leadership*. Boston: Allyn and Bacon.

Bolman, L. G., & Deal, T. E. (1984). *Modern approaches to understanding and managing organizations*. San Francisco: Jossey-Bass.

Bossert, S. T., Dwyer, D. C., Rowan, B., & Lee, G. V. (1982, Summer). The instructional management role of the principal. *Educational Administration Quarterly*, 18(3), 34–64.

Boyan, N. J. (1951). *A study of the formal and informal organization of a school faculty*. Unpublished doctoral dissertation, Harvard University.

Boyan, N. J. (1981). Follow the leader: A commentary on research in educational administration. *Educational Researcher*, 10(2), 6–13, 21.

Boyan, N. J. (1982). Administration of educational institutions. *Encyclopedia of Educational Research* (5th ed.). New York: Free Press.

Boyd, W. L. (1974). The school superintendent: Educational statesman or political strategist. *Administrator's Notebook*, 22(9).

Boyd, W. L. (1976). The public, the professionals, and educational policy making: who governs? *Teachers College Record*, 77(4), 539–577.

Boyd, W. L., & Crowson, R. L. (1981). The changing conception and practice of public school administration. *Review of Research in Education*, 9, 311–373.

Brennan, B. (1973). Principals as bureaucrats. *Journal of Educational Administration*, 11(2), 171–178.

Bridges, E. M. (1965). Bureaucratic role and socialization. *Educational Administration Quarterly*, 1(2), 19–28.

Bridges, E. M. (1970). Administrative man: Origin or pawn in decision making. *Educational Administration Quarterly*, 6(1), 7–25.

Bridges, E. M. (1982, Summer). Research on the school administrator: The state of the art, 1967–1980. *Educational Administration Quarterly*, 18(3), 12–33.

Brookover, W. B., Beady, C., Flood, P., Schweitzer, J., & Wisenbaker, J. (1979). *School social systems and student achievement*. New York: Praeger.

Brown, J. S. (1970). Risk propensity in decision-making: A comparison of business and public school administrators. *Administrative Science Quarterly*, 15, 473–481.

Button, H. W. (1966). Doctrines of administration: A brief history. *Educational Administration Quarterly*, 2, 216–223.

Callahan, R. (1962). *Education and the cult of efficiency*. Chicago: University of Chicago Press.

Callahan, R. E., & Button, H. W. (1964). Historical changes of the role of the man in the organization: 1865–1950. In D. E. Griffiths (Ed.), *Behavioral science and educational administration*. 63rd Yearbook of the National Society for the Study of Education, Part II. Chicago: University of Chicago Press.

Campbell, M. V. (1959). Teacher-principal agreement on the teacher role. *Administrator's Notebook*, 7(6).

Campbell, R. F., Fleming, T., Newell, L. J., & Bennion, J. W. (1987). *The history of thought and practice in educational administration*. New York: Teachers College Press, Columbia University.

Campbell, R. F., & Gregg, R. T. (1957). *Administrative behavior in education*. New York: Harper.

Campbell, R. F., & Newell, L. J. (1973). *A study of professors of educational administration: Problems and prospects of an applied academic field*. Columbus, OH: University Council for Educational Administration.

Carlson, R. O. (1961). Succession and performance. *Administrative Science Quarterly*, 6(2), 210–227.

Carlson, R. O. (1972). *School superintendents: Careers and performance*. Columbus, OH: Merrill.

Carlson, R. O. (1979). *Orderly career opportunities*. Eugene: Center for Educational Policy and Management, University of Oregon.

Carvver, F. D., & Sergiovanni, T. J. (1969). Some notes on the OCDQ. *Journal of Educational Administration*, 7(1), 78–81.

Charters, W. W., Jr. (1963). The social background of teaching. In N. L. Gage (Ed.), *Handbook of research on teaching*. Chicago: Rand McNally.

Clark, D. L., Lotto, L. S., & Astuto, T. A. (1984). Effective schools and school improvement: A comparative analysis of two lines of inquiry. *Educational Administration Quarterly*, 20(3), 41–68.

Clear, D. K., & Seager, R. C. (1971). The legitimacy of administrative influence as perceived by selected groups. *Educational Administration Quarterly*, 7, 46–63.

Cohen, E., Deal, T. E., Meyer, J. W., & Scott, W. R. (1979). Technology and teaming in the elementary school. *Sociology of Education*, 52(1), 20–33.

Congreve, W. J. (1957). Administrative behavior and staff relations. *Administrator's Notebook*, 6(2).

Conway, J. A. (1976). Test of linearity between teachers' participation in decision-making and their perception of schools as organizations. *Administrative Science Quarterly*, 21, 130–139.

Conway, J. A. (1978). Power and participatory decision making in selected English schools. *Journal of Educational Administration*, 16, 80–96.

Conway, J. A. (1984, Summer). The myth, mystery, and mastery of participative decision making in education. *Educational Administration Quarterly*, 20(3), 11–39.

Corwin, R. G. (1965). Professional persons in public organizations. *Educational Administration Quarterly*, 1(3), 1–22.

Corwin, R. G. (1970). *Professionalism: A study of organizational conflict in high schools*. New York: Appleton-Century-Crofts.

Crespo, M., & Haché, J. B. (1982, Winter). The management of decline in education: The case of Quebec. *Educational Adminis-*

tration Quarterly, *18*(1), 75–99.

Croft, J. C. (1965). Dogmatism and perceptions of leader behavior. *Educational Administration Quarterly*, *1*, 60–71.

Croft, J. C. (1968). The principal as supervisor: Some descriptive findings and important questions. *Journal of Educational Administration*, *6*(2), 162–171.

Crowson, R. L., & Porter-Gehrie, C. (1980). The discretionary behavior of principals in large-city schools. *Educational Administration Quarterly*, *16*(1), 45–69.

Cuban, L. (1976). *Urban school chiefs under fire*. Chicago: University of Chicago Press.

Culbertson, J. A. (1983). Leadership horizons in education. *Educational Administration Quarterly*, *19*(3), 273–296.

Deal, T. E., & Celotti, L. D. (1980). How much influence do (and can) educational administrators have on classrooms? *Phi Delta Kappan*, *61*, 471–473.

De Good, K. C. (1959). Can superintendents perceive community viewpoints? *Administrator's Notebook*, *8*(3).

Dill, W. R. (1958). Environment as an influence on managerial autonomy. *Administrative Science Quarterly*, *2*(4), 409–443.

Dufty, N. F., & Williams, J. G. (1979). Participation in decision-making. *Journal of Educational Administration*, *17*, 30–38.

Duignan, P. (1980). Administration behavior of school superintendents: A descriptive study. *Journal of Educational Administration*, *18*(1), 5–26.

Dwyer, D. C. (1985, April). *Contextual antecedents of instructional leadership*. Paper presented at the Annual Meeting of The American Educational Research Association, Chicago.

Dwyer, D.C., Lee, G. V., Barnett, B. G., Filby, N. N., & Rowan, B. (1984). *Methodology: A companion volume for the Instructional Management Program's field study of principals*. San Francisco: Far West Laboratory for Educational Research and Development.

Erez, M., & Goldstein, J. (1981). Organizational stress in the role of the elementary school principal in Israel. *Journal of Educational Administration*, *19*(1).

Erickson, D. A. (1967). The school administrator. *Review of Educational Research*, *37*(4), 417–432.

Erickson, D. A. (1972). Moral dilemmas of administrative powerlessness. *Administrator's Notebook*, *20*(8).

Erickson, D. A. (Ed.). (1977). *Educational organization and administration*. Berkeley, CA: McCutchan.

Erickson, D. A. (1979). Research on educational administration: The state-of-the-art. *Educational Researcher*, *8*, 9–14.

Farkas, J. P. (1983). Stress and the school principal: Old myths and new findings. *Administrator's Notebook*, *30*(8).

Feldvebel, A. M. (1964). Organizational climate, social class, and educational output. *Administrator's Notebook*, *12*(8).

Fiedler, F. E. (1967). *A theory of leadership effectiveness*. New York: McGraw-Hill.

Fiedler, F. E., & Chemers, M. M. (1974). *Leadership and effective management*. Glenview, IL: Scott, Foresman.

Firestone, W. A. (1975–1976). Between two communities: External pressures on the direction of educational change. *Administrator's Notebook*, *24*(6).

Firestone, W. A., & Herriott, R. E. (1982a). Prescriptions for effective elementary schools don't fit secondary schools. *Educational Leadership*, *40*(3), 51–54.

Firestone, W. A., & Herriott, R. E. (1982b). Two images of schools as organizations: An explication and illustrative empirical test. *Educational Administration Quarterly*, *18*(2), 39–59.

Fogarty, B. M., & Gregg, R. T. (1966). Centralization of decision making and selected characteristics of superintendents of schools. *Educational Administration Quarterly*, *2*, 62–71.

Foskett, J. M. (1967). *The normative world of the elementary school principal*. Eugene, OR: Center for the Advanced Study of Educational Administration.

Foskett, J. M., & Wolcott, H. F. (1967). Self-images and community images of the elementary school principal. *Educational Administration Quarterly*, *3*, 162–181.

Gaertner, K. N. (1978–1979). The structure of careers in public school administration. *Administrator's Notebook*, *27*(6).

Garland, P., & O'Reilly, R. R. (1976). The effect of leader-member interaction on organizational effectiveness. *Educational Administration Quarterly*, *12*, 9–30.

Getzels, J. W. (1952). A psycho-sociological framework for the study of educational administration. *Harvard Educational Review*, *22*, 235–246.

Getzels, J. W., & Guba, E. G. (1957). Social behavior and the administrative process. *School Review*, *65*, 423–441.

Glasman, N. S. (1978–1979). The effects of governmental evaluation mandates. *Administrator's Notebook*, *27*(2).

Glasman, N. S. (1981). Increased centrality of evaluation and the school principal. *Administrator's Notebook*, *30*(7).

Glasman, N. S. (1982). The school principal as evaluator. *Administrator's Notebook*, *31*(2).

Glasman, N. S. (1986). *Evaluation-based leadership: School administration in contemporary perspective*. Albany: State University of New York Press.

Glasman, N. S., & Paulin, P. J. (1982). Possible determinants of teacher receptivity to evaluation. *Journal of Educational Administration*, *20*(2), 148–171.

Glasman, N. S., & Sell, G. R. (1972). Values and facts in educational administrative decisions. *Journal of Educational Administration*, *10*(2), 142–163.

Glatthorn, A. A., & Newberg, N. A. (1984, February). A team approach to instructional leadership. *Educational Leadership*, 60–63.

Goldhammer, K. (1983). Evolution in the profession. *Educational Administration Quarterly*, *19*(3), 249–272.

Goldman, P., & Gregory, S. (1977). PPBS and teachers: Responses to an educational innovation. *Journal of Educational Administration*, *15*(2), 249–263.

Greenfield, T. B. (1975). Theory about organization: A new perspective and its implication for schools. In M. Hughes (Ed.), *Administering education: International challenge*. London: Athlone.

Greenfield, W. D. (1982). *Empirical research on principals: The state of the art*. Paper presented at the Annual Meeting of the American Educational Research Association, New York City. (ERIC ED 224 178)

Greenfield, W. D., Jr. (1977a). Administrative candidacy: A process of new-role learning—Part I. *Journal of Educational Administration*, *15*(1), 30–48.

Greenfield, W. D., Jr. (1977b). Administrative candidacy: A process of new-role learning—Part II. *Journal of Educational Administration*, *15*(2), 170–193.

Griffiths, D. E. (1958). Administration as decision-making. In A. W. Halpin (Ed.), *Administrative behavior in education*. New York: Harper & Row.

Griffiths, D. E. (1959). *Administrative theory*. New York: Appleton.

Griffiths, D. E. (1964). The nature and meaning of theory. In D. E. Griffiths (Ed.), *Behavioral science and educational administration*. 63rd Yearbook of the National Society for the Study of Education, Part II. Chicago: University of Chicago Press.

Griffiths, D. E. (1969). Administrative theory. In R. L. Ebel (Ed.), *Encyclopedia of educational research* (4th ed.). New York: Macmillan.

Griffiths, D. E. (1979). Another look at research on the behavior of administrators. In G. L. Immegart & W. L. Boyd (Eds.), *Problem-finding in educational administration: Trends in research and theory*. Lexington, MA: Heath.

Griffiths, D. E. (1983). Evolution in research and theory: A study of prominent researchers. *Educational Administration Quarterly*, *19*(3), 201–222.

Griffiths, D. E., Goldman, S., & McFarland, W. J. (1965). Teacher mobility in New York City. *Educational Administration Quarterly*, *1*, 15–31.

Gronn, P. C. (1982). Methodological perspective: NeoTaylorism in educational administration? *Educational Administration Quarterly*, *18*(4), 17–35.

Gronn, P. C. (1983). Talk as the work: The accomplishment of school administration. *Administrative Science Quarterly*, *28*, 1–21.

Gronn, P. C. (1984a). "I have a solution...": Administrative power in a school meeting. *Educational Administration Quarterly*, *20*(2), 65–92.

Gronn, P. C. (1984b). On studying administrators at work. *Educational Administration Quarterly*, *20*(1), 115–129.

Gross, E., & Popper, S. H. (1965). Service and maintenance orientation in a junior high school organization. *Educational Administration Quarterly*, *1*, 29–41.

Gross, N. C., & Herriott, R. E. (1965). *Leadership in public schools*. New York: John Wiley.

Gross, N. C., Mason, W. S., McEachern, A. W. (1958). *Explorations in role analysis*. New York: John Wiley.

Hallinger, P., & Murphy, J. (1982). The superintendent's role in promoting instructional leadership. *Administrator's Notebook*, *30*(6).

Hallinger, P., & Murphy, J. (1983). Instructional leadership and school socio-economic status: A preliminary investigation. *Administrator's Notebook*, *31*(5), 1–4.

Halpin, A. W. (1957). A paradigm for research on administrator behavior. In R. F. Campbell & R. T. Gregg (Eds.), *Administrative behavior in education*. New York: Harper & Row.

Halpin, A. W. (1966). *Theory and research in administration*. New York: Macmillan.

Halpin, A. W., & Croft, D. B. (1963). *The organizational climate of schools*. Chicago: The Midwest Center, University of Chicago. A slightly abridged version now appears as Chapter 4 in A. W. Halpin, *Theory and research in administration*. New York: Macmillan.

Hannaway, J., & Sproull, L. S. (1978–1979). Who's running the show? Coordination and control in educational organizations. *Administrator's Notebook*, *27*(9).

Hanson, E. M. (1972). The emerging control structure of schools. *Administrator's Notebook*, *21*(2).

Hanson, E. M. (1973). On social systems theory as a predictor of educational change: The adoption of classroom innovations. *Journal of Educational Administration*, *11*(2), 272–277.

Hanson, E. M. (1975). The modern educational bureaucracy and the process of change. *Educational Administration Quarterly*, *11*(3), 21–36.

Hanson, E. M. (1976). The professional/bureaucratic interface: A case study. *Urban Education*, *11*, 313–332.

Hanson, E. M. (1985). *Educational administration and organizational behavior* (2nd ed.). Boston: Allyn and Bacon.

Hemphill, J. K. (1958). Administration as problem solving. In A. W. Halpin (Ed.), *Administrative theory in education*. Chicago: The Midwest Center, University of Chicago.

Hemphill, J. K. (1964). Personal variables and administrative styles. In D. E. Griffiths (Ed.), *Behavioral science and educational administration*. 63rd Yearbook of the National Society for the Study of Education, Part II, Chicago: University of Chicago Press.

Hemphill, J. K., Griffiths, D. E., & Frederiksen, N. (1962). *Administrative performance and personality*. New York: Teachers College Press, Columbia University.

Herriott, R. E., & Firestone, W. A. (1984, Fall). Two images of schools as organizations: A refinement and elaboration. *Educational Administration Quarterly*, *20*(4), 41–57.

Hess, F. (1983). Evolution in practice. *Educational Administration Quarterly*, *19*(3), 223–248.

Hodgkinson, C. (1970). Organizational influence on value systems. *Educational Administration Quarterly*, *6*, 46–55.

Holloway, W. H., & Niazi, G. A. (1978). A study of leadership style, situation favorableness, and the risk-taking behavior of leaders. *Journal of Educational Administration*, *16*, 160–168.

Hoy, W. K. (1972). Some further notes on the OCDQ. *Journal of Educational Administration*, *10*(1), 46–51.

Hoy, W. K., & Miskel, C. G. (1987). *Educational administration: Theory, research, and practice* (3rd ed.). New York: Radom House.

Hoy, W. K., Newland, W., & Blazovsky, R. (1977). Subordinate loyalty to superior, esprit, and aspects of bureaucratic structure. *Educational Administration Quarterly*, *13*, 71–85.

Hoy, W. K., & Rees, R. (1974). Subordinate loyalty to immediate superior: A neglected concept in the study of educational administration. *Sociology of Education*, *47*, 268–286.

Hoy, W. K., Tarter, C. J., & Forsyth, P. (1978). Administrative behavior and subordinate loyalty: An empirical assessment. *Journal of Educational Administration*, *16*(1), 29–38.

Hoy, W. K., & Williams, L. B. (1971). Loyalty to immediate superior at alternate levels in public schools. *Educational Administration Quarterly*, *7*(2), 1–11.

Iannaccone, L. (1958). *The social system of an elementary school faculty*. Unpublished doctoral dissertation, Columbia University.

Iannaccone, L. (1962). Informal organization of school systems (Chap. 14), Leadership in Whitman (Chap. 15), and The stability of informal organizations (Chap. 16). In D. E. Griffiths, D. L. Clark, D. R. Wynn, & L. Iannaccone (Eds.), *Organizing schools for effective education*. Danville, IL: Interstate.

Iannaccone, L. (1964). An approach to the informal organization of the school. In D. E. Griffiths (Ed.), *Behavioral science and educational administration*. 63rd Yearbook of the National Society for the Study of Education, Part II. Chicago: University of Chicago Press.

Iannaccone, L., & Lutz, F. W. (1970). *Politics, power and policy*. Columbus, OH: Charles E. Merrill.

Immegart, G. L. (1977). The study of educational administration, 1954–1974. In L. L. Cunningham, W. G. Hack, & R. O. Nystrand (Eds.), *Educational administration: The developing decades*. Berkeley, CA: McCutchan.

Inbar, D. E. (1977). Perceived authority and responsibility of elementary school principals in Israel. *Journal of Educational Administration*, *15*(1), 80–91.

Kmetz, J. T., & Willower, D. J. (1982, Fall). Elementary school principals' work behavior. *Educational Administration Quarterly*, *18*(4), 62–78.

Koff, R., Laffey, J., Olson, G., & Cichon, D. (1979–1980). Stress and the school administrator. *Administrator's Notebook*, *28*(9).

Kunz, D. W., & Hoy, W. K. (1976). Leadership style of principals and the professional zone of acceptance of teachers. *Educational Administration Quarterly*, *12*(3), 49–64.

Lally, J. (1974). Staff cliques, "Peter" principals, and parochialism. *Journal of Educational Administration*, *12*(1), 76–83.

Larson, L. L., Bussom, R. S., & Vicars, W. M. (1981). *The nature of a school superintendent's work* (Final Technical Report). Carbondale: Southern Illinois University, College of Business and Administration, Department of Administrative Sciences.

Licata, J. W., & Hack, W. G. (1980,). School administrator grapevine structure. *Educational Administration Quarterly*, *16*(3), 82–99.

Lightfoot, S. L. (1983). *The good high school: Portraits of character and culture*. New York: Basic.

Lipham, J. M. (1960). Personal variables of effective administrators. *Administrator's Notebook*, *9*(1), 1–4.

Lipham, J. M. (1964, October). Organizational character of education: Administrative behavior. *Review of Educational Research*, 435–454.

Lortie, D. C. (1969). The balance of control and autonomy in elementary school teaching. In A. Etzioni (Ed.), *The semiprofessions and their organization*. New York: Free Press.

Lyons, D. S., & Achilles, C. M. (1976, Winter). The principal as a professional decision maker. *Educational Administration Quarterly*, *12*(1), 43–53.

MacPherson, R. J. S. (1984, Fall). On being and becoming an educational administrator: Some methodological issues. *Educational Administration Quarterly*, *20*(4), 58–75.

Mann, D. (1976). *The politics of administrative representation: School administrators and local democracy*. Lexington, MA: Heath.

March, J. G. (1978). American public school administration: A short analysis. *School Review 86*, 217–249.

March, J. C., & March, J. G. (1977). Almost random careers: The Wisconsin school superintendency, 1940–1972. *Administrative Science Quarterly*, *22*, 377–409.

Martin, W. J., & Willower, D. J. (1981). The managerial behavior of high school principals. *Educational Administration Quarterly*,

17, 69–90.

Martin, Y. M., Isherwood, G. B., & Lavery, R. E. (1976, Spring). Leadership effectiveness in teacher probationary committees. *Educational Administration Quarterly, 12*(2), 87–99.

McCarty, D. J., & Ramsey, C. E. (1968). Community power, school board structure, and the role of the chief school administrator. *Educational Administration Quarterly, 4*, 19–33.

McCarty, D. J., & Ramsey, C. E. (1971). *The school manager*. Westport, CT: Glenwood.

McGivney, J. H., & Haught, J. M. (1972). The politics of education: A view from the perspective of the central office staff. *Educational Administration Quarterly, 8*, 18–38.

McKague, T. (1970). LPC: A new perspective on leadership. *Educational Administration Quarterly, 6*, 1–14.

McVey, R. C. (1957). Personality: A key to administrative success. *Administrator's Notebook, 5*(8).

Metz, M. (1978). *Classrooms and corridors*. Berkeley: University of California Press.

Mintzberg, H. (1973). *The nature of managerial work*. New York: Harper & Row.

Miskel, C. G. (1977a). Principals' attitudes toward work and co-workers, situational factors, perceived effectiveness, and innovation effort. *Educational Administration Quarterly, 13*(2), 51–70.

Miskel, C. G. (1977b, Winter). Principals' perceived effectiveness, innovation effect, and the school situation. *Educational Administration Quarterly, 13*(1), 31–46.

Moore, H. A., Jr. (1957). *Studies in school administration*. Washington, D.C.: American Association of School Administrators.

Morris, V. C., Crowson, R. L., Hurwitz, E., & Porter-Gehrie, C. (1981). *The urban principal: Discretionary decision-making in a large educational organization*. Chicago: University of Illinois at Chicago Circle, College of Education.

Mooris, V., Crowson, R., Porter-Gehrie, C., & Hurwitz, E. (1984). *Principals in action*. Columbus, OH: Charles E. Merrill.

Ortiz, F. I. (1982). *Career patterns in education*. New York: Praeger.

Parsons, T. (1958). Some ingredients of a general theory of formal organization. In A.W. Halpin (Ed.), *Administrative theory in education*. Chicago: The Midwest Center, University of Chicago.

Peterson, K. D. (1984). Mechanisms of administrative control over managers in educational organizations. *Administrative Science Quarterly, 29*, 573–597.

Pfeffer, J., & Salancik, G. R. (1974). Organizational decision making as a political process: The case of a university budget. *Administrative Science Quarterly, 19*, 135–151.

Pitner, N. J., & Ogawa, R. T. (1981). Organizational leadership: The case of the school superintendent. *Educational Administration Quarterly, 17*, 45–65.

Pitner, N. J., & Russell, J. (1985–1986). Structured observation of school administrator work activities: Methodological limitations and recommendations for research. *Educational Research Quarterly, 10*, 13–24.

Prince, R. (1957). Individual values and administrative effectiveness. *Administrator's Notebook, 6*(4).

Punch, K. F. (1969). Bureaucratic structure in schools: Toward redefinition and measurement. *Educational Administration Quarterly, 5*, 43–57.

Punch, K. F. (1970). Interschool variation in; bureaucratization, *Journal of Educational Administration, 8*(2), 124–134.

Rogers, D. (1968). *110 Livingston Street*. New York: Random House.

Rosenblum, S., Jastrzab, J., Brigham, N., & Phillips, N. (1980). *The role of the principal in change: The teacher corps example*. Cambridge, MA: Abt.

Rowan, B., Bossert, S. T., & Dwyer, D. C. (1983). Research on effective schools: A cautionary note. *Educational Researcher, 12*, 24–31.

Salley, C. (1979). Superintendents, job priorities. *Administrator's Notebook, 28*(1).

Salley, C., McPherson, R. B., & Baehr, M. E. (1979). What principals do: A preliminary occupational analysis. In D. A. Erickson & T. L. Reller (Eds.), *The principal in metropolitan schools*. Berkeley, CA: McCutchan.

Sara, N. G. (1981, Winter). A comparative study of leader behavior of school principals in four developing countries. *Journal of Educational Administration, 14*(1), 21–31.

Sarason, S. B. (1971). *The culture of the school and the problem of change*. Boston: Allyn and Bacon.

Schutz, W. (1961). *Procedures for identifying persons with potential for public school administrative positions*. Berkeley: University of California.

Schutz, W. (1977). *Leaders of schools: FIRO theory applied to administrators*. La Jolla, CA: University Associates.

Scott, L. K. (1978). Charismatic authority in rational organizations. *Educational Administration Quarterly, 14*(2), 43–62.

Silver, P. F. (1975, Autumn). Principals' conceptual ability in relation to situation and behavior. *Educational Administration Quarterly, 11*(3), 49–66.

Silver, P. (1983). *Educational administration: Theoretical perpectives on practice and research*. New York: Harper & Row.

Sletten, V. O. (1958). Policy questions—board members and superintendents agree. *Administrators's Notebook, 7*(4).

Sproull, L. S. (1981). Response to regulation: An organizational process framework. *Administration and Society, 12*, 447–440.

Summerfield, H. L. (1971). *The neighborhood-based politics of education*. Columbus, OH: Charles E. Merrill.

Sweitzer, R. E. (1958). The superintendent's role in improving instruction. *Administrator's Notebook, 6*(8).

Thomas, A. R. (1986). Seeing isn't believing? Neither is hearing! In defense of observational studies. *Educational Administration Quarterly, 22*(1), 29–48.

Thomas, J. A. (1963). Educational decision-making and the school budget. *Administrator's Notebook, 12*(4).

Thomas, J. A., Kemmerer, F, & Monk, D. H. (1978). Educational administration: A multi-level perspective. *Administrator's Notebook, 27*(4).

Thomas, M. P., Jr., & Gregg, R. T. (1962). The interaction of administrators and school boards. *Administrator's Notebook, 10*(6).

Tronc, K. C. (1967). *Journal of Educational Administration, 5*(2), 107–123.

Tyack, D. B. (1976). Pilgrim's progress: Toward a social history of the school superintendency, 1860–1960. *History of Education Quarterly, 16*, 257–294.

Tyack, D. B., & Hansot, E. (1982). *Managers of virtue: Public school leadership in America, 1820–1980*. New York: Basic.

Valverde, L. A. (1974). *Succession socialization: Its influence on school administrative candidates and its implications for the exclusion of minorities from administration*. Washington, DC: National Institute of Education (ERIC ED 098 052).

Watkins, J. F. (1968, Spring). The OCDQ—An application and some implications. *Educational Administration Quarterly, 3*, 46–60.

Weick, K. E. (1976). Educational organizations as loosely coupled systems. *Administrative Science Quarterly, 21*, 1–19.

Williams, L. B., & Hoy, W. K. (1971). Principal-staff relations: Situational mediator of effectiveness. *The Journal of Educational Administration, 9*(1), 66–73.

Willower, D. J. (1983, Winter). Analogies gone awry: Replies to Hills and Gronn. *Educational Administration Quarterly, 19*(1), 35–47.

Willower, D. J. (1984, Fall). Self-critical inquirers. *Educational Administration Quarterly, 20*(4), 107–109.

Wolcott, H. F. (1973). *The man in the principal's office: An ethnography*. New York: Holt, Rinehart, & Winston.

Zeigler, L. H., & Jennings, M. K. (1974). *Governing American schools*. North Scituate, MA: Dubury.

CHAPTER 5

The Study of Administrator Effects and Effectiveness

Nancy J. Pitner

The belief that administrators as agents of educational policy are potentially highly influential has generated research into their activities, behavior, and managerial structures. What does this research tell us about administrator effects?

The administrator's contribution to a school's functioning has been studied from two conceptual positions. The first has attempted to test verifiable propositions about the association of administrator effects with carefully measured, and presumably manipulable, social phenomena and indicators. Several conceptual frameworks regarding administrator influence and effects, which extend and elaborate upon the works of Barnard (1938), Halpin (1966), and Likert (1967), have appeared relatively recently in the literature. As a result, these models have not yet spawned much research. Most of the research reviewed in this chapter was conducted prior to their development and does not reflect their complexity, either in the number of variables included or in the types of relationships portrayed. The alternative research position has focused on trying to understand the social life of administrators—their attitudes, feelings, and conceptual awareness—and how these conditions influence what happens in schools. Much of this research may be classified as exploratory field work, and as thick as the description might be, it contributes modestly to an answer to the question of administrator effects.

These contrasting positions necessarily shape the

Consultant/reviewers: Richard O. Carlson, Bowling Green State University; and Donald A. Erickson, University of California—Los Angeles

questions asked, the methods used, and the meanings attached to research findings. To understand the state of the art, the first section of this chapter reviews four theoretical formulations regarding the influence of administration on the school social system. The second section considers available empirical data, treating separately correlational and qualitative studies. The third section proposes directions for future research and theory building on the study of administrator effects and effectiveness.[1]

ADMINISTRATOR EFFECTS AND EFFECTIVENESS: CONCEPTUAL AND ANALYTICAL CONSIDERATIONS

Connections across the institutional, managerial, and technical levels of school organizations (Parsons, 1960) and among the five commonplaces of schools—subject matter, learners, teachers, administrators, milieu (Haller & Knapp, 1985)—are portrayed in frameworks developed by Bossert, Dwyer, Rowan, and Lee (1982), Duckworth (1983), Ellett and Walberg (1979), and Pitner (1982a). Each model is discussed here in terms of its conceptual components and the type of causal relationship it depicts (i.e., direct, indirect, nonrecursive, mediating effects, or moderating variables).

Bossert Framework

Bossert et al. (1982) portray the connection between principal behavior and student learning as an antecedent system of causal relationships, with school climate and instructional organization variables standing in a

Figure 5.1   The Bossert model of the principal's influence on student learning .

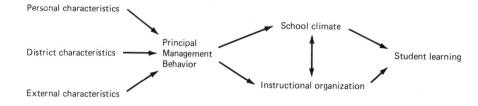

NOTE: S. Bossert, D. Dwyer, B. Rowan, G. Lee, "The Instructional Management Role of the Principal," *Educational Administration Quarterly*, Vol. 18, #3 (1982), pp. 34–64. Copyright © 1982 by copyright holder *Educational Administration Quarterly*. Reprinted by permission of Sage Publications, Inc.

mediated position (see Figure 5.1). According to this model, the antecedents hypothesized to influence or shape the instructional management behavior of principals include (a) personal characteristics (intelligence, skills, orientations, preparation); (b) district characteristics (rules and policy, community expectations, teacher collective bargaining agreements); and (c) external characteristics (demographics, state mandates, federal program requirements). Principal behavior, operating through influence mode and activities, directly affects patterns of climate and instructional organization, the two basic features of the school's social organization.

The authors hypothesize that the principal shapes student learning indirectly by attending to school-level factors such as student time in classrooms, instructional class size and composition, and grouping of teachers (e.g., teams, department) rather than by directly supervising individual teachers. In sum, the administrator influences student achievement indirectly by manipulating structural-technical relationships. Bossert et al. (1982) identify as particularly strategic school-level analogs of factors identified as critical in research on effective teaching.

Ellett and Walberg Framework

Ellett and Walberg (1979) portray the relationship between principal behavior and student outcomes as nonrecursive (see Figure 5.2). In contrast with the Bossert model, Ellett and Walberg argue that the causal linkages across all four variables—principal behavior, within-school conditions (teacher and student behavior), without-school conditions (including parent behavior), and student outcomes—are reciprocally related in such a way that each affects and depends on the others. Thus, the functional relationships among all variables are portrayed as bidirectional.

Ellett and Walberg further specify that individuals other than principals (e.g., teachers, parents, community) serve as mediators because they intervene between the principals' functioning and student outcomes such as attendance, learning, and achievement.

Principals may direct their behavior at any moment toward teachers, students, or factors outside the school. Or, the more immediate effects on other persons may mediate still longer-term effects. The model assumes that principal behavior (as well as that of teachers, students, and parents) reflects perceptions and intentions. As Ellert and Walberg (1979) explain:

> For example, the principal who perceives and acts on a student discipline problem with the intention of changing the student's behavior may do so by discussing the matter with the student's teacher. The teacher's subsequent perception, intention, and behavior impact on the student can mediate the principal's original intention. Similarly, principal behavior directed toward changing parent and community attitudes toward the school may be direct (for example, in a PTA meeting), or indirect and mediated by teachers (parent-teacher conferences), depending upon the original perception and intention. (p. 148)

According to Ellett and Walberg, all principal effects are "indirect, largely mediated by factors within and external to the school environment" (p. 147).

Pitner Framework

In reaction to the "one best way to lead" emanating from effective schools research, Bossert et al. (1982) and Pitner (1982a) point to contemporary leadership theory, which holds that no single style of management is appropriate for all organizations. In other words, specific administrator behaviors may have different effects in different contexts. Extending the situational leadership concept, Kerr and Jermier (1978) suggest that leadership variables often account for only a small portion of criterion variance in many empirical studies because of situational characteristics that render hierarchical leadership unimportant or impossible.

Following Kerr and Jermier's observation, Pitner (1982a) has questioned the assumption coming out of effective schools findings that "strong principal leadership" is always necessary. Pitner (1982a) contends that this assumption may contribute to the inconsistent findings regarding the effects of the administrator on

Figure 5.2   The Ellett and Walberg framework of the reciprocal nature of the influence relationship between the principal and other school variables

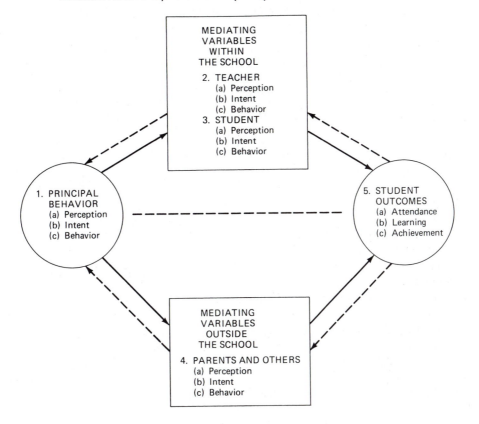

NOTE: Reprinted by permission of the publisher from Herbert J. Walberg: *Educational Environment and Effects.* © 1979 by McCutchan Corporation, Berkeley, California 94704.

the school's technical core activities. She has reconceptualized the question to this: Under what conditions can, or must, a principal lead?

The Bossert model also recognizes the effect of context. However, instead of portraying the relationship between context variables and principal behavior as directly as do Bossert et al, Pitner and Charters (1984) suggest that the relationship is best conceptualized as an interaction effect. The Pitner framework posits that the effect of principal (or superintendent) leadership on productivity depends on characteristics of the faculty and staff, the conception of the teaching task, and the organization. These characteristics influence whether a given leadership style enables the principal to motivate, direct, and control teacher performance.

Twelve characteristics have been identified as potential substitutes for leadership: experience-training, professional orientation, indifference to organizational rewards, task clarity, task-provided feedback, intrinsically satisfying tasks, formalization, rule inflexibility, active advisory staff, cohesive work groups, low position power, and spatial distance between principal and

teacher (Kerr & Jermier, 1978). This conceptualization invokes two widely cited dimensions of leadership: instrumental (or initiating structure) and supportive (or consideration) behaviors (Halpin & Winer, 1957). According to the scheme, the presence of a substitute can influence the effectiveness of leader behavior in one of three ways. Specifically, Pitner (1986) states that a characteristic may:

1. substitute for instrumental, but not supportive, leader behavior;

2. substitute for supportive, but not instrumental, behavior; or

3. substitute for both instrumental and supportive behaviors. (p. 25).

Examples of the operation of substituting characteristics and relationships follow. In a school organized into functioning work teams, principal behaviors to control task or provide support may be redundant. Likewise, lack of control over valued resources/rewards (e.g., pay raises, promotions, materials and supplies, preferred teaching assignments) may negate principal leadership efforts. Simply stated, the underlying assumption in applying the notion of substitutes for leadership to the position of the principal is that principal behaviors likely to affect the work performance of teachers may vary from school to school depending on the presence of personal or impersonal sources of leadership. The notion of substitutes is akin to that of institutionalized leadership identified by Charters (1964). An important aspect of the substitutes model is that leadership may be institutionalized in school policies, rules, and procedures, and the relationship between leader behavior and outcomes may change in degree from time to time and context to context (see Packard, Charters, Duckworth, & Jovick, 1978).

Duckworth Framework

Duckworth (1983) also asserts that principal effects are indirect: "The impact of school and district policy and management processes is to be found primarily in changes in the conditions of teaching and learning rather than learning itself" (p. 3). Duckworth begins with student work and the conditions that influence student achievement and then deductively moves backward from research on effective schools and teaching practices to identify teacher and principal work structures and school district policy believed to cause student achievement. Duckworth represents these pre-

dicted relationships in a series of three schematic models: teacher work, school organization and climate, and principal work (see Figures 5.3, 5.4 and 5.5). These models are regarded as operating concurrently and depict a series of reciprocal causal relationships.

> Any notion of a single row of dominoes—changes in the principal's work, which changes the school organization and climate, which alters teacher work conditions, thus leading to different patterns of work—is inadequate to the intricate networks of effects included in the models. Instead, the three models might be conceived in terms of relationship between a hierarchy of biological orientation such as an organ within the body. In looking at the performance of an organ, one would need to maintain concurrent measures of intraorganic chemical and cellular processes, the chemical environment of the organ, the simultaneous function of the other organs and the messages sent to the organs by the body's activity and stress. These messages would vary with the information possessed by the more inclusive structure about the less inclusive structures and thus allow for the organ to influence the body as well as vice versa. (Duckworth, 1983, p. 51)

Duckworth states that changes in any one dimension initiate subsequent changes in the others.

Everything seems to influence everything else in what appears to be a model of mutual simultaneous shaping. Many elements comprise the complex array of

Figure 5.3   Duckworth's model of the determinants of teachers' work conditions.

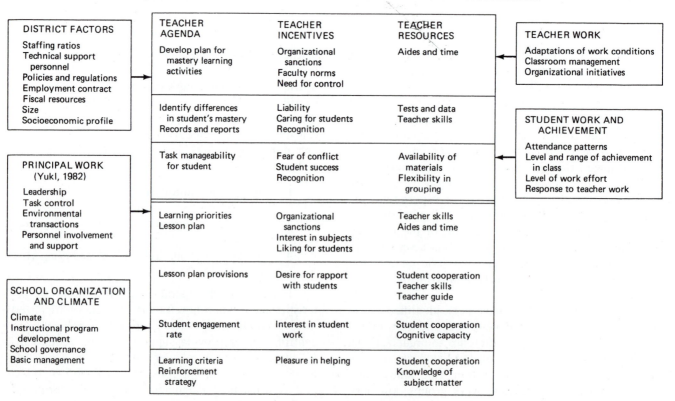

Figure 5.4 Duckworth's model of the determinants of school organization and culture.

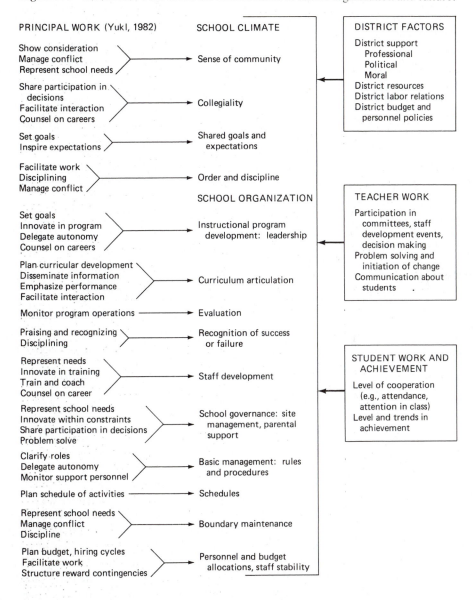

social and psychological processes attendant to the production of student learning. From the perspective of causality, because so many variables are included in the model, the potential for misspecification is great; that is, important independent or dependent variables may be omitted or extraneous ones included. On the other hand, Duckworth attempts to integrate at least the central ideas of the aforementioned three models.

Summary

The four analytical frameworks hypothesize how the principal contributes to the school's functioning. Each model depicts somewhat differently the causal ordering between principal behavior and valued outcomes. Each builds on research findings, primarily in the areas of teaching and school effects, and theoretical understandings of organizations and their processes. Two models (Duckworth, 1983; Pitner, 1982a; Pitner & Charters, 1984) build explicitly on existing measures of leader behavior. Duckworth (1983), for example, uses Yukl's (1981) taxonomy of managerial behavior to identify specific administrator activities and behaviors that are likely to influence teacher work agenda and conditions. Pitner and Hocevar (1986) have confirmed the superiority of this multidimensional operation of leadership in comparison with the traditional two-dimensional approach.

The four frameworks variously represent principal influencing as (a) perception, intention, and behavior

Figure 5.5   Duckworth's model of the determinants of principals' work conditions.

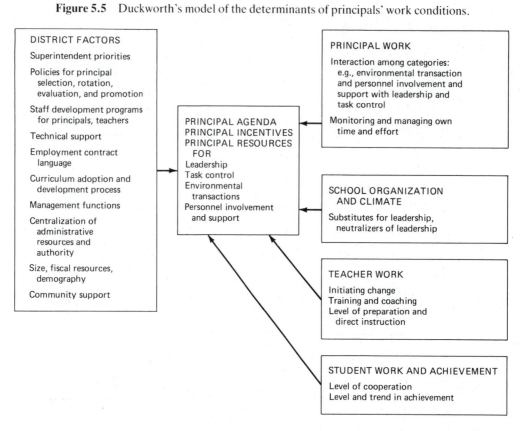

NOTE: Figures 5.3, 5.4, 5.5 from SPECIFYING DETERMINANTS OF TEACHER AND PRINCIPAL WORK, (pp. 23, 31, 48) by Kenneth Duckworth, 1983,
         Eugene: Center for Educational Policy Management, University of Oregon. Copyright 1983 by the Center for Educational Policy Management, University of
         Oregon. Reprinted by permission.

(Ellett & Walberg, 1979); (b) mode and activity (Bossert et al., 1982); (c) instrumental and supportive behaviors (Pitner, 1986; Pitner & Charters, 1984); and (d) principal work structure—agenda, incentive, resources (Duckworth, 1983). All suggest that personal attributes, district characteristics, and external characteristics shape principal behavior. Bossert et al. (1982) portray the attributes as antecedents to principal behavior. Ellett and Walberg (1979) and Duckworth (1983) represent principal behavior as affected by the school context along the lines of a nonrecursive (or reciprocal) relationship, which is often incorrectly referred to as an interaction effect (see Cohen & Cohen, 1983). Pitner (1982a, 1986) and Pitner and Charters (1984), departing radically from the other perspectives, hypothesize an interaction effect among variables. In assuming a radical contingency approach, Pitner and Charters (1984) suggest that the influence of leader behavior depends on other factors but assert that sometimes there will be an effect and sometimes there will not. The other models imply there will always be some effect, albeit sometimes indirect.

These frameworks offer the field a number of benefits. First, the assumptions, variables, and hypothe-sized relationships regarding administrator effects are made explicit. Second, the causal models provide a framework for constructing and testing the internal consistency of theories and their measurement, in addition to determining the degree of correspondence between theories and observations. Third, these models provide a basis from which to consider how adminis-tration effects and effectiveness have been studied and verified empirically.

THE EMPIRICAL EVIDENCE

Investigators have employed quantitative and qualita-tive methods to study the issue of administrator in-fluence. Van Maanen (1979) has noted that support for the use of qualitative methods has resurfaced, in part because of growing concern about the shortcomings of quantitative methods for revealing organizational dynamics. Attention to issues of administrator in-fluence requires consideration of the value of both methodological approaches.

Of the four major categories of social-science research—laboratory experiments, field experiments, field studies, and survey research (Kerlinger, 1973)—

research in educational administration clusters in the last two categories (Bridges, 1982). The general pattern also holds for inquiry on administrator effects, including some cases where researchers apply the logic of scientific empiricism to data collected through interviews and observations (e.g., Martinko & Gardner, 1984; K. Peterson, 1984), methods often associated with more interpretive analytic schemes.

Survey Research

Differences among administrators and the effect of these differences on aspects of the school context (e.g., learning environment, student achievement, teacher satisfaction) occupy center stage in research that attempts empirically to predict, clarify, or discover relations between administrator behavior and style and specified criteria of effect or effectiveness. If all school organizations were the same, for example, there would be little interest in studying the determinants of teacher commitment, in predicting teacher commitment, or in measuring teacher commitment. Yet individual teachers and entire school faculties do vary in commitment to their workplaces.[2] One hypothesis about variation in teacher commitment is that the leadership style and behavior of a principal makes a difference: in short, that the two variables covary. Correlational research seeks to determine how accurately administrator scores on leadership instruments [e.g., Leader Behavior Description Questionnaire (LBDQ), Least Preferred Coworker scale (LPC), Management Behavior Survey (MBS)] can predict scores of other participants on different measures (e.g., standardized achievement tests, Organizational Commitment Questionnaire). Often the same reporters (i.e., teachers) provide ratings for both independent (e.g., principal behavior) and dependent (e.g., commitment) variables.

Causal models present predicted relationships between administrator behavior and outcome variables in a variety of ways. Their respective treatments, severally and in connection with the four formulations examined in the previous section, enlighten the complex relationships between administrator behavior and valued organizational outcomes and educational effects. First to be considered are those models that provide correlational evidence on predicted administrator effects and effectiveness. The total set includes models of direct effects, mediated effects, antecedent effects, reciprocal effects, and moderated effects. All except the models of moderated effects appear in the form of path analytic diagrams that portray administrator behavior and work activities as a_1 and a_2, antecedents as b_1 and b_2, mediators as c_1 and c_2, and outcomes as y_1 and y_2.

Figure 5.6 Model of direct effects of administrator behavior.

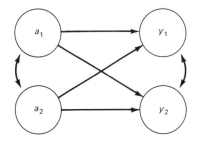

Direct Effects

Figure 5.6 represents the model of direct effect between administrator behavior and an outcome variable. Direct-effects models of administrator behavior involve only two variables: administrator behavior that is assumed to be a cause and an outcome that is presumed to result from administrator behavior. Direct-effects models are just what the name implies; the administrator effect is not mediated or moderated by a third variable. A wide variety of research predicting that the principal either directly influences student achievement or teacher attitudes and perceptions comes out of this theoretical base.

Evidence regarding the influence of the principal on student achievement is provided in studies by Brookover, Schweitzer, Schmeider, Flood and Wisenbaker (1978); Copeland, Brown and Hall (1974); Gall, Fielding, Shalock, Charters, and Wikzynski (1985); and Rasmussen (1976). Some of the studies belong to the genre of school effectiveness research; others do not. For specific studies of effective schools, see Austin (1979); Ogden, Folwer, and Kunz (1982); Ramey, Hillman, and Matthews (1982); Weber (1971); and Wellisch, MacQueen, Carriere, and Duck (1978).

Rasmussen (1976) investigated the influence of principal leadership behavior on school success in a random sample of 25 outlier elementary schools in California in which students were achieving markedly better or worse than would be explained by student socioeconomic characteristics. Principal leadership behavior was assessed by the LBDQ, and student achievement data on a standardized test served as the measure of school performance. Rasmussen found no statistically significant relationships between LBDQ scores and elementary school performance.

In contrast, Copeland, Brown, and Hall (1974) had earlier investigated the effect on the behavior of 79 children of principal-initiated procedures (one-on-one verbal praise for student attendance, tutoring and praise in the principal's office for selected low-achieving students, and verbal praise in the classroom for academic work). The application of multiple baseline designs revealed a functional relationship between the children's behavior and the actions taken by the principal. In all three "experiments," the target behaviors of pupils moved in the desired directions when the principals applied the treatment contingencies.

The extent of principal influence on the behaviors, perceptions, and attitudes of teachers has received more attention than the influence of principals on pupils. Natriello (1984) investigated teachers' perceptions of administrator evaluation activity and teachers' assessments of their own effort and effectiveness in a sample of 182 teachers in six inner-city middle schools. He found a positive relationship between the frequency of evaluation and teacher leverage (defined as degree of effort applied to teaching tasks). In 41 secondary schools, Hoy, Newland, and Blazovsky (1977) studied the relationship between school centralization and formalization on one side and on the other, teachers' loyalty to the principal and esprit as measured by the OCDQ. Hierarchy of authority emerged as the single most important factor in the principal's ability to command loyalty; and the more carefully that rules and regulations specified the job, the higher the esprit among teachers. Kunz and Hoy (1976) investigated in 50 randomly selected secondary schools the relationship between principals' leadership style as measured by the LBDQ and the professional zone of acceptance of teachers. The teachers' zone of acceptance was significantly greater when principals scored high on both the measures of Initiating Structure (IS) and of Consideration (C) as well as when principals were high on IS and low on C. The findings prompted the researchers to conclude that instrumental leadership covaries with zone of acceptance. Caldwell and Lutz (1978) investigated the rule-administration behavior (Gouldner, 1970) of school principals in compliance with collective-bargaining contracts and found an association between teachers' reports of executive professional leadership and selected principal behaviors. Specifically, punishment-centered rule administration and mock patterns drew low leadership scores.

Deal and Celotti (1980) examined the influence of district- and school-organization policies, roles, and relationships over time on team teaching and individualized instruction in 103 randomly selected elementary schools in 34 San Francisco Bay area school districts. They could discern no systematically significant influence from the district level on classroom practices but were able to detect the influence of physical arrangements and state program initiatives on classroom practices.

Gall et al. (1985) used a quasi-experimental design to investigate the relationship between principal involvement in teacher in-service training on student achievement and on-task behavior in mathematics. The

data supported belief that involving principals in a staff development program positively affects implementation of program objectives. Hall and Rutherford (1983) studied the relationship in nine elementary schools between a principal's leadership style (innovator, responder, or manager) and the success of improvement efforts. The innovator style was associated with success in introducing change at the classroom level more than either of the other two styles.

Although most of the research on the influence of the administrator predicts and/or tests for direct effects, the more recent theoretical formulations represent the administrator's relationship in the social system as more complex. These formulations seek relationships across three or more variables and either explicitly or implicitly employ mediated-, antecedent-, reciprocal-, or moderated-effects models to illustrate and explain the extent of complexity. Unfortunately, however, protagonists of the more complex models often retreat to the use of simple analytical procedures, so their theories do not receive full, empirical testing.

Antecedent Effects

In the antecedent-effects model (Figure 5.7), antecedent variables influence administrator behavior, which in turn influences organizational outcomes (y). Not only do antecedent variables account for differences in administrator behavior, but also the administrator variable stands as both a dependent and an independent variable. The Bossert framework (Figure 5.1) presents a model of antecedent effects. Bossert et al. (1982) posit that personal, district, and external characteristics affect the instructional management behavior (and by implication, other behaviors) of principals.

Earlier empirical work provides support for the applicability of the model. Nirenberg (1977) studied the influence of alternative versus traditional organizational structures on management systems in 15 public high schools. He found that structure influenced administra-

Figure 5.7   Model of antecedent effects of administrator behavior.

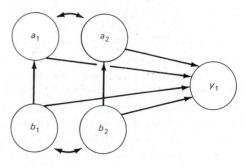

tive climate, extent of bureaucratization, teachers' sense of power, and degree of professionalization. He did not, however, search for any organizational outcomes as such. Bidwell (1975) examined the relationships between pupils' reading achievement and a combination of environmental variables (size of district, resources available, percentage of disadvantaged students, parental education), and school-district organization (pupil-teacher ratio, administrative intensity, professional support, staff quality). He found a negative effect of size on administrative intensity (ratio of administrators to teachers) and subsequently on student achievement. In a different vein, Silver (1975) investigated the relationship between the level of principals' conceptual development and their leadership style (flexible and responsive versus rigid and authoritarian) as perceived by others. Principals with a more complex conceptual structure interacted more frequently with staff members, performed more varied functions in their schools, and headed schools in which teachers were more professionally oriented.

Reciprocal Causation Model

The relationship between administrator behavior and outcomes may involve reciprocal causation between pairs of variables, a nonrecursive condition. A nonrecursive model (Figure 5.8) stipulates that the administrator causes certain outcomes (y) that in turn influence subsequent administrator behavior. As noted earlier (see Figure 5.2) Ellett and Walberg (1979) propose a reciprocal relationship between administrator behavior, teacher behavior, and student outcomes. Although the reciprocal relationship is mentioned frequently in the literature, few empirical tests exist. An example appears in a study by Wiggins (1972) of the influence of principals' behavior (as measured by FIRO–B) on school climate (as measured by OCDQ) in 31 randomly selected elementary schools. Wiggins initially found no statistically significant relationship between a principal's behavior and school climate. A re-analysis of the data revealed that as the length of the

principal's incumbency increased, the level of significance of the relationship between behavioral characteristics and school climate increased. Also, school climates did not change immediately with change in principals. Wiggins (1972) concluded that over time the school climate socializes the principal and the principal influences school climate.

Mediating Effects

In addition to stipulating reciprocal effects, Ellett and Walberg (1979) view teachers and parents as mediators of administrator intentions (see Figure 5.2). Bossert et al. (1982) also assert that school climate and instructional organization mediate a principal's management behavior (see Figure 5.1).

In a model representing mediating effects, administrator influence is divided into an indirect effect that is mediated by a third variable and a direct effect that operates independent of a third variable (see Figure 5.9). Examples of research that invokes a mediated-effects model include a study by Weil, Marshalek, Mitman, Murphy, Hallinger, and Pruyn (1984) of characteristics of effective and typical schools and an often-cited study by Keeler and Andrews (1963) of principals' leadership behavior as a factor in staff morale and in level of student achievement.

In rural Alberta, Keeler and Andrews (1963) investigated a complex mediated relationship in 42 schools selected for their productivity. The independent variable—leader behavior—was measured with the LBDQ; the mediating variable—teacher morale—was measured with instruments developed for the study; and the dependent variable—school productivity—was based on scores on Grade 9 examinations, adjusted for student aptitude. The investigators found that leader behavior was positively related to productivity; teacher morale was positively related to productivity; leader behavior was negatively related to teacher morale in highly productive schools; and the relationship of the Initiating Structure score of the

Figure 5.8 Model of reciprocal (nonrecursive) effects of administrator behavior.

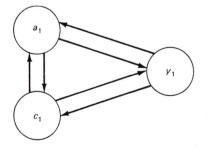

Figure 5.9 Model of mediated effects of administrator behavior.

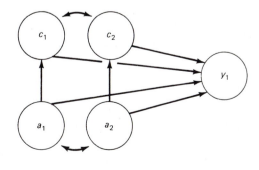

LBDQ was stronger than that of the Consideration score (but each score was related independently as well as jointly). In their test of a mediated-effects model, Ellett and Walberg (1979) report that teachers' perceptions of principals' effectiveness were related to teachers' attitudes about their schools, which in turn were related to student attendance. High student test performance and positive teacher attitudes were often associated with a low frequency of direct contact between principal and students (Ellett & Walberg, 1979, p. 151).

Moderated Effects

In contrast to other models, a moderated-effects model (Figure 5.10) specifies that administrator effects are moderated by a third variable. Typically, researchers hypothesize that administrator effects occur under one set of conditions but not under other, less favorable conditions.

The substitutes-for-leadership model (Pitner, 1982a) is an example of the perspective that the effects of administrator behavior are moderated by characteristics of the staff, the task, or the organization. Garland and O'Reilly (1976), however, were unable to establish that group atmosphere moderated the relationship between leadership style and group effectiveness. Miskel (1977a, 1977b) studied the relationship between innovation effort, perceived principal effectiveness, interpersonal climate, and technology level. Although Miskel found a number of statistically significant relationships, there was no evidence that situational variables moderated these relationships. In contrast, Brookover et al. (1978) conducted a large-scale study of the effect of school social structure and school climate on student outcomes (mean school achievement in reading and mathematics, student self-concept of reading ability, and student self-reliance). The two-pronged research project included surveys of three random samples of schools (for a total of 159 schools) and a follow-up observation study of four schools. The activities of the principal emerged as one

of the conditions that contributed to differences in the performance of outlier schools.

In another moderated-effects study, Rowan and Denk (1984) investigated the effect of change in principal (executive succession) on achievement in basic skills in 149 schools in the San Francisco Bay area. Changes in school organization following a change in principal led to effects that were not uniform across all types of schools. The socioeconomic status of the school (SES) moderated the effect of the principal. Schools of lower socioeconomic status were more likely to have higher academic achievement in the second year following a change in principal, but the improvement was short-lived. Low-performing schools were more likely to change principals. Still, succession effects, on the average, tended to be associated with decrease in performance.

Summary

Beyond the category system, it is extremely difficulty to integrate the extant correlational literature on administrator effects because most of the empirical research includes variables and measures peculiar to one or a limited number of studies. To illustrate, investigators use a diverse set of independent variables, including principal style, principal behavior, centralization, administrator succession, and the like. The array of dependent variables is equally diverse, including teacher effectiveness, administrator effectiveness, student achievement, staff morale, and more.

The foregoing differences notwithstanding, there is some commonality across the correlational studies of the relationships between school administration and school outcomes. First, in all but a few the principal (as opposed to other administrative positions) is the subject of study, and principal behavior is treated as an independent variable. Bridges (1982), among others, has noted the striking absence of significant research on the superintendency and other administrative positions in both the public and private sectors. Meanwhile, some researchers have shifted attention to technostructural variables, which Erickson (1979) recommended as a new and promising research area in educational administration.

Second, investigators continue to use the LBDQ to measure the behavior of leaders despite longstanding criticism of its shortcomings (Charters, 1979; Schreisheim & Kerr, 1977). Other researchers have turned to surrogates for administrator behavior, such as principal succession, because "existing quantitative measures of principal behavior have lacked the requisite validity and reliability for testing assertions about instructional leadership" (Rowan & Denk, 1984, p. 518). It appears that useful measures lag behind theoretical models and

Figure 5.10 Model of moderated effects of administrator behavior.

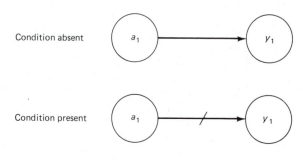

available statistical procedures for testing stipulated relationships.

Third, administrator effect is measured "freeze frame." Data are collected at a particular moment and judged against a uniform normative standard. If administrators contribute to an organization's functioning, the contribution should be detectable over time. Establishing the effect of leaders on organizations requires longitudinal study, a commitment made by few researchers. Observing change in the organization associated with change in administrator (e.g., Rowan & Denk, 1984) represents a useful alternative to conventional cross-sectional inquiry.

Fourth, in contrast to an earlier observation by Rowan, Dwyer, and Bossert (1982), theory does appear to have driven most studies in the sense that it is possible to identify notions about which variables were causes and which variables were effects. Assessment of the value of the "theories" is quite another matter, given that the investigators often left implicit their notions about causes and effects and either omitted altogether or stated only vaguely their hypotheses. Future researchers, it is hoped, will state hypotheses explicitly and use path analytic diagrams to represent their causal models. Doing so will allow for better integration of research findings and enhance the possibility of useful meta-analysis in lieu of the typical discursive review.

Fifth, collectively, the data analytic techniques (Table 5.1) typically used in the correlational studies are simplistic. To illustrate, although multiple-regression techniques (Cohen & Cohen, 1983; Pedhazur, 1982) best serve the analysis of antecedent-effects models and mediated-effects models, multiple regression was not used in a single study that invoked those models. Similarly, while the moderated-effects model requires that statistical interactions be analyzed, interactions were sometimes ignored or inappropriately analyzed.

Finally, despite the acknowledgment of the possibility of reciprocal effects at work, they were not analyzed in a single study. Recent advances in nonrecursive analysis and the increasing popularity of LISREL VI, a software package that can analyze reciprocal effects, may redress this condition.

A large number of the correlation studies shared three methodological problems. First, few investigators attempted to incorporate and measure logically chosen control variables. Those studies that did employ statistical controls appeared to select variables on the basis of convenience. Second, in respect to choice of unit of analysis, many researchers created school-level indexes from data collected from and averaged across teachers in the school. Such an approach will work only if teachers' ratings, say, of principal behaviors, demonstrate a reasonable level of agreement. Although level of agreement can be easily assessed, researchers in general either did not compute or failed to report inter-rater reliability, even when the data were clearly available. Third, investigators have continued the practice of requesting the same subjects, usually teachers, to provide ratings for both independent and dependent variables, thus increasing the likelihood of their correlation. Given the likelihood of correlation across the assorted mental states of teachers, using one to predict the other is not particularly illuminating.

Qualitative Studies

Some qualitative studies have explored administrator behavior and processes without preconceived notions about what administrators do or should do. Others have attempted to generate concepts and hypotheses (or confirm them) in programmatic research and/or to complement statistical findings yielded by survey research. Investigators watch what people do and say (observation), and/or they ask people to report on their actions and those of others (interview).

Many qualitative studies assert that their interest is in providing rich, detailed descriptions devoid of evaluations of administrator behavior or its effectiveness. Wolcott's (1973) caveat is indicative of this posture. "This study was not designed to provide an evaluation of the role of the principal but to provide a description of what a principal does..." (p. 319).

Two groups of studies are relevant to this discussion. One group focuses on the administrator's role and either attempts to capture everything an administrator does (e.g., Martin & Willower, 1981; Morris, Crowson, Porter-Gehrie, & Hurwitz, 1984; Peterson, 1977–1978;

Table 5.1   Analytic Procedures for Studying Administration Effects

MODEL OF EFFECTS	DATA ANALYSIS PROCEDURE REQUIRED TO TEST THE THEORY
1. Direct	Path analysis
2. Moderated	Regression with product vectors
3. Antecedent	Path analysis
4. Reciprocal (nonrecursive)	LISREL analysis
5. Mediated	Path analysis

Pitner, 1981; Pitner & Ogawa, 1981; Wolcott, 1973) or attends to a particular aspect of role performance (e.g., Blumberg, 1985; Blumberg & Greenfield, 1980; Dwyer, Lee, Rowan, & Bossert, 1983). A second group (e.g., Lightfoot, 1983; Metz, 1978) looks at an entire school and then turns to descriptions and interpretations of the administrator, usually the principal, to help explain and understand the whole. Nine studies of the qualitative genre will receive detailed review here, with others brought in occasionally, to illuminate the nature of the research questions asked, the evidence supplied, and the conclusions drawn by field investigators.

A common standard of comparison for other observation studies is Wolcott's study of an elementary school principal in a medium-sized school district in a city in the Northwest. Wolcott (1973) spent a full year observing one principal, with follow-up visits in a second year. He describes and analyzes a broad range of the principal's social behavior in close detail, as, for example, the socializing influence of the principal on teachers' work. The centrality of formal evaluation in the socialization process stands clear in Wolcott's (1973) description:

> The observation and evaluation process produced considerable apprehension among teachers as well as among principals. No teacher at Taft could ignore the feeling that Ed's classroom visits in January and early February lacked their usual casualness. Among their colleagues, the principals expressed the discomfort they felt in performing a task so judgmental in nature, one which conflicted blatantly with the ideal of democratic administration in which most principals preferred to present themselves among their teacher colleagues as a first among equals. The evaluation procedure emphasized the hierarchical position of the principal both in terms of the subordinates whom he evaluated and the superordinates who held him responsible for completing the assignment. (p. 246).

Wolcott notes, however, that evaluation served more ritual functions than real ones, a general observation about the socialization of teachers that he further enhances through reports on two probationary teachers. In neither report does Wolcott suggest that principals affect classroom processes or individual teachers so as to improve instruction.

Wolcott reflects at some length on how the role and functions of the principalship limit possible effects. The principal's commitment is to resolve or prevent problems in a situation in which every problem is important. Preoccupation with unprioritized problems "mitigates the principal's opportunity for constructive accomplishment" (p. 318). The efficiency and effectiveness of bureaucratic organizations for bringing large numbers of people together to accomplish their goals

implies that "whatever pride and proprietary interest Ed Bell felt for 'his' school, he could not have created it by himself" (p. 320).

Wolcott concludes that researchers pay too little attention to the varied circumstances of teachers and notes that in the principal's treatment of teachers, "we see him acting consistently on behalf of the institution to organize the diversity that he confronted, both real and imagined, in terms of its tolerances for that diversity as he assessed it" (p. 322). Although many envision principals as agents of change, principals contribute to the school organization as "monitors of continuity of institutions and society. The real change agents of schools are young teachers and young parents" (p. 321). Wolcott suggests that because principals are not recognized for their contribution to continuity and are, instead, viewed as resisting change, "they have become ritually preoccupied with talk about change and expert at initiating continual minor reorganization within their own domain" (p. 321). Finally, within a complex system of interrelationships, the principal is a mediator—preventing and resolving conflict—which makes it impossible for him to "attend in any depth to the educational process itself" (p. viii).

Another study involving sustained observation explored life in two recently desegregated urban junior high schools. Metz (1978) spent almost a year in the field collecting data—observation, document analysis, and interviews. The concept of authority and definitions by a principal of the character of a school receive central consideration within a larger study of differences between the two schools in behavior, attitudes, and social relationships of students and adults. In her report, Metz noted that many of the teachers thought the principal's role to be key to the character of the whole school. However, she concludes:

> Principals appear to be caught between having direct responsibility without direct control over events. The principals...were keenly aware that they were responsible both for imaginative academic education and for safety and order in every part of the school. They were also aware that this double responsibility entailed practical contradictions and the necessity for choice. (p. 189)

Metz uses the strands of her interview data and observations to weave reality. She skillfully juxtaposes the principal's rhetoric, his actual practice, and teachers' perceptions of that practice to create a whole tapestry. For example, if a principal said he was going to do something, Metz confirmed whether he carried out his intentions. In one instance, a principal indicated the intention to transfer a teacher who did not adopt the principal's vision and demonstrate commitment to it by accepting extra responsibilities. However, in a subsequent interview the principal confessed that it was very difficult to transfer a teacher.

According to Metz (1978) search for and insistence on acceptance and support for the principal's definition of the situation was a repeated theme. For example, the deployment of teachers to achieve one principal's agenda was evident in his appointment and use of department chairs. He selected energetic teachers who were informal leaders, gave them heavy responsibilities and kept them busy at tasks he identified, and used personal contacts to increase their understanding of the administrative problems of running the school (p. 194). Metz cites several instances of the principal's invoking of rules and using communication channels to secure teachers' acceptance of the principal's interpretation of problems and their solutions. For example:

> Mr. Brandt saw to it that communication within the school flowed hierarchically wherever possible. He used various devices to underscore his own position as the source of authoritative statements. Unlike the other principals, he issued all faculty and student bulletins over his signature as communications from him, though the bulk of notices were contributed by other staff members. (p. 193)

The idiosyncratic constellations of principal behavior appear in the comparison of how each conceived and responded to an identical problem: student refusal to recite the pledge of allegiance. Each principal was able to assume a particular style and to adopt a particular stance, Metz argues, because of context (more specifically, the history of the school and the recruitment and assignment of teachers to it). Once an authority pattern took form at the school, Metz concluded, there was no way to reverse it (p. 189).

In contrast to the carefully documented, longitudinal work of Wolcott (1973) and Metz (1978), Lightfoot (1983) drew quick sketches of culture in six high schools with reputations as fine institutions. In exploring the reasons for prevailing "goodness," Lightfoot adopts a broader perspective of the good than is commonly used by "effective" schools researchers:

> My first assumption about goodness was that it is not a static or absolute quality that can be quickly measured by a single indicator of success or effectiveness...goodness [is not achievement scores, numbers of graduates attending college, literacy rates, or attendance records...[it refers to] the school's "ethos," not discrete additive elements. (p. 23)

In drawing her portraits, Lightfoot "explored and described competitive and dissonant perspectives and searched for their connections to other phenomena" (p. 15). The administrator is a figure in each portrait. For example:

Hogan's ultimate and uncompromising power is not without focus or reason. Certainly his temperamental tendencies appear to be authoritarian, and he has a large measure of personal ambition. But more important, he believes that he will only be able to realize his goals for Carver if he runs a tight ship. Discipline and authority have become the key to gaining control of a change process...Schools must provide the discipline, the safety, and the resources that these students are not getting at home...Hogan believes they must be strictly disciplined and mannerly...There is a preoccupation with rules and regulations.... (p. 35)

Other descriptions of principals emanate from the perspectives of other actors, such as teachers.

From Lightfoot's (1983) unique portraits of widely different schools, several organizational themes emerge:

> Good high schools reveal a sustained and visible ideological stance that guards them against powerful and shifting social intrusions; that what is often perceived as solitary leadership in schools is fueled by partnerships and alliances with intimate, trusted associates. We discover that the qualities traditionally identified as female—nurturance, receptivity, responsiveness to relationships and context—are critical to the expression of noncaricatured masculine leadership. Good leaders redefine the classic male domain of high school principals. We also discover that good high schools offer teachers the opportunity for autonomous expression, a wide angle on organizational participation and responsibility, and a degree of protection from the distorted stereotypes that plague their profession. (p. 25)

These themes are expressed, according to Lightfoot, through the interactions, ideology, rituals, and symbols of a school.

Where Lightfoot and Metz located the principal as only one element in a larger social system, Morris et al. (1984) focused specifically on principals' role performance. Using structured and unstructured approaches, they observed 16 elementary and secondary principals in an urban district for up to 12 days each over the course of 3 years. Concerned with the image of principals as powerless, Morris and his colleagues set out to study discretionary behavior without regard either for the motivation therefor or legitimacy thereof:

> Administrators...function partly as transmission boxes; they transmit information from higher echelons to the school, and, in reverse, transmit information from the school to higher authorities....But since performance in this area is, by definition, pro forma, it is not susceptible to school managers' discretionary judgment... Accordingly, we concentrated our attention on everything else a principal does: the spheres of activity which are not routine or merely clerical, not dictated by strict rules, mandatory procedures, or the severe, even if unstated, expectations of immediate supervisors. (pp. 28–29)

Principals work constantly at balancing the needs for improvement and enhancement in programs, stability and control in student behavior, parent and community involvement, and teacher performance (p. 77). Maintenance of discipline structures to ensure pupil safety and classroom efficiency is central. Some principals find it possible to extend the maintenance of control in ways to enhance the school's learning environment. Anticipating problems, managing events, and enforcing rules consumes much time and energy. Morris et al. (1984) sprinkle behavioral descriptions throughout their report to support their conclusions, as illustrated by the following excerpt on event management:

> Principal Smith learned that a rock had been thrown through a second floor window, spraying the room with glass. His initial response, after making sure there were no injuries, was not to send people to look for those who threw the rock. Instead, he sent staff to the second floor to enter classrooms and explain the incident, quiet things down, return pupils in the hall to class, and enforce order. (p. 79)

The authors also describe in crisp action and process language the strategies principals use to balance constituent interest and parent involvement against the stability demanded by the school's values.

One criticism of previous studies of administrator work activities is that they have not discriminated between the behaviors of effective and ineffective executives (e.g., Pitner & Russell, 1985–1986). Neither antecedents of work activity patterns nor their consequences for the organization and its members have received systematic attention. Martinko and Gardner (1984) set out to fill this void by differentiating among the performance levels of principals and concentrating specifically on the activities of effective performers. Forty-one principals—22 high-performing and 19 moderately performing principals—were observed for a total of 270 days using a structured observation approach.

The investigators used multiple criteria for selecting the sample, including measures of school performance, superintendent ranking of the school, superintendent ranking of the principal, and tenure of the principal (each of whom had completed a minimum of 3 years in the present assignment). The schools in the sample met most of the selection criteria. In addition, the researchers incorporated environmental characteristics into the research design (staff size, geographic size, socioeconomic status). Chi-square analysis and t tests yielded statistically significant differences between high and moderate performers on each of four criterion variables.

Martinko and Gardner sought to identify the behaviors that characterize effective school managers. Over 30,000 discrete behavioral incidents were coded into communication and structure categories in the Mintzberg (1973) tradition, and the data were also analyzed according to seven other category systems. The post hoc analysis included coding according to (a) the purpose of verbal contact and managerial roles (Mintzberg, 1973); (b) the Leader Observation System (Luthans & Lockwood, 1983); (c) leadership style (Yukl & Nemeroff, 1979); (d) functional area of responsibility (Martinko & Gardner, 1984); (e) the McBer categories (of Martinko & Gardner, 1984); and (f) several category systems generated by observers. Each coding system, with the exception of leadership style, permitted the coding of multiple categories simultaneously.

The researchers employed frequency analysis and inferential contrasts of behavioral frequencies, with t tests and profile analysis of observational data. The profile analysis provided an overall test of coincidence that indicated whether there were any significant differences in the overall profiles of the coding systems related to the independent variables under study. Whenever statistically significant differences appeared, the researchers tested for interactions.

Martinko and Gardner (1984) found few systematic differences between high and moderately performing principals. Where significant differences in behavior existed, they were accompanied by differences in grade level, organization type, staff size, and school's SES. Principals spent more time managing change in high SES schools, managing human relations in middle SES schools, and visiting classrooms in low SES schools. The authors conclude that the relationships between principals' behaviors and their environments are unique. "These cases suggest that the normative statements regarding behaviors which will be universally effective in a variety of environments are unlikely" (p. 17). Further, the "failure to find differences which are robust enough to be detected despite environmental variation suggests that, if differences do exist, they are relatively small and may be of little practical significance" (p. 20). In support of a contingency and symbolic approach to leadership, Martinko and Gardner conclude that environmental variables are more closely associated with principal behavior than are their administrator performances and school performance levels.

Eschewing a wide-angle study of administration, Dwyer et al. (1983) concentrated on how principals influence school climate and instruction organization. They observed each of five principals of reputedly effective schools (four elementary and one junior high school) for 3 full work days over an 8-week period, for a total of 15 days of field contact. Subjects were nominated by superintendents and screened by researchers as to interest in the study, variation in personal characteristics, and deficiencies in school contexts. Antecedents to principal behavior (personal attributes, district and external characteristics) and the consequences of administrator behavior on school climate and organization and student achievement are described. For example, Dwyer et al. (1983) note the influences of the community on principal behavior as follows:

> The nature of the McDuffy neighborhood prescribes much of Hudson's work. He declared that visits by police to his schools "are so common that they might as well open a substation at McDuffy." He estimates that 60 percent of his time is spent on problems of child abuse, drug abuse, abandonment, and runaways. Community violence and family turmoil impinge upon his school. An important aspect of greeting children in the morning, he believes, is detecting unrest and defusing potential problems before they erupt. (p. 10)

The investigators also note how, they believe, principal actions influence climate and instructional organization:

> By design, Hudson expects his activities to improve school climate, a concept that seems to include a host of factors external to children that enhance their readiness for learning. At McDuffy, he recounts improving the climate through a variety of specific activities: painting walls; carpeting floors; feeding hungry students; personally reading to students in the lower grades; making frequent visits to upper grade classrooms; pitching balls to youngsters at recess; replacing harsh, corporal discipline procedures with patient counseling; talking with individual students about their work and progress; and serving as the school's ambassador at community meetings. In his mind, these efforts signal students that their school is interested in them and prepared to help them. (p. 12)

According to the variation of the Bossert et al. (1982) model (see Figure 5.1) used by Dwyer et al. (1983), attention to climate and instructional organization translates into effect on student outcomes. The authors describe how at the first faculty meeting of the year one of the principals outlined the year's agenda and indicated his intention to observe each teacher three times during the year. His statement of intention to make a better effort at observing more than in the previous year drew some laughter from the teachers.

Narrative case studies identified the idiosyncratic models at work in each of the five sites that incorporated contexts, activities, and expected outcomes of management behaviors. These five models served as

reality checks against the general instructional management model proposed by Bossert et al. (1982). Their data led Dwyer et al. (1983) to conclude that instructional management is a high priority for successful principals.

Blumberg and Greenfield (1980) used still another approach to study principals who enjoyed reputations of being effective and serving in effective schools. Their sample included four elementary school (one female) and four secondary school (two female) principals. The researchers interviewed each principal at length, using an unstructured format without suggesting topics or probing in an attempt to ensure the veracity of each principal's testimony and to avoid contamination of the data by researcher bias.

The authors use direct quotations liberally to present each principal's social construction of reality. All principals discussed their relationships with teachers; thus, an examination of principals' conversations provides an entré into the evidence supplied by Blumberg and Greenfield (1980).

One principal discussed the demands to be an instructional leader as follows:

> I think in the area of leadership, real leadership, the principal has a free hand. For example, nobody's pushing the principal to a new curriculum, nobody's pushing for a new schedule or a new program for students. There is no push for new budgeting techniques. You don't have a parent come in and say, "Hey, let's get X program started at the high school." The faculty doesn't push you either. Even if one department has an out-of-proportion slice of the budget, there's very little pressure to change it from other departments because they see it as just too big a task. (p. 69)

The building of a mutually supportive administrative-faculty relationship starts with the ability and willingness of a principal to listen to teachers:

> They made it obvious to me what they expected. They wanted more strict enforcement of student discipline codes. They wanted to be sure kids were not loitering in the halls. They wanted administrators around the building; they wanted you to be visible. They did not want you in the office working on schedules or other such things. As you fulfill their expectations, also taking into consideration your own priorities, you build one hell of an alliance with your faculty. You really get them in your corner, so that when the time comes for you to ask them to do something they would not normally do, they'll do it. (p. 111)

A different approach is taken by an administrator who lived by one of the terms of the teachers' collective bargaining agreement and evaluated tenured and non-tenured teachers despite the norms and informal agreements of the school:

...people are probably a little more secure and accepting now. No tenured teachers were fired and I think they're coming to understand that evaluation has two purposes: to make judgments about continued employment and for professional development. Maybe it's the professional development part that they're a bit more accepting of now. (p. 142)

The specifications for the job of principal, as found in the teacher contract, were burdensome for another administrator:

> I think principals have done themselves in. They don't know if they have any power, don't feel they have a lot of administrative power, and yet feel the responsibility is overwhelming. So, they can never get out of the building because in order to feel good, in order not to be feeling guilty, they feel they've got to be running the whole show. And, they do it. No wonder they don't have the time. For example, if the teachers' contract says that the teachers can't do hall duty. So, the principals say, "I'll have to do it." Well, I don't do hall duty and I don't intend to unless everybody does it. (p. 60)

The authors conclude that a generic description of effective principal behavior and activities cannot be constructed due to the idiographic nature of principal behavior.

> Each...seemed to have his/her own theory of the principal's role that stemmed from his/her personality, experience, and training...illustrat[ing] the many forms that leadership in a school can take and still produce a productive learning environment. (p. 5)

Although effective principals have "in common" an idiosyncratic perspective toward their work, Blumberg and Greenfield (1980) identify three factors to explain principal success. These principals (a) wanted to make their schools over in "their" image, (b) assumed a proactive and initiating stance in their schools, and (c) structured their roles and responsibilities to permit them to pursue their personal objectives as principals (p. 201).

As in the case of the correlational research, field research that focuses specifically on superintendents or district organizational structure is sparse. Descriptions of superintendents do appear in (a) a study of three big city superintendents during the late 1950s and 1960s (Cuban, 1976), (b) studies of superintendent work activities (e.g., Duignan, 1980; Larson, Bussom, & Vicars, 1981; Pitner & Ogawa, 1981), (c) the meanings superintendents attach to their work (Blumberg, 1985), and (d) organizational control mechanisms used by district personnel to control the work of principals (Peterson, 1984).

Pitner and Ogawa (1981) combined three data sets (two structured observation studies and one elite interview study) to describe and analyze superintendent work. They document the strategic location of the superintendent in the flow of information and portray the superintendent as mediator:

> The superintendent's position grants access to a variety of networks, which lead to more information about what is happening within, as well as external to, the school district. The superintendent puts available pieces of information together to adjust conflicting claims, to persuade others to accept his or her decisions, and to impose decisions when necessary. (p. 57)

Given the superintendent's limited control over processes contributing to student achievement and his or her attributed responsibility for goal achievement, Pitner and Ogawa emphasize the symbolic dimension of superintendents' leading behavior and activities. Superintendents must respond to and reflect external influences. They serve as mediators—managers of meaning—in the social systems of which they are a part.

To understand the relationship between the managerial structures in school districts, Peterson (1984) investigated the use of control mechanisms to influence the work of principals. He interviewed a random sample, stratified by size of district, of 113 principals in 59 elementary districts (with a range of 2 to 20 schools per district). Peterson sought to determine to what extent principals perceived the relative use and salience of six control mechanisms: supervision, input, output, behavior, selection-socialization, and environmental controls. The study was avowedly exploratory; statistical presentation is limited to central tendencies and distributions.

Peterson confirmed that all six control types are used and found that the magnitude of their use varied with district size and school status. Supervision by superintendent and central-office personnel tended to decrease with increasing school status and school size. Input controls were evident in administrative and instructional areas. Administrative input controls were aimed at financial allocations (i.e., per capita budgeting, availability of contingency funds, ability to transfer funds among budget categories). Instructional input controls included discretion in the initial hiring and transfer of teachers. Principals were more constrained in administrative areas; even so, higher status schools and smaller districts enjoyed more autonomy. Behavior controls included rules, procedures and directives, specification of curriculum content, central adoption of texts, written job descriptions, and programmed management systems. Higher status schools experienced fewer input controls; larger districts exercised more control over principals. Output controls included standardized student achievement tests and public reaction. Higher status schools faced greater output controls. Selection and socialization controls included principal recruitment and hiring from within the district. Environmental controls referred to feedback from parents.

Control appears to be zoned, with tighter exercise over administrative areas and substantial autonomy granted in the instructional process.

> The patterns of control we find point to a subtle balancing of control and autonomy, with principals constrained through the evaluation of outputs and the mandatory accomplishment of administrative tasks, but permitted considerable autonomy in the selection of means to achieve ends, in the choice of tasks to attend to, and in the selection of faculty. (p. 39)

Peterson concludes that multiple controls provide a broad-based and pervasive influence on principal work.

Summary

The focus of the qualitative studies is describing what administrators do *qua* administrators, as well as identifying their beliefs and perceptions about the work they do. Often, administrators talk about what they perceive their influence to be in the social system of which they are a part. Still, the studies vary in respect to their methods of data collection as well as the presentation and interpretation of these data. The data across the set of studies includes a mixture of summaries of researchers' observations, verbatim records of administrators' talk, and summaries and quotes secured through interviewing administrators (and less frequently other actors in the school). Because management is essentially an oral occupation, verbatim records of transactions comprise valuable data for describing the process of administering and allocating the influence of administrators (Gronn, 1984; Pitner, 1982b; Pitner & Russell, 1985–1986).

One of the issues that the qualitative studies present for serious consideration is the discrepancy between the action language of subjects and the summaries of researchers' observations. The principal's construction of reality is sometimes reported in words lacking precision and open to interpretation, such as notation of an administrator's style as "tight-reined." Also, discrepancies between principal intention and behavior are noted and described by some (e.g., Metz, 1978) but largely ignored by others (e.g., Dwyer et al., 1983). In many instances, the reported evidence does not support conclusions reached about administrator behavior or influence. For example, one researcher

concluded that instructional leadership was a priority for a principal without verifying whether the principal actually visited classrooms or whether he met the standard of three observations he proclaimed in a faculty meeting. Contradictions between principals' talk and situational reality receive neither sufficient notation nor careful exploration. However valuable a principal's social construction of reality, inconsistencies are certainly worth noting and exploring.

Halpin (1966) long ago discussed the problem of observing and reporting administrator behavior:

> Obviously, an administrator can seduce himself into believing that he has achieved his purpose, simply because he says that he has. This is not uncommon. Although this type of blind faith in his own accomplishments may comfort the administrator, the social scientist engaged in research on administrator behavior requires more tangible evidence than this for evaluating the organization's achievement. (p. 51)

Qualitative studies provocatively suggest the influence of administrator processes and structure on the organization. Still, it is difficult to separate the effect of the principal from the effects of other factors. It is even more difficult to detect from the data typically provided the effect of a given principal over time or the effect of a succession of administrators. Such determinations require a longer exposure to the natural setting than is typical. For the most part, researchers who use qualitative approaches to describe and analyze administrator behavior report administrator "impact," "influence," and "affect," *not* "effect." Most use a language of process, not outcomes.

Researchers who rely on qualitative methods, which often use limited and small samples, tend to be modest and cautious about their findings and gingerly draw conclusions about administrator effects:

> Although not employing any explicit measures for tracking this possibility [of a principal's effect on student achievement] we did come to appreciate in a general way the influence that the principal's behavior has on the total learning community. (Morris et al., 1984 p. 30)

Unfortunately, however, others tend to overstate the findings and overgeneralize, perhaps unaware of the original data. Qualitative research should be taken and appreciated for what it is; no more should be expected of it than it can deliver. The detailed descriptions provide a basis for the refinement of concepts and the development of hypotheses to be tested in larger-scale studies. The findings are not the end of the journey; they represent a rough map to guide future travelers.[3]

DISCUSSION

Scholarly inquiry into the effects and effectiveness of educational administrators provides fertile ground for criticism and commentary (e.g., Bidwell, 1975; Boyan, 1982; Boyd & Crowson, 1981; Burlingame, 1979; Erickson, 1979; Greenfield, 1968; Griffiths, 1979; Immegart & Boyd, 1979; Rowan, 1984; Rowan et al., 1982; Silver, 1981). For the most part, the critical comments have centered on the nature of the questions asked (the research problem) and the methods used to illuminate the problems.

The Questions Asked

Much of the work on administrator effects employs a social-psychological perspective, although anthropological and sociological approaches have gained popularity. Boyd and Crowson (1981) have summarized the status of the field:

> The question of what site-level administrators do or could do with what effects on student outcomes remains to be answered. Clear linkages between the on-the-job behaviors of school managers and varying kinds of schooling outcomes have not yet been documented. Conceptual and methodological difficulties abound in this quest...and are exacerbated by the principals' indirect and mediatory relationship to classroom instruction.... Still, preliminary evidence that is available suggests that such old, but still ill-defined, concepts as school "climate" do after all have some meaning for the educational program....Moreover, there is reason to believe administrator effects need not necessarily be so indirect. Administrators can "make a difference" through control over such matters as the shaping of the allocation of time on instruction. (p. 349)

Some scholars have suggested that the relevant research question is, but should be less "What are administrator effects?" and should be more "What are the consequences of different organizational arrangements and structures?" In place of emphasis on administrator behavior, Bidwell (1975), Erickson (1979), and Silver (1981) focus on organizational variables at the classroom and school levels (e.g., setting organizational arrangements and structures as independent variables with student outcomes as dependent variables). The theoretical framework proposed by Bossert et al. (1982), Duckworth (1983), Ellett and Walberg (1979), and Pitner (1982b) suggests the linkages from macrostructure to microprocess (i.e., classroom activities) and microorganizational conditions. The frameworks provide suggestions for investigating the operation of schools at the technical, managerial, and institutional levels and for testing presumptions of looseness and tightness of coupling between these levels. Instead of explaining coupling by labeling it as such, the several frameworks consider it more productive to treat coupling as a variable to be studied, as urged by Herriott and Firestone (1984).

Despite a general interest in studying the linkages between managerial structure and technology, a number of scholars have retained specific interest in administrators and leadership. They have urged (a) studying the daily events of administrative practice in organizations (Burlingame, 1979; Pitner & Russell, 1985–1986); (b) examining the linkages between policy and the practices of administrators and teachers (Immegart & Boyd, 1979); (c) investigating the relationship of applied science to pragmatic action (Rowan, 1984); (d) considering the cognitive and information processes involved in administrator work (Pitner & Russell, 1985–1986; Yukl, 1984); (e) investigating the symbolic and expressive aspects of leadership and attributions of leader effects and effectiveness (e.g., Firestone & Wilson, 1983; Pitner & Ogawa, 1981); and (f) viewing cases of school improvement and effectiveness as organizational stories and legends with administrators as heroes and investigating nonhierarchical (e.g., faculty, department chairs, and teacher unions) sources of leadership (e.g., Pitner, 1986; Purkey & Smith, 1983).

Review of the literature says, however, that the relationship between what administrators do (and aspects of administration like organizational arrangements) and other commonplaces is not fully understood. The complexity of the linkages is well recognized in theory but less well taken into consideration in empirical research. In addition to inadequate study of the complexity of linking relationships, the research relevant to administrator effects has taken a narrow conception of effects and effectiveness. Researchers were long preoccupied with organization effects on administrators, teachers, and administration rather than on instruction or student outcomes (Erickson, 1979). Although the field has moved somewhat away from teacher performance ratings of principals as measures of effectiveness, the more subjective indicators have given way to single "objective" measures, such as academic achievement scores or other dependent variables often lacking empirical and theoretical significance as signals of "productivity." Researchers predominantly settle for only one criterion of effectiveness, usually a conveniently available indicator.

The difficulties in studying administrator effects noted by Boyd and Crowson (1981) remain:

> Indeed, one difficulty is that there is no widely agreed upon definition of what "administrator effects" really are. To the degree, for example, that elements of school "climate," staff morale, curriculum emphasis, reward

and punishment strategy, school social organization, and the like, can be found to affect student learning, one may or may not be able to attribute effects to the school administrator. But, how, for instance, does one separate out the unique contribution of a building administrator to the "climate" found in effective schools—if indeed this climate is not merely a by-product but contributes to the effectiveness of the schools? (p. 345)

A multidimensional approach to the study of effects and effectiveness and longitudinal research design have been advocated to capture the complexity of factors that influence the achievement or nonachievement of the goals of schooling (Erickson, 1967; Halpin, 1957; Morphet & Schutz, 1966; Rowan, 1984). Empirical work has typically ignored the advice, even by investigators who offer it in their conceptual pieces.

Methods Used to Answer the Questions

The Griffiths-Greenfield debates (Herda, 1978) centered on legitimate ways of inquiring and knowing about organizations and people within them. Although the arguments did not center exclusively or centrally on the relative value of quantitative and qualitative methodology, controversy still flares on methodological preferences and contributions.

Quantitative Methods

The condition in the mid-1980s of correlational research on administrator effects and effectiveness corroborates McNamara's earlier observation that inquiry in educational administration is distinguished by a naive use of statistics. McNamara (1979) observed that researchers often did not clearly state their independent and dependent variables; they often used inappropriate analytical procedures to test hypotheses; and they too often based dependent and independent measures on the reports and perceptions of only one group of observers, usually teachers. Conditions over the past decade have not changed markedly, even though Charters (1979) has identified several methodological advances in educational administration. The field still stands in need, for example, of more rigorous development of path analysis tools to assist theory building and meta-analysis.

In addition to problems of modeling and statistical analysis, research studies on administrator effects may be suspect because of sampling problems. Clark, Lotto and Astuto (1984) have shown the heavy loading of effective-schools studies in urban elementary schools with large proportions of low SES students and the loading of school-improvement studies in schools with large proportions of high SES students. To further illustrate the long-standing issue of sample and general-

izability, Keeler and Andrews (1963) fully acknowledged the limitations of their findings about the effect of principals on teachers' morale in rural junior high schools in Alberta, Canada, but subsequent citations seldom mention the sample and typically ignore problems of generalizability. In somewhat the same vein, Rowan (1984) has noted a tendency in some of the effective-schools literature to disregard empirical data that are counter to the reporter's ideology. Rowan characterizes the use of research findings in school-effectiveness research as shamanistic rituals designed to promote organizational health. Research findings that are contrary to effective-schools ideology are discarded, and fugitive materials and reviews of research reviews are cited to support preferred claims. Rules of quantitative evidence appear to be disregarded.

To counteract sampling problems, an effort should be made to increase the variation in the phenomena studied. The tendency has been of late, both in quantitative and qualitative work, to study sameness and uniformity, not to account for variation. Samples should be selected that capture more diversity. This recommendation is made recognizing that incumbents of administrative positions and perhaps schools as organizations may be rather indistinguishable (March & March, 1977). Similarly, Pitner and Charters (1984) found little variation in the number and magnitude of substituting conditions in a sample of 47 elementary schools. Thus, purposive samples may be in order and should perhaps include nonpublic institutions, which may not be subject to the same filters and configurations of substitutes.

Qualitative Methods

Disappointment with the contributions of quantitative approaches to illuminating organizational life and administrator effect has evoked calls for more emphasis on qualitative modes of inquiry (see Griffiths, 1979; Willower, 1979). Griffiths (1979) asserted that

there should be a way of describing organizations that tries to determine, not *a priori* but in actuality, what the particular organization is attempting to do, and in particular, what the people in it are attempting to do. (p. 46)

Researchers have responded positively to the calls by increasing the flow of case studies, ethnographies, structured observations, and interview reports that had started to build in the early and mid-1970s.

Review of and commentary on qualitative studies reveal several pertinent themes. First, use of qualitative methods, in and of itself, does not guarantee the presence of a hermeneutical perspective among investigators, as some argue it should (see Smith & Heshusius, 1986). Second, the tradition of behaviorism is favored over interpretive or explanatory-comparative modes, even in ethnography (see Sanday, 1979, for elaboration of the differences between these anthropological schools). Third, studies continue to over-rely on "reality" as presented by one informant and do not distinguish between presentational and operational data (see Goffman, 1967; Van Maanan, 1979). Fourth, researchers tend to restrict themselves to the use of a single method for collecting data as opposed to combining methods.

The tenets of positivism continue to provoke argument within the set of users and protagonists of qualitative methods. On one side, Sanday (1979) points out the variation in the ethnographic paradigm evident in both primary focus and data analysis. Investigators, says Sanday, may set themselves either to capture the whole, to establish meaning, or to isolate behavior. Their analytic goal may be diagnosis or explanation (e.g., see Peterson, 1984; Martinko & Gardner, 1984). In brief, the ethnographic paradigm is "internally differentiated" and the approach taken appears to be a "matter of taste and not dogma" (Sanday, 1979, p. 34). Smith and Heshusius (1986), however, argue differently. They express concern over the evidence of positivistic hegemony exhibited in the recent focus on standardizing qualitative data-collection and analysis procedures (e.g., Lincoln & Guba, 1985; Miles & Huberman, 1984). They argue that qualitative and quantitative methods differ essentially and fundamentally on both philosophical assumptions and techniques (Smith & Heshusius, 1986). Their argument, however, ignores internal differentiation in the application of the ethnographic paradigm in anthropology. The degree to which anthropologists interpret and/or seek verifiable propositions varies (Sanday, 1979). Extant variability in the ethnographic paradigm should encourage its use for inquiries into educational administration.

Still, qualitative methods appear to be problematic in the search for the "truth" about the influence of the school administrator. Qualitative findings do not accumulate in the same way quantitative findings do (although some argue that correlational research to date has not added too much either). Also, investigators only loosely apply the rules that could strengthen both the collection and analysis of qualitative data. These characteristics of qualitative methodology make it difficult to draw conclusions confidently about administrator behavior and effectiveness. And despite arguments about the nature of extreme variation "out there," many of the studies reviewed exhibit a peculiar sameness. Only a few qualitative studies are as distinctive as Wolcott's *The Man in the Principal's Office* (1973) for its admirable use of description, interpretation, and theoretical analysis. Blumberg and Greenfield (1980) and Morris et al. (1984) treat their data in a similar way.

The argument by Smith and Heshusius (1986) that positivist rules of evidence are inappropriate for qualitative research does not mean that no applicable rules of evidence exist. The desire of Smith and Heshusius to ensure maintenance of distinctions between qualitative and quantitative approaches may be sensible as long as it is recognized that *qualitative* is not synonymous with *hermeneutical* or *phenomenological*. Intuitive and artistic approaches to research do not have to be undisciplined. Technical mastery is essential for the researcher (as for artist or scientist) to be able to create and interpret. Ansel Adams, known for his dramatic black and white photographic landscape studies of the West and Southwest, provides an apt metaphor. Adams was known for his ability to look at a scene and visualize how a photograph of it would come out in the development process; that is, he could predict the effect of emulsions and time exposure on a final print.

The controversy over choice of appropriate research methodology or methodologies, like the related debates about appropriate conceptual schemes, have thus far proved more divisive than centripetal. As Morey and Luthans (1984) put it, "The potential and real disagreements among organizational researchers over these contrasting approaches are unfortunate and can lead to neglect of common interests and interests on both sides" (p. 28). They add that the dichotomy between the perspectives of the subjective-qualitative-idiographic outsider and the objective-quantitative-nomothetic outsider is unproductive. Along the same line, Boyd and Crowson (1981) have suggested that both perspectives should be embraced on the grounds that the two approaches complement and, indeed, presuppose each other (p. 319). They point out that the use of multiple perspectives to analyze and explain organizational behavior and policy has proved useful (e.g., Allison, 1971; Firestone, 1980; Peterson, 1976). Whether multiple ways of constructing reality can or need to be integrated into a gestalt remains unanswered.

Final Comment

The position advocated here is that both quantitative and qualitative methods should be used continuously to inform and reformulate research problems. On this point, Morey and Luthans (1984) suggest taking an emic perspective and using the techniques of ethoscience in organizational research to gain more knowledge of subject understandings, perceptions, cognitive processes, meanings, and intentions, and then to use this information to develop survey instruments (p. 34). In brief, they call for objectifying subjective data and producing quantifiable data for traditional techniques of statistical analysis (p. 35). Their position squares with the suggestion to move beyond either tolerance of or advocacy for qualitative methods in favor of support for the enhanced use of multiple designs and analytic designs.

Does urging rapproachement deny the technical and philosophical differences between positivist and hermeneutical paradigms? Not at all, but it does encourage the use of information gained from one mode of inquiry to help formulate the research questions pursued with another. For example, the specific behavioral incidents unearthed by work activity and interview studies could be used to develop instruments to assess leader behavior that derive from direct observation of behavior (and its meanings as existentially expressed by participants) rather than from abstract notions about leader behavior.

A useful analog for the preferred posture exists in the graphics of Mauritis Escher. When viewing an Escher drawing, the observer feels the sensation of seeing the plane simultaneously from above, below, and at the same level and being tricked about reality, illusion, and abstraction. For example, his lithograph "Three Worlds" shows a woodland pond comprising three elements: the autumn leaves floating on the surface of the water; the reflection of three barren trees in the background; and in the foreground, a large Japanese goldfish seen through the translucent water (Escher, 1967, p. 14). Using the water's surface as a mirror, Escher creates a more complete view of the pond than direct observation might yield.

Similarly, the portrayal of the administrator in research can be likened to the artist's representation of figures in a drawing. When the artist focuses on a particular object, everything else recedes into the background and supports the figure. If the artist makes all component parts equal in size, no more than a fragment of the whole can be represented on the drawing plane. On the other hand, if the artist attempts to represent the whole, the size of the figures must be gradually reduced until they reach "the limit of infinite smallness" (Escher, 1967, p. 11). The metaphor is relevant for both qualitative and quantitative researchers. Rendering always involves distorting reality. The review of research on administrator effects reveals a significant and continuing problem of rendering.

NOTES

[1] The emphasis here is on how investigators have thought about and inquired into the problems of administrator effects and effectiveness since approximately 1970, with special attention to research that has examined in some detail the relationship between administrator behavior, organizational processes and structures, and other significant participants and conditions. The relatively limited scope seems appropriate in light of previous general and focused reviews and critiques of research in educational administration (general: Boyan, 1982; Bridges, 1982, Clark, Lotto, & Astuto, 1984; Erickson, 1967, 1977, 1979; T. B. Greenfield, 1968; Immegart, 1977; focused: Anderson, 1982; Charters, 1964; W. D. Greenfield, 1982; Leithwood & Montgomery, 1982; Persell, 1982; Purkey & Smith, 1983; Rowan, Bossert, & Dwyer, 1983). By attending to research that has examined the administrator in detail, certain works have been excluded; for example, see Pitner (1982b) regarding limitations of Rutter, Maugham, Ouston, and Smith (1979) for understanding principal effect.

[2] The distinction between effects and effectiveness is largely semantic. Statements about both depend on the accumulation of data, so in that sense they are empirical constructs. "Effects" conveys more limited meaning than "effectiveness." The latter projects an evaluative sense that the former does not. Further, it is possible for the evaluator (e.g., teacher, superintendent, researcher) to attribute an effect to the administrator when the administrator is not the causal agent.

Several problems attend the measurement of effects and effectiveness: (a) effectiveness criteria may change over time due to fashion and fads; (b) different groups may have different conceptions and perceptions of effectiveness; (c) the concept varies at different levels of analysis; (d) effectiveness criteria may vary with different types and levels of schools; (e) relationships between intermediate criteria and ultimate outcomes may be weak or nonexistent; (f) effects may be felt initially in one variable but over time in another requiring longitudinal study to detect effects; (g) potentially there is a variety of causes for any effect, so it is often difficult to isolate a single cause.

[3] This metaphor was suggested to me by Leland Stuart.

REFERENCES

Allison, G. (1971). *Essence of decision: Explaining the Cuban missile crisis*. Boston: Little, Brown.

Anderson, C. S. (1982). The search for school climate: A review of the research. *Review of Educational Research, 52*(3), 368–420.

Austin, G. R. (1979). Exemplary schools and the search for effectiveness. *Educational Leadership, 37*(1), 10–14.

Barnard, C. (1938). *The Functions of the Executive*. Cambridge, MA: Harvard University Press.

Bidwell, C. E. (1975). The relationship between school district organization and student achievement. *Administrator's Notebook, 23*(2), 1–4.

Blumberg, A. (1985). *The school superintendent: Living with conflict*. New York: Teachers College Press, Columbia University.

Blumberg, A., & Greenfield, W. (1980). *The effective principal: Perspectives on school leadership*. Boston: Allyn and Bacon.

Bossert, S., Dwyer, D., Rowan, B., & Lee, G. (1982). The instructional management role of the principal. *Educational Administration Quarterly, 18*(3), 34–64.

Boyan, N. J. (1982). Administration of educational institutions. In H. E. Mitzel (Ed.), *Encyclopedia of educational research* (pp. 22–49). New York: Free Press.

Boyd, W., & Crowson, R. (1981) The changing conception and practice of public school administration. In D. Berliner (Ed.), *Review of Research in Education, 9,* 311–373. Washington, DC: American Educational Research Association.

Bridges, E. (1982). Research on the school administrator: The state of the art, 1967–1980. *Educational Administration Quarterly, 18*(3), 12–33.

Brookover, W. B., Schweitzer, J., Schmeider, R., Flood, P., & Wisenbaker, J. (1978) Elementary school, social climate and school achievement. *American Educational Research Journal, 15*(2), 301–318.

Burlingame, M. (1979) Some neglected dimensions in the study of educational administration. *Educational Administration Quarterly, 15*(1), 1–18.

Caldwell, W. E., & Lutz, F. W. (1978) The measurement of principal rule administration behavior and its relationship to leadership. *Educational Administration Quarterly, 14*(2), 63–79.

Charters, W. W., Jr. (1964). *Teacher perceptions of administrator behavior.* (Final Report, Cooperative Research Project No. 927) Washington, DC: U.S. Office of Education, HEW.

Charters, W. W., Jr. (1979). Administrator success: An artifactual finding. *American Educational Research Journal, 16*(2), 197–199.

Clark, D., Lotto, L. S., & Astuto, T. A. (1984). Effective schools and school improvement: A comparative analysis of two lines of inquiry. *Educational Administration Quarterly, 20*(3), 41–68.

Cohen, J., & Cohen, P. (1983). *Applied multiple regression and correlation analysis for the behavioral sciences* (2nd ed.). Hillsdale, NJ: Erlbaum.

Copeland, R., Brown, R., & Hall, R. (1974). The effects of principal-implemented techniques on the behavior of pupils. *Journal of Applied Behavioral Analysis, 7*(1), 77–86.

Cuban, L. (1976). *Urban school chiefs under fire.* Chicago: University of Chicago press.

Deal, J. E., & Celotti, L. D. (1980). How much influence do (and can) educational administrators have on classrooms? *Phi Delta Kappan, 61*(7), 471–473.

Duckworth, K. (1983). *Specifying determinants of teacher and principal work.* Eugene. OR: Center for Educational Policy and Management, University of Oregon.

Duignan, P. (1980). Administration behavior of school superintendents: A descriptive study. *Journal of Educational Administration, 18*(1), 5–26.

Dwyer, D. C., Lee, G. V., Rowan, B., & Bossert, S. T. (1983). *Five principals in action: Perspectives on instructional management.* San Francisco: Far West Laboratory for Educational Research and Development.

Ellett, C. D., & Walberg, H. J. (1979). Principal competency, environment, and outcomes. In H. J. Walberg (Ed.), *Educational Environments and Effects* (pp. 140–167). Berkeley: McCutchan.

Erickson, D. A. (1967). The school administrator. *Review of Educational Research, 37*(4), 417–432.

Erickson, D. A. (1977). An overdue paradigm shift in educational administration, or, how can we get that idiot off the freeway? In L. L. Cunningham, W. G. Hack, & R. O. Nystrand (Eds.), *Educational administration: The developing decades* (pp. 119–146). Berkeley: McCutchan.

Erickson, D. A. (1979). Research in educational administration: State-of-the-art. *Educational Researcher, 8*(3), 9–13.

Escher, M. (1967). *The graphic work of M. C. Escher.* New York: Ballantine.

Firestone, W. (1980). Images of schools and patterns of change. *American Journal of Education, 88*(4), 459–487.

Firestone, W., & Wilson, B. (1983). *Substance and symbolism: An analysis of the work of the secondary school principal.* Eugene, OR: Center for Educational Policy and Management, University of Oregon.

Gall, M., Fielding, G., Shalock, D., Charters, W. W., Jr., & Wikzynski, J. (1985). *Involving the principal in teachers, staff development: Effects on mathematics instruction and achievement.* Eugene, OR: Center for Educational Policy and Management, University of Oregon.

Garland, P., & O'Reily, R. R. (1976). The effect of leader-member interaction in organizational effectiveness. *Educational Administration Quarterly, 12*(3), 9–30.

Goffman, E. (1967). *Presentation of self in everyday life.* New York: Doubleday.

Gouldner, A. W. (1970). About the functions of bureaucratic rules. In W. Scott (Ed.), *Social processes and social structures* (pp. 320–328). New York: Holt, Rinehart, & Winston.

Greenfield, T. B. (1968). Research on the behavior of educational leaders: Critique of a tradition. *Alberta Journal of Educational Research, 14*(1), 55–76.

Greenfield, W. D. (1982). Empirical research on principals: The state of the art. Paper presented at the Annual Meeting of the American Educational Research Association, New York City (ERIC ED 224–178).

Griffiths, D. E. (1979). Another look at research on the behavior of administrators. In G. Immegart & W. Boyd (Eds.), *Problem-finding in educational administration* (pp. 41–62). Lexington, MA: Lexington.

Gronn, P. (1984) On studying administrators at work. *Educational Administration Quarterly, 20*(1), 115–129.

Hall, G. E., & Rutherford, W. L. (1983, April). *Three change facilitator styles: How principals affect improvement efforts.* Paper presented at the Annual Meeting of the American Educational Research Association, Montreal, Canada.

Haller, E. J., & Knapp, T. R. (1985). Problems and methodology in educational administration. *Educational Administration Quarterly, 21*(3), 157–168.

Halpin, A. (1957). *The leadership behavior of the school superintendent* (School Community Development Study Monograph #4). Columbus, OH: Ohio State University.

Halpin, A. (1966). *Theory and research in administration.* New York: Macmillan.

Halpin, A., & Winer, B. J. (1957). A factorial study of leader behavior descriptions. In R. M. Stogdill and A. E. Coons (Eds.), *Leader behavior; Its description and measurement* (pp. 38–51). Columbus, OH: Bureau of Business Research, Ohio State University.

Herda, E. (1978). *Implications of a critical discussion in educational administration theory: The Griffiths-Greenfield debate from a philosophy of science perspective* (Doctoral dissertation, University of Oregon).

Herriott, R. E., & Firestone, W. A. (1984). Two images of schools as organizations: A refinement and elaboration. *Educational Administration Quarterly, 20*(4), 41–57.

Hoy, W., Newland, W., & Blazovsky, R. (1977). Subordinate loyalty to superior, espirit, and aspects of bureaucratic structure. *Educational Administration Quarterly, 13*(1), 71–85.

Immegart, G. L. (1977). The study of educational administration, 1954–1974. In L. Cunningham, W. Hack, & R. Nystrand (Eds.), *Educational administration: The developing decades* (pp. 298–328). Berkeley: McCutchan.

Immegart, G., & Boyd, W. L. (1979). *Problem finding in educational administration.* Lexington, MA: Lexington.

Keeler, B. T., & Andrews, J. H. M. (1963). The leader behavior of principals, staff morale and productivity. *Alberta Journal of Educational Research, 9*(3), 179–190.

Kerlinger, F. (1973). *Foundations of behavioral research.* New York: Holt, Rinehart, & Winston.

Kerr, S., & Jermier, J. M. (1978). Substitutes for leadership: Their meaning and measurement. *Organizational Behavior and Human Performance, 22*(3), 375–403.

Kunz, D. W., & Hoy, W. K. (1976). Leadership style of principals and the professional zone of acceptance of teachers. *Educational Administration Quarterly, 12*(3), 49–64.

Larson, L. L., Busson, R. S., & Vicars, W. M. (1981). The nature of superintendents's work: Final technical report. Carbondale, IL: Southern illinois University.

Leithwood, K. A., & Montgomery, D. J. (1982). The role of the elementary school principal in program improvement. *Review of Educational Research, 52*(3), 309–339.

Lightfoot, S. L. (1983). *The good high school: Portraits of character and culture.* New York: Basic.

Likert, R. (1967). *The human organization: Its management and values.* New York: McGraw-Hill.

Lincoln, I, & Guba, E. (1985). *Naturalistic inquiry.* Beverly Hills, CA: Sage.

Luthans, F., & Lockwood, D. L. (1984). Toward an observational system for measuring leader behavior in natural settings. In J. G. Hunt & C. A. Schreisheim (Eds.), *Leaders and managers: International perspectives on managerial behavior and leadership.* (pp. 117–141). New York: Pergamon.

March, J. C., & March, J. G. (1977). Almost random careers: The Wisconsin school superintendency, 1940–1972. *Administrative Science Quarterly, 22*(3), 377–409.

Martin, W. J., & Willower, D. J. (1981). The managerial behavior of high school principals. *Educational Administration Quarterly, 17*(1), 69–80.

Martinko, M., & Gardner, W. (1984). The behavior of high performing educational managers: An observational study. Tallahassee, FL: Department of Management, Florida State University.

McNamara, J. F. (1979). Practical significance and statistical models. *Educational Administration Quarterly, 14*(1), 48–63.

Metz, M. (1978). *Classrooms and corridors.* Berkeley: University of California Press.

Miles, M. B., & Huberman, A. M. (1984). *Qualitative data analysis.* Beverly Hills, CA: Sage.

Mintzberg, H. (1973). *The nature of managerial work.* New York: Harper & Row.

Miskel, C. G. (1977a). Principals' attitudes toward work and co-workers, situational factors, perceived effectiveness, and innovation effort. *Educational Administration Quarterly, 13*(2), 51–70.

Miskel, C. G. (1977b). Principals' perceived effectiveness, innovation effort, and the school situation. *Educational Administration Quarterly, 13*(1), 31–46.

Morey, N., & Luthans, F. (1984). An emic perspective and ethno-science methods for organizational research. *Academy of Management Review, 9*(1), 27–36.

Morphet, E. L., & Schutz, W. C. (1966). *Procedures for identifying persons with potential for public school administrative positions.* U.S. Dept. of Health, Education and Welfare, Office of Education Cooperative Research Project No. 1076. Berkeley: University of California Press.

Morris, V., Crowson, R., Porter-Gehrie, C., & Hurwitz, E. (1984). *Principals in action.* Columbus, OH: Charles E. Merrill.

Natriello, G. (1984). Teachers' perception of the frequency of evaluaton and assessments of their effort and affectiveness. *American Educational Research Journal, 21*(3), 579–595.

Nirenberg, J. (1977). A comparison of the management systems of a traditional and alternative public high school. *Educational Administration Quarterly, 13*(1), 86–104.

Ogden, E. H., Fowler, W. J., & Kunz, D. W. (1982). *A study of strategies to increase student achievement in low achieving schools.* Paper presented at the Annual Meeting of the American Educational Research Association, New York.

Packard, J. S., Charles, W. W., Jr., Duckworth, K., & Jovick, T. (1978). *Management implications of team teaching.* Eugene, OR: Center for Educational Policy and Management, University of Oregon.

Parsons, T. (1960). *Structure and process in modern society.* Glencoe, IL.: Free Press.

Pedhazur, E. J. (1982). *Multiple regression in behavioral research.* New York: Holt, Rinehart, & Winston.

Persell, C. (1982). *Effective principals: What do we know from various educational literatures?* Washington, DC: National Institute of Education.

Peterson, K. (1977–1978). The principal's tasks. *Administrator's Notebook, 26*(8), 1–4.

Peterson, K. (1984). Mechanisms of administrative control over managers in educational organizations. *Administrative Science Quarterly, 29*(4), 573–597.

Peterson, P. (1976). *School politics, Chicago style.* Chicago: University of Chicago Press.

Pitner, N. J. (1981) Hormones and harems: Are the activities of superintending different for a woman? In P. Schmuck, W. W. Charters, Jr., & R. O. Carlson (Eds.), *Educational policy and management: Sex differentials* (pp. 273–296). New York: Academic.

Pitner, N. J. (1982a, April). *Principal influence of teacher behavior: Substitutes for leadership.* Paper presented at the Annual Meeting of the American Educational Research Association, New York.

Pitner, N. J. (1982b). *Training of the school administrator: State of the art.* Eugene, OR: Center for Educational Policy and Management, University of Oregon.

Pitner, N. J. (1986). Substitutes for principal leadership behavior: An exploratory study. *Educational Administration Quarterly, 21*(2), 23–42.

Pitner, N. [J.], & Charters, W. W., Jr. (1984). *Principal influence on teacher behavior: Substitutes for leadership.* Eugene, OR: Center for Educational Policy and Management, University of Oregon.

Pitner, N. J., & Hocevar, D. (1986, April). An empirical investigation of the multidimensional nature of principal leadership. Paper presented at the annual meeting of the American Educational Research Association, San Francisco.

Pitner, N. J., & Ogawa, R. T. (1981). The school superintendent: A case of organizational leadership. *Educational Administration Quarterly, 17*(2), 45–65.

Pitner, N. J., & Russell, J. (1985–1986). Structured observation of school administrator work activities: Methodological limitations and recommendations for research, Parts I and II. *Educational Research Quarterly, 10*(2) 13–24.

Purkey, S. C., & Smith, M. S. (1983). Effective schools—A review. *Elementary School Journal, 83*(4), 427–452.

Ramey, M., Hillman, L., & Matthews, T. (1982). *School characteristics associated with instructional effectiveness.* Paper presented at the Annual Meeting of the American Educational Research Association, New York.

Rasmussen, R. L. (1976). The principal's leadership behavior in unusually successful and unsuccessful elementary schools. *Educational Research Quarterly, 1*(1), 18–29.

Rowan, B. (1984). Shamanistic rituals in effective schools. *Issues in Education, 2*(1) 76–87.

Rowan, B., Bossert, S., & Dwyer, D. (1983). Research on effective schools: A cautionary note. *Educational Researcher, 12*(4), 24–31

Rowan, B., & Denk, C. (1984). Management succession, school socioeconomic context, and basic skills attainment. *American Educational Research Journal, 21*(3), 517–537.

Rowan, B., Dwyer, D., & Bossert, S. (1982, April). Methodological considerations in studies of effective principals. Paper presented at the annual meeting of the American Educational Research Association, New York.

Rutter, M., Maugham, B., Ouston, J., & Smith, A. (1979). *Fifteen thousand hours: Secondary schools and their effects on children.* Cambridge, MA: Harvard University Press.

Sanday, P. R. (1979). The ethnographic paradigm. In J. Van Maanen (Ed.), *Qualitative Methodology* (pp. 19–36). Beverly Hills, CA: Sage.

Schreisheim, C. A., & Kerr, S. (1977). Theories and measures of leadership: A critical appraisal. In J. G. Hunt & L. L., Larson (Eds.) *Leadership: The cutting edge* (pp. 9–44). Carbondale, IL: Southern Illinois University Press.

Silver, P. (1975). Principals' conceptual ability in relation to situation and behavior. *Educational Administration Quarterly, 11*(3), 49–66.

Silver, P. (1981). The development of a knowledge base for the practice of educational administration. *Administrator's Notebook, 29*(2), 1–4.

Smith, J. R., & Heshusius, L. (1986). Closing down the conversation: The end of the quantitative-qualitative debate. *Review of Educational Research, 15*, 4–12.

Van Maanen, J. (1979). Reclaiming qualitative methods for organizational research. *Qualitative Methodology* (pp. 9–18). Beverly

Hills, CA: Sage.

Weber, G. (1971). Inner city children can be taught to read: Four successful schools. (Occasional Paper 18). Washington, DC: Council for Basic Education.

Weil, M., Marshalek, B., Mitman, A., Murphy, J., Hallinger, P., & Pruyn, J. (1984, April). Effective and ineffective schools: How different are they? Paper presented at the Annual Meeting of the American Eductional Research Association, New Orleans.

Wellisch, J. B., MacQueen, A. H., Carriere, R. A., & Duck, G. A. (1978). School management and organization in effective schools. *Sociology of Education*, *51*(3), 211–226.

Wiggins, T. (1972). A comparative investigation of principal behavior and school climate. *The Journal of Educational Research*. *66*(3), 103–105.

Willower, D. (1979). Some issues in research on school organiza-
tions. In G. Immegart & W. Boyd (Eds.), *Problem-finding in educational administration* (pp. 63–86). Lexington, MA: Lexington.

Wolcott, H. (1973). *The man in the principal's office: An ethnography*. New York: Holt, Rinebart, & Winston.

Yukl, G. (1981). *Leadership in organizations*. Englewood Cliffs, NJ: Prentice-Hall.

Yukl, G. (1984). Assessment of alternative methods for measuring leader behavior. Paper presented at the Annual Meeting of the American Psychological Association, Toronto, Canada.

Yukl, G. A., & Nemeroff, W. (1979). Identification and measurement of specific categories of leadership behavior: A progress report. In J. G. Hunt & L. L. Larson (Eds.), *Crosscurrents in leadership*. Carbondale, IL: Southern Illinois University Press.

CHAPTER 6

Women in Educational Administration

Flora Ida Ortiz and Catherine Marshall

FOUR THEMES: PATTERNS IN THE DEVELOPMENT OF EDUCATIONAL ADMINISTRATION

Educational administration has developed as a profession occupied by men rather than women even though the number of women in teaching far exceeds the number of men. Examination of the historical record, research reports, and school practices reveals that four themes dominate the development of educational administration as a field for men but not for women.

The first theme is that teaching and administration have become separate but mutually dependent professions. The second is that schools followed the lead of the turn-of-the-century municipal reform to become more hierarchical as well as professional (Callahan, 1967; Tyack & Hansot, 1982; Waldo, 1955). Heavy emphasis on efficiency and, essentially, a misreading of Taylor's scientific management turned schools into competitive bureaucracies, rather than collaborative service organizations, emphasizing control over instruction. The third theme is that careers in school administration rested on sponsorship rather than on open competition (Griffiths, Goldman, & McFarland, 1965; Turner, 1960; Valverde, 1974). Finally, knowledge, theory, research, and policy in educational administration coalesced into a social and political structure that discouraged discussion of gender and power issues.

Consultant/reviewers; Judith Adkison, North Texas State University; Patricia Schmuck, Lewis and Clark University; and Laurence Iannaccone, University of California–Santa Barbara

Separate, Mutually Dependent Professions

Teaching has been and continues to be primarily a women's profession, with a static career potential. In contrast, educational administration is primarily staffed by men, who enjoy highly differentiated career possibilities. Over time, the structure of school organizations has become characterized by the emergence and growth of two mutually dependent professions: teaching and administering. The ranks of teachers are large, occupied more by women than men, all remaining near the bottom of the policy-making hierarchy. The ranks of administrators are much smaller, occupied almost exclusively by men, who control the structure and the values in the organizations. In brief, the general pattern in schools is that many women teach and a few men supervise, evaluate, and manage. The pattern took stronger form as bureaucratization increased in schools.

Historically, several factors contributed to structuring schools along the male endeavors of administering and the female services of instructing. Influential commissions like the Committee of Ten of 1892, as well as other bodies established to draft proposals on the superintendency, included only men. Recommendations like those made by Mowry (1895) stressed the importance of adopting a business model for education and employing professional experts as school administrators, by implication at the time limiting the field to men. As Callahan (1967) reported, the Draper report stressed the importance of managing the business and supervising instruction as the two fundamental tasks of superintendents, again by implication the work of men. The domination of graduate education and textbook writing by schoolmen during the early 1900s, when school administrators "centered their attention almost exclusively upon the financial, organizational and mechanical problems of schooling" (Callahan, 1967, p. 208), further supported task differentiation by gender.

A characteristic instance of the historical development of men's control of the educational establishment appear in the records of the National Education Association (NEA). As of 1857 the constitution extended membership to gentlemen occupied in teaching and "ladies were eligible to honorary membership only, and were not allowed to speak from the Association's platform, but it was permitted that they have papers presented for them by gentlemen who were members" (Schmid, 1963, p. 23).

By 1866 women had gained admission to full membership primarily to cure the financial problems of the NEA. In 1870, the NEA added two new departments (Normal School and Superintendence) to the existing ones (Elementary Education and Higher Education). Eventually, the Department of Superintendence, composed almost entirely of men, gained the most influence and power.

Gender conflict within the NEA emerged among (a) an old guard consisting of W. T. Harris, Nicholas Murray Butler, Aaron Gove, James M. Greenwood, Newton C. Dougherty, and F. Louis Soldan; (b) insurgents representing educational journalists such as Carrol G. Pearse, E. O. Vaile, S. Y. Gillan, and A. E. Winship; and (c) classroom teachers led by Margaret A. Haley, Grace Strachan, and Katherine Blake. "For a time," according to Schmid (1963), "Ella Flagg Young lent her support" (p. 51). The conflict centered around the leadership's neglect of classroom teachers' welfare and the preoccupation of the NEA's leaders with controlling the membership and offices of the most influential units. In 1904, Margaret Haley, leader of the Chicago Teachers' Federation, gained a place on the NEA's convention platform during a session on democracy in education. Schmid (1963) writes, "She was, so far as can be determined, the first classroom teacher to deliver a major address before the Association. It was titled, 'Why Should Teachers Organize?'" (p. 125). But the tactics of NEA leaders, including creating situations in which women speakers were ridiculed and nominating women candidates who were unprepared for the public speaking required in the election process, temporarily undermined the credibility of both women leaders and the movement to open the NEA to full discussion of teachers' concerns.

By 1915, the insurgents had wrested control of the NEA from the old guard. Callahan (1967), Tyack and Hansot (1982), and Schmid (1963) have described the successful challenge to the old guard and the rise of Ella Flagg Young to the presidency of the NEA. Schmid recounts: "The actual planning and the execution of the campaign was largely accomplished by Margaret Haley, Grace Strachan, and A. E. Winship" (p. 173), supported by the journalists and a coalition of active classroom teacher members from New York and Chicago. An old-guard account of events of 1910 includes a comment that "the one regrettable feature of the meeting was the election of Mrs. Ella Flagg Young of Chicago to the presidency" (Schmid, 1963, p. 178). In 1911, Pearse was elected President, Katherine Blake, Treasurer, and Young became a member of the Executive Committee. The insurgents strengthened their control over the next few years, when James Y. Joiner was elected to the Board of Trustees.

The changing of the guard led to openly expressed fears that the NEA would come to be completely dominated by women classroom teachers. Schmid notes that "Pearse forestalled this by a series of manipulations the first of which was to change the meeting place for the 1912 convention" (p. 191). Holding the convention in Chicago instead of New York served to "stop the drive of the New York teachers to make Grace Strachan president of the Association" (p. 192). Pearse's strategy effectively took from the women their potential control when the choice of Fairchild, "acceptable to all men, including the old guard, was clearly aimed at returning to the men, albeit a different group of men, the control of the body they had so long enjoyed" (pp. 203–204). Thus, the control of the NEA remained with men, at least for several more years.

Subsequently, the NEA did reorganize. Margaret Haley successfully promoted the establishment of a new Department of Classroom Teachers, a structural change that enhanced opportunities for women to play more prominent and politically visible roles in NEA affairs. Mary C. Bradford assumed the presidency in 1917, a year when only women competed. After 1917, there was a tacit agreement that every other year the president would be a woman. The NEA has scrupulously observed the agreement.

When George Strayer became President in 1918, the NEA shifted its concerns to the growth of the association and school administration. Appeals to "professionalism" by NEA's leadership successfully diverted the membership's attention from emphasis on teacher welfare. Schmid (1963) argues that the NEA's promulgation of a strong ethos of professionalism, heightened and sharpened by its struggle against the American Federation of Teachers (AFT), promoted teachers' subservience to administrators and school boards and acceptance of conditions of hierarchical control.

The history of the formative years of education uncovers the processes and the meaning of the development of a social system in which men secured and continue to retain control of the power structures, women's roles are undermined, and administration is separated from teaching. The story also reveals how municipal reform and admiration for the corporate executive model helped to establish administration as the more valuable, powerful, and responsible of the two mutually dependent professions. Reform and adoption of the business model, in which administrators and professors of administration controlled the structure, the knowledge, and the values for education, took place without much interference from the community, minority groups, teachers, or even from school boards.

Municipal Reform and the Increased Emphasis on Efficiency, Control, and Hierarchy

At the turn of the 20th century, the municipal reform movement gave rise to increased hierarchical administration. The movement aimed to replace political influences with the leadership of experts in city and school governance. Emphasis on professionalism, expertise, and scientific-management ideologies displaced concern for representing constituents. Callahan (1967) and Tyack and Hansot (1982) report how business managers, school board members, and other social groups encouraged school administrators to become more professional, to apply scientific-management ideologies in their work, and to build power on neutral, apolitical expertise separate from the politics of the community. Iannaccone (1982) comments:

> The municipal reform movement reveals social class bias both with composition of its leadership and in its political ideology. The same class bias characterized its educational reform membership and its ideology of educational governance reflected the same corporate model. Its administrative image reflected the same corporate model and its delivery system was based on factory analogies. (p. 298)

Callahan (1967) wrote, "America in 1925 was a business society. Americans wanted their schools run in a businesslike way" (p. 6). He further explains that during the period from 1865 to 1910 the superintendent was seen and saw himself as a scholar-educator type, an educational leader, and a teacher of teachers. From 1910 to 1929 the superintendent was seen and saw himself as a combination business manager-school executive type.

The office of the superintendent was established because of the "sheer increase in the number of schools [and, of course, of teachers and of students] and the continuously increasing complexity of the educational task" (Callahan, 1967, p. 12). Graduate schools of education, especially Teachers College, Columbia University, state and national associations, and educational journals promulgated uniform understandings about how to deal with common problems.

Administrators created the myth of neutral professional competence, adopting the scientific management movement, as described by Waldo (1955), "to discover the One Best Way to perform complex human operations" (p. 18), and emphasizing in schools the operational goals of efficiency, financial savings, standardization, and control of complex operations.

It was in the cities, with their high schools, their longer school years, and greater population growth and mix, that the superintendency really flourished. Callahan (1967) cites "the sheer numbers of students to be educated, the increasing effort to provide a better quality of education, plus the inadequate financial arrangement we have had for supporting our schools" (pp. 32–33) as the factors that most contributed to the shaping of the superintendency.

Access Through Sponsorship

The separation of administration from teaching that evolved during the late 19th and early 20th centuries has been maintained by informal selection and socialization processes for administrators. State credential requirements have established teaching experience as a prerequisite for an administrator license, but the sponsorship of other administrators and/or strategically located professors of educational administration commonly decides who moves into a particular post. Griffiths et al. (1965), Valverde (1974), and Wolcott (1973), among others, have described how applicants become administrators. They report that sponsorship plays a deciding role in administrative careers and that it limits the play of open competition. Valverde (1974) specifically shows how sponsorship has operated to exclude women and minorities. Marshall (1979), Ortiz (1982), and others have demonstrated how even fully qualified women have been denied access to administrative positions because they were unable to obtain suitable sponsorship.

As a practice, sponsorship has historical roots as well as modern applications. Tyack and Hansot (1982) report how Cubberly "sponsored" many practitioners, including his students. Callahan (1967) describes how Strayer placed his students in administrative or university posts. The study of the NEA by Schmid (1963) shows how organization leaders supported and drew each other into prominent administrative posts across the country as well as in the association itself. In brief, educational administration has a well-developed history of sponsoring both new entrants and the further mobility of experienced participants. Women have not enjoyed the benefits of the sponsorship process, a condition that contributed materially to distinguishing teaching from administration by gender.

Educational institutions, like many other complex organizations, have taken hierarchical form, displaying varying degrees of bureaucratization and emphasizing control and competition rather than the form and character of collaborative or cooperative service organizations. The work of administrators who maintain hierarchical control is valued over that of educators who view collaboration and cooperation as more suitable in the operation of schools. To the extent that women fall in the latter group, they run the risk of being overlooked by sponsors, historically male, who adhere to the dominant view of control and competition.

Past and current operation of the traditional sponsorship process has contributed not only to structural tension between instructional goals and school management but also to the related exclusion of women from administration. Renewed emphasis in the 1980s on instructional leadership, stimulated by the "excellence movement," may redress the balance of value between teaching and managing. Also, given the historical accent by women on the former and by men on the latter, it may reorient the direction and operation of sponsorship. To date, however, sponsorship has contributed to the perpetuation of school-based professions divided by gender into separated instruction and management camps.

The Management of Knowledge

The final theme in the development of educational administration is the management of knowledge. As explicated by Bates (1983), Greenfield (1979), and Iannaccone (1982), knowledge in educational administration passes through the filters of professors and practitioners, who maintain control by judging the relevance, credibility, adequacy, and fit of theory, research, and interpretations.

Therefore, the transformation of school systems to acceptance of the myth of control of apolitical professional administrators and the separation of administration from teaching was accompanied by an acceptance of knowledge emphasizing hierarchical control and efficiency. Theory, research methods, structures, and people that challenged the dominant goals or sought to open the system to alternative views tended to be discredited or denied access to the system. As Bates (1983) says, "the selection and organization of knowl-

edge by subordinate cultural groups is inevitably evaluated as inferior, inadequate, or irrelevant" (p. 18). The dominant thought in educational administration emphasized organization of work into hierarchies and techniques for social control, reflecting the dominant societal values for schools "to act as agencies of behavioral control and agencies of vocational allocation" (Bates, 1983, p. 39). Theory, research, and training in educational administration has focused on issues like organizational size and structure and incentive systems for increased productivity of teachers, separating such issues from pedagogy and from questions about the fundamental goals of schooling. Foster (1980) notes that the texts in educational administration present school management itself as a fundamental purpose, with little attention to the goals of schooling, with little discussion of fundamental conflicts of class, power, and politics, and with no discussion of the function of schooling in controlling such conflicts.

The traditional management of knowledge in educational administration has had the combined effects of (a) separating educational administration from education; (b) blinding educators to inequities and incongruities that have become part of the accepted system of schooling; and (c) promoting a base of theory, research, and knowledge disconnected from the voices, needs, and realities of individuals who do not comply with or benefit from the ethos of hierarchical control. Conventional management knowledge has also inhibited the exploration or explanation of social-system characteristics that have maintained the separation of men from women in education and, particularly, the unequal access of women to significant administrative careers.

Thus, the management of knowledge has effectively contained and prevented educational administration from exploring fundamental questions or resolving fundamental systemic problems. Incongruities like supporting inequity in the system, displaying the fundamental work of schooling (teaching and learning), and making the maintenance of order predominant has left educational administration unprepared to deal with persistent social problems and emerging instructional demands.

This chapter is organized around these four themes: the development of two separate professions, the impact of municipal reform and the emphasis on hierarchical control, the importance of sponsorship, and the management of knowledge. The themes not only help to explain the status, the careers, and the research on women in education; they also place the issue of women in the field in the middle of the emerging critique of theory, research, and practice of educational administration.

THE STATUS OF WOMEN IN EDUCATIONAL ADMINISTRATION

Researchers have sought to explain the extent and character of women's participation by exploring women's status, career decision-making processes, experiences in organizational socialization and sponsorship, attitudes affecting their own careers, and their performance in groups and in leadership positions. Several scholars have also critically analyzed theory and research and have demonstrated the blindness of organizational theorists to the perspectives and contributions of women in organizations.

Women in Administrative Positions

Available historical data on women principals show a steady decline. Women constituted 55 percent of elementary principals in 1928, 41 percent in 1948, 38 percent in 1958, 22.4 percent in 1968, and 19.6 percent in 1973 (Johnson, 1973). In 1979, the American Association of School Administrators (AASA) reported that women held 18 percent of elementary principalships in 1978 and projected a level of 11 percent in 1980. Data on women in other administrative positions, such as the superintendency and high school principalship, were not consistently recorded in the first half of the 20th century.

In the decades of the 1970s and 1980s, the greatest number of women in educational administration occupied central-office positions. NEA data for 1970–1971 show the following participation rates for women: 37.5 percent of all central-office administrators; 38.3 percent of administrators in instructional and supervisory areas; and 48.2 percent in general administration (that is, administration of matters other than personnel or finance). The 1972–1973 NEA report reveals a drop in the overall figure to 35 percent, but an increase from 2.9 percent in 1970–1971 to 5.3 percent in 1972–1973 in the proportion of women assistant superintendents. However, the percentage of women deputy superintendents and general superintendents declined from 7.5 percent and 0.6 percent respectively in 1970–1971 to 6.2 percent and 0.1 percent in 1972–1973. In 1980, of some 16,000 district superintendents, only 154 (less than 1 percent) were women. The Women's National Advisory Council on Women (1981) projected a slight increase, to 169 by April 1981, and 173 by July 1981, in the number of women superintendents. Another recent report (AASA, 1981) shows that 9 percent of superintendents were women in 1950, 1 percent in 1972, and an estimated 0.5 percent for 1980.

Even where gains have occurred or are projected, care must be exercised in viewing the data (see *Educa-*

tion Week, 1984; *Quality Education Data*, 1984). For example, J. W. Jones has identified the importance of looking at the specifics of district size, type of population, and budget. As she documents, the recent increase in the number of women superintendents has occurred primarily in very small districts or involves minority women in urban districts that enroll predominantly minority students.

Data from the Equal Employment Opportunity Commission (EEOC) (1977) delineate differences among minority and majority populations as well as between men and women in administrative positions. Table 6.1 reveals that minority men were more likely in the 1970s to attain line administrative positions than were minority women. Table 6.2 updates the earlier report and confirms continuation of the patterns of more minority men than women and the overwhelming dominance of white men in number and proportion of administrative positions.

Even the most generous analysis of recent trends says that women have remained, and are likely to remain for some time, predominantly in teaching and in administrative posts most closely connected with instruction. Recent decades have witnessed advancement of exceptional individuals but no reversal of the pattern strongly established long ago in the social system of the professions. Even the minute movement that has occurred in the special cases of large urban districts and of the smallest districts does not represent a significant change in the predominant pattern. Given the persistently large number of women who teach, women who manage represent a trace element in administration. Women, especially minority women but even minority men, continue to occupy the lowest positions in the administrative hierarchy, white males the higher and the more powerful positions. This long-standing pattern has, in turn, shaped the sponsorship process that is so crucial for women and minorities who seek administrative careers. In sum, no significant alteration of prevailing organizational structures and dynamics has occurred.

Women's Career Decisions and Advanced Degrees

The examination of the career choices and directions of women educators provides a view of women's responses to a system where sponsored mobility provides differential access and where competition and control displace instructional goals. Griffiths et al. (1965) identified the importance of GASing (Getting the Attention of Superiors) for promoting mobility. GASing involves affiliating with superiors, exhibiting like attitudes and abilities, and taking extra responsibilities to demonstrate readiness for administrative assignment. But Valverde (1974) demonstrated that spon-

Table 6.1   Percentages of Women, Minority Women, and Minority Men by Ethnicity in Selected Administrative Positions in Public Elementary and Secondary Schools, 1974, 1976, and 1978

SUBGROUPS	CENTRAL-OFFICE EXECUTIVE POSITIONS			PRINCIPALS			NONTEACHING ASSISTANT PRINCIPALS			CONSULTANTS/ SUPER. INST.		
	1974	1976	1978[a]	1974	1976	1978[a]	1974	1976	1978[a]	1974	1976	1978[a]
Percentage women	14.1	16.6	17.5	12.7	13.0	13.3	18.5	18.3	22.2	50.4	51.6	54.6
Percentage minority women	2.3	3.0	3.2	2.2	2.6	2.8	5.1	5.4	5.4	9.3	11.0	11.0
Black women	1.9	2.4	2.4	2.0	2.3	2.4	4.7	4.8	4.7	7.8	8.7	8.1
Hispanic women	0.3	0.5	0.5	0.1	0.2	0.3	0.3	0.4	0.6	1.2	1.7	1.9
Asian women	*	0.1	0.1	*	*	0.1	0.1	0.1	0.1	0.2	0.3	0.4
Native American women	*	0.1	0.2	*	*	0.1	*	*	*	0.1	0.3	0.9
Percentage minority men	5.0	5.8	5.8	7.1	7.6	7.3	12.7	13.6	13.8	4.8	5.0	5.4
Black men	3.6	3.7	3.6	5.7	5.8	5.6	11.0	11.4	11.4	3.5	3.5	3.6
Hispanic men	1.0	1.6	1.7	1.0	1.3	1.3	1.2	1.8	2.0	1.0	1.1	1.1
Asian men	0.1	0.1	0.2	0.1	0.1	0.1	0.2	0.2	0.2	0.1	0.2	0.6
Native American men	0.3	0.4	0.3	0.1	0.4	0.3	0.2	0.2	0.2	0.1	0.2	0.2

* Less than 0.05 percent.
[a] These percentages are estimated because data are not included for several large school systems.
NOTE. Percentages may not add to subgroup total percentages because of rounding errors.
NOTE. From *Employment Opportunity in the Schools: Job Patterns of Minorities and Women in Public Elementary and Secondary Schools* by the Equal Employment Opportunity Commission, 1977, Washington, DC: U.S. Government Printing Office. Copyright 1977 by U.S. Government Printing Office. Reprinted by permission.

Table 6.2   Racial/Ethnic and Sex Percentage Distribution of School administrators, 1981–1982

POSITION	MALE				FEMALE			
	White	Black	Hispanic	Other	White	Black	Hispanic	Other
Superintendents	96.5	0.7	1.1	0.4	1.2	0.1	0.1	0.0
Assistant superintendents	82.3	5.3	3.3	0.6	7.0	1.2	0.3	0.1
Principals	75.4	5.2	2.8	0.8	12.5	2.5	0.6	0.2
School administrators	68.2	5.1	2.2	0.8	18.9	3.6	0.8	0.3

NOTE. From *Recent Trends in the Representation of Women and Minorities in School Administration and Problems in Documentation* by Effie H. Jones and Xenia Montenegro, 1982, Arlington, VA: Office of Minority Affairs, American Association of School Administrators. Reprinted by permission.

sorship is not readily available to minorities and women. So, as Marshall (1979) showed, women must create substitutes for sponsorship while they create alternate role definitions to make entry into administrative roles that are male-normed. It is in this context that women already in education make career choices.

Despite the consistent pattern of increase in numbers of women seeking the doctorate in educational administration, there are indications of shifts in women's choices of careers in the 1980s. Roberson, Keith, and Page (1983) and Schlecty and Vance (1981) document the fact that fewer women with high academic qualifications are choosing to make their careers in education. In addition, Jones and Montenegro (1982) found that women involved in programs intended to help them overcome barriers to entering school administration sometimes decide to leave public education as they learn more about the system and career possibilities.

In 1980, women earned 48 percent of all masters degrees and 20 percent of all doctorates (Neidig, 1980). The largest proportion of the latter group majored in educational administration. Table 6.3 shows that the number of doctorates in educational administration awarded to women has increased dramatically since 1955. By 1981–1982, women earned 555, or 39 percent, of all doctoral degrees awarded in the field, compared to only 11 percent in 1972 (Fishel & Pottker, 1975; National Research Council, 1973). In the period 1960–1969, only 13 percent of the doctorates in educational administration went to women, as compared to 26 percent in educational psychology and 21 percent in counseling (Council for University Women's Progress at the University of Minnesota, 1971; Pottker & Fishel, 1977).

Recent studies report that women doctoral students in educational administration, unlike their male counterparts, typically do not use their degrees to

Table 6.3 Educational Administration Degrees Granted

YEAR	DEGREE	TOTAL NUMBER	MALES	FEMALES
1955–1956	Educational administration	505	437	68
	Supervision			
	Comparative education			
	Curriculum			
	Counseling and guidance			
	Finance			
	Other nonteaching areas			
1960–1961	(Same categories as above)	483	413	70
1965–1966	Educational administration	633	574	59
	Supervision and finance			
1970–1971	Educational administration	957	875	82
1975–1976	Educational administration	1,497	1,204	293
1976–1977	Educational administration	1,497	1,171	326
1977–1978	Educational administration	1,432	1,073	359
1978–1979	Educational administration	1,381	969	412
1979–1980	Educational administration	1,468	984	484
1980–1981	Educational administration	1,593	977	616
1981–1982	Educational administration	1,423	858	555

NOTE. From: *Digest of Education Statistics*, 1975 and 1980. Washington, DC: National Center for Education Statistics, U.S. Department of HEW.

further careers in public school administration but instead find employment as consultants and researchers or in government service (McCarthy, 1979; Oller, 1979a, 1979b). As for credential programs, Edson (1979) found men overrepresented both in 1974–1975 and in 1978–1979, even though the proportion of women had increased significantly. "Thus, to enhance women's representation in school administration, it may be important for women to enter credential programs with the same frequency as men" (Edson, 1979, p. 86). A study by Marshall (1984) found that male doctoral students in educational administration were more likely than women to expect to use their degrees to move up in their current school organizations, whereas women expected the degree program to help them move to a new organization or to shift career focus. Still, some women view the university as a potential substitute for sponsorship that is problematic where they work (Marshall, 1979). These studies imply that women more than men depend on degree programs as sources of future sponsorship, whereas men more than women view credential programs as relevant because they can rely on traditional sponsorship arrangements.

Women in Education Policy Positions

The status of women in education policy positions mirrors their status in administration and reflects the four themes. A recent dramatic increase in the number of women school board members may, however, signal a shift in values toward instructional concerns and away from the dominance of control and efficiency.

The National School Boards Association (1974) reported in 1974 that women held 11.9 percent of the nation's school board positions, barely more than the 10.5 percent held by women in 1962, and that incumbent school board members, school administrators, and political parties were far more likely to discourage women than men from seeking office. However, a recent survey revealed that the presence of women on America's school boards rose by nearly 9 percent (28.3 percent to 37.1 percent) from 1982 to 1983 (*School Board News*, 1984). If the shift truly reflects women's concerns with instruction, it may signal the beginning of new conceptions of leadership, including a higher valuation of women's abilities. The increase may also set the stage for conflict over control of positions and knowledge similar to the struggle within the NEA in the early 1900s.

No comparable shifts have occurred in other education policy positions. Few women have occupied top positions in the U.S. Office of Education: In 1972 no women held Grade 18 positions, only two held Grade 17 positions, and only one held a Grade 16 position. The average grade for women was GS 7; the average grade for men was GS 14. The 1984 roster of the Department of Education confirms continuation of the preponderance of men in top positions (*Federal Staff Directory*, 1984), even though at a point during the 1970s women headed the Department of Health, Education and Welfare, the Department of Education, and the National Institute of Education.

Only 20 percent of the members of state boards of education were women in 1972, and 2 percent of the top state education positions (chief state school officer and deputy, associate, and assistant state superintendents) were women (Fishel & Pottker, 1974). In 1973, only two states, Montana and Wisconsin, had women state superintendents of public instruction (Taylor, 1973); by 1985, the number had increased to five states (S. Bailey & R. Smith, personal communication, July 1985).

Marr's study of state departments of education found that the number of women in policy-making positions had declined, from 14.5 percent in 1950 to an average of 6.8 percent in 1972 (Marr, 1973). The California State Department of Education, for one, had channeled women into positions, like nutrition, library services, and homemaking, that reflected women's traditional roles. Unfortunately, the status of women in state departments of education has not received recent study.

In 1973, even teachers associations were led by men, with both the AFT and the NEA headed by men, and with men serving as executive secretaries in all 50 state associations. Women made gains as state association presidents in 1973, occupying 33 percent of these positions (Taylor, 1973). By 1984, 12 of 43 AFT state chapters were headed by women presidents, and more than 50 percent of the senior officers and 33 percent of the national field staff were women (*AFT Fact Sheet*, 1983). On the NEA side, women occupied 56 percent of the state affiliate presidencies and 7 percent of the executive directorships (C. Elvin, personal communication, August 14, 1984; S. P. Taylor, personal communication, August 5, 1984). Thus, despite some gains by women, men remained in firm control of major policy positions in education.

Women in Educational Administration Professorships

The 1983–1984 *Educational Administration Directory*, which enumerates the faculties in departments granting degrees in educational administration, identifies approximately 200 women professors of educational administration in a listing of 2,553 professorships. Detailed information on some 196 of the 200 positions reveals that (a) 63 were temporary and 133 were permanent; (b) of the 133 permanent positions, 49 were at the assistant professor level, 50 at the associate professor level, and 34 at the full professor level. Of two females with Spanish surnames, one was listed as part time and one as a full-time associate professor (Lilley, 1984). Table 6.4 portrays the gender change

that occurred in the professorship from 1975 to 1983, indicating a 6 percent increase, but reflecting that more than half the 8 percent women faculty listed in 1983 were temporary and assistant professors.

Thus, the university, where educational administrators receive their formal training, presents a picture consistent with the pattern in schools; only trace numbers of women have secured positions that place them in a position to shape the goals of educational administration.

Overall, then, educational administration continues as a male profession. The strength of the traditional pattern suggests that women as trace elements in administration have become a social-system characteristic that has taken "constitutional" form (Sarason, 1982): that is, a part of organizational assumptions deeply rooted in society.

RESEARCH ON WOMEN

Organizational Socialization

The research on organizational socialization has tended to focus either on person-centered or organization-centered explanations. In the person-centered explanations, personal behavioral patterns, traits, and attitudes are described in terms of differential sex-role socialization in childhood and adolescence (Hennig & Jardim, 1977; Riger & Galligan, 1981).

The organization-centered explanations describe behaviors and attitudes in the work place as being conditioned by organizational structures (Kanter, 1977; Lockheed, 1975; Mayes, 1979; Riger & Galligan, 1981). Kanter's study suggests that "the critical factor for women may not be their gender but their number" (cited in Riger & Galligan, 1981, p. 905). When so few women are promoted within organizations, women overemphasize the job at hand, making it their major source of satisfaction and self-esteem. A competing notion is that women's emphasis on being well liked by co-workers is the result of the job situation they face. Having little chance of advancement, their sources of satisfaction do not come from the job itself but from the quality of their relationships with their co-workers. According to Kanter (1977), "Being well liked becomes

Table 6.4   Status of Women Professors of Educational Administration

PRIOR TO 1975	1975	1983
No available information; no evidence of research on, or concern for, the status.	Women constitute 2% of all professors of educational administration.	Women constitute 8% of all professors of educational administration. However, 56% of these women are in low-level and unstable positions.

another meaning of success to people in dead-end work" (p. 59).

Organizational socialization, the process of finding satisfying ways of fitting in, has profound implications for education and teaching. Lortie (1975) found, for example, that women teachers derive their greatest satisfaction from students' learning. The cellular structure of classroom teaching provides a setting for individuals to work alone but to engage informally in other relationships. The organization provides a structure that protects satisfying work for women teachers. Another body of literature has reported that leaving teaching for administration is more traumatic for women than for men (Blood, 1966; Marshall, 1979). Persistence in teaching represents satisfaction. Women value instruction and accept membership in the teacher work group that tends to resist male and administrator norms and to work divorced from instructional goals.

Marshall (1979) considers the interaction between the need for self-role congruence and institutional characteristics in her study of women school administrators' career decision making. Her work describes the processes encountered by women who persist in climbing the ladder to educational administration. The study identifies the transition phase, a crucial process in which women must create techniques, supports, and new definitions of self in order to fit the norms for administration. If successful in this endeavor, they must still convince organizational members of their worth. Hence, women's socialization for administration requires not only redefining administrative roles but also redefining self.

Given the relevance of the process to accessing administrative work, it is not surprising that much of the research dealing with women in educational administration focuses on socialization. The general conclusion drawn from the research is that different organizational incentives and values for men and women make for different patterns of socialization, both in process and results (Marshall, 1979; Ortiz, 1982). The data square with the themes of the separate but mutually dependent structures of teaching and administration and the practice of sponsorship.

Attitudes of and Toward Women

Examination of attitudes regarding women in school administration contributes to understanding both the socialization process and the sponsorship system. Some studies have sought to determine attitudes toward women administrators. Other studies have attempted to identify underlying beliefs that generate negative attitudes toward women. Still other studies present findings that illuminate the effects of negative attitudes toward women.

Taylor (1977) concluded that "the assumption that attitudes toward women in administrative positions represent a male-female issue is true" (p. 309). In her study she used two instruments: an Attitude Research Instrument (ARI) and a Background Data Questionnaire (BDQ). The subject sample included superintendents and school board members from 107 of Connecticut's 133 school districts. The usable returns included responses from 84 superintendents and 321 school board members. Taylor analyzed the data with one-way analysis of variance (p. 300). She found that "opportunities for women to pursue administrative careers were limited. Given a choice between men and women for line administrative positions, men would be selected" (p. 310).

Other attitudinal studies demonstrate the pervasive bias for men over women for school administrative positions. The preference manifests itself in less encouragement from superiors, less preparation and motivation on the part of women themselves, less self-selection by women, and the belief that women who progress in the administrative ranks must be "superhuman superwomen" bordering on the unearthly or unnatural (Fishel & Pottker, 1975; Johnston, Johnston, & Yeakey, 1977; Lahner, 1972; Sandorff & Nieto, 1979; Tipple, 1972). The attitudes of fellow workers toward females may also impede women's mobility (O'Leary, 1974). Basse, Krusell, and Alexander (1971) reported that men's negative attitudes toward women did not rest on beliefs that women are less competent or qualified but on the sentiment that the presence of women as colleagues or bosses upsets the traditional relationships between men and women (cited in Riger & Galligan, 1981).

Fishel and Pottker (1975) reviewed nine studies that addressed (a) teacher attitudes toward women principals, (b) the recruitment and hiring of women principals, and (c) the attitudes of women principals toward their jobs. The investigators found a consistent pattern of prejudice expressed by most male teachers, school superintendents, and school board members.

Women's aspirations reflect their realization of these attitudes. Nixon and Gue (1975) reported that more than 90 percent of a sample of women administrators in place expressed willingness to spend additional time on the job as compared to 70 percent of two samples of women teachers, one younger and one more experienced. They found no relationship between marital status and willingness to apply for administrative positions. The administrators also considered a career in school administration an interesting professional challenge, a view not shared widely by the teachers. The study suggests that women educators sense barriers and little opportunity, and they respond with lowered aspirations. Those who aspire to administration have undergone processes that separate them from women teachers in attitudes and aspirations. In a later and related study, Ortiz (1982) found that female teachers are cautious about showing ambition and that they learn not to show that they aspire to administration until they have gained tenure. The research on attitudes, then, identifies both values of the society and values of the educational system as sources of discouragement to women who consider the desirability of moving into administration.

Mobility

Schein's (1971) conceptualization of career mobility in organizations specifies the simultaneous availability of movement in three different directions: vertical, lateral, and radial. Vertical movement includes hierarchical advancement, title change, and salary increase; lateral movement includes task change (for example, from directing children to directing adults); and radial movement includes drawing closer to those who matter in the organization. Career movement is physical (e.g., a change of office closer to the superintendent); interaction patterns change (e.g., exchange with the superintendent, cabinet members, and school board members); and the new work may involve decision making and policy formulation and implementation. Most organizational movement is vertical and lateral, but ascension to the top organizational position requires radial movement as well.

Researchers looking at women's mobility in educational administration have applied Schein's notions in their analyses. The pertinent studies illustrate how career patterns influence the way individuals behave in a given organizational position.

Ortiz (1982) observed how school administrators follow the pattern Schein identified by moving simultaneously in three different directions: vertically, laterally, and toward the center of the organization. She used the difference between line and staff positions to identify specifically positions that halt and those that propel movement. She divided administrative positions into the categories of line or staff, site or central office, and secure or insecure. Then Ortiz delineated the sequence of positions that lead to the superintendency and identified the factors that determine how and why obtaining the superintendency eludes women. The potency of the secondary principalship becomes clear; even minority women ascend from it. The study also reveals the interdependency of personal attributes,

organizational characteristics, and the operative socialization processes for advancement into and within school administration.

Other inquiries into career mobility have emphasized either personal attributes, individual initiative and action, or institutional positions and their characteristics. Gaertner (1981) looked at the last of these. She used data collected in Michigan, "where between 1968 and 1973 extensive records were kept concerning the public schools ($n = 520$) and the people employed therein" (p. 204). Gaertner discovered that the two critical assessment points occurred at the entrance to a long career path and near the top. Both points share the characteristic of visibility, the need to demonstrate skills required at a higher level, and the potential for attracting sponsors. She reported that "people beginning as administrative specialists are more likely to leave the system rather than to move to another position within the system" (p. 205). The two exceptions to this trend were people who moved into principalships from assistant elementary and secondary principal positions.

Specifically, Gaertner (1981) found the following patterns of mobility into the superintendency: (a) specialist in instruction to administrator of instruction to assistant superintendent; (b) secondary assistant principal to principal; and (c) elementary assistant principal to principal. The third path, however, was weakly connected to the superintendency. She also identified three exit positions: (a) the superintendency itself; (b) the elementary principalship; and (c) the lowest-level instructional or curricular supervisor. The critical assessment positions included the posts of lowest-level instructional or curricular supervisor and assistant superintendent. Gaertner's perception that the patterns she discovered are deterministic is particularly pertinent because women are found in larger proportions in the more vulnerable exit and assessment positions.

Wheatley's (1981) study shows how individuals' behaviors, self-esteem, and investment reflect their sense of being in a stuck or a moving position. Organizational placements of individuals, then, become self-fulfilling prophecies.

Prolman (1983) concluded from her study of elementary principals that sex-role socialization does influence career choice and career pattern. It is the career pattern, though, and not the sex of the individual that influences differences in behavior, a condition also reported by Levinson (1982) for men.

Mobility from teaching to administration and within administration remains problematic for women despite research that shows them as successful as men in administrative work. The research findings are consistent with the long-standing bifurcation of education by gender that has routed women to instruction and men to administration. The institutional memory of education has confined women, despite changing patterns of experience, preparation, and aspiration, to instructional and child-centered units.

Study of mobility into and within school administration says that the process of reaching the superintendency is not, of itself, gender related. What is gender related, however, is the relaxation of efforts to encourage and support women in seeking the superintendency on the grounds of the modest improvement that has occurred in participation rates at lower-level positions. Because sponsorship is so necessary for career mobility, for men as well as women, full incorporation of women into a truly gender-unrelated sponsorship process remains critical. Significant movement on this front remains problematic as long as teaching and administration remain so characteristically related to gender. The available research convincingly establishes that men still move into and through the administrative career sequence in greater numbers and proportions than women.

Female School Administrators at Work

The studies that have contrasted the effectiveness of men and women school administrators have consistently reported several areas in which women do as well as or better than men. Over 20 years investigators have reported that women school administrators contribute to higher teacher performance and student achievement (Clement, Di Bella, Eckstrom, & Tobias, 1977; Fishel & Pottker, 1973; Gross & Trask, 1964, 1976; Manassee, 1982; Meskin, 1974; Pallante & Hinton, 1977; Tibbets, 1980; Wheatley, 1981). Wheatley (1981) concluded that women administrators "take a more active stance toward instructional leadership" (p. 269). Several investigators have observed that it is the use of more desirable supervisory practices that yields higher ratings for teachers in schools with women principals (Berman, 1982; Frasher & Frasher, 1979; Grobman & Hines, 1956; Sandorff & Nieto, 1979; Tibbets, 1980). Meskin (1974) and Fishel and Pottker (1975) found that women principals were more concerned than men with students' individual differences. Women principals have also demonstrated superior knowledge of teaching methods and have exhibited more concern with the objectives of teaching (Hemphill, Griffiths, & Fredericksen, 1962, cited in Cirincione-Coles, 1975; Fishel & Pottker, 1975; Lupini, 1975). In brief, the research has documented that women's educational leadership concentrates heavily on areas most closely aligned with the instructional tasks.

Work Styles

The work styles of school administrators have also received systematic attention, with appropriate distinctions between principals or school-site administrators and superintendents or central-office officials. Most of the studies on principals have concentrated at the elementary school level. Gilbertson (1981), for example, contrasted interaction patterns among male and female school administrators and found that male teachers were involved more frequently than female teachers in principal-teacher interaction. The male-male combination was particularly conducive to interaction, and the principal's office was the most common site of interaction. Male principals tended to consider the staff room a good place for interaction, whereas female principals did not. Most interactions were very brief, and principals, regardless of sex, initiated them more often than did teachers. The most popular topics of the interactions were organizational matters, particularly among males, who concerned themselves less with student affairs.

The Gilbertson findings illuminate two important themes. First, men incline more than women to "GAS" principals, regardless of gender. Conversely, principals, regardless of gender, initiated the interactions that provide the context of potential sponsorship. Second, males tend to interact more than women over organizational matters. The focus of women's interaction is more diffuse. Thus, the structure and the pattern of teacher-principal interaction, even where principals are women, serve to confirm traditional perceptions of organizational leadership potential.

Levinson (1982) found that, regardless of gender, principals who had taught in elementary schools emphasized instruction whereas principals who had taught in secondary schools emphasized administrative tasks like budgeting and school plant management. Given the disproportionate loading of women school administrators in the elementary school principalship, Levinson's data raise the question of whether women's concern with instruction may be as much dependent on experience as on gender, an interpretation supported by Gross and Trask (1976) that women's experience in teaching is much lengthier than men's. The additional experience may also contribute to women's greater facility in instruction and in dealing with supervision of matters related to instruction.

Two studies by Pitner (1978, 1981) have identified gender-related differences among superintendents (Pitner, 1981). In the first study, she observed three male superintendents in the suburbs of a large midwestern city; in the second, three female superintendents in the suburbs of two large cities on the West

Coast. Both studies focused on the "observed behavior rather than on the traits and capacities of superintendents and both focused on descriptions of types of behavior and frequency of occurrence rather than on evaluation of behavior" (1981, p. 274).

Pitner (1981) found the following: (a) Female superintendents interacted more with female groups such as the predominantly female Parent-Teacher Association, whereas the male superintendents communicated more with male groups such as the Elks, the Rotary and the Lions Clubs. (b) Female superintendents took care of their written correspondence and dictation in the evening at home, but males rarely did paper work at home. (c) Female superintendents averaged seven tours per week, each lasting about 30 minutes, whereas males averaged five tours per week, each lasting about 12 minutes. (d) Female superintendents visited classrooms and teachers to remain abreast of the instructional program, whereas male superintendents walked through the halls with the principals and the head custodians, requesting that they follow up on particular concerns. (e) Female superintendents expressed concern over the specific ideology and activities that dominated the district's curricular program, whereas the males attended more to issues of organizational structure. (f) Females differed in the way they established contact in four respects: they were more informal; they spent more time with community members who were not parents, such as the president of a local corporation; they interacted more frequently with their professional peers and almost exclusively with their female counterparts; and they formally involved themselves in the training of administrators as adjunct professors in local universities and in sponsoring women teachers in their districts for leadership positions within and outside their districts. Women also spent their unscheduled time handling curriculum and instructional matters, whereas men dealt with political activities such as campaigning for a candidate for office in the state affiliate of AASA, eating lunch in local restaurants, maintaining liaisons with the state department of education, and trying to capture the state teacher-of-the-year award for the district. (g) Female superintendents also tended toward greater informality. They were addressed by subordinates by their first names, whereas the male central-office administrators and principals were addressed by their last names. Informality was also evident during meetings with administrative staff; women assumed a more limited control of the agenda than did their male counterparts. They used an instant agenda, which they were willing to change to neutralize status differences, whereas males typically stayed with an agenda distributed several days in advance.

The differences between male and female superintendents that Pitner (1981) describes appear to derive from differences in previous work experiences, but her data neither confirm nor disconfirm such an interpretation. However, her findings do square with other reports about a heavier emphasis on organizational matters among men and a heavier emphasis on instruction among women. Pitner's data also suggest a stronger tendency on the part of women to ameliorate status differentiation.

Clark (1983) identified other gender differences in her study of men and women presidents of educational unions. More women (83 percent) than men (50 percent) classified governance activities as maintenance rather than leadership. Half the women presidents claimed to have spent more time on person-oriented activities, whereas one-third of the men said that they spent more time on task-oriented ones. All the female presidents but only one-half the male presidents preferred to avoid confrontation. Two-thirds of the men but only one-third of the women participated in political activities external to the role of association president. Women used more objective judgments in evaluating their own effectiveness, whereas men more often used subjective personal judgments.

Two major conclusions flow from the studies of superintendents and union presidents. First, men exert their leadership both within and without the organization; women, in contrast, exert their leadership within the organization and in those activities most closely associated with their roles. Second, men administer their organizations by interacting with influentials; women interact with members who bear primary responsibility for the conduct of organizational functions.

Summary

The study of women's attitudes toward career mobility reveals a pattern of devaluation in the attitudes of relevant others, avoidance of separation from instructional concerns, and a corresponding lowering of aspiration. The literature on organizational socialization and mobility confirms the problematic nature of sponsorship but also points to the potential of examining women's socialization more closely to uncover how women redefine administrative roles. What is learned may provide useful insights into alternative perspectives on school administration. The literature on female administrators' performance not only highlights their emphasis on instruction but calls loud attention to the promise of more tightly coupling managing and teaching by emphasis on instructional leadership. Finally, invocation of the four themes of the development of educational administration has enlarged the meaning of the study of women's status and problems of access and inextricably tied that study to the larger issues in the field.

THE GENDER QUESTION
AND EDUCATIONAL POLICY

To what extent are the assumptions of policy makers and policy implementers associated with the persistence of theories, values, and structures that have kept women in teaching and out of administration? Policy is formulated within the context of policy makers' sense of what is appropriate, necessary, valued, and possible. Myths, beliefs, traditions, and customs make up the main architecture of policy makers' assumptive worlds (Raab, 1982). Operative assumptions in education appear to have included bureaucratic control, the tradition of male leadership, and reliance on the existing system for implementation of policy. All formal policies have the legitimacy conferred by the authority of the governing body that enacted them. Not all policies have moral legitimacy, however (Habermas, 1975). When a policy conflicts with the ideological assumptions, values, and needs of powerful and/or large numbers of people, it will probably not earn moral legitimacy. Policy also is formulated within the framework of the prevailing theory and assumptions about the nature of the problem and appropriate mechanisms and supports for solving the problem. Policy makers' incorporation of theory and research depends upon whether theory and research fit with past experience (Lindblom & Cohen, 1979).

Therefore, analysis of sex-equity policy requires examination of the political pressures, the prevailing assumptions about the problem and the traditional solutions, and the power and values of those affected by the problem. Policy makers and implementers, from legislators to site administrators, "lay meaning" on the policy, redefine the value of the problem, and determine the amount of resources devoted to solving it (Sproull, 1981; Weatherley & Lipsky, 1977; Wirt & Kirst, 1972). Accordingly, policy analysis must include consideration of the value system of the people entrusted with administering the implementation of the policy, the amount of resources allocated, and the level of monitoring and enforcement.

Policies, Policy Assumptions, Translations,
and Implementation

Federal, state, and school-district policies for sex equity in education have received systematic review and analysis elsewhere (Adkison, 1982; Bailey & Smith, 1982; Marshall & Grey, 1982; Segal, 1982). The pro-grams established by the policies generally provide special training to small groups of women to enable them to fit into educational administration. Sex-equity policy enforcement depends on the complaint of an individual grievance or on a class action suit. No federal, state, or local government agency is required to assess the efficacy of policy implementation. Another serious drawback is that the political support for women's equity in schools often comes from groups outside the network of education interest groups.

The National Advisory Council on Women's Educational Programs reported that "at its highest level, federal support for sex equity in education was infinitesimal compared to its support for education in general, or even other equity needs of the handicapped, and racial and ethnic minority populations. For example, in FY 1980 at $33.9 million, its highest level of support, the Office of Education spent only 0.2 percent of its budget on sex equity" (cited in Klein & Dauito, 1982). Funding for the WEEA (Women's Educational Equity Act) programs has declined in recent years, and the Reagan administration proposed total elimination of WEEA funding in 1982 and 1983. The WEEA program publishes materials for staff development, some targeted for training, support, and monitoring to enable women to advance in school administration (WEEA, 1984).

Implementing Measures, Options, and Agencies

Title IX is implemented by local school districts. They decide on appropriate efforts, resources, and personnel to devote to the policy; they have the option to apply for federal grants under Title VII of WEEA. Thus, implementation is left to the decision-making and prioritizing processes of local administrators. The legislation does not require or make implementation resources readily available.

Adkison (1982) found that all the districts she studied had taken the required steps to eliminate discriminatory policies and practices and to assure equal access to courses and activities, but only those districts with "advocates" achieved real movement toward substantive equal opportunity. Also, Marshall and Grey (1982) reported how the legal rights of women seeking administrative positions can be circumvented by ambiguity in job specifications, lack of uniform preparation standards for school administrators, professional norms of loyalty, and difficulty in proving that superiors' assessments are in error.

Recent research on university programs, scholarly publications, and textbooks indicates that institutions of higher education have not, for the most part, taken the leadership for sex equity. For example, analysis by

Tietze and Davis (1981) of best-selling educational administration textbooks found that the texts "provide little or no understanding of sexism, its impact in education, approaches for redress, or practical techniques to eliminate sexism, nor do they provide inspiration or motivation to combat sexism" (p. 10). Schmuck, Butman, and Person (1982) and Marshall (1984) analyzed journals addressed to school administrators. Both studies revealed a notable lack of articles about the implementation of sex equity. Stockard and Kempner (1981) found that most educational administration programs report little or no use of formal or informal recruiting procedures that make special efforts to help women find positions.

A review of special programs for women (see National Advisory Council on Women's Educational Programs, 1984) leaves unanswered a set of important questions.

1. Why have the programs reached such small numbers?

2. Why have the programs focused attention on the *women* rather than on educational systems?

3. Why, in spite of almost a decade of implementation of Title IX and more years of the application to education of federal policy for sex equity in employment, do so few women attain high positions and equal pay in educational administration?

4. Why have there been so few law suits, and no withdrawal of federal funds, for noncompliance with Title IX?

5. How have educational organizations been able to assert compliance with affirmative action while continuing to show little increase in the number of women in high positions?

6. Why have the loud calls of the 1980s for reforming education so singularly overlooked the continuation of sex stereotyping and a sex-structured employment model?

7. What values undergird policies that support programs to prepare women to fit into educational systems that stress hierarchical control when those systems have left unsolved so many educational problems?

A Critique of Policy Assumptions

Analyses of sex-equity policy suggest that it has not yet achieved the status of morally legitimate policy; instead, it continues to be viewed as a vehicle for providing a compensatory benefit to a special interest group. Policy makers and implementers have failed to see that placing the burden of making the necessary changes on the organizational systems that have contributed to the underrepresentation of women in administration does not constitute a promising approach to achieving sex equity. Federal, state, and local policy

systems and policy outcomes have left women with little alternative except to work within, and to try to change from within, systems that have perpetuated sex structuring and placed little or no value on the enforcement of sex-equity policy.

Alternative Explanatory Framework: The Maintenance of Power

The judgment of elders and power brokers prevails in determining what is good, correct, legitimate, and valuable in theory, research publication, practice, behavior, and even sentiment. Questioning fundamental values and structures to explain gender inequity could not be expected to occur without extraordinary challenge because of the threat to existing practice and the distribution of power in educational institutions. As Minogue (1983) put it, "nothing gets done which is unacceptable to dominant or influential political groups, which may be defined to include the 'bureaucratic leadership' group" (p. 73).

Perhaps policymakers were never able to conceive or create policies that would alter belief systems and structures in education to value sex equity and to reconceptualize educational leadership in a way to value the contribution of women. Perhaps those already in charge would not permit themselves and strategically located policy makers to consider new forms and structures that would challenge existing patterns of control and distribution of power. Merton (1964), in his analysis of the self-fulfilling prophecy, helps to explain this phenomenon. Borrowing from Malinowski's (1922) observations of Trobriander chieftains, Merton states:

> The moral virtues remain virtues only so long as they are jealously confined to the proper in-group. The right activity by the wrong people becomes a thing of contempt, not of honor. For clearly, only in this way, by holding these virtues exclusively to themselves, can the men of power retain their distinction, their prestige, and their power. No wiser procedure could be devised to hold intact a system of social stratification and social power. (p. 483)

Thus, an alternative explanation for the failure to see the potential value of women's contributions to educational administration is that the chiefs want to retain the power inherent in defining what is valuable, good, and proper. *Different* values and behaviors can simply be defined as deficient, devalued, and wrong when they are displayed by people who appear to pose threats to those in control. Dominance is maintained, and the actions of the powerful are seen as the virtuous, valued actions.

To allow women expanded participation in school administration could undermine the exclusive power and values of incumbent administrators. The insight into the process of maintaining power recalls the power struggle of the early 1900s in the NEA. Considerations of maintaining power and seeking power can help explain the gender issue in educational leadership. Analysis focused on power calls for investigations into the ability and willingness of power brokers and elders to explore critically long-standing assumptions in educational administration if the exploration poses a challenge to the existing distribution of power.

An alternative explanation for the continuation of the underrepresentation of women in leadership positions comes from analysis of the decline in legitimacy of education as an institution in the United States. Women may associate a general decline in legitimacy with a pervasive loss of hope that education may ever be able to value their contributions as professional educators. If so, they may simply exit the system. Hirschman (1970) has offered a provocative discussion of "exit, voice, and loyalty." When an organization's service deteriorates, organization members express their dissatisfaction: "The decision whether to exit will be taken in the light of the prospects for the effective use of voice" (p. 37).

Well-trained, motivated, intelligent women *are* exiting from education. Speculation about why they are exiting include several plausible factors: (a) lack of political clout to secure desired changes, including sex equity; (b) sense of treatment as interchangeable, replaceable parts in organizations that do not value their services; (c) sense of exclusion from deliberations about policy; (d) belief that organizational response to their expression of voice is to seek to silence them by asserting bureaucratic rationales and implying women's deficiency in administration and policy making; (e) a market response to better employment opportunities elsewhere. As noted earlier, Jones and Montenegro (1982) found that a number of women who had participated in specially supported administration preparation programs had decided to leave public education after they learned more about realistic career opportunities.

Hypotheses about the relevance of power considerations and of the decline-exit phenomenon to the current and future status of sex equity need both careful statement and thoughtful investigation. Particularly, the pertinent hypotheses require exploration by way of paradigms and models that guarantee serious and systematic attention to issues of gender.

NEW PERSPECTIVES AND CHALLENGES TO EDUCATIONAL ADMINISTRATION

Fruitful analysis of women's participation requires not only posing strategic questions but also employing new perspectives. Beard (1962) recognized the "duality of women's position in society—women [as] subordinated, yet central; victimized, yet active" (p. xxi). She argued "that an accurate understanding of the past required women's experience to be analyzed with as much care as historians had normally devoted to the experience of men" (cited in Kerber & Matthews, 1982, p. 3). Lerner (1979) observed that the central question about women's roles has progressed from Who are the women missing from history? Who are the women of achievement and what did they achieve? What have women contributed to abolition, to social reform, to the progressive movement, to the labor movement, to the New Deal? Who oppressed women and how were they oppressed? How did women respond to such oppression? Why and how were women victimized? The central question now is: What would history be like if it were seen through women's eyes and ordered by [the] values they define (pp. 145, 178)? Scholarship in educational administration has not seriously and systematically attended to these questions. From this perspective the logical questions include: What would the educational system be like if it were ordered by values, needs, and priorities of women?

Shakeshaft (1982) has offered an approach in her rubric of four theoretical frameworks through which the issues of female administrators have been and can be studied. The symbolic interaction framework is concerned with how schools appear to the women who administer them. The feminist framework focuses on female leadership as community building, which increases levels of job satisfaction. The revisionist framework calls for a rethinking of organizational theory that adds women's experience to the equation (Tietze & Shakeshaft, 1982). The structural framework explores the effects of the structure of the organization, as well as the numerical distribution of women in both administrative and teaching positions, on behavior.

Gilligan's work extends the line of strategic questioning into the area of morals and values. Gilligan (1977), as well as Bussey and Maughan (1982) found that men differ from women in moral orientation. Men are oriented toward "rights"; women are oriented toward "caring." These studies demonstrate the need for an expanded developmental theory that makes room for expression in the feminine voice, not only for explaining the development of women but also for understanding, in both sexes, the characteristics and precursors of adult moral views and their consequences in organizational contexts. Specifically, serious attention to differentiated moral development might illuminate issues of whether, via group norms and leader behavior, schools should emphasize and enforce rules, principles, and rights over caring and helping.

The gender segregation of administration and teaching can be challenged in light of research on men and women in groups. Findings include the following: (a) Men and male groups compete with each other and seldom express feelings (Mehrabian, 1971). (b) A differentiated division of labor was more characteristic of all-male than all-female groups (Fennel, Barchos, Cohen, McMahan, & Hildebrand, 1978). (c) Interpersonal relations, intimacy, and concern are more characteristic of all-female than all-male groups (Aries, 1974; Safilios-Rothschild, 1979). (d) In mixed groups men developed a more personal orientation, with increased one-to-one interaction and less aggression (Aries, 1974; Safilios-Rothschild, 1979). (e) Familiarity with the task and prior opportunity to achieve competence increased women's task-oriented initiation behavior in mixed groups (Lockheed & Hall, 1976). Such findings challenge analysts of educational administration to examine critically the group norms that have evolved in a system segregated by gender.

Interestingly, more recent studies and texts have advocated leadership as a means for engaging and mobilizing human needs and followers' aspirations and countering the effects of bureaucratic control (e.g., see Burns, 1978; Ouchi, 1981; Peters & Waterman, 1982; Ramos, 1981). Leaders would be intensely involved in the actual production units of the organization (teaching and learning) and serve the organizational workers by resolving conflicts and coordinating resources. These "new" ideas echo the theory of integrative leadership of Mary Parker Follett (1924).

The debates and challenges to the dominant paradigm in educational administration open up questions about the validity of theory developed without considering women's experience. For example, two professions occupied primarily by women, teaching and nursing, show women resisting hierarchical ranking. And yet, theories of bureaucracy and the structuring of organizations rest on hierarchical control and ranking. Women are more apt to develop lateral relationships and crossrelationships, whereas men look to their superiors (Archibald, 1971; Corwin, 1966; Fennel et al., 1978; Follett, 1924; Gross & Trask, 1976; Kramer, 1974; Mayo, 1933; Metz, 1978; Ortiz, 1982; Roethlisberger & Dickson, 1939; Shakeshaft, 1982; Wolcott, 1977).

It is important to question the capacity of organizational theorists to consider gender issues critically. For instance, the able and astute theoretician George Homans (1950, 1952), in his analysis of the Hawthorne studies, failed to recognize differential recruitment and control based on gender. Others have noted these differences (Acker & Van Houten, 1967; Parsons, 1977; Pennock, 1930; Viteles, 1954). The need for edu-

cational administrators to examine critically organizational theories and their research bases for validity in the representation of women's experience persists.

Three frameworks of feminism use women's status as an issue of power and politics. As women have sought inclusion in occupational arenas, in some instances their efforts have adopted the cast of feminism. Feminism declares that women's issues are political issues: that to be feminist not only defines the problems as political but also gives primacy to political solutions. Liberals, socialists, and radicals assign feminism different emphasis, with the radicals most strongly committed to an entirely female-oriented movement—but all make it the practical center of their political action. Liberals blame the system of learned sex roles; socialists blame the economic and cultural exploitation of capitalism; radicals blame men (Bouchier, 1984).

IMPLICATIONS FROM THE FOCUS ON WOMEN IN EDUCATIONAL ADMINISTRATION

This chapter has used four major themes in the development of the field of educational administration to frame the context in which women's status was established and in which theory, research, knowledge, values, policies, and structures have emerged. The education system developed, in response to societal assumptions, "constitutional" elements so fundamental that they pervade theory, practice, and policy and so sedimented in organizational assumptions that they have become almost unnoticed. The notion of administration as politically neutral, technical practice focused on efficiency and hierarchical control continues. The prevailing notion entered the scene in the early 1900s and obscured the political realities of education and downplayed the conflicts of values that riddled the system. The effective separation of education into two professions, based considerably on gender, placed status and power in the hands of relatively few male administrators, who attended more to managing the enterprise than enhancing the technical core practiced by the many. The separation is perpetuated in best-selling textbooks on school administration, in research that uses frameworks derived from theory on organizational control, and in long-standing reward systems and distributions of power that favor the managers over the instructors. The management of knowledge and control of access by powerful elders both discouraged new perspectives and discoveries and denied access to people and groups who raised questions about the fundamental structure of the field. The ease with which organization theorists have ignored gender differences and the apparent unwillingness of policy makers to examine critically the system's exclusion of women from full participation offer eloquent testimony to the postulated discouragement and denial.

Locating the gender issue within the major developmental themes in educational administration has helped to identify not only long-standing problems but also potential gains both for women in education and for education. Sharpened focus on women in education may provide useful answers to several fundamental questions:

1. What are the costs of continuing the separation between teachers and administrators in preparation, functions, values, and loyalties?

2. To what extent does a system of hierarchical control enhance teaching and learning?

3. What are the costs and benefits of maintaining an aura of politically neutral, technical competence in educational administration, with its attendant attempts to buffer schools from social conflicts?

4. To what extent do traditional ranking and emphasis on competition square with the enhancement of educators as people and of instructional services?

5. What are the consequences for the learning environment of administrative reliance on rationalizing beliefs and actions?

6. What are the significant gaps in the knowledge base of educational administration? Do the dominant paradigm in organizational theory—research—and the dominant practice in training and recruitment in educational administration meet the essential needs of and provide useful explanations for the major problems in the field?

REFERENCES

Acker, J., & Van Houten, D. R. (1974). Differential recruitment and control: The sex structuring of organizations. *Administrative Science Quarterly, 19*(2) 152–163.

Adkison, J. A. (1982). *Local response to federal mandates: The implementation of Title IX*. Paper presented at the Annual Meeting of the American Educational Research Association, New York.

AFT Fact Sheet. (1983). Washington DC: Women's Rights Commission of the American Federation of Teachers.

American Association of School Administrators. (1979). Survey shows male attitudes may hinder advancement. *The School Administrator, 46*(5), 6.

American Association of School Administrators. (1981). *Survey: Attitudes toward women as school district administrators*. Newton, MA: WEEA Publishing Center.

Archibald, K. A. (1971). The supply of professional nurses and their retention and recruitment by hospitals. AS36R83, No. 834–837 of the *Rand Report*. New York: New York City Rand Institute.

Aries, E. (1974). *Interaction, patterns and themes of male, female and mixed groups*. Paper presented at the American Psychological Association Annual Convention, New Orleans.

Bailey, S., & Smith R. (1982). *Policies for the Future: State policies, regulations and resources related to the achievement of educational equity for females and males*. Washington, DC: Council of the Chief State School Officers.

Basse, B. M., Krussell, J., & Alexander, R. A. (1971). Male managers' attitudes toward working women. *American Behavioral Scientist, 15*, 221–236.

Bates, R. (1983). *Educational administration and the management of knowledge*. Geelong, Australia: Deakin University Press.

Beard, M. K. (1962). *Women as a force in history*. New York: Collier Books.

Berman, J. (1982). *The managerial behavior of female high school principals: Implications for training*. Paper presented at the American Educational Research Association, New York.

Blood, R. E. (1966). *The functions of experience in professional preparation: Teaching and principalship*. Unpublished doctoral dissertation, Claremont Graduate School, Claremont, CA.

Bouchier, D. (1984). *The feminist challenge: The movement for women's liberation in Britain and the U.S.A.* New York: Schocken.

Burns, J. M. (1978). *Leadership*. New York: Harper & Row.

Bussey, K., & Maughan, B. (1982). Gender differences in moral reasoning. *Journal of Personality and Social Psychology, 42*(4), 701–706.

Callahan, R. E. (1967). *The superintendent of schools: An historical analysis, Final Report, S–212*. Washington, DC: U.S. Office of Education, HEW.

Chion-Kenney, L. (1984). Coalition seeks urban-education policy for women and minorities. *Education Week, 16*, 5.

Cirincione-Coles, K. (1975). The administrator: Male or female? *Journal of Teacher Education, 26*(4), 17–22.

Clark, P. P. (1983). *A leadership study of local education association presidents in Maryland*. Unpublished master's thesis, University of Maryland, Baltimore.

Clement, J. P., Di Bella, C. M., Eckstrom, R. B., & Tobias, S. (1977). No room at the top? *American Education, 13*(5), 20–23, 26.

Corwin, R. G. (1966). The professional employee: A study in conflict in nursing roles. *American Journal of Sociology, 6*, 604–615.

Council for University Women's Progress at the University of Minnesota. (1971). *Proportion of doctorates earned by women by area and field, 1960–1969*. Washington, DC: Association of American Colleges.

Edson, C. H. (1979). To seek America: A history of ethnic life in the United States. *Urban Education, 13*(4). 519–521.

Equal Employment Opportunity Commission. (1977). *Employment opportunity in the schools: Job patterns of minorities and women in public elementary and secondary schools*. Washington, DC: U.S. Government Printing Office.

Federal Staff Directory. (1984). Mt. Vernon, VT: Congressional Staff Directory, Ltd.

Fennell, M. L., Barchos, P. R., Cohen, E., McMahan, A. M., & Hildebrand, P. (1978). An alternative perspective on sex differences in organizational settings: The process of legitimation. *Sex Roles, 4*(4), 589–604.

Fishel, A., & Pottker, J. (1973). Women lose out: Is there sex discrimination in school administration? *The Clearinghouse, 47*, 387–391.

Fishel, A., & Pottker, J. (1974). Women in educational governance: A statistical portrait. *Educational Researcher, 3*(7), 4–7.

Fishel, A., & Pottker, J. (1975). Performance of women principals: A review of behavioral and attitudinal studies. In J. Pottker & A. Fishel (Eds.), *Sex bias in the schools: The research evidence* (pp. 300–310). London: Associated Universities Press.

Follett, M. P. (1924). *Creative Experience*. London: Longman, Green.

Foster, W. P. (1980). Administration and the crisis of legitimacy: A review of Habermasian thought. *Harvard Education Review, 50*(2) 496–565.

Frasher, J. M., & Frasher, R. S. (1979). *Educational Administration Quarterly, 15*(2), 1–13.

Gaertner, K. M. (1981). Administrative careers in public organizations. In P. A. Schmuck, W. W. Charters, Jr., & R. O. Carlson (Eds.), *Educational policy and management: Sex differentials* (pp. 199–217) New York: Academic Press.

Gilbertson, M. (1981). The influence of gender on verbal interactions among principals and staff members: An exploratory study. In P. A. Schmuck, W. W. Charters, Jr., & R. O. Carlson (Eds.), *Educational policy and management: Sex differentials* (pp. 297–306). New York: Academic Press.

Gilligan, C. (1977). In a different voice: Women's conceptions of self and morality. *Harvard Educational Review, 47,* 481–517.

Greenfield, T. B. (1979). Organization theory as ideology. *Curriculum Inquiry, 9*(2), 97–112.

Griffiths, D. E., Goldman, S., & McFarland, W. J. (1965). Teacher mobility in New York City. *Educational Administration Quarterly, 1,* 15–31.

Grobman, H., & Hines, V. A. (1956). What makes a good principal? *NAASP Bulletin, 40*(223), 5–16.

Gross, N., & Trask, A. (1964). *Men and women as elementary school principals (Final Report No. 2, Cooperative Research Project No. 853).* Cambridge, MA: Graduate School of Education, Harvard University.

Gross, N., & Trask, A. (1976). *The sex factor and the management of schools.* New York: John Wiley.

Habaermas, J. (1975). *Legitimation crisis.* London: Heinemann.

Hemphill, J. K., Griffiths, D. E., Frederickson, N. (1962). *Administrative performance and personality.* New York: Bureau of Publications, Columbia University.

Hennig, M., & Jardim, A. (1977). *The managerial woman.* Garden City, NY: Doubleday.

Hirschman, A. O. (1970). *Exit, voice, and loyalty: Responses to decline in firms, organizations, and states.* Cambridge, MA: Harvard University Press.

Homans, G. C. (1950) *The human group.* New York: Harcourt, Brace & World.

Homans, G. C. (1952). Group factors in worker productivity. In G. E. Swenson, T. M. Newcomb, & E. L. Hartley (Eds.), *Readings in Social Psychology.* New York: Harcourt, Brace & World.

Iannaccone, L. (1982). Changing political patterns and governmental regulations. In R. Everhart (Ed.), *The public school monopoly: A critical analysis of education and the state in American society.* Cambridge, MA: Ballinger.

Johnson, J. J. (1973). Why administrators fail. *Clearing House, 48,* 3–6.

Johnston, H. S., Johnston, G. S., & Yeakey, C. C. (1977). A study of the attitudes of male graduate students. *Journal of Educational Administration, 15,* 310–318.

Jones, E. H., & Montenegro, X. (1982). *Recent trends in the representation of women and minorities in school administration and problems in documentation.* Arlington, VA: Office of Minority Affairs, American Association of School Administrators.

Kanter, R. M. (1977). *Men and women of the corporation.* New York: Basic.

Kerber, L., & Matthews, J. D. (Eds.). *Women's America: Refocusing the past.* New York: Oxford University Press.

Klein, S., & Dauito, K. (1982). *What's left of federal funding for sex equity in education?* Washington, DC: U.S. Government Printing Office.

Kramer, M. (1974). *Reality shock.* St. Louis: Mosby.

Lahner, L. J. (1972). *Contrast of high school students, attitudes toward men and women department heads in a large city secondary school.* Unpublished doctoral dissertation, University of North Carolina, Chapel Hill.

Lerner, G. (1979). *The majority finds its past: Placing women in history.* New York: Oxford University Press.

Levinson, R. M. (1982). *Administrative task orientation of school principals.* Unpublished doctoral dissertation, University of California, Santa Barbara.

Lilley, M. E. (1984). *Educational administration directory, 1983–84.* Morgantown, WV: West Virginia University Press.

Lindblom, C. E., & Cohen, D. K. (1979). *Usable knowledge: Social science and social problem-solving.* New Haven, CT: Yale University Press.

Lockheed, M. E. (1975). Female motive to avoid success: A pychological barrier or a response to deviancy? *Sex Roles, 1*(1), 41–50.

Lockheed, M. E., & Hall, K. P. (1976). Conceptualizing sex as a status characteristic: Applications to leadership training strategies. *Journal of Social Issues, 32,* 111–124.

Lortie, D. C. (1975). *Schoolteacher: A sociological study.* Chicago: University of Chicago Press.

Lupini, D. (1975). Women in administration: Where are they now? *Education Canada, 15*(4), 17–22.

Malinowski, B. (1922). *The argonauts of the western Pacific.* London: Routledge & Kegan Paul.

Manassee, A. L. (1982). Effective principals: Effective at what? *Principal, 62,* 10–15.

Marr, J. (1973). Women in state departments of education. *Phi Delta Kappan, 55,* 142–143.

Marshall, C. (1979). *Career socialization of women in school administration.* Unpublished doctoral dissertation, University of California, Santa Barbara.

Marshall, C. (1984). Men and women in university educational administration programs. *Journal of the National Association of Women Deans, Administrators, and Counselors, 48*(1), 3–12.

Marshall, C., & Grey, R. (1982). Legal rights of women seeking administrative positions in local school districts. *Journal of Educational Equity and Leadership, 2,* 253–259.

Mayes, S. S. (1979). Women in positions of authority: A case study of changing sex roles. *Signs: Journal of Women in Culture and Society, 4,* 556–568.

Mayo, E. (1933). *The human problems of an industrial civilization.* New York: Macmillan.

McCarthy, M. M. (1979). Characteristics and attitudes on doctoral students in educational administration. *Phi Delta Kappan, 61,* 200–203.

Mehrabian, A. (1971). Seating arrangement and conversations. *Sociometry, 34*(2), 281–289.

Merton, R. (1964). *Social theory and social structure.* London: Free Press.

Meskin, J. (1974). The performance of women school administrators: A review of the literature. *Administrators Notebook, 23*(1) 21–24.

Metz, M. (1978). *Classrooms and corridors.* Berkeley: University of California Press.

Minogue, M. (1983). Theory and practice in public policy and administration. *Policy and Politics, 11*(1), 63–85.

Mowry, W. A. (1895). Powers and duties of school superintendents. *Educational Review, 9,* 38–51.

National Advisory Council on Women's Educational Programs. (1984). S. S. Klein, C. K. Tittle, P. A. Schmuck, P. B. Campbell, P. J. Blackwell, L. N. Russo, S. R. Murray, & C. A. Dwyer (Eds.), *Handbook for achieving sex equity through education.* Baltimore: Johns Hopkins University Press.

National Research Council (1973). *Summary Report: 1972 Doctoral Recipients from United States Universities.* Washington, DC: Author.

National School Boards Association (1974). *Women on School Boards.* Evanston, IL: Author.

Neidig, M. B. (1980). *The other half of the talent bank: Woman administrators.* Paper presented at the annual meeting of the National Association of Secondary School Principals, Miami Beach.

Nixon, M., & Gue, L. R. (1975). Women administrators and women teachers: A comparative study. *Alberta Journal of Educational Research, 21*(3), 196–206.

O'Leary, V. E. (1974). Some attitudinal barriers to occupational aspirations in women. *Psychological Bulletin, 81,* 809–826.

Oller, S. K. (1979a). Female graduates in educational administration: Myths and realities. *Sex Equity in Educational Leadership Report.* Eugene, OR: University of Oregon.

Oller, S. K. (1979b). *Differential experiences of male and female aspirants in public school administration: A closer look at perceptions within the field.* Paper presented at the Annual Meeting of the American Educational Research Association, San Francisco.

Ortiz, F. I. (1982). *Career patterns in educational administration: Women, men and minorities in educational administration.* New

York: Praeger.

Ouchi, W. G. (1981). *How American business can meet the Japanese challenge*. Reading, MA: Addison-Wesley.

Pallante, J. J., & Hinton, C. L. (1977). Authority positions for women: Principalships in public education. *Contemporary Education, 48*(4), 206–214.

Parsons, H. M. (1977). What happened at Hawthorne? In R. L., Hamblin & J. H. Klunkel (Eds.), *Behavioral theory in sociology: Essays in honor of George C. Homans*. New Brunswick, NJ: Transaction.

Pennock, G. A. (1930) Industrial research at Hawthorne. *Personnel Journal, 8*, 296–313.

Peters, T. J., & Waterman, R. H. (1982). *In search of excellence: Lessons from America's best-run corporations*. New York: Harper & Row.

Pitner, N. J. (1978). *Descriptive study of the everyday activities of suburban school superintendents: The management of information*. Unpublished doctoral dissertation. Ohio State University, Columbus.

Pitner, N. J. (1981). Hormones and harems: Are the activities of superintending different for a woman? In P. A. Schmuck, W. W. Charters, Jr., & R. O. Carlson (Eds.), *Educational policy and management sex differentials* (pp. 273–295). New York: Academic.

Pottker, J., & Fishel, A. (1977). *Sex bias in the schools: The research evidence*. London: Associated University Press.

Prolman, S. (1983). *Gender, career paths and administrative behavior*. Paper presented at the annual meeting of the AERA, Montreal.

Raab, C. (1982). *Elite interviewing as a tool for political research: The case of Scottish educational policy-making*. Paper presented at the European Consortium for Political Research, University of Nijmegen, Netherlands.

Ramos, A. G. (1981). *The new science of organizations: A reconceptualization of the wealth of nations*. Toronto: University of Toronto Press.

Riger, S., & Galligan, P. (1981). Women in management: An exploration of competing paradigms. *American Psychologist, 35*(10), 902–910.

Roberson, S., Keith, T., & Page, E. (1983). Now who aspires to teach? *Educational Researcher, 2*(6), 13–21.

Roethlisberger, F. J., & Dickson, W. J. (1939). *Management and the worker*. Cambridge MA: Harvard University Press.

Safilios-Rothschild, C. (1979). *Sex role socialization and sex discrimination: A synthesis and critique of the literature*. [Microfiche document]. Washington, DC: National Institute of Education.

Sandorff, P., & Nieto, C. (1979). Administrator bound women. *Emergent Leadership, 3*(3), 3–19.

Sarason, S. (1982). *The culture of the school and the problem of change*. (2nd ed.). Boston: Allyn and Bacon.

Schein, E. H. (1971). The individual, the organization, and the career: A conceptual scheme. *Journal of Applied Behavioral Science, 7*(4), 401–426.

Schlecty, P. C., & Vance, V. S. (1981). Do academically able teachers leave education? The North Carolina case. *Phi Delta Kappan, 63*, 106–112.

Schmid, R. D. (1963). *A study of the organizational structure of the National Education Association, 1884–1921*. Unpublished doctoral dissertation, Washington University, St. Louis, MO.

Schmuck, P. A., Butman, L., & Person, L. (1982). *Analyzing sex bias in "planning and changing."* Paper presented at the annual meeting of the American Educational Research Association, New York.

School Board News. (1984). Washington, DC: National School Boards Association, 4(1).

Segal, P. N. (1982). State constitutional equal rights provisions:

Legal tools for achieving sex equity in education. *Journal of Educational Equity and Leadership, 2*(2), 85–99.

Shakeshaft, C. (1982, March). *A framework for studying schools as work settings for women leaders*. Paper presented at the annual meeting of the American Educational Research Association, New York.

Sproull, L. S. (1981). Response to regulation: An organizational process framework. *Administrative Science Quarterly, 12*(4), 447–470.

Stockard, J., & Kempner, K. (1981). Women's representation in school administration: Recent trends. *Educational Administration Quarterly, 17*(2), 81–91.

Taylor, S. S. (1973). Educational leadership: A male domain. *Phi Delta Kappan. 55*, 124–128.

Taylor, S. S. (1977). The attitudes of superintendents and board of education members toward the employment and effectiveness of women as public-school administrators. In J. Pottker & A. Fishel (Eds.), *Sex bias in the schools: The research evidence* (pp. 300–310). London: Associated University Press.

Tibbets, S. (1980). The woman principal: Superior to the male? *Journal of the National Association of Women Deans, Administrators, and Counselors, 43*(4), 15–18.

Tietze, I. N., & Davis, B. H. (1981). *Sexism in texts in educational administration*. Paper presented at the annual meeting of the American Educational Research Association, Los Angeles.

Tietze, I. N., & Shakeshaft, C. (1982). *Toward a reconstruction of organizational theory: Androcentric bias in A. H. Maslow's theory of human motivation and self actualization*. Paper presented at the annual meeting of the American Educational Research Association, New York.

Tipple, M. E. (1972). *Sexual discrimination: Attitudes toward the hireability of women for professional administrative positions in public education*. Unpublished doctoral dissertation, University of Michigan.

Turner, R. H. (1960). Sponsored and contest mobility and the school system. *American Sociological Review, 25*, 855–867.

Tyack, D., & Hansot, E. (1982). *Managers of virtue: Public school leadership in America, 1820–1980*. New York: Basic.

Valverde, L. A. (1974). *Succession socialization: Its influences on school administration candidates and its implications for the exclusion of minorities from administration*. (Project 3–0813). Washington, DC: National Institute of Education.

Viteles, M. S. (1954). *Motivation and morale in industry*. London: Staples.

Waldo, D. (1955). *The study of public administration*. New York: Random House.

Weatherley, R., & Lipsky, M. (1977). Street level bureaucrats and educational innovation. *Harvard Educational Review, 47*, 171–197.

WEEA. (1984). *Catching up: A review of the Women's Educational Equity Act programs*. Washington, DC: The Citizens' Council on Women's Educational Equity.

Wheatley, M. (1981). The impact of organizational structures on issues of sex equity. In P. A. Schmuck, W. W. Charters, Jr., & R. O. Carlson (Eds.), *Educational policy and management: Sex differentials* (pp. 255–271). New York: Academic.

Wirt, F., & Kirst, M. (1972). *The political web of American schools*. Boston: Little, Brown.

Wolcott, H. F. (1973). *The man in the principal's office: An ethnography*. New York: Holt, Rinehart, & Winston.

Wolcott, H. F. (1977). *Teachers versus technocrats: An education innovation in anthropological perspective*. Eugene, OR: Center for Education Policy and Management, University of Oregon.

Woman's National Advisory Council on Women. (1981). *Woman's National Advisory Council on Women's Educational Programs*. Washington, DC: U.S. Government Printing Office.

CHAPTER 7

Influences on Leadership Development Among Racial and Ethnic Minorities

Leonard A. Valverde and Frank Brown

A discussion of salient issues involving minority school administrators in elementary and secondary schools reveals that in every phase of the process of moving into educational administration, many minorities may and usually do encounter experiences different from whites'. The search by ethnic- and racial-minority teachers for administrative positions leads to a discussion of socialization and role conflict, sponsorship and upward mobility, the content and availability of preparation programs, and policies and philosophies that affect their career aspirations.

For clarity of understanding, the referent for the term "minority" used here follows a definition by Lenski. In *Power and Privilege: A Theory of Social Stratification*, Lenski (1966) states that whenever "membership in a group begins to have an appreciable influence on one's access to important rewards...an individual becomes a minority, a member of a disadvantaged racial and ethnic group" (pp. 396–397). Membership in certain racial or ethnic groups in America plays a significant role in the distribution of power and therefore in minority group status. Lenski (1966) and Ogbu (1977) believe that blacks, Hispanics, Native Americans, and some Asian Americans have minority status in the United States. The minority status results in a pattern of inequality in virtually every aspect of an individual's life, including education,

economics, and social mobility. This condition holds particularly true for minorities who seek administrative positions and associated power and prestige. Even though school administrators, on average, do not earn as much as managers in private industry (U.S. Bureau of the Census, 1983), the former have job security and prestige similar to or greater than their counterparts in the private sector.

Because it is important to gaining membership in the managerial and professional classes, education "has...become a much more valuable resource; and therefore, higher educational institutions are more important in the distribution of power and privilege by providing access to administrative positions" (Lenski, 1966, pp. 396–397). Minority-group membership and level of education, in general, influence one's chances of becoming a school administrator as well as of gaining membership in a managerial and professional class. For detailed analysis of racial- and ethnic-group status in America, see the discussions by Franklin (1968), Marden and Meyer (1968), Orleans and Ellis (1971), and Carnoy (1974).

Also relevant to the participation of minorities in educational administration are assumptions, and related concepts, about leadership and organizational behavior. Several writers (Contreras, 1979; Hanson, 1984; Jackson, 1978; Scott, 1980; Shakeshaft & Nowell, 1984; Stanley, 1979) have argued that most theories of leadership behavior in educational organizations assume that schools consist of academically and racially homogeneous pupil groups managed by white males.

Consultant/reviewers: Tomas Arciniega, California State College-Bakersfield; and David Carter, University of Connecticut

However, many schools have diverse pupil populations and nonwhite male administrators and female administrators. Therefore, some observations on the educational experience of racial- and ethnic-minority group members in a diversified society are pertinent.

HISTORICAL OVERVIEW

A focused discussion of the role and participation of members of ethnic and racial minorities in the management and leadership of schools requires a brief historical overview of the education of minorities in the United States. Treatment of bias in any such review remains a problematic matter both with respect to the selection of content and source materials and to interpretation and reporting. It also depends on the assessment of other scholars. The discussion that follows focuses almost exclusively on two major groups, black Americans and Americans of Latin ancestry, with attention to American Indians wherever possible. Concentration on blacks and Hispanics is strictly a function of the amount of documentation and research available. Even so, the paucity of research regarding minority populations and their participation in educational administration has required insertion of interpretation as well as straightforward reporting. The requirement holds for data as well as for examination of the underlying assumptions pertinent to the management of public educational enterprises by minorities. Careful unraveling of the incorporation of minorities into the management of education starts with an understanding of the acculturation process for different racial, ethnic, linguistic, national, and religious groups and the varying consequences for each.

Ethnocentric School Philosophy: Genesis for Discrimination

Besides providing instruction, the other major mission of schools is the socialization of young people. The role of acculturation—to promote individual assimilation into U.S. society—became more central in schools following the American Revolution. The primary concern of U.S. political leaders at the time was to ensure the establishment of a patriotic citizenry and a common national identity. Because the political leadership wanted moral values to guide the behavior of citizens and because most were of the Protestant faith, the ethics of Protestantism were promoted in schools as a way of building moral character. The ethnocentric aim of promoting the Protestant ethic via the public schools lasted for a century.

A second and related phase of ethnocentrism in schools began around 1880 as a response to accom-

modate the greatest immigration in U.S. history. "Facing public education was the task of transforming these millions of newcomers—speaking dozens of languages, clinging to diverse folkways, owing multiple loyalties—into one people" (Tyack, 1967, p. 228). The aim of acculturation shifted from promoting the Protestant ethic to Americanization, as witnessed in the 1906 pronouncement by the superintendent of the New York City schools: "We mean by Americanization an appreciation of the institutions of this country, absolute forgetfulness of all obligations with other countries because of descent or birth" (Gordon, 1964, p. 100). Coincident with the press for Americanization came the emergence of the common school and mandatory attendance. Thus, the common school, which all children were required to attend, became an institution for fashioning immigrants into a homogeneous group characterized by white Anglo-Saxon, Protestant values.

At the start of the 20th century, then, the dominant American civic philosophy was the "melting pot." In his play *The Melting Pot*, Zangwill (1909) offered the metaphor of the United States as a large furnace, a crucible where all cultures, both immigrant and native, merged into one. The melting-pot thesis dictated that only the best traits in each culture would contribute to the new American identity. However, as the major immigrant flow began to come from southern and eastern Europe, the public schools frequently distorted in their curricula the contributions of some immigrant groups and also of colored native groups by omitting or negatively interpreting their cultural heritage and the parts they had played in the building of America.

In the 1920s, Horace Kallan led an important movement to turn away from the dominant ethnocentric orientation. Kallan (1924), invoking Dewey's beliefs in democracy, individualism, and diversity, publicly acknowledged the reality of the United States' pluralistic society. He argued that cultural pluralism allowed individuals to retain their ethnic identities without suffering adverse consequences from doing so (Kallan, 1924, p. 86). However, he also maintained that each person needed to learn the mainstream culture in order to function adequately. Kallan, then, was indirectly recommending acceptance of a bicultural identity, even though the duality was to remain unequal. Unfortunately the concept of cultural pluralism gathered little momentum at this time and did not take hold in the schools for three reasons: (a) the general inertia that prevails in the schools; (b) the Great Depression, which turned the concern of schools, like many other institutions, to sheer economic survival; and (c) World War II, which focused attention in the United States on the free world's life-and-death struggle against totali-tarianism (Itzkoff, 1969, p. 59).

The decade of the 1950s was a prologue to the turbulent 1960s. The focus of the 1950s was on de-segregation, particularly on ensuring the access of black youngsters to the same facilities and opportunities as white students. The Supreme Court decision *Brown v. Board of Education of Topeka* (1954) heralded the start of desegregation. Partially as a result of very little and slow response by school districts to the *Brown* decision, the strife-riddled 1960s witnessed acceleration of the national movement for civil rights and equality of treatment for all racial, ethnic and socioeconomic groups. The schools, as social institutions most acces-sible to minority communities, became prime targets for change, especially because the *Brown* case made them seem legally reachable and accountable. Further-more, because schools were located in neighborhoods, their proximity made them accessible. Parents and community leaders could establish physical contact with the local authorities, particularly principals and teachers. Minorities not only demanded educational equity for their children but also insisted on quality education. Hispanics and Asian Americans pushed for bilingual education, American Indians lobbied for bicultural education, and blacks demanded implemen-tation of school desegregation and Afro-American studies.

These minority groups sought these specific remedies in order to extinguish long-standing but erroneous popular beliefs that they were really not interested in full assimilation into U.S. society. Given the generally available evidence that ethnic and racial groups of non-European descent had not assimilated as readily as European immigrants and given the broadly based majority belief that nonwhite and non-European minorities did not really want to move into the main-stream, minority activists considered it important to establish that there had been significant differences in earlier times in opportunities for and conditions of acculturation. For example, white immigrants with few exceptions came to the United States by their own choice and, for the most part, sought assimilation into U.S. culture (Handlin, 1959). Even where they resisted specific features of the new society (for example, Germans insisting on their native language in the curriculum, Catholics and Jews establishing private schools, and Southern Italians holding their children out of schools), the resistance involved relatively free choice (Tyack, 1967). Such had not been the case for minorities who moved to the front and center in the 1960s. The phenomenon of lack of full assimilation into U.S. society by nonwhite groups implicated much more than a strategy of self-imposed exclusion.

Exclusionary Policies

Some historians (McWilliams, 1968; Rivera, 1972) have described how American Indians and Mexican Ameri-cans were entrapped in white America's development and how blacks and Asian Americans were brought to North America as slaves and indentured servants. Already established groups first resisted the integration of these particular groups, then sought to limit their participation in society (Acuna, 1972). Snapshots of the experiences of several minority groups in the schools substantiates the history of exclusion and limited participation.

American Indians

The dominant policy for American Indian assimilation, coercive acculturation with only a brief episode of relief, is best described by the then popular phrase "Kill the Indian, save the child." During the era of ascendance of the Protestant ethic, Native Americans were placed in Christian missions in order to indoctri-nate them to take up farming, appreciate private prop-erty, and assume English names (Meriam, 1928). Bilingual education, the only positive feature of the missionary schools, was eliminated after the Civil War when the federal government decided to accelerate the pace of transforming Indians. In 1881 bilingual mis-sionary schools were displaced by English-only govern-ment schools at which attendance was mandatory. Indian children from the same tribe were separated in order to force them to speak English. The new federal facilities were overcrowded, poorly maintained board-ing schools, in which children were separated from their homes and parents. Thus, Indian children were kept away from public schools, kept to themselves in boarding schools set up for Indians only, and the major goal was to de-Indianize them. In 1928, the Meriam Committee, funded by the federal government to evaluate the effectiveness of its Indian education policies, repudiated such policies and recommended programs that would provide increased cultural free-dom for Indians. However, it was not until 1934 that the U.S. Congress legislated the reinstatement of bilin-gualism, Native American teachers, and emphasis on the preservation of Indian cultural heritage. However, implementation was brief, for in 1950 the government returned to its boarding-school policy. It was not until President L. B. Johnson's administration that coercive assimilation was again repudiated.

Black Americans

Whereas the government proceeded to force the accul-turation of the Native American through a conscious and systematic process of de-Indianizing, black people were denied assimilation into society by exclusion via segregation and institutionalized inequality. Most blacks were excluded from public schools until after the Civil War. Prior to that time, only a few blacks acquired some form of education, usually as house servants, artisans, tailors, and carpenters. A few attended "underground" schools taught by blacks. Public education for blacks, most of whom lived in the South, really began with Reconstruction. Mission schools solely for blacks were started and mostly taught by teachers trained in New England. Although a network of mission schools did develop, the number was too small to meet the large demand. Mandatory attendance was not initially required and later, when enacted, was not enforced.

After first suffering total exclusion, black students were later denied equitable distribution of school funds. For example, the average class size in southern black schools in 1912–1913 was 67 (Tyack, 1967, p. 269). School buildings for blacks were miserable shacks, sparsely furnished and housing a few outdated books. Tyack (1967) documents that the inequities showed no improvement over time. In 1932 a South Carolina county spent $8 on each black student in public school and $178 for each white student; a Mississippi county that enrolled 4,016 black children and only 917 white children allocated only 18 cents per black student for school supplies as compared to $25 for each white student (Tyack, 1967, p. 268). Clearly, neither equity nor justice prevailed in the education of southern blacks.

From southern communities and states, blacks migrated in large numbers to the big cities in the North in search of a better life. They congregated in large urban areas such as northern Philadelphia, southern Chicago, and Harlem in New York City, where industrial growth had created jobs. As the migration of blacks to the North grew in numbers, contacts between whites and blacks in northern schools actually declined, partly due to housing patterns, partly due to gerrymandering of school boundaries, and partly due to state and local policies requiring segregation.

Although slavery had been legally abolished, segregation became the legal national policy. The U.S. Supreme Court ruled in *Plessy v. Ferguson* (1896) that the provision of "separate but equal" facilities was constitutional. As a result, southern states passed a multitude of "Jim Crow" laws. As late as 1957, 21 states and the District of Columbia either compelled or permitted the separate education of the races. It was not until 1954 that 8-year old Linda Brown of Topeka, Kansas, challenged the 1896 Plessy decision and won.

Hispanics

To discuss the Hispanic experience in a historical way consistent with that of blacks and Native Americans and because of the information that is available, emphasis is on Mexican Americans in the Southwest. On a delayed and shorter timeline, Puerto Ricans experienced similar treatment in the Northeast and Cubans in the Southeast.

The educational experience of Mexican Americans recalls the treatment of American Indians and blacks. Carter (1970) has labeled their experience as "a history of educational neglect." Like their American Indian cousins, Mexican Americans were first educated by Catholic missionaries. The mission schools in some states, for example New Mexico, offered bilingual instruction. In still other southwestern states, bilingual education was permissible but rarely available. As in the case of blacks, schooling was not available to many Mexican American youngsters until the late 19th century. Although school attendance was compulsory across the nation, school officials found it convenient not to enforce the law for children of Mexican descent. Also, maintenance of segregated schools squared with the *Plessy v. Ferguson* separate-but-equal doctrine still in force. In the 1930s the no-Spanish-speaking-on-school-grounds rule was invoked in California and Texas, with corporal punishment and school expulsion used for enforcement. During the early years of desegregation, until 1970, school districts in the Southwest and Northeast expediently classified Mexican Americans and Puerto Ricans as white in order to prevent mixing Anglo-Saxon white students with black youngsters. Not until the *Cisneros* ruling (1970) in Texas were Chicanos (Mexican Americans) identified as a distinct ethnic group for desegregation purposes. Where Native Americans suffered under the reservation policy and blacks under the institution of slavery, Mexican Americans in the 1800s and 1900s, and Puerto Ricans and Cubans in the 1900s, experienced the suppression of colonization. Mexicans were entrapped by the War of 1846–1848 between Mexico and the United States and by the subsequent adoption of the conquerer's mentality on the part of the U.S. government. Even though Mexicans who became American citizens under the Treaty of Guadalupe Hildago (1848) (ending the War of 1846) were guaranteed certain rights, such as bilingualism, many of the rights were rarely honored.

History reveals that blacks, Native Americans, and Hispanics had long suffered the violation of their educational and other civil rights, as a direct consequence of both *de jure* and *de facto* national, state, and local policies and practices. Sufficient grounds existed for these minority groups to demand equitable treatment. Their demands, abetted by growing national awareness, reached a crescendo in the 1960s. In a series of legislative enactments, the federal government responded with new policies and categorical funding of programs intended to repair previous inequities. The rationale adopted by the federal government to justify federal assistance to special populations downplayed the long-standing public policies and practices that had resulted in exclusion and highlighted instead the argument of cultural and educational disadvantage. The minority children in question, went the argument, were educationally behind in academic achievement due to deprived and disadvantaged home conditions, which were caused by an inferior cultural background. Hence, minority children entered school culturally deficient and had to be compensated with additional instruction. Students were at fault because they possessed a different culture from a white middle-class culture. Consequently, traditional curricula, methodologies, and structures were to stay intact. Furthermore, Anglocentrism went unchallenged. What was required to educate minorities were additional funds to provide remedial instruction. In general, instructional and support programs designed for minority students were viewed as negative and inappropriate for white students.

Some educators shared society's view of blacks, Indians, and Hispanics as outsiders, groups not expected to participate fully in the U.S. lifestyle. These attitudes were tinged with racial prejudice, and literature on the subject emphasized the inadequacies of such groups. The typically low IQ test scores of minority children were considered evidence of intellectual inferiority, which in turn was thought to justify low academic achievement. Low grades and early withdrawal from school were additional indexes to educators of such children's inability and disinterest in school. However, from the perspective of minority parents, their children were miseducated and mistreated, resulting in low school achievement and high drop-out rates. Although the preceding discussion has shown that national education policies and practices for minority groups have changed over time from harsh to less harsh, the lack of full and thorough historical analysis of relevant policy decisions and their connections with changing philosophies and dynamic movements over time stands in the way of real understanding of the forces at work and their effects. Repair of the holes in the data deserves serious attention.

ANTECEDENTS FOR INCLUSION

The inclusion of traditionally excluded minorities (American Indians, blacks, and Hispanics) into administrative roles in public school systems followed significant actions by the three branches of the federal government: (a) congressionally funded instructional and support programs targeted at poor and minority students, (b) federal court decisions aimed at resolving issues affecting racial or ethnic minorities, and (c) orders by the executive branch. The substantial involvement of the federal government in education, commencing seriously in the mid-1960s, constituted not only a significant attempt at upgrading the educational experience of minority youngsters but also a major effort on the part of minority leaders to realize a new policy of equal educational opportunity, mostly via the federal court system. The ensuing reforms comprised the educational side of the larger civil rights movement, which materially advanced the educational condition of ethnic and racial minorities, particularly enlarging the proportion of blacks and Hispanics in the teacher pool as well as increasing the number (albeit to a minor extent) of nonwhite administrators. The latter increase became entangled, however, with the desegregation movement in the South.

The unprecedented attempt to provide federal support for the education of disadvantaged and poor minority students began seriously during the administration of President L. B. Johnson (following initial efforts to start the process by the Kennedy administration) with the passage of the Elementary and Secondary Education Act (ESEA) in 1965. Title I of the ESEA provided federal dollars to school districts that enrolled high concentrations of poor children in an attempt to break the long-standing negative association of poverty and school achievement. Given the equally long-standing association between poverty and nonwhite ethnic and racial status, the effective target for Title I funds was underachieving, poor minority children. Most of the funds went to support compensatory instructional programs for these children. Reauthorization of Title I extended its provision to migrant children in 1966 and to institutionalized, neglected, and delinquent children in 1969. Other Titles of ESEA directed funds to other populations and efforts. For example, a 1968 amendment of the 1965 ESEA (Public Law 90–247) created Title VII of the Bilingual Education Act. Title VII addressed five purposes, including the establishment of training programs to increase the number and quality of bilingual education personnel. Even before ESEA, Title IV of the Civil Rights Act of 1964 made provision for training and offering technical assistance to school personnel to cope with problems incident to school desegregation. In 1972 Title VI of ESEA established the Emergency School Aid Act (ESAA) to meet the special costs incurred by school districts in their efforts to eliminate segregation and discrimination against minorities, both students and faculty. These federal actions, and others in the same vein, not only addressed the improvement of elementary and secondary education for minority children but also contributed to a substantial increase in the number of minority adults in the nation's schools and the importance of their work.

At the college level, the federal government passed legislation to aid youth from low-income families to attend college and to assist traditionally black colleges. The Higher Education Act (HEA) of 1965 also created Upward Bound and the Talent Search Program. In 1972 amendments to Title IV of the HEA funded the Basic Education Opportunity Grant Program; in 1973 further amendments authorized the National Direct Student Loan Program and the Guaranteed Student Loan Program; in 1974 the Supplemental Educational Opportunity Grant Program; and in 1978 the Training Program for Special Programs Staff and Leadership Personnel, and the Graduate and Professional Educational Opportunities Program. Title II of the HEA created the Fund for the Improvement of Postsecondary Education (FIPSE), which, although not targeted exclusively for traditionally black colleges, did provide those institutions substantial financial support to upgrade faculty, programs, and facilities. In sum, federal funding for postsecondary education enabled more minority persons to attend college. In turn, a large number of these students entered the field of education as teachers. Additionally, one federally funded initiative, the Teacher Corps (Title V–A of the HEA), sought directly to identify persons who could, after appropriate training, enhance the educational opportunities available to children in areas with high concentrations of low-income families. The Teacher Corps attracted primarily minority candidates, who added materially to the number of minority professionals working to improve the educational lot of minority children and youth.

While the Congress responded to demands for equity by funding experimental projects and compensatory educational programs and by providing financial assistance to expand minority access to higher education, the judicial branch of the federal government also acted. At the highest level, the U.S. Supreme Court contributed in case after case to the reform of educational policies and practices by requiring governments at all levels to meet minimal constitutional standards. The Court overthrew a body of state case law developed between 1850 and 1950 that permitted, if not actually sanctioned, educational practices and policies that failed to meet federal constitutional tests. Specifically, the Court's action in *Brown v. Board of Educa-*

tion of Topeka in 1954 began a long period of redefining the meaning of equal educational opportunity. Prior to 1850, a state's responsibility to provide its citizenry with education was generally interpreted by educators to mean making available a common school and a uniform curriculum (Zettel & Abeson, 1978, p. 189). In 1896 the Supreme Court ruled that separate but equal facilities and/or resources met the constitutional test of equality of treatment.

After the *Brown* decision, courts began to take into consideration factors such as the composition of the student body and the impact of the school on student achievement and engagement. In the late 1960s, a third definition of equal educational opportunity unfolded, with emphasis on establishing the connection between inputs and outcomes. Two important court cases contributed to the new definition, the Serrano case in California (*Serrano v. Priest*, 1971) and the Rodriguez case in Texas (*Rodriguez v. San Antonio*, 1973). Both cases addressed the issue of equitable state financing of public schools on constitutional grounds. Although the advocates who sought reform of school finance based on the 14th Amendment of the U.S. Constitution lost their arguments before the Court, the legislative and professional attention that the two cases drew, plus similar cases in other states, recast the case for equality in terms of equal results rather than equal resources and/or equal opportunity. The new line of argument sought to establish constitutional guarantees at the state level for differential resources for low-wealth school districts, which could not hope to match the levels of expenditures in high-wealth districts and which, therefore, could never hope to achieve equivalent levels of school performance. Given the high concentration of minority students in low-wealth school districts, it is obvious that this line of argument was eminently pertinent for enhancing equality of education for minorities.

Another Supreme Court ruling that helped to redefine equal educational opportunity appeared in *Lau v. Nichols* (1974). The Lau family sued the San Francisco school district, on behalf of their child and other children who did not understand English, on the grounds that the district did not provide the children a proper education because instruction was offered only in English. The Court ruled that the school district must provide instruction to non-English speakers in ways to ensure that they learned both English and the school curriculum. The direct consequence of the *Lau* decision was to require some form of bilingual or English-as-a-second-language instruction. But indirectly the ruling advanced the definition of equal educational opportunity one step further by requiring of schools not only different resources for achieving similar curricular objectives but now also different curricular objectives.

Judicial redefinition of equal educational opportunity, then, recognized that minority students received inadequate resources for their education and ruled that schools must provide adequate educational programs for minority populations. In addition, the accumulation of court cases revealed ever more clearly dire historical conditions, inadequate contemporary educational practices, and enormous challenges facing the educational community and the society as a whole.

The executive branch of the federal government now moved to improve minority education, and that movement stimulated organized social activism. Education itself had come under severe attack from ethnic and racial minorities because of these historical, and continuing, wrongs. Along with other political activists and society in general, minorities had brought under attack the "educational bureaucracy" for perpetuating a closed system of governance. Education had become, argued out-of-power groups and supportive observers, the exclusive domain of educational experts. The dissidents included minorities, feminists, advocates for the handicapped, advocates of tax reform and students, rights, and a number of elected officials. These diverse groups found common cause in the pursuit of a more humane, responsive, efficient, and effective school system.

In response to the entreaties of civil rights activists and especially their focus on employment discrimination, President Johnson signed Executive Order 11246, which laid the foundation for "affirmative action." Even though Executive Order 11246 applied to employment generally, it did not materially contribute to increasing the number of ethnic and racial minorities in school-district administrative positions. Although the intent of affirmative action applied also to the size and composition of the teaching pool, federal dollars and the specified purposes of the ESEA Title I and Title VI Programs in particular proved much more effective for opening teaching ranks to minorities outside the South. Meanwhile, another federal initiative—the press for

desegregation—actually negatively affected the employment of black teachers and administrators, particularly in the South.

THE STATUS OF MINORITIES IN ADMINISTRATIVE POSITIONS

Prior to school desegregation in the southern and border states, minority school administrators in segregated schools comprised a substantial proportion of the executive force. However, one of the unanticipated consequences of desegregation was a large reduction in the number of black school principals and teachers in those states (Abney, 1978; Arney, 1978; Butler, 1974; Haney, 1978). For example, during the 3-year period from 1967 to 1970, the number of black principals in North Carolina declined from 670 to 170; in Alabama from 250 to 40; in Mississippi from 250 to almost zero (Haney, 1978, p. 92). Also, in Louisiana between 1966 and 1971 the number of black principals fell from 512 to 363, a decrease of 29.1 percent. In Florida, Georgia, Louisiana, and Mississippi between 1968 and 1970, the percentage of decline in number of black principals was 27, 19.7, 19.6 and 21.4 respectively (Weinberg, 1977). (See Tables 7.1 and 7.2).

The 1970 national figures for minorities in the principalship reflect the historical lack of affirmative action that had long prevailed in administrative advancement: 0.3 percent were American Indians, 0.1 percent Asian American, 7.7 percent black, and 1.1 percent Hispanic, whereas 87.9 percent were white (Moody, 1973).

Again, at the principalship level nationally, Table 7.3 shows that between 1974 and 1982 the percentage of whites declined from 90.7 to 87.9; American Indians remained constant at 0.3 percent; Asian Americans rose from 0.1 to 0.6 percent; blacks remained constant at 7.7 percent; and Hispanics rose from 1.1 to 3.4 percent.

The figures for superintendents (Table 7.4) and for assistant, associate, and deputy superintendents (Table

Table 7.1　Changes in Number of Black and White Principals in Four States, 1968 and 1970

STATE	NUMBER OF SCHOOL DISTRICTS REPORTING, 1968 AND 1970	NUMBER OF BLACK PRINCIPALS			NUMBER OF WHITE PRINCIPALS		
		1968	1970	PERCENTAGE CHANGE	1968	1970	PERCENTAGE CHANGE
Florida	49	211	154	−27.0	1,026	1,082	+5.2
Georgia	123	342	276	−19.1	894	969	+7.7
Louisiana	49	366	298	−19.6	741	781	+5.1
Mississippi	74	199	158	−21.6	332	288	−13.3
Total	295	1,118	886	−21.4	2,993	3,120	+4.0

NOTE. From *U.S. v. State of Georgia, Brief Amicus Curiae for the National Education Association*, March 8, 1971, U. S. Court of Appeals for the Fifth Circuit No. 30,338, p. 39. Cited in *A Chance to Learn* (p. 130) by M. Weinburg, 1977, New York: Cambridge University Press.

Table 7.2   Percentage of Black and White Principals in Louisiana, 1966–1971

YEAR	TOTAL PRINCIPALS	WHITE PRINCIPALS	PERCENTAGE OF TOTAL	BLACK PRINCIPALS	PERCENTAGE OF TOTAL
1966–1967	1,452	940	64.7	512	36.3
1967–1968	1,470	960	65.3	510	34.7
1968–1969	1,464	973	66.5	492	33.5
1969–1970	1,432	1,009	71.4	413	29.0
1970–1971	1,480	1,043	74.1	363	25.9

NOTE. From "Black Education in Louisiana: A Question of Survival" by J. S. Butler, 1974, *Journal of Negro Education*, Vol. 43, No. 1, 1974, p. 23. Copyright 1974 by the *Journal of Negro Education*. Reprinted by permission.

Table 7.3   Percentage Representation of Principals by Race and Sex, 1974–1982

SURVEY DATE	WHITE MALE	WHITE FEMALE	TOTAL WHITE	AMERICAN INDIAN MALE	AMERICAN INDIAN FEMALE	TOTAL AMERICAN INDIAN	ASIAN MALE	ASIAN FEMALE	TOTAL ASIAN
1982	75.4	12.5	87.9	0.3	0.05	0.35	0.5	0.1	0.6
1979	77.3	11.7	89.0	0.3	0.1	0.4	0.2	0.1	0.3
1978	78.2	11.0	89.2	0.3	0.1	0.4	0.1	0.1	0.2
1975	79.8	10.4	90.2	0.3	0.05	0.35	0.1	0.05	0.15
1974	80.3	10.4	90.7	0.3	0.05	0.35	0.1	0.05	0.15

Table 7.3   (continued)

SURVEY DATE	BLACK MALE	BLACK FEMALE	TOTAL BLACK	HISPANIC MALE	HISPANIC FEMALE	TOTAL HISPANIC	NUMBER OF PRINCIPALS IN SAMPLE
1982	5.2	2.5	7.7	2.8	0.6	3.4	43,008
1979	6.1	2.6	8.7	1.4	0.3	1.7	67,262
1978	5.7	2.6	8.3	1.4	0.3	1.7	66,530
1975	5.8	2.2	8.0	1.1	0.2	1.3	72,285
1974	5.7	2.0	7.7	1.0	0.1	1.1	70,455

Table 7.4   Public School Superintendents by Race and Sex, 1981–1982

ETHNICITY	MALE NUMBER	MALE PERCENTAGE	FEMALE NUMBER	FEMALE PERCENTAGE	TOTAL NUMBER	TOTAL PERCENTAGE
American Indian	24	0.3	0	0	24	0.3
Asian, Pacific Islander	9	0.1	0	0	9	0.1
Black	51	0.7	6	0.1	57	0.7
Hispanic	84	1.1	4	0.1	88	1.1
White	7,417	96.5	93	1.2	7,510	97.7

NOTE 1. Total school superintendents in sample with *both* ethnicity and sex data = 7,688 from 28 states and Washington, DC; total districts reporting = 13,715 for 50 states and Washington, DC.

NOTE 2. Percentages in columns are based on total number of school superintendents in sample with *both* ethnicity and sex data.

NOTE 3. Tables 7.3 and 7.4 from *Recent Trends in the Representation of Women and Minorities in School Administration and Problems in Documentation* by Effie H. Jones and Xenia P. Montenegro, 1982, Arlington, VA: Office of Minority Affairs of the American Association of School Administrators, pp. 4, 16. Copyright 1982 by The Office of Minority Affairs of the American Association of School Administrators. Reprinted by permission.

7.5) reveal that by 1981–1982, the percentages of minorities in high administrative offices were even lower than for principals. The numbers in Tables 7.4 and 7.5 reveal the gross underrepresentation of racial and ethnic minority persons in executive positions in education.

Table 7.6 shows change status for all public school administrative positions between 1974 and 1982. The proportion of whites declined minimally, from 92.6 to 87.1 percent; American Indians declined, from 0.35 to 0.3 percent; Asians rose, from 0.15 to 0.8 percent; blacks rose, from 5.5 to 8.7 percent; and Hispanics rose, from 1.3 to 3.0 percent. Overall, between 1974 and 1982, there was an actual increase in the proportion of administrative positions held by blacks, Hispanics, and Asians, in that order, and a slight decrease in the percentages for whites and American Indians. However, the increases for blacks, Hispanics, and

Table 7.5   Deputy, Assistant, and Associate School Superintendents by Race and Sex, 1981–1982

	MALE		FEMALE		TOTAL	
ETHNICITY	NUMBER	PERCENTAGE	NUMBER	PERCENTAGE	NUMBER	PERCENTAGE
American Indian	4	0.1	0	0	4	0.1
Asian, Pacific Islander	16	0.5	4	0.1	20	0.6
Black	164	5.3	36	1.2	200	6.5
Hispanic	101	3.3	8	0.3	109	3.6
White	2,545	82.3	216	7.0	2,761	89.3

NOTE 1. Total deputy, assistant, and associate superintendents in sample with *both* ethnicity and sex data = 3,094 from 23 states and Washington, DC; total in the sample = 5,229.

NOTE 2. Percentages in columns are based on total number of deputy, assistant, and associate school superintendents in sample with *both* ethnicity and sex data.

Table 7.6   Representation in Administrative Positions by Race and Sex, 1974–1982

SURVEY DATE	WHITE MALE	WHITE FEMALE	TOTAL WHITE	AMERICAN INDIAN MALE	AMERICAN INDIAN FEMALE	TOTAL AMERICAN INDIAN	ASIAN MALE	ASIAN FEMALE	TOTAL ASIAN
1982	68.2	18.9	87.1	0.2	0.1	0.3	0.6	0.2	0.8
1979	74.1	16.5	90.6	0.3	0.2	0.5	0.2	0.1	0.3
1978	75.7	14.9	90.6	0.3	0.2	0.5	0.2	0.1	0.3
1975	79.6	12.6	92.2	0.3	0.1	0.4	0.1	0.1	0.2
1974	80.8	11.8	92.6	0.3	0.05	0.35	0.1	0.05	0.15

Table 7.6   (continued)

SURVEY DATE	BLACK MALE	BLACK FEMALE	TOTAL BLACK	HISPANIC MALE	HISPANIC FEMALE	TOTAL HISPANIC	NUMBER OF PRINCIPALS IN SAMPLE
1982	5.1	3.6	8.7	2.2	0.8	3.0	85,308
1979	3.8	2.5	6.3	1.7	0.6	2.3	44,944
1978	3.8	2.6	6.4	1.8	0.6	2.4	42,850
1975	3.5	2.0	5.5	1.4	0.4	1.8	43,208
1974	3.6	1.9	5.5	1.0	0.3	1.3	38,990

NOTE 1. Administrative positions include superintendents, associate, deputy, and assistant superintendents, and principals.

NOTE 2. Table 7.5 and 7.6 from *Recent Trends in the Representation of Women and Minorities in School Administration and Problems in Documentation* by Effie H. Jones and Xenia P. Montenegro, 1982, Arlington, VA: Office of Minority Affairs of American Association of School Administrators, pp. 9 and 22. Copyright 1982 by The Office of Minority Affairs of the American Association of School Administrators. Reprinted by permission.

Asians occurred in the context of a very rapid increase in the total number of administrative positions (from 38,990 in 1974 to 85,308 in 1982). Furthermore, the increase in the number of black administrators that occurred in the large urban areas of the North and of Hispanic administrators in the Southwest compensated for sharp reductions that took place in the southern and border states (Nieto & Valverde, 1976). As to the future, the increase in the size of the pool of black teachers (Weinburg, 1977) may presage continued expansion in the number of minority administrators, especially in large urban areas.

UPWARD MOBILITY

Sponsorship

Recent research offers an alternative explanation to the commonly held notion that the small size of the available pool explains the underrepresentation of minorities in public school administration. After the desegregation movement began in earnest, a notable influx of ethnic and racial minorities into administration started during the mid-1960s and continued into the mid-1970s. Prevailing sentiment has long supported the view that advancement into administrative ranks is a competitive process, encompassing formal preparation and state certification. Even the salience of competition within the selection process entered the scene only as late as the 1930s. Alongside a pattern of school administration based on preparation and merit has grown a system of sponsorship by university faculty and organizational superiors that some observers believe more significantly influences promotion than open competition. In fact, Tyack and Hansot (1982, p. 7) argue that sponsorship existed long before disinterested merit in educational administration. Studies of organizational advancement by Schein (1968, 1971) and of professionalization by Becker (1952, 1956, 1962) also document the pervasiveness of sponsorship in both education and other professions.

Sponsorship sometimes starts with recruitment, sometimes after individuals signal their interest in advancement. In either case the process of sponsorship commences with the determination by a cohort of administrators or university faculty that a recruit possesses desired qualities. Early on, and for some time, the operative criteria were based on personal attributes, specifically that "the man had accepted the Protestant ethic, and that he had some feeling of loyalty to the American dream" (Campbell, 1972, p. 13). As late as the 1940s and 1950s, according to Campbell, educators in a position to sponsor career mobility were not fully aware or supportive of cultural pluralism and loyalties. Valverde (1974) has empirically verified that administrators in one large urban school district concluded that minorities and women did not possess to the same extent as white males the personal attributes considered important for administration and were either discouraged from pursuing advanced studies in administration or were shunted into quasi-administrative posts.

Young (1973) and Ortiz (1982) found that minority teachers are typically assigned to schools with a high percentage of minority students. In addition, minority teachers often experience further separation from white teachers because of assignments to remote rooms such as bungalows; to courses in bilingual education, ethnic studies, remedial reading; and to duties in study and disciplinary halls. The crucial feature of the customary pattern of work activities is that it has deprived many minority teachers of opportunities for sponsorship. The connection between physical and social isolation is significant because it reduces chances for getting the attention of superiors, the GASing phenomenon discovered by Griffiths, Goldman, and McFarland (1965). (Blood, 1966, confirmed that GASing also existed on the West Coast.) Aspirants benefit from sponsorship only to the extent that they gain the respect, as well as the attention, of superiors. The process obviously favors those who are positioned, or who find ways to position themselves, to be visible to colleagues, principals, and central-office personnel.

The selection of minority teachers for administrative assignments shows still another significant difference from the pattern that applies to white males. Mascaro (1973), Valverde (1974), Contreras (1977), and Ortiz (1982) found that school districts commonly permit members of the minority community to participate in the selection process of minority administrators for posts of symbolic and/or practical significance to the community, such as director of bilingual educa-

tion programs and principals who "understand" the students' culture. Consistent with this practice of segregating teachers, minority administrators are placed in minority schools and assigned to direct programs identified with minorities. Such placements, again, reduce opportunities for interaction with potential sponsors.

Role Conflict

Not only have minority administrators found themselves required to manage very difficult situations; overcome stereotyping and segregation; gain much-needed exerience; and respond to minority constituents (students, parents, and community leaders). They also have had to demonstrate loyalty to superiors, fellow administrators, and teachers; explain dysfunctional practices of school districts in the education of minorities; and help district personnel to understand what is important to minority groups. All the while they serve as agents of change on behalf of policies and practices considered appropriate to the enhancement of minority children and youth. Given the unusual variety of demands and expectations placed on them, it comes as no surprise that minority administrators experience significant role conflict.

Problematic sponsorship also contributes to the conflict. Because of the entanglement of sponsorship with organizational socialization (that is, the phenomenon of adopting an administrative perspective about expectations, organizational values, and acceptable behaviors) and because of differences between the upward mobility of minority administrators and white males, organizational dissonance on the part of the former usually emerges. Hodgkinson (1970) offers additional explanation for role conflict via dissonance by postulating that values also vary with status in the organization. In addition, age, sex, and length of service in a particular organization, irrespective of minority status, appear to affect value orientation. Thus, the biographical approach suggests that minority administrators, especially when new in service and young in age, may not see the school world like older and more experienced white male administrators. The Getzels and Guba model (1957; see also Chapter 9) helps further to explain the role conflict in minority administrators. The minority experience has shaped the idiographic dimension of the minority administrator differently from that of white males and, to varying degrees, in opposition to the nomothetic needs of the administrative hierarchy of the organization. The organizational culture and climate (value structures, attitudes, and expected behaviors) established and maintained by white male administrators often promote in minority administrators not only role conflict but also intrapersonal conflict.

Differential assessment also has promoted conflict in cases when superordinates, colleagues, and subordinates evaluate minority administrators without taking into consideration the extent of multiple and conflicting agendas and the particularly heavy workload carried by the minority administrators. Evaluation according to standards that do not consider appropriately their work circumstances often leads to judgments that minority administrators are less competent than white counterparts (Casso, 1976; Escobedo, 1981). Inequity in assessment of performance reinforces historical attitudes about the worth of ethnic and racial minorities, thereby heightening role conflict.

So historical events, societal values, minority attitudes and attitudes toward minorities, organizational policies, and the nature of selection and participation of minorities all contribute to role conflict. Despite conceptual and empirical explanations for minority administrators' attitudinal dissonance and behavior in conflict with established organizational expectations and actions, observers' failure to appreciate these explanations has led to charges that many minority administrators are disloyal to the school's administration. The recent documentation by minority researchers of the extent and severity of the role conflict encountered by minority administrators in white institutions has helped to quiet those charges (Acevedo, 1979; Lopez, 1978, 1984).

A final contributor to the sense of role conflict derives from the difficulty minorities have in establishing claims of discrimination or social victimization (Lewis, 1978, p. 23). In the distribution of power and prestige in an information society like the United States, members of managerial and professional classes play important roles (Lenski, 1966). Unequal representation in managerial and professional positions by members of minority groups constitutes a vast inequality in the distribution of power in the United States. However, because so many Americans have believed that success or failure depends on individual merit and worth, it has been difficult to secure acceptance of the view that individual and/or institutional racism accounts for minority school administrators' behavior and depreciation of their performance (Lewis, 1978). An assertion of social victimization by a minority individual may bring only damage to his or her self-respect and the label of whiner or complainer.

PLACEMENT AND PREPARATION

Changing demographic trends have accelerated the need for recruiting, preparing, and placing minority candidates in administrative positions. More and more, minorities will become the majority in large urban school districts and in some suburban districts as well. If, at the same time, racism fades, then nonminority school districts may also seek the services of minority administrators. The long-standing practice of assigning minority administrators to schools primarily serving minorities, which reflected a racist orientation, may yield to a pattern of assignments that represents a pluralistic perspective. Together, the certain demographic trends and hopeful social conditions ensure an increasing demand for minority administrators.

How can more minorities be recruited into, and be appropriately prepared in, administration programs? Brooks (1984) recommends the use of a crosscultural and social perspective for recruiting minority candidates for advanced-degree programs. The recommendation applies with particular force to school administration because of the difficulties any candidate is likely to encounter in multiracial school communities plagued by inadequate financial resources and other difficult conditions. However, adoption of an authentic crosscultural and social perspective by preparation programs is particularly important for improving their success rates in socializing minorities into school administration (Lane, 1972; Rokeach, 1970; Seasholes, 1973).

If stronger invocation of a crosscultural and social perspective in recruitment proves successful in increasing the flow of minorities, change in the content of preparation programs must keep pace to equip potential administrators (and not only minorities) for the reality of existing multicultural schools. However valid and useful are the components of most existing educational administration preparation programs, a number of observers agree on the need for including new components that offer students opportunities to explore schools and their communities as unique cultural systems (Contreras, 1979; Jackson, 1978; Shakeshaft & Nowell, 1984; Stanley, 1979; Valverde, 1976). Renovation of preparation is crucial also because the theoretical constructs that dominate preparation programs figure into the difference between the recruitment, selection, advancement, and socialization of minority and white administrators.

Given the manner in which school districts select top executives, it is imperative that minority school administrators receive experience in a wide variety of settings to increase their chances of obtaining senior-level positions, especially in settings that have not consistently employed minorities. Currently, most minority superintendents are employed in districts with large minority pupil populations (Moody, 1973; Scott, 1980). Because of the nature of the socialization and networking processes that foster access to higher-level positions generally, minority administrators must find more opportunities for placement at the lower level in the mainstream if they are to progress in increasing numbers to the top.

As for the substantive side of preparation programs, several studies strongly suggest the importance of more stress on the presence and operation of informal friendship patterns, coalitions, and networks (Bass, 1984; Forsyth & Hoy, 1978; Gladstein, 1984; Gronn, 1983; Hanson, 1984; Licata & Hack, 1982). These studies take on increased meaning in the light of data from Lincoln and Miller (1979) and Ortiz (1982) that race influences the level and degree of communication among colleagues within an organization. Thus, minority status may influence the pattern of communication in an organization and, therefore, sponsorship and socialization.

Other findings with implications for preparation come from (a) Herriott and Firestone (1984), who suggest that educational administrators must take into account that their organizations fall on a continuum between anarchy and a loosely coupled state; (b) Peterson (1984), who argues that a school's size and social status as well as selected socialization practices affect the district's control over principals; (c) Crowson and Porter-Gehrie (1980), who support the notion that schools are highly decentralized and loosely coupled organizations; and (d) Smircich (1983), who urges that educational organizations be viewed as cultural systems rather than as solely rational organizations existing in a social milieu that influences administrative effectiveness (see also Fiedler & Chemers, 1976; Lane, 1972; Lewis, 1978; Lincoln & Miller, 1979; Myrdal, 1944). But the research does not indicate how strongly minority membership influences communications, friendship, and sponsorship.

In sum, incorporation of what can be learned from the studies cited above promises to enhance the recruitment, retention, preparation, and placement of minority candidates for educational administration.

CONCLUSIONS AND A LOOK TO THE FUTURE

It is highly desirable in a multicultural and multiracial society to tap the resources of talented individuals from all racial and ethnic groups to improve the effectiveness of our schools; to expose everyone connected with our schools to diverse social values; and to improve our democratic system of government through participation by minorities at all levels in an important social organization, the school. To accomplish these objectives, school districts of every type and size and in every part

of the nation must increase the employment of minority administrators; colleges and universities must improve efforts to increase enrollment of minority students in educational administration programs and must add to the preparation of administrative candidates systematic study of schools as cultural systems. Improved understanding of the culture of schools will contribute not only to improved administrative practice but also to opportunities for participation in sponsorship networks.

The importance of increasing the number and percentage of minority school administrators goes beyond the issue of underrepresentation and the need to enhance the influence and status of minority educators. Although individual achievement is important, the long-term benefit remains the potential for minority administrators to contribute to the improvement of educational opportunities for minority school pupils. Coleman (1974) offers a clue to how the school administrator may make his or her contribution. In his treatise on *Power and the Structure of Society*, Coleman concludes that in modern societies power is separated from its sources, that individuals have lost power to "corporate" actors, including school administrators (p. 53). Corporate actors can hire specialists (for example, in schools, counselors, psychologists, and curriculum specialists) to assist them in dealing with pupils and their parents, whereas parents typically cannot hire such specialists. Therefore, in a transaction with a pupil or parent the advantage lies with school administrators (p. 61). But minority school administrators, as corporate actors, may sensitize schools to the value of providing improved educational opportunities for minority pupils. Preparation programs that emphasize the concept of schools as cultural systems can enhance the capability of both minority and nonminority administrators to serve as corporate actors in behalf of minority and nonminority pupils alike.

Edelson (1980) and Sennett (1978) have both argued that most administrative actions taken on behalf of the disadvantaged are symbolic and serve primarily to protect the interest of elites. Thus, educational administrators must be taught to understand value-laden symbols within social systems in order to improve their effectiveness as administrators. The future will surely need minority school administrators employed in a wider variety of school systems and aided by preparation programs that view schools as cultural systems in which effective leadership involves the use of symbols to motivate pupils, teachers, and parents (Cunningham & Payzant, 1984). Administrators will need to analyze schools as cultural systems that contain informal networks and friendships and will need to use wisely the symbols that are valued by the membership.

Because schools are generally loosely coupled, with decentralized decision-making structures, educational administrators will need to learn how to manage routine organizational matters and how to understand formal and informal organizational communication in different ways than before, as well as how to form coalitions among peers in multicultural settings.

On the research side of the coin, it is pertinent to recognize that race and ethnicity appear not only in particular conditions and events, such as the denial of voting rights but, more significantly, in the way in which individuals use epistemological categories, usually ethnocentric ones (Johnson, 1975), to construct their own cultural and social realities. So it is that researchers who examine educational issues pertinent to minority populations must utilize broader ideological frameworks to insure that heretofore seemingly unrelated problems come together in recognizable patterns. To be specific, researchers will need to redefine problems of race and ethnicity in education so that new solutions to lasting problems, such as upward mobility, can be generated.

Along with adoption of a more comprehensive ideological framework, researchers should find it rewarding to make more extensive use of the qualitative methodology when investigating conditions and elements associated with prospects of minorities in education. Because race and ethnicity exist in a cultural and social context as well as in an organizational environment, the use of a field methodology, as advocated by Miles and Huberman (1984), may prove particularly fruitful: that is, utilizing a research scheme that requires intense observation, scrupulous recording of naturally occurring social interactions, and the drawing of patterns in the inductive tradition. Researchers who are interested in studying the conditions of minorities will find that scholars in other fields—for example policy analysis, program evaluation, public administration, organizational studies, linguistics, psychology, sociology, and urban planning—have already blazed a useful trail for them.

Beyond preparation and beyond research, however, remains the strategic issue of restructuring educational institutions to eliminate inequity and social injustice. A fundamental task for leaders, today and tomorrow, is to restate the purpose of school in ways that promote meaningful dialogue and debate, even controversy, and that attempt to establish goals broad enough to foster and encompass cultural pluralism as well as the common wealth. The preparation of educators, administrators in particular, has long emphasized the prevention or deflection of organized opposition by stressing consensus, by coopting external groups, by abstaining from organizational conflict. But school administrators must learn to cope with conflict and create new organizational arrangements necessary to integrate all administrators into the social networks in organizations. Educational leaders, minority and majority, will need to develop skills in coping with differing social networks, formal and informal, within school districts. In the past organizational members sought accommodation in order to avoid conflict, but this is no longer true in most instances. It appears that the future will continue to see groups competing with each other to see whose power and philosophy will succeed.

REFERENCES

Acevedo, B. A. (1979). *Socialization: The Mexican American mid-level administrator in Texas institutions of higher education.* Unpublished doctoral dissertation, University of Texas at Austin.

Acuna, R. (1972) *Occupied America: The Chicano's struggle toward liberation.* San Francisco: Canfield.

Abney, E. E. (1978). The effects and consequences of desegregation on the professional job status of Black public school principals employed in Florida. *Cross Reference, 1*(3), 239–258.

Arney, N. L. (1978). Implementation of desegregation as a discriminary process. *Journal of Negro Education, 47*(1), 28–45.

Bass, D. J. (1984). Being in the right place: A structural analysis of individual influence in an organization. *Administration Science Quarterly, 29*(4), 518–539.

Becker, H. S. (1952). The career of the Chicago public school teacher. *American Journal of Sociology, 52,* 470–477.

Becker, H. S. (1956). The elements of identification with an occupation. *American Sociological Review, 21,* 341–348.

Becker, H. S. (1962). The nature of a profession. In *Education for the Profession* (pp. 27–46). 61st Yearbook of the National Society for the Study of Education. Chicago: University of Chicago Press.

Blood, R. (1966). *The functions of experience in professional preparation: Teaching and the principalship.* Unpublished doctoral dissertation, Claremont Graduate School, Claremont, CA.

Brooks, L. (1984). Counseling special groups: Women and ethnic minorities. In D. Brown, L. Brooks, & Associates (Eds.), *Career choice and development: Applying contemporary theories and practice.* San Francisco: Jossey-Bass.

Brown v. Board of Education of Topeka, 347 U.S. 483 (1954).

Butler, J. S. (1974). Black educators in Louisiana: A question of survival. *Journal of Negro Education, 43*(1), 9–24.

Campbell, R. F. (1972). Educational administration: A twenty-five year perspective. *Educational Administration Quarterly, 8*(2), 1–15.

Carnoy, M. (1974). *Education as cultural imperialism.* New York: David McKay.

Carter, T. (1970). *Mexican Americans in schools: A history of educational neglect.* New York: College Entrance Examination Board.

Casso, H. (1976). *Chicanos in higher education.* Albuquerque: University of New Mexico Press.

Cisneros v. Corpus Christi ISD Civil action no. 68-C-95 (S.O. Texas, June 4, 1970).

Coleman, J. (1974). *Power and the structure of society.* New York: Norton.

Contreras, R. A. (1977). *The role of the Spanish-surnamed administrator in the school-community relationship.* Unpublished doctoral dissertation, Stanford University, Stanford, CA.

Contreras, R. A. (1979). Spanish-surnamed educational administrators. *Emergent Leadership, 3*(2), 33–47.

Crowson, R. L., & Porter-Gehrie, C. (1980). The discretionary behavior of principals in large-city schools. *Education Administration Quarterly*, *16*(1), 45–69.

Cunningham, L., & Payzant, T. (1984). *Understandings, attitudes, skills and symbols: Leadership in the future*. Phoenix, AZ: University Council of Educational Administration.

Edelson, M. (1980). *The symbolic uses of politics*. Urbana, IL: University of Illinois Press.

Escobedo, T. (1981). *Education and Chicanos: Issues and research*. Los Angeles: Spanish Speaking Mental Health Research Center, UCLA.

Fiedler, F., & Chemers, M. (1976). *Improving leadership effectiveness: The leader match concept*. New York: John Wiley.

Forsyth, P. B., & Hoy, W. K. (1978). Isolation and alienation in educational organizations. *Education Administration Quarterly*, *14*(1), 80–96.

Franklin, J. H. (Ed.). (1968). *Color and race*. Boston: Beacon.

Getzels, J. W., & Guba, E. G. (1957). Social behavior and the administrative process. *School Review*, 65, 423–441.

Gladstein, D. L. (1984). Groups in context: A model of task groups' effectiveness. *Administration Science Quarterly*, *29*(4), 499–517.

Gordon, M. M. (1964). *Assimilation in American life*. New York: Oxford.

Griffiths, D. E., Goldman, S., & McFarland, W. J. (1965). Teacher mobility in New York City. *Educational Administration Quarterly*, *1*, 15–31.

Gronn, P. C. (1983). Talk as the work: The accomplishment of school administration. *Administration Science Quarterly*, *28*(1), 1–22.

Handlin, O. (1959). *Immigration as a factor in American history*. Englewood, Cliffs, NJ: Prentice-Hall.

Haney, J. E. (1978). The effects of the Brown decision on Black eductors. *Journal of Negro Education*, *47*(1), 88–95.

Hanson, M. (1984). Exploration of mixed metaphors in educational administration research. *Issues in Education*, *2*(3), 167–185.

Herriott, R. E., & Firestone, W. A. (1984). Two images of schools as organizations: A refinement and elaboration. *Education Administration Quarterly*, *20*(4), 41–57.

Hodgkinson, C. (1970). Organizational influence on value systems. *Educational Administration Quarterly*, *7*(3), 46.

Itzkoff, S. (1969). *Cultural pluralism and American education*. Scranton, PA: International Textbook.

Jackson, B. L. (1978). Preparation of educational leaders from a Black perspective. *Emergent Leadership*, *2*(2), 67–93.

Johnson, H. C. (1975). Educational policy study and the historical perspective. *Educational Administration Quarterly*, *11*(2), 38–54.

Jones, E. H., & Montenegro, X. P. (1982). *Recent trends in the representation of women and minorities in school administration and problems in documentation*. Arlington, VA: American Association of School Administrators.

Kallan, H. (1924). *Culture and democracy in the United States*. New York: Boni & Liveright.

Lane, R. E. (1972). *Political man*. New York: Free Press.

Lau v. Nichols, 414 U.S. 563 (1974).

Lenski, G. E. (1966). *Power and privilege: A theory of social stratificaton*. New York: McGraw-Hill.

Lewis, M. (1978). *The culture of inequality*. New York: Meridian.

Licata, J. W., & Hack, W. G. (1980). School administrator grapevine structure. *Education Administration Quarterly*, *16*(3), 82–99.

Lincoln, J. R., & Miller, J. (1979). Work and friendship ties in organizations: A comparative analysis of relational networks. *Administration Science Quarterly*, *24*(2), 244–266.

Lopez, A. F. (1979). *Role conflict specific to Chicano administrators in higher education*. Unpublished doctoral dissertation, University of Arizona, Tucson.

Lopez, H. (1984). *The management of ethnic role conflict by Chicano chief executive officers*. Unpublished doctoral dissertation, University of Texas at Austin.

Marden, C. F., & Meyer, G. (1968). *Minorities in American society*. New York: Van Nostrand Reinhold.

Mascaro, C. (1973). *The early on the job socialization of first year elementary school principals*. Unpublished doctoral dissertation, University of California, Santa Barbara.

McWilliams, C. (1968). *North from Mexico: The Spanish-speaking people of the United States*. New York: Greenwood.

Meriam, L. (1928). *Meriam report*. Washington, DC: Brookings Institute.

Miles, M., & Huberman, A. M. (1984). Drawing valid meaning from qualitative data: Toward a shared craft. *Educational Researcher*, *13*(5), 20–30.

Moody, C. D. (1973). The Black superintendent. *School Review*, *81*(3), 373–382.

Myrdal, G. (1944). *An American dilemma* (Vols. 1–2). New York: Harper & Row.

Nieto, C., & Valverde, L. (1976). A momentous leap: From survival to leadership. *Consortium Currents*, *3*(1), 2–10.

Ogbu, J. (1977). *Minority education and caste*. New York: Academic.

Orleans, P., & Ellis, W. R., Jr. (Eds.). (1971). *Race, change, and urban society*. Beverly Hills, CA: Sage.

Ortiz, F. I. (1982). *Career patterns in education: Women, men, and minorities in public school administration*. New York: Praeger.

Peterson, K. D. (1984). Mechanisms of administrative control over managers in educational organizations. *Administration Science Quarterly*, *24*(4), 573–597.

Plessy v. Ferguson, 163 U.S. 537 (1896).

Rivera, F. (1972). *The Chicanos: A history of Mexican Americans*. New York: Hill and Wang.

Rodriguez v. San Antonio ISD 36 L. Ed. 2d. 45. (1973).

Rokeach, M. (1970). *Beliefs, attitudes, and values*. San Francisco: Jossey-Bass.

Schein, E. H. (1968). Organizational socialization and the profession of management. *Industrial Management Review*, *9*, 1–15.

Schein, E. H. (1971). The individual, the organization and the career: A conceptual scheme. *Journal of Applied Behavioral Science*, *7*(4), 401–426.

Scott, H. (1980). *The Black school superintendent*. Washington, DC: Howard University Press.

Seasholes, B. (1973). Political socialization of Blacks: Implications for self and society. In J. A. Banks & J. D. Grombs (Eds.), *Black Self-Concept* (pp. 71–92). New York: McGraw-Hill.

Sennett, R. (1978). *The fall of the public man*. New York: Random House.

Serrano v. Priest 5 Cal. 3d 584, 96 Cal. Rptr. 601, 487 P 2d 1241. (1971).

Shakeshaft, C., & Nowell, I. (1984). Research on theories, concepts, and models of organizational behavior: The influence of gender. *Issues in Education*, *2*(3), 186–203.

Smircich, L. (1983). Concepts of culture and organizational analysis. *Administration Science Quarterly*, *28*(3), 339–358.

Stanley, H. D. (1979). Rockefeller foundation program for training minority-group school administrators at the superintendent level: Perceptions of skills and value. *Cross Reference*, *2*(2), 86–95.

Treaty of Guadalupe Hidalgo, 1848. (1968) Sacramento, CA: Telefact Foundation.

Tyack, D. (1967). *Turning points in American educational history*. Waltham, MA: Blaisdell.

Tyack, D., & Hansor, E. (1982). *Managers of virtue*. New York: Basic.

U.S. Bureau of the Census. (1983). *Detailed occupation and years of school completed by age, for civil labor force by sex, race, and Spanish origin*. 1980. Washington, DC: U.S. Department of Commerce.

Valverde, L. A. (1974). *Succession socialization: Its influence on school administrative candidates and its implication on the exclusion of minorities from administration*. Washington, DC: National Institute of Education Project 3–0813. ERIC ED 098 052.

Valverde, L. A. (1976). Why are so few women and minorities in educational administration? *Emergent Leadership*, *1*, 7–10.

Weinberg, M. (1977). *A chance to learn: A history of race and education in the U.S.* New York: Cambridge University Press.

Young, D. (1973). The socialization of American minority peoples. In D. Goslin (Ed.), *Handbook of Socialization Theory and Research* (pp. 1103–1140). Chicago: Rand McNally.

Zangwill, I. (1909). *The melting pot.* New York: Macmillan.

Zettel, J., & Abeson, A. (1978). The right to a free appropriate public education. In C. P. Hooker (Ed.), *The courts and education.* The 77th Yearbook of the National Society for the Study of Education. Chicago: University of Chicago Press.

CHAPTER 8

The Search for Equity in Educational Administration: A Commentary

Craig Richards

It is no simple task to write a commentary on a field of research whose findings hold profound consequences for our society. The temptation is to want to comment on everything. Chapters 6 and 7, by Ortiz and Marshall and by Valverde and Brown are excellent examples of the diversity of the literature. Before proceeding with my discussion of their work and the larger body of research it surveys, one caveat is in order: Commentaries are commonly critical; this one is not. It is, however, intended to complement their work within the constraints of my own disciplinary perspective as a political economist.

As my colleagues have demonstrated in their literature reviews, the research on women and racial and ethnic minorities in educational administration is eclectic, embracing the spectrum of methodological possibilities, from descriptive narrative to complex causal models. It has found many disciplinary homes as well: anthropology, economics, organizational psychology and sociology, and political science. The research is characterized not only by methodological and disciplinary diversity but also by sharp differences in ideological perspective and a concomitant narrowing of the distance between the normative and positive aspects of the research. If, indeed, such distinctions are falsely held in the social sciences, as some would argue, then it is crucial that the ideological assumptions we

Consultant/reviewers: Jacqueline Jordan Irvine, Emory University; John H. Maxey, Georgia State University; and Charlotte Robinson, Georgia State University

hold be even clearer. They must be clear not only to our readers but to ourselves. It is to this problem that I want to address my comments. In particular, I want to focus on the causal assumptions we bring with us when we prescribe solutions for the problems of inequality and discrimination in educational administration.

Educational researchers—even the least action-oriented among them—are dually charged: first, to seek and describe accurately the truth about inequality and discrimination; and second, to pursue vigorously policies that would ameliorate both the practices and their destructive effects. Unfortunately, the poverty of theory attending most of the research on inequality and discrimination impedes policy prescription. For example, what in the research explains the current level of hostility toward affirmative action by major federal institutions whose charge it is to encourage it, and at the same time explains the resistance of many state and local agencies and firms in the private sector to the conservative signals being sent from Washington? It appears that the "good guys" and the "bad guys" have switched hats. But one cannot be sanguine about why they have done so.

Why should we continue to be concerned about the participation of minorities and women in positions of educational leadership? For one, our legal responsibilities require it: Title VII of the Equal Employment Opportunity Act prohibits discrimination in employment because of race or sex; desegregation mandates and sex-discrimination decrees by the courts mandate compliance; affirmative action guidelines encourage more hiring; Executive Order 11246 makes federal contract compliance applicable to institutions of higher education. But there are more compelling reasons.

Educational insitutions are visibly situated at the crossroads of American life. Public schools, the foundation of our educational system, are collectively owned enterprises that retain their currency not only because they transmit skills valued in the reproduction of the economic life of U.S. society but also because they provide our children with an implicit curriculum that transmits civic values and symbolizes, in microcosm, the fundamentals of U.S. democracy. Ideally, public schools project an archetypal vision, a prototype, of U.S. society. At their worst, a "hidden curriculum" imbedded in the organization of school life leads to less than ideal learning experiences for children (Apple, 1982; Carnoy & Levin, 1985; Sharp & Green, 1975). One feature of the hidden curriculum can be the deleterious effects associated with the absence of minority and female role models in positions of educational leadership.

If affirmative action is a legitimate concern in public schools, it is more so in our nation's public colleges and universities. Whereas the public school is most deeply rooted in the norms of its local community, in collegiate institutions the normative frame of reference takes on a larger, less parochial cast; it shifts from community to region, region to state, and state to nation, depending only on the type of institution and its vision. Our best institutions reach beyond the normative demarcation of the nation-state to inspire in their students a sensitivity to a multicultural society in a world community.

Yet, however parochial or global the vision of a school or college, it signals to its community, through daily institutional practice, the intensity of its commitment to democratic ideals. When its daily practice too severely contradicts the public weal, the legitimacy of the institution is undermined.

Thus, our schools and colleges figure prominently in the compulsion for legitimacy because they are the *sine qua non* of legitimacy. Indeed, educational institutions manufacture legitimacy at a rate that rivals their manufacture of knowledge. The ultimate symbol of their legitimacy is a certificate of completion, a diploma. Because our society ascribes to meritocracy and individualism with great enthusiasm, the legitimizing power of the diploma—and thus, the school—is magnified. The symbolic terrain of schools and colleges becomes contested when educators and citizens disagree on the legitimacy of particulars—allocating scarce resources, energy, and time. This contest becomes particularly keen when educational practice and national ideals clash.

The tumult of the 1960s recalls many such clashes: over desegregation, student First Amendment rights, school prayer. The tension between love of tradition and the impulse to pursue a reconstructive vision of education frequently pits those whose place in U.S. society is enhanced by the status quo against those who aspire to enter into the mainstream.

Schools and colleges, in their daily institutional practices, possess great symbolic value because they can either recreate anew the ideals of democracy or perpetuate the gulf of despair built on caste and class. The affirmative employment of women and minorities in leadership positions in schools and colleges speaks directly to the possibilities of bridging of this gap. In a sense, our nation's schools and colleges present our collective public self.

For these reasons, people who believe that public education should promote racial and gender equality express concern not only that institutional resources be equitably distributed and that textbooks present role models of minorities and women in leadership positions but also that the employment practices of the institution reflect these values. In short, public institutions of education should serve as ideals—institutional role models—of the democratic principles of the society.

Nowhere is the disparity between ideal and practice more damaging to the meritocratic charter of educational institutions than in the underrepresentation of women and minorities in administrative positions. These positions are highly visible; they signal institutional commitment to equity for all other units within the organization. Furthermore, when women and minorities secure highly visible leadership positions in educational institutions, the organization signals the legitimacy of affirmative action and equal employment opportunity to the wider society, diminishes the power of stereotypes, provides role models for children and young adults, and confirms experientially the democratic ideals taught in the classroom. To put it simply, schools and colleges nourish democratic values when they practice what they teach.

So how have public schools and colleges fared in establishing women and minorities in visible positions of educational leadership? A reasonable answer to this question must address a complex definitional problem: namely, what constitutes a legitimate level of representation? Should, for example, the percentage of minority administrators in a given institution reflect the percentage of minority students, the percentage of minority advanced-degree holders, the percentage of minority graduates from administrative-degree-granting institutions in the region, or should all such benchmarks be rejected as "reverse discrimination"? Are suburban school districts in affluent white communities exempt from affirmative action considerations because there is no community-inspired "crisis of legitimacy"? No compelling rejoinder to these questions leaps to the fore, but the questons must be raised because the choice of yardstick supplies meaning to the facts. The selection process itself is profoundly political; it defines the legitimate level of representation of women and minorities in educational administration. Indeed, a great deal of the current political dissension surrounding alternative definitions (and social policy) derives from a lack of consensus about how affirmative public schools and colleges should be in their employment practices.

The politics involved in forging a policy of public consensus are further complicated by competing theories, each claiming to explain better *why* women and minorities are statistically underrepresented in the professional sectors of the labor market.

The chapters by Ortiz and Marshall and by Valverde and Brown in this book provide excellent, concrete examples of competing explanatory approaches in the literature. Ortiz and Marshall's review on women in educational administration develops four themes in the historical development of the profession. These four themes indeed dominate the literature as causal explanations for the underrepresentation of women in educational administration. They are (a) the bifurcation of the education profession into teaching (female-dominated) and administrative (male-dominated) components; (b) the municipal reform movement at the beginning of the 20th century, which encouraged efficiency and scientific management (male ideology); (c) the importance of sponsorship, not open competition, to career mobility in educational administration (patriarchal exclusion); and finally, (d) the ability of male-dominated faculties of educational administration to discourage research and discussion of gender and power issues. Although Ortiz and Marshall's paper does not do so explicitly, presumably the causal linkages between these four themes could be summed as follows: The ideology of the day held that efficient and scientific management were things that men did better than women; thus, the municipal reform movement encouraged school boards to hire male principals and superintendents. Male administrators, pursuing efficiency and scientific management, bureaucratized the schools, making it difficult for women to manage them. Finally, men—through the "old boy" network—sponsored other men into the key positions required to advance into the principalship and superintendency. And if all the foregoing didn't serve to keep women out of the profession, then departments of educational administration, also dominated by men, were insensitive to the aspirations of women educators and some-

times openly hostile. Furthermore, such institutions avoided discussing in their classes or conducting research on the problem of discrimination against women in educational administration. For Ortiz and Marshall, the glass has been clearly more empty than full.

The chapter by Valverde and Brown, on the other hand, strikes a more optimistic note. Their history would summarize something like this: During the early years of public education, the white, Anglo-Saxon, Protestant elite was primarily concerned with the Americanization and mainstreaming of the flood of immigrants pouring into the country. Thus, it could not permit the schools in the mainstream to be run by racial and ethnic minorities for fear that such school leaders would fail to appropriately acculturate the children under their charge. (Segregated schools in the South remained an exception.) Opportunities for minority educators in leadership positions became possible only after Congress, the courts, and the executive branch took strong legislative, legal, and fiscal action to improve the education of minorities. One result of their collective intervention, in what we now call the Civil Rights Era, was to enlarge the number of minorities in the teacher labor force. These new minority teachers, hired in the 1960s, would form the pool from which the future supply of minority administrators would be drawn. Valverde and Brown see continued problems with the recruitment, selection, and sponsorship of minority administrators, but they are hopeful that the demand for minority administrators will continue to increase and that eventually minority administrators will be assigned to schools in a color-blind fashion. Valverde and Brown see the glass less than half full, but filling.

While both Ortiz and Marshall and Valverde and Brown take historical perspectives in their analyses of the literature, their reviews are also implicitly infused with a liberal dose of social-science explanatory schemas and methodological suggestions. For example:

> The judgment of elders and power brokers prevails in determining what is good, correct, legitimate, and valuable in theory, research publication, practice, behavior, and even sentiment. Questioning fundamental values and structures to explain gender inequity could not be expected to occur without extraordinary challenge because of threat to existing practice and the distribution of educational institutions. As Minogue (1983) put it, "nothing gets done which is unacceptable to dominant or influential political groups, which may be defined to include the 'bureaucratic leadership' group" (p.73). (Ortiz & Marshall, p.136)

> Because race and ethnicity exist in a cultural and social context as well as an organizational environment, the use of a field methodology as advocated by Miles and Huberman (1984) may prove particularly fruitful: that is, utilizing a research scheme that requires intense

observation, scrupulous recording of naturally occurring social interactions and the drawing of patterns in the inductive tradition. (Valverde & Brown, p.155.)

Yet it is not obvious to readers what kind of policy conclusions can flow from the social-science constructs and methodologies that undergird their analyses. The following taxomony, although it has limited usefulness, suggests a method for locating the causal locus of the researcher, and thus, where the researcher would be likely to encourage strategic interventions. Subsequent to this discussion, I will return to the two literature reviews and discuss their policy implications in light of my taxonomy.

MODELS OF INEQUITY

Explanations for the underrepresentation of women and minorities in positions of professional leadership fall loosely along a continuum of themes resting on separate bodies of research. At one end of the continuum, the research emphasizes existential themes; in the middle, institutional themes; at the other end, macrostructural themes. The research associated with existential themes examines variation related to gender and race in individual choices, attitudes, and motivations. Studies that explore the middle range focus on women and minorites in specific institutional settings. The research on macrostructural themes includes a literature that emphasizes the broad cultural and social forces shaping both individuals and institutions.

Existential Themes

One body of research on women and minorities emphasizes motivational and attitudinal characteristics to explain the observed differences in participation rates in administrative posts. These studies tend to highlight personality factors—intrapersonal experiences—that condition minorities and women to values and behavior patterns that are inimical to success in occupations traditionally dominated by white males. Personality traits such as low self-esteem, low expectations of success, self-derogation, and an external locus of control have received attention (Herner, 1971; Laws, 1976; Schmuck, 1975; Sutherland, 1978).

Another approach, in the economics literature, looks at differences in individual investments in education and training. The human-capital approach explains observed differences in the participation rates or wages secured by minorities and women as a function of their comparatively lower investments in education and training. That is, compared to white males, the model predicts that women and minorities will offer, on average, fewer years of investment in education and training or that the quality of their education and training will be lower. Thus, because women and minorities are less competitive in the labor market, they earn less. The human-capital approach dominates contemporary approaches to labor economics and rests upon the assumptions of rational market behavior (Ehrenberg & Smith, 1982).

The psychological and human-capital approaches both emphasize individual differences, whether of motivation, self-perception, or training and education. Thus, the existential literature focuses on individual choices, behaviors, and psychological states. Although this line of research frequently documents that women and minorities make poor choices, lack motivation, and have problems with their self-esteem, it fails to address, for the most part, why it is that women and minorities, *in particular*, have less education or an inferior education, have lower self-esteem, and have poor work habits compared to the white males with whom they compete. It is only by implication that minorities and women appear to be victims of a culture of poverty or patriarchy and thus make the kinds of choices that lead to failure in the labor market.

Institutional Themes

Institutional research shifts emphasis from the responses of individual women and minorities toward their social environment to the impact upon them of institutions like the family and the workplace. Institutional researchers use concepts like role expectation, institutional racism and sexism, and employer discrimination to explain why women and minorities are underrepresented (Blau & Justenius, 1976; Knowles & Prewitt, 1969; Lloyd & Niemi, 1979). For minorities, this argument frequently shows itself in terms of the role the family plays in sustaining "a culture of poverty," and for women, as sex-role socialization (Gross & Trask, 1976; Moynihan, 1965; Schmuck, 1975; Stansbury, Thomas, & Wiggens, 1984).

Some researchers have proposed that institutional discrimination occurs because of race and gender stereotyping. One form of this argument in the economic literature is called "signaling" theories of discrimination (Arrow, 1973; Schiller, 1980). The argument proceeds as follows: Collecting and maintaining information about prospective employees costs money; employers statistically associate certain risks with ascriptive characteristics (e.g., race, gender, age); employers use those characteristics to screen *all* applicants to reduce information costs.

Another economic explanation focuses on wage differentials. The "monopsony model," applicable where the employer has monopoly power in the labor market, makes it profitable for the employer to separate his labor force into distinguishable groups according to how they respond to changes in wages offered. For example, at the institutional level women tend to have less job mobility than men, restricting women's ability to seek competitive wages. Their job mobility is lower because their careers stand second in importance to the careers of male heads of households. Women, it is argued, will therefore continue to offer their services at a lower wage (Lloyd & Niemi, 1979, p. 158).

Most neoclassical economists draw a sharp distinction between market and nonmarket discrimination. The former occurs when some economic agent, whether an individual or a firm, places a negative valuation on a worker because of ascriptive characteristics unrelated to that worker's productivity (Arrow, 1973; Becker, 1957). In addition, the agent must be both willing and able to pay a discrimination coefficient, an additional wage paid, for example, to a male worker to avoid hiring a female worker. Nonmarket discrimination occurs when a group, based on ascriptive characteristics, has unequal access to education, the courts, or housing and it is frequently an important source of observed differences in occupational attainment and wages received.

The most profound implication of the neoclassical approach to labor-market discrimination is that the discriminator maximizes utility rather than profit. That is, discriminators value their personal satisfaction higher than additional profits; thus, they maximize their utility (satisfaction), not profits. However, according to neoclassical theory, when an employer satisfies the desire to discriminate, it should lead to higher average labor costs. (For example, in black-white racial discrimination, this would be the equivalent of a wage premium for white workers.) Thus, discriminatory employers should, over the long run, be driven from the marketplace by nondiscriminatory employers, who are more competitive because they do not discriminate.

The empirical persistence of labor-market discrimination over "the long run" has undermined the validity of the traditional economic optimism that discrimination is untenable in a free market society. It has also encouraged the development of alternative explanations. One of the earliest of such efforts linked disenfranchised groups to separate labor markets (Kerr, 1954). Kerr argued that the labor force had become "balkanized," with the poor, the uneducated, and women and minorities trapped in a secondary labor market with little hope of obtaining employment in the primary market. Doeringer and Piore (1971) elaborated on Kerr's ideas and carefully documented how women and minorities were relegated to secondary labor markets while white male workers secured employment in protected primary labor markets.

The proponents of an institutionally segmented labor-market model have argued that supply and demand did not apply inside the large monopoly firm in the allocation of human resources. Rather, administrative rules and procedures determined job placement and promotion. These rules and procedures (e.g., seniority) were collusive in that they protected the jobs of white males at the expense of women and minorities, reenforcing the structural duality of the labor market.

Macrostructural Explanations

Although the internal-labor-market theorists drew attention to the statistical underrepresentation of minorities and women in the primary labor market, they, like the human capitalists, failed to provide an adequate explanation for the origins of the observed differences, their persistence over time, and the possibilities for changing the status quo. A radical perspective on labor-market discrimination emerged in the 1970s in response to these deficient explanations. The radical theorists agreed that the existence of labor-market segments was bound up in the structures of institutions rather than in individual inadequacies, but they criticized the dual-market theorists for failing to analyze why women and minorities were systematically underrepresented in the primary labor market. Influenced by the Marxian tradition of class analysis, radical labor-market theorists located the roots of discrimination in the efforts of the capitalist class to keep the working class divided. Capitalists were willing to forgo profit maximization in the short run to secure their class interests over the long run (Edwards, 1979; Reich, Gordon, & Edwards, 1973, 1982).

As minority and female intellectuals began to examine the social causes of their own conditions more systematically, the neo-Marxian analyses struck them as formalistic and uncompelling in explaining the logic of race and sex discrimination. As a result of these new criticisms of Marxism, two additional and noteworthy macro-structural approaches took form. The first focused on racism in the United States and proposed a model of internal colonialism. Carmichael and Hamilton (1965) argued that only a very small group of black people would be allowed higher education by a society as racist and capitalistic as the United States. The function of this small educated group would be to exercise social control over the large masses of unemployed, underemployed, and poorly educated minorities. Furthermore, a small number of educated minority persons would provide ideological leverage against minorities attempting to challenge the structure of the system as fundamentally racist (Charmichael & Hamilton, 1965). The logic of the colonial view placed racial divisions above class divisions. Thus, it was an explicit critique of the Marxian perspective, which many black nationalists felt placed too much emphasis on class dynamics and not enough on race (Baron, 1977). A similiar approach was developed by Barrera (1979) to explain discrimination against Chicanos in the Southwest.

The second radical addition to the macrostructural literature was also critical of the Marxist superordination of class divisions. Feminists, disenchanted with attempts to account for the persistence of both occupational and wage discrimination against women (England, 1982), sought to explain the observed differences through a patriarchical model. Strober (1982), for example, argues, "Although the profit motive may explain employers' desire to augment the division of labor, it does not explain why that division turns into one based on gender" (p. 4). Although specific definitions of patriarchy vary, they tend to share a common view that men, irrespective of their class background or class position in society, benefit materially and ideologically from the exploitation of women's labor (Keohane, Rosaldo, & Gelpi, 1981; Sokoloff, 1980).

The internal colonial model and the patriarchy model both argue for a strong cultural component in explanations for race and sex discrimination. The models simultaneously attack the rationalist and market assumptions of the neoclassical model and the primacy of class offered by the Marxist model. From the perspective of race, both white men and women benefit from the exploitation of minorities; from the perspective of gender, both white men and minority men benefit from the exploitation of women.

The Models and the Public Sector

The preceding summary of perspectives on the statistically observed underrepresentation of women and minorities in the strategic dimensions of the labor force points to the theoretical complexity involved in reaching a simple conclusion about what causes underrepresentation and how to ameliorate it. Furthermore, and importantly, most of the sociological and economic models, whether mainstream or radical, have drawn their evidence on discrimination from the private sector, where presumably the market place for labor operates relatively freely. Yet, the largest employer of both women and minority professionals and semi-professionals remains the public sector. Maximizing

profits does not motivate public institutions (e.g., schools, universities, social-welfare agencies). Indeed, whether government agencies are motivated to maximize the common good, their own legitimacy, or anything whatsoever is the subject of serious debate. The social analyst's position on these matters has serious implications, both for assessing past employment practice and for assessing various strategies for reform.

Another literature has attempted to construct alternative models to explain and analyze public-sector employment patterns without relying on traditional private-sector supply and demand models. One approach seeks to account for the decisions of public institutions in terms of utility maximizing (Downs, 1957; Tullock, 1967). More recently, an effort has been made to predict government actions, and particularly employment patterns, as a way to maximize political support among voting constituencies (Borjas, 1982; Lindsey, 1976). According to Borjas, "the voter-maximization hypothesis predicts that the economic status of minorities in federal agenices depends on how important minorities are to the political support generated by the particular agency" (1982, p. 272). The central premise of the voter-maximization approach is that various agencies within government cater to constituencies and that these constituencies (consumers) have a taste for discrimination; they prefer to see certain groups representing them in particular agencies. Thus, for example, a predominantly white suburban school system might prefer to exclude racial minorities from administrative positions and a predominantly minority school system might prefer to exclude white male administrators.

The use of a voter-maximization approach involves a basic theoretical indeterminancy. As Ehrenberg and Smith (1982) observe, institutional decision makers may be sensitive to voter preferences, but in a multi-issue environment it is difficult to establish just how voter preferences are communicated and enforced (p. 405).

Most recently, research has shown that schools alter their employment practices in response to a complex social environment. Using a notion called "compensatory legitimacy," Richards (1983) and Richards and Encarnation (1985, 1987) document that race and ethnicity are important predictors of teacher placement patterns in public and private schools. In the earlier study, Richards demonstrates how the racial composition of the school and the race or ethnicity of the teacher jointly influence the probable assignment of the teacher. In the latter report, Richards and Encarnation develop an open-systems model and empirically test the model using data from a six-county study of public, Catholic, and private schools in the San Francisco Bay area. Their findings indicate that both Catholic and public schools respond to legitimacy claims to employ minority teachers when the schools serve minority clients and when the schools are involved in state and federal compensatory education programs designed to serve poor students. Furthermore, their research found that racially homogeneous public schools in the suburbs are no more likely than similar Catholic or private schools to hire minority teachers. This datum is consistent with their model, which predicts that schools will attempt to maximize their legitimacy with their constituents within the constraints of the status quo, at the same time compensating interest groups who are contesting the status quo, and thereby sustaining legitimacy with them as well. Although Richards and Encarnation have looked only at the employment of teachers, their research contains implications for the employment of minority and women administrators as well. Perhaps the most important implication is that the model theoretically explains the conditional responses of educational institutions to the equity-employment claims of minorities and women in both the public and private sectors while controlling for variations in client, fiscal, and regulatory characteristics.

The preceding sections have offered a justification for public concern about the underrepresentation of women and minorities in positions of educational leadership and a brief review of several explanations for why that underrepresentation persists. Let us now return to what Ortiz and Marshall and Valverde and Brown have discussed in this book in order to assess their policy prescriptions in light of the preceding discussion.

CAUSAL AGENCY AND POLICY

Not only do Valverde and Brown have differing perspectives on the willingness and capacity of the democratic political and juridical systems to intervene on behalf of women and minorities, they have differing perspectives on the policies required to rectify the inequities they describe. Ortiz and Marshall, for example, say that permitting women administrators access to positions of educational administration would "undermine the exclusive power and values of incumbent administrator" p.136. Thus, Ortiz and Marshall argue that sex-equity policy has not achieved the status of a morally legitimate policy because to do so would require challenging the moral legitimacy of the existing school system based on competition and bureaucratic rationality and replacing it with one based on nur-

turance and cooperation. Their policy recommendations, however, seem largely to call for more research and an increased willingness of a male-dominated system to hear the feminist voice that labors in it. The solutions they pose are strikingly passive given the trenchant tone of their critique. I am reminded of a quote by Wilhelm Reich when he was asked why juvenile delinquency was becoming such a problem. He answered, "The real question is why are there so few juvenile delinquents?"

One cannot help but wonder why perfectly capable and dynamic women have not long ago taken over the administration of a school system in whose ranks they have toiled so faithfully for so many years. Ortiz and Marshall provide a clear window from which we can view the structures and psychology of women's subordination but only a glimpse into the history of women's resistance to their exclusion from power in educational administration. Valverde and Brown note both the early history of racial exclusion and the legislative, judicial, and executive actions that contributed to the recent historic opening of the system during the Civil Rights Era. Yet, they too do not report the history of student strikes and walkouts that challenged the legitimacy of segregated schools run by white teachers and administrators. Nonetheless, they are optimistic: "The future will surely need minority school administrators employed in a wider variety of school systems and aided by preparation programs that view schools as cultural systems..." (p. 154). In short, Valverde and Brown are much more hopeful that the system will continue in the direction of inclusion and participation. Unfortunately, the solutions to the problems of inequality remain unclear. Programs that have successfully expanded the participation of women and minorities in educational administration are hard to find, and their results have been modest, as the statistics testify.

What about the prospects for the future? As Valverde and Brown state, there "remains the strategic issue of restructuring educational institutions to eliminate inequity and social injustice" (p.155). I would argue that the prospects for improvement are in the mid-1980s threatened as much by structural factors and benign neglect as by overt discrimination.

Any hope of improving the representation of women and minorities requires an adequate supply of incoming women and minority teachers in graduate programs of administration. Obviously, in the absence of an adequate supply of women and minorities with advanced degrees, efforts at affirmative action for positions of educational leadership will be futile (Foster, 1982).

Evidence suggests that there have been substantial improvements in the available supply of women who hold advanced degrees. In 1970, 37 percent of all bachelor's degrees, 29 percent of all master's degrees, and 14 percent of all doctorates were awarded to women; in 1980, 44 percent of all bachelor's degrees, 36 percent of all master's degrees, and 27 percent of all doctorates were awarded to women (National Center for Education Statistics [NCES], 1982, p. 130, Table 119).

Improved college attendance among blacks began to be consistently recorded in the 1968–1969 academic year, when 370,000 blacks, or 5.8 percent of the total student population of 6,401,000, were estimated to be in higher education. A sustained increase continued until 1973–1974, when black enrollment dropped to 7.4 percent, with the largest decline occurring among black males. In 1976 college enrollment of blacks was about 8 percent, with blacks representing 12 percent of the U.S. population. By 1980 about 9.2 percent of the first-time college students were black; however, 50 percent of all college-bound black students are enrolled in community colleges. Furthermore, the number of black graduate students dropped by 3 percent between 1978 and 1980 (NCES, 1982).

An examination of the current educational pipeline for minorities nationally found that 72 percent of blacks and only 55 percent of all Hispanic (Chicano and Puerto Rican) children complete high school, compared to 83 percent for white students. At the college level, 12 percent of black students and 7 percent of Hispanic students receive bachelor degrees. This compares with 23 percent for white students. At the graduate and professional levels, only 4 percent of all black students and 2 percent of Hispanic students in their age cohort obtain degrees. This compares with 8 percent for white students (Himes, 1982).

Of those who received doctorates in 1980, 76.4 percent were white, 4.6 percent black, 0.5 percent Mexican-American, 1.9 percent other Hispanic, 8.4 percent Asian, and 7.8 percent other and unknown (NCES, 1982, p. 133, Table 121). Minority women have recorded significant gains in both college attendance and in completion rates when compared with minority men. Sharp differences remain, however, in the career choices selected by minority and nonminority women. Men continue to dominate the growth professions, the physical sciences, life sciences, engineering, and mathematics (Marrett & Matthews, 1984). This fact continues to constrain the prospects for women to assume leadership positions in these fields.

Does this mean that there is a shortage of women and minorities available for positions in educational administration? Not necessarily. Shortages are a func-

tion of the interaction between supply and demand. If school districts and colleges get enough pressure to increase their demand for women and minority administrators, I am confident the labor market will respond. Nonetheless, if women and minorities are structurally underrepresented in certain fields, as they are in mathematics and the sciences, when positions of administrative leadership do open, in the absence of an aggressive effort at affirmative action, both minorities and women are unlikely to be represented among the pool of eligible candidates.

Recommendations

Any effort to remedy the patterns of inequity described in the preceding pages will require a countercausal strategy at least as multifaceted as the causal linkages that currently bind us to the present patterns. Such a strategy must include leadership training and mentoring to overcome the psychologically debilitating effects of the legacy of discrimination, changes in institutional structures and resource allocations to increase participation, and concerted political and economic pressure on the educational system.

Following are some suggestions and examples of what might be done in each of the cited domains to remedy the inequalities described:

1. At the individual level, as Kathryn Moore's research has demonstrated, minority and women leaders need mentors in order to break into the traditional "old-boys'" network (Moore, 1982, 1983a, 1983b; Moore & Sagaria, 1981). The development of mentor programs will facilitate the movement of minority and women leaders into positions of educational leadership. One such program, Castle Hot Springs, in Arizona, has had remarkable success in mentoring potential women administrators at the elementary and secondary level. Between 1979 and 1983 between 40 and 50 women participated each year. In the 4-year period from 1980 to 1984, the number of female principals in Arizona increased from 121 to 217. Thirty-two percent (70) of those hired were participants in the Castle Hot Springs mentoring program (Metzger, 1985).

2. At the institutional level, the available supply of minority and women college graduate students, particularly in the fields of rapid growth and in the quantitative sciences (to the extent that these are not synonymous), can be increased through scholarships and by withholding funds from departments that do not demonstrate affirmative action. In order for this plan to be successful, however, a concerted effort is required to ensure that elementary and secondary schools receive resources necessary to increase the participation rates of minority and female youth in advanced programs in math and

science. Exposure to successful role models in these fields is also quite important.

3. Special 5-year programs must be sponsored by flagship universities. Such a program has been instituted by Bernard Gifford, Dean of the Graduate School of Education at the University of California, Berkeley. It is designed to increase the supply of minority teachers who can pass the growing number of teacher-competency exams states require for certification (Hechinger, 1984) and at the same time help such students compensate for academic weaknesses inherited from unequal educational opportunities in their elementary and secondary education.

4. Affirmative-action programs as presently constructed are limited in effectiveness due to the current resource constraints of schools and colleges. Furthermore, affirmative action is implicitly predicated on the assumption of institutional growth. When departments and schools are losing enrollment, it is difficult enough to sustain present levels of representation, let alone to increase them. Nontraditional avenues of advancement must be created to further the representation of minorities and women in positions of educational leadership. This would include, for example, federally funded exchange programs between predominatly black colleges and leading public and private universities, similiar exchange programs between suburban and urban school systems, and internships in administrative positions in both public schools and institutions of higher education. State leadership can also make a difference. The Commissioner of Higher Education in New Jersey has put the state's colleges on notice that they will lose their state aid for disadvantaged students unless they significantly increase minority enrollments.

5. At the macrostructural level, there is no substitute for concerted political action. This has been demonstrated time and again, from the suffragette movement during the early part of the 20th century and the struggles of women in the NEA to the more recent efforts of the civil rights movement. As the labor organizer John Lewis once said, "The National Guard cannot mine coal." It probably cannot collect school taxes or teach students either.

Women and minorities in positions of educational leadership are at the very top of a professional pyramid, but by any reasonable criterion they are underrepresented in both elementary and secondary schools and in institutions of higher education. The causes are many and related. As must be self-evident, whether one's disciplinary perspective leads to an investigation of the existential, institutional, or macrostructural causes and consequences of employment discrimination in educational administration, each of these various levels of analysis alone explains only a part of the story. Together, I suspect they explain most of it.

REFERENCES

Apple, M. W. (Ed.). (1982). *Cultural and economic reproduction in education: Essays on class, ideology and the state.* London: Routledge & Kegan Paul.

Arrow, K. (1973). The theory of discrimination. In O. Ashenfelter & A. Rees (Eds.), *Discrimination in labor markets.* Princeton, NJ: Princeton University Press.

Baron, H. (1977). Racial domination in advanced capitalism: A theory of nationalism and divisions in the labor market. In R. Edwards, M. Reich, & D. Gordon (Eds.), *Labor market segmentation.* Lexington, MA: Heath.

Barrera, M. (1979). *Race and class in the Southwest: A theory of racial inequality.* Notre Dame, IN: University of Notre Dame Press.

Becker, G. (1957). *The economics of discrimination.* Chicago: University of Chicago Press.

Blau, F. D., & Justenius, C. L. (1976). Economists' approaches to sex segregation in the labor market: An appraisal. In M. Blaxall & B. Reagan (Eds.), *Women and the workplace.* Chicago: University of Chicago Press.

Borjas, G. (1982). The politics of employment discrimination in the federal bureaucracy. *Journal of Law and Economics, 25*(2), 271–299.

Carmichael, S., & Hamilton, C. (1965). *Black power.* New York: Harper & Row.

Carnoy, M., & Levin, H. (1985). *Schooling and work in the democratic state.* Stanford, CA: Stanford University Press.

Doeringer, P. B., & Piore, M. J. (1971). *Internal labor markets and manpower analysis.* Lexington, MA: Heath.

Downs, A. (1957). *An economic theory of democracy.* New York: Harper.

Edwards, R. (1979). *Labor market segmentation.* Lexington, MA: Heath.

Ehrenberg, R. G., & Smith, R. S. (1982). *Modern labor economics.* Glenview, IL: Scott, Foresman.

England, P. (1982). The failure of human capital theory to explain occupational sex segregation. *Journal of Human Resources, 3,* 358–370.

Foster, S. (1982). For black administrators, little progress and few openings. *Education Week.* 6(1), (17).

Gross, N., & Trask, A. E. (1976). *The sex factor and the management of schools.* New York: John Wiley.

Hechinger, F. (1984, November 6). Minority teacher plan aims for excellence. *New York Times.*

Herner, M. S. (1971). Femininity and successful achievement: A basic inconsistency. In M. Garskof, (Ed.), *Roles women play: Readings toward women's liberation.* Berkeley, CA: Wadsworth.

Himes, J. A. (1982). *Hispanic participation in higher education: A focus on Chicanos and other Hispanics in California.* Princeton, NJ: Woodrow Wilson National Fellowship Foundation.

Keohane, N., Rosaldo, M. Z., & Gelpi, B. C. (Eds.). (1981). *Feminist theory: A critique of ideology.* Chicago: University of Chicago Press.

Kerr, C. (1954). The Balkanization of labor markets. In E. Bakke, et al., *Labor mobility and economic opportunity.* New York: John Wiley.

Knowles, L., & Prewitt, K. (1969). *Institutional racism in America.* Englewood Cliffs, NJ: Prentice-Hall.

Laws, J. (1976). Work aspiration of women: False leads and new starts. In M. Blaxall & B. Reagan (Eds.), *Women and the workplace.* Chicago: University of Chicago Press.

Lloyd, C. B., & Niemi, B. T. (1979). *The economics of sex differentials.* New York: Columbia University Press.

Lindsey, C. M. (1976). A theory of government enterprise. *Journal of Political Economy, 84*(5), 1061–1077.

Marrett, C., & Matthews, W. (1984). The participation of minority women in higher education. In E. Fennema & M. Ayer (Eds.), *Women and education*. Berkeley, CA: McCutchan.

Metzger, C. (1985, December). Helping women prepare for principalships, *Phi Delta Kappan*, 292–296.

Moore. K. (1982). The role of mentors in developing leaders for Academe. *Educational Record*, *63*(1), 23–28.

Moore, K. (1983a). *Leaders in transition. A national study of higher education administrators. The top line: A report on presidents', provosts' and deans' careers*. College Park, MD: Center for the Study of Higher Education.

Moore, K. (1983b). *Leaders in transition. A national study of higher education administrators. Women and minorities*. College Park, MD: Center for the Study of Higher Education.

Moore, K., & Sagaria, M. (1981). Women administrators and mobility: The second struggle. *Journal of the National Association for Women Deans, Administrators and Counselors*, *44*(2), 21–28.

Moynihan, P. (1965). *The Negro family: The case for national action*. Washington, DC: Government Printing Office.

National Center for Education Statistics. (1982 and 1984). *Condition of education*. Washington, DC: Government Printing Office.

Reich, M., Gordon, D., & Edwards, R. (1973). A theory of labor market stratification. *American Economic Review*, (2), 359–363.

Reich, M., Gordon, D., & Edwards, R. (1982). *Segmented work, divided workers: The historical transformation of labor in the United States*. Cambridge, England: Cambridge University Press.

Richards, C. (1983). *Race and educational employment: The political economy of teacher labor markets*. Unpublished doctoral dissertation, Stanford University, Stanford, CA.

Richards, C., & Encarnation, D. (1985). Social policy and minority employment in public, private and Catholic schools." Stanford, CA: Institute for Research on Educational Finance and Governance, Stanford University.

Richards, C., & Encarnation, D. (1987). Teaching in public and private schools: The significance of race. In H. Levin & T. James (Eds.), *Comparisons of public, Catholic, and private schools*. London: Falmer Press.

Schiller, B. (1980). *The economics of poverty and discrimination*. Englewood Cliffs, NJ: Prentice-Hall.

Schmuck, P. (1975). *Sex differentiation in public school administration*. Unpublished doctoral dissertation, University of Oregon, Eugene.

Sharp, R., & Green, A. (1975). *Education and social control: A study in progressive primary education*. London: Routledge & Kegan Paul.

Sokoloff, N. (1980). *Between money and love: The dialectics of women's home and market work*. New York: Praeger.

Stansbury, K., Thomas, L., & Wiggens, T. (1984). Women in leadership and implications for affirmative action. *Journal of Educational Equity and Leadership*, *4*(2), 99.

Strober, M. (1982). "Segregation by gender in public school teaching: Toward a general theory of occupation segregation in the labor market." Unpublished paper, Stanford University, Standford, CA.

Sutherland, S. (1978). The unambitious female: Women's low professional aspirations. *Signs: Journal of Women in Culture and Society*, *3 & 4*, 778–793.

Tullock, G. (1967). *Towards a mathematics of politics*. Ann Arbor, MI: University of Michigan Press.

PART

II

Organizations

CHAPTER 9

Getzels's Models in Educational Administration

James M. Lipham

The theoretical models of Jacob W. Getzels provide especially powerful perspectives for improving theory, research, and practice in education—whether at the level of the classroom, school, district, community, or society at large. Here the focus is on application of the models in educational administration, since this is the field that has felt the greatest impact of his work.

Three dominant themes characterize Getzels's theoretical conceptualizations; each has contributed to substantial bodies of continuing research regarding the educational process. First and foremost is the focus on the complexity of the human personality—its nature, structure, development, creativity, expression, perception, and influence on individual, interpersonal, group, and organizational relationships, particularly in educational institutions. Second is the analysis of formal and informal roles, expectations, perceptions, relationships, conflicts, and behaviors in educational organizations. Third is the thrust on the analysis, description, formation, and expression of individual and group values, particularly in the American culture. Also derived from these three themes are clear conceptual contributions that are useful in the analysis of leadership, conflict, morale, and educational change. Underlying the three themes is a continued concern for bridging the gap between theory and practice in education.

Getzels's several models are presented here in the order of their development, beginning with his early

attention to the use of theory in educational administration. The models include Getzels's (1952) psychosociological framework for the study of educational administration, the Getzels-Guba (1957) model of the administrative process, the Getzels-Thelen (1960) model of the classroom as a social system, and Getzels's (1978b) model of the communities of education. Each model is described, followed by illustrative research studies and selected references that examine and utilize the concepts and relationships posited. The chapter concludes with a critique of current criticisms concerning the models and shows the continued vitality and utility of the models for improving our understanding of the administration, operation, and outcomes of schools.

GETZELS'S PSYCHOSOCIOLOGICAL FRAMEWORK

In a pioneering paper that Culbertson (1981) has credited as the first published theory for the study of educational administration, Getzels (1952) presented a psychosociological framework that "*appears* to offer fruitful dimensions and concepts for the study and analysis of significant problems and processes in educational administration [italics added]" (p. 246). Observing that surveys, ad hoc testimonials, and untested principles constituted much of the material that passed as research in administration at that time, Getzels stressed the intimate, interactive relationship between theory and practice, showing that they can illuminate each other.

Consultant/reviewer: Max G. Abbott, University of Oregon; and Jacob W. Getzels, University of Chicago

The psychosociological framework (Getzels, 1952) begins with the following observation:

> The administrative relationship is enacted in two separate situations, one embedded in the other. On the one hand is the relationship as perceived and organized by the superordinate member in terms of his needs and goals; on the other, the relationship is perceived and organized by the subordinate member in terms of his needs and goals. The interactions are related through the existential objects and symbols which have to some extent a counterpart in both situations. (p. 236)

In analyzing the administrative relationship, Getzels, influenced by Weber (1947) and Parsons (1951), posited three major dimensions. The first is the authority dimension—the source of the superordinate's dominance and the subordinate's acceptance of this dominance. The second dimension is the scope of the relationship—the effective range of roles and facilities covered by the relationship. The third is the affectivity dimension—the nature of the "personal" interaction between the participants in the relationship. Definitions of the dimensions follow.

Regarding authority, the administrative relationship in education is founded more in rational than traditional or charismatic grounds. Thus, the administrator must possess the technical knowledge and the competence for allocating and integrating roles and facilities for attaining the institutional goals of both parties in the administrative relationship. Since both members of this institutional dyad occupy professional status, an essential feature of the rational administrative relationship is its reciprocality, wherein both members make functional claims on each other. Hence, it is appropriate to investigate how leader-follower relations are affected by the exercise of authority in specific school situations.

The scope of administrative roles may be defined with reference to two types of interpersonal interaction: functionally diffuse and functionally specific. In the functionally diffuse type of interaction, the members of the dyad are bound in such a way that the obligations of the one to the other are taken for granted and are in a sense limitless. In the functionally specific type, the obligations are restricted to those elements in the relationship that are defined by the technical competence and the institutional status of the participants. Hence, the need exists to determine the extent and effect of functional diffuseness and functional specificity on administrative relationships in the educational setting.

Regarding affectivity, an important variable in the administrative relationship is the quality of the personal interaction. Affectivity may be neutral (impersonal) or charged with meaning for the individuals involved (personal). Interactions are impersonal when they are expected to have the same quality for all participants and are based on constant behavioral norms—hence they are universalistic. Interactions are personal when they are expected to have varying qualities depending on the identity of particular participants and are based on differential behavioral norms—hence the relationship is particularistic. In the universalistic relationship, the important issue is *what* is involved; in the particularistic relationship, the important issue is *who* is involved. Thus, it is helpful to examine those personality and situational factors that impel the administrative relationship in the school toward predominantly universalistic or particularistic considerations and the relative effect of such patterns of interaction on the administrative process.

Many research studies have been conducted drawing directly or indirectly on the psychosociological framework. These studies examine not only the expectations mutually held for organizational roles but also the effects of selective interpersonal perception of value orientations and personal variables on organizational outcomes. In an early study, for example, Ferneau (1954) found that the extent to which consultants and administrators mutually perceived complementary role expectations was directly related to the effectiveness of the consultation. Similarly, Savage (1959) examined the consultant relationship, identifying consultant roles as expert, resource person, and process person. Regarding mutual expectations for leadership in local schools, Moyer (1954) found agreement between teachers and principals to be related to favorable attitudes toward the work situation. Maire (1965) found that congruence in expectations for the consultative role of school architects was related to the effectiveness of the services provided. Reed (1973) examined the consultative role of middle-school learning coordinators, finding that mutuality in expectations among administrators, consultants, and teachers was related to the perceived effectiveness of the learning coordinators. Similar results were reported by Davis (1977) regarding the agreement on perceptions of the role and the effectiveness of school psychologists. Paul (1974, 1977) found that mutual agreement on the consultative relationships of research and development centers and state departments of education to local schools was systematically related to the diffusion of educational innovation. These and other studies have directed sustained attention to the examination of interpersonal and interorganizational linkage relationships in fostering educational change and improvement (Lieberman, 1977; Lipham, 1977).

The reciprocality of relationships posited in the

psychosociological framework also highlights the phenomenon of selective interpersonal perception. Thus, the administrative relationship is affected not only by direct differences in expectations but also by differences in the mutual perceptions of role, value, and personality elements in interaction. Regarding perceptual differences in roles, for example, Hencley (1960) discovered several systematic types of perceptual error in administrators' perceptions of others' expectations. Regarding perceptual differences in values, Abbott (1960) concluded that conflict in the school superintendency may result not so much from differences in values that are "out in the open" and understood as from those that are misperceived and misunderstood. Regarding the perception of personal variables, Gilberts (1961) and Evers (1974) found the mutuality of interpersonal need-dispositions to influence working relationships in team teaching situations. Further studies are needed regarding the mechanisms whereby the selective perception of role, value, and personal elements affect administrative relationships.

The psychosociological framework also served as the stimulus for examining the integrity of the theory-practice relationship in education. Citing the framework as a major example, Coladarci and Getzels (1955) stated:

> On the grounds of both the definition and the universality of theorizing, then, the theory and practice functions can be seen as necessarily interrelated aspects of professional behavior. We can dislike this state of affairs but we cannot avoid it. Theorizing and practicing can and do co-exist. Each is an aspect of the process of inquiry and, intelligently pursued, *each constantly redefines the other* [italics in the original]. (p. 6)

The symbiotic relationship between theory and practice was further stressed by Getzels (1960) when he identified how prevailing theories of the human being as a learner affected classroom interaction and the structure of the learning environment of the school throughout the 20th century. In subsequent papers Getzels (1975, 1979) stressed problem finding in research as a creative, personal process wherein important research problems are not so much presented as they are discovered as one draws upon and moves between theory and practice. Recent research (Getzels & Smilansky, 1983) on individual differences in pupils' perceptions of school problems is enlightening; similar studies are needed of individual differences in how administrators and teachers perceive school problems.

THE GETZELS-GUBA MODEL

Building on the psychosociological framework, the Getzels-Guba (1957) model of the administrative process examines observed behavior within a social system. The social system can range from the community to the school to classrooms and groups within it. This model, shown in Figure 9.1, conceives of the social system as involving two major classes of phenomena that are at once conceptually independent and phenomenally interactive. There are, first, the institutions with certain roles and expectations that will fulfill the goals of the system. Second, inhabiting the system there are the individuals with certain personalities and need-dispositions whose interactions comprise what is generally called "social behavior." Social behavior may be apprehended as a function of the following major elements: institution, role, and expectation, which together constitute the normative or nomothetic dimension of activity in a social system; and individual, personality, and need-disposition, which together constitute the personal or idiographic dimension of activity in a social system.

Regarding the normative dimension, the school as an institution is purposive, peopled, and structured into roles that are complementary, interlocking, and

Figure 9.1 The Getzels-Guba model of the dimensions of social behavior.

NOMOTHETIC DIMENSION

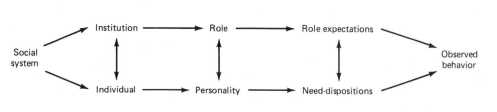

IDIOGRAPHIC DIMENSION

SOURCE. From "Social behavior and the administrative process" by J. W. Getzels and E. G. Guba, 1957, *School Review, 65*, p. 429. Copyright 1957 by University of Chicago Press. Reprinted by permission.

sanction bearing. Roles are defined in terms of expectations, which are the normative rights and duties of a role incumbent. Role expectations can range from required to prohibited, from specific to diffuse, and from impersonal to personal. Regarding the personal dimension, each individual in the school has his or her own personality, which is defined as one's need-dispositions that determine a person's unique interactions with the environment. Behavior in a social system, therefore, results from the interaction between a given institutional role, defined by the expectations attached to it, and the personality of a particular role incumbent, defined by one's need-dispositions; it can be represented by the general equation $B = f (R \times P)$.

The proportion of role and personality factors determining behavior vary with the specific act, role, and personality involved. The amount of behavior dictated by role expectations may be quite large (as in the military, where much behavior is prescribed). By contrast, the proportions may be reversed if behavior is dictated largely by personality (as in an artists' colony, where much is left to individual choice). In schools, the proportion of role and personality considerations probably is balanced somewhere between these two extremes. When role is maximized, behavior still retains some personal aspects because no role is ever so closely defined as to eliminate all individual latitude. When personality is maximized, social behavior still cannot be free from some role prescription. Congruence between the role and the personality dimensions can be increased through the personalization of roles or the socialization of personalities. Thus, the unique task of administration is to integrate the demands of the institution and the demands of the staff in a way that is at once organizationally productive and individually fulfilling.

The three distinct leadership styles derived from the model by Getzels and Guba include the nomothetic, the idiographic, and the transactional. The nomothetic leadership style emphasizes the requirements of the institution, role, and expectations. It stresses defining roles clearly, following appropriate procedures, reducing role conflicts, achieving integration through the socialization of personalities, and judging the excellence of leadership in terms of organizational effectiveness. The idiographic leadership style emphasizes the requirements of the individual, personality, and need-dispositions. It stresses providing latitude in roles, encouraging individual initiative and contributions, reducing personality conflicts, achieving integration through the personalization of roles, and judging the effectiveness of leadership in terms of individual efficiency. The transactional leadership style emphasizes moving from one style to the other, depending on

contingencies and circumstances in the particular situation. It stresses taking into account both the expectations for roles and the personalities of people; showing awareness of the limits of institutional and individual resources; reducing role, role-personality, and personality conflicts; achieving integration through either the socialization of personalities or the personalization of roles; and judging the excellence of leadership in terms of both organizational effectiveness and individual efficiency.

The Getzels-Guba model served to clarify the major types of conflict that occur in the administrative setting: role-personality conflict, role conflict, and personality conflict. Role-personality conflicts occur as a function of discrepancies between the pattern of expectations attaching to a given role and the need-dispositions characteristic of the incumbent of the role. Role conflicts occur whenever a role incumbent is required to conform simultaneously to a number of expectations that are mutually exclusive, contradictory, or inconsistent, so that adjustment to one set of requirements makes adjustment to the other impossible, or at least difficult. Role conflicts can result from disagreement within a reference group defining the role; from disagreement among several reference groups, each having a right to define the same role; or from contradiction in the expectations of two or more roles an individual is occupying at the same time. Personality conflicts occur as a function of opposing needs and dispositions within the personalities of role incumbents. Personality conflicts may occur either between people or within an individual. In addition to these major types, conflict can also result from discrepancies between the real behaviors actually exhibited (what one does) and the ideal behaviors that are desired (what one should do). Furthermore, conflict in social systems also often results from the misperception of role, personality, and value elements on the part of self and others.

The Getzels-Guba formulation clearly defined the major dimensions of morale. In terms of the model, effectiveness is a function of the congruence of behavior with role expectations; efficiency, the congruence of behavior with need-dispositions; and satisfaction, the congruence of institutional role expectations with individual need-dispositions. When the goals of the social system are considered, rationality represents the extent to which expectations placed upon a role are logically appropriate to the achievement of institutional goals; identification represents the degree to which an individual can integrate the goals and actions into his or her own structure of needs and values; belongingness represents the anticipation that one will be able to achieve personal satisfaction within the institutional framework. Hence, the interaction of effectiveness, efficiency, and satisfaction, together with rationality, identification, and belongingness, help in understanding and improving morale in social systems.

The Getzels-Guba model represents a landmark in the application of social-science theories to the field of educational administration. A multitude of studies have been conducted that draw on the concepts and relationships posited. Only some exemplary studies are cited here.

In an early study of instructors in Air Force schools, Getzels and Guba (1954, 1955a) found differences in many personality variables to be systematically related to felt conflict in the teaching situation. A subsequent study (Getzels & Guba, 1955b), based on extensive interviews with public school teachers, likewise identified felt conflicts in the socioeconomic, citizen, and professional roles of teachers; moreover, these conflicts were discovered to differ in the extent to which they were situationally independent, situationally variant, or situationally specific. Campbell (1959), also assessing the personal need-dispositions of teachers in public schools, the expectations held for teachers by their principals, and the teachers' perceptions of the principals' expectations, found that teachers low in role-personality (self-role) conflict expressed significantly greater satisfaction with teaching. In a study of the self-role conflict of school principals, Lipham (1960) discovered the personal variables of activity drive, achievement drive, social ability, feelings of security, and emotional control to be significantly and positively related to the effectiveness of principals. Similar results were reported for public school superintendents by Semrow (1965). The examination of role-personality conflict continues to constitute a major research thrust in education. Martin (1970), for example, found self-role conflict to be systematically related to teachers' adaptation to change and innovation. Woods (1977) found significant differences in felt and perceived expectations for the administrative role between black and white school administrators.

Many of the studies derived from the Getzels-Guba model have examined actual or potential conflict in expectations and perceptions held for a variety of educational roles. These include studies of classroom teachers (Heyerdahl, 1967; Ingraham, 1979); departmental chairpersons (Dean, 1975; Payne, 1971; Pedicone, 1981); principals (Aho, 1971; Muhm, 1968; Wallace, 1969); school superintendents (Tornow, 1965; Waier, 1970); and school board members (McCarty, 1959; Thorson, 1966). In addition to clarifying organizational roles, the studies have generally shown that extent of agreement on role expectations and perceptions is meaningfully related to a wide variety of organizational processes, relationships, and outcomes.

Other investigators have examined the relationship of personal variables to interaction within the school. Andrews (1958), for example, discovered personality differences among teachers grouped by subject fields, and he suggested that these differences have direct implications for staff supervision and involvement. In an experimental study, Brown (1962) demonstrated differential effects of stress-inducing supervision, according to the personality characteristics of the teachers being supervised. Meyer (1964) found the personality variables of teachers to influence their perceptions of the same administrative behavior, even when observed in a controlled, simulated situation. Evers (1974) found the personal needs of teachers to influence their ratings of the effectiveness of team teaching in elementary schools.

Studies of nomothetic, idiographic, and transactional leadership styles have also been revealing. Moser (1957), for example, found that superintendents and teachers expect different styles of leadership from principals, concluding that "the principal is in a delicate leadership position as a member of two organizational families (p. 4)." Substantiating the leader-follower relations proposed by the model, Baldwin (1979) subsequently reported that transactional leadership behavior generates higher teacher morale than does either nomothetic or idiographic leadership behavior.

The Getzels-Guba model is widely treated in textbooks in educational administration. Introductory texts in eductional administration (Campbell, Corbally, & Nystrand, 1983; Kimbrough & Nunnery, 1976; Sergiovanni & Carver, 1980) typically depict the model and show how the derivations from it regarding leadership, conflict, and morale are useful in the study and practice of administration. Textbooks on the school principalship (Faber & Shearron, 1970; Hencley, McCleary, & McGrath, 1970; Hughes & Ubben, 1984; Lipham, Rankin, & Hoeh, 1985; Roe & Drake, 1980) not only describe the model and its derivations but also stress its particular relevance for helping principals provide leadership in the personnel functions of recruitment, selection, assignment, orientation, supervision, development, and evaluation of staff. References on organizational theory and behavior in educational administration (Hoy & Miskel, 1982; Owens, 1981; Silver, 1983) compare and contrast the model with other theoretical formulations, summarize extant research related to the model, and show its particular relevance for stimulating further productive research regarding the administration of educational organizations.

THE GETZELS-THELEN MODEL

In describing and depicting the classroom as a unique social system, Getzels and Thelen (1960) integrated previous conceptualizations and incorporated additional dimensions to show (a) that the climate of the school and the classrooms within it represents a "way of life" wherein organizational, individual, and group intentions are achieved; (b) that the biological states of learners and others, as living human organisms, condition and affect goal behavior; and (c) that the school operates within a culture having certain traditions, laws, and symbols that constitute an ethos defined by prevailing latent and manifest value orientations. These additional three dimensions to the basic Getzels-Guba (1957) model are shown in the Getzels-Thelen (1960) model in Figure 9.2. The definitions of and interactions among rationality, identification, and belongingness in relation to goal behavior are also indicated to the right in this model.

Getzels and Thelen (1960) stressed that the school is an open system, embedded in a historical, physical, and social environment, stating, "There is nothing that goes on in the classroom that is not of ultimate consequence for the social order; and there is not much that is of immediate consequence for the social order that is not reflected in the classroom" (pp. 60–61). They also indicated that a change in one part of the classroom as a system is reflected in changes in all other parts of the system and ultimately, however tenuously, in all other systems in a society.

The "group climate" dimension, shown in the center of the model in Figure 9.2, was relevant to much research regarding the organizational climate of classrooms and schools that has been summarized elsewhere (Getzels, 1969) and is beyond the scope of treatment here.

The "biological" dimension figures prominently in much recent research in teaching and learning regarding the preferred learning styles of students (Dunn &

Dunn, 1978; Klausmeier, Lipham, & Daresh, 1983) wherein such preference variables as temperature, light, sound, time of day, persistence, mobility, and other physical and emotional conditions and states of students are examined. In educational administration, many researchers have analyzed the variable of male-female sex differences and stereotypes in relation to effective leadership and performance in administrative roles (Adkison, 1981); Fishel & Pottker, 1973; Gross & Trask, 1976; Kobayashi, 1974; Morsink, 1970). Recently, studies (Voss, 1983; Wallich, 1985) in educational administration have also focused on the variable of age as a biasing factor in the selection of candidates for various types of teaching positions. Additional studies (Gilbert, 1985) not only of sex and age but also of the capacities, potentialities, and physical states of administrators and teachers in relation to effective role performance are needed.

The *Values* or "anthropological" dimension, shown in the top line of Figure 9.2, indicates that the school as an institution is embedded in a culture with certain mores and values that influence goals, roles, and social behavior. Thus, conflicts in values can occur both among groups in the larger environment and between the cultural values outside the classroom and the institutional expectations within the classroom. Moreover, in regard to the school, values are held not only by those "out there" but also by individuals "in here." Hence, a composite model of the school as a social system (Getzels, Lipham, & Campbell, 1968) was constructed to depict educational administration as a social process; it is shown in Figure 9.3. The bottom line in this model stresses that the values held by individuals in the school explain and predict much goal-oriented social behavior. This composite model also clearly indicates that any social system, whether a group, classroom, school, or school district, must operate within and articulate with its larger environment.

In a penetrating analysis of American cultural

Figure 9.2 The Getzels-Thelen model of the classroom as a social system.

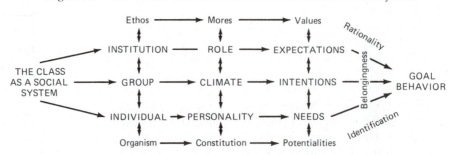

Figure 9.3 General model of behavior in social systems.

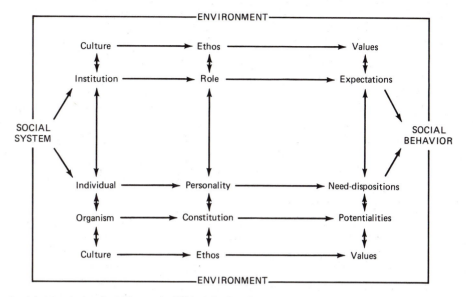

SOURCE. From *Education Administration as a Social Process* (p. 105) by J. W. Getzels, J. M. Lipham, and R. F. Campbell, 1968; New York: Harper & Row. Copyright 1968 by Harper & Row. Reprinted by permission.

values, Getzels, (1957, 1958a, 1972, 1978b, 1980) drew a distinction between the national core or "sacred" values that constitute our relatively stable ideals and beliefs and the more transient down-to-earth or "secular" values that are subject to change and wide interpretation at the operational level of the school. The four sacred values that he defined as being at the core of the American ethos included democracy, individualism, equality, and human perfectability. It is to these values that we appeal when we wish to undertake significant national action. The traditional secular values that governed one's down-to-earth beliefs regarding work, time, relation to others, and personal morality were the work-success ethic, future-time orientation, independence, and Puritan morality.

Although the sacred values remain stable—we still go to war for democracy—the secular values undergo transformation or at least changes in emphasis over time as reactions to the major themes of the traditional values. Thus, in the 1950s, the emergent values stressed sociability, present-time orientation, conformity, and moral relativism. In a sense, the change was from the self-made Horatio Alger hero of Main Street to the "Young Man in a Gray Flannel Suit" of Madison Avenue as the exemplar for youth. Subsequently, as conditions changed in the 1960s, these emergent values themselves underwent modification to a transitional set of values including social consciousness, relevance, authenticity, and moral commitment. One may recall the political activism, civil rights demonstrations, and school sit-ins of the period. In due course these values

too gave way to what became known as the narcissism and "me" values of the 1970s, including self-concern, career-orientation, security, and moral disengagement. The avant-garde abandoned the sit-in for the School of Business. The dates, as Getzels points out, are of course only rough bench marks, the categories in fours are more or less arbitrary, and the changes were by no means as sharp as the necessarily schematic account may imply. Yet the secular values continue to change and, in the 1980s, portend a possible recycling toward the traditional values, albeit not in the original form. In any case, the fact that values do shift at least in emphasis and that individuals and groups do differ in the expression of the values may make for strains between generations and between school and community, with consequent problems and implications for the educational administrator.

Many studies of individual values in educational administration have derived from Getzels's formulations. In an early study regarding student-teacher relations, Prince (1957) devised the *Differential Values Inventory* to assess traditional and emergent secular values, and he used it to discover significant differences in value orientations of teachers and students in public, private, and religious schools. Moreover, the value differences between teachers and students were found to be systematically related to student performance, grades, and career choices. Similar results were obtained in a subsequent study by Stone (1961). Rose (1967) discovered that the traditionalism of teachers is reflected in increased formality of the school and high aspiration and achievement levels of students. Regarding the secular values of superintendents and school board members, Abbott (1960) found that direct differences in individual values, as well as indirect differences in the mutual perception of values, significantly affect superintendent-school board working relationships. Subsequently, Rock (1975), building on Getzels's (1972) reformulation of secular values, developed the *Revised Differential Values Inventory* to ascertain the extent to which differences in traditional, transitional, and emergent values held by administrators, teachers, and students impact on the administration and operation of schools.

Although the studies cited immediately preceding have tended to highlight the climate, biological, and individual values dimensions of the Getzels-Thelen and composite models, one must recognize that many of the studies cited previously as derived from Getzels's psychosociological framework and the Getzels-Guba model may also have been stimulated by the more complete models, depending on the time at which the studies were designed and conducted. To reiterate, the Getzels-Thelen and composite models directed major attention to the relationship of the school to its larger environment and the impact of cultural and individual values on the operation of the school. Getzels's (1978a) theoretical formulation regarding the communities of education illuminates further these important relationships.

GETZELS'S MODEL OF THE COMMUNITIES OF EDUCATION

Educators often use the concept of community in a variety of confusing ways, such as in referring to the local community, the school district community, the political community, the educational community, and the like. Noting this confusion Getzels (1978a) described and drew distinctions among the various communities of education. He defined communities as groups of people conscious of a collective identity characterized by common cognitive and affective norms, and he delineated the following taxonomy of communities, which ranges from most to least dependent on a particular locality

1. *Local community.* The collective identify is founded in a particular neighborhood or region: for example, the local neighborhood or school community.
2. *Administrative community.* The collective identity is founded in a particular politically determined identity: for example, the city, country, or school district community.
3. *Social community.* The collective identity is founded in a particular set of interpersonal relationships without regard to local or administrative boundaries: for example, all the people in one's community of friends.
4. *Instrumental community.* The collective identity is founded in direct or indirect engagement with others in performance of a particular function of mutual concern: for example, a professional group, such as the educational community; a union community; or a philanthropic community.
5. *Ethnic, caste, or class community.* The collective identity is founded in affinity to a particular national, racial, or cultural group: for example the Irish, black, or upper-class community.
6. *Ideological community.* The collective identity is founded in a particular historic, conceptual, or sociopolitical community that stretches across the local, administrative, social, instrumental, or ethnic communities: for example, the Christian, scholarly, or socialist communities.
(p. 671)

As shown in Figure 9.4, the taxonomy of the communities of education clarifies both the cultural-values dimension and the individual-values dimension of the school as a social system. The model also shows that individual and institutional norms and values

Figure 9.4 Getzels's model of the communities of education.

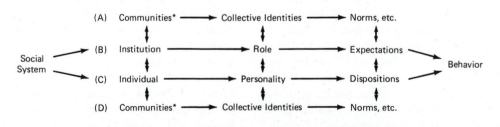

*Includes (1) local community, (2) administrative community, (3) social community, (4) instrumental community, (5) ethnic community, (6) ideological community.

NOTE. From "The communities of education" by J. W. Getzels, 1978, *Teachers College Record, 79*, p. 673. Copyright 1978 by Teachers College, Columbia University. Adapted by permission.

interact continually, affecting personality dispositions, role expectations, and resultant behavior in educational institutions.

Getzels's (1978a) model of the communities of education calls attention to the fact that many discontinuities result from one's simultaneous membership in the overlapping "variety of communities" (pp. 676–677) and that this lack of congruence affects both individual and organizational relationships and outcomes. Such discontinuities also help explain change or the lack of it in educational institutions.

Earlier, Getzels (1970, 1973) developed a fruitful taxonomy of change in education, based on the sources of and reactions to change. Three types of change result: enforced, expedient, and essential. When the source of a change is from the cultural dimension outside an organization, then the type of change is enforced (one that would not have occurred if it were not for external pressures), and the mechanism of change in the organization is accommodation. Enforced change is the type referred to when one says that most change in schools is from the outside, not from within. Expedient change is a corollary of enforced change. Change brought on from the outside creates pressures for alteration in the internal system, and the mechanism of change is reaction (wherein expedient alterations may be made) to maintain the existing system rather than to change it in substance. Essential change is neither merely an accommodation to external pressures nor a reaction to internal forces but derives from the voluntarism, abilities, interests, and insights of individuals inhabiting the organization. The result is neither the faddism of enforced change nor the rigidity of expedient change but creative transformation based on commitment and principle. In a recent private conversation (July, 1984), Getzels suggested a fourth type of change, extruded change, wherein essential change within the organization is diffused upward and outward to the larger instrumental community and other communities and to society in general. Extruded change calls to mind the early challenge by Counts (1932), *Dare the School Build a New Social Order?*

Through the years a substantial body of research has been conducted that examines the impact of cultural and community differences on expectations for the school as an institution. Although these studies were largely derived from the Getzels-Thelen model and composite models, they relate conceptually and can be better appreciated according to Getzels's model of the communities of education. Observing that schools typically are expected to achieve multiple, often conflicting, goals and objectives, Downey, Seager, and Slagle (1958) constructed the *Task of Public Education Opinionnaire* to measure expec-

tations held across the nation for the task of public elementary and secondary schools regarding the intellectual, social, personal, and productive dimensions of education. Somewhat surprisingly, they found expectations for the task of the schools to be similar between members of the educational community and citizens in general (Downey, 1960). But they also discovered substantial differences in expectations according to respondents' occupational status, educational level, geographic region, age, religion, and race. Other researchers (Carver, 1966; Hartrick, 1962; Hills, 1961) documented the extent of these differences, and still others (Levine, 1963; McPhee, 1959) analyzed the relationships among subpublic differences in values, educational viewpoints, and school approval by the local community. During the 1970s, under the sponsorship of Phi Delta Kappa, the task items were revised and used in both English and Spanish versions to ascertain expectations for schools throughout the nation (Spears, 1973). Most of these studies were of immediate practical value in helping administrators and boards of education reach a reasonable degree of consensus on educational goals and priorities in the local and administrative communities of the school.

As with the other formulations, Getzels's model of the communities of education is also cited in recent textbooks in educational administration (Lipham, Rankin, & Hoeh, 1985; Roe & Drake, 1980). The model is particularly helpful in delineating the principal's responsibilities for relating simultaneously to the local and the administrative communities, which often hold divergent goals, priorities, and expectations for effective performance in the principalship, as, for example, in the closing of a local school. Moreover, the model is also useful in helping principals exert leadership in linking the local school to consultants and others in the larger administrative and instrumental communities to effect essential educational change. In summary, this model assists administrators in fulfilling the important leadership functions of community analysis, communication, and involvement; it also helps them in resolving conflicts deriving from their own and others' simultaneous membership in the multiple communities of education.

CRITIQUE OF GETZELS'S MODELS

In the search for new paradigms to guide administrative theory, research, and practice, it has become popular during the past few years to criticize, if not castigate, the so-called Theory Movement in educational administration, to which Getzels contributed significantly and with which his work has been closely associated. In these reviews and perspectives (Culbertson, 1981; Griffiths, 1979a, 1979b, 1983; Hoy, 1982), the work of Getzels and other theorists is often cited as (a) communicating grandiose claims about the validity of the theoretical models; (b) representing a closed-system approach; (c) subscribing to a behavioristic view of the human being; (d) avoiding or eschewing values; and (e) slavishly adhering to logical positivism. The validity of each of these charges can be evaluated by consulting and considering direct quotations that provide a veridical history of what was written, and presumably intended, at the time.

Regarding the "strong assurances," "unrealistic expectations," and "undesirable excesses" mentioned by Culbertson (1981), Getzels (1952) initially presented the psychosociological framework, stating that it "*appears* [italics added] to offer fruitful dimensions and concepts" (p. 146). Concerning the Getzels-Guba (1957) model, the authors wrote, "In conclusion, we wish to disown any implication that the improvement of administrative practice will automatically ensue from a knowledge or manipulation of the concepts and variables of the sort proposed in this model" (p. 440). Again, regarding the Getzels-Guba model, Getzels (1958b) wrote, "Finally we should like to make clear that the model presented here is not, of course, the only possible framework or, indeed, that it is even a good one—whatever the term good means in this context. We suggest, however, that it is at present useful for stimulating and guiding what seems to be a fruitful line of inquiry into the administrative process" (p. 165). In a review of the Getzels-Guba model published in the *Administrative Science Quarterly*, Trow (1959) stated, "Getzels is becomingly *modest* [italics added] about his efforts, but his work at once connects with major lines of theory in social science and is also likely to be useful to administrators, both in their thinking and practice" (p. 124). Regarding the composite social-systems model, Getzels, Lipham, and Campbell (1968) concluded, "Not only our research and practice but also our conceptualizations must be open-ended" (p. 411). In ending the presentation of the model of the communities of education, Getzels (1978a) stated, "The intent of these observations has not been to offer, much less urge, a particular conceptual or methodological solution to the complexities in understanding the relations between community and education" (p. 682). It is, therefore, hard to comprehend how the foregoing statements could be construed as "communicating strong assurances, unrealistic expectations, undesirable excesses, and grandiose claims" for the models, as now charged.

Hoy (1982), citing Griffiths (1979a, 1979b), characterized the Getzels-Guba social-process model as a closed-system theory that does not permit one to describe either organizations or the people in them. This is quite puzzling since the normative and personal dimensions of the model deal precisely with both institutions and the individuals in them. Instead, Hoy urged that open-system theories be used that stress the interdependence of the school with the larger environment. Although the Getzels-Guba model dealt primarily with internal organizational relationships, it is erroneous to call it a closed-system theory. In fact, the model was introduced (Getzels & Guba, 1957) by describing a social system as follows: "Within our framework, for one purpose a given community may be considered a social system, with the school a particular organization within the more general social system; for another purpose the school itself, or even a class within the school may be considered a social system in its own right" (p. 424). As indicated earlier in this chapter, the overlapping, dynamic, open-systems view of classrooms was also stressed in the Getzels-Thelen and composite models. Moreover, Getzels's model of the communities of education deals precisely with one's simultaneous membership in multiple, interactive educational communities ranging from local to global. How better could one try to communicate the "openness" of the school?

In characterizing the Getzels-Guba model as a theory no longer productive, Griffiths (1979a, 1979b) focused mainly on relationships posited in the normative dimension, while ignoring the personal dimension of the model. Subsequently, Culbertson (1981) agreed with Griffiths, stating that theorists working at the time were behavioristic and did not take into account that an "important difference between human and natural phenomena is that mental perceptions, thought processes, and communication via language operate...within the former but not within the latter" (p. 242). As indicated earlier in this chapter, Getzels's initial psychosociological framework stressed the importance of idiosyncratic perceptions of needs, goals, and symbols in defining situations in which human beings interact. This point of view is continually reiterated in subsequent works (Coladarci & Getzels, 1955, p. 26; Getzels, 1958b, pp. 159–161; Getzels et al., 1968, pp. 286–317, 381–382). In *Educational Administration as a Social Process*, moreover, behaviorism was explicitly rejected. The behavioristic conception of human beings, as proposed by Watson, was considered and discarded in favor of a conception such as that of Allport, who devoted a lifetime to impeaching positivism and behaviorism and advocating humanism and intentionalism. Far from excluding mental perception and thought processes in their conceptions of individuals in organizations, Getzels, Lipham, and Campbell (1968) went further to include the very stuff of the humanness of human beings and wrote of individuals in organizations as "living people with hates and loves, fears and aspirations" (p. 65). Hates, loves, fears, aspirations, symbols, values, perceptions—these surely are not the words of writers who, as is now said, were behaviorists who could not distinguish between human and nonhuman phenomena.

The following quotations from Getzels speak directly to the charge (Culbertson, 1981, pp. 40–42) that Getzels's work ignores or eschews values:

> The central serious issue facing the school today, as it always has been, is the problem of values...[for] whether we will it or not—in fact, whether we know it or not—the choices we teachers and parents make with respect to objectives, curriculum, methods, personnel, and even the buildings we construct, are founded in some system of values, however subliminally these may function in any particular case. The specific forms that our child-rearing and educational practices take from among the almost infinite range of possibilities cannot be understood outside the context of our dominant values and the shifts and cleavages these values are presently undergoing. (1957, p. 92)

> Surely, it is a truism that education is not merely the dissemination of facts but a preparation for life. And preparation for life, as life itself, requires not only the technological wisdom of *how* to do, that is, the wisdom of means, but also the greater wisdom of *what* to do, that is, the wisdom of ends and of values [italics in original]. (1958a, p. 146)

> Indeed, I wonder whether we can achieve intellectual neutrality any more than we can achieve moral or political neutrality. And I would wonder whether even if we could, it would be an unequivocal blessing. *I myself doubt that we can truly neutralize ourselves either morally, politically, or intellectually without ceasing to be* [italics added]. (1960, p. 37)

> The objectives, curricula, methods, and administrative policies and procedures...must be understood in the context of the culture and the component values to which they are inevitably related. (Getzels, Lipham, & Campbell, 1968, p. 102)

How, in the face of the above, is it possible to suggest that Getzels's models avoided value issues and eschewed value inquiry in educational administration?

To say that logical positivism or hypothetico-deductive modes of theorizing did not influence Getzels's models would be inaccurate; to state that they were the dominant influences (Culbertson, 1981), however, is equally wrong. Getzels's (1952) psycho-sociological framework stated, "The debt of the present formulations to the work of Max Weber and Talcott Parsons...will be self-evident throughout the paper" (p. 2). Surely, Weber and Parsons were not logical positivists whose concepts and modes of inquiry were drawn from mathematics, physics, or chemistry. The monograph by Coladarci and Getzels (1955) stated:

> As was noted earlier, the particular framework partially outlined here is presented for the purpose of *illustrating one process of theorizing* [italics added] about educational administration. One may of course suggest other frameworks. In fact, we would argue that, if we are to make progress in understanding and improving administrative practice, *we must devise alternative formulations and construct competing theoretical frames-of-reference* [italics added]. (p. 26)

This monograph also stated that theory is *induced* from the world of everyday events:

> One searches for before-after relationships among the facts, observations, and events of every-day existence on the assumption that they are not independent, non-controllable events and their future occurrence can be predicted and their past understood...In this *inductive* [italics added] aspect of theory construction no identifiable line can be drawn between the observed events and the hypothesized explaining or predicting principle. (p. 4)

Reiterating this view, Getzels (1960) subsequently stated:

> In the long run the relevance of the respective [conceptual] choices will be settled by the fruitfulness of the explanatory, research, and practical applications to which each choice gives rise. Always, however, we think and work within some conceptual framework, some theoretical *bias* [italics added], some intellectual stance, which is of course to be held lightly, but nonetheless held, however provisionally, until a better one comes along. We are in a more strategic position to move forward both in our own thinking and in communicating with others if we make this bias explicit to ourselves and to others than if we keep it implicit under the guise of self-proclaimed neutrality. (p. 41)

Again, far from the uncritical and wholehearted acceptance of the tenets of logical positivism, the views of other philosophers were brought to bear on various aspects of Getzels's work. For example, the views of Dewey were cited concerning the problem of theory and practice, and the philosopher of science whose conception of theory and practice was cited with approval was Toulmin, who explicitly disagreed with, as he said, the "answers and solutions" of logical positivism (Getzels, 1960, pp. 28, 31, 43). Thus, it is apparent that no single epistomology guided or dictated Getzels's theoretical formulations.

That Getzels's models of the school, community, and educational administration continue to be relevant to theory, research, and practice in education today is evident in the scholarly exegeses and controversies that still center on them (Campbell, 1981; Culbertson, 1981; Griffths, 1983; Hoy, 1982); the substantial space devoted to them in current textbooks (Campbell, Corbally, & Nystrand, 1983; Hoy & Miskel, 1982; Lipham, Rankin, & Hoeh, 1985; Silver, 1983), and recent research on such issues as effective schooling, as well as criticisms of the "effectiveness schooling movement." As does Getzels, most of the researchers of "effective schools" view them as social systems (Austin, 1979; Brookover, Beady, Flood, Schweitzer, & Wisenbaker, 1979; Edmonds, 1979; Rutter, Maugham, Mortimore, & Outson, 1979); they have attempted to determine the specific values, goals, roles, expectations, dispositions, and behaviors that contribute to the increased academic achievement, or lack of it, on the part of students.

Although such studies of effective schooling have been helpful, they have been criticized not only on methodological grounds (Clark, Lotto, & Astuto, 1984; Mackenzie, 1983) but also on the ground that they have isolated and prescribed a particular set of goals, roles, behaviors, and outcomes to be emulated no matter what the community context of the school and its pupils (Cuban, 1983; Ralph & Fennesey, 1983). Hence, most critics of this movement (Purkey & Smith, 1983) argue that in determining educational effectiveness, one must consider the total culture of the school. This brings us full course, suggesting that we return, reexamine, and reconsider the three dominant themes that characterize Getzels's work in educational administration—the complexity of the human personality, the interaction of personality with the formal and informal roles in schools as social systems, and individual and group values in the variety of communities to which the school is related—if essential educational change ever is to be implemented to enhance the effectiveness of schools.

In conclusion and as a personal note, through the years it has been stimulating, as a student and colleague of Getzels, to understand, utilize, and share appreciation of the power of the concepts and constructs posited by his several models and their derivations. They are useful in formulating theory, conducting research, and preparing educational administrators. Even so, much remains to be done. Thus, it will be interesting to observe the extent to which Getzels's models continue to challenge critics and colleagues to present equally fruitful formulations and frameworks for improving administrative research and education, both now and in the years ahead.

REFERENCES

Abbott, M. G. (1960). Values and value-perceptions in super-intendent-school board relationships. *Administrator's Notebook*, 9(4), 1–4.

Adkison, J. A. (1981). Women in school administration: A review of the research. *Review of Educational Research*, 51, 311–343.

Aho, A. A. (1971). Urban school decentralization and the role of the junior and senior high school principal (Doctoral dissertation, University of Wisconsin-Madison, 1971). *Dissertation Abstracts International*, 32/06–A, 2931.

Andrews, J. H. M. (1958). A deterrent to harmony among teachers. *Administrator's Notebook*, 6(7), 1–4.

Austin, G. R. (1979). Exemplary schools and the search for effectiveness. *Educational Leadership*, 37(1), 10–14.

Baldwin, J. E. (1979). Role perception and teacher morale: A study of their relationship in secondary schools (Doctoral dissertation, Brigham Young University, 1979). *Dissertation Abstracts International*, 40/10–A, 5256.

Brookover, W., Beady, C., Flood, P., Schweitzer, J., & Wisenbaker, J. (1979). *School social systems and academic achievement*. New York: Praeger.

Brown, A. F. (1962). Conflict and stress in administrative relationships. *Administrator's Notebook*, 10(7), 1–4.

Campbell, M. V. (1959). Teacher-principal agreement on the teacher role. *Administrator's Notebook*, 7(6), 1–4.

Campbell, R. F. (1981). The professorship in educational administration—a personal view. *Educational Administration Quarterly*, 17(1), 1–24.

Campbell, R. F., Corbally, J. E., & Nystrand, R. O. (1983). *Introduction to educational administration* (6th ed.). Boston: Allyn & Bacon.

Carver, F. D. (1966). Relationships between educational level, family income and expectations of citizens for the role of the school board (Doctoral dissertation, University of Wisconsin-Madison, 1967). *Dissertation Abstracts International*, 28/07–A, 2472.

Clark, D. L., Lotto, L. S., & Astuto, T. A. (1984). Effective schools and school improvement: A comparative analysis of two lines of inquiry. *Educational Administration Quarterly*, 20(3), 41–68.

Coladarci, A. P., & Getzels, J. W. (1955). *The use of theory in educational administration*. Stanford, CA: Stanford University Press.

Counts, G. S. (1932). *Dare the schools build a new social order?* New York: Day.

Cuban, L. (1983). Effective schools: A friendly but cautionary note. *Phi Delta Kappan*, 64, 695–696.

Culbertson, J. A. (1981). Perspective: Antecedents of the theory movement. *Educational Administrative Quarterly*, 17(1), 25–47.

Davis, K. P. (1977). Perceived role and effectiveness of school psychologists in IGE schools (Doctoral dissertation, University of Wisconsin-Madison, 1977). *Dissertation Abstracts International*, 38/12A, 7045.

Dean, G. W. (1975). Role conflict among community college chairpersons and its relationship to satisfaction and effectiveness (Doctoral dissertation, University of California, Los Angeles, 1975). *Dissertation Abstracts International*, 36/09A, 5677.

Downey, L. W. (1960). *The task of public education*. Chicago: The Midwest Center, University of Chicago.

Downey, L. W., Seager, R. C., & Slagle, A. T. (1958). *Task of Public Education Opinionnaire*. Chicago: The Midwest Center, University of Chicago.

Dunn, R. D., & Dunn, J. J. (1978). *Teaching students through their individual learning styles: A practical approach*. Reston, VA: Reston.

Edmonds, R. (1979). Effective schools for the urban poor. *Educational Leadership*, 37(1), 15–24.

Evers, N. A. (1974). An analysis of the relationship between the effectiveness of the multiunit elementary school's instruction and research unit and interpersonal relations (Doctoral dissertation,

University of Wisconsin-Madison, 1974). *Dissertation Abstracts International, 35/06A*, 3336.

Faber, C. F., & Shearron, G. F. (1970). *Elementary school administration*. New York: Holt, Rinehart, & Winston.

Ferneau, E. F. (1954). Which consultant? *Administrator's Notebook, 2*(8), 1–4.

Fishel, A., & Pottker, J. (1973). Women lose out: Is there sex discrimination in school administration? *Clearing House, 47*, 387–391.

Getzels, J. W. (1952). A psycho-sociological framework for the study of educational administration. *Harvard Educational Review, 22*, 235–246.

Getzels, J. W. (1957). Changing values challenge the schools. *School Review, 65*, 91–102.

Getzels, J. W. (1958a). The acquisition of values in school and society. In F. S. Chase & H. A. Anderson (Eds.), *The high school in a new era* (pp. 146–161). Chicago: University of Chicago Press.

Getzels, J. W. (1958b). Administration as a social process. In A. W. Halpin (Ed.), *Administrative theory in education* (pp. 150–165). Chicago: The Midwest Center, University of Chicago.

Getzels, J. W. (1960). Theory and practice in educational administration: An old question revisited. In R. F. Campbell & J. M. Lipham (Eds.), *Administrative theory as a guide to action* (pp. 37–58). Chicago: The Midwest Center, University of Chicago.

Getzels, J. W. (1969). A social psychology of education. In G. Lindzey & E. Aronson (Eds.), *Handbook of Social Psychology* (rev. ed.) (pp. 459–537). Reading, MA: Addison-Wesley.

Getzels, J. W. (1970). Creative administration and organizational change: An essay in theory. In L. J. Rubin, (Ed.), *Frontiers of school leadership* (pp. 69–85). Chicago: Rand-McNally.

Getzels, J. W. (1972). On the transformation of values: A decade after Port Huron. *School Review, 80*, 505–519.

Getzels, J. W. (1973). Theory and research on leadership: Some comments and some alternatives. In L. L. Cunningham & W. J. Gephart (Eds.), *Leadership: The science and the art today* (pp. 16–25). Itasca, IL: Peacock.

Getzels, J. W. (1975). Problem finding and the inventiveness of solutions. *Journal of Creative Behavior, 9*, 12–18.

Getzels, J. W. (1978a). The communities of education. *Teachers College Record, 79*, 659–682.

Getzels, J. W. (1978b). The school and the acquisition of values. In R. W. Tyler (Ed.), *From youth to constructive adult life: The role of the school* (pp. 43–66). Berkeley, CA: McCutchan.

Getzels, J. W. (1979). Problem finding and research in educational administration. In G. L. Immegart & W. L. Boyd (Eds.), *Problem-finding in educational administration* (pp. 5–22). Lexington, MA: Heath.

Getzels, J. W. (1980). *Alternative directions for research in educational administration*. In R. H. Farquar & I. E. Housego (Eds.), *Canadian and comparative educational administration* (pp. 354–378). Vancouver, Canada: The University of British Columbia Centre for Continuing Education.

Getzels, J. W., & Guba, E. G. (1954). Role, role conflict, and effectiveness: An empirical study. *American Sociological Review, 19*, 164–175.

Getzels, J. W., & Guba, E. G. (1955a). Role conflict and personality. *Journal of Personality, 24*, 74–85.

Getzels, J. W., & Guba, E. G. (1955b). The structure of roles and role conflict in the teaching situation. *Journal of Educational Sociology, 29*, 30–40.

Getzels, J. W., & Guba, E. G. (1957). Social behavior and the administrative process. *School Review, 65*, 423–441.

Getzels, J. W., Lipham, J. M., & Campbell, R. F. (1968). *Educational administration as a social process*. New York: Harper & Row.

Getzels, J. W., & Smilansky, J. (1983). Individual differences in pupil perceptions of school problems. *British Journal of Educational Psychology, 53*, 307–316.

Getzels, J. W., & Thelen, H. A. (1960). The classroom group as a unique social system. In N. B. Henry (Ed.), *The dynamics of instructional groups*. The 59th Yearbook of the National Society for the Study of Education (pp. 53–82). Chicago: University of Chicago Press.

Gilbert, K. M. (1985). Candidate experience and administrative orientation in selecting secondary school principals. (Doctoral dissertation, University of Wisconsin-Madison, 1984). *Dissertation Abstracts International*.

Gilberts, R. D. (1961). The interpersonal characteristics of teaching teams (Doctoral dissertation, University of Wisconsin-Madison, 1961). *Dissertation Abstracts International, 22/06*, 1882.

Griffiths, D. E. (1979a). Another look at research on the behavior of administrators. In G. L. Immegart & W. L. Boyd (Eds.), *Problem finding in educational administration* (pp. 41–62). Lexington, MA: Heath.

Griffiths, D. E. (1979b). Intellectual turmoil in educational administration. *Educational Administration Quarterly, 15*(3), 43–65.

Griffiths, D. E. (1983). Evolution in research and theory: A study of prominent researchers. *Educational Administration Quarterly, 19*, 201–221.

Gross, N., & Trask, A. (1976). *The sex factor and the management of schools*. New York: John Wiley.

Hartrick, W. J. (1962). Perceptions of the task and program of the public schools (Doctoral dissertation, University of Chicago, 1961). *Dissertation Abstracts International, X 1962*, 71.

Hencley, S. P. (1960). The conflict patterns of school superintendents. *Administrator's Notebook, 8*(9), 1–4.

Hencley, S. P., McCleary, L. E., & McGrath, J. H. (1970). *The elementary school principalship*. New York: Dodd, Mead.

Heyerdahl, L., Jr. (1967). Teachers' perceptions of expectations for their role and membership in teacher organizations (Doctoral dissertation, University of Wisconsin-Madison, 1967). *Dissertation Abstracts International, 28/11–A*, 4412.

Hills, R. J. (1961). Social classes and educational views. *Administrator's Notebook, 10*(2), 1–4.

Hoy, W. K. (1982). Recent developments in theory and research in educational administration. *Educational Administration Quarterly, 18*(3), 1–11.

Hoy, W. K., & Miskel, C. G. (1982). *Educational administration: Theory, research, and practice* (2nd ed.). New York: Random House.

Hughes, L.W., & Ubben, G. C. (1984). *The elementary principal's handbook* (2nd ed.). Boston: Allyn & Bacon.

Ingraham, M. J. (1979). Role conflict of teachers with the principal and team members and the relationship of role conflict to perceived climate and rated effectiveness (Doctoral dissertation, Boston University, 1979). *Dissertation Abstracts International, 40/05–A*, 2386.

Kimbrough, R. B., & Nunnery, M. Y. (1976). *Educational administration: An introduction*. New York: Macmillan.

Klausmeier, H. J., Lipham, J. M., & Daresh, J. C. (1983). *The renewal and improvement of secondary education*. Lanham, MD: University Press of America.

Kobayashi, K. J. (1974). A comparison of organizational climate of schools administered by female and male elementary school principals (Doctoral dissertation, University of the Pacific, 1974). *Dissertation Abstracts International, 35/01–A*, 129–130.

Levine, D. U. (1963). Liberalism, conservatism, and educational viewpoint. *Administrator's Notebook, 11*(9). 1–4.

Lieberman, A. (1977). Linking processes in educational change. In N. Nash & J. A. Culbertson (Eds.), *Linking processes in educational improvement* (pp. 149–188). Columbus, OH: University Council for Educational Administration.

Lipham, J. M. (1960). Personal variables of effective administrators. *Administrator's Notebook, 9*(1), 1–4.

Lipham, J. M. (1977). The administrator's role in educational linkage. In N. Nash & J. A. Culbertson (Eds.), *Linking processes in educational improvement* (pp. 118–148). Columbus, OH: University Council for Educational Administration.

Lipham, J. M., Rankin, R. E., & Hoeh, J. A., Jr. (1985). *The principalship: Concepts, competencies, and cases*. White Plains, NY: Longman.

MacKenzie, D. (1983). Research for school improvement: An appraisal of some recent trends. *Educational Researcher, 12*(4),

5–31.

Maire, M. H. (1965). Expectations for the architect's role in school plant development programs and the effectiveness of architectural services (Doctoral dissertation, University of Wisconsin-Madison, 1965). *Dissertation Abstracts International, 20/09,* 5166.

Martin, W. M. (1970). Role conflict and deviant adaptation as related to educational goal attainment: A social systems approach (Doctoral dissertation, University of California, Los Angeles, 1970). *Dissertation Abstracts International, 30/07–A,* 3221.

McCarty, D. J. (1959). School board membership: Why do citizens serve? *Administrator's Notebook, 8*(1), 1–4.

McPhee, R. F. (1959). Individual values, educational viewpoint, and local school approval. *Administrator's Notebook, 7*(8), 1–4.

Meyer, G. V. (1964). Role perception in a problem situation (Doctoral dissertation, Oklahoma State University, 1964). *Dissertation Abstracts International, 26/03,* 1456–57.

Morsink, H. M. (1970). Leader behavior of men and women principals. *National Association of Secondary School Principals Bulletin, 54* (347), 80–87.

Moser, R. P. (1957). The leadership patterns of school superintendents and school principals. *Administrator's Notebook, 6*(1), 1–4.

Moyer, D. C. (1954). Teachers' attitudes toward leadership as they relate to teacher satisfaction (Doctoral dissertation, University of Chicago, 1954). *Dissertation Abstracts International, W 1955,* 180.

Muhm, J. B. (1968). A study of the relationship between the organizational climate of elementary schools and the occupational characteristics of principals as perceived by teachers (Doctoral dissertation, University of Illinois, 1968.) *Dissertation Abstracts International, 30/03–A,* 961.

Owens, R. G. (1981). *Organizational behavior in education* (2nd ed.). Englewood Cliffs, NJ: Prentice-Hall.

Parsons, T. (1951). *The social system.* New York: Free Press.

Paul, D. A. (1974). The diffusion of an innovation through inter-organizational linkages: A comparative case study (Doctoral dissertation, University of Wisconsin-Madison, 1974). *Dissertation Abstracts International, 35/09–A,* 5740.

Paul, D. A. (1977). Change processes at the elementary, secondary, and post-secondary levels of education. In N. Nash & J. A. Culbertson (Eds.), *Linking processes in educational improvement* (pp. 7–73). Columbus, OH: University Council for Educational Administration.

Payne, N. M. (1971). Perceptions of the actual and ideal role of mathematics department chairmen in selected Georgia schools (Doctoral dissertation, University of Georgia, 1971). *Dissertation Abstracts International, 32/09–A,* 4926.

Pedicone, J. J., Jr. (1981). Role expectations of department chairpersons in Wisconsin senior high schools (Doctoral dissertation, University of Wisconsin-Madison, 1981). *Dissertation Abstracts International, 42/10–A,* 4238.

Prince, R. (1957). Individual values and administrative effectiveness. *Administrator's Notebook, 6*(4), 1–4.

Purkey, S. C., & Smith, M. S. (1982). Effective schools—a review. *Elementary School Journal, 83,* 427–452.

Ralph, J. H., & Fennesey, J. (1983). Science or reform: Some questions about the effective schools model. *Phi Delta Kappan, 64,* 689–694.

Reed, R. K. (1973). The middle school learning coordinator in Wisconsin: The role and relationship between leader behavior and effectiveness (Doctoral dissertation, University of Wisconsin-Madison, 1973). *Dissertation Abstracts International, 34/10–A,* 6324.

Rock, D. J. (1975). The revision, redevelopment and field test of the Differential Values Inventory: A methodological study (Doctoral dissertation, University of Wisconsin-Madison, 1975). *Dissertation Abstracts International, 36/03–A,* 1226.

Roe, W. H., & Drake, T. H. (1980). *The principalship* (2nd ed.). New York: Macmillan.

Rose, G. W. (1967). Organizational behavior and its concomitants in schools. *Administrator's Notebook, 15*(7), 1–4.

Rutter, M., Maugham, B., Mortimore, P., & Outson, J., with Smith, A. (1979). *Fifteen thousand hours: Secondary schools and their effects on children.* Cambridge, MA: Harvard University Press.

Savage, W. W. (1959). *Consultative services to local school systems.* Chicago: The Midwest Center, University of Chicago.

Semrow, J. J. (1965). Personal variables and their relationship to self-role conflict and administrator effectiveness (Doctoral dissertation, University of Wisconsin-Madison, 1965). *Dissertation Abstracts International, 25/12,* 7053.

Sergiovanni, T. J., & Carver, F. D. (1980). *The new school executive: A theory of administration* (2nd ed.). New York: Harper & Row.

Silver, P. F. (1983). *Educational administration: Theoretical perspectives on practice and research.* New York: Harper & Row.

Spears, H. (1973). Kappans ponder the goals of education. *Phi Delta Kappan, 60,* 29–32.

Stone, S. C. (1961). A study of the relationships among values, family characteristics, and personality characteristics of adolescents (Doctoral dissertation, University of Chicago, 1960). *Dissertation Abstracts International, X 1961,* 57.

Thorson, J. R. (1966). Expectations for the school board role as related to level of local financial support and allocation of expenditures (Doctoral dissertation, University of Wisconsin-Madison, 1966). *Dissertation Abstracts International, 28/03–A,* 924.

Tornow, E. W. (1965). A study of teachers' perceptions of decision points and the interactions of the superintendent of schools, director of instruction, and the high school principal (Doctoral dissertation, University of Wisconsin-Madison, 1965). *Dissertation Abstracts International, 37/03–A,* 643.

Trow, M. (1959). Book review: Administrative theory in education. *Aministrative Science Quarterly, 4*(1), 122–126.

Voss, G. C. (1983). The effect of age, position, and amount of résumé information on the selection of teacher candidates (Doctoral dissertation, University of Wisconsin-Madison, 1983). *Dissertation Abstracts International, 44/05A,* 1288.

Waier, R. D. (1970). The role of school superintendents in the negotiation process (Doctoral dissertation, University of Wisconsin-Madison, 1970). *Dissertation Abstracts International, 31/09–A,* 4438.

Wallace, R. W., Jr. (1969). Teacher identification of a potential for conflict and role expectations for the elementary principal. (Doctoral dissertation, Case Western Reserve University, 1969). *Dissertation Abstracts International, 31/06–A,* 2670.

Wallich, L. R. (1985). The effects of age and sex on the prescreening for selection of teacher candidates (Doctoral dissertation, University of Wisconsin-Madison, 1984). *Dissertation Abstracts International.*

Weber, M. (1947). *The theory of social and economic organization* (A. M. Henderson & T. Parsons, Trans.). New York: Oxford University Press.

Woods, J. D. (1977). A study of differences between black and white school administrators in role expectations, role conflict, and organizational mobility (Doctoral dissertation, Syracuse University, 1977). *Dissertation Abstracts International, 38/06–A,* 3208.

CHAPTER 10

The Pupil Control Studies

John S. Packard

This chapter examines the lines of inquiry that have used either or both the pupil control ideology questionnaire (PCI) and the pupil control behavior rating form (PCB). PCI is the older of the two instruments and has enjoyed much more use and subsequent influence. Some 200 original studies have employed PCI; several hundred publications have reported the results. The first report on PCI appeared in 1965 (Eidell, 1965). Reference to PCB appeared in 1973 (Helsel & Willower, 1973). Both measures include 20 items scored on a five-point Likert scale. Each measure has high internal stability (reliability estimates are often reported to exceed 0.90) and through-time stability (all reported correlations save one exceed 0.70). The developers claim that PCI measures an ideology about or an orientation toward how to enact pupil control. Scoring is bipolar, ranging from custodial to humanistic. High scores (maximum of 100) signal a custodial orientation, and low scores (minimum of 20) a humanistic orientation. The PCB instrument, which requires students to report on the pupil control behaviors of teachers, is scored in the same way. Teachers who receive high scores are considered to behave in a custodial fashion.

ORIGINS

The lines of inquiry that employ PCI and PCB originated in a field study conducted by Willower and Jones in a single junior high school. Their reports

Consultant/reviewers: Norman J. Boyan, University of California-Santa Barbara; and Thomas Fleming, University of Victoria.

(Willower & Jones, 1963, 1967) emphasized the pervasiveness of concern among the faculty and staff about pupil control. The investigators depicted these concerns as the most visible thread woven through the fabric of school life. The observation that public school educators constantly think, speak, and act in lines dominated by pupil deportment prompted Willower and Jones to formulate and advance the organizing concepts that led to the development first of PCI and second of PCB. The particular form that the two instruments took, short and easily scored questionnaires, made them readily available for survey-based, hypothesis-testing inquiry quite in keeping with the Theory Movement in educational administration that was gaining momentum in the early 1960s.

Willower and his associates (Eidell, 1965; Hoy, 1965; Willower, Eidell, & Hoy, 1967, 1973) argued that the preoccupation of public school educators with pupil control required more systematic examination and exploration than it had previously received, and that the works of Gilbert and Levinson and Carlson (cited by Willower et al.) provided theoretical notions for illuminating and extending the findings of the junior high school study. Gilbert and Levinson had earlier reported that staff members in mental hospitals were often preoccupied with controlling patients but that variations in the attitudes and actions of hospital staff ranged from custodial to humanistic. The more custodial staff members thought about and treated patients as if they were not fully deserving of respect and humane treatment. The conduct of the more humanistic staff suggested a belief that patients were fully or almost fully human and deserved common courtesies and more open forms of therapies. Carlson (1964) speculates that schools are like prisons and mental hospitals in the respect that in none of these institutions do staff members and clients choose to interact in pursuit of common goals. The "clients" are more or less constrained to avail themselves of the offerings of professional and nonprofessional staff members. Carlson reasoned that in such "domesticated" organizations, both clients and staff members often come into conflict over issues of client control and, therefore, remain preoccupied with those issues. Willower and his colleagues also found support for their observations of the overriding salience of pupil control in the work of Willard Waller (1932) and the prose of Mark Twain. The intellectually respectable backdrop against which Willower and his associates elaborated their discussions of the findings of a single study, as well as the fit of the discussion with the personal experiences of many school workers and observers, contributed effectively to setting pupil control ideology in place as a popular heuristic.

When Eidell (1965) set about developing the PCI measure, he regarded the "category of normative literature about discipline in schools quite irrelevant to the theoretical scientific study of pupil control" (p. 14). Results of early field trials of a first draft of the measure persuaded Eidell to drop from the scale almost all items worded in a humanistic fashion on the basis that they were "mere pedagogy" (Eidell, 1965, p. 34). Use of PCI in the field by Eidell and, close on his heels, Hoy (1965) yielded findings that they and Willower (1967) regarded as eminently sensible and promising. Elementary teachers were more humanistic than secondary school teachers, females more humanistic than males, administrators more humanistic than teachers, counselors more humanistic than administrators, and teachers with less than 5 years' teaching experience more humanistic than teachers with 5 or more years' teaching experience. The repetition of these findings over time and location has created a sense of empirical regularity that encouraged developers of the instrument to believe in its theoretical soundness. Hoy (1965) added another dimension to the discourse by reporting an apparent association between PCI and dogmatism (using Rokeach, Form E). At the end of his dissertation, Hoy listed nine questions that in large measure framed the next 20 years of PCI work, including queries about the relationships between PCI and behavior, PCI and personality, PCI and role, PCI and educational innovation, PCI and student alienation, and PCI and effective teaching.

THE STUDIES

So, soon after their initial appearances, the PCI and PCB measures, especially the former, gained wide-spread use, sometimes by investigators who did not invoke explicit theory and/or rigorous methods. The investigations that have accumulated over the years fall into four major categories: (a) search for personality correlates, (b) search for organizational correlates, (c) search for experience correlates, and (d) search for behavioral connections and outcomes.

Personality Correlates

Approximately 100 studies have attempted to answer the question often posed only implicitly: "What sorts of educators lean toward custodial or humanistic modes of thought?" Sometimes guided by reference to a roughly defined pupil control theory, sometimes not, a large number of investigators searched with intermittent discipline for personality correlates of PCI.

The most striking finding from this line of inquiry confirms that PCI correlates well with itself. Internal consistency correlations range from .61 to .95 (Eidell, 1965; Murad, 1974; Zak & Horwitz, 1978; Zelei, 1971). Estimates of through time stability in PCI scale scores are also quite high, with calculated values running from .86 to .65 (Docking & Docking, 1984; Glasnapp & Guenther, 1973; Halpin & Goldenberg, 1973; Kiss, 1981; Lundin, 1980). The single notable exception in the data on through time stability is a correlation of −.06 reported by Franklin (1976) in a study of an apparently successful, deliberate attempt to destabilize the PCI of student teachers. Taken together, the findings support a conclusion that the PCI instrument possesses high reliability; responses to PCI items align very well with each other, and over time a respondent's total score is predicted by an earlier one.

Tables 10.1, 10.2, and 10.3 report, respectively, high ($r = .60$ and above), low ($r =$ approximately .20 and below), and medium ($r =$ between approximately .20 and .60) correlations between PCI and measures of other personal variables.

The High Correlations

The highest correlation of .92 is reported by Henderson (1982), between PCI and a measure of locus of control. The very high correlations present something of a mixed blessing for PCI. To find that PCI correlates as well with several other measures as it correlates with itself suggests either that PCI taps into the same characteristics as the other instruments or that the respondents fall into response habits. For example, the items on the Minnesota Teacher Attitude Inventory (MTAI) and on Student/Teacher Attitudes of Human Relations (STAHR) are very much like those on PCI. The similarity of item form and structure between PCI and several other personality instruments, then, leaves

Table 10.1   High PCI—Personality Correlates

R	VARIABLE MEASURE	SOURCE	
.92	Locus of control	Henderson	1982
.84	Authoritarianism, principals	Nachtscheim & Hoy	1976
−.79	(−.66 to −.72) feelings of inadequacy	Henderson	1982
.78	Attitudes about corporal punishment	Bogacki	1981
.77	Traditional family values	Nachtscheim & Hoy	1976
.77	Perception of informal group PCI feelings	Henderson	1982
−.78	MTAI	Caffee	1979
.77	Other teachers in close contact	Salerno	1975
.76	STAHR (human relations)	Murad	1974
.76	Use of corporal punishment	Bogacki	1981
.76	Dogmatism	Heineman	1971
.71	Dogmatism	Franklin	1976
.68	Dogmatism	Lundin	1980
.69	Imaginativeness	Enochs	1982
.68	Subject matter emphasis	Bartlett	1976
.67	Aloofness (OCDQ)	Hoy & Appleberry	1970
−.63	Progressive educational attitudes	Voege	1979
.64	Status obeisance	Helsel	1971b
.63	Emphasis on classroom order	Bartlett	1976
.63	Authenticity of principal leadership	Hoy & Henderson	1982
.62	Teacher anxiety	Docking & Docking	1984
−.61	Closed climate (OCDQ)	Appleberry & Hoy	1969
−.61	Open (OCDQ)	Hoy & Appleberry	1970
−.60	Thrust (OCDQ)	Hoy & Appleberry	1970
−.66 to +.31	Venturesomeness	Henderson	1982
−.62 to +.29	Toughmindedness	Henderson	1982
−.61	Emotional stability	Henderson	1982

Table 10.2   Low PCI—Personality Correlates

R	VARIABLE MEASURE	SOURCE	
.23	Teacher warmth	McCaskill	1979
.21	Orderliness	Leppert & Hoy	1972
−.20	Knowledge of student rights	Horowitz	1980
−.17	Intellectual interests	Leppert & Hoy	1972
.17 to .06	Professional orientation	Willower & Landis	1970
−.17	Sense of power	Rose	1974
.18	Interpersonal aggression	Winberg	1982
−.16	Attitudes about handicapped	Rouse	1978
.14	Freedom	Heineman	1971
−.12	Job satisfaction	Heckert	1976
.11	Need for order	Winberg	1982
−.09	Rating of principal	Long	1979
.08	Liberalism	Primeaux	1979
.08	Knowledge of adolescents	McCaskill	1979
−.08	Progressivism (India)	Chawla	1977
−.08	Professionalism (India)	Chawla	1977
.08	Sense of bureaucracy	Hamalian	1979
−.07	Accept self	Brenneman	1974
−.07	Need for people	Winberg	1982
.06	Equality	Heineman	1971
.06	Satisfaction with supervisor	Krohn	1979
−.06	Need to help	Winberg	1982
N.S.	Principled moral reasoning	Bloom	1978
N.S.	Prefer middle school	Hardesty	1978
.04	Need for social acceptance	McAndrews	1971
.03	Self-esteem	McAndrews	1971
−.03	Divine fate control	Winberg	1982
−.02	Teacher militancy	Stoops	1980
00	Professional role orientation	Browning	1979

Table 10.3   Moderate PCI—Personality Correlates

R	VARIABLE MEASURE	SOURCE	
.59	Teacher direction	Bartlett	1976
−.57	Student autonomy	Bartlett	1976
−.55	Teacher attitude inventory	Hoy & Jalovick	1979
.54	Decentralization (−)	Zelei	1971
.54	Toughness	Zelei	1971
.54	Traditional family values	Nachtscheim & Hoy	1976
−.54	Skills orientation	Glasnapp & Guenther	1973
.52	Authority	Nachtscheim & Hoy	1976
−.51	Self-actualization	Jury	1973
−.51 to −.68	Assertiveness	Henderson	1982
−.49	Leadership authenticity	Hoy & Henderson	1982
−.49	Self-actualization	Noll	1976
.49	Conservatism	Primeaux	1979
.49	Dogmatism	Keefe	1969
−.49	Esprit (OCDQ)	Hoy & Appleberry	1970
.47	Traditional values	Helsel	1971b
.47	Status obeisance	MacMillan	1973
.46	Dogmatism	Williams; Drozda	1972a; 1972b
−.44	Climate (OCDQ)	Hoy & Henderson	1982
.44	Dogmatism	Longo	1974
.43	Emotional disengagement	Bartlett	1976
.40	Disengagement (OCDQ)	Hoy & Appleberry	1970
.39	Low self-esteem	McAndrews	1971
−.38	Sense of PCI of principal	Blust	1977
.38	Educational preference scale	Murad	1974
−.37	Self-actualization	Jury	1973
.36	Conservative security (U.S., India)	Chawla	1977
.35	Traditionalism (India)	Chawla	1977
.34	Local cosmopolitan	Williams	1972
−.34	Personal adjustment ideology	Bartlett	1976
−.34	Concerns about education	Ford	1976
.33	Dogmatism	Helsel	1974
−.33	Attitudes about student rights	Horowitz	1980
−.33	Self-report class management	Docking & Docking	1984
−.31	Verbal fluency	Halpin & Goldenberg	1973
.30	Sense of threat	Willower & Lawrence	1979
−.28	Perception of modernity of community attitudes	Gipp	1974
−.28	Accept others	Brenneman	1974
−.28	Humanistic philosophy	Barrick	1981
−.28	Creative personality	Halpin & Goldenberg	1973
−.27	Verbal flexibility	Haplin & Goldenberg	1973
.27	Dogmatism	Heineman	1971
−.26	Verbal originality	Halpin & Goldenberg	1973
.26	Employee role orientation	Browning	1979
.25	Job satisfaction	Krohn	1979
−.25	Progressivism	Chawla	1977
.24	General pessimism	Winberg	1982
−.24	Expect students to accept responsibility	Barrick	1981
−.23	School as source of discipline problems	Barrick	1981
−.23	Believe students penalized for bad behavior	Barrick	1981
.23	Perception of others' PCI	Salerno	1975
−.21	Sense of power	Zelei	1971

unsettled the issue of PCI's validity. Correlated method variance may be as much at work here as validity. Also, even if the operational concept of PCI does vary meaningfully with the concepts of dogmatism, traditionalism, and progressive teacher attitudes, until PCI scores are fully established as reasonable representa-

tions of pupil control ideology, the question of response bias in the questionnaire studies cited in Table 10.1 remains.

Despite the similarity in appearance of several measures of dogmatism, surprisingly, the correlations between PCI and those measures are not uniformly high. In addition to the set reported in Table 10.1, others range from $r = .49$ to $r = .27$ (Keefe, 1969, $r = .49$; Williams, 1972, $r = .46$; Drozda, 1972, $r = .46$; Longo, 1974, $r = .44$; Helsel, 1974, $r = .33$; Heineman, 1971, $r = .27$). After using analysis of variance, Lunenberg (1972) reports that dogmatism has no main effect on PCI. Given the comparability of research methods and conditions across the several dogmatism studies, some reporting high and some reporting moderate to low correlations, uncertainty remains as to the theoretical soundness of a postulated relationship between PCI and dogmatism. Helsel (1974) and Williams (1972) both expressed surprise at the low correlations they found and speculated that the relationship between PCI and personality is not well understood. Helwig (1973) and Helwig and Smallie (1973), with rather tortured reasoning about the relationship between PCI and the standard measure of dogmatism, agree. In a study not directly implicating dogmatism, Leppert and Hoy (1972) expressed similar thoughts about the uncertainty of the association between PCI and other personality characteristics.

Low Correlations

Why PCI does not correlate well with the measures identified in Table 10.2 is not at all clear. Not only do the measures range across a variety of characteristics that seem as closely related to pupil control ideology as the measures identified in Table 10.1, but the investigators chose the characteristics with high anticipation that strong correlations would materialize. In addition, the researchers often administered the other instruments at the same time as PCI and in the same general fashion as the researchers who reported high correlations (see Table 10.1). If correlated method variance applies at all to the search for personality correlates, it obviously did not have any strong effect here.

Moderate Correlations

In the intermediate range (Table 10.3), some combination of correlated method variance and true agreement may be at work. Also, there is no explicit rationale that suggests what these various measures have in common and why they relate with PCI in approximately the same fashion. Because correlations between measures are reported only once or twice, the question of stability of the association remain unanswered. The various correlates of PCI seem to have something, and yet little, in common. Some, for example, address personality traits, say, conservatism, dogmatism, authoritarianism, and traditionalism. Others appear to attend to personality states; for example, local-cosmopolitan orientation, self-actualization, emotional disengagement, and personal adjustment. Others seem to focus on school-related phenomena such as status obeisance, decentralization, teacher directiveness, class management practices, threat, and the Organizational Climate Description Questionnaire, OCDQ. Perhaps these measures like little magnets of different names, shapes, and sizes point more or less toward one "pole" when brought into contact with PCI.

As Helsel (1974) suggests, general personality might manifest itself in particular personal states, which take on more specific interpretations in the context of the school and school language. For example, the argument goes that conservative persons are also typically dogmatic and authoritarian, traditional in outlook. They tend to be low in self-actualization, provincial in deciding where to work and live, attentive to the directives of their organizational superiors, uncreative. They have little need for social interaction, and they feel somewhat powerless. As educators, they sense that their school is relatively closed interpersonally and find little to recommend about their coworkers. They see others displaying the same sort of conservative educational attitudes as themselves; they distrust, feel threatened by, and believe they must control children. The data, to the extent they confirm these patterns, tend to support the ideal type description of the custodial personality, as noted by Nachtscheim and Hoy (1976). PCI, then, appears to be valid at least in the sense that whatever it measures aligns reasonably with whatever is measured by other instruments that seek to probe a general personality state. In this connection, one observes that the PCI items lean disproportionately in a custodial direction. Other reviewers have observed that PCI seems to be a better measure of custodial than of humanistic orientation (Anderson, 1982; Boyd, 1981; Mann, 1970; Savage, 1981).

At the same time, low levels of association with PCI (Table 10.2) suggest that a custodial orientation does not include (a) lack of personal warmth, (b) militant or nonmilitant leanings, (c) negative or positive predisposition toward the handicapped, (d) absence or possession of formal knowledge of adolescence, (e) particular notions about equality and freedom or liberalism, and (f) reasoning about moral issues in principled or unprincipled ways.

Gender and Age

One of the most frequently reported PCI findings is that females are more humanistic or less custodial than males. In 27 separate studies, investigators report either statistically significant differences between male and female PCI mean scores or statistically significant correlations between gender and PCI. In only two cases were the females significantly more custodial than the males. The statistical differences were typically not large, ranging from 2 to 8 scale points. With few exceptions the mean scores of both groups fall below 60, which can be regarded as possible demarcation between humanistic and custodial orientations. Indeed, the majority lie close to 55. However, there are 27 other reports in which differences in group means between gender failed to reach statistical significance. Only a few of the latter set of studies even identified females as falling toward a more custodial orientation. Despite the tendency to promote the view that males are more custodial than females, the full array of available data reveals that the two sexes, at least among educators, score for all intents and purposes about the same on PCI.

The PCI studies also persistently report a link between PCI and age: the younger are more humanistic, the older more custodial. The age variable, however, is hopelessly interrelated with experience and position, as well as with the sex of the respondent. The problem of similar interrelatedness receives systematic attention below. Meanwhile, the problem still remains of clarifying and making sense of whatever conceptual and empirical regularity may exist in the vast body of literature on the relationship betwen PCI and a host of personal and personality correlates.

Organizational Correlates

A number of studies have addressed the question "Under what conditions will people most likely display custodial and humanistic scores on the PCI?"

Threat

The most obvious rationale is that threatening conditions contribute to higher PCI scores, but there have been few genuine attempts to define threat in clear, operational terms. Investigators have treated threat in terms of student, community, and organizational characteristics. High schools may be more threatening because they are larger and more complex and have bigger and more dangerous students than elementary schools. Similarly schools in center city areas may be more threatening than schools in suburban and rural areas due to differences in student composition, interests, and behavior patterns. Within schools, individual educators may feel more or less threatened by objective circumstances, including how closely they must work with students, the dominant nature of their role relationships with students, and the sorts of students with whom they interact. Educators whose roles bring them into less frequent contact with students, into contact with students who are eager to be in school and agreeable when there, and/or into contact with students who actively seek assistance are likely to

be more humanistic. To what extent do PCI studies support this line of reasoning?

There is some evidence that educators in more threatening circumstances have more custodial PCI scores. For example, Gossen (1969), assuming an inverse relationship between socioeconomic status and threat, reports that teachers in low SES schools are more custodial than teachers in middle and high SES schools. Rausch (1974) observes that the PCI of educators in schools with only boys is greater than that of educators in schools with only girls and in coeducational schools. Boys are more threatening than girls but less threatening when combined with girls. Rausch also reports that the PCI of public school educators is more custodial than that of Catholic school educators. In neither case, however, does Rausch include tests of statistical significance. Duggal (1969) shows in high schools that had experienced student unrest, PCI is greater than in comparison schools. Hoy (1971) documents that PCI is higher where community population density is greater and where the proportion of minority staff members is higher. Mitchell (1974) reports that small schools have lower PCI scores.

Contrary evidence, however, shakes support for the hypothesis about a direct relationship between custodialism and organizational structures and circumstances that appear threatening. Kelton (1976) reports that PCI of educators is unrelated to the race and SES of students. Barfield and Burlingame (1974) show that teachers of low SES schools have lower (more humanistic) scores than faculties in middle and high SES schools. Even Gossen (1969) notes that principals' PCI scores are lowest in the low SES settings and higher in the middle and high SES settings. A similar unexpected pattern appears in other studies exploring ethnicity. Williams (1972) shows that PCI is unrelated to changes in ethnic distribution of students due to court-ordered busing and to pupil density. Foley and Brooks (1978) also document that the number of students in a classroom does not affect PCI. Abrams (1971) reports that the PCI of elementary school principals is unrelated to the proportions of black, Spanish, Oriental, and white students or to the type of neighborhood from which pupils come. Hoy (1971) also reports that teacher PCI shows no relationship to the number of minority pupils in school. Smith, Reinhartz, Oshima, and Smith (1982) a decade later found higher PCI scores among teachers in white middle class schools than among teachers in urban, ethnically diverse schools. Voege (1979) discovered slightly higher (but not significantly so) PCI scores among teachers who worked in secondary schools that could select students than among their counterparts in nonselective schools.

Nor does working with handicapped children offer

support for the threat relationship. Salerno and Willower (1975) report that teachers of special education classes score lower on PCI than teachers of regular classes. Rouse (1978) found that teacher PCI scores vary inversely with the number of handicapped pupils in class, noting that special education teachers are less custodial than teachers of academic and vocational subjects. In a similar vein, Tippeconnic (1975) indicates that teachers in schools operated by the Bureau of Indian Affairs have lower PCI scores than teachers in public schools. Primeaux (1979) shows that PCI of educators is unrelated to the number of Native American children they teach. Finally, Appleberry (1969) shows that the PCI of educators in rural settings is more custodial than the PCI of educators in suburban and urban settings.

Conventional wisdom holds that large schools are more difficult to work in than small schools, in part because higher levels of bureaucracy and student alienation seem to vary directly with size. So, size and its correlates could convey some sense of threat that might relate to PCI. In support of this proposition, Mitchell (1974) and Brayboy (1981) report that the PCI of teachers in small schools is lower (less custodial) than the PCI of teachers who work in large schools. Racine (1980) shows that principal PCI does vary directly with school size. However, these are the only findings that corroborate the relationship between size and PCI. Studies that report absence of a statistically significant positive association include Ford (1976), who even allows the implication of an inverse relationship, Appleberry (1969), Day (1973), Hoy (1971), Jones (1969), Kozakewich (1973), MacMillan (1973), Racine (1980), Voege (1979), and Williams (1972). The weight of the evidence clearly indicates that school size and PCI generally do not go together and that size, therefore, does not constitute a source of threat linked with PCI.

Another line of thought implies that secondary schools are more threatening than elementary schools, because they contain students who are both physically larger and more difficult to control. More than a little evidence supports this view. The following studies identify secondary educators as more custodial than their elementary counterparts: Barfield and Burlingame (1974), Brenneman (1974), Docking and Docking (1984), Eidell (1965), Gipp (1974), Hamalian (1979), Hoy (1965), Jury (1973), Krohn (1979), Leppert and Hoy (1972), McAndrews (1971), Noll (1976), Ross (1980), Salerno (1975), Smith et al. (1982), Williams (1972), Willower and Lawrence (1979), Yuskiewicz (1971), and Zelei (1971). Several of the studies cite the association between level and PCI score only incidentally; none exercise controls for personality correlates.

Secondary schools may well attract or select teachers who lean toward a custodial orientation. In addition, a number of studies have found no statistically significant difference in PCI between teachers at the elementary and secondary school levels: Barfield and Burlingame (1974), Hardesty (1977), Helsel (1976), Hoy and Jalovick (1979), Kozakewich (1973), and Murad (1984). In any case, the data do not permit a firm conclusion as to whether the levels of schooling contribute to or reflect initial custodial predisposition.

Moreover, the findings themselves are equivocal. Barfield and Burlingame (1974), Blust (1977), Brooks (1977), Hardesty (1977), Kozakewich (1973), Mitchell (1974), and Rexford (1970) report that junior high school educators are more custodial than senior high educators; and Longo (1974), for example, reports that college teachers are less custodial than public school teachers. So, something other than student size, age, and maturity seems to be at work. Given the commonly held views of pupil behavior in junior high school, the studies offer support for the view that the issue centers on the nature and extent of problems that students pose for teachers rather than on age, level, and maturity as such. These findings, then, offer some support for the threat hypothesis, adding to its force in refined ways; that is, junior high schools are more threatening because of objective student realities. Even here the matter is not all settled because several studies cite important PCI differences among educators at the same level: Blust (1977), Brayboy (1981), Dobson, Goldenberg and Elsom (1972), Ferguson (1972), Fritz (1973), Licata (1974), Lunenberg (1972), Shearin (1981), and Tippeconnic (1975). Nor does the only quasi-longitudinal study of the relationship between PCI and school level add a sense of confidence. Warrell (1969) happened upon a school where a ninth grade faculty moved to the senior high school. Using an after-only nonequivalent control group design, he was unable to show that the ninth grade faculty who had moved differed in PCI from other junior high school faculty.

Given the contradictory findings, considerable caution seems highly appropriate in treating the assumption that something about the nature of schools at different levels, including students, accounts for differences in the PCI of educators. The results are not uniform; investigators have not controlled for personality correlates of PCI, and reliance on cross sectional design has led to much too easy conclusions that teachers in elementary schools differ importantly from secondary school counterparts with respect to PCI.

Threat has also figured in yet another important way: position. Here the reasoning holds that within the organization the adults most responsible for pupil control, and correspondingly most threatened by pupils, will score the highest on PCI. The direct prediction is that teachers exhibit more custodial orientation than principals and counselors on the grounds that the latter two positions stand more removed from the "battle zone." The following studies support the predictions that teachers are more custodial than principals and that principals are more custodial than counselors: Appleberry (1969), Bowen (1975), Brayboy (1981), Eidell (1965), Fritz (1973), Horowitz (1980), Hoy (1965), Kozakewich (1973), Levine (1976), MacMillan (1973), Packard (1971), Rausch (1974), Salerno (1975), Shirley (1974), Voege (1979), Williams (1972), and Willower et al. (1973).

Again, however, several contradictory findings have surfaced. Seefa (1981) and Fritz (1973) find no differences between teachers and administrators, a condition possibly related to the locale of their studies (Thailand and Canada). MacMillan (1973) reports no difference between female elementary teachers and principals. Eidell (1965), Murphy (1977), and Voege (1979) conclude that the differences between teachers and principals is not statistically significant. Still, the loading of the findings on the relationship of PCI and position supports the central proposition, even if the studies all employ a cross-sectional methodology.

One investigation does trace individuals moving from one position to another and documents that PCI changes correspondingly. Lundin (1980) studied a group of Australian teachers who became librarians. Their PCI scores dropped over the course of a year-long preparatory period away from classrooms and schools. Lundin argues, however, that the respondents' original PCI scores and, next, their dogmatism scores serve as stronger predictors than change in position itself. In the absence of a control group, Lundin remains appropriately cautious about attributing change in PCI to time away from teaching and assumption of a new school role. No study that specifically traces shifts across the positions of teacher, counselor, and principal has been found.

Other data raise questions about the relationships of position, threat, and PCI. Fritz (1973) and Ciaglia (1980) each report that students are as custodial as teachers. They and Murphy (1977) also report that parents are more custodial than teachers. Voege (1979) found that in a sample of religious schools, board members are more custodial than teachers and principals. Murphy (1977) also reports that janitors and like employees are more custodial than either parents or teachers. Even if there are grounds for believing that parents are closer to the "battle line" than teachers are, the condition hardly holds for board members and non-professional support staff. So, anomalies remain in

establishing an unequivocal relationship between threat and PCI scores.

Due to these anomalies, however, the heavy loading offered by the cross-sectional studies on differences in pupil control ideology related to position requires further attention. To what extent do respondents report what they consider to constitute socially acceptable and expected PCI responses? A clue to the answer comes from consideration of the estimates of the PCI scores of various role incumbents. Dunkerly (1979), Heckert, 1976, McAndrews (1971), Packard (1971), Salerno (1975), and Yuskiewicz (1971) demonstrate that teachers and principals rate themselves much lower on PCI than do others; that is, teachers and principals deem themselves much less custodial than independent observers deem them to be. For example, Bean (1972) shows that students rate teachers more custodial than teachers report themselves. The difference is especially pronounced for female teachers. Bean further reports that student perceptions of teacher PCI and of teacher authoritarian behavior correlate almost perfectly. In the other direction, Packard (1971) notes that educators generally rate counselors even more humanistic than the counselors rate themselves. These studies suggest that (a) it is very difficult to estimate a person's self-reported PCI (the phenomenon of pluralistic ignorance, as reported by Packard and Willower, 1972); and (b) very few observers regard teachers and principals to be as humanistic as they claim to be. The discrepancies between self and others' reports cannot discount altogether the accumulated findings of the cross-sectional studies, but the discrepancies do weaken support for the threat hypothesis. Altogether, the data leave unsettled and equivocal the relationship between PCI and size, location, community type, student race and wealth, school level, student educability, and organizational position.

Even in studies of subjective organizational features that might systematically covary with PCI, the results are mixed. Washington (1981) reports differences in teacher PCI between open and conventional or traditional schools. Krohn (1979) notes that elementary and secondary teachers tend to view their schools as differentially emphasizing various bureaucratic tendencies and that these different perceptions do relate to PCI. Barfield and Burlingame (1974) find lower PCI scores for teachers who view the political efficacy of their schools to be high. Appleberry and Hoy (1969) document some very high correlations between school-level PCI scores and subscales on the OCDQ, and Hoy and Henderson (1982) report a high correlation between PCI and leadership authenticity of the principal. But Day (1973), Ferguson (1972), and Holzwarth (1974) all indicate no consistent or simple relationship between PCI and OCDQ. Batista (1973) sought unsuccessfully to establish a relationship between organizational press and PCI. Again, and equivocal set of findings prevails. So, on both the objective and subjective sides, efforts to operationalize threat in organizational terms have failed to produce convincing findings about a consistent association with PCI.

Experience Correlates

The threat hypothesis appears again in examination of the effect of initial experience on PCI. The line of reasoning runs that as individuals move into the role of teacher and find themselves confronted with threatening students in a threatening atmosphere, they will assume over time a more custodial ideology. Neophytes also learn from experienced teachers to view the environment, particularly students, as threatening. In addition, official and informal group expectations induce new teachers to act in more custodial ways. Presumably, then, the teacher adjusts ideology to remain consonant with acting more strictly. The school, in turn, is assured of the continuation and maintenance of custodialism as a dominant ideology. Some evidence supports the theme in PCI research that new teachers become more custodial with initial experience and a corollary that PCI does not change after initial experience. But other evidence casts doubts on the universality of the theme. Pertinent studies include both cross-sectional and longitudinal investigators.

At least 23 cross-sectional studies document higher (more custodial) scores among more experienced teachers (Bowen, 1975; Brenneman, 1974; Brooks, 1977; Budzik, 1971, Eidell, 1965; Gardiner, 1975; Heineman, 1971; Helsel, 1971b; Holzwarth, 1974; Hoy, 1965; Hoy & Jalovick, 1979; Jury, 1973; Lawrence, 1977; MacMillan, 1973; Martin, 1976; McAndrews, 1971; Murad, 1974; Salerno, 1975; Spearly, 1979; Voege, 1979; Williams, 1972; Yuskewicz, 1971; Zelei, 1971). Many of the investigators report significant (statistical and otherwise) mean differences between the more and less experienced groups, where usually the cutting point is 5 years' experience. In some instances the strength of the evidence seems overwhelming. Several mean differences approach six PCI "units"; more often, the mean differences fall in the 2- to 3-unit range, and statistically significant differences depend on sample size. The evidence appears persuasive: Initial experience covaries with increases in custodial orientation.

However, several of the studies cited above offer only weak support for the postulated variation of PCI scores with experiences. Eidell (1965), Hoy (1965), Noll (1976), and Spearly (1979) all report statistically

nonsignificant correlations, even if in the "anticipated" direction. Heineman (1971) provides some contradictory evidence. Hoy and Jalovick (1979) find a curvilinear relationship: PCI higher among teachers with moderate levels of experience, lower among the least and most experienced.

Other cross-sectional studies offer qualified support for or contradictory evidence on the experience-PCI relationship. A number report positive, statistically nonsignificant correlation (Appleberry, 1969; Blust, 1977; Fritz, 1973; Hassan, 1979; Helsel, 1971b; Horowitz, 1980; Jones, 1969; Keefe, 1969; Krohn, 1979; Leppert & Hoy, 1972; Noll, 1976; Seefa, 1981; Shirley, 1974; Tippeconnic, 1975). A few provide weak, contradictory findings (Ens, 1975; Kozakewich, 1973; Mitchell, 1974; Stoops, 1980). Several note negative correlations: Abrams (1971) shows a strong negative association between experience and PCI among elementary school principals; Noll (1976) also documents a negative correlation among teachers with more than 5 years' experience; Foley and Brooks (1978) report a negative, statistically nonsignificant relationship between PCI and experience.

Altogether, the evidence from the cross-sectional studies favors an inference that PCI scores rise after initial experience, but the large number of studies that report statistically nonsignificant findings and the few that offer contradictory data urge cautious interpretation. Longitudinal studies shed further light on the influence of experience on teachers' orientations.

Hoy (1967, 1968, 1969) describes a panel of new teachers who report an increase in PCI scores after student teaching and again after a first year of teaching experience, but not a year later. A naturally occurring nonequivalent control group who did not teach after student teaching also reported a higher mean PCI score after student teaching but not a year later. McArthur (1975, 1978, 1979, 1980, 1981) corroborates in part Hoy's findings in a study of a panel of new teachers who reported higher mean PCI scores after a first year of teaching but not 5 years later. A naturally occurring nonequivalent control group did not show a higher mean PCI score after the first year. Drozda (1972) and Wsiaki (1974) also report higher (but not significantly so) mean PCI scores at the end of the first year of teaching. Neither used a control group.

Many studies of student teachers document increases in PCI scores over the period of student teaching (Caffee, 1979; Campbell & Williamson, 1978; Fink, 1979; Glasnap & Guenther, 1973; Hoy & Rees, 1977; Jones, 1982; Jones & Harty, 1981; McCullough, 1980; Murad, 1974; Phillips, 1976; Preston, 1974; Roberts, 1969; Roberts & Blankenship, 1970; Smith et al., 1982; Templin, 1978). Jones and Harty (1980) specifically note a statistically significant positive correlation between level of increase of score and amount of time spent in student teaching, although Jones (1982) later found that the relationship held for secondary school student teachers but not for elementary school student teachers.

Despite empirical and common-sense grounds for expecting early job experience to alter attitudes and behavior and to induce many new teachers to accept and express the dominant sentiments of their workplaces, the longitudinal PCI studies leave several doubts. Are the reported changes in PCI scores important? Are the changes predictable? Can these changes be attributed to experience?

Are the Changes Important?

PCI scores can range from 20 to 100, but rarely do self-reports fall below 30 or above 80. Mean scores range mostly between 45 and 55. Changes in mean scores from the beginning to the end of initial experience rarely exceed five PCI units. Statistically significant differences between before and after PCI mean scores have been reported when the mathematical difference was less than two PCI units (Hoy, 1967) and slightly greater than six (McArthur, 1979). The exact meaning of a PCI unit remains problematic. It is not certain if the difference, say, between scores of 45 and 47 is comparable to the difference between 55 and 57. The great majority of mean scores reported (except in cases of unorthodox scoring) fall below 60, a theoretical if unannounced division between custodial and humanistic orientations. In those longitudinal studies that employed contrast groups (by Hoy and by McArthur) the controls were not strictly comparable. Thus, a regression effect has to be taken seriously, particularly the possibility that the *before* measure reflects artificially low scores. Zeichner and Tabachnick (1981) give the popular account that college education results in a thin, liberal veneer that is quickly removed afterward. One senses in Yee's (1969) review of research on student teachers a begrudging realization that the liberal influence of the university vanishes with but the slightest provocation. Reverse causality is also a distinct possibility. Those with low PCI scores who enter teaching may be more disposed to give up their artificially extreme humanistic orientation than those who do not. Experience, thus, may not cause the shift to custodialism; rather, the propensity to shed (or maintain) a humanistic orientation may result in a decision to enter (or not) the workforce. Given these considerations, the reported PCI changes used to illustrate the effects of socialization seem unimpressive.

Are the Changes Predictable?

The longitudinal studies document rather consistently an upward movement in PCI mean scores associated with early experience that does not appear in the absence of comparable initial teaching experience. The evidence suggests also that after some time (5 years is often cited) no further change in PCI occurs, and in the absence of teaching experience, change in PCI does not take place. At least some PCI researchers seem to regard matters in this fashion. Yet overlooked evidence and interpretation deserve consideration in the matter of the predictability of PCI changes in conjunction with teaching experience.

Roberts (1969) first reported a substantial number of student teachers who did not have higher scores and some of whom actually reported lower scores after experience. Roberts and Blankenship (1970) explain this in two ways. Some apprentices encounter only weak socialization pressures, and others are immune due to extreme disparities between their own and their perception of the pupil control orientations of supervising teachers. Drozda (1972) shows that the most dogmatic, closed-minded first-year teachers report lower PCI scores after 1 year in the classroom. He explains this by arguing that the most closed-minded who enjoyed "easy" classes adjusted their PCI downward based on their actual encounters with students! Jones and Harty (1980) report but do not explain a slight decline in the PCI of female student teachers. Wsiaki (1974) observes that approximately one-quarter of a sample of beginning teachers had lower PCI scores on especially relevant items after their first year of teaching. Ten new teachers moved away from the median scores of groups of experienced teachers with whom they interacted frequently, and seven of these showed an overall decrease in PCI. Ross (1980) reports that elementary teacher trainees had lower PCI scores after a fieldwork assignment.

Yee (1969) and Wsiaki (1974) indicate that the attitudes of supervising teachers change to comport with the orientations of the new teachers. Enochs (1982) reports a decline in mean PCI among science teachers after several months of in-service training. Templin (1978) shows that the mean PCI scores of a group of supervising teachers increased during the period in which they worked with student teachers, *and* that the mean scores of the most custodial group of supervising teachers declined more than five PCI units. Templin (1978) also administered PCI twice to a group of college freshmen enrolled in physical education courses. These were neither teachers nor teacher trainees. Yet the second PCI mean was greater than the first.

In short, within the prevailing pattern of increase in PCI scores accompanying early teaching experience, there are pieces of evidence showing that changes in PCI scores are not always in a custodial direction. In some cases there is no change, and in other cases, the change is toward the humanistic pole. Also there is evidence that the PCI of experienced teachers is unstable and that in the absence of teaching experience, change may yet occur in a custodial direction. Changes in PCI thus seem less than confidently predictable, even in light of evidence suggesting that with initial experience, change is routine and custodial in direction.

What Can Be Said about the Effects of Experience?

Early on Willower, Eidell, and Hoy (1967, 1973) suggested that the influence of experienced teachers may account for the custodial shift in PCI on the part of beginning teachers. This view is supported in Yee's (1969) review of research on student teachers that identified supervising teachers as the most influential source of change in the attitudes of apprentice teachers about teaching, classroom management, and pupils. PCI researchers in other quarters offer somewhat different explanations of the forces that induce new teachers to change in a custodial direction. Some agree with Yee that the influence of the supervising teachers is paramount, and by extension, so is the effect of the experienced teachers on those new to their teaching jobs (Drozda, 1972; Roberts and Blankenship, 1970; Smith et al., 1982; Wsiaki, 1974). Drozda (1972), Campbell and Williamson (1978), and Fink (1975), however, report data to suggest that pupil behavior and the sorts of problems pupils might or do create constitute more important influences on the shift of the new teachers toward a more custodial orientation. Templin (1978) offers something of a combined interpretation by suggesting that supervising, and by implication experienced, teachers mediate the association of pupil behavior and PCI change by attributing particular social meanings to the behaviors of pupils in school. In addition, or as a result, Templin (1978) observed that "all student teachers exercised an inflexible will to control and dictate student behavior" (p. 135). Hoy and Rees (1977) imply that something about the bureaucratic nature of the school contributes to change in new and student teacher PCI scores. Yet Drozda (1972) does not find much support for supposing that new teachers change in response to the PCI of those in the school hierarchy. Hoy (1969) and Hoy and Rees (1977) also argue that PCI change is related to the bureaucratic nature of schools; institutional norms urge the beginning employee to emphasize orderliness and compliance with rules, and equate good teaching with the

ability to control pupils. The influence of these conditions seems so plausible that few researchers in the area doubt that the forces somehow operate to push all new teachers in the direction that prompts many of them to record a shift toward a custodial orientation after early experience.

There have been several efforts to counteract the effects of initial experience. Some failed (Afolayan, 1975; Armer, 1976; McCullough, 1980; Uncapher, 1974), either because they employed weak or contradictory treatments or because they confused ideology with efficacy. There have been several successes, intended or not, and these seem to support the view that initial experience unchecked leads to a more custodial orientation. Griepenstroh and Miskel (1975–1976, 1976) exposed a nonrandom sample of student teachers to T Group sessions. The treatment group reported a lower mean PCI and the control group a higher mean PCI after student teaching. The researchers exerted statistical controls for gender and dogmatism but did not control for variations in the experience itself or for the initial level of PCI (the experimental group began with a considerably higher PCI mean). Nonetheless T Group sessions may blunt the effects of early experience or at least help maintain an initial humanistic orientation. Luster (1980), using a small sample (other details are missing) reports that student teachers who received training in class management techniques emerged from student teaching with a lower PCI mean score than a control group. Henderson (1982), using an *after*-only nonequivalent control group design, reports a lower PCI mean for a group of experienced elementary teachers enrolled in an assertive discipline program. Lundin (1980) reports three sets of mean PCI scores for moderately experienced teachers who spent a year in training to become teacher librarians and later assumed that role. The PCI mean after training was lower than the mean before training; the mean moved slightly higher after the subjects had taken their new positions, but the third mean was lower than the first. These several studies seem to indicate that when some elements of experience are removed or when they are counteracted by a novel sort of armament, the effects of initial experience may not be pronounced or recorded. The findings may, therefore, be regarded as supporting the "socialization" line of reasoning.

Whereas many studies may be interpreted as producing evidence of the custodial effects of early experience, the explanation is squarely challenged by other evidence also resulting from PCI inquiry. Few PCI researchers have attended explicitly or satisfactorily to the rival hypothesis that derives from evidence suggesting that the best predictor of a PCI score is the previous PCI score. The next best predictors are measures of closely related attitudes. (See discussion in section on personality correlates.) For example Glasnap and Guenther (1973) report a correlation of .65 between *before* and *after* measures of PCI in a sample of 33 secondary school teachers. Lundin (1980) reports autocorrelations ranging from .73 to .84. Docking and Docking (1984), Halpin and Goldenberg (1973), Kiss (1981), and Zeichner and Grant (1981) also report very high through-time PCI correlations. In the Lundin (1980) study noted above, the best predictor of any PCI score is the previous PCI score and the next best predictor is a concurrent dogmatism score. The same holds for change in PCI scores. Caffee (1976) reports a high correlation between scores on PCI and on the MTAI and also a strong relationship between changes in the scores of the two measures. Franklin (1976) and Kiss (1981) control for the initial PCI score and find no evidence that the final PCI score can be explained by measures of experience. Drozda (1972), Keefe (1969), Longo (1972), Williams (1972), and others had noted the strong relationship between PCI scores and dogmatism measures. The autocorrelation data and the data on personality correlates point rather straightforwardly to the suggestion, if not the conclusion, that the best predictor of a PCI score is the previous score and that the next best predictors are personality measures that appear to tap equivalent features. Early experience may well stand further down the list of predictors of changes in PCI scores.

Fink (1975) finds no evidence of the "planned socialization" of student teachers. Preston (1974) studied intensively four first-year teachers and concluded that the significant element in the development of a control ideology is the individual's initial beliefs about discipline. Both Fink (1975) and Templin (1978) observe that new teachers adopt stricter disciplinary measures than they had intended or were aware of, so natural is the process of fitting in.

In short, the PCI "socialization" data do not really provide overwhelming evidence of a reality shock that results in a sudden, intense change in attitudes concerning pupil control. Nor is there much support for an impression of loss of innocence as a consequence of sharp socialization pressure. Recent studies of work stress among teachers indicate that stress and burnout appear disproportionately among new workers (Gmelch, 1984). The "burnout" period seems to parallel the "socialization" phase, suggesting that speedy alienation from their work may be as operative among new teachers as establishing a routine made comfortable by adopting a more custodial attitude promoted by senior colleagues. Quite possibly both the alienating and the socializing conditions reinforce each other.

Questioning the inference that initial experience contributes materially to changes in PCI scores is not the same as questioning the conclusion that experience affects attitudes, perspectives, and behavior. The issue is identifying the scale on which a particular set of experiences operates. Certainly sudden, dramatic events have altered people permanently, but such events are not especially prominent in teachers' careers. Rather, the experience at stake is the experience of historicity, living in a particular culture, at a particular time, with a particular dominant socially constructed sense of reality taken for granted. The PCI studies take for granted schools as conceived in a common social ethos that values civility, that views society as a kind of meritocracy, and that considers schools the instruments by which merit is encouraged or denied and attached predictably to some, but not all, individuals. Good behavior is easy to distinguish from bad behavior. A dominant control ideology, of which a PCI may be but a facet, helps undergird and justify a particular way of maintaining order in both school and society. Both ideologies, the larger and the smaller, have developed over a long period of time spent as a member of one's society, as well as a shorter time of serving as apprentice teacher. That incontrovertible evidence of the effects of short-term job socialization is missing should not come as a surprise. Rather, the mixture of evidence on change in PCI scores following early experience suggests that PCI does not measure a simple personality state or trait but does document cultural continuity manifest in the experience of living in a particular culture at a particular time.

Pupil Control Ideology and Behavior

Several researchers have attempted to trace the relationships between PCI and PCB as well as other measures of teacher behavior. For some, there seems to be an explicit moral agenda: to show that custodial attitudes lead to custodial behaviors that lead to undesirable classrooms and education. For others, the agenda remains the advancement of knowledge. In both instances, PCI research has produced evidence that school people who tilt in a custodial direction on PCI and PCB also influence students in different ways. However, the evidence is somewhat shaky and the evaluation paradigm remains vague and implicit.

PCI and PCB

The PCB consists of 20 items describing what teachers might or might not do in classrooms. The typical observers and reporters are students. They report how frequently their teacher engages in each particular event; for example, "smiles when students are around," "is 'bossy' with students," and "gets angry with students." Higher scores, as in the PCI, signal more custodial behavior. A teacher's or a principal's PCB score is the average of all student responses. Estimates of internal consistency range from .89 to .93 (Browning, 1979; Forlenza & Willower, 1980; Pritchett & Willower, 1975; Smedly, 1980). Estadt (1974) reports that the correlation of PCB scores on two separate classes of the same teacher is .66. Forlenza and Willower (1980) show a rank-order through-time correlation of .87. Franklin (1976) notes a correlation of .71 between two separate administrations of the same measure in the same classes but also comments that the correlation may fall as low as .45. Thus, the data say that PCB possesses high reliability without addressing the issue of validity.

Evidence of a rather believable relationship between PCI and PCB does exist. Correlations between the two measures range from .59 (Templin, 1978) to .08 (Brayboy, 1981). Most correlations fall around the .25 level: $r = .31$ (Blust, 1977; Heckert, 1976, who used the same sample); $r = .29$ (Browning, 1979; Helsel, 1974; Helsel & Willower, 1974); $r = .26$ (Ens 1975; Estep, 1979, who also report ranges in school-level r from .58 to .12); $r = .21$ (Multhauf, 1977; Rose, 1974); $r = .20$ (Noll, 1976). Littrell (1980) reports weaker levels of association, but the general pattern is that the higher an educator's self-reported PCI score, the higher the student-reported PCB score. The temptation is to conclude that the more custodial the teacher's ideology, the more custodial the teacher's classroom behavior.

Other Behaviors

There is corroborating evidence. For example, Bogacki (1981) reports a correlation of .76 between teacher PCI and self-reports on the use of corporal punishment. Horowitz (1980) reports correlations of .70 between PCI of principals and .32 between PCI of teachers and the number of suspensions in their schools. Horowitz also noted a positive correlation between principals' PCI and number of discipline cases documented in the school. Foley and Brooks (1978) observe a correlation of .65 between teacher PCI and records of discipline reports filed by the teachers. Hoy and Jalovick (1979) display a correlation of $-.42$ between PCI and open classroom behavior reported by pupils. Ens (1975) reports that teachers who rank themselves low on PCI and PCB make the fewest discipline referrals. In brief, to the extent that PCI represents an attitudinal disposition, it also seems related in discernible ways to the behavior of school personnel. When they report themselves to think in ways that are labeled custodial, they engage in behaviors that, it is assumed, students consider punitive.

Furthermore, investigators have found evidence that PCI covaries with selected teaching behaviors. Rexford (1970) reports that persons who score very high and very low on PCI score differently on the Flanders classroom observation guide. Less custodial teachers use indirect teaching methods much more frequently; more custodial teachers use direct teaching methods more frequently. Dobson, Goldenberg, and Elsom (1972) report similar findings on particular subscales of the Flanders instrument. Kayden (1976) reports that the classrooms of teachers with higher PCI scores exhibit greater momentum. Salerno and Willower (1975) observe that innovative teachers score significantly lower on PCI than do conventional teachers. But Forman (1971) notes that teachers who score higher on PCI are more likely to have their proposals for classroom innovations accepted. Jones (1970) finds that students report different classroom and laboratory practices among science teachers who score at the extremes of PCI. For example, the more custodial teachers stress tests and teacher directiveness.

Conceptually, these findings seem to make sense. Custodial educators behave in ways roughly coincident with their attitudes. However, only a few studies document the relationship, and there are several bits of disquieting evidence. Foley and Brooks (1978) estimate that PCI was higher where teachers had more students. However, they conclude that the number of students for whom a teacher is responsible is an inadequate explanation for the differences in discipline referrals between the most and least custodial teachers where the ratio was about 10 to 1. On the other hand, Ferguson and Miskell (1973) conducted a similar study some years earlier and reported different results; namely, that the most and least custodial teachers, in a quartile distribution, made equally high numbers of discipline referrals. Teachers in the middle range of PCI made the fewest discipline referrals and were also apt to score high on either the Consideration or Initiating Structure subscales of the LBDQ. Kozakewich (1973) reports that teacher PCI is higher in schools that have fewer rather than more severe discipline problems. Furthermore, Hinojosa (1974) and McCaskill (1979) were unable to confirm the relationship between differences on the Flanders instrument and differences in PCI scores noted earlier by Rexford (1970) and by Dobson et al. (1972). In a different vein, Brayboy (1981) found a weak, negative relationship between principal ratings of teacher discipline effectiveness and teacher PCI. Caffee (1976) reports a statistically nonsignificant relationship between teacher PCI and scores or effectiveness scales completed by students. Seidell

(1982) finds no relationship between teachers' use of control language and their PCI. Bean (1972) shows that student reports of teacher classroom behaviors are unrelated to the teachers' PCI score, but are related to the students' estimates of teachers' PCI score. In addition, Bean (1972) documents an almost perfect correlation between students' perceptions of teachers' PCI and students' ratings of the teachers' authoritarian behavior. These scattered bits of evidence suggest that much remains unexplained in the relationship between PCI and behavior.

Even so, the relative stability of association between PCI and PCB is impressive. With few exceptions, correlations are strong and in the right direction. Correlated method variance hardly accounts for the consistency in relationship. The two scores are separated in time, measure, and unit of measurement. The care exercised in these studies makes it unlikely that the researchers influenced student responses.

Although PCB was not involved, the reports of Bean (1972) and Bean and Hoy (1974) may provide a clue about the nature of the observed association between PCI and PCB. They report that students' estimates of their teachers' PCI correlated almost perfectly with student reports of the teachers' authoritarian behavior; $r = .92$ for male teachers and .90 for female teachers. However, the association between student-estimated and teacher-reported PCI is not as strong; $r = .48$ for male teachers and .08 for female teachers. If, for the purpose of argument, it is assumed that the measure of authoritarian behavior used by Bean and Hoy is a proxy for PCB, then it is possible that students literally equate their sense of teacher PCI with authoritarian teacher behavior. PCB, with this special assumption, could well be the same as the students' perception of teacher PCI. However, the link between teacher PCI and student sense of teacher PCI is strong for male and nonexistent for female teachers. Over all teachers, a PCI–PCB association of about .25 would normally appear. A question arises: When students report teacher PCB, might they not actually report their perception of teacher PCI? Perhaps PCB is really not a measure of teacher behavior.

In addition, evidence indicates that the PCI–PCB relationship itself is linked to the gender of the teacher. Bean and Hoy (1974) show that student estimates of teacher PCI exceed female teacher self-reports by 6.0 units but fall short of male teacher self-reports by 1.7 units. The difference between student estimates and teacher reports is significant for females. The differences between the means of female and male teacher self-reports are not significant. Ens (1975) reports that students rate female teacher PCB higher than male teacher PCB. In his sample, female teacher PCI was 2.6

PCI units less than the male PCI. For female students, the PCB rating of female teachers was 4 units greater than their PCB scores for male teachers. Overall, the correlation between PCI and PCB is .34 for male teachers and .13 for female teachers. Ens (1975) also reports that the correlation between PCI and PCB is higher ($r = .26$) for experienced than for inexperienced ($r = .11$) teachers. Noll (1976) repeats the experience finding of Ens but shows the PCI–PCB relationship is stronger for female (and elementary) teachers than for male (and secondary) teachers. If it is the case that men stay in teaching more years than women, the apparent influence of teacher gender on the PCI–PCB association may itself be a function of time on the job, wherein behavior and ideology may become better aligned (Ens, 1975). Whatever the case, there is additional reason to doubt that PCB is strictly a measure of teacher behavior.

On the relationship between PCI and student sentiments, several reports identify an association of student alienation with teacher PCI. Rafilides and Hoy (1971) cite the following correlations: .35, total alienation; .42, normlessness; .34, powerlessness; .31, isolation; .20, self-estrangement; and −.27, meaninglessness. In subsequent analyses using multiple regression, Hoy (1971, 1972) confirmed the findings between PCI and student scores on total alienation, normlessness, and powerlessness. Shearin (1981) also shows that students report lower alienation scores in schools with more humanistic faculty. Waple (1974) notes a direct relationship between teacher PCI scores and student statements of resentment. Hassan (1979) calculates a correlation of −.54 between teacher PCI and student sense of support. Stouten (1974) and Seidell (1982) report that students respond more favorably to humanistic teachers. Deibert (1978) and Deibert and Hoy (1977) report moderate negative correlations between PCI and student self-actualization. Day (1973) observes that student attitudes are more positive in small schools where teachers are more humanistic and where students rate the school more open on the OCDQ. Ford (1976) notes a correlation of .63 between pupil perception of teacher power and teacher self-reported PCI.

Similar reports appear for PCB. Ju (1983) reports correlations between PCB and student alienation as follows: .40, total alienation score; .43, disaffection; .40, powerlessness; .38, normlessness; .35, isolation; .35, self-estrangement; and .09, meaninglessness. Pritchett and Willower (1975) present the following correlations between PCB and *negative* attitudes about: school work, .23; the school program, .12; social acceptance, .14; social context, .13; school, .18; teachers, .35. Brown and Licata (1978) cite a correlation of .47 between PCB and disliking the teacher.

In sum, the several studies indicate that the higher the PCI and PCB of teachers, the less positive are student attitudes. Some investigators see a snowball effect here. Custodial teachers think, believe, and act in ways that arouse in students such undesirable reactions that the students feel compelled to act out. As they do so, more custodial teachers respond more punitively. Thus the number of discipline problems and referrals is notably greater for teachers who score higher on PCI. The same general relationship holds, it appears, for entire schools. The more a school's staff score tilts toward a custodial orientation, the more likely the school will experience serious problems with students. The direction of the relationship, however, remains uncertain. Does a custodial orientation provoke student behavior problems, or vice versa? A provocative and somewhat puzzling set of studies had its origin in the observation that students may prefer teachers who are more custodial. To his surprise Licata (1974) found that students in a school whose teachers were quite custodial were more euphoric about school than students in another school whose teachers were significantly less custodial. This led to the speculation that the drama of the struggle for control between teachers and students may be more enlivened where the teachers are more custodial. Several studies pursued this possibility, adding PCB to the search and replacing the measure of euphoria with a measure of robustness. The original observation was not confirmed. Multhauf (1977), Estep (1979), and Smedley (1980) each report significant negative correlations between robustness and PCB; $r = -.64, -.72$, and $-.51$, respectively. Where PCI was used, the correlations were also negative but smaller. Smedley measured the PCB of the principal. These findings fall opposite Licata's. All the researchers seem to agree, however, that humanistic schools and classrooms are more interesting to students because they are more varied and less routinized.

Once again, teacher gender seems to have some influence on the findings. Multhauf (1977) and Estep (1979) show that the relationship between PCB and robustness is stronger for female than for male teachers. This might be explained if female teacher PCI scores were consistently higher than the PCI of men. However, PCI differences by gender do not follow this pattern consistently. One should not expect that students would uniformly prefer classes with female teachers. Furthermore, the robustness findings pertain to PCB. As noted, the PCI–PCB relationship is confounded by teacher and student gender and by student perceptions of teacher attitudes. Ens (1975) reports that female teacher PCB is higher than that of males. Estep (1979) reports the opposite.

Furthermore, the relationships between PCB and other teacher characteristics do not necessarily connote uniform attractiveness. Williams (1979) reports a correlation of $-.38$ between PCB and teacher warmth. Heckert (1976) reports a correlation of $-.28$ between PCB and job satisfaction. PCB has been shown to be uncorrelated with dogmatism (Helsel, 1974), sense of power (Rose, 1974), and conservatism and liberalism Primeaux (1979).

Estadt (1974) and Marshall (1977) both find essentially no association between PCB and the teachers' sense of bureaucracy in the school. Noll (1976) reports that PCB and teacher self-actualization are uncorrelated. Browning (1979) reports weak correlations between PCB and employee and professional role orientations. Brayboy (1981) finds weak associations between PCB and teacher sex, age, experience, education, and race. PCB seems unrelated to many teacher characteristics that might otherwise be related to the way students might regard classrooms and teachers. Moye's (1975) findings about PCB and student alienation contradict those reported by Hoy (1971, 1972) concerning PCI. Sweeting (1975) reported that students prefer teachers with higher PCB scores than those they attributed to their own teachers. Subsequently, Davis (1979) and Forlenza and Willower (1980) reported just the opposite. Ju (1983) reports that boys, low achievers, and students in higher grades give higher PCB scores. Brown (1973) finds no relationship between PCB and students' SES and race. Most interesting is Smedley's (1980) finding that there is a weak negative relationship ($r = -.17$) between the PCB of the principal and the students' avowed knowledge of the principal. Other than those few clues gleaned from Bean (1972) and Ens (1975), it is very difficult to know what students have in mind when they make PCB reports.

On this very matter the findings relating PCI and student and classroom characterisitics are more compelling and uniform. Humanistic teachers seem to connect better with children than do custodial teachers. How the attitude or ideology is translated into more positive student characteristics if not by behavior is not revealed in the pupil control studies. But to the extent PCI may be an imperfect index of a bundle of personal teacher attitudes and outlooks, pupils may apprehend these directly in a manner not necessarily contingent upon or clearly mediated by teacher behaviors. On the other hand, humanistic teachers may actually treat children in a caring, sensitive, and just fashion, and students may respond to these actions favorably. Perhaps the PCB instrument just cannot capture such dimensions of behavior.

SUMMARY OF THE STUDIES

Personal and Personality Correlates

The PCI instrument exhibits high reliability. Its construct validity is less secure. Correlations with various personal characteristics and personality measures fall into three groups; high, moderate, and low. For the high group, a question of correlated method variance arises. Do PCI and the personality instruments where correlations fall in the range of $r = .60$ and above really measure the same personality state or trait, or are two substantively different variables related? The very nature of the several personality measures with which PCI shows a strong relationship suggests that correlated method variance could indeed have been at work. This suggestion raises, in turn, questions about the validity of the PCI instrument, especially as to whether PCI scores reasonably represent a fully operational concept and whether responses represent patterns of how respondents believe they should reply. Yet PCI seems to be valid in the sense that whatever it measures aligns reasonably with whatever the instruments probing the same personality traits and/or states also measure.

The reasons for the low correlations are not apparent, particularly because a number of these constructs appear as closely related conceptually to PCI as those that show strong association. For the correlations that fall in the range of $r = .20$ to $r = .60$ (the moderate group), some combination of real agreement and correlated method variance may be at work; but the several inquiries seldom offer explicit rationale for the selection of the correlates and why they should covary with PCI. What the correlates have in common is loosely suggested by the concept of PCI.

As for the correlations of PCI with age and gender, the former appear seriously interrelated with a number of other variables, and there are as many data one way as the other for the latter.

In sum, the sizable body of evidence on the relationship of PCI with personal and personality correlates has not yet made definitive conceptual sense or exposed sure empirical regularity. A case in point is the wandering and uncertain relationship between PCI scores and dogmatism.

Organizational Correlates

The central theme of threat suffers from few genuine attempts to define the construct operationally. The evidence of structural and organizational sources of threat loads modestly on the nonsupportive side, but findings vary. Investigators have too quickly drawn overly confident inferences regarding persistent differences between elementary and secondary schools in respect to the presence of threatening conditions that matter. Despite some minor contradictory evidence and design weakness, the interpretation that the variation of PCI scores with position (that is, teacher, counselor, principal) derives from difference in the levels of threat seems reasonable. Overall, the loading of evidence in the expected direction is heavy, but important anomalies remain. The data leave unsettled and equivocal the relationship between PCI and various "objective" indicators of threat (size, location, community type, student race and SES, and educability) and also several "subjective" features of organizations. The results are not uniform and depend heavily on cross-sectional studies. So, on both the objective and subjective sides, efforts to make operational the construct of threat (other than in the instance of organizational position) fail to produce convincing findings and consistent association with PCI.

Experience Correlates

The notion of threat presumably operates on the experience side as well as for organizational correlates; that is, as an individual moves deeper and deeper into the role of teacher, threat from pupils promotes custodial leanings, a condition reinforced early by supervising teachers and continued by experienced colleagues. Evidence from a substantial number of cross-sectional and several longitudinal studies appears to make a persuasive case that early experience covaries with increase in custodial orientation, but several of the investigations offer only qualified support or contradictory evidence. Even the supportive longitudinal studies leave doubts about whether the changes in PCI over job tenure are (a) important, (b) predictable, and (c) related specifically to job experience. Overall, the evidence supports the explanation of individual internal consistency. Contradictory results and the extent of statistically nonsignificant correlations urge caution in accepting universality in the theme of influence of early experience. The influence of the experience of living for some time in a particular culture deserves consideration as a rival hypothesis to the salience of the effects of short-term socialization on the job. The rival hypothesis suggests the PCI could reflect cultural continuity as least as much as it reflects a sensitive personality state.

Ideology and Behavior

The relative stability of association between PCI and PCB scores is impressive. With rare exception, the correlations are strong and in the anticipated direction; that is, the more custodial is PCI, the more custodial is PCB. PCI also covaries with selected teacher behaviors assessed by methods other than PCB in ways that seem to make conceptual sense. In addition, both PCI and PCB scores covary inversely with student sentiments; the higher the scores, the less positive are student attitudes and reports of relationships with teachers. Still, the evaluation paradigm for assessing the relationship between ideology and behavior remains vague and implicit, and some of the evidence is shaky. Only a few studies actually document the relationship, and several present bits of disquieting evidence. Much still remains unexplained about the relationship between PCI and behavior, including some puzzling findings on gender differences that raise questions about the issue of whether and to what extent the association between PCI and PCB is related to actual teacher behavior.

SOME FURTHER COMMENTS ON MEASUREMENT ISSUES

The PCI and PCB instruments appear highly reliable according to conventional estimates, but several measurement issues warrant mention. The first, noted briefly earlier, pertains to the assumption of equal intervals between scale points and the assumption that the difference between any adjacent scale points conveys the same meaning as the difference between any other adjacent points. Unfortunately, there does not really exist any straightforward way to probe the equal-interval assumption for PCI and for PCB, or for the hundreds of instruments used in social and behavioral research that invoke that assumption. The relevance for PCI and PCB research is twofold: (a) the need to exercise caution in accepting tests of statistical significance that treat scores as if they do fall along a continuum of equal intervals; (b) the need to exercise equal caution in accepting conclusions that groups whose average scores differ by, say, 4 to 6 PCI "units" really represent different populations.

A second measurement issue pertains to interpreting the meaning of a total score. If on PCI a respondent selects the "undecided" alternative on all 20 items, the item score would be 3 in each instance, and the total score would be 60. But, is this person custodial or humanistic? How does an investigator compare, conceptually or theoretically, the first person to a second who selects a scale point of 4 on 10 items and a scale point of 2 on 10 items and whose total score is also 60? On half the items, the second person tilts toward a custodial orientation; on the other half, toward a humanistic orientation. But is this person really one or the other? Again, the problem identified here for PCI (and PCB) plagues all research that uses similar instruments.

An issue related to the two cited above hinges on the instructions to respondents. The PCI instructions stipulate that there are no "correct" answers and ask respondents to offer only their "frank" opinions. The PCI instrument, however, limits the opportunity to express opinion freely by forcing indication of extent of agreement with each of 20 statements, which even the developers of the instruments admit load more heavily on the custodial side. The more problematic feature is that there are at least three different bases for responding to an item. The instrument developers seem to have had in mind that respondents would rest opinions on their emotional states, thus revealing ideologies. However, there are also a factual basis and a moral basis to consider. For example, Item 4 reads "Directing sarcastic remarks toward a defiant pupil is a good disciplinary technique." A respondent could choose an alternative on the basis of actual experience (factual); or a respondent could choose on the basis of right belief (moral); or a respondent could choose on the basis of feeling (emotional). The likelihood that a respondent will consistently rest selection of responses on any one basis throughout the instrument, and particularly on an emotional basis, remains undetermined and uncertain.

Equally, if not more, important is the difficulty of relating a particular response to the basis or combination of bases that may be operative. A respondent could "disagree" with Item 4 on at least three grounds: (a) Factually; sarcasm does not work well with defiant pupils; (b) morally, use of sarcasm is not considered good teaching practice; (c) emotionally, sarcasm is not a severe enough reaction to defiant behavior. But a "disagree" response loads on the humanistic side, raising once again the question of interpreting patterns of responses. Independent analysis for this chapter has revealed singular difficulty in identifying exactly the basis for a respondent's extent of disagreement in no less than 18 of 20 PCI items. For PCB the problem of interpretation is perhaps more severe. Student reports of teacher behavior are surely colored by student ideations, which as many studies suggest, operate independently of "objective" matters. In sum, because the scoring of PCI (and PCB) provides little opportunity for understanding the reasoning, or absence thereof, that influenced responses, the meaning of item and total scores remains equivocal. So, the ability of the two instruments to offer an unequivocal interpretation of the concepts they intend to measure remains open to question.

One additional point deserves consideration; namely, search for an answer to the question of whether the entire ideological force of the instruments operates to capture respondents in a web of particular assumptions about schools. Specifically, the instruments place the respondent in a role in an organization characterized by (a) the unequal distribution of power between adults and children that favors the former and (b) the continuous threat of the redistribution of that power. The PCI and PCB items take on meaning only within conventions of schooling that share a particular set of characteristics centered on the distribution of power. Even if only dimly seen, then, PCI and PCB items and the concept(s) behind them come into contact with only one conventional form of socially constructed reality.

These several concerns direct attention again to the issue of validity. Both PCI and PCB seem to exhibit good face validity and reasonable content validity; estimates of concurrent validity are not as convincing. Willower, Eidell, and Hoy (1967, 1973) reported some 20 years ago the first, and regularly cited, effort to estimate the validity of PCI. The investigators distributed to principals written descriptions of ideal-type custodial and humanistic instances of PCI and asked the principals to name teachers who were most like each extreme conceptual description. The mean PCI scores of the different sets of teachers identified by the principals were statistically different. The PCI scores agreed with principals' estimates. The investigators concluded that the PCI instrument met the appropriate test of validity. Unfortunately, however, the test does not answer the question of whether individuals with different PCI scores really hold different control ideologies, for reasons cited just above, particularly the difficulty of identifying and interpreting the basis on which the principal could infer ideology and on which respondents choose their responses to specific items.

FINAL COMMENT

In addition to issues of measurement that have surfaced after review of literally hundreds of PCI and PCB studies, both published and still unpublished, the question of the extent to which theory has driven the line of inquiry receives different answers. In 1979 Willower and Lawrence published an explication of PCI theory, building on an earlier piece by Willower alone (1978). Erickson (1977) has opined that the line of inquiry contained in PCI and PCB research represents a significant contribution, both conceptually and empirically, to the understanding of schools as complex organizations. (Willower's 1977 chapter in the Erickson volume reviews pupil control studies through 1975, with an emphasis on theoretical origins.) Griffiths (1983), on the other hand, observes that PCI studies lack strong theory, an estimate with which the current review concurs. There is less than full unanimity on the

answer to the question of the theoretical strength of PCI and PCB research.

The most basic, and perhaps the really significant, pupil control hypothesis generated by the theoretical apparatus undergirding PCI and PCB is that when an educator senses an increase in threat, the educator will respond both ideologically and behaviorally in a custodial manner. The basic hypothesis has received support in about half the cases of empirical test. The data suggest, then, that (a) the central construct of threat remains unspecified and (b) there has not yet appeared an adequate explanation of just why the construct of threat relates to the concept of control ideology and of just why control ideology tilts toward a custodial orientation under conditions of threat.

The long and voluminous research on PCI and PCB, generated by the work of Willower and his associates in the mid-1960s, needs in the late 1980s (a) reconsideration and more explicit statement of the theoretical and conceptual framework behind PCI and PCB empirical inquiry; (b) reanalysis of the measurement properties of the PCI and PCB instruments; and (c) secondary analyses of the hundreds of studies, published and otherwise, to determine just how they fit into the existing theoretical apparatus and/or how they might contribute to a reconstruction of a guiding conceptual scheme. Toward this end, Pennsylvania State University, where the line of inquiry started, would be well advised to bring together in one place all known studies and commentaries of the PCI genre to facilitate the next round of effort and also to pay fitting tribute to a most productive and influential scholar, Donald J. Willower.

REFERENCES

Adrams, J. D. (1971). *Relationships among responses of elementary school principals in the New York City public school system to school decentralization, their perceptions concerning teacher professionalism and their pupil control orientation.* Doctoral dissertation, New York University, New York, NY.

Afolayan, A. O. (1975). *The effects of participation in the "basics" program on the self-concept, experimental beliefs, dogmatism, and pupil control ideology of inservice elementary school teachers.* Doctoral dissertation, North Texas State University, Denton.

Anderson, C. S. (1982). The search for school climate: A review of the research. *Review of Educational Research, 52*(3), 368–420.

Appleberry, J. B. (1969). *The relationship between organizational climate and pupil control ideology of elementary schools.* Doctoral dissertation, Oklahoma State University, Stillwater.

Appleberry, J. B. & Hoy, W. K. (1969). The pupil control ideology of professional personnel in "open" and "closed" elementary schools. *Educational Administration Quarterly, 5*(3), 74–85.

Armer, W. M. (1976). An affective curriculum and its effects on teachers and learners. *Dissertation Abstracts International, 36*, 8A.

Barfield, V. M., & Burlingame, M. (1974). The pupil control

ideology of teachers in selected schools. *Journal of Experimental Education*, 42(4), 6–11.

Barrick, D. A. S. (1981). *A study of the relationship between teacher-pupil control ideology and discipline effectiveness*. Doctoral dissertation, George Peabody College for Teachers, Nashville, TN.

Bartlett, V. L. (1976). Teacher attitudes as a function of pupil control ideology. *Journal of Educational Administration*, 14(2), 211–219.

Batista, D. M. (1973). *The relationship of environmental press and the pupil control ideology of teachers in flexibly modular and conventionally scheduled high schools*. Doctoral dissertation, New York University, New York, NY.

Bean, J. S. (1972). *Pupil control ideologies of teachers and certain aspects of their classroom behavior as perceived by pupils*. Doctoral dissertation, Rutgers University, New Brunswick, NJ.

Bean, J. S. & Hoy, W. K. (1974). Pupil control ideology of teachers and instructional climate in the classroom. *High School Journal*, 58(2), 61–69.

Bloom, R. B. (1978). Discipline: Another face of moral reasoning. *College Student Journal*, 12(4), 356–359.

Blust, R. S. (1977). *Perceived organizational press, personal ideology and teacher-pupil control behavior*. Doctoral dissertation, Pennsylvania State University, University Park.

Bogacki, D. F. (1981). *Attitudes toward corporal punishment: Authoritarian personality and pupil control ideology of school personnel*. Doctoral dissertation, Temple University, Philadelphia, PA.

Bowen, J. M. (1975). *Relationships between components of work motivation and the pupil control ideology of public high school teachers and principals*. Doctoral dissertation, State University of New York, Albany.

Boyd, A., Jr. (1981). *A study of a direct measure of the concept of humanism and its relation to the pupil control ideology form*. Doctoral dissertation, University of Iowa, Iowa City.

Brayboy, L. R. (1981). *Teacher pupil control ideology and behavior and principals' ratings of teachers' discipline effectiveness*. Doctoral dissertation, Pennsylvania State University, University Park.

Brenneman, O. N. (1974). *Teacher self-acceptance, acceptance of others, and pupil control ideology*. Doctoral dissertation, Pennsylvania State University, University Park.

Brooks, R. C. (1977). *A study to establish behavioral and other correlates of the pupil control ideology form at the junior and senior high school level*. Doctoral dissertation, University of Iowa, Jowa City.

Brown, L. H. (1973). *Student socio-economic status and teacher-pupil control behavior*. Doctoral dissertation, Pennsylvania State University, University Park.

Brown, R. E. & Licata, J. W. (1978). Pupil control behavior, student brinkmanship and environmental robustness. *Planning and Changing*, 9(4), 195–202.

Browning, M. E., Jr. (1979). *The relationships among secondary school teacher role orientation, pupil control ideology, and pupil control behavior*. Doctoral dissertation, Northern Illinois University, De Kalb.

Budzik, J. M. (1971). *The relationship between teachers' ideology of pupil control and their perceptions of administrative control style*. Doctoral dissertation, University of Michigan, Ann Arbor.

Caffee, B. S. (1979). *The effects of the student teaching experience on student-teacher attitudes and relationships between attitudes and teacher effectiveness*. Doctoral dissertation, East Texas State University, Commerce.

Campbell, L. P., & Williamson, J. A. (1978). Inner-city schools get more custodial teachers. *Clearing House*, 52(3), 140–141.

Carlson, R. O. (1964). Environmental coustraints and organizational consequences: The public school and its clients. In D. E. Griffiths (Ed.), *Behavioral science and educational administration*. The 63rd Yearbook of the National Society for the Study of Education, Part II. Chicago: The Society.

Chawla, S. S. (1977). *A comparative study of Bharati and American teachers' educational attitudes, pupil control ideology, and motivation to work*. Doctoral dissertation, University of Kansas, Lawrence.

Ciaglia, A. F. (1980). *Parents' social background and pupil control attitudes and pupil control attitudes of students and teachers*. Doctoral dissertation, Fordham University, New York.

Davis, J. L. (1979). *American Indian students' perceptions of actual and ideal dormitory aides' pupil control behavior, and students' attitudes regarding their dormitory aides*. Doctoral dissertation, Pennsylvania State University, University Park.

Day, H. W., Jr. (1973). *A study of the relationships between organizational climate, teachers' pupil control ideology and pupils' attitude toward learning in elementary schools*. Doctoral dissertation, Memphis State University, Memphis, TN.

Deibert, J. P. (1978). Pupil control ideology and teachers and student self-actualization in the public schools. *Dissertation Abstracts International*, 38(7A).

Deibert, J. P., & Hoy, W. K. (1977). "Custodial" high schools and self-actualization of students. *Educational Research Quarterly*, 2(2), 24–31.

Dobson, R., Goldenberg, R., & Elsom, B. (1972). Pupil control ideology and teacher influence in the classroom. *Journal of Educational Research*, 66(2), 76–80.

Docking, R. A., & Docking, E. (1984). Reducing teacher stress, *Unicorn* (Bulletin of the Australian College of Education), 10(3). 261–274.

Drozda, D. G. (1972). *The impact of orgnizational socialization on the pupil control ideology of elementary school teachers as a result of the first year's teaching experience*. Doctoral dissertation, University of Oregon, Eugene.

Duggal, S. P. (1969). *Relationship between student unrest, student participation in school management, and dogmatism and pupil control ideology of school staff in the high school*. Doctoral dissertation, University of Michigan, Ann Arbor.

Dunkerly, R. D. (1979). *An examination of alternative explanations for pluralistic ignorance among teachers*. Doctoral dissertation, Pennsylvania State University, University Park.

Eidell, T. L. (1965). *The development and test of a measure of the pupil control ideology of public school professional staff members*. Doctoral dissertation, Pennsylvania State University, University Park.

Enochs, L. G. (1982). Implementation proneness in terms of teacher factors relating to inservice on selected science education trends: A case study. *Dissertation Abstracts International*, 42(11A).

Ens, J. (1975). *The ideology-behavior interface: A comparison of high school teachers' pupil control ideology and behavior as perceived by themselves and their students*, Doctoral dissertation, University of Oregon, Eugene.

Erickson, D. A. (Ed.) (1977). *Educational organization and administration*. Berkeley. CA: McCutchan.

Estadt, G. J. (1974). *The relationship between the rule administration behavior of the secondary school principal and the pupil control behavior of secondary teachers*. Doctoral dissertation, Pennsylvania State University, University Park.

Estep, L. E. (1979). *Teacher pupil control ideology and behavior and classroom environmental robustness in the secondary school*. Doctoral dissertation, Pennsylvania State University, University Park.

Ferguson, J. S. (1972). *The relationship between pupil control ideology and observed leader behavior of public secondary school teachers*. Doctoral dissertation, University of Kansas, Lawrence.

Ferguson, J. S., & Miskel, C. G. (1973). *The relationships among pupil control ideology, observed behavior, and discipline referrals of public secondary school teachers*. Paper presented at the Annual Meeting of the American Educational Research Association, New Orleans.

Fink, C. H. (1975). *The impact of student-teaching on attitudes and behaviors relating to pupil control and teacher authority for a group of secondary social studies student-teachers*. Doctoral dissertation, University of Maryland, College Park.

Foley, W. J., & Brooks, R. (1978). Pupil control ideology in predicting teacher discipline referrals. *Educational Administration Quarterly*, 14(3), 104–112.

Ford, C. B. (1976). *A study of the relationships among pupil perception of teacher social power base, teacher-pupil control ideology, and teacher concern level in teachers of secondary mathematics.* Doctoral dissertation, University of Houston, TX.

Forlenza, V. A., & Willower, D. J. (1980). Students' perceptions of ideal and actual teacher-pupil control behavior and reading achievement. *Child Study Journal*, 10(1), 49–57.

Forman, N. (1971). An investigation of personality and situational factors associated with teacher innovativeness. *Dissertation Abstracts International*, 32(6A).

Franklin, W. J. (1976) *The effect of T-groups on pupil control ideology and pupil control behavior of student-teachers in secondary schools.* Doctoral dissertation, University of Kansas, Lawrence.

Fritz, J. O. (1973). Views of schooling in Alberta high schools. (Mimeo, part 5.) Calgary, Canada: University of Alberta.

Gardiner, D. E. (1975). *An examination of the differences between and among teacher responses to the pupil control ideology form and the Runner studies of attitude patterns and administrative judgments of teachers' potential.* Doctoral dissertation, Temple University, Philadelphia, PA.

Gipp, G. E. (1974). *The relationship of perceived community educational viewpoints and pupil control ideology among teachers.* Doctoral dissertation, Pennsylvania State University, University Park.

Glasnapp, D. R., & Guenther, J. E. (1973). Humanistic and skills orientation change during student teaching. *College Student Journal*, 7(3), 43–47.

Gmelch, W. H. (1984). *Educators' response to stress: Towards a coping taxonomy.* Paper presented at the Annual Meeting of the American Educational Research Association, New Orleans.

Gossen, H. A. (1969). *An investigation of the relationship between socioeconomic status of elementary schools and the pupil control ideology of teachers.* Doctoral dissertation, Oklahoma State University, Stillwater.

Griepenstroh, G. D., & Miskel, C. (1975–1976). Training groups and student teachers' pupil control ideology. *Planning and Changing*, 6(3–4). 177–184

Griepenstroh, G. D., & Miskel, C. (1976). *Changing the custodial socialization of teachers' pupil control ideology.* Paper presented at Annual Meeting of the American Educational Research Association, San Francisco.

Griffiths, D. E. (1983). Evolution in research and theory: A study of prominent researchers. *Educational Administration Quarterly*, 19(3). 201–248

Halpin, G., & Goldenberg, R. (1973). *Relationships between measures of creativity and pupil control ideology.* Paper presented at the Annual Meeting of the American Educational Research Association, New Orleans.

Hamalian, A. (1979). Pupil control ideology: Comparative perspectives—United States and Canada. *Alberta Journal of Educational Research*, 25(1), 37–47.

Hardesty, L. F. (1978). *Pupil control ideology of teachers as it relates to middle-school concepts.* Doctoral dissertation, University of Kansas, Lawrence.

Hassan, H. A. (1979). *Pupil control ideology and the science classroom environment in the secondary schools of Khartoum, Sudan.* Doctoral dissertation, Indiana University, Bloomington.

Heckert, J. W. (1976). *Pupil control ideology—pupil control behaviour congruence and the job satisfaction of public school teachers.* Doctoral dissertation, Pennsylvania State University, University Park.

Heinman, R. J. (1971). *Relationships among selected values, levels of dogmatism, and pupil control ideologies of high school principals.* Doctoral dissertation, New York University, New York, NY.

Helsel, A. R. (1971a). Value orientation and pupil control ideology of public school educators. *Educational Administration Quarterly*, 7(1), 24–33.

Helsel, A. R. (1971b). Status obeisance and pupil control ideology. *Journal of Educational Administration*, 9(1), 38–47.

Helsel, A. R. (1974). *Personality and pupil control behavior.* Paper presented at the Annual Meeting of the American Educational Research Association, Chicago.

Helsel, A. R. (1976). Personality and pupil control behaviour. *Journal of Educational Administration*, 14(1), 79–86.

Helsel, A. R. & Willower, D. J. (1973). *Toward definition and measurement of pupil control behavior.* Paper presented at Annual Meeting of the American Educational Research Association, New Orleans.

Helsel, A. R., & Willower, D. J. (1974). Toward definition and measurement of pupil control behavior. *Journal of Educational Administration*, 12(1), 114–123.

Helwig, C. (1973). Authenticity and individual teacher interpersonal needs. *Journal of Educational Administration*, 11(1), 139–143.

Helwig, C., & Smallie, R. C. (1973). Openness-closedness as a viable concept. *California Journal of Educational Research*, 24(2), 52–60.

Henderson, C. B. (1982). *An analysis of assertive discipline training and implementation on inservice elementary teachers' self-concept, locus of control, pupil control ideology and assertive personality characteristics.* Doctoral dissertation, Indiana University, Bloomington.

Hinojosa, D. (1974). *A study of the relationship between the organizational climate and the pupil control ideology and the self-esteem and power dimensions of the students' self-concept in selected elementary schools in the Corpus Christi Independent School District.* Doctoral dissertation, University of Houston, TX.

Holzwarth, J. F. (1974). *The relationship of pupil control ideology of teachers to student alienation in two school environments.* Doctoral dissertation, University of Rochester, Rochester, NY.

Horowitz, D. (1980). *Relationships between the attitudes toward student rights and the pupil control ideology of New York State public school teachers and administrators.* Doctoral dissertation, State University of New York at Albany.

Hoy, W. K. (1965). *Dogmatism and the pupil control ideology of public school professional staff members.* Doctoral dissertation, Pennsylvania State University, University Park.

Hoy, W. K. (1967). Organizational socialization: The student teacher and pupil control ideology. *Journal of Educational Research*, 61, 153–155.

Hoy, W. K. (1968). The influence of experience on the beginning teacher. *School Review*, 76(3) 312–323.

Hoy, W. K. (1969). Pupil control ideology and organizational socialization: A further examination of the influence of experience on the beginning teacher. *School Review*, 77, 257–265.

Hoy, W. K. (1971). An investigation of the relationships between characteristics of secondary schools and student alienation. (Final Report, RMQ66004, DHEW May 1971), Office of Education. Washington, DC: Bureau of Research.

Hoy, W. K. (1972). Dimensions of student alienation and pupil control orientations of high schools. *Interchange*, 3(4), 38–52.

Hoy, W. K., & Appleberry, J. B. (1970). Teacher-principal relationships in "humanistic" and "custodial" elementary schools. *Journal of Experimental Education*, 39(2), 27–31.

Hoy, W. K., & Henderson, J. R. (1982). *Principal authenticity, school climate, and pupil-conrol orientation.* Paper presented at American Educational Research Association, New York.

Hoy, W. K., & Jalovick, J. M. (1979). Open education and pupil control ideologies of teachers. *Journal of Educational Research*, 73(1), 45–49.

Hoy, W. K., & Rees, R. (1977). The bureaucratic socialization of student teachers. *Journal of Teacher Education*, 28(1), 23–26.

Jones, D. R. (1982). The influence of length and level of student teaching on pupil control ideology. *High School Journal*, 65(7), 220–225.

Jones, D. R., & Harty, H. (1980). Secondary school student teacher classroom control ideologies and amount of engaged instructional activities. *High School Journal*, 64(1), 13–15.

Jones, D. R., & Harty, H. (1981). Classroom management-pupil control ideologies before and after secondary school science student teaching. *Science Education*, 65(1), 3–10.

Jones, P. L. (1970). *An analysis of the relationship between biology teachers' pupil control ideology and their classroom practices.* Doctoral dissertation, Oklahoma State University, Stillwater.

Jones, T. E. (1969). *The relationship between bureaucracy and the pupil control ideology of secondary schools and teachers.* Doctoral dissertation, Oklahoma State University, Stillwater.

Ju, J. (1983). *Student perceptions of teachers' pupil control orientation and student alienation in junior high schools of Taipei, the Republic of China.* Doctoral dissertation, University of Northern Colorado, Greeley.

Jury, L. E. (1973). *Teacher self-actualization and pupil control ideology.* Doctoral dissertation, Pennsylvania State University, University Park.

Kayden, M. G. (1976). *Teachers' pupil control ideology and classroom management behavior.* Doctoral dissertation, Pennsylvania State University, University Park.

Keefe, J. A. (1969). *The relationship of the pupil control ideology of teachers to key personal and organizational variables.* Doctoral dissertation, Boston University, Boston, MA.

Kelton, B. A. (1976). *An analysis of the relationship between pupil control ideology held by professional staff and children's beliefs in internal-external control.* Doctoral dissertation, University of Connecticut, Storrs.

Kiss, S. H. (1981). *The influence of content area, school location, and cooperating teacher on change in the pupil control ideology of secondary-level student teachers.* Doctoral dissertation, New York University, New York, NY.

Kozakewich, E. J. (1973). *An analysis of the pupil control ideologies and pupil control structures in elementary, junior high, and senior high schools.* Master's thesis, University of Alberta, Canada.

Krohn, E. W. (1979). *Perceived organizational structure and the pupil control ideology and job satisfaction of elementary and secondary school teachers.* Doctoral dissertation, University of North Carolina at Chapel Hill.

Lawrence, J. D. (1977). *Teacher perception of student threat to teacher status and teacher/pupil control ideology.* Doctoral dissertation, Pennsylvania State University, University Park.

Leppert, E. J., & Hoy, W. K. (1972). Teacher personality and pupil control ideology. *Journal of Experimental Education, 40*(3), 57–59.

Levine, L. R. G. (1976). *The organizational learning climate, pupil control ideology and goals actualization as perceived by special day school administrators and teachers.* Doctoral dissertation, Fordham University, New York.

Licata, J. W. (1974). *A study of the systemic function of student brinkmanship.* Doctoral dissertation, Pennsylvania State University, University Park.

Littrell, D. M. (1980). *Teachers' pupil control ideology, pupil control behavior, and student discipline.* Doctoral dissertation, University of Missouri at Columbia.

Long, J. N. (1979). *Pupil control ideology, executive professional leadership and pluralistic ignorance in elementary schools.* Doctoral dissertation, Pennsylvania State University, University Park.

Longo, P. B. (1972). *Pupil control attitudes of public school cooperating teachers and education instructors affiliated with the Queens College teacher training program.* Doctoral dissertation, New York University, New York NY.

Longo, P. B. (1974). Pupil control as an institutional pattern. *Contemporary Education, 45*(2), 143–146.

Lundin, R. (1980). *The selection and preparation of teacher librarians.* Doctoral dissertation, Monash University, Clayton, Victoria, Australia.

Lunenburg, F. C. (1972). *The influence of organizational climate and dogmatism of pupil control ideology.* Doctoral dissertation, University of Ottawa, Ontario.

Luster, J. T. (1980). *The effect of classroom management training on the interactive process of student teachers and pupils.* Doctoral dissertation, University of Pittsburgh, Pittsburgh, PA.

MacMillan, M. R. (1973). *Pupil control ideology and status obeisance of teachers and principals in elementary schools.* Doctoral dissertation, University of Alberta, Canada.

Mann, J. B. (1970). *Dimensions of teacher ideology and their relationship to aspects of perceived work environment and job satisfaction in crisis secondary schools.* Doctoral dissertation, University of Michigan. Ann Arbor.

Marshall, C. E. (1977). *The relationship between the rule administration behavior of the elementary school principal as perceived by teachers and the pupil control behavior of teachers as perceived by pupils.* Doctoral dissertation, Pennsylvania State University, University Park.

Martin, L. S. (1976). *An investigation of pupil control ideology and personality characteristics of high- and low-achieving pupils.* Doctoral dissertation, University of Connecticut, Storrs.

McAndrews, J. B. (1971). *Teachers' self-esteem, pupil control ideology and attitudinal conformity to a perceived teacher peer group norm.* Doctoral dissertation, Pennsylvania State University, University Park.

McArthur, J. T. (1975). *Teacher socialization: The influence of initial teaching experience on the pupil control ideology of beginning secondary teachers.* Doctoral dissertation, Monash University, Clayton, Victoria, Australia.

McArthur, J. T. (1978). What does teaching do to teachers? *Educational Administration Quarterly, 14*(3) 89–103.

McArthur, J. T. (1979). Teacher socialization: The first five years. *Alberta Journal of Educational Research, 25*(4), 264–274.

McArthur, J. T. (1980). *The first five years of teaching, their effect on PCI, and commitment to teaching.* Paper presented at the Annual Meeting of the American Educational Research Association Conference, Boston.

McArthur, J. T. (1981). The first five years of teaching. Australian Government Publication Service, Educational Research and Development Committee, No. 30, Canberra, Australia.

McCaskill, R. H. (1979). *The relationship between teacher knowledge of adolescent development, teacher warmth, and teacher educational ideology, with teacher overt verbal behavior in selected junior high classrooms.* Doctoral dissertation, University of Maryland, College Park.

McCullough, K. L. (1980). *An experimental study of the effect of seminars on attitudes of elementary student teachers toward pupil control.* Doctoral dissertation, Oklahoma State University, Stillwater.

Mitchell, C. W. (1974). *Pupil control ideologies of teachers and principals in small and large schools.* Doctoral dissertation, University of Illinois at Urbana-Champaign.

Moye, N. (1975). *An investigation of the relationship between student perceptions of pupil control behavior orientation of teachers and student alienation in selected secondary schools.* Doctoral dissertation, University of Georgia, Athens.

Multhauf, A. P. (1977). *Teacher-pupil control ideology and behavior and classroom environmental robustness.* Doctoral dissertation, Pennsylvania State University, University Park.

Murad, B. J. (1974). *A study of the effects of a teacher education program on dimensions of teacher trainees' professional ideology, attitudes and values.* Doctoral dissertation, University of Kentucky, Lexington.

Murphy, S. A. (1977). *A comparison of the pupil control ideology of parents and school staff.* Doctoral dissertation. University of Arkansas, Fayetteville.

Nachtscheim, N. M., & Hoy, W. K. (1976). Authoritarian personality and control ideologies of teachers. *Alberta Journal of Educational Research, 22*(2), 173–178.

Noll, R. L. (1976). *Teacher self-actualization and pupil control ideology—behavior congruence.* Doctoral dissertation, Pennsylvania State University, University Park.

Packard, J. S. (1971). *Pluralistic ignorance and pupil control ideology.* Doctoral dissertation, Pennsylvania State University, University Park.

Packard, J. S., & Willower, D. J. (1972). Pluralistic ignorance and pupil control ideology. *Journal of Educational Administration, 10*(1), 78–87.

Phillipps, B. K. (1976). *Pre-education practicum: Its influence upon the student's pupil control ideology.* Doctoral dissertation, University of Iowa, Iowa City.

Preston, S. M. (1974). *Development of the pupil control ideology of novice teachers: A descriptive research project.* Doctoral dissertation, Harvard University, Cambridge, MA.

Primeaux, A. F. (1979). *The relationship between pupil control ideology, pupil control behavior and the political attitudes of elementary school teachers.* Doctoral dissertation, Pennsylvania State University, University Park.

Pritchett, W., & Willower, D. J. (1975). Student perceptions of teacher-pupil control behavior and student attitudes toward high school. *Alberta Journal of Educational Research, 21*(2), 110–115.

Racine, C. S. (1980). *A study of the relationship between pupil control ideology of high school teachers and principals and alienation and structured role orientation of high school students.* Doctoral dissertation, State University of New York at Albany.

Rafilides, M., & Hoy, W. K. (1971). Student sense of alienation and pupil control orientation of high schools. *High School Journal, 55*(3) 101–111.

Rausch, C. J. (1974). *Pupil control ideology of educators in the nonpublic Catholic secondary schools of the Twin City area.* Education specialist dissertation, St. Thomas College, St. Paul, MN.

Rexford, G. E. (1970). *The relationship between pupil control ideology and observed verbal behavior of selected secondary teachers.* Doctoral dissertations, Pennsylvania State University, University Park.

Roberts, R. A. (1969). *The relationship between the change in pupil control ideology of student teachers and the student teacher's perception of the cooperating teacher's pupil control ideology.* Doctoral dissertation, Oklahoma State University, Stillwater.

Roberts, R. A., & Blankenship, J. S. (1970). *The relationship between the change in pupil control ideology of student teachers and the student teacher's perception of the cooperating teacher's pupil control ideology.* Paper presented at the Annual Meeting of the National Association for Research in Science Teaching, Minneapolis.

Rose, K. R. (1974). *Teachers' sense of power and pupil control ideology and behavior congruence.* Doctoral dissertation, Pennsylvania State University, University Park.

Ross, R. W. (1980). *The effects of an early field experience program on the pupil control ideology of teacher trainees.* Doctoral dissertation, Northern Arizona University, Flagstaff.

Rouse, H. W. (1978). *Teacher control ideology and their attitudes towards the handicapped.* Doctoral dissertation, Rutgers University, New Brunswick, NJ.

Salerno, L. J. (1975). *Faculty informal structure and pupil control ideology.* Doctoral dissertation, Pennsylvania State University, University Park.

Salerno, L. J., & Willower, D. J. (1975). Faculty informal structure, pupil control ideology and pluralistic ignorance. *Journal of Educational Administration, 13*(2), 81–89.

Savage, M. H. (1981). *The relationship of teachers' perceptions of organizational structure and pupil control ideology to teacher alienation in New York City public high schools.* Doctoral dissertation, New York University, New York NY.

Seefa, D. (1981). *An analysis of the pupil control ideology of principals and teachers in public elementary schools in the Province of Sukhothai, Thailand.* Doctoral dissertation, North Texas State University, Denton.

Seidell, S. L. (1982). *Perceptions of teachers' control language—authority, power, and persuasion.* Doctoral dissertation, University of California at Santa Barbara.

Shearin, W. H., Jr. (1981). *The relationship between student alienation and extent of faculty agreement on pupil control ideology.* Doctoral dissertation, University of North Carolina at Chapel Hill.

Shirley, T. W. (1974). *An analysis of the leader behavior, values and pupil control ideologies of school principals.* Doctoral dissertation, Northwestern University, Chicago.

Smedley, S. R. (1980). *Principals' pupil control behavior and school environmental robustness.* Doctoral dissertation, Pennsylvania State University, University Park.

Smith, S. D., Reinhartz, J., Oshima, L., & Smith, W. D. (1982). *The development of student teacher discipline beliefs: Patterns and contexts.* Unpublished report, The University of New Mexico.

Spearly, D. J. (1979). *Teacher inbreeding and pupil control ideology.* Doctoral dissertation, Pennsylvania State University, University Park.

Stoops, C. E. (1980). *The relationship between militancy and pupil control ideology among public secondary school teachers.* Doctoral dissertation, Pennsylvania State University, University Park.

Stouten, J. W. (1974). *Pupil control ideology and certain demographic variables of teachers in relationship to children's expressions of affection or rejection toward their teachers.* Education specialist dissertation, institution unknown.

Sweeting, L. M. (1975). *Black students' perceptions of ideal and actual teacher-pupil control behavior and attitudes regarding their teacher and school.* Doctoral dissertation, Pennsylvania State University, University Park.

Templin, T. J. (1978). *Pupil control ideology and behavior and selected socialization factors influencing the physical education student-teacher.* Doctoral dissertation, University of Michigan, Ann Arbor.

Tippeconnic, J. W. (1975). *The relationship between teacher-pupil control ideology and elementary student attitudes in Navajo schools.* Doctoral dissertation, Pennsylvania State University, University Park.

Uncapher, K. J. (1974). *An investigation of the effect of feedback information during simulation on the Getzels-Guba decision-making style and the level of pupil control ideology.* Doctoral dissertation, Bowling Green State University, Bowling Green, OH.

Voege, C. C. (1979). *Personal values, educational attitudes, and attitudes toward pupil control, of staffs and boards of religious-affiliated schools, in relationship to staff retention.* Doctoral dissertation, New York University, New York NY.

Waller, W. (1932). *The sociology of teaching.* New York: John Wiley. (Paperback publication authorized by Russell & Russell, Inc.)

Waple, C. C. (1974). *Relationship between the existence of "Ressentiment," student perception of internal-external control and pupil control ideology of certificated high school staff in selected Ohio public schools.* Doctoral dissertation, Bowling Green State University, Bowling Green, OH.

Warrell, C. J. (1969). *The relationship of organizational patterns and pupil control ideology of teachers in selected junior and senior high schools.* Doctoral dissertation, New York University, New York NY.

Washington, N. (1981). *Teacher-pupil control ideology and school organizational climate in open education and traditional elementary schools.* Doctoral dissertation, Pennsylvania State University, University Park.

Williams, J. M. (1979). *Relationship of organizational climate and socioeconomic status to pupil control behavior.* Doctoral dissertation, University of Kansas, Lawrence.

Williams, M. (1972). *The pupil control ideology of public school personnel and its relationship to specified personal and situational variables.* Doctoral dissertation, University of Georgia. Athens.

Willower, D. J. (1967). *Schools as organizations—some illustrated strategies for educational research and practice.* Paper presented at West Virginia University Social Science Colloquium, Morgantown, WV.

Willower, D. J. (1977). Schools and pupil control. In D. A. Erickson (Ed.), *Educational organization and administration.* Berkeley, CA: McCutchan.

Willower, D. J. (1978). Inquiry on school organizations: Some hunting stories. *Studies in Educational Administration and Organization,* 43–55.

Willower, D. J., Eidell, T. L., & Hoy, W. K. (1973). *The school and pupil control ideology.* Penn State Studies No. 24, 1st ed. 1967; 2nd Ed. University Park, PA: Pennsylvania State University.

Willower, D. J., & Jones, R. G. (1963). When pupil control becomes an institutional theme. *Phi Delta Kappan, 45*(2), 107–109.

Willower, D. J., & Jones, R. G. (1967). Control in an educational organization. In J. D. Raths et al. (Eds.), *Studying teaching* (pp. 424–428). Englewood Cliffs, NJ: Prentice-Hall.

Willower, D. J., & Landis, C. A. (1970). Pupil control ideology and professional orientation of school faculty. *Journal of Secondary Education*, *45*, 118–123.

Willower, D. J., & Lawrence, J. D. (1979). Teachers' perceptions of student threat to teacher status and teacher-pupil control ideology. *Psychology in the Schools*, *16*(4), 586–590.

Winberg, K. R. (1982). *The relationship between home economics teachers' conceptual systems levels and classroom discipline ideologies*. Master's thesis, South Dakota State University, Brookings.

Wsiaki, M. T. (1974). *Colleague influence on the control ideology of novice elementary school teachers*. Doctoral dissertation, University of Oregon, Eugene.

Yee, A. H. (1969). Do cooperating teachers influence the attitudes of student teachers? *Journal of Educational Psychology*, *60*(4), 327–332.

Yuskiewicz, V. D. (1971). *Pupil control ideology and job satisfaction of public school teachers*. Doctoral dissertation, Pennsylvania State University, University Park.

Zak, I., & Horowitz, T. R. (1978, May). Developmental transitions in the professional growth of teachers. Based on the Proceedings of the 1978 Conference of the International Association for Educational Assessment. F. Octobre (Ed.). Baden, Austria.

Zeichner, K. M., & Grant, C. A. (1981). Biography and social structure in the socialization of student teachers: A re-examination of the pupil control ideologies of student teachers. *Journal of Education for Teaching*, *7*(3), 298–314.

Zeichner, K. M., & Tabachnick, B. R. (1981). Are the effects of university teacher education "washed out" by school experience? *Journal of Teacher Education*, *32*(3), 7–11.

Zelei, R. A. (1971). *Relationship between pupil control ideology and sense of power of teachers in selected public schools*. Doctoral dissertation, University of Akron, OH.

CHAPTER 11

School as Workplace: Structural Constraints on Administration

Ronald G. Corwin and Kathryn M. Borman

This chapter discusses some structural constraints that limit the capacity of administrators to control the work of teachers and students in schools. Our decision to focus on the structural parameters of administration departs from a dominant tradition in the educational literature, which treats administration almost synonymously with the personal actions and behavior of administrators. Consequently, this body of literature tends to dwell on those variables that can be manipulated. However, we believe that it is also important to understand the social context that frames administrative choices and sets the parameters of managerial power and authority.

Our thesis is that because of the way power and authority are distributed within school districts, normative conflicts are systematically patterned into their structures. Merton (1976) calls this condition *sociological ambivalence*. Ambivalence can take different forms. In the most extreme case, it can constitute a *paradox*, defined as a seemingly contradictory assertion that yet may be true. Or, it may exist as a *structural incompatibility*, defined simply as contradictory norms. Although incompatibility is a potential source of problems, it need not constitute an eminent problem. Finally, ambivalence can be the source of a *dilemma*, which implies the need to make *choices* among socially structured alternatives. Merton maintains that making such choices is the basic process that governs social

structure. In the case of school districts, tensions arise because their members have been socialized into distinctive occupational roles and confront dissimilar problems in their respective formal positions.

We have identified six types of structural incompatibilities applicable to school districts, the source of which is the way power and authority are distributed. Each is capable of producing tensions or conflict. Although perhaps they do not always become dilemmas as we have defined the term, we have taken the liberty of using that term throughout this chapter because it is so crucial to the administrative process. To provide a quick overview of the chapter, the six structural incompatibilities will be very briefly summarized at this point, although this cryptic treatment does not do justice to the complexity of issues involved.

1. *The Dilemma of Control.* Central-office administrators are legally and politically responsible for the actions of schools, but total centralization is neither administratively nor technically feasible. Chain-of-command protocols help preserve administrative control, but they can interfere with the ability of schools to solve local problems, whereas decentralization and slippage can interfere with coordination and with administrators' official responsibilities.

2. *The Dilemma of Autonomy.* In order to acquire discretion within the classroom, teachers have relinquished some of their claims to exercise control over fundamental parameters of their work, some of which were dictated by curricular forms. Teachers are subordinates, but they are also members of

Consultant/reviewers: Robert Dreeben, University of Chicago; and Kenneth Duckworth, University of Oregon.

powerful unions. As they have gained collective bargaining power, it often has been at the expense of their personal autonomy.

3. *The Dilemma of Occupational Status*. Compliance with administrative policies and procedures can interfere with professional norms. The most compliant teachers are not necessarily responsive to the circumstances of their students. The teachers' work has become routinized, but lesson plans, precise schedules and deadlines, required textbooks and standardized tests, and the like are not equally appropriate for all students. The goals of service are also constantly jeopardized by pragmatism and the requirements of survival.

4. *The Dilemma of Career*. It has been difficult to provide incentives for teachers because of the way the teaching career is structured. Those teachers who choose to make a lifelong vocational commitment do so at the expense of formal advancement after midcareer, and in any event promotion requires leaving the classroom. Moreover, opportunities for achieving informal professional recognition among peers are minimized by a high degree of segmentation within the occupation.

5. *The Dilemma of Order*. Schools exist to educate students, but they also must keep order. Arrangements necessary to maintain order can subvert the goals of instruction.

6. *The Dilemma of Equity*. For purposes of instruction, students must be classified into different schools, classrooms, programs, tracks, and learning groups. Each classification must be treated in a special way and requires different types of resources, but tradeoffs that must be made are so complex as to produce almost certainly some inequities.

Although these dilemmas overlap, the first two are associated with the administrative context of work in schools, the third and fourth with the occupational structure of teaching, and the last two with classrooms as social systems and work settings. These three dimensions, we believe, constitute the main parameters of work in schools. We emphasize that what we are calling dilemmas exist at the level of the social system, and hence they are not necessarily experienced uniformly from one school to another. Each dilemma, we submit, is a consequence of structural incompatibilities within school systems and cannot be resolved without extensive organizational reforms. Although we do not claim to have answers, some brief speculations are offered at the end of the chapter under the section entitled Implications.

We recognize that schools differ widely from one another. The administration of school districts, of secondary schools, and of elementary schools varies greatly. There is the large, poorly maintained inner-city high school patrolled by police and characterized by high rates of truancy and delinquency, and there is the small suburban elementary school attended by largely compliant and enthusiastic students. There are of course some commonalities, but the differences are conspicuous. This diversity, we suspect, accounts for much of what seems problematic about school systems and about schools, but our discussion will be confined to the dilemmas themselves.

SOME CASES

Some of the themes found in the discussions in this chapter are apparent in numerous case studies documenting efforts to introduce planned change programs into schools. Our interest here is not in innovation per se but in what such studies reveal about schools as workplaces. Consider for example Wacaster's (1973) account of the life and death of differentiated staffing at Columbia High School. Lauded as a relatively new idea in American education, differentiated staffing was touted by its supporters in the district as the path to the improvement of the education process, a way to combat the disenchantment of students and the disillusionment of teachers in the wake of growing student enrollments. It promised to establish a career ladder that would make better use of teachers and provide new sources of individualized instruction and guidance leading to the education of the whole child. However, less than a month after these claims were announced, staff members of the pilot high school voted to discontinue the project. A process that had taken over 2 years of planning and training prior to 8 months of attempted implementation had come to an abrupt end. What happened?

The staff had decided to offer an interdisciplinary curriculum divided into three "domains" that were to supersede the customary departmental organization. For over 2 weeks committees met to prepare a set of job descriptions, only to learn that the administrative cabinet rejected them because positions were not clearly ranked by levels of authority and responsibility. Rejecting the idea of authority, differentiation, or anything to do with hierarchy among teachers, the staff voted to discontinue the project. In the meantime other problems arose, as teachers tried to organize interdisciplinary courses. Since there was little time for instructional development during the previous summer, teachers had to write their own courses of study as they went along, and that had to be done cooperatively with other team members. But, the domains simply did not function; only four poorly attended meetings were held during the fall. Consequently, project goals gradually shifted further into an indefinite future. It was decided that differentiated staffing was a three-step process, and that actually it was only a "concept," not a model. In fact, it really meant only that each teacher does what he or she does best.

Several properties of schools were operative: (a) the resilience of the traditional classroom teaching role; (b) role overload and the tendency for immediate problems and short-run decisions to take precedence in the press of day-to-day duties; (c) the widespread faith that teachers are self-sufficient and that problems will "work themselves out" in time; (d) and the pervasive influence of teacher autonomy and the reluctance of individual teachers to relinquish their control over the teaching process. The case thus illustrates, among other things, some features associated with the dilemma of autonomy and the dilemma of status. The innovation impinged on traditional status and authority relationships among teachers in ways they disapproved, and they were able to mobilize the power necessary to defeat it. Also, the teachers' resistance to a differentiated staffing hierarchy is relevant to the dilemma of career in a way that we shall try to make clear later in the chapter.

Gross, Giacquinta, and Bernstein (1971) reported an attempt to change an urban elementary school. This innovation was supposed to redefine the traditional role of the elementary school teacher. The classroom was to become an environment where the students would have maximum freedom to choose among activities and materials that might interest them. The teacher was to become a person assisting children to learn according to their interests throughout the day in self-contained classrooms. Emphasis was to be placed on the process, not the content, of learning. It was expected that the motivation and academic achievement of low-income children would improve.

When first informed of this innovation, many teachers were positively predisposed toward it; some were neutral; there was no opposition. Teachers recognized that they were not adequately meeting all the varied needs of the disadvantaged pupils in their classrooms, and they had some hope that the innovation would improve the situation. Moreover, funding was assured and more than ample to cover the project's substantial budget. Nonetheless, 7 months after it was introduced, the teachers had become thoroughly disillusioned. The change effort was judged an abysmal failure and abandoned.

This case touches on some issues that are central to the dilemma of control. Administrators, who must rely upon subordinates to carry out programs lose some control in delegating responsibility. Moreover, sub-ordinates do not have the capacity to provide the necessary resources and conditions. A number of factors contributed to the failure: (a) teachers were unclear about their new role, and they lacked the skills required to perform it; (b) essential instructional materials and professional services were not made available; (c) adjustments were not made in other aspects of the educational program as required to implement this innovation; (d) and teachers were exposed to role overload. Also, the strategy followed by the director of the effort consisted primarily of explaining the philosophy and objectives of the innovation through several written documents, giving teachers maximum freedom to carry it out and delegating responsibility for it to an administrative subordinate. Although he was able to get it started in this way, it was not an effective way to implement it. No one took into account or made provisions for training to provide staff with the necessary skills to change their roles, materials and assistance necessary to implement the innovation, monitoring and feedback procedures, a means of compensating teachers for the overload required of them for additional duty in after-school planning meetings, and the like. But the problems cannot be blamed entirely on the administration either, because no one was in a position to foresee all the potential pitfalls; and even if they had been anticipated, the capabilities of administrators to respond were limited by the available resources, time, skills, and means of control. For example, because they were so basic to social control, it would have been very time consuming and perhaps infeasible to suspend rules regulating freedom of movement throughout the school even after it became evident that some of these rules were interfering with the program.

Sussman (1977) studied still another attempt to introduce individualized instruction into a school. The objective of this program was to enhance the child's sense of competence. However, it was found that more typically children were given work too difficult for them to accomplish. The children adapted by withdrawing or engaging in compulsive copying. The innovations attempted were constantly plagued by rigid scheduling of school time, the fact that pupils were assigned to classrooms exclusively according to their age, the use of subject-oriented report cards, and stubborn allegiances to the traditional teacher-directed classroom with its focus on specific subjects. The net effect of the changes was to make the teachers' job more difficult. Not only did they have to cope with new curricula and materials, but they also with a new classroom organization and new roles. Yet, they received little assistance. They tried to cope with the high rate of pupil failure by denying the fact, by falsifying the evidence, and by teaching specific information known to be covered on the test. Sussman found that even those teachers who initially subscribed to the spirit of the program and tried to create a great deal of free time for children, later shifted back to a more structured classroom environment because they had observed that the children could not use the free time wisely.

The dilemmas of order, equity, and control are all involved in this case. The impression one gets from Sussman's discription of this and three other innovations at the school is that the staff were so concerned about maintaining order and good public relations that they could not admit low pupil achievement was the real problem. Consequently, the innovations were used as facades, not as realistic ways to improve basic skills. Moreover, when teachers made proposals for other ways to improve basic skills, their ideas were quietly squelched by the administration. With little support from the administration, teachers carried the burden of implementing the program. There was never enough assistance or enough time.

Such studies provide very fragmentary glimpses into some of the strains associated with work in schools. We now shall address these strains more systematically.

THE DILEMMA OF ADMINISTRATIVE CONTROL

The dilemma of administrative control is that central office administrators are officially in charge of school districts, but actually many policies are determined by the actions of local schools. Consequently, in effect, district administrators are held accountable for things they cannot always control. This condition is a product of decentralization processes within formally centralized school districts. School districts are organized officially as hierarchies. Implementing educational policy is legally and politically the responsibility of high-level school district administrators. However, in practice only certain decisions are centralized. Many others have been decentralized, and administrators can never fully control such responsibilities.

Delegation or Slippage?

Decentralization can mean one of two things. First, many types of decisions have been formally *delegated* to schools and other lower-echelon units. Second, some decisions have been absorbed by lower-echelon units through the process of *slippage* (Selznick, 1948). Delegation is required due to the large size of modern school districts, their division of labor, and diversity in their environments. Slippage, however, is a function of the power of lower participants, the influence of external constituencies, and the discretion inherent in

some jobs. It prevails because subordinates must interpret policies, because they often have the power to resist some directives, and because administrators must rely on them to take the initiative necessary to make an organization work (Bendix, 1942; Gouldner, 1954).

Parsons (1956) questioned whether it is even accurate to speak of "delegation" because the functions of each level are so essentially different, operating under diverse pressures and varying sources of support. The central office has its agenda, principals have their turf to protect, and teachers desire to protect their autonomy within the classroom. Although designed as a mechanism for coordinating activities, the hierarchy is an anomaly. It is a means of coordination, but the separate layers of authority create further divisiveness, which only contributes to the problem the hierarchy was designed to remedy (Corwin, 1970, p. 214). Thus, slippage is one of the constraints that central administrators must live with.

Zones of Autonomy or Contested Terrain?

According to some writers, a well-defined division of labor has been worked out among central administrators, principals, and teachers, who seem to have agreed upon zones, or areas of decision domains, over which each group exercises independent control (Barnard, 1938; Lortie, 1969). The term *zones of control* connotes an imagery of a deliberate plan or at least a carefully worked out accommodation. However, another view is that domains are tentative outcomes of hotly contested power struggles, informal compromises, and negotiated union contracts. Boundaries of domains are never fixed because the hierarchy is always vulnerable and negotiable, not absolute (Crozier, 1964; Simmel, 1950). So-called decision domains in many school districts are at best only vaguely and tentatively defined, and in any case they are subject to continual renegotiation. The consequent ambiguities sometimes can act as another constraint on administrative control.

Hierarchy or Protocol?

However, administrators have an important political tool available to use in these negotiations: namely, *chain-of-command protocols* requiring teachers, citizens, and outside experts to obtain permission through the district hierarchy to communicate with teachers and other subordinates. We have found that it is often difficult for an outsider to talk directly with a classroom teacher without first securing permission from appropriate administrators at several levels of the hierarchy (Corwin & Dentler, 1984). One explanation is simply that the chain of command facilitates coordination by channeling information to the appropriate echelons where decisions will be made. But it seems that these protocols are adhered to even when central offices are not where the decisions will be made or even the most effective points of contact.

Instead, we suggest that protocols have other, more important functions, not the least of which is to solidify administrative control. Administrators have reason to be concerned about any independent action taken by a teacher that might inadvertently set precedent for which the administration will be held responsible. A closely related function is to insulate teachers from external pressures by restricting the public's access to them, which in turn minimizes the opportunities for teachers to develop constituencies. Still another function of the protocols of hierarchy is to preserve certain myths about authority in school districts. One myth is that administrators control the educational process. Another is that they are instructional leaders. In helping to maintain the appearance of administrative control, then, protocols serve as strategies in the dialectic between centralization and decentralization.

School Autonomy or Constraint?

If decentralization is a product of ongoing negotiations, then how significant is the autonomy so often attributed to schools? Lortie (1969) says that schools sometimes exhibit a remarkable degree of autonomy from the central administration, which he traces to a unique "cellular" pattern of growth that originated with the single classroom and evolved in a "bottom up" pattern. As one example, Corwin and Dentler (1984) interviewed a curriculum coordinator in a small school district who was able to secure the cooperation of only one of four principals in the district about having the faculties participate in a series of workshops. The other three principals refused to sponsor the workshops, notwithstanding the fact that the central administration backed the curriculum coordinator's program.

However, autonomy is a variable. Whereas schools sometimes seem to have a lot of autonomy, they also seem severely constrained in many important ways. Their discretion is necessarily circumscribed by school district policies ratified by school boards, and moreover their priorities must be hammered out through negotiations with constituencies (e.g., see Rogers, 1968). To understand the role of organizational autonomy in school districts, it must be recognized that organizational autonomy is not merely a historical product of the unique circumstances of American education; it is also a predictable outcome of organizational principles. School districts are not substantially different from many other complex systems.

They are made up of federations of schools, which in turn represent federations of classrooms. The *rational* basis for school-level autonomy is rooted in the work ideology that technical aspects of work are best served by providing latitude to the technical subunit responsible for instruction (Thompson, 1967). The *political* basis for school autonomy is implicit in the view of organizations once proposed by Barnard (1938): "All complex organizations are built up of 'working' or 'basic' organizations overlaid with units of autonomy" (p. 113).

Autonomy represents an accommodation to systematic variations in the degree to which different units of an organization depend on one another. Thus, school-level autonomy fluctuates widely from school to school, issue to issue, and time to time. At best, school autonomy is fluid and tenuous. Although some delegation is required in large school districts, the amount and type of delegation also depend in large part upon very volatile, personal relationships between principals and central offices (Sarason, 1971). Unlike teachers, principals are not usually unionized, and the concessions they gain are not secured by contracts. Principals' personal willingness to challenge protocols, their ability to cultivate personal constituencies, and their initiative and idiosyncratic relationships with the central office are at best shaky bases on which to build a strong case for the ubiquity of school autonomy (Gross & Herriott, 1965; Morris, Crowson, Hurwitz, & Porter-Gehrie, 1981; Sarason, 1971).

Bureaucracy or Loosely Coupled System?

Some scholars think of the tensions between centralization and decentralization as byproducts of more basic differences between what are sometimes regarded as two types of organization called *bureaucracy* and *loosely coupled system*. It seems that schools and school districts have some of the characteristics of bureaucracy—hierarchy, division of labor, formal rules, supervision, and the like—but they are not "really" bureaucracies. They are, say these authorities, loosely coupled systems (Bidwell, 1965; Weick, 1976). Indeed, Pellegrin (1976) believes that the image of schools as bureaucracies has been so grossly exaggerated as to obscure their "structural looseness" and the "undifferentiated" cellular structure of classrooms within schools (see also Lortie, 1977). With many other writers Pellegrin subscribes to the conclusion that schools can be more accurately viewed as loosely coupled systems than as bureaucracies. The misplaced reverence sometimes displayed toward this notion is reflected in the comment made by Abramowitz and Tenenbaum (1977):

Thus, although school policies that avoid direct control and coordination seem insufficient at first blush, these *new* [italics added] theorists [i.e., the "loose coupling" theorists] suggest an interesting twist: The looseness affords a vitality and organizational flexibility that allows schools to better serve the changing needs of their diverse clientele. (p. 38–39)

However, the idea that certain patterns of organizational structure promote flexibility is *not* new (Corwin, 1981; Gouldner, 1959). Nor is it accurate to think of school districts and schools merely as loosely coupled systems. Schools can and do assume many different patterns (Firestone & Herriott, 1982). Some resemble bureaucracies more than others do. Indeed, it would be preposterous to contend that school districts are not organized as bureaucratic hierarchies having a division of labor, rules and supervision, records, career and tenure, and related properties.

There has been some confusion over the term *loose coupling* because it has been used in at least two different ways, by social psychologists and by sociologists. From an individualistic, sociopsychological perspective, loose coupling refers to inconsistent and vaguely defined preferences of individuals. The decision process is central in this usage of the term. Decisions are regarded as the product of cognitive processes individuals use to cope with ambiguity (Cohen, March, & Olson, 1972; Weick, 1976). However, within the sociological tradition the stress usually has been on relationships among component parts of a natural social system. A natural system is one in which goals are ambiguous, hierarchies of authority are not closely integrated, technologies are unclear, participation is fluid, and organizational units are partially autonomous from their social environments. These relationships are products of both conflict and impersonal evolutionary accommodations (see Corwin, 1981, 1983).

We propose that the crude distinction between bureaucracy and loosely coupled systems has not been useful, and in fact it has been misleading. The popularity of the loose coupling imagery can be explained as a misunderstanding of an overreaction to Weber's model of bureaucracy. A bureaucracy is a means of organizing *administration*; it was not intended to be applied to all aspects of an organization. Moreover, the ideal type is by definition an extreme, polar type of administrative organization not intended to be representative of most actual organizations. The bureaucratic model has been and continues to be useful to the extent that it suggests important *variables*. The model can be likened to a yardstick. The objective is to compare the relative differences between two or more organizations. Criticizing the ideal type because it does not precisely comply with a given school district is as

ridiculous as criticizing a yardstick for being too short or too long. Of course, the bureaucratic model is not sufficient in itself, but the alternative to both the bureaucratic model and the loose coupling imagery already exists. It is the *complex organization* model that has been in the social-science literature for decades. Complex organizations are composites of bureaucratic, professional, and political variables (see Corwin, 1973; 1975a). This model, which is fully applicable to schools, can easily accommodate notions as diverse as bureaucracy, informal organization, and loosely coupled systems.

We acknowledge that schools have some unique characteristics, but that does not mean they operate on idiosyncratic laws that can be explained only with a specially contrived model. On the contrary, we would expect, for example, that subunit autonomy and decentralization are functions of variables such as organizational size, division of labor, professionalization and specialization, technology, supervision patterns, environments, organizational demography, and the like. However, a circle of scholars in education seems to operate on the opposite premise, which is unfortunate if true, because it will tend to divorce the literature on educational organizations from the mainstream of organization theory.

Summary

The tensions between school district administration and schools are products of a complex balance of power. On one side of the equation, administrators' responsibilities sometimes have become separated from administrators' ability to control the conditions necessary to fulfill those responsibilities. Administrative control is constrained not only by the need to delegate certain decisions but also because subordinate units can independently exert influence over spheres that are still the official responsibility of administrators. On the other side of this equation, however, it must be recognized that schools are also constrained not only by school district policy but also by variable and often limited capacities of principals to protect the independence of their schools. Ultimately, the relationships between schools and central administration are products of negotiation. The hierarchy is an important political tool in these relationships, for in addition to being a rational means of coordination it helps administrators protect their ability to control, and it helps shield teachers from pressures exerted by their constituencies.

THE DILEMMA OF TEACHER AUTONOMY

Three dilemmas can be included under this heading:

1. *The Dilemma of Teacher Discretion.* This dilemma refers to the apparent contradiction between the subordinate status teachers occupy within the formal hierarchy and the discretion available to them in classrooms.

2. *The Dilemma of Subordination.* This dilemma refers to the inconsistencies in teachers' power as subordinates in the hierarchy compared to their collective power as members of a teacher organization.

3. *The Dilemma of Collective Power.* This dilemma refers to the sacrifice that teachers sometimes must incur in their personal discretion in order to achieve collective power.

The inconsistencies among their positions helps explain why teachers have been variously portrayed as minor functionaries, autonomous directors of classroom activities, and influential decision makers. Undoubtedly, the autonomy and influence of teachers varies considerably within and among schools and school districts. In addition, the way one thinks of teachers depends on whether one is considering their personal discretion within classrooms, their authority within a school, or their collective power within a school district.

After examining the literature, Lortie (1969) concluded that the central problem school administrators must resolve is how to achieve an optimal balance between control and autonomy. Their solution, he said, was to grant teachers a high degree of autonomy in some spheres but to constrain them in others. Thus, although administrators dominate administrative matters, they have relinquished control to teachers in instructional areas, except at points of possible trouble. However, this answer is not entirely adequate. In the first place, the distinction between "instructional" and "administrative" decisions is itself subject to dispute. Moreover, Lortie did not consider how personal discretion within classrooms might be related to either teachers' personal or collective influence.

Administrative Control or Support?

After examining the literature on managerial relationships in schools, Firestone and Wilson (1985) concluded that there is evidence suggesting principals can contribute to instruction either through control or by giving support. However, existing theory suggests that it is difficult to use both tactics at once (Mintzberg, 1983). Bossert, Dwyer, Rowan, and Lee (1982) identify several types of decisions that are controlled by the principal and that can shape instruction, and Wellisch, MacQueen, Carriere, and Duck (1978) concluded from their study that students learn more when principals communicate their strong views about the importance of instruction, take responsibility for decisions, and

actively coordinate the instructional program. However, Firestone and Wilson (1985) also cite Rosenholtz (1985), who suggests that the principal's influence is due not to control but to supportive actions, such as the following:

> providing opportunities for learning new skills and refining old ones;
>
> protecting teachers from outside interference and wasted time by providing clerical support, reducing paper work, and keeping announcements and other classroom interruptions to a minimum;
>
> and setting and maintaining clear expectations about student behavior to provide the kind of climate that is conducive to learning.

Data analyzed by Firestone and Wilson from 107 schools indicate that principal support contributes positively to student learning outcomes and that the measure of control was inversely related to learning. A path model revealed that support was positively associated with teaching quality, which in turn contributes to student learning. Control modestly but directly reduced both the amount of support in the school and the amount of student learning. The ability of principals to provide support was constrained by the socioeconomic status of the students and by the level of the school. There was more support in higher SES elementary schools than in lower SES high schools.

Administrative Control or Autonomy?

Pellegrin (1976) is among those who have chosen to emphasize the autonomy teachers have gained over instructional decisions within classrooms. They decisively control the scheduling of classroom activities, homework assignments, grading, pupil promotion, choices regarding teaching methods, grouping practices, scope and sequencing of subject matter, content, supplementary materials, and the like. Huberman (1983) shares this view, noting:

> The key to understanding the situation is the realization that in classroom-related matters teachers have great power regardless of their lack of legal organizational authority. Our empirical evidence indicates that the teacher plays a highly significant role in decisions precisely at the critical junction where teaching and learning takes place—in the instructional situation. (p. 479)

Moreover, it is clear that teachers are not closely inspected by administrators (Abramowitz & Tenenbaum, 1978; Dornbusch & Scott, 1975; Meyer, Cohen, Brunetti, Molnar, & Lueders-Salmon, 1971; Meyer & Rowan, 1978). Surveillance is impeded by the sheer complexity of school districts, by self-contained classrooms, by the ambiguities of teaching and disputes about which outcomes to measure, by contracts with teacher organizations, and by professional ideologies (Corwin, 1965; Kerchner, 1984; Miles, 1975).

But personal autonomy within classrooms is only one part of a larger equation. From other writers we learn that teachers have little voice in the most fundamental policies pertaining to school districts and schoolwide practices, such as attendance requirements; discipline policies; assignments of students to schools, classes, and ability groups; the processes of credentialing teachers; and codifying knowledge in the forms of courses, programs, credit hours, and required textbooks (Corwin, 1965; Hammersley, 1977; McNeil, 1982). Such policies are dictated by state law, tradition, local school boards, and district administrators, with little input from teachers. Although some of these areas have been subjected to collective bargaining in recent years, teachers do not yet control the most important parameters of education or of their work.

Wayland (1964) once identified various ways in which teachers' discretion is restricted, including (a) rules (e.g., governing discipline procedures, field trips, etc.); (b) standard lesson plans and curriculum guides; (c) the use of standardized tests; (d) common textbooks; (e) periodic evaluations based on specific hiring and promotion and dismissal criteria; (f) institutional patterns, such as age-grading based on annual promotions and uniform grading policies; (g) gossip, feedback, and pressure from students, parents, and other teachers about assignments and achievement levels; (h) school-specific traditions and ideologies (e.g., about whether teachers should "teach to the test," how much experimentation is permissible in classrooms, the appropriateness of corporal punishment, and whether it is permissible to assign controversial books). In addition, Meyer and Rowan (1978) maintain that social control over teachers is assured by their conformity to widely shared societal values. Still other constraints include union contracts; student resistance (McNeil, 1982; Metz, 1978; Waller, 1932); compulsory attendance (Packard, Charters, & Duckworth, 1978; Willower, 1970); students' abilities (Barr & Dreeben, 1983); rigid and busy teaching schedules; state laws governing the curriculum; shortages of supplies and equipment; and time-consuming, detailed record keeping (Cusick, 1973).

The problem of assessing teachers' power is compounded by three types of issues: (a) whether teachers have as much control over classrooms as some writers have contended; (b) whether teacher autonomy necessarily leads to power; and (c) whether collective power necessarily enhances personal autonomy.

Discretion or Routinization?

One issue is whether teachers really do control classroom processes to the extent some observers believe. With the evolution of large school districts, administrators assumed responsibility for conceptualizing policies governing teachers' work, and teachers took responsibility for the execution of those policies. Teachers' work, like that of their counterparts in industry, became simplified, fragmented into distinct tasks (such as lessons), and routinized (see Braverman, 1974). As McNeil (1983) says, the teachers' main job is to facilitate the curriculum, not to question its premises. But, more important for this discussion is the fact that the control of work has shifted even from the administration to the work process itself. Demands on teachers are no longer defined exclusively by higher authorities because the job is embedded in school technologies such as pacing and sequencing of subject matter, precise schedules, and standardized tests, all of which make it difficult for either teachers or administrators to affect the parameters of work (see Gitlin, 1983). This is not to say that teachers have no influence on their classrooms. Indeed, as the case studies at the beginning of this chapter suggest, teachers can effectively combat policies they don't like and they can effect instructional decisions. But perhaps the amount and significance of the teacher's discretion has been overestimated. In any event, routinization places definite limits on the amount of control that administrators can exercise over the work process.

Autonomy or Power?

In discussions about the discretion of teachers, autonomy has sometimes been confused with power. Lortie (1969) describes the relationship between power and autonomy succinctly: "Succeeding layers of administration may narrow the range of goal selections possible at the teacher level, but persons at that level may be free to choose among the goals that remain" (pp. 12–13). Autonomy refers to the goals that remain as well as the means to effect those goals. But power is the ability to establish the goals and to effect the means of achieving them.

How important are the decisions that remain to be made by classroom teachers? In view of the highly ubiquitous constraints, it would seem that there are few important policy options that teachers can control within their classrooms. They can perhaps determine when to administer a standardized test, but the decision that it will be administered has already been made at a higher level. It appears that the autonomy of teachers within their classrooms is inversely correlated with their influence over schoolwide and districtwide policies. They have purchased discretion within the classroom by relinquishing their opportunity to influence policy at higher levels. Of course as already noted, it is still possible that within these narrow limits the instructional decisions teachers do control—such as time allocations, pacing, and grouping—can have important consequences for student learning outcomes.

Individuals or Collectivity?

To the distinctions we have made between discretion and routinization on the one hand and between autonomy and power on the other we must add another: the difference between teachers acting as individuals and acting collectively. These three dimensions produce several types of power and autonomy, including individual autonomy, individual power, collective autonomy, and collective power. An *individual's discretion* represents one extreme, which can be compared with *collective power* at the other extreme. It appears that collective power (in the form of collective bargaining agreements) has reduced the autonomy of individual teachers. Kerchner (1984) found that during the evolution of union-management relations teachers came to perceive their work as more rationalized and structured than they did in the earlier stages of labor relations. As Braverman (1974) has noted for other occupations, with bureaucratization teaching begins to lose autonomy, and the teacher's work becomes less flexible and more rigidly preplanned and closely inspected. Collective power accentuates this trend. In effect, Kerchner concludes, teaching has become less like a profession or an art and more like *labor*. This tradeoff between the autonomy of individual teachers on the one hand and their collective power on the other was also observed by Pellegrin (1970). He found that teachers who had formed teaching teams were exercising more influence, but the *locus* of authority had shifted from teachers acting individually to teachers as a *group* who, as committees, made decisions that affected other teachers. He concluded that this increase in the authority of the collegial group in effect reduced the discretion available to individual teachers as well as reducing the authority of the principal and school district officials.

Solidarity or Segmentation?

On the one hand teacher organizations are large and potentially very powerful. The National Educational Association (NEA) is one of the largest labor organizations in the world. Moreover, the occupation as a whole has been growing more militant with each passing decade. The percentage of teachers believing it is right for teachers to strike rose sharply during the 1960s. By 1970, nine out of 10 teachers supported some type of group action, and three out of four believed that at least in some circumstances teachers should strike (Corwin, 1975b). In addition, teachers in the mid-1980s overwhelmingly support political activity. A survey in 1957 revealed that the majority of teachers at that time thought it inappropriate to attempt to persuade others to vote for the political candidate of the teacher's choice, serve as party precinct workers, conduct partisan elections, or give political speeches. By 1968, most teachers favored campaign work.

More important, during the last two decades teacher organizations have become very active politically. Many NEA state affiliates have developed political arms, and in some cases teachers have been asked to donate substantial sums for the purpose of lobbying. Some observers claim that teacher support has been an important factor in several congressional, state legislative, and gubernatorial races. Moreover, a number of studies over the years have pointed to the distinct possibility that teacher militancy is ultimately targeted at controlling educational *policy* (Corwin, 1970; Goldschmidt, Bowers, Riley, & Leland, 1983; Kerchner, 1984). Teachers have bargained for textbooks, discipline practices, new courses, and special programs.

Nevertheless, teacher unions do not yet control educational policy, and as a general practice it is not clear that they are prepared to exercise this type of leadership. Notwithstanding the collective power of teacher organizations, high school principals in Abramowitz and Tenenbaum's (1978) survey said that teacher organizations as a distinct entity rarely participate in decisions on any of the issues considered. Their professional associations are not a primary source of new information for teachers in comparison to other sources. Conventions and professional-association meetings were mentioned by teachers as relatively infrequent sources of knowledge in a survey conducted by Hood and Blackwell (1976). Considering the amount of resources the NEA devotes to collective-bargaining activities, one must conclude that instructional leadership is not one of the NEA's major priorities. More than a decade ago the NEA disbanded the unit primarily responsible for teacher preparation and standards, apparently in order to concentrate more of its resources on wage negotiations.

One obstacle to more effective united action, already discussed, is the autonomy of schools. Kerchner's (1984) study of three school districts revealed that teachers engage in local bargaining with their principals in such a way as to compromise contract provisions; consequently, schools operating under the same contract varied greatly in the way it was implemented. For example, all contracts specified the length of the work day; one principal monitored the times that teachers arrived at school by walking through the teachers' parking lot at the contractually stated hour, but another intervened "only if somebody's late all the time," and another enforced the rule differentially, ignoring occasional infractions by those who sometimes arrived before 7:00 A.M. to make up for being late on other occasions.

Fragmentation of the occupation as a whole is still another source of weakness, for even while teacher *organizations* have grown more powerful, the *occupation* of teaching in the United States has remained highly segmented. Consequently, many individual teachers seem relatively content with things as they are, whereas others want more authority. In 1970, Corwin estimated that only 15 percent of high school teachers in a midwestern sample were "militant professionals"; that is, *both* professionally oriented and involved in disputes with the administration. The majority thought they should be prepared to adjust their teaching to the administration's views of good educational practice, and approximately half of them believed that teachers who are openly critical of the administration should be encouraged to leave. Although these figures may have changed, in some specifics the acceptance of the status quo among many rank-and-file teachers continues to restrain the militant leadership of teacher organizations from being more assertive about policy issues. For example, the NEA has lagged in taking an assertive leadership position with respect to school integration, partially to avoid alienating conservative local affiliates.

The occupation is divided along several other dimensions as well, including the following:

1. The extent of segmentation within the profession is reflected in the more than three dozen departments and organizations affiliated with the NEA and in numerous other organizations for school administrators. In addition, there are approximately two dozen independent associations and councils explicitly dealing with specialized problems in teaching (Corwin, 1975b).

2. There are fundamental differences between elementary, junior high, and secondary schools in their norms, division of labor, communication patterns, and authority structures (Firestone, Herriott, & Wilson, 1983). Firestone and Wilson (1983) concluded that goal consensus and communication are lower in high schools than in elementary schools. It seems to us that these differences in working conditions virtually preclude any significant communication among teachers across school level. Elementary and secondary teachers seldom meet together within school districts, seldom attend the same meetings, and don't read the same professional literature (Corwin & Dentler, 1984). Although

undoubtedly schools vary in this regard (Packard et al., 1978), fewer than one in five principals included in a survey of schools in the San Francisco area had observed daily working relationships between teachers of different grade levels, and most said that teachers in the same grade level did not communicate on a daily basis (Meyer & Rowan, 1978, p. 84).

3. Teachers are further divided on the basis of subject matter taught, their specialized training, and their experience. There are nearly 100 publications in education. The influence of a journal tends to be limited to a particular audience.

It can be concluded that although teacher organizations have amassed considerable influence, various categories of teachers do not talk frequently among themselves about their craft or even share the same information. Those in different categories seem not to associate, attend different meetings, and read different journals. These cleavages weaken their collective power. In this respect teachers appear to be no different from physicians and other specialized professionals. The similarities suggest that diversity is an inherent feature of modern organizations, not easily overcome. Later in the chapter we shall suggest that different staffing patterns might help to promote solidarity.

Cooperation, Isolation, or Competition?

As a result of the inviolate status of the classroom, teachers are very much alone in their work (Goodlad, Klein, & Associates, 1970, p. 94). They seem reluctant to trade off their personal autonomy for collective goals, and moreover they are highly competitive in certain areas. Consequently, even if instruction were regarded philosophically as a cooperative venture, the coordination of instruction is problematic. One way coordination can be achieved is for teachers to arrive at a consensus among themselves about how to work together. However, it seems that teachers are not inclined to cooperate within formally structured settings such as in team-teaching arrangements. Research on team teaching only reinforces how much teachers value their autonomy (see Cohen, 1981). "The privatization of teachers," as Lortie (1975) calls it, is also a major obstacle to teaming. From years of isolation in classrooms, observe Packard et al. (1978), teachers have evolved a "basic rule"—only one teacher will supervise a given student in a designated subject area at a time. Belonging to a teaching team requires the individual to give up ownership and control over domains that once were exclusively his or hers (Wolcott, 1973). When teams do function, they tend to focus on administration rather than instruction. Few teams in the research reviewed by Cohen (1981) discussed instruction; most met together to plan, schedule, and coordinate their activities.

In a system where personal autonomy is so highly valued, it can be expected that competition and jurisdictional disputes will abound. There is probably no greater blow to a teacher's status than when another teacher violates implicit agreements about "territorial rights." Encroaching can occur in various ways—principals interrupting classes, teachers covering content belonging to a related course, or a teacher assigning too much homework. Corwin (1970) once published an account of routine disputes reported in a sample of over 300 teachers in 28 high schools in three midwestern states. We have no reason to believe that the issues revealed have become irrelevant today. Several colleagues in that study expressed concern because a teacher was assigning so much homework their students missed class to work on his assignments, and one coach became especially irritated when his athletes began to skip practice to work on this teacher's courses. Taking students out of class was an even more frequent source of controversy, because when one teacher is able to take students out of another's class, it reflects on the relative status of the two teachers. One teacher said, "That teacher just detained her, a student, to clean up the room. . . She was assuming that her work was more important than my class." Some teachers developed effective defensive strategies to protect themselves from class disruptions. One proudly reported that she assigned homework to any student who missed her class for an extracurricular activity.

A teacher summed up very succinctly a major source of tension: "I don't care what department it is, they all want the good students." Teachers used a variety of ideologies to justify their competition for desirable students, including the utility of certain courses, the difficulty of teaching less desirable students, the stigma of teaching low-achieving students, and the advantages of specializing with students having different ability levels. They also devised a number of strategies to help them grab the students they wanted. They competed to have their courses required or scheduled at a desirable hour, tried to impose difficult course prerequisites and entrance requirements, and pressured counselors to steer better students into their courses (or at least refrain from advising students not to take their courses). Many advocated rules to regulate the competition for students, such as a policy that would distribute less desirable students equally among all teachers instead of assigning them to a few courses. In a suburban high school observed by Finley (1984) teachers did adopt such a policy, agreeing to share the chore of teaching remedial classes. However,

dissension arose when some of the teachers found ways to avoid the responsibility. Some created new courses that, by virtue of the content and the way they were advertised, attracted only the desirable students. Others encouraged undesirable students to transfer out of their courses. Still others failed many remedial students and gained a reputation of being hard on low achievers, which discouraged them from enrolling. Finley concluded that this competition among teachers for high-status students in essence is what shaped the tracking system, not teachers' concerns for helping the students.

Thus, again we find a mixed picture. On the one hand, as we have said, as the curriculum has become more rationalized, teachers have lost some of their control over the classroom. But on the other hand, even rational plans for instruction are in practice negotiated among teachers with different philosophies, specialties, and constituencies of students and citizens. Inundated with a host of demanding responsibilities and operating within the constraints of rigid schedules, vague goals, and a structured curriculum, teachers have come to prize the few degrees of freedom still available to them. This is an occupation where the major parameters of work have been decided by others, but the remaining autonomy provides a buffer against colleagues as well as against the administration. Teachers use their discretion defensively to temper the rules, to establish their own priorities and specialties, to obtain small concessions from the administration, and to jockey with fellow teachers for a slight competitive edge. Thus, the technology of teaching may require teachers to share students and to take collective responsibility for the outcomes, but teachers nonetheless have the means to vie for the good students. Some teachers gain virtual monopolies over the most desirable students, others being left with the least desirable ones.

According to McNeil (1982), in order to overcome pervasive administrative restraints, teachers also have learned to teach defensively, sometimes by simplifying assignments and reducing requirements, at other times by increasing them. Such teaching strategies are rooted less in theories of learning than in the need to satisfy the requirements of the system—to cover material on time, to get students successfully through exams, and to maintain order. Teachers simplify and omit material, gloss over controversial subjects, and fragment lessons into definitive lists of facts.

Rational Division of Labor or Idiosyncratic Specialization?

Another way to achieve coordination—in addition to cooperation—is by creating a rational division of labor, or what Durkheim (1893/1960) referred to as contractual forms of cooperation. He postulated that while the division of labor erodes consensus, it somehow promotes another form of solidarity based on functional interdependence. He was vague about how this occurs, however, and there is some evidence (Corwin & Herriott, 1986) that in fact it might not occur in quite the way he predicted it would. In any event, the formal division of labor in schools is minimal. It is based on the content and level of difficulty of subject matter, teacher certification and specialized training, age and ability of students, and classroom designations. Within these broad parameters, the formal structure of schools is not highly differentiated. Formal staffing patterns are generally very simple. Indeed, job descriptions would suggest that all teachers perform essentially the same duties (Pellegrin, 1976). Nearly one half of the high schools have only one specialist or counselor, and 40 percent have fewer than nine subject-matter departments (Abramowitz & Tenenbaum, 1978).

But, putting the formal structure aside for the moment, in practice teachers have informally absorbed a host of unspecified and vaguely defined responsibilities that are only occasionally recognized as part of their official assignments. Their formal roles do not reflect the actual diversity of their responsibilities. Nor are there usually clear policy goals and rules (Miles, 1975) establishing priorities among competing demands upon the teacher's time. In the absence of clear policy goals and rules (Miles, 1975), teachers are forced to establish their own priorities among competing demands upon their time. In the words of one teacher, "Time is the worst enemy of the public schools" (Corwin & Dentler, 1984, p. 241). Teachers complain that they are bombarded with all sorts of new materials and in-service programs they do not have time even to consider. With multiple preparations, and often taking work home, their priorities are shaped by the press of immediate demands on their time.

From this situation an "idiosyncratic" division of labor seems to have evolved, which fluctuates widely within and among school districts (Pellegrin, 1976). With the important exception of instruction, the teacher's work has not been fully rationalized. A task to which one teacher devotes considerable time and energy will be virtually ignored by another teacher with essentially the same official status in the school. There is little agreement as to what the main dimensions of the teaching job are, the importance of a given task, or the amount of time that should be devoted to it. It is Pellegrin's belief that schools employ persons to perform a variety of general and amorphous duties, and as now organized, the typical school system does not operate to insure that all these functions will be performed. Instead, teachers do what they feel they can do or should do, based on the knowledge, objectives, and interests of each individual rather than organizationally or professionally planned and prescribed job descriptions. Consequently, idiosyncratic specialization cannot take advantage of the coordination potentials that Durkheim (1893/1960) saw in a more formalized role structure. Moreover, these idiosyncratic specialties do not have counterparts in the structure of professional associations, and consequently there are few formal channels to facilitate communication among such specialists.

Summary

As in the case of the relationship between schools and the central administration, the balance of power between teachers and local education agencies fluctuates tenuously. On the one hand, administrators must share their authority with teachers. Teachers are not closely supervised, and they can exercise discretion within their classrooms over crucial instructional decisions. This discretion also gives them the opportunity to resist administrative initiatives, the leverage to compete among themselves for status and resources, and the capacity to teach defensively in order to circumvent certain types of administrative restraints. This autonomy necessarily places limits on administrative control. Moreover, the same traditions and organizational patterns, the routinization of classwork, and other forces that constrain teachers also limit the options available to administrators. And of course, in addition to their personal discretion, teachers can collectively exercise influence over some policy areas through collective bargaining. Unions and labor contracts impose further limitations on the power of administrators.

Nonetheless, we do not wish to overstate the case. In the final analysis, teachers are subordinate employees of school districts subject to districtwide and schoolwide policies, rules, and procedures. Hence, their autonomy is never absolute but always subject to negotiation. Indeed, as a group they seem to have purchased some of their autonomy at the price of exercising even more authoritative control over school district policy than they have thus far achieved. Their collective power probably has been further weakened by role overload, by their preference for isolation, by fragmentation into recognized and implicit specialties and into grade levels, and by interpersonal competition and jurisdictional disputes. Thus, although their autonomy and collective power are significant, neither has altered their basic status as subordinate employees.

THE DILEMMA OF OCCUPATIONAL STATUS

In the preceding section, the discussions were focused on the position of teachers within school districts. The same themes will be pursued under this heading, except that we shall now take more systematically into account the normative characteristics of the occupation as a whole. We shall argue that although some teachers subscribe to norms that would impose further impediments to administrative control, these norms are muted by other, more pervasive norms that have the opposite effect and thus facilitate administrative control. The dilemma involved is a product of the contradictions between professional and employee roles. Teachers subscribe to professional norms. Professional norms can reinforce teacher autonomy in ways that were already discussed, and to that extent they will sometimes tend to act as a constraint on administrative control. At the same time, teachers are subordinate employees, and thus expected to obey administrative superiors and to comply with organizational rules.

Profession or Labor?

A profession is a work group that has acquired a legal monopoly over expertise associated with an abstract body of knowledge. It can police members and control licensing standards. And it endorses independent occupational norms that may be in conflict with certain policies and practices of the work organizations that employ members of the profession.

The occupation of teaching is partially professionalized. A license is required, and there are a substantive body of knowledge and formal training programs. Moreover, some teachers subscribe to norms that require them to exercise independent judgment about matters that may be controlled by administrative policies. As professionals, teachers must support standards endorsed by the occupation as a whole, and they must exercise independent judgment on behalf of the welfare of their students. To Seeley and Schwartz (1981) these contradictions between bureaucracy and profession are absolute: "Bureaucracy and professionalism are like oil and water; they don't mix" (p. 63). They see a dilemma in the fact that teachers are at the bottom of the bureaucracy even though teaching is the "heart of the process."

Professional ideologies do survive in large, bureaucratized school districts, and there is evidence that professional and bureaucratic principles of organization are incompatible in many respects (Corwin, 1970; Darkenwald, 1971). Consequently, bureaucratization has been problematic for many teachers. There is a body of research suggesting that interpersonal conflict

in schools increases with organizational size, hierarchy, division of labor, close supervision and rule enforcement (Beck & Betz, 1975; Corwin, 1969; Corwin & Herriott, 1986). Moreover, some research supports the notion that in the most bureaucratic schools conflict becomes accentuated when teachers espouse professional ideologies (Corwin, 1970).

However, teaching is not a "fullfledged" profession, because the occupation has been shaped by a strong tradition of local, lay control over education and the growth of complex school districts (see Pellegrin, 1976; Simpson, 1969). As employees of bureaucracies, teachers are servants of the public, principals, and school boards. They do not yet have major policy-making roles. Moreover, in his remarkable account of the history of public education in the United States, Curti (1959) documents the submissiveness of leading educators to various groups that have dominated each era and the vocation's willing complicity in its low stature. A profession requires an effective technology controlled by members of the occupations. Although teachers have developed a few relatively effective techniques for maintaining classroom control, motivating some children, and conveying certain types of information, the technologies are not codified or highly rationalized (Dreeben, 1970; Lortie, 1969, p. 9), and the consequences of most alternative teaching methods remain ambiguous and immeasurable (Miles, 1975). Moreover, there is only a modest degree of specialization among teachers (Corwin, 1975b). Teaching is still carried on primarily according to traditional practices, accumulative experience, and craft wisdom. Some observers describe teaching as an art, labor, or a craft (Kerchner, 1984). A firm foundation of knowledge and technology would provide teachers with a powerful defense against administrative control. But without it, they remain highly vulnerable, notwithstanding the way individual teachers may think of themselves.

Service or Survival?

Teaching in the public schools is a public service, and teachers seem to espouse service ideologies. Nevertheless, many of the norms and beliefs subscribed to by teachers more closely resemble self-interested, profit-making occupations, manual labor, and clerical work than one would associate with a service-oriented profession. Some of the norms often mentioned in the literature are outlined below.

Service
Lortie (1975) maintains that the traditions of teaching have emphasized the service ideal so much that teachers have become suspicious of money, prestige,

power, and other extrinsic rewards. Moreover, those who are personally ambitious for recognition and money may be frowned upon by their colleagues, and they eventually leave teaching. But to compensate for a rudimentary career ladder, he concludes, teachers emphasize various kinds of intrinsic, "psychic" rewards derived from the work itself, especially relationships with students (Spuck, 1974).

However, the importance teachers attach to psychic rewards has been disputed. The research of Chapman and Lowther (1982), for example, does not support the thesis that teachers derive their primary satisfactions from their relationships with students or from the work itself. Mann (1976, p. 329) observes that feedback from pupils is not of equal importance to elementary and secondary teachers because of the latter's segmental interaction with pupils, and more generally Miles (1975) notes that Lortie's data do not indicate whether teachers are *actually* rewarded by student learning. In this regard Chapman and Lowther (1982) and Silver (1973) found that teachers' relationships with peers and administrators, leadership opportunities, classroom autonomy, and participation in running the school were more highly related to their job satisfaction than was the quality of students' work. Aside from the question of psychic rewards, one must ask if teachers do not give priority to students, then are they disinclined to challenge administrative policies and practices or materials that could prove harmful to particular students?

Pragmatism and Experience

Somewhat in contrast to the portrait of service and idealism sometimes painted for teaching, other writers portray the subculture as being pragmatic and practice oriented. Teachers are known to be very receptive to practical tips, techniques, guides, lists, and other operational measures that can be immediately applied in the classroom, but they seem less concerned about understanding the underlying concepts and reasons why certain things work and others do not (Corwin & Dentler, 1984). As Huberman (1983) has noted, research evidence is an unlikely source of information for teacher-practitioners because the theoretical, scientific framework collides with their experience-based reality. Hargraves's (1984) account of curriculum meetings in an English middle school reinforces the conclusions reached by McNeil (1982). Most of the teachers did not value educational theory or use it as an authoritative guide for insights related to their curriculum decisions. Having rejected theory in their initial training, they continued to have little acquaintance with it, and they made little use of it in their current practice. They did not refer even to careful and detailed scholar-

ship into the very questions most central to their effort to redesign the curriculum. Hargraves concluded that neither scholarship nor other kinds of experience outside of the classroom are admissible in conversations among teachers because of the extreme emphasis they place on their personal classroom experience. Thus, this research again causes us to question the existence of overarching occupational norms that constitute a real challenge to administrative control. If such norms exist, we propose they apply to only a small, albeit influential, group of teachers.

Mutual Support and Administrative Backing

There seems to be an unwritten rule among teachers that they should never disagree with each other in front of students or parents. Public criticisms or making unfavorable comparisons about one another's courses can be regarded as "unprofessional" (Corwin, 1970). In the same vein, many observers have commented on the importance teachers attach to being supported and protected by the school administration in the face of criticism from parents and pressure groups outside the school (Becker, 1953). Corwin (1970) found teachers very critical of any principal who seemed more concerned with pleasing parents and the general public than defending the authority of teachers. The dominant ideology was expressed by one administrator, who said simply, "I always stick up for the teacher because I think this is the best for the child and the school." It seems that administrative support is part of a system of reciprocity that creates a closer bond between teachers and administrators. Again, there is little reason to suppose that occupational norms are an important source of constraint on administrative control; on the contrary, they often facilitate it.

Role Conflict or Accommodation?

On balance, then, it appears that professional and bureaucratic principles have become accommodated in a variety of ways. First, some *individual* teachers seem to be able to maintain loyalty to both bureaucratic and professional ideologies simultaneously, even though their split loyalties might involve them in more interpersonal conflicts (Corwin, 1965). Secondly, there is an implicit division among groups of teachers, with some segments emphasizing professional norms and others their employee roles (Corwin, 1965; 1970). Typically, a small leadership group spearheads collective actions; other segments of the occupation remain more compliant. Third, collective bargaining has become a vehicle for accommodating professional and employee role conflicts. The form of the accommodation depends upon which stage of the labor-relations cycle a school district is in (Kerchner, 1984). Districts still in the "meet-and-confer" stage operate on the assumption that teachers and administrators share common interests, the function of the teacher organization being primarily to communicate teachers' views on policy issues to the authorities. Not until the second generation, the "good-faith bargaining" era, does it become legitimate for teachers to try to alter their working conditions. The third stage is concerned with negotiating policy pertaining to the way schools are run; it appears that by the mid-1980s many school districts are in or are entering this stage. A study by Goldschmidt et al. (1983) indicates that recent contracts tend to place more emphasis on policy concerns. What is still problematic is how much support teacher organizations will give to professional norms. At present, professionalism remains only a potential restraint on administrative control, at best confined to a few restricted policy areas.

Summary

While professional norms constitute a potential threat to administrative control, they seem to be endorsed by only a small, although perhaps influential, group of teachers. On the whole, teachers seem compliant and more interested in pragmatic considerations. At present, professional norms seem to have accommodated to administrative constraints rather than posing a real challenge to administrative control.

THE DILEMMA OF CAREER

Stages in the teaching career are denoted by both formal recognition within the school district bureaucracy and by an informal prestige system subscribed to by members of the occupation. The dilemma of career is a consequence of teachers' making lifelong commitments to an occupation with a primitive, formal career ladder. The career ladder is truncated. The lack of promotion opportunities enormously complicates the task of rewarding teachers and providing incentives adequate to attract and retain competent people. On the one hand, the occupation is organized around principles characteristic of occupations with orderly career patterns: that is, experience and seniority, tenure, full-time employment, and formal training programs lasting 4 to 6 years. On the other hand, the career is, to use Spilerman's (1977) term, "chaotic." Teachers hold undistinguished and homogeneous formal positions, and substantial promotion opportunities are relatively limited. With the exception of narrow ranges of salary gradations based on experience and education, the occupation provides relatively few

formal career steps. Compared to some other kinds of middle-class work, there is less opportunity for movement upward into more specialized, higher paying positions or positions of higher authority, responsibility, or social prestige. Consequently, the career progression is less orderly than, for example, government civil service or even university teaching. Lortie (1975) describes the career profile of teachers as unpredictable, comparatively unstaged, and "front loaded," in that one begins at a high level relative to the ultimate earning potential.

Career or Job?

This chaotic career pattern attracts particular kinds of people and affects the vocational commitment they are willing to make, which in turn limits the options of administrators. Teaching is often considered to be a low-commitment occupation, largely because teachers still have conflicting allegiances to their families and to part-time jobs (Cusick, 1981; Lortie, 1975). Although substantial numbers of experienced teachers do remain in the occupation for much of their career, young teachers exhibit intermittent careers, high rates of turnover among school districts, and low survival rates. Studies of the demography of teachers indicate they are generally recruited from the middle class—with professional and managerial families contributing significantly more teachers than would occur by chance and working-class and manual-occupation families contributing less than would be expected by chance (Dworkin, 1980). For a period of time between 1940 and 1970, a relatively high proportion of younger teachers were recruited from blue-collar and service-work families (Betz & Garland, 1974). However, from a sample of 3,500 public school teachers in one major southwestern metropolis, Dworkin concludes that since the mid-1970s new cohorts of both black and white teachers are fully entrenched in the middle class. The new teachers from middle-class families in that study, regardless of their race, were significantly more likely to quit teaching if they perceived their assignment as undesirable, than were individuals from working-class backgrounds. The author concluded that school districts tend to develop a bifurcated faculty: one from lower occupational origins, who are not subject to high turnover rates, and a sizable faculty from higher occupational origins, who continue in their careers only a year or two.

Chapman and Hutcheson (1982) concluded that as teaching is presently organized, those teachers who value salary are progressively selected out, and those who remain are the ones oriented to the recognition and approval of family, close friends, and supervisors. Teachers in their sample who left teaching for other careers attached a high value to salary as a criterion of occupational success. For those who remained, however, recognition and approval were important precisely because salary and other extrinsic rewards are relatively fixed. Those remaining were also characterized as having greater "organizational" skills (ability to organize time, develop new approaches, plan and organize activities). Those leaving were characterized as having greater "analytic" skills (ability to analyze and evaluate and to interpret numerical data) and assigning more importance to salary increases, job challenge, and autonomy.

Good or Bad Teachers?

The quality of the teaching labor force constitutes one of the most fundamental constraints on administrative control, since we must assume that the options open to administrators are in large part a function of the quality and commitment of the teachers within a district and, more generally, within the labor pool as a whole. Certainly any effort to improve the quality of teaching must be framed within the constraints of this variable. Since teachers represent a selected segment of the population, many critics have asked how good they are. During 1983, a wave of more than 20 reports and studies of schools in the United States promoted an environment of dissatisfaction with public education seemingly of crisis proportions. The reports are critical of the quality of teachers and filled with some strong indictments of schools. One panel of distinguished Americans warns that the "educational foundations of our society are presently being eroded by a rising tide of mediocrity that threatens our very future as a nation and as a people" (National Commission on Excellence in Education, 1983). This group concluded that too few academically able students are being attracted to teaching; that teacher preparation programs need substantial improvements; and that the professional working life of teachers is, on the whole, unacceptable. The subsequent debates have produced a long list of recommendations for the reform of school curriculum and teaching practices, the time students spend in school, and ways to attract and retain competent teachers.

However, the evidence—that the problems are actually as serious as claimed—is frail, uneven, and dated (Peterson, 1983). And, in particular, the evidence regarding a favorite remedy—performance-based pay schemes used in the private sector—is mixed and inconclusive. Indeed, "merit-pay" recommendations are based on assumptions whose application to schools are at best dubious. Generally speaking, three types of recommendations have been made: (a) in-

creasing teachers' salaries across the board to make teaching more competitive with other professions; (b) tying salary increments to assessments of the merit of individual teachers; and (c) developing some type of career ladder for teachers in order to distinguish specialized responsibilities and to recognize distinctive contributions. Each type of recommendation is based on different models of how labor markets function.

The across-the-board and merit-pay plans are based on a conventional *human resource* labor market theory, which assumes that the income earned by any group of workers reflects the demand for their skills in relation to the supply. Job mobility is defined as an *individual* status attainment process. Workers compete with all other workers for the highest wage, and employers compete for desired skills by meeting the current wage rates. Pay is the mechanism responsible for attracting the most competent individuals to some jobs and allocating the less competent to others. Employees can increase their earnings only by improving their skills and performance. It follows from this perspective that to attract into and retain competent people in teaching, as in any occupation, salary levels must be made competitive with comparable occupations, and the most competent individuals must be rewarded through a mechanism, such as merit pay, that recognizes superior skill.

This model has attracted much criticism because it provides little insight into important cultural and organizational mechanisms, other than pay, that are responsible for attracting and retaining individuals in various occupations. These other factors are important because wages, and hence the supply of labor, are not controlled exclusively by impersonal economic forces of the marketplace. Pay is instead strongly influenced by the policies of large, powerful corporations and public bureaucracies (such as school districts) partially insulated from conventional economic market forces. The evolution of large-scale organizations has produced another type of labor market, an *internal* market, in which the supply and use of labor are regulated through the creation of job hierarchies and the elaboration of *rules* governing access to these jobs. Earnings are dictated by (a) workers' positions in the internal administrative structure, rather than by going wages; (b) the job, rather than the skills and abilities of the incumbent; and (c) job vacancies and other opportunities. There is no automatic relationship between one's level of personal skill and one's wages. Instead, salaries and wages are linked to job descriptions, and promotions come routinely with seniority and vacancies. As long as workers perform at or above a minimum level, their wages are more dependent on the job they hold than on exceptional performance in comparison to other workers. Rewards include many types of organizational status considerations in addition to money.

Since the early 1970s, there have appeared hundreds of articles, books, position papers, and other writings examining the idea of a career ladder as it might apply to teachers. In education, career ladders are sometimes referred to as "differentiated staffing models" (see Edelfelt, 1979, 1985). In this same spirit several special "commission reports" have recently advocated establishing career ladders. Within levels, teachers would be assigned specialized responsibilities of varying degrees of difficulty and importance. Different salaries and responsibilities would be associated with each job and with each step on the career ladder.

Writers disagree about the functions of career ladders. One view is that they provide a rational way to fix and reward responsibility on grounds that many of the skills needed by employees are acquired informally, only with experience on the job, and hence experienced workers cannot be easily replaced on the open labor market. Employers, therefore, find it necessary to create hierarchies tied to seniority in order to retain people with these intangible skills. But another view is more critical in that career ladders are seen to evolve from struggles for control over the labor process. Stone (1975) believes that employers implemented hierarchical systems of authority to compensate for the fact that traditional techniques of controlling workers had lost effectiveness. She maintains that if it were not for the need of employers to maintain discipline, some other system—perhaps based on job rotation or on the principle of workers allocating work among themselves—would have been just as rational and as effective. "Revisionist" critics of education such as Katz (1975) echo this criticism, maintaining that public school administrators have bureaucratized American schools in order to serve the interests of elites and thus to maintain the existing inequities in the society. In Katz's words, school district bureaucracy represents the "crystalization of bourgeois social attitudes" (p. xxi).

However, both apologists for and critics of career ladders seem to agree that they are important but largely untapped souces of incentives that administrators might use profitably. The number of steps in a hierarchy reflects opportunities for promotion. The existence of few promotion opportunities creates a large pool of low-level candidates who have relatively little visibility or distinction among themselves. A study of state civil service employees found that advancement in a job chain (as indicated by the proportion of managers to employees) explained retention and quit rates in several different occupations. Members of early-ceiling occupations, reaching their peak earnings and responsibilities early in their career, were more likely to change jobs because of lack of advancement, and minor differences in pay and working conditions were not enough to insure retention. Opportunity for advancement was more important than worker characteristics (Smith, 1979).

Such findings help explain the research results of Chapman and Lowther (1982), which seem to indicate the morale problems of American teachers are more closely related to what they call "internal" factors—namely, the lack of potential for personal growth, for opportunities to learn, and for leadership responsibilities—than to "external" ones such as low salaries. Teachers were predictably unhappy with their salary levels, but what they rated especially low was their prospect of achieving eventually "at the level of my potential capability." Morale problems were more closely tied to bureaucratic pressures, a negative public image, and the lack of recognition and rewards than to either relations with students or salary per se. The amount of recognition and approval teachers believed they had received from their administrators or supervisors was positively related to the career satisfaction of those who remained in teaching.

The human resource labor market, which currently dominates the teaching career pattern, has not been effective, only partially because of the low salary levels in teaching and lack of effective mechanisms for recognizing individual merit. What is more significant is that the model is simply inappropriate for an occupation that operates in the context of large-scale, complex systems like school districts. Teachers seem to be at least as responsive to wage differentials between their teaching jobs and alternative occupations as are other workers, and they are more responsive to the salaries of other occupations than to differentials among teaching jobs (Blaug, 1976). Although there may be some exceptions, the internal labor market for classroom teachers is at best rudimentary and primitive. As currently organized, teaching is an anomalous occupation straddling both internal and external labor market forces but not consistently using the principles of either model. Until more effective career ladders are developed, the teaching career will continue to be an anomaly.

Summary

We maintain that the way the labor market for teaching has been structured imposes serious impediments to administrative control. The options available to administrators for providing the kinds of incentives needed to recruit and reward good teachers have been drastically restricted because of the truncated career ladders within school districts and within the occupation as a whole. We suggest that the creation of job hierarchies within school districts would resolve more problems than would merit-pay plans because job hierarchies are more compatible with the conditions of the modern school district's organization.

THE DILEMMA OF ORDER

So far we have not said much about student-teacher relationships in classrooms. But each of the dilemmas considered to this point impinges on classrooms, and indeed, they form the basis for still other dilemmas, one of which is the dilemma of order. On the tension between keeping order in the classrooms and providing education for a diverse student population, Metz (1978) observes:

> Public schools have a dilemma at their heart. They exist to educate children, but they must also keep order. Unless the children themselves are independently dedicated to both these goals, the school will find that arrangements helpful for one may subvert the other. (p. 243)

This dilemma has implications for administrative control, for student resistance, like teacher autonomy, limits the options available to administrators. Policies must be formulated and applied consistently in order to establish order and to maintain control over students (see Gottfredson, 1985), which may be inconsistent with the policies needed to assure and reward good academic performance.

Teaching or Overcoming Resistance?

The theme of student resistance to school is prominent in recent studies of children and adolescents. Resistance becomes especially apparent as students mature and enter junior high and high school. Strategies used by students include joking, diverting discussions to peripheral topics, using covert forms of communication such as note passing and "socializing" in class, and smoking, skipping school, and other forms of defiance (Everhart, 1983). McNeil (1982, 1983) maintains that much of what teachers do in classrooms is guided by their hope of eliciting minimal levels of cooperation and overcoming waves of adversarial relationships. For example, she suggests student resistance helps explain the prevalence of lecturing. Lectures are an effective way to satisfy the goals of simplifying complex topics in a limited amount of time for skeptical students.

The ultimate form of resistance is dropping out. Nearly one-third of ninth graders nationally leave school before completing their senior year in high school (Ordorensky, 1987). Issues related to school leaving begin to crystallize during the years of junior high school. The junior high school has been the subject of two recent ethnographies. One is Everhart's (1983) study of Harold Spencer Junior High, a blue-collar, predominantly white school of about a thousand students. The other is Schofield's (1982) study of Wexler, an interracial junior high school enrolling blacks from predominantly working-class families and whites from middle-class and professional families. According to Everhart's (1983) informants, work in classrooms includes such components as having to write on paper, do assignments, memorize, do exercises and other things that teachers require. Nonwork consists of experiments, listening, art, science, watching films and the like. Work was particularly distasteful because it is passive and discourages interaction. Classrooms were punctuated by acts designed to "bug" teachers who were disliked because they enforced many trivial rules and treated students "like babies." Teachers who were not the targets of these laughing episodes, gum chewing, and pencil tapping were those who varied the curriculum and allowed students to talk among themselves. The favored teachers at Harold Spencer were similar to the "developmental" teachers in the junior high schools studied by Metz (1978). However, her developmental teachers were most successful with higher-track students who enjoyed class discussion and a lively classroom atmosphere, whereas lower-track students liked teachers who provided highly structured seatwork, kept students quiet and busy, and didn't yell.

Classroom organization at Wexler Junior High, the site of Schofield's (1982) research, was dictated by the school's mission of promoting racial integration and status equality. The school was designed to attract middle-class whites by providing an outstanding academic program, yet was also structured to provide integrated schooling. It was to serve as "a model of interracial harmony" in a district that remained racially segregated except for Wexler. As a result of the school's overall objectives, classes were racially mixed. Because of the differing backgrounds and varied academic performances of white and black students, the racial integration of classes led to uneven student outcomes in most classrooms. Teachers, however, were able to juggle class composition to accommodate their own teaching preferences. For example, teachers often grouped students within classes to make them more academically homogeneous, in spite of the fact that this practice fostered resegregation.

Teacher Tyranny or Accommodation?

Gouldner (1954) once distinguished between "authoritarian" and "representative" types of organization. In the former the manager makes decisions unilaterally, whereas in the latter subordinates have a voice. Various writers have portrayed classroom management in both ways (Willower, Eidell, & Hoy, 1973). On the one hand, many have emphasized the unilateral authority of teachers and the finality of their decisions. These writers maintain that students are at the mercy of the teacher's perceptions and values (Rosenthal & Jacobson, 1968). Waller (1932) saw traces of despotism in the teacher-student relationship, and Henry (1963) portrayed classrooms as literal tyrannies.

But are teachers so forcefully in control? Mehan (1979) maintains that while students seldom have the upper hand, they do participate in shaping the curriculum. Lessons, he says, are "mutually constitutive" events in that they are negotiated between teachers and students (see also McNeil, 1981). Metz (1978) carries the possibility another step in suggesting that teachers are forced to accommodate their teaching styles to student subcultures. There is not much tension between order and diversity in those schools where most students arrive wanting to learn what the school teaches. But in the numerous schools where this is not the case, the adults strive to prevent students from openly challenging the worth of what is being taught and the rules and routines supporting social order (Cusick, 1983). Much of what happens in school, Metz (1978) believes, can be interpreted on the basis of rival philosophies about how to cope with such tensions. She proposes a typology of student-teacher relationships in classrooms based on two dimensions: (a) whether it is presumed that teachers and students share the same goals, and (b) whether the teacher acts autonomously or shares decision-making authority with students. At the one extreme, an authoritarian teacher directs all activities in the classroom. At the other extreme, the teacher adopts a nondirective developmental approach in cooperation with the students. Through a combination of on-the-job socialization and selective migration, certain types of teachers become matched up with certain types of student bodies. From this process of working out authority relationships, idiosyncratic specializations emerge and distinctive school subcultures evolve.

The actual prevalence of the various types of teachers suggested in the typology remains to be documented, but the notion that teaching roles are shaped by student subcultures requires caution about some popular views of teaching, such as the notion that the teacher's actions inevitably produce a "self-fulfilling prophecy." This notion may attribute to teachers more influence than they have. It seems entirely possible that students are not so passive and they often thwart teachers' expectations through overt and covert resistance. The limits of the ability of teachers to control their classrooms, in turn, necessarily limit administrative control.

Adult or Childhood Values?

Indeed, in some of the recent research the image of the teacher as the dominant classroom figure has given way to another image, of classrooms dominated by the students. The impression one gets from some authors is that the truly fundamental forces of socialization are controlled by the world of childhood, not by teachers nor by administrative policy. Davies (1982) maintains that the most distinctive and important feature of the experience of children in all nations in the Western hemisphere is not social class, nationality, or even belonging to a particular age group. It is simply being a child. Access to childhood culture is gained through friendships and peer groups. Friendships can shelter a child from the traumas associated with the transition between the home and the dramatic event of attending school. Such friendships occasionally develop from groups of peers organized by teachers for instructional purposes (Borman, 1979; Bossert, 1979; Slavin, 1983). Outside the classroom, peer groups take on importance in reinforcing the rules governing childhood culture. In the context of playground games, children organize themselves most frequently into groups segregated between members of the same sex.

Davies's conclusions come from interviews with Australian school children in an effort to learn children's ideas about the meaning of friendship and the rules governing the culture of childhood. These rules, it seems, are based on children's experiences with one another during play quite apart from the supervision of adults. Several types of norms were discerned. Behaviors that were defined as wrong by one's friends (though not necessarily wrong by others) were getting the "snobs," or "cranks," teasing, lying, showing off, "getting too full of yourself," bashing people up, being "piss weak," wanting everything your way, being spoiled, being stupid, and "dobbing" (i.e., telling tales). Sticking up for friends, being tough, sharing, and being aware of each other's feelings were appropriate behaviors correlative to the inappropriate ones. Davies (1982) found that *events* have a discernible, factual quality in childhood culture. The children's arguments frequently centered on "what happened," and indicated that they believed strongly in the "facility of events" at any single point in time. But in contrast to the single truth they adhered to in explaining events, they assumed that *people* have a plastic or existential quality. For example, they observed that actions with friends that might seem inappropriate in one context may be viewed as appropriate in another. The tone of voice provided important cues to the children as to how they should respond to one another in different situations.

The children Davies studied were well aware that they must manage two sets of agendas within classrooms: their own, as defined by rules of their subculture, and those of the adults who manage schools. They firmly expected adults to take resolute lead in defining the rules governing their behavior, but what they feared was uncertainty and inconsistency in adult expectations. The author concluded that children prefer to work with those teachers who are sensitive both to the adult-child rules the children have already gone to some trouble to learn *and* to the culture of childhood.

Paralleling the studies of childhood values in elementary schools is a legacy of case studies describing adolescent subcultures in high schools. The concept of an adolescent subculture governed by the value system of a "leading crowd" has been modified considerably since Coleman's (1961) early study of adolescent social life. Coleman concluded that athletic skill (for boys) and being a cheerleader and having good looks (for girls) determined status in high school. Such characteristics as intellectual ability and interests in the arts were of little importance in the status hierarchies in the high schools Coleman examined. However, more recent studies of adolescent subcultural values and hierarchies suggest that there is considerable diversity in student groups and that although male athletes and female cheerleaders may enjoy superior status by virtue of their close alliance with administrative staffs, students as a whole are reluctant to identify these groups as opinion leaders or even as the most popular crowds in many high school settings (Cusick, 1973). Male athletes and female counterparts are still active on the scene and frequently function as they did in Coleman's schools, as liaisons between the front office and the rest of the students (Cusick, 1973; Varenne, 1983). However, other groups with their own clearly perceived identities and status in school are also prominent.

Many adolescents today seem to be reluctant to see themselves as members of a group or clique, preferring to identify themselves with a number of friends (Larkin, 1979; Varenne, 1983). One of Larkin's more articulate informants, a self-identified freak, described the natural history of crowd formation as a process of expansion and splitting. Once a clique grows larger in scope than eight members, the point where it becomes difficult to maintain face-to-face contact, it splits into smaller groups.

Studies conducted in the 1970s of three diverse high school settings, a suburban working-class school 25 miles from New York (Varenne, 1983), a semirural midwestern high school near Detroit (Cusick, 1973), and a large, elite high school in an affluent suburb of Boston (Larkin, 1979) reveal similar configurations of student cliques or crowds. In the smaller school observed by Varenne, although there were self-identified groups of jocks, freaks, drama buffs, a loose confederation of loners, the stage crew, and the audio-visual crowd, there seemed to be fluidity and interpenetration of memberships, particularly among "marginal" jocks and freaks. Of particular interest is the similarity both of group interests and of patterns of group structure across all settings. For example, in each school the freaks were students who tended to use marijuana and to display a high degree of skepticism toward the established official goals of the school. They displayed particular disdain for jocks and cheerleaders and espoused a fairly well-developed political ideology, as well as demonstrating considerable insight into their own and their peers' mores. Other groups included the time-honored jocks and their female followers, members of a music-drama clique, and in the more affluent and larger school settings, politicos and intellectuals. Cusick (1973) provides the most poignant analyses of the loners who drifted through the corridors and classrooms attempting to maintain a guarded isolation from other students.

The system of rules and regulations in many high schools operates according to the principle of get the pupils in, keep them busy and get them out (Cusick, 1983). Students, in Varenne's term, often sense they are "done to." Crowd membership in high school, like the tentative friendships formed during the early elementary school years, functions to provide adolescents with a buffer against what they perceive as the hostile, or at best indifferent, world of adults.

Segmental Participation or Total Institution?

In their quest for order, educators have sought to expand their control over many aspects of students' personal lives—through codes and rules regulating dress, language, study habits, use of tobacco, drugs, and alcohol, manners, and the like. Corwin (1970) found that numerous disputes in high schools concerned dress codes; one teacher even succeeded in getting a student fired from a part-time job because he had defied the school's dress code. Another frequent source of tensions involved homework assignments. Homework can be a sensitive issue to students because although they typically do not expect to participate in decisions about the management of classrooms, they are inclined to view homework as an encroachment on their personal time and therefore a decision area in which they want to participate.

The personal lives of students have become regulated as a consequence of leisure-time, so called "extracurricular," activities. Frederick (1959) has traced the status of extracurricular activities in public schools through at least four stages of development: (a) *abstinence* during the Colonial period, when students were expected to attend to their lessons; (b) *tolerance*, as religious influence declined and students were encouraged to organize dances, parties, and other activities under faculty leadership; (c) *capitalization*, in the 1950s, when extracurricular activities flourished and became part of the school program; and (d) *institutionalization*, in recent years, as teachers started supervising extracurricular activities on a part-time basis and later as such assignments were added to their normal full-time duties. Such activities were sometimes granted the status of a required course. Music, typing, homemaking, physical education, and other courses that have achieved over required status time have evolved through such stages.

The teachers who are responsible for different extracurricular activities struggle to gain favored status for their activities. Band directors in Corwin's (1970) study, wanting new uniforms and instruments, complained that athletic teams were receiving too much money for uniforms, and music directors and coaches often tried to persuade the same student to come to an after-school practice. In one case a chorus director was holding rehearsals before school in order to avoid an after-school conflict with athletic practice, only to find that some coaches had also scheduled the same early morning hours. A chorus teacher complained that the administration was putting pressure on students to take speech as well as supporting proposals for additional physical education requirements, and as a result many students were not able to enroll in her music class. In one school district, the board announced a policy that said in effect, if there is a conflict between an athletic tournament and any other extracurricular activity, the student should go to the tournament.

Prestige hierarchies of leisure-time activities have evolved from the rivalries. Schools officially endorse certain activities such as athletics and music, which thereby gain dominance in the program, crowding out other activities like the Latin club, the rifle team, or art. From such structures children vicariously learn which leisure activities are "good" (i.e., approved) and which are not. The prominence of certain activities may also encourage some students to compete excessively in many activities in search of approval and popularity.

Administrative control has been enhanced as a consequence of rules encroaching on the personal aspects of students' personal lives, but ironically administrators' control has been simultaneously circumscribed as student activities and behavior codes have become more fully institutionalized and bound up with status hierarchies among teachers and students, and subject to laws and court decisions not readily open to change by administrative policy.

Uniformity or Diversity?

The dilemma of order is in part a consequence of strains arising from trying to impose uniformity within and among classrooms on a diversified body of students and variable conditions of teaching. It seems ironic that according to many observers, the discretion so often attributed to teachers has not produced schools and classrooms that are more diversified than appears to be the case. Classrooms are often portrayed as being highly uniform, routinized, and rigidly scheduled (Jackson, 1968, pp. 5–17). Schools seem to be a place where things happen solely because it is time for them to happen (Jackson, 1968; Pellegrin, 1976). The authority of teachers is described as tenuous and precarious in the face of student resistance (Everhart, 1983; McNeil, 1983). To compensate, teachers become preoccupied with order, control, and survival, pursuing their stated objectives only ritualistically (Abramowitz & Tenenbaum, 1978; Carlson, 1965; Meyer & Rowan, 1978; Miles, 1975; Packard et al., 1978; Waller, 1932; Willower, Eidell, & Hoy, 1973). In contrast to the teachers' discretion, *students* are closely supervised and have little freedom or influence (Packard et al., 1978).

A study of 1,000 classrooms in 38 schools by Goodlad (1984) found little variation in classroom management styles. Much of what goes on, he believes, is conditioned by the need to maintain orderly relationships among 20 to 30 or more students in a relatively small space. Each student essentially works and achieves alone within a group setting. Although a class may be praised for its performance, this recognition is typically accorded to the average of individual performances, not some shared collaborative achievement. Moreover, even in the early elementary years there were strong indications that students did not have time to finish their lessons or did not understand what the teacher wanted them to do. A significant percentage of them believed that the teacher was not giving them sufficient help with mistakes and difficulties.

The observations of Goodlad's (1984) research team support the popular image of an authoritarian teacher sitting in front of a class and imparting knowledge to a group of students. The teacher is almost always the central figure in determining classroom activities, as well as in setting the tone of the classroom. Explaining and lecturing monopolized teaching activities at all grade levels but especially in the senior high school years. Teachers also spent a substantial amount of time observing students at work or monitoring their seatwork, especially at the junior high school level. Student work was divided into three categories—written work, listening, and preparing for assignments—all of which were marked by passivity.

Goodlad (1984) concludes that despite the fact that during the last two decades teachers have been exhorted to provide for student individuality in learning rates and styles, the chances are little better than 50–50 that if an observer were to walk into any of the classrooms in that sample, he would see one of these three activities underway and being closely monitored by teachers. On the basis of her observations of four high schools, McNeil (1982) speculates that teachers deliberately try to reduce students to passive recipients of information in order to minimize adversarial relations.

However, in contrast to this image of monotonous uniformity, passivity, and rigid control, one can find in the literature glimpses of diversity among teachers in the way they fulfill their roles and in their classroom management practices (Barr & Dreeben, 1983; Packard et al., 1978; Pellegrin, 1976; Simpson, 1969). Some classrooms are pictured as lively, intense, and busy places where there is a persistent threat of relationships becoming emotionally charged. In these classrooms students are divided into "batches," and the more routinized procedures are tempered with flexible, mediating technologies. According to Barr and Dreeben (1983), a day in a given elementary-level classroom might consist of complex tradeoffs between different kinds of instructional arrangements that range from close relationships between small groups of children and a teacher, to unsupervised individual seatwork, to plenary sessions where the instruction is directed to the class as a whole. These researchers present an illuminating scenario in which during one part of the day the teacher explains assignments to the total class; while the children are working on these tasks independently, the teacher assembles the first reading group for work in a basal reader; after assigning that group work to be completed following the teacher instruction, works with other small groups in turn.

Cusick's (1983) account of life in three large public high schools explored student life in a biracial urban context and the professional lives of teachers in a suburban and a small city high school. Teachers in both Factory High and Suburban High were relatively free to tailor their subject matter specialties to fit their own

unique sets of personal assessments, interests, and predictions. All, nonetheless, argued that they were making adjustments in their teaching for the good of the students.

Cusick also observed great variations both in the curriculum and in the enthusiasm teachers put into their teaching in these high schools. He concluded that the differences resulted from organizational structures, or rather, the lack of structures, in these schools. First, teachers were provided considerable freedom. Their only constraints were an occasional meeting (often poorly attended and little regarded) and the understanding classes would be conducted during appointed hours. Second, even though one of the schools had undertaken massive revisions of the curriculum in line with new state requirements, no standard curriculum was followed by members of a particular academic department. Elective courses predominated, and these were designed by teachers to correspond to their individual interests and perceptions of what appealed to students. Further, a number of factors served to dissipate a collective understanding of goals and methods among the staff, including the lack of supervision, the weakness of departments, the isolation of teachers in the classroom, and the lack of common values among teachers regarding student behavior and achievement, biracialism, and appropriate educational goals.

Again, there seems to be no simple answer. The tensions between order and learning have produced a variety of educational settings. Uniformity may be the prevailing pattern, as some observers maintain, but it appears that many teachers and administrators are equally determined to create alternative learning environments. A case study of classrooms reported by Gracey (1972) contains an agonizing account of the tension between order and diversity in classrooms. One group of teachers was committed to a nontraditional, student-centered, educational approach, but they were strait-jacketed by parents' and administrators' expectations of the skills that ought to be imparted through the curriculum, by students' desires for grades, by the school's requirements for order and quiet in the classroom, and by the large size of classes. Some teachers tried to work out a compromise by allowing most children to work at their individual desks under a highly structured system of control. This would permit the teacher to spend much of his or her day working with individuals or small groups of children; however, this compromise proved not acceptable to all.

The degree of uniformity among classrooms has implications for the effects of administrative policies on classroom behavior. One can ask to what extent do administrators use the discretion available to them to promote diversity and, to be more specific, how much of the uniformity is an intended or unintended consequence of administrative control?

Summary

Student resistance and the salience of childhood values are important sources of constraint on administrative control. The limits imposed by student subcultures must be at least as important as the autonomy and power of teachers. Research on childhood values, we maintain, should become an important component of research on educational administration as well, because of the implications for administrative control.

Again, the literature exposes a fluid balance of power between teachers and students. On the one hand, there is reason to believe that what young children learn from one another, apart from adults, is an important ingredient of their school. And, moreover, teachers often negotiate the curriculum with students, adapting their teaching practices as well as administrative and instructional policies to the condition of the students and the demands of their various subcultures. On the other hand, the adults certainly have not relinquished control. On the contrary, student activities have been institutionalized and student conduct has been legislated in the form of codes administered by school districts. The adults are confronted with the problem of simultaneously adapting professional norms and administrative policies to student subcultures while trying to overcome student resistance and providing quality education.

The tensions have left a legacy of mixed portraits of classrooms with pockets of diversity in a prevailing pattern of uniformity. In the final analysis, the demands of maintaining order often dictate classroom teaching practices and undoubtedly some administrative policies as well. In many cases the requirement of order seems more important than concern for how students learn. Moreover, it is possible that what students do learn is determined more directly by the values of their own subcultures than by what teachers or administrators do.

THE DILEMMA OF EQUITY

The dilemma of order just discussed grows out of tensions involving the management of authority relationships within classrooms. A related dilemma concerns possible inequities in the way students are organized for learning. Some of the most profound administrative choices entail compromising strongly ingrained ideologies favoring egalitarian treatment and individualized attention with the practical requirements of teaching students in small and large groups. The sheer number of students in schools and school districts is one of the most fundamental constraints on administrative control, and the problem of managing size is compounded by an egalitarian ideal that blames schools when children fail (Cusick, 1983). In the 1880s, only a small percentage of the adult population had completed high school. In the 1980s, the assumption is that everyone must graduate in order to be a competent member of society. Although the structure of high schools has been altered somewhat from the classical academic program of the 19th century, principally through the introduction of vocational and technical training, a central mission of most high schools is to prepare students for further education, either in a general way or in a manner not unlike the classical model of education for future college or university studies. Faced with this set of restrictions, high schools accommodate or resist, modify, and rechannel the pressures constraining them.

The dilemma is that most learning theories and many teaching practices as well are based on the individual learner, whereas schools are organized around batch-processing technologies. Many critics have charged that some students are disadvantaged by the practice of assigning students to ability groups for instructional purposes. There are three related issues: (a) Is it possible for teachers to be fully sensitive to individual differences within classroom settings? (b) To what extent are assignments to ability groups based on ascriptive criteria, such as the students' social skills and family backgrounds, as opposed to their academic abilities? (c) Does the practice of assigning students to instructional groups on the basis of their past academic performance consign them to a social caste from which there is no escape or otherwise disadvantage some students?

Individual Attention or Grouping?

The diversity and uniquenesses among students would seem to require personal attention—tailoring of teaching strategies to fit the needs, abilities, and interests of each individual. However, school is a place where "students learn to live in crowds" (Jackson, 1968; Packard et al., 1978; Pellegrin, 1976). Teachers must work with students in large and small groups as well as individually. The constraints inherent in comprehensive classrooms make it difficult for teachers to provide much individualized instruction. As a practical necessity students are allocated to programs, or "tracks," within schools and to groups within classrooms. Barr and Dreeben (1983) conclude that even when the elementary teachers in their study were conscientious about how they created instructional groups, they did not appear to be primarily concerned with adapting instruction to individual differences. Grouping seemed more directly related to how abilities and other characteristics are distributed in classrooms. Grouping involves complex tradeoffs between different kinds of instructional arrangements, and consequently Barr and Dreeben (1983) found it difficult to determine which situation is more individualized—when a teacher spends 30 minutes working closely with a few children or when the children work by themselves at their own pace in order to permit teachers to work with small groups.

Achievement or Ascription?

Social status in most social systems, including classrooms, is based on a mix of ascriptive and achievement criteria, of contest and sponsorship. There is debate about the *relative* importance of the mix of these two factors within schools, but one theme is that ascriptive criteria often take precedence over merit as the basis of grouping and instructing students. A related theme is that even when students are *initially* assigned to groups on the basis of their proven abilities, they become stereotyped and stratified in such a way that there is little opportunity to transfer to other groups as their performance improves or diminishes. Rist (1970) is among those who believe that students tend to be stereotyped. He observed a kindergarten teacher assign students to a permanent seating arrangement after only 1 week on the basis of socioeconomic criteria and the way they interacted in the classroom. Rist felt that the teacher treated these groups differently in respect to the way she used her time, gave praise, asserted social control, and permitted students to use autonomy; he concluded that because of stereotyping, students in low-ability groups suffer, whereas high-ability students profit from grouping. If so, then in the long run grouping would tend to have the effect of increasing, rather than diminishing, differences in academic performance levels among students.

Class or Caste?

However, other writers have questioned whether stereotyping is as rigidly imposed and as prevalent as often pictured. Barr and Dreeben (1983) found some elementary schools in which teachers were conscientious about grouping children on the basis of their aptitudes and then matching available materials to the ability levels of the groups by varying the amount and difficulty of material covered. Not only were students assigned to low-ability groups solely on the basis of their performance, but the teachers moved children promptly from one group to another as their performance improved. Although there is no way to deter-

mine how many teachers are as conscientious as these, the authors do make a fundamental point: namely, that grouping in itself is a *neutral* act.

Advantage or Disadvantage?

Nevertheless, some researchers maintain that even if assignments to ability groups were based solely on objective assessments of each student's ability and even if effective administrative procedures existed to ensure transfer among groups as performance improved, the practice of ability grouping would continue to have seriously detrimental latent side effects because students learn about their *social* identities in such groups. These identities are formed early in the elementary school career, and by the time students reach high school they increasingly see their educational and job opportunities reflected in their location in the tracking system (Rosenbaum, 1976). Moreover, they readily identify themselves with members of segregated social crowds formed on the basis of ability, which in turn helps crystallize their classroom status (Coleman, 1961; Cusick, 1973; Varenne, 1983).

The commingling of academic and social identities is graphically evident in the junior high studied by Schofield (1982), where black and white students were mixed in order to achieve racial balance within classrooms. Since the black students generally performed less well than whites on academic criteria, when academic tasks were differentiated according to ability level, little interaction between whites and blacks occurred no matter how the curriculum was organized. However, when teachers formed groups on other than academic criteria, interracial interaction increased. According to a black female in the school:

> In reading, [blacks] stay on one side of the room and the whites stay on the other... Now in language arts, [the teacher] puts us together. So it's more like we talk in language arts and we hate each other in reading. (Schofield, 1982).

Moreover, when academic ability was stressed, white students came to hold increasingly negative views of their black counterparts. Blacks were disadvantaged because children frequently assisted their friends by providing "academic favors," such as the opportunity to copy answers during a test or the chance to get the correct spelling of a difficult word. Friendships were in large part formed on the basis of children's perceptions of their similarity in achievement; as a consequence, their social relationships and hence their cooperation in acquiring information in class were almost always racially homogeneous.

Faculty members were rarely, if ever, observed to

wonder about the impact of great academic disparity on either intergroup relations or the academic motivation of the slower students (Schofield, 1982). They believed that merely by being in contact in classrooms and hallways and during extracurricular activities, children of both races would develop increasingly better relations. This ideology helped justify teachers' emphasis on organizing their classrooms so as to enhance students' academic achievements, even though in fact this goal overwhelmed matters related to the improvement of intergroup interaction.

There is a great deal of evidence that teachers do tailor lessons to the level of a groups' collective ability, especially in reading, science, and social science (Rosenholtz & Rosenholtz, 1981; Rosenholtz & Simpson, 1984; Rowan & Miracle, 1982). There is also some evidence that teachers interact differently with students of different ability levels. For example, teachers are more likely to give perceived high-achieving students a second chance to respond to an incorrect answer (Good & Brophy, 1973) and to wait longer for them to answer questions (Rowe, 1969). Using a microanalytic technique to analyze teacher-student interactions during classroom lessons in the first grade, Eder (1981) determined that low-ability groups were characterized by more frequent disruptions, more inattentiveness, and more concern shown by the teacher about disciplinary issues than was the case for groups of higher ability. After examining data on third-grade students grouped within classrooms to maximize homogeneity of achievement, Leiter (1983) concluded that one's ability group takes on special importance when instruction is accomplished by dividing entire classes into instructional groups. The higher the mean ability level of a group, the greater the mathematics gains of students in the class. He concluded that the ability composition of the classroom influences the benefit students receive from mathematics instruction in the third grade. The ability level of a given classroom is, to a greater or lesser extent, an important administrative policy decision.

But whether grouping is detrimental to students would also seem to depend primarily on how grouping is related to the *context* and overall task structure of the classroom. On this point Rosenholtz and Simpson (1984) distinguished between "unidimensional" and "multidimensional" classrooms. In the former they found academic ability to be both narrowly and publicly defined and usually contingent on performance in a reading group. In such classrooms students perceived greater inequity in the ability levels of their classmates than they did in the multidimensional classroom. Unidimensional classrooms have several organizational features in common, including an undifferentiated academic task structure which allows all students who

are simultaneously using the same materials to accomplish the same task; low student autonomy with the teacher in charge of the curricular program; student grouping patterns allowing public identification of poor and good performers; and formal performance evaluation during recitations before the class. Multidimensional classrooms have the opposite characteristics.

These conclusions are consistent with Bossert's (1979) earlier findings from a study of classroom organization patterns within the same grade levels in the same school. Classroom task structure, he concluded, affected the moral socialization of third- and fourth-grade students and hence their achievement. In unidimensional classrooms organized to accomplish student learning by recitation, teachers relied on top performers to keep the class discussion moving along. In multitask classrooms, on the other hand, students were freer to participate in group activities on the basis of their own interests rather than the teacher's perception of their abilities. Friendship patterns and children's social status systems were, as a result, fluid and not hierarchically organized, as they were in classrooms dominated by recitation.

It appears then that the ideology of individualized attention notwithstanding, it is extremely difficult to provide individualized instruction within the present structure of elementary and secondary schools. In many cases teaching involves the class as a whole, dominated by recitations from a segment of the students. Grouping, a compromise between these extremes, entails other dilemmas related to finding ways to (a) assign students to such groups and yet prevent individuals from becoming victims of a rigid stratification system on the basis of their prior achievement, and (b) minimize the adverse social and moral consequences associated with ability hierarchies. Perhaps multidimensional classrooms provide an answer, as they seem to minimize the ascriptive tendencies often associated with grouping and tracking.

IMPLICATIONS

Each of the dilemmas we have discussed here, we submit, is a consequence of structural incompatibilities within school systems and therefore cannot be resolved without extensive organizational reforms along the lines suggested below.

The control dilemma necessitates continual negotiations between district administrators and principals, which in turn would be facilitated by creating a more effective bargaining structure. For example, principals could increase their leverage by forming collective bargaining units and by trying to obtain legal authority to create administrative cabinets in school districts. The resolution of the autonomy dilemma seems to require nothing short of a reorganization of schools to replace self-contained classrooms with more interdependent technologies and work structures. Within the present structure of schools, teachers have reason to value personal autonomy because it does provide them with some protection from the system, and they will continue to rely on personal autonomy until new structures facilitate collective forms of action.

The need for structure to facilitate formal and informal negotiations between teachers and administrators is also implied by the status dilemma. Negotiations can become more fully institutionalized if, for example, teacher representatives were to be included on policy-making bodies such as administrative cabinets and school boards. However, the prospects for improving the teaching career solely through collective wage negotiations seem limited, partially because of the unprecedented volume of resources required to increase the salaries in this huge vocation and partially because money is not the only appropriate incentive in complex school districts. The resolution for the career dilemma can come only through a more formalized division of labor enabling career ladders to be incorporated within the official administrative structure of school districts.

The dilemma of order is rooted in laws mandating compulsory education, but it is greatly compounded by the extensive reliance in the United States on comprehensive schools. The comprehensive school was deliberately erected as a barrier to specialization, but although there might have been good historical reasons for avoiding specialization, the consequences have been devastating. Prevented from specializing in explicit ways, schools and teachers have developed idiosyncratic forms of specialization to cope with the different requirements of students of low ability, alienated students, and talented and motivated students. Moreover, comprehensive classrooms promote rigid exterior uniformities. Although specialization may produce uniformities *within* a classroom, the comprehensive school, based on the philosophy that all students can be treated uniformly irrespective of circumstances, is responsible for much of the uniformity across classrooms and schools.

If specialization has failed, it is because it has not been seriously incorporated into the structure of school systems. Indeed, specialized classrooms and schools at best usually have been marginal, ceremonial efforts, often only vaguely disguised dumping grounds for managing difficult students. Specialization can work only if the proper incentives and sanction are provided to reward successes with various kinds of students.

The source of the equity dilemma is not inequity per se but rigid stratification. Stratification would be minimized if all students had an opportunity to be part of some highly esteemed groups, which would be facilitated if multiple criteria were used to form learning groups and again to assign students to them. Students with different types of abilities and interests and different levels of motivation could then participate in different ways in various types of learning groups.

We are not convinced that our proposals are the only correct ones, but we are sure that solutions to these and other dilemmas will be found only through continuing analysis addressed to revamping the archaic structure of American school systems. We hope we have demonstrated that the topical concerns of educational administration necessarily reach through all levels of a school district and into the classroom itself.

REFERENCES

Abramowitz, S. & Tenenbaum, E. (1977, November). National high school study: A conceptual framework. Working paper, School Finance and Organization Division. Washington, DC: National Institute of Education.

Abramowitz, S., & Tenenbaum, E. (1978). *High school '77: A survey of public secondary school principals*. Washington, DC: National Institute of Education.

Barnard, C. I. (1938). *The functions of the executive*. Cambridge, MA: Harvard University Press.

Barr, R., & Dreeben, R., with N. Wiratchal. (1983). *How schools work*. Chicago: University of Chicago Press.

Beck, E. M., & Betz, M. (1975). A comparative analysis of organizational conflict in schools. *Sociology of Education, 48*, 59–74.

Becker, H. S. (1953). The teacher in the authority system of the public schools. *Journal of Educational Sociology, 27*, 128–144.

Bendix, R. (1942). Bureaucracy: The problem and its setting. *American Sociological Review, 12*, 502–504.

Betz, M., & Garland, J. (1974). Integenerational mobility rates of urban school teachers. *Sociology of Education, 47*, 511–522.

Bidwell, C. E. (1965). The school as a formal organization. In J. March (Ed.), *Handbook of organizations* (pp. 972–1022.) Chicago: Rand-McNally.

Blaug, M. (1976). The empirical status of human capital theory: A slightly jaundiced survey. *Journal of Economic Literature, 14*, 827–855.

Borman, K. (1979, September). *Children's interpersonal relationships, playground games and social cognitive skills*. Paper presented at the Annual Meeting of American Sociological Association, Boston.

Bossert, S. (1979). *Tasks and social relationships in classrooms*. Cambridge, England: Cambridge University Press.

Bossert, S. T., Dwyer, D. C., Rowan, B., & Lee, G. V. (1982). The instructional management role of the principal. *Educational Administration Quarterly, 18*, 34–64.

Braverman, H. (1974). *Labor and monopoly capital*. New York: Monthly Review Press.

Carlson, R. O. (1965). Barriers to change in public schools. In R. O. Carlson et al. (Eds.), *Change processes in the public Schools*. Eugene, OR: Center for Education and Policy Management, University of Oregon.

Chapman, D. W., & Hutcheson, S. M. (1982). Attrition from teaching careers: A discriminate analysis. *American Educational Research Journal*, *19*(1), 93–105.

Chapman, D., & Lowther, M. (1982). Teachers' satisfaction with teaching. *Journal of Education Research*, *75*, 241–247.

Charters, W. W., Jr., & Jones, J. E. (1975). On neglect of the independent variable in program evaluation. In J. V. Baldridge & T. E. Deal (Eds.), *Managing change in educational organizations*. Berkeley, CA: McCutchan.

Charters, W. W., Jr. (1963). The social background of teaching. In N. L. Gage (Ed.). *Handbook of research on teaching*. Chicago: Rand McNally.

Cohen, E. G. (1981). Sociology looks at team teaching. In Ronald G. Corwin (Ed.), *Research in sociology of education and socialization: Research on educations*. (Vol. 2). Greenwich, CT: JAI.

Cohen, M. D., March, J. G. & Olson, J. P. (1972). A garbage can model of organizational choice. *Administrative Science Quarterly*, *17*, 1–25.

Corwin, R. G. (1965). Professional persons in public organizations. *Educational Administration Quarterly*, *1*, 1–22.

Corwin, R. G. (1970). *Militant professionalism: A study of conflict in high schools*. New York: Appleton-Century-Crofts.

Corwin, R. G. (1973). *Reform and organizational survival*. New York: John Wiley.

Corwin, R. G. (1975a). *Education in crisis*. New York: John Wiley.

Corwin, R. G. (1975b). The new teaching profession in teacher education. In Kevin Ryan (Ed.), *The 74th Yearbook of the National Society for the Study of Education*, Part II Chicago: University of Chicago Press.

Corwin, R. G. (1981). Patterns of organizational control and teacher militancy: Theoretical continuities in the idea of "loose coupling." In A. C. Kerchoff & R. G. Corwin (Eds.), *Research in sociology of education and socialization* (Vol. 2). Greenwich, CT: JAI.

Corwin, R. G. (1983). *The entrepreneurial bureaucracy: Biographies of two federal programs in education*. Greenwich, CT: JAI Press.

Corwin, R. G., & Dentler, R. A. (1984). *Structural barriers to dissemination in exchanging ideas: The communication and use of knowledge in educational settings*. In K. S. Louis, D. G. Kell, R. A. Dentler, R. G. Corwin, & R. E. Herriott (Eds.). Prepared for the National Institute of Education.

Corwin, R. G. & Herriott, R. E. (1986). *Interpersonal conflict in mechanical and organic social systems: An empirical study of elementary and secondary schools*. Unpublished manuscript.

Crozier, M. (1964). *The bureaucratic phenomenon*. Chicago: University of Chicago Press.

Curti, M. (1959). *The social ideas of American educations*. Paterson, NJ: Tuttlefield, Adams.

Cusick, P. A. (1973). *Inside high school*. New York: Hope.

Cusick, P. (1983). *The egalitarian ideal and the American high school*. New York: Longman.

Darkenwald, G. G. (1971). Organizational conflict in college and universities. *Administrative Science Quarterly*, *16*, 407–412.

Davies, B. (1982). *Life in the classroom and playground*. London: Routledge & Kegan Paul.

Dornbusch, S., & Scott, R. A. (1975). *Evaluation and the exercise of authority*. San Francisco: Jossey-Bass.

Dreeben, R. (1970). *The nature of teaching: Schools and the work of teachers*. Glenville, IL: Scott, Foresman.

Durkheim, E. (1960). *The Division of Labor in Society*. T. George Simpson, Ed. Glencoe, IL: Free Press. (Original work published 1893)

Dworkin, A. G. (1980, April). Changing demography of public school teachers: Some implications for faculty turnover in urban areas. *Sociology of Education*, *53*, 65–73.

Edelfelt, R. (1985, November). Career and ladders: Then and now. *Educational Leadership*, *42*, 62–66.

Edelfelt, R. A. (1979, April). In service education: A concept and an overview. National Council of States on In Service Education Newsletter (pp. 4–11, 15) Syracuse, NY: Syracuse University.

Eder, D. (1981, July). Ability grouping as a self-fulfilling prophecy: A micro-analysis of teacher-student interaction. *Sociology of Education*, *54*, 151–162.

Everhart, R. B. (1983). Classroom management, student opposites, and the job process. In M. W. Apple & L. Weis (Eds.), *Ideology and practice in schooling*. Philadelphia, PA: Temple University Press.

Everhart, R. B. (1983). *Reading, writing and resistance: Adolescence and labor in a junior high school*. Boston: Routledge & Kegan Paul.

Finley, M. K. (1984, October). Teachers and tracking in a comprehensive high school. *Sociology of Education*, *57*, 233–243.

Firestone, W. A., & Herriott, R. E. (1982, December). *An empirical study of the applicability of images of organization to schools*. Philadelphia, PA: *Research for Better Schools*. Unpublished manuscript.

Firestone, W. A., Herriott, R. E., & Wilson, B. L. (1983). *Explaining differences between elementary and secondary schools: Individual, organizational and institutional perspectives*. Unpublished manuscript.

Firestone, W. A., & Wilson, B. L. (1983). *Using bureaucratic and cultural linkages to improve instruction: The high school principal's contribution*. Eugene, OR: Center for Educational Policy and Management. University of Oregon.

Firestone, W. A., & Wilson, B. L. (1985, July). Management organizational outcomes: The effects of approach and environment in schools. [Mimeo]. Philadelphia, PA: *Research for Better Schools*.

Frederick, R. W. (1959). *The third curriculum: Student activities in American education*. New York: Appleton-Century-Crofts.

Gitlin, A. (1983). School structure and teachers's work. In M. W. Apple & L. Weis (Eds.), *Ideology and practice in schooling*. Philadelphia: Temple University Press.

Goldschmidt, S., Bowers, B., Riley, M., & Leland, S. (1983). *The extent and nature of educational policy bargaining*. Eugene, OR: Center for Educational Policy and Management, University of Oregon.

Good, T., & Brophy, J. (1973). *Looking in classrooms*. New York: Harper & Row.

Goodlad, J. I. (1983). *A place called school*. McGraw-Hill.

Goodlad, J. I. & Klein, M., & Associates. (1970). *Behind the classroom door*. Worthington, OH: Charles A. Jones.

Gottfredson, D. C. (1985). *School size and school disorder*. Baltimore, MD: Center for Social Organization of Schools, Johns Hopkins University.

Gouldner, A. W. (1954). *Patterns of industrial bureaucracy*. Glencoe, IL: Free Press.

Gouldner, A. W. (1959). Organizational analysis. In R. K. Merton, L. Bloom, & L. S. Cottrell, Jr. (Eds.), *Sociology today*. New York: Basic.

Gracey, H. L. (1972). *Curriculum or craftsmanship*. Chicago: University of Chicago Press.

Gross, N., Giacquinta, J. B., & Bernstein, M. (1971). *Implementing organizational innovations: A sociological analysis of planned educational charge*. New York: Basic.

Gross, N., & Herriott, R. E. (1965). *Staff leadership in public schools: A sociological inquiry*. New York: John Wiley.

Hammersley, M. (1977). *The social location of teacher perspectives*. Milton Keynes: Open University Press.

Hargraves, A. (1984, October). Experience counts, theory doesn't: How teachers talk about their work. *Sociology of Education*, *57*, 244–254.

Henry, J. (1963). *Culture against man*. New York: Random House.

Hood, P., & Blackwell, L. (1976). *The educational information market study*. San Francisco: Far West Laboratory for Educational Research and Development.

Huberman, M. (1983). *Recipes for busy kitchens: A situational analysis of routine knowledge use in schools. Knowledge: Creation, diffusion, utilization*, Vol. 4. Beverly Hills, CA: Sage.

Jackson, Philip. (1968). *Life in classrooms*. New York: Holt, Rinehart, & Winston.

Katz, M. B. (1975). *Class, bureaucracy and schools; The illusion of educational change in America*. New York: Praeger.

Kerchner, C. T. (1984). *Labor policy in school districts: Its diffusion and impact on work structures*. Eugene, OR: Center for Educational Policy and Management, University of Oregon.

Larkin, P. (1979). *Suburban youth in cultural crisis*. New York: Oxford University Press.

Leiter, J. (1983, July). Classroom composition and achievement gains. *Sociology of Education, 56*, 126–132.

Lortie D. C. (1969). The balance of control and autonomy in elementary school teaching. In A. Etzioni (Ed.), *The semi professions and their organization*. New York: Free Press.

Lortie, D. C. (1975). *School teacher: A sociological study*. Chicago: University of Chicago Press.

Lortie, D. C. (1977). Two anomalies and three perspectives on school organization. In R. G. Corwin & R. Edelfelt (Eds.), *Perspectives on organizations: The school as a social organization*. Washington, DC: American Association of Colleges for Teacher Education.

Mann, D. (1976). The politics of training teachers in schools. *Teachers College Record, 77*(3), 323–338.

McNeil, L. M. (1982, June). *Contradictions of control: Organizational context of social knowledge*. Madison, WI: Wisconsin Center for Public Policy.

McNeil, L. M. (1983). Defensive teaching and classroom control. In M. A. Apple & Lois Weis (Eds.), *Ideology and practice in schooling*. Philadelphia, PA: Temple University Press.

Mehan, H. (1979). *Learning lessons*. Cambridge, MA: Harvard University Press.

Merit Pay Task Force Report. (1983). Report No. 98 (pp. 1–9). Washington, DC: Government Printing Office.

Merton, R. K. (1976). Sociological ambivalence. In *Sociological ambivalence and other essays*. New York: Free Press.

Metz, M. H. (1978). *Classrooms and corridors*. Berkeley, CA: University of California Press.

Meyer, J. W., Cohen., E., Brunetti F., Molnar, S. & Lueders-Salmon, E. (1971). The impact of the open-space school upon teacher influence and autonomy: The effects of an organizational innovation. *Technical Report* 21: Stanford, CA: Stanford Center for Research and Development in Teaching.

Meyer, J. W., & Rowan, B. (1978). The structure of educational organizations. In M. Meyer & Associates (Eds.), *Environments and organizations: Theoretical and empirical perspectives*. San Francisco: Jossey-Bass.

Miles, M. B. (1975). Mapping the common properties of schools. In R. Lehming and M. Kane (Eds.), *Improving schools*. Beverly Hills, CA: Sage.

Mintzberg, H. (1983). *Structure in fives: Designing effective organizations*. Englewood Cliffs, NJ: Prentice-Hall.

Morris, V. C., Crowson, R., Hurwitz, E., Jr., & Porter-Gehrie, C. (1981). *The urban principal: Discretionary decision-making in a large educational organization*. Chicago: University of Illinois at Chicago Circle.

National Commission on Excellence in Education. (1983). *A nation at risk: The imperative for educational reform*. Washington DC: U.S. Department of Education.

Ordoransky, P. (1987, Feb. 11). U.S. schools 'holding ground.' *Cincinnati Enquirer*, A–1.

Packard, J. S., Charters, W. W., Jr., & Duckworth, K. E., with T. D. Jovich. (1978). *Management implications of team teaching: Final Report*. Eugene, OR: Center for Educational Policy and Management, University of Oregon.

Parsons, T. (1956). Suggestions for a sociological approach to the theory of organizations—1, 2. *Administrative Science Quarterly, 1*, 63–85, 225–239.

Pellegrin, R. J. (1970). *Professional satisfaction and decision making in the multi-unit schools*. Technical Report No. 7, Center for the Advanced Study of Educational Administration, University of Oregon, Eugene.

Pellegrin, R. J. (1976). Schools as work settings. In R. Dubin (Ed.), *Handbook of work, organization and society*. Skokie, IL: Rand McNally.

Peterson, P. E. (1983, Winter). Did the education commission say anything? *Brookings Review*, 3–11.

Rist, R. C. (1970). Student's social class and teachers' expectations: The self-fulfilling prophecy in ghetto education. *Harvard Education Review, 40*, 411–450.

Rist, R. C. (1973). *The urban school: Factory for failure*. Cambridge, MA: MIT Press.

Rogers, D. (1968). *110 Livingston Street*. New York: Holt, Rinehart, & Winston.

Rosenbaum, J. E. (1976). *Making inequality*. New York: John Wiley.

Rosenholtz, S. J. (1985). Effective schools: Interpreting the evidence. *American Journal of Education, 93*(3), 352–388.

Rosenholtz, S. J., & Rosenholtz, S. H. (1981, April). Classroom organization and the percentage of ability. *Sociology of Education, 54*, 132–140.

Rosenholtz, S. J., & Simpson, C. (1984). Classroom organization and student stratification. *Elementary School Journal, 85* (1), 21–37.

Rosenthal, R. & Jacobson, L. J. (1968). *Pygmalion in the classroom*. New York: Holt, Rinehart, & Winston.

Rosenthal, R. & Jacobson, L. J. (1968). *Pygmalion in the classroom: Teacher expectations and pupils' intellectual development*. New York: Holt, Rinehart and Winston.

Rowan, B. & Miracle, A. W. (1983, July). Systems of ability grouping and stratification of achievement in elementary school. *Sociology of Education. 56*, 133–144.

Rowe, M. (1969). Science, silence and sanctions. *Science in Children, 6*, 11–13.

Sarason, S. (1971). *The culture of the school and the problem of change*. Boston: Allyn and Bacon.

Schofield, J. (1982). *Black and white school: Trust, tension or tolerance*. New York: Praeger.

Seeley, D., & Schwartz, R. (1981). Debureaucratizing public education. In D. Davies (Ed.), *Communities and their schools*. New York: McGraw-Hill.

Selznick, P. (1948). Foundations of the theory of organizations. *American Sociological Review, 13*, 25–35.

Silver, C. B. (1973). *Black teachers in urban schools*. New York: Praeger.

Simmel, G. (1950). *The sociology of Georg Simmel* (Curt Wolf, Trans.). Glencoe, IL: Free Press.

Simpson, R. (1969). *The school teacher: Social values, community role, and professional self-image*. Final Report to the U.S. Office of Education.

Slavin, R. (1983). *Cooperative learning*. New York: Longman.

Smith, C. B. (1979, September). Influence of internal opportunity structure and sex of workers on turnover patterns. *Administrative Science Quarterly, 24*, 361–381.

Smith, R. B. (1979). Cumulative social science: Paradigms, social research theory and development. In R. B. Smith & P. K. Manning (Eds.), *Handbook of social science methods*: Vol. 1. *Qualitative Social Research*, New York: Irvington.

Spilerman, S. (1977). Careers, labor market structure, and socio-economic achievement. *American Journal of Sociology, 83*, 551–593.

Spuck, D. W. (1974). Reward-structures in the public high school. *Educational Administration Quarterly, 10*(1), 18–34.

Stone, K. (1975). The origins of job structures in the steel industry. In R. Edwards, M. Reich, & D. Gordon (Eds.), *Labor market segmentation*. Lexington, MA: Heath.

Sussman, L. (1977). *Tales out of school*. Philadelphia, PA: Temple University Press.

Thompson, J. D. (1967). *Organizations in action*. New York: McGraw-Hill.

Varenne, H. (1983). *American school language*. New York: Irvington.

Wacaster, C. T. (1973). The life and death of differentiated staffing at Columbia high school. In W. W. Charters, Jr., R. B. Everhart, J. E. Jones, J. S. Packard, R. J. Pelligrin, L. J. Reynolds, & L. T. Wacaster (Eds.), *The process of planned change in the school's instructional organization*. Monograph No. 25. Eugene,

OR: Center for Advanced Study of Educational Administration, University of Oregon.

Wayland, S. (1964). Structural features of American education as basic factors in innovation. In M. B. Miles (Ed.), *Innovation in education*. New York: Teachers College Press, Columbia University.

Weick, K. E. (1976). Educational organizations as loosely coupled systems. *Administrative Science Quarterly, 21*, 1–19.

Waller, W. (1932). *The sociology of teaching*. New York: John Wiley.

Wellisch, J. B., MacQueen, A. H., Carriere, R. A., & Duck, G. A. (1978). School management and organization in successful schools–*Sociology of Education, 51*(3), 211–226.

Willower, D., Eidell, T. W., & Hoy, W. (1973). *The school and pupil control ideology*. Penn State Studies No. 24, (2nd ed.). University Park, PA: Pennsylania State University.

Wolcott, H. F. (1973). *The man in the principal's office: An ethnography*. Prospect Heights, IL: Waveland.

CHAPTER 12

Power, Authority, and Bureaucracy

Max G. Abbott and Francisco Caracheo

INTRODUCTION

Eisenstadt's (1959) two definitions of bureaucracy, (a) as an instrument of power and (b) as a mechanism for accomplishing purposes, summarize succinctly an issue that has been controversial for years. Those who view bureaucracy primarily as an instrument of power focus on Max Weber's studies of German society and point to his essays on the world's great religions. Those who perceive bureaucracy primarily as a mechanism for accomplishing purposes focus on Weber's specification of the elements that constitute the "ideal" bureaucracy.

In fact, the two definitions are not incompatible. Weber spent most of his life studying the phenomenon of "domination" (power) in human interaction. As a result he came to a firm conclusion about acceptable modes of domination, and he formulated a series of principles to ensure the application of those acceptable modes. In his later years, Weber set about to apply his principles to a specific institution. The institution he chose was bureaucracy, and the result was a detailed definition of what Weber considered to be the most effective mechanism for accomplishing purposes.

In this chapter we elaborate on the definition of bureaucracy as a mechanism for accomplishing purposes, and we clarify the concepts of power, authority, and prestige, concepts that are especially relevant to an understanding of bureaucracy. The ultimate purpose of the chapter, of course, is to provide information that can be used to enhance our understanding of schools.

Consultant/reviewers: Norman J. Boyan, University of California-Santa Barbara, and Wayne K. Hoy, Rutgers University

Of all those who have written about domination (power, authority, and bureaucracy), Weber remains the most influential. To understand bureaucracy, as that term is used today, it is necessary to know something about Weber. We begin the chapter, therefore, by discussing Weber's influential role in shaping and elucidating modern concepts of power and bureaucracy.

Contemporary studies on social organization are replete with confusing terminology related to the phenomenon of domination. This confusion exists because the terms *power*, *authority*, *control*, *leadership*, and *influence* tend to be used interchangeably. Later we offer a suggestion for reducing the confusion, and we develop a conceptual framework to clarify relationships among the key concepts.

We then discuss the conceptualization of bureaucracy, retaining as nearly as possible Weber's original formulation. In the concluding section, we report and discuss the research related to this conceptualization.

WEBER'S ROLE AND INFLUENCE

Economy and Society (Roth & Wittich, 1968)[1] may well be considered the crowning achievement in Weber's lifelong study of the origins and development of social structure and social organization in the modern world. His treatment of the concept of bureaucracy, as it appears in that volume, was destined to have a major impact on the thinking of organizational theorists for generations to come.

Weber's treatise on bureaucracy grew out of a series of investigations of social institutions, ranging from the German agrarian culture and the stock exchange to the world's major religions. An understanding of the values that stimulated his interest in such institutions, as well as the convictions that grew out of his studies of those institutions, may help us to understand more clearly his model of bureaucracy.

To gain insight into his later works, it is useful to review briefly his early life and his developing intellectual interests. An excellent source of information for this purpose is Reinhard Bendix's (1960) *Max Weber: An Intellectual Portrait*. In our discussion we draw heavily from that volume; much of our material is paraphrased from Bendix without citation.

Weber's Early Life and Intellectual Interests

Max Weber was born in 1864 and lived at home with his parents until the age of 29. His father was a lawyer and a member of parliament. As a result of his father's connections, Weber came to know the prominent politicians of the time, as well as the leading academicians at the University of Berlin. At the age of 19, he enrolled in the University of Heidelberg as a student of law. He took his law examination at the age of 22.

In Heidelberg, Weber manifested signs of conflicting desires, which characterized both his personal life and his academic work. Lured by the promise of an academic career, and at the same time wanting to play an active role in the practical affairs of political life, Weber eventually withdrew from both to become an independent scholar. Displaying a combination of commitment and detachment, Weber was able to identify with and reflect upon the contradictory conditions of German society; he was able to transcend the limitations of such conditions and see them as universal phenomena.

Weber's Early Scholarly Works

Shortly after passing the bar examination, Weber undertook graduate study at the University of Berlin. His dissertation, published in 1891, was his first treatise: *A Contribution to the History of Medieval Business Organization* (noted in Bendix, 1960, p. 25). Shortly thereafter he published a second book in 1891: *Roman Agrarian History and Its Significance for Private and Public Law* (noted in Bendix, 1960, p. 26). An outgrowth of these publications was Weber's involvement in an investigation of two major national problems of the time: agrarian labor practices east of the Elbe river and the economic impact of the stock exchange.

His involvement in the investigation of labor practices was to have a profound influence on his intellectual perspective. The landholders of the time had access to two sources of labor: day laborers, who worked only in the seasons of high labor demand; and contract laborers, who, with their families, were bound to a landowner throughout the year. These two groups of workers had conflicting interests in labor practices. Contract workers had a personal stake in the maintenance and productivity of estates. Day laborers, on the other hand, had self-interests that were counter to the interests of the landholders: They were interested in maximum wages and minimum prices.

Contract workers enjoyed economic security for themselves and their families, but in return they were subjected to the patriarchal rule and arbitrary demands of the landlords. Day laborers lacked this financial security, but they enjoyed more personal freedom and had greater opportunities for mobility. Weber was impressed by the fact that over time contract workers gradually relinquished their secure economic position in order to enjoy the freedom of day laborers. In Weber's view, the trend away from patriarchal rule and personal servility toward personal freedom and rule by law was clear. The last vestiges of a feudal system that had for so long prevailed in the Occident were giving way to a capitalistic economy and to the general principles of democratic government.

Weber had a particular interest in the impact that membership in status groups had on the beliefs and values of members of those groups. Noting this relationship between membership in groups and personal view, and persisting in his commitment to rationality in human affairs, Weber began investigations of the relationship between religion and society.

Initially, his attention focused on the interaction of religious beliefs and economic views. For example, he observed a close relationship in German culture between Protestant religious beliefs and views that favored a rational pursuit of economic interests, or capitalism.

Weber's emphasis on the relationship between religious beliefs and attitudes toward economic interests soon expanded into an investigation of the relationship between religious views and other social processes. He was particularly interested in understanding the process by which "the charismatic inspirations of the few became first, the 'style of life' of a distinct status group, and eventually the dominant orientation of a whole civilization" (Bendix, 1960, p. 266). Later, Weber's emphasis shifted from a general notion of society as a collection of status groups to a more limited focus on modes of domination in human affairs.

POWER AND ITS CORRELATES

Bureaucracy is a type of domination; domination is a form of power. But what is domination and what is power? Is domination identical to authority or leadership or imperative coordination, as has so often been claimed in English translations of Weber's writings? To place Weber's concepts and terminology in a current perspective and to avoid much of the confusion that is prevalent in current literature on organizations, we propose a framework for understanding *power* and its associated terms. Although this framework is not derived directly from Weber, it is consistent with his views.

It is important to make clear that we are discussing power in an institutional setting. We are not talking about power in informal groups, nor are we considering power as a psychological phenomenon. The meaning of power in reference to a dyadic relationship would not be the same as its meaning in a formal organization or in society as a whole.

Since Weber's time, terminology related to the concept of power has become increasingly equivocal. On the one hand, a variety of words is used to express a single concept; the terms *power, authority, influence,* and *leadership* are used interchangeably to refer to the ability to move other people. On the other hand, a single term is used to refer to a variety of concepts. For example, *authority* may indicate the ability to influence others, it may refer to the source of that ability, or it may be equated with the term *leadership*, or personal power. The issue becomes further complicated if we add such terms as *dominance, dominion, headship, influence, expertise,* and *control*, all of which at times refer to identical concepts, whereas at other times each is used to express a unique idea. At this point, we propose a way to clarify the key terms and to eliminate much of the confusion that now exists.

Definitions from Weber

According to Bendix (1960), "Weber defined power as the possibility of imposing one's will upon the behavior of other persons, and he pointed out that in this general sense power is an aspect of most, if not all, social relationships" (p. 294). Weber identified two sources of power that he considered to be important for the social scientist: "power derived from a *constellation of interests* that develops on a formally free market, and power derived from *established authority* that allocates the right to command and the duty to obey [italics in the original]" (p. 294).

From this definition it is clear that Weber considered the term *power* to be the general, all-encompassing concept. Constellation of interests in a free market and established authority were viewed as more limited and more specific concepts.

As he shifted from a discussion of the general term

power (*macht*) to the more specific term domination (*herrschaft*), Weber excluded situations in which power is derived from a constellation of economic interests in a free market and limited his definition to power that is derived from established authority. Although he did not use the term *authority* as a separate technical term, the relationship between authority and domination in his writing was so close that Bendix (1960) concluded that the two terms could be used interchangeably (p. 296).

Regardless of the terms used, Weber considered power *to be derived from* established authority. Therefore, authority (legitimate domination) was viewed as a source of power, not a derivative of power.

TOWARD A CONCEPTUAL FRAMEWORK

Essential Elements of Power

There are three essential elements related to the phenomenon of social power: (a) a general conceptualization, a definition in the broadest sense, which establishes the limits for further consideration of the phenomenon; (b) a specification of the bases or sources of power; and (c) an elaboration of the ways in which power is exercised.

Basic Definition

We consider power to be the generic and most encompassing term in a conceptualization of domination in social interaction. We define power as a force that determines behavioral outcomes in an intended direction in a situation involving human interaction. From this definition we would not say that an individual or group *has* power; rather, we would say that an individual or group is able to exercise power when... The *when* would specify the conditions under which power might be exercised. In proposing this definition, we follow Weber, who stated that power includes "every conceivable quality of a person and every combination of circumstances that may put someone in a situation where he can demand compliance with his will" (Roth & Wittich, 1968, p. 117).

Bases of Power

In discussing the bases or sources of power we again specify the context in which the discussion occurs. We are not talking about power in informal groups, nor are we considering power as a psychological phenomenon. We are discussing power in an institutional setting. In doing so, our discussion is consistent with that of Weber, Simmel (1961), Merton (1957), and others.

Within this context, we conceive of two, and only two, sources of power: authority and prestige. Any consideration of power can be undertaken with reference to one or the other of these concepts, or to some combination of the two.

Authority The term *authority* refers to the capability of exercising power by virtue of the fact that an individual occupies a legally established position within a social institution. Thus, authority is conceived as a relationship between subordinates and superordinates; or, as Bendix put it, authority "involves a reciprocal relationship between rulers and ruled" (p. 295).

Prestige Whereas authority refers to the institutional element of power, prestige refers to the personal element. It can be defined as the capability of exercising power by virtue of the fact that an individual possesses personal characteristics, either natural (candor, energy) or acquired (knowledge, expertise), that are valued by others. Unlike authority, which must be delegated by the institution but cannot be earned, prestige must be earned; it cannot be delegated.

Although there is considerable historical precedent for the term *prestige* as we have used it, Weber did not elaborate on this personal dimension of power. Does this mean that Weber did not consider this dimension to be important in his conception of power? The answer is not simple, but there is considerable evidence that he did not ignore the issue.

Throughout most of his works, Weber's attention was directed primarily toward groups, not individuals. Prestige is a concept related to the individual; consequently, it did not appear frequently in his writings. However, Weber did at times distinguish between the individual and the institution. In particular he distinguished between the term *charismatic leadership*, in which the person is basic, and *charismatic authority*, in which the person is merely a symbol.

Weber's use of the term *charisma* is not equivalent to our use of the term *prestige*. For Weber, "charisma means magical power as a unique and hence transient attribute of an individual" (Bendix, 1960, p. 306). Charisma refers to superhuman qualities; prestige refers to human qualities. Charisma is fleeting and unstable; prestige is enduring and stable. Charisma is an all-or-nothing concept; prestige refers to a number of human characteristics that exist in varying degrees in different individuals.

In our formulation, true charisma represents the one exception to the general rule that power is derived from two sources. In the case of true charisma, the individual *is* the institution; therefore, the institutional and individual dimensions converge to become a single dimension.

The relationships among the concepts of power, authority, and prestige can be represented as in Figure 12.1.[2]

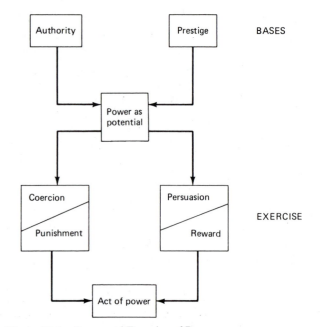

Figure 12.1 Bases and Exercise of Power

In this formulation authority and prestige are considered to be complementary concepts. The amount of power (force) available to a role incumbent can be increased if the individual simultaneously occupies an authoritative position and enjoys the esteem of others.

Exercise of Power

So far, in developing a framework related to power and its correlates, we have proposed a basic definition of the term *power*, and we have identified the two sources of power in an institutional setting. We turn now to a consideration of the third essential element of power, its exercise. We have said that power is a potential whose force is derived either from authority (legitimate position) or from prestige (personal attributes). The actualization of power, a power act, is what we call its exercise.

Once again, the confusion regarding this "force" has come about because of the tendency of social scientists to use different terms for the same concept. Regardless of the terms used, the concept can be reduced to two major components: a coercive-compelling component or a persuasive-rewarding component. The exercise of power, then, ultimately becomes either an act of coercion or an act of persuasion Each of these acts can stem from either authority or prestige. Authority is not equivalent to coercion, and prestige is not equivalent to persuasion. A power act based on authority can be either persuasive or coercive; likewise, a power act based on prestige can be either coercive or persuasive.

The discussion to this point can be summarized as

follows: Institutional power, the potential to elicit intended behaviors from others, is based either on authority or on prestige; and its exercise takes the form of either coercion or persuasion. These ideas can be clarified by comparison with a contrasting formulation. We have chosen the influential study by French and Raven (1960) in which the authors distinguish among five "especially common and important" bases, or types, of power; reward, coercive, legitimate, referent, and expert.

According to French and Raven (1960), "reward power is defined as power whose basis is the ability to reward" (p. 263). Logically, this is equivalent to saying that rewarding is based on the ability to reward. The problem is the confusion between an action—rewarding—and the source of the ability to perform that action. In fact, an individual has the ability to reward if that individual has either authority or prestige. These are the bases or sources of the ability to reward. Thus, rewarding is an expression of power, the exercise of power; it is not a basis of power.

The same reasoning applies to coercive power. Reward power and coercive power are expressions of power, ways in which power is exercised. Both are actions that must be based on something; in an institutional setting, that "something" can be either authority or prestige or both.

French and Raven's treatment of legitimate power is also confusing. Legitimacy, a key term for Weber, is an essential element of acceptable domination in social interaction. Conceptually, legitimacy cannot be separated from legal-rational domination, nor from traditional domination, nor from charismatic domination. These types of domination constitute power because they are accorded legitimacy by those who are ruled. Within an institutional setting, therefore, authority *is* legitimate power.

The last two types of power identified by French and Raven, referent power and expert power, are in fact elements of what we have termed here *prestige*. Prestige is a comprehensive concept and could arise from a number of sources, including identification (referent power) and expertness (expert power). Other factors that contribute to prestige could be named. For example, Peabody (1962) listed professional competence, experience, and human-relations skills as sources of functional authority (prestige); and Fayol (1949) identified intelligence, experience, moral worth, ability to lead, and past services as contributors to personal authority (prestige). The list could go on, but we contend that all of the characteristics that contribute to prestige can be encompassed in four basic elements: knowledge, moral character, physical attributes, and human-relations skills.

DOMINATION AND BUREAUCRACY

Weber wrote extensively about domination in social interaction. His conclusions about that phenomenon led him to a reconceptualization and a reformulation of bureaucracy as a significant social institution.

Types of Domination

From his studies of governments and religions, Weber identified three types of legitimate domination in social interaction. One was *legal* domination, derived from a belief in rule by law. Under legal domination, superiors are obligated to support the rules, which constitute a *legal order*. In such an order, the subjects are considered to be the *legal equals* of their superiors; their duty is to obey the *rules*, not the *rulers*. Superiors may dominate subordinates only in the spheres of life covered by the rules. They can undermine the beliefs sustaining the law (legitimacy) by manipulating their "subjects" to extend the domination of the superiors indefinitely.

The second was *traditional* domination, which differs from legal domination in that legitimacy is derived not from a system of rules but rather from a belief in sacred traditions that have vested in authoritative positions the right to rule. The individuals who occupy those positions usually inherit the right of domination. Since they are constrained only by historical customs, and since in many cases their interpretations of those customs prevail, there is no mechanism for limiting arbitrary behavior on their part. However, they can undermine the belief in sacred tradition (legitimacy) if they use their arbitrary powers to place themselves above the traditions.

The third was *charismatic* domination. This type of domination achieves legitimacy from a belief in the supernatural powers of a leader. Such a leader (prophet, hero, demagogue) possesses charisma through magical qualities, revelations from a deity, uncommon heroism, or other extraordinary gifts. Followers of such a leader are "disciples," who consider the leader's commands to be inviolable. Decisions of the leader are not bound by either rules or tradition; constraints are imposed solely by the leader's judgment and self-discipline. The beliefs that sustain charismatic leaders (legitimacy) may disappear (a) if these leaders fail to prove themselves in the eyes of their disciples or (b) if the original leaders die.

As noted earlier, Weber made a distinction between charismatic leadership and charismatic authority. Charismatic leadership refers strictly to heroic qualities: it represents a response to crisis, and it approximates its pure type only at the time of its origin.

Thus, charismatic leadership is fragile and unstable. Because of this instability, attempts are made to transform charismatic leadership into a more stable form of dominance. This is achieved by institutionalizing charisma, by attaching it to a position and thus converting it to charismatic authority. Charisma may then be conferred upon successors through some type of magical ceremony, which is designed to assure the retention of the charismatic qualities of the original leaders. Charismatic leadership may also be transmitted by converting it to some form of traditional domination, such as patrimonialism, and by having successors chosen on the basis of ascription, such as heredity.

To summarize, we have noted that the concept of legitimacy is central to Weber's concept of domination. In the case of charisma, legitimacy stems from a belief in revelation, and power is concentrated in the hands of a *prophet*. In the case of tradition, legitimacy is derived from a belief in the sacredness of tradition, and power is concentrated in the hands of the occupant of a *traditionally sanctioned position*. In contrast, legal domination derives its legitimacy from the exercise of reason and the enactment of *laws*. In the case of charismatic and traditional domination, the ability to rule depends on the acquiescence of the ruled to the wishes and commands of the ruler. In the case of legal domination, the ability to rule rests on the willingness of free individuals to enter into a contract or to conform to orders based upon a prior agreement.

Weber was adamant in his belief in the superiority of legal domination over other forms. The rule of law was the only means by which people or their representatives could control. Thus, *rule of law* was synonymous with *democracy*. It prohibited arbitrary rule, and it protected a right that had been won through a long struggle against the absolutism of a monarchical form of government. The test of the efficacy of the principles of rationality as expressed in legal domination would be to apply it to a specific case. For Weber, the specific case was bureaucracy.

Bureaucracy and Bureaucratization

Bendix (1960) points out that Weber actually dealt with four related but conceptually distinct aspects of bureaucracy (p. 418). First, he analyzed the historical and technical reasons for the process of bureaucratization, which he listed as (a) the development of an economy based on money, (b) the expansion of administrative tasks in a developing society, and (c) the superiority of bureaucracy as a means of carrying out those tasks.

Second, he considered the impact of the rule of law

upon the functioning of bureaucratic organizations. His conclusions regarding this issue constituted a major portion of his description of the "ideal" form of bureaucracy.

Third, he developed specifications for the occupational position and professional orientation of bureaucratic officials. Among the conditions he stipulated were the separation of management from ownership and the limitation of official authority by rules.

Fourth, he analyzed the consequences of bureaucracy in a modern world. Central to this issue was Weber's contention that only within the rule of law is it possible to "calculate" the results of a decision.

Confusing Terminology

One of the troublesome terms Weber and his interpreters used is *ideal type*. Although the term appears in virtually every English translation of Weber's essays, rarely does one encounter its definition, and the definitions that do appear are vague. Apparently, Weber himself used the term without clarifying its meaning. Even so, a sense of the meaning it had for him can be obtained by drawing on a number of his essays. In "Types of Authority" (Weber, 1965b), Weber stated that "all ruling powers, profane and religious, political and apolitical, may be considered as variations of, or approximations to, certain pure types" (p. 129). Those pure types could be determined in relation to the basis of their legitimacy (charisma, tradition, law, and reason).

In "Subjective Meaning in the Social Situation" (Weber, 1965a), Weber said, "For the purpose of a typological scientific analysis it is convenient to treat all irrational, affectually determined elements of behavior as factors of deviation from a conceptually *pure type* of rational action [italics added]" (p. 238). Using examples of panic on the stock exchange and an analysis of political or military campaigns, Weber argued that one should determine in each case what would have happened if no irrational affects had entered into the action. In this way it would be possible to identify the irrational elements and to assess the significance of those elements in accounting for the *deviations* of the actions from *pure* types. As Weber noted, "The construction of a purely rational course of action in such cases serves...as a type ('ideal type') which has the merit of clear understandability and lack of ambiguity" (1965a, p. 238).

In "Legitimate Order and Types of Authority" (Weber, 1961), Weber discussed his three *pure* types of legitimate authority. "The fact that none of these three ideal types...is usually to be found in historical cases in 'pure' form," he said, "is naturally not a valid objection to attempting their conceptual formulation in the sharpest possible form" (p. 235).

For Weber, then, the ideal type was a conceptualization. His use of the terms *ideal* and *pure* interchangeably clearly indicates that he was describing a set of conditions toward which officials should strive. Deviations from these ideal conditions were the result of human fallibility and should not be allowed to divert attention from the conceivable "ideal."

And what were those conditions that constituted the ideal type? In virtually all translations of his works into English, three basic elements appear: (a) rule by law (legal domination), (b) acceptance by the governed of the norms upon which the laws are based (legitimation), and (c) elimination of irrational elements from the actions of officials (rationality).

From this brief summary of Weber's conceptualization of the "ideal" form of bureaucracy, we turn to a review of the research on schools as bureaucracies.

RESEARCH

The amount of research on bureaucracy as it relates to schools is relatively modest. Much of the literature in this field consists of essays in which the authors describe bureaucracy and then, by inference, attempt to demonstrate the ways in which school organizations conform to the bureaucratic model.

Since our primary interest is in research, we generally have not referenced essay literature in this chapter. Instead, we conducted a thorough review of the research literature on schools as bureaucracies, and we have supplemented that review with findings from selected studies in the more general field of organizational theory. We have included nonschool studies that are relevant to schools or that have stimulated research on schools.

We have organized the research into four broad categories. The first has to do with measurement issues; the second deals with the nature of bureaucracy; the third includes research on the intended and unintended consequences of bureaucratic organization; and the fourth includes research on the relationships between bureaucratic principles and various organizational variables.

Measurement Issues in Research on Bureaucracy

Over the years a number of questions have been raised about the issue of measurement in research on bureaucracy. One such question has to do with appropriate methods for collecting data. Some have argued for the use of case studies that allow an in-depth analysis of a single organization. Others have contended that survey methods should be used so that comparisons might be made among a variety of organizations.

Questions have also been raised about the concept of dimensionality in bureaucracies. Should measuring scales reflect the assumption that bureaucracy is a unidimensional concept? Or should those scales be based on the assumption that bureaucracy is a multi-dimensional concept?

A third measurement issue, closely related to the second, has to do with the source of data to be used when employing survey techniques. Should the data reflect the perceptions of employees, should the data come from official descriptions of the organizational structure, or should the data be collected from both sources?

Early challenges to the concept of unidimensionality were lodged by Gouldner (1948) and Udy (1959). Both recommended that the ideal-typical attributes of bureaucracy should be viewed as variables to be investigated. Hall (1963) acted on that recommendation, arguing that "bureaucracy is a form of organization which exists along a number of continua or dimensions" (p. 33).

To carry out his research, Hall used the six dimensions of bureaucracy that he had identified earlier (Hall, 1962). Those six dimensions were (a) a division of labor based on functional specialization, (b) a well-defined hierarchy of authority, (c) a system of rules covering the rights and duties of positional incumbents, (d) a system of procedures for dealing with work situations, (e) impersonality of interpersonal relations, and (f) promotion and selection based on technical competence.

Hall (1963) collected data by interviewing organizational participants. Although he acknowledged the possibility that "the perceptions of participants of their organizations may well be at variance with the officially described structure" (p. 35), he contended that the official structure is important only to the extent that it is adhered to. He argued that accurate measurements of perception would yield a reliable and valid representation of the actual structure. From his research Hall (1963) came to the following conclusions:

> First, the bureaucratic dimensions are meaningful organizational structural attributes. Second, when measured quantitatively, the dimensions exist in the form of continua rather than as dichotomies. Third, the magnitude of the dimensions varied independently to the organizations studied. (p. 39)

Hall's research, including his measurement scale, the Organizational Inventory, has had a significant impact on the subsequent investigations related to schools and bureaucracy. MacKay (1964), adapted

Hall's inventory to make it applicable to schools, and he used it in an investigation that yielded results similar to Hall's. Punch (1969) further refined MacKay's instrument, using data collected by MacKay and others, until he could say that the "Organizational Inventory appears adequate on technical grounds for the task of mapping the domain of bureaucratic structure" (p. 49). He then used the refined instrument to conduct research on this question: Is bureaucratic structure in schools realistically conceptualized as a unitary, homogeneous variable?

Punch collected data from 48 schools in southern Ontario, Canada. Based on an analysis of the intercorrelations among the six dimensions, as well as the results of factor analysis, Punch demonstrated that the six dimensions combined to produce two major factors. The first, which accounted for 81 percent of the common variance among the schools, was composed of hierarchy of authority, rules for incumbents, procedural specifications, and impersonality. The other, which accounted for 10 percent of the common variance, was composed of specialization and technical competence. In answer to his own question Punch stated: "Bureaucratic structure in schools is realistically conceptualized as a unitary, homogeneous variable only if restricted to the dimensions [that constitute the major factor.] If, as usual, specialization and technical competence are included, then bureaucratic structure is a two-factor and not a unitary concept" (p. 53).

Sousa and Hoy (1981) took note of Punch's work and set about to develop and test a still more refined measure of bureaucratic structure in schools. They pointed out that the original Organizational Inventory developed by Hall depended exclusively on the perceptions of organizational participants for data on bureaucratic dimensions. They argued that although such data should be taken into account in explaining behavior, other sources of information should be sought to provide a more accurate description of the phenomenon under investigation.

The other source of information for Sousa and Hoy was an interview schedule developed by researchers at the University of Aston in England (Pugh, Hickson, & Hinnings, 1968). Using modified versions of both the School Organizational Inventory and the Aston interview schedule, Sousa and Hoy collected data that enabled them to interpret the interrelationships among the scales that were used.

Factor analysis yielded four underlying dimensions of school structure (Sousa & Hoy, 1981): "*Organizational Control*, consisting of hierarchy of authority, rules, procedural specifications, and standardization; *Rational Specialization*, comprising technical competence and specialization; *System Centralization*, encompassing centralization and autonomy; and *Formalization of Routine*, consisting of formalization of role performance" (p. 36). Sousa and Hoy (1981) concluded that the "present research identifies two distinct loci of power, Organizational Control and System Centralization" (p. 35). They contended that organizational control refers to control exercised within a school building, whereas system centralization refers to control exercised by the broader system. They also concluded that "schools may be bureaucratic in a large number of ways" (p. 36).

Moeller and Charters (1966) reported an investigation into the relationship between degree of bureaucratization and the feeling of powerlessness among classroom teachers. Their measurement scale was based on an assumption of unidimensionality. The degree of bureaucratization of the school systems was determined by having knowledgeable individuals rate the districts as either high or low on a list of eight dichotomous statements. The investigation demonstrated that it is possible to differentiate among school districts using dichotomous measures of bureaucracy.

The research has demonstrated that it is possible to use a variety of research methods to investigate formal organizations, including case studies and survey techniques. If survey techniques are used, it is possible to develop instruments based on either unidimensional or multidimensional concepts; moreover, either descriptive or perceptual data can be used. However, a fundamental issue remains: Are we in fact investigating bureaucracy? That is a conceptual issue, not a measurement issue.

The Nature of Bureaucracy

There is considerable disagreement regarding the appropriate interpretation of the concept of bureaucracy. We noted earlier that for Weber the fundamental purpose of bureaucracy was to insure domination based on law and reason. There was no equivocation in his elaboration of the elements that were necessary to achieve that goal; all of the elements had to be present, and together they constituted an entity. To the extent that any of those elements was not found in a specific organization, the organization fell short of conforming to the ideal model.

Litwak (1961) challenged that conceptualization. He argued that Weber's model is most efficient "when an organization deals primarily with uniform events and with occupations stressing traditional areas of knowledge rather than social skills" (p. 177). He also contended that emphasis on rules, hierarchy, specialization, impersonality, and the separation of policy and administrative decisions all apply to situations involving uniform events. According to Litwak, where organizations deal with nonuniform events

> a model of bureaucracy may be more efficient which differs in degree from Weber's in at least six characteristics: horizontal patterns of authority, minimal specialization, mixture of decisions on policy and administration, little a priori limitation of duty and privileges to a given office, personal rather than impersonal relations, and a minimum of general rules. (p. 179)

Litwak characterized this model as a "human-relations" model of bureaucracy. To build a case for a third model, Litwak referred to the work of Pelz (1960), who had investigated a large industrial firm in which workers in one section dealt with nonuniform events whereas workers in another section dealt with relatively uniform events. Pelz had reported that the correlation between decision making and motivation varied depending on the nature of the tasks performed. In those groups that dealt with uniform, relatively routine tasks, the correlation between motivation and productivity was higher when the workers were *restricted* in making decisions. The reverse held true for those groups that dealt with nonuniform tasks.

This phenomenon, the existence of work involving two different types of tasks within the same organization, creates a dilemma for organizational structure. In Litwak's terms, Weber's model is appropriate when dealing with work involving uniform tasks, and a human-relations model is appropriate when dealing with work involving nonuniform tasks. But, how does one incorporate both models into the same organization?

To deal with the dilemma, Litwak (1961) proposed a third model, which he called "professional bureaucracy." A fundamental issue for this model, according to Litwak, is to determine procedures by which potentially contradictory social relations might be coordinated. His response was to "segregate" incompatible work units. In this way nonuniform events could be handled by workers within a unit, separated from regular hierarchical channels. Litwak contended that "a key area for advancing the theory of complex organizations is the study of ways by which contradictory forms of organizational structure exist side by side without ruinous friction" (p. 87).

Following the publication of Litwak's paper, Hall (1962) designed an empirical investigation to test Litwak's theoretical propositions. Hall proposed using a simpler, more direct method of testing the propositions than the one implied by Litwak's three models. Hall suggested the use of a single bureaucratic model. His proposal was based on his earlier assumption that Weber's characteristics of bureaucracy were in fact separate dimensions of bureaucracy and that it would be possible to measure the degree to which each dimension existed within a specific organization. Such measures would make it possible to identify and describe differences among organizations. To carry out that investigation, Hall developed his Organizational Inventory.

Hall found that departments dealing with nonuniform events were significantly less bureaucratic on three of the six dimensions than were those dealing with uniform events. Those three dimensions were hierarchy of authority, division of labor, and presence of external procedural specifications. However, no significant differences were found on the other three dimensions.

Litwak and Hall called attention to three issues that were to receive considerable attention in subsequent research on bureaucracy. First, they raised the possibility that the term *bureaucracy* could be used to describe organizations that differed substantially in a number of ways. Second, they called attention to the seeming incompatibility between bureaucratic norms and professional norms in respect to control structure. Third, they suggested the possibility that different decision-making structures could exist simultaneously within the same organization.

Regarding the first issue, a number of investigators have suggested ways in which the term *bureaucracy* could be applied to different types of organization. In his study of management at a gypsum mine, Gouldner (1954) concluded that management employed a "punishment-centered bureaucracy." In contrast, he contended that it would be possible to identify situations in which management might employ "representative bureaucracy." (It should be noted that Gouldner was referring more to the way that officials use authority than he was to characteristics of bureaucracy.)

From an investigation of decision making related to university budgets, Hills and Mahoney (1978) defined two models of organization: bureaucratic and coalitional. They contended that the two models could be differentiated in terms of the major assumptions underlying each. A bureaucratic model assumes the existence of a unitary, stable goal; a decision maker who can elucidate that goal; and an optimal allocation of resources among the various units of the organization. On the other hand, the coalitional model assumes that goals are relatively independent constraints on resource allocation; that allocation decisions are based on arbitrary rules; and that the rules sustain the relative position of units found among the coalitions. Hills and Mahoney's first model follows the classical definition of bureaucracy, whereas their second model conforms to a political model of organizations.

Isherwood and Hoy (1973) developed a typology of organizations using a two-dimensional grid. The two dimensions were derived from the School Organizational Inventory. The first dimension was labeled *bureaucratic* and consisted of items related to hierarchy of authority, rules for incumbents, procedural specifications, and impersonality. The second dimension was labeled *professional* and consisted of items related to technical competence and specialization.

By dichotomizing the two dimensions (low or high) and by placing them on a grid, Isherwood and Hoy derived a four-part organizational typology. The first, a Weberian type, is one that ranks high on both the bureaucratic and the professional dimensions. The second, an authoritarian type, is one that ranks high on the bureaucratic dimension but low on the professional dimension. The third, a professional type, is one that ranks high on the professional dimension but low on the bureaucratic dimension. The fourth, a chaotic type, is one that ranks low on both dimensions. These investigators demonstrated empirically that it is possible to classify schools as either professional or authoritarian.

The research reviewed in this section clearly demonstrates that two or more decision-making structures may exist simultaneously within a given organization. Stated more generally, *multidimensional* is an accurate adjective to use in describing complex organizations. Whether this means that *bureaucracy* is a multidimensional concept depends on whether one views bureaucracy as structure or as a conceptualization. We hold to the view that Weber's formulation was a conceptualization. Where the investigators cited here use the word *bureaucracy*, therefore, we would substitute the word *organization*.

Intended versus Unintended Consequences

In applying his general principles of social order to the concept of bureaucracy, Weber focused his attention on the intended, desirable consequences of legal-rational domination. He said nothing about the limitations of bureaucracy; he evidenced no concern about the unintended consequences of adherence to bureaucratic principles.

The earliest of Weber's critics responded to this issue. Three of the most articulate of those critics were Merton, Selznick, and Gouldner. Their findings have received extensive treatment in the literature, including a succinct presentation of the implications of those findings in the widely quoted theoretical work by March and Simon (1958). In this section, therefore, we present only brief résumés of those criticisms.

Merton (1940) pointed out that in a bureaucracy there is an emphasis on the use of rules and procedures to assure reliable behavior on the part of organizational members. Such behavior is necessary to assure the coordination of various task units. In addition, by adhering to the rules and procedures, individuals are protected from unjust demands. Thus, rules and procedures constitute a defense mechanism for organizational members.

Simultaneously, however, adherence to rules also leads to rigidity on the part of employees. To avoid punishment, organizational members adhere closely to the rules; in those cases where it is necessary to choose between exercising judgment and adhering to rules, the rules tend to win. The increased rigidity that results from strict adherence to rules tends to increase the amount of conflict between members and clients, and the increased conflict leads in turn to an increase in the felt need for defense on the part of employees. The increased need for defense tends to lead to a proliferation of rules, which leads once again to increased rigidity, and the cycle is repeated.

Selznick (1949) focused attention on the need for delegation to assure control and to increase organizational efficiency. Delegation brings about increased training and thus increased competencies in specialized functions. Specialization is accompanied by departmentalization, which results in a bifurcation of interests. Participants within departments come to view their specializations as ends rather than means. This means-ends reversal creates increased conflict among subunits, and the increased conflict detracts from the effectiveness of the organization.

Gouldner (1954) discussed the use of general and impersonal rules as a response to demands for organizational control. The use of rules is intended to reduce the visibility of power relations, which then reduces the level of interpersonal tension and conflict. However, rules increase the participants' awareness of minimally acceptable behavior, which tends to lead to less than optimal performance. Since organizations are not satisfied with less than optimal performance, this tendency toward the minimum results in an increase in personal supervision, the condition that the rules were intended to eliminate. The increase in closeness of supervision leads to an increase in the visibility of power relations, which leads in turn to an increase in the level of interpersonal tension and conflict.

A more recent elaboration of the intended versus unintended consequences of the use of rules was developed by Anderson (1969). In his discussion of bureaucracy and the school, Anderson argued that organizational authority becomes imbedded in a set of rules and that the use of rules as "bearers of authority" leads to both functional and dysfunctional consequences.

Among the functional consequences, Anderson listed the following: First, rules give direction to organizational behavior. They communicate expectations for role performance, and they clarify relationships among roles. Second, rules make it possible to decentralize authority. As rules come to be known and accepted at all levels of the organization, behavior can be controlled from a distance, making frequent surveillance unnecesary. Third, rules depersonalize authority relationships and thus serve as a buffer between administrators and subordinates; they also legitimize administrative authority by specifying the conditions under which such authority may be exercised. Fourth, rules legitimize punishment by giving advance notice of possible sanctions for noncompliance; at the same time, rules protect subordinates from unjust punishment. Fifth, rules provide the means for administrators to bargain with subordinates. Through selective enforcement of the rules, administrators accumulate "chips," which they can use to bargain with subordinates over issues that are not covered by the rules. Finally, rules serve as a buffer between employees and external demands. Thus, the rules provide security by minimizing the risks and reducing the anxiety associated with role performance.

Among the dysfunctional consequences, Anderson listed the following: First, rules lead to goal displacement and role distortion. Unquestioning compliance with rules rather than their judicious enforcement becomes the norm. The rules take on an aura of compulsion, and what were intended to be means become ends. Second, rules tend to reinforce apathy and foster legalistic thinking. Creative efforts to respond to problems are discouraged, whereas minimal performance, justified by a legalistic interpretation of the rules, is encouraged. Third, rules lead to avoidance behavior. The rules become substitutes for personal judgment; problems that are difficult to resolve tend to be ignored since the inability to resolve them could be interpreted as failure. For those concerned about their careers, the message received is that promotion comes to those who adhere to the rules, not to those who question the rules.

The notion of unintended consequences has by now become almost universally understood and accepted. This is true whether we are talking about organizational structure or problem solving and decision making. This phenomenon is vividly conveyed by Wildavsky (1979), who says that every action taken to solve a problem creates new problems. The question to ask in such a situation is: Are the new problems more or less acceptable than the problem we are trying to solve?

Relationships Among Organizational Variables

In the section on the nature of bureaucracy, we discussed the relationships that exist among the variables implied by Weber's elements of bureaucracy. And we reported evidence to show that those variables cluster to form major organizational dimensions. In this section we discuss the research on the relationships between elements of bureaucracy and other organizational variables. The other variables are divided into five categories: organizational size, attitudinal variables, authority relationships, bureaucratic versus professional norms, and linkages and coupling.

Organization Size

Kimberly (1976) conducted an extensive review of the research on organizational size and concluded that conceptual and empirical problems exist regarding this concept. First, the concept of size is too global to permit a specification of its role. Second, the effects of size may vary depending on the type of organization. Third, current approaches to studying this phenomenon are far too static; they do not consider the extent to which a change in size over time affects an organization. Keeping these cautions in mind, it is still important to examine the available evidence regarding relationships between organizational size and other variables.

Meyer (1968) examined the commonly accepted assumption that bureaucratic authority consists only of the authority of office. He concluded that such an assumption seems not to be warranted in light of current research findings. As an alternative assumption, he argued that written regulations, as well as less formalized conventions, are also sources of bureaucratic authority.

To test his alternative assumption, Meyer investigated the ways in which labor might be divided. Two contrasting methods were noted: vertical division, which Meyer termed *hierarchical* differentiation, and horizontal division, which he termed *functional* differentiation. Functional differentiation is generally associated with small organizations, whereas hierarchical differentiation increases as organizations increase in size. Treating organizational size as one variable, Meyer examined the ways in which rules and regulations relate to the authority dimension in organizational structure. He concluded that rules and regulations can be used either to centralize authority or to decentralize authority.

A key finding reported by Meyer was that hierarchically differentiated (vertical) structures are most compatible with decentralization of decision making, whereas functionally differentiated (horizontal) structures tend to maintain patterns of centralized authority. Stated differently, in flat organizations authority tends to be centralized; in pyramidal organizations authority tends to be decentralized.

Meyer's findings received considerable support

from findings reported by Mansfield (1973). From his research on different types of organizations in England, Mansfield concluded that increasing organizational size forces managers to create rules to govern behavior and hence to reduce the range of possible day-to-day problems. Contrary to generally accepted views, this increase in the use of rules, with a concomitant delegation of authority, results in decentralization rather than centralization of decisions.

Although he did not address himself explicitly to the issue of organizational size, Anderson made a similar point in his discussion of rules as bearers of organizational authority. One use of rules, according to Anderson (1966), "is as a decentralizing mechanism" (p. 14). Where direct supervision of behavior is difficult, rules may be used to control behavior from a distance.

Attitudinal Variables

A number of investigations of the relationship between bureaucracy and *attitudinal* (psychological) variables in educational organizations have been reported. Variables included in those investigations are feeling of powerlessness, loyalty, esprit, and alienation.

An early investigation on this issue was reported by Moeller and Charters (1966). Their research concerned the relationship between a sense of powerlessness among classroom teachers and the degree of bureaucratization of the school systems in which they worked. It was hypothesized that "teachers in highly bureaucratized school systems would have a much lower 'sense of power' than teachers in less bureaucratic systems" (p. 448). The logic was that when teachers are constrained by elaborate systems of rules and regulations that have been developed with little input from them, they will respond with a sense of powerlessness to control their lives at work.

This hypothesis was not confirmed. In fact, teachers in highly bureaucratic systems had a lower sense of powerlessness than did teachers in the less bureaucratic systems. Moeller and Charters also found that the degree of bureaucratization was not related to the size of the school system. The largest system in the study was one of the three lowest on the measure of bureaucratization.

Isherwood and Hoy (1973) also investigated the relationship between bureaucratization and teachers' feelings of powerlessness. Unlike Moeller and Charters (1966), who used the school district as the unit of analysis, Isherwood and Hoy used the individual school as the unit of analysis. Moreover, where Moeller and Charters used a dichotomous scale to measure the degree of bureaucratization, Isherwood and Hoy used two of the four categories derived from their two-

dimensional grid. Those two categories defined schools as authoritarian or collegial. (The terms *authoritarian* and *collegial* more accurately refer to management style than to degree of bureaucratization.)

Isherwood and Hoy included another variable in their investigation, work value. The inventory they used enabled them to categorize teachers as holding either professional, organizational, or social work values. Therefore, they were able to examine differences between teachers in authoritarian schools and those in collegial schools; they were also able to examine differences among teachers who held different work values, regardless of school type.

Isherwood and Hoy (1973) found that teachers in authoritarian schools had a greater sense of powerlessness than did their counterparts in collegial schools. They also found that "professionally oriented teachers have the greatest sense of powerlessness in the authoritarian school, while organizationally and socially oriented teachers have the greatest sense of powerlessness in collegial schools. Furthermore, authoritarian schools seem to have a greater alienating effect, in terms of powerlessness, on more teachers than do collegial schools" (pp. 137–138).

Hoy, Newland, and Blazovsky (1977) noted the differences between the findings of Moeller and Charters and those of Isherwood and Hoy. They also noted that Hoy and Rees (1974) had reported that "authoritarian" supervision decreased the loyalty of teachers toward school principals. To learn more about these issues, Hoy et al. (1977) investigated further the relationship of structure to subordinate loyalty; they also investigated the relationship between structure and esprit.

Their measures of structure included two elements of the concept of centralization: an index of hierarchy of authority and an index of participation in decision making. Their measures also included two elements of the concept of formalization: an index of job codification and an index of rule observation.

Contrary to their expectations, Hoy et al. (1977) did not find a significant relationship between participation in decision making and loyalty. What they did find was that the "autonomy to execute assigned tasks unimpeded by supervisors is more important in generating subordinate loyalty than participation in school-wide decisions" (p. 80).

The findings on the relationship between esprit and the two measures of formalization were somewhat contradictory. Esprit was positively related to job codification but negatively related to rule observation. Hoy et al. (1977) interpreted this finding to mean that "teachers seem to want rules and regulations to reduce job uncertainty, but they resent excessive supervision and the tight enforcement of those rules" (p. 83).

Further support for this finding comes from research reported by Cox and Wood (1980), in which they investigated the relationship between structure and professional alienation among public school teachers. All four of their measures of structure—participation in decision making, hierarchy of authority, job codification, and rule enforcement—correlated positively with alienation. The factors that contributed most to their findings were (a) increased professional training of teachers and (b) concomitant demands from teachers for greater professional autonomy.

Hoy, Blazovsky, and Newland (1983) carried out a follow-up to their 1977 investigation to examine more directly the relationship between bureaucratization and alienation. They developed two measures of alienation: alienation from work and alienation in expressive relationships (from fellow workers). They used the measures of bureaucracy that they had employed in their earlier study, except that the indexes of centralization and formalization were combined to form the single concept, *hierarchy*. They reported a positive relationship between bureaucratization (hierarchy) and both alienation from work and alienation in expressive relationships. On the other hand, they observed a negative relationship between participation in decision making and the two measures of alienation.

Authority Relationships

The concept of authority is an essential element in the broader conceptualization of bureaucracy. A key issue in the study of bureaucracy, therefore, is the nature of authority relationships in the hierarchy.

Much, if not most, of the writing about hierarchy is based on the assumption that it is a monistic concept. A common interpretation of the meaning of hierarchy, therefore, is that in a bureaucracy, decision making is centralized. This interpretation creates a dilemma that was enunciated by Thompson (1961) when he said that "*the most symptomatic characteristic of modern bureaucracy is the growing imbalance between ability and authority* [italics in the original]" (p. 6).

In recent years a growing number of writers have called attention to the inevitable conflict between the monistic assumption and the facts of organizational life. Specifically, it has been argued that occupants of hierarchical positions frequently do not have the technical competence to make decisions about issues that involve specialized (professional) knowledge.

One writer who makes this point is Corwin (1961), who observed that research on the relationships between hospital administrators and physicians had shown that there was potential conflict between the hierarchical organization and the essence of professional knowledge. The conflict had been largely avoided, however, by separating spheres of authority: that is, by delegating strictly administrative decisions to those in hierarchical positions, while allowing physicians to make decisions requiring professional knowledge. Based on those research findings, Corwin (1965) set about to investigate the same issue in schools.

Information for the investigation was obtained from two sources. First, teachers were asked to respond to a scale that differentiated between professional and bureaucratic role conceptions (norms). Second, a number of teachers were randomly selected for open-ended interviews about incidents of tension (conflict).

Corwin found that almost half of all incidents of conflict involved teachers in opposition to administrators; about one-fourth of all such incidents involved issues such as proper teaching techniques and procedures, curriculum changes, and selection of textbooks. He also found that there was a significant correlation between professional orientation and conflict. Persons who held high professional and low bureaucratic perceptions had higher rates of conflict than did those who held high bureaucratic and low professional perceptions. Corwin (1965) concluded "that there is a consistent pattern of conflict between teachers and administrators over the control of work" (p. 15).

Boyan (1966) conducted an extensive review of the literature dealing with the role of teachers in the authority structure of the schools. Based on that review, Boyan called attention to two major issues. First, he noted that teachers consistently have differentiated between administrative and supervisory authority. They agree that they should defer to decisions related to administrative authority, but they feel that they should resist administrative attempts to exercise supervisory authority. Second, he pointed out that if current trends continue, increased professionalism of teachers would exacerbate the conflict over supervisory authority. According to Boyan (1966):

> The need for two separate structures for teacher participation in school government is compelling...The first would permit teacher involvement via a bargaining or negotiations model in the development of organizational legislation addressed to general employment conditions. The second would extend the classical participatory model to include *the right, as a right*, of teachers to participate in organizational decisions on educational programs [emphasis in the original]. (pp. 16–17)

These recommendations, as well as Corwin's, are consistent with Mansfield's (1973) conception of hierarchy. In our earlier discussion we referred to Mansfield's investigation on the relationship between bureaucracy and centralization. In the discussion of his research findings, Mansfield stated that there were misconceptions in the literature regarding Weber's concept of authority. He pointed out, for example, that although a system of hierarchical authority was a vital characteristic of Weber's bureaucracy, at no point did Weber suggest "that centralization of decision making in such a hierarchy was a characteristic of bureaucracy" (p. 478). On the contrary, Mansfield quoted Weber's comment that "the notion of authority within a bureaucratically administered organization does not mean that the 'higher' authority is simply authorized to take over the business of the 'lower'" (p. 478).

The most extensive and definitive empirical findings on the issue of authority relationships in schools have been reported by Charters (1981). Charters and his colleagues designed a program of research to determine what effects, if any, the adoption of a new teaching technology, team teaching, would have on the control structure of schools. The term *control structure* referred to those types of decisions made by school personnel that had the intent of regulating directly the task performance of teachers. According to Charters, "to map a school's control structure from this perspective is to locate the individuals or groups formally responsible for various kinds of decisions and to specify the class of teaching personnel whose behavior is affected by them" (p. 230). We might add that to map a control structure this way is to describe the role of the teacher in the authority structure of the school.

The investigators identified five types of decisions: those made by individuals completely outside the school, with no involvement of any individuals inside the school; those made by school principals alone; those in which at least one individual (teacher) affected by the decision took part; those made by groups of individuals (teachers) affected by the decision, with no others involved; and those made by individuals regarding their own behavior, with no involvement of either colleagues or administrators.

Using content analysis the investigators identified three decision *domains*. The first included issues that are left to the teachers' discretion: that is, decisions that teachers make independently, with no involvement of others. Included were such matters as when and how long subjects would be taught, the particular lessons that would be presented, teaching methods that would be used, and disciplinary practices to be followed. This was termed the *instructional-processes domain.*

The second included decisions as to which teachers were to teach which classes or which groups of pupils, and how such groupings would be determined. These are decisions in which the building administrator ordinarily plays the leading role; the domain was termed the *pupil and teacher deployment domain.*

The third, which was termed the *systemic-decisions domain*, included issues related to the school's curriculum, textbook adoption, and procedures for reporting pupil progress to parents. Decisions in this domain are generally made outside the particular school.

The results of this investigation clearly call into question the monistic conception of hierarchy. That conception does not apply to schools, at least not to elementary schools. Authority can be, and is, centralized or decentralized depending on the type of decision to be made.

Bureaucratic versus Professional Norms

In our discussion of the work of Pelz (1960) and Litwak (1961), we noted that the concepts of bureaucracy and professionalism may refer not to different types of organizations but rather to different patterns of structuring work within the same organization. The two most common patterns are those based on bureaucratic norms, where authority resides in the hierarchy, and those based on professional norms, where authority is derived from technical competence. A number of studies have investigated the conflict that occurs in organizations in which structures based on these two contrasting sets of norms exist simultaneously in the same organization. An early and influential study in a nonschool setting was undertaken by Scott (1965). He investigated employees' reactions to supervision in a public welfare agency in which professional employees were subordinated to an external authority system. Scott found that workers generally accepted the system; however, the degree of acceptance was found to vary with the professional orientations of both workers and supervisors. Professionally oriented workers were more critical of the system than were nonprofessionally oriented workers, and workers supervised by professionally oriented supervisors were less critical of the system than were workers serving under less professionally oriented supervisors.

Hall (1968) extended Scott's findings in a study of the attitudes of professionals toward elements of bureaucracy in three different types of professional organizations. The first type included organizations in which the work of professionals was subject to their own jurisdiction rather than to that of external or administrative sources. The second included organizations in which professional employees were subjected to an external authority system. The third included organizations in which professionals worked in departments that were embedded in a larger bureaucratic system.

Hall's elements of bureaucracy were hierarchy, division of labor, technical competence, elaborated procedures, and impersonality. His indicators of professionalism were identification with a professional reference group, a commitment to providing a service, a belief in self-regulation, a sense of calling, and a feeling of autonomy.

Hall found positive correlations between the bureaucratic element of technical competence and the following professional indicators: identification with a professional reference group, belief in service, belief in self-regulation, and a sense of calling. He found negative correlations between the bureaucratic element of elaborated procedures and the professional indicator, identification with a professional reference group. He also found negative correlations between the professional indicator, feeling of autonomy, and the following bureaucratic dimensions: hierarchy, division of labor, elaborated procedures, and impersonality.

By demonstrating that certain elements of bureaucracy correlated positively with certain indicators of a professional orientation, Hall questioned the contention of an inherent conflict between bureaucracy and professionalism. According to Hall (1968), "An assumption of inherent conflict between the professional or professional group and the employing organization appears to be unwarranted" (p. 104).

Engel (1970) also investigated relationships between elements of bureaucracy and indicators of professionalism. He identified three types of organizations in which professionals—medical practitioners—carried out their work. The first, which Engel defined as a low-hierarchy organization, was one in which solo practitioners worked in offices obtained and equipped with their own funds and in which they attended to patients who had voluntarily chosen them as their physicians on a fee-for-service basis. The second, a moderately bureaucratic organization, was one in which physicians worked in an integrated clinic and/or hospital. A physician could become a profit-sharing partner, as well as a salaried employee, after 3 years of full-time employment. The third, a highly bureaucratic organization, was one in which physicians worked in a governmental-associated organization that provided medical care for a select group of individuals who qualified under federal regulations.

On all measures, the physicians in the moderately bureaucratic, physician-owned facility reported higher degrees of professional autonomy than did either of the other groups. In contrast, there was little difference in sense of professional autonomy between the low-hierarchy and highly bureaucratized groups. Engel concluded that bureaucracies can service the needs of professionals by providing funds, equipment, technical personnel, and a stimulating intellectual climate in which those professionals can exchange information and control the quality of services.

Corwin (1961) investigated the role conflicts that professionally oriented nurses experienced in a bureaucratically structured hospital. He began with the assumption that professional and bureaucratic orientations would differ in respect to (a) the standardization of tasks and procedures, (b) the degree of authority delegated to workers, and (c) the relationship that exists between means and goals. He found that nurses who held high professional norms *and* high bureaucratic norms expressed a greater discrepancy between those two aspects of their roles than did nurses who held either professional *or* bureaucratic norms.

In a subsequent investigation involving teachers, Corwin (1965) found that there was a basic conflict in educational organizations between authority based on hierarchy and authority based on professional norms. He also noted that since there is a relationship between increased professionalization of teaching and increased militancy of teachers, the amount of conflict is likely to increase.

From his findings in the study of dimensionality, discussed earlier, Punch (1969) came to a conclusion that supports the findings of Corwin. According to Punch, "the central notions of bureaucratization and professionalization are logically incompatible" (p. 54).

Research carried out in a school setting by Balderson (1977) and by Marjoribanks (1977) supports the no-conflict thesis of Hall and Engel. Balderson concluded that both bureaucratic and professional elements are found in the behavior of elementary school teachers; Marjoribanks asserted that bureaucratic orientations and professional attitudes need not conflict if teachers are provided with sufficient autonomy to carry out their work.

It is clear from the findings reported here that hierarchy is neither a monistic nor an exclusive concept. Authority and responsibility can be delegated vertically, where the right to make decisions is based on office incumbency. Authority and responsibility can also be delegated horizontally, where the right to make decisions is based on the possession of specialized knowledge.

This conclusion represents more than a reaffirmation of the concepts of line and staff, where decisions are made in line positions, influenced by recommendations from staff positions. It means that alternative structures for decision making may exist simultaneously within a given organization. The structure employed in the case of a specific decision will be determined by the nature of the issue involved.

Linkages and Coupling

The reference to autonomy by Marjoribanks (1977) leads to a consideration of another perspective that has emerged only recently but that has generated a great deal of discussion in the theoretical and research literature. That perspective has to do with the notion of linkages in the hierarchy.

One point of view about linkages has been enunciated most clearly by Weick (1976) and has come to be associated with the term that he used, *loose coupling*. According to Weick the image conveyed by coupling is "that coupled events are responsive, but that each event also preserves its own identity and some evidence of its physical or logical separateness" (p. 3). As it is applied to schools, Weick's thesis is that there are weak linkages among the units that make up the school organization. Thus it is argued, for example, that administrative decisions within a school have little effect on the decisions made by teachers within the classrooms of that school; in their day-to-day contacts with students, teachers enjoy almost total autonomy.

Another point of view about linkages has emerged from the growing body of literature on "effective schools." Although this point of view is less sharply focused than is the work on loose coupling, the literature associated with effective schools has received wide attention. A summary treatment of this literature is found in *The Structure of School Improvement* by Joyce, Hersh, and McKibbin (1983).

The effective-schools literature directs attention to the organizational attributes of schools that have been characterized as effective. According to the research, effective schools are those in which a great deal of emphasis is placed on sharing: shared understanding of purpose, shared role expectations, shared attitudes toward pupils, and shared conceptions of effective instruction. Such sharing is viewed as necessary to assure "adherence to *common* sets of values, norms, beliefs, expectations, rules, and sanctions" (Joyce, Hersh, & McKibbin, 1983, p. 24). This sharing of understandings creates bonds among occupants of different roles, which constitute tight linkages or tight coupling.

Wilson and Corbett (1983) investigated the relationships between linkages and the implementation of new practices in schools. Linkages were defined as the interrelatedness of behavior patterns among school personnel. These investigators identified three types of linkages: structural, cultural, and interpersonal. Structural linkages consist of the exercise of formal control by direct authority, by enforcement of rules, or by limiting the discretion (autonomy) of teachers. Cultural linkages consist of teachers' shared views of the school's primary goals. Interpersonal linkages consist of opportunities for teachers to communicate about work-related activities or to observe each other at work.

Wilson and Corbett (1983) reported a positive relationship between tight linkages and the implementation of new practices. They concluded that "if certain practices are effective and deemed worthy of widespread use, then tighter linkages are apparently the structural conditions that can best promote their implementation" (p. 102).

Miskel, McDonald, and Bloom (1983) conducted an investigation to determine the relationships between structural and expectancy linkages on the one hand and indicators of school effectiveness on the other. Structural linkages were work interdependence, communication, discipline procedures, and teacher isolation. Expectancy linkages were teachers' estimates of the relationship between effort expenditure and success. Included were teachers' expectations for their own efforts as well as the expectations they held for pupils' performance.

To examine structural linkages the investigators used Mintzberg's (1979) classification of organizational units. Of the five units proposed by Mintzberg, this investigation included three: a technostructure—general supervisors and directors of special programs; a middle line—school principals; and an operating core—the teachers.

The investigators concluded that there was a relationship between linkages and perceived effectiveness: tightly linked schools tended to be viewed by teachers as more effective. They advised caution in the interpretation of their results, however. Even in the tightly linked schools the linkages were weak. The investigators predicted that considerable increase in the tightness of the linkages would result in a decline in the teachers' perceptions of school effectiveness.

Miskel, McDonald, and Bloom reported two findings that are of particular interest in a discussion of bureaucracy. In contrast to the general pattern of weak linkages, in matters of discipline the linkage between teachers and principals was strong. The strength of that linkage made a distinct contribution to the teachers' perceptions of school effectiveness. The factor of teacher isolation also contributed to the teachers' perceptions of school effectiveness. The freedom to carry out instruction without outside interference apparently led teachers to perceive the school as more effective.

Firestone and Wilson (1985) reviewed the research literature to identify linkages that would increase the principals' influence over instruction. They defined linkages as mechanisms that coordinate the activity of school personnel, and they divided those mechanisms into two categories. The first was called *bureaucratic linkages*, and it included the direct supervision of teachers and the establishment of plans and schedules. The second was called *cultural linkages*, and it included shared views of effectiveness, students' commitment to task, and the sharing and communication of certain symbols and rituals.

Although they argued that the use of bureaucratic and cultural linkages could be used by principals to influence instruction, Firestone and Wilson concluded that currently both linkages are weak. External influences on the development of plans and schedules and the norm of freedom from interference in instructional affairs make it virtually impossible for the principal to have much influence over the teachers' conduct in classrooms.

CONCLUSIONS

In preparing this chapter we reviewed the research literature to determine the extent to which the concept of bureaucracy has generated inquiry in the field of educational administration. If we consider only research that specifically refers to bureaucracy, we find that the amount is limited. However, if we expand our definition to include research generated by previous findings related specifically to bureaucracy, or if we include research related to bureaucratic ideology, it is obvious that the impact of this concept has been considerable.

From our review of the research we have identified a number of cautions that should be observed by those who continue to do research related to the concept of bureaucracy. First, care should be exercised in defining bureaucracy and in developing measures to determine its presence or absence. When a measurement consists of the degree of centralization of decision making, for example, what is being measured is not bureaucracy. That is not to say that centralization is not an important variable for investigation. It is only to say that in a "bureaucratic structure," decision making can be either centralized or decentralized. The important question is not whether centralized decision making constitutes bureaucracy. The important question is what the consequences are of centralizing decision making.

This observation points to another caution about decision making. Decision making is obviously an important concept in studying organizations. To identify points at which decisions are made is to take a big step toward understanding the nature of an organization. However, research on decision making must take into account the type of decision under consideration. As we reported earlier, Charters and his colleagues identified three distinct decision domains in elementary schools. To ignore the differences among those domains, including differences with respect to the

locus for decision making, is to ignore a major feature of the decision-making process.

We have contended that the research we reviewed was not research on bureaucracy but rather was research on formal organizations. To clarify that contention, we return briefly to Weber's conceptualization.

Bureaucracy may be viewed as encompassing two major dimensions. The first, a structural dimension, consists of elements that can be identified and defined operationally. Such concepts as rules, hierarchy, contract, and separation of ownership and management are illustrative. At the same time, there is an attribution of purpose or intent associated with each of those concepts. Rule by law, acceptance of the norms on which laws are based, and the elimination of irrationality from the conduct of officials are the purposive and intentional aspects of bureaucracy. These elements constitute an ideological dimension.

These two dimensions combined make up Weber's "ideal" type of bureaucracy. This ideal type is a construct whose usefulness can "only be judged by its results in promoting systematic analysis" (Roth & Wittich, 1968, p. 216). The error that most of Weber's interpreters have made is that they have "mistakenly assumed that he provided a description of concrete bureaucracies rather than an abstract conceptual scheme" (Coser & Rosenberg, 1965, p. 463). When researchers study only one dimension, they are studying organizations, not bureaucracy.

From the concept of bureaucracy, investigators have identified a number of important organizational variables to be studied. Virtually all those variables have been related to the structural dimension, however. Concepts related to this dimension have been operationalized, measures have been developed, and data have been collected to test a number of hypotheses about the nature of bureaucracy, as well as relationships between the elements of bureaucracy and other variables. There is also a normative dimension to bureaucracy, and one does not have to reify the concept to derive norms that can be compared with those underlying alternative conceptualizations.

It is our contention that the ideological, or normative, dimension of bureaucracy has had a greater impact on both research and practice than has the structural dimension. America discovered Weber at a relatively late date. By the time his work was translated into English, organizational studies in this country had gone through a number of phases, including scientific management and human relations. A great deal of effort had already been directed toward the study of what we have called the structural dimension of bureaucracy.

It was the ideology behind bureaucracy that struck

a responsive chord in this country. Rule by law, rationality in social behavior, and equality under the law were an integral part of the American creed. The application of those principles to organizations met with ready acceptance. It is not difficult to understand, therefore, why scholars have used the concept of bureaucracy to lend force to their efforts. At the same time, there is an invidious connotation to bureaucracy, and that connotation has provided a convenient foil for those who are calling for a new approach to conceptualizing organizations.

The time has come to stop using bureaucracy as an object of inquiry and instead to use the concept as a means of furthering our understanding of schools. Most of the research reviewed in this chapter involves variables and relationships that have little to do with what schools are about: student learning. We do not contend that it is necessary to show a direct relationship between an organizational variable and student learning to justify conducting research on that variable. We do contend that there is little to be gained from further research on such issues as the number of dimensions that constitute an organization or the conflict that exists between bureaucratic and professional norms.

Future research should be directed toward the connections that exist between organizational structure and organizational outcomes. The reason for structure is to achieve coordination. The reason for coordination is to increase effectiveness. In schools, effectiveness is determined by student learning. We have much yet to learn about the relationships among structure, coordination, and learning.

NOTES

[1] *Economy and Society* is a translation of pages 1–550 and 559–882 of *Wirtschaft und Gesellschaft, Grundriss der Verstehenden Soziologie*, 4th German edition, Johannes Winckelmann (ed.) Tubingen: J. C. B. Mohr (Paul Siebeck) (1956). *Economy and Society*, edited by Roth and Wittich, includes partial translations of Fischoff, Gerth, Henderson, Kolegar, Mills, Parsons, Rheinstein, Roth, Shils, and Wittich.

[2] This conceptualization was developed initially by Guba (1960) and presented at a conference titled Theory into Action, held at the University of Chicago in 1959. We acknowledge our indebtedness to Guba for the original formulation. We accept full responsibility for the interpretation of the concepts as used in this chapter.

REFERENCES

Anderson, J. G. (1966). Bureaucratic rules: Bearers of organizational authority. *Educational Administration Quarterly, 2*, 7–34.

Anderson, J. G. (1969). *Bureaucracy in education*. Baltimore: Johns Hopkins University Press.

Balderson, J. H. (1977, April). *The bureaucratization of teacher behavior scale and the measurement of school organization structure*. Paper presented at the Annual Meeting of the American Educational Association, New York City.

Bendix, R. (1960). *Max Weber: An intellectual portrait*. Garden City, NY: Doubleday.

Boyan, N. J. (1966). The emergent role of the teacher and the authority structure of the school. In R. Allen and J. Schmid (Eds.), *Collective negotiations and educational administration*. Fayetteville, AR: University of Arkansas Press.

Charters, W. W., Jr. (1981). The control of micro-educational policy in elementary schools. In S. E. Bacharach (Ed.), *Organizational behavior in schools and school districts*. New York: Praeger.

Corwin, R. G. (1961). The professional employee: A study of conflict in nursing roles. *American Journal of Sociology, 66*, 605–615.

Corwin, R. G. (1965). Militant professionalism, initiative, and compliance in public education. *Sociology of Education, 38*, 310–331

Coser, L. A., & Rosenberg, B. (Eds.). (1965). *Sociological theory: A book of readings*. New York: Macmillan.

Cox, H., & Wood, J. R. (1980). Organizational structure and professional alienation: The case of public school teachers. *Peabody Journal of Education, 58*, 1–6.

Eisenstadt, S. N. (1959). Bureaucracy, bureaucratization, and debureaucratization. *Administrative Science Quarterly, 4*, 302–320.

Engel, G. V. (1970). Professional autonomy and bureaucratic organization. *Administrative Science Quarterly, 15*, 12–21.

Fayol, H. (1949). *General and industrial management*. Translated by C. Starrs. London: Pitman.

Firestone, W. A., & Wilson, B. L. (1985). Using bureaucratic and cultural linkages to improve instruction: The principal's contribution. *Educational Administration Quarterly, 21*, 7–30.

French, J. R. P., Jr., and Raven, B. (1960). The bases of social power. In D. Cartwright & A. Zander (Eds.), *Group dynamics: Research and theory*. New York: Harper & Row.

Gouldner, A. (1948). "Discussion" of industrial sociology. *American Sociological Review, 13*, 396–400.

Gouldner, A. (1954). *Patterns of industrial bureaucracy*. New York: Free Press.

Guba, E. (1960). Research in internal administration—what do we know? In R. Campbell & J. Lipham (Eds.), *Administrative theory as a guide to action*. Chicago: The Midwest Center, University of Chicago.

Hall, R. H. (1962). Intraorganizational structural variations: Application of the bureaucratic model. *Administrative Science Quarterly, 7*, 296–308.

Hull, R. H. (1963). The concept of bureaucracy: An empirical assessment. *American Journal of Sociology, 69*, 32–40.

Hull, R. H. (1968). Professionalization and bureaucratization. *American Sociological Review, 33*, 92–104.

Hills, F. S., & Mahoney, T. A. (1978). University budgets and organizational decision making. *Administrative Science Quarterly, 23*, 454–465.

Hoy, W. K., Blazovsky, R., & Newland, W. (1983). Bureaucracy and alienation: A comparative analysis. *Journal of Educational Administration, 21*, 109–120.

Hoy, W. K., Newland, W., & Blazovsky, R. (1977). Subordinate loyalty to superior, esprit, and aspects of bureaucratic structure. *Educational Administration Quarterly, 13*, 71–85.

Hoy, W. K., & Rees, R. (1974). Subordinate loyalty to immediate superior: A neglected concept in the study of educational administration. *Sociology of Education, 47*, 268–286.

Isherwood, G. B., & Hoy, W. K. (1973). Bureaucracy, powerlessness, and teacher work values. *Journal of Educational Administration, 11*, 124–137.

Joyce, B. R., Hersh, R. H., & McKibbin, M. (1983). *The structure of school improvement*. White Plains, NY: Longman.

Kimberly, J. R. (1976). Organizational size and the structuralist perspective: A review, critique, and proposal. *Administrative Science Quarterly, 21*, 571–597.

Litwak, E. (1961). Models of bureaucracy which permit conflict. *American Journal of Sociology, 67*, 177–184.

MacKay, D. A. (1964). A empirical study of bureaucratic dimensions and their relations to other characteristics of school organization (Doctoral dissertation, University of Alberta, Alberta,

Canada.

Mansfield, R. (1973). Bureaucracy and centralization: An examination of organizational structure. *Administrative Science Quarterly, 18,* 477–488.

March, J. G., & Simon, H. A. (1958). *Organizations.* New York: John Wiley.

Marjoribanks, K. (1977). Bureaucratic orientations, autonomy, and the professional attitudes of teachers. *Journal of Educational Administration, 15,* 108–113.

Merton, R. K. (1940). Bureaucratic structure and personality. *Social Forces, 23,* 405–415.

Merton, R. K. (1957). *Social theory and social structure,* New York: Free Press.

Meyer, M. W. (1968). The two authority structures of bureaucratic organizations. *Administrative Science Quarterly, 13,* 211–228.

Mintzberg, H. (1979). *The structuring of organizations.* Englewood Cliffs, NJ: Prentice-Hall.

Miskel, C., McDonald, D., & Bloom, S. (1983). Structural and expectancy linkages within schools and organizational effectiveness. *Educational Administrative Quarterly, 19,* 49–82.

Moeller, G. H., & Charters, W. W., Jr. (1966). Relation of bureaucratization to sense of power among teachers. *Administrative Science Quarterly, 10,* 444–465.

Peabody, R. L. (1962). Perceptions of organizational authority. *Administrative Science Quarterly, 6,* 463–482.

Pelz, D. C. (1960). Conditional effects in the relationship of autonomy and motivation to performance. Mimeographed paper.

Pugh, D. S., Hickson, D. J., & Hinnings, C. R. (1968). Dimensions of organizational structure. *Administrative Science Quarterly, 13,* 65–105.

Punch, K. F. (1969). Bureaucratic structure in schools: Towards redefinition and measurement. *Educational Administration Quarterly, 5,* 43–57.

Roth, G., & Wittich, C. (Eds.). (1968). *Max Weber, economy and society: An outline of interpretative sociology.* New York: Bedminster.

Simmel, G. (1961). On subordination and superordination. In T. Parsons, E. Shils, K. D. Naegle & J. R. Pitts (Eds.), *Theories of society: Foundations of modern sociological theory.* New York: Free Press.

Scott, W. R. (1965). Reactions to supervision in a heteronomous professional organization. *Administrative Science Quarterly, 10,* 63–81.

Selznick, P. (1949). *TVA and the grass roots.* Berkeley, CA: University of California Press.

Sousa, D. A., & Hoy, W. K. (1981). Bureaucratic structure in schools: A refinement and synthesis in measurement. *Educational Administration Quarterly, 17,* 21–39.

Thompson, V. A. (1961). *Modern organization.* New York: Knopf.

Udy, S. H., Jr. (1959). "Bureaucracy" and "rationality" in Weber's organization theory: An empirical study. *American Sociological Review, 24,* 791–795.

Weber, M. (1961). Legitimate order and types of authority. In T. Parsons, E. Shils, K. D. Naegle, & J. R. Pitts (Eds.), *Theories of society: Foundations of modern sociological theory.* New York: Free Press.

Weber, M. (1965a). Subjective meaning in the social situation. In L. A. Coser & B. Rosenberg (Eds.), *Sociological theory: A book of readings,* New York: Macmillan.

Weber, M. (1965b). Types of authority. In L. A. Coser, & B. Rosenberg (Eds.), *Sociological theory: A book of readings.* New York: Macmillan.

Weick, K. E. (1976). Educational organizations as loosely coupled systems. *Administrative Science Quarterly, 21,* 1–19.

Wildavsky, A. (1979). *Speaking truth to power: The art and craft of policy analysis.* Boston: Little, Brown.

Wilson, B. L., & Corbett, H. D. (1983). Organization and change: The effects of school linkages on the quality of implementation. *Educational Administration Quarterly, 19,* 84–104.

CHAPTER 13

Leadership and Leader Behavior

Glenn L. Immegart

Leaders and leadership have long been subjects of study, analysis, and reflection. The descriptors *leader*, *leadership*, and *leadership behavior* consistently reveal a sizable number of treatments of this topic area from any card catalogue, indexing system, or bibliographical listing. The 1974 compendium of research on leadership by Stogdill (1974) drew on over 3,000 selected sources, and the revision of that volume by Bass (1981) added another 2,000 references. In addition, the general literature on administration and organization leads one to conclude that there is much to illuminate this topic under other areas of activity such as administrative behavior (Bridges, 1982; Dill, 1984), organizational behavior (Applewhite, 1965; Schein, 1985), decision making (Conway, 1984; Vroom & Yetton, 1973), change (Huberman & Miles, 1982), and even the recent instructional management and effective schools rubric (Clark, Lotto, & Astuto, 1984). Further, because of the importance and pervasiveness of the domain, any number of reviews or critiques of activity on leadership and leader behavior are also readily available (Barrows, 1977; Bass, 1981; Cunningham & Gephart, 1973; Gibb, 1954, 1969; Greenfield, 1968; Hollander & Julian, 1968; House & Baetz, 1979; Jago, 1982; McCall & Lombardo, 1978; Stogdill, 1948, 1974; Stout & Briner, 1969; and Vroom, 1976).

Not wanting for material and operating in a well-worked arena, a reviewer is confronted with a number of problems in choosing how to proceed. Several

approaches to the review were considered and rejected at the outset. For example, a detailed review of individual studies was not deemed appropriate because of the existence of a number of such reviews over the years (Gibb, 1954; Greenfield, 1968; House & Baetz, 1979; Jago, 1982; and Vroom, 1976) and because of the volume of leadership studies (Bass, 1981; Stogdill, 1977) and space restrictions of a handbook chapter. It was also decided not to restrict the review solely to the field of education because of the amount of important work on leadership in a number of social-science areas. As appealing as a qualitative assessment of research might have been, this was reluctantly ruled out because of the time involved in doing, and obtaining the materials for, such a task. Meta-analysis, also very promising and used in one leadership study (Crehan, 1984), was not attempted because of obvious problems that loomed as insurmountable in moving across varying conceptualizations, differing operational definitions, and a variety of methodological and analytical approaches. Although meta-analysis might be possible with some lines or sectors of leadership inquiry (Crehan, 1985, p. 273), this approach necessarily would have been selective and would have eliminated much work deserving citation.

It was, however, decided not only that the review ought to consider inquiries into leadership and leader behavior generally, but also that the analysis should not be limited to a particular time frame. It was also early seen as advisable to consider more than just the findings of studies as such and to include some scrutiny of conceptualizations of leadership and leader

Consultant/reviewers: Luvern L. Cunningham, The Ohio State University; and Thomas J. Sergiovanni, Trinity University

behavior as well as research methodology. Further, given the definitional variation noted by Stogdill (1974, p. 16), a loose rather than a precise definition of leadership was adopted in selecting pieces to review. It was simply assumed that, regardless of conceptualization or operational definitions, those engaged in the study of leadership and leader behavior were, more or less, directing their efforts toward the same kind of phenomenon. (This can be debated, but the fact remains that although operational definitions for theoretical or research purposes may vary a great deal, there is general agreement on what is commonly meant by the term or the concept *leadership*.)

The foregoing decisions did not delimit the task in any sense and served in some ways to broaden it. As a result, it was necessary to establish some boundaries for the review and to select an approach that kept the work in manageable proportions. First, it was decided to focus on material that could be identified by the descriptors of *leadership* and *leader behavior* and that by intent clearly were directed to those topics at hand. This eliminated the material on other topics, such as administration or change, that might be related to leadership. Second, it was decided to limit the review to studies or research that followed the standard definition of research as being a systematic process of inquiry engaged in for the purpose of generating knowledge. This, of course, ruled out a large volume of material on the topic from perspective or thought pieces (e.g., Kellerman, 1984; Morris, 1985) to other nonempirical treatments of the topic (Burns, 1978; Cunningham & Payzant, 1983; Sergiovanni & Corbally, 1984). Treatments such as those cited certainly are important aspects of the literature, and they represent rigorous efforts to grapple with the topic, but the purpose here is unabashedly to focus on investigative efforts and the results of inquiry. Third, because of the existence of a number of excellent, detailed reviews over the years, as cited above, a general or macroscopic perspective was chosen in order to provide new insights. It was thus decided to concentrate on selected existing reviews, supplemented by a consideration of reviews in general and an overview of the published research literature on the topic.

In settling on a broad, holistic perspective for the review—basically a review of reviews, augmented by an overview and somewhat more detailed analysis of research—it was held as more important to account for the accumulation of knowledge about leadership and leader behavior than to deal with studies in the more typical microscopic sense.

Thus, the first step was the analysis of existing reviews of research on leadership, followed by a more detailed analysis of periodical and other published research literature over the past decade (including the *Administrative Science Quarterly*, *Academy of Management Journal*, *Academy of Management Review*, *Educational Administration Quarterly*, *Journal of Educational Administration*, and *Planning and Changing*). This was complemented by a general overview of major studies and sources in the research literature, including encyclopedia (Boyan, 1982; Cooper, 1982; Runkel & Schmuck, 1982; and Stout & Briner, 1969) and other compendia or summaries (Bass, 1981; Stogdill, 1974, 1977) covering an extended period of time. Following subsequent reanalysis of the selected reviews (Cunningham & Gephart, 1973; House & Baetz, 1979; Jago, 1982; and Vroom, 1976), final analysis was directed toward identification of (a) corroborated results or findings that have stood the test of time or that have been confirmed in the research literature and (b) reasonably well-agreed-upon or established outcomes of the inquiry on leadership. In spite of an essentially positivistic approach, impressions and feelings about the collective activity in this area of inquiry were not ignored in the overall effort to assess critically the larger picture with respect to research on leadership and leader behavior.

The reader is reminded that, in dealing with a general review of reviews, it is important to refer back to basic sources—both reviews and particular studies as well as lines of inquiry. Detail has been eschewed here in favor of a broad view. The cost of operating at a general level is loss of much detail. Consultation of the basic evidence not presented here could lead other analysts to different conclusions. As a summary device, this review is intended as a starting point for understanding leadership inquiry, not as a source of all the knowledge from or about it. This is an effort to look at the results of empirical activity and its directions over time and to assess "where we are" in that regard. What is known about leadership and leader behavior with some certainty will be set forth first. Some general outcomes, methodological concerns and issues, and problems with conceptualization will be treated next. The review will conclude with suggestions for future inquiry on the basis of this analysis.

THE STUDY OF LEADERSHIP

The focus of investigative efforts in the study of leadership has shifted over the last several decades from a concentration on the leader to a broadened concern for an increasing number of variables and their interactions. The heavy emphasis on the "scientific" study of leadership since the late 1940s ushered in an era when a number of aspects of the phenomenon, related interpersonal dynamics, and contextual factors have been incorporated in empirical activity. The approach has shifted from an essentially personal and/ or historical perspective to a number of disciplinary views—including first the pyschological, then the sociological and political, and more recently, other specialized and interdisciplinary perspectives—on leadership. Put another way, the study of leadership has moved from an analysis of the so-called "great man" to the exploration of traits, styles, behaviors, situations (contingencies), and a variety of other related concerns, including the interaction of multiple variables and sets of variables.

Empirical efforts, individually and collectively, in this area of study have not been without their detractors (Guba, 1973; McCall and Lombardo, 1978; Pfeffer 1977). As a result, there is a range of opinion about individual studies, lines of inquiry, and the field as a whole, with the most accurate assessment in all probability being somewhere between the views at the extremes of those propounding a given thrust and their critics. It was clear in this analysis of research activity that the level at which one operates in making observations or coming to conclusions about research and research findings is important. Although one loses data and encounters other problems in moving to more general or macroscopic levels, at least with respect to the leadership and leader behavior research, the degree of confidence for observations at such levels is much greater. For example, in scrutinizing particular types of studies or lines of inquiry, one is often beset by conflicting evidence and unresolvable dilemmas, but in terms of the "weight of evidence" across several lines of inquiry and a variety of studies, observations and conclusions tend to be much less tenuous. Thus, the general conclusions and observations that follow, based on macroscopic levels of analysis, can be stated with some confidence.

Major Findings on Leadership and Leader Behavior

In attending to the archival function of a research review, this section is directed toward a summary of major findings from the research on leadership and leader behavior. The goal is to set forth the more conclusive, if not always the most definitive, findings on the topic. Detail is bypassed in favor of a balanced picture of the present state of knowledge as gleaned from leadership and leader behavior inquiry. Beginning with the consideration of whether leadership makes a difference, the summary then will deal with findings about leadership by moving chronologically from the earlier trait studies through current investigative emphases.

Findings on the Impact of Leaders and Leadership

The question of whether leadership or leader behavior makes a difference is a logical point of departure. If it does not, then inquiry in this domain may indeed be of marginal value and there would be little point in going further. If leadership has been demonstrated to make a difference, then the results of research will have greater usefulness as well as pertinence. Although there are some who would contend that this question has not been adequately addressed (Pfeffer, 1977, p. 105), one review has briefly summarized a number of studies supporting the impact of leadership (House & Baetz, 1979, pp. 346–348). There it has been noted that a number of studies have demonstrated that leadership styles and certain combinations of behaviors contribute significantly to important effects. Most such studies are laboratory studies or field-longitudinal investigations at lower organizational levels; there are, nevertheless, a couple of inquiries at higher organizational levels that confirm the findings of the more prevalent studies and reveal that changes in leader behavior precede changes in relevant outcomes. House and Baetz (1979) also point out that a few studies contradict these results and other studies show a reverse effect— that leader behavior is a result of or can be attributed to other variables, including the performance of group members. Nonetheless, House and Baetz (1979) have concluded that "leadership has an effect under some conditions and not under others" and that the leader-group performance linkage is a two-way street (p. 349). The weight of the evidence to date, then, does indicate what most people seem to feel, if only experientially: Leadership and leader behavior can make a difference. (The caveats of the House and Baetz review, 1979, only serve to underscore the situational nature of leadership and the present utility of pursuing contingency approaches in its study.)

Findings on the Traits of Leaders and Leadership

Despite long argument and some evidence to the contrary, the consistency with which some traits have been linked to leaders and leadership situations, along with the magnitude of their correlations in studies, indicates that certain traits are associated with leaders in leadership situations. Depending on the analyst—that is, who is adding up the evidence and how it is done—there is some slight difference in opinion as to which specific traits are most relevant (House & Baetz, 1979, pp. 348–352; Jago, 1982, pp. 316–318; Stogdill, 1974, pp. 35–91). The traits of *intelligence*, *dominance*, *self-confidence*, and *high energy/activity level* are most often mentioned and are commonly agreed on across reviewers. That others possess such traits but are not leaders does not refute the evidence in this regard, any more than does the fact that some leaders in some situations do not possess such characteristics.

As House and Baetz (1979, p. 352) have noted, studies of emergent leaders and more recent contingency studies employing traits as one of a number of multiple variables or sets of variables both confirm results of earlier trait-focused inquiry and establish the situational nature of traits themselves. As a matter of fact, Stogdill's equivocation in this regard (House & Baetz, 1979, p. 352) can be resolved through a serious consideration of differences in earlier studies (in terms of populations and measures) and the results of recent studies that have explored the interaction of several variables as opposed to the presence or absence of a single variable or the simple relationship of two variables (e.g., a trait and behavior or performance). It seems clear that current contingency or situational approaches will identify more context-bound or -determined traits and that the interaction of leader personality and other kinds of variables, including the situation, still offers a fertile arena for inquiry (House & Baetz, 1979, p. 352; Jago, 1982, p. 318). Together, the durability of certain traits and the results of recent efforts support both the linkage of such traits as those mentioned earlier with leaders and the notion that these traits are moderated by the task or leadership situation at hand (Jago, 1982, p. 318).

Findings on the Style of Leaders and Leadership

Another major emphasis in the relatively early scientific study of leadership was that of leadership style. Style refers to the action disposition, or set or pattern of behaviors, displayed by a leader in a leadership situation. It has been the concern of any number of investigators, and a variety of conceptualizations of style have been explored. Style conceptualizations have taken a number of forms from nominal idealized categories (such as heroes, princes, and supermen [Jennings, 1960]) to typological categorizations (such as highly participative, mildly participative, and non-participative [Bass and Valenzi, 1974]) and to the most popular of all—the either dichotomous or continuous style categorizations of initiating structure and consideration (Stogdill & Coons, 1957), the nomothetic and idiographic (Getzels & Guba, 1957), or that of democratic and autocratic leadership (White & Lippitt, 1960). (The latter are all plagued by their varying usage as both discrete and continuous variables.)

Furthermore, style conceptualizations overall vary in rigor and differ, often greatly, in substance. As a result, the conclusions one can arrive at in this respect are less precise than is the case with the study of traits. Nevertheless, the goal and direction of many early studies of style—to find the "right" or "best" style or to find the leadership style that was the most effective—have, for the most part, long been abandoned. Amid much conflicting evidence and drawing from most lines of inquiry using pure or continuous categorizations of style (e.g., initiating structure and consideration), it has become apparent that most effective or successful leaders demonstrate style variability: that is, they score high on both or all style dimensions employed in studies.

The implications of these results from research are twofold: first, effective leaders exhibit a repertoire of styles; and second, style is related to situation, both context and task (Jago, 1982, p. 320; Stogdill, 1974, p. 140).

Further, studies in this vein also have underscored the importance of the congruence between leadership style and group expectations in leader success and effectiveness (Cooper, 1982, p. 1830; Jago, 1982, p. 322). In addition, the effect of task per se on leadership style has been summarized by House and Baetz (1979, pp. 356–359). House's own line of inquiry related to the initiating-structure and consideration categorization of leadership style has pointed out the value of the latter style in terms of tasks that are stressful, frustrating, or dissatisfying and the value of the former in terms of tasks that are clear and routine in nature (House, 1971; House & Dessler, 1974). The data reveals that highly considerate leaders tend to have more satisfied subordinates and fewer subordinate absences (Fleishman & Harris, 1962), but the relationship of a considerate leader style to group productivity seems to vary greatly (House & Baetz, 1979, pp. 362–363). However, a leadership style high on initiating structure is related to productivity (Schriesheim, House, & Kerr, 1976), even if such leaders have been found to experience higher grievance rates and more turnover among subordinates (Fleishman & Harris, 1962). Style is, from inquiry to date, highly situational, and it has been found to be related to leadership success and effectiveness in a highly situational or contextual sense. Vroom (1976) has, in fact, expressed the opinion that leadership style is completely situational.

Some research in this vein has been less definitive and even somewhat contradictory on the matter of leadership style. For example, research on the relationship of permissive and restrictive leadership styles and productivity has been quite inconclusive (Stout & Briner, 1969, p. 704). There is also little empirical support for either democratic or autocratic leadership styles in terms of productivity (Jago, 1982, p. 321). Still, leaders do tend toward a democratic style when subordinates exercise initiative and set goals and a more autocratic style when subordinates are passive, seek instructions, or are unquestioning. In terms of these particular styles, it appears that they are perhaps more the result of certain kinds of situations than they are the determinant of outcomes in those situations.

In any event, this particular notion of style might better be considered a dimension of participative leadership in decision making and supervision, as has been discussed by House and Baetz (1979, pp. 263–270). In this sense, participative leaders do not necessarily eschew leading, initiating structure, or providing task direction. Instead, they involve others. But the work of House (1971; House & Dessler, 1974) indicates that participative leadership is not likely to be of value when tasks are clear or routine. Its value is greater with complex and ambiguous tasks and when subordinates are ego-involved. Inquiry has also revealed that the effects of participation are moderated by the predisposition to participate, the perceived costs and benefits of participation, and the satisfaction that subordinates gain from participation (Duke, Showers, & Imber 1980; House & Baetz, 1979). Related to leadership style and the involvement of others, the inquiry on participative approaches has been a bit more revealing than that directed toward the investigation of democratic-autocratic styles of leadership as such.

From another perspective, the Michigan studies of Likert (1961; Likert & Katz, 1948) and others (Katz, 1960; Katz, Maccoby, Gurin, & Floor, 1951) have indicated that, in terms of behavior patterns or style, highly productive supervisors are employee centered, exercise general supervision, and differentiate their own and workers' roles. Studies of this genre have also reported that, effective leaders are stylistically supportive and set high performance goals.

Finally, it should be noted that Bales's work on task-facilitative and socioemotional leadership (parallel to initiating structure and consideration) in the small groups supports some of the foregoing conclusions, but it is at odds at least in one respect (Bales, 1958; Bales & Slater, 1955). It is supportive in identifying leadership roles as important and provides further evidence of the importance of task-oriented leadership for effective performance. However, Bales's line of inquiry has indicated that the two roles or styles need to be integrated (as opposed to employed situationally) for effective or successful leadership. The findings may, of course, may be a function of the small group context of this line of research and the fact that role integration may be necessary in small groups because members of such groups must play multiple roles. Or, the findings may be generalizable; namely that an integrated leadership style is necessary quite apart from the context or size of the performing group.

In any event, the exploration of leadership style has resulted in ascertaining its situational nature and the importance of situation—context and task—in understanding leadership. In spite of some mixed evidence, the matters of style variation and fit (situationally with respect both to expectations and task) appear important in providing leadership. There is also strong support for employing a variety of styles based on situations (contingencies), and certain styles seem to make a difference in that sense. Further clarification of the effect of leadership style might well come from inquiry that explores the interaction of a number of variables, including style, in currently popular contingency types of models (see below).

Findings of Behavioral Studies of Leaders and Leadership

In moving to the results of behavioral studies of leadership and leaders, several preliminary observations are in order. First, there is a fine line between much of the research on leadership style and the inquiry into leader behavior. "Behavioral research" as used here refers to attempts to focus on the effects of particular or specific leader behaviors as opposed to the generic notion or behavioral pattern type of definition of style. In this sense, the style focus preceded the focus on behavior(s), and approaches to the study of behavior took many cues, conceptualizations, and definitions from the style perspectives. In fact, the study of leader behavior to some degree can be viewed as an attempt to operationalize earlier style conceptualizations, and it represents a move toward greater specificity as well as a desire to get at what leaders do (behavior). It represents an effort, in other words, to link the behavior of leaders to a variety of other variables, from success and performance to satisfaction and motivation. Second, it must be noted that much of the "behavioral" study of leadership has been reputational in nature, relying on questionnaires and other after-the-fact reported perceptions of what a leader did, or even in some cases would do. It is, thus, quite legitimate to question whether such investigations really got at behavior or what leaders did. Only some laboratory studies and a few field investigations observed actual behavior; many of the inquiries relied on reputed or reported data. Further, the subjects in such studies often were in lower-level positions, and the use of convenience samples and students or training-program participants seems to abound in this line of inquiry. Although additional variables were, in fact, explored through this approach, little beyond specificity was added to the leadership equation, and the variables were characteristically limited to two or three factors in particular studies. There have also been endless replications of such studies.

Similar to and in harmony with the style studies, leader behavior research has revealed that leaders who exhibit a variety of behaviors (e.g., initiating-structure and consideration behaviors, nomothetic and idiographic behaviors, and so forth) are more effective than those who do not (Stogdill, 1974, p. 140). And, again, the situational nature of leadership has been corroborated as well as the matter of fit with respect to subordinate expectations and task.

It can also be concluded from this line of inquiry that leader behavior is related to a number of organizational variables (Hencley, 1973, pp. 150–151). These variables include such factors as satisfaction and productivity, the nature of the task at hand, organizational structure and climate, occupational level of employees, group cohesiveness and harmony, motivation, organizational conflict, group characteristics, bureaucracy, and innovation (Hencley, 1973; House & Baetz, 1979; Stogdill, 1974).

It is further apparent that preferences and expectations for leader behavior vary among reference groups and that perceptions of leader behavior also vary similarly (Hencley, 1973, pp. 148–149). In the latter respect, leaders' perceptions of their own behavior differ from those of superordinates and subordinates, which also differ from each other. Perceptions of leader behavior, however, loom as very important considerations. They influence not only leader-subordinate fit, as noted, but also as Hencley (1973, p. 150) has pointed out, incongruous perceptions or misperceptions (and value differences) may seriously compromise leadership effectiveness. The potential of attribution theory (Calder, 1977; Hollander, 1964; House & Baetz, 1979, pp. 401–403) and the import of leader-follower linkages are supported by the study of leader behavior and continue to offer fruitful avenues for multiple variable studies of leadership.

In a more specific sense, a number of findings have been reasonably well supported in studies of the behavior of leaders. Pelz (1952) reported that the leader must be successful in obtaining resources from other parts of the organization and in representing subordinates to superordinates in order to be considered effective. The finding of the importance of upward influence has been corroborated (Hills, 1963; Nahabetian, 1969); it represents one of the more definitive outcomes from inquiries along this line. Other studies have also revealed the importance of work facilitation, task skill, and task facilitation by the leader (Bales, 1958; House & Baetz, 1979, pp. 356–359; Stout & Briner, 1969, pp. 702–703). As with the case of leadership style, the many behavioral investigations employing initiating structure and consideration (or their numerous parallels) have produced some

supported results but also results that are mixed and often linked to the instrument used (House & Baetz, 1979, pp. 360–363). For example, there is support for the finding that initiating-structure behaviors are positively related to performance and negatively related to satisfaction. However, with the revised LBDQ, initiating-structure behaviors have low positive correlations with satisfaction in relation to routine tasks. Also, employees of higher occupational levels react more favorably than do others to initiating-structure behaviors (Schriesheim et al., 1976). Considerate behavior is most positively correlated with the satisfaction of subordinates on ambiguous, stressful, and dissatisfying tasks, and highly considerate behaviors are related generally to satisfaction but not always with performance.

An interesting and very important outcome of studies in the behavioral vein has to do with the direction of effect with respect to leader behavior. It is clear from this line of investigation that leader behavior affects and is affected by other variables such as performance. Leaders do respond differently to competent subordinates (they are more considerate) than to others; and they are more supportive to, and are perceived as more sensitive and nonpunitive by, high performers (Jago, 1982, p. 321). Further, organizations have been found to create climates favoring certain behaviors on the part of leaders (Jago, 1982, p. 322). Leaders, in addition, have revealed a tendency to model their behavior after that of their superiors and to conform behaviorally to expectations of superiors and preferences of subordinates (House & Baetz, 1979, p. 370–374). Their behavior is also shaped by environmental factors, the interaction of individual characteristics and environmental variables, and situationally, such as by stress and ambiguity in the group setting (House & Baetz, 1979, p. 370–374). An important outcome of behaviorally oriented investigations of leaders has been the identification of the reciprocal effect of such behavior and other variables. The reciprocity clouds the issue with respect to understanding leadership success and effectiveness, and it makes inquiry using behavioral variables more tenuous in respect to ascertaining the direction of effect when studying the behavior of leaders.

In sum, the behavioral study of leadership has strongly affirmed the situational nature of the phenomenon; has been parallel to and extends, but is somewhat less definitive overall than, inquiry on style; and has revealed the reciprocal effect between leader behavior and other organizational or situational variables. Leader behavior does appear to make a difference in a situational sense and in the light of moderating variables, but it must be remembered that

conflicting evidence and mixed results remain somewhat characteristic of this area of leadership inquiry.

Findings of Situational or Contingency
Studies of Leaders and Leadership

Turning to current emphases in the study of leaders
shifts the focus to situational or contingency studies, to
studies that explore the interaction of multiple variables, and to other recent efforts that are being established as valid approaches to the investigation of
leadership. Following the already documented situational nature of leadership from the earlier trait, style,
and behavioral research, the work of Fiedler (1967,
1971; Fiedler & Chemers, 1974) initiated the era of the
situational or contingency studies. Fiedler hypothesized
in his work that group productivity was dependent on
the match of leadership orientation (task versus relationship oriented) and situational favorableness (a
mix of personal-trait, group, and situational variables).
In his research, Fiedler operationalized leadership
orientation in terms of high and low scores on his Least
Preferred Co-worker Scale (LPCS). Situational favorableness was determined in terms of eight categories
indicated by high and low scores on the three dimensions of degree of task structure, amount of power, and
quality of interpersonal relationships. In many studies,
Fiedler found that task-oriented leadership was related
to effectiveness in situations of high and low favora-
bility and that relationship-oriented leadership was
related to effectiveness in moderately favorable situations. He has concluded from his line of work that one
cannot speak of effective or ineffective leadership, only
of effective or ineffective leadership in one situation or
another. His work confirms the situational nature of
leadership and posits leadership effectiveness as being
situational in nature as well. Put another way, the
Fiedler line of inquiry clearly has challenged the idea
that there is one best way to lead.

Fiedler's work, however, has itself been challenged on a number of fronts. First, it is not clear what
the scores from the LPCS really mean relative to the
matter of leadership style. The problem is with the
meaning of high versus low scores and with the derivation of a leadership characterization from a personality
test. Vroom (1976) also has noted that relationships
between these scores and leader behavior have been
weak and that correlations reveal reversals in direction
(p. 1534). Furthermore, the conception of leadership in
the model is immutable. Second, at best there has been
mixed support for the findings from this approach relative to existing full model tests (House & Baetz,
1979, p. 380). Third, concern has been expressed about
the restricted nature of the variables—leader orientation from a single scale and situational favorableness

from only three dimensions—and whether they, in
fact, add up to what they purport to represent. Fourth,
despite contradictory evidence and the inability to determine the meaning of scale scores, the outcomes of
this line of inquiry have not been moderated by Fiedler,
who has been quick to make pronouncements about
the selection and recruitment of leaders (Vroom, 1976,
p. 1535). Nevertheless, as Jago (1982, p. 323) has
noted, Fiedler clearly questioned the notion that there
is one best way to lead, and he took the first important
direct step toward the study of leadership in terms of
situational dependencies. While extending the results
of earlier lines of inquiry, he also moved to an explicit
consideration of situation and greater complexity in the
exercise of leadership in terms of the use of several
situational variables. All in all, Fiedler's work, its
arguable aspects aside, served to establish the value of
the contingency approach for the study of leadership.

Work employing the decision-analysis model of
Vroom and Yetton (1973) is often considered as inquiry
related to leadership. It must, nevertheless, be noted
that this model focuses on decision-making activity,
and it is really a diagnostic tool for managers or
designated leaders that is intended to be used in specific decision situations in order to determine the appropriate degree of participation in decision-making
activity. Although clearly in the participation domain,
the model may well have limited usefulness for
informing leadership in a general sense. In this contingency type of context, the manager (leader) must
choose from five styles by analyzing seven attributes of
problems. Not only does the model lack a degree of
parsimony, it also lacks validation (House & Baetz,
1979, pp. 396, 398), for much of its support to date has
come from training applications. Few rigorous studies
have been conducted, and the work thus far offers, at
best, weak verification of the contingency notion.
There have been, however, two interesting results of
extant tests of this deduced theory: (a) subjects
(managers and managers in training) are less flexible
than the model predicts and (b) the model prescribes
extremes (low and high participation) more than
managers and those in training situations choose them.
These results could well speak more to managerial
decision-making behavior than to leader behavior, especially since effective leaders have been shown to vary
their styles and behavior. The decision-analysis model
has really not yet been very productive in substantively
advancing understanding about leadership.

The work of House and his colleagues (Filley,
House, & Kerr, 1976; House, 1971; House & Mitchell,
1974) related to the use of path-goal theory in the study
of leadership represents a very important step in
situational or contingency investigations. Using a situa-

tional theory, the theory of expectancy motivation (Evans, 1970; Vroom, 1964), House and others have suggested that the leader's strategic functions are to enhance motivation and performance, subordinates' job satisfaction, and acceptance of the leader. The conceptualization derived by House involves two categories of situational variables: the personal characteristics of subordinates and the enrivnoment with which they must deal. In this view, leader behavior is accepted and satisfying to the extent that it is a source of satisfaction or is instrumental in gaining satisfaction, and leader behavior is motivational to the extent that it makes satisfaction contingent on performance and provides the coaching, guidance, support, and rewards necessary for effective performance. The findings of House's work and more recent tests have supported the hypotheses that (a) only when tasks are unambiguous and not ego-involving will subordinate personality or predisposition moderate the effects of participative leadership and (b) the effects of leader consideration on performance and subordinate satisfaction will be most positive when subordinates are engaged in dissatisfying tasks, are fatigued, are frustrated, or are under stress (House & Baetz, 1979, pp. 388–390). This line of work has corroborated the situational nature of leadership, has lent considerable credence to the general direction and nature of Fiedler's contentions, and has established leader-task competence as an important variable in leadership effectiveness. Others have supported the findings of House and his colleagues and have added more variables (such as intragroup conflict, organizational size, and structural variables) to the model, but to date, the results of investigations overall are somewhat mixed (Jago, 1982, p. 326). It has also been argued that path-analytic approaches should be used in testing the theory (Dessler & Valenzi, 1977). More time will be required to ascertain fully the value of this promising line of activity, but House and others have contributed greatly to the study of leadership by including more variables, refining the contingency approach, and supporting the addition of potentially powerful variables to the leadership equation. Perhaps the real import of this work lies in expanding the conceptualization used in inquiry and in getting at more complex interactions of variables for a domain that has been empirically revealed to be quite complex itself.

Another promising recent focus following the contingency thrust toward leadership inquiry has drawn on operant conditioning. Such investigations have explored the effect of rewards and punishment on reinforcing particular behavioral patterns of followers (Jago, 1982, p. 326). These studies follow from the premise that because leaders are significant sources of reward contingencies and reward administration, leadership can best be explained in terms of the principles of operant conditioning. Leadership is thus viewed in terms of leaders' motivational activity and the shaping of behavior by controlling consequences (Mawhinney & Ford, 1977; Scott, 1977; Sims, 1977). These investigations have demonstrated consistent results for positive rewards and inconsistent results for punitive consequences. Positive rewards contingent on high levels of performance are associated with high overall levels of performance and higher levels of satisfaction (House & Baetz, 1979, p. 403; Jago, 1982, p. 326). Punitive rewards are, however, related to low levels of performance and satisfaction in some studies but to higher performance and satisfaction in other studies. Nevertheless, it can be concluded that positive rewards have been revealed by this line of inquiry as motivating subordinates and providing for need satisfaction. Also, these results are consistent with those from work employing the path-goal approach, and they support the notion that the leader can be instrumental in determining subordinate responses and task-related behaviors. These studies as well add another class of leader behavior (reward behavior) to the overall list of variables related to leadership.

In sum, the recent advances using contingency or situational models in the study of leadership represent a promising direction for future inquiry. Although results are more or less definitive, and mixed, depending on the scientific approach employed, it is apparent that Fiedler's work suggested the value of the contingency approach and the path-goal and operant-conditioning studies have indicated its viability. Not only do these studies clarify earlier findings but also, and most importantly, they have extended the number of variables employed in studies of leadership and have better attended to the complexity of leadership than had many earlier, more simplistic, and restricted approaches to inquiry. In fact, the matters of traits, styles, and leader behavior have been given fresh perspective by these studies.

Summary

It can be concluded at the general level of analysis employed in this review that the study of leadership is neither the barren ground nor the frustrating arena portrayed by some critics (McCall & Lombardo, 1978; Minor, 1975). Although the accumulation of empirical data has not produced an integrated understanding of leadership (Stogdill, 1974, p. vii) and a lot is known about a few aspects of leadership (Jago, 1982, p. 332), there have been both an accumulation of knowledge and a progression of investigations that have built upon prior empirical activity and findings about leadership.

Studies have revealed the complexity of leadership, the situational nature of leader behavior, and the importance and effect of an increasing number of related variables. That some might expect more from so much activity or that the domain of inquiry might be characterized by more chaff than wheat is not to take away from the progress that has been made. Indeed, current efforts in terms of rigor and sophistication are clearly of a different order than the early subjective or simplistic "studies" of leadership. The prevalence and continuation of the latter kinds of studies—two variable investigations, mindless replications and endless repeated pursuits, and conceptually and methodologically inadequate efforts—do cloud the situation and serve to mask the advances that have been realized. That the developments do not sufficiently inform practice or represent major breakthroughs or increments to knowledge also should not detract from the positive nature of developments. Decades are not long periods of time in science, and the needs of practice and related science and knowledge do not correlate very well for any number of phenomena in a wide variety of fields. The foregoing conclusions do appear to provide a sound base for further empirical activity and represent reasonable results, given inquiry to date.

On two counts, however, the results of empirical work are not as heartening. First, the study of educational leaders or leadership and the efforts by those in the field of education and others studying the field present several dilemmas. Second, empirical evidence on the effects of leadership training is clearly limited and beset with problems.

In the first respect, as a result of careful examination of research in the educational literature on leadership and leader behavior, it can safely be concluded that there has not been very much priority for such study, at least over the last decade or so. There have, of course, been some excellent studies of educational leaders (Gross & Herriott, 1965; Halpin, 1959) and reviews of work in the educational field (Cunningham & Gephart, 1973; Greenfield, 1968; Stout & Briner, 1969), but these kinds of activity have clearly waned. This is especially curious in the light of circumstances in this field, particularly the well-noted decline in educational settings that in fact offers interesting prospects for the study of leadership, as noted by Bass (1981). Educational studies of leadership and research on educational leaders appear to be dwindling in number, not increasing. This observation is supported by the facts that, based on search of the journal literature on the topic, recent studies of educational leadership are relatively few and far between and leadership as a review topic was dropped in the most recent *Encyclopedia of Educational Research* (1982). It can be added that

this reviewer's experience as editor of the *Educational Administration Quarterly* for a period of 6 years, from 1980 through 1985, further supports this observation. Of over 1,000 manuscripts submitted to that journal in that time, only a small percentage were empirical efforts directed toward leadership and leader behavior. Such efforts were typically of poor quality and were repetitive, not ground breaking, in nature. In fact, the only piece on the topic published over the period was a perspective (not research) article (Morris, 1985), and material on leadership in *EAQ* over the period came from byproduct treatment derived from other investigative emphases. This is not to say that there has been no activity in the field of educational administration relative to leadership, but research activity on leadership has not recently appeared to enjoy a very high priority.

In any event, at the general level of analysis employed for this review, studies of educational leaders and investigations by those in the field have for the most part corroborated and replicated other inquiry. Although educational studies have reported some differences, as noted by Stogdill (1974) and Hencley (1973), the general findings on leadership reported above pertain to work on and in the educational context. There are only a few minor differences between education and in other areas, and it is also quite apparent that studies in education tend to mirror other work and to lag behind the empirical, conceptual, and methodological advances realized elsewhere (e.g., there are few contingency-type educational studies). Further, just as activity relative to leadership inquiry is not prominent in sources covering education, educational studies receive scant mention in extant reviews, including modest sections in the Stogdill (1974) handbook and Bass's 1981 revision.

Despite the number and visibility of educational leaders, they have rather perplexingly failed to attract greater interest on the part of researchers. In wondering why they have not, both Burlingame (1973) and Stogdill (1974) have suggested less than flattering reasons. The former noted that "leaders in education have been lesser [persons] attempting to maintain schools. . .They are not on the frontier, reconnoitering virgin territory" (Burlingame, 1973, p. 64). The latter, in reflecting on interviews with educational leaders, observed that they led him to surmise that there was "a passive commitment throughout the profession to a *laissez faire* style of leadership" that resulted not only in a permissive style open to examination and challenge but also in a view that saw structuring as autocratic and as suppressing sensitivity to group processes (Stogdill, 1974, p. 98). There may well be more favorable explanations of the recent paucity of research on the topic in the field of education, but the activity level relative to leadership and the number of educational leadership studies of the 1960s (Cunningham & Gephart, 1973; Greenfield, 1968; Stout & Briner, 1969) stand in stark contrast to the record of the past decade or so.

In the second respect and in relation to the effect of leadership training, there has been a pronounced preoccupation with moving hastily from the conceptualization of some aspect of leadership through a "field test" or "test with a small number of trainees" to a range of findings on the topic and a full-blown leadership training program. These kinds of efforts have really provided meager evidence about leadership and the effectiveness of leader or leadership training. Stogdill (1974, pp. 198–199) observed in his handbook of leadership research that no effort was found that was designed to see whether or not leadership trainees were more effective than nontrainees. Problems simply abound in this regard. First, many really untested models, like the Vroom and Yetton (1973) model or the Blake and Mouton (1964) managerial grid, are moved rather quickly into training settings. Second, what has been labeled leadership training ranges from lectures, films, and discussions more or less related to the topic to equally more-or-less-related models, exercises, simulations, and programs and even sensitivity training (Bass, 1981, pp. 553–583). Some of these have an effect on trainees, but an on-the-job effect of leadership training really has not yet been ascertained. Third, as noted elsewhere, "the research on leadership training is generally inadequate in both design and execution" (Stogdill, 1974, p. 199). It is, therefore, difficult to determine the value of leadership training from the available evidence, and one should be extremely cautious of the claims (and the empirical work) in this regard. The difficulty of developing training for something as complex and imperfectly understood as leadership must be taken into account in considering the claims of many training studies.

Despite the dilemmas about the study of leadership and leader behavior in education and the problems with the work on leadership training, the major findings on the review topic remain encouraging and represent significant strides in the study and understanding of leadership.

GENERAL OBSERVATIONS AND METHODOLOGICAL CONSIDERATIONS

Turning more explicitly to the assessment function of a review, a number of general observations about empirical activity related to leadership warrant explication. Further, some critical consideration of inquiry methodology, including the conceptualization of leadership for research purposes, should be undertaken. In this section, the general observations, including concerns and uneasiness, will be explored first. Then methodological matters and problems will be discussed. Finally, the section will address what are held to be important issues in the conceptualization of leadership for research purposes.

General Observations

The careful review and analysis of any body of inquiry, regardless of the level at which one is operating, leads to certain conclusions like those reported in the preceding results section. Review and analyses also lead to a number of more general observations as well as impressions and feelings about the domain at hand. These observations and impressions about leadership research are reported because they appear to be appropriate and important concerns in looking toward next steps in the study of leadership and leader behavior.

The study of leadership unfortunately can be generally characterized by an overreliance on looking backward and the extensive use of reputational data. Although the study of leadership has moved away from a historical perspective because of inquiry rooted in a number of disciplines and professional fields, research has, nevertheless, maintained an after-the-fact quality. It is curious that students of leadership have tended to avoid studying actual unfolding situations and have opted so frequently to focus on what has already happened. It is evident in the literature that, although there are exceptions to the rule, investigating real situations has not been a high priority for very many researchers. Some kinds of research cannot be done using real-world situations, but if the goal is to get at behavior or to gain knowledge about what leaders do and how they do it, then more studies of actual situations are needed. The call of Motowidlo (1976) for building a bank of data from actual situations and subjecting such data to several different kinds of analysis is very well taken. It is only in field studies, some laboratory studies, and other relatively circumscribed investigations (such as with training situations) that actual leadership or leader behavior has been explored. The use of contrived or controlled situations may well have limited utility for a complex phenomenon like leadership, and the emphasis on approaches that rely on reputational and questionnaire data, regardless of the type of study, further confounds the situation.

A nagging concern throughout the course of this review activity was whether scientific inquiry itself was getting in the way of advancing what is known about leadership. Although research has contributed to understanding, as has already been pointed out, it is also possible that normal processes of inquiry have unduly delimited and restricted what has been investigated. Through operational definitions, the selection of variables for study, the delimitation and control of those variables, and the determination of the focus of inquiry, the very same studies that have continued to demonstrate the complexity and situational nature of leadership and the need to look at a greater number of variables have tended to remain relatively restricted or selective themselves, and thereby have not very greatly expanded what has been considered. A number of things that can be gleaned from case accounts and biographies that warrant the attention of leadership researchers have escaped conscious and systematic attention: for example, the cultural or environmental aspects of situations (House & Baetz, 1979, p. 374; Sergiovanni & Corbally, 1984); the goals and motivation of leaders in various situations (House & Baetz, 1979, pp. 410, 411); the role of second-level or subordinate leaders ("lieutenants") or leadership structures (Broad, 1963); how leaders use resources and array organizations and their members to achieve results (Bennis & Nunus, 1985; Peters & Waterman, 1982); and how leaders get "from here to there" (Kearns, 1976). Perhaps what has been studied has been explored in part because of convenience or because it has been more readily operationalized and measured. If so, other things, in spite of their import, may have been neglected or avoided because they are not as amenable to scientific inquiry and are, in fact, more subjective and elusive. All in all, normal scientific inquiry may have contributed to oversimplification of the notion of leadership and, in so doing, may have limited advances in what is known about it. If this is the case, there is a need to consider other approaches to collecting and analyzing data about leadership and leader behavior as well as other sources of data and even broader perspectives on what should be investigated.

Another observation about leadership research is that, in the general literature on leadership, inquiry and empirical efforts for advancing understanding are somewhat subservient to other kinds of concerns. Not only are there almost endless opinion, perspective, point of view, and thought pieces on the topic, along with numerous descriptive and prescriptive treatments, but also the more pressing and popular matters of the selection and training of leaders often seem to take precedence over the study of leadership generally. Perhaps the importance and centrality of the phenomenon in a variety of social-science areas and pursuits have contributed to impatience with research and have

served to compromise inquiry for other goals. Nowhere is this more obvious than in effort, some supposedly empirical, in the literature that are directed toward leadership selection and training. These efforts are quickly turned toward the more immediate concerns of choosing or preparing leaders, and in the process inquiry is compromised. Leadership appears to be a topic of great concern and one on which there are a lot of opinions and ideas; it is somewhat less a general arena for rigorous investigation.

A persistent uneasiness in the course of this review activity concerned the degree to which what is generally considered research on leadership really covers the full range of knowledge about the topic. As was noted in the first paragraph of this chapter, the discrepancy is notable. This problem is compounded when something that is said to be about the topic of leadership has little to say about it, while inquiry identified as attending to other topics increase understanding of the phenomenon. Clearly the biographical material on political figures such as Winston Churchill (1948; Broad, 1963) or Lyndon Johnson (Kearns, 1976) speak to the topic. Even popular sources such as *In Search of Excellence* by Peters and Waterman (1982) or Lee Iaccoca's autobiography (Iaccoca & Novak, 1984) contain relevant material. A nonrandom sample of practicing leaders was asked at one point in the course of this review whether they had read any recent studies of leadership. None could recall reading any research on the topic, but when asked what they had read, each did name two or more biographical accounts of people who could easily be classified as leaders. Further, when asked why such sources were read, the respondent noted that the readings revealed how the subjects accomplished what they achieved. Opening up the domain of material so broadly would certainly make a review task such as this impossible. In looking to other sources of data on leadership, there may be a variety of rich arenas that might well be advantageously brought into the fold, no matter how difficult the task may be. The collation and synthesis of such knowledge may be neither so glamourous nor exciting an undertaking as breaking new ground, but it is clearly part of the enormous task of establishing what is known about leadership and accumulating the full range of understanding about the topic.

Finally, it should be observed that there is no shortage of experts on the topics of leadership and leadership research. The area is not wanting for those who wish to advise it or who seem to know where inquiry should be tending. On this score, however, close review was exceedingly sobering. The data reveal that there may be really only a number of experts on a limited number of facets of leadership. It is almost incomprehensible that anyone could begin to qualify as an expert over the entire domain. And, expertise in an area where there is a wide variety of views should be subjected to constant scrutiny. As well, less frequent visitors to and casual observers of the area warrant greater suspicion by all, but judgment that takes on more meaning as one becomes more familiar with the territory.

Methodological Considerations

In the course of the analysis activity for this review, a number of problems related to research methodology were identified. These problems have, in fact, been variously recognized. That is, although there is general agreement in the research reviews on methodological problems, the problems are seldom taken into account by many who conduct "going fare" or "run of the mill" studies. This condition contributes to the repetitious nature of much leadership research as well as the suspect nature of many inquiries that simply are not "state of the science" efforts. The problems with methodology in leadership research range from those of conceptualization and study design to those of instrumentation, variables and subjects, and approaches to the analysis of data.

One of the most curious things about leadership research is the previously mentioned reliance of researchers on reputational and questionnaire approaches, even in attempts to study leadership behavior. This has led at least one observer to raise the issue of whether this arena is developing a science of questionnaire behavior as opposed to one of leadership behavior (Karmel, 1978). The extensive use of questionnaire data and/or data from constructed, simulated, or hypothetical (or otherwise contrived or controlled) situations raises serious problems of validity with much inquiry. At a surface level, although reputational data might be justified in getting at something such as leadership style, these kinds of data are not as defensible in studying behavior, particularly in the sense of trying to ascertain what leaders actually do. In addition, the flaws of self-report data, perceptual data, and after-the-fact data are all too well documented in the general research literature. At an even more telling level, however, given what is known from inquiry about leadership and leader behavior—its complexity, its situational nature, and the two-way nature of effects— this approach to data collection without corroboration or the support of observational data is more than just suspect. The need is not only to investigate (and collect data about) actual leadership situations but also to systematically accumulate a large number of incidents portraying actual examples of leader behavior and leadership situations (House & Baetz, 1979,

p. 412). If the goal is to understand and illuminate behavior, only the use of data from real settings will move the study of leadership beyond the presumptuousness of attempting to ascertain what leaders do from reputational approaches. This is not to argue against such approaches or what they can contribute; it is, rather, to focus on their limitations and encourage movement to even more valid approaches for inquiry on the behavior of leaders.

A related issue recognized in the review literature is that there are problems with particular instruments that are used in leadership studies (Bass, 1981, pp. 391–392; House & Baetz, 1979, pp. 360–363, 380–381; Jago, 1982, pp. 319, 322–323, 325–326; Stogdill, 1974, pp. 142–156). Such problems are related to the results that can be obtained from use of the instruments, item content, and often the nature and stage of development of instruments. This can be illustrated with reference to the LBDQ. House and Baetz (1979, pp. 360–363) point out clearly that results differ with the early and later forms of the LBDQ. In particular, the newer form (LBDQ–12) has different item content for initiating structure (Stogdill, 1963), and the results of its use are more consistent both with other lines of inquiry and with logic. Thus, Stogdill (1974, p. 155) on the basis of his analysis encourages the use of the LBDQ–12 rather than earlier forms of the instrument, and he suggests that all items on the scale should be employed in research (in contrast to the prevalent use of just the consideration and initiating-structure items). There is little justification for using a portion of the instrument or earlier versions of it when, as in this case, the value of the revised scale is so apparent (House & Baetz, 1979, pp. 362–363). The problems with other well-used instruments are documented both in other reviews and in lines of inquiry where they have been employed. Greater care in the selection and use of data collection instruments in leadership research is clearly called for, and it behooves investigators to scrutinize past experience with instruments along with their content and what can be expected from their use.

Study design also represents a sizable methodological problem in leadership inquiry. Copied designs or replications with and without variation are all too common, and studies often appear to be raw empiricism or the haphazard and uncritical linking of variables with a less than rigorous design, if there is a design at all. As a result of the current state of conceptualizations or theory about leadership (a matter to be treated in the next section) and varying definitions of the phenomenon (as already noted), there are few well-established constructs for specifying and linking variables and otherwise guiding inquiry. This problem is compounded somewhat by the complexity and nature of leadership and, hence, the design of inquiry is not the easiest task facing a leadership researcher. Conscious and rigorous effort on the part of the investigator are required in selecting or formulating a conceptual base for the study of leadership, in operationalizing that base and the variables to be studied, in generating research questions or hypotheses, and in determining an appropriate study design. This is apparent in the work of some (Fiedler, 1967; Filley et al., 1976; Hollander, 1964; Mawhinney & Ford, 1977; Scott, 1977; Sims, 1977; Sims & Szilagyi, 1975). Many others, however, seem to fall into a design as a result of the arbitrary selection of instrumentation or the variables to be investigated, the convenient selection of subjects, or the accidental choice of analytic procedures. All too often, when everything else fails, rigorous quantitative procedures for analysis seem to be assumed to be adequate to correct for all flaws in study conceptualization. A sufficient quantity of leadership research unfortunately is atheoretical, even aconceptual, and clearly lacks a conscious, well-thought-out design. It behooves those operating in this area of inquiry to be more rigorous, in the full sense of the word, in conceptualizing and designing studies.

There is a clear need in leadership research to broaden the number of variables investigated. This is so well established that it need not be developed or dwelled upon here (Bass, 1981; House & Baetz, 1979; Jago, 1982; Motowidlo, 1976; Vroom, 1976). Unfortunately, some variables have been pursued endlessly (e.g., initiating structure and consideration, or satisfaction), and others have been almost totally ignored (e.g., cultural and environmental aspects of situations or the motivation and goals of the leader). The already ascertained complexity and situational nature of leadership together argue strongly for expanding the numbers of variables examined in this arena. At the very least, it is rather indefensible at this point in the study of leadership not to include four kinds or sets of variables in studies: (a) personal characteristics of the leader—including traits; (b) behavior or patterns of behavior—style: (c) the situation—context, task, and environment; and (d) outcomes—performance or effects (House & Baetz, 1979; Vroom, 1976). Put another way, these variables should be viewed in combination in order to determine their relationships and the nature of their effects on outcomes in a situational sense. It is apparent from studies thus far that a lot of things are correlated with leadership (Hencley, 1973, pp. 150–151) and that there are reciprocal effects (House & Baetz, 1979, p. 348; Jago, 1982, pp. 321–322). However, the linkage of variables in a directional sense and in terms of variance explained is an important consideration from the time of study conceptualization and

design to variable selection and the analysis of data. Simple correlational studies of limited and restricted variables are no longer appropriate.

There are several problems with respect to the subjects of leadership inquiry. First, it is hard to find a category of possible subjects that has not been studied by someone. This variety or proliferation of kinds of subjects has done little to advance the understanding of leadership, but the problems of subjects of investigations also have to do with the prevalence of restricted samples, convenience samples, and questionable subjects in leadership research. With respect to questionable subjects, it seem curious indeed to try to generalize about leaders or a category of leaders from those in preparation or in training situations. Although certain aspects of leadership might be explored with these kinds of subjects, they do not offer the potential for broad generalization or for illuminating very fully the phenomenon at hand. In another respect, the convenience sample is just that, and in leadership research it has often included those in classes, training programs, or whomever else the investigator can readily get data from. Problems here are considerably greater because there is little that can be said for such samples, and they offer limited value even for exploratory efforts. Finally, the restricted sample—such as that from an organization, an area, a portion of a state, or a state—has similar problems, even though such a sample is better in some respects than the other problematic ones. Needed as subjects for leadership research are actual leaders, purposively and systematically sampled when necessary, in adequate numbers for the research purposes at hand.

In turning to the matter of analysis, it has been indicated that simple correlational approaches to the analysis of data currently are of limited utility. Given the need for more rigorous investigative designs with more complex conceptualizations of variables, increasingly sophisticated analytic procedures are called for in studies of leadership. The need is not for quantification or rigor as such but for analytic schemes that fit the designs and conceptualizations employed. The role of the methodologist in leadership study is increasing, and a high level of analytical expertise will be required in future studies. Illustrative of the problems related to data analysis in leadership studies are the following. First, there is an obvious unit-of-analysis problem in much of the leadership research. In this regard, the unit of analysis is all too often not specified, and variables involving different units of analysis (e.g., the individual and group) are indiscriminately mixed and lumped together in analyses. For example, leader behavior (individual unit), satisfaction (individual unit), and productivity (group unit) are correlated by aggregating data from subjects without attention to the unit of analysis or its meaning for the statistical or analytic approach utilized (Knapp, 1982; Miskel & Sandlin, 1981; Sirotnik, 1980). Second, as noted by Jago (1982, p. 331) and Graen and his associates (Dansereau, Graen, & Haga, 1975; Graen & Cashman, 1975; Graen & Schiemann, 1978), the "average style" approach is common in leadership research. In this sense, departures from the average are treated as random error and, thus, explained away. Based on what is known about leadership, an analytic approach involving the vertical dyad or the one-to-one leader-follower relationship is more appropriate—not only in individual leader-follower situations but also in shedding light on dynamics and differences in one-to-many situations. It has been demonstrated by Graen and Cashman (1975) that, when using this approach to analysis, departures from an average are not random and are predictive of subsequent phenomena. Third, as a result of activity related to path-goal investigations of leadership, the value of path-analytic approaches in such studies has been ascertained (Dessler & Valenzi, 1977; House & Baetz, 1979, pp. 390–391; Sheridan, Downey, & Slocum, 1975). Such advances in methodology ought not be disregarded and should be taken into account in future investigations drawing on path-goal theory. Fourth, it seems obvious that the blind pursuit of regularities in leadership studies ought to be abandoned in favor of the more systematic exploration of variations. Regardless of whether the preoccupation with regularities has been prompted by the early pursuit of the "best way to lead" or the desire to come to firm conclusions and generalizations, accumulated knowledge seems to argue for greater attention to variation and more explanation of variations and "exceptions." From mounting evidence and inquiry activity to date, issues and problems related to the analysis of data in leadership research are neither casual nor elementary concerns. Instead, they warrant explicit attention and an increasing level of methodological expertise.

Finally, it must be noted with respect to methodological problems in the study of leadership that, at least from this review activity, some effort ought to be invested in adjudicating the quality and adequacy of investigations. The sheer volume of and problems noted with the empirical activity in this area of study speak to the need. Many efforts at reviewing, collating, and synthesizing leadership research simply collect and summarize the results of investigations. Few go so far analytically and critically as do House and Baetz (1979) or Jago (1982) in their reviews, and it seems unwise to continue to assemble and synthesize uncritically the many studies of no or limited utility. It may well be

time to identify clearly and discard from consideration studies of suspect quality or those that have been ascertained as inadequate. Although a huge task, such an effort would (a) reduce the volume of work to which inquirers must attend, (b) facilitate the synthesis of knowledge about leadership, and (c) make meta-analysis, such as Crehan's (1984) study, or other analysis across lines of study more feasible. The value of clearly separating adequate inquiry from suspect or inadequate work appears to be essential from the point of view of clarifying what is known and directing the way toward most viable next steps for research activity.

The Conceptualization of Leadership

Much attention has been given by researchers to the definition of leadership. In fact, over a decade ago, Stogdill (1974, pp. 7–16) reported and classified more than 70 definitions from inquiry efforts up to that time. With the attention to definition given by researchers and the large amount of material on thought about leadership and the study of it, one might expect rather well established conceptualizations and constructs for and used in leadership research. That is not the case. There really are no commonly accepted conceptualizations, and there is very little of what could really be called leadership theory to guide inquiry. Instead, there are a number of more or less rigorous competing notions about the phenomenon and a number and variety of definitions devised for several purposes, including research, with little agreement among them (Stogdill, 1974, pp. 15, 16).

As a result, there are a number of problems with extant conceptualizations of leadership for inquiry. Early theories and conceptualizations tended to be about individuals (leaders) or about the leader and the group. Efforts have moved thinking beyond this point, but problems remain. One is the limited or restricted nature of most conceptualizations of leadership. Rather than logically embracing the totality of what is known about the phenomenon, many conceptualizations seem to be derived from, or to be developed to justify, particular variables or aspects. Thus an "invented" character to many conceptualizations used in leadership inquiry. Further, formulations tend to be partial and incomplete. Because they are concerned with specific aspects of the phenomenon of leadership—and there are a lot of aspects to any complex phenomenon—conceptualizations tend not to approach the full picture or range of even the known dimensions. Few conceptualizations cover even the earlier mentioned set of variables (personal characteristics, behavior or style, situation, and outcomes) that, from inquiry to date, ought to be included in a study. Not only are there, therefore, a variety of incomplete conceptualizations, but also many existing ones overemphasize personal and interpersonal dimensions at the expense of environmental and cultural considerations and a range of potentially heuristic concerns from goals and resources to work structures.

A consequence of the present state of the conceptualization of leadership is the aconceptual and atheoretical nature of all too many studies. In numerous instances, there is simply no conceptualization guiding the inquiry. This is typical of many correlational studies of style and any other of a number of variables that strike investigators as worth investigating or linking to style. These studies have certainly proved their lack of value in the leadership arena and represent the antithesis of what is needed.

To some degree, the more recent contingency approaches have moved conceptualization and theory past the work of Hollander (1964) and Fiedler (1967) to the somewhat more theoretically sophisticated path-goal and reward-theory notions of other scholars (Evans, 1970; House, 1971; Scott, 1977). These efforts are, nevertheless, still recognizably restricted or limited, and many such conceptualizations rely heavily on borrowed theory or theory from other areas or about other phenomena. As such, theory is incorporated into leadership conceptualizations, but it is not leadership theory in and of itself. In any event, the latter conceptualizations of leadership represent movement beyond earlier, more simplistic ones and have already resulted in evidence of the value of more adequate theory and conceptualization in empirical work.

Perhaps the real problem with respect to leadership theory and conceptualization has been the lack of attention to theoretical development. Rigorous attempts at theory building and conceptualization are somewhat scarce. Many existing efforts are merely attempts to theorize or conceptualize *about* leadership as opposed to being serious work directed toward developing theories or conceptualizations *of* leadership. There are a number of routes to constructing concepts and theory for research purposes, from borrowing or generating them from what is known to following the purely logical approaches of deduction and induction. Improved conceptualizations of leadership seem critical at this time for further advancing inquiry and the understanding of leadership. Such activity should be directed toward expanded formulations and should include consideration of the full range and complexity of the phenomenon.

It may well be, however, that efforts thus far have focused on the wrong thing. Griffiths (1979, pp. 44, 45–46) and others (Haller & Knapp, 1985) have already indicated the advantage for the study of administrative behavior of shifting to a focus on "doing administration." In fact, Griffiths's lucid example in this regard is directly relevant for the study of leadership as well, and it suggests the advantage not only of examining real situations but also of focusing on the act of *leading*, or what leaders do. Shifts in the focus of leadership study over the years have already been noted, and it may well be time to move on to the investigation of *leading* rather than *leadership*. This notion has heuristic potential and could, perhaps, enhance conceptualization for leadership study.

Much remains to be done in mapping the leadership domain, in identifying dimensions and variables critical to the phenomenon (as well as their linkages), and in developing viable conceptualizations and constructs to guide research. Both positivistic and naturalistic approaches warrant attention in this regard. Given the current state of knowledge and available case, biographical, and historical accounts of leaders, certainly some effort should be directed toward the development of grounded theory utilizing the naturalistic paradigm. From the positivistic perspective, efforts directed toward expanded formulations of the phenomenon would seem most valuable. This kind of activity could well be moved ahead by focusing on leading or the act of providing leadership. For example, if leadership is invoked or leading is attempted in order to get something done, then the leader's goals or what the leader wants to get done, his or her values and motivation as well as what is done by the leader and others in the leadership setting, and the results or outcomes of that activity all seem to be important for inclusion in the conceptualization of the phenomenon. In very broad strokes, the outlines of such a conceptualization could take the form of the model in Figure 13.1. This kind of model for a conceptualization of leadership, or maybe more appropriately lead*ing*, has the potential for further development using what is known about leadership, theory from other areas, and logical reasoning. It is also consistent with emerging empirical activity in the contingency vein but extends conceptualization into a broader and more comprehensive realm.

At this point, treatment of the conceptualization of leadership is getting beyond the task of a review. However, the weaknesses in this respect noted in the review activity, and in reflecting on prevailing research conceptualizations of leadership, well indicated the need to treat explicitly the matter of conceptualization, to note existing problems in that regard, and to indicate on that basis possible ways of alleviating a very problematic aspect of leadership inquiry. The conceptualization of leadership has been a somewhat

Figure 13.1 Model of a Broad Conceptualization of Leadership

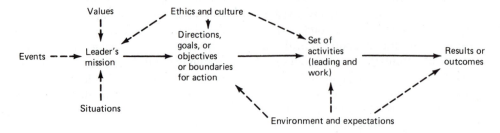

underattended area, but it is one important to research activity and, hence, one worthy of greater attention by those involved in the study of leadership.

SUGGESTIONS FOR THE FUTURE STUDY OF LEADERSHIP

Although there is some presumptuousness on the part of anyone charting the future for an area as complicated as the study of leadership, and one who undertakes that task does so with trepidation, the suggestions that follow have some support in a number of quarters. On the basis of the review and in summary, they are intended as broad, general guidelines.

First, from a methodological perspective, it is suggested that inquiry proceed in two distinct directions. The current work along the contingency approach to inquiry merits further activity, including efforts to refine methodology, to clarify conflicting findings, to resolve existing problems, and to expand the sets of variables explored. Such lines of possible activity are well indicated by Jago (1982) and House and Baetz (1979). As well, other studies revealing a promising direction for inquiry, such as operant conditioning and goal theory, should be pursued further. In addition to such a science-as-usual approach, it is also clear that extensive efforts along case study lines and using the naturalistic paradigm are called for. Given the need to expand the aspects, dimensions, and variables of leadership studied, to account more fully for leadership's complexity, to examine actual leadership situations, and to expand conceptualizations, case study and analysis seem potentially very useful. If an investigator really wants to get at leading and what is involved in leadership, real-world situations offer the best prospects. Building a bank of such data could prove to be very beneficial in ascertaining important dynamics and variables as well as their linkage and in pinpointing priorities for subsequent study. Such data bases should also provide rich material for generating grounded theory, thereby contributing to the conceptualization of

leadership. Longitudinal and comparative case studies should not be ignored in this kind of inquiry. For example, leaders should be studied over time in a number or series of cases and with a variety of situations—different kinds of tasks or goals. Also, in given contexts such as a school district or state, the responses of several leaders to the same policy or need-for-leadership initiative should be investigated and subjected to scrutiny. Further, an effort could be made through a series of cases to ascertain the effect of different magnitudes of situations on leadership and across leaders. All in all, a number of rigorous strategies for case and naturalistic study appear promising.

Second, although not inquiry per se, conceptualization of the domain of leadership merits greater priority and more attention than it has received. The importance of theory and viable constructs for inquiry has been demonstrated in the contingency approach to the study of leadership. Conceptualization and theory development can logically proceed in two directions. Positivistic theory building should be undertaken to guide research using that paradigm, and the generation of grounded theory from naturalistic studies has potential utility for explaining leadership and in generating research hypotheses and contributing to other theory-building activities. Extant conceptualizations of leadership appear to present distinct problems in terms of facilitating the kinds of investigations that appear to be needed.

Third, it is suggested that the focus of the study of leadership ought to shift clearly to one on *leading*, or the act of providing leadership. The import of behavioral study and getting at what leaders do has been established for quite some time. Inquiry must, however, go further in attempting to reach that goal, and both case study and more rigorous conceptualizations will facilitate movement toward the goal of understanding better what leaders do.

Fourth, the number of aspects, dynamics, and variables that are examined in leadership research must be increased. This, too, can be fostered through more rigorous and comprehensive conceptualizations. In addition, the matter of the linkages of variables must be more systematically explored, and variations across leaders and situations must not continue to ignored. Potentially important but neglected variables—those from the environmental and cultural arenas and the matters of resources, values, and goals—should also be included in studies.

Fifth, leadership researchers are well advised to take cues from the leads of others, including both investigators and reviewers. The repetitious nature of much work, the seemingly unending "reinvention of the wheel" approach of many, and the lack of awareness of activity in the domain all inhibit the advancement of knowledge. It behooves anyone embarking on a leadership study to become more than casually cognizant of what has been going on. There has been a lot of activity, and greater priority must be placed on building upon existing work.

Sixth, it is time for a massive effort to adjudicate the adequacy of extant investigations and, as a result, to discard useless or marginally useful work in order to better focus on and accumulate sound inquiry. This is essential because of the volume problem with leadership research. Further synthesis of findings and evaluation of where we are and where we can go with leadership inquiry would be facilitated by such qualitative assessment and the sorting out of deficient work. Then meta-analysis, currently a problem as noted earlier and by Crehan (1985), and other analyses across lines of inquiry might also be more feasible and usefully employed.

Finally, it seems important for those in education and educational administration to give greater priority to the study of leadership. The decline in such activity over the past decade or so was, in all fairness, somewhat to be expected, but the meager quantity of empirical work related to education and educational leadership was completely unanticipated. This is hard to fathom, much less explain, given the impact of decline on education in the 1970s and the challenges to education in the 1980s; this reviewer is not alone in such an assessment of the scene (Morris, 1985). The picture related to the field is fragmented, and although studies continue to appear, they do not reflect very well the developments in the larger leadership arena. In education efforts are lagging far behind efforts elsewhere. Concern about educational leadership ought to be a matter of greater import to researchers and the profession at large.

In conclusion, leadership study has moved ahead over the past few decades despite its not being a very high priority to many and despite problems that are both inherent in the territory and in research activity more generally. Instead of chastising leadership re-searchers and blindly seeking more fertile or more easily tackled domains, the fact is that the optimism of House and Baetz (1979) and Bass (1981) about leadership research remains justified. The continued advancement of the understanding of leadership is, in any case, contingent on sound empirical activity, including renewed interest and work on the part of those in the field of education.

REFERENCES

Applewhite, P. B. (1965). *Organizational behavior*. Englewood Cliffs, NJ: Prentice-Hall.

Bales, R. F. (1958). Task roles and social roles in problem-solving groups. In E. S. Maccoly, T. M. Newcomb, & E. L. Hartley (Eds.), *Readings in social psychology*. New York: Holt, Rinehart, & Winston.

Bales, R. F., & Slater, P. E. (1955). Role differentiation in small decision-making groups. In T. Parsons et al., *Family, socialization, and interaction processes*. Glencoe, IL: Free Press.

Barrows, J. C. (1977). The variables of leadership: A review and conceptual framework. *Academy of Management Review, 2*, 231–251.

Bass, B. M. (1981). *Stogdill's handbook of leadership*. New York: Free Press.

Bass, B. M. & Valenzi, E. R. (1974). Contingent aspects of effective management styles. In J. G. Hunt & L. L. Larson (Eds.), *Contingency approaches to leadership*. Carbondale, IL: Southern Illinois University Press.

Bennis, W. G., & Nunus, B. (1985). *Leaders: Strategies for taking charge*. New York: Harper & Row.

Blake, R. R., & Mouton, J. S. (1964). *The managerial grid*. Houston: Gulf.

Boyan, N. J. (1982). Administration of educational institutions. In *Encyclopedia of educational research* (5th ed., Vol. 1). New York: Free Press.

Bridges, E. M. (1982). Research on the school administrator: The state of the art, 1967–1980. *Educational Administration Quarterly, 18*(3), 12–33.

Broad, L. (1963). *Winston Churchill*. New York: Hawthorne.

Burlingame, M. (1973). The great man approach to the study of American educational leadership. In L. L. Cunningham & W. J. Gephart (Eds.), *Leadership: The science and the art today*. Itasca, IL: Peacock.

Burns, J. M. (1978). *Leadership*. New York: Harper & Row.

Calder, B. J. (1977). An attribution theory of leadership. In B. Stark & G. Salancik (Eds.), *New directions in organizational behavior*. Chicago: St. Clair.

Churchill, W. S. (1948). *The second world war* (Vols. 1–6). Cambridge, MA: Riverside.

Clark, D. L., Lotto, L. S., & Astuto, T. A. (1984). Effective schools and school improvement: A comparative analysis of two lines of inquiry. *Educational Administration Quarterly, 20*(3), 41–68.

Conway, J. A. (1984). The myth, mystery, and mastery of participative decision making in education. *Educational Administration Quarterly, 20*(3), 11–40.

Cooper, J. M. (1982). Supervision of teachers. *Encyclopedia of Educational Research* (5th ed., Vol. 4). New York: Free Press.

Crehan, P. (1984). *A meta-analysis of Fiedler's contingency model of leadership effectiveness*. Doctoral dissertation, University of British Columbia, Vancouver.

Crehan, P. (1985). An exploration of the usefulness of meta-analysis in educational administration. *Educational Administration Quarterly, 21*(3), 263–279.

Cunningham, L. L., & Gephart, W. J. (1973). *Leadership: The science and the art today*. Itasca, IL: Peacock.

Cunningham, L. L., & Payzant, T. W. (1983). *Preparing leaders to anticipate and manage the future: Part 3, Understandings, attitudes, skills, and symbols: Leadership in the future.* Columbus, OH: University Council for Educational Administration.

Dansereau, F. G., Graen, G., & Haga, W. J. (1975). A vertical dyad linkage approach to leadership within formal organizations. *Organizational Behavior and Human Performance, 13,* 46–78.

Dessler, G., & Valenzi, E. R. (1977), Intitiation of structure and subordinate satisfaction: A path analysis test of path-goal theory. *Academy of Management Journal, 20*(2), 251–259.

Dill, D. D. (1984). The nature of administrative behavior in higher education. *Educational Quarterly, 20*(3), 69–100.

Duke, D. L., Showers, B. K., & Imber, M. (1980). Teachers and shared decision making: The costs and benefits of involvement. *Educational Administration Quarterly, 16*(1), 93–106.

Encyclopedia of Educational Research (5th ed.), Vols. 1–4. (1982). New York: Free Press.

Evans, M. G. (1970). The effects of supervisory behavior on the path-goal relationship. *Organizational Behavior and Human Performance, 5,* 277–298.

Fiedler, F. E. (1967). *A theory of leadership effectiveness.* New York: McGraw-Hill.

Fiedler, F. E. (1971). *Leadership.* New York: General Learning Press.

Fiedler, F. E., & Chemers, M. M. (1974). *Leadership and effective management.* Glencoe, IL: Scott, Foresman.

Filley, A. C., House, R. J., & Kerr, S. (1976). *Managerial process and organizational behavior.* Glenview, IL: Scott, Foresman.

Fleishman, E. A., & Harris, E. F. (1962). Patterns of leadership behavior related to employee grievances and turnover. *Personnel Psychology, 15,* 43–56.

Getzels, J. W., & Guba, E. G. Social behavior and the administrative process. *School Review, 55,* 423–441.

Gibb, C. A. (1954). Leadership. In G. Lindzey (Ed.), *Handbook of Social Psychology.* Cambridge, MA: Addison-Wesley.

Gibb, C. A. (1969). Leadership. In G. Lindzey & E. Aronson (Eds.), *The Handbook of Social Psychology* (2nd ed., Vol. 4). Reading, MA: Addison-Wesley.

Graen, G., & Cashman, J. F. (1975). A role-making model of leadership in formal organizations: A developmental approach. In J. G. Hunt & L. L. Larson (Eds.), *Leadership frontiers.* Kent, OH: Kent State University Press.

Graen, G., & Schiemann, W. (1978). Leader-member agreement: A vertical dyad linkage approach. *Journal of Applied Psychology, 63;* 206–212.

Greenfield, T. B. (1968). Research on the behavior of educational leaders: Critique of a tradition. *Alberta Journal of Educational Research, 14,* 55–76.

Griffiths, D. E. (1979). Another look at research on the behavior of administrators. In G. L. Immegart & W. L. Boyd (Eds.), *Problem finding in educational administration.* Lexington, MA: Heath.

Gross, N., & Herriott, R. E. (1965). *Staff leadership in public schools: A sociological inquiry.* New York: John Wiley.

Guba, E. G. (1973). Reaction. In L. L. Cunningham & W. J. Gephart (Eds.), *Leadership: The science and the art today.* Itasca, IL: Peacock.

Haller, E. J., & Knapp, T. R. (1985). Problems and methodology in educational administration. *Educational Administration Quarterly, 21*(3), 157–168.

Halpin, A. W. (1959). *The leadership behavior of school superintendents.* Chicago: The Midwest Center, University of Chicago.

Hencley, S. P. (1973). Situational behavioral approach to the study of educational leadership. In L. L. Cunningham & W. J. Gephart (Eds.), *Leadership: The science and the art today.* Itasca, IL: Peacock.

Hills, R. J. (1963). The representative function: Neglected dimensions of leadership behavior. *Administration Science Quarterly, 8,* 83–101.

Hollander, E. P. (1964). *Leaders, groups, and influence.* New York: Oxford University Press.

Hollander, E. P. & Julian, J. W. (1968). Leadership. In E. F. Borgatta & W. W. Lambert, *Handbook of personality theory and research.* Chicago: Rand-McNally.

House, R. J. (1971). A path-goal theory of leader effectiveness. *Administrative Science Quarterly, 16,* 321–338.

House, R. J., & Baetz, M. L. (1979). Leadership: Some empirical generalizations and new research directions. In *Research in Organizational Behavior,* Vol. 1. Greenwich, CT: JAI.

House, R. J., & Dessler, G. (1974). The path-goal theory of leadership: Some post hoc and a priori tests. In J. G. Hunt & L. L. Larson (Eds.), *Contingency approaches to leadership.* Carbondale, IL: Southern Illinois University Press.

House, R. J., & Mitchell, T. R. (1974). Path-goal theory of leadership. *Journal of Contemporary Business, 5,* 81–97.

Huberman, A. M., & Miles, M. B. (1982). *People, policies and practices: Examining the chain of school improvement, Vol. 4: Innovation up close: A field study in twelve school settings.* Andover, MA: The Network.

Iacocca, L., & Novak, W. (1984). *Iacocca: An autobiography.* New York: Bantam.

Jago, A. G. (1982). Leadership: Perspectives in theory and research. *Management Science, 28*(3), 315–336.

Jennings, E. E. (1960). *An anatomy of leadership: Princes, heroes, and superman.* New York: Harper.

Karmel, B. (1978). Leadership: A challenge to traditional research methods and assumptions. *Academy of Management Review, 3*(3) 475–482.

Katz, D. (1960). Leadership practices in relation to productivity and morals. In D. Cartwright & A. Zander (Eds.), *Group dynamics* (pp. 612–628). Evanston, IL: Row Peterson.

Katz, D., Maccoby, N., Gurin, G., & Floor, L. G. (1951). *Productivity, supervision, and morale among railroad workers.* Ann Arbor: Institute for Social Research, University of Michigan.

Kearns, D. (1976). *Lyndon Johnson and the American dream.* New York: Harper & Row.

Kellerman, B. (1984). *Leadership—multidisciplinary perspectives.* Englewood Cliffs, NJ: Prentice-Hall.

Knapp, T. R. (1982). The unit and the context of analysis for research in educational administration. *Educational Administration Quarterly, 18*(1), 1–13.

Likert, R. (1961). *New patterns of management.* New York: McGraw-Hill.

Likert, R., & Katz, D. (1948). Supervisory practices and organizational structures as they affect employee productivity and morale. *American Management Association Personnel Services.*

Mawhinney, T. C., & Ford, J. D. (1977). The path-goal theory of leader effectiveness: An operant interpretation. *Academy of Management Review 2,* 398–411.

McCall, M. W. Jr., & Lombardo, M. M. (1978). *Leadership: Where else can we go?* Durham, NC: Duke University Press.

Minor, J. B. (1975). The uncertain future of the leadership concept: An overview. In J. G. Hunt & L. L. Larson (Eds.), *Leadership frontiers* (pp. 197–208). Kent, OH: Kent State University Press.

Miskel, C., & Sandlin, T. (1981). Survey research in educational administration. *Educational Administration Quarterly, 17*(4), 1–20.

Morris, G. B. (1985). A futuristic cognitive view of leadership. *Educational Administration Quarterly, 21*(1), 7–28.

Motowidlo, S. J. (1976). Needed: New variables for the contingency paradigm of leadership effectiveness. Paper presented at the Canadian Psychological Association, Toronto.

Nahabetian, H. J. (1969). The effects of a leader's upward influence on group member satisfaction and task facilitation. Unpublished doctoral dissertation. Rochester, NY: University of Rochester.

Pelz, D. C. (1952). Influence: A key to effective leadership in the first-line supervisor. *Personnel, 29,* 209–217.

Peters, T. J., & Waterman, R. H., Jr. (1982). *In search of excellence.* New York: Harper & Row.

Pfeffer, J. (1977). The ambiguity of leadership. *Academy of Management Journal, 2,* 104–112.

Runkel, P. J., & Schmuck, R. A. (1982). Group processes. In *Encyclopedia of Educational Research* (5th ed, Vol. 2, pp. 747–749). New York: Free Press.

Schein, E. H. (1985). *Organizational culture and leadership*. San Francisco: Jossey-Bass.

Schriesheim, C. S., House, R. J., & Kerr, S. (1976). Leader initiating structure: A reconciliation of discrepant research results and some empirical tests. *Organizational Behavior and Human Performance, 15*, 197–321.

Scott, W. C. J. (1977). Leadership: A functional analysis. In J. G. Hunt & L. L. Larson (Eds.), *Leadership: The cutting edge*. Carbondale, IL: Southern Illinois University Press.

Sergiovanni, T. J., & Corbally, J. (1984). *Leadership and organizational cultures*. Champaign, IL: University of Illinois Press.

Sheridan, J. E., Downey, H. K., & Slocum, J. W., Jr. (1975). Testing causal relationships in House's path-goal theory of leadership effectiveness. In J. G. Hunt & L. L. Larson (Eds.), *Leadership frontiers*. Kent, OH: Kent State University Press.

Sims, H. P., Jr. (1977). The leader as a manager of reinforcement contingencies. In J. G. Hunt & L. L. Larson (Eds.), *Leadership: The cutting edge*. Carbondale, IL: Southern Illinois University Press.

Sims, H. P., & Szilagyi, A. D. (1975). Leader reward behavior and subordinate satisfaction and performance. *Organizational Behavior and Human Performance, 14*, 426–438.

Sirotnik, K. A. (1980). Psychometric implications of the unit-of-analysis problem. *Journal of Educational Measurement, 17*, 245–282.

Stogdill, R. M. (1948). Personal factors associated with leadership: A survey of the literature. *Journal of Psychology, 25*; 35–71.

Stogdill, R. M. (1963). *Manual for the leader behavior description questionnaire—Form 12*. Columbus, OH: Bureau of Business Research, The Ohio State University.

Stogdill, R. M. (1974). *Handbook of leadership: A survey of theory and research*. New York: Free Press.

Stogdill, R. M. (1977). *Leadership: Abstracts and bibliography 1904 to 1974*. Columbus, OH: College of Administrative Science, The Ohio State University.

Stogdill, R. M., & Coons, A. E. (1957). *Leader behavior: Its description and measurement*. Columbus, OH: Bureau of Business Research, The Ohio State University.

Stout, R., & Briner, C. (1969). Leadership. In *Encyclopedia of Educational Research* (4th ed., pp. 699–706). New York: Macmillan.

Vroom, V. H. (1964). *Work and motivation*. New York: Wiley.

Vroom, V. H. (1976). Leadership. In M. Dunnette (Ed.), *Handbook of industrial and organizational psychology*. Chicago: Rand-McNally.

Vroom, V. H., & Yetton, E. W. (1973). *Leadership and decision making*. Pittsburgh: University of Pittsburgh Press.

White, R. K., & Lippitt, R. (1960). *Autocracy and democracy: An experimental inquiry*. New York: Harper

CHAPTER 14

Work Motivation, Job Satisfaction, and Climate

Cecil Miskel and Rodney Ogawa

In this chapter current theory and research on work motivation, job satisfaction, and climate will be reviewed and evaluated. Each concept is reviewed separately, with particular attention given to the literature most germane to educators and school organizations. Two sets of constraints for the reviews should be noted. Due to the wide-ranging body of literature surrounding the three concepts, only selected models are considered, and emphasis is given to empirical studies. Published literature receives the primary focus; less attention is accorded to dissertations and other unpublished research.

WORK MOTIVATION

Given the constraints on space the better-known theories are not presented in detail.[1] Although Steers and Porter (1983) observe that during the early 1960s scholarly interest in motivational work problems of organizations increased significantly and were continuing at high levels at the time of the report, a similar emphasis does not appear in educational organizations. The literature in educational administration dealing with educator motivation remains limited in quantity and dominated by static cognitive content theories developed by Maslow and Herzberg that look at what energizes human behavior. However, cognitive process theories focusing on factors that channel or direct

Consultant/reviewers: Lloyd Bishop, New York University; and Eddy Van Meter, University of Kentucky

behavior are appearing in the literature increasingly often. For example, expectancy motivation is receiving some attention, and two other perspectives—goal theory and job characteristics—are gaining recognition. In considering work motivation, the basic concepts and postulates, empirical tests, and criticisms of these cognitive models will be presented. Understanding the dynamics of employee motivation is important because a knowledge of when people will work hard offers the prospect of developing work conditions to maximize productivity (Miner, 1980).

Needs Hierarchy Model

Theory

Mazlow's (1943, 1954, 1970) theory of an internal hierarchy proposes five levels of needs. Physiological needs are the basic biological functions of the human organism. Safety and security needs, the second level, relate to a desire for a peaceful, smoothly run, stable society. Belonging, love, and social needs comprise the third level. The fourth level, esteem needs, contains the desire for high regard by others. Achievement, competence, status, and recognition satisfy this needs level. Finally, self-actualization as the highest level remains a subject of discussion. An unambiguous meaning of self-actualization remains elusive. However, the definition offered by Campbell and Pritchard (1976) is acceptable: "An individual's need to self-actualize is the need to be what one wants to be, to achieve fulfillment of one's life goals, and to realize the potential of one's personality" (p. 97). The needs hierarchy theory contains two fundamental postulates. First, individuals are wanting creatures, and needs constitute the main driving force behind human behavior. Second, needs are universal across individuals and are arranged in a hierarchy of prepotency. In other words, as relative gratification of a given need occurs, it submerges and it activates the next higher need in the hierarchy.

Research

The longest line of research based on Maslow's theory evolved from Porter's work (1961, 1962, 1963). He modified the hierarchical paradigm to include autonomy needs that lie between esteem and self-actualization. Porter reasoned that concepts such as authority, independent thought and action, and participation are logically distinct from more common esteem items such as prestige. This distinction, coupled with the assumption that physiological needs are adequately satisfied for managerial and professional employees, enabled Porter to develop the needs satisfaction questionnaire (NSQ). In his investigations of managers, Porter found that self-actualization was most critical. Moreover, esteem, security, and autonomy needs were more often satisfied in middle- rather than in bottom-management positions. Similar findings have resulted with respect to inquiries in educational organizations.

Using an adapted NSQ for the school setting, Trusty and Sergiovanni (1966) reported that the largest deficiencies for professional educators were esteem, autonomy, and self-actualization needs. Administrators, when compared to teachers, had fewer deficiencies of esteem needs and more of self-actualization needs. In fact, Trusty and Sergiovanni concluded that the lack of self-esteem received from school positions represented the largest source of needs deficiency for teachers. Anderson and Iwanicki (1984) compared scores of teachers in the late 1970s on the NSQ with the earlier results of Trusty and Sergiovanni. The deficiencies were similar, but the later findings indicated larger deficiencies in the higher-level needs than the earlier results. To examine teacher and administrator needs, Chisolm, Washington, and Thibodeaux (1980) employed the NSQ with a sample of administrators and teachers. Administrators exhibited fewer needs deficiencies than teachers on all five subscales—security, social, esteem, autonomy, and self-actualization. The greatest area of deficiency for both administrators and teachers was autonomy needs.

Critique

An interesting paradox exists for Maslow's work: The theory is widely accepted, but little research evidence supports it. The five needs areas, or six in Porter's

modification, have not been verified empirically. Moreover, the basic premise of prepotency—that higher-level needs become activated as the lower-level needs become satisfied—has mixed empirical support. Wahba and Bridwell (1973, 1976) concluded that the best studies testing the prepotency proposition indicated no support.

Two explanations for the lack of support include definitional clarity and methodological rigor. The concepts comprising the model are vague and general. The higher-order needs, in particular, represent complex variables with multiple definitions. Self-actualization may not be a need at all but a socially desirable response resulting from certain cultural values. The research purporting to test the theory also exhibits shortcomings. Many of the questionnaires designed to measure the needs categories have severe psychometric weaknesses. The NSQ, which has been the most popular measure, does not accurately reflect Maslow's needs classification scheme (Schneider & Alderfer, 1973; Wahba & Bridwell, 1973, 1976).

Maslow's theory continues to enjoy wide acceptance in education despite growing criticism that it lacks empirical support. There can be little doubt that the needs hierarchy framework requires revision and additional research.

The Two-Factor Theory

Theory

Another popular content theory of motivation—the two-factor or motivation-hygiene theory—was proposed by Herzberg, Mausner, and Snyderman (1959). It is based on findings from a study that used a critical-incidents interview procedure with 203 accountants and engineers. The data collection technique essentially asked each respondent to describe critical events experienced at work that had resulted, first, in a marked improvement in job satisfaction and, second, in a significnt reduction in job satisfaction. The interview transcripts were content analyzed.

Herzberg et al. concluded that positive events were dominated by references to achievement, recognition, the work itself, responsibility, and advancement. Negative events were dominated by considerations of interpersonal relations with superiors and peers, technical supervision, company policy and administration, working conditions, and personal life. Based on these findings, the researchers drew the basic postulate that one set of factors (motivators) produces satisfaction, and another set (hygienes) produces dissatisfaction. Therefore, work satisfaction and dissatisfaction are not opposites; rather, they are separate and distinct dimensions of work orientation.

Research

A large number of replications of the original study have been made. In the educational setting, studies by Sergiovanni (1967) with teachers and Schmidt (1976) with administrators are representative. Both used the critical-incidents interview approach and content-analysis procedures. With faculty in colleges and universities, Moxley (1977) used a similar set of questions in a mail questionnaire format. Overall, the replications have supported the original findings of Herzberg et al. (1959). With some variations, industrial employees, teachers, and administrators tend to relate one set of factors with job satisfaction and a different set with job dissatisfaction.

Using a questionnaire based on the content of the two-factor theory, Miskel (1973) found that principals have a greater tolerance for work pressure than do elementary teachers and that central-office administrators have less desire for security than do elementary teachers. In addition, those educators who aspired to administrative positions exhibited a greater desire for risk and motivator rewards. An extrapolation of these findings suggests that people who aspire to rise to membership in the next higher group tend to adopt the attitudes of people of the next level or group before gaining the promotion or membership. In another study by Miskel (1974), the results supported a conceptual continuum for risk, motivator, and hygiene factors for different business and educator groups. Business managers exhibited high-risk propensity with less concern for hygiene factors; teachers showed low-risk propensity with high concern for hygiene factors. Two groups of educational administrators appearing in the middle of the continuum were similar to teachers in that they had a high concern for hygiene factors and security; however, when risk was attached to the motivator factors, they resembled business managers.

Critique

The motivation-hygiene model has been the target of severe criticism. King (1970) has pointed out that a major portion of the difficulty stems from the lack of an explicit statement of the theory. He found five distinct versions of the two-factor theory in the literature. Only limited support existed for any of the five versions.

The most devastating criticism, however, has been that the theory is method-bound. The results produced by Herzberg et al. (1959) can be replicated only when the critical-incidents technique is used. Both King (1970) and Soliman (1970) concluded that most studies using the Herzberg technique support the motivation-hygiene theory, but most studies using a different method do not.

These and other criticisms have produced a growing consensus among scholars that the two-factor theory should be abandoned. Salancik and Pfeffer (1977) observed that the formulation is currently regarded as theoretically weak. Campbell, Dunnette, Lawler, and Weick (1970) stated: "The most meaningful conclusion that we can draw is that the two-factor theory has now served its purpose and should be altered or respectfully laid aside" (p. 381). Steers and Porter (1979, pp. 394–395) were somewhat more moderate. They believe that Herzberg deserves a great deal of credit because his ideas filled a void in the late 1950s by calling attention to the need for improved understanding of the roles played by motivation in work organizations. The approach was systematic and the language was understandable. Even if this moderate view is accepted, scholars in educational administration should reduce their reliance on the model and move to use process models such as expectancy theory.

Expectancy Theory

Theory

Since the mid-1960s expectancy theory as a cognitive-process approach has occupied a prominent place in the study of motivation to work. Originally popularized by Vroom (1964) and modified by others (Galbraith & Cummings, 1967; Graen, 1969; Porter & Lawler, 1968), the approach is also called valence-instrumentality expectancy, VIE, and value theory.

Expectancy theory rests on the assumptions that motivation is a conscious process in which decisions lawfully relate to psychological events that accompany behavior and that forces in the individual and the environment combine to determine behavior. The theory builds on these assumptions with the concepts of valence, instrumentality, and expectancy. *Valence* refers to the perceived positive or negative worth or attractiveness of potential outcomes, rewards, or incentives for working in an organization. *Instrumentality* refers to the perceived probability that an incentive with a valence will be forthcoming after a given level of performance or achievement. *Expectancy*, resembling *instrumentality*, refers to the subjective probability that a given effort will yield a specified performance level.

The overall multiplicative formulation for the relationships is that the force of motivation (*FM*) is the product of expectancy (*E*) and the sum of the cross products for instrumentality (*I*) and valence (*V*) items. Stated symbolically by Galbraith and Cummings (1967), the equation is $FM = E(\Sigma IV)$. Therefore, motivation to behave in a certain way changes as the level of each variable increases or decreases. Because the relationships are multiplicative, if one of the variables is zero, effort is zero.

Until recently, a widely ignored aspect of Vroom's expectancy theory was the postulate for a within-subjects, choice model. In other words, the individual should have motivational forces, $E\Sigma(IV)$, for a whole series of effort levels and will choose the effort level with the highest $E(\Sigma IV)$ (Mitchell, 1980). Most scholars have used an across-subjects or between-subjects model that uses a single effort level. For example, a between-subjects study typically poses a single generalized situation, such as working as an educator or working in your present job, and asks a single set of expectancy, instrumentality, and valence questions of the respondent. In contrast, a within-subjects design specifies a number of alternatives, such as working with regular, special, and extracurricular classes of students, and asks separate expectancy and instrumentality questions of each respondent for each alternative. Valence usually is assumed to be constant because the outcomes will be valued the same regardless of how they are attained. The within-subjects model should be a more powerful predictor of effort than the between-subjects model because it taps different levels of motivational forces. Thus, in a within-subjects design, the individual selects the level of effort at which he or she desires to work from among a set of alternative levels. The model hypothesizes that the individual will choose the level with the highest $E(\Sigma IV)$.

Since the original statement by Vroom, expectancy theory has been revised, modified, and extended by a number of authors (Arnold, 1981). Distinctions have been made between types of outcomes, task goals and outcomes, and intrinsic rewards. Most of the suggested changes essentially add variables to the model or provide specification and differentiation of various classes of expectancies and valences.

Research

Several authors (Campbell & Pritchard, 1976; Heneman & Schwab, 1972; Mitchell, 1974, 1980; Schwab, Olian-Gottlieb & Heneman, 1979) have systematically reviewed the literature that reports research based on expectancy motivation theory. Their conclusions are similar. Force of motivation based on between-subjects expectancy models has been demonstrated repeatedly to be positively correlated with both job satisfaction and performance across a variety of settings. However, the magnitude of the relationship between force of motivation and independent ratings of effort appear to be stable and to have a ceiling correlation of about .30, or about 9 percent of the criterion's variance.

Investigations in educational organizations based on expectancy theory began to be published during the 1970s. Mowday (1978) found that school principals with higher expectancy motivation were more active in attempting to influence district decisions. As reported by Herrick (1973), schools with high centralization and stratification levels are staffed with teachers having low forces of expectancy motivation. In a dissertation study using Halpin's definitions, Pulvino (1979) found principal consideration was significantly related to expectancy motivation of teachers.

In a study of secondary and higher education teachers, Miskel, Defrain, and Wilcox (1980) found the force of motivation to be significantly related to job satisfaction and perceived performance for both groups. However, the magnitudes of the relationships exhibited great diferences. For force of motivation and job satisfaction, the correlations were .56 and .59, but for force of motivation and performance, they were both .19. Similar results emerged from studies by Zaremba (1978), Oades (1983), and Lincoln, Graham and Lane (1983).

Using a longitudinal approach, the findings by Miskel, McDonald, and Bloom (1983) suggest that expectancy motivation of teachers is positively related to student achievement, student and teacher attitudes, and communication among educators. Moreover, the relationships were stable over a 7-month time period.

Support for expectancy theory in educational organizations is similar to support found in other organizations. Motivational force is positively associated with effectiveness indicators, but the magnitudes are limited. In general, people work hard when they think that working hard is likely to lead to desirable organizational rewards.

Critique

Excellent summaries are available that detail several weaknesses in the expectancy theory and in research purporting to test the theory (Campbell & Pritchard, 1976; Mitchell, 1974, 1980). One alleged shortcoming is that expectancy theory lacks the power to explain large percentages of variance in criterion variables such as effort and performance. This problem may be, however, a function of the expectancy model being tested. In recent years, a number of within-subjects tests has been completed (Arnold, 1981; Dillard, 1979; Muchinsky, 1977). As postulated, the relationships are much stronger for the within-subjects choice models than for the between-subjects models. But Mitchell (1980) concluded that even at its best the model seldom explains more that 50 percent of the variance in the criterion indicators. A second weakness is that the theory overintellectualizes the cognitive processes that individuals use when selecting alternative actions (Schwab et al., 1979, p. 146). The hypothesized process is too complex an exercise for anyone to believe that people actually calculate probabilities and values, multiply them together, and then decide how to act.

Issues involving methodology seemed to abate somewhat during the 1970s. General support was found for using a limited number (5–10) of valence and instrumentality outcomes, employing diverse sets of outcomes (intrinsic and extrinsic) for measuring the components, and defining appropriate criterion variables (Mitchell, 1980). The development of improved measures also was reported (Ilgen, Nebeker, & Pritchard, 1981). A persistent problem is the mathematical operations used to combine variables. Strictly speaking, variables must be measured on ratio scales if scores are to be multiplied together (Campbell & Pritchard, 1976, p. 94). Schmidt (1973) showed that the correlations can be changed drastically by transformations that would be invariant when the scales exhibited ratio properties. This problem may not be too serious because Mitchell (1980, p. 17) cited evidence that demonstrated that under some conditions interval-level scales are appropriate.

In sum, expectancy theory has emerged as a popular model to explain work motivation. Although it exhibits several shortcomings, expectancy theory does offer useful insights to explain educator effort. To develop an improved understanding of employee motivation, the repertoire of theories that guide research and practice in educational administration should be expanded. Other process theories of motivation have recently shown popularity in the organizational behavior literature—models hardly mentioned in educational administration. Two emerging models will be presented and examined: goal theory and the job-characteristics model.

Job-Characteristics Model

Theory

Based on expectancy theory, Hackman and Lawler (1971) started the developmental work on the job-characteristics model. The theory was presented formally in 1976 by Hackman and Oldham. By the early 1980s it was considered the most popular approach (Roberts & Glick, 1981) and one of the most elaborate and widely accepted theories of job design (Kiggundu, 1983). The model was constructed with three concepts or psychological states. Experienced meaningfulness of the work is the degree to which the individual experiences the job as being valuable and worthwhile. Hackman and Oldham (1980) believe that for work to be meaningful the job must have skill variety, task identity, and task significance. The second concept is experienced responsibility for work outcomes, or the degree to which the individual feels personally accountable for the results of the work she or he performs. The third concept, knowledge of results, or feedback, is the degree to which the individual knows and understands on a continuous basis how effectively he or she is performing the job. The overall generalization of the job-characteristics model is that the motivating-potential score (MPS) is the product of meaningfulness, autonomy, and feedback. Stated symbolically, the equation is the following:

$$MPS = \frac{skill\ variety + task\ identity + task\ significance}{3} \times$$

$$autonomy \times feedback$$

Hackman and Oldham (1980) later emphasized that the MPS of a job does not cause employees to be internally motivated, to perform well, or to experience job satisfaction. But jobs that are high in motivating potential do create conditions that reinforce employees who have high performance levels. Therefore, the characteristics of a job set the stage for the internal motivation of individuals. Oldham (1976) found support for this basic generalization.

Research

To operationalize the variables in the model, Hackman and Oldham (1975, 1980) developed the job diagnostic survey (JDS) questionnaire. Even though the model and measure are relatively new, a number of studies have been published. The initial field research by Hackman and Oldham (1976) supported the major generalizations of the theory. Other investigations that buttress the theory include those by Terborg and Davis (1982), Kiggundu (1980), Bhagat and Chassie (1980), Orpen (1979), Oldham and Miller (1979), and Sims and Szilagyi (1976). In contrast, the findings of Arnold and House (1980), and Farh and Scott (1983) indicated no support for the formulation. Similarly, Evans, Kiggundu, and House (1979) found, at best, only partial support for the job-characteristics model. No studies were found that fully tested the model in educational settings. Pastor and Erlandson (1982) used the portion of the JDS called the higher-order-need strength. They concluded that the needs of secondary teachers are predominantly higher order in nature and that the needs are positively related to job satisfaction.

Critique

Hackman and Oldham (1980) acknowledged several shortcomings in their theory. Individual differences exist among people, and how best to define, measure, and include variations among individuals in the model remains open to question. The model treats variations as though they were independent or uncorrelated, but jobs that are high on one characteristic tend to be high on others. Similarly, the links between job characteristics and psychological states are apparently not as strong as was suggested in the original formulation. Another problem involves the lack of independence of the job characteristics. Similarly, O'Connor, Rudolf, and Peters (1980) make the following argument: Additional objective measures of task characteristics are needed; research should be directed toward precise specification of complementary levels of individuals and task characteristics; and larger sample sizes or less rigid significance criteria should be used to test adequately the hypothesized individual-differences moderating effects. The concept of feedback as used in the model is also not adequately defined. It is difficult to determine what is and is not job-based feedback. Finally, how the objective properties of a job relate to an individual's perceptions of those properties is not clear. The model does not consider the inevitable redefinition of the tasks that employees will make to draw more consistent relationships between their jobs and their needs, values, and attitudes.

In sum, the job-characteristics model as now formulated is not a complete theory of motivation. In fact, Roberts and Glick (1981) concluded that there are substantial inconsistencies in the area of task design across the theory, measurements, analyses, and interpretations. Although the evidence is somewhat mixed, the model should be viewed as a guide to further research and theory development.

Goal Theory

Theory

Locke (1968) and his associates (Locke, Cartledge & Knerr, 1970; Mento, Cartledge & Locke, 1980) originally stated goal theory or the technique of goal setting in 1968. Elaborated 2 years later, goal theory became increasingly popular during the 1970s as a cognitive-process approach to work motivation. Even though the model is not fully developed, several important school practices implicitly use goal theory. Evaluation systems for teachers and administrators often are modifications of a management-by-objectives (MBO) technique, and behavioral objectives are frequently used to guide decisions on instructional procedures and course content.

Goal theory is not complex. A goal is what an individual is consciously trying to achieve. To elaborate the cognitive processes that explain goal theory, Locke et al. (1970) proposed a model with seven components.

The first five serve to energize behavior, and the last two maintain and regulate behavior. The goal-setting process begins with the assumption that the individual knows something about the nature and properties of things that exist in the work environment. This knowledge is gained through perceptions and the exercise of reason. Since action or behavior is required to fulfill personal needs, it becomes necessary to judge elements in the environment to determine which actions will enhance the individual's well-being. The basis of choosing among alternative courses of action is value judgments. Using a code of values or set of standards, the individual judges which behaviors serve his or her personal interests. This evaluation is made by estimating the relationship between perceptions of the environment and personal value standards. Based on the alternative selected, the individual anticipates new conditions in the work environment and projects instrumentality for the anticipated behavior and satisfaction. As in expectancy theory, instrumentality refers to a probability that an outcome will occur. At this point in the goal model, behavior is ready to be energized.

Goal theory assumes that most human action is purposive; behavior is regulated and maintained by goals and intentions. The most fundamental effects of goals on mental or physical actions are directive. They guide thoughts and overt behavior to one end rather than another. Because some goals require greater mental concentration and physical effort to pursue than others, goals also regulate energy expenditure in the process of directing action. For example, if a principal decides to develop a new set of discipline policies rather than using the existing ones, the action necessarily requires more effort than administering the available policies.

Research

Early support for goal theory came primarily from a series of laboratory experiments. Most of the studies used college students who performed relatively simple tasks for short periods of time. Overall, the experiments indicated that goal theory provided good descriptions and predictions of behavior. In fact, Locke, Shaw, Saari, and Latham (1981) claim that the goal-setting approach to work motivation has shown a positive effect on performance in 90 percent of the reported studies.

Later support for the goal model came from both laboratory and field research methods (Campbell & Pritchard, 1976; Garland, 1982; Latham & Yukl, 1975; Mento et al., 1980; Mitchell, 1979). Three generalizations drawn from goal theory gained substantial support. First specific performance goals elicit higher performance than general goals or the absence of goals. Telling an individual generally to do his or her best produces low effort. Second, the more difficult the performance goal, if it is accepted by the individual, the higher the effort. Apparently, the generalization holds even when the goal is so difficult that virtually no one can achieve it. Third, subordinate participation in goal-setting activities, as opposed to having goals assigned by the supervisors, leads to employee satisfaction, but it may not increase performance. However, Beehr and Love (1983) note that participation in goal setting leads to goal acceptance. Available evidence also suggests that participation may increase the difficulty of the set goals. If this occurs, performance might be higher because of the goal difficulty and acceptance effects.

Critique

Goals represent a major source of work motivation, and strong support exists for the basic propositions of goal theory. The greatest deficiency in the model is the failure to specify the determinants of goal acceptance and commitment. Latham and Yukl (1975) believe that expectancy theory provides promising directions for elaborating goal theory; that is, goal acceptance is correlated with one's expectancy that effort will lead to goal attainment. From a slightly different perspective, the expected value of accepting a goal is a function of two concepts: the expectancy that attainment of the goal will lead to outcomes and the value of the outcomes to the individual (Erez & Kanfer, 1983). Dillard (1981) has attempted to integrate the two theories. A similar shortcoming concerns the mechanisms that explain how goal acceptance, goal difficulty, and other variables combine to determine effort. Currently, effort and performance can be predicted with some success, but understanding why goal setting affects employee behavior has just started to emerge. For example, Campion and Lord (1982) have added the concepts of self-set goals and environmental feedback. The concepts are then incorporated into a performance-monitoring and performance-determining motivational system. Another problem with goal theory, particularly for educational applications, involves the moderating effects of task complexity and accuracy of performance measures. Another area in the model that requires further explanation is the role of feedback or knowledge of results for the goal setter (Ivancevich & McMahon, 1982; Matsui, Okada, & Inoshita, 1983).

Even with the foregoing reservations, goal theory offers powerful predictions for simple jobs with concrete, countable outcomes. It may be less effective when tasks are complex and dimensions cannot be measured quantitatively; nevertheless, goal theory shows promise for testing with educators because goal-

setting techniques complement and enhance other theories of work motivation, including expectancy theory and the job-characteristics model.

Conclusions and Recommendations Regarding Work Motivation

Although this review, as noted in the opening paragraph, has covered a broad area of work motivation theory and research, it certainly is not exhaustive. The material related to the topic is vast. A number of models, not widely cited in the literature on educational administration, were not considered, e.g., attribution (Frasher & Frasher, 1980), equity (Adams, 1963), existence relatedness-growth (Alderfer, 1972; Alderfer & Guzzo, 1979), and behaviorism (Luthans & Kreitner, 1975; Miller, 1978; Skinner, 1974).

To advance the knowledge base, the levels of scholarly effort for developing and testing work motivation theories in educational administration will need to increase significantly. Relatively few efforts were found which attempted to integrate or test existing theories for educators. Moreover, the models appearing in the educational administration literature tend to be the weaker content theories of Maslow and Herzberg. Given the stated intensity of the practical problems associated with the work motivation of educators, scholars in educational administration should heighten their emphasis on providing useful and broadly based theoretical explanations of work behavior in educational organizations.

Differing perspectives also should be considered directly and openly. To be useful to scholars, extrinsic and intrinsic distinctions (Broedling, 1977; Deci, 1975; Dyer & Parker, 1975; Guzzo, 1979) require careful definitions and consistent applications. Both cognitive and behavioral approaches have potential utility in educational administration, and neither should be rejected on ideological or emotional grounds alone. In addition, content and process theories should be viewed and employed as complementary approaches to understanding work behavior. The field of educational administration has focused too narrowly on content theories.

A promising area is to synthesize the models that have compatible concepts and generalizations. Expectancy and goal theories, for instance, both contain the concept of instrumentality as a probability that an outcome or reward will occur. Similarly, instrumentality and its relationship to contingent conditions offers an area for exploring the application of behaviorism. Also, the job-characteristics model and expectancy, goal, and behavioral theories all suggest or employ the concepts of reinforcement and feedback. In sum, varied opportunities to build explanatory frameworks are available to enterprising scholars.

Research also is needed to test the process theories in educational settings. Initial studies can be made to test the job-characteristics model and attribution theory. Additional investigations based on expectancy theory should be conducted with diverse samples of educators and a wide range of criterion variables. Specifically, across-subjects models and within-subjects models of expectancy motivation should be compared. In regard to goal theory, several important and costly practices in schools embody a goal or objective component. Given the lack of published findings for the education setting, the characteristics and effects of programs based on goal setting represent fruitful areas for research. One approach to the study of goal setting employs school district files and other artifacts of a program. Personnel evaluation procedures containing a variant of MBO, curriculum development programs incorporating behavioral objectives, and community processes for developing districtwide goals illustrate goal-setting activities that produce records that can serve as important data sources. A second approach could be the use of questionnaire procedures. Steers (1975) and Ivancevich and McMahon (1977) have developed measures that ask respondents, such as teachers and administrators, to describe the goals of an organization on several characteristics.

Methodological considerations need to be addressed (Campbell & Pritchard, 1976). Measurement of the variables is crude in all the models. Instruments with high reliability estimates and diverse validity indicators are absent from the literature. Compounding the measurement problem is the lack of systematic data regarding the precise nature of the job outcomes that educators value. To date, scholars cannot describe the outcomes for which educators work. Content models such as Herzberg's provide some hints, but additional work is required to design methodologically rigorous tests of the various theories of adult motivation in educational settings.

Overall, some encouraging signs provide evidence that work motivation theory is a viable and growing area. Even though some disappointment must be expressed about the low quantity and lack of diversity characterizing the research in educational administration, the opportunity exists for scholars to make significant advances in understanding educators' work effort. This final optimism is based on the review findings that the larger field of organizational behavior has moved ahead in conceptualizing individual work motivation and in testing a variety of theoretical formulations. Therefore, the opportunity exists for scholars in educational administration to build on the

work in related areas and to synthesize the models, improve their measurement, and test them on the educational organizations.

JOB SATISFACTION

Before beginning the discussion of job satisfaction, its connection to work motivation must be considered. As Gunn (1984) observes, the distinction between the closely related concepts of motivation and job satisfaction is not clearly made by many writers. Depending on the scholar, major theories, such as expectancy, equity, need fulfillment, and two factor, are discussed in chapters titled either motivation or job satisfaction. The fundamental difference between the concepts is their relationship to behavior. Motivation is a direct cause of behavior; job satisfaction is not. Stated differently, rewards that fill important needs satisfy people but do not necessarily motivate them. Rewards motivate people only if their behavior is necessary in getting the rewards. As Gunn concludes, rewards as the determinants of job satisfaction may also be determinants of motivation, but only if rewards are contingent on certain behavior.

Since the 1930s job satisfaction has been of intense interest to scholars. Locke (1976), for example, estimated that a minimum of 3,350 articles were published on the topic by early 1972 and that number was growing by over 100 new publications per year. A similar emphasis is evident in educational administration, with more research studies being conducted on job satisfaction than motivation. Despite the multitude of studies, however, the understanding of job satisfaction has not increased substantially (Lawler, 1973). Two reasons are offered by Lawler for this failure: The research has typically been atheoretical and has not tested causal relationships. Two approaches typify the literature on job satisfaction—general relationships, or facet models, and discrepancy hypotheses. In an effort to upgrade the knowledge base for job satisfaction, Lawler (1973) proposed a model that integrates both approaches. To make an orderly presentation, the research definition and measurement issues will be considered first and then three approaches to the study of job satisfaction will be reviewed.

Definition and Measurement

One of the earliest explicit definitions of job satisfaction was any combination of psychological, physiological, and environmental circumstances that cause a person to say, "I am satisfied with my job" (Hoppock, 1935). Later attempts to define the concept have tended to use similar ideas of emotional states and feelings toward the job (Locke, 1976; Smith, 1967; Vroom, 1964). For educational settings Hoy and Miskel (1982) defined job satisfaction as a present- or past-oriented affective state that results when educators evaluate their work roles. Although the foregoing definitions are acceptable the measurement of job satisfaction remains problematic.

The most common methods of measuring job satisfaction employ survey questionnaires that vary primarily in their directness in assessing the concept. The most direct method is a single global question such as "How satisfied are you with your job?" A number of researchers have argued that this approach is useful, e.g., Gunn (1984), Kyriacou and Sutcliffe (1979), Porter and Lawler (1968), and Rice (1978). Nevertheless, this procedure is not entirely adequate because the reliability of a single item cannot be assessed adequately. Another problem of using one item to measure job satisfaction is the probability of receiving a socially biased response set. Educators have always been told that they should derive satisfaction from serving children. Consequently, it may be socially unacceptable for a professional educator to voice low job satisfaction (Hoy & Miskel, 1982). Support for this contention is found when the data from direct and indirect measures of job satisfaction are compared. Fuller and Miskel (1972) measured satisfaction level with a single item with the responses scaled from 1 to 5. The mean value was 4.15. In contrast, Miskel, Glasnapp, and Hatley (1975) used an indirect measure with similarly scaled responses and found the average to be substantially lower.

As noted by Hoy and Miskel (1982), a somewhat less direct approach uses a series of items that probe a variety of components or indicators of teachers' job satisfaction. A widely used indirect measure of overall satisfaction is the job-descriptive index (JDI) developed by Smith, Kendall, and Hulin (1969). The JDI is a carefully developed instrument that has been demonstrated repeatedly to yield high reliability and validity estimates (Golembiewski & Yeager, 1978).

General Relationships Model

The primary hypothesis from the general relationships model is that combinations of variables or facets such as job, organization, personality and motivation, and demographic characteristics correlate with job satisfaction. Based on the general model, several reviews of the job satisfaction literature have been published (e.g., Carroll, 1973; Gruneberg, 1976, 1979; Gunn, 1984; Holdaway, 1978b; Locke, 1969, 1976).

In a review of the literature focused on school structure, Ratsoy (1973) concluded that teacher job satisfaction, in general, is lower in schools where teachers perceive a high degree of bureaucracy. Later evidence, however, suggests that Ratsoy's conclusion may be too general. When specific bureaucratic dimensions of schools are related to job satisfaction, a complex picture emerges. Bureaucratic factors that enhance status differences among the professionals, such as the hierarchy of authority and centralization, produce low levels of satisfaction. But factors that clarify the job and yield equal applications of school policy promote high levels of satisfaction (Carpenter, 1971; Grassie & Carss, 1973; Miskel, Fevurly, & Stewart, 1979; Miskel & Gerhardt, 1974). For example, fair application of the rules that help delineate job responsibilities probably enhances the job satisfaction of employees. Recently, Bacharach and Mitchell (1983) reinforced the importance of organizational factors in the study of satisfaction. Focusing on superintendents and principals, they found that differences between the sources of dissatisfaction for the administrator groups are role specific. Bureaucratization, supervision, decision-making power, district environment, and work demands, for example, can be used to develop a relatively detailed description of a given role that relates systematically to the level of job satisfaction.

Work motivation is also consistently correlated with job satisfaction. Motivator and hygiene factors, needs, and expectancy contribute to teacher and administrator satisfaction (Anderson & Iwanicki, 1984; Chisolm, Washington, & Thibodeaux, 1980; Friesen, Holdaway, & Rice, 1983; Haughey & Murphy, 1983; Miskel et al., 1975; Miskel et al., 1980; Miskel, et al., 1983; Oades, 1983; Sergiovanni, 1967; Trusty & Sergiovanni, 1966; Zaremba, 1978).

As the organizational climates of schools become more open or participative, the level of teacher satisfaction increases (Grassie & Carss, 1973; Miskel et al., 1979; Miskel et al., 1983). In an earlier study, Coughlan (1971) used a relatively objective procedure to define closed and open schools. He found a directional trend that as schools become more open, job satisfaction increases. The relationship tends to be so strong that the frequently implied assumption is that organizational climate is a causal factor in job satisfaction (LaFollette & Sims, 1975). In an even stronger statement, Johannesson (1973) hypothesized that organizational climate, measured perceptually, was redundant with job satisfaction because describing the environment is directly affected by individuals' satisfaction with that environment. However, LaFollette and Sims (1975) found little support for the redundancy hypothesis. Hellriegel and Slocum (1974) and Payne, Fineman, and Wall (1976) identify three factors that distinguish the concepts. First, the unit of analysis is the individual for job satisfaction and the group or organization for organizational climate. Second, the element of analysis for satisfaction is the job and for climate the group or organization. Third, the nature of measurement of satisfaction is affective and for climate descriptive.

Leadership, decision making, and communication processes influence educator job satisfaction as well. The effects of the leadership styles of school administrators on teacher job satisfaction have long been recognized (Blocker & Richardson, 1963; Chase, 1951), and a recent study reaffirms the relationship (Nelson, 1980). The quality of teacher-administrator relationships and the quality of leadership correlate highly with teacher satisfaction: The better the relationship and the higher the quality of leadership, the higher teacher satisfaction tends to be. More recent findings affirm earlier assertions to this effect. Greater participation in decision making, especially concerning instructional methods, yields enhanced teacher job satisfaction (Belasco & Alutto, 1972; Mohrman, Cooke, & Mohrman, 1978). Moreover, the lack of opportunities to participate in decision making is the greatest source of teacher dissatisfaction (Holdaway, 1978a, 1978b). However, teacher militancy was found not to be related to the job satisfaction of principals (Johnston, Yeakey, & Winter, 1980). Finally, the quality of communication processes relates to overall teacher job satisfaction (Nicholson, 1980). Communicating clearly to employees the scope of the job, how their contributions are related to the school's goals, and how they are being judged, for instance, are positively correlated with job satisfaction.

Discrepancy Model

Smith et al. (1969) posited that job satisfaction is best explained by a discrepancy between the work motivation of job holders and the rewards offered them by the organization. Similar explanations are offered by inducements-contributions theory (March & Simon, 1958) and cognitive dissonance theory (Festinger, 1957). These approaches hypothesize a direct positive relationship between the level of job satisfaction and the perceived difference between what is expected or desired as fair and what is actually experienced in the job situation.

If the needs that motivate an individual to work are satisfied exactly by the organization's incentives, no dissonance exists and job satisfaction is high. If an individual's needs are greater than the rewards received for work, a discrepancy exists that leads to dissatisfaction. But if the rewards exceed needs, the discrepancy

yields positive job satisfaction. Examples of research in educational settings based on discrepancy models and supporting the discrepancy hypothesis include Miskel et al. (1975) and Ortloff (1980). Using a discrepancy approach with the concept of status congruence, Arikado (1976) found no relationship between the correspondence of personal status and leadership position with satisfaction. Similarly, Koopman-Boyden and Adams (1974) found little relationship between role consensus of the head teacher and teachers and job satisfaction. However, Willower and Heckert (1977) found a significant direct relationship between teacher job satisfaction and the congruence or lack of discrepancy of teacher-pupil control ideology and behavior.

An Integrated Model

Lawler (1973) proposed a model of facet satisfaction that incorporates both the general relationships and discrepancy hypotheses. The model is shown in Figure 14.1. Lawler intended the model to be applicable to explaining what determines personal satisfaction with any aspect of the job.

As depicted in Figure 14.1, Lawler's formulation includes a discrepancy model because satisfaction is the difference between *a*, what individuals feel they should receive, and *b*, what individuals perceive that they actually receive. Note in Figure 14.1 that the perceptions of what the reward levels should be are influenced by a number of facets—job input based on skills (experience, training, effort, and so forth) and job characteristics such as level of demands, difficulty, timespan, and responsibility. In addition, the model includes a key generalization from Adam's (1963) equity theory that stresses the idea that people compare inputs and outcomes of others to determine what their own outcome level should be.

Conclusions and Recommendations Regarding Job Satisfaction

Gruneberg (1979) observes that a number of scholars have doubted the value of the job-satisfaction concept. The criticisms focus on the lack of a generally accepted theory of job satisfaction, contradictory research findings, vague definitions of the concept itself, and, for the most part, an overreliance on common sense. Gruneberg provides three persuasive arguments disputing the pessimistic view that job satisfaction is not a useful concept.

First, job satisfaction as common sense is clearly at variance with what actually happens. For example, if people are asked what they think the relationship is between satisfaction and productivity, the great

Figure 14.1 Model of the determinants of satisfaction

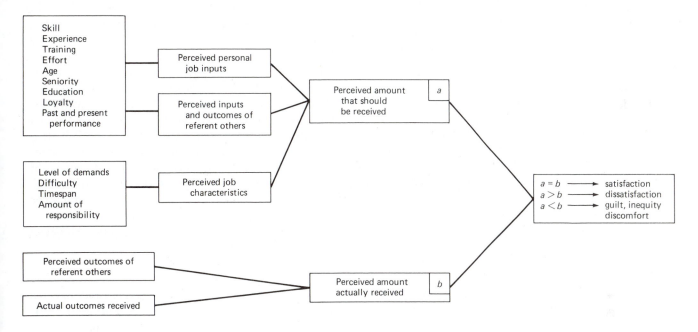

NOTE. Adapted from *Motivation in Work Organizations* by E. E. Lawler, III, 1973, Monterey, CA: Brooks/Cole. Copyright 1973 by Wadsworth. Reprinted by permission.

majority speculate that the two concepts are directly related (Gruneberg, 1979, p. 149). This belief was relatively unchallenged until a critical review by Brayfield and Crockett (1955) revealed that the relationship is not a simple, direct one. Further doubt was cast on the satisfaction-causes-performance hypothesis when Vroom (1964, p. 183) found that the size of the median correlation between the variables across a number of studies was small at .14. He concluded that this magnitude of association was of little theoretical or practical importance. Even the modest relationship produces a controversy over which variable causes the other (Greene & Craft, 1979). A reasonable explanation for the actual lack of relationship between the two variables is that people often derive job satisfaction from parts of the job, such as social interactions, that have little to do with productivity. Therefore, additional research seems necessary to understand this counterintuitive relationship.

Second, the argument that job satisfaction is characterized by contradictory findings and is not helpful, Gruneberg believes, is unreasonable. While acknowledging that many studies do produce contradictory findings, Gruneberg maintains that scholars must remember that the research is dealing with complex human behavior in social, organizational, and technological situations that vary subtly across investigations. He is optimistic that further research will clarify why the inconsistencies are occurring.

Third, the charge that job satisfaction only produces vague conclusions is understandable if one considers the complexity of the phenomenon being investigated and the practical difficulties involved in undertaking the research. Gruneberg concludes that of course conclusions based on field studies are likely to be vague because the research cannot be carefully controlled. From a practical point of view, vagueness may not necessarily be critically important as long as the combined effect of job changes is to increase both productivity and satisfaction.

Regardless of Gruneberg's strong defense of job satisfaction as an important concept for administrators, the knowledge of job satisfaction remains fragmented, though it is a topic of great interest. A reason for the fragmentation is that many if not most investigations lack theoretical foundations and produce only isolated facts. Work is needed to provide and test coherent theories of job satisfaction. Lawler's (1973) model serves as a sound starting point for research in educational administration.

ORGANIZATIONAL CLIMATE

People often sense that there are differences in the overall atmosphere of schools and that these differences somehow affect how people behave. Social and behavioral scientists have not been immune to this intuitively compelling notion. They have developed the concept of climate to describe the set of internal characteristics (Tagiuri, 1968) that distinguishes one organization from another. Subsequently, climate has found wide use as both a descriptive metaphor and an explanation of differences in the performance of schools.

The broad, intuitive appeal of climate as a descriptive term and as an explanatory factor as well has led to some confusion in the educational literature regarding what constitutes school climate. This problem is reflected in the wide variety of school characteristics, ranging from buildings and facilities to attitudes toward pupil control, that have been described as elements of schools' climates. The confusion results from the all-encompassing nature of the concept of climate and from the varied perspectives from which climate has been examined. Anderson (1982) has noted that contributions to the literature on the climate of schools are rooted in two traditions: the study of organizational climate and the examination of school effects. Since the educational administration literature has typically treated school climate as a specific type of organizational climate, we will focus upon the contributions of theorists and researchers who have worked in that tradition.

Because of the large amount of literature on the organizational climate of schools, the existence of previously published reviews of that literature, and constraints on chapter length, we will not attempt yet another comprehensive review.[2] Instead, we will address two related issues concerning limitations of the treatment of climate in the literature on the organizational climate of schools. The more general issue concerns the narrowness of the approaches that have been taken toward the examination of climate by scholars of educational administration. The second issue is nested in the first. It involves comparing the views of school climate as seen from the perspectives of organizational climate and school effects. Such a comparison illustrates at least some of the sources of the narrowness of the conceptualization of climate evident in the organizational-climate perspective adopted by scholars of educational administration. Our discussion of these issues will be based on the foundation established by works of Tagiuri (1968) and James and Jones (1974).

The Framework

In her comprehensive review of the school climate literature, Anderson (1982) noted that Tagiuri provided a useful breakdown of the dimensions comprising an organization's climate. Tagiuri (1968) argued that climate is a summary concept concerned with the total environmental quality within an organization. He further proposed that climate is comprised of four dimensions: ecology, milieu, social system, and culture. Ecology, he said, includes the physical and material aspects of an organization's climate, such as the physical plant. Milieu involves the presence of individuals or groups who possess particular attributes, such as social class. Social system concerns the pattern of relationships that exist between individuals or groups or both. Culture involves belief systems, values, cognitive structures, and meaning. We will employ this taxonomy of the dimensions of organizational climate to guide our examination of the ways in which scholars have operationalized the concept of climate in the study of schools; that is, the ontological tendencies reflected in the existing literature.

James and Jones (1974) identified three approaches to the measurement of organizational climate employed by researchers: multiple measurement-organizational attribute, perceptual measurement-organizational attribute, and perceptual measurement-individual attribute. The first of these approaches treats climate as a set of organizational attributes or main effects measurable by a variety of methods. The second treats climate as a set of perceptual variables that are seen as organizational main effects. The third approach treats climate as perceived and an attribute of the individual members of the organization. This categorization of approaches to the measurement of organizational climate can serve as a framework for the identification of tendencies among researchers to measure the climate of schools in certain ways. Thus, just as Tagiuri's taxonomy can serve as a guide to the examination of ontological biases in the literature on school climate, so the work of James and Jones can serve to identify epistemological patterns.

The matrix that synthesizes Tagiuri's and James and Jones's perspectives provides a framework for an examination of the ontological and epistemological tendencies reflected in research on the organizational climate of schools in the form of a 4×3 matrix: four dimensions of climate by three approaches to the measurement of climate (see Figure 14.1).

The Organizational Climate of Schools

The literature on the organizational climate of schools is largely rooted in four conceptualizations (Hoy & Miskel, 1982): Halpin and Croft's (1963) concept of open and closed climates; Likert's (1961) concept of managerial systems that range from exploitive-authoritative to participative; Steinhoff's (1965) and Stern's (1970) needs-press model; and Willower, Eidell, and Hoy's (1967) concept of pupil-control orientation. Each has led to the development of measurement instruments and subsequent research on schools. These conceptualizations of climate share two important features: They are extensions of theories or perspectives concerning what Tagiuri (1968) has called the social-system dimension of climate, and they operationalize climate as the average of organizational members' perceptions.

Halpin and Croft (1963) developed what is probably the most widely known conceptualization and measurement of the organizational climate of schools. Based on Halpin's previous work in leadership (Anderson, 1982), school climate is conceptualized as the quality of faculty-principal relations and the relative presence of two organizational dimensions derived from the precedent leadership model: consideration and initiation of structure. Halpin and Croft developed the Organizational Climate Description questionnaire (OCDQ) based on this conceptualization. It contains 64 items.

A factor analysis of data collected using the OCDQ in 71 elementary schools resulted in the identification of eight climate factors. Four of the factors are concerned with teacher relationships and attitudes: the amount of "hindrance" experienced by teachers as the result of their principal burdening them with busywork; the level of "intimacy" among teachers; the extent of teachers' "disengagement" from tasks; and the level of "esprit" experienced by teachers as the result of the satisfaction of social needs and the accomplishment of tasks. The four other factors are concerned with principal-teacher relations: the extent to which a "production emphasis" is evident in the close supervision of teachers by the principal; the amount of "aloofness" or impersonality and formality that characterizes the principal's behavior; the extent to which the principal expresses "consideration" through warm and friendly behavior; and the amount of "thrust" that exists, as indicated by the extent to which the principal sets an example of the direction in which she or he wishes to move the school.

Halpin and Croft found that six types of climate characterized the schools in their sample. The climates fall on a continuum from open to closed: open, autonomous, controlled, familiar, paternal, and closed. Where a given school falls on the continuum depends on the configuration of its overall profile on the eight climate factors. For example, an open climate is characterized by high degrees of esprit, consideration, and thrust; an average degree of intimacy; and low degrees of hindrance, disengagement, production emphasis, and aloofness. The OCDQ is typically administered to the entire faculty of a school. A school's climate is determined by calculating the average score of its faculty on the eight dimensions and examining its climate profile.

Halpin and Croft's conceptualization of climate clearly falls into the social-system dimension of our matrix. The eight climate factors and, hence, the six types of climate identified by Halpin and Croft, are largely concerned with the nature of the relationships of teachers to teacher and teachers to the principal. Note, for example, that intimacy involves the degree to which close, personal relationships exist among teachers and that consideration is concerned with the extent to which the principal acts in a warm and friendly manner toward the faculty. Even disengagement and production emphasis are concerned with the quality of relations between faculty and principal. A review of the OCDQ items shows that disengagement is manifested by teachers rambling "when they talk in faculty meetings." Production emphasis is manifested in the close supervision of teachers.

It is even clearer that Halpin and Croft employed a perceptual-measurement–organizational-attribute approach to measuring climate. They designed the OCDQ expressly to determine the perceptions of the members of a school's staff with regard to the climate factors outlined above. Further, a school's profile is obtained by calculating the staff's average score on each climate factor. It is assumed that such an average reflects the overall climate of a school.

Two other general limitations of the OCDQ have been identified. First, questions have been raised about the usefulness of the six discrete climates described by Halpin and Croft (Andrews, 1965; R. Brown, 1965; Watkins, 1968). Also, Carver and Sergiovanni (1969) have questioned the adequacy of the OCDQ in measuring the climate of urban and large secondary schools.

Despite these limitations, the OCDQ has spawned a long list of studies in educational administration. The OCDQ has spawned a long list of studies. What has all this work produced? One study has established that there is a link between the openness of the climate of high schools and the absence of student alienation (Hartley & Hoy, 1972). Other studies have found that principals of open schools tend to be more confident, sociable, and resourceful than their counterparts in closed schools (Anderson, 1964); teachers are more satisfied with and loyal to principals of open schools (Kanner, 1974); and teachers in open schools tend to be more confident about their own and the school's effectiveness (Andrews, 1965). On the other hand, research has not established the existence of a link between climate as measured by the OCDQ and student achievement (Hoy & Miskel, 1982).

To summarize, Halpin and Croft's conceptualization and operationalization of climate led a generation of researchers to examine climate and its relationship to a variety of factors. Although this research contributed to our understanding of educational organizations, the OCDQ falls into the social-system–perceptual-measurement–organizational-attribute cell of our matrix. This, as we will show, is generally true of scholarship on the organizational climate of schools.

Likert (1961) posited a conceptualization of organizational climate that, like Halpin and Croft's, was based on a theory concerned with the relationship of superordinates and subordinates. He argued that organizations fall on a continuum of four types of managerial systems: exploitive-authoritative, benevolent-authoritative, consultative, and participative. Likert also identified eight crucial organizational characteristics: leadership processes, motivational forces, communication process, interaction-influence process, decision-making process, goal setting, control processes, and performance goals and training. Placement of an organization on the managerial continuum is based on its profile of eight organizational characteristics. For example, a participative system is characterized by the following: supportive leadership; highly motivated employees; communications that flow throughout the organization, including upward; warm and friendly interpersonal relationships; shared decision making; shared goal setting; collegial control processes; and high performance goals.

The Likert measure of organizational climate has not been applied to schools as widely as has the OCDQ. The findings of research do seem to show that ratings of effectiveness and excellence are associated with the participative system (Ferris, 1965) and that both students and teachers tend to be most satisfied in participatory schools (Wagstaff, 1969).

Likert's conceptualization of climate is another that is concerned primarily with the social-system dimension of climate. Note that each one of the eight organizational characteristics that he identified as being important in determining an organization's managerial style is concerned with relationships between superordinates and subordinates. For example, leadership process is concerned with the supportiveness of superiors in their actions toward subordinates, and decision-making process involves the extent to which the entire organization is involved in the making of decisions.

The instrumentation based on Likert's conceptualization is another example of what James and Jones (1974) have called the perceptual-measurement–organizational-attribute approach to measuring climate. Likert and his colleagues developed a 51-item questionnaire to which organizational members re-

spond. An organization's score on each of eight characteristics is determined by calculating the mean across corresponding items and across respondents. The organization's location on the managerial-style continuum is then established by an analysis of the profile of characteristics.

Thus, as was the case with Halpin and Croft's work, Likert's conceptualization and instrumentation place it in the social-system–perceptual-measurement–organizational-attribute cell of our matrix. Beyond that, both Halpin and Croft's and Likert's conceptualizations of climate are largely concerned with the relationship of superordinates, or managers, to subordinates. That these views of climate have found their way into the educational administration literature is not surprising. Scholars of educational administration have quite naturally been concerned with the influence that administrators exert on schools. It only follows that scholars would be drawn to conceptualizations of organizational climate that focus on administrator-faculty relations as the determinant of climate. The final two conceptualizations of organizational climate that will be examined depart to different degrees from this administrator-centered view of climate.

Stern and Steinhoff, building on the ideas of Lewin (1935) and Murray (1938), developed a conceptualization and an instrumentation of climate that have found their way into the literature on educational administration. Basically, Lewin and Murray took the position that human behavior is the result of the relationship between an individual and the environment. In articulating this model, Murray developed the notion of environmental presses, the conditions of the external situation that correspond to internal personality needs. He posited that behavior will occur when environmental presses and individual needs are congruent. Murray identified 30 basic needs that individuals seek to satisfy and 30 corresponding environmental presses.

After a variety of iterations, Steinhoff (1965) developed the Organizational Climate index (OCI). The OCI is a questionnaire that contains 300 items and is aimed at determining the environmental press, or climate, that exists in organizations. A factor analysis of data from public schools indicates that the 30 press scores cluster the six first-order factors: intellectual climate, achievement standards, practicality, supportiveness, orderliness, and impulse control.

It was further determined that these factors collapse into two second-order factors: development press and control press. The development press is characterized by the following first-order factors: intellectual climate, achievement, practicality, respect for individual integrity, and orderliness. The control press is characterized by the relative absence of these five factors and the presence of the one remaining factor, impulse control. According to this conceptualization, four types of organizational climate are theoretically possible: high-development and high-control presses; low-development and low-control presses; high-development press but low-control press; and low-development press but high-control press. Research indicates that most schools are characterized by one of the latter two types of climate (Owens & Steinhoff, 1969).

The concept of environmental press includes both the cultural and social-system dimensions of climate. Recall Tagiuri's (1968) point that culture includes belief systems, values, general cognitive structures, and meaning and that social system is the patterned relationships of persons and groups. At one level the concept of environmental press depicts organizations as rewarding and sanctioning certain values and beliefs. For example, a school characterized by a development press would encourage or facilitate intellectual activity, achievement, practicality, integrity of the individual and order; that is, the school would reinforce these values. At another level the concept of environmental press focuses on the social-system dimension of climate. It is the social system that serves as the vehicle by which values are reinforced. For example, Silver (1983, p. 211) suggested that a school with an intellectual press might be characterized by an emphasis on "musical and theatrical performance, art and science exhibits and political activism."

The measurement of environmental press, like its conceptualization, can take two forms. First, one can infer the nature of a school's environmental press from observations of school-related activities. Second, one could employ the OCI to determine a school's environmental press. The mean of individual respondents' scores is calculated to obtain the school's score on each press dimension. This latter approach to the description of a school's environmental press is more commonly used. Thus, in most cases researchers have employed a perceptual-measurement–organizational-attribute approach to the measurement of environmental press.

The OCI has been used in few studies of schools. Attempts to link climate, as measured by this instrument, to academic achievement have resulted in inconsistent findings (Hamaty, 1967; McDill, Meyers & Rigsby, 1967). However, because the OCI has consistently differentiated among climates of schools, it promises to be a useful instrument for measuring climate in future studies (Hoy & Miskel, 1982).

Willower and his associates developed a fourth conceptualization of the organizational climate of schools that has gained prominence in the educational administration literature. This conceptualization is based on the widely shared observation that the control of student behavior is an important aspect of schools (Waller, 1932; Willower & Jones, 1963).

Willower et al. (1967) developed a continuum of staff orientations toward pupil control. The pupil control ideology (PCI) names a continuum that ranges from custodial to humanistic. A custodial orientation is characterized by the stereotyping of students by appearance, behavior, and parents' socioeconomic status (SES); a tendency to view the school as autocratic with a rigid hierarchy of pupil-teacher status; the unilateral and downward flow of power and communication; and the expectation that students will unquestioningly accept teachers' decisions. In sharp contrast to the custodial orientation, the humanistic orientation views learning and behavior in psychological and sociological terms, emphasizes self-discipline, and is characterized by two-way communication between students and teachers. (See Chapter 10.)

Much of the research that has employed the PCI has focused on predictors of individuals' PCIs (Willower, 1977). These cannot be considered to be studies of climate, which is an organizational characteristic. For the same reason, studies of the relationship of individual teachers' ideologies and student outcomes such as self-esteem or achievement are not studies of climate. Closer to the issue of climate are studies that have linked schools' SES with the PCIs. Schools with students from lower socioeconomic background were found to be more custodial in PCI than middle or high SES schools (Andrews, 1965; Gossen, 1969). One of the few studies that can truly be considered a climate study was a large-scale study of high schools that employed the PCI to determine, among other things, the relationship between schools' PCIs and student alienation (Hoy, 1972). The findings of the study generally supported the hypothesis that more custodial schools would have higher levels of student alienation.

Unlike the conceptualizations of Halpin and Croft and Likert, the concept of PCI does not emphasize faculty-principal relations. Instead, it draws attention to the relationship of teachers and their pupils. However, like the other three conceptualizations of climate reviewed here, PCI is primarily concerned with the social-system dimension of the organizational climate of schools. For example, two dimensions that distinguish a humanistic orientation from a custodial orientation are a de-emphasis of hierarchical structure and an internal rather than external form of social control. Both deal with patterns of interaction.

The measurement of PCI is of the perceptual-measurement–organizational-attribute type. The PCI form was developed to operationalize the concept of pupil control orientation. The instrument is a 20-item Likert-type scale. The pupil control orientation of a school is measured by pooling the responses of its professional staff members.

In summary, the four most prominent conceptualizations of organizational climate in the educational administration literature basically fall into one cell of our climate-dimension-measurement matrix. The conceptualizations focus primarily on the social-system dimension of climate (Anderson, 1982). Two emphasize the relationship of administrators and their staffs. Halpin and Croft's conceptualization is concerned with faculty and faculty-principal relationships. Likert's work is based on his concept of a continuum of managerial systems that range from exploitive-authoritative to participative. Stern and Steinhoff's concept of environmental press, while bringing in an element of the cultural dimension, treats social systems as the vehicle for reinforcing and facilitating the pursuit of values. Finally, Willower, Eidell, and Hoy's concept of PCI departs from the others in that it draws attention to the relationship of teachers and students. However, like the other conceptualizations, it emphasizes the relationship of persons and groups, or the social system, with its focus on the hierarchical structure of teacher-student relations.

All four of these conceptualizations have led to the development of instruments that record respondents' perceptions. Further, in all cases school-level scores are obtained by aggregating the scores of individual respondents. Thus, all employ what James and Jones (1974) have categorized as perceptual-measurement–organizational-attribute approaches to the measurement of climates.

Another way to look at the apparent narrowness of the conceptualization of climate in the educational administration literature is to consider the untapped potential that exists for the examination of climate. We found that three dimensions of climate (ecology, milieu, and culture) and two methods of measuring climate (multiple-measure–organizational-attribute and perceptual-measure–individual-attribute), or 11 of 12 cells of our matrix, have virtually been ignored. Since the selection of research method is driven as much by the conceptualization of the phenomenon to be examined as by the availability of instruments, the remainder of the discussion will focus on the three climatic dimensions, as described by Tagiuri (1968), that have been ignored, with particular attention to the possibilities for research on organizational culture.

However, before turning to the discussion of the three climatic dimensions, we will digress a bit to consider an issue that has received little attention: the

difference in the treatment of school climate by research rooted in the organizational climate and school-effects traditions. This is an important issue because it touches on both the confused state of the literature on school climate and the narrowness of the conceptualization of climate in the literature on educational administration and organizational climate.

Organizational Climate and School Effects

The broad appeal of climate as both a descriptive metaphor and an explanation of differences between schools has resulted in some confusion in the education literature. The term *climate* has been applied to so many different school characteristics that it is not really clear what climate is. Researchers have at various times considered everything from physical facilities to the SES of students' families and the quality of teacher-administrator interaction to be elements of school climate. This confusion is in part due to the fact that scholars who have applied the term *climate* to describe school-level characteristics have done so from different perspectives.

Anderson (1982) concluded that most research on school climate has been conducted from two perspectives: school climate as a form of organizational climate or the effect of school-level characteristics on student performance. A systematic comparison of these two perspectives has not been undertaken. Although a long and comprehensive comparison lies beyond the scope of this chapter, we will offer a brief comparison of the research that has grown out of these two perspectives in order to make two points. The first is that some of the confusion that characterizes the literature on school climate is the result of research rooted in conceptually distinct perspectives. The second is that the literature on school effects illustrates that the adoption of different perspectives can overcome the narrowness evident in the literature on organizational climate.

As we noted above, the four conceptualizations that have guided much of the work on the organizational climate of schools are focused on only one of four climate dimensions: the social system. Since each of the conceptualizations that we described led to the development of an instrument to measure climate, it follows that research rooted in these conceptualizations would also focus on the social-system dimension. Thus, the organizational climate of schools has been conceptualized as some aspect of the social-system dimension in a variety of studies that either sought to determine the adequacy of a given conceptualization as a descriptor of climate (A. Brown, 1965; Hall, 1972; Halpin & Croft, 1963; Owens & Steinhoff, 1969; Steinhoff, 1965; Willower et al., 1967) or examined the extent to which climate is associated with (a) other aspects of a school's social system (Anderson, 1964; Andrews, 1965; Kanner, 1974; Licata & Willower, 1975; Wagstaff, 1969), (b) with other types of school characteristics (Flagg, 1964; Herr, 1965; Mitchell, 1968; Watkins, 1968), or (c) with school achievement (Feldvebel, 1964; Hale, 1965; Maxwell, 1967; Miller, 1968).

The treatment of climate in the school-effects literature departs quite markedly from its treatment in the organizational-climate literature. Whereas research on the organizational climate of schools is rooted in predetermined conceptualizations and subsequent operationalizations of organizational climate, the approach taken to the examination of climate in school effects research is less conceptually constrained. Rather than examining narrow conceptualizations of climate, school-effects researchers have sought to identify school-level factors, including elements of schools' climates, that affect academic performance. This broad approach has led to the examination of school characteristics that fall into each of the four climate dimensions posited by Tagiuri (1968): ecology, milieu, social system, and culture. A series of selected examples follows.

Ecology, it will be recalled, involves the physical and material aspects of organizations (Tagiuri, 1968). At least three studies have considered the effect of schools' physical facilities on academic performance. Weber (1971) considered the age of buildings in his study of four American inner-city schools, as did Rutter, Maugham, Mortimore, Ouston, and Smith (1979) in their study of 12 secondary schools in London. Rutter et al. also studied the effect of the decoration and upkeep of facilities on student achievement. Similarly, a study of American schools commissioned by Phi Delta Kappa (1980) considered the effect of the appearance of facilities on academic performance.

School-effects research has also considered the impact of factors that fall into the milieu dimension of climate on academic achievement. Milieu is concerned with the actual presence of persons or groups in an organization. For example, several studies have examined the effect of teacher characteristics or student characteristics or both on achievement. McDill and Rigsby (1973) considered level of teacher salary and the percentage of teachers with bachelor's degrees as predictors of both student achievement and plans. With regard to student characteristics, McDill and Rigsby (1973) and Brookover, Beady, Flood, Schweitzer, and Wisenbaker (1979) examined the relationship of student bodies' racial and socioeconomic composition to achievement. Focusing on other student characteristics, Schneider, Glasheen, and Hadley

(1979) studied family background and academic skills at intake as predictors of grade point average and performance on achievement tests.

Like research conducted from the organizational-climate perspective, research on school effects has considered the social-system dimension of climate. Researchers have considered the influence of many variables on student achievement, including the administrative organization of schools (Anglin, 1979; Rutter et al., 1979), the extent to which teachers are involved in decision making (Phi Delta Kappa, 1980; Rutter et al., 1979; Wynne, 1980) and teacher-teacher relationships (Phi Delta Kappa, 1980; Rutter et al., 1979; Wynne, 1980), and the extent to which the incumbents of a variety of roles in schools are involved in instructionl activities (Brookover & Lezotte, 1979; Edmonds, 1979; McDill & Rigsby, 1973; Phi Delta Kappa, 1980; Weber, 1971), on student achievement.

Finally, school-effects researchers have generally found that various elements of the cultural dimension of climate influence student achievement. Culture includes the beliefs, values, meanings, and basic cognitive structures that characterize an organization. The results of a variety of studies indicate that the following cultural elements affect academic achievement: the expectations that teachers and administrators hold for the academic performance of students (Brookover & Lezotte, 1979; Brookover & Schneider, 1975; Edmonds, 1979; Phi Delta Kappa, 1980; Rutter et al., 1979; Weber, 1971), the emphasis placed on academics by the school staff (Brookover & Lezotte, 1979; Edmonds, 1979; McDill & Rigsby, 1973; Phi Delta Kappa, 1980; Weber, 1971), the commitment of teachers to improving students' academic performance (Brookover & Lezotte, 1979; Phi Delta Kappa, 1980), and norms shared by students (Brookover & Schneider, 1975; McDill & Rigsby, 1973; Rutter et al., 1979).

Research conducted from the school-effects perspective has employed more methods of examining, or measuring, climate than has research from the organizational-climate perspective. Whereas the dominant conceptualizations of organizational climate gave rise to questionnaires to measure climate, school-effects researchers have employed a variety of methods to assess climate. Questionnaires have also been the dominant means for collecting data in school-effects research (Brookover & Lezotte, 1979; Brookover & Schneider, 1975; Edmonds, 1979; McDill & Rigsby, 1973; Phi Delta Kappa, 1980; Rutter et al., 1979). However, school-effects researchers have also employed observation (Brookover & Schneider, 1975; Weber, 1971) and school records (Edmonds & Fredericksen, 1978; Lezotte & Passalacqua, 1978). In terms of the types of approaches to measuring climate identified by James and Jones (1974), then, school-effects research has tended to employ perceptual-measurement–organizational-attribute methods of measurement but has occasionally employed multiple-measure–organizational-attribute methods.

To summarize, research rooted in the school-effects tradition has employed a variety of methods to examine the extent to which elements of four dimensions of climate affect student achievement. The treatment of climate in the school-effects literature falls into 8 of the 12 cells of our measurement-dimension matrix. Both perceptual-measurement–organizational-attribute and multiple-measure–organizational-attribute methods have been employed in school-effects research, and all four dimensions of climate—ecology, milieu, social system, and culture—have been examined. Research rooted in the organizational-climate tradition, it will be recalled, fell into only one cell of the matrix: perceptual-measurement–organizational-attribute–social system.

As Anderson (1982) has observed, the literature on the climate of schools presents a confusing array of research findings. The confusion can in part be traced to the divergent approaches taken to the examination of climate in the educational literature. The research rooted in the organizational-climate literature is based on conceptualizations that depict climate as the nature of social relationships between and among incumbents of various hierarchical levels of schools: principals, teachers, and students. Note that Halpin and Croft's (1963) and Likert's (1961) conceptualizations both focus on principal-teacher relationships, whereas that of Willower et al. (1967) focuses on an aspect of the relationship between students and members of the instructional staff.

In contrast, the research rooted in the school-effects tradition is more eclectic. Anderson (1982) noted that researchers have typically embraced one of three types of theory in examining the effect of school-level factors on achievement: input-output, sociological, and ecological. Each type of theory focuses researchers' attention on different sets of variables. Research driven by input-output theory, with its emphasis on the inputs processed by schools, emphasizes the ecological dimension of climate. Research based on sociological theory, with its focus on the social relations of the various actors in school settings, typically examines the influence of the social system and cultural dimensions on academic performance. Finally, research rooted in ecological theory, with its inclusion of both input factors and social relationships, tends to consider the influence of a wide variety of variables, including the ecological, social-system, and cultural dimensions of climate.

What has occurred, then, is that scholars have rather loosely applied the term *climate* to conceptually distinct aspects of the overall environment of schools. Those working in the organizational-climate tradition have applied the term to broad conceptualizations that are based on the assumption that the character of organizations' social systems is what is intuitively experienced as climate. On the other hand, the term has been applied in the school-effects literature to a broad set of school characteristics that might influence academic performance.

The comparison of research rooted in the organizational-climate and school-effects traditions also suggests a solution to the problem of the narrow treatment of school climate in the educational administration literature. School-effects research illustrates what can happen when a variety of approaches are taken to the examination of phenomena: A variety of pictures emerge. In the concluding section, we will discuss the potential for research on the three dimensions of climate largely ignored in the organizational-climate literature, with particular attention being given to the dimension of culture.

Implications for Future Research

Although the failure of educational administration scholars to attend to three of four climate dimensions indicates a narrowness of perspective, it also marks potentially fertile fields of future research. It perhaps is not a coincidence that discussions of the ecology, milieu, and culture of organizations have recently cropped up in the literature on organizations. We will turn to these developments to guide our discussion of the potential for educational research on these three dimensions of climate.

Ecology

The ecology dimension of an organization's climate involves its physical and material aspects (Tagiuri, 1968). That the ecological dimension has not been the focus of research on the organizational climate of schools is consistent with Pfeffer's (1982) assertion that physical structures have generally escaped the notice of organizational analysts. Pfeffer identifies six qualities of organizations' physical facilities that he argues might influence organizational behavior: size, quality, flexibility, arrangement, privacy, and location. Further, he posits that these physical properties might influence the following behaviors: amount of interaction, affective reaction to job and organization, and affective reaction and orientation toward others.

Research on the effects of the physical properties of schools on the behavior of staff members and students is lacking in the educational administration literature. Although studies of school facilities are part of the educational administration tradition, they have tended to focus on cost, capacity, and architectural features but have not examined relationships between the characteristics of facilities and behavior. Although the findings of school-effects research regarding the influence of the age and physical appearance of facilities on academic performance are contradictory (Anderson, 1982), research on the relationship between other characteristics of buildings and achievement and other organizational behaviors could generate information useful to practitioners.

One aspect of the narrowness of research on the organizational climate of schools is illustrated by the absence of research on the influence of ecological characteristics on organizational behavior in the educational administration literature. Pfeffer (1982) has argued that organizational analysts have forsaken concrete and directly measurable structural variables for nondiscrete variables that lie hidden in the minds of people to explain organizational behavior. The reliance of educational administration scholars on perceptual measures of climate rather than on more tangible aspects of climate such as the ecological dimension is consistent with Pfeffer's point.

Milieu

The milieu dimension of organizational climate is concerned with the people and groups in organizations. Again, Pfeffer (1982) provides direction for the examination of this overlooked set of organizational factors. He suggests the importance of considering the demographic characteristics of organizational members. Specifically, Pfeffer discusses the possible importance of the distribution of length of service of organizational workforces in explaining organizational behavior. He argues that there is some evidence to suggest that four factors—unionization, personnel practices, growth, and technology—affect the distribution of length of service, which in turn affects other organizational variables including innovativeness, type of control system, intraorganizational conflict, career processes, and administrator succession.

Clearly, Pfeffer's identification of possible relationships between distribution of length of service and other organizational variables can be useful in guiding research on public schools as well as other types of educational organizations. For example, examinations of the influence of length of service on administrator succession and career processes could contribute to the current discussion on the structures of professional careers in public education. Miskel and Cosgrove (1985) have outlined the set of factors that research

suggests can influence the effects of administrator succession in schools.

Further, beyond distribution of length of service lie additional aspects of organizational demography that might be plumbed fruitfully by scholars of educational administration. Consider that both the staffs and student bodies of schools bear demographic characteristics, something that school-effects researchers fully appreciate. Add to that the many demographic characteristics, such as distribution of staff training, distribution of the SES of students' families, and distribution of gender of staffs and student bodies, whose relationship to other school variables, such as academic achievement, conflict levels, and control systems, could be examined. Pfeffer's (1982) point that it is the distribution and not simply the mean that is important in considering the influence of demographic factors on organizational behavior is well taken. The nature of the particular mix of schools' staffs and student bodies on a particular demographic characteristic may be the telling variable and could be masked by simply calculating school averages. For example, the average age of teachers in one school could be identical to the average age of teachers in another school. However, in the first school teachers' ages may be normally distributed about the mean, whereas in the second the ages of teachers cluster about two modes. If these different patterns are associated with differences in climate, analysis in which school means are employed would miss the connection. One need only turn to research at the classroom level to find the effects of the demographic composition of groups on achievement (Beckerman & Good, 1981).

The failure of educational administration researchers to examine the milieu dimension of the organizational climate of schools again illustrates the general tendency to overlook tangible, directly measurable aspects of climate.

Culture

The final dimension of organizational climate that has received scant attention in the educational administration literature is culture. There are signs, however, that culture is one dimension of climate that will be more closely examined in the future. This is reflected in the recent attention given to organizational culture and qualitative research methods in the literature both of organizations and of educational administration.

Culture involves the systems of beliefs, values, meanings, and cognition of organizations (Tagiuri, 1968). Smircich (1983) has identified five views of culture represented in the organizations literature. Three of these views focus on particular conceptualizations of culture: culture as cognition, culture as symbol, and culture as unconscious processes and organization. Although educational administration scholars have begun to discuss what amount to cultural views of school organization (Allison, 1983; Greenfield, 1975; Guba & Lincoln, 1981), few studies of the cognitive, symbolic, or unconscious cultures of schools have appeared in the educational administration literature. Again, although this exposes the narrowness of the conceptualizations that have driven research in educational administration, it also points to areas for future research.

The cognitive perspective of organizational culture views culture as a system of shared cognitions or a system of knowledge and beliefs (Smircich, 1983). A few studies have been published in the educational administration literature that deal with the way administrators think about their work (Dwyer, Bossert, Rowan, & Lee, 1983; Pitner & Ogawa, 1981), and there exists an extensive literature on teacher cognition. However, little, if any, attention has been given to the patterns of cognition that characterize schools as organizations. Recently, researchers have begun to apply the cognitive perspective to the analysis of organizations other than schools. For example, Bougon, Weick, and Binkhorst (1977) studied the cognitive maps of the members of a jazz orchestra. They found that the similarity of orchestra members' beliefs about causal linkages between orchestral elements was statistically significant. Thus, the foundation for the examination of the cognitive culture of schools rests firmly in previous work in organizational analysis and teacher and administrator cognition. Since educators have been characterized as professionals, or at least semiprofessionals, and since control in the professions is self-imposed and based upon knowledge (Hoy & Miskel, 1982), it seems that the cognitive perspective would provide an appropriate way for examining the organizational nature of schools.

The symbolic perspective treats organizations as systems of symbolic discourse (Smircich, 1983). Organizations must be interpreted or read in order to be understood. Researchers working from this perspective attempt to describe the ways in which meaning is attached to experience by organizational members. Again, some work has been done on the symbolic dimension of school administration. Wolcott's (1973) study of an elementary school principal is an excellent example of that type of work. Cusick's (1973) study of student culture in a high school and his more recent description of the "egalitarian ethic" of the American high school (1983) and Gronn's (1983) work on the use of talk by a principal as an instrument of social control are among the few notable studies of the symbolic culture of schools. There is also Meyer and Rowan's

(1977) insightful explication of the structural attributes of schools as "myth and ceremony." Perhaps the recent interest shown by educational administration scholars in ethnographic research methods signals the beginning of additional efforts to examine the symbolic dimension of schools.

Students of organizations have already begun to apply the symbolic perspective to the analysis of other types of organizations. The bestsellers *Corporate Cultures* by Deal and Kennedy (1982) and *In Search of Excellence* by Peters and Waterman (1982) describe the cultures of successful corporations. Each book recounts the rituals, ceremonies, stories, and heroes that transmit the fundamental values of highly productive organizations to both employees and the public. The symbolic perspective apparent in these popular books is also evident in the scholarly organizations literature. Bolman and Deal (1984) describe four "frames," one of which is the symbolic, within which organizations are and can be understood. Researchers have begun to examine such aspects of organizations' symbolic systems as stories (Martin, Feldman, Hatch, & Sitkin, (1983), ceremonies (Gephart, 1978), signs (Barley, 1983), and social dramas (Pettigrew, 1979).

The third perspective on culture reflected in the organizations literature focuses on unconscious processes and organization (Smircich, 1983). It depicts organizations as the projections of deeply embedded psychological structures. For example, Mitroff (1983) explains that managerial behavior reflects the information-processing tendencies of individuals and that organizations manifest Freudian ego characteristics and are the projections of Jungian archetypes. This perspective is not represented in the educational administration literature. However, the almost spiritual investment that Americans have made in their system of public education (Tyack & Hansot, 1982; Waller, 1932) is consistent with Mitroff's point that individuals project archetypes, the deepest, most basic symbols that the human mind can form, onto organizations. This suggests that the examination of the unconscious processes and organization of schools may produce important insights into their organizational nature.

Beyond simply marking potentially fertile fields for research on the organization of schools, consideration of the cultural dimension of climate exposes two general limitations of conventional treatments of the organizational climate of schools. First, the notion of culture suggests the possible existence of subcultures (Gregory, 1983). The idea of subculture suggests that an organization may not be experienced in the same way by all participants. Yet, we have noted that the organizational climate of schools has typically been operationalized as the arithmetic average of the staffs' or student bodies' scores on a survey instrument. This does not take into account the strong possibility that individuals or groups may experience a school's climate differently.

A second limitation of conventional treatments of the organizational climate of schools that becomes apparent from the cultural perspective is that climate has been treated as a static phenomenon. Researchers have typically measured climate by having staff members or students complete a questionnaire on one occasion. However, an important aspect of the cultural view of organizations is that beliefs, values, meanings, and patterns of cognition are negotiated and renegotiated through social interaction. This process of negotiation is ignored in most existing studies of the organizational climate of schools. The work of researchers and theorists who have examined organizations from a political perspective is instructive. An excellent example is Allison's (1971) study of the Cuban missile crisis. Recently, Pfeffer (1981) and Bolman and Deal (1984) have articulated variations on the political model.

Summary and Conclusions

An examination of the educational administration literature revealed that four conceptualizations have spawned much of the research on the organizational climate of schools. Employing a matrix constructed from the four dimensions of climate described by Tagiuri (1968) and the three types of approaches to the measurement identified by James and Jones (1974), we found that the research rooted in the four dominant conceptualizations fell into one cell. All the studies employed perceptual-measurement–organizational-attribute approaches to measure some aspect of the social-system dimension of climate, the dimension dealing with the patterned relationships of persons or groups. Two approaches to the measurement of climate—multiple-measure–organizational-attribute and perceptual-measure–individual-attribute—and three dimensions of climate—ecology, milieu, and culture—have been virtually ignored.

A comparison of research on school effects with research on the organizational climate of schools underscored the narrowness of the conceptualization of climate in the organizational-climate literature. Whereas organizational-climate researchers employed only one approach to measuring climate and focused on one dimension of climate, school-effects researchers had employed a variety of methods to examine the extent to which elements of four dimensions of climate affect student achievement. The broader approach taken to examine climate in the school-effects research seems to have resulted from the application of more than one theory regarding what school characteristics affect achievement. This suggests that educational administration scholars could fruitfully employ conceptualizations of climate other than those that have dominated previous research.

Finally, the potential for studying the three dimensions of climate ignored by the educational administration literature—ecology, milieu, and culture—was discussed. Consideration of these three dimensions exposed further aspects of the narrowness of conventional conceptualizations of climate. It was noted that the failure of educational administration scholars to study elements of the ecology and milieu of schools reveals a tendency to ignore tangible, directly measurable, structural variables in explaining organizational behavior. On the other hand, the lack of attention given to the cultural dimension has resulted in the failure to consider both how climate is negotiated by organizational members over time and that climate may not be experienced in the same way by all subgroups and individuals.

NOTES

[1] For a discussion of the basic assumptions and generalizations of the models, see C. G. Miskel (1982) and Chapter 7 in W. K. Hoy and C. G. Miskel (1982). These sources also served as the basis for portions of the general discussion in the present review.

[2] For comprehensive reviews of the literature on organizational climate the reader is referred to the following sources, all listed in References: C. S. Anderson (1982); L. R. James and A. P. Jones (1974); D. Hellriegel and J. W. Slocum, Jr. (1974); and G. H. Litwin and R. A. Stringer (1968).

REFERENCES

Adams, J. S. (1963). Toward an understanding of inequity. *Journal of Abnormal and Social Psychology*, 67, 422–436.

Alderfer, C. P. (1972). *Existence, relatedness, and growth: Human needs in organizational settings*. New York: Free Press.

Alderfer, C. P., & Guzzo, R. A. (1979). Life experiences and adult's enduring strengths and desires in organizations. *Administrative Science Quarterly*, 24, 347–361.

Allison, D. J. (1983). Toward an improved understanding of the organizational nature of schools. *Educational Administration Quarterly*, 29, 7–34.

Allison, G. T. (1971). *Essence of decision: Explaining the Cuban missile crisis*. Boston: Little, Brown.

Anderson, C. S. (1982). The search for school climate: A review of the research. *Review of Educational Research*, 52, 368–420.

Anderson, D. P. (1964). *Organizational climate of elementary schools*. Minneapolis: Educational Research and Development Council.

Anderson, M. B. G., & Iwanicki, E. F. (1984). Teacher motivation and its relationship to burnout. *Educational Administration Quarterly*, 20, 109–132.

Andrews, J. H. M. (1965). School organizational climate: Some validity studies. *Canadian Education and Research Digest*, 5, 317–334.

Anglin, L. W. (1979). Teacher roles and alternative school organizations. *Educational Forum*, *43*, 439–452.

Arikado, M. S. (1976). Status congruence as it relates to team teacher satisfaction. *Journal of Educational Administration*, *14*, 70–78.

Arnold, H. J. (1981). A test of the validity of the multiplicative hypothesis of expectancy-valence theories of work motivation. *Academy of Management Journal*, *24*, 128–141.

Arnold, H. J., & House, R. (1980). Methodological and substance extensions to the job characteristics model of motivation. *Organizational Behavior and Human Performance*, *25*, 161–183.

Bacharach, S. B., & Mitchell, S. M. (1983). The sources of dissatisfaction in educational administration: A role-specific analysis. *Educational Administration Quarterly*, *19*, 101–128.

Barley, S. R. (1983). Semiotics and the study of occupational and organizational cultures. *Administrative Science Quarterly*, *24*, 570–589.

Beckerman, T. M., & Good, T. L. (1981). The classroom ratio of high and low aptitude students and its effect on achievement. *American Educational Research Journal*, *18*, 317–327.

Beehr, T. A., & Love, K. G. (1983). A meta-model of the effects of goal characteristics, feedback, and role characteristics in human organizations. *Human Relations*, *36*, 151–166.

Belasco, J. A., & Alutto, J. A. (1972). Decisional participation and teacher satisfaction. *Educational Administration Quarterly*, *8*, 44–58.

Bhagat, R. S., & Chassie, M. B. (1980). Effects of changes in job characteristics on some theory-specific attitudinal outcomes: Results from a naturally occurring quasi-experiment. *Human Relations*, *33*, 297–313.

Blocker, C. E., & Richardson, R. C. (1963). Twenty-five years of morale research—a critical review. *Journal of Educational Sociology*, *36*, 200–210.

Bolman, L. G., & Deal, T. E. (1984). *Modern approaches to understanding and managing organizations*. San Francisco: Jossey-Bass.

Bougon, M., Weick, K., & Binkhorst, D. (1977). Cognition in organizations: An analysis of the Utrecht Jazz Orchestra. *Administrative Science Quarterly*, *22*, 606–631.

Brayfield, A. H., & Crockett, W. H. (1955). Employee attitudes and employee performance. *Psychological Bulletin*, *52*, 396–424.

Broedling, L. A. (1977). The uses of the intrinsic-extrinsic distinction in explaining motivation and organizational behavior. *Academy of Management Review*, *2*, 267–276.

Brookover, W. B., Beady, C., Flood, P., Schweitzer, J., & Wisenbaker, J. (1979). *School social systems and student achievement*. New York: Praeger.

Brookover, W. B., & Lezotte, L. W. (1979). Changes in school characteristics coincident with changes in student achievement. Occasional Paper No. 17, East Lansing, Michigan: Michigan State University, Institute for Research on Teaching.

Brookover, W. B., & Schneider, J. M. (1975). Academic environments and elementary school achievement. *Journal of Research and Development in Education*, *9*, 82–91.

Brown, A. F. (1965). Two strategies for changing climate. *CAS Bulletin*, *4*, 64–80.

Brown, R. J. (1965). *Organizational climate of elementary schools*, Research Monograph No. 2. Minneapolis: Educational Research and Development Council.

Campbell, J. P., Dunnette, M. D., Lawler, E. E., III, & Weick, K. (1970). *Managerial behavior, performance, and effectiveness*. New York: McGraw-Hill.

Campbell, J. P., & Pritchard, R. D. (1976). Motivation theory in industrial and organizational psychology. In M. D. Dunnette (Ed.), *Handbook of industrial and organizational psychology* (pp. 63–130). Chicago: Rand-McNally.

Campion, M. A., & Lord, R. G. (1982). A control systems conceptualization of the goal-setting and changing process. *Organizational Behavior and Human Performance*, *30*, 265–287.

Carpenter, H. H. (1971). Formal organizational structural factors and perceived job satisfaction of classroom teachers. *Administrative Science Quarterly*, *16*, 460–465.

Carroll, B. (1973). *Job satisfaction: A review of the literature*. Ithaca, NY: New York State School of Industrial and Labor Relations.

Carver, F. D., & Sergiovanni, T. J. (1969). Notes on the OCDQ. *Journal of Educational Administration*, *7*, 71–81.

Chase, F. S. (1951). Factors for satisfaction in teaching. *Phi Delta Kappan*, *23*, 127–132.

Chisolm, G. B., Washington, R., & Thibodeaux, M. (1980). *Job motivation and the need fulfillment deficiencies of educators*. Paper presented at the Annual Meeting of the American Educational Research Association, Boston.

Coughlan, R. J. (1971). Job satisfaction in relatively closed and open schools. *Educational Administration Quarterly*, *7*, 40–59.

Cusick, P. A. (1973). *Inside high school*. New York: Holt, Rinehart, & Winston.

Cusick, P. A. (1983). *The egalitarian ideal and the American high school*. White Plains, NY: Longman.

Deal, T. E., & Kennedy, A. A. (1982). *Corporate Cultures*. Reading, MA: Addison-Wesley.

Deci, E. L. (1975). *Intrinsic motivation*. New York: Plenum.

Dillard, J. F. (1979). Applicability of an occupational goal-expectancy model in professional accounting organizations. *Decision Sciences*, *10*, 161–176.

Dillard, J. F. (1981). An update on the applicability of an occupational goal-expectancy model in professional accounting organizations. *Decision Sciences*, *12*, 32–38.

Dwyer, D. C., Bossert, S., Rowan, B., & Lee, G. V. (1983). *Five principals in action: Perspective on instructional management*. San Francisco: Far West Laboratory for Educational Research and Development.

Dyer, L., & Parker, D. F. (1975). Classifying outcomes in work motivation research: An examination of the intrinsic-extrinsic dichotomy. *Journal of Applied Psychology*, *60*, 455–458.

Edmonds, R. R. (1979). Some schools work and more can. *Social Policy*, *9*, 28–32.

Edmonds, R. R., & Fredericksen, J. R. (1978). *Search for effective schools: The identification and analysis of city schools that are instructionally effective for poor children*. Cambridge, MA: Harvard University, Center for Urban Studies.

Erez, M., & Kanfer, F. H. (1983). The role of goal acceptance in goal setting and task performance. *Academy of Management Review*, *8*, 454–463.

Evans, M. G., Kiggundu, M. N., & House, R. J. (1979). A partial test and extension of the job characteristic model of motivation. *Organizational Behavior and Human Performance*, *24*, 354–381.

Farh, J., & Scott, W. E., Jr. (1983). The experimental effects of "autonomy" on performance and self-reports of satisfaction. *Organizational Behavior and Human Performance*, *31*, 203–222.

Feldvebel, A. M. (1964). Organizational climate, social class and educational output. *Administrator's Notebook*, *12* (8).

Ferris, A. E. (1965). *Organizational relationships in two selected secondary schools: A comparative study*. Unpublished doctoral dissertation, Columbia University, New York NY.

Festinger, L. (1957). *A theory of cognitive dissonance*. Evanston, IL: Row, Peterson.

Flagg, J. T. (1964). *The organizational climate of schools: Its relationship to pupil achievement, size of school, and teacher turnover*. Unpublished doctoral dissertation, Rutgers University, New Brunswick, NJ.

Frasher J. M., & Frasher R. S. (1980). *Verification of administrative attribution theory*. Paper presented at the Annual Meeting of the American Educational Research Association, Boston.

Friesen, D., Holdaway, E. A., & Rice, A. W. (1983). Satisfaction of school principals with their work. *Educational Administration Quarterly*, *19*, 35–58.

Fuller, R., & Miskel, C. G. (1972). *Work attachments and job satisfaction among public school educators*. Paper presented at the annual meeting of the American Educational Research Association, Chicago.

Galbraith, J., & Cummings, L. L. (1967). An empirical investigation of the motivational determinants of task performance. *Organizational Behavior and Human Performance*, *2*, 237–257.

Garland, H. (1982). Goal levels and task performance: A compelling replication of some compelling results. *Journal of Applied Psychology, 67*, 245–248.

Gephart, R. (1978). Status degradation and organizational succession. *Administrative Science Quarterly, 23*, 553–581.

Golembiewski, R. T., & Yeager, S. (1978). Testing the applicability of the JDI to various demographic groupings. *Academy of Management Journal, 21*, 514–519.

Gossen, H. A. (1969). *An investigation of the relationship between socioeconomic status of elementary schools and the pupil control ideology of teachers.* Unpublished doctoral dissertation, Oklahoma State University, Stillwater, OK.

Graen, G. (1969). Instrumentality theory of work motivation: Some experimental results and suggested modifications. *Journal of Applied Psychology Monograph, 53*, 1–25.

Grassie, M. C., & Carss, B. W. (1973). School structure, leadership quality, teacher satisfaction. *Educational Administration Quarterly, 9*, 15–26.

Greene, C. N., & Craft, R. E., Jr. (1979). The satisfaction-performance controversy—revisited. In R. M. Steers & L. W. Porter (Eds.), *Motivation and Work* (2nd ed., pp. 270–287). New York: McGraw-Hill.

Greenfield, T. B. (1975). Theory about organization: A new perspective and its implications for schools. In M. Hughes (Ed.), *Administering education: International challenge* (pp. 71–99). London: Athlone.

Gregory, K. L. (1983). Native-view paradigms: Multiple cultures and culture conflicts in organizations. *Administrative Science Quarterly, 28*, 359–376.

Gronn, P. C. (1983). Talk as work: The accomplishment of school administration. *Administrative Science Quarterly, 28*, 1–21.

Gruneburg, M. M. (Ed.). (1976). *Job satisfaction—a reader.* New York: John Wiley.

Gruneburg, M. M. (1979). *Understanding job satisfaction.* London: Macmillan.

Guba, E. G., & Lincoln, Y. S. (1981). *Effective evaluation.* San Francisco: Jossey-Bass.

Gunn, J. A. (1984). *Job satisfaction of senior high school principals and their perceptions of school effectiveness, their leadership and their bases of influences.* Unpublished doctoral dissertation, University of Alberta, Edmonton.

Guzzo, R. A. (1979). Types of rewards, cognitions, and work motivation. *Academy of Management Review, 4*, 75–86.

Hackman, J. R., & Lawler, E. E. (1971). Employee reactions to job characteristics. *Journal of Applied Psychology, 55*, 259–286.

Hackman, J. R., & Oldham, G. R. (1975). Development of the job diagnostic survey. *Journal of Applied Psychology, 60*, 159–170.

Hackman, J. R., & Oldham, G. R. (1976). Motivation through the design of work: A test of a theory. *Organizational Behavior and Human Performance, 16*, 250–279.

Hackman, J. R., & Oldham, G. R. (1980). *Work redesign.* Reading, MA: Addison-Wesley.

Hale, J. (1965). *A study of the relationship between selected factors of organizational climate and pupil achievement in reading, arithmetic, and language.* Unpublished doctoral dissertation, University of Alabama, Tuscaloosa, AL.

Hall, J. W. (1972). A comparison of Halpin and Croft's organizational climates and Likert and Likert's organizational system. *Administration Science Quarterly, 17*, 586–590.

Halpin, A. W., & Croft, D. B. (1963). *The organizational climate of schools.* Chicago: University of Chicago Press.

Hamaty, C. G. (1967). *Some behavioral correlates of organizational climates and cultures.* Unpublished doctoral dissertation, Syracuse University, Syracuse.

Hartley, M., & Hoy, W. K. (1972). Openness of school climate and alienation of high school students. *California Journal of Educational Research, 23*, 17–24.

Haughey, M. L., & Murphy, P. J. (1983). Quality of work life: Rural teachers' perceptions. *The Canadian Administrator, 23*, 1–6.

Hellriegel, D., & Slocum, J. W., Jr. (1974). Organizational climate: Measures, research and contingencies. *Academy of Management Journal, 17*, 255–280.

Heneman, H. G., III, & Schwab, D. P. (1972). An evaluation of research on expectancy theory predictions of employee performance. *Psychological Bulletin, 78*, 1–9.

Herrick, H. S. (1973). *The relationship of organizational structure to teacher motivation in multiunit and non-multiunit elementary schools.* (Technical Report No. 322). Madison, WI: Wisconsin Research and Development Center for Cognitive Learning, University of Wisconsin.

Herzberg, F., Mausner, B., & Snyderman, B. (1959). *The motivation to work.* New York: John Wiley.

Holdaway, E. A. (1978a). *Job satisfaction: An Alberta report.* Edmonton: University of Alberta.

Holdaway, E. A. (1978b). Facet and overall satisfaction of teachers. *Educational Administration Quarterly, 14*, 30–47.

Hoppock, R. (1935). *Job satisfaction.* New York: Harper.

Hoy, W. K. (1972). Dimensions of student alienation and characteristics of public high schools. *Interchange, 3*, 38–51.

Hoy, W. K., & Miskel, C. G. (1982). *Educational administration: Theory, research and practice* (2nd ed.). New York: Random House.

Ilgen, D. R., Nebeker, D. M., & Pritchard, R. D. (1981). Expectancy theory measures: An empirical comparison in an experimental simulation. *Organizational Behavior and Human Performance, 28*, 189–223.

Ivancevich, J. M., & McMahon, J. J. (1977). A Study of task-goal attributes, higher order need strength, and performance. *Academy of Management Journal, 20*, 552–563.

Ivancevich, J. M., & McMahon, J. J. (1982). The effects of goal setting, external feedback, and self-generated feedback on outcome variables: A field experiment. *Academy of Management Journal, 25*, 359–372.

James, L. R., & Jones, A. P. (1974). Organizational climate: A review of theory and research. *Psychology Bulletin, 81*, 1096–1112.

Johannesson, R. E. (1973). Some problems in the measurement of organizational climate. *Organizational Behavior and Human Performance, 10*, 118–144.

Johnston, G. S., Yeakey, C. C., & Winter, R. A. (1980). *A study of the relationship between the job satisfaction of principals and the perceived level of teacher militancy.* Paper presented at the annual meeting of the American Educational Research Association, Boston.

Kanner, L. (1974). *Machiavellianism and the secondary schools: Teacher-principal relations.* Unpublished doctoral dissertation, Rutgers University, New Brunswick, NJ.

Kiggundu, M. N. (1980). An empirical test of the theory of job design using multiple job ratings. *Human Relations, 33*, 339–351.

Kiggundu, M. N. (1983). Task interdependence and job design: Test of a theory. *Organizational Behavior and Human Performance, 31*, 145–172.

King, N. (1970). Clarification and evaluation of the two-factor theory of job satisfaction. *Psychological Bulletin, 74*, 18–31.

Koopman-Boyden, P. G., & Adams, R. S. (1974). Role consensus and teacher job satisfaction. *Journal of Educational Administration, 12*, 98–113.

Kyriacou, C., & Sutcliffe, J., (1979). Teacher stress and satisfaction. *Educational Research, 21*, 89–96.

LaFollette, W. R., & Sims, H. P., Jr. (1975). Is satisfaction redundant with organizational climate? *Organizational Behavior and Human Performance, 13*, 257–278.

Latham, G. P., & Yukl, G. A. (1975). A review of research on the application of goal setting in organizations. *Academy of Management Journal, 18*, 824–845.

Lawler, E. · E., III (1973). *Motivation in work organizations.* Monterey, CA: Brooks-Cole.

Lewin, K. (1935). *A dynamic theory of personality.* New York: McGraw-Hill.

Lezotte, L. W., & Passalacqua, J. (1978). Individual school buildings: Accounting for differences in measured pupil performance. *Urban Education, 13*, 283–293.

Licata, J. W. & Willower, D. J. (1975). Student brinksmanship and the school as a social system. *Educational Administration Quarterly, 11*, 1–14.

Likert, R. (1961). *New patterns of management*. New York: McGraw-Hill.

Lincoln, Y.S., Graham, L. L., & Lane, E. P. (1983). *Expectancy theory as a predictor of grade-point averages, satisfaction, and participation in the college environment*. Paper presented at the annual meeting of the Association of the Study of Higher Education, Washington, DC.

Litwin, G. H., & Stringer, R. A. (1968). *Motivation and organizational climate*. Boston: Harvard University Press.

Locke, E. A. (1968). Toward a theory of task motivation and incentives. *Organizational Behavior and Human Performance, 3*, 157–189.

Locke, E. A. (1969). What is job satisfaction? *Organizational Behavior and Human Performance, 4*, 309–336.

Locke, E. A. (1976). The nature and causes of job satisfaction. In M. D. Dunnette (Ed.), *Handbook of industrial and organizational psychology* (pp. 1297–1349), Chicago: Rand-McNally.

Locke, E. A., Cartledge, N., & Knerr, C. S. (1970). Studies of the relationship between satisfaction, goal-setting, and performance. *Organizational Behavior and Human Performance, 5*, 135–139.

Locke, E. A., Shaw, K. N., Saari, L. M., & Latham, G. P. (1981). Goal setting and task performance: 1969–1980. *Psychological Bulletin, 90*, 125–152.

Luthans, F., & Kreitner, R. (1975). *Organizational behavior modification*. Glenview, IL: Scott, Foresman.

March, J. G., & Simon, H. A. (1958). *Organizations*. New York: John Wiley.

Martin, J., Feldman, M. S., Hatch, M., & Sitkin, S. B. (1983). The uniqueness paradox in organizational stories. *Administrative Science Quarterly, 28*, 438–453.

Maslow, A. H. (1943). A theory of human motivation. *Psychology Review, 50*, 370–396.

Maslow, A. H. (1954). *Motivation and personality*. New York: Harper & Row.

Maslow, A. H. (1970). *Motivation and personality* (2nd ed.). New York: Harper & Row.

Matsui, T., Okada, A., & Inoshita, O. (1983). Mechanism of feedback affecting task performance. *Organizational Behavior and Human Performance, 31*, 114–122.

Maxwell, R. E. (1967). *Leader behavior of principals: A study of ten inner-city elementary schools of Flint, Michigan*. Unpublished doctoral dissertation, Wayne State University, Detroit.

McDill, E. L., Meyers, E. D., Jr., & Rigsby, L. C. (1967). Institutional effects on the academic behavior of high school students. *Sociology of Education, 40*, 181–199.

McDill, E. L., & Rigsby, L. C. (1973). *Structure and process in secondary schools: The academic impact of educational climates*. Baltimore, MD: Johns Hopkins University Press.

Mento, A. J., Cartledge, N. D., & Locke, E. A. (1980). Maryland vs. Michigan vs. Minnesota: Another look at the relationship of expectancy and goal difficulty to task performance. *Organizational Behavior and Human Performance, 25*, 419–440.

Meyer, J. W., & Rowan, B. (1977). Institutionalized organizations: Formal structure as myth and ceremony. *American Journal of Sociology, 83*, 340–363.

Miller, H. E. (1968). *An investigation of organizational climate as a variable in pupil achievement among 22 elementary schools in an urban school district*. Unpublished doctoral dissertation, University of Minnesota, Minneapolis, MN.

Miller, L. M. (1978). *Behavior management*. New York: John Wiley.

Miner, J. B. (1980). *Theories of organizational behavior*. Hinsdale, IL: Dryden.

Miskel, C. G. (1973). The motivation of educators to work. *Educational Administration Quarterly, 9*, 42–53.

Miskel, C. G. (1974). Intrinsic, extrinsic, and risk propensity factors in the work attitudes of teachers, educational administrators, and business managers. *Journal of Applied Psychology, 59*, 339–343.

Miskel, C. G. (1982). Motivation in educational organizations. *Educational Administration Quarterly, 18*, 65–88.

Miskel, C. G., & Cosgrove, D. (1985). Leader succession in school

settings. *Review of Educational Research, 55*, 87–105.

Miskel, C. G., DeFrain, J. A., & Wilcox, K. (1980). A test of expectancy motivation theory in educational organizations. *Educational Administration Quarterly, 16*, 70–92.

Miskel, C. G., Fevurly, R., & Stewart, J. W. (1979). Organizational structures and processes, perceived school effectiveness, loyalty, and job satisfaction. *Educational Administration Quarterly, 15*, 97–118.

Miskel, C. G., & Gerhardt, E. (1974). Perceived bureaucracy, teacher conflict, central life interests, voluntarism, and job satisfaction. *Journal of Educational Administration, 12*, 84–97.

Miskel, C. G., Glasnapp, D., & Hatley, R. V. (1975). A test of the inequity theory for job satisfaction using educators' attitudes toward work motivation and work incentives. *Educational Administration Quarterly, 11*, 38–54.

Miskel, C. G., McDonald, D., & Bloom, S. (1983). Structural and expectancy linkages within schools and organizational effectiveness. *Educational Administration Quarterly, 19*, 49–82.

Mitchell, J. V., Jr. (1968). The identification of student personality characteristics related to perceptions of the school environment. *School Review, 76*, 50–59.

Mitchell, T. R. (1974). Expectancy models of job satisfaction, occupational preference, and effort: A theoretical, methodological, and empirical appraisal. *Psychological Bulletin, 81*, 1053–1077.

Mitchell, T. R. (1979). Organization behavior. *Annual Review of Psychology, 30*, 243–281.

Mitchell, T. R. (1980). *Expectancy-value models in organizational psychology*. Unpublished manuscript, University of Washington.

Mitroff, I. (1983). *Stakeholders of the organizational mind*. San Francisco: Jossey-Bass.

Mohrman, A. M., Jr., Cooke, R. A., & Mohrman, S. A. (1978). Participation in decision making: A multidimensional perspective. *Educational Administration Quarterly, 14*, 13–29.

Mowday, R. T. (1978). The exercise of upward influence in organizations. *Administrative Science Quarterly, 23*, 137–156.

Moxley, L. (1977). Job satisfaction of faculty teaching higher education: An examination of Herzberg's dual factor theory and Porter's need satisfaction research. ERIC Document ED 139–349.

Muchinsky, P. M. (1977). A comparison of within- and across-subjects analyses of the expectancy-valence model for predicting effort. *Academy of Management Journal, 20*, 154–158.

Murray, H. (1938). *Explorations in personality*. New York: Oxford University Press.

Nelson, M. A. E. (1980). *Leader behavior and its relationship to subordinate behaviors as moderated by selected contingency factors in Minnesota schools: A path-goal approach*. Unpublished doctoral dissertation, University of Minnesota, Minneapolis, MN.

Nicholson, J. H. (1980). *An analysis of communication satisfaction in an urban school system*. Unpublished doctoral dissertation. Vanderbilt University, Nashville.

Oades, C. D. (1983). *Relationship of teacher motivation and job satisfaction*. Unpublished doctoral dissertation, University of Manitoba, Winnipeg.

O'Connor, E. J., Rudolf, C. J., & Peters, L. H. (1980). Individual differences and job design reconsidered: Where do we go from here? *Academy of Management Review, 5*, 249–254.

Oldham, G. R. (1976). Job characteristics and internal motivation: The moderating effect of interpersonal and individual variables. *Human Relations, 29*, 559–569.

Oldham, G. R., & Miller, H. E. (1979). The effect of significant other's job complexity and employee reactions to work. *Human Relations, 32*, 247–260.

Orpen, C. (1979). The effects of job enrichment on employee satisfaction, motivation, involvement, and performance: A field experiment. *Human Relations, 32*, 189–217.

Ortloff, W. G. (1980). *The use of the equity theory in predicting job satisfaction among high school administrators*. Unpublished doctoral dissertation, Oklahoma State University, Stillwater, OK.

Owens, R. G., & Steinhoff, C. R. (1969). Strategies for improving inner-city schools. *Phi Delta Kappan, 50*, 252–263.

Pastor, M. C., & Erlandson, D. A. (1982). A study of higher order need strength and job satisfaction in secondary public school teachers. *Journal of Educational Administration, 20*, 172–183.

Payne, R. L., Fineman, S., & Wall, T. D. (1976). Organizational climate and job satisfaction: A conceptual synthesis. *Organizational Behavior and Human Performance, 16*, 45–62.

Peters, T. J., & Waterman, R. H., Jr. (1982). *In Search of Excellence.* New York: Harper & Row.

Pettigrew, A. M. (1979). On studying organizational culture. *Administrative Science Quarterly, 24*, 570–589.

Pfeffer, J. (1981). *Power in organizations.* Marshfield, MA: Pitman.

Pfeffer, J. (1982). *Organizations and organization theory.* Marshfield, MA: Pitman.

Phi Delta Kappa (1980). *Why do some urban schools succeed? The Phi Delta Kappa study of exceptional urban elementary schools.* Bloomington, IN: Author.

Pitner, N. J., & Ogawa. R. T. (1981). Organizational leadership: The case of the school superintendent. *Educational Administration Quarterly, 17*, 45–65.

Porter, L. W. (1961). A study of perceived need satisfactions in bottom and middle management jobs. *Journal of Applied Psycholgoy, 45*, 1–10.

Porter, L. W. (1962). Job attitudes in management: I. Perceived deficiencies in need fulfillment as a function of job level. *Journal of Applied Psychology, 46*, 375–384.

Porter, L. W. (1963). Job attitudes in management: II. Perceived importance of needs as a function of job level. *Journal of Applied Psychology, 47*, 141–148.

Porter, L. W., & Lawler, E. E., III. (1968). *Managerial attitudes and performance.* Homewood, II: Dorsey.

Pulvino, C. A. F. (1979). *Relationship of principal leadership behavior to teacher motivation and innovation.* Unpublished doctoral dissertation, University of Wisconsin, Madison.

Ratsoy, E. W. (1973). Participative and hierarchical management of schools: Some emerging generalizations. *Journal of Educational Administration, 11*, 161–170.

Rice, A. W. (1978). *Individual and work variables associated with principal job satisfaction.* Unpublished doctoral dissertation, University of Alberta, Edmonton.

Roberts, K. H., & Glick, W. (1981). The job characteristics approach to task design: A critical review. *Journal of Applied Psychology, 66*, 193–217.

Rutter, M., Maugham, B., Mortimore, P., Ouston, J., & Smith, A. (1979). *Fifteen thousand hours: Secondary schools and their effects on children.* Cambridge, MA: Harvard University Press.

Salancik, G. R., & Pfeffer, J. (1977). An examination of need-satisfaction models of job attitudes. *Administrative Science Quarterly, 22*, 427–456.

Schmidt, F. L. (1973). Implications of a measurement problem for expectancy theory research. *Organizational Behavior and Human Performance, 10*, 243–251.

Schmidt, G. L. (1976). Job satisfaction among secondary school administrators. *Educational Administration Quarterly, 17*, 68–86.

Schneider, B., & Alderfer, C. P. (1973). Three studies of measures of need satisfaction in organizations. *Administrative Science Quarterly, 18*, 489–505.

Schneider, J. M., Glasheen, J. D., & Hadley, D. W. (1979). Secondary school participation, institutional socialization, and student achievement. *Urban Education, 14*, 285–302.

Schwab, D. P., Olian-Gottlieb, J. D., & Heneman, H. G., III, (1979). Between-subjects expectancy theory research: A statistical review of studies predicting effort and performance. *Psychological Bulletin, 86*, 139–147.

Sergiovanni, T. (1967). Factors which affect satisfaction and dissatisfaction of teachers. *Journal of Educational Administration, 5*, 66–82.

Silver, P. (1983). *Educational administration: Theoretical perspectives on practice and research.* New York: Harper & Row.

Sims, H. P., Jr., & Szilagyi, A. D. (1976). Job characteristic relationships: Individual and structural moderators. *Organizational Behavior and Human Performance, 17*, 211–230.

Skinner, B. F. (1974). *About behaviorism.* New York: Knopf.

Smircich, L. (1983). Concepts of culture and organizational analysis. *Administrative Science Quarterly, 28*, 339–358.

Smith, P. C. (1967). The development of a method of measuring satisfaction: The Cornell studies. In E. A. Fleishman (Ed.), *Studies in personnel and industrial psychology* (pp. 343–350). Homewood, IL: Dorsey.

Smith, P. C., Kendall, L. M., & Hulin, C. L. (1969). *The measurement of satisfaction in work and retirement.* Chicago: Rand-McNally.

Soliman, H. M. (1970). Motivation-hygiene theory of job attitudes: An empirical investigation and an attempt to reconcile both the one- and the two-factor theories of job attitudes. *Journal of Applied Psychology, 54*, 452–461.

Steers R. M. (1975). Task-goal attributes, achievement, and supervisory performance. *Organizational Behavior and Human Performance, 13*, 392–403.

Steers, R. M. & Porter, L. W. (1979). *Motivation and work behavior* (2nd ed.). New York: McGraw-Hill.

Steers, R. M. & Porter, L. W. (1983). *Motivation and work behavior* (3rd ed.). New York: McGraw-Hill.

Steinhoff, C. R. (1965). *Organizational climate in a public school system.* Washington, DC: U.S. Office of Education, Cooperative Program Contact No. OE–4–225, Project No. S–083, Syracuse University.

Stern, G. G. (1970). *People in context: Measuring person-environment in education and industry.* New York: John Wiley.

Tagiuri, R. (1968). The concept of organizational climate. In R. Tagiuri & G. H. Litwin (Eds.), *Organizational climate: Explorations of concept.* Boston: Division of Research, Graduate School of Business Administration, Harvard University.

Terborg, J. R., & Davis, G. A. (1982). Evaluation of a new method for assessing change to planned job redesign as applied to Hackman and Oldham's job characteristic model. *Organizational Behavior and Human Performance, 29*, 112–128.

Trusty F. M., & Sergiovanni, T. J. (1966). Perceived need deficiencies of teachers and administrators: A proposal for restructuring teacher roles. *Educational Administration Quarterly, 2*, 168–180.

Tyack, D., & Hansot, E. (1982). *Managers of virtue: Public school leadership in America, 1820–1980.* New York: Basic.

Vroom, V. H. (1964). *Work and motivation.* New York: John Wiley.

Wagstaff, L. H. (1969). *The relationship between administrative systems and interpersonal needs of teachers.* Unpublished doctoral dissertation, University of Oklahoma, Norman, OK.

Wahba, M. A., & Bridwell, L. G. (1973). Maslow reconsidered: A review of research on the need hierarchy theory. *Proceedings of the 33rd Annual meeting of the Academy of Management* (pp. 514–520).

Wahba, M. A., & Bridwell, L. G. (1976). Maslow reconsidered: A review of research on the need hierarchy theory. *Organizational Behavior and Human Performance, 15*, 212–240.

Waller, W. (1932). *The sociology of teaching.* New York: John Wiley.

Watkins, J. F. (1968). The OCDQ-An application and some implications. *Educational Administration Quarterly, 4*, 46–60.

Weber, G. (1971). *Inner city children can be taught to read: Four successful schools.* Occasional Paper 18. Washington, DC: Council for Basic Education.

Willower, D. J. (1977). Schools and pupil control. In D. A. Erickson (Ed.), *Educational organization and administration.* Berkeley, CA: McCutchan.

Willower D. J., Eidell, T. L., & Hoy, W. K. (1967). *The school and pupil control ideology.* University Park, PA: Pennsylvania State University.

Willower, D. J., & Heckert, J. W. (1977). *Teacher pupil control ideology-behavior congruence and job satisfaction.* Paper presented at the annual meeting of the American Educational Research Association, New York.

Willower, D. J., & Jones, R. G. (1963). When pupil control becomes an institutional theme. *Phi Delta Kappan, 45*, 107–109.

Wolcott, H. F. (1973). *The man in the principal's office: An ethnography*. New York: Holt, Rinehart, & Winston.

Wynne, E. A. (1980). *Looking at schools: Good, bad and indifferent.*

Lexington, MA: Heath.

Zaremba, J. P. (1978). *Relationship of teacher motivation to innovativeness and job satisfaction*. Unpublished doctoral dissertation, University of Wisconsin, Madison.

CHAPTER 15

Decision Making

Suzanne E. Estler

INTRODUCTION

Decision–making processes in educational organization look and operate differently under different conditions. Some of these differences can be illustrated through simple cases.

1. The purchase of supplies and materials and scheduling of classes can typically be done relative to clear objectives, identification of alternatives and their consequences, and choice of the alternative that best meets the objectives. In large part, elements of these processes can be routinized through standard operating procedures. Standardized forms can be used to gather information or place orders because the task is such that relevant information can be clearly identified. The computer can be used to analyze information since the issues are clear. The information can be passed through fixed and regular reporting channels because it is clear who will need or use the information. The process is marked by task specialization and coordination; that is, a teacher typically identifies needed supplies and the business manager approves the purchase-ordering from the most cost-efficient source.

2. Revision of a high school history curriculum is more likely to call for discussion among history teachers and other relevant personnel. Such a discussion would likely be marked by shared goals, expertise, and information, with final choice based on con-

sensus. Once the relevant curricular decisions are made, implementation occurs both through the bureaucratic structure in, for example, the ordering of books and supplies, and under the professional autonomy of the teacher, for the classroom aspects. The emphasis in this case is on human interaction resulting in consensus among relative equals.

3. We can imagine another case involving initiation of a sex education curriculum that has drawn strong and conflicting community attention. Various groups, including subunits within the school, church-affiliated groups, and the ACLU, have different rationales for wanting or not wanting the curriculum. Individuals and groups join forces to pressure the school board and administrators to decide consistent with their particular interests. The goals are clear to the participants. However, these goals differ depending on the particular points of view and interests of the participants. The latter vary as well in the amount and sources of power they bring to bear on the process. The process is marked by the normality of conflict and the use of bargaining and compromise as varying interests attempt to achieve their desired ends.

4. Finally, there are situations where neither goals nor the means to achieve them are clear. On a daily basis, a classroom teacher decides on specific instructional strategies adapted (or not) to the needs of two dozen or more students. General school-board goals are not prioritized nor specific. They may include such diverse items as literacy, problem-solving skills, good citizenship, the acquisition of good work habits, and social skills. On a given morning the teacher has had a domestic disagreement prior to leaving home, a phone call from

Consultant/reviewers: Jane Hannaway, Princeton University; and Dale Mann, Teachers College, Columbia University[1]

an upset parent, a sick child, disruption among students when attending to the sick child, notice that the principal will observe the class that afternoon to show a district administrator the innovative teaching occurring in the school, and a notice that a film ordered for the class had arrived in the resource center. As the students go to lunch, the teacher ponders the allocation of time for the afternoon. The general school board and building goals offer minimal operational direction for the teacher.

Each of these examples poses decision problems under different conditions. The research related to decision making reflects a number of different assumptions applicable to varying decision conditions. This chapter evaluates past research and future directions in order to assess the degree to which various models have, or might, serve to improve decision making in schools and school systems. Specifically, we want to address the question of how well various models expand our knowledge of decision making and the degree to which they provide useful implications for practice. Consistent with other commentaries, the emphasis is not on which model is "right," but on how each helps to identify different aspects and applications of decision-making processes (Allison, 1971; Bolman & Deal, 1984; Elmore, 1978; Peterson, 1976).

From the turn of the century to the present, the literature on decision making in education has been successively and cumulatively built on assumptions of choice based on the following:

1. rational calculation to achieve specified goals within a highly integrated bureaucratic structure (rational-bureaucratic);
2. consensus among relevant participants to achieve shared goals (participatory);
3. bargaining among interest groups and coalitions to maximize their separate goals (political); and
4. the confluence of streams of choice opportunities, participants, problems, and solutions at a given point in time and under conditions of ambiguity in goals, technology, and participation (organized anarchy).

The first of the models reflecting these assumptions, the rational-bureaucratic, provided the normative base for the development of modern school systems during the industrial revolution. The second, the participatory, reflected both democratic and professional norms dating to the work of Mary Parker Follett and the general reaction to the impersonality of scientific management beginning in the 1920s (Gross, 1964). The third, a political perspective, began to appear in the 1960s when federal court decisions, legislation, and regulation and demands for community participation in school policy made the realities of multiple demands on school goals impossible to ignore. Finally, the contextual, or organized-anarchy perspective, appeared in the 1970s, when the hopes and promises for education's role in solving innumerable social problems in the 1960s proved unrealistic despite the committed efforts of policy makers and educators across the country. The organized-anarchy perspective made the leap beyond assumptions of goal-driven behavior to address observations of decision-making reality left unexplained by traditional models. In so doing, it addressed the limits to the power of an individual decision maker in dealing with a complex world only partially understood and only partially within his or her control.

Although these perspectives emerged successively, each is very much alive in current literature. Viewed in historical context, these various models have served to inform subsequent ones. Thus, over time, rather than a denial of prior thinking, successive models have re-integrated elements of earlier traditions in new ways, yielding fuller explanations for the reality of educational decision making. Furthermore, earlier traditions have become modified to reflect interaction with newer perspectives. This evolution has produced a number of substantial shifts in the decision-making literature over time.

1. Models are moving from normative or prescriptive formulas for decision-making processes to descriptive theories with greater focus on explaining and predicting the everyday realities of educational decision making.
2. The view of the role of goals in decision making is shifting from that of a precondition and driving force for choice to a more complex one where goals may serve a number of purposes but are not necessarily a precondition to choice.
3. The view of the decision-making context is shifting from that of an exclusively tightly coupled, integrated structure insulated from its environment to that of a structure varying in the looseness of the coupling among its components, many of which are highly vulnerable to the outside environment.
4. The view of the decision maker has become fuller. From the impersonal rational actor functioning in terms of a specified role, the newer views reflect a sometimes fallible and sometimes heroic human being subject to competing role demands, tradition, duty, experiential learning, human affect, and a need for meaning in life.
5. The normative view of decision making itself has shifted from one associated primarily with science and technology to one often associated with art and drama.

THEORETICAL THEMES IN EDUCATIONAL DECISION MAKING

Each of these shifts reflects a movement toward greater congruence between theory and practice. In this section each of the perspectives underlying these shifts is reviewed in greater depth. Attention is paid to the historical context from which they emerged, the assumptions and key concepts associated with them, and the nature of related research supporting them.

Rational-Bureaucratic

The rational-bureaucratic view of decision making has its roots in the development of modern schooling during the Industrial Revolution. Schools were faced with unprecedented urban growth, perceived meddling by lay boards in school affairs, and questions of efficiency in school management by growing, powerful business communities. Under these pressures, the tenets of "scientific management" and professionalization provided a basis for school administrators to lay claim to autonomy in the administration of schools (Callahan, 1962; Cuban, 1984; Tyack, 1974). The distinction between the "politics" of policy setting at the board level and the internal "administration" of school systems was clearly an artificial one in practice, for administrators were not independent of community pressures or goal-setting processes. Yet the facade of the distinction stood well after it had fallen in the private sector. It survived because it served to protect both the internal functioning of school systems from the buffeting of the political environment and the influence of administrators who headed them (Mann, 1975).

A number of authors equate administration in education with rational-bureaucratic decision making (Campbell, Corbally, & Nystrand, 1974; Gregg, 1957, Griffiths, 1959). These authors only partially reflect the scientific-management heritage in educational administration. They more thoroughly represent the emphasis on developing theory and related empirical research in educational administration that grew out of the Kellogg Foundation Cooperative Program in Educational Administration (CPEA) in the 1950s (Griffiths, 1969). In its concern for improving the quality of educational administration, the CPEA sought to bring the best of the behavioral sciences to the study of schools. Decision making was an attractive target for such study because it incorporated work from economics, sociology, political science, and psychology, among others (Dill, 1964). Despite relatively limited empirical research related to the application and effectiveness of the rational-bureaucratic model, its assumptions continue to dominate the literature, such as the text by Hoy and Miskel (1982), to which aspiring administrators are exposed.

Assumptions

The rational view assumes decisions are the outcome of choice among alternatives with regard to objectives. Spelled out more fully, the steps include the specification of goals and objectives with a ranking based on organizational values (preferences), identification of alternatives, evaluation of the consequences of alternatives, and choice based on goal optimization. This view assumes structural aspects when placed in the context of a bureaucracy marked by task specialization, a formal control system, high integration with component parts contributing in separate ways to the achievement of organizational goals with decision-making responsibility at the apex of the hierarchy, and a closed system buffered from the environment (Firestone & Herriott, 1981; Simon, 1976; Weber, 1947). Implicit in the structural assumptions are the use of clear rules for organizational roles and behavior, separation of personal passions and interests from the formal work role, and activity in support of centralized decision making at the apex of the hierarchy (e.g., information, communication, and coordination).

Though this perspective deals structurally with organizational decision making, it does so as though decisions were made by a single rational actor. Through assumptions related to common preferences, goals, and knowledge, groups of individuals who may be involved in decision making are still viewed as acting as one (Allison, 1971).

Research

Corwin (1981) notes an interesting puzzle regarding the literature on organizations: "Writer after writer seems to believe that everyone *else* assumes that organizations are actually coordinated rationally in accordance with Weber's ideal type bureaucracy" (p. 270). The literature related to decision making reflects this puzzle. Despite normative literature based on rational bureaucratic assumptions (Cunningham, 1982; Hoy & Miskel, 1982; Odiorne, 1979), empirical research has been more focused on the problems implicit in the idealized model. The model has profoundly affected the research in providing a framework for highlighting key issues related to decision making such as centralization, rules, specialization, and authority (Anderson, 1968; Corwin, 1970; Firestone & Herriott, 1981; Lortie, 1969; Meyer & Rowan, 1978).

The research has identified a number of problems associated with the pure application of the rational-bureaucratic model including, the following.

Goals   Central goals are multiple and too general for

guiding school-level decisions, making them subject to competing interpretations and prioritization (Firestone & Herriott, 1981; Mann, 1975; Sieber, 1975). Assumptions of goal-driven behavior do not explain elements of decision-making behavior that is not goal driven (Corwin, 1970; March & Olsen, 1976; Perrow, 1982).

Participation The rational-bureaucratic model deals with participation based on the formal structure of the organizations. It does not deal effectively, however, with the effects of human attributes on the behavior of participants (Corwin, 1970), nor with the competing demands on the attention of participants that affect the nature of their involvement in a given decision (March & Olsen, 1976; Weiner, 1976). Studies dealing with the conflict between bureaucratic and professional orientations have been particularly important in identifying some of the problems related to participation (Corwin, 1970; Lortie, 1969). Studies such as these draw on the theoretical base provided by Getzels and Guba (1957) in defining the school as a social system characterized by both nomothetic (structural) and idiographic (individual psychological) dimensions (Griffiths, 1969).

Information Work in the more general literature of organizations discusses limitations to human rationality in decision making, focusing specifically on the limitations to human information processing (March & Simon, 1958; Simon, 1976). More recent literature deals as well with organizational limitations to information access and processing (Estler, 1980; Feldman & March, 1981; Kennedy, 1984; Lindblom & Cohen, 1979).

Structure and Technology Educational organizations do not appear to fit totally into the assumptions of a tightly integrated hierarchy. Although schools are formally characterized by a hierarchy of authority, decisions related particularly to the technical core of schooling, that is, teaching and learning, occur within the classroom with relatively loose coupling with the formal structure (Meyer & Rowan, 1978). Despite the trappings of standardization such a syllabuses, curriculums, materials, and schedules, teaching itself is a relatively unstandardized activity with ambiguity in outcome measurement (Willower, 1982). In other words, the multiplicity of goals, differences among students, and lack of clarity in what produces a "more educated" student lends difficulty to the assessment of success or failure.

The persistence of the rational-bureaucratic tradition suggests it has served a basic function in the field. Some of that function may be, as more recent literature suggests, largely symbolic. The image of scientific management has helped protect the internal functioning of the educational enterprise from outside meddling; it provides a kind of legitimation by providing the appearance of rationality to processes necessarily surrounded by ambiguity; it lends meaning to the lives of participants who live in a world valuing rationality; and it provides a sense of order to participants in an environment that is often disorderly (March, 1982; Meyer & Rowan, 1978).

Perhaps, most simply, rational-bureaucratic assumptions accurately reflect the context of many educational decisions. School systems can, in fact, be seen as formal hierarchies with clear chains of command and defined responsibilities. Many decision problems faced by those bureaucracies can be characterized in terms of clearly defined goals, knowable alternatives, and identifiable consequences for those alternatives. Particularly tasks typically considered as managerial can be defined in those terms, such as the development and monitoring of budgets, ordering of supplies, formal hiring processes, facility maintenance, scheduling, and development of new facilities. In these areas the normative tools reflecting rational-bureaucratic assumptions, such as management by objectives (MBO), management information systems, and associated models for decision analysis, are useful to the administrator in providing a structure for decision making that is explainable, sensible, and efficient in the use of staff time and organizational resources.

Application of rational-bureaucratic assumptions becomes more problematic, and can produce organizational pathology, under conditions (fitting many educational decisions) that do not meet those assumptions. Wise (1983), for example, discusses the dangers of "hyperrationalization" in educational organizations as a result of attempts to impose rational standards on nonrational processes.

Whereas the rational-bureaucratic approach is the most expansive in viewing the purpose of administration as decision making, it provides the narrowest view of decision making in the specific variables it defines. By defining decision making as rational choice made at the apex of a hierarchy, it does not deal effectively with multiple and ambiguous goals, multiple interests and participants, scarce or inaccessible information, and quirks of human nature, all often observed in reality.

Participatory

Consensual views of decision making in formal organizations share many assumptions with rational-bureaucratic models. Assumptions of shared goals, goal-driven choice based on information, professional expertise, and organizational structure make participatory models a subset of rational-bureaucratic models. Although later discussion in this chapter will so treat participatory models, the ongoing tension between bureaucratic and professional values in educational organizations, reflected in the research and at bargaining tables, calls for separate discussion.

Like the rational-bureaucratic model, the literature related to participatory decision making has, historically, been largely normative in nature. Based on the history of schooling and claims to professionalism among teachers, the theme of participatory decision making has continued to re-emerge at various times since the turn of the century (Cuban, 1984). More recently, the tension between bureaucratic and professional values related to school decision making has been identified in empirical studies reflecting the movement toward unionization in the 1960s (Corwin, 1970; Lortie, 1969) and in later analyses of the effects of unionization (Mitchell, Kerchner, Erck, & Pryor, 1981).

Perhaps more than any other tradition within the decision-making literature, the participatory model is rooted more in values and beliefs than in empiricism. Greenberg (1975) categorizes the literature related to participatory decision making into four major schools of thought reflecting different value orientations: (a) the management school, valuing participation as a means for increasing productivity; (b) the humanistic psychology school, valuing participation based on ethics and human growth potential; (c) the democratic school, valuing participation as an end in itself; and (d) the radical left, valuing participation as a means of educating participants toward a revolutionary consciousness. In each case, the benefits of participation are viewed as given rather than as an empirical question.

Despite the limited empirical support linking participation and decision outcomes, the continuing tensions created by the conflicting values implicit in bureaucratic and professional authority make questions related to participatory decision making important practical and research concerns.

Assumptions

Participatory decision making assumes decisions are the outcome of consensus among relevant participants. Typically applied to professional settings, organizational preconditions for consensual decision making include shared goals or values, influence based on professional expertise, and reason among participants. The model places high emphasis on communication and status equalization among participants. The organization is viewed as a closed system (Scott, 1981). Thus, decisions are still assumed to be goal optimizing, but the emphasis is on human processes rather than on structure to reach them (Baldridge, 1971; Bolman & Deal, 1984; Slater & Bennis, 1964).

These assumptions suggest that participatory decision processes are most applicable to professional organizations and professional work units within large organizations. Thus, the revision of the history curriculum in the second example reflects this perspective. There, peers with professional expertise reached consensus through the sharing of information and expertise.

Research

Reviews of research related specifically to the relationship between participation and decision outcomes consistently note ambiguity or nonsupport for related hypotheses (Conway, 1984; Dunn & Swieczek, 1977; Giaquinta, 1973; Locke & Schweiger, 1979). Much of the work in this area focuses on factors affecting teacher participation, taking the benefits of participation as a given (Bridges, 1967). Firestone (1977) found that standard operating procedures and unequal distribution of time and skills between administrators and teachers are barriers to teacher participation in decision making. The question of benefits may lie not in direct effects on decision outcomes but in indirect effects associated with morale and satisfaction (Duke, Showers, & Imber, 1980; Hoy & Miskel, 1982). Even this assumption, however, is subject to conflicting research conclusions. The weakness of positive results when found and of methodological questions related to much of the research leave many questions related to the effects of participation still very much in need of further research (Firestone & Herriott, 1981).

As a model to explain decision-making processes in organizations, the participatory model has yet to prove itself except under limited conditions. It does not deal with external influences nor aspects of structure and bureaucratic authority that affect the reality of most educational decision problems. However, in the normative focus on the values underlying participation, questions of participatory decision making cannot be ignored. Though rational models deal with decision-making processes in terms of their relationship to outcomes, work that will be discussed later deals with other ways in which to view decision making. These later views take into account the importance of beliefs, symbols, and unintended consequences of the process itself. Within such a framework, participatory decision making and the associated research issues take on a new light.

Political

As illustrated by the case of the conflict-ridden sex-education curriculum described at the beginning of this chapter, not all educational decisions fit within a closed system framework or a neatly structured hierarchy of authority. Outside interests with no hierarchical authority can and do influence school decision making.

The political model takes into account competing, and often equally legitimate, interests; formal and informal power; and the effect of the external environment on internal processes.

The political view of decision making in education is a product of the 1950s and 1960s. The environment of the schools, traditionally buffered from the outside, became increasingly complex and volatile as a result of such divergent circumstances as the effects of the Supreme Court's *Brown* decision; the civil rights movement and related demands for decentralization and citizen participation in school policy; concerns about schooling triggered by the Soviet launch of Sputnik, resulting in federal legislation and funding affecting state and local levels; and teacher unionization (Atkin & House, 1981; Mosher, Hastings, & Wagoner, 1979). The high visibility of outside interest groups and constituencies made the fact of environmental influences and multiple goals irrefutable. Gross's (1958) study of influences on school-board and superintendents' decisions was important for empirically affirming this observation.

Mann (1975) and Wirt and Kirst (1982) discuss at length the application of a political-systems model to the analysis of educational policy. Taking political concepts to the organizational level, Allison (1971) articulated a bureaucratic-politics model for the analysis of intraorganizational decision-making processes in his important study of the Cuban missile crisis. Baldridge (1971) brought a similar, if less clearly developed, model to bear on decision making in his study of New York University.

Assumption

Assuming decision as the outcome of bargaining among competing interests, the political model remains rational in assuming intentionality on the part of participants. It differs from the rational-bureaucratic model in viewing organization coalitions with multiple goals and inconsistent preferences associated with various interests as opposed to unitary, overarching goals. Scarce resources and multiple interests set up a framework where conflict is the norm and where bargaining is the basic process producing decisions. The rules and channels specified through the formal structure define usual action channels, participants, and decision arenas where the political process occurs. Access to formal or informal power weights the degree of influence an individual or group brings to the bargaining process. Position authority and budgets represent examples of formal power; ability to mobilize a constituency and political clout within the community are examples of informal power. Structure further affects the process in influencing the perspective and information access of various actors in the process. Their positions affect their perceptions of priorities and problems (Allison, 1971). Decisions, often in response to deadline pressures, reflect compromise and tradeoffs aimed toward goal maximization of separate groups with differential access to power.

Research

Much of the research based on political assumptions has involved case studies of the policy process at the level where school systems intersect with external forces (Boyd, 1976; Fantini, Gittell, & Magett, 1970; Gittell, 1980; Peterson, 1976; Wirt, 1974). However, the notions have been extended into studies of intraorganizational decision-making processes, the focus of this review. The extension has occurred particularly in studies involving unionization and professionalization in schools.

Corwin's (1970) study of the relationship between bureaucracy and conflict resolution in 24 midwestern high schools in the early 1960s explicitly modified rational bureaucratic assumptions to recognize the effects of professional socialization and external influences on internal decision-making processes. Mitchell et al. (1981) and Kerchner and Mitchell (1981) specifically focused on the effects of collective bargaining on school management and policy in their in-depth study of collective bargaining in California and Illinois. They found that the centralization promoted by the bargaining process modified the decision-making authority available to school principals and other middle managers. Johnson (1983) elaborated on this theme by identifying variations in principal accommodation to the reduction in formal authority based on informal factors including teacher interests, educational consequences, administrative leadership, and staff allegiance. Similar results were found in a study of discretionary decision making in the Chicago schools by Morris, Crowson, Hurwitz, & Porter-Gehrie (1981). In each of these studies, recognition of multiple interests and both formal and informal structural effects allowed the researchers to see outcomes that could have been overlooked if they had employed rational-bureaucratic assumptions, which view the organization as a unitary actor.

These kinds of studies have been important in moving the decision-making literature from more normative approaches toward those addressing the very real balancing of multiple interests involved in educational decision making. While taking structural elements into account, they go beyond rational-bureaucratic and consensual models in viewing school decision making in the context of multiple external influences and the exercise of formal and informal power. Combining a range of methods, they capture the complexity of decision making, often raising questions that are simply not addressed through other models.

The political model provides a clearer understanding of the process of decision making among competing interests, as in the selection of a school superintendent. Although the rational model may provide a useful means for structuring the process, such as identification of job requirements or candidates or the analysis of information regarding a pool of candidates, the action within that framework is likely to be political in nature. Various participants representing different interests within the community and the schools will bargain about the desired attributes and the job description. The relative power participants bring with them may affect the outcome in the job description and the final choice, after a process of coalition building and tradeoffs. At the level of interest groups, the process will be rational in terms of maximizing goals under constraints. By opening up the rational model to an open-systems perspective and recognizing multiple goals, the political model expands the vision of the participant in understanding the decision process and planning a more realistic strategy.

The normative implications of the political model will not, however, prepare the practitioner for surprises in the choice process resulting from nonrational aspects of human behavior and the effects of beliefs, competing problems, solutions, and demands on participant time. Some key participants may be involved by virtue of duty, finding the occasion one in which interests may be discovered; particularly important actors may be absent by virtue of crisis or illness at particularly important junctures; and others with no identifiable power base may accrue influence in the final choice simply by being there most often. Mitchell et al. (1981), for example, found both teachers and management had strong and different beliefs about what constituted a "good contract." These beliefs were often rooted in external sources unrelated to their respective interests, such as prior training, personal beliefs, settlements in surrounding districts, and contracts in the private sector. Elements not brought to attention through a rational view of the decision process nevertheless suggest a certain reality that can have profound effects on outcomes. These realities, unexplained by the political model, spurred the empirical research and theory development, yielding nonrational views of organizations and decision making.

Organized Anarchy

The teacher planning afternoon activities in our fourth example was faced with several factors that could influence her decision: parental concerns expressed in a morning phone call regarding a return to basics; an unanticipated visit by the principal, who wished to demonstrate the innovative teaching occurring in the school to a district administrator; the arrival of a film relevant to the scheduled social studies class; and signs that the class's conduct was less than optimal that day. The particular set of problems, solutions, and participants that could affect the choice of teaching strategy was highly contextual. It could be very different on another day. The specific mix coming together at this particular time may lead to a choice that would not be the same if the teacher were faced with a similar problem on another day. The final outcome might be more likely to reflect how an innovative teacher or disciplined students are expected to appear rather than conscious attention to optimizing student learning. Furthermore, an optimizing decision becomes unknowable given that there is no single "right way" to teach social studies and limited understanding of how any single method influences learning outcomes. The example demonstrates elements of decision making under ambiguity in goals, technology, and participation.

These circumstances do not fit easily into any of the rational perspectives on decision making. Consistent with a growing body of literature that may be labeled *postrational*, the organized-anarchy view considers decision making not only relative to rational means-ends chains but, in terms of symbolism, myths and rituals (March, 1982; Meyer & Rowan, 1977; Weick, 1982). Decision making is viewed as a process having many effects unrelated to outcomes rather than as a technology focused only on goal achievement. It is a point of view suggesting that decision making should be understood and described more as we would understand art or poetry than as we would science and technology (March, 1982).

Among other things, March and Olsen (1976, p. 11) describe the choice process as providing an occasion for

> executing standard operating procedures and fulfilling role expectations, duties, or earlier commitments;
>
> defining truth and virtue, during which the organization discovers or interprets what happens to it, what it has been doing, what it is going to do, and what justifies its actions;
>
> distributing glory and blame for what has happened in the organization, thus, becoming an occasion for exercising, challenging, or reaffirming friendship, trust relationships, antagonism, power, or status relationships;
>
> expressing and discovering "self-interest" and "group interest" for socialization and an occasion for recruiting (to organizational positions or informal groups);

having a good time, for enjoying the pleasures of taking part in a choice situation.

Feldman and March (1981) acknowledge the importance of instrumental aspects of choice but see choice also as "an arena for developing and enjoying an interpretation of life and one's position." The rituals of choice, then, provide meaning in an ambiguous world. As such, the legitimacy of those processes to the organization and its environment are important for lending meaning. Thus, consistent with Edelman (1964) and Meyer and Rowan (1978), they view the trappings of rationality associated with decision making as symbolically important in a society placing high value on rationality.

By focusing on the significance of the process itself and by recognizing the loose coupling and even reversal between goals and action, this perspective moves beyond rational assumptions of goal-based decision making. These general ideas form the background for a contextual model of choice to describe decision making under conditions of ambiguity in goals, technology, and participation, labeled a *garbage-can model* (Cohen & March, 1974; Cohen, March, & Olsen, 1972; March & Olsen, 1976). The model focuses specifically on decision making in educational organizations. Its full development incorporates many familiar elements of rational approaches to decision making such as structure, standard operating procedures, participants, and goals. However, they are put together in a different way, representing a conceptual leap from the assumption that decision making is a process for achieving goals to one in which decision making is often a process only loosely connected to organizational outcomes or individual intention.

The garbage-can and organized-anarchy terminology is most likely useful as vivid metaphor. However, the literature that has evolved in response to much of this work often shows misunderstanding of the model, perhaps in response to the labels. For example, it has been simplified to "anarchy" (Firestone & Herriott, 1982), and described as "totally random" (Kennedy, 1984). In contrast, March (1982) argues that rather than chaos, "there is order, but it is not the conventional order" (p. 5), and elaborates the relationship to temporal ordering of problems and solutions and the role of rules and routines in decision outcomes.

Assumptions

The model addresses choice processes under conditions of ambiguity in organizations that the authors label "organized anarchies" (Cohen et al., 1972; Cohen & March, 1974; March & Olsen, 1976). These are organizations characterized by (a) problematic goals involving inconsistent and ill-defined preferences; (b) unclear technology in which processes for producing organizational outcomes, such as a more educated student, are unclear; and (c) fluid participation by decision makers in response to competing demands on attention and energy. They identify public, educational, and illegitimate organizations as conspicuous examples of organized anarchies, while noting that all organizations demonstrate these characteristics in part part of the time (March & Olsen, 1976).

In a garbage-can process, decisions are the product of the confluence of four relatively independent streams at a given time:

1. *Choice opportunities:* occasions in which the organization is expected to produce a decision, such as the signing of contracts, hiring, firing, approval of budgets, and allocation of responsibilities. They represent metaphorical garbage cans, which attract available problems, solutions, and participants, depending on availability and the existence and attractiveness of competing choice opportunities.

2. *Problems:* the concerns of people inside and outside the organization, including nonchoice-related issues such as family problems, career and status, interpersonal conflicts, and ideology.

3. *Solutions:* somebody's product or an answer looking for a question, such as computers, a management information system, a new employee, and, in the world at large, Velcro.

4. *Participants:* those entering and leaving a decision arena as dictated by competing demands on time, "rights of participation" as determined by organizational structure, norms, interest, and duty.

The choice process is one in which problems, solutions, and participants constantly move from one choice opportunity to another. Thus, the nature of the choice, the time it takes, and the problems it solves all depend on the intersection of the mix of available choices, the mix of problems that have access to the organization, the mix of solutions looking for problems, and the competing demands on decision makers at a specific time.

Elements of structure influence outcomes of the garbage-can process by (a) affecting the time pattern of the arrival of problems, choices, solutions, or decision makers; (b) determining the allocation of energy by potential participants in the decision; and (c) establishing linkages among the various streams (March & Olsen, 1976).

The model further defines three kinds of decision styles that can occur through the garbage-can process: oversight, flight, and resolution. This terminology is frequently confusing because it applies not to the choices but the problems in the garbage can. Thus, oversight occurs when potentially confounding problems are attached to other choices and energy is available to make the choice at the time it is activated. In other words, potential problems do not "see" the new choice, allowing it to be made without complication. Returning to the example, oversight might occur if the irate parent of the morning phone call had afternoon commitments preventing his intended visit to the teacher to further vent his concerns about basic education.

Flight occurs when a long-standing problem leaves a choice for a more "attractive" choice, allowing a decision to be made that incidentally does not solve that particular problem. A high-level meeting to discuss curriculum innovation could, in our example, call the district administrator away from the intended visit to the classroom, allowing the choice about teaching activities for the afternoon to be made independently from the issue of innovative teaching.

Finally, resolution occurs when a choice solves problems attached to it. A teaching strategy that at once calms the class, thus taking care of discipline, and provides an example of new teaching methods, thus satisfying the principal's problem, would represent resolution in the example.

Research

There is irony in the garbage-can model in that it could be considered a rational (logical, deductive) model to explain nonrational processes. Based on college and university data, it was originally tested through a computer simulation, yielding a number of observations about the process (Cohen et al., 1972):

1. Flight and oversight are far more typical decision styles than resolution, which is more likely where flight is severely limited or under a few conditions of light load.

2. The process is extremely sensitive to variations in load. Increased energy-load generally increases problem activity, decision maker activity, decision difficulty, and the uses of flight and oversight. Given load variations dictated by the varying pace within the school year, this observation may explain why the same choice may see a very different response at different times of the year.

3. Decision makers and problems tend to track each other through choices. This observation may explain why participants with very different roles continually see one another in different arenas as they pursue problems of mutual interest.

4. The decision process is sharply interactive. Many outcomes are produced by the particular time phasing of choices, problems, and participant availability.

5. Important problems are more likely to be solved than unimportant ones. Early-arriving problems are more likely to be solved that later ones.

6. Important choices are less likely to resolve problems than unimportant ones, and they are more likely made by oversight and flight. Unimportant choices are more often made by resolution. This observation reflects the fact that important choices, such as the selection of a superintendent, often have to be made. Whereas the choice may attract difficult problems, such as district goals, collective-bargaining issues, staff relationships, and philosophical differences, the choice will ultimately be made without solving these problems. Unimportant choices may simply be sufficiently low in visibility that they do not attract irrelevant problems that could confound the decision.

7. Choices of intermediate importance are almost always made. Choice failures that do occur are primarily among the most and least important choices. Least important choices may simply get lost in the face of more pressing demands on the system; the most important choices are more likely to draw the most "garbage" interfering with a choice.

The simulation study was followed by a series of case studies, mostly within educational organizations or policy arenas within the United States and Scandinavia, exploring aspects of the garbage-can process. Twelve different cases by 10 authors were presented in connection with March and Olsen's (1976) major treatment of the theory. The cases dealt with issues such as the perception of power, socialization, interpretation of organizational history, reorganization, factors related to participation, deadlines, status, norms, and ideology in the context of the garbage-can model. Sproull, Weiner, and Wolf's (1978) study of the National Institute of Education followed in this tradition. Especially taken as a whole, these cases show the power of this perspective in making sense of behaviors and processes that would be unexplained variance in or simply unidentified by other models. At the same time, they suffer the weaknesses of generalizability inherent in case studies.

Several other studies that have not come out of the organized-anarchy tradition per se address some of the assumptions of the model. Studies of administrative activities in educational organizations are consistent in identifying the demands on the administrator as fragmented, rapid fire, and difficult to prioritize (Kmetz & Willower, 1982; Morris et al., 1981; Sproull, 1981). Morris et al., 1981), for example, noted specifically that the fragmented and unpredictable workday of the 16 principals in their study was not conducive to either ordered thoughtful decision making or ranked priorities.

A number of recent studies (Chaffee, 1980; Firestone & Herriott, 1981; and Padgett, 1980) have specified and tested comparative models, using organized anarchy as one of several. This direction of research is promising for identifying empirical conditions under which one or another of various decision models may operate. Firestone and Herriott (1981), for example, found that high schools were more likely to resemble organized anarchies than were elementary schools, which more closely resembled the structural characteristics of the rational bureaucracy. High schools, which were typically departmentalized and characterized by more diverse goals, showed looser coupling among components.

As a normative model, the notion of a garbage-can decision process is discomforting. It is not neat or simple. It does not provide straightforward imperatives for action. But it does provide a picture that captures the contextual realities of decision processes. Unlike many of the reviewers of this model, I will not argue that it portrays a process of chaos. Yet the order that may be perceived here has limits.

The garbage-can model permits the practitioner to look at a given decision context in a broader way than do rational models while using many of the variables presented in those models. It suggests an order to things but an order that is situational. Thus, for example, the practitioner hoping to influence the choice of superintendent could look at (a) how the structure would affect participation in a given decision. (b) competing issues that might draw participants and problems to or from the superintendent choice, (c) personal agendas associated with individuals in the process, and (d) environmental influences that may affect problems and solutions associated with the choice and their interpretation. Such an analysis provides a basis for the development of a strategy for influencing the choice. It also acknowledges the limitations inherent in influencing final outcomes.

In some senses the preceding analysis deals in a rather traditional way with only a portion of the notions associated with garbage-can decision making. It directs attention to the decision or organizational outcome as the result of the process. Taken in a broader perspective, the model would direct the attention of both practitioner and researcher to effects of the process having little to do with organizational outcomes. Another view of the choice of superintendent is that of an organization ritual having important symbolic significance. The choice of participants in the process has effects separate from the decision outcome in signaling who in the district matters. The appearance of rationality in the process serves as a signal of technical competence and impartiality even if the reality of the process involves complex interests, competing goals, and some random events.

This perspective brings us back to a reinterpretation of the literature related to participatory decision making. Despite the limited support for the effects of shared decision making on effectiveness, this line of research and practice may remain so persistent because of effects undefined from rational perspectives. The organized-anarchy perspective draws attention to the symbolic role decision making plays for both individuals and groups in organizations. Inclusion in the process signals importance and status within the organization. Though educational organizations can be viewed as structured as hierarchical bureaucracies, educators have consistently defined themselves as professionals. As stated earlier, this has been a consistent argument for the exclusion of lay citizens from internal decision-making processes. However, exclusion of teachers from decision-making processes has the effect of challenging what Lortie (1969) calls the "myth of professionalism" in schools. Thus in many cases it is not the reality of participation that is important but the appearance of participation.

Given the conditions of decision making related to teaching and learning, the organized-anarchy perspective helps explain observations that the technical core of schooling is the area most subject to nonrational decision processes (Hannaway & Sproull, 1979; Meyer & Rowan, 1978). The student is, in effect, the product of schooling. The product enters, goes through a process, and becomes the output. The goals of the process are extensive and subject to differing interpretations—literacy, values, citizenship, intellectual development, problem-solving ability, work skills, and so forth—all meant to produce an "educated" person. Although we can measure changes in some of these goals from entry to exit, others defy clear measurement. Further, given environmental effects, we do not know the extent to which schooling produces given outcomes. Finally, our knowledge of human cognition is sufficiently limited that there is ambiguity regarding the processes producing those outcomes we can attribute to schooling. In other words, the goals are diverse and often ambiguous and the technology for achieving them unclear. Yet teachers and administrators daily juggle the contextual variables to make hundreds of decisions affecting students in ways that show stability over time.

DISCUSSION: APPLICATIONS AND IMPLICATIONS

The research and theory related to educational decision making has blossomed since Griffiths (1959) published

Table 15.1 Perspectives on Decision Making

	RATIONAL-BUREAUCRATIC	PARTICIPATORY	POLITICAL	ORGANIZED-ANARCHY
Organizing Concept:	Choice based on optimizing goals in the context of hierarchical system	Choice based on consensus . . . discussion to achieve common goals	Choice based on bargaining among interests	Choice is the outcome of the contemporaneous confluence of choice opportunities, problems, solutions, participants
View of Decision Making:	Organizational goal achievement	Organizational goal achievement	Interest-group goal achievement	Symbolism: reaffirmation of worth, competence and legitimacy; opportunity for discovery of goals
Organizational Preconditions:	Bureaucracy, centralization	Professionalism, equalization of status	Competing interests accentuated by scarce resources	Ambiguity in goals, technology, and participation
Role of Rationality:	Central to decision in both structure and process	Central at individual level with assumed effects on the organization	Central to the decision process at the interest-group level	Symbolically important but does not necessarily drive decision
View of Organization in Environment:	Closed system	Closed system	Open system	Open system with ambiguity in feedback
View of Structure:	Hierarchical, highly integrated	Assumed present but not central to decision process; establishes relevance of participation	Defines action channels, "rules of game," and participation	Defines access, roles, duty; loose coupling produces structural ambiguity
Role of Information:	Clarification of alternatives, consequences, feedback	Clarification of alternatives and consequences	Clarification of alternatives and consequences; persuasion and influence	Legitimation of decision process
Nature of Theory:	Normative	Normative	Descriptive	Descriptive

his major attempt to move work from a primarily normative enterprise to one reflecting solid theorizing and empirical research. His model of decision making drew heavily on the works of Barnard and Simon to illustrate the applicability of the social sciences to educational decision making.

Dill (1964) called for a continuation of interdisciplinary research but with particular attention to the nature of schools as organizations. He was concerned that concepts applied to educational decision making were derived from those developed for business and industry. He noted inherent ambiguities in mission and heterogeneity in composition as examples of elements of schools that should be considered in decision-making research. Dill's vision has to some extent been realized. Decision-making research originating with a focus on the specific characteristics of educational organizations has come, in the 1980s, to influence the research related to business and industry (Peters & Waterman, 1982).

Boyan (1982), in his thorough review of research in educational administration, notes the evolution in the range of images that are now applied to educational decision making. This chapter has detailed those images and metaphors that appear to have had the most

significant impact on the research on decision making in education. They are by no means the only views of decision making. Neither do they represent the only way to structure the literature. However, they do represent dominant themes that have emerged over time and illustrate some of the key variables in considering a variety of models. These variables and how they differ across the models discussed in the chapter are summarized in Table 15.1. The models are reviewed in terms of organizing concepts, views of decision making, organizational preconditions, the role of rationality, the view of the organization in relation to the environment, the view of structure, the role of information, and the normative or descriptive nature of the theory.

This chapter began with the question of how well these models expand our knowledge of educational decision making. Whereas individual sections have addressed this question relative to each model, Table 15.1 helps us to consider the aggregate effects of the models on our knowledge of decision making.

Beginning with the rational-bureaucratic and moving across the table to the organized-anarchy view, these models represent the evolution of thinking about educational decision making. That thinking has been very much a product of the political context of both schools and related academic research over time. For example, the rational-bureaucratic view evolved in the context of concerns for a theoretical base for research and practice in educational administration in order to lend the field greater legitimacy for graduate study (Gross, 1964).

The models have not supplanted one another but have been complementary in expanding the range of decision-making processes and variables that they explain. In combination, they acknowledge a more sophisticated understanding of the complexity of educational decision making and its role in organizational life. As new models and associated research have developed, earlier models have evolved to respond to some of the questions they raised. Thus, the more current research based on rational-bureaucratic assumptions, for example, has become less normative, more qualified, and often focused on variables suggested by newer models. Much of the attention to loose coupling in structure represents such an approach.

As schools have drawn increasing attention from scholars from different fields, research in educational decision making has become more interdisciplinary. From perspectives reflecting either sociological or psychological bases, newer research can genuinely be viewed as a product of the social sciences rather than a single discipline. This, too, has added to the richness of explanations for understanding decision making in schools and has, in turn, influenced the general field of decision research.

Perhaps as a consequence of the recent interdisciplinary nature of the research, and a common focus on the schools as a specific type of organization there seems to be an increasing confluence in thinking. This confluence is reflected in the increasing difficulty in categorizing current research and in signs of the development of a common language among scholars who focus on educational decision making. Where even a few years ago terms like *loose coupling* and *organized anarchy* generated competitive fervor, they seem to have become part of the language of educational decision making.

The study of decision making has reached a level of maturity such that we might expect to see more comparative studies across perspectives, more than those bound by a single view. Firestone and Herriott (1982), Chaffee (1980), and Padgett (1980) offer promising beginnings in this direction. Such comparative studies would allow more in-depth understanding of the similarities, as well as the differences, among various models. The discussion of the models seems to be moving from the earlier debates on superficialities of metaphors more to an extension of our understanding

of the basic processes they address. In particular, there is much we can learn about the conditions under which one model might be more applicable than another, and vice versa.

A second question raised at the beginning of this chapter was the degree to which the models provide useful implications for practice. Although each offers concrete guidance for decision makers, that guidance is conditional to specific circumstances. For example, the rational-bureaucratic model offers useful tools for decision making when goals are well defined and the means for achieving them well understood and where organizational components are well integrated. The political model helps in dealing with multiple goals and interests, again assuming a relatively integrated structure for implementing decisions once made. The garbage-can model is more effective for understanding decision making under conditions of ambiguity in goals, technology, and participation.

Over time, the prescriptions offered by each of the perspectives have become more contextual and realistic, in acknowledgment of the situational nature and ambiguities inherent in educational organizations. This condition is probably both a relief and a frustration to the practicing administrator. On the one hand, it may be a relief to see a breakdown in the previously existing discrepancy between rational decision-making theory and the realities of decision making among conflicting interests: a frenetic and fragmented work place, limited information, an unpredictable sequence of problems and solutions, and the ambiguity of goals, technology, and human nature. On the other hand, it may be frustrating to lose the security of straightforward recipes for rational decisions.

This suggests that in training administrators, we might replace recipes with skills in analysis of organizational dynamics and contexts. Though the ambiguities of educational decision making cannot be eliminated, they can be made more understandable and less threatening. By understanding a variety of approaches to decision making and the range of organizational conditions under which they may be applicable, the administrator can be better prepared to respond to, and even enjoy, organizational ambiguity and complexity.

Fortunately, many administrators have been ahead of the literature in realizing both rational and nonrational dimensions of decision making. However, the growing body of research particularly related to decision making under ambiguity can provide a framework for practicing administrators to understand, validate, and improve on what they are already doing to respond to and tolerate complexity. Finally, knowledge of this research can allow administrators to enter school systems with a more realistic sense of the possibilities for and limitations on their ability to guide and influence educational decision making.

A Note on the Diffusion of Ideas: Metaphorical Cautions

The literature related to decision making increasingly reflects research resulting in variations on or the development of new images of decision making and organizations (Boyan, 1982). Although images and metaphors can be valuable in providing simple conceptual frameworks, they and the words used to convey them can draw more attention than the complex organizational processes and assumptions they are meant to represent. The garbage-can model is an example at hand. Based on a complex, carefully developed set of theories, the images of the garbage can and organized anarchy startle readers into thinking about decision making in a different way. Yet this shift in thinking, in response to the images, often seems to be shaped at least partially by the images rather than the underlying theory.

An alternative metaphor for the garbage-can process may offer a clear example of the phenomenon. We can think of it as the "decision making as drama" metaphor. It shares the assumptions of the garbage-can model in viewing decisions as the outcome of the confluence of choice opportunities, participants, problems, and solutions at a given time. The setting is a large and active theater district. The degree of activity depends on a number of factors—the time of year, the degree to which the economy provides an audience with discretionary income, tastes of the public, and the range of scripts and producers. We can think of an organizational choice opportunity as a production within a single theater that draws participants (actors, directors, producers, stage designers, writers, and support personnel), problems (concerns for careers, quality, status and interpersonal relations, staging, the physical constraints of the theater, props, acoustics, etc.), and solutions associated with both individual participants.

The outcome of the process, or opening night and a full-scale production, looks fairly straightforward to the audience. But, the production, or outcome, could have looked quite different and still appear straightforward to the audience. The choice of script was affected by other productions, popular taste, and the producer's personal taste. Actors were a product of a market, personal tastes, and career concerns. They move from theater to theater depending on scripts and their own skills and interests and the tastes of the production staff. Perhaps most of all, the composition of the cast is constrained by possible actors' competing commitments. Thus, the cast of a given production is

the product of individuals acting in perceived rational ways but within a total system that may function within constraints that are less than rational in nature. To the actors, the drama itself assumes a life of its own. The same production, offered in different cities, may appear similar to the audience but represent a very different experience for the cast. The chemistry created by the mixture of problems, solutions, participants, and competing plays at a given point in time makes each production different. To the observer, the important variable is the final production. To the cast and production staff, the process of delivering the production is central and looks different to each participant. The outcome assumes very different, symbolic importance to each observer and participant, just as the outcome does in a garbage-can process. As with the garbage-can process, some problems get solved through the production, some do not, and others leave before the production opens, in some cases relieving an impediment to the production schedule.

Though the drama and garbage-can metaphors can address similar assumptions about decision-making processes, they conjure different images for the reader. Organizational processes viewed as garbage, as opposed to drama, elicit different emotional responses affecting the way the process is seen. The point of the analogy is not that authors should change their metaphors or that we should adopt yet another name for garbage-can processes. Instead, it is a reminder that we should see beyond any metaphor to the meaning and structure of the underlying assumptions. The literature, particularly responding to the garbage-can and organized-anarchy models and the notion of loose coupling, seems to be marked by a simple response to the metaphors that fails to envision the complexity of the assumptions.

NOTE

[1] In addition to the editor and consultant/reviewers, I am indebted to students at the University of Washington and the University of Maine at Orono for helpful comments in developing and improving this chapter. I am especially grateful to Bruce Haulman for his contributions to the conceptualization of the chapter and for research assistance.

REFERENCES

Allison, G. T. (1971) *Essence of decision: Explaining the cuban missile crisis*. Boston: Little, Brown.

Anderson, J. G. (1968). *Bureaucracy in education*. Baltimore, MD: Johns Hopkins University Press.

Atkin, J. M., & House, E. R. (1981). The federal role in curriculum development. *Educational Evaluation and Policy Analysis*, *3*(5), 5–36.

Baldridge, J. V. (1971). *Power and conflict in the university*. New

York: John Wiley.

Bolman, L. G., & Deal, T. E. (1984). *Modern approaches to understanding and managing organizations*. San Francisco: Jossey-Bass.

Boyan, N. J. (1982). The administration of educational organizations. In H. E. Mitzel, J. H. Best, & W. Rabinowitz (Eds.), *Encyclopedia of educational research* (5th ed.). New York: Macmillan.

Boyd, W. L. (1976). The public, the professionals, and educational policy making: Who governs? *Teachers College Record, 77*, 56.

Bridges, E. M. (1967). A model of shared decision making in the school principalship. *Educational Administration Quarterly, 3*, 49–61.

Callahan, R. E. (1962). *Education and the cult of efficiency*. Chicago: University of Chicago Press.

Campbell, R., Corbally, J. E., & Nystrand, R. O. (1983), *Introduction to educational administration*. Boston: Allyn and Bacon.

Chaffee, E. E. (1980). *Decision models in university budgeting*. Unpublished doctoral dissertation. Palo Alto, CA: Stanford University.

Cohen, M. D., & March, J. G. (1974). *Leadership and ambiguity: The American college president*. New York: McGraw-Hill.

Cohen, M. D., March, J. G., & Olsen, J. P. (1972). A garbage can model of organizational choice. *Administrative Science Quarterly, 17*, 1–25.

Conway, J. A. (1984). The myth, mystery and mastery of participative decision making in education. *Educational Administration Quarterly, 20*(3), 11–40.

Corwin, R. G. (1970). *Militant professionalism*. New York: Meredith.

Corwin, R. G. (1981). Patterns of organizational control and teacher militancy: Theoretical continuities in the idea of "loose coupling." In R. G. Corwin (Ed.), *Research in the sociology of education and socialization* (Vol. 2, pp. 261–291). Greenwich, CT: JAI.

Cuban, (1984). *How teachers taught*. New York Longman.

Cunningham, W. G. (1982). *Systematic planning for educational administration*. Palo Alto, CA: Mayfield.

Dill, W. R. (1964). Decision-making. In D. E. Griffiths (Ed.), *Behavioral science and educational administration*. The 63rd Year-book of the National Society for the Study of Education, Part 2 (pp. 199–222). Chicago: University of Chicago Press.

Duke, D. L., Showers, B. K., & Imber, M. (1980). Teachers and shared decision making: The costs and benefits of involvement. *Educational Administration Quarterly, 16*, 93–106.

Dunn, W. N., & Swierczek, F. W. (1977). Planned organizational change. Toward grounded theory. *Journal of Applied Behavioral Science, 13*(2), 135–157.

Edelman, M. (1964). *The symbolic uses of politics*. Urbana, IL: University of Illinois Press.

Elmore, R. (1978). Organizational models of social program implementation. In D. Mann (Ed.), *Making change happen* (pp. 185–223). New York: Teachers College Press, Columbia University.

Estler, S. E. (1980). Systematic analysis and university decision making: The case of sexual equity. Paper presented at the Annual Meeting of the Association for the Study of Higher Education, Washington, DC (ERIC No. ED 187 211).

Fantini, M., Gittell, M., & Magat, R. (1970). *Community control and the urban school*. New York: Praeger.

Feldman, M. S., & March, J. G. (1981). Information as signal and symbol. *Administrative Science Quarterly, 26*, 171–186.

Firestone, W. A. (1977). Participation and influence in the planning of educational change. *Journal of Applied Behavioral Science, 13*(2), 167–187.

Firestone, W. A., & Herriott, R. E. (1981). Images of organization and the promotion of educational change. In R. Corwin (Ed.), *Research in sociology of education and socialization* (Vol. 2, pp. 221–260). Greenwich, CT: JAI.

Firestone, W. A., & Herriott, R. E. (1982). Two images of schools as organizations: An explication and illustrative empirical test. *Educational Administration Quarterly, 18*(2), 39–59.

Getzels, J. W., & Guba, E. G. (1957, Winter). Social behavior and the administrative process. *School Review, 65*, 423–441.

Giaquinta, J. (1973). The process of change in schools. In F. N. Kerlinger (Ed.), *Review in education research* (Vol. 1). Itasca, IL: Peacock.

Gittell, M. 1980. *Limits to citizen participation: The decline of community organization*. Beverly Hills, CA: Sage.

Greenberg, E. S. (1975). The consequences of worker participation: A clarification of the theoretical literature. *Social Science Quarterly, 56*, 12–21.

Gregg, R. T. (1957). The administrative process. In R. F. Campbell & R. T. Gregg (Eds.), *Administrative behavior in education*. New York: Harper.

Griffiths, D. E. (1959). *Administrative theory*. New York: Appleton.

Griffiths, D. E. (1969). Administrative theory. In R. L. Ebel (Ed.), *Encyclopedia of educational research* (4th ed.). New York: Macmillan.

Gross, B. M. (1964). The scientific approach to administration. In D. E. Griffiths (Ed.), *Behavioral science and educational administration*. The 63rd Yearbook of the National Society for the Study of Education (Part 2, pp. 33–72). Chicago: University of Chicago Press.

Gross, N. (1958). *Who runs our schools?*. New York: John Wiley.

Hannaway, J., & Sproull, L. S. (1979). Who's running the show? Coordination and control in educational organizations. *Administrator's Notebook, 27*(9).

Hoy, W. K., & Miskel, C. G. (1982). *Educational administration: Theory, research and practice* (2nd ed.). New York: Random House.

Johnson, S. M. (1983). Teacher unions in schools: Authority and accommodation. *Harvard Educational Review, 53*(3), 309–326.

Kennedy, M. M. (1984). How evidence alters understanding and decisions. *Educational Evaluation and Policy Analysis, 6*(3), 207–226.

Kerchner, C. T. & Mitchell, D. (1981). *The dynamics of public school collective bargaining and its impacts on governance, administration and teaching*. Washington, DC: National Institute of Education.

Kmetz, J. T., & Willower, D. J. (1982). Elementary school principals' work behavior. *Educational Administration Quarterly, 18*(4), 62–78.

Lindblom, C. E. (1980). *The policy-making process* (2nd ed.). Englewood Cliffs, NJ: Prentice-Hall.

Lindblom, C. E., & Cohen, D. K. (1979). *Usable knowledge: Social science and social problem solving*. New Haven, CT: Yale University Press.

Locke, E. A., & Schweiger, D. M. (1979). Participation in decision making: One more look. *Research in Organizational Behavior, 1*, 265–339.

Lortie, D. C. (1969). The balance of control and autonomy in elementary school teaching. In A. Etzioni (Ed.), *The semi-professions and their organization* (pp. 1–53). New York: Free Press.

Mann, D. (1975). *Policy decision-making in education: An introduction to calculation and control*. New York: Teachers College Press, Columbia University.

March, J. G. (1982). Emerging developments in the study of organizations. *The Review of Higher Education, 6*(1), 1–18.

March, J. G., & Olsen, J. P. (1976). *Ambiguity and choice in organizations*. Bergen, Norway: Universitetsforlaget.

March, J. G., & Simon, H. (1958). *Organizations*. New York: John Wiley.

Meyer, J. W. & Rowan, B. (1977). Institutionalized organizations: Formal structure as myth and ceremony. *American Journal of Sociology: 83*(2), 440–463.

Meyer, J. M., & Rowan, B. (1978). The structure of educational organizations. In M. W. Meyer (Ed.), *Environments and organizations* (pp. 78–109). San Francisco: Jossey-Bass.

Mitchell, D. E., Kerchner, C. T., Erck, W., Pryor, G. (1981). The impact of collective bargaining on school management and policy. *American Journal of Education, 89*(2), 147–188.

Morris, V. C., Crowson, R. L., Hurwitz, E., Jr., & Porter-Gehrie, C. (1981). *The urban principal: Discretionary decision-making in a large educational organization.* (Research report.) Chicago: University of Illinois at Chicago Circle.

Mosher, E., Hastings, A. & Wagoner, J. (1979). *Pursuing equal educational opportunity.* New York: Columbia Teachers College Clearinghouse on Urban Education.

Odiorne, G. S. (1979). *MBO II: A system of managerial leadership for the 80's.* Belmont, CA: Pitman.

Padgett, J. F. (1980). Managing garbage can hierarchies. *Administrative Science Quarterly, 25,* 583–604.

Perrow, C. (1982). Disintegrating social sciences. *Phi Delta Kappan, 63*(10), 684–688.

Peters, T. J., & Waterman, R. H. (1982). *In search of excellence.* New York: Harper & Row.

Peterson, P. E. (1976). *School politics Chicago style.* Chicago: University of Chicago Press.

Scott, R. W. (1981). *Organizations: Rational, natural and open systems.* Englewood Cliffs, NJ: Prentice-Hall.

Sieber, S. D. (1975). Organization influences on innovative roles. In J. V. Baldridge & T. E. Deal (Eds.), *Managing change in educational organizations.* Berkeley, CA: McCutchan.

Simon, H. (1976). *Administrative behavior.* New York: Free Press.

Slater, P. E., & Bennis, W. G. (1964, March-April) Democracy is inevitable, *Harvard Business Review, 42,* 51–59.

Sproull, L. S. (1981). Managing education programs: A microbehavioral analysis. *Human Organization, 40,* 113–122.

Sproull, L. S., Weiner, S. S., & Wolf, D. B. (1978). *Organizing an anarchy.* Chicago: University of Chicago Press.

Tyack, D. B. (1974). *The one best system.* Cambridge, MA: Harvard University Press.

Weber, M. (1947). *The theory of social and economic organization.* (A. M. Henderson & T. Parsons, Trans.). Oxford: Oxford University Press.

Weick, K. E. (1982). Administering education in loosely coupled systems. *Phi Delta Kappan, 63* (10), 673–676.

Weiner, S. S. (1976). Participation, deadlines and choice. In J. G. March & J. P. Olsen (Eds.), *Ambiguity and choice in organizations* (pp. 225–250). Bergen, Norway: Universitetsforlaget.

Willower, D. J. (1982) School organizations: Perspectives in juxtaposition. *Educational Administration Quarterly, 18*(3), 89–110.

Wirt, F. M. (1974). *Power in the cities: Decision making in San Francisco.* Berkeley, CA: University of California Press.

Wirt, F. M., & Kirst, M. W. (1982). *Schools in conflict.* Berkeley, CA: McCutchan.

Wise, A. (1983). Why educational policies often fail: The hyper-rationalization hypothesis. In J. V. Baldridge & T. Deal (Eds.), *The dynamics of organizational change in education* (pp. 93–113). Berkeley, CA: McCutchan.

CHAPTER 16

Planned Organizational Change

William A. Firestone and H. Dickson Corbett

No educational observer, to our knowledge, has ever begun a paper with the comforting thought that "these are calm times indeed for education." More typically, the claim is that educators now face a challenge more intense than any that preceded it. This stylistic uniformity may simply indicate limited imagination, but the kernel of truth contained in the oft-used opening is that education does seem to face repeated reforms—from curriculum reform in the late 1950s to the Great Society in the late 1960s to individualized instruction in the 1970s to "back to basics" in the late 1980s, to name a few. Whether these waves of reforms reflect public whimsy or the schools' inability to sustain significant improvements, responses to them have yielded a steadily growing storehouse of knowledge about how to change schools. We simply know more now about how to improve schools, including both what not to do as well as what to do.

This chapter examines the accumulated research knowledge about planned organizational change in schools—that is, intentional efforts to modify some aspect of the organization or practice of schooling. It focuses on what has been learned about how to manage the change process. Although the problems of what should be changed in schools and what practices or arrangements are really improvements are crucial ones (Fullan, 1982), the scope of this effort is limited to a review of research on *how* change happens. It is organized into four major sections. The first traces the

Consultant/reviewers: Terrance E. Deal, Vanderbilt University; Michael Fullan, Ontario Institute for Studies of Education; and Karen S. Louis, University of Massachusetts–Boston

history of research on planned organizational change from the late 1960s to the present, identifying major themes and highlighting conclusions on which there is agreement and debate. Since planned change has become a matter of both motivating from without and orchestrating from within, the next two sections examine what has been learned about external and internal tactics to manage the change process. Section two focuses on three policy tools: mandates, grants, and dissemination efforts. Section three examines leadership tasks that support planned change, the utility of participation in the change process, and local contingencies that influence how change efforts progress. Section four identifies one research area that we believe is crucial for the future understanding of planned change in education: how to modify organizational cultures.

PLANNED CHANGE AND CHANGE RESEARCH IN THE 1970s

Studying research into planned change in education became a mainstream concern for educational researchers in the 1970s because of dissatisfaction with efforts to reform American schools. Its major discovery was the complexity of the processes of change at the school and district level. This discovery contributed first to massive pessimism about the feasibility of external efforts to improve schools. Later, as realistic expectations for what could be changed in schools became clearer, feasible strategies and better knowledge of how local conditions would enhance improvement also began to appear.

Major Initiatives for Change

Two distinct initiatives promoted innovation in postwar American schools. The first was the modernization of curriculums in a variety of content areas, including mathematics, science, foreign languages, and social studies. For example, university scientists began projects such as the Physical Science Study Committee (PSSC) and the University of Illinois Committee on School Mathematics (UICSM) to upgrade high school curriculums (Atkin & House, 1981). By "upgrading," developers meant both updating the content to be taught to reflect recent disciplinary advances and introducing more active, discovery-oriented teaching techniques to raise student interest. Development typically proceeded through a highly rational process that is captured by Clark and Guba's (1967) RDDU model. In this model improvement begins with *research* on a generally recognized problem and moves through *development* in progressively more realistic settings to *dissemination* and then local *utilization*. The programmatic intent was often to "install" the best ideas about what and how to teach, with school staff being passive receptors. Developers gave little thought to school-based realities that reinforced existing practice and could undercut the use of new approaches (Sarason, 1971).

The second initiative concerned equality of educational opportunity, with the Elementary and Secondary Education Act (ESEA) of 1965 a major cornerstone. By far the major provision of that act was Title I, which provided financial assistance to school districts to operate programs for children from low-income families. Other provisions of the act funded (a) the local development of exemplary educational programs (Title III); (b) research on the improvement of educational practice—and development, demonstration, and dissemination models to use the research (Title IV); and (c) monitoring and enforcement of the act by state government (Bailey & Mosher, 1968).

The several provisions reflected different assumptions about how to promote local change. Title I began with broad assistance objectives, based on optimism that, given resources, local districts would extend themselves to support low-income students. As subsequent studies and complaints contradicted this assumption, policy makers strengthened and enforced "targeting" requirements to ensure that funds would be concentrated on serving low-income and minority students (McLaughlin & Elmore, 1982). On the other hand, Titles III and IV assumed that practice could be improved by creating new knowledge about education and sharing it with educators who would be willing to use it. Title IV in particular borrowed the RDDU approach prevalent in the curriculum development efforts. University-based centers supported by the act concentrated on research, while private, unaffiliated regional laboratories focused on developing new products for school use. Neither dissemination nor training was a key component in the federal role in promoting change in those days (Chase, 1970).

Discovery of Local Implementation

School improvement practice and research at this time underestimated the difficulties of change at the local level. Prior to this period, educational change research (e.g., Mort & Cornell, 1941) followed a diffusion-of-innovations paradigm developed in agriculture and drug marketing (see Rogers & Shoemaker, 1971). This simplistic paradigm assumed a unitary decision maker, such as a farmer buying seed corn or a doctor prescribing a drug (Baldridge & Deal, 1975). Its mismatch with education became apparent in the late 1960s and the early 1970s as researchers and practitioners found that formally adopted innovations were not being implemented. For instance, in the Follow Through Planned Variation study (Rivlin & Timpane, 1975), unexpected negative findings about program outcomes prompted evaluators to inquire about whether the programs had been implemented as planned; otherwise they risked evaluating "nonevents" by looking for differences between "groups" that had not actually received different treatments expected by the program designers (Charters & Jones, 1973). Investigating program implementation was a strategic shift so fundamental that it was viewed as "a Copernican revolution in analytic thinking" (Schick, cited in Cronbach et al., 1980, p. 129).

As quantitative evaluations began to demonstrate that innovative programs were not being implemented in the same way in different sites, ethnographic studies illustrated the dynamics of the change process that contributed to cross-site variation. Three of the most important of these appeared in 1971. Sarason in *The Culture of the School and the Problem of Change*, reflected on efforts to get teachers to use the "New Mathematics" curriculum and identified the regularities of school life that worked against implementation. Gross, Giacquinta, and Bernstein's *Implementing Organizational Innovations* (1971) described the mismanagement of a new program for minority students funded by ESEA and showed that limited implementation resulted from more than teachers' irrational "resistance to change." Smith and Keith's *Anatomy of an Educational Innovation* (1971) chronicled in great detail the traumas of starting a new school. Together, these studies graphically illustrated the effects of local context on externally initiated change efforts. The major reviews of the planned change literature in education during this period also focused on the dynamics of change within the school (e.g., Fullan & Pomfret, 1977; Giacquinta, 1973).

Three Perspectives on Implementation

Research attention shifted to the dynamics of change at the local level, and a number of perspectives emerged to interpret these forces. House (1981) identified three: the technological, the political, and the cultural. The technological perspective views implementation as a technical task, subject to rational analysis. This perspective identifies problems stemming from a failure of systematic planning, including ambiguity in a program's purposes, the unavailability of key materials, unrealistic expectations for immediate results, role overload for participants, and failure to adjust organizational arrangements like schedules and rules to support proposed changes (Charters & Pellegrin, 1973; Gross et al., 1971). Fundamentally optimistic, the perspective assumes that barriers to innovation can be anticipated and managed. However, change is rarely a rational process (Clark, 1981). Instead, program purposes are often clarified by action (Weick, 1976). The benefits of an innovation occasionally become apparent only through trial and use—so too with the costs and barriers. One may not know what rules need to be changed until after experimentation. Finally, a host of "routine critical events," such as turnover of key staff, can have drastic effects on a program (Huberman & Miles, 1984; Louis, Rosenblum, & Molitor, 1981). Thus, the technological perspective often fails to capture many complexities of implementation.

The political perspective proposes that rational analysis of planned innovation is impossible because of the divergent interests of the many actors in the process. How those interests are played out given the power and authority relationships in school districts and their environs creates considerable uncertainties for project leaders. This perspective also highlights the role of available incentives for change (Sieber, 1981). For instance, administrators' desires for career advancement may lead to the frequent adoption of innovations without regard to quality (House, 1974; Nelson & Sieber, 1976); yet few incentives are available to encourage teachers to innovate even though their cooperation is critical for successful implementation (Lortie, 1975; Weatherley & Lipsky, 1977). As a result, there typically are more incentives to adopt a change than to implement it. Finally, this perspective argues that because local educators and external policy makers have different interests, promoting innovation from afar will lead to substantial conflict (Herriott & Gross, 1979).

The political perspective is basically pessimistic. Its careful analysis of incentives and balances of power clarifies both fundamental limitations to rationality and the range of interests likely to be arrayed for and against any specific change effort. Nevertheless, this perspective also suggests ways to design programs to make them more attractive to the groups who must use them, as well as implementation strategies that will make change agents more effective (Baldridge, 1975).

The political and technological perspective dominated the 1970s, but there is now growing interest in the cultural perspective. It reinterprets divergent interests as the result of differences stemming from enduring values and cognitions of those involved in change processes. Generated by the behavioral regularities of the settings in which people live (Sarason, 1971), over time these values assume a life of their own and continue even after those regularities change (Metz, 1984). Culture is fundamentally conservative, establishing a set of long-standing and often unstated evaluation criteria that an innovation must meet to be accepted without a struggle.

An early contribution of the cultural perspective was to point out the divergence between the cultures of schools and of the organizations that house external reformers. Sarason (1971) contrasts the cultures of schools and universities to illustrate how members of each organization talk past the other. Wolcott (1977) views the educational world as comprised of two moities or subgroups: teachers and technocrats, with the second group including both administrators and external experts. Although these groups are mutually interdependent, the refusal of the former to implement the latter's ideas stems from divergent world views. Gideonse (1980) suggests that the "federal establishment" has its own culture—replete with special hierarchies, symbols, and language like "scopes of work," "contract officers," and "requests for proposals" (RFPs)—and is at least as foreign to the schools' culture as the university is.

Such basic differences in world view do not bode well for externally motivated planned change efforts. However, cultural analyses have also identified cultural features of organizations that promote innovation and effectiveness (Berman & McLaughlin, 1979; Peters & Waterman, 1982) and have suggested new ways to think about what and how to change in schools. Through these suggestions, the cultural perspective may prove to be much more optimistic than the political. More will be said on this topic in the last section of the chapter.

FPSEC and the Problem of Development

Among the many studies completed during the 1970s, the one that received the greatest attention was the massive Rand study of Federal Policies Supporting Educational Change (FPSEC). Its first wave consisted of a survey of 293 projects, including interviews at all levels of the district, from superintendent to teacher, with intensive visits to 29 sites (Berman & McLaughlin, 1975). A second wave looked at the institutionalization of change in 100 of the original 293 projects (Berman & McLaughlin, 1977). FPSEC's findings were pessimistic in two regards. First, the study documented a failure of innovation. It identified three outcomes of implementation efforts: *nonimplementation, cooptation*—where an innovation accommodates the local context so much that its fundamental features are lost, and *mutual adaptation*—where both the innovation and the local context are modified. This typology generated considerable interest in how to facilitate mutual adaptation and debate about whether such an outcome was good or bad. However, the fundamental point was that even mutual adaptation—a far cry from the "high-fidelity implementation" hoped for by those who developed new curriculums and other innovations—was exceedingly rare (Berman & McLaughlin, 1975).

Second, most of the centrally controllable policy variables examined in the study—such as program support or level of funding—had little impact on ultimate implementation and institutionalization. Instead, implementation strategies (such as the quality of training and the amount of staff participation) and institutional characteristics (including both the extent of administrative support and teachers' sense of efficacy) had greater impacts on the final levels of implementation. Thus, there seemed to be little that central policy agencies at the state or federal level could do to promote educational reform.

FPSEC helped to sound the death knell for development work on new curriculums. The proposition that centrally developed innovations would not be implemented locally became widely accepted and publicized by academics, policy makers, and even the popular press (Datta, 1981), and federal funding for such efforts dropped dramatically (Welch, 1979). In its place emerged a "let a thousand flowers bloom" theory that stressed local invention and reinvention (reinventing the wheel) and the development of a built-in "capacity" to improve at the school or district site. The possibility that materials could be developed in one place and used successfully elsewhere fell into wide disrepute.

In spite of FPSEC's importance, later studies suggest that its stress on the immutability of local districts and the weakness of external interventions overstates the case. FPSEC studied grants programs that provided relatively small amounts of money with very broad guidelines to schools and districts on a competitive basis. Local educators were expected to find effective products and quality technical assistance on their own (Datta, 1981). Programs offering greater support to educators, such as the Pilot State Dissemination Program (PSDP) (Sieber, Louis, & Metzger, 1972), the National Diffusion Network (NDN) (Crandall & Loucks, 1983; Emrick et al., 1977), and the Research and Development Utilization demonstration program (RDU) (Louis, Kell, Dentler, Corwin, & Herriott, 1981) were generally more successful. Studies of these programs found positive relationships between product quality and local improvement, and one investigation uncovered a negative association between local development and beneficial outcomes (Louis et al., 1981). These studies concluded that centrally supported assistance strategies combining a mix of quality products and effective assistance in a manner responsive to local concerns would promote local change.

The Legacy of the 1970s

In retrospect, the optimism that girded the reform programs of the 1960s was as excessive as the pessimism of most of the planned change research through the mid-1970s. Yet, this research contributed to a deep appreciation of the difficulties in promoting change that should be shared by both those who study change and those who seek to bring it about. Organizations are fundamentally conservative about their basic purposes, understandings about the world, and ways of doing their work (Deal & Kennedy, 1982). That conservatism is often functional for schools, given their frequent buffeting by waves of externally initiated reform efforts that may not be based on a firm understanding of the regularities of school life (James & Tyack, 1983).

The current state of knowledge about planned organizational change in education has been summarized by Fullan (1982) as follows:

> Being at the early stages of a complex undertaking, we have an obligation to be neither insultingly optimistic nor boringly pessimistic. We have seen many failures, but also some successes even under adverse circumstances. What is more, we understand better why things turn out as they do. (p. 288)

This view recognizes the difficulties of planned change without becoming fatalistic. It also acknowledges that more is known now about how external actors can promote school change and how local conditions and actions affect change processes than 20 years ago. The next two sections review some of what has been learned in those two areas.

EXTERNAL EFFORTS TO SHAPE LOCAL CHANGE

A growing body of research about how those outside the schools go about contributing to constructive local change identifies three major policy tools: mandates, grants, and dissemination. This research clarifies their assumptions, the conditions under which they work well, and some of their associated difficulties. Research also throws some light on the advantages and disadvantages of combining the policy tools.

Mandates

Mandates are rules or regulations that specify what shall or shall not be done. Their power derives from the sanctions that will be imposed if local educators do not comply. The assumption behind mandates is that schools or districts do not want to do whatever is required; the problem is one of willingness to comply (Elmore, 1980). To overcome this unwillingness, mandates make the costs of noncompliance higher than the costs of compliance and provide for a system of surveillance to ensure that mandates are in fact followed. Mandates have been used to desegregate schools, to govern the education of the handicapped, and in conjunction with grants (through Title I ESEA, now Chapter 1 of the Educational Consolidation and Improvement Act) to strengthen the education of students with low levels of achievement.

Mandates work best when the goals to be met and their attainment are clear, there is a balance of public and professional support or neutrality for the change, and the target sites can feasibly achieve mandated ends. Clarity is important because enforcement is possible and more effective where there are well-defined indicators of compliance. For example, desegregation requirements are easier to monitor because the racial distribution of students in a school can be readily determined and verified. By contrast, the regulations governing the education of the handicapped (Public Law 94–142) are more ambiguous. One regulation requires that children be placed in the "least restrictive environment" feasible for their condition. Specification of the least restrictive environment must be done case by case, and professionals often disagree on what constitutes such an environment for a specific student. As a result, enforcement is difficult (Hargrove et al., 1981).

Some form of public support is an important ingredient of the mandating process, as Orfield (1969) illustrates in his discussion of the early history of desegregation in this country. In spite of local opposition by both citizens and elected officials, federal efforts to achieve desegregation in the South were quite successful in the late 1960s in part because of massive public support in the North. However, public acceptance in that region—and the backing of key elected officials—declined substantially when desegregation initiatives moved north. Not all mandates are as controversial as desegregation. When the public is neutral on an issue and professionals are neutral or positive, mandates are relatively effective in inducing change. Rowan (1982) has shown how such mandates promoted the spread of ancillary health and other special personnel in California schools in the 1930s and 1940s.

Finally, the change must be feasible. Desegregation of southern—and especially rural—schools was initially feasible because there were enough black and white children in the same district to have integrated schools. (The expansion of private schools in the South and the departure of white students has changed this in some areas.) By contrast, many urban districts had such segregated housing patterns and high concentrations of minority students that it proved difficult to create integrated educational settings (Bullock, 1976).

The risks associated with mandates parallel the conditions that promote their use. First, the need for clarity often leads to a goal displacement in enforcement. Those charged with enforcement develop measurable indicators of compliance, and both enforcers and local educators tend to focus narrowly on those indicators rather than on the act's broader purposes. For example, after an initial period of drift between 1965 and 1969, federal and state enforcement of Title I attended to provisions such as the "targeting" of funds or ensuring that a district used federal funds in a concentrated enough way to have an impact on students rather than as general aid. Yet, federal evaluations indicated that enforcement activities did not, in themselves, encourage high-quality service. Thus, the balance of enforcement shifted to seeing that rules were followed rather than that students were better educated (McLaughlin & Elmore, 1982).

Second, enforcement can reduce a mandate's popularity, especially when it expands to a broader population, establishes more specific enforcement criteria, or monitors the criteria more carefully. Eventually, this can lead to a backlash or legitimacy crisis where public confidence in educational institutions declines markedly. American education experienced such a crisis in the 1970s (Weiler, 1982). Although the reasons for this crisis were numerous, the expanded role of regulatory bodies in determining the conduct of local education seemed to contribute to it.

Finally, policy makers often confuse lack of knowledge or capacity to comply with lack of willingness to comply (Elmore, 1980). For instance, in spite of recent advances in knowledge about how to improve education in the basic skills for low-achieving students (e.g., Rosenholtz, 1985), serious limits to our knowledge about how to overcome the effects of race and SES on student learning remain. Under these circumstances, local variation in practice becomes a useful laboratory for discovering and validating more effective approaches. If, however, policy makers view variation as lack of compliance, they will specify regulations in more detail and have them monitored more closely. The result is greater uniformity and a loss of learning opportunities (Elmore, 1980).

Grants

Grants provide financial incentives to help local educators change or continue valued activities. The assumption in this case is that two parties share a common interest that can be met when one gives money to the other. For instance, Title III (later Title IVc) of ESEA offered funds to local school districts for a limited time to develop innovative educational projects or products. This program assumed that local educators had the capacity to develop practice-based approaches for themselves and perhaps others as well.

Grants work well to support changes that recipients want to make anyway, primarily because they rely so heavily on the recipient's goodwill. As a result, grants are best suited for promoting modest changes that are well accepted by professionals and the public. More radical changes will not be advanced by grants alone (Hargrove, 1982). Thus, grants are not particularly useful for pushing changes that threaten teachers' professional autonomy, such as team teaching and "teacher-proof curriculums." Similarly, programs to redistribute educational benefits among various student populations—such as the handicapped, bilingual students, or other minority groups—will not progress far unless grants are combined with other policy tools. Grants also work well in situations where there is considerable tolerance for variation and even for failure (Elmore, 1980). Hence, they are an appropriate tool for supporting demonstration projects or for projects that encourage people to experiment, as the old Title IVc did.

The risk is that grants will be used "opportunistically"—that is, educators will seek the grant money with no serious intent to follow through on the purposes for which the money was awarded. This was a frequent

pattern of grant use among the programs studied by FPSEC (Berman & McLaughlin, 1975) and also occurred often with Title I funds in its early days (Murphy, 1971). Whether opportunistic use is inherent in the grants strategy is not entirely clear. Datta (1981) argues that the kinds of grants programs examined in FPSEC were especially prone to opportunism because they were experimental or demonstration programs with broad missions and ambiguous goals. When funding agencies better specify what they want accomplished, they may be better able to identify grant requirements for schools and to identify which schools are willing to comply.

Dissemination

A third policy tool is the *dissemination* of knowledge-based products.[1] This can be accomplished through special dissemination programs (like the NDN), the creation of demonstration programs (e.g., the PSDP), or attaching a dissemination component to a major educational initiative—as was done with the Title I Technical Assistance Centers (TACs). The dissemination strategy makes two assumptions: First, a knowledge base is available somewhere that will help to improve education and that can be shared with educators in a useful form; second, educators are willing to take steps necessary to improve education but, without the dissemination program, they lack the knowledge necessary to make the requisite changes. The objectives of agencies employing this strategy are usually rather general when compared to agencies using mandates; in some cases the end sought is nothing more specific than "educational improvement."

At one level, we know that dissemination works under the same conditions that grants do. It is useful for encouraging changes that are generally acceptable to educators and do not threaten any powerful interest groups. It is also useful where there is tolerance for variation because, as will be discussed below, educators in different schools will adopt different innovations and are likely to modify them further during implementation.

More specifically, effective dissemination programs require a combination of implementable innovations and direct personal assistance. To be implementable, an innovation must meet four criteria (Fullan, 1982): It must be needed, clear, complex, and practical. The irony is that only some of these characteristics can be built into an innovation in advance. Others come through the selection of an innovation to fit local conditions (i.e., correct match) or through a learning process that takes place during implementation. Just this learning that the perfect innovation cannot be designed in a context-free way in advance, although almost commonplace knowledge today, is one of the great advances of the last 30 years.

The first characteristic of an implementable innovation is that it must be needed. In a study of 10 rural school districts receiving support for change from the federal Experimental Schools program, Rosenblum and Louis (1981) found formal recognition of unmet district needs associated with greater project implementation. The success of programs like NDN and RDU is an indication of the importance of matching changes to needs; both programs take schools through a change process that encourages them to examine possible innovations in light of local conditions. (See also Berman & McLaughlin, 1975.) The importance of the need for the product is one reason why the agency using an assistance strategy must tolerate considerable local variation; needs of schools vary.

The second characteristic is clarity of the innovation's purposes and procedures. According to Fullan (1982), "problems related to clarity have been found in virtually every study of significant change" (p. 57). Lack of clarity can result from the way policy makers design a program. For instance, the purpose of the Experimental Schools program was to explore the feasibility of "comprehensive," districtwide change. However, the program never developed a definition of comprehensiveness that was clear to participating districts; the result was great distress in the districts and much conflict with the funding agency (Herriott & Gross, 1979).

Lack of clarity can also result from poor design at the school or district level. For instance, one Experimental Schools district adopted an approach to individualized instruction as the centerpiece of its project. When the project began, the idea was clear only to the project consultant; no materials or training designs existed to help teachers and administrators understand. The resulting confusion contributed to the eventual redirection of the project and firing of the superintendent who initiated it (Firestone, 1980).

Adequate preparation and materials along with technical assistance will contribute to positive outcomes to the process, but an initial period of confusion is apparently inherent in the change process (Huberman & Miles, 1984). This confusion is overcome only through a process of trial-and-error learning, which is most effective when it is guided.

The third characteristic is complexity, that is, the amount of change required by an innovation, the difficulty of change, and the extent of the difference between new practices and old ones. Simpler changes will be cosmetically more successful but will achieve less. Huberman and Miles (1984) concluded that early implementation was much smoother and less traumatic in projects that adopted simple innovations; but because less was attempted, less was learned; concomitantly there was less real change. Their findings agree with Crandall and Loucks (1983), Louis and colleagues (1981), and Berman and McLaughlin (1977). Berman and McLaughlin found that a greater percentage of project goals was achieved in small projects, but more ambitious projects led to greater change in teacher practice.

Although complex changes are inherently more difficult to implement than simpler ones, obstacles are surmountable when the change project can be broken into a large number of separate parts (Fullan, 1982). Rosenblum and Louis (1981) found that three of the four Experimental Schools districts that achieved the highest levels of implementation had projects with many separate components. Each component was geared to a different part of the district's identified problem, and each was phased in through schedules that minimized the shock of change. When some components did not work, they were dropped.

Fullan's (1982) final characteristic is practicality, or the extent to which an innovation is capable of being put into practice. One aspect of practicality is the adequacy of the materials describing the innovation. Fullan (1982) cites a number of U.S. and Canadian studies where teachers faulted the innovations for lacking tangible relevance to classroom concerns. The innovations contained insufficient guidance on what teaching strategies, instructional activities, or materials should be used. Practicality changes with the stage of innovation. During early adoption and awareness stages, practitioners need concise overview materials. More detailed "how-to" oriented materials are appropriate during early implementation.

The practicality of an innovation also depends on its fit with the organizational realities of the school. A school's formal rules or unwritten understandings create expectations that a change may violate. For instance, innovations intended to allow students to progress as far as possible every year will face problems in schools that group children by age and insist on providing letter grades at fixed times (Gross et al., 1971). In such cases, either the innovation or the rules must be changed. Additionally, changes can be impractical just because they are too time consuming for teachers (Charters & Pellegrin, 1973). Such impracticality is hard to assess at the start, however. Learning new practices and incorporating them into teachers' repertoires, requires considerable time and energy (Huberman & Miles, 1984). Thus, it is not always wise to terminate an innovation too soon just because it takes too much time initially.

Because some of the characteristics that facilitate the use of innovations emerge only through local involvement, dissemination benefits from direct, on-site assistance (Louis, 1981). This conclusion becomes clear from a comparison of dissemination programs that use on-site help with those that develop products but do not offer such help (Emrick & Peterson, 1977). Thus, the NDN and RDU, which provided assistance, were quite successful in getting innovations implemented (Crandall & Loucks, 1983; Emrick et al., 1977; Louis et al., 1981). By contrast, Program Information Packages did not have nearly as much success, in large measure because it did not offer on-site help (Stearns & Norwood, 1977).

The reason for these findings is relatively clear. The press of everyday events typically encourages teachers and principals to be more concerned with organizational maintenance than with change (Fullan, 1982; Lortie, 1975). Whether the need is for special knowledge about the content of the innovation, skill with the change process, or an extra pair of hands to get coffee or doughnuts for a meeting, it must usually be met from outside the building.

When one pushes beyond this basic finding to determine how on-site assistance contributes to change, three problems arise. The first is that relationships between assistance activities and their outcomes are dependent upon other factors. For instance, the conditions under which different kinds of expertise actually help depend on the stage of the change process. The recurring question here is whether those who provide assistance should be generalists—that is, experts at managing the change process—or specialists who have mastered a particular innovation's content. Neither one is universally more useful. Generalists are more important in the early stages of the change process when educators are searching for information and need to be encouraged to select quality innovations that meet local needs. During implementation, content specialists become more important because teachers need to understand how to carry out the innovation in practice (Louis & Sieber, 1979; Louis et al., 1981).

The second problem stems from a series of unresolved inconsistencies in the research on assistor time spent on site. Some studies find more time on site leads to greater change—at least up to a point (Louis et al., 1981; Louis et al., 1984). Others find no appreciable relationships between time spent and results (Firestone & Corbett, 1981). There are also of tradeoff indications: More time on site facilitates the implementation of the innovation but minimizes the learning of the teachers involved (Crandall & Loucks, 1983; Louis et at., 1981).

It is possible that all these studies mistake the direction of causality. Corbett (1981) suggests that school events determine what the person providing assistance does. Where projects are in trouble, that person is likely to spend more time on site just to keep the change effort alive. Where things proceed more smoothly, less external assistance is required. The contribution of the assistor comes from an ability to use time, knowledge, and other resources to respond to local conditions in ways that facilitate change. Yet, even this explanation does not cover all situations because some differences in the amount of time on site result from program design rather than local contingencies (Rosenblum & Louis, 1981).

The third problem is that assistors are often assigned different purposes or goals. Their employing agency has its own mission that determines what purposes assistors must serve. A number of typologies have been developed that differentiate these purposes. One frequently cited (Butler & Paisley, 1978) identifies three roles:

> the *resource finder*, who conducts information searches to answer a school's questions but does not conduct analyses of client problems;
>
> the *process helper*, who becomes involved in the school's problems by helping to collect data and analyze conditions but who remains neutral with respect to the substantive problem or the decisions made; and
>
> the *solution giver*, who is familiar with one or more alternative practices and advocates their use in a school.

Each of these implies different definitions of success. Resource finders are "successful" if they locate information that satisfies the concerns of the client, but solution givers succeed only if innovations are adopted and actually implemented. Thus, some of the discrepancies among studies of assistance activities and change outcomes derive from designed differences in what assistors do.

The importance of on-site assistance points up the major difficulty of the dissemination strategy: It is very expensive and there does not seem to be substantial political interest in making that kind of investment in planned change efforts. Most dissemination programs that incorporate on-site assistance into the implementation phase are relatively marginal to major educational policies. They include temporary demonstration programs, small ongoing federal programs like the NDN, and small offices in state departments of education and intermediate service agencies. None of them have the resources to provide the intensity of assistance that seems to effectively boost local improvement. Moreover, these programs serve a wide range of constituent districts. This forces a choice between "depth" and "breadth"—that is, between giving enough assistance to a few districts to facilitate significant change and serving all interested districts even though dramatic improvement may not ensue (Firestone & Rossman, 1983).

Combinations of Policy Tools

In practice, there is a growing tendency to combine grants, mandates, and assistance in various combinations. The advantages and disadvantages of doing so have not been fully explored, but there are some hints available as to what the issues might be.

One would expect that grants would complement a dissemination program. Certainly the selection and implementation of an innovation require staff time for joint planning and training; funds targeted for those purposes should help and in some instances seem to (Roberts, Kenney, Buttram, & Wolf, 1982). On the other hand, Louis et al. (1981) found some negative associations between the size of grants awarded to the RDU schools implementing new programs and overall outcomes. They speculate that the availability of large amounts of funds gives the project a special external status. People in the school are less likely to see it as a part of their everyday life and may be less committed to making the change happen. Thus, large grants possibly lead to a reverse Hawthorne effect.

Grants and mandates have also been combined with three kinds of effects. First, the specification of requirements for the use of grant funds can help to avoid opportunism. A progressive tightening of requirements on the use of Title I funds through 1981 did in fact minimize misuse (Kirst & Jung, 1980). Second, grant funds can soften the shock of implementing mandates. Emergency School Aid Act funds that went to desegregating districts eased the transition into new organizational patterns after the integration order had been followed. Finally, regulation in the use of grants funds can lead to resentment of the regulator, especially when recipients have been accustomed to having greater discretion.

There have been few efforts to tightly integrate mandates and dissemination. Many mandating programs do provide technical assistance, but this is usually limited to assistance with the interpretation of regulations (McLaughlin & Elmore, 1982). Designers of implementation systems fear that the combination of functions will be mutually contaminating. That is, if monitors also help local educators identify new practices, they may be coopted by their own advice. If the proposed remedies do not have the desired effect, it is feared that the monitors will not impose sanctions on those who took their advice; they may even be held to

blame for the failure to achieve those effects. At the same time, monitors cannot develop the trust relationships necessary to assist in the dissemination process (Firestone & Wilson, 1983).

To summarize, research over the last 15 years on the strengths and weaknesses of various external policy tools for encouraging school and district change indicates some of their limits. For instance, no external strategy can get too far out in front of public opinion and the range of accepted occupational practice. Even (or perhaps especially) mandates require a certain level of support to be implemented successfully. In addition there is a growing recognition that local variation in how a new practice or policy goal is implemented is not always a sign of noncompliance but instead a very reasonable response to contextual differences across schools. In addition, researchers have come to a greater appreciation and a more nuanced understanding of when to use different policy tools and what to expect from them. This new understanding leads to a substantial diminution of expectations from the 1960s, when there was a greater belief in the ability to cause major reforms in education. Many currently implemented changes are not so much reforms as incremental adjustments in practice. On the other hand, those responsible for helping schools make those adjustments know better how to proceed in doing so.

INTERNAL ISSUES IN THE CHANGE PROCESS

The major "discovery" of the planned organizational change research in the 1970s was the complexity of the dynamics of change implementation and incorporation at the local level. In time researchers began to clarify the central issues that had to be addressed in managing the change process and the local conditions that affected it. To review what has been learned about how change takes place in schools, this section addresses three issues: leadership tasks that support change, factors that determine the usefulness of participation in decision making, and local contingencies that shape the change process.

Leadership Tasks that Support Change

According to Arends (1982), one clear message of the planned organizational change research is that change efforts succeed with active principal support. A variety of studies (e.g., Berman & McLaughlin, 1977; Hall & Hord, 1984; Huberman, 1981) buttress this position. Yet there are exceptions. Rosenblum and Louis (1981) conclude that the superintendent seems to play an extremely crucial role, and Carnine, Gersten, and Green (1982) identify leadership functions that teachers can perform effectively. The sources of change leadership have not been fully explored because most analyses have focused on specific roles—especially the principal and the superintendent (Fullan, 1982)—rather than necessary tasks. To determine how important the contributions of any role or position is, it is first imperative to clarify the tasks that promote implementation and incorporation. Then one can determine who in a school system is best placed to accomplish these tasks.

Central Tasks

The performance of four tasks facilitates any change effort: (a) obtaining resources, (b) buffering the project from outside interference, (c) encouraging staff, and (d) adapting standard operating procedures to the project. Most discussions of resources focus on money. Frequently, districts do not make additional contributions to a project after funds from outside sources have run out (Berman & McLaughlin, 1976). As a result, staff enthusiasm and energy can decline because the necessary support the outside funds bought is no longer available. Money is important only for what it can buy, however. If support can be obtained in other ways, the presence or absence of external funding becomes less critical.

Additional needed resources include time, clerical help, and adequate facilities. The availability of slack time for new ventures is an identifying characteristic of instructionally effective schools (Clark, Lotto, & Astuto, 1984) and of excellent corporations (Peters & Waterman, 1982). Slack time makes room for formal planning meetings, initial training in new techniques, teachers to talk with one another about both routine and unusual problems (Joyce & Showers, 1982), demonstration classes conducted by experts, and the development and/or customizing of appropriate materials. Such time can be created by hiring substitutes, but this arrangement seldom proves satisfactory for teachers or students (Corbett, Rossman, & Dawson, 1984). Two preferable alternatives are also less expensive. First, administrators can arrange teaching assignments so that project participants have common planning periods that can be used for project purposes. Second, since teachers usually have little opportunity to discuss instruction with their peers, creating new work groups or encouraging existing ones to use their available meeting times for that purpose rather than "administrivia" can surmount this considerable obstacle to the spread of change.

Another important resource is the availability of clerical help and physically comfortable facilities for project participants. Whether participants are comfortable, have refreshments, can get plans typed, and have documents reproduced for all members seem mundane and routine. However, if staff do not have unlimited slack time, then switching meeting rooms, heating up a coffee pot, looking for a secretary, or running hastily to make photocopies can slice deeply into the meeting. And as trivial as these issues appear, they can be time consuming, distracting, and discouraging—especially to participants who are not fully committed to an innovation (Corbett, Dawson, & Firestone, 1984).

The second key leadership task is buffering the project from external interference. Staff rarely begin a project with the skill, understanding, or commitment necessary to make it go. Commitment and understanding follow behavioral changes, and all of this takes time (Fullan, 1985). Implementation is in large part a learning process (Huberman & Miles, 1984). Even with innovations that seem clear, people experience substantial ambiguity—along with feelings of confusion, frustration, anger, and exhaustion—when they begin using new practices. Where implementation is successful, users go through a series of steps, including initial undifferentiated use and day-to-day coping, stepwise and disjointed use, initial coordination and consolidation of basic routines, coordinated practice and differentiated use, and finally refinement and extension. It may take up to 18 months for staff to achieve higher mastery levels.

Buffering the process minimizes interruptions. The most bothersome distraction usually comes from the school system itself in the form of competing projects. Too often principals revamp discipline policies at the same time they revise lesson plan formats; superintendents standardize curriculums and concurrently initiate special reading projects in all academic subjects; state agencies launch new testing programs while altering graduation requirements and curriculum standards. Each person looking up at this array of activities and "priorities" coming from higher levels in the system has a difficult time determining what is most important and what will last long enough to be worthwhile. Trying to allocate scarce time effectively and efficiently among these activities becomes impossible.

The third leadership task is providing encouragement and recognition to staff for their efforts. The importance of this task cannot be underestimated (Sieber, 1981). Offering appropriate recognition requires finesse because individuals want to stand out from the crowd while also being part of a winning team (Peters & Waterman, 1982). Both sides of this paradox of individual recognition and belonging underscore the significance of encouragement and recognition from peers, experts, and supervisors. The most critical incentive during the change process is social support and recognition. And providing this encouragement need not be time consuming (Corbett, Dawson, & Firestone, 1984). In fact it is easily incorporated into the everyday schedule, assuming that the leader has frequent interactions with staff—a suspect assumption in many schools, to be sure. Peters and Waterman (1982) identify an effective management style as "MBWA," or "management by wandering around." Rather than relying on formal visits, the manager circulates to learn what staff are doing and to reinforce positively desired behaviors. The length of the encounter is not critical but the message is; and, in excellent companies, the message is consistently related to the organization's "core value." Applying this to schools, the supportive leader frequently inquires about and emphasizes the priority of new practices throughout the day. The heart of this activity is the signaling of organizational objectives and the reinforcement of attempts to enact them.

The final leadership task is to adjust standard operating procedures to fit with the innovation. Standard operating procedures include a whole array of formal arrangements in the school or district, such as rules, staff and student evaluation procedures, staff and student assignments, and so forth. This task may begin at the earliest stages of the change process if the proposed innovation is incongruent with existing procedures. For instance, certain "open classroom" techniques that emphasize the intrinsic rewards of schooling and allowing children to progress through the curriculum at their own rate are incompatible with report cards, letter grades, and grouping the student body by age (Gross et al., 1971). The problem of modifying standard operating procedures always becomes acute at the point when the successfully implemented innovation must be incorporated into the school or district on a permanent basis (Huberman & Miles, 1984; Yin, Quick, Bateman, & Marks, 1978). Until that time, projects may operate as temporary systems somewhat protected from the pressures of everyday school life (Miles, 1964). If the innovation is to be built into the organization on a regular and permanent basis, adjustments must be made in at least five ways (Huberman & Miles, 1984):

The new practices must be codified as rules;

the curriculum must be revised to accommodate the innovation;

training programs must be established for newcomers to the district;

evaluation procedures have to reflect the new practice;

and finally, project-related activities must be supported as line items in the regular district budget.

Tasks and Positions

The responsibility for performing these four tasks may fall to any of three positions: district office staff (including the superintendent), principals, or teachers. In most cases more than one position must make a contribution in order for the desired consequences to ensue. In others, the appropriate position to carry out a task depends on special local conditions and thus can vary from school to school and district to district.

Locating resources is typically an administrative task. For example, fund seeking is usually done by the district office, often by a special director of federal programs (Corbett, Rossman, & Dawson, 1984), whereas the creation of slack time can be accomplished by both district staff or the principal. The same is true with clerical and facilities support, although external assistors also can make a significant contribution (Corbett, 1981).

Buffering is an administrative task as well. Principals use a variety of tactics—ranging from conveniently interpreting district-office communications to creative disobedience—to protect a change project from potentially disruptive district directives (Morris et al., 1981) or parental opposition. The district's contribution is to avoid inundating schools with competing programs and to screen changing state and federal priorities.

All positions can assume a leadership role for offering encouragement. The ability of teachers to do so will depend in part on how the internal flow of collegial communication is shaped by grade or departmental organization. Corbett, Dawson, & Firestone, (1984) identify four types of school subunits that vary in how well they facilitate collegial interactions: (a) the Social Club, where teachers frequently but informally discuss instruction among themselves; (b) the Professional Team, where teachers not only talk with one another frequently but also specify curriculum guidelines for all members to follow; (c) the Administrator's Delight, where collegial interaction is rare but conformity to administrative expectations and established procedures is high; and (d) the Egg Crate—the modal situation for teachers—where teachers are isolated from other staff. In both Social Clubs and Professional Teams, teachers become available sources of incentives. If these groups support a proposed change, encouragement occurs naturally. Such subunits are rarely present, however; so this task often falls to someone else.

The principal is uniformly placed well to provide encouragement. Indeed, the principal's day is typically organized into a great many brief, unstructured encounters with staff and students (Kmetz & Willower, 1982). These provide an excellent opportunity for the principal to learn what is happening in the school and to find opportunities to encourage teachers. The reverse is true as well. When the principal frequently communicates dislike of a change, that message discourages teachers (Firestone, 1980).

The superintendent has less opportunity to interact with teachers and therefore fewer chances to provide encouragement. For that very reason, however, superintendents' active and visible support for an innovation can have greater symbolic value when it occurs. Moreover, principals need encouragement too if they are to reinforce teachers.

Finally, although many people, including the principal, can propose and campaign for changes in standard operating procedures, such modifications must be made by authorized decision makers. Decisions on most of the key procedures required for incorporation must be made by the district office or even school boards.

Thus, it is too simplistic to say that the support of the principal is the key to successful change. Success depends upon the accomplishment of four tasks. The principal can play a major role, but important contributions can also be made by district staff and—in the case of encouragement—by teachers. Success is most likely when all positions combine to make substantial contributions to accomplishing the tasks.

Participation and Decision Making

"Participation" refers to formal opportunities for teachers to be present during the process of making decisions about school improvement (Firestone, 1977). The literature contains three major underlying reasons for involving local participants in planning. First, participation increases people's commitment (or at least willingness) to spend the time and effort required to implement new practices and to continue them after initial incentives are withdrawn (Berman & McLaughlin, 1977). Second, participation helps develop local capacity for implementation; that is, people will acquire the knowledge and skills needed to change their behavior (Gross et al., 1971; McLaughlin & Marsh, 1978). Third, local participation in project planning heightens the possibility that changes will be appropriate in a particular setting (Bartunek & Keys, 1979; Berman & McLaughlin, 1977).

According to Conway (1984), "The notion that participation is essential to the acceptance and implementation of change decisions has practically become a law in the literature on educational change" (p. 23). He argues that such exhortations may be based more on myth than fact and that there is no overwhelming evidence that involving "two or more actors in the process of reaching a choice" (p. 19) produces greater productivity or job satisfaction. Instead, there are conditions under which participation seems to work and not work. The administrative challenge is deciding when and in what form participation will be most efficacious.

Three issues are particularly salient for making this determination. First, one reason that participation does not routinely build ownership and a sense of commitment to change is that it takes time (Corbett, Dawson, & Firestone, 1984). When innovation planning and decision making infringe on other staff obligations, participation becomes a cost rather than a benefit. That this happens in schools should not be surprising. Few staff members have slack time. With the exception of a planning period, lunch, or after school hours, teachers generally have classroom responsibilities. Any meeting is likely to impinge on other valued activities—for example, preparing for classes, socializing with peers, evaluating student performance, or instructing students. Moreover, freeing the teacher from classroom duties through proctors or substitutes does not necessarily reduce this cost; it is exacerbated if the teacher is concerned about resentment from colleagues covering the class or a substitute's incompetence. In such cases the project becomes a source of dissatisfaction, and commitment to it will drop concomitantly. Thus, the relationship between participation and its touted benefits is likely curvilinear (Conway, 1984). That is, commitment to change will be difficult to generate with no, or only token, staff participation, but it likewise will suffer if participation competes too strongly with regular duties.

Second, the content of change decisions also affects teachers' perceptions of participation's value. Essentially, there is a zone of acceptance within which staff grant an administrator the freedom to make decisions without consulting them (Kunz & Hoy, 1976). This zone seems to be bounded by the amount of organizational trust (Driscoll, 1978) and whether a decision is related to the technical content of what teachers do (Conway, 1984). Berman and McLaughlin (1977) concluded that teachers were more interested in participating in decisions affecting day-to-day implementation (their zone) than in selecting the innovation (the administrators' zone).

Third, the structure of participation affects staff sentiments about change. It is necessary to avoid both overcontrolling and undercontrolling the process. Overcontrol leads to mock participation (Firestone, 1980), which occurs when teachers are told they will influence the innovation's design and implementation—and input may actually be solicited, but the final plan does not reflect their input. This tactic provokes anger and distrust that flow over to actual implementation activities. Participation often requires a real sharing of control.

Undercontrol results when administrators announce an innovation's adoption but drop planning and execution in the teachers' laps. Teachers, then, plan in a vacuum, with insufficient understanding of the innovation's purposes and the required new behaviors. Often they cannot contact key administrators to obtain clarification, resources, or changes in rules to make organizational conditions congruent with the innovation. Such undercontrol leads to confusion, frustration, and bad technical planning, all of which undermine the implementation effort (Gross et al., 1971).

Addressing these latter two issues, Conway (1984) proposes a contingency model for the form of participation required in certain situations. The form is a function of the quality of the decision needed and the extent to which staff acceptance is likely and necessary. When decision quality needs to be high but staff acceptance is easily obtained, the leader can make the decision but should informally gather some staff input; when quality is of less importance but acceptance is absolutely necessary, a staff group with or without an administrative leader is the most effective form; when neither quality nor acceptance is critical (i.e., a routine matter), the important guideline is not to overburden anyone with decision-making responsibilities; and, finally, when both quality and acceptance are paramount, a formal staff committee coupled with pressure from administrators is the best form.

This discussion of participation paves the way for a general point about the change process: *There are no universal rules for changing organizations.* Participation is useful—sometimes; and even though administrative support is critical, its form will vary across schools. Thus, one cannot assert that any particular change strategy is most effective. It depends on the situation and the nature of the decision. The next section expands on this contingency theme.

Contingencies in the Change Process

Recent research on change indicates that a systematically planned, high-quality innovation can be put in place successfully with good technical assistance and strong administrative support. Sometimes a top-down process can succeed; at other times, a grassroots approach is more appropriate. But given the millions of dollars and countless energy devoted to studying and carrying out the change process, what has really been learned? Essentially this: Some efforts succeed in some settings and not in others; and the setting is the critical factor.

This section examines the interaction between the change process and the setting. It asks: How can the variability in success across similar projects be explained? Or, put another way, is there a pattern to the spotty success of planned change projects? The answer to the second question is yes; and to the first, it is contingent on local context.

There are three answers to why the same change strategy yields desired outcomes in School A but not in School B. First, the strategy was not really enacted in School B. This explanation is similar to that proposed for why many curriculum innovations in the past decade were not successful. They simply were never implemented. Second, in School B, the strategy had unintended side effects that negated desired outcomes. Third, the strategy just did not have the desired effect, even though it was enacted faithfully. All three explanations suggest that School B had extenuating circumstances not present in School A.

These extenuating circumstances reside in the social and organizational context of the school. There is an inevitable intertwining of strategies with the context that produces varying outcomes from school to school. Categories of events that are most salient for understanding a school's context are referred to as "contingencies"; that is, the enactment and consequences of a change strategy are contingent on these contextual characteristics.

A contingency approach makes several assumptions about change strategies. First, they are bounded by time and place. There are no universally successful strategies. Knowledge about the relationship among events in one setting is not fully predictive of what will happen in another (Berman, 1981). Second, there is limited generalizability of event relationships. As Hanson (1979) notes about contingency approaches to school management, "contingency theory stresses the view that…there is some middle ground between the existence of universal principles of management that fit all organizational types, and that…each organization is unique and therefore must be studied as unique" (p. 102). Third, interaction between a change strategy and a contextual condition tints subsequent events (Schoonhoven, 1981). Thus, a school affects and is affected by the initiation of a change strategy, and the ensuing change process is partially the consequence of this interaction.

The usefulness of contingency approaches for understanding human action has been asserted in business management (Lorsch, 1979), in understanding the relationship between organizational structure and technology (Perrow, 1970), in promoting organizational change (Zaltman & Duncan, 1977), in choosing field-agent strategies (Litwak & Meyer, 1966; Louis, 1977), and in school management (Hanson, 1979, 1981). More recently, this approach has been suggested for school improvement research. As Berman (1978) notes concerning FPSEC, "it became apparent that the same technology was implemented in very different ways in different institutional settings with very different results" (p. 161). In school improvement efforts, contingencies belong to that class of events referred to by Hall, Zigarmi, and Hord (1979) as "unsponsored interventions"; that is, they are "not intended to influence use of the innovation, although, in fact, they do (p. 16). The same authors point out that when such intrusions repeat themselves over time, they can be called "themes"—themes that frequently force themselves into the spotlight, occasionally echo hauntingly in the background, and disappear, only to suddenly return to the forefront depending on the change strategy being examined.

Related issues arose in the 1970s concerning site readiness: that is, the preconditions necessary for a site to be able to change (Rosenblum & Louis, 1981). But, the influence of contextual factors was not tracked throughout the process. Herriott and Gross (1979) argued, in fact, that these conditions were largely unknowable ahead of time. However, the Corbett, Dawson, and Firestone (1984) study of curriculum change in 14 schools identified eight specific features of a school's context that partially determined a change project's success:

> existing school goals and priorities;
>
> the nature and extent of faculty factions and tensions;
>
> turnover in key administrative and faculty positions;
>
> patterns of knowledge use and current instructional and administrative practices;
>
> the prior history of change projects;
>
> the extent of organizational linkages among school subunits;
>
> the availability and nature of incentives and disincentives for innovative behavior; and
>
> the availability of school resources.

The better the fit between a change project's objectives and school and/or district priorities, the greater the likelihood that change will result; and the more similar the change objectives are to a district's goals, the better the chance that changes will be continued (Berman & McLaughlin, 1976). With a match, little disruption occurs in the flow of change activities. Problems arise when change objectives fall below a district's top two priorities. Then, sudden resource shortages are more apt to interrupt the change process and require adjustments in it.

From a political perspective, the often-competing interests of different factions within a faculty are an important local condition (Firestone, 1980). Tensions between teachers and administrators are obvious foci, to investigate but teachers do not constitute a homogeneous body of interests (Deal, 1985). Instead, a faculty often presents an array of formal and informal coalitions of varying intensities and endurance. If not appeased or coopted, these can sidetrack, stall, or stop the change process.

Schools vary in the amount of staff turnover. It is perhaps not too common to encounter a situation where a teacher with the least seniority has taught in the building for 12 years. It may be equally uncommon to find a school where staff come and go so frequently that names are generally unknown and faces only vaguely familiar. Nevertheless, turnover varies widely between these extremes. Its consequences for change efforts can be considerable, especially if a supportive principal leaves and is replaced by another with different priorities. Similarly, the departure of a respected teacher who is an ardent project advocate may dampen other teachers' enthusiasm (Fullan, 1982).

A project has to strike a balance in how much an innovation and the change process depart from existing staff practices. For example, most projects encourage the use of research-based knowledge to make decisions; yet school personnel rarely seek this type of knowledge in their day-to-day work (Hood & Blackwell, 1976). Thus, the fit among an innovation, its associated activities, and current practices has considerable implications for the change process.

There has been little investigation of the carryover effects of prior change initiatives to subsequent ones, yet this can also have an impact (Kozuch, 1979; Paul, 1977). The cumulative residue of prior projects creates a legacy of change. This legacy partially sets a staff's expectations for subsequent school improvement efforts and tempers staff members' willingness and ability to participate.

Aspects of school organization closely touch the day-to-day operation of a school and, as a result, the change process. Of these, the most important are linkages, or coordination mechanisms. These tie action in one part of the organization to action in another. Discussions of this issue in education abound, especially in recent literature on loose coupling—the situation in which one person's or subunit's behavior is mostly independent of another's behavior (Firestone & Wilson, 1985; Weick, 1982). In loosely coupled systems, an individual can easily initiate changes, but these rarely spread. The reverse is the case in more tightly linked systems. Given that most schools are loosely coupled (Miles, 1981), special efforts probably will have to be made to stimulate schoolwide change.

Teachers have very few rewards available to them,

and the ones that are available offer little material advantage (Lortie, 1975). Nevertheless, the provision of incentives is the most crucial local contribution to successful implementation and continuation. Encouragement and recognition from peers and administrators are the most salient of these.

The availability of resources influences strategies more than any other local condition. If staff time and materials are scarce, change activities will not make much, if any, headway. Where the resources come from is also critical. External support helps to initiate a project, but only when a school contributes the major portion of the resources does lasting change ensue (Berman & McLaughlin, 1976; Chabotar, Louis, & Sjogren, 1981).

NEXT STEPS: EXPANDING THE CULTURAL PERSPECTIVE

This review has indicated a wide range of topics on planned organizational change in education that could be explored in future research. However, with increasingly limited resources for both research and planned change projects, energy should be concentrated on directions that are most likely to enhance understanding of how to manage educational change in the foreseeable future.

Our view is that the most profitable direction is to apply more systematically the cultural perspective to understanding the change process. This perspective is underrepresented in current thinking and practice; indeed, many state and federal policy makers, program developers, school administrators, and program evaluators seem wedded to a technological perspective, which poses the major process objective in bringing practitioners into contact with new knowledge. When teachers and administrators are confronted with compelling evidence, this perspective assumes that they will alter their behavior willingly (see also Sarason, 1982). Some researchers and practitioners have also incorporated into their interpretations and management of the change process the political perspective that takes into account the conflict and search for personal advantage that surrounds planned change. However, change takes more than rational planning and persuasion. The cultural perspective goes beyond the political one to suggest that the differences among those engaged in the change process are more fundamental than personal interest or gain. Instead, these differences reflect deeply ingrained sets of values, beliefs, and norms.

There are at least three reasons for extending the cultural perspective at this time. First, a great deal of effort is being devoted right now to applying the cultural perspective to the study of organizational behavior in general (e.g., see Jelinek, Smircich, & Hirsch, 1983). This work will provide an extended range of conceptual and methodological tools for examining planned organizational change as a cultural phenomenon. Second, this work is addressing a central issue for the study of planned organizational changes: how to manage cultural change. Until recently, those who have looked at schools from a cultural perspective have emphasized the immutability of organizational cultures (e.g., Sarason, 1982). Although there is considerable debate right now as to how changeable such cultures are, there are indicators that managers can in fact shape them (e.g., Peters & Waterman, 1982). Finally, as will be discussed later, research on instructionally effective schools suggests that the cultures of those schools do contribute to the quality of learning that takes place there (Deal, 1985).

To indicate the direction that such research might take, this section offers a definition of organizational culture and indicates how it influences school effectiveness. It then introduces two issues central to the study of planned organizational change: the examination of dissemination from a cultural perspective and the study of school improvement as cultural transformation.

Organizational Culture

Culture is "socially shared and transmitted knowledge of what is, and what ought to be, symbolized in act and artifact" (Wilson, 1971, p. 90). It is "social heredity [and] the precipitate of learned human adjustments" (Williams, 1970, p. 25). Culture provides a normative structure for a social group; it is the wellspring from which flow recurrent and predictable behavior patterns. Indeed, "culture points to those common elements in behavior that are derived from individuals' having been reared in the same tradition" (Williams, 1970, p. 26). This normative structure defines both "what is"—knowledge, beliefs, and technology—and "what ought to be"—values and norms—for successive generations. Such definitions provide points of order and stability in the blooming, buzzing confusion of everyday life. Culture helps to clarify what is important and what is not, as well as what to do about both. Culture is, then, conservative, although not immutable. It carries the past to the present, yields grudgingly to the cumulative impact of concurrent social conflicts, and long outlasts the lives of particular individuals.

"Culture" and "normative structure" are basic conceptual tools for analyzing societies; yet they have also been fruitfully applied to smaller social groups. For example, Lortie (1975) and Sarason (1982) have analyzed the occupational culture of teachers and point to the behavioral commonalities evident in classroom after classroom after classroom. Equally important, a number of authors have emphasized the idea of an "organizational culture" (Deal & Kennedy, 1982; Peters & Waterman, 1982). They use the term to denote the emergence of distinct systems of knowledge, beliefs, technology, values, and norms in a particular organization. They argue further that organizational culture is what separates well-run firms from those that perform poorly. The most effective companies have a well-integrated culture that clearly defines "core values" (Peters & Waterman, 1982). These widely shared values drive behavior and guide the settlement of disputes, thereby enabling united devotion to attaining major organizational goals.

Culture in Effective Schools

In a more subtle way, the literature on effective schools parallels the emphasis on culture in excellent companies (Rossman, 1985). The terminology has not been so directly transported, but similar social phenomena can be seen. For example, as one examines the lists of characteristics of effective schools that have emerged in the last decade, what comes through as significant is not the specific characteristics themselves; indeed, individual characteristics or practices often have little explanatory value alone. Their power comes from the way they combine to form a common "ethos," or culture (Rutter, Maugham, Mortimer, Ousten, & Smith, 1979). This culture is a widely shared understanding of what is and what ought to be symbolized in student, teacher, and administrator acts as well as in the school's artifacts, like billboards, wall charts, documents, awards, and use of space. The literature highlights the content of values for behavior in effective schools. One of these is that all students can learn at least the basic skills that schools teach—in other words, high expectations for all students (Brookover, Beady, Flood, Schweitzer, & Wisenbaker, 1979). Others include high commitment to work, an action orientation, professional autonomy, meaningful and salient recognition for good performance, and available slack time (Clark et al., 1984).

Traces of these characteristics are found in some quantity in any school, for example, within an energetic grade-level team or department. What sets the highly achieving school apart from the less effective one is not simply the presence of particular norms and values but the fact that most members espouse them in word and deed. Thus, the most productive schools have a distinctive normative structure that supports quality instruction.

Dissemination as Cultural Reconstruction

Most studies that have looked at external efforts to promote change from a cultural perspective have emphasized the conflicts between the cultures of teachers and those of university researchers, developers, or policy makers. More work needs to be done to trace the distinctive differences between the organizational cultures of schools and of universities, research-and-development agencies, state and federal education agencies, and other organizations committed to educational reform. Yet, a professional culture is constructed out of elements borrowed from others. This is especially true of subcultures, including organizations, that draw upon the larger society (Metz, 1984). Even subcultures in opposition extract the material for expressing that opposition from the dominant culture, as Willis (1977) has shown in his study of working-class youth. Thus, an important issue for future research is to clarify how this borrowing and sorting of cultural elements takes place.

One step in that enterprise will be to clarify educators' truth and utility tests. These tests constitute a set of values or criteria used to evaluate new knowledge and ideas. Weiss and Bucuvalas (1980) have shown the differences between the truth and utility tests of researchers and policy makers. Policy makers look not only at the research quality of the study but also at how well it conforms to their past experience. Teachers apparently rely even more upon their experience, especially in the classroom, than policy makers do (Lortie, 1975). Outsider emphasis on theory often leads to teacher rejection of research or innovations that are too "theoretical" (Hargreaves, 1984).

Yet, products that strike teachers as being realistic demonstrate that they incorporate the practical suggestions of educators, are compatible with the social context of prospective users, minimize jargon in their explanations, and have a strong inspirational thrust; and such products are quite likely to be used (Louis et al., 1984). Available research is just beginning to clarify the truth and utility tests used by educators, the differences in the tests used by teachers and various kinds of administrators, and the implications of those tests for the design of products to be used in schools.

Research on planned organizational change from a cultural perspective is a useful way to extend what has been learned about the field in the last 15 years. Although it provides new perspectives for viewing external efforts to guide change efforts, it is most obviously a way to reexamine the local dynamics of the process. In so doing it mixes a healthy respect for the conservative, stable nature of the schools as organizations with an interest in how they can be changed.

By focusing on the underlying values that promote stability, the research draws attention not only to the factors that affect how discrete change projects will progress but also to the conditions that contribute directly to school effectiveness.

School Improvement as Cultural Transformation

The cultural perspective suggests that most efforts to alter some behavioral or procedural regularity in a school will reshape its normative structure, intentionally or not. On the surface, an improvement project may seem to tinker only with discrete behaviors, for example, encouraging teachers to use small groups often to increase time-on-task. More deeply, such suggestions may strike at the heart of the tradition of grouping students for reading or math instruction. The fact that some research on time-on-task favors whole-group instruction for raising test scores may pale considerably beside years of teachers' having been taught in groups when they were students, having watched other teachers teach in groups, and using groups in their own classrooms—not to mention their devaluing test scores as indicators of successful teaching and valuing relief from always being "on stage." Treating the issue as simply a technological problem without understanding the knowledge and values supporting small-group instruction can lead to the use of totally inappropriate change strategies.

This is the takeoff point for future research on school improvement. For example, the literature on effective schools portrays the characteristics of excellent schools. Although these can be reinterpreted as cultural elements fairly easily, there is still little guidance as to how they were created or transported. The core research question is this: What are the processes by which values and norms that support effective school performance become a part of a school's normative structure?

To begin to answer this question, several scholarly activities are required—four of which are described below. First, we should reexamine the major contributions to the planned change literature to date from a cultural perspective. This perspective will provide a coherent framework for understanding why what is already known about changing schools works. For example, Kirst and Jung's (1980) description of eventual success of the Title I program for improving schools' services to disadvantaged children highlights the importance of creating an occupational subculture of Title I directors who were committed to supporting the aims of the act. In addition, the fact that the program attained this milestone over a 13-year period indicates the conservative character of culture and

suggests that fundamental change comes slowly, not through a "quick fix." Similarly, principals may be central to successful change because they are best placed structurally to establish, or at least affirm, norms for the whole school. Underlying the behaviors that make up the amorphous term *administrative support* is the importance of signaling to school staff what is and is not necessary for them to address.

Second, we need additional investigations of the norms and values that support and inhibit change and improvement. A major concern here is to understand how norms and values are distributed. Common sense suggests that adherence to every norm cannot be expected of every person. Such a system would be much too rigid and constraining. Norms vary as to their explicitness, specificity, and flexibility; some proscribe and others prescribe; and some are technical whereas others are conventional, esthetic, or moral (Williams, 1970). In excellent organizations there is a core set of norms everyone is expected to observe, whereas other behavioral expectations have more narrow applications (Peters & Waterman, 1982). Research on planned organizational change should clarify the norms that accompany improvement and that promote student learning. The effective schools research provides a useful start in this direction, but we need cultural analyses that better specify the types of norms in effective schools, the content of those norms, and how they are distributed, transmitted, and enforced.

Third, although cultural conflict can be inferred from existing studies, we need to put together a collection of in-depth, detailed studies of that process at work. Researchers must capture the ongoing clash of competing norms and values in the school setting (for one of the few existing studies like this, see Wolcott, 1977). Examinations solely of the planning process when only a small number of actors are involved or reconstructions of now-distant events are of little use. The former depicts the present normative structure, not its transformation. The latter is an excellent way to describe cultural maintenance, but interpretations, ceremonies, and myths constructed subsequent to the transformational period tell more about the current culture than the transformation process.

Excellent opportunities to study cultural conflict reside in the first several years after (a) the appearance of a new administrator; (b) the initiation of a new state or local graduation, curriculum, or testing requirement; (c) the transfer of staff when schools have been closed; and (d) the recovery from a teachers' strike. Such events create a clash among competing values in a school. Moreover, Williams (1970) observes that "norms are rarely produced unless there is some important motivation to behave in ways other than those specified by the norm" (p. 33). The situations cited above create such motivations and, thus, are more likely to provide glimpses of cultural transformation.

Fourth, we need to examine current intentional efforts to shape a school's culture. Willard Waller (1967) once said about sociology, "A sociological writer cannot, in the present state of our science, hope to get very far ahead of common sense, and he is usually fortunate if he does not fall behind it" (p. 3). Although educational administration researchers are just now rediscovering the cultural side of school life, there are certainly practitioners who have long realized that staff perceptions of what is and what ought to be are inescapably involved with school performance, and they seek to change those perceptions. Others create such changes without even knowing it. In other words, not having a label for a behavior does not preclude its existence. This research activity becomes, then, a search for exemplars. Deal (1985) details at least five ways businesses shape organizational cultures: (a) frequently espousing core values in credos and using the values visibly as guides to decision making; (b) anointing heros and heroines; (c) establishing rituals; (d) holding and emphasizing certain ceremonies; and (e) promulgating positive stories of organizational exploits. Effective school administrators already do these things; researchers should seek them out, build a storehouse of rich examples, and detail the conditions under which culture shaping proves effective or ineffective.

CONCLUSION

After 15 years of systematic research about and experience with improving schools, educators know substantially more about planned organizational change. There is greater respect for the complexities of the process, more realism in expectations, and enhanced understanding of strategies that work in different situations. Yet much remains to be learned about how potential changes challenge underlying values, beliefs, and norms. Cultural elements of a school or district are what hold the organization together and will continue to do so in the face of initiatives that may alter them. Greater emphasis on understanding school culture, its formation, and how to shape it currently holds the greatest promise for building on the momentum of current educational reforms.

NOTE

[1] One generally speaks of the dissemination of "knowledge" that has been defined and categorized in a variety of ways. Weiss (1978) has identified a wide range of possible outcomes of the dissemination of knowledge, from "enlightenment," where one sees or conceptualizes a problem or phenomenon differently, to engineering, where one changes one's ways of doing things. Although there have been efforts to disseminate research studies to educators through the Education Research Information Clearinghouse (ERIC) for a whole range of purposes, most dissemination efforts in education focus on some sort of "product" that transforms some kind of research or craft-based knowledge in some way. One tends to think of such products as curricula, but they can include a broad range of phenomena, such as ways to supervise teachers or organizational arrangements like team teaching. The intended outcome, however, is usually some change in daily practice or organizational arrangements that is expected to contribute to student learning.

REFERENCES

Arends, R. I. (1982). The meaning of administrative support. *Educational Administration Quarterly, 18*(4), 79–92.

Atkin, J. M., & House, E. R. (1981). The federal role in curriculum development: 1950–1980. *Educational Evaluation and Policy Analysis, 3*(5), 5–36.

Bailey, S. K., & Mosher, E. K. (1968). *ESEA: The office of education administers a law.* Syracuse, NY: Syracuse University Press.

Baldridge, J. V. (1975). Rules for a Machiavellian change agent: Transforming the entrenched professional organization. In J. V. Baldridge & T. E. Deal (Eds.), *Managing change in educational organizations.* Berkeley, CA: McCutchan.

Baldridge, J. V., & Deal, T. E. (1975). Overview of change processes in educational organizations. In J. V. Baldridge & T. E. Deal (Eds.), *Managing change in educational organizations.* Berkeley, CA: McCutchan.

Bartunek, J., & Keys, C. B. (1979). Participation in school decision making. *Urban Education, 14*(1), 52–75.

Berman, P. (1978). The study of macro- and micro-implementation. *Public Policy, 26*(2), 157–184.

Berman, P. (1981). Toward an implementation paradigm. In R. Lehming & M. Kane (Eds.), *Improving schools: Using what we know.* Beverly Hills, CA: Sage.

Berman, P., & McLaughlin, M. W. (1975). *Federal programs supporting educational change: Vol. 4. The findings in review.* Santa Monica, CA: Rand.

Berman, P., & McLaughlin, M. W. (1976). Implementation of educational innovation. *Educational Forum, 40*(3), 345–370.

Berman, P., & McLaughlin, M. W. (1977). *Federal programs supporting educational change: Vol. 7. Factors affecting implementation and continuation.* Santa Monica, CA: Rand.

Berman, P., & McLaughlin, M. W. (1979). *An exploratory study of school district adaptation.* Santa Monica, CA: Rand.

Brookover, W. B., Beady, C., Flood, P., Schweitzer, J., & Wisenbaker, J. (1979). *School social systems and student achievement: Schools can make a difference.* New York: Praeger.

Bullock, C. S. (1976). Desegregating urban areas: Is it worth it? Can it be done? In F. H. Levinson & B. D. Wright (Eds.), *School desegregation: Shadows and substance.* Chicago: University of Chicago Press.

Butler, M., & Paisley, W. (1978). *Factors determining roles and functions of educational linking agents.* San Francisco: Far West Laboratory for Educational Research and Development.

Carnine, D., Gersten, R., & Green, S. (1982). The principal as instructional leader: A second look. *Educational Leadership, 40*(3), 47–50.

Chabotar, K. J., Louis, K. S., & Sjogren, J. (1981). *Relationships between local contributions and the success of a federal school improvement program.* Cambridge, MA: Abt.

Charters, W. W., & Jones, J. E. (1973). On the risk of evaluating non-events in program evaluation. *Educational Researcher, 2*(11), 5–7.

Charters, W. W., & Pellegrin, R. (1973). Barriers to the innovation process: Four case studies of differentiated staffing. *Educational Administration Quarterly, 9*(1), 3–14.

Chase, F. S. (1970). The laboratories: 1970 and beyond. *Journal of Research and Development in Education, 3*(2), 104–120.

Clark, D. (1981). In consideration of goal-free planning: The failure of traditional planning systems in education. *Educational Administration Quarterly, 17*(3), 42–60.

Clark, D., & Guba, E. (1967). An examination of potential change roles in education. In *Rational planning in curriculum and instruction.* Washington, DC: National Education Association.

Clark, D., Lotto, L., & Astuto, T. (1984). Effective schools and school improvement: A comparative analysis of two lines of inquiry. *Educational Administration Quarterly, 20*(3), 41–68.

Conway, J. (1984). The myth, mystery, and mastery of participative decision-making in education. *Educational Administration Quarterly, 20*(3), 11–40.

Corbett, H. D. (1981). School impacts on technical assistance roles: An in-depth analysis. *Knowledge: Creation, Diffusion, Utilization, 3*(2), 249–267.

Corbett, H. D., Dawson, J. A., & Firestone, W. A. (1984). *School context and school change: Implications for effective planning.* New York: Teachers College Press.

Corbett, H. D., Rossman, G. R., & Dawson, J. A. (1984). The meaning of funding cuts: Local context and coping with Chapter 2 of ECIA. *Educational Evaluation and Policy Analysis, 6*(4), 341–354.

Crandall, D. P., & Loucks, S. F. (1983). *People, policies, and practices: Examining the chain of school improvement, Vol. X: A roadmap for school improvement.* Andover, MA: The Network.

Cronbach, L. J., Ambron, S. R., Dornbusch, S. M., Hess, R. D., Hornick, R. C., Phillips, D. C., Walker, D. F., & Weiner, S. S. (1980). *Toward reform of program evaluation.* San Francisco: Jossey-Bass.

Datta, L. (1981). Damn the experts and full speed ahead: An examination of the *Study of Federal Programs Supporting Educational Change* as evidence against directed development and for local problem-solving. *Evaluation Review, 5*(1), 5–32.

Deal, T. E. (1985). The symbolism of effective schools. *Elementary School Journal, 831*(5), 601–620.

Deal, T. E., & Kennedy, A. A. (1982). *Corporate cultures: The rites and rituals of corporate life.* Reading, MA: Addison-Wesley.

Driscoll, J. W. (1978). Trust and participation in organizational decision making as predictors of satisfaction. *Academy of Management Journal, 21*(1), 44–56.

Elmore, R. E. (1980). *Complexity and control: What legislators and administrators can do about implementing public policy.* Washington, DC: National Institute of Education.

Emrick, J. W. & Peterson, S. A. (1977). *A synthesis of findings across five recent studies of educational dissemination.* Menlo Park; CA: Stanford Research Institute.

Emrick, J. W., with Peterson, S. M., & Agarwala-Rogers, R. (1977). *Evaluation of the National Diffusion Network.*, Menlo Park, CA: Stanford Research Institute.

Firestone, W. A. (1977). Participation and influence in the planning of educational change. *Journal of Applied Behavioral Science, 13*(2), 163–183.

Firestone, W. A. (1980). *Great expectations for small schools: The limitations of federal programs.* New York: Praeger.

Firestone, W. A., & Corbett, H. D. (1981). Schools vs. linking agents as contributors to the change process. *Educational Evaluation and Policy Analysis, 3*(2), 5–17.

Firestone, W. A., & Rossman, G. R. (1983). *You can lead a horse to water...limits to state control over technical assistance agencies in education.* Philadelphia: Research for Better Schools.

Firestone, W. A., & Wilson, B. L. (1983). Assistance and enforcement. *Knowledge: Creation, Diffusion, Utilization, 4*(3), 429–452.

Firestone, W. A., & Wilson, B. L. (1985). Using bureaucratic and cultural linkages to improve instruction: The principal's contribution. *Educational Administration Quarterly, 20*(2), 7–30.

Fullan, M. (1982). *The meaning of educational change.* New York: Teachers College Press, Columbia University.

Fullan, M. (1985). Change processes and strategies at the local level. *Elementary School Journal, 85,* 391–421.

Fullan, M., & Pomfret, A. (1977). Research on curriculum and instruction implementation. *Review of Educational Research, 47*(1), 335–397.

Giacquinta, J. (1973). The process of organizational change in schools. In F. N. Kerlinger (Ed.), *Review of research in education.* Itasca, IL: Peacock.

Gideonse, H. D. (1980). Improving the federal administration of education programs. *Educational Evaluation and Policy Analysis, 2*(1), 61–70.

Gross, N., Giacquinta, J. B., & Bernstein, M. (1971). *Implementing organizational innovations.* New York: Basic Books.

Hall, G., & Hord, S. (1984). Analyzing what change facilitators do. *Knowledge: Creation, Diffusion, Utilization, 5*(3), 275–307.

Hall, G., Zigarmi, P., & Hord, S. (1979). *A taxonomy of interventions: The prototype and initial testing.* Paper presented at the annual meeting of the American Educational Research Association, San Francisco.

Hanson, E. M. (1979). School management and contingency theory: An emerging perspective. *Educational Administration Quarterly, 15*(2), 98–116.

Hanson, E. M. (1981). Organizational control in educational systems: A case study of governance in schools. In S. Bacharach (Ed.), *Organizational behavior in schools and school districts.* New York: Praeger.

Hargreaves, A. (1984). Experience counts, theory doesn't: How teachers talk about their work. *Sociology of Education, 57*(4), 244–254.

Hargrove, E. (1982). Strategies for the implementation of federal education policies: Compliance and incentives. *Peabody Journal of Education, 60*(1), 20–33.

Hargrove, E. C., Scarlett, G. G., Ward, L. E., Abernethy, V., Cunningham, J., & Vaughn, W. (1981). School systems and regulatory mandates: A case study of the implementation of the education for all handicapped children act. In S. B. Bacharach (Ed.), *Organizational behavior in schools and school districts.* New York: Praeger.

Herriott, R. E., & Gross, N. (1979). *The dynamics of planned educational change.* Berkeley, CA: McCutchan.

Hood, P. D., & Blackwell, L. (1976). Key educational information users and their styles of information use. In *The educational information market study: Vol. 1.* San Francisco: Far West Laboratory for Educational Research and Development.

House, E. R. (1974). *The politics of educational innovation.* Berkeley, CA: McCutchan.

House, E. R. (1981). Three perspectives on educational innovation: Technological, political, and cultural. In R. Lehming & M. Kane (Eds.), *Improving schools: Using what we know.* Beverly Hills, CA: Sage.

Huberman, M. (1981). *ECRI, Masepa, North Plains: Case study.* Andover, MA: The Network.

Huberman M., & Miles, M. B. (1984). *Innovation up close: How school improvement works.* New York: Plenum.

James, T., & Tyack, D. (1983). Learning from past efforts to reform the high school. *Phi Delta Kappan, 64*(6), 400–406.

Jelinek, M., Smircich, L., & Hirsch, P. (1983). Introduction: A code of many colors. *Administrative Science Quarterly, 28*(3), 331–338.

Joyce, B., & Showers, B. (1982). The coaching of teaching. *Educational Leadership, 40*(1), 4–10.

Kirst, M., & Jung, R. (1980). The utility of a longitudinal approach in assessing implementatioon: A thirteen year view of Title I, ESEA. *Educational Evaluation and Policy Analysis, 2*(5), 17–34.

Kmetz, J. T., & Willower, D. J. (1982). Elementary school principals' work behavior. *Educational Administration Quarterly, 18*(4), 62–78.

Kozuch, J. A. (1979). Implementing an educational innovation: The constraints of the school setting. *High School Journal, 62*(5), 223–231.

Kunz, D. W., & Hoy, W. K. (1976). Leadership style of principals and the professional zone of acceptance of teachers. *Educational Administration Quarterly, 12*(3), 49–64.

Litwak, E., & Meyer, H. (1966). A balance theory of coordination between organizational and community primary groups. *Administrative Science Quarterly, 11,* 31–58.

Lorsch, J. W. (1979) Making behavioral science more useful. *Harvard Business Review, 57*(2), 171–180.

Lortie, D. C. (1975). *Schoolteacher: A sociological analysis.* Chicago: University of Chicago Press.

Louis, K. S. (1977). Dissemination of information from centralized bureaucracies to local schools: The role of the linking agent. *Human Relations, 30*(1), 25–42.

Louis, K. S. (1981). External agents and knowledge utilization: Dimensions for analysis and action. In R. Lehming & M. Kane (Eds.), *Improving schools: Using what we know.* Beverly Hills, CA: Sage.

Louis, K. S., Kell, D. G., Dentler, R. A., Corwin, R. G., & Herriott, R. E. (1984). *Exchanging ideas: The communication and use of knowledge in education.* Boston: Abt.

Louis, K. S., Rosenblum, S., & Molitor, J. A. (1981). *Strategies for knowledge use and school improvement.* Washington, DC: National Institute of Education.

Louis, K. S., & Sieber, S. D. (1979). *Bureaucracy and the dispersed organization: The educational extension agent experiment.* Norwood, NJ: Ablex.

McLaughlin, M. W., & Elmore, R. L. (1982). Implementaton of federal education programs: Implications for future federal policy. *Peabody Journal of Education, 60*(1), 8–19.

McLaughlin, M. W., & Marsh, D. (1978). Staff development and school change. *Teachers College Record, 80*(1), 69–94.

Metz, M. H. (1984). *Faculty culture: A case study.* Paper presented at the annual meeting of the American Sociological Association, San Antonio.

Miles, M. B. (1964). On temporary systems. In M. B. Miles (Ed.), *Innovation in education.* New York: Teachers College Press, Columbia University.

Miles, M. B. (1981). Mapping the common properties of schools. In R. Lehming & M. Kane (Eds.), *Improving schools: Using what we know.* Beverly Hills, CA: Sage.

Morris, V. C., Crowson, R. L., Hurwitz, E., & Porter-Gehrie, C. (1981). *The urban principal: Discretionay decision-making in a large educational organization.* Chicago: University of Illinois at Chicago Circle.

Mort, P. R., & Cornell, F. G. (1941). *American schools in transition.* New York: Teachers College Press, Columbia University.

Murphy, J. T. (1971). Title I of ESEA: The politics of implementing federal education reform. *Harvard Educational Review, 41*(1), 35–63.

Nelson, M., & Sieber, S. (1976). Innovation in urban secondary schools. *School Review, 84,* 213–231.

Orfield, G. (1969). *The reconstruction of Southern education.* New York: John Wiley.

Paul, P. (1977). Change processes at the elementary, secondary, and post-secondary levels of education. In N. Nash & J. Culbertson (Eds.), *Linking processes in educational improvement: Concepts and applications.* Columbus, OH: University Council for Educational Administration.

Perrow, C. (1970). *Organizational analysis: A sociological view.* Belmont, CA: Wadsworth.

Peters, T., & Waterman, R. (1982). *In search of excellence.* New York: Harper & Row.

Rivlin, A. M., & Timpane, P. M. (Eds.). (1975). *Planned variation in education.* Washington, DC: Brookings Institute.

Roberts, J. M. E., Kenney, J. L., Buttram, J., & Wolf, B. (1982). *Instructional improvement in Maryland: A study of research in practice.* Philadelphia: Research for Better Schools.

Rogers, E. M., & Shoemaker, F. F. (1971). *Communication of innovations: A cross-cultural approach,* (2nd ed.). New York:

Free Press.

Rosenblum, S., & Louis, K. S. (1981). *Stability and change.* New York: Plenum.

Rosenholtz, S. J. (1985). Political myths about education reform: Lessons from research on teaching. *Phi Delta Kappan, 65*(5), 349–355.

Rossman, G. R. (1985). *Studying professional cultures in improving high schools.* Paper presented at the annual meeting of the American Educational Research Association, Chicago.

Rowan, B. (1982). Organizational structure and the institutional environment: The case of public schools. *Administrative Science Quarterly, 27*(2), 259–279.

Rutter, M., Maughan, B., Mortimer, P., Ouston, J., & Smith, A. (1979). *Fifteen thousand hours: Secondary schools and their effects on children.* Cambridge, MA: Harvard University Press.

Sarason, S. B. (1971). *The culture of the school and the problem of change.* Boston: Allyn and Bacon.

Schoonhoven, C. B. (1981). *Problems with contingency theory: Testing assumptions hidden within the language of contingency "theory."* Administrative Science Quarterly, 26, 349–377.

Sieber, S. (1981). Knowledge utilization in public education: Incentives and disincentives. In R. Lehming & M. Kane (Eds.), *Improving schools: Using what we know.* Beverly Hills, CA: Sage.

Sieber, S., Louis, K., & Metzger, L. (1972). *The use of educational knowledge* (Vols. 1–2). New York: Columbia University, Bureau of Applied Research.

Smith, L. M., & Keith, P. M. (1971). *Anatomy of an educational innovation: An organizational analysis of an elementary school.* New York: John Wiley.

Stearns, M. S., & Norwood, C. R. (1977). *Evaluation of the field test of the project information packages.* Menlo Park, CA: Stanford Research Institute.

Waller, W. (1967). *The sociology of teaching* (3rd printing). New York: John Wiley.

Weatherly, R., & Lipsky, M. (1977). Street-level bureaucrats and institutional innovation: Implementing special-education reform. *Harvard Educational Review, 47*(2), 171–191.

Weick, K. E. (1976). Educational organizations as loosely coupled systems. *Administrative Science Quarterly, 21,* 1–19

Weick, K. E. (1982). Administering education in loosely coupled schools. *Phi Delta Kappan, 63*(10), 673–676.

Weiler, H. N. (1982). Education, public confidence, and the legitimacy of the modern state: Do we have a crisis? *Phi Delta Kappan, 64*(1), 9–14.

Weiss, C. H. (1978). Improving the linkage between social research and public policy. In L. E. Lynn (Ed.), *Knowledge and policy: The uncertain connection.* Washington, DC: National Academy of Sciences.

Weiss, C. H., & Bucuvalas, M. J. (1980). *Social science research and decision-making.* New York: Columbia University Press.

Welch, W. W. (1979). Twenty years of science curriculum development: A look back. In D. C. Berliner (Ed.), *Review of research in education.* Washington, DC: AERA.

Williams, R. M. (1970). *American Society.* New York: Knopf.

Willis, P. (1977). *Learning to labour; How working class kids get working class jobs.* Westmead, England: Gower.

Wilson, E. K. (1971). *Sociology: Rules, roles, and relationships.* Homewood, IL: Dorsey Press.

Wolcott, H. F. (1977). *Teachers vs. technocrats.* Eugene, OR: Center for Educational Policy and Management, University of Oregon.

Yin, R., Quick, S., Bateman, P., & Marks, G. (1978). *Changing urban bureaucracies: How new practices become routinized, executive summary.* Santa Monica, CA: Rand.

Zaltman, G., & Duncan, R. (1977). *Strategies for planned change.* New York: John Wiley.

CHAPTER 17

School Effects

Steven T. Bossert

The concept of school effectiveness is important to both the theory and practice of educational administration. Educators and the public constantly judge the success of school programs, and the premise of many studies of school management lies in some theory about important determinants of school effectiveness. Yet the concept of effectiveness is like a Rorschach test for educational researchers. Just about anything can become a predictor of effectiveness, given a particular image of the school as an organization. Effectiveness studies in educational administration focus on everything from the job satisfaction of teachers to the equity of policies on student discipline. What is treated as an "effect" in one study may be seen as a factor that produces effects in another study. This relativism in the definition of school effectiveness partly reflects the multiple goals attached to schools as social agencies. More than any other social institution, schools have been asked to accomplish a wide variety of complex and often contradictory missions for our society—from creating the conditions for equitable social participation to the moral inculcation of our youth.

Despite this multiplicity of organizational goals, one key "effect" always is associated with the charter of our public schools: to provide children with the opportunities to learn reading, writing, and arithmetic. Instruction constitutes the productive, or technical, core of the school. Yet, the field of educational administration has been criticized for its lack of attention to the effects that administrative leadership and school

organization have on instruction and student learning (Bidwell, 1979; Erickson, 1978).

It is important to focus on instruction for several reasons. First, public demand for improving student achievement is making school administrators more accountable for the "products" of schools. The push for instructional leadership requires an understanding of the interplay among organizational structures, management, and instructional activities that enhance student achievement. Second, the rationale for many studies in educational administration rests on an assumed but indirect link between certain organizational characteristics and student learning. For example, many researchers have studied the determinants of school climate because climate factors are supposed to be related to student achievement (Brookover, Beady, Flood, Schweitzer, & Wisenbaker, 1979; Miskel, Fevurly, & Stewart, 1979; Sergiovanni & Starratt, 1979). Yet, climate effects on student learning, although often statistically robust, are loosely defined and have no clear basis in a theory of schooling or few identifiable links to children's learning experiences (Anderson, 1982). It is important to identify frameworks that can assess directly the relationships among organizational factors that affect what students accomplish in school. Third, organizational theory has consistently acknowledged the fundamental relationship between an organization's productive technology and its administrative functioning (Thompson, 1967). Research on educational administration must adequately characterize the productive technology of the school and map its relationship to administrative organization and processes.

Consultant/reviewers: David L. Clark, University of Virginia; and Donald A. Erickson, University of California—Los Angeles

This review of research will focus on several major lines of inquiry that have influenced thinking about school effectiveness. First, the long tradition of research that questions the effects schools have on student learning will be reviewed briefly. Although this research casts doubts on school effectiveness, it has spawned a number of studies that have tried to overcome certain methodological and conceptual flaws, providing some evidence for school effects. Several important examples of these latter studies also will be examined. Third, the recent research on "effective schools" will be summarized. This research has been exceedingly influential in shaping school improvement programs, administrative training, and research agendas. One result of the effective schools research has been a renewed interest in the instructional management role of school principals; several recent investigations of this role will also be described. Finally, the review will summarize recent studies that may chart the future for school effectiveness research.

QUESTIONING SCHOOL EFFECTS

There is a long tradition of research that questions the effect that schools have on the achievements of students. School environments have been described alternatively as structures of resources, roles, expectations, and values; yet, links between these structures and students' attainments have eluded many educational researchers. Even studies of teaching methods have, until recently, produced inconsistent findings about effective instructional processes (Berliner & Koehler, 1983). Two major types of studies have contributed to the skepticism concerning the issue of school effects: input-output research and analyses of institutional systems.

Input-Output Research

Perhaps the most cited educational input-output study is the report entitled *Equality of Educational Opportunity* (*EEOR*), produced by James Coleman et al. (1966). Although primarily a study of the distribution of educational resources, the *EEOR* became associated with the phrase "schools don't make a difference" because of its finding that school characteristics account for an extremely small proportion in student achievements once the social composition of students is statistically controlled.

Like subsequent input-output studies, the *EEOR* reported that the physical facilities, level of expenditure, curriculum, and other quantifiable characteristics did not vary substantially among schools, nor did they affect students' performance on standardized achievement tests. The overall estimate of a "school effect" was small. Only about 10 percent of the variance in children's standardized test scores was attributed to the "unique" contribution of schools. The one factor that seemed to make a difference in children's aggregate test scores was the social composition of the student body. In schools where children from affluent homes were educated, all students benefited academically.

Coleman's study did confirm that black and white students attended different schools. Racial segregation was clear, not only in the South but also in the Northeast and urban, industrial areas of the Midwest. However, this segregation did not appear to produce wide differences in school expenditures. Once the social-class composition of the school was controlled, race as an independent variable became insignificant.

These findings stimulated a flurry of reanalyses of Coleman's data and many new studies of school effects. One of the most notable studies was completed by Jencks (1972b). He also found that the variance among schools in resources was very slight; that differences among schools accounted for a small proportion of the variance in students' achievements, especially when family background was controlled; and that the social composition of the school was the most important school-level factor associated with student performance on standardized tests. However, Jencks noted that the causal ordering among factors was questionable. He wrote, "It is almost never clear whether a school characteristic affects student achievement or vice versa" (Jencks, 1972a, p. 83). Because greater differences in childrens' achievement scores occurred within rather than between schools, Jencks suggested that it was important to examine how the same school treats different children. In other words, the source of inequality may not lie in the allocation processes that distribute resources to schools but in the ways schools put those resources to use.

In reviewing input-output studies, Spady (1973) lists several additional drawbacks. First, these studies rarely control for students' prior achievements. At any point, a student's performance is shaped by current resource allocations, by exposure to past allocations, and by past achievements. The cumulative effects of resource allocations are not measured directly by most input-output studies. Second, the effect of family background on student performance is likely to be overinflated due to the joint variance shared by socioeconomic status (SES), student motivation, and instructional experience. Third, the resources measured by input-output studies may not be the ones that really make a difference in student achievement, or they may not be measured at the level of student use. For example, the number of books in the school's library does not reflect students' reading habits. Spady argues that studies must be able to document the influence processes that work within schools.

Despite this call for an analysis of within-school processes that shape opportunities for students to learn, numerous studies of resource allocation between schools have been produced. (For reviews, see Averch, Carroll, Donaldson, Kiesling, & Pincus, 1972; Madaus, Airasian, & Kelleghan, 1980). The major findings have been the same—differences among schools account for an extremely small proportion of variance in students' achievements. Many researchers and policy makers feel that this means that schools, as organizations, do not have an effect on students' learning; others have contested this interpretation.

Two additional methodological concerns add fuel to the school effects debate. First, the reliance on norm-referenced achievement tests may result in an underestimation of schooling effects. When criterion-referenced tests are used to measure subjects that actually are taught, between-school variance increases substantially (Madaus, Kelleghan, Rakow, & King, 1979). Rutter (1983) suggests that effectiveness estimates often are based on items that are unrelated to what schools attempt to teach. Second, common aggregation procedures also may lead to inaccurate estimates of school effects. Regression models typically combine items measured at units within the school (e.g., classroom student-teacher ratios) to construct school-level variables, while using other items (e.g., student social class) that are treated as individual variables. Bidwell and Kasarda (1980) show that this use of mixed variables causes biased parameters for both school and individual variables: School effects are considerably lower and background effects are higher than those estimated by using data that are aggregated appropriately. (Also see Leucke & McGinn, 1975.)

Awareness of these problems has not slowed the use of inaccurately modeled input-output research designs. For example, Coleman and his associates recently have completed a study purporting to show that students in private schools achieve at higher levels than students in public schools (Coleman, Hoffer, & Kilgore, 1982). Again, this report has been soundly criticized for its conceptual and measurement errors. (For an excellent summary, see *Sociology of Education*, 1982.)

These input-output studies suffer many of the problems that have plagued other research on organizational effectiveness. Cameron and Whetten (1983) suggest that effectiveness studies have not been productive because they have failed to develop a comprehensive model or framework for defining effectiveness and for specifying important independent variables for study. (Also see Goodman & Pennings, 1979.) It is not unfair to say that many studies of school effects have adopted a "dustbowl" empiricism in their search for statistical relationships. Convenience or common-sense myths about educational practice seem to dictate the choice of variables included in these studies rather than any verifiable theory of schooling effects.

Bidwell and Kasarda (1980) also indicate that a particular set of unstated assumptions underlies most of the studies of school organization. They characterize this approach as the "radical individualist" model of schooling: The effects that formal education has on students are primarily a function of students' individual goals, levels of motivation, and inherent aptitudes. This approach focuses attention on social and intellectual dimensions, especially on how students who differ along these dimensions varyingly utilize school resources. This ignores the fact that schools may structure children's perceptions of, access to, and participation in learning activities of various types. The organizational outcomes of schools lie not simply in the way resources are allocated but in the mechanisms that specify students' access to and participation in different types of learning opportunities.

Institutionalization

The weak and inconsistent findings from input-output and teaching studies caused some social scientists to look elsewhere for the organizational effects of schools. Meyer (1977), for example, concludes that the influence that schools have does not accrue from their socialization or training of students. Because of the loose coupling between stated goals and instructional processes, the power of the school rests in its relationship to other institutions of social selection.

Meyer (1977) argues that schools produce graduates who are subject to social definitions about their worth and capabilities. He states that "educational systems involve large-scale public classification systems, defining new roles and statuses for both elites and members. These classifications are new constructions in that the newly defined persons are expected (and entitled) to behave, and be treated by others, in new ways" (p. 56). Classifications are not related directly to the social or technical competency produced in schools but rather to the currency placed by society on a diploma obtained from an particular institution. Therefore, the effects of schools are linked to their distinctive missions—technical-vocational, professional, elite liberal arts colleges, and the like. The important organizational outcomes of schools are associated with their function to legitimize social status: "Education allocation rules...give to the schools social *charters* to define people as graduates and as therefore possessing distinctive rights and capacities in society" (Meyer, 1977, p. 59).

Collins's (1971) analysis of the relationship between advances in the technical requirements of occupations and increasing educational credentials for entry into these occupations supports Meyer's theory. From a purely functional perspective, educational requirements for an occupation should reflect the training needed to successfully accomplish job demands. In analyzing over 1,500 different occupations, Collins found that educational requirements increased more rapidly than the technical requirements of the job. In fact, many jobs showed no increase in requisite skills but considerable increases in grade-level attainments required of job applicants.

Collins also cites research by Berg (1970) that indicates that individual work productivity does not increase with level of educational attainment. In general, better educated employees are not more productive and overeducated employees, ones whose school attainments are higher than the average worker in a job, have higher than average absentee rates. The rise in educational requirements, Collins concludes, cannot be linked to employers' desires to obtain more technically qualified employees. Rather, higher standards for educational attainment operate as a social control mechanism, limiting the numbers and types of applicants for positions within occupational sectors.

Collins argues that education is regarded as a "mark of membership in a particular group." The rise in general education attainment of all groups in the United States makes historical educational requirements incapable of discriminating among individuals and thus limiting access to certain jobs. Status groups in control of occupational sectors raise educational requirements to correspond to their own educational advancements, thus restricting access to occupants of lower status.

Schools, as organizations, therefore serve to legitimize the status distinctions among groups in our society. Like Meyer, Collins emphasizes the classificatory power of schools and not their socialization functions.

Meyer's and Collins' arguments are important because they focus attention on the relationship between schools and other institutions that process adults. Their arguments hint at how social categories are attributed to schools rather than recognized as arising from the technical functions of socialization and learning provided by schools. However, their argument does not really speak to the nature of production processes within schools but rather to the selection mechanisms used by other social institutions. Schools may have a substantial effect on students' socialization and learn-

ing, but other institutions simply may not be willing to assess that effect.

EVIDENCE FOR SCHOOL EFFECTS

When studies have examined directly the processes and resources that shape students' experiences in schools, school effects are quite evident. Three areas of research on school resources and structures are illustrative—time allocations, tracking structures, and classroom effects. Although the studies reviewed here help to bolster the idea that schools have effects, they are not models for school effectiveness research because of some clear limitations.

Time in School

A major criticism of input-output studies has been that they do not consider how students actually use resources that are available in the school. When researchers began looking for indicators of resource use, one of the most obvious of these is amount of education—amount not in the sense of years of schooling but in a more proximal measure of actual exposure to school resources at the school level.

Wiley (1976) noted, "If schooling has an influence on a child, it does so on a day-by-day basis, when he is present and subject to that influence, and cannot influence him when he is not there" (p. 228). By analyzing a subsample of the *EEOR* data for the sixth grades in the Detroit metropolitan area, Wiley found that background characteristics, especially social class, were strongly associated with school attendance. He questioned whether the amount of variance attributed to family background in Coleman's (1966) analysis was actually shared variance with attendance.

When he separated the unique and shared contributions that attendance accounted for in student achievements, Wiley found some significant school effects. For example, an increase in the length of the school year by 10 days could increase student achievement on the average of 1.00, 1.97, and 1.00 grade equivalent months in verbal ability, reading comprehension, and mathematics achievement, respectively. A 10 percent increase in the school day, from an average of 5 hours, could produce 14-percent increases in reading and mathematics performance and a 27-percent increase in reading comprehension.

An overly simplistic interpretation of these results implies that "more school is better." However, Wiley's analysis indicates that even a gross measure of students' exposure to school resources and involvement in learning activities—their attendance—demonstrates that schools have effects. Although Karweit (1976) has questioned the generalizability of Wiley's analysis, the issue of student time in school has become an important area of research and policy analysis (Denham & Lieberman, 1980).

Another study indicates the importance of school time. Heyns's (1978) analysis of student achievement gains during the school year and during summer suggests that schooling diminishes the effect of family background on learning. The achievement "gap between black and white children, and between low- and high-income children, widens disproportionately during the months when school is not in session" (Heyns, 1978, p. 187). Moreover, children who attend summer school programs or extensively use public library facilities learn more rapidly than those who are not involved in these programs. This effect was true for all children and all types of measured cognitive skills, but it was especially strong for relatively disadvantaged students. Heyns concludes that although schooling does not equalize the influence of status differences among students, it does have a significant independent effect on cognitive growth.

Although Wiley's and Heyns's studies create optimism about the effects that schools can have on their students, both are essentially "black box" studies. They argue that something happens when children are attending school, but they cannot identify the nature of the instructional activities and resources that actually affect learning.

Tracking Studies

A number of studies have tried to identify the within-school structures that affect students' learning opportunities. At the high school level, the focus has been on tracking because of perceived curricular differences among tracks and the relationship between track placement and future educational attainment.

Rosenbaum (1975, 1976) has pointed out that most tracking studies ignore the structural aspects of the tracking system and the social composition of the student body in tracked schools. For example, the distinctiveness of track boundaries and the amount of courses unique to a particular track may vary from school to school. A tracking system that separates students for only one or two courses should have only a minimal effect on students. Moreover, because track placement is highly correlated with students' social class, the separate effects of class and track cannot be disentangled.

Fortunately, Rosenbaum found a high school in which the student population was fairly homogeneous, where social class was unrelated to track placement, and where five distinctive curricular tracks existed.

Using student IQ as a dependent measure, Rosenbaum analyzed the effects of track placement on student learning gains. Track placement accounted for 5 percent of the variance in IQ gain. The effect of track on IQ change was independent of initial IQ.

Rosenbaum argues that the socialization experiences of children in different tracks varied substantially, thus causing the tracking effect. Although he did not examine these differences directly, there is evidence that students receive considerably different learning opportunities in various tracks. For example, Metz (1978) found that students in upper, college-preparatory tracks were given more opportunities for self-directed learning. (Also see Peterson, Wilkerson, & Hallinan, 1984.)

Classroom Effects

When input-output designs examine the proximal environments where pupils actually are exposed to instruction, resources that appear to have little effect at the school level actually can be shown to be important determinants of learning. One of the first production function studies that disaggregated school-level data and examined the influences that various resources had on different subgroups of children was Summers and Wolfe's (1975) analysis of Philadelphia schools.

They found that differences in class size, school size, teacher experience, and attendance had significant effects on low-income and racial minority students. For example, they confirmed that class size on the average does not affect student achievement. However, for students who were achieving below grade level, classes larger than 28 students had a negative effect on performance. Summers and Wolfe also reported that teacher experience had different effects on high- and low-achieving children. High-achieving pupils performed best with more experienced teachers, but low achievers did best with new, relatively inexperienced teachers. An interesting anomaly to this finding was that junior high school math teachers with 3 to 9 years of experience produced the highest math achievements, whereas math teachers with more than 10 years' experience had a negative effect on learning math (Summers & Wolfe, 1975, p. 12).

EFFECTIVE SCHOOLS RESEARCH

One of the latest and most popular entries into the quest for school outcomes has been the research on "effective schools." Comparisons of effective and ineffective schools have begun to identify specific school-level factors that promote higher student achievements, particularly in the basic skills (Armor et al., 1976;

Brookover et al., 1979; Clark, Lotto, & McCarthy, 1980; Rutter, Maugham, Mortimore, Ouston, & Smith, 1979; Venesky & Winfield, 1979; Wellisch, MacQueen, Carriere, & Duck, 1978). Studies consistently report that successful schools have the following characteristics (for reviews, see Bossert, Dwyer, Rowan, & Lee, 1982; Good & Brophy, 1985; Purkey & Smith, 1983):

> a school climate conducive to learning—one free of disciplinary problems and vandalism;
>
> a schoolwide emphasis on basic skills instruction;
>
> teachers who hold high expectations for all students to achieve;
>
> a system of clear instructional objectives for monitoring and assessing students' performances; and
>
> a school principal who is a strong programmatic leader and who sets high standards, observes classrooms frequently, maintains student discipline, and creates incentives for learning.

This research revived hopes among many researchers and practitioners that there are tractable aspects of school organization and culture that can affect the instructional attainments of children. Moreover, the message to school administrators is clear. It is embodied in the phrase "effective principal, effective school" (Lipham, 1981), which often means that school principals should become instructional leaders.

This research and its practical implications also have substantial appeal to educational administration because they mirror many of the findings from past leadership studies. Effective school principals, like other effective leaders, exhibit the following characteristics:

1. *Goals and Production Emphasis*: Effective principals are actively involved in setting instructional goals, emphasizing basic skills instruction, developing performance standards for students, and expressing the belief that all students can achieve (Brookover et al., 1979; Wellisch et al., 1978).

2. *Power and Strong Decision Making*: Effective principals are more powerful than their colleagues, especially in the areas of curriculum and instruction. They are seen as leaders and are effective in maintaining the support of parents and the local community (Blumberg & Greenfield, 1980; Lipham, 1981).

3. *Effective Management*: Principals in effective schools devote more time to the coordination and management of instruction and are more skilled in instructional matters. They observe their teachers at work, discuss instructional problems, support teachers' efforts to improve, and develop evaluation procedures that assess teacher and student per-

formance (Clark et al., 1980; Wellisch et al., 1978).

4. *Strong Human Relations Skills*: Effective principals recognize the unique styles and needs of teachers and help teachers achieve their own performance goals. They instill a sense of pride in the school among teachers, students, and parents (Brookover et al., 1979; Rutter et al., 1979).

Few would disagree with the desirability of these traits. In fact, studies of business, the military, and other organizations show that successful managers exhibit these same characteristics. If they exemplify these traits, the promise to school administrators is that their schools will become more effective. There are more than 39 major programs, involving 1,750 school districts, that promulgate this promise (Kyle, 1985; Miles, Farrar, & Neufeld, 1983).

Unfortunately, a number of troubling questions arise when one tries to apply these findings as prescriptions for school management. For example, if an effective school principal helps to set high expectations for students, how high should those expectations be? Should they be set at grade level or above? Should all students be held accountable to the same standard? Studies of motivation, as well as common sense, indicate that effort may decrease when standards are set too high, just as achievements may decrease when standards are too low. The research has not specified at what level expectations should be set or how they can be communicated effectively.

Effective principals emphasize instruction in basic skills. But how much time should be devoted to elementary decoding and numeracy tasks? What about important reasoning and social skills? Most schools have goals that go beyond the learning of basic skills. And too much time spent on basic tasks may detract from the higher-order thinking capacities that are necessary for success in the secondary grades (Peterson & Janicki, 1979). The most productive balance of various skill tasks has not been described.

Effective schools have strong principals. But teachers in effective schools also have high levels of autonomy so that they can provide instruction appropriate to the immediate needs of their students. How are strong leadership and autonomy managed simultaneously?

These dilemmas from the studies of effective schools and principals are due largely to limitations of their research designs. Several problems have plagued these studies (see Rowan, Bossert, & Dwyer, 1983). First, they are correlational. That is, after a small number of effective schools are identified, researchers catalog school characteristics, hoping to find a list of shared factors among the schools. This post hoc method cannot readily separate those factors that caused effectiveness from other inconsequential but shared items. Nor can these studies chart how important factors shaped success because the process of becoming successful is never studied. For example, it is unclear whether changes in school climate cause schools to become more effective or whether climate naturally improves as effectiveness increases. Likewise, it is unknown what characteristics and behavior are exhibited by principals when they are trying to change school structures as compared to when they are maintaining an effective organization (see Fiedler, 1967).

Second, the research has used a very circumscribed definition of effectiveness, and the techniques used to select effective schools are unreliable. Usually, effectiveness is defined by a school's average level of achievement on standardized basic-skills tests. Schools are considered effective if they score higher than expected given the SES of their students. In other words, two schools that have identical average achievement scores may not be equally effective. This definition of success is unstable: The likelihood of a school being successful for 2 consecutive years is nearly 50 percent—not much better than pure chance (Rowan & Denk, 1984).

Moreover, important school goals are not assessed. The studies never examine problem solving, social, or other types of schooling outcomes. In fact, most effective school studies use only one achievement score at two grade levels (e.g., reading in the third and sixth grades) to measure effectiveness. Therefore, there is no guarantee that schools that are identified by this technique are also excellent in attaining all, or even most, important goals set by schools at all grade levels. (For an expanded list of relevant schooling outcomes, see Rutter, 1983.)

These problems do not suggest that findings from the effectiveness studies should be ignored. The cumulative evidence, as well as the practical experience of educators, supports the importance of having high expectations for students, developing a positive school climate, improving instruction, and demonstrating leadership. These are necessary but probably not sufficient elements of effective instructional management. The effective schools research does provide a glimmer of hope for charting school effectiveness. However, because it maintains the "black box" and correlational approach without providing a conceptual framework that identifies and links important elements of school structure, its usefulness both for future research and for administrative practice is severely limited.

INSTRUCTIONAL MANAGEMENT

Recent examinations of the instructional management role of school principals have begun to describe the relationship between school structure, administrative action, and instructional practices. Although earlier work suggested that principals may have little influence on teaching practices (Deal & Celotti, 1980; Morris, Crowson, Porter-Gehrie, & Hurwitz, 1984; Wolcott, 1973), newer studies are beginning to uncover the important activities that principals can use to shape instruction and student learning in their schools.

One framework for analyzing instructional management (Bossert et al., 1982) focuses attention on how organizational forms and management practices affect the concrete, day-to-day experiences of teachers and students. Instruction is considered as the core technology of the school. Therefore, an effective school principal manages a school in the same way as any other production manager (Thompson, 1967), by crystallizing production goals, managing interdependencies in the workflow, and "buffering" production processes from external influences.

By drawing on recent research on instructional effectiveness, the framework suggests six important factors that can link management activities to instructional practice: instructional time, class size and composition, instructional grouping, curriculum pacing and articulation, student evaluation, and classroom task characteristics. Studies indicate that good teachers seem to know, plan, and construct their classrooms and lessons using these six factors. Although these factors operate primarily at the classroom level, Bossert et al. (1982) hypothesize that effective school-level management activities should affect these elements. Two examples follow.

Instructional Time

Studies show that the amount of time a student is engaged in a learning activity affects achievement and that teachers can be trained in classroom management practices that increase students' engagement rates (Fisher et al., 1980; Stallings, 1980). And even at levels far removed from classroom time-on-task, time allocations influence students' achievements (Wiley, 1976). At the school level, numerous things can determine instructional time in classrooms. Schools have yearly, weekly, and daily cycles that specify not only how much time can be allotted to instruction in various curricular areas but also when evaluations and tests must be given before students can progress to new subjects and materials. Housekeeping, reporting requirements, transition time needed for special classes, and other tasks may seriously cut into students' time-on-task. The degree of coordination within the school may heighten or lessen interruptions of classroom lessons. For example, pullout programs for children with learning problems can fragment a child's day, interrupt important practice time provided in the regular classroom and thus perpetuate that child's underachievement unless the program is carefully coordinated with regular classroom activities.

Studies of managers in business and industry demonstrate that successful managers "buffer" their workers during key production periods in order to guarantee maximum efficiency (Thompson, 1967). Although schools are not factories, school principals can be mediators of organizational and environmental forces that determine the amount of engaged time and student productivity (Noli, 1980). For example, the principal's role as disturbance handler, as school gatekeeper, and as intermediary in disputes between parents and teachers buffers classrooms from disturbances that can interrupt the flow of instruction. Principals can guarantee that all classrooms have the resources necessary to carry out the school's instructional goals so that teachers do not have to use valuable class time to secure needed materials (Venesky & Winfield, 1979, Wellisch et al., 1978).

Curriculum Pacing and Articulation

Research on the curriculum shows that the pacing, sequencing, and content coverage in classroom lessons influence both individual students' achievement and the distribution of performance among classrooms (Barr, 1975; Barr & Dreeben, 1983; Dalhoff, 1971). School principals can be involved in a variety of school-level decisions about the curriculum that shape what and how much students learn. Textbook choices, for example, may largely determine the pace of instruction and hence the level of performance students attain. One study of first-grade reading groups found that identical groups of children were exposed to very different amounts of material (Barnett & Filby, 1984). One group learned about two new basal words each day, whereas another group learned nearly five new words with equal success. When questioned about the differences in curriculum pacing, the teachers referred to the guidelines supplied by the textbooks.

Another area of schoolwide curricular management that can be addressed by the principal concerns the articulation of the curriculum across grades. For example, in schools that have numerous programs for children with special needs, principals can play a crucial role in assisting teachers to coordinate these pro-

grams with regular classroom activities. Because of the lack of coordination, some children may experience a fragmented instructional program, and they are not provided opportunities to practice and accomplish the various learning tasks they are assigned. Often the competing demands of regular and special-program teachers need to be addressed by the school principal, and not simply in terms of the teachers' convenience. (For additional examples, see Bossert, 1985.)

Case studies of effective school principals support these notions. Using techniques of detailed interviewing and ethnographic observation, Dwyer and his associates (Dwyer, Lee, Rowan, & Bossert, 1983) have analyzed the instructional management activities of elementary and junior high school principals. They find that two common management activities involve principals in "buffering" and instructional coordination.

The successful principals in this study continually screen their schools from external intrusions and internal disruptions. They have effective ways of handling clerical chores so that important instructional periods are not interrupted. And they schedule conferences with parents so that teachers remain in their classrooms during school time. Moreover, the principals are highly visible in their schools. Usually the principals begin each day by roaming their buildings and greeting children and staff as they arrive. As classes begin, the principals return to their offices for short planning meetings with assistants or to resolve student problems. But they are back into the hallways and classrooms to monitor events and communicate with staff and students. The principals are systematic about observing, and being seen, in just about every locale and context within their schools—hallways, classrooms, recesses, libraries, and lunchrooms. Afternoons bring these principals back to their offices to handle student problems, paperwork, and parents. Dwyer et al., (1983) argue that this daily cycle serves as a maintenance function for the school. It allows the principals to assess the working status of their organizations and circumvent minor difficulties before they become major problems.

In addition, this daily cycle is consciously linked to improving instruction within their schools. All the principals can articulate direct and remote links between their actions and the instructional system. It seems as if the principals always ask themselves how a particular decision affects the learning environment within their schools and classrooms. Although each principal expresses his or her own instructional philosophy, the elements of that guiding philosophy are strikingly similar to the factors that derive from effective instructional research. The principals are concerned about instructional time, class size and composition, instructional grouping arrangements, curriculum pacing and articulation, student evaluation, and classroom task demands. And they are actively involved in instructional improvement either as "master teachers" modeling effective practices or as coordinators of school efforts.

For these principals, effective instructional management does not imply the adoption of new, highly visible and costly programs. Rather it means systematically linking everyday management activities to the important factors that shape excellent instructional practices in all classrooms within the school.

Leithwood and Montgomery (1982) present a similar picture of effective principals. After reviewing research on school effectiveness and planned change and interviewing school principals about the salience of the review categories, they conclude that successful principals place a high priority on student achievement, influence a complex set of classroom-based and school-related factors that affect teaching, and establish cooperative relationships with the school staff. Among the factors they include in a principal's management activities are supporting procedures that maximize student time-on-task, selecting curriculum materials, scheduling pullout and other special programs, and setting evaluation and homework policies for the school. (For a similar assessment, see Mackensie, 1983.)

The frameworks described by Bossert (1982) and by Leithwood and Montgomery (1982) focus on instruction as the school's key productive structure. Their analyses of instructional leadership examine how certain management activities shape the nature of instructional practice, which in turn influences students' achievements. This shifts the attention of school effectiveness studies away from the allocative processes that distribute resources to schools or the static structural properties of schools and onto the productive processes in which those resources are varyingly put to use.

CONCEPTUALIZING SCHOOL EFFECTS

Recently, attention has been given to how productive processes at each level of school organization actually transform resources into school "products." As Barr and Dreeben (1983) point out, "School systems are divided into distinct levels of organization—district, school, class, group, and individual—each one of which has a particular and characteristic productive agenda. The central problem, then, is to identify each agenda, to determine what takes place at each organizational level and how it fits into the larger enterprise" (p. 153).

This idea has been labeled the *multilevel perspective*. It derives from March and Simon's (1958) classic discussion of decision making in organizations and Thompson's (1967) propositions about managerial control. Higher levels of organization and management place constraints on lower levels. As currently developed among educational researchers, the multilevel perspective addresses the constraints imposed by resource allocation decisions. It questions the nature of resources that come into play at each organizational level, asks how decisions about these resources affect other decision makers, and examines how these various reciprocal decisions affect the productive activities of the school (Barr & Dreeben, 1983).

The value of this perspective is that it shifts the focus of research on organizational outcomes away from the morphology of the school to the production processes themselves. That is, the social structure of schools cannot simply be characterized as the resource stocks attached to various school-system positions. Rather it is the emergent frame within which resources are put to use (Bidwell & Kasarda, 1980). Although no coherent picture of this emergent frame has been developed, a number of conceptual papers have begun to outline possible parameters of a multilevel model (Monk, 1981; Thomas, 1977).

Barr and Dreeben provide the most carefully framed analysis of multilevel processes. They argue that an understanding of school production must include the division of labor and the allocation of resources to various subunits within the school. Schools are not really the units of instruction. Barr and Dreeben (1983) liken them to "switching yards where children within a given age range and from a designated geographical area are assigned to teachers who bring them into contact with approved learning materials, specified as being appropriate to age or ability, during certain allotted periods of time" (p. 6). The school's main task, therefore, is the assignment of materials, children, and teachers.

The productive technology, where materials are actually put to use, occurs in the classroom. But Barr and Dreeben do not suggest that simple aggregations of individual data to the classroom mean are justified. They note that instruction often is provided at a subgroup level, for example, in ability-based reading groups. It is important to characterize how these subgroups are formed and how they affect the learning experiences of children in them. Moreover, Barr and Dreeben discount an analysis of school production at the level of the individual because "teachers attend more to the *distribution of aptitudes* in a class and its transformation into instructible groups than to the particular aptitudes of individual children [italics in the original]" (p. 66).

Barr and Dreeben carry their analysis to 15 first-grade classrooms, where they demonstrate how outcomes at one level of organization constitute the productive conditions at the next lower level. First, they show that the grouping arrangements constructed by teachers vary with the distributional structure of class aptitudes, not with the individual attributes of students. Class size determines the number of reading groups created in the classrooms, but this relationship is mediated by teachers' preferences for particular types of grouping strategies. The discreteness among reading groups and the aptitude range of group means is related to the dispersion of aptitudes within the class. And the concentration of low-achieving pupils in a classroom affects the relative size of reading groups. Classes with a more equal mix of aptitudes allow teachers to choose among various grouping options, whereas classes with a high proportion of poor performers constrain teachers' options about groupings and typically force them to create a traditional stratified grouping structure.

Second, Barr and Dreeben (1983) examine variations in the instructional treatments offered to each reading group. Using indicators of content coverage, they find that instructional pace is related to the mean aptitude of instructional groups. That is, higher achievers received more new words and phonics training. However, considerable differences exist even among groups with similar mean aptitudes. The level of difficulty in phonic materials has a major effect on instructional pace and time. Obviously, more time is needed to teach more difficult materials. But group mean aptitude does not necessarily determine the difficulty of materials—similar groups are often taught materials at different levels of difficulty.

Finally, Barr and Dreeben assess individual learning as a result of group placement and instruction. Instructional pace turns out to be the most powerful predictor of a student's reading performance, even when initial aptitude is taken into account. First graders who encounter more new words and phonics instruction achieve at higher levels. Barr and Dreeben argue that "the association between the mean aptitude of a child's group and the pace of instruction does not really reflect two characteristics of the child but rather the fact that each individual in a group gets carried along at the pace of the group itself" (p. 151).

Barr, Dreeben, and their students are replicating this study at other elementary-school grade levels. However, other studies of classroom instruction also support their findings. Barnett and Filby (1984), for example, report that pacing differences among reading groups in first- and fifth-grade classrooms can be substantial, even when comparable groups of children are compared. These differences affect children's oral reading performance.

This work is important because it demonstrates how potent curriculum factors are imbedded in choices about materials. Moreover, it highlights that a single decision at one organizational level, school-level assignments of children and teachers to classrooms, can have a large effect on student learning. One clear implication of this for administrative research is that the search for managerial control over instruction should not confuse the relative frequency of control behavior with its effect on the organization of instruction. Mintzberg-type studies, and other analyses that point to the infrequency of direct, instructional management activities in schools as a sign of no administrative effects on learning ignore the potential power of one-time-only decisions (Deal & Celotti, 1980; Mintzberg, 1979).

Barr and Dreeben's analysis, however, may not universally describe the productive processes and interlevel constraints that shape school effectiveness. For example, it cannot be used directly to model the complex functions that determine the assignment of teachers and students to curricular tracks in secondary schools. Yet it does begin to offer a framework for assessing school effectiveness that captures the interdependencies among levels of the school's productive system.

THE FUTURE FOR RESEARCH ON SCHOOL EFFECTIVENESS

A classical model of bureaucratic organization underlies much of the thinking about school effectiveness. It characterizes the school as a goal-oriented, hierarchically organized structure in which the level of resource allocations determines the quantity of learning. Administration, in this view, consists of central managers who closely monitor subordinates' behavior and deliberately adapt organizational procedures and resource allocations in order to meet clear performance criteria.

Input-output studies, governed by this bureaucratic perspective, measure the aggregate stocks of resources available at the district or school level, assuming that the internal distribution of resources and their use is homogeneous and that certain resources have equal value to all students. Because these assumptions are not true, measured differences in students' aptitude or family background become the only source of variance available to explain student learning, thus eliminating the case for school effects.

Likewise, studies of school administrators, in their search for bureaucratic controls over teaching, find little evidence of frequent and direct instructional intervention. School principals, district supervisors, and superintendents do not inspect school production closely, and instructional decision making seems more symbolic than instrumental. The conclusion that schools are loosely coupled systems reflects the bureaucratic ideal. Schools should exhibit formal, tight controls over instruction. Because they do not, organizational control does not exist. This stance devalues the argument for any type of organizational control over school outcomes (Cohen, 1983).

Effective schools studies have tried to resurrect the bureaucratic ideal by stating that strong principal leadership is needed in order to structure schools for effectiveness. But this prescription is weak because little is said about what processes must be structured or what structures need to be imposed in order to create success.

The multilevel perspective seems to chart the future for research on school organization effects by overcoming the biases of the bureaucratic model and the loosely coupled formulation. It focuses attention on how the organizational milieu shapes the nature of instructional activities in which teachers and students engage and the way in which resources are made available to and used by teachers and students in these instructional activities. When the processes that constitute the technical core of the school are described, linkages between organizational structure, administration, and student learning will become apparent.

Some time ago, Bidwell (1979) foreshadowed several of the central questions that the multilevel perspective must address. He noted that the "form of the process through which multiple resources are combined into instruction, how the combinational process may be conditioned by values of the organizational context of schooling, and the conceptualization of the student as a factor in educational production are scarcely touched" (p. 127). He lists three key issues for study: how decision making is affected by organizational structure and vice versa; the relationship between administrative processes or decisions and the technology of teaching; and how educational organizations assess the effectiveness of their actions and organizations. These issues still provide an untapped agenda for research on school effectiveness.

Even if the productive technology of instruction is not well codified, variations in its structure and effects can be described. And investigations of how administrative organization and control shape what teachers and children accomplish are necessary for understanding school effectiveness. This perspective leads to several questions for future research: What specific decisions can principals make concerning instructional

organization at the school level? Can certain school decisions constrain instructional organization at the classroom level, and can these constraints facilitate student learning? What role does the overall coordination of instruction play in enhancing school effectiveness?

Advances in research on instruction hold promise for helping to specify the productive dimensions of classrooms. The task for future research on school effectiveness, then, is to begin to elaborate the linkages between administrative organization and decisions and those productive instructional processes that occur within schools.

REFERENCES

Anderson, C. S. (1982). The search for school climate: A review of the research. *Review of Educational Research*, *52*, 368–420.

Armor, D., Conry-Oseguera, P., Cox, M., King, N., McDonnell, L., Pascal, A., Pauly, E., & Zellman, G. (1976). *Analysis of the school preferred reading program in selected Los Angeles minority schools.* Santa Monica, CA: Rand.

Averch, H. A., Carroll, S. J., Donaldson, T. S., Kiesling, H. J., & Pincus, J. (1974). *How effective is schooling? A critical review and synthesis of research findings.* Santa Monica, CA: Rand.

Barnett, B., & Filby, N. N. (1984). *Effects of the presentation of reading material and instructional pacing on first graders' reading fluency.* Paper presented at the annual meeting of the American Educational Research Association, Montreal.

Barr, R. (1975). How children are taught to read: Grouping and pacing. *School Review*, *83*, 479–498.

Barr, R., & Dreeben, R. (1983). *How schools work.* Chicago: University of Chicago Press.

Berg, I. (1970). *Education and jobs: The great training robbery.* New York: Praeger.

Berliner, D. C., & Koehler, V. (Eds.) (1983). Research on teaching [Special issue]. *The Elementary School Journal*, *83*, 261–499.

Bidwell, C. E. (1979). The school as a formal organization: Some new thoughts. In G. L. Immegart & W. L. Boyd (Eds.), *Problem-Finding in Educational Administration.* Lexington, MA: Heath.

Bidwell, C. E., & Kasarda, J. D. (1980). Conceptualizing and measuring the effects of school and schooling. *American Journal of Education*, *88*, 401–430.

Blumberg, A., & Greenfield, W. (1980). *The effective principal: Perspectives on school leadership.* Boston: Allyn and Bacon.

Bossert, S. T. (1979). *Tasks and social relationships in classrooms: A study of instructional organization and its consequences.* New York: Cambridge University Press.

Bossert, S. T. (1981). Understanding sex differences in children's classroom experiences. *Elementary School Journal*, *81*, 254–266.

Bossert, S. T. (1985). Effective elementary schools. In R. Kyle (Ed.), *Reaching for excellence: An effective schools sourcebook.* Washington, DC: U.S. Government Printing Office.

Bossert, S. T., Dwyer, D., Rowan, B., & Lee, G. V. (1982). The instructional management role of the principal. *Educational Administration Quarterly*, *18*, 34–64.

Brookover, W. B., Beady, C., Flood, P., Schweitzer, J., & Wisenbaker, J. (1979). *School social systems and student achievement: Schools can make a difference.* New York: Praeger.

Brophy, J. E., & Good, T. (1974). *Teacher-student relationships: Causes and consequences.* New York: Holt, Rinehart, & Winston.

Cameron, K. S., & Whetten, D. A. (1983). Organizational effectiveness: One model or several. In K. S. Cameron & D. A. Whetten (Eds.), *Organizational effectiveness.* New York: Academic.

Clark, D. L., Lotto, L. S., & McCarthy, M. M. (1980). Factors associated with success in urban elementary schools. *Phi Delta Kappan*, *61*, 467–470.

Cohen, M. (1983). Instructional, management and social conditions in effective schools. In A. Odden & L. Webb (Eds.), *School finance and school improvement: Linkages for the 1980's*. Cambridge, MA: Ballinger.

Coleman, J. S., Campbell, E., Hobson, C., McPartland, J., Mood, A., Weinfield, F., & York, R. (1966). *Equality of educational opportunity*. Washington, DC: U.S. Department of Health, Education, and Welfare.

Coleman, J. S., Hoffer, T., & Kilgore, S. (1982). *High school achievement: Public, Catholic and other private schools compared*. New York: Basic.

Collins, R. (1971). Functional and conflict theories of educational stratification. *American Sociological Review*, *36*, 1002–1032.

Dalhoff, U. (1971). *Ability grouping, content validity, and curriculum process analysis*. New York: Teachers College Press, Columbia University.

Deal, T., & Celloti, L. (1980). How much influence do (and can) administrators have on classrooms? *Phi Delta Kappan*, *61*, 471–473.

Denham, C., & Lieberman, A. (Eds.) (1980). *Time to learn*. Washington, DC: U.S. Department of Education.

Dwyer, D. C., Lee, G. V., Rowan, B., & Bossert, S. T. (1983). *Five principals in action: Perspectives on instructional management*. San Francisco: Far West Laboratory for Educational Research and Development.

Erickson, D. A. (1978). Research on educational administration: The state-of-the-art. *Educational Researcher*, *8*, 9–14.

Fiedler, F. E. (1967). *A theory of leadership effectiveness*. New York: Free Press.

Fisher, C. W., Berliner, D. C., Filby, N. N., Marliave, R., Cahen, L. S., & Dishaw, M. M. (1980). Teaching behaviors, academic learning time, and student achievement: An overview. In C. Denham & A. Lieberman (Eds.), *Time to learn*. Washington, DC: U.S. Department of Education.

Good, T., & Brophy, J. (1985). School effects. In M. C. Wittrock (Ed.), *Handbook of research on teaching* (3rd ed.). New York: Macmillan.

Goodman, P. S., & Pennings, J. S. (Eds.). (1979). *New perspectives on organizational effectiveness*. San Francisco: Jossey-Bass.

Heyns, B. (1978). *Summer learning and the effects on schooling*. New York: Academic Press.

Jencks, C. (1972a). The Coleman report and the conventional wisdom. In F. Mosteller & D. Moynihan (Eds.), *On equality of educational opportunity*. New York: Vantage.

Jencks, C. (1972b). *Inequality*. New York: Basic.

Karweit, N. (1976). A reanalysis of the effect of quantity of schooling on achievement. *Sociology of Education*, *49*, 236–246.

Kyle, R. (Ed.) (1985). *Reaching for excellence: An effective schools sourcebook*. Washington, DC: U.S. Government Printing Office.

Leithwood, K. A., & Montgomery, D. J. (1982). The role of the elementary school principal in program improvement. *Review of Educational Research*, *52*, 309–339.

Leucke, D. F., & McGinn, N. F. (1975). Regression analyses and educational production functions: Can they be trusted? *Harvard Educational Review*, *45*, 325–350.

Lipham, J. (1981). *Effective principal, effective school*. Reston, VA: National Association of Secondary School Principals.

Mackenzie, D. (1983). Research for school improvement: An appraisal of some recent trends. *Educational Researcher*, *12*, 5–16.

Madaus, G. F., Airasian, P. W., & Kelleghan, T. (1980). *School effectiveness: A reassessment of the evidence*. New York: McGraw-Hill.

Madaus, G. F., Kelleghan, T., Rakow, E. A., & King, D. J. (1979). The sensitivity of measures of school effectiveness. *Harvard Educational Review*, *11*, 207–230.

March, J. G., & Simon, H. (1958). *Organizations*. New York: John Wiley.

Metz, M. H. (1978). *Classroom and corridors*. Berkeley, CA: University of California Press.

Meyer, J. W. (1977). Education as an institution. *American Journal of Sociology*, *83*, 55–77.

Miles, M. B., Farrar, E., & Neufeld, B. (1983). *The extent of the adoption of effective schools programs*. Cambridge, MA: Huron Institute.

Mintzberg, H. (1979). *The structuring of organizations*. Englewood Cliffs, NJ: Prentice-Hall.

Miskel, C., Fevurly, R., & Stewart, J. (1979). Organizational structures and processes, perceived school effectiveness, loyalty, and job satisfaction. *Educational Administration Quarterly*, *15*, 97–118.

Monk, D. H. (1981). Toward a multilevel perspective on the allocation of educational resources. *Review of Educational Research*, *51*, 215–256.

Morris, V. C., Crowson, R., Porter-Gehrie, C., & Hurwitz, E. (1984). *Principals in action: The reality of managing schools*. Columbus, OH: Merrill.

Noli, P. (1980). A principal implements BTES. In C. Denham & A. Lieberman (Eds.), *Time to learn*. Washington, DC: U.S. Department of Education.

Peterson, P., & Janicki, T. (1979). Individual characteristics and children's learning in large-group and small-group approaches. *Journal of Educational Psychology*, *71*, 677–687.

Peterson, P., Wilkerson, L., & Hallinan, M. (Eds.). (1984). *The social context of instruction: Group organization and group processes*. New York: Academic.

Purkey, S. C., & Smith, M. S. (1983). Effective schools: A review. *Elementary School Journal*, *83*, 427–453.

Rosenbaum, J. E. (1975). The stratification of socialization processes. *American Sociological Review*, *40*, 48–54.

Rosenbaum, J. E. (1976). *Making inequality: The hidden curriculum of high school tracking*. New York: John Wiley.

Rowan, B., Bossert, S. T., & Dwyer, D. C. (1983) Research on effective schools: A cautionary note. *Educational Researcher*, *12*, 24–31.

Rowan, B., & Denk, C. (1984). Management succession, school socioeconomic context, and basic skills achievement. *American Educational Research Journal*, *21*, 517–538.

Rutter, M. (1983). School effects on pupil progress: Research findings and policy implications. In L. S. Shulman & G. Sykes (Eds.), *Handbook of teaching and policy*. New York: Longman.

Rutter, M., Maugham, B., Mortimore, P., Ouston, J., & Smith, A. (1979). *Fifteen thousand hours: Secondary schools and their effects on children*. Cambridge, MA: Harvard University Press.

Sergovanni, T. & Starratt, R. (1979). *Supervision: Human perspectives* (2nd ed.). New York: McGraw-Hill.

Sociology of Education, (1982). 55.

Spady, W. G. (1973). The impact of school resources on students. In F. Kerlinger (Ed.), *Review of research in education*. Itasca, IL: Peacock.

Stallings, J. (1980). Allocated learning time revisited, or beyond time on task. *Educational Researcher*, *9*, 11–16.

Summers, A. A., & Wolfe, B. L. (1975). *Equality of educational opportunity quantified: A production function approach*. Philadelphia: Federal Reserve Bank of Philadelphia.

Thomas, J. A. (1977). *Resource allocation in classrooms*. Chicago: Department of Education, University of Chicago.

Thompson, J. D. (1967). *Organizations in action*. New York: McGraw-Hill.

Venesky, R. L., & Winfield, L. (1979). *Schools that succeed beyond expectations in teaching reading* (Tech. Rep. No. 1). Newark, DE: Department of Educational Studies, University of Delaware.

Wellisch, J. B., MacQueen, A., Carriere, R., & Duck, C. (1978). School management and organization in successful schools. *Sociology of Education*, *51*, 211–226.

Wiley, D. E. (1976). Another hour, another day: Quantity of schooling, a potent path for policy. In W. H. Sewell, R. M. Hauser, & D. L. Featherman (Eds.), *Schooling and achievement in American society*. New York: Academic.

Wolcott, H. (1973). *The man in the principal's office: An ethnography*. New York: Holt, Rinehart, & Winston.

PART
III
Economics and Finance

CHAPTER 18

Economics of Education: The U.S. Experience

Charles S. Benson

Economic analysis of educational data is intended to yield practical, useful results. These results fall into three main categories. First, economic analysis establishes a monetary return to the resources used in producing learning. This process of measurement is otherwise called "computing the yield from the creation of human capital." It attributes increments of lifetime income to the possession of a hierarchical set of educational qualifications. Second, economic analysis of educational data helps to match the work skills created in educational institutions and the requirements for particular skills in labor markets. The shorthand label for this process is anachronistically but resolutely sexist: "manpower planning." Obviously, the first and second processes are related. If manpower planning is done effectively, the economic value of education should be greater than if manpower planning is done ineffectively or not at all. Hence, the second process is sometimes described as a means for improving the "external efficiency" of an educational system.

The third analytical process in economics of education sets out to give guidance on the way to allocate resources more wisely in educational institutions. Resources are the means to produce educational outcomes. Some resources, such as the time devoted to learning by elementary school children, may be regarded as costless or free. Nevertheless, the careful administrator will pay careful heed to the proper allocation of children's time to instructional activities in the school and in the home as well.

For the most part, however, resources, such as text books, the services of teachers, and equipment for science laboratories, cost money. In the short run, almost any educational budget is more or less fixed or stable. If, then, local administrators would like to do something substantial to improve the achievement of the students in their charge and if they find it necessary to spend some money to meet that objective—hiring specialized teaching services, obtaining improved instructional materials, installing devices of educational technology, and the like, they almost certainly will need to rearrange the pattern of expenditures in that more or less fixed budget. The treatment of what are called "educational production functions" is intended to inform the local administration how best to make that rearrangement of the budget to reveal what kinds of expenditures are powerful in affecting student achievement and what kinds are weak. Once this information is available, wise administrators will withdraw some of the money being spent in the weak items and shift it over to the strong. Thus, by means of this third process one seeks to raise the "internal efficiency" of educational activities.

Though the three topics noted above comprise the main content of economics of education, researchers in this field often turn their attention to complementary or related subjects of inquiry. Perhaps the largest of these related subjects, at least in terms of books and papers published, is educational finance (See Chapters 19 and 20.) Additionally, economists have studied the relationship between farmer literacy and farm productivity (Jamison & Lau, 1982; Moock, 1973) and the effects of early mild malnutrition on school perfor-

Consultant/reviewer: Henry M. Levin, Stanford University

mance (Balderston, Wilson, Freire, & Simonen, 1981). Some economists view educational systems as instruments to reproduce social conditions to maintain the capitalist mode of production rather than as instruments to produce human capital (Bowles & Gintis, 1976; Carnoy & Levin, 1976). Other economists employ the techniques of cost-benefit analysis to evaluate educational programs (Zodhiates, 1980). Regrettably, limits of space do not permit these specialized forms of research to be covered here.

ESTIMATING RETURNS ON EDUCATIONAL INVESTMENTS

Economics has what is generally recognized to be a birthyear—1776—for it was then that Adam Smith, a Scottish philosopher later recognized as the first great economist, published his monumental work, *The Wealth of Nations*. It is here that one finds the strongest statement ever made of the doctrine of *laissez faire*, the idea that unfettered individual action improves the economic welfare of everybody and that government controls impede economic growth. Because Smith is the best-known proponent of free enterprise, it is interesting to note that he advocated public support of education; indeed, public support by the central government.

More to the present concern, Smith (1776/1937) formulated the concept of valuation of human capital:

> When any expensive machine is erected, the extraordinary work to be performed by it before it is worn out, it must be expected, will replace the [money] laid out upon it, with at least the ordinary profits. A man educated at the expense of much labor and time to any of those employments which require extraordinary dexterity and skill, may be compared to one of those expensive machines. The work which he learns to perform, ...over and above the usual wages of common labor, will replace to him the whole expense of his education, with at least the ordinary profits of an equally valuable capital. It must do this, too, in a reasonable time, regard being had to the very uncertain duration of human life, in the same manner as to the more certain duration of the machine. The difference between the wages of skilled labor and those of common labor is founded upon this principle. (p. 101)

What are the main ideas in this important paragraph? (a) Something called "capital" is useful in production. (b) Capital takes two main forms: machinery and skilled labor. In present-day terms, "machinery" is a shorthand expression for all devices created by human labor that enter into production, from steel mills through computers to communications satellites. (c) The creation of capital is costly, and the costs of creating capital must be borne by deferring resources that would be used for the immediate satisfaction of consumers' desires. (d) The creation of human capital is costly, both in ordinary outlays (instructors' salaries, etc.), and in time of the student (time has value!). (e) Capital enhances production over a period of time. (f) Nevertheless, both material and human capital eventually wear out and need to be replaced. (g) Only those who expect to get their money back, plus some profit, all within the expected productive life of the given investment, are likely to pay for the creation of capital. (h) This requirement to obtain a reasonable return for an investment applies to human capital as well as material. In a free market, it is what explains the salary and wage differentials between people with higher skills, representing a greater investment of money and time, and those with lower skills, representing a lesser investment.

Those ideas comprise the essence of the economic valuation of an educational experience. This ancient bit of economic wisdom is reported here to demonstrate that when an educator and an economist join hands today and say that investment in education yields a valuable return, they need not be seen to speak as a special interest; rather, they are speaking in a grand and early tradition of economic analysis.

Processes of Measurement

In capitalist nations it is assumed that the primary beneficiary of investment in education is the individual worker, not the worker's employer and not society at large (though it is also customary to assume that education creates a certain amount of widely diffused "social benefits" as well). Hence, we measure returns to education in terms of the extra lifetime income that a worker earns as a result of having completed a given stage of schooling. This extra amount of lifetime income can then be compared with the costs of acquiring the education of the given stage and one can then establish the yield of education as a rate.

Rates of return to education can be set alongside the yields available to households in such things as money market accounts or buying or expanding a business. Thus, this kind of information can be helpful in weighing the worth of particular educational credentials—a high school diploma, a BS in engineering, a teaching certificate, a law degree—against alternative investment opportunities. These kinds of analytical results are also used in the planning offices of private educational institutions.

To construct a set of rate-of-return estimates, an analyst needs first of all information about the incomes of people who hold different kinds of educational certificates. Preferably these estimates would represent earned, not total, income. Total income includes the money that a person gets from investments, and the assets so invested might have been acquired through inheritance. To assess the yield of educational investments in a given person—or group of persons—we naturally want to confine our attention to wages and salaries; that is, earned income. Estimates are provided from time to time by the U.S. Bureau of the Census as well as by professional societies, like the American Medical Association. Survey research firms can also provide these kinds of data for a particular occupational group. The three essential elements to be obtained from respondents are educational level and type of certificate, if any; income; and age.

From the data so obtained, the analyst establishes a kind of average lifetime income profile for workers of different educational levels. These profiles are then "discounted" by a compound rate of interest to obtain "present discounted values" of lifetime income streams. There is a potentially easier way to think of this kind of calculation: Imagine two hypothetical individuals, each having a total earned lifetime income of $5 million. Let one be a successful professional basketball player who gains most of his earned income early in his working life. Let the other be a college professor who lives on her standard, 9-month salary for most of her life but has a big income in the last few working years by producing a best-selling book. Are these two people equally well off? No, because the athlete can put the money he gets early in his working life out to earn interest, thus receiving a higher total income (earned plus investments) than the professor. Adjusting the two income streams by a compound rate of interest discounts the value of the income received late in her career by the college professor and renders the two income streams comparable. (For a full discussion of rate-of-return analysis, see Cohn, 1978.)

It is next required to estimate the costs of acquiring different amounts of education. As Adam Smith noted, one of the costs of acquiring education is the time of the student. It is common practice to include the "forgone income" of students as an element of educational costs. This factor represents the average amount of money students of different ages could be expected to earn if they were gainfully employed instead of spending time in their studies. In this regard, distinctions are made as to whether students are full- or part-time. Forgone income is a significant cost of education for college and university students, and it is also substantial at the high school level.

Other major elements of cost are the running expenses of educational institutions and depreciation of their plant and capital equipment. These are ordinarily expressed in a per-student, per-year form, but at this point, the analyst must decide whether to estimate private costs, social costs, or both. Private costs refer to outlays borne individually, not collectively, by households. For example, when a family sends a young person to a state university, it pays out a certain amount of money in tuition, but that fee does not cover the entire running expenses of the university. Fees plus room and board, transport, books, and special clothing, together with forgone income, represent private costs, and these estimates are relevant to a household's decision about whether education is a good investment. Social costs include all the costs mentioned above, plus that part of the institutional instructional budget not met by fees. Social costs are useful in evaluating the public commitment to education.

Net benefits of education can be expressed as

$$NB = \sum_{t=0}^{m} \frac{b_t}{(1+i)^t} - \sum_{t=0}^{m} \frac{c_t}{(1+i)^t}$$

where b_t = income earned in any year, t, c_t = educational costs in any year, t, i = an appropriate rate of interest (discount rate), m = year in which normal work span is closed, and Σ = a summation. Earnings can be intermittent; that is, in a given year earnings may be zero on account of voluntary or involuntary unemployment. Likewise, training costs can be intermittent during the workspan. It would be unusual, however, to find that workers incurred large amounts of expenditure for training near the end of that span, because they would have only a short period of time to recoup the outlay.

The analyst must choose the discount rate, and there is no general agreement on the basis for that choice. Higher rates make any longer-term investment, including education, look less profitable, other things being equal. For the calculation of private returns to education, a suitable discount rate might be the average yield of high-grade corporate bonds.

An alternative approach is to calculate an "internal rate of return;" that is, to let the flows of benefits and costs themselves dictate the percentage yield of educational investment. By the process of iteration (trial and error), the analyst computes a value for r in the formula

$$\sum_{t=0}^{m} \frac{b_t}{(1+r)^t} = \sum_{t=0}^{m} \frac{c_t}{(1+r)^t}.$$

The internal rate of return, r, adjusts the discounted values of benefits and costs to equality. Accordingly, it represents a concept of yield that matches the most common, conventional notion. If one knows that the internal rate of return for acquiring a BS in engineering is, say, 14 percent, one can compare that figure with the yield one might obtain from investments in stocks, real estate, or the foreign-exchange market.

Whether computing net benefits of education or internal rates of return (or both), the analyst ordinarily makes a set of measurements, showing the value of investments in education of different lengths and types. Naturally, the calculations assume that the relationships among earnings of people who hold different kinds of educational qualifications will be relatively stable and will conform reasonably well to what they have been in the past.

These notions represent in brief outline the theory of human capital as developed by such scholars as Becker (1975), Mincer (1974), Schultz (1961), and Walsh (1935).

Some Estimates of Educational Returns

A preliminary view of returns to educational investment can be obtained by examining expected lifetime earnings of persons who possess different amounts of schooling. Using data from the 1980 census, the U.S. Bureau of the Census has estimated a set of present discounted values of earned incomes for persons from age 18 to age 64, considering males and females separately. These projections are in "constant dollars," meaning that they reflect price levels in a base year of 1981. The estimates take into account mortality and the statistical probability of a person of given educational level and sex being unemployed at different ages in the work span.

The particular estimates shown in Table 18.1 were calculated on a "real" interest rate (the difference between an assumed interest rate and the projected rate of inflation) of 5 percent, and they are based on the assumption that productivity (average output per worker) will rise at an annual compound rate of 2 percent. The resulting estimates in Table 18.1 are startling on two counts. First, the returns to education for women are notably smaller than they are for men. Suppose a school district was engaged in a program of drop-out prevention and suppose further that the district had reason to believe that any given $1,000 applied to drop-out prevention was equally effective with male and female students. How, then, would the

district maximize the human capital returns from the program? Obviously, by concentrating its efforts on male students and ignoring the female. A sex-fair policy may be by far the best social policy, but from the data at hand, it is not a policy with the highest economic justification.

Second, Table 18.1 indicates that returns to *completion* of programs are especially strong. For males, the extra lifetime income for completing 4 years of high school over being a dropout is $128,000. Since most students attend high school for the first 2 years anyway, the extra amount of education to qualify for the additional lifetime income of $128,000 is likely to be no more than 2 years. Costs of 1 year of high school, including forgone income, hardly exceed $15,000; hence, the benefit-cost ratio of the last 2 years of high school appears to be extraordinarily high.

On the other hand, if a male continues beyond high school into college but does not complete 4 years of college, the extra projected income is only $27,000, no great bargain. If the male completes 4 years of college, he can expect to earn $125,000 more than a male who stops at the end of high school. And last, note that the yield of continuing in college beyond 4 years is not very great. These same relationships are found in returns to education of women, except that the extra yield of completing 4 years of college is not so pronounced and the yield of continuing beyond 4 years of college is relatively greater than for males.

To go beyond describing the average level of lifetime incomes associated with different amounts of educational attainment takes the analyst into the calculation of rates of return. This requires recognizing the diversity of educational enterprises in the United States. Calculation of rates of return is a process of relating extra income attributed to a particular kind of schooling with the costs of acquiring that schooling, as noted above. Educational costs vary a great deal from one type of educational institution to another. Table 18.2 offers some estimates of private rates of return for educational investment of white males, based upon a sample of 2,765 students who were surveyed in 1972 and could have completed their bachelor's degrees in 1976 and their advanced degrees by 1980.

The returns shown in Table 18.2 are based on

Table 18.1   Projected Lifetime Earnings from Year 1979 for Males and Females by Educational Level, Constant 1981 Dollars

EDUCATIONAL LEVEL	MALES	FEMALES
Less than 12 years	291,000	105,000
High school, 4 years	419,000	192,000
College, 1–3 years	446,000	229,000
College, 4 years	534,000	258,000
College, 5 years or more	576,000	326,000

NOTE. From *Current Population Reports*, Series P–60, No. 139, 1982, U.S. Bureau of the Census.

Table 18.2 Percentage Private Rates of Return to Educational Investment of White Males by Degree Level and Type of Institution Attended

| Degree | RESEARCH UNIVERSITY | | COMPREHENSIVE FOUR-YEAR COLLEGES | | LIBERAL ARTS COLLEGES |
	Public	Private	Public	Private	Private
Bachelor's	19.0	26.0	21.0	18.5	8.7
Master's	9.6	17.3	6.2	−0.7	7.7
Doctorates, Other Professional	19.3	11.6	9.0	−1.8	10.3

NOTE. From Walter W. McMahon and Alan P. Wagner, "The Monetary Returns to Education as Partial Social Efficiency Criteria," in Walter W. McMahon and Terry G. Gerke (Eds.), *Financing Education: Overcoming Inefficiency and Inequity*, Urbana: University of Illinois Press, 1982, p. 167.

earnings figures that represent expected earnings of students who attended as undergraduates one of the five types of institutions and on cost estimates that reflect net costs to the student based on detailed budgets of income (part-time earnings, grants, scholarships, tuition waivers) and outgo (fees, books and supplies, forgone earnings). The returns indicate values of increments of education—the amount of extra income a college graduate from a particular type of institution receives, on the average, as compared with costs to the student of obtaining the given degree.

In 8 of the 15 cells of Table 18.2, the internal rate of return to educational investment exceeds 10 percent. This return compares favorably with the level of return most people receive from investments in the stock and bond markets, the money markets, and real estate. Returns to the higher-yielding educational investments compare not very favorably with returns from successful entrepreneurship, but by no means is it true that everyone who starts up a business makes a success of it. It should also be noted in Table 18.2 that returns to educational investments in advanced degrees may be less than returns to first degrees; however, this tapering off of returns is not apparent in two cases: students who attend undergraduate programs in (a) public research universities and (b) private liberal arts colleges.

It is also possible to develop a set of figures to show expected rates of return by intended occupation. McMahon and Wagner (1982) report that the expected return for an MD or DDS is 14 percent. An undergraduate degree in engineering is expected to yield 25.5 percent and a master's in engineering has an estimated return of 12 percent. For persons who expect to enter elementary or secondary school teaching, the return for the BA is 12.3 percent and for a master's degree 0.8 percent. That is, in education, getting a master's degree over and beyond acquiring a certificate, and accumulating graduate credits doesn't count for all that much (McMahon & Wagner, 1982).

Work continues apace in analyzing and estimating the economic value of education. With regard to general reviews of the field, see Chapter 19 and Berger, 1983;

Bowman, 1976, 1985; Chamberlain and Griliches, 1975, Corman and Davidson, 1984; Griliches, 1977; Hill, 1981; Mincer, 1979, 1984; Ribich & Murphy, 1975; Welch, 1974; and Wise, 1975. In recent years, considerable attention by economists has been attached to the effects of race and sex on education-related income differentials (Blakemore & Low, 1984; Kenny, 1983; Levine & Moock, 1984; Mincer & Polachek, 1974; Smith, 1984; Welch, 1973; and Weiss & Williamson, 1972). Another topic that has attracted attention is the relationships among education, migration, and income (Bowles, 1970b; Lynch, 1983; Schultz, 1975; and Winkler, 1984). Economists have also begun to explore the contribution of educational quality to the production of human capital. (Note that most of the work discussed above relates income differences to length of schooling, not to the quality of the educational experience.) Some important papers are Behrman and Birdsall, 1983; Borus and Carpenter, 1984; Fleisher, 1974; Hill and Stafford, 1974; Johnson and Stafford, 1973; Link & Ratledge, 1975; Rizzuto and Wachtel, 1980; Solomon and Wachtel, 1972; and Wachtel, 1974. Intriguing and challenging as these topics are, they are too specialized to be considered here.

The Special Case of Vocational Education

Much of the work in computing financial returns to educational investments shows an emphasis on postsecondary programs (as in Table 18.2 above). Notwithstanding this fact, considerable work has been done in the last few years in estimating returns to vocational education at both the secondary and postsecondary levels. Here, the concentration is on returns to programs at the high school level.

In assessing the economic worth of vocational education, the analyst tends to ignore costs of program and instead compares the labor market success of vocational graduates with the labor market success of graduates of other school programs (academic, general, etc.). If the analyst is examining strictly the economic value of vocational programs at the high school level, the comparison is among groups of graduates who choose not to take up postsecondary studies. A standard form of analysis is to predict hourly earnings, weeks employed, and hours worked, in a multiple regression model that uses as independent variables high school program (vocational, academic, general) and such control variables as are relevant and available—sex, previous part-time employment, SES of family, race, grade point average in high school, and the like (Gustman & Steinmeier, 1982).

Ordinarily, expectations would lead to the belief that vocational graduates should have better labor market experiences than graduates of other programs. In the usual case, they have been taught specific, marketable skills. The content of their programs of study is presumably informed by advisory committees of local employers. Faculty members are said to be prepared to perform placement services for their graduates. Nevertheless, the evidence about the economic worth of vocational education is at best mixed.

For example, Grasso and Shea (1979a, 1979b), after analyzing data from four major national longitudinal surveys of American youth, reported the following:

> With respect to wages and earnings, findings...differed by *sex*. Among males, enrollment in an occupational program during high school was on average unrelated to rate of pay and annual earnings...Indeed, some evidence suggests that vocational graduates enjoyed slower rates of growth in wages over time than did general graduates. Among the females, business and office graduates *were* found to enjoy higher rates of pay and annual earnings than were general graduates. (p. 183)

A similarly ambiguous assessment of the economic value of vocational education has been given by Meyer (1981). He reports that there is no net gain in lifelong benefits of earned income across all programs of occupational training for high school students. However, taking business or office courses gave young women some advantage in the marketplace for the first 8 years of their working lives. Likewise, young men who take courses in trade and industry show higher initial gains in income than do graduates of business courses, but the gains for young male graduates of trade and industry programs are, however, rather short lived. After the first few years of working life, earnings of general academic program graduates tend to catch up with or exceed earnings of vocational graduates.

The general finding that a strong, positive case for the economic worth of vocational education cannot be made must be viewed with some caution. Here are some reasons. Imperfections in the labor market may allow employers to seize the economic benefits by paying wages to vocational graduates that fail to reflect their differential productivity. This condition is especially likely to occur when the employing firms are large and the unions are weak. Thus, the programs could be economically beneficial even though the graduates were not themselves the gainers. Also, enrollment in vocational programs is a voluntary act, which poses two unresolved problems for the research. (a) Some students may enroll in the programs to acquire skills for home production. The skills so acquired may have economic value that is never reflected in market wage differentials. (b) Characteristics of students that affect their potential in the labor market may be systematically different between those who enroll in vocational programs and those who do not. If these characteristics work to the disfavor of vocational students, then no one can be sure that the control variables in the regression models describe them adequately. In addition, the labor market experience of vocational graduates may be affected by the quality of programs in which they studied and the intensity of their involvement. These variables are not yet described adequately in the regression models. The models, that is, show an average of the labor market experience of vocational graduates. The returns to high-quality vocational education are not shown separately, and those returns may indeed be handsome.

The economists' interest in vocational education has taken new and interesting directions. Mertens (1982) has provided an excellent study of the relationship between studying vocational education and dropping out of high school. Stern (1982, 1984) has proposed an integration of work and education for students of high school age in a form radically different from conventional vocational education. Both Mertens and Stern defend their propositions with empirical evidence.

A Qualification and a Contrary View

There exists a clear positive relationship between length of schooling and earned income. But does education "cause" the extra earning power to come into being, or is the extra earning power simply a return to the inborn capacity or ability of persons who also happen to have a lot of schooling? A great deal of work has been done in trying to distinguish between the effects on wages of family background and ability (IQ) of workers, on the one hand, and length of schooling on the other. A lot of reliance has been placed on data regarding persons who share a common family background: siblings or twins.

The various studies show conflicting and inconsistent results, but the predominant opinion is that education accounts for something over half of earnings differentials (a common rule of thumb is to attribute 60 percent of earnings differentials to education and 40 percent to other factors, such as family background and IQ). As Mincer (1979) has stated,

> I think it fair to say, based on the predominant evidence thus far, that employers pay for characteristics and efforts of the workers, not of their parents. The economic analysis of human capital investment decisions suggests that the effects of background variables are *indirect* by influencing the accumulation of human capital [italics in the original]. (p. 27)

But not, presumably, in the process of its pricing!

Another attack on the propositions of human capital theory must be taken more seriously. It is known as the "labor queue theory," or the "screening hypothesis." To understand the significance of this alternative approach, it is necessary to review some central assumptions of conventional theory. In mainstream economic theory, any trained person can always find employment in his or her specialty because in a highly competitive economy unemployed workers will offer their services to employers at reduced wages. Employers' hiring decisions under "pure competition" respond quickly and thoroughly to changes in wage rates. On the other hand, mainstream economic theory holds that workers can always find a new employer who will want to take on additional workers up to the point where the wage cost of the workers is equal to the value of their contribution to the firm. Markets are in a perpetual process of adjustment to assure full employment and a correspondence between pay and productivity.

What human capital theory adds to this model of wage competition is the assertion that education creates skills that raise productivities of workers. It should follow, then, that to increase the average level of education of workers is to create two favorable events. (a) The average level of pay of workers will rise because the average level of productivity is higher. (b) Inequality of income will be reduced; an increase in the supply of highly skilled workers puts downward pressure on their pay, and a decrease in the supply of less skilled persons helps to raise their incomes.

Thurow (1975) attacks this whole line of argument on the ground that workers do not compete for wages but for jobs. Put another way, the number of jobs an employer offers is little affected by changes in wage levels in the short run but greatly affected by the amount of capital goods under the employer's control. For example, suppose it happened that there was an increase in the supply of commercial airline pilots and that the executives of the airlines sensed that they could

hire pilots at less than prevailing wages. Pilots' pay is a rather small (though not insignificant) factor in airline costs. The executives would hire a significantly larger number of pilots only if they were in the process of buying more airplanes, a decision that would be based on estimates of future ticket sales. Estimates of ticket sales would in turn be based on many variables, among which pilots' pay would be a relatively minor one.

In the "job competition" model, moreover, most skills are assumed to be acquired on the job, not in institutions of formal education. How does education influence earned income? Thurow (1975) asserts that employers use education to screen applicants for jobs. Employers are looking for persons who are stable, take their work seriously, are careful of the equipment, and are easily trained. Employers assume that length of schooling is a good proxy measure of these desired qualities. Hence, people with the highest degrees or the longest schooling experience go to the head of the line for jobs, without regard to whether the content of their formal education is in any way related to the specific skills they will use on the job.

Under this theory, once people sense what is happening to them, they will pursue education defensively. Bank telling formerly was a job for high school graduates. Now, people with AA degrees from community colleges apply and get preferential treatment. Students who think there is a chance they will want to be tellers are then likely to see the need to continue education through the community college level. The education system is thus used as an expensive way to reduce an employer's need for a ready means to choose among applicants for jobs.

An alternative version to Thurow's model is the dual labor market theory (Doeringer & Piore, 1971; Gordon, Edwards, & Reich, 1982). Dickens and Lang (1985) state the essence of the theory:

> Human capital has tended to emphasize differences among people, rather than among jobs, as a determinant of the distribution of income. Workers in low-wage jobs are viewed simply as low-productivity workers who are unwilling or unable to obtain the skills that are necessary for access to higher paying jobs. It follows from this approach that the way to eliminate poverty is to provide individuals with more skills, or with incentives to obtain skills...Dual market theorists have maintained that jobs can roughly be divided into two groups: those with low wages, bad working conditions, unstable employment, and little opportunity for advancement (secondary jobs), and those with relatively high wages, good working conditions, and opportunities for advancement into higher paying jobs (primary jobs)...Advocates of this view have argued that primary sector jobs are rationed and that, in particular, women, blacks, and other minorities find it difficult to obtain primary employment. Since...it is unlikely that rationing can be

eliminated, training programs will not be successful in eliminating proverty. (p. 792)

Which theoretical model is more descriptive of the way labor markets in America actually work? No one can say for certain. Thurow (1982) is able to point out, in defense of his own position, that the distribution of years of schooling among members of the work-force has become considerably more equal, absent any noticeable reduction in inequality of income distribution. There well may be industries that conform to the screening hypothesis in their labor market behavior, but almost surely there are other industries in which the concepts of human capital theory apply.

Uses of Human Capital Theory in the Local Setting

Educational administration may make use of human capital theory in the local setting. Not all people who take an interest in local school matters are aware that investment in education offers quantifiable returns. Reports appear from time to time, published by the U.S. Bureau of the Census, the U.S. Department of Education, and various research centers, that bring the data on returns to particular forms of education up to date. Educational administrators can explain and interpret these reports to the local citizenry; ordinarily, the reception will be favorable. It is important, however, for the administrators to know how the data are analyzed, for otherwise their presentations of the findings may not be convincing.

Also, local administrators can prepare their own surveys to show, for example, the economic value to students of completing high school; the appropriate data base would be students in the local district. It would be necessary to keep in touch with a reasonable sample of high school graduates and school leavers, but this is not a difficult task. Periodically, one would need to ask these school leavers about their employment status (whether they were working, how many weeks they had worked during the year), and about their earnings. It is not necessary in such a study to record employment status and earnings for the entire working lives of the sample; indeed, 3 to 5 years' worth of data would be sufficient to establish whether high school completion carries economic value. From the data presented above, presumably it does.

In the kind of study just mentioned, primary attention would be given to persons who left high school—with or without a diploma—to enter the labor market. A more ambitious study would attempt to follow a cohort of local high school graduates into college and thence into the labor force. These two approaches to measuring the economic value of local

investments in education would be complementary to each other.

LABOR FORCE REQUIREMENTS AND THE EXTERNAL EFFICIENCY OF EDUCATION

The second main topic of economics of education is the elucidation of the relationship between the demand for and the supply of work skills. Regardless of whether students enter the labor market directly after high school or after a period of further education, elementary and high schools shape differential capacities of young people to acquire the skills they will use in their work. If our economy needs more scientists, for example, then it is important that our elementary and secondary schools do a good job of teaching mathematics. Projection of labor market requirements gives directions to school systems in these regards.

What is the difference between human capital theory and manpower planning? Human capital theory provides a set of benefit-cost ratios that give general guidance about the relative worth of different educational levels and the relative worth of different types of degrees, but it does not inform us about the numbers of persons with specific skills who will be needed at given dates in the future. This latter kind of information is what exercises in manpower planning offer. Hence, manpower planning establishes the opportunity, if it is done well, to adjust the flows of students through different occupational programs closely to their future employment opportunities.

All manpower planning exercises are quantitative. Some are highly mathematical, using large-scale "input-output" models (Adelman, 1966). Instead of a full discussion of these models, which is beyond the scope of this chapter, a type of quasi-judgmental model chiefly associated with the economist Herbert Parnes, widely used throughout the world, will receive attention here.

The Parnes Model for Manpower Forecasting and Educational Planning

The Parnes method consists of a series of steps of data collection and analysis (see Parnes, 1962). The process begins with the preparation of a "manpower inventory"; the data in the inventory are used in several of the subsequent steps. The inventory arrays data to show numbers of employed and unemployed persons in the economy, the numbers of persons who work in the different industries (agriculture, mining, fisheries, manufacturing, banking, finance, insurance, retail trade, wholesale trade, government, and many different types of services), and the occupations of the persons in these different industries. The data are crossclassified by occupation and industry, by occupation and education, and by educational attainment and age.

Next, the analyst projects the size of the labor force 5, 10, and 15 years into the future. The two chief elements in this projection are change in total population and change in the rate of labor force participation. (In the United States, the large influx of women into the labor force has caused the labor force to increase more rapidly than the population.) The analyst estimates the future size of the national product. This is done by (a) estimating a rate of productivity change per worker, using recent trend data, and (b) multiplying productivity per worker in the target years by projected size of labor force.

The future estimates of national product are divided into shares for each specific industry, using recent data on relative industrial growth and judgmental estimates of shifts in consumer demand and of technological change. The analyst proceeds to assign shares of the future labor force to different industries, based on industry-specific rates of growth or decline and on estimated future changes in worker productivity by industry.

Using data from the manpower inventory, the analyst divides up the labor force assigned to each industry into occupational categories. To each occupational category is assigned an educational qualification. A total is then derived for the numbers of persons of each educational qualification that the economy requires in the future.

From the manpower inventory the analyst can see that certain persons hold educational qualifications today and, under normal circumstances, can project that a majority of these trained people will still be working at their jobs in the target dates 5, 10, and 15 years into the future. However, a certain proportion will die or retire. The manpower inventory includes data on age of worker by educational qualification, so it is possible to estimate the numbers of people by educational qualification who will leave the labor force; a certain number of qualified people will be needed to replace them. "Replacement demand" for trained labor is always a positive number. Total demand for educated workers is the sum of replacement demand and "new demand." New demand can be positive or negative, depending on whether the industries in which people of particular skills are concentrated are expected to grow or decline.

Knowing the future demand for people of particular educational qualifications—the sum of replacement demand and new demand—the analyst estimates the flows of students through various parts and branches

of the educational system to produce graduates in a "correct number." The correct number of graduates is the one that meets but does not exceed the estimates established under the processes of manpower planning for persons of different educational qualifications to enter the labor force in the future target dates. In estimating the flows through the educational system to produce the correct number of graduates, the analyst must take account of drop-out and grade repetition rates as well as the possibilities that some students will fail their final examinations and that some successful graduates will decline to enter the line of work for which they have been trained.

Certain deficiencies of this approach as to the external efficiency of the educational system should be noted (Blaug, 1973). The estimates of future needs for persons of different educational qualifications is grounded almost entirely in past relationships between job and educational level. There is no assurance that this relationship, being affected by many considerations beside economic efficiency, is the proper one. Thoroughgoing job analysis, which is not part of conventional manpower planning exercises, might reveal that persons who are going to hold certain jobs in the future should have either more or less education or training than their predecessors if they are to perform well while not being overqualified. However, thoroughgoing job analysis is a slow and expensive process. Also, manpower planning taken seriously means that large units of government must control programs offered in local schools and colleges. Manpower planning is not an activity that fits well into small local governments in the first place, because firms and workers are mobile and because labor markets overlap small, local public jurisdictions. Hence, manpower planning implies an interference with local autonomy in education that goes against the grain of American ideology. Even so, it is interesting to note that vocational education is subject to a greater degree of federal and state planning than are academic or general programs.

Current National Concerns About the External Efficiency of the Educational System

From time to time public concern about whether the schools are helping students to find satisfying work careers mounts to a high pitch. There is, in the mid-1980s, great interest in the issue of quality education and educational excellence. Basic to this interest is a doubt that U.S. schools are doing as well as those in other advanced nations to prepare students for careers in mathematics and science, fields seen as central to maintaining a dominant position for U.S. manufactured products in world markets. Education thus becomes a source of economic strength.

The National Academy of Sciences has addressed two other issues that are more specific. In its report, *Education for Tomorrow's Jobs* (Sherman, 1983), the Academy took up the problem of youth unemployment. Rates of youth unemployment tend to be high in recession, of course, but they remain high in good times as well. Further, youth unemployment is concentrated—it affects particularly minority youth and youth who grew up in low-income families.

Improving education is not an especially powerful way to create jobs, but the Academy concluded that employers, nevertheless, were prepared to hire larger numbers of young people if they were better prepared for work. The Academy recommended that vocational education programs make closer contacts with employers and that strong efforts be made to help vocational education teachers stay up to date in their fields. Also, the Academy suggested that the federal government establish "vocational incentive grants," or training vouchers, that would be fully portable. These grants could be used to purchase training in any bona fide institution, public or private, and they would carry a substantial dollar value. In awarding them, the government would give priority to low-income students. This provision would be combined with a "truth-in-training" act requiring training institutions to provide full disclosure to prospective students about the rigor of the program, completion rates, job prospects, actual placement rates of graduates, and earnings of graduates.

In a companion report, *High Schools and the Changing Workplace* (National Academy of Sciences, 1984), the Academy turned to the question of what employers want to find when they go into the hiring market for labor: "The sole object [of this report] is to identify, from the employers' perspective, the basic education needed for effective, upwardly mobile, life-long participation in the American work place (p. viii). The panel responsible for the preparation of the report concluded that the ability of workers to learn and adapt to change is of the utmost importance. Second the panel stressed the usefulness, even in so-called menial jobs, of academic skills: reading, writing, mathematical problem solving, and basic concepts of scientific inquiry. Indeed, the panel asserted that high school graduates who plan to enter the work force right after leaving high school require virtually the same level of academic competence as students who seek admission to four-year colleges.

A recent assessment of the current state of manpower planning is to be found in Psacharopoulos and Woodhall (1985) and also in Psacharopoulos, Hinch-

liffe, Dougherty, and Hollister (1983). In the United States, concern has been expressed about a possible oversupply of college-educated persons (Freeman, 1976). In the developing world, manpower issues are now becoming focused on requirements for skills in rural areas (International Labor Office, 1972; King, 1977) and on the contributions that skills training for women make in the program for economic growth (Buvinic, Lycette, & McGreevey, 1983; Clark, 1979; Smock, 1981). A search for a solution to the problem of educated unemployment in the third world continues strongly (Coombs, 1985; Dore, 1976; and Simmons, 1980). The basic techniques of manpower planning appear in Davis (1980).

Uses of Concepts of Manpower Planning in the Local Setting

Local administrators can find advantage in studying labor market trends in their regions and in the nation. As for the regional labor market, most students who leave the high schools of a given school district to enter the labor market will seek employment locally. These young persons, high school graduates and dropouts, are dependent on the regional labor market for their livelihood, and the employers in the region likewise are dependent on the local schools to supply workers for entry-level positions. When the superintendent and high school principals take the trouble to talk to employers about job needs, they accomplish several things at once: (a) They engender goodwill toward the schools; (b) they obtain information that should be of use to the counselors in advising students about jobs and job prerequisites; (c) they improve the chances that the counselors themselves will have easy access to local employers; and (d) by demonstrating an interest in conditions in the local labor market, administrators reinforce in counselors' minds the idea that counselors have responsibilities to serve all school leavers, not just the graduates who are going directly to college.

A note of caution. Sometimes the chief executive officers of business firms will report exaggerated claims about their future needs for workers and relay exaggerated doubts about the potential performance of newly hired persons (reflecting generalized doubts about public institutions, including schools). If possible it is always good in assessing conditions in the regional labor market to talk to people in the firm who have current, first-hand information to offer, such as production managers, office supervisors, and personnel chiefs.

There are, likewise, gains to be made when school administrators keep themselves up to date on national labor market trends. Here, the clients are students who expect to go to college and possibly to graduate or professional school—and their parents. Students and parents should be informed that prediction of career prospects for future scientists, doctors, engineers, business administrators, and the like often lacks precision. The administrators can then explain that they try to keep in touch with the most reliable agencies (e.g., the U.S. Bureau of the Census, the National Science Foundation, and the major schools of business administration)—and "here are the findings."

SPENDING MONEY WISELY AND THE INTERNAL EFFICIENCY OF EDUCATION

The third main topic in the field of economics of education deals with internal allocations of resources: how to accomplish more for the benefit of students within the constraints of a more-or-less fixed budget. The chief technique of research is the education production function, and the chief technique of management is cost-effectiveness analysis.

Educational Production Functions

The educational production function is intended to offer information on the relative power of different kinds of educational resources (teachers, facilities, materials of instruction, technological devices), called "inputs," to raise student achievement. Knowing the relative power of inputs to affect achievement and also knowing the costs of the inputs permits arranging the patterns of resource use to maximize outputs. Educational production functions deal with the first of these questions, the relative power of inputs. The research attempts to cast light on the question of whether reducing class size is more powerful in affecting student achievement than is increasing the proportion of teachers in the district who score well in subject-matter tests—or vice versa. How much do expenditures on textbooks and materials of instruction matter? Does changing the amount of time spent in teaching different subjects have a strong or weak influence on achievement? Is size of school an important variable?

The general form of the educational production function is a linear multiple regression model of the following type:

$$A_{it} = f(F_i^{(t)}, P_i^{(t)}, S_i^{(t)})$$

where A_{it} = quantitative measures of attainment of the ith student at time t; $F_i^{(t)}$ = set of family and neighborhood characteristics of the ith student cumulative to time t; $P_i^{(t)}$ = set of student-body characteristics (peer influence) cumulative to time t; and $S_i^{(t)}$ = set

of school inputs received by the ith student cumulative to time t.

The intent is to evaluate the power of different school inputs, taking account of the influence on a given student of home, neighborhood, and classroom peers. Suppose it turns out that achievement rises 10 points (on whatever scale) for each additional year of experience of classroom teachers, and it rises 5 points for each reduction of 10 students in class size. Let the cost of hiring more experienced faculty in the school be $10,000 and the cost of reducing class size be $100,000. Raising the experience level of teachers yields a 1-point gain in achievement for $1,000; doing it by reducing class size (hypothetically) costs $20,000.

The earliest production function studies, dating from the mid-1960s, were rather crude. They used achievement scores at one point in time. The unit of analysis was the school, or even the school district, and the consequent averaging of results weakened the power of the findings. Each variable on the right-hand side of the regression was treated as if wholly independent of the other variables. In considering the effects of teacher characteristics on achievement, no account was taken of the fact that a child's progress in school is not determined by his or her current teacher alone but is the result of the cumulative actions of all the teachers in the child's school career.

More recent studies have been better prepared. Change in achievement scores is used as a dependent variable, along with scores at a given time. The unit of analysis is the individual student, allowing the analyst to show how different types of students respond differently to different combinations of inputs. The independent variables are treated interactively. For example, it is possible to consider the combined effects of increasing (reducing) class size and placing in the classroom a teacher whose own education is of higher (lower) quality. As becomes clear in the more recent studies, the responses of students from high SES homes to these combinations of resource changes can be quite different from the responses of students from low SES homes. A further improvement made in the educational production function studies has been the use of data that are "longitudinal," that is, with regard to which the school resources available to a student are tracked year by year during the student's entire school experience. Information is included not just on the characteristics of the teacher a child has when the study is made, for example, but also on the characteristics of teachers the student had in earlier years.

In some cases, it is possible in principle to make costless transfers of resources within a district to improve the performance of students in that district. A major study of the Philadelphia public schools indicated that high-achieving students did best with experienced teachers, whereas low-achieving students performed best when taught by younger teachers who had themselves been educated in elite colleges and universities (Summers & Wolfe, 1974). Further, low-income students were helped especially by having teachers who took their baccalaureate work in a high-prestige college and by having small classes (fewer than 28). Middle-income students did almost as well regardless of the type of college their teacher attended and were unaffected by being in classes up to size 33. An administrator who had a free hand in making teacher assignments and in regulating class sizes could readily use such information to reorder the resources placed before students of different characteristics, to the end that student performance goes up absent any noticeable financial cost to the district.

Unfortunately, the instances in which educational production function studies have yielded policy-relevant findings are rare. Though something approaching 100 such studies have been made, the results generally are ambiguous, inconsistent, and contradictory—in short, not robust. One possibility is that available data do not describe the process of learning with sufficient completeness, a problem of "omitted variables." Another possibility is that schools are operated with considerable inefficiency. It is difficult to draw conclusions about the true effects of resource tradeoffs on achievement from a mass of data in which resources are combined without serious regard to maximizing the output included in the studies (Levin, 1976).

The classic review of the earlier vintage of educational production function studies is Averch, Carroll, Donaldson, Kiesling, and Pincus (1972). A more recent and very comprehensive review of studies is Bridge, Judd, and Moock (1979). Two examples of thorough analysis are Burkhead, Fox, and Holland (1967), referring to academic achievement in large-city high schools, and Cohn, Millman, and Chew (1975), in which the authors examine the processes of educational production in schools in Pennsylvania. Unfortunately, neither of the last two studies provides much in the way of clear guidance or efficient patterns of resource allocation; in both, rather, the findings are ambiguous. A study with stronger conclusions regarding the power of school inputs to affect student achievement is Winkler (1975). Using longitudinal data from schools of a large California district, Winkler reported that both teachers' salaries and quality of teacher training were significantly related to student performance. Similar conclusions about the importance of teacher variables were reached by Bowles (1969, 1970a).

An excellent critique of the methods used in educational production function studies is provided by Hanushek and Jackson (1977). Murnane (1981), emphasizing the positive, offers a contemporary assessment of what we have learned from the studies. He suggests that the educational production function approach can truly be used to inform educational policy, provided researchers take account of the responses that "key actors" make to policy changes, with "key actors" being defined as parents, students, teachers, union leaders, and administrators.

Cost-effectiveness Analysis

Cost-effectiveness analysis is similar in basic concept to the use of educational production functions, but it is far more useful to school administrators. The steps in using cost-effectiveness analysis include the following. Identify a discrete program or activity in the local district. Describe two or more alternative processes of production for the given program. Establish a means to estimate the product or output of the program in quantitative terms. Measure (a) the output and (b) the cost of each alternative process. Compute the ratio of output/cost for each process. The process showing the highest ratio is the most cost-effective one and should be made the preferred mode of operation in the particular program.

Consider a hypothetical example. Suppose for a program in English as a Second Language there is one class a day and the course runs 3 months. Within that framework, assume the availability of four alternative processes. The first is a full morning of instruction with an ESL teacher (4 hours); 20 students can be accommodated. The second is a half morning of instruction (2 hours) with an ESL teacher; again, 20 students can be accommodated. The third process is a full morning divided between 2 hours of instruction by the ESL teacher and 2 hours of handicraft (cottage industry) instruction, taught by refugee peers—18 students can be accommodated. The fourth method is 2 hours per day of self-paced, computer-assisted instruction; 15 students can be served.

Assume now that the objective measure of program performance is the average number of new English words learned by the students during the 3-month period. Let us estimate the number of new words learned in each of the four processes, as shown in Table 18.3. Let us also estimate the dollar cost of each process. Taking the ratio of cost to total new words learned, we see in Column 6 of Table 18.3 that process 3—half ESL instruction and half work experience (handicrafts)—is the most cost-effective, providing 36 new words for each dollar of expenditure.

Cost-effectiveness analysis is extremely useful when the goal of policy is getting the most for the

Table 18.3   Hypothetical Example of Cost-Effectiveness Analysis: English as a Second Language

(1) PROCESS	(2) CLASS SIZE	(3) AVERAGE NUMBER OF NEW WORDS PER STUDENT	(4) TOTAL NEW WORDS	(5) TOTAL COST	(6) COST PER WORD
1. Full morning	20	5,000	100,000	$4,000	$0.040
2. Half morning	20	3,000	60,000	$1,800	$0.030
3. Half ESL, half work experience	18	4,000	72,000	$2,000	$0.028
4. Self-paced computer assisted	15	2,000	30,000	$1,700	$0.057

money—and this is often the goal of policy! However, Table 18.3 offers other bases for choosing among processes. If one cares little for refugees, one might opt for process 4, the cheapest one (but not the most cost effective). Or, if one thought it very important that refugees learn as many words as possible in the 3-month period, one would opt for process 1. It offers the most learning, and it is the most expensive. Process 2 has nothing to recommend it. It is not cost effective, it is not the cheapest process, nor does it provide the most learning.

To conduct cost-effectiveness analysis requires investigation of the output of alternative processes. These processes generally are specific, and often they are small in scale—unlike the processes that educational production functions attempt to describe. Often it is possible to estimate yields of alternative processes by actual observation, though it is important to be wary of conditions under which yield is especially high or low because of the personality of commitment of the particular operator who is in charge of the process at the moment. In other cases, it may be possible to estimate outputs of alternative processes by assembling a panel of experts.

In any case, it is generally wise to apply sensitivity analysis in the cost-effectiveness calculations, a means of seeing how sensitive the results are to changes in the values of the outputs. Suppose, after having performed the calculation shown in Table 18.3, the analyst is not sure whether the output figures are correct, that is, whether the yield of 3 months of full morning instruction (Process 1) is 5,000 words. Might it be more or less? The procedure is to recompute Table 18.3, allowing the output figures to vary up or down by, say, 20 percent. If Process 3, the most cost-effective process, continues to be ranked as the most cost effective after these changes in values are made, the analyst can be reasonably sure that small errors in measurement cannot distort the results. If, on the other hand, the cost-effective ranking of processes is highly unstable under sensitivity analysis, then experiments should

be conducted with the different projects to try to improve the estimates of outputs.

The other analytical task is estimation of the costs that the alternative processes entail. This is best dealt with in a straightforward, common-sense way. In most educational processes, the largest item of expenditure is for personnel salaries and benefits. The salary price should not ordinarily be the salary paid to the person who is conducting the process at the moment, because that person may hold unusually high or low seniority status. The analyst wants a typical salary for the position; for example, the midpoint of the position's salary scale. Often, the persons engaged in a process work only part time in the given activity, so the analyst must prorate salaries as a percentage of time worked. If overtime is involved, the value should be added in, as should the costs of personnel benefits. These are ordinarily simple matters to deal with.

Somewhat more complicated is the estimation of time value of volunteers. Since the educational agency does not pay money for their help, then the value of their time might well be excluded from calculations of cost-effectiveness of public expenditure. A related question is whether to include estimates of the value of student time. Some processes may require a lot of student time and other processes may not. Time definitely has value to high school students and adults. Unless there is evidence that students are eager to ignore the value of their time—like volunteers—then the cost of student time should be included, priced at or slightly above minimum wage.

Cost of supplies and materials should be estimated, but it is not always necessary to go into great detail about these items. If costs of supplies and materials are a small part of the overall budget, then a general estimate is sufficient. Prorating costs of central administration is not advisable unless expansion or contraction of the processes under study would have a marked effect on the expenses of central administration. Sometimes, however, central administration costs are indeed "lumps." Suppose that one or more of the processes under consideration make use of the agency's central computing facility, and suppose that facility is near capacity. Expansion of the process under question could then require a major addition to the computer facilities although the specific process itself used only a small part of the new capacity.

Long-lived facilities should be costed under a depreciation schedule, taking account of the expected lives of the various assets. Procedures for dealing with long-lived assets, as well as procedures for conducting cost-effectiveness analysis in total, are shown in Levin's *Cost-Effectiveness Analysis: A Primer* (1983).

An early study that applied cost-effectiveness analysis to prevention of high school dropouts is Weisbrod (1965). A more recent application to the question of optimum school size is Chambers (1981). Cost-effectiveness analysis is used in educational planning in the third world; an example is Cochrane and Jamison (1982).

Cost-Effectiveness Analysis in the Local Setting

The foregoing discussion is intended to indicate that cost-effectiveness analysis is eminently feasible in the local setting. Not only is it feasible, but it offers important benefits to administrators and their staffs. First and foremost, cost-effectiveness analysis allows educational agencies to obtain more desired outcomes from the expenditures at their command. Second, the analysis stimulates educators to think about alternative processes by means of which instructional tasks can be carried forward. The mentality that assumes that "there is only one good way to do anything" is conducive to neither vitality nor efficiency in organizations. Third, cost-effectiveness analysis offers different bases for choices of preferred processes. Table 18.3 illustrated three: maximization of output, minimization of expenditure, or maximum yield per dollar of expenditure (the cost-effective solution). Each kind of choice can be appropriate under certain circumstances, but it is important to know rationally which choice one is making and why. The process of cost-effectiveness encourages people to be rational in their decisions.

ECONOMICS OF EDUCATION AND PUBLIC SUPPORT OF EDUCATIONAL INSTITUTIONS

The analysis of returns to education, as described in the first section of this chapter, emphasizes a relationship between incremental income attributable to some educational experience and the cost of obtaining that educational experience. Education as viewed in human capital theory has value because it helps the participant to become richer, just like any other successful in-

vestment. In the general case, government does not subsidize private investment, there being no particular reason why the masses of people should pay taxes to support the creation of privately held wealth. If education is simply a process of creating privately held wealth, and wealth that is unequally distributed (MDs versus high school dropouts), all as human capital theory might indicate, one may reasonably ask why governments—federal, state, and local—appear to pay for most of elementary-secondary schooling and for a large share of post-secondary education.

The answer to this important question emerges in several parts. The first part is to note that the public contribution to education is not as overwhelmingly great as some people might suppose. Education is supplied as between schools and colleges on the one side and students and parents on the other. In the case of public elementary and secondary schools (the closest common example of "full" public support), the taxpayer supplies the schoolhouse, pays the teachers and other staff, and provides some of the necessary materials of instruction. Parents may make voluntary cash contributions to the school, give time to the school, provide supplementary learning materials for their children, pay for supplementary classes, arrange transport thereto, help with homework, and so on. Students supply great amounts of time, which has value. Generally speaking, the students who acquire the greatest amounts of educational capital are those who make the greatest amount of private investment in its acquisition—from both parental and their own sources.

The second part of the answer as to why we do not place the financing of education fully in the private sector is grounded in the concepts of "externalities" and "social goods." In some cases, actions motivated strictly by private gain of a given individual yield benefits external to that person, which is to say benefits accruing to others, even strangers. When people are inoculated against life-threatening, contagious diseases, they themselves receive a benefit, but so do people with whom they come in contact. People who acquire an education benefit themselves but also give pleasure to people who prefer to live in an educated, literate society. Certain actions, then, create value beyond private rewards, but the initiators of these actions—those who get inoculated or who become educated—cannot, as private citizens, demand a contribution from their beneficiaries. Government steps in to levy a tax, the proceeds of which supplement the costs of creating externalities, thus assuring an appropriate supply of them (Musgrave & Musgrave, 1980).

A similar argument is found in the treatment of the distinction between private goods and social goods. A person who wishes to enjoy private goods—an automobile, a pair of shoes, a sandwich—must either meet the supplier's price or be excluded from that satisfaction. Thus, in private markets, suppliers are guaranteed sales receipts for all goods and services in demand. Forces of competition assure that sales receipts cover costs plus a reasonable profit. But for some goods or services, it is not possible to exclude anyone from sharing in consumption. Defense is an example. All citizens are protected from foreign aggression by the defense forces, and no one can be excluded from that protection. Hence, defense, in the sense of national defense, could not be sold in any private market. Everyone would know that the effectiveness of defense would be approximately the same regardless of whether any one individual made his or her own contribution because each is only one of a very large number of citizens. Each one would also know that he or she could not be denied whatever protection is given. Accordingly, knowing that his or her contribution would yield nothing of value, that individual can become a "free rider" as far as national defense is concerned (Shoup, 1969).

Goods characterized by "nonexcludability" are defined as social goods. In the provision of social goods, market mechanisms fail to work. If social goods are to be provided, they must be paid for through compulsory levies, called taxation. Education offers social goods as well as private. Examples are living in a democracy of educated voters and living in a society that is characterized by scientific advances. Yet another is growth in artistic appreciation. No one can be excluded from these benefits. Measurement of social goods created by education has proven to be difficult, but some progress has been made (Lazear, 1983; Weisbrod, 1964). In any case, the presumed existence of social goods created by education establishes a case for public support of educational programs.

Last, the question at hand may be viewed in the context of comparing private and social returns to education (Jallade, 1977). In estimating private returns to education, benefits are counted as incremental earning minus taxes—in short, the return to education that the individual gets to keep. Costs are those that are paid by the individual to acquire the education—fees, books, transport, and forgone income. Social returns are computed on more inclusive data. Benefits include gross incremental income including taxes; costs include the public subsidy toward the increment of education. Governments can "make money" on education by collecting more back in taxes from the recipients of education than is paid in subsidies toward that schooling. Whenever social returns exceed private returns, the government is making money.

Concluding Observations

It is always appropriate at the end of a chapter like this to warn about the limitations of the analytical processes discussed. Some people might contend that education is so good and precious that to measure its value in economic terms and to show how acquiring educational certificates raises one's lifetime income is crass. Likewise, some people may feel that the attempt to manipulate educational processes by efficiency criteria is misguided. They prefer to say that education possesses so much cultural, social, and personal value that the public should be willing to subsidize inefficiency in educational operations.

In the author's view, these attitudes are too politically idealistic. There are, nevertheless, some serious problems in the economic analysis of education.

Extreme reliance upon estimates of returns to human capital to determine resource allocations in education could mean a slighting of certain fields of training that are important to our social welfare, such as nursing and teaching, relative to other fields whose graduates have a chance to make a lot of money. Similarly, blind reliance on economic returns might dictate a possibly excessive shift of resources toward the more gifted students and away from slower learners. The market economy responds to short-term opportunities for profit, accepting the distribution of household income and the character of consumers' tastes as they are. Schools exist, in part at least, to change the intergenerational distribution of incomes and to raise both the cultural tone and the social awareness of the population. To regulate flows to educational resources solely on a set of signals from the market economy would rob the system of schooling of its most creative responsibilities. It is important to continue to maintain a certain distance between the values of the private market for human services and the values of educational institutions.

As applied to education, there are serious deficiencies in the techniques of economic analysis. Take one example from the search for external efficiency: projections into the future of skills requirements. Skills require years to produce, counting both instruction in schools and colleges and on-the-job training. Thus, the analyst cannot be content to know what the demand for different kinds of skills are today; rather, he must forecast or project the demand for skills 5, 10, and 20 years into the future. But skill demand is strongly affected by shifts in consumer tastes and by technological change. It is the pride of a dynamic capitalistic economy that it responds swiftly to changes in consumer tastes and that it keeps itself in the forefront of technological discovery. Those kinds of changes, however, are inherently unpredictable, thus introducing an element of uncertainty in the projections of skills requirements. Manpower planning is more successfully performed in a more controlled economy, such as the Soviet Union.

To take a second example of methodological inadequacy, consider the effort to improve the internal efficiency of school systems. The processes by which students learn are complex. Students seem to display a lot of individual differences, and the processes are not easily observed. The opportunities for controlled experimentation are limited, both by concern for the rights of human subjects and by a certain bureaucratic inflexibility in educational institutions. Thus, the economic analyst falls back upon a multiple regression model that relies upon data generated for administrative purposes and is uninformed by learning theory in any significant manner. For these and possibly other reasons, the policy advice generated in educational production function studies is most often general rather than specific.

The third problem with using economic analysis to guide educational policy can be stated more briefly. The processes of analysis rely strongly upon quantification. Certain educational outcomes cannot easily be cast in quantitative terms, as, for example, the development of the altruistic spirit. Those outcomes that cannot be quantified are likely to be downgraded in economic studies.

We have described three main components of the economics of education: valuation of human capital, projection of skills requirements in the economy, and estimation of efficient means of educational production. Each component draws upon a well-established base in economic literature, reaching back to the founding of the discipline of economics. Each main component in economics of education receives the continued serious interest of some members of the economics profession.

That education is deemed worthy of study by members of such an analytical and powerful tribe as economists may be a good thing for the ego of educationists. The contributions of the tribe indicate that the techniques of economic analysis as applied to educational processes can be *used* by educational administrators to the benefit of the systems for which they are responsible. There is more than ego burnishing involved.

Ideally, the application of techniques of analysis from the discipline of economics to the solution of real educational problems will be a collaborative effort. Educators know a lot more about their organizations, their processes, and their products than economists will ever learn, but the other side of that statement is that

economists have a better grasp of analytical methods than administrators are likely to acquire. The best hope is to find a happy meeting ground of interests.

REFERENCES

Adelman, I. (1966). A linear programming model of educational planning: A case study of Argentina. In I. Adelman & E. Thorbecke (Eds.), *The theory and design of economic development* (pp. 385–417). Baltimore: Johns Hopkins University Press.

Averch, H. A., Carroll, S. J., Donaldson, T. S., Kiesling, H. J., & Pincus, J. (1972) *How effective is schooling?: A critical review and synthesis of research findings*. Santa Monica, CA: Rand.

Balderston, J., Wilson, A., Freire, M., & Simonen, M. (1981). *Malnourished children of the rural poor: The web of food, health, education, fertility, and agricultural production*. Boston: Auburn.

Becker, G. S. (1975). *Human capital* (2nd ed.). New York: National Bureau of Economic Research.

Behrman, J. R., & Birdsall, N. (1983). The quality of schooling: Quantity alone is misleading. *American Economic Review*, 73(5), 928–946.

Berger, M. C. (1983). Changes in labor force composition and male earnings: A production approach. *Journal of Human Resources*, 18(2), 177–196.

Blakemore, A. E., & Low, S. A. (1984). The high-school dropout decision and its wage consequences. *Economics of Education Review*, 3(2), 111–119.

Blaug, M. (1973). *Education and the employment problem in developing countries*. Geneva: International Labor Office.

Borus, M. E., & Carpenter, S. A. (1984). Factors associated with the college attendance of high-school seniors. *Economics of Education Review*, 3(3), 169–176.

Bowles, S. S. (1969). *Educational production function: Final report*. Washington, DC: Office of Education, U.S. Department of Health, Education, and Welfare.

Bowles, S. S. (1970a). Toward an educational production function. In W. L. Hansen (Ed.), *Education, income, and human capital* (pp. 11–70). New York: Columbia University Press.

Bowles, S. S. (1970b). Migration as investment: Empirical tests of the human investment approach to geographical mobility. *Review of Economic Statistics*, 52(4), 356–362.

Bowles, S., & Gintis, H. (1976). *Schooling in capitalist America*. New York: Basic Books.

Bowman, M. J. (1976). Through education to earnings? *Proceedings of the National Academy of Education*, 3, 221–292.

Bowman, M. J. (1985). Education, population trends and technological change. *Economics of Education Review*, 4(1), 29–44.

Bridge, R. G., Judd, C. M., & Moock, P. R. (1979). *The determinants of educational outcomes: The impact of families, peers, teachers, and schools*. Cambridge, MA: Ballinger.

Burkhead, J., Fox, T. G., & Holland, J. W. (1967). *Input and output in large-city high schools*. Syracuse: Syracuse University Press.

Buvinic, M., Lycette, M. A., & McGreevey, W. P. (Eds.). (1983). *Women and poverty in the third world*. Baltimore: Johns Hopkins University Press.

Carnoy, M., & Levin, H. M. (1976). *The limits of educational reform*. New York: McKay.

Chamberlain, G., & Griliches, Z. (1975). Ability, schooling, and the economic success of brothers. *International Economic Review*, 16(2), 422–450.

Chambers, J. (1981). An analysis of school size under a voucher system. *Educatonal Evaluation and Policy Analysis*, 3(2), 29–40.

Clark, N. (1979). *Education for development and the rural woman*. New York: World Education.

Cochrane, S., & Jamison, D. T. (1982). Educational attainment in rural Thailand. In A. Summers (Ed.), *New directions for testing and measurement: Productivity assessment in education* (pp. 43–

59). San Francisco: Jossey-Bass.

Cohn, E. (1978). *The economics of education* (rev. ed.). Cambridge, MA: Ballinger.

Cohn, E., Millman, S. D., & Chew, I. (1975). *Input-output analysis in public education.* Cambridge, MA: Ballinger.

Coombs, P. H. (1985). *The world crisis in education: The view from the eighties.* New York: Oxford University Press.

Corman, H., & Davidson, P. K. (1984). Economic aspects of postsecondary schooling decisions. *Economics of Education Review, 3*(2), 131–139.

Davis, R. (Ed.). (1980). *Planning education for development.* Cambridge, MA: Harvard Graduate School of Education.

Dickens, W. T., & Lang, K. (1985). A test of dual labor market theory. *American Economic Review, 75*(4), 792–805.

Doeringer, P. B., & Piore, M. J. (1971). *Internal labor markets and manpower analysis.* Lexington, MA: Lexington.

Dore, R. (1976). *The diploma disease: Education, qualification and development.* Berkeley: University of California Press.

Fleisher, B. (1974). *Mother's home time and the production of child quality.* Unpublished paper, The Ohio State University, Columbus.

Freeman, R. B. (1976). *The overeducated American.* New York: Academic.

Gordon, D. M., Edwards, R. C., & Reich, M. S. (1982). *Segmented work, divided workers: The historical transformation of labor in the United States.* Cambridge, England: Cambridge University Press.

Grasso, J. T., & Shea, J. R. (1979a). Effects of vocational education programs: Research findings and issues. In National Institute of Education, *The planning papers for the vocational education study.* Washington, DC: U.S. Government Printing Office.

Grasso, J. T., & Shea, J. R. (1979b). *Vocational education and training: Impact on youth.* Berkeley, CA: Carnegie Council on Policy Studies in Higher Education.

Griliches, Z. (1977). Estimating the returns to schooling. *Econometrica, 45*(1), 1–22.

Gustman, A. L., & Steinmeier, T. L. (1982). The relation between vocational training in high school and economic outcomes. *Industrial and Labor Relations, 36*(1), 73–87.

Hanushek, E. A., & Jackson, J. E. (1977). *Statistical methods for social scientists.* New York: Academic Press.

Hill, C. R. (1981). Education and earnings: A review of the evidence. *Economics of Education Review, 1*(4), 403–420.

Hill, C. R., & Stafford, F. P. (1974). Allocation of time to preschool children and educational opportunity. *Journal of Human Resources, 9*(3), 323–341.

International Labor Office. (1972). *Employment, income and equality: A strategy for increasing productive employment in Kenya.* Geneva: Author.

Jallade, J. P. (1977). *Basic education and income inequality in Brazil: The long term view.* Washington, DC: World Bank.

Jamison, D. T., & Lau, L. J. (1982). *Farmer education and farm efficiency.* Baltimore: Johns Hopkins University Press.

Johnson, G. E., & Stafford, F. P. (1973). Social returns to quantity and quality of schooling. *Journal of Human Resources, 8*(2), 139–155.

Kenny, L. W. (1983). The accumulation of human capital during marriage by males. *Economic Inquiry, 21*(2), 223–231.

King, K. (1977). *The African artisan.* New York: Teachers College Press, Columbia University.

Lazear, E. (1983). Intergenerational externalities. *Canadian Journal of Economics, 16*(2), 212–228.

Levin, H. M. (1976). Concepts of economic efficiency and educational production. In J. Froomkin, D. T. Jamison, & R. Radner (Eds.), *Education as an industry* (pp. 149–191). Cambridge, MA: Ballinger.

Levin, H. M. (1983). *Cost-effectiveness: A primer.* Beverly Hills, CA: Sage.

Levine, V., & Moock, P. R. (1984). Labor force experience: Women with children. *Economics of Eduction Review, 3*(3), 183–193.

Link, C. R., & Ratledge, E. C. (1975). Social returns to quantity and quality of education: A further statement. *Journal of Human*

Resources, *10*(1), 78–89.

Lynch, L. M. (1983). Job search and youth unemployment. *Oxford Economic Papers, 35,* 71–82.

McMahon, W. W., & Wagner, A. P. (1982). The monetary returns to education as partial social efficiency criteria. In W. W. McMahon & T. G. Geske (Eds.), *Financing education: Overcoming inefficiency and inequity* (pp. 150–187). Urbana: University of Illinois Press.

Mertens, D. M. (1982). *Vocational education and the high school dropout.* Columbus: National Center for Research in Vocational Education, The Ohio State University.

Meyer, R. H. (1981). *An economic analysis of high school vocational education, IV: The labor market effects of vocational education.* Washington, DC: The Urban Institute.

Mincer, J. (1974). *Schooling, experience and earnings.* New York: Columbia University Press.

Mincer, J. (1979). Human capital and earnings. In D. M. Windham (Ed.), *Economic dimensions of education.* New York: National Academy of Education.

Mincer, J. (1984). Human capital and economic growth. *Economics of Education Review, 3*(3), 195–205.

Mincer, J., & Polachek, S. (1974). Family investments in human capital: Earnings of women. *Journal of Political Economy, 82*(2), S76–S108.

Moock, P. R. (1973). *Managerial ability in small-farm production: An analysis of maize yields in the Vihiga Division of Kenya.* Unpublished doctoral dissertation, Columbia University, New York.

Murnane, R. J. (1981). Interpreting the evidence on school effectiveness. *Teachers College Record, 83*(1), 19–35.

Musgrave, R. A., & Musgrave, P. B. (1980). *Public finance in theory and practice* (3rd ed.). New York: McGraw-Hill.

National Academy of Sciences. (1983). *Education for tomorrow's jobs.* Washington, DC: National Academy Press.

National Academy of Sciences. (1984). *High schools and the changing workplace: The employers' view.* Washington, DC: National Academy Press.

Parnes, H. S. (1962). Manpower analysis in educational planning. In H. S. Parnes (Ed.), *Planning education for economic and school development* (pp. 79–94). Paris: Organization for Economic Cooperation and Development.

Psacharopoulos, G., Hinchliffe, K., Dougherty, K., & Hollister, R. (1983). *Manpower issues in educational investment: A consideration of planning processes and techniques.* Washington, DC: World Bank.

Psacharopoulos, G., & Woodhall, M. (1985). *Education for development: Analysis of investment choices.* New York: Oxford University Press.

Ribich, T. I., & Murphy, J. L. (1975). The economic returns to increased educational spending. *Journal of Human Resources, 10*(1), 56–77.

Rizzuto, R., & Wachtel, P. (1980). Further evidence on the returns to school quality. *Journal of Human Resources, 15*(2), 240–254.

Schultz, T. W. (1961). Education and economic growth. In N. B. Henry (Ed.), *Social forces influencing American education.* Chicago: University of Chicago Press.

Schultz, T. W. (1975). The value of the ability to deal with disequilibria. *Journal of Economic Literature, 13*(3), 827–846.

Sherman, S. (Ed.). (1983). *Education for tomorrow's jobs.* Washington, DC: National Academy Press.

Shoup, C. (1969). *Public finance.* Chicago: Aldine.

Simmons, J. (Ed.). (1980). *The education dilemma.* New York: Pergamon.

Smith, A. (1937). *An inquiry into the nature and causes of the wealth of nations.* New York: Modern Library Edition, Random House. (Original work published 1776)

Smith, J. P. (1984). Race and human capital. *American Economic Review, 74*(4), 685–698.

Smock, A. C. (1981). *Women's education in developing countries: Opportunities and outcomes.* New York: Praeger.

Solomon, L. C., & Wachtel, P. (1972). *Effects of school quality on earnings.* New York: National Bureau of Economic Research.

Stern, D. (1982). *Managing human resources: The art of full employment*. Cambridge, MA: Auburn.

Stern, D. (1984). School-based enterprise and the quality of work experience: A study of high school students. *Youth and Society*, *15*(4), 401–427.

Summers, A. A., & Wolfe, B. (1974). *Intradistrict distribution of school resources to the disadvantaged: Evidence for the courts*. Philadelphia: Federal Reserve Bank of Philadelphia.

Thurow, L. C. (1975). *Generating inequality: Mechanisms of distribution in the U.S. economy*. New York: Basic Books.

Thurow, L. C. (1982). The failure of education as an economic strategy. *American Economic Review*, *72*(2), 72–76.

Wachtel, P. (1974). *The effect of school quality on achievement, attainment and earnings*. New York: New York University.

Walsh, J. R. (1935). Capital concept applied to man. *Quarterly Journal of Economics*, *49*(2), 255–285.

Weisbrod, B. (1964). *External benefits of public education*. Princeton, NJ: Princeton University Press.

Weisbrod, B. (1965). Preventing high school dropouts. In R. Dorfman (Ed.), *Measuring benefits of government investments* (pp. 117–149). Washington, DC: Brookings Institution.

Weiss, L., & Williamson, J. (1972). Black education, earnings, and interregional migration: Some new evidence. *American Economic Review*, *62*(3), 372–382.

Welch, F. (1973). Black-White differences in returns to schooling. *American Economic Review*, *67*(5), 893–907.

Welch, F. (1974). Relationships between income and schooling. *Review of Research in Education*, *2*(1), 179–201.

Winkler, D. R. (1975). Education achievement and school peer group composition. *Journal of Human Resources*, *10*(2), 189–205.

Winkler, D. (1984). The fiscal consequences of foreign students in public higher education: A case study of California. *Economics of Education Review*, *3*(2), 141–154.

Wise, D. (1975). Academic achievement and job performance. *American Economic Review*, *65*(3), 350–366.

Zodhiates, P. (1980). Project analysis: Benefit-cost and cost-effectiveness. In R. Davis (Ed.), *Planning education for development* (Vol. 2). Cambridge, MA: Harvard Graduate School of Education.

CHAPTER 19

Educational Finance: The Lower Schools

James W. Guthrie

This chapter describes the social and economic scope of and governmental practices associated with financing the lower schools in the United States; it reviews major dimensions of school finance research which have evolved since the midpoint of the 20th century; and it comments on components of a research agenda that deserve the future attention of analysts. Identification of several general conditions serves as an introduction.

SCHOOL FINANCE AND PUBLIC VALUES

The constitutional provisions, statutes, court decisions, regulations, and administrative guidelines shaping the financing of U.S. schools are remarkably complicated. Moreover, they vary substantially from state to state. The complexity and variation are consequences of major social and economic conditions that have operated differentially as the nation grew. A state's financial provisions at any given time represent both previous and current efforts to insert into public policy society's expectations for the functions of schools and the performance of students. The policy analyst recognizes both that school financing is complex and that it varies because it reflects the unusual value diversity that exists across the United States and the populations within each state.

The U.S. political system must accommodate individuals and groups who hold values that at their roots often conflict with one another. However valid

their positions, some people believe schools should spend more money and others believe spending levels are already excessive. There are advocates for and opponents of aid to nonpublic schools. Some people believe that public school spending should be absolutely equalized; still others propose that school spending, however unequal, should be completely a matter of local choice. Some groups propose far-reaching property tax revisions, yet others want education funded only from state sources or desire that lotteries and gambling revenues be used for school support. Somehow, this vast spectrum of beliefs must be consolidated, compromised, and codified. That is the function of the political system, and the resulting crazy-quilt pattern among states is but a reflection of the constantly shifting diversity of public opinion throughout the United States.

Space does not permit detailed description here of the school finance systems of each of the 50 states. Accordingly, only general concepts related to the understanding of any state's specific arrangements will receive emphasis.

MAGNITUDE OF THE U.S. SYSTEM OF PUBLIC SCHOOL FINANCE

Not only is the United States' pattern of decentralized school financing more complex than that of any other developed nation, but also it affects more individuals. Approximately one out of every six members of the U.S. population is enrolled in a public school, and the absolute number of enrollees is growing. Delivery of public education services to a vast student population

Consultant/reviewers: Charles S. Benson, University of California—Berkeley; Walter I. Garms, University of Rochester; Richard A. Rossmiller, University of Wisconsin–Madison

Figure 19.1   Public School Expenditures per Pupil, 1965–1986 in Current and Constant Dollars

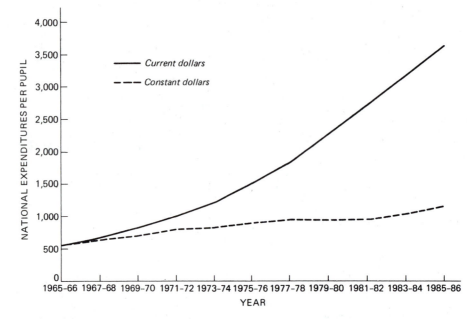

NOTE. Compiled from data in *Inflation Measures for Schools and Colleges* (Washington, DC: Research Associates of Washington, 1982, *1984 Report of the President's Council of Economic Advisers*, and *Statistical Abstract of the United States* (U.S. Bureau of the Census, various years).

(approximately 42 million in 1987) employs over 4 million individuals, 3 million of whom are licensed education professionals. In addition, the United States's approximately 15,000 local school districts annually purchase literally millions of tons of supplies (fuel, food, paper, paint, vehicles, and so on). Public education, kindergarten through 12th grade, is one of the nation's largest governmental undertakings, of the same order of magnitude as other publicly subsidized human services such as health delivery, welfare, arrangements, and transportation. The enterprise requires awesome levels of financial resources to maintain. For example, total spending for U.S. public schools (K–12) stood at $126 billion in 1985 ($3,006 per pupil). Figure 19.1 displays per-pupil expenditures for the period 1965–1966 through 1985–1986.

Within the nationwide pattern, variation among the 50 states is substantial. For example, in 1980 the highest average annual current expense per pupil across the 48 contiguous states was $3,452 in New York State; the lowest was $1,564 in Arkansas. The annual spending differential between these two states, $1,888 per pupil, approximated 80 percent of the national average. Moreover, states differ in their projected rates of population growth, adaptation to high-technology industries, access to inexpensive energy sources, and preferences for the quality of schooling. Thus, existing per-pupil spending differences are predicted by the National Institute of Education's School Finance Project to increase over time unless there is enacted a

massive federal aid program intended to reduce interstate disparities (Geske, 1984; Sherman, 1982). In light of projected U.S. federal budget deficits, such legislation appears highly unlikely.

Whether the total of $126 billion in expenditures is sufficient for the nation's K–12 needs is arguable. Historical comparison does, however, reveal rapid growth over four decades. For example, in 1940, at the end of the Great Depression and before formal declaration of World War II, the nationwide average annual expenditure per pupil was $100.[1] Even when discounting for inflation by statistically holding dollar purchasing power constant, expenditures per pupil have increased almost 500 percent since that time. This rate of growth is greater than that for any other major public service, with the exception of subsidized health care. Table 19.1 depicts spending trends, adjusts them for changes in the consumer price index (CPI), and, for selected years since 1960, displays per-capita public school spending as a percentage of national mean personal income (a rough measure of the national "effort" to support schools).

Tables 19.2 and 19.3 report school spending as a percentage of gross national product (GNP) from 1940 through 1980, and compare U.S. spending in this regard to selected other nations. Table 19.2 documents the long-term trend of education spending, identifying the extraordinary expansion of schooling and associated funding needed from 1950 to 1970 in order to serve the World War II baby boom. From 1970 to the

Table 19.1   Education Expenditures per Capita for Selected Years from 1960 to 1983

	PER-CAPITA EXPENDITURE		CURRENT DOLLAR PER-CAPITA EXPENDITURE AS % OF PERSONAL INCOME
YEAR	CURRENT $	1980 $	
1960	87	230	3.9
1970	200	411	5.1
1976	328	459	5.1
1978	374	464	4.8
1980	424	424	4.5
1981	447	401	4.2
1982	491	420	4.4
1983	516	427	4.4

NOTE. The data are from *Statistical Abstract of the United States: 1984* and *Statistical Abstract of the United States: 1985*, by the U.S. Department of Commerce, Bureau of the Census, Washington, DC.

Table 19.2   Public School Expenditures as a Percentage of GNP for Selected Years from 1940 to 1983

YEAR	K-12	GNP (BILLIONS OF $)	% OF GNP	TOTAL PUBLIC EXPENDITURE (IN BILLIONS)	% OF GNP
1940	2.3	100.0	2.3	2.6	2.6
1945	2.9	212.4	1.4	3.4	1.6
1950	5.9	286.5	2.1	7	2.4
1955	10.1	400.0	2.5	11.7	2.9
1960	15.9	506.5	3.1	19.7	3.9
1965[a]	26.5	691.1	3.8	35.3	5.1
1970	41.0	992.7	4.1	56.8	5.7
1975	65.0	1549.2	4.2	91.3	5.9
1977	76.8	1918.3	4.0	107.6	5.6
1978	81.2	2163.9	3.8	114.6	5.3
1979	87.1	2417.8	3.6	123.5	5.1
1980	96.4	2631.7	3.7	137.8	5.2
1981	102.9	2957.8	3.5	149.5	5.1
1982	110.0	3069.3	3.6	160.5	5.2
1983	117.6	3304.8	3.6	172.2	5.2

NOTE. The data are from *Statistical Abstract of the United States*, various years, U.S. Bureau of the Census and from *Historical Statistics of the United States, Colonial Times to 1970, Part 1*, p. 393, Department of Commerce, U.S. Bureau of the Census, Washington, DC.
[a] 1966 data.

Table 19.3   Public School Expenditures, International Comparisons

COUNTRY	YEAR	EXPENDITURES (MILLIONS OF $)	% OF GNP	% OF TOTAL PUBLIC EXPENDITURES
United States	1977	120,700	6.3	17.7
Australia	1977	6,402	6.5	16.2
Austria	1978	3,280	5.7	8.0
Brazil	1979	1,043	5.6	(NA)
Canada	1978	16,153	8.1	18.5
Colombia	1978	513	2.3	19.9
France	1978	25,301	5.3	(NA)
Germany (Fed. Rep.)	1979	34,699	4.6	(NA)
India	1977	2,923	2.9	9.9
Japan	1978	55,563	5.7	16.1
Mexico	1979	6,103	5.2	(NA)
Saudi Arabia	1979	4,841	7.8	10.2
Soviet Union	1978	47,431	7.4	12.0
Sweden	1978	7,850	9.1	13.1
United Kingdom	1976	14,177	6.3	14.3
Zaire	1979	363	5.0	25.8

NOTE 1. The spending and GNP figures differ from those in Table 19.2 because of different bases used by different government agencies.
NOTE 2. The data are from *Statistical Abstract of the United States: 1983*, by the U.S. Department of Commerce, Bureau of the Census, Washington, DC.

early 1980s, a declining school-age population, a "surplus" of teachers, increased competition from other public sector services, and uncertainty in the nation's economy decreased education's share of GNP. Even so, compared to many nations, the United States allocates a large proportion of its GNP to support the lower schools.

GENERAL SCHOOL FINANCE PRINCIPLES

In the absence of a national system of education in the United States, state-level government has ultimate responsibility for financing public schools. The federal government contributes, as of the late 1980s, approximately 6 to 7 percent of total K–12 spending. Thus, the major practices involved in state-level revenue generation and distribution are of central importance.

Revenue Generation

For more than a century the property tax served as the revenue mainstay for the support of local government operations and for schools particularly (Walker, 1984). Since 1977, however, the share of the school dollar contributed by the local property tax, as a national average, has fallen to 46 cents, while the states have assumed a substantially larger role in financing schools. By the late 1980s, state general funds, again as a national average, contributed more than 47 cents to each school dollar. The federal government contributes between 6 and 7 cents.[2]

Distributing School Dollars

No two states have established an identical school finance distribution system. Each is the product of a unique mixture of historical development, taxation schemes, preferences for quality of schooling, and governmental arrangements. At one end of a continuum is Hawaii, which depends almost exclusively on state school financing, plus federal categorical aids, using no local property tax revenues for school operation. At the other end is New Hampshire, which depends almost exclusively on locally generated property tax revenues for school support. In between are the majority of states, which depend heavily upon both state and local funding. Even though a generally modal pattern exists, it remains impossible to present a single descriptive model. An alternative is to explain several school finance distribution formulas, which together cover most states.

These distribution schemes cover "general aid" money, which can be spent at the discretion of local school authorities. General aid funds contributed by the states and raised at the local level together comprise approximately 75 percent of most school expenditures. "Categorical aid" funds complement general funds. Categorical aids come from both the federal and state governments for specified purposes (e.g., aid for handicapped students). An additional major classification of school revenues is funds for capital outlay, primarily school construction. Here mechanisms for the distribution of general aid receive particular attention.

Allocation Units

Every state relies on a measure of students to be schooled as a means for allocating general funds to local school districts (Guthrie, Garms, & Pierce, 1987). Approximately half the states utilize a measure of actual attendance, usually *average daily attendance* (ADA) as an allocation unit. Other states utilize a measure of *average daily enrollment* or *membership* (ADE or ADM). Attendance, ADA, is an attractive measure from a state policy point of view because it induces local officials to encourage pupils to come to school. Conversely, local school administrators contend they incur expenses whether or not a student actually attends. Once a student is enrolled, teachers must be paid, fuel bills still arrive, and so on. A few states try to compromise in this controversy by combining ADA and ADE into an average figure.

States frequently use pupil weightings in their allocation processes. The term WADA or WADM denotes *weighted average daily attendance* or *membership*. Assigning an added weight to a category of pupils is a means for more closely approximating what state officials believe ought to be spent for such pupils. Most commonly, weighting schemes appear in categorical aid programs. For example, states frequently weight handicapped pupils proportionate to the severity of the disability (e.g., 1.1 for speech impairment and 2.5 for an orthopedic or neurological handicap). Similarly a state may assign an added weight to youngsters from low-income households or who are low achieving. Weightings are derived from past practice, professional judgment, available finances, and political compromise. They are seldom an outcome of rigorously scientific analysis. They represent a politically practical and acceptable estimate of the additional costs of educating classes of students on whom arguably more should be spent.

States typically provide added funding for secondary students because smaller and more specialized high school classes involve higher labor and supply costs. Elementary educators frequently contend, however, that if more money were spent in the early years of schooling, the need for later remedial spending would be reduced. Florida, for example, recognizes this argument by providing added pupil weighting in grades 1 through 4 as well as 9 through 12.

Distribution Schemes

States have assumed at least partial responsibility for the financial support of local school districts since the 19th century (Walker, 1984). Initially, state aid took the form of flat grants, that is, a specified dollar amount to a local jurisdiction. The grant was intended to pay total school operating costs. Subsequently, the flat grant was altered to a flat grant per pupil. Flat-grant arrangements frequently continue today as an anachronistic and insignificant feature of many state school finance plans. By itself, the flat grant provision is insufficient to cover full operating costs. Fortunately for schools, states have introduced other financing features over time.

In the 1920s, two school finance experts, George Strayer and Robert Haig, advocated a distribution system that came to be widely adopted throughout the nation. Their scheme revolved around (a) the establishment of a minimum spending floor, or foundation expenditure, per pupil, to be reached through a combination of local revenues and state aid and (b) the introduction of a system of equalizing the assessed valuation of property within school districts to ensure that districts would make equivalent efforts to generate

their fair shares of revenues required to meet the foundation level.

In brief, *foundation plans* specify a state-established minimum per-pupil spending level. This dollar amount is intended to serve as a floor below which no student, irrespective of personal or district wealth, has less spent on him or her. The foundation amount is also intended to represent the level of resources that policy makers consider the minimum needed to enable students to succeed personally and occupationally. It further signifies the amount thought necessary to ensure the state's need for an educated citizenry. The foundation amount, or minimum spending level, is established by legislative action. As with pupil weighting schemes, past practice, political feasibility, and the state's fiscal condition shape the choice of a foundation spending figure more than does rigorous scientific analysis.

Foundation plans Figure 19.2 illustrates graphically the operation of a foundation distribution scheme. The asterisk and horizontal line depict the dollar amount of the foundation guarantee (i.e., $2,400), supposedly representing the cost of a minimal program. The section labeled *Required Local Effort* is the amount raised by the local property tax at, say, a required rate of 15 mills against assessed valuation. The section labeled *State Aid* is contributed by the state. To meet

Figure 19.2 Foundation Plan

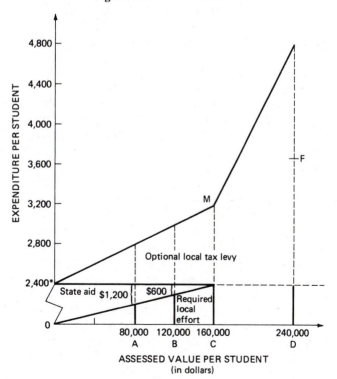

the foundation level of $2,400, District A's required
local effort (RLE) raises only half ($1,200), and the
state contribution ($1,200) is high. District B raises
more of the guaranteed minimum ($1,800) than the
state-contributed subsidy ($600). District C raises the
full guaranteed amount ($2,400) and receives nothing
from the state.

The solid sloping line above the $2,400 level
identifies the dollar increment that would be raised if all
districts chose to levy an optional local tax at the rate of
5 mills above the required 15-mill tax. Because of
differences in assessed valuation, District B can raise
more than District A, and District C can raise more
than District B. The slope becomes steeper at point *M*
because districts (like D) beyond that point already
raise more than the required minimum by levying only
the required rate, thus making the total property tax
revenue they collect that much higher.

It may be argued that it is unfair that some districts, because they happen to be rich in property, have
more money to spend from levying the required tax
rate than do property-poor districts. If the required tax
truly represents a state tax, then the amount raised
above the guarantee should be returned to the state to
be used elsewhere. This concept is called recapture or
recycling. Its effect is shown by the dashed lines in
Figure 19.2. District D would raise, at the required
rate, the amount shown by the line *DF*. It would return
to the state the amount *EF*, leaving it exactly as much
as every other district.

Percentage Equalizing and Power Equalizing   Historically, most states exhibited intense reluctance to
equalize educational expenditures across districts beyond the minimum foundation level. Districts with the
advantage of higher levels of property wealth were able
to spend more per pupil, to levy lower property tax
rates, or to do both. Over time, the continuation of
conditions that produced great disparities in expenditures, however much justified as supportive of "local
control" of school decisions, triggered substantial reform efforts. However, even before the 1970s' era of
equal protection reform began in earnest, several states
had set in place a distribution mechanism that reduced
the potential for unequal spending and taxing, namely,
percentage equalizing or its variant, *power equalizing.*

Percentage and power equalization commonly
guarantee to each of a state's local school districts the
same amount of assessed valuation per pupil. (This
condition sometimes leads to use of the label, *guaranteed yield plans.*) Equalization is accomplished mathematically, not by redrawing district boundaries so as
geographically to encompass the same amounts of
property wealth. Figure 19.3 illustrates the manner in
which a percentage or power equalizing plan operates.

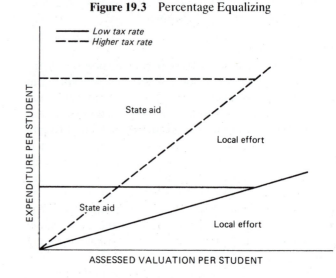

Figure 19.3   Percentage Equalizing

Within the boundaries of a state-specified spending
minimum and maximum, local school officials select a
per-pupil spending level that they deem appropriate.
Spending levels can be differentially established by
legislation to vary by grade levels, or even to accommodate weighted pupil costs.

Once a local spending level is selected, a district's
property tax rate is scheduled accordingly. If the local
application of the attendant tax rate does not raise the
per-pupil amount specified, then state general funds
subsidize the district for the difference. If an excess
amount is raised, then, logically speaking, the surplus
should be "recaptured" by the state and recycled to
other districts. Such recycling is highly visible and
politically unpopular (Perrin & Jones, 1984). States
generally have not engaged in recapture and where it
has happened, it has been at less than the full rate. In
the early 1970s, the Florida legislature was artful in
designing such a plan around the state's wealthiest
district, Dade County. In this fashion, all counties were
free to select their pupil spending levels, but there was
no recapture since application of a scheduled tax rate
never generated a per-pupil funding level in excess of
the amount specified.

Full State Funding   Yet another highly equitable means
for financing schools is simply to mandate that the state
specify per-pupil funding levels for each classification of
student and thereafter impose a statewide uniform
property tax to fund the plan. In those districts in which
the uniform statewide property tax rate generates insufficient revenue for the specified per-pupil spending
level, then the state makes up the difference. If the
tax rate generates more than specified funding levels,
then the state recaptures the excess for distribution
elsewhere.

Categorical Aid Program

State-appropriated general funds are intended to cover whatever are judged to be the educational needs of "average" students. However, not all districts are alike in respect to their concentrations of students in need of services that cost more than the average. Also, it is frequently the case that some districts may have unusual geographic features or extremes of population sparsity or density that render delivery of educational services more expensive. To compensate for such conditions, state legislatures authorize payment of *categorical funds* intended to cover added costs of specified programs. Handicapped students, students from low-income households, low-achieving students, gifted and talented students, and vocational students are among the categories most frequently included in state categorical funding programs.

Additionally, some school districts judged to be necessarily small in terms of their enrollment (e.g., in rural areas) frequently receive extra funds per pupil to compensate for diseconomies of scale. Conversely, city school districts sometimes receive additional compensation for the high density of the populations from which their enrollments are drawn. School construction funds, school lunches, and preschool programs are other examples of categorically funded undertakings.

Cost Differential

Within the boundaries of a state it is frequently the case that the cost of delivering an equivalent education program will differ from district to district. For example, cost-of-living differences may increase labor prices in urban school districts (Garms, Guthrie, & Pierce, 1978). Similarly, long distances and isolation may elevate delivery and fuel costs for rural areas. State school finance distribution formulas have become increasingly sensitive to these cost differentials. One approach, limited to states that undertake periodic regional cost-of-living analyses, is to index spending levels, possibly for both general and categorical aid, to whatever price differences exist throughout the state. A more sophisticated approach involves carefully analyzing regional cost variations in delivering a standardized set of education services. The funding per pupil in each district is then adjusted in accord with these regional education cost differentials (Chambers, 1980).

POST-WORLD WAR II SCHOOL FINANCE RESEARCH

United States public policy is heavily influenced by interactions among proponents of three values: equality, efficiency, and liberty. All three values are embedded deeply in the American ethos and are taken as conditions to be fostered or secured by government. At their logical roots the values can be antithetical. Moreover, concern for each of the dimensions is neither constant across constituencies, calculable in its intensity, nor consistent through time. Periodically, public attention to equality will exceed that for efficiency or liberty and, subsequently, the converse will be the case. The political system is engaged constantly in achieving a new equilibrium among the three values.

Because of its cost, complexity, and crucial social significance, education is a major part of the fabric of public policy. Consequently, school finance research has been and undoubtedly will continue to be influenced by the dynamic tensions connecting the three major value streams. Hence, equality, efficiency, and liberty (or choice) offer a useful rubric for classifying school finance research efforts, even though some degree of arbitrariness is inevitable in assigning specific publications and analyses to the several categories. Moreover, some scholarly efforts address more than one value stream.

The relevant work on equality, efficiency, and liberty fits within the substantial expansion of school finance research that has occurred since 1955. What once was almost the exclusive province of professors of school administration has productively expanded to include a wide range of social science and legal scholars. Probably the most significant change in school finance practices since 1980 has been the incorporation of research findings into state school finance distribution policies, including schemes that increasingly specify instructional practices at the local level. The volume of pertinent research prohibits exhaustive review and dictates only the citation of signal studies to illustrate the consequences for school finance of influential scholarship.

Equality

Decisions in *Brown v. Board of Education* and other racial desegregation court cases in the 1950s materially influenced school finance research. The desegregation decisions displayed the judicial utility of applying "equal protection" logic to education problems. Wise (1968) and Coons, Clune, and Sugarman (1970) were the first to apply the new line of legal reasoning to school finance reform. The arguments they developed served as underpinnings for court challenges to existing finance arrangements in dozens of states and at the federal level.

The centerpiece of the legal argument is that state school finance plans resulting in widely unequal spending and taxing violate the equal protection clause contained in the U.S. Constitution's Fourteenth Amendment and comparable provisons of state constitutions in at least two ways. First, school financing arrangements result in uneven delivery of services to individuals in three so-called suspect classifications: race, income stratum, and geographic location. Second, equal protection claimants contend that uneven delivery of educational services violates rights of citizens crucial to the fulfillment of a so-called fundamental interest. Freedom of speech, the right to vote, and freedom of assembly are among the civil liberties classified constitutionally as fundamental interests because of their crucial significance to the fulfillment of democratic processes.

Violation of a suspect classification or of a fundamental interest separately may be sufficient to trigger a particularly strict constitutional test, a compelling-interest test. Taken together, such alleged violations necessitate proof on the part of state governments that they possess more than a rational basis for their school finance plans. This latter test is a less intense justification in that the court need only concur that the justification is rational, rather than capricious.

The legal logic did not prevail in all court cases that challenged existing state finance systems. For example, the highest courts in Oregon, New York, Maryland, Georgia, and Colorado were not persuaded that school taxing and funding disparities were unconstitutional.[3] One the other hand, courts in California, Connecticut, Washington, and West Virginia were moved by the equal protection logic, and reforms were mandated.[4] The most visible case to reach the Supreme Court, *Rodriguez v. San Antonio*,[5] eventually was decided in favor of defendants (the state of Texas) and the status quo. However, the United States Supreme Court based the decision on the federal Constitution and thus left states free to come to different conclusions based on their own constitutions.

Despite several unfavorable state and federal court decisions, school finance litigation exerted significant pressures for reform. The period between 1970 and 1980 saw more and more far-reaching changes in school finance distribution formulas and associated taxation plans than any other decade in U.S. history. Inequities remain in the manner in which states generate and distribute school revenues. Indeed, some critics assert that disparities are as grave as ever or even more intense in the late 1980s. In some states, the assessment may be accurate. On balance, however, it appears that invocations of the equal protection judicial strategy proved practically useful (*Journal of Education Finance*, 1983).

School Finance Reform: Revenue Distribution

From the equal protection suits and other efforts to reform school finance through the judicial system there emerged the *principle of fiscal neutrality*. This negatively stated standard provides a measure against which the equity of a school finance system can be appraised. The operative principle (also the intellectual contribution of Wise, 1968, and of Coons, Cline, and Sugarman, 1970) is that *the quality of a child's schooling should not be a function of wealth, other than the wealth of the state as a whole.* Note that the standard does not specify what the quality of schooling should be. A satisfactory answer to that philosophically difficult question might forcefully lift the lid off the state's treasury. However, by stating the principle in the negative it is possible to judge what a school finance system should not do. It should not tie school service quality, translated into dollar resource level per pupil, to measures of local property wealth.

Three major plans have emerged to render a state school finance system compatible with the principle of fiscal neutrality. Two of these plans, full state funding and district power equalizing, have proved politically more practical than the third, a system of state subsidized vouchers.

Full State Funding California, Washington, New Mexico and West Virginia have effectively adopted full state funding in the wake of equal protection suits. Hawaii had adopted the system at the time of its 1969 entry into the union. Complexities are legion, but the essence of full state funding (as noted earlier) is that the state specifies spending levels per pupil and thereafter subsidizes districts directly whenever a state-mandated property tax rate applied at the local level generates insufficient revenue to meet the stipulated minimum level of expenditure. Such a system ensures that each district receive the level of revenue deemed appropriate by the state regardless of the ability of local tax sources to generate the desired revenue level. This solution to the problem of achieving equity stresses equality of expenditure and taxing capacity. In order to maximize the value of equality, full state funding trades a large degree of local discretion. School district officials find themselves without taxing authority and with no choice regarding the level of spending in their jurisdictions.

District Power Equalizing As noted previously, the state guarantees each district the effective availability of an equal amount of property wealth to be taxed for education. Districts may choose various spending levels, and at any specified taxing level any two districts within a state will receive identical per-pupil revenues. Hence, the principle of fiscal neutrality is met because local wealth is not a determinant of school quality. Power equalizing does not yet exist in its pure form. However, Maine, Michigan, California, and Florida have implemented it in part. The system forgoes a measure of equality on school spending and taxing in order to preserve a degree of local decision-making authority.

Vouchers Adoption of a voucher plan by any state would not only alter school financing but also would dramatically change school governance patterns. While no state has ever enacted a full voucher plan, Congress did so following World War II (Servicemen's Readjustment Act, P.L. 78, 346) to assist returning military veterans to further their college education. The now-defunct federal Office of Economic Opportunity attempted in the 1970s to induce school districts to experiment with voucher alternatives. Only the Alum Rock District, near San Jose, California, took the offer. Alum Rock dropped the plan within 3 years (Weiler, 1974). The idea, usually espoused by fiscal conservatives and political libertarians, sometimes by those who view it as a means of empowering school choice among the poor, has not yet proven attractive to a political majority either nationally or in a particular state.

Despite the fact that no state has seen fit to adopt a voucher plan, protagonists continue to advance the proposal. In 1983, a presidentially appointed national school finance panel recommended that federal categorical aid programs for low-income students be transformed into a voucher plan. In 1985, Secretary of Education William Bennett also advocated enactment of voucher plans.

Tuition tax credits constitute a version of the voucher scheme. President Reagan has espoused tuition tax credit plans, the U.S. Senate has passed tuition credit bills six times, and the House of Representatives once supported such a bill in 1979. The threat of veto by President Carter was then sufficient to discourage Senate approval. In a complicated 1984 decision, the U.S. Supreme Court appears to have diluted previous First Amendment objections and supported the constitutionality of tuition tax credit plans enacted by states.[6] The political climate at both state and national levels is such that voucher and tax credit proposals (which receive subsequent mention in the discussion of liberty) are likely to surface and be hotly debated for years to come. Public concern for equity issues appears to have diminished since 1980 and has been replaced by an emphasis on school productivity and higher student performance. (See Griesemer & Butler, 1983, for a comparative review of seven major reform proposals.) Nevertheless, in focusing public attention on the issue

and developing pragmatic solutions to problems of disparity, the school finance research of the 1960s and 1970s has generated a legacy of sophisticated analytic concepts and techniques that renders it easier to record the extent of progress toward school resource equality.

Early school finance research connected with equal protection litigation was of a relatively simple nature. Disparities in school district tax rates and per-pupil revenue levels were compiled as evidence for court cases (Berke, 1974). Such analyses were generally accurate and in some instances persuasive for trial purposes. However, over time, understanding of relationships between school financing and public finance and economics expanded substantially. School finance distribution formulas have been developed which can more effectively compensate for disparities in local school district property wealth (Garms et al. 1978) and consumer price index (Governor's Citizens' Committee on Education, 1972) or cost of education differences (Chambers, 1980) throughout a state. In addition, helpful refinements have sharpened pupil weighting mechanisms and introduced more accurate proxies for representing pupil needs in distribution formulas (Leppert & Routh, 1980).

Early equal protection analyses of state formula operation generally relied upon simple distributional displays of per-pupil spending and corresponding local district property tax rates. Attention to important definitions of equality and subsequent application of sophisticated measurement technologies have resulted in more powerful statistical gauges of equality (Berne & Stiefel, 1979). The more precise instrumentation that has become available has contributed not only to public policy and litigation purposes but has also shaped federal fund allocations to states under impact aid statutes.[7]

Not only is distribution better understood as a result of school finance research but so also is the revenue side of the financial equation. Aaron (1975), Musgrave (1974), and Netzer (1971) have substantially advanced understanding of the property tax. Garms et al. (1978) describe means for mitigating property tax regressivity. Benson (1978) has expanded the understanding of school tax-rate capitalization in residences and the interaction between overall economic conditions and property tax yield.

Efficiency

The link between economic growth and education has long been touted by educators and economists alike (Bowman, 1975; Denison, 1962; Schultz, 1961). However, early efforts by educators to understand the mechanisms by which schooling imparted added value to an individual and a society were conceptually and procedurally oversimplified and rooted in improperly specified models (Mort, 1952). Somewhat ironically, it was the search for equality in the 1960s that initiated much of the later research on school efficiency and productivity. The federal Civil Rights Act of 1964 included authorizations for a survey of equal educational opportunity. The study, undertaken under the overall direction of sociologist James S. Coleman, focused on equality of school inputs and outcomes and produced a highly controversial report (Coleman et al., 1966). Because the Coleman Report was the most comprehensive analysis of U.S. education made to that time, its seminal nature justifies substantial explanation even though it was completed over two decades ago.

The Coleman team surveyed and tested thousands of students, teachers, and school officials throughout the United States. Data were collected regarding resource inputs (e.g., school revenues, facilities, and teachers' experience) and outputs (e.g., student attitudes and academic achievement). Also, sophisticated statistical techniques were utilized in an effort to assess relationships between the two.

The report's three major findings did not receive a warm reception. Within geographic regions, no disparity was uncovered in the quality of school resources available to white and minority students. Conversely, substantial disparity was found along racial lines in pupil performance. The report's conclusion regarding school productivity was, if anything, even more contentious. Coleman and his colleagues were careful to circumscribe their position in stating that no significant school effects could be found independent of students' social-class background. Press and public interpretations of this finding were nowhere near so restrained. The widespread popular understanding was that schools, or added financing for schools, was irrelevant to student achievement.

The Coleman Report was thoroughly criticized for its methodological shortcomings, and its findings were declared by academicians to be irrelevant for purposes of guiding public policy (Bowles & Levin, 1968; Cain & Watts, 1968a, 1968b; Kain & Hanushek, 1968). No matter; policy makers, including courts, were influenced by the findings, and schooling went through a prolonged period when its utility as a significant instrument of social policy was intensely questioned (Jencks et al., 1972; Madaus, Airasian, & Kelleghan, 1980).

Still, the Coleman Report has had consequences for research far outlasting its influence on public policy. Previous school effectiveness studies had been conducted almost exclusively by professors of education who had attempted to deduce connections between school revenues and pupil performance without adequately controlling for student background variables such as SES (Mort, 1952). The Coleman Report attempted, albeit crudely, in retrospect, to control for student characteristics and thus contributed to a substantially more useful model of education production. Moreover, controversy surrounding the findings and methods of Coleman and his colleagues attracted wide and sustained academic attention (Mosteller & Moynihan, 1972). A large number of social scientists became interested in questions of school effectiveness and subsequently contributed to construction of more precise models of school production. In addition to defining input variables with greater accuracy, control measures of students were more carefully drawn, output measures of pupil performance became more creative, and the "black box" of education production itself was described more completely (Dreeben & Thomas, 1980; Madaus et al., 1980).

By the 1970s and 1980s, researchers had succeeded in developing more sophisticated models of schooling and instruction that led to new findings about the relationship between schooling and student achievement (Murnane, 1975; Rutter, Maugham, Mortimore, Ouston, & Smith, 1979). These findings assisted in rebuilding public confidence in schooling. However, the restoration took two decades to accomplish.

Whereas the finance reform era spawned productive research regarding models of school effectiveness, other endeavors in the name of efficiency in education were not particularly useful, either practically or analytically. The so-called accountability movement of the 1960s and 1970s marked yet another effort to apply private-sector technocratic processes to public education. Reformers displayed an intensity not witnessed since the 1920s era of scientific management and time and motion efficiency experts (see Callahan, 1962; Tyack, 1974).

An assortment of well-meaning academics and school administrators, with the aid of a large contingent of entrepreneurial consultants, proclaimed the public-sector utility of modern management applications such as program performance budgeting systems (PPBS), program evaluation and review technique (PERT), management by objectives (MBO), performance contracting, and competency-based teacher education (CBTE) training programs. However well intentioned, the proclamations suffered from questionable assumptions (Guthrie, 1972; Wise, 1979). The various plans assume an agreement on and ability to measure school outcomes and the existence of techniques to control for outside influences that far exceed reality. Careful research on the utility for education of the several programs generally yielded negative results and revealed the ineffectiveness of technocratic strategies and in some cases their dismal disutility (Kirst, 1975).

The accountability movement did, however, leave a useful research residue in the general area of achievement testing and assessing pupil performance. Though far from what might ideally be useful for public policy purposes, nationwide and state testing programs such as the National Assessment of Education Progress (NAEP) and the California and New York assessment programs have contributed usefully to the ability to measure school outcomes (Madaus et al., 1980).

Even if the accountability movement was politically naive, by the mid-1980s economic research techniques were being applied to education practices with increasing ingenuity. Results from these analyses have shaped state school finance policies and practices, and portend even greater future influence. For example, the research of Levin, Glass, and Meister (1984) determined the relative cost effectiveness of four instructional improvement strategies. Their results revealed that cross-age tutoring, using higher-grade-level or older students to assist in the instruction of younger or lower-grade-level students, was substantially more cost effective than three other practices: computer-assisted instruction, class size reduction, and increases in time allocated to instruction.

Liberty

In education, concern for "liberty" frequently translates to interest in institutional responsiveness and choice among instructional alternatives. Several practical efforts were begun in the 1960s to induce greater responsiveness; for example, "community control" of schools, administrative decentralization, school-site management and school-site advisory councils, and "alternative schools" (Ravitch, 1983). The only lasting consequences of these reforms appear to be school-site advisory councils. Their numbers have dwindled and, though perhaps still politically popular in some quarters, their utility has always been subject to question. Much advocacy accompanied these organizational reform efforts, but it is difficult to deduce a stream of research results that has had lasting effects.

Efforts to expand the range of choices available to pupils and parents have received substantial publicity since the 1950s. Research on the several proposals has centered on the voucher plans and tuition credit arrangements cited previously. Contemporary interest in educational vouchers appears to stem from Milton Friedman's 1962 volume *Capitalism and Freedom*, which advocates a simplified unregulated voucher plan. In the mid-1960s, social scientists and social reform advocates, searching for means more fully to enfranchise the poor, gave substantial attention to a more complicated choice mechanism, compensatory vouchers, which weighted low-income and low-achieving pupils more heavily for financing purposes (Manley-Casimir, 1982). Subsequently, even more complicted versions of regulated vouchers were developed, which attempted to balance public policy concern for social cohesion and due process with liberterian concerns for choice (Coons & Sugarman, 1978).

Actual experimentation with vouchers in the United States has been modest, and evaluations of such efforts have results in mixed findings (Cohen & Farrar, 1977; Weiler, 1974). Nevertheless, attention to vouchers gave rise to two useful research streams, one quite practical, the other more abstract.

Research on voucher proposals has produced an uncommon degree of pragmatic lore regarding their potential liabilities and advantages (James & Levin, 1983; Manley-Casimir, 1982). At a more abstract level, a small cadre of economists, legal scholars, and historians has honed the philosophic argument for choice to a far sharper point than was previously the case (Coons & Sugarman, 1978; Michaelson, 1980). Voucher plans still nowhere exist in the United States as public policy. However, a 1983 Gallup poll asserted that a majority of U.S. adults favors some sort of voucher mechanism, and interest in tuition tax credits has surfaced repeatedly at the federal level, in both executive and legislative branches (Catteral, 1983; James & Levin, 1983).

A SCHOOL FINANCE RESEARCH PARADIGM

Whereas much of the research related to school finance is aimed at promoting public policy consistent with equality, efficiency, or liberty, the specific studies themselves range over a broad spectrum of topics, utilize different units of analysis, employ a variety of research methods, and occasionally are inconsistent in their findings. Moreover, the number of such studies has proliferated to the point where it no longer is possible for an individual to be expert across the board about all of them or for a single journal to report all research results. The field has expanded and now draws often from economics, public finance, political science, sociology, law, and public administration. A means is needed to order the field. A paradigm for doing so is presented in Figure 19.4.

The paradigm is adopted from several system models that have been in fashion with social scientists since the 1960s. Even though the selected models are considerably misunderstood and offer little by way of

Figure 19.4   A Model of School Finance Research

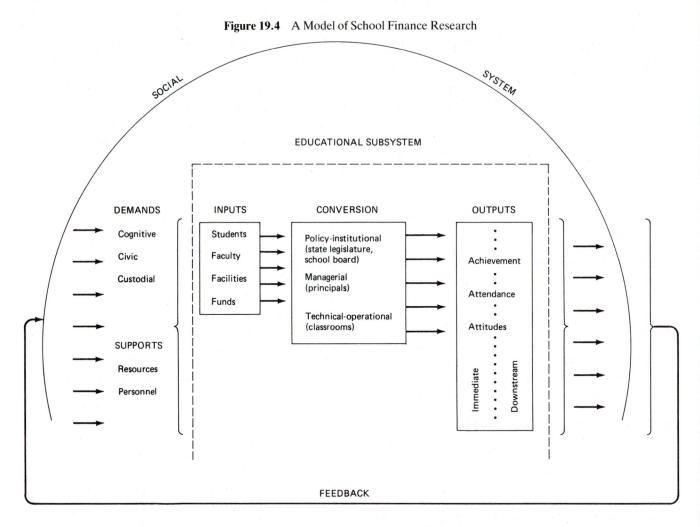

causal explanation, they are frequently useful for classifying phenomena. Hence, with due acknowledgment to theorists such as David Easton (1965) and Talcott Parsons (1960), the model that appears in Figure 19.4 represents an effort at categorizing the world of school finance related research.

The model is not at all as tidy as the boxes and lines suggest. What is sometimes an education input can also be classified on occasion as an instructional variable. For example, the student socioeconomic composition of a school or class appears in Figure 19.4 as an input into the conversion process. However, it is widely held that peer influences are a significant contribution to student learning. Thus, student socioeconomic makeup can also be taken as a policy variable for organizational or instructional purposes. The position of a particular line of research within the paradigm may depend on the definition of the education phenomenon under consideration. Withal, the brief categorization of school finance research that follows is organized in keeping with the model as presented. (See Rossmiller & Geske, 1977, for a similar model.)

Research Regarding the Social Environment

Research on the environment is often of a descriptive nature and when analytic tends to be at the macro level. It involves the gathering and presentation of data in forms such as the annual Gallup poll regarding public perceptions of education, the U.S. decennial census, demographic projections, and various indexes and forecasts pertaining to the overall economy. Collections of data of this genre suggest the nature of present or future inputs, both demands and resources, exchanged between the education system and the larger society (e.g., Osman, 1985).

Research Regarding Interactions Between the Social Environment and the Education System

Included here are at least two types of analyses, the first those that attempt to explain linkages between societal conditions and resources allocated for the education system. Research on relationships between local property wealth and per-pupil expenditures is an example

(Guthrie, Kleindorfer, Levin, & Stout, 1971; James, Kelly, & Garms, 1966).

In 1963 James fashioned a paradigm that categorized relationships between school finance and the larger environment. The model specifies the existence of (a) expectations for educational services (demand), (b) ability to "pay" (supply), and (c) governmental arrangements that act as a market mechanism to mediate supply and demand. In a research study involving more than 100 of the nation's largest school districts, James et al. (1966) employed regression analysis to assess the relationship between demand, supply, governmental arrangements, and school expenditures. Their findings confirmed the explanatory power of the model. Major correlates of per-pupil expenditures for city school districts were median family income, median years of schooling in the adult population, and property value per pupil. These variables accounted for more than 50 percent of the variance in spending per pupil. Also, these three variables when combined with 14 additional proxies for supply and demand explained almost 75 percent of per-pupil spending differences among city school districts in the 107-city study sample. Interestingly, proxies for governmental arrangements were not systematically correlated with per-pupil spending differences. It appears that government is the mediator between supply and demand, and the details of government organization (e.g., whether school boards are elected or appointed) do not exert a powerful influence on the outcome.

A second set of studies regarding environmental influences explores the relationship between education system outputs and the nature of the larger society. Illustrative analyses include (a) studies by economists of the contribution of education to economic productivity and industrial development (Bowman, 1975; Schultz, 1961); (b) analyses by political scientists of the link between schooling and levels and character of citizen political participation and of regime norms (Almond, 1965; Easton, 1963; Wirt & Kirst, 1982); and (c) studies of the influence of economic conditions on education and education policy (Guthrie, 1986a).

Input Research

Analyses of resource input provided influential evidence in equal protection litigation and in shaping distribution policies such as Title I of the Elementary and Secondary Education Act of 1965 and its successor, Chapter One of the 1981 Education Consolidation Improvement Act. Typically, input studies entail a mapping of demand or resource inputs and a comparison over time or over states and districts, as well as an analysis of the relationship between demands and resource availability (Guthrie, Pierce, Garms & Kirst, 1975).

Output Research

Output research encompasses surveys of student achievement such as undertaken regularly by the NAEP and through mechanisms such as the Scholastic Aptitude Test (SAT). Research on outputs entails attempts to create or develop more comprehensive or precise measures of pupil performance. Also, *outputs* can be defined as client satisfaction as assessed, for example, by the annual Gallup polls of parent and public opinion regarding schools.

Conversion Process Research and Interactions

Herein reside the most complex and in many ways the most significant lines of research. Much social-science inquiry during the late 1970s and 1980s has centered on understanding interactions between resource inputs and instructional procedures and outputs. This research has begun to inform school finance policy. For example, the relationship between time spent on instruction and student achievement received research attention during this period (Bloom, 1974; Karweit, 1982). The reform efforts begun in many states in the mid-1980s relied heavily on such research as a justification for offering school finance incentives to districts to extend the length of their school day and school year.

Input-output interaction research is crucial if school finance policy is to continue to provide incentives for added educational effectiveness. It is important to understand relationships between various inputs (institutional policies, organizational arrangements, and instructional strategies and teaching techniques) and educational outputs. Particularly useful to enhancing the desired understanding are education production function studies (e.g., Dreeben & Thomas, 1980; Levin, 1975), cost benefit analysis (Levin, Glass, & Meister, 1984), and analyses of organizational variables such as school-site decision making (Guthrie, 1986b) or districtwide collective-bargaining arrangements (Eberts & Pierce, 1980).

What About the Future?

The research model described above offers a matrix for locating and ordering existing studies related to school finance and for considering areas that would benefit from future study. Projection from past research to future inquiry must take into account not only the fund of accumulated knowledge but also several crucial policy conditions. Over the next 5 to 10 years the following conditions appear particularly salient: (a) the impact of public values on public policy; (b) state domination of educational policy; and (c) limited resources.

Public Policy and Public Values
It is virtually impossible to predict the valence of public concern for a policy-related value at a particular point in the future. The intensity of interest for any one value stream will undoubtedly continue to shift in a kaleidoscopic fashion. Nevertheless, it is reasonable to assume that general concern for the three central values of equality, efficiency, and choice will persist. Thus, research related to all three will continue to be appropriate, though from time to time more emphasis may be accorded one value area over another.

State Dominance of Educational Policy
The centrality of the state will persist, at least in the short run, not only because of historic patterns but also because of revenue availability. Whereas federal revenue sources may be more elastic, pressures of existing and projected federal deficits will dampen prospects of major federal funding initiatives. The historic shift toward state funding for and control over local operating districts will continue (Walker, 1984). Reforms initiated in 1983 that were intended to render schooling more rigorous and productive appear again to strengthen state decision making (Knapp, 1983).

Limited Resources
Educational institutions generally and research agencies particularly are unlikely in the near future to regain fully the levels of funding that characterized the mid-1970s. When controlling for inflation, the United States, on average spent $7,000 per classroom less in 1982–1983 than in 1977–1978. Whereas the economic upturn of the mid-1980s restored resources for education (Guthrie, 1986a), it nevertheless seems likely that efficient utilization of resources will be a persistent concern among the public, elected and appointed officials, and educators. There will be continued emphasis on identifying means by which educational institutions can be rendered more productive. Increasing enrollment in some segments of the nation and public perceptions of economic competition from other countries will only intensify concern for school productivity.

What to Do Next
Given the projected policy conditions, the following research emphases appear strategic.

Continue a Diversified Portfolio
Whereas research on educational productivity and schooling efficiency rose to high favor politically in the 1980s and is likely to remain popular in the foreseeable future, there continues to be a need to monitor conditions of equity. Moreover, public concern for liberty or choice is so sufficiently fluid that this issue could become salient quickly. The practical outcome of these conditions is to undertake continued analyses of equity relationships among inputs and to sponsor state-of-the-art reports and efforts to develop more creative and comprehensive measures of output. Even if studies of inputs and outputs comprise only a relatively small portion of the school finance research agenda, it is important that they not be neglected.

Concentrate on "Conversion Processes"
Major research attention should be concentrated on studies of interaction effects among conversion processes themselves and across conversion processes, inputs, and outputs. This recommendation is substantially easier to make than to implement. There is still much to learn about instruction. Researchers often treat schools and teaching as if there were direct cause-and-effect relationships that lend themselves to rational manipulation. The logic of systematic empirical inquiry often demands that research questions be framed in terms of independent and dependent variables in a quest for generalization. However, an individual instructor is constantly struck by the complexity of interactions, the ambiguity of instructional settings, the inconsistency of procedural outcomes, and the seeming caprice of pupil performance. All that may persist is uncertainty.

In striving for scientific rigor and precision, researchers often elevate their measures to levels of abstraction that are devoid of meaning for practitioners. Thus, the latter are suspicious of social-science research about conversion processes. What is necessary is substantial and continued attention to description and the construction of ever more comprehensive models that encompass more of the complexity of conversion.

Given the high probability of continued resource constraints, focusing research attention on interactions with relatively low cost consequences is also important (Kirst, 1984). This agenda suggests more analyses inside the school and the classroom. Research of the kind undertaken at the University of Chicago, at Stanford University, and at the University of Wisconsin on school productivity continues to be in order (Dreeben & Thomas, 1980; Levin et al., 1984; Rossmiller, 1978). Increased research is certainly in order on topics

Table 19.4 "Inexpensive" Reforms In Need of Further Research

1. INCREASE TIME ALLOCATED TO INSTRUCTION.

Lengthen school day and school year.
Eliminate high school electives and improve coordination of instructional content in elementary schools.
Increase amount of homework and tie content of homework more closely to classroom instruction.
Raise requirements for college entrance.

2. INCREASE TIME ACTUALLY DEVOTED TO INSTRUCTION.

Review programs and school procedures that interrupt instruction.
Improve teachers' classroom management skills so as to minimize interruptions and more fully utilize start-up time and transition roles.
Evaluate school schedules (in terms of lengths of periods, recess, lunch) to minimize lost time for instruction.

3. INCREASE AMOUNT OF TIME STUDENTS SPEND ACTIVELY LEARNING.

Decrease unsupervised learning activities.
Increase peer tutoring.
Trade off large and small group instruction.
Evaluate utility of classroom aides in terms of their contributions to instruction.

4. REDUCE TIME NEEDED FOR LEARNING.

Increase clarity and challenge of textbooks.
Improve teachers' ability to diagnose learning problems, sequence instruction, and keep students working at a fast pace.
Utilize computers and other technology for instruction where appropriate.

related to instructional time, curriculum content, graduation requirements, college entrance standards, instructional materials, teacher performance, organizational arrangements, and the interplay of these variable dimensions with differing kinds of inputs.

Kirst (1984) has proposed a rather comprehensive array of relatively inexpensive reforms (Table 19.4) as potential routes to achieving greater school productivity. He suggests that the cost-effectiveness and equity consequences of each of the enumerated policy options should be assessed through sophisticated inquiry with an educational production cast.

In brief, research about conversion processes should span a broad continuum. On one hand there continues to be an intense need for studies to map the domain of converting inputs to outputs. Such studies will assist in time to inform us better about what variables are significant and on what dimensions more data should be collected. On the other end of the continuum there continues to be a need for the practical studies related to school finance such as those illustrated by Kirst's (1984) list of proposed routes to increased efficiency.

Select Research Strategies That Illuminate More Than One Value

Research focused on greater efficiency, for example, can also assist in promoting greater equality. Better understanding of education production might assist in enhancing achievement of pupils from low-income households, gifted students, or handicapped students. Similarly, it is not out of the realm of reason to expect that inquiry into means for enhancing choice can also assist in creating greater equality of opportunity.

The systematic collection and distribution of a wider range of data regarding education inputs, conversion processes, and outputs would greatly advantage research aimed at equality, efficiency, and liberty. The federal government need not itself collect and disseminate all such information. It would also be of use to seek the collection of better examples for local and state officials to use for modeling their own data-gathering efforts. A state-of-the-art volume describing and assessing a variety of data dimensions important both for policy and research purposes could guide the information collection and distribution strategies of federal, state, and local officials. The federally developed guide to uniform school financial accounting has been instrumental in systematizing the collection by states and local districts of useful statistics regarding education revenues and expenditures (Roberts & Lichtenberger, 1973). A similar venture addressed to collection of additional education input, conversion, and output data could also contribute materially to promoting more informed policy and more useful research.

NOTES

[1] The U.S. mean-per-pupil expenditures at the beginning of the 20th century were $25.00 (Walker, 1984).

[2] Figures taken from *Finances of public school systems; 1982 census of governments*, 4(1). Washington DC: U.S. Government Printing Office.

[3] *Olsen v. Oregon*, 270 Or. 9, 554 p. 2d. 139 (1976); *Levittown v. Nyquist*, 453 NYS 2d 643 (1982); *Hornbeck v. Somerset County*, 485 A. 2d 758 (1983); *Lujan v. Colorado Board of Education*, 649 p. 2d 1005 (1982).

[4] *Serrano v. Priest*, 5 Cal. 3d 584, 487 p. 1241 (1971); *Horton v. Meskill*, 172 Conn. 615, 376 A. 2d 359 (1977); *Seattle v. State of*

Washington, 90 Wash. 2d 476, 585 p. 2d 71 (1978); *Pauly v. Kenny*, 255 S.E. 2d 859 (1979).

[5] *Rodriguez v. San Antonio*, 411 U.S. 1 (1973).
[6] *Mueller v. Allen*, 103 S. CT. 3062 (1983)
[7] See P.L. 81-874, 246.

REFERENCES

Aaron, H. J. (1975). *Who pays the property tax?: A new view.* Washington, DC: The Brookings Institution.

Almond, G. A. (1965). A developmental approach to political systems. *World Politics*, *17*(2), 183–215.

Benson, C. S. (1978). *The economics of public education* (3rd ed.). Boston: Houghton-Mifflin.

Berke, J. S. (1974). *Answers to inequity: An analysis of the new school finance.* Berkeley, CA: McCutchan.

Berne, R., & Stiefel, L. (1979). Concepts of equity and their relations to state school finance plans. *Journal of Education Finance*, *5*(2), 109–132.

Bloom, B. S. (1974). Time and learning. *American Psychologist*, *29*(9) 682–688.

Bowles, S. S., & Levin, H. M. (1968). The determinants of scholastic achievement: An appraisal of some recent findings. *Journal of Human Resources*, *3*(1), 3–24.

Bowman, M. J. (1975). Education and opportunity: Some economic perspectives. *Oxford Review of Education*, *1*(1), 73–84.

Cain, G., & Watts, H. (1968a). The controversy about the Coleman Report: Comment. *Journal of Human Resources*, *3*(3), 389–392.

Cain, G., & Watts, H. (1968b). Problems in making inferences from the Coleman Report. (Mimeographed working paper.) Madison: The Institute for Research on Poverty, University of Wisconsin.

Callahan, R. E. (1962). *Education and the cult of efficiency.* Chicago: University of Chicago Press.

Catteral, J. S. (1983). *Tuition tax credits: Fact and fiction.* Bloomington, IN: Phi Delta Kappa Education Foundation.

Chambers, J. G. (1980). The development of a cost of education index: Some empirical estimates and policy issues. *Journal of Education Finance*, *5*(3), 262–281.

Cohen, D. K., & Farrar, E. (1977). Power to the parents? The story of educational vouchers. *Public Interest*, *48*, 72–97.

Coleman, J. S., Campbell, E. Q., Hobson, C. J., McPartland, J., Mood, A., Weinfeld, F., & York, R. L. (1966). *Equality of educational opportunity.* Washington, DC: U.S. Government Printing Office.

Coons, J. E., & Sugarman, S. D. (1978). *Education by choice.* Berkeley: University of California Press.

Coons, J. E., Clune, W. H., & Sugarman, S. D. (1970). *Private wealth and public education.* Cambridge, MA: Harvard University Press.

Denison, E. (1962). *The sources of economic growth in the United States and the alternatives before us.* New York: Committee for Economic Development.

Dreeben, R., & Thomas, J. A. (1980). *The analysis of educational productivity, Vol. 1: Issues in microanalysis.* Cambridge, MA: Ballinger.

Easton, D. (1963). *The political system: An inquiry into the state of political science.* New York: Knopf.

Easton, D. (1965). *A framework for political analysis.* Englewood Cliffs, NJ: Prentice-Hall.

Eberts, R. W., & Pierce, L. C. (1980). *The effects of collective bargaining in public schools.* Eugene, OR: Center for Educational Policy and Management, University of Oregon.

Friedman, M. (1962). *Capitalism and freedom.* Chicago: University of Chicago Press.

Garms, W. I., Guthrie, J. W., & Pierce, L. C. (1978). *School finance: The economics and politics of education.* Englewood Cliffs, NJ: Prentice-Hall.

Geske, T. G. (1984). Financing the public schools in the Great Lakes states: Declining revenues in the 1980's. *Journal of Education Finance*, *9*(3), 358–383.

Governor's Citizens' Committee on Education (1972). *Improving Education in Florida.* Tallahassee: State of Florida.

Griesemer, J. L., & Butler, C. F. (1983). *Education under study: An analysis of recent major reports on education.* Chelmsford, MA: Northeast Regional Exchange.

Guthrie, J. W. (1972). Emerging federal role in finance education. *Theory Into Practice*, *11*(2), 137–143.

Guthrie, J. W. (1986a). The educational policy consequences of economic instability: The emerging political economy of American education. *Educational Evaluation and Policy Analysis*, *7*(4), 319–332.

Guthrie, J. W. (1986b). School-based management: The next-needed education reform. *Phi Delta Kappan*, *68*(4), 302–307.

Guthrie, J. W., Garms, W. I., & Pierce, L. C. (1987). *School Finance: The Economics and Politics of Education.* Englewood Cliffs, NJ: Prentice-Hall.

Guthrie, J. W., Kleindorfer, G., Levin, H. M., & Stout, R. T. (1971). *Schools and inequality.* Cambridge, MA: MIT Press.

Guthrie, J. W., Pierce, L. C., Garms, W. I., & Kirst, M. W. (1975). *State-school finance alternatives: Strategies for reform.* Eugene, OR: Center for Educational Policy and Management, University of Oregon.

James, H. T., Kelly, J. A., & Garms, W. I. (1966). *Determinants of educational expenditures in large cities of the United States.* Stanford, CA: School of Education, Stanford University.

James, H. T., Thomas, J. A., & Dyck, H. J. (1963). *Wealth expenditure & decision-making for education.* Stanford, CA: School of Education, Stanford University.

James, T., & Levin, H. M. (Eds.) (1983). *Public dollars for private schools: The case of tuition tax credits.* Philadelphia: Temple University Press.

Jencks, C., Smith, M., Acland, H., Bane, J. J., Cohen, D., Gintis, H., Heyns, B., & Michelson, S. (1968). *Inequality: A reassessment of the effect of family and schooling in America.* New York: Basic.

Kain, J. F., & Hanushek, E. A. (1968). *On the value of equality of educational opportunity as a guide to public policy.* (Mimeo. working paper No. 36.) Cambridge, MA: Program on Regional Urban Economics, Harvard University.

Karweit, N. (1982). *Time on task: A research paper.* Prepared for the National Commission on Educational Excellence.

Kirst, M. W. (1975). the rise and fall of PPBS in California. *Phi Delta Kappan*, *56*(8), 535–538.

Kirst, M. W. (1984). A new school finance for a new era of fiscal constraint. In *School finance and school improvement: Linkages for the 1980s* (4th Annual Yearbook of the American Education Finance Association). Cambridge, MA: Ballinger.

Knapp, M. (1983). *The state education reform movement and the practice of policy research.* (Unpublished research paper.) Menlo Park, CA: Stanford Research Institute.

Leppert, J., & Routh, D. (1980). *Policy guide to weighted pupil/education finance systems: Some emerging practical advice.* Washington, DC: National Institute of Education.

Levin, H. M. (1975). Cost effective analysis in evaluation research. In E. L. Streuning & M. Guttentag (Eds.), *Handbook of evaluation research: Vol. 1.* Beverly Hills, CA: Sage.

Levin, H. M., Glass, G. V., & Meister, G. R. (1984). *Cost effectiveness of four educational innovations.* Stanford, CA: Institute for Research on Educational Finance and Governance, Stanford University.

Madaus, G. F., Airasian, P. W., & Kelleghan, T. (1980). *School effectiveness: A reassessment of the evidence.* New York: McGraw-Hill.

Manley-Casimir, M. W. (Ed.) (1982). *Family choice in schooling.* Lexington, MA: Lexington.

Michaelson, J. B. (1980). Efficiency, equity, and the need for new educational policy. In J. W. Guthrie (Ed.), *School finance policies and practices: The 1980's, a decade of conflict.* Cambridge, MA: Ballinger.

Mort, P. R. (1952). Cost quality relationships in education. In R. L. Johns & E. L. Morphet (Eds.), *Problems and issues in public school finance.* New York: National Conference of Professors of

Educational Administration.

Mosteller, F., & Moynihan, D. P. (Eds.) (1972). *On equality and educational opportunity*. New York: Random House.

Murnane, R. J. (1975). *The impact of school resources on the learning of inner city children*. Cambridge, MA: Ballinger.

Musgrave, R. A. (1974). Is a property tax on housing regressive? *American Economic Review, 64*(2), 222–229.

Netzer, D. (1971). Property taxes. *Municipal Finance, 44*(2), 36–39.

Osman, J. (1985). *Projections of education expenditures and revenues in California to 1990*. Berkeley: Policy Analysis for California Education, University of California.

Parsons, T. (1960). *Structure and process in modern societies*. New York: Free Press.

Perrin, A. F., & Jones, T. H. (1984). Voter rejection of a school finance recapture provision. *Journal of Education Finance, 9*(4), 485–497.

Ravitch, D. (1983). *The troubled crusade: American education, 1945–1980*. New York: Basic.

Roberts, C. T., & Lichtenberger, A. R. (1973). *Financial accounting: Classifications and standard terminology for local and state school systems*. (Handbook II, rev. ed., Department of Health, Education, and Welfare, No. OE 73–11800). Washington, DC: U.S. Government Printing Office.

Rossmiller, R. A. (1978). *Input-output relationships in IGE schools*. (Tech. Rep. No. 451.). Madison: Research and Development Center for Individualized Schooling, University of Wisconsin.

Rossmiller, R. A., & Geske, T. G. (1977). *Economic analysis of education: A conceptual framework*. (Theoretical paper No. 68.) Madison: Research and Development Center for Individualized Schooling, University of Wisconsin.

Rutter, M., Maugham, B., Mortimore, P., Ouston, J., & Smith, A. (1979). *Fifteen thousand hours: Secondary schools and their effects on children*. Cambridge, MA: Harvard University Press.

Schultz, T. W. (1961). Education and economic growth. In *Social forces influencing American education*. The 60th Yearbook, National Society for the Study of Education. Chicago: University of Chicago Press.

Sherman, J. D. (Ed.) (1982). *New dimensions of the federal-state partnership in education*. Washington, DC: Institute for Educational Leadership.

Tyack, D. B. (1974). *The one best system*. Cambridge, MA: Harvard University Press.

Walker, B. D. (1984). The local property tax for public schools: Some historical perspectives. *Journal of Education Finance, 9*(3),265–288.

Weiler, D. (1974). *The public school voucher demonstrations: The first year at Alum Rock*. Santa Monica, CA: Rand.

Wirt, F. M., & Kirst, M. W. (1982). *Schools in conflict: The politics of education*. Berkeley, CA: McCutchan.

Wise, A. E. (1968). *Rich schools, poor schools: A promise of equal opportunity*. Chicago: University of Chicago Press.

Wise, A. E. (1979). *Legislated learning: The bureaucratization of the American classroom*. Berkeley: University of California Press.

CHAPTER 20

Educational Finance: Higher Education

Larry L. Leslie and Paul T. Brinkman

In the mid-1980s the direction of the financing of higher education in the United States is unclear. Financing policy, both public and private, seems to be on hold. The various fiscal resources now being generated are primarily products of a momentum created as much as a decade or more ago. Financing policy for higher eduction is floating along with the current of a slow-moving summer stream. In short, financing policy for higher education in the United States is at a hiatus.

Individuals are uncertain of the degree to which college pays off. Potential students face ever-higher prices, while they are uncertain of the short- and long-term availability of government and often even parental support. Many slip in and out of the collegiate system as the job market changes, taking with them their badly needed tuition dollars. The declining numbers of potential students in the traditional age group adds to the worries of already financially troubled institutions.

Governments, too, appear ambivalent. The enormous growth of federal student aid during the 1970s seems to have come to an end, although the states still add some student aid money in most years. The federal student-aid programs, which grew from almost nothing to about $10 billion by the early 1980s, are now declining, at least in constant dollars.

State governments, always the primary benefactors of public institutions, cannot seem to settle on their priorities. During the difficult years of the early 1980s recession, many states slowed their rates of higher education increases; a few actually reduced institutional aid in current dollar terms. It was not only that resources were scarcer than usual; higher education as a public priority had declined too. Then, as prosperity returned, most states set out to reverse the recent pattern, and the financing of higher education increased in real terms. Still, the enterprise had not regained its favored position in the competition for state funds; indeed, a good part of the rebound in public favor had been based not on a return of public faith in traditional collegiate activities but on the belief that public universities could lead the charge out of the economic doldrums by creating or attracting new, high-technology industries. Now, although funding for higher education in most states has recovered, relatively, from near-depression levels, it could scarcely be said that prosperity has returned. One wonders whether the recent recovery in postsecondary funding has not been a mere interlude in a modest but continuing downward spiral. When hard times for higher education arrive in Texas, can any other state be far behind?

Another recent trend in search of a new direction is found in tuition pricing. Due to shortfalls in state appropriations, but also to incentives found in student aid policies, tuition increases well beyond inflation became commonplace by the early 1980s. With some recoveries in state appropriations plus declines in inflation, those increases began to moderate but were still beyond increases in general price levels by the mid-1980s for both public and private schools. Like

Consultant/reviewers: Richard E. Anderson, Teachers College, Columbia University; and Lewis B. Solmon, University of California—Los Angeles.

other financing sources, those who set tuition policy seem to be awaiting the dropping other shoe.

That "shoe" probably will be released by the federal government as it grapples with $200 billion deficits. Will higher education funding, especially need-based student aid, be cut? If so, how much? If the cuts are major and continue, will the states again increase their student aid funding as they have recently? If so, will these funds be taken ultimately from general institutional aid? If so, will institutions be forced again to raise tuitions to recover the lost state revenues? Will the states force this action anyway in order to retain present competitive price between the public and private sectors? If the federal government does not act, what will this mean for state and institutional actions?

These questions bring us back to individuals. Are we approaching the limit that students can or will pay? What is good private (i.e., personal) financing policy? At what price level does higher education no longer represent a good investment?

Clearly, the pieces to the puzzle of higher education financing are tightly interrelated. Many private and public policy decisions have been based, directly or indirectly, on empirical research or at least impressions gained from that research. Studies attempting to contribute to enlightened public and private finance policy are the focus of this chapter.

INTRODUCTION TO THE REVIEW

When addressing a topic as broad as research in higher education finance, it is necessary at the outset to set some limitations. First, an attempt is made to limit the review to empirical work. This is neither a fully satisfactory decision nor a simple task, as many important nonempirical works exist. Second, the number of topics addressed is limited so that they can be treated relatively thoroughly. In short, the content herein is confined to major policy topics on which a significant amount of empirical work has been completed.

Also, we wanted to follow the principles suggested by G. B. Jackson (1978) to avoid the common failings of review articles and the advice found in the meta-analytical work of Glass and associates (Glass, McGaw, & Smith, 1981). Simply put, our objective was to examine the literature systematically and, where possible, to reach definite conclusions. Thus, samples of studies were arrayed in comparative matrixes. In three of the most important areas, a neo-meta-analysis was undertaken.[1]

Studies were included unless they were obviously flawed. In other words, conformity with our notions of suitable methods and analytical techniques was not required. The approach was to include all studies located after a thorough search of computerized data bases, bibliographies, abstracts, and citation archives, as suggested by Glass et al. (1981, Chap. 3). Matrixes were formed (Glass et al., 1981, Chap. 4) and are included as space allows. In all cases some matrix categories were eliminated, and in several cases the number of studies located was too large for total inclusion. When this occurred, representative studies were listed, and summary results report both covered and uncovered works. In sections where the number of studies is relatively small, the review follows somewhat more traditional approaches.

It is hoped that these efforts yielded a more concise determination of effects and relationships. The "maybe yes, maybe no" conclusions of most other reviews are largely avoided. It is also hoped that conclusions are more valid than often is the case in review essays because reviewer judgments and other potential sources of bias are reduced. For example, it has been found that in concentrating on published works, most reviews are likely to sample studies that find statistically significant results (Glass et al., 1981, pp. 64–67) and to undersample dissertations, which in general appear to be at least as well designed as published research (Glass et al., 1981, p. 67).

On the other hand, in avoiding qualitative judgments, meta-analytical approaches ignore the fruits of the constant methodological and analytical improvements assumed to occur over the years as a topic is researched. That is, the quality of research within a field of study is presumed to improve constantly; however, meta-analysts generally treat all studies as equally valid or simply segregate studies into more and less valid categories. Clearly, equal weighting of all studies is not totally satisfactory either. Yet, the fact remains that most researchers can and do make strong cases for their designs and analytical approaches. Choosing methodological and statistical methods is often more a matter of taste than of clear scientific superiority.

Accordingly, the chapter takes a middle road between meta-analytical and traditional approaches. A complete meta-analysis would have demanded more in the way of human resources than were readily available;[2] most topics have been too little researched to permit full application of this technique anyhow.

The chapter is separated into five major sections, each dealing with an important research topic on the financing of higher education. The first four sections address the major, finance-related, public policy issues of the past decade: (a) How do higher education prices affect student demand? (b) Is there over- or under-investment in higher education by individuals and by society? (c) Given the distribution of higher education benefits, is the present system of higher education financing progressive or regressive? (d) Does the major recent financing emphasis, need-based student aid, achieve its stated objectives? The remaining section addresses a problem of importance primarily to higher education institutions, rather than to the public at large: (e) What is the relationship between cost and size?

PUBLIC POLICY QUESTIONS

What happens when colleges and universities raise their prices? Who, if anyone, is sent away? What is the net impact of higher prices and reduced enrollments on institutional financial ledgers? Does higher education "pay off" for society and for individuals? Should society and individuals spend less for higher education? In what fields are the returns the greatest? Who pays for higher education, and who benefits? Does the cost-benefit calculus favor the low-income student or the high? Does student aid further access to college, choice of institutions, the likelihood that matriculants will persist and graduate? These are the major questions of public policy as it relates to higher education finance. The following subsections are organized in much the same way researchers in higher education financing conceptualize and attack the related issues.

Student Demand

Student-demand studies, investigations into the economic factors that affect student enrollment, are probably the second most ubiquitous of all studies in higher education finance, for two basic reasons, with an important corollary. First, expanding and equalizing student access long has been a major public policy goal, and the goal of student choice of institutions has been emphasized since the 1970s. Both goals have become pre-eminent national higher education policy priorities. Whereas the major instrument of recent federal policy has been direct subsidies to students, the states address student access largely through tuition policy. Whether direct through student aid or indirect through low tuition, obviously the effectiveness of public subsidies in meeting the access and choice goals becomes an important public policy issue. Second, there is a very practical reason for the large number of student-demand studies: Such issues conform nicely with the applied research capabilities developed in econometrics. The corollary is that with declining enrollments, real or expected, institutions too have a keen interest in the effects of price upon enrollments.

The Neo-Meta Analysis

Obviously, there are many prices in higher education. The particular price researchers have selected for study has changed, along with changing public policy strategies. Most early studies estimated the effects of tuition prices or, less frequently, total price or some other price variant such as commuting cost. A relatively few and recent studies have addressed the access and choice issues by examining the enrollment effects of student aid.

Approximately 50 empirical investigations and seven or eight review articles have considered this important question of price and the relationship to enrollment. Twenty-five studies containing useful quantitative estimates are presented in Table 20.1. They were selected because they contained estimates that could be transformed into a common value, a student price response coefficient (SPRC)—specifically, the change in first-time, full-time enrollment per $100 change in price. The major problems of comparability of results in Table 20.1 have been greatly reduced or eliminated.[3] The studies summarized cover or include public and private schools; 2-year and 4-year institutions; national, state, individual, district, and institutional samples; experiments, hypothetical situations, and secondary analysis; old data and new (from 1927 to the 1980s); well-controlled and (a few) poorly controlled designs; published results from dissertations, journals, and reports; cross-sectional and time-series designs; regression, logit, Bayesian, descriptive, discriminant, and correlational statistics; and more.

The results of all studies in Table 20.1 are in the expected direction: Enrollment declines when prices are raised (negative coefficients) and vice versa (positive coefficients). Adjusted to 1982–1983, the overall mean price response is about 0.75 percentage points. That is, for every $100 increase in tuition price, one would expect a first-time, full-time participation *rate* drop among 18- to 24-year-olds of about three-quarters of 1 percent. Since the national higher education participation rate is about 33 percent, U.S. enrollments would decline by about 2.3 percent for each $100 price increase, all other factors equal. The estimate is rough and is drawn from very disparate studies.

However, the degree of consistency among many of the estimates is reassuring. The modal result is 0.6 percentage points per $100 and a 1.8 percent enrollment decline, and these results come mostly from studies that should give the most valid results for the nation overall. Further, many other studies show results in the very close range of 0.5 to 0.8 percentage points. Results markedly above or below the modal responses tend to balance each other out, except that there are more results above the mode than below,

Table 20.1 Student Demand and Price

(1) I.D. NO.	(2) AUTHOR, YEAR	(3/4) DATA YEAR/POPULATION[a]	(5/6) PUBLICATION SOURCE[b]/ STUDY TYPE[c]	(7/8) PRICE SPECIFICATION/DEGREE OF CONTROL
01	AASCU, 1977	1973/WI	R/CS	Tuition Low
02	AASCU, 1977	1976/WI	R/CS	Tuition/Low
03	Barnes, 1975	1970/NC	S/CS	Tuition/High
04	Berne, 1980	1975/NY	J/CS	Student aid/High
05	Bishop, 1977	1960/Project Talent, U.S.	J/CS	Tuition, room & board, travel/ High
06	Campbell & Siegel, 1967	1927–1963 U.S.	J/TS	Tuition/Low
07	Clotfelter, 1976	1970/U.S.	J/CS	Tuition/High
08	Corrazzini et al., 1972	1963/Project Talent, U.S.	J/CS	Tuition/High
09	Funk, 1972	1959–1970 Creighton U.	J/TS	Tuition/Low
10	Ghali et al., 1977	1970/HA	J/CS	Tuition, total cost/High
11	Hight, 1975	1927–1972/U.S.	J/TS	Tuition/Middle
12	Hoenack, 1968	1967/U. CA	R/CS	Commute cost/High
13	Hoenack & Feldman, 1969	1963/Project Talent, U.S.	R/CS	Tuition/High
14	Hoenack & Weiler, 1975	1958–1972/MN	J/CS, TS	Commute cost/High
15	Hopkins, 1974	1963–1964/49 states	J/CS	Net tuition/High
16	G. A. Jackson, 1978	1972 U.S.	J/CS	Student aid/High
17	Knudsen & Servelle, 1978	1970/U.S.	J/CS	Tuition, net tuition/Middle
18	Kohn et al., 1976	1966/IL, NC	J/CS	Tuition, room & board, commute cost/High
19	Lehr & Newton, 1978	1960–74/OR	J/TS	Tuition/Middle
20	Orvis, 1975	1970/MN	D/CS	Commute cost/High
21	Radner & Miller, 1970	1966/IL, CA	J/CS	Cost income ratio/High
22	Sulock, 1982	1969/U.S.	J/CS	Tuition/Middle
23	Tannen, 1978	1959, 1969/U.S. Census	J/CS	Forgone income, net tuition, room & board/High
24	Tauchar, 1969	1966/CA	J/CS	Cost/NA
25	Wilson, 1977	1972/MN	D/CS	Commute cost/High

[a] States are indicated by Zipcode abbreviations.
[b] D = dissertation, J = journal, R = report, S = secondary source.
[c] CS = cross section, TS = time series.
[d] *e* signals that the individual student was used as unit of analysis in the study cited.
[e] *e* signals that financial aid was considered in the study cited.
[f] SPRC–P = student price response, participation rate effect.
[g] SPRC–E = student price response, enrollment effect.

Table 20.1 (continued)

(9/10) STATISTICS/INDIVIDUAL STUDENTS[d]	(11/12) FINANCIAL AID CONSIDERED/ INSTITUTIONAL TYPE[c]	(13) NOTES	(14) SPRC P[f]	E[g]
Descriptive	2-year	Experiment	+1.3	+4.1
Descriptive	2-year	Experiment	−1.0	−3.0
Linear probability	x		−.6	−1.8
x	All			
Regression	x	Applicants only	+.5	+1.5
x	2-year			
Logit	x	11th graders	−.4	−1.2
x	All	Minimum cost college		
Regression	4-year		−.6	−1.7
Regression	Public		−.5	−1.5
Regression		10th graders	−.5	−1.5
x	All			
Regression	4-year private	Average SPRC over time	−.2	−.5
Logit	x	Hawaii	−.6	−1.8
x	Public			
Regression	x	Identification problem	−1.1	−3.3
	Public and private			
Regression	4-year public	12th graders, total cost	−.6	−1.8
Regression		10th graders, "indifferent"	−1.0	−3.0
x	All			
Regression	4-year public	Own price response only	−1.3	−4.1
Regression	x	Rate = % of enrollment to high school grads in 4 yrs.	−.6	−1.8
	Public, private			
Discriminant, regression	x	Aid is dependent variable	−.2	−.6
x	All			
Regression		Midselective privates, average weighted values	−.6	−1.9
x	Private			
Logit		Estimates calculated, average, 12th graders	−.6	−1.8
x	All			
Discriminant, regression	x	Oregon	−.7	−2.2
	All			
Regression		11th graders	−1.1	−3.3
	Public			
Logit, Regression		Average	−.3	−.9
x	All			
Regression	x	Community colleges	−2.4	−7.4
	Community colleges			
Regression	x	14–24 age rates, males only	−.8	−2.5
	All			
Descriptive		Catholic high schools	−.3	−.8
x	Roman Catholic			
Regression, logit		Distance is dependent variable	−.8	−2.5
	All			

yielding the slightly higher mean result. As a best estimate for public policy purposes, a $100 tuition price increase appears to be associated with a 0.6 percentage point decline in the first-time, full-time 18- to 24-year-old participation rate and an enrollment decline of 1.8 percent (1982–1983 values).

Although space constraints prohibit extensive discussion, a descriptive word or two on the studies tabled is necessary for understanding and interpreting the results. The first two studies tabled (AASCU, 1977) report on the single known tuition experiment. Tuition was reduced experimentally at two 2-year centers of the University of Wisconsin and then was raised again to its previous level a few years later. There occasionally has been a strong inclination to attach extra meaning to the results of the Wisconsin studies because experiments generally show causal effects; however, the results here really are not much different from other studies, if at all. Students in the Wisconsin sample tend to be more responsive to price than are students overall. The reasons are two: (a) 2-year schools attract more lower-income and older students, both of whom are known to be particularly responsive to price, and (b) the tendency is strong for 2-year students to attend 4-year public institutions when 2-year prices are raised and vice versa. Although the Wisconsin report states that very little of this substitution occurred, the first of the two reasons alone easily could explain the relatively large price response. Finally, it is worth noting that the effects of tuition declines were greater than the countereffects of tuition increases. This is a result that has been suggested by other studies; none have shown the opposite.

The Berne (1980) study considered applicants to two New York community colleges. For reasons similar to those in Wisconsin, higher SPRCs might have been expected here. But the effects of adjustments made to render the applicant data comparable to the data for the overall age group (18–24) and the fact that $100 in aid, rather than tuition, was the independent variable apparently balanced out. Another generalization arises from Berne: In all cases reviewed save one, the award of aid had a lesser effect than a tuition price change of the same value.

The Bishop (1977) results, which relatively are slightly low, are based on a model that reflected only the (educational) alternative of selecting the lowest-cost nearby college. Next, the Campbell and Siegel (1967) study, which utilized 1927–1963 time-series data and generally is considered to be the first on this topic, yielded modal results.

Based on a reanalysis of the Campbell and Siegel (1967) data, Hight (1975) obtained relatively high price-response estimates, probably reflecting the sub-

stitution problem already discussed. (McPherson, 1978, p. 182, shows Hight's crosselasticity of demand between public and private institutions to be unusually high.) Hight's work also appears to demonstrate the econometrician's most common identification problem, difficulty in separating the respective effects of supply and demand.

Other results that require special comment include those of Funk (1972), who examined tuition price response in a single private university. Funk's results square with the general trend for private schools to show less student price response than public schools. This undoubtedly is due in part to the average higher family incomes of students attending private schools. Low-income students typically demonstrate the highest price response, followed by middle-income and then high-income youth.

Another special case is that of Ghali, Miklius, and Wada (1977), whose case study was of the University of Hawaii, an institution with few nearby competitors. The studies by Hoenack (1968) and Hoenack and Weiler (1975) use distance elasticities (percentage variation in commuting costs in relation to percentage change in enrollments) to generate tuition SPRCs. The results reported by them in Table 20.1 are for the University of California and the University of Minnesota, respectively, and do not consider substitution (see Note 1). Therefore, these results, which are accurate from the perspectives of the institutions' own enrollments, are biased upward in terms of effects on participation rates. Hoenack and Feldman (1969) conceptualize the problem in a unique way, by postulating individuals who are "indifferent" to attendance and then observing effects of price changes.

G. A. Jackson's (1978) study considers the effects of student aid. His conclusion that the mere awarding of aid is far more significant than the amount of aid is of major importance to policy. His apparent confirmation of the relative insensitivity of students to aid in comparison to tuition is tempered by a recognition that methodological differences may explain the result.

The results reported by Knudsen and Servelle (1978) appear high. Their use of *net* tuition increases (tuition increases net of student aid) should yield smaller SPRCs for private institutions. (Note that some other studies have also used net tuitions.) The most likely explanation for the high estimates involves the unusual design, which chose only moderately selective private colleges having a nearby "true" competitor, public or private.

Lehr and Newton's (1978) study is for Oregon only; Orvis's (1975) and Wilson's (1977) results derive from distance elasticities in Minnesota, and the results tabled are converted own-price tuition elasticities only.

Radner and Miller's (1970) results are on the low side, undoubtedly because the price variations in their sample were inadequate—a potentially biasing influence constantly mentioned in the literature. Sulock's (1982) high results are for community colleges; he also shows the expected high crossprice elasticity (substitution) with 4-year public schools. Tauchar's (1969) study is for Roman Catholic high school students queried about their likely attendance behaviors as prices of Roman Catholic colleges are hypothetically raised.

There are many constraints in comparing and interpreting the results of the studies arrayed in Table 20.1. Ideally, an analyst desires SPRCs in the *ceteris paribus* (all other factors equal) case. Most but not all results documented in the table reflect instead price response in the natural environment: that is, in light of prices charged by competitors. This condition implicitly is true in the case of time-series studies where tuition prices are juxtaposed with enrollments in the natural market setting. To seek comparable results, cross-sectional studies should (as many do) include prices charged by competitors; otherwise, the observed effect of own tuition and other included variables may be biased upward, as in any (regression) case of omitted variables. In these important regards, the degree of compatability of results often is not easily assessed with certainty. Analysts may not, for example, apply some simple correction. What they must do is return to the particular environmental setting of each study, examine the controls, and apply judgment to interpretation of the results. They may not simply directly net out SPRCs for omitted variables because the allocation of covariances to included (and excluded) variables is not really possible. In short, meta-analysis relies heavily on the assumption that the reader will examine the matrix closely and make appropriate discriminations.

Nevertheless, examination of studies yielding somewhat disparate results reveals quite consistent findings when the variations are taken into account. Modal results appear to be good estimates for higher education overall. From an institutional perspective, the enrollment effect of tuition price changes varies considerably, depending on the institution's own price level, the characteristics of its students, its student-aid structure, its applicant pool, and its competitors. The figures in column 14 should prove quite accurate in predicting enrollment from a national aggregate level, but each institution will need to assess its own student price environment.

Subordinate Issues

The policy issues involved and the institutional concerns often require greater elaboration than that presented in Table 20.1. Many of these issues and concerns are discussed in greater depth in several reviews already published. Jackson and Weathersby's (1975) controversial review was the first effort to render comparable the results of student-demand studies; McPherson (1978) extends the analysis by Jackson and Weathersby and particularly emphasizes effects of price changes in private institutions. Weinschrott (1977) analyzes eight studies utilizing five evaluative criteria he believes to be critical to valid conclusions. Cohn and Morgan (1978) and especially Hyde (1978) provide broad, commentary-type reviews of studies completed. The California State Postsecondary Education Commission (1982) offers a more recent but less detailed summary. Finally, Chisolm and Cohen's (1982) useful review blends methodological and analytical commentary with a brief treatment of previous studies.

There are four fairly discrete and simple findings and issues that require only brief mention. One, where broad studies have considered more than economic effects on enrollment rates, sociological variables invariably have turned out to be most potent. In other words, the determinants of college attendance are associated more with such traits as social class and parents' education than with college price. Two, student-demand studies almost always concentrate on freshman enrollments. Therefore, the immediate effects of a tuition increase at a given institution will be less than estimated in Table 20.1 because at least 4 years are required for freshman effects to impact total undergraduate (not to mention graduate) enrollments. Three, and again from an institutional perspective, tuition effects on enrollments generally are most usefully viewed from an institutional revenue basis. Tuition elasticities (which can be calculated directly from SPRCs) of less than 1.0 suggest increased revenues when tuitions are increased; elasticities greater than 1.0 yield revenue reductions. For revenue purposes, institutions should calculate their own price elasticity values and monitor them closely. Four, reducing tuitions will have a more positive enrollment effect than increasing tuitions will have a negative effect.

Next, further comment on price forms is required. Analysts should not assume that all price changes impact enrollments equally. It is often suggested that of all prices, tuitions consistently show the greatest enrollment effect. Bishop (1977), for example, found the price effect of tuition increases to be roughly five times greater than the effect of opportunity cost changes, and room and board and travel costs to be about 60 percent greater, although he acknowledges that the true differences probably are much less. On the other hand, Hoenack's (1968) work has assumed that effects of various costs are similar. Hoenack holds, for example, that when the value of one's time is included, commuting cost effects are comparable to those of tuition. In any case the tuition coefficients of Kohn, Manski, and Mundel (1976) are at least five times greater than their commuting cost coefficients and are about twice as great as their room and board coefficients. Chapman's results (1979) for tuition versus commuting costs for Carnegie Mellon University are consistent with the findings of Kohn et al., as are those of Wilson (1977) and Orvis (1975). Nevertheless, researchers' opinions are rather sharply divided as to whether effects of various prices differ.

The most critical related issue from a public policy perspective is the relative potency of student aid versus tuition subsidies. The policy direction since the early 1970s has been to favor need-based student aid over low tuition as a vehicle for expanding opportunities. Results of empirical work seem to show that students are more sensitive to tuition changes than to equivalent per-student aid changes (Carlson, Farmer, & Weathersby 1974; Fife & Leslie, 1976; G. A. Jackson, 1978; Leslie & Fife, 1974), although Tierney's (1980b) results for individuals who apply to both public and private institutions do not show much difference. Hyde (1978, pp. 35–42) elaborates on this matter.

Low tuitions are, of course, subsidies provided to everyone, whereas need-based student aid is more restrictive; therefore, per dollar of subsidy, if carefully targeted, aid programs should be more effective than low tuition policies. G. A. Jackson (1978) put the cost of such aid at $3,048 for each new low-income student enrolled, compared to $9,223 for a universal aid program of $500 per student. Due to inflation and some additional depletion of the potential college-eligible aspirant pool over time, the cost would be significantly higher in the mid-1980s.

Finally, most research indicates some superiority of grants over other forms of student aid in encouraging enrollments (Carlson et al., 1974, pp. 14, 25; Carlson, 1975, p. 62) although again, for Tierney's (1980b) special population, little difference is observed.

Several efforts have been aimed at comparing the price responsiveness of special categories of students, especially categories by income class. The reason for this interest, of course, is rooted in the need-based student aid programs of the 1970s and 1980s. Results across such studies are generally consistent. Bishop's (1977) estimates show atypically high price sensitivity only for the lowest income quartile; the Kohn et al. (1976) results for Illinois are generally similar except the middle-income group also shows considerable price sensitivity. The Kohn et al. results for North Carolina, however, yield a low-income coefficient that is positive.

Radner and Miller (1970) also find student responsiveness inversely related to family income, as does Hoenack (1968). When stratifying their data by institutional type, Corazzini, Dugan, and Grabowski (1972), however, show a mixed pattern, with the greatest responsiveness demonstrated by the two higher income quartiles in private institutions and the greatest responsiveness among the second lowest income quartiles in both 2- and 4-year public institutions. In his study of students who apply to both public and private institutions, Tierney (1980b) actually shows slightly lower tuition responsiveness for the lowest income group. In a later study (1982) using the same data set, he finds greater responsiveness in the lowest income group except for the case of low-cost institutions, where elasticities by income group are essentially equal. One would anticipate a reduction in price response differences among the various income groups as more and more need-based student aid has become available to offset price increases for the low-income group. No verification of this expectation as yet exists.

One study (Bishop & VanDyk, 1977) examines price response among adult students (older than 25). Although rate SPRCs are low due to very small participation rates for the adult group, enrollment response actually is very high. A $100 tuition decrease is estimated to raise enrollments by roughly 25 percent, and the cost of enrolling one additional adult student is estimated to be only one-third as high as it is for traditional-age students.

By institutional type, price-related enrollment declines seem to be lower in private institutions than in public, and lower in 4-year than in 2-year public institutions. Table 20.1 shows the public-private pattern rather convincingly, although some exceptions can be noted. (See Funk, Tauchar, and Knudsen-Servelle versus Clotfelter, Ghali et al., Hoenack, Hoenack and Weiler, Orvis, and Wilson.) Corazzini et al. (1972) corroborate the public-private pattern and the 4-year, 2-year differences. The AASCU and Sulock studies show very large effects in 2-year schools; Berne's results are more modest. Within the public sector, relative price responsiveness is less clear than it is between the two sectors.

The fact that SPRCs do not vary more than they do by institutional type may come as a surprise to some readers. Note first that the discussion centers on own-price response, not effects on participation rates. The distinction is important because of the substitution effect already discussed—a student who leaves an independent college, for example, typically does not leave higher education altogether. Further, for reasons obviously important to institutions themselves, tuition response rates should be viewed not as responses to change in tuition but as responses to change in overall price. When researchers employ their student-demand models, the effects of tuition price changes are estimated in the context of overall prices facing the student. A $100 tuition increase should be viewed not as a $100 change on a tuition base of, say $1,500 but on an overall cost of tuition, forgone earnings, books, room and board, commuting, and so forth. Hence a $100 tuition increase, although proportionally less in private than in 4-year and 2-year public colleges, is not as much less, proportionately, when all costs are considered as it is when only tuition is considered.

In sum, there is little doubt that the general results reported in and about Table 20.1 improve markedly on the accuracy of previous literature reviews, despite some unease about study comparability. Weinschrott (1977) was correct when he warned about the difficulties in achieving consistency across studies so disparate in character.

Rates of Return

Studies aimed directly at calculating the economic benefits to schooling and especially at solving the many related analytical problems probably constitute the most numerous set of all empirical work in higher education finance research. Although the rates-of-return studies frequently are characterized by questionable assumptions, poor data, and analytical shortcomings, the topic is so important that inquiries do not seem to diminish in number over time.

Why Study Return to Education?
Among the several reasons for examining the economic returns to higher education, the foremost is allocative efficiency, the cardinal concern of public finance: Where will society gain the maximum benefit from its investment? The corollary question to the individual is: Where will one's investment yield the highest return? Both questions divide into three parts. First, how do the benefits from higher education compare with those of noneducational alternatives? Second, how do the benefits from higher education compare with those of educational alternatives? Third, how do the benefits compare by field of study within higher education? If it can be shown that the returns to one alternative are greater than from another, then society's and the individual's choice is clear, and resources can be directed accordingly.

How Are the Returns to Be Measured?
Calculation of the "yield" on higher education investment requires determination of costs and of benefits, each of which must be discounted to reflect the fact that

the present value of money is greater than the future value ("A dollar isn't worth what it used to be"). The returns to education most commonly are stated either in terms of income differentials, which reflect benefits only; cost-benefit ratios; net present values (NPV); or internal rates of return (IRR).

Debate in the literature has centered on NPV and IRR. NPV is simply the worth in dollar terms of the difference between the cost of education and the associated monetary gain, each properly discounted to reflect "present value." IRR is that rate of interest or discount that sets one's stream of lifetime earnings back to its present value and equates this value to one's total educational costs compounded forward to educational termination. Proponents of the NPV approach would seem to have the best of the technical arguments but not the practical ones. As Joy and Bradley (1973) point out, IRR generally are satisfactory when one is facing a simple go, no-go decision; besides, they say, IRR are more easily understood. Here, Psacharopoulos (1973, p. 19) makes the practical choice for us by observing that rates of return are by far the most commonly reported. Detailed discussions of the use of IRR versus NPV are contained in Hirshleifer (1958), Bailey (1959), Cohn (1972), and Joy and Bradley (1973). Calculations of IRR as used here are clearly laid out in Eckaus (1973, p. 71).

IRR may be assessed in two ways, the choice depending on whether it is the relative efficiency of society's or the individual's educational decision that is at issue. The former involves calculation of a social IRR, the latter a private IRR. To the educator, the economist's standard specification of costs and benefits will appear dubious, to say the least.

Rate of return studies, at least under ideal conditions, identify private costs as the student's tuition and fees, books and supplies, net forgone income, and other education-related expenditures; private benefits are defined in most cases as after-tax earnings. Social costs are defined most commonly as educational expenditures of institutions plus private costs, and benefits are defined as before-tax earnings of individuals. Many issues surround these definitions (see Becker, 1975, pp. 194–200). Some of the most serious related difficulties are addressed below. Suffice it to say here that these definitions include only the nonconsumption pecuniary benefits.

Finally, by way of introduction, analysts also need data on interest rate standards against which the (pecuniary) returns to higher education may be compared; that is, the yield that can be expected from comparable, alternative investments. Although Taubman and Wales (1975, p. 42) set a relatively high 13 to 15 percent standard for evaluating social IRR, most analysts select a 10 percent social and private IRR as suitable for the degree of risk represented by investment in education.[4]

Methodological Issues

Of some 130 references examined, less than one-third specifically attempted to provide rate-of-return estimates. The remainder in some fashion or other addressed related methodological problems. Pertinent methodological issues fall into five classes: (a) standardizing reporting of IRRs—are marginal or average rates reported and what does marginal, in this context, mean? (b) specifying the dependent variable—should earnings or income be used and if the former, which earnings? (c) adjusting to enhance data compatibility—what adjustments are necessary for differences due to mortality, taxes, secular growth, unemployment, and hours worked? (d) assessing the advantages of cross-sectional versus time-series data bases—which yields more valid results? and (e) interpreting the residual—what conclusions may be reached about the sources of unexplained variance? The implications of these and other issues to the validity and application of study results are considered later.

Results

Besides cost-benefit approaches such as IRR analysis, there are two other useful ways of viewing the contribution to earnings from education. One is the contribution of education to growth in the economy, and the other is the share of earnings differences that can be explained by education.

Denison (1962) ascribed 23 percent of the growth in total real national income to education and another 20 percent to the advancement of knowledge and "change in lag in the application of knowledge" over the period 1929–1957. Later Denison found that education accounted for 15 percent of national economic growth between 1957 and 1962, and his projection for 1960–1980 was that education would account for 19 percent of total real income growth. A related approach to this issue is described in Psacharopoulos (1973, Chap. 7), who puts the percentage of growth from education at 17.9 percent (p. 116).

More common in assessing the impact of education on earnings are studies that offer estimates of an "alpha factor," the portion of earnings differences that is explained by education. Almost all such studies have controlled for ability, which generally is considered to be the largest source of bias on earnings differentials by educational level; and most studies have controlled for additional variables, such as parents' education, income, and occupation, marital status, family size, health, religion, and region of the country.

The average alpha value for 13 studies of the BA degree is .79. Values tend to be lower for 2-year and technical degrees. Alpha values of .90 are found for the graduate level. Altogether the 17 studies examined support the generalization in the literature that the alpha factor increases with educational level. Coefficients for schooling levels below higher education are consistently lower.

Neo-Meta Analysis

Table 20.2 displays rate-of-return estimates from 25 studies. The results are not strictly comparable because of varying data sources; populations; time periods; social and private cost specifications, controls, and adjustments; dependent-variable specification; inclusion or exclusion of nonpecuniary variables; and whether the data were cross-sectional or time series. Primarily because of differences in controls and adjustments (Column 10), the results could not be standardized as readily as the data on student demand. The most important factors to note for comparing results are listed in Column 12.

The *Private IRR* and *Social IRR* rows of the table present average estimates by level of higher education. Careful review of the 25 empirical reports and over 100 conceptual and methodological papers dealing with analytical issues generates the sense that, especially for the BA degree, the averages roughly reflect pecuniary rates of return to higher education over the past 20 years or so. Table 20.2 reveals that the average private rate (22 studies) and social rate (14 studies) of return are 11.8 percent and 11.4 percent, respectively. The social rate of return probably is upwardly biased by about 1.0 percent in relation to the private rate. Both rates compare favorably to conventional benchmark rates for alternative investments, especially against the ups and downs of the equities market. (See McMahon & Wagner, 1982, p. 161, Figure 2.)

The lower return for less than the BA (10.1 percent) is consistent with generalizations in the literature. Though not tabled here, the returns to elementary and secondary education tend to be higher than those for the postsecondary level. The major reason is that both private and social costs increase by level, not that benefits decrease.

Graduate Education   The private rates of return tabled for graduate education in general, the MA, and the PhD at 8.3, 7.6, and 8.1 percent, respectively, also support the generalizations in the literature: Returns within graduate education tend to increase as one moves upward toward the PhD.[5] The variation in results for the graduate school studies is relatively large, ranging from a negative value (Maxwell, 1970) to as high as 20 percent or more (Curtis & Campbell,

1978). The principal reason for this high variation is that most IRR studies of graduate education are of special groups, as opposed to the broad national samples characteristic of undergraduate IRR studies. Also, costs of graduate education vary more widely. Ashenfelter and Mooney (1968, 1969) obtained quite high results by studying the early earnings of Woodrow Wilson fellows who were graduates of prestigious universities. Not only were these graduates highly able, but their costs were low because they received stipends, increasing rates of return by roughly a factor of two (Siegfried, 1972–1973). At the other extreme, Maxwell (1970) obtained negative results (rates of return) in considerable part because he oversampled education students at a nonprestigious midwestern university (Wessel, 1971). Bailey and Schotta (1972) observed very low returns (0.8 percent) by studying persons who entered the academic profession later and who studied longer, and thus incurred costs over longer periods of time. Weiss (1971) showed that returns are greater, within every graduate field and level, for persons later employed in private industry and management than in academia. Curtis and Campbell (1978) reanalyzed the Bailey and Schotta data and, showing the importance of regional markets for graduates, proper corrections for risk and for taxes and leisure time, reported that graduate IRR could vary between 0.04 and 20 percent and more.

By Field   Although space does not permit elaboration here, several studies have compared rates of return by field of study (Eckaus, 1973; Hanoch, 1967; Koch, 1972; Seeborg, 1975; Taubman & Wales, 1974; Thurow, 1968; Wilkinson, 1966). McMahon (1981) and McMahon and Wagner (1981, 1982) have calculated expected rates of return by occupation. Returns tend to be highest in the mature professional fields and lowest in the striving professions, such as education and nursing, and in the humanities and fine arts. Problems in conducting rate-of-return studies by field are discussed in Eckaus (1973, pp. 17–21). Among the problems cited are selecting the appropriate comparison group (to whom should the IRR of a physician or history major be compared?), difficulties in separating education from noneducation sources of knowledge and skills, psychic income differences, and worker movement among occupations. Seeborg (1975) points out that the various curricula attract persons of quite different abilities, thus again raising comparability questions.

By College Type and Quality   One of the more interesting questions addressed in the IRR studies is whether returns vary by type of college and by college quality. The only known extensive study comparing rates of return across institutional types is a carefully controlled effort by McMahon and Wagner (1982, pp. 161–169). The authors show that community and junior colleges, which offer many technical courses of study, yield high returns, as do private and public research universities and public and private comprehensive colleges. Graduates of liberal arts colleges do not fare as well, except for those who go on to graduate school.

Determining what constitutes institutional quality is itself a complex matter, but regardless of the measure, a positive association with earnings uniformly is found. Using the Project Talent index of freshmen attitudes, Reed and Miller (1970) reported a generally linear relationship between college quality and earnings. Based on the quality values of the Gorman Report (1967), Taubman and Wales (1973) concluded that the contribution of college quality to earnings was large but only for the top quality one-fifth, whereas Solmon (1975) found differences for only the bottom and top quality quartiles. Ribich and Murphy (1975) reported a positive relationship between school quality and later earnings but primarily because of the additional quantity of education induced by higher quality institutions. On the other hand, Johnson and Stafford's (1973) findings were strong enough to allow them to conclude that institutional quality was more important to earnings than was educational quantity (years of schooling), a conclusion supported by Link and Ratledge (1975). A very thorough discussion of the related issues and research is contained in Solmon (1975).

Over Time   One of the most contentious and important issues to arise in higher education finance in recent years is the alleged decline in the value of a college education. Freeman in a series of publications (1975a, 1975b, 1975c; 1977; 1979; 2980) and Freeman and Holloman (1975) purported to show that the private rate of return had declined markedly between 1969 and 1974, to a point (about 7.5 percent) that the investment in higher education was not justified. McMahon and Wagner (1982, pp. 152, 155), Schwartz and Thornton (1980), Smith and Welch (1978a, 1978b), and Witner (1980) wrote critiques in which, among other things, it is pointed out that Freeman's calculations were only for males in their very early employment years and that Freeman's cost estimates were badly flawed. Freeman's response (1980) made a strong case for the general pattern of his results over time; that is, his results do appear to be biased downward,[6] but since his method is consistent over time, a decline probably did occur. Whether Freeman's IRR was below benchmark levels is another matter.

In retrospect, Freeman's findings were neither unexpected nor alarming. It had been known for some time and has since been verified, both theoretically (Psacharopoulos, 1973, p. 9) and empirically (Ashen-

Table 20.2   Rates of Return

(1) ID NO.	(2) AUTHOR, YEAR	(3/4) DATA YEAR/ POPULATION	(5/6) PUBLICATION SOURCE[a]/ STUDY TYPE[b]	(7/8) DATA SOURCE[c]/ COST SPECIFICATION[d]	(9/10) GRADE LEVELS/ CONTROLS, ADJUSTMENTS[e]
01	Ashtenfelter & Mooney, 1968	1966/Woodrow Wilson Fellows	J/CS	Woodrow Wilson Fellows/ FI + ?	All graduate/A, not M, Ta
02	Becker, 1975	1939, 1949/census	B/CS	Census/.75 FI + DC	High school and college/M/ S, Ta
03	Becker & Chiswick, 1966	1959/White males	J/CS	Census/FI + DC (?)	0–8, 8–12, > 12/NA
04	Carnoy & Marenbach, 1975	1939, 1949, 1959, 1969/ Whites	J/ CS, TS	Census/Pvt. = 75% of FI; Soc. = "institutional cost" + FI	Elementary, high school, college graduates/Ta (men only), U, not M, S
05	Danielson, 1969–1970	1956–1966/Males	J/TS	CPS 1956–1966/Woodrow Wilson files/FI (perceived) + DC	BA–PhD/M, S, Ta
06	Duncan, 1976	1970–1971, 1973/ Working white nonfarm males age 21–65	J/CS	Quality of Employment Survey, panel study of income dynamics/none	All/A + others
07	Eckaus, 1973	1959/White males, age 14–64	B/CS	Census/FI + DC	Elementary-college/H, Ta, M, U, S
08	Freeman, 1975b	1959, 1969, 1972, 1974/ Males	J/CS	Census, CPS/Soc. = E + G ÷ enrollments; Pvt. = T − scholarships	High school v. 4-year college/T
09	Greer, 1976	1960, 1970/Census	J/CS	Census/FI, T	College v. high school/T, M
10	Hanoch, 1967	1959/Males	J/CS	Census/Assumes student earnings = DC	K–17/Demographic variables + M, S, Ta, U
11	Hansen, 1963	1949/Males	J/CS	Census/Soc. = institutional + FI + incidentals; Pvt. = same except T for institutional	1–16/M, T
12	Hunt, 1963	1947/College graduates	J/CS	*Time* magazine 1947 survey of college graduates/"Expense per pupil," graduate is 2 × undergraduate	College/A + others
13	Johnson & Stafford, 1973	1965/White, male, urban employed	J/CS	Survey Research Center/ "Soc. Cost" .75 FI	12, 16
14	Koch, 1972	1968–1969/Graduates	J/CS	Illinois State/Undergraduate cost at Illinois State	Undergraduate/A, Ta, others
15	Liberman, 1979	1958–1976	S		
16	Mattila, 1982	1956–1979/Males	J/TS	CPS/.75 × wages of high school graduates + net T	High school, some college, continuing college/ Business cycle
17	McMahon & Wagner, 1982	1976/BA graduates	B/CS	ACT College Investment Decision Study/FI, books, net of scholarships & institutional expenditures	BA/A, S, others, (∝ = .66)
18	Mincer, 1958	1950/Census	J/CS	Census/FI + DC	College/Not A, S, U; a correction factor; part-time employment
19	Raymond & Sesnowitz, 1975	1969/Census	J/CS	Census/.75 FI net of taxes, T, books & supplies	College/A, S, T, PT workers
20	Solmon, 1975	1969/Male air cadets	J/CS	NBER–TH/FI	Some college/College quality, other

Table 20.2   (continued)

(11) DEPENDENT VARIABLE SPECIFICATION	(12) SPECIAL NOTES	(13) INCLUDES PSYCHIC?	(14) RESULTS (%)	
			PRIVATE	SOCIAL
Annual income by graduate level/ Years	Early income, high ability, prestige colleges, fellowships	No	9.1	
Earnings	Results after all adjustments	Somewhat	10	13
Earnings in South, non-South	Average IRR to all college years	No	8.5	
Annual income, earnings	No DC, whites only	No	14.3	9.3
Annual income	BA IRR for GA	No	16.2	
Wage rates	Nonpecuniary, pecuniary items	Yes		
Hourly wage	Excellent adjustments	No	11.5	
Annual earnings	E & G, no FI, 10% discount rate	No	10.4	9.7
Net annual earnings	Low cost estimate	No	16.1	
Annual earnings	Study highly regarded	No	10	
Income		No	10.1	10.2
	Very small N, old data; not really Pvt. RR; ignore		6	
Hourly earnings		No		8.8
Annual earnings by discipline	Illinois State		7	
Pretax income				14
Annual earnings	Mixed earnings-income	No	12	
Annual earnings	Pvt. − expected IRR	No	18	13.3
Pretax income	Downward biased	No	11	13
Annual income		No	15.7	14.3
Annual earnings		No	9.7	

(continued)

Table 20.2   **(continued)**

(1) ID NO.	(2) AUTHOR, YEAR	(3/4) DATA YEAR/ POPULATION	(5/6) PUBLICATION SOURCE[a]/ STUDY TYPE[b]	(7/8) DATA SOURCE[c]/ COST SPECIFICATION[d]	(9/10) GRADE LEVELS/ CONTROLS, ADJUSTMENTS[e]
21	Taubman & Wales, 1973	1955, 1969/Male air cadets	J/CS	NBER–TH/Soc. = 71% of E & G + FI + plant; Pvt. = T + FI + incidental	High school & college/A + others
22	Wachtel, 1976	1955, 1969/Male air cadets	J/TS	NBER–TH/School expenditures, T + (.75) FI	High school, some college, college graduates/A + others, ∝ factor
23	Weiss, 1971	1966/NSF scientific & technical personnel	J/CS	National Register of Scientific & Technical personnel, NSF, 1966/FI & academic expenses	Graduate/S + demographic variables
24	Witmer, 1983	1967–1982/Men, women	J/TS	Census/Pvt. = full cost net of aid; Soc. = full cost	High school, college/A, M, Ta, U, other
25	Witmer, 1980	1961–1972/Men, women	J/TS	CPS/E & G net of research & public service	Higher education/NA

IRR[f]	2 YEARS OR SOME COLLEGE	BA 4 YEARS	GRADUATE	MASTERS	PhD/ PhD-PROFESSIONAL
Private	10.1	11.8	8.3	7.6	8.1
Social	NA	11.4	NA	NA	NA

[a] J = journal, B = book, S = secondary source
[b] CS = cross section, TS = time series
[c] CPS = current population surveys, NBER–TH = National Bureau of Economic Research—Thorndike
[d] DC = direct costs, FI = forgone income, Pvt. = private cost, Soc. = social cost, E & G = educational and general, T = tuition
[e] A = ability, H = hours worked, M = mortality, S = secular growth, Ta = taxes, U = unemployment, ∝ = % of earnings attributed to education, NA = not applicable
[f] IRR = internal rate of return

felter & Ham, 1979; Bartlett, 1978; Cline, 1982; Mattila, 1982; Miller, 1960; Psacharopoulos, 1973, pp. 95–97; Welch, 1970, 1979), that cohort size (the so-called vintage effect) and business cycles affect earnings.[7] In the past the growth of college-educated cohorts essentially had been matched by growth in technical and related labor markets (Welch, 1979).[8] Freeman's data covered a period in which both cohort size and business recession placed a dampening effect on earnings of new college-educated entrants into the workforce. Indeed, Freeman (1975b, 1979) explained his results as reflecting the interaction of recessions and the vintage effect and suggested that the observed effects might be only temporary. One could observe that, at worst, even if the trend had persisted, the value of a college degree had not declined so much as cohort sizes had grown—a temporary phenomenon that would begin to pass by the early 1980s.

Regardless, more recent works have shown either that Freeman's decline did not really occur (Witmer, 1983) or that the decline was temporary (Liberman, 1979; Mattila, 1982; Rumberger, 1980); rates appear now to have returned to near their historic level. Smith and Welch (1978a) were prophetic when they wrote, "If the size of cohort produces only a temporary decline until the market absorbs the new workers, it remains plausible that this recent 'depression' is only 'market indigestion'" (p. 19). Cline (1982) argues that what has changed over time is the composition of the college-educated group; those who graduate from college in the 1980s are quite different kinds of persons from those who graduated in decades past, and their earnings reflect that fact.

International Studies   Rate-of-return studies are by no means unique to the United States, and much can be learned about relationships between earnings and education in other countries. The book by Psacharopoulos (1973) is by far the most complete work on this subject. He shows, for example, that the returns to education are greater in developing than in developed countries; that primary education yields the highest returns in most countries; that differences in national incomes are more a function of human than physical capital differences; that education contributes importantly to the rate of growth of output, particularly in developing countries; that earnings inequalities asso-

Table 20.2 (continued)

(11)	(12)	(13)	(14)	
DEPENDENT VARIABLE SPECIFICATION	SPECIAL NOTES	INCLUDES PSYCHIC?	RESULTS (%)	
			PRIVATE	SOCIAL
Deflated, before-tax monthly earnings		Adjustment for teachers	9	8
Monthly earnings	Pvt. = per year RR, Soc. = return to expenditures	No		10
Annual earnings	Registered time	No		
Annual earnings	Average per year	No	16	13
Estimated earnings		No		14

ciated with education are greatest in less developed countries; and that labor substitution among workers of varying educational levels is great, arguing for education cost-benefit analysis for education over manpower planning programs as devices of public policy. Other and more recent though more limited works in this area include those by Belanger and Lavalée (n.d.), Dougherty and Psacharopoulos (1977), Okachi (1983), and Ziderman (1973).

Issues and Problems: What Do the IRR Studies Tell Us?
The rate-of-return studies are held up as a way of judging optimal investments in education. But do they succeed in doing so? Very large questions arise on both the cost and the benefit sides.

As noted earlier, rates of return are particularly sensitive to cost variations. Mention of rates of return usually prompts most persons to think of benefits to education, not the cost side. Yet, differences in rates of return (especially private rates) by educational levels primarily reflect differences in costs rather than in earnings. Private rates of return to elementary education are very high, sometimes approaching infinity, because the elementary student pays very little of the direct costs, and forgone earnings (indirect costs) are almost nil (Carnoy & Marenbach, 1975). At the other extreme, direct and indirect costs of higher education are relatively high. Social costs vary in the same fashion, although not as drastically. From the perspective of the utility of public policy, a rate-of-return result generally will tell policy makers more about relative public subsidies of the students' costs at each educational level than it will tell about benefits of

education. Low private IRR may be increased most easily by lowering costs to the student, and the cost reduction need not be very large to impact IRR substantially. Or, put another way, subsidies to alternative educational levels may be reduced if rates are found to be high. The point is that private IRR are artificial in that they do not represent the value of education in some absolute sense; rather, more than anything they represent the degree of public subsidy obtained or simply a low cost of educational production. For example, Wachtel (1975, pp. 158–162) estimates that the rate of return on higher education for those receiving the GI Bill after World War II was almost double the rate for nonrecipients. Similarly, Siegfried (1972–1973) shows that graduate economics students on fellowships realize rates of return ranging from 11.4 to 23.6 percent, compared to 13 percent for those solely on private funds.

Therefore, a vital issue is the accuracy of cost estimates in rate-of-return studies. In regard to social costs, Becker (1975, pp. 192–193) points out the arbitrariness and inconsistency in determining what will be included in college costs. Although typically authors do not clearly specify the social costs they employ, many appear to utilize, for the large institutional contribution, total educational and general expenditures.[9] This category includes all components of the annual operating budget including organized research and public service, even though the implicit *benefit* measured is earnings from instruction.

Private cost estimates are even more problematic. First, for direct cost, researchers almost exclusively employ national averages of student expenditures. As

Eckaus (1973) notes, "The use of such averages introduces strong qualifications in the interpretation of the internal rates of return associated with college especially" (p. 84). He observes: "Although I have no more to apologize for in this respect than other investigators, the procedure is felt to be particularly unsatisfactory" (p. 84). One of the more obvious "qualifications" is that expenditures vary tremendously between the public and independent sectors, so that utilizing an "average" cost significantly understates the IRR to the student enrolled in the public sector. Studies employing aggregate data that obscure variations in postschool investment even may understate aggregate rates of return (Knapp & Hansen, 1976).

Based on actual numbers of hours worked by students, Parsons (1974) shows that most studies err seriously in imputing opportunity costs by ignoring or misstating student earnings. Discussing the five ways of estimating forgone earnings used in the literature, he shows (from hours worked by students) that the errors range from −28 percent to +31 percent (pp. 262–264). Becker's (1975) and Hanoch's (1967) technique of using three-fourths of the earnings of nonstudents to impute forgone income seems to yield the most accurate results. Less accurate estimates fail to reflect the greater sacrifice of leisure for work by students than nonstudents (Parsons, 1974). The data of Freiden and Leimer (1981), however, seem to suggest that the three-fourths estimate is too high and thus biases rate-of-return estimates downward. Again, the reason is that students earn a good deal. Freiden and Leimer estimate that 18- to 21-year-old males earn from 53 to 68 percent of the amount earned by comparable male nonstudents, and females earn from 32 to 46 percent of female nonstudents. The earnings of 18- to 24-year-olds are even higher. Using the National Longitudinal Study of 1972, Crary and Leslie (1978) controlled for ability and SES to equate college-goers and nonattenders in order to assess forgone earnings directly. Only Becker's 1964 estimates were found to approximate actual total average costs, whereas others have overestimated costs (and thus understated IRR) by 16 to 56 percent. Further, it was found that the annual amounts forgone in 4-year schools were several times greater than in 2-year and proprietary schools. Crary and Leslie also shed considerable light on variations by ability and SES. Surprisingly, high-ability students have the lowest opportunity costs, often very much lower, suggesting a very high IRR; the reverse is true for low-ability students.

Finally, and most importantly from the cost side, by assuming that all costs are paid by the student, analysts have greatly understated private rates of returns. From an individual's perspective, the judgment

as to whether higher education represents a good investment is based not on some published gross price, as commonly used in rate-of-return studies, but on the student's actual net cost. As already noted, IRR calculations are sensitive to cost estimates. Very few IRR studies take student aid into account, and of the 130 or so references found, none acknowledged that parents often pay a large part of the costs of higher education. If indeed the *student's* net cost is much less than the published price or the total cost paid from whatever sources, then the student realizes a much higher IRR than essentially all studies show. Thus, from a student's perspective, if student aid or family support is substantial, on average, higher education represents an investment almost without equal. Using data that for the first time allow comparisons of comparable student and nonstudent earnings, Crary and Leslie (1978) showed that student indirect costs actually are much less than generally thought. Further, Leslie (1984) has found that the net cost to the student is only some 32 to 40 percent of total private direct costs in 1980, having declined by about 10 percentage points between 1973 and 1980. Parents and governments directly subsidize the remainder. For most individuals, IRR must be much higher than reported earlier. Perhaps it is not surprising that higher education participation rates have been maintained at high levels during a period when it was anticipated that the rate would decline.

There are also factors on the benefits side that bias rate-of-return estimates downward. The major omission is the nonpecuniary benefits of education. As defined, neither the measures of the social nor the private benefits employed in IRR analysis extend beyond the pecuniary or dollar earnings realized. Indeed, it may have struck the reader as bizarre that social benefits would be defined as *private* earnings, before taxes are paid. This matter did not escape Becker (1975), who labeled the before-tax definition as only "a first approximation" (p. 195) to rate-of-return estimation. He recognized the "common criticism" that earnings greatly understate the social productivity of college graduates. McMahon and Wagner (1982) are quite direct on this point, often glossed over:

> This should not imply that the incremental taxes paid by college graduates are a fully adequate measure of the external benefits of education, or of education's overall contribution to equity, but they are the best measures of society's estimate of the value of these social contributions. (p. 152)

Becker (1975) estimates that the total return to higher education may be as much as twice the private return obtained from conventional IRR analyses (pp. 117–120).

The nonpecuniary benefits may be subdivided into

consumption benefits and postcollege, psychic benefits. Consumption benefits are those benefits that the student enjoys as a part of student life, including, for example, the pleasures of living in college housing, belonging to collegiate organizations, attending athletic and cultural events, and the pleasure component of learning: in short, all activities from which a later "return" will not be realized. Wachtel (1975, p. 160) makes the interesting observation that the substantially higher IRR on direct cost investments over the IRR on indirect cost investments demonstrates that full-time study, in comparison to part-time study, yields largely a consumption benefit.

Postschooling Psychic Benefits There exists a substantial literature regarding the "psychic" or nonpecuniary benefits that follow higher education enrollment. It is known that education, especially that of females who become wives and mothers, is associated with better health; each additional year of schooling appears to extend life by 0.4 percentage points, or almost 3 percent for a college graduate over a high school graduate (Grossman, 1976). The better educated also experience less work disability (Lando, 1975); the children of better educated women are generally more healthy (Grossman, 1982); and when combined with the mother's "home investment" (reading, writing, story-telling), her education appears to raise children's IQ considerably (Leibowitz, 1974).

Rosen (1975, p. 23) reports that people often accept lower-paying jobs for the opportunity to advance their education. McMahon (1976, p. 322) finds that parents' education contributes to the number of years of college planned by their children.

Education is related positively to savings, investment management, and the willingness to take financial risks (Solmon, 1975). The better educated tend to be wiser spenders, indirectly enhancing their incomes by between 10 and 50 percent (Michael, 1975), and to have fewer children, especially "unwanted" births (Michael, 1982). Schooling is known to be correlated positively with the selection of a spouse whose earnings potential is relatively high (Michael, 1982). A wife's schooling has been found to raise her husband's earnings (Welch, 1974), but divorce rates are higher for educated women. The work of the better educated is more interesting and challenging and is more likely to lead to advancement (Beaton, 1975). Unemployment is less likely (Erlich, 1975), and depreciation of one's human capital as well as obsolescence of job skills is slower or less likely (Rosen, 1975). The better educated tend to place less importance on "luck" and "connections" in their employment behaviors.

Efforts to quantify these benefits for inclusion in IRR estimates have been creative, though modest in number. Dunn (1977) surveyed textile plant workers and asked them to identify dollar and hours-of-work values they would trade off for certain fringe benefits, such as sick leave and retirement. Lucas (1977) showed that the omission of psychic job considerations, such as repetitiveness and the physical conditions of the work place, understates the returns to education. The reader is referred to McMahon (1982a) for a current and broad summary of all nonpecuniary benefits of education, to Witmer (1970), and to Michael (1982).

Externalities There is also considerable literature on the external benefits of education: that is, the "spill-overs" or benefits gained by society from the education of individuals. The direct pecuniary benefits of that education presumably are captured in the social rate-of-return calculations that reflect extra taxes paid by the more highly educated. However, productivity gains realized through a highly educated workforce and nonpecuniary gains that spill over from individuals to society must be taken into account. Becker (1975, p. 32) observes that the omission of consideration of these particular gains is the main reason rate-of-return studies have not been well accepted.

Again, McMahon (1982b) has written a concise review of the externalities of education, as have Bowen (1982), Weisbrod (1964, 1966), and Witmer (1970). Empirical work in this area depends on imputing dollar values and using shadow prices.

Education, especially inequality in education, has been observed to have an effect on the crime rate, the theory being proven when crimes of "profit" are separated from other crimes. That is, the relationship of education to crime can be demonstrated for crimes of profit but not for profitless crimes when other factors are controlled. The better educated also are more able to prevent crimes (Erlich, 1975). Education reduces juvenile delinquency (Spiegleman, 1968). The cost of crime that can be associated with educational deficiencies of adult prison inmates was put at $19.8 billion for 1982 (McMahon, 1982b).

High welfare and Medicaid costs have been associated with low educational levels (Garfinkle & Haveman, 1977, p. 53). Higher levels of education seem to yield greater liberality on issues such as integration and freedom for youth (Beaton, 1975), and many community agencies enjoy voluntary assistance and leadership that come heavily from more highly educated groups (Weisbrod, 1962).

A reading of this literature leaves the distinct impression that traditional rate-of-return estimates almost invariably and rather decisively understate the true social rates of return.

Conclusion

What then does all of the foregoing say about rate-of-return studies? First, the rates presented in Table 20.2

should not be considered as a sufficient basis for allocative decision making on higher education. These rates understate the true return to education by a substantial, probably a wide, margin. Berg (1981, p. 102) is quite right when he observes that rate-of-return studies capture only a few of the elements in educational productivity.

Raymond and Sesnowitz's (1975) statement that it is better to have imperfect information than none at all is problematic. Suppose that imperfect information leads to a conclusion contrary to that reached with complete knowledge. The experiences from 1975 to 1985 or so in American higher education seem clearly to say that this is precisely what has happened. Governments have shifted funding priorities away from higher education to areas such as prisons and welfare, and they have done so on grounds that, if completely and accurately represented, would have led to contrary conclusions. In a similarly misguided way, individuals have reduced their propensity to enroll in higher education. It seems clear that the so-called declining value of a college education has been greatly oversold.

Present rate of return studies can offer a go decision; they cannot yield a no-go decision. If pecuniary rates of returns, as presently constructed, show that the returns are greater than benchmark rates, additional educational investment is supported. If such benchmarks are not exceeded, additional information is required.

An analyst could argue that the rate-of-return issue should be viewed solely from the perspective of specific fields of study. In a sense, the policy question is not whether higher education pays off; clearly and overwhelmingly it does pay off financially in many fields of study, and it clearly does not pay off financially in some others. Yet, it is a fact of life that governments, at least, tend to think generically in terms of support of higher education. Society might benefit more by making public allocations on a field-by-field IRR basis, but practically such an approach would raise other serious issues. Would the public allocate less money to fields such as teacher education, nursing, theology, and social work by knowing that rates of return are small there? Clearly not. Perhaps this sort of field-by-field analysis points up most clearly the inadequacy of traditional IRR analyses that neglect the nonpecuniary benefits to society and to the individual.

Wealth Redistribution Effects of Higher Education Finance

In 1969, Hansen and Weisbrod set off what came to be known as the Hansen-Weisbrod-Pechman debate. Simply put, the central issue was whether the poor,

through the combination of regressive state and local tax structures and low rates of participation in higher education, subsidized the higher education of the rich.

Hansen and Weisbrod's (1969) conclusion that public higher education in California had a regressive effect was based on the following logic. First, the amount of public subsidies received by students of the University of California is higher than that received by state university and college students, who in turn receive more than those enrolled in junior colleges, in part because student persistence declines in the same order as do public subsidies among the three systems. Second, as one moves up through the three systems, attendance rates are positively associated with family income, partially because of relative selectivity criteria and the correlation of ability with income. The result was that average per-student public subsidies were higher where average family incomes were higher. Third, certain state and local tax rates (though not average taxes paid) were highest for the lowest two income categories and were more or less constant over the seven highest income categories. When averages for all three of these parts of the analysis were combined, the result was that families without children enrolled realized a net negative transfer of $650. Transfer for those with children enrolled was as follows: junior colleges +$40, state colleges +$630, and universities +$790. Hansen and Weisbrod (1969) concluded that the system yielded greater rather than less inequality. The conclusion Hansen and Weisbrod reached, a conclusion often cited in the arena of public policy making, was that higher education redistributes wealth from the poor to the rich.

Pechman (1970) reviewed the Hansen-Weisbrod work and conducted a reanalysis of their data. His compelling results were that the very poor and the very rich pay for the higher education of the middle class. Pechman pointed out that Hansen and Weisbrod (1969) compared *average* benefits and taxes paid, and he showed, using their own data, that the findings reveal progressivity, not regressivity, when distributions by income levels are used in the analysis. Pechman argued that only a selected portion of state and local taxes should enter into the calculation because higher education lays claim to only a particular share of certain revenues. Further, he found that Hansen and Weisbrod ignored sources of important taxes used to support higher education, leaving out two of the more progressive forms—the corporate income tax and the estate and gift tax. Pechman observed that the entire Hansen-Weisbrod exercise essentially was useless since benefits properly can be measured only through lifetime earnings, that many benefits are transferred to subsequent generations, and that tax regressivity is poorly addressed through singling out a single government activity. Separately, one could observe that essentially every public service favors one group or another. Highways and welfare are two obvious examples.

In 1970, Windham considered the redistribution question in Florida. Employing essentially the Pechman method, his results confirmed those of Hansen and Weisbrod—regressivity. About the same time, Hansen (1970) replicated the Hansen-Weisbrod study for the University of Wisconsin and Wisconsin State Universities, finding overall that the Wisconsin system was "more egalitarian" than California's but still favored higher income groups. Hartman (1972), too, seemed to suggest that public higher education had a regressive effect when he observed that between 57 and 66 percent of the costs of higher education were financed by "nonusers" and that users were considerably more likely to come from the upper 50 percent of the income distribution. Zimmerman (1973) found very slight regressivity in the St. Louis community college district, with cost-benefit differentials amounting to $50 at most. As in almost every study reviewed, the redistribution observed by Zimmerman was primarily to the middle-income categories.

But there have been at least as many and somewhat more compelling results on the other side (see Table 20.3). Hight and Pollack (1973) attempted to reconcile some of the conflicting evidence by applying a uniform analytical method and measure to the states where most of the conflict had arisen. Using essentially the Pechman and Windham method, but comparing instead absolute dollar redistributions, Hight and Pollock contrasted tax burdens with benefits (enrollment rates) by income group not only for their own state of Hawaii but also as had Hansen and Weisbrod and Pechman for California, and as had Windham for Florida. Though this method clearly did not respond to all of Pechman's criticisms of the

Table 20.3 Redistribution of Wealth

(1) ID NO.	(2) AUTHOR, YEAR	(3/4) DATA YEAR/ PUBLICATION SOURCE[a]	(5/6) POPULATION/DATA SOURCE	(7/8) PROGRESSIVE OR REGRESSIVE/SPECIAL NOTES
01	Crean, 1975	1961–62/J	Canadian universities/Canadian government	Progressive
02	Hansen, 1970	1964–65/J	University of Wisconsin, Wisconsin State Universities/WI universities and government data	Regressive/Same data and method limitations as in Hansen & Weisbrod, 1969
03	Hansen & Weisbrod, 1969	1964/J	CA undergraduates/CA Coordinating Council for Higher Education	Regressive/Compared only averages, numerous methodological problems
04	Hartman, 1970	1970 $/J	CA/Secondary analysis of Hansen & Weisbrod and Pechman data	Progressive
05	Hartman, 1972	1965/J	100,000 high school seniors/Census	Regressive/Students traced through college and employment
06	Hight & Pollock, 1973	1968/J	CA, FL, HI/Secondary analyses of data from other authors	CA, mixed; FL, regressive; HI, neutral/Tax share and university enrollment rates assessed
07	Jencks, 1968	1965/J	U.S./Census	Progressive/Taxes paid versus BAs received
08	Judy, 1970	1959, 1965/B	Canadian universities/Dominion Bureau of Statistics, Canada	Progressive
09	Machlis, 1973	1968 $/J	CUNY 18–24 year olds/Census	Progressive
10	Machovec, 1972	1970/J	CO 2-year, 4-year, universities/Census	Progressive
11	McGuire, 1976	Inflated to 1971 $/J	Undergraduates, graduates/Census, CA government	Progressive/Families whose head was 35–60, student aid included
12	Moore, 1982	1974 $/J	SUNY/Census	Progressive/Families whose head was 35–59, student aid considered
13	Pechman, 1970	1964/J	CA undergraduates/Secondary analysis of Hansen & Weisbrod data	Progressive
14	Zimmerman, 1973	1969/J	St. Louis area/St. Louis County Junior College	Slightly regressive/Community college only

[a] J = journal, B = book.

Hansen and Weisbrod's work, Hight and Pollock did show that the percentage gainers in California were limited to two of the lower three income groups and that by far the largest loser was the high income group, thus supporting Pechman's conclusions. In Florida the middle four groups were relative gainers, whereas the highest and especially the lowest income groups were relative losers. In Hawaii the lowest two and the highest income groups yielded resources to the third, fourth, and fifth highest of the six income groups. An example of the importance of values and associated comparative techniques can be seen readily in the Hight and Pollock (1973) study, which offered alternative ways of viewing the data. Results differ markedly when *tax rates* by income category are used in place of *tax payments* as a percentage of taxes paid by income category. Generally, employment of tax rates yields a conclusion of regressivity; however, when the analyst speaks literally of income redistribution, the latter definition seems to be more appropriate, and progressivity typically is observed.

Probably the most important methodological refinement in the wealth redistribution studies has been introduction of the life-cycle approach. This issue has been addressed by several persons (Crean, 1975; McDonald, 1980; McGuire, 1976; Moore, 1982; Pechman, 1970), who have pointed out the fallacy of designating as nonbeneficiaries those taxpayers who happen not to have family members enrolled in higher education at a particular time. When analysis is limited to families whose heads are roughly of ages 35 to 60, the age of most parents of college students, tax payments are seen to be at higher levels than when all families are included. By eliminating other age groups from the calculations, usually wealth is seen to be transferred progressively. Proponents of this method reason that calculations for younger persons can properly be done when their children reach college age and the time for calculating cost and benefits for older persons has passed.

Applying life-cycle methods to a Canadian sample, Crean (1975) first demonstrated the relatively high earnings of the 35 to 54 age group and then proportionately higher collegiate participation among lower-income students. Overall, the less wealthy pay lower taxes and receive more benefits, whereas the wealthier pay more and receive less.

McGuire (1976), who returned to the original California data sources of Hansen and Weisbrod (1969) to employ the life-cycle correction, found that an absolute dollar margin favoring lower-income groups was essentially linear across all three systems of higher education in California. McGuire added student financial aid to tuition subsidy, included graduate students in his study, and limited the sample to California families whose heads of household were between 35 and 60 years of age. When student financial aid was added to tuition subsidy, again low-income students fared best.

Moore (1982) added yet another refinement to the life-cycle method in examining the income redistribution effects in New York. Showing that Crean (1975) and McGuire (1976) understated the effect of limiting the analysis to the 35 to 60 age group, Moore found that the redistribution effects were positive for all income groups except the highest, with the greatest shift again being noted to the middle categories.

In other works, Machovec (1972) found that the benefits to the poor in Colorado approximately equaled their share of costs; the middle-income cost-to-benefit ratio was 30:45, and the high-income ratio was 61:47, clearly suggesting that the wealthy were not benefiting at the expense of the poor. Machovec observed that if student aid, which is highly progressive, were included, it would be seen that the poor benefited directly from higher education.

Like most others, Machlis's (1973) results for City University of New York showed the greatest redistribution from the upper- to the middle-income group, with notable differences by type of college. Overall, the distributional effects clearly were progressive. In another Canadian study, Judy (1970) found modest progressivity resulting from higher education, with almost symmetrical net wealth gains and losses for the lowest and highest income categories, respectively. In this study the major benefits did not accrue to middle-income groups. Finally, Jencks (1968) in a study of social stratification, reported that although the rich pay higher taxes, they do not realize a commensurate proportion of (public college) BA degrees granted.

Summary

In most populations that have been studied, public higher education apparently acts to redistribute income in a progressive manner. Most careful analyses support this conclusion, although the reverse may be true where political subdivisions tax in a particularly regressive manner. Varying methods and decision rules occasionally may lead to contrary conclusions, but when further adjustments are made for need-based student aid received, in most cases progressivity seems to exist. Yet, probably no more accurate, concise, and informative conclusion can be made than Hartman's (1970) observations:

(1) Poor people pay taxes and very few of them use public higher education. Those who do, gain thereby; those who don't, don't.
(2) Middle income people are heavy users of the system. Their taxes don't cover the costs.

(3) A few rich people use the system and gain handsomely thereby. The rest of the rich pay substantial taxes and get no direct return. (p. 521)

The prime beneficiaries of state and local financing policies under conditions that predate the need-based student aid programs of the 1970s appear to be middle-income groups. If this is so, student aid programs actually may have redressed an imbalance, instead of their having punished the middle class, as has been widely alleged.

Student Aid

Does student financial aid make a difference? From the empirical evidence available, the answer seems to be yes, but the impact is less than might be expected. Judging on the basis of the three traditional student aid goals of access, choice, and retention and completion, the report card reads quite favorably in all regards.

Access

There exist three forms of evidence concerning the relationship of student aid to the achievement of access. None of these is a completely satisfactory valid measure.

First, the analyst may question college students or potential students as to their perceptions of the role aid plays in inducing enrollments. The problem with this approach, of course, is that actions may belie words. The large disparity between self-reports and the results of more direct observations suggests that students may overstate the importance of aid. Another factor is that self-report studies typically only query aid recipients, not all potential applicants, thereby creating the impression that the effect is greater than it really is.

Table 20.4, Part A, shows that roughly 50 percent of recipients of student aid programs in California, Illinois, Pennsylvania, and New York reported that they would not have attended college without state aid (Fenske, Boyd, & Maxey, 1979; Leslie & Fife, 1974). Although the figure for Virginia (Schwartz & Chronister, 1978) is only about one-half as high, the Virginia sample included only matriculants at private institutions. Private college enrollees are known to be less marginally enrolled than are students overall; they have a propensity to substitute public colleges when personal resources are lacking. The final study in Part A, that of Leslie, Johnson, and Carlson (1977), surveyed high school seniors and reported that 25 percent of the respondents identified aid as crucial to their attendance decision. Given that the sample included nonrecipients as well as recipients of aid, the figure is not inconsistent with other studies. Nevertheless, it seems unlikely that as many as 50 percent of state aid recipients matriculate

solely because of the state awards. It seems plausible that, out of self-interest, recipients overstate the significance of aid. Further, it should be remembered that even if the true figure approaches 50 percent, aid recipients are only a portion of enrolled students.

A second approach assesses the impact of aid directly by comparing matriculation decisions of aid recipients to those of suitable comparison groups, for example, to applicants who applied for but did not receive aid and to nonapplicants. The major problem with this strategy is that it is difficult to track nonrecipients who may enroll elsewhere.

Two studies that have taken the second tack are presented in Part B of Table 20.4. Crawford (1966) followed National Merit Scholars of 1958–1959 and learned that among the 16 percent classified as needy, only 2 percent of those offered aid failed to matriculate, compared with 24 percent of those not offered aid. Crawford, however, gave no indication regarding the extent to which each group sought aid. It may be that nonrecipients were disinclined to attend college. Fields and LeMay (1973) compared Oregon State University freshman applicants and found average matriculation rates of 83 percent, 50 percent, and 72 percent, respectively, for aid recipients, aid-applicant nonrecipients, and nonapplicants for aid. Unfortunately, Fields and LeMay did not determine to what extent nonmatriculants enrolled elsewhere; therefore, the findings are of specific use only to Oregon State University.

G. A. Jackson (1978), on the other hand, in a carefully controlled study was able to estimate that college enrollments were 8.5 percent less among National Longitudinal Study (NLS) aid-applicant nonrecipients than among recipients. He then calculated that without aid, matriculation among recipients would have declined from 80 to 78.4 percent, leading him to conclude that the effect of aid is "not large," although it is the only factor apparently able to modify inclinations toward college attendance or nonattendance. In another important observation that generally holds across other studies, Jackson concluded that it is the receiving of aid, not the amount, that seems to have an important impact on the attendance decision.

The third approach is to attempt to relate aid awards and amounts to higher education participation rates in the larger environment: That is, do enrollment rates grow along with amounts of student aid awarded? Often, this is the form of practical political test used to assess public policy initiatives. Progress in this regard may be seen as offering a *prima facie* case that the initiative has worked, whereas stable or declining rates may be viewed as failures of policy. The shortcoming of this strategy, of course, is that although it is possible to separate out those groups to whom aid has been

Table 20.4   Access and Choice

(1) ID NO.	(2) AUTHOR, YEAR	(3/4) DATA YEAR/ POPULATION	(5/6) PUBLICATION SOURCE[a]/ STUDY TYPE[b]	(7) FORM OF AID	(8/9) RIGOR OR DEGREE OF CONTROL/STATISTICS
Part A					
01	Fenske, Boyd, & Maxey, 1979	1967–1977/Illinois Scholarship Commission recipients	J/TS	Grants, scholarships	Low/Descriptive
02	Leslie & Fife, 1974	1972–1973/5 states, 1st-time recipients of state aid	J/CS	Grants, scholarships	Low/Descriptive
03	Leslie, Johnson, & Carlson, 1977	1974/High school seniors in NY and PA	J/CS	All	Low/Descriptive
04	Schwartz & Chronister, 1978	1976–1977/VA state student-aid recipients	J/CS	Grants, loans	Low/Descriptive
Part B					
05	Crawford, 1966	1958–1959, 1961/Needy National Merit Scholars	R/CS	All	Low/Descriptive
06	Fields & LeMay, 1973	1969, 1970/OR aid applicants	J/CS	All	Low/Descriptive
07	G. A. Jackson, 1978	1972/NLS	J/CS	All	High/Discriminant, regression
08	Kehoe, 1981	PA high school seniors	J/CS	All	High/Discriminant
09	Shaut & Rizzo, 1980	NY TAP recipients	J/CS	Grants	Low/X^2, coefficients of variation
10	Tierney, 1980b	1975/CIRP freshmen	J/CS	All	High/Regression

[a] J = journal, R = report.
[b] TS = time series, CS = cross-section.

targeted and compare their participation rates to those who have not been targeted, it is impossible to be sure to what extent other social dynamics may have caused the rate changes.

The conclusion from the third form of evidence is only modestly encouraging. In a volume titled *Higher Education Opportunity*: *A Decade of Progress*, Leslie (1977) showed that between 1967 and 1975, when student aid was increasing from $400 million to $1.4 billion, low-income enrollment rates—the object of the aid programs—actually declined from 23.0 to 22.6 percent, although rates of other groups declined even more—from 54.8 to 54.1 percent for the high income and 39.4 to 34.1 percent for the middle income (p. 16). Student aid growth may have prevented a deeper decline in low-income enrollment rates; aid clearly did not raise those rates as expected. Suter (1977) of the Bureau of the Census came to the same conclusion as Leslie after viewing data relating to approximately the same time period. These data many simply reflect different impacts of the Vietnam war, and its ending, on youth of the various income groups.

More recently, Hansen (1982) essentially updated

the work of Leslie and Suter and found that conditions had not changed greatly. Hansen observed that the massive growth in governmental student aid over the 1970s had a "modest" impact on enrollment rates.

Critics vehemently attacked Hansen's paper but took far more exception to his conclusions than to his findings. The critics argued that aid programs have assisted middle-income youth as well as low-income youth and have been targeted more on enhancing choice than access. Thus, they say, it comes as no surprise that low-income participation rates have not risen sharply. These exceptions would seem to be well grounded, but it remains that there is no direct evidence that this form of student support clearly promotes higher education access for low-income students. Mullen's (1982) insight from observing the effects of the New York Tuition Assistance Program (TAP), may be instructive. In essence, he concluded that the TAP may have done little for student access because numerous aid programs of substantial amounts were already in place when the TAP was instituted. Mullen implied that the amount of aid already available for needy students may have been adequate to meet

Table 20.4   (continued)

(10)	(11)
SPECIAL NOTES	RESULTS
Self-perceptions, state-aid recipients	Induced enrollments of ~ 20% of aid recipients in 1967 to ~ 50% in 1977. Would enroll at different college without aid: 1967, 23.2%; 1977, 15.6%.
Self-perceptions, state-aid recipients	Induced enrollment of ~ 50% of aid recipients, especially low income; 68–88% of students in first-choice institution.
Self-perceptions, all 12th graders	Induced enrollment of ~ 25% of aid recipients, especially low income. One-third cite aid as allowing attendance at first-choice college.
Self-perceptions, state-aid recipients, private colleges only	Induced enrollment of 13–41% of aid recipients; 19.4% would attend public colleges if no aid.
Unique population, needy only, differences in aspiration (?)	98% of those awarded aid attended; 76% of those not awarded aid attended.
Nonmatriculants may have enrolled elsewhere	% of applicants who matriculated = 83% for aid recipients, 50% nonrecipients, 72% applicants.
Broad based, well-designed, well-controlled study	Aid recipients 8.5% more likely to enroll than nonrecipients; without aid, applicant participation rates 78.4% v. 80% with aid.
	Aid variables useful in predicting migration of students.
	TAP awards promoted choice of higher cost institutions.
Pertains only to those accepted at a public and private college	Aid significantly accounts for public-private choice among those who consider both options.

the demand for those who wanted to attend college.

Most recently, Leslie and Brinkman (1988) conducted a thorough review of the evidence at the same three levels of analysis. They estimated that grant aid is responsible for the enrollment of more than a million full-time, low- and middle-income students. Fully 20 to 40 percent of low-income enrollments are estimated to be due to grant aid alone.

Choice

Public student aid from the mid-1970s to the mid-1980s seems to have been less successful in promoting access than in assisting students in attending higher-cost institutions, particularly private ones. The motives of policy makers in expanding the need-based aid programs have comprised a mixture of desires to allow low-income and minority students opportunities to attend higher-cost colleges, to assist a private sector that has at times been financially troubled, and to reduce the need for a costly further expansion of the public sector.

Returning to the perceptual studies (Part A, Table 20.4), Fenske et al. (1979) reported that approximately one-quarter of 1967 recipients of Illinois State Scholarship Commission grants or scholarships would have en-

rolled in another institution if the aid had not been available and that the comparable figure for 1977 was about 16 percent. Fenske et al. attribute the decline to the growing tendency of award winners to enroll in lower-cost institutions. Essentially all students who report that aid changed their behavior regarding choice between the public and private sectors identify the latter sector as the beneficiary of the public policy. Leslie and Fife (1974) reported that from 68 to 88 percent of the state aid recipients in the four states studied were attending their first-choice institutions and that 40 percent of the remainder cited reasons that were not financial. In a study of high school seniors, Leslie et al. (1977) found that approximately one-third cited student aid as a critical factor in their ability to attend their first-choice school. As anticipated, the percentage was inversely a function of family income. In the Virginia sample of private college enrollees (Schwarz & Chronister, 1978), 19.9 percent indicated they would switch to public colleges if aid were withheld.

G. A. Jackson's (1978) and Tierney's (1980b) well-designed statistical examinations of attendance patterns of aid recipients and nonrecipients yield the most useful results in examining the college choice goal. Jackson concluded that student aid impacts choice much more than it does access. He found that whereas $100 of aid increased the likelihood of applicant attendance (access) by 0.1 percentage point, the same $100 increased the likelihood that the applicant would attend the institution offering aid by 1.5 percentage points (choice). Tierney's approach was to identify students who applied to and were accepted by at least one public and one private institution. Forcing student aid variables last into multiple regression equations after institutional and student variables were entered, Tierney found that the aid variables added 7 to 22 percent to the explanation of college choice, with the largest additions being for low-income students and for those who initially had preferred public colleges. For low- and middle-income groups, of the personal variables only student aid and tuition were significant in predicting college choice. For low-income youth, the size of grant and work-study coefficients was almost twice that of loans. Two other studies (Kehoe, 1981; Shaut & Rizzo, 1980) support the importance of aid in affecting college choice but are less decisive. Shaut and Rizzo found that both the award and the amount of a TAP grant in New York significantly affected choice, and Kehoe utilized discriminant analysis to show that financial aid variables were useful in predicting in-state versus out-of-state matriculation.

Finally, employing the technique of relating growth in student aid to enrollment flows among institutions over time, Leslie (1977) concluded that aid had raised private college enrollments of low-income students but had not been associated with shifts within the public sector, especially from community colleges to universities. He found that during an era of growth in student aid, median incomes of the families of freshmen had declined in community colleges and had increased in universities, but he also found that median incomes had declined by $600 in private institutions and that the low-income share of private enrollments had grown from 15.5 to 22.0 percent. All in all, student aid seems to have enhanced choice of institution when choice is measured by enrollment in private schools (Leslie, 1977, pp. 20–25).

The recent Leslie-Brinkman (1988) analysis at the same three levels of evidence shows that state student · aid particularly has been effective in promoting choice and that students believe strongly that aid has contributed to their institutional selection. The results of econometric studies support this conclusion, but results are somewhat mixed.

Retention and Completion

In his 1977 study, Leslie could find in the literature very little solid evidence regarding the impact of aid on student persistence in college or on degree completion (p. 28). By the mid-1980s more studies have addressed this topic than they have either access or choice.

The conclusion reached is that much depends upon the criterion employed. At first glance it appears that student aid generally impacts student persistence very little, in that persistence rates for aid recipients are not usually greater than for nonrecipients. However, if it is reasoned that aid was intended only to *equalize* opportunity, then conclusions are more positive.

Of four national studies found, two are particularly well designed, promising good internal and external validity (see Table 20.5). The study by Peng and Fetters (1978), which reports no relationship between aid and persistence, is probably the most valid, although students are followed for only 2 years. The study by Kohen, Nestel, and Karmas (1978) of male students found that aid recipients are from 8 to 14 percent more likely than nonrecipients to complete a year of study but that the differences disappear when the observation is extended to 2 years. Astin's work (1975) shows small positive relationships between persistence and grants, and especially work study, and a negative relationship to loans; however, his conclusions rely heavily on student perceptual data or planned decisions and are for freshmen only. Riccobono and Dunteman (1975) conclude there is a strong relationship between aid and persistence, but their analysis is uncontrolled, and their results run counter to those of Peng and Fetters (1978), who examined the same data using a controlled design.

For specific institutions, the results are more encouraging, although such studies seldom are rigorously designed. Among the seemingly more valid studies, Blanchfield (1971) showed that aid was a significant discriminator between dropouts and graduates at Utica College when important variables were controlled. Jensen's (1981) study of Washington State freshmen of 1970–1971 was controlled somewhat, and his use of number of semesters completed as the dependent variable is superior to most approaches, which simply consider number who drop out in a semester or two. Jensen concluded that the award of aid had a small positive association with persistence and that denial of aid had a small negative relationship, as did the amount of aid awarded. McCreight and LeMay (1982) sought to institute some control through a recipient-nonrecipient matching process, and they extended the persistence measure broadly to include 6 subsequent years for the Oregon State (resident) freshman class of 1975. They showed modestly superior persistence by recipients of Basic Educational Opportunity Grants (BEOGs, or Pell Grants) over nonrecipients. At the University of

Wyoming, Bergen and Zielke (1979) also matched BEOG recipients with nonrecipients and obtained mostly statistically nonsignificant results: Although recipients completed more credits each semester, nonrecipients were more likely to graduate and were less likely to drop out. The remaining studies are more limited in degree of control and in terms of breadth of the persistence measure. In an earlier study at Oregon State, Fields and LeMay (1973) found no differences in recipient-nonrecipient freshman withdrawal or returning sophomore rates; Hochstein and Butler (1983) found higher loan rates but lower grant, work-study, and scholarship rates among those who completed a semester at the University of Nebraska–Omaha, than those who did not. Iwai and Churchill (1982) concluded that persisters at Arizona State University rely on more sources of aid than nonpersisters, and Taylor and Raffetto (1983) showed mixed and statistically nonsignificant persistence among BEOG recipients at a small rural Texas community college.

Murdock (1986) completed a thorough meta-analysis of the persistence studies. Essentially she found that persistence rates among recipients and nonrecipients did not vary. Utilizing the criterion that aid is intended only to equalize opportunity, she concluded that the persistence goal of student aid was achieved.

Summary and Discussion

Student aid is a politically acceptable form of transfer payment in a democratic society with a mixed economy. It seems not to be a reasonably efficient form of enhancing low-income access to college, choice of college, and of insuring completion and retention. The reasons for its less than full success include the fact that student aid is spread among various income groups and is not exclusively targeted on low-income students. Because aid is awarded on a cost-need basis, much of it goes to improving institutional choice and, in reality, to subsidizing private institutions. Cope (1978) mentions a general consensus that financial problems alone probably do not cause students to drop out. The same conclusion most likely pertains to college access as well. Finally, there is evidence that aid received by undergraduates may lead to higher participation rates in postbaccalaureate study (Golladay & Noell, 1978; Sanford, 1980; Wight, 1936) and only slight evidence to the contrary (Davis, 1964).

INSTITUTIONAL ISSUES

Is there an optimally efficient institutional size? Are economies of scale more probable for some institu-

tional functions than others? Where can resources be saved to be used elsewhere?

Cost and Scale

Educational cost is not one theme but many, due in part to the nature of costs. Costs may be direct or indirect, average or marginal, fixed or variable, long run or short run. They may be measured in terms of actual outlays (expenditures) or expressed in terms of forgone opportunities. They may be allocated by function or by object of expenditure. They may be aggregated at any number of levels, and various combinations by type and level of aggregation are possible. The fact that institutions of higher education are themselves so various increases the overall complexity.

Within this multilayered structure, two questions are pervasive: How much are the costs, and what determines them? The first question is essentially a matter for accountants to answer, at least when costs are restricted to actual expenditures. The second question, to be addressed in part in this section, can also be understood from an accounting perspective, in that the prices and quantities of inputs do determine costs (again in the sense of expenditures) by virtue of a simple accounting relationship. For analytical purposes, however, the more interesting perspective addresses the ways in which outputs (products and services rendered) determine cost. Either econometric or engineering approaches can be used, indirectly by examining the relationship between inputs and outputs (the production function) or directly by examining the immediate relationship between costs and outputs (the cost function). An aspect of the latter relationship that has been investigated with some regularity is the way in which costs are affected by the scale of operation. Here the emphasis is on summarizing the results of the economy-of-scale investigations.

Background

In higher education, the idea of economies of scale—larger institutions having lower unit costs—generated considerable interest in the 1960s as a result of massive growth in enrollments. In the mid 1980s, the threat of enrollment declines and the relatively high cost of maintaining small institutions have led to renewed interest in the cost-scale relationship, scale typically being defined in terms of enrollment or student credit hours and costs being defined most often in terms of average expenditures per student or per credit hour.

There is good reason to believe that colleges and universities would experience a decrease in unit costs as they enroll more students. In instruction, the possibilities for larger class sizes and higher student-faculty

Table 20.5 Persistence

(1) ID NO.	(2) AUTHOR, YEAR	(3/4) DATA YEAR/ POPULATION[a]	(5/6) PUBLICATION SOURCE[b]/STUDY TYPE[c]	(7/8) PERSISTENCE SPECIFICATION/ FORM OF AID[d]	(9/10) RIGOR OR DEGREE OF CONTROL/STATISTICS[e]
01	Astin, 1975	1968–1972/U.S. freshmen	B/TS	1st year/All	High/Descriptive
02	Bergen & Zielke, 1979	1973–1977/U. Wyoming freshmen	J/TS	Credits completed, graduation, dropping out/BEOGs	Middle/t, X^2
03	Blanchfield, 1971	Not reported/Utica College	J/CS	"Dropouts"/Grants and loans	Middle/Discriminant
04	Fields & LeMay, 1973	1969–1970, 1970–1971/Oregon State freshmen	J/CS	Freshman withdrawal, credits completed, sophomore returnees/All	Low/Descriptive
05	Hochstein & Butler, 1983	Fall, 1981–1982/U. Nebraska, Omaha	J/CS	Semester completion/All	Low/Descriptive
06	Iwai & Churchill, 1982	1975–1976/Arizona State U.	J/CS	1 semester/All	Middle/ANOVA
07	Jensen, 1981	1970–1971/Washington State freshmen	J/CS	Semesters attended/All	Middle/ANCOVA, path analysis
08	Kohen, Nestel, & Karmas, 1978	1966–1970/Males, U.S., NLS1	J/TS	Completing 1 year of study in 2 years or less/Scholarships	High/Regression
09	McCreight & LeMay, 1982	1975–1981/Oregon State U.	J/TS	Earned degree or enrolled after 6 years/BEOGs	Low/Descriptive
10	Peng & Fetters, 1978	1973–1974/U.S., NLS2	J/TS	Two years (academic programs)/All	High/Regression
11	Riccobono & Dunteman, 1975	1973–1974/U.S., NLS2	R/TS	Enrolled 1 year later and planned beyond/All	Low/Descriptive
12	Taylor & Raffetto, 1983	Not reported/Temple, TX, Junior College	J/TS	Graduation (AA degree)/BEOGs	Low/X^2

Symbols, by column
[a] NLS1 = National Longitudinal Survey, NLS 2 = National Longitudinal Study
[b] J = journal, B = book
[c] TS = time series, CS = cross section
[d] BEOG = Basic Equal Opportunity Grant
[e] t = *t* test, X^2 = chi square, ANOVA = analysis of variance, ANCOVA = analysis of covariance

ratios suggest opportunities for scale-related economies. Similarly, larger enrollments allow some administrative services to be better utilized, resulting in lower average costs. The same can be said for some aspects of maintaining buildings and providing library resources.

At the same time, at least some countervailing forces can be expected. Generally speaking, the larger the institution, the larger the array of its courses and programs. Surely more offerings must add to the unit costs of instruction. The sizable bureaucracies at many large institutions suggest that administrative and support functions also have a tendency to grow in conjunction with enrollment increases, thereby negating at

least some potential economies of scale. Furthermore, salaries tend to increase along with the size of the institution, particularly for administrators.

Although seldom recognized explicitly, two different questions have been addressed in the research literature on economies of scale. One has to do with the "pure" effects of scale on unit costs, that is, the effects when other things remain constant. The other question is simply whether large institutions spend less per student than do small institutions regardless of other factors. Some studies fall in between. Their data and methodologies reflect the latter approach, but the investigators acknowledge the presence of the inter-

Table 20.5 (continued)

(11)	(12)
SPECIAL NOTES	RESULTS
Freshmen only, limited persistence measure, data limitations	Scholarship/grants small + correlation, loans −, work study −, GI Bill −, ROTC +
Matched recipients with nonrecipients	Recipients completed more credits each semester, but nonrecipients dropped out less and graduated more.
One private institution	% of costs financed by grants, significant; loans not significant.
No controls	No differences except academic suspension rates lower for recipients.
No controls, 1 semester	Persisters: loans 44.6%, grants 64.0%, scholarships 18.3%, work study 5.1%; Nonpersisters: loans 72.8%, grants 43.4%, scholarships 2.3%, work study 2.9%.
Very low response rate, 1 semester	Persisters rely on more sources of support than nonpersisters.
Limited sample	Aid has small + impact; denial of aid, small −; amount of aid, small −.
Well designed	Recipients 8–14% more likely to complete a year of study in 1 year. No difference when 2 years allowed.
Weak controls (matching), limited sample, long-term	30% of BEOG recipients and 34% of nonrecipients did *not* return for sophomore year; 17% and 14% graduated in 4 years. After 6 years, 51% and 42% had graduated or still enrolled.
Well designed, limited to 2 years	No significant differences. Standardized regression coefficients small but − for loans.
Lack of control; from same data with controls Peng & Fetters show the reverse	"Strong relationship" of aid to persistence.
Community college, not controlled	In 5 of 6 years, graduation rates 1–15% higher for BEOG recipients than nonrecipients. No significant differences. Scholastic probation greater for recipients in 4 of 6 years. No significant differences.

vening variables even though not controlling for them mathematically. This was the case, for instance, in the extensive work done on economies of scale by the Carnegie Commission on Higher Education (1971, 1972).

Method

Most studies deal separately with 2-year, 4-year, and university-level institutions and with one or more functional areas. Thus, studies such as those by Broomall, Mahan, McLaughlin, and Patton (1978) and McLaughlin, Montgomery, Smith, and Broomall (1980), which deal collectively with a great variety of institutional types, are not included in the analysis that follows. Also excluded are studies that relate size to inputs, such as Trueheart and Weathersby (1976), or to the utilization of inputs, such as Hungate, Meeth, and O'Connell

(1964). The material covered deals directly with the size-cost issue. All studies that were known and were available have been included. Previous reviews can be found in Bowen (1980) and Reichard (1971).

Aspects of the relationship between scale and cost are reported in several ways: the shape of the average or marginal cost curves, the difference between average and marginal costs, the sign and magnitude of correlation or regression coefficients, or costs in relation to scale (enrollment) intervals. Cost data by enrollment intervals are by far the most frequently reported findings. Typically, the procedures used in such studies involve no direct control over intervening variables, other than stratification by institutional type, and thus the studies address the second of the two economy-of-scale questions. In any case, there were enough interval studies to warrant the derivation of average values. Also, it was possible on occasion to use reported regression results to calculate predicted costs at various enrollment levels, thus increasing the number of interval-type data points.

The enrollment range can be divided into intervals in a variety of ways. Conventional percentiles are occasionally used, but more often investigators simply create intervals to suit their own purposes. For example, the interval from 1 to 500 students may be chosen to represent the smallest institutions by one investigator; another may choose the range from 200 to 600. In order to provide some degree of standardization of the findings, percentage changes in unit cost were calculated on the basis of from three- to fourfold differences in enrollment, using whatever interval was

provided for the smallest institutions as the starting point. The extent of the enrollment difference is indicated for each percentage change in unit costs shown in Table 20.6. For example, in the study by Meeth (1975), the average cost dropped 20 percent where the midpoint of the interval for large institutions was four times larger than the corresponding midpoint for the interval representing the smallest institutions. Intervals for extremely small institutions (less than 200 students) were ignored in calculating percentage changes; in those instances, the interval for the next larger institution was chosen instead as the base interval. Table 20.6a helps in assessing the meaningfulness of the average values derived from the interval data.

Table 20.6 Cost and Size

(1) ID NO.	(2) AUTHOR, YEAR	(3/4) DATA YEAR/ POPULATION	(5/6) PUBLICATION SOURCE/STUDY TYPE	(7/8) DATA SOURCE/ LEVEL OF ANALYSIS	(9/10) TYPE OF CONTROL/ STATISTICS
01	Bowen, 1980	1976–1977/268 P&I, RU&DU,CU,LA,CC	B/CS	NCES (HEGIS)/I	IS,IT/Descriptive
02	Brinkman, 1981a	1976–1977/50 P&I RU	J/CS	NCES (HEGIS)/I	IT,CD,SF,CL,FS,SL,IS/ Regression
03	Brinkman, 1981b	1977–1978/P RU,DU, CU,BD,CC	D/CS	NCES (HEGIS)/I	IT,IS,CD,CL,SD,IP,SL,RE, FS/Regression
04	Brovender, 1974	1968–1969/1 P RU	J/CS	I/P	SL,IS,IT/Regression
05	Buckles, 1978	1963–1964 to 1969–1970/ 1 P RU	J TS/CS	I/D	FS,FL,CS,IT,IS/Regression
06	Butter, 1966	1964–1965/12 P&I RU	R/CS	AS/D	IT,SF,FS,RE,CD/Regression

2-Year Colleges

For 2-year colleges, the data in Table 20.6 suggest that most scale-related economies for educational and general expenditures are typically realized by the time these institutions reach an enrollment level of about 1,000 to 1,500 full-time-equivalent (FTE) students (Carnegie Commission on Higher Education, 1971; Kress, 1977; Mullen, 1981). For instructional expenditures, the "breakpoint" probably occurs a little earlier than 1,000 FTE students; for administrative expenditures it appears to occur later, perhaps in the 1,250 to 1,500 range (Mullen, 1981).

On a percentage basis, scale-related economies for 2-year colleges are greatest for administrative expenditures. Across nine data points, administrative unit costs at the larger institutions were, on average, 38 percent lower than at smaller institutions (using, as always, three- to fourfold differences in enrollment). By contrast, the corresponding decrease in instructional unit costs at larger institutions was only 12 percent. Measured in similar fashion, economies in the operation and maintenance of the physical plant came to 24 percent, the same as for educational and general expenditures, the aggregate functional expenditure category.

Studies that provide correlation or regression coefficients offer supporting evidence for the presence of economies of scale in 2-year colleges and for the countervailing effects of curriculum diversity. For instance, Wallhaus (1981) reports coefficients of $-.30$

Table 20.6 (continued)

(11/12) COST SPECIFICATION/ SCALE SPECIFICATION	(13) % DECREASE IN AC	(14/15) SHAPE OF LAC CURVE MC:AC	(16/17) BREAKPOINT/ESTIMATED COEFFICIENT
(I + pro rata share of support costs) per S		RU; DU LA—S P—S I—S CC	
S (FTE, W)		P—S CU&BC I—S P—S I—S	
I per S	(4x) 26	$.51^a$	(C) I per S w 1 per S = .731 (all institutions)
S (FTE)			(C) I per S w 1 per S = .203 (public institutions)
I		^{b} LD UD G RU DD DD DD DU DD DD U	^{b} LD UD G RU 4000 6000 6000 DU 4000 4000
S (FTE)		CU DD IU DD BC DD L CC DD	CU 2000 1800 BC 1200 1000 CC 1000
		RU .99 DU .83 CU .83 BC .82 CC .90	$(R)^c$
Total Salaries SCH	$(4x)^d$ HUM 27 NAT SCI 26 SOC SCI 14	HUM .66 NAT SCI .66 SOC SCI .81	$Dept.^d$ $Prog.^d$ HUM 8.13 10.66 NAT SCI 11.44 11.64 SOC SCI 18.76 13.88 (all Sig)
T per SCH SCH	(4x) 34	DD	(R) log T per SCH = a log SCH + FS + FL + CS + CC $a = -.301^c$ (Sig)
T per S S (HC, PhD level)	(3x) Physics 62 Sociology 69		(R) T per S$_{Physics}$ = aS + RE + CD $a = -218^f$ (Sig) (R) T per S$_{Sociology}$ = aS + CD + FS $a = -164^f$ (Sig) (C) T per S S$_{Physics}$ S$_{Sociology}$ $-.23$ $-.21$

(continued)

Table 20.6   (continued)

(1) ID NO.	(2) AUTHOR, YEAR	(3/4) DATA YEAR/ POPULATION	(5/6) PUBLICATION SOURCE/STUDY TYPE	(7/8) DATA SOURCE/ LEVEL OF ANALYSIS	(9/10) TYPE OF CONTROL/ STATISTICS
07	Cage & Manatt, 1969	1967–1968/15 P CC&IA area schools	J/CS	AS/P	IT,IS/Correlation
08	California Coordinating Council for Higher Education, 1969	1968–1969/17 P CU&BC	R/CS	State/I	IT/Descriptive
09	Calkins, 1963	1954–1955/145 LA	D/CS	USOE, O/I	IT,CC,IS,CD,FS,Q/ Regression
10	Carlson, 1972	1967–1968/668 P&I RU& DU,CU,BC,LA	R/CS	NCES (HEGIS)/I	IS,IT,CD,CC,SL,F/Frontier analysis
11	Carnegie Commission, 1972	1967–1968/1,550 P&I RU&DU,CU,BC, LA,CC	R/CS	NCES (HEGIS)/I	IT,IS/Descriptive
12	Carnegie Commission, 1971	1967–1968/1,550 P&I RU&DU,CU,BC, LA,CC	R/CS	NCES (HEGIS)/I	IT,IS/Descriptive
13	Cirino & Dickmeyer, 1981	1979–1980/403 P CC	R/CS	NACUBO S/I	IT,IS/Descriptive
14	Corrallo, 1970	1961–1962, 1963–1964, 1965–1966, 1966–1967/363 P&I RU& DU,CU&BC,LA,CC	D/CS	USOE/I	IT,IS,SF,SL,SD/Regression
15	Dickmeyer, 1980	1978–1979/187 P CC	R/CS	NACUBO S/I	IT,IS/Descriptive
16	Dickmeyer, 1982	1977–1978/568 LA	J/CS	NCES (HEGIS)/I	IT,IS/Regression
17	Dickmeyer & Cirino, 1982	1980–1981/420 P CC	R/CS	NACUBO S/I	IT,IS/Descriptive

Table 20.6 (continued)

(11/12) COST SPECIFICATION/ SCALE SPECIFICATION	(13) % DECREASE IN AC	(14/15) SHAPE OF LAC CURVE MC:AC	(16/17) BREAKPOINT/ESTIMATED COEFFICIENT
T per S/S (FTE)			(C) T/S w S = $-.72^g$
E&G (excluding debt service) per S/S (FTE)	(4x) 40	DD	(C) E&G Rev/S w S = $-.018$ (NSig) (PC) E&G Rev/S w S, controlling for CD, CC, and FS, = $-.36$ (Sig) (R) E&G Rev/S on aS + CS + CC + FS a = $-.28^h$ (Sig)
E&G revenues per S/S (FTE)	(4x) 33		
E&G per S/Total revenue	(1.5x) P RU&DU 6 (1.5x) I RU&DU 11 (1.5x) P CU 7 (1.5x) I CU 1 (2x) P BC 26 (2x) SEL LA 3 (1.5x) NSEL LA 1		

E&G (excluding research), I, A (including student) services), O&M, L, all per S/S (FTE, W, UW)	(4x) E&G I A O&M L
	RU&DU:
	  I 13 36 43 43 34
	CU:
	  P 27 25 24 33 40
	  I 35 27 40 24 25
	LA1 28 24 56 39 38
	LA2 39 19 43 51 36
			RU/DU—5000 FTES
			CU —2000–2500
			BC —2500
			LAI —900–2000
			LAII —1000–1500
			P CC —2000
			I CC —1000–1500

E&G (excluding research), I, A (including student services) O&M, L, all per S/S (FTE, W, UW)		RU&DU—DD CU —DD&F BC —DD&L LAI —DD LAII —DD P CC —DD I CC —DD	

Various E&G per S/S (FTE, credit, noncredit)	(4x) E&G 19
	     I 7
	     A 22
	   O&M 15
		DC	(R) E&G per S on aS + Q:
			P RU&DU a = $.05^i$ (Sig)
			I RU&DU a = $.01^i$
			P BC a = $.03^i$ (Sig)
			(Nonsec) LA a = $-.05^i$ (Sig)
			(Religious) LA a = $-.28^i$ (Sig)
			P CC a = $.01^i$
			I CC a = $-.54^i$ (Sig)

E&G, A&G, I, O&M, L per S/S (FTE)			

Various categories in E&G per S/S (FTE, credit, noncredit)	(4x) E&G 17
	     I 6
	     A 26
	   O&M 34
		DD	

E&G per S/S (FTE)		L	

Various categories in E&G per S/S (FTE, credit, noncredit)	(4x) E&G 23
	     I 19
	     A 30
	   O&M 23
		DD	

(continued)

Table 20.6   (continued)

(1) ID NO.	(2) AUTHOR, YEAR	(3/4) DATA YEAR/ POPULATION	(5/6) PUBLICATION SOURCE/STUDY TYPE	(7/8) DATA SOURCE/ LEVEL OF ANALYSIS	(9/10) TYPE OF CONTROL/ STATISTICS
18	Dukiet, 1974	1972–1973, 1973–1974/ 791 P&I CU&BC&LA.CC	J/CS	AS/I	IT/Descriptive
19	Jenny & Wynn, 1970	1959–1960—1967–1968/ 48 LA	R/CS	AS/I	IT,IS/Descriptive
20	Jenny & Wynn, 1972	1967–1968/48 LA	R/CS	AS/I	IT,IS/Descriptive
21	Jordan, 1965	1962–1963/31 P CC in TX	D/CS	AS/I	IT,IS,CD/Regression
22	Kress, 1978	1975–1976/68 P CC districts in CA	D/CS	State district	IT,IS,CD,SD/Regression
23	Leslie & Brinkman, 1980	1976–1977/31 P&I RU	J/CS	NCES (HEGIS)/I	IT,IS,SL,CD,FS,SF/ Regression
24	Magee, 1931	±1930/15 P BC	B/CS	AS/I	IT,IS,CD/Correlation
25	Marks, 1980	1971–1972, 1976–1977/ 134 P CC	D/TS,CS	NCES (HEGIS)/I	IT,IS/Descriptive
26	Maynard, 1971	1967–1968/123 P CU&BC,CC	B/CS	AS/I	IT,IS/Regression
27	Meeth, 1975	1970–1971/66 LA	B/CS	AS/I	IT,IS/Descriptive
28	Metz, 1964	1963–1964/404 P CU, BC,CC	B/CS	AS/I	IT,IS/Descriptive
29	Millett, 1952	1948–1949/80 LA	B/CS	AS/I	IT,IS/Descriptive

Table 20.6 (continued)

(11/12) COST SPECIFICATION/ SCALE SPECIFICATION	(13) % DECREASE IN AC	(14/15) SHAPE OF LAC CURVE MC[:]AC	(16/17) BREAKPOINT/ESTIMATED COEFFICIENT

T,I,A,O&M,L per S/S
   HC
	(3x) CC: *1972–73 1973–74*
	         T 24 8
	         I 15 19
	         A 51 65
	        O&M 12 27
	         L 35 (9)
	
	CU;BC;LA:
	         T 14 13
	         I 2 1
	         A 46 44
	        O&M 21 15
	         L 2 (2)		

A,I,O&M,L per S/S
   (FTE)
	(3.5x) I 20
	               A 35
	              O&M 25
	               L 16		

I,A,O&M per S/S (FTE)	(3.5x) I 18
	               A 35
	              O&M 24
	               L 19
			(R) T per S = aFTES
			           $a = -.06^j$ (NSig)
			       T per S = aFTE + CD_1
			           $a = -.64^j$ (Sig)
			       T per S = aFTE + CD_2
			           $a = -.35^j$ (Sig)

T,I,A,O&M, per S/S (FTE)	(3.8x) T (5)
	               I (4)
	               A 29
	              O&M 21
		T per S = aFTES
		   $a = -.06^k$ (NSig)
		T per S = aFTE + CD_1
		   $a = -.64^k$ (Sig)
		T per S = aFTE + CD_2
		   $a = -.35^k$ (Sig)
			1,000 to 1,500 (ADA)
			
			(R) $T = a_1 ADA + a_2 (ADA)^2$
			     $a_1 = 1,114$ (Sig)
			     $a_2 = .00152$ (NSig)
			     (constant = 250,189)

T, numerous others, per
   S/S (ADA)
	(4x) 23
	(500 to 2,000 ADA)
		U^l	(C) E&G per S w S = $-.65$
			(C) I per S w S = $-.67$
			(R) I per S = aS + CL + FS + CD
			         $a = -.27^l$ (Sig)
			(R) I per S = aS + CL + FS + CD
			         $+ \dfrac{GS}{US} + SF : a = -.03^l$ (NSig)

E&G, I per S/S (FTE)			(C) I per SCH w SCH = $-.24$ (NSig) (PC) I per SCH w SCH controlling for CD = $-.63$ (Sig)
I, per SCH/SCH			

T per S/S (FTE)	(2.89x) 29		(R) CU&BC:
			         E&G per S = $a_1 S + a_2 S^2$
			             $a_1 = -.244$
			             $a_2 = .000002275$

E&G (excluding organized
   research, extension, and
   public services) per S/S
   (FTE)
	(4x)
	CU&BC 20^p
	CC 30^p
		CU&BC—L^m, U^n	

E&G (excluding organized research) per S/S (FTE)	(4x) E&G 20		
E&G,A&G,I,O&M,L per S/S (FTE)	(4x) E&G A&G I O&M L CU 41 63 29 26 38 BC 25 38 16 14 24 CC 18 53 (4) 31 18	CC—DD (E&G)	
A&G per S/S (FTE)	(4x) 23		

(continued)

Table 20.6   **(continued)**

(1) ID NO.	(2) AUTHOR, YEAR	(3/4) DATA YEAR/ POPULATION	(5/6) PUBLICATION SOURCE/STUDY TYPE	(7/8) DATA SOURCE/ LEVEL OF ANALYSIS	(9/10) TYPE OF CONTROL/ STATISTICS
30	Millett, 1980	1977–1978/18 P CC in MN	R/CS	State/I	IC,IT/Descriptive
31	Mullen, 1981	1976–1977/900 P CC	D/CS	NCES (HEGIS)/I	IT,IS/Regression
32	NFCUBOA, 1955	1953–1954/60 LA	R/CS	AS/I	IT,IS/Descriptive
33	NFCUBOA, 1960	1957–1958/56 LA	R/CS	AS/I	IT,IS/Descriptive
34	Razin & Campbell, 1972	1964–1965—1968–1969/ 1 P RU	J/TS,CS	Institution	IT,IS,SL/Regression
35	Reeves, Russell, Gregg, Brumbaugh, & Blauch, 1932	1929–1930/34 LA	B/CS	AS/I	IT,IS/Descriptive
36	Russell & Doi, 1955	1954–1955/6 P CU&BC in NM	J/CS	State/I	IT,IS/Descriptive
37	Russell & Reeves, 1935	1930–1931/44 P&I DU& CU&BC&LA&CC	B/CS	AS/I	Q/Correlation
38	Shymoniak & McIntyre, 1980	1978–1979/69 P CC districts in CA	R/TC,CS	State/District	IT,IS/Regression
39	Tierney, 1980a	1972–1973—1975–1976/ 31 LA	J/TS; CS	AS/D	IT,IS,Q/Regression
40	Wallhaus, 1981	1978–1979/38 P CC in IL	R/CS	State/I	IT,IS/Correction

Table 20.6 (continued)

(11/12) COST SPECIFICATION/ SCALE SPECIFICATION	(13) % DECREASE IN AC	(14/15) SHAPE OF LAC CURVE MC[:]AC	(16/17) BREAKPOINT/ESTIMATED COEFFICIENT
E&G per S/S (FTE)	(4x) 30		E&G—1,000 FTES I—600 to 800 A—2,000 O&M—1,000 L—1,200 to 1,500
Various categories in E&G, total and per S/S (FTE)	(3x) (4x) E&G 22 35 I 18 32 A&G 26 37 O&M 22 32 L 30 47	DD^q	(R)^r
E&G,A,I,O&M,L per S/S (FTE)	(3x) E&G 17^s 36^t I 23 15 A&G 41 52 O&M 33 38 L 7 20		
E&G,A,I,O&M,L per S/S (FTE)	(3x) E&G (2)^s 11^t I 0 5 A&G 30 31 O&M 29 19 L (26) (4)		
Faculty salaries/SCH	(3x) 28^u (4x) 34^u		
Educational, noneducational per S/S (FT)	(4x) Educ. 12 Noneduc. 50		
A per S/S (FTE)	(4x) 34	L^v	1,000 FTES (C) T per S w S = −.426^w (Sig) (C) T per S w S = −.08 (NSig)
T,E&G,I per S/S (FTE)			3,000 ADA
T, various categories in E&G per U/ADA,SHC, FHC,Plant sq. ft.		I per ADA .90 SS per SHC .64 A per SHC .72 T per ADA .85 O&M per sq. ft. .86	
Direct cost by department/ S (FTE,W)		U Bio .10 Phil .23 Chem .32 Gov .48 Engl .54 Psy .50 Math .40 Mean=.37	R^x
I,O&M per S/S (FTE)			(C) I per S w S = −.30 (C) O&M per S w S = −.33

Symbol key appears on next page

(continued)

KEY. *Symbols by column*

(4) RU = research university, DU = doctoral university, CU = comprehensive university, BC = baccalaureate college, LA = private liberal arts college, CC = community or junior college, P = public, I = independent.

(5) B = book, D = dissertation, J = journal, R = report

(6) CS = cross section, TS = time series

(7) S = survey, AS = author survey, O = other

(8) D = department, I = institution, P = program

(9) CC = curriculum content, CD = curriculum diversity, CL = cost of living, CS = class size, F = number of faculty, FL = faculty load, FS = faculty salaries or compensation, IS = institutional sector, IT = institutional type, Q = quality, RE = research expenditures, SD = student demographics, SF = student faculty ration, SL = student level

(11) A = administrative, A&G = administrative and general, E&G = educational and general, I = instructional, L = library, O&M = operation and maintenance of plant, per S = per student

(12) ADA = average daily attendance, FT = full-time, FTE = full-time equivalent, HC = headcount, S = student, SCH = student credit hours, W = weighted by student level, UW = unweighted by student level

(13) *nx* = midpoint of scale interval for large institutions is *n* times greater than midpoint for small institutions

(14) IU = inverted U, DC = decreasing at a constant rate, DD = decreasing at a decreasing rate, F = flat, L = rectangular hyperbola, S = sawtooth, U = U shape, LAC = long-run average cost

(15) AC = average cost, MC = marginal cost

(16) Breakpoint (BP) = scale level at which the bulk of economies of scale are typically realized

(17) C = simple correlation, PC = partial correlation, R = regression, w = with

NOTES. [a] Publics only, holding FS, CL, RE, CD, F and number of staff constant.

        [b] Marginal cost curves; thus BP for AC would come at somewhat higher enrollment levels in each instance.

        [c] Numerous regression coefficients on logarithmic transformations and higher order terms.

        [d] Values = $s per additional SCH.

        [e] AC declines .3% for each 1% increase in SCH.

        ID No. 06: Coefficient on S not significant for zoology and English department equations.

        [f] AC declines $213 or $164 for each additional PhD student in department.

        [g] By curriculum.

        [h] E&G revenue per student declines by $.28 for each additional student.

        ID No. 09: Data are for "least cost" institutions only.

        ID No. 10: Percentages are based on unweighted enrollment figures.

        ID No. 11: Curves and breakpoints reflect behavior of E&G expenditures.

        ID No. 12: Percentages are based on credit enrollments.

        [i] AC increases (decreases) by $.05, $.01, $.03, $.05, $.28, $.01, or $.54 for each additional student enrolled.

        ID No. 14: Percentages are based on credit enrollments.

        ID No. 16: Percentages are based on credit enrollments.

        [j] AC declines by $.06, $.64, or $.35 for each additional student enrolled.

        [k] Very shallow after initial sharp decline.

        ID No. 21: Various equations with alternative dependent variables and controlling for CD and SD; little evidence of scale-related economies or disceconomies, except for individual curricula.

        [l] AC declines $.27 or $.03 for each additional student enrolled.

        ID No. 25: 2.89x = growth in FTE enrollment over 5 years.

        [m] Authors' interpretation.

        [n] Authors' estimated function.

        [o] Across 13 states.

        [p] Average for 2 states.

        [q] For all expenditure categories.

        [r] Various regression estimates with logarithmic and higher-order terms.

        [s] Median expenditure

        [t] Mean expenditures.

        [u] ID No. 34: Implied by MC:AC.

        [v] For various expenditures.

        [w] S < 1,200.

        [x] Various regression coefficients on first and second order FTES, by department.

p.20.36

CHB 4

Table 20.6a   Average Cost Associationed with Threefold to Fourfold Increases in Enrollment[a]

EXPENDITURE TYPE[b]	2-Year Institutions				4-Year Institutions			
	E & G	A	I	O & M	E & G	A	I	O & M
Minimum	17	22	(4)	12	(2)	23	0	14
Maximum	35	65	32	34	41	63	29	51
Mean	24	38	12	24	26	40	16	28
Median	23	30	15	25	27	41	19	26
Standard deviation	6.6	15.1	11.8	7.6	12.2	10.9	9.8	10.2
n	8	9	9	9	14	17	16	14

[a] Supplementary data on the results of the economy-of-scale studies in Table 20.6.
[b] E & G = educational and general; A = administrative; I = instruction; O & M = operation and maintenance of the plant.

and −.33 for enrollment correlated with instructional unit costs and unit costs for plant operation and maintenance, respectively, with no controls, whereas Cage and Manatt (1969) report a coefficient of −.72 for the correlation of enrollment with total contact hour costs per student by curriculum. Similarly, Jordan (1965) found no statistically significant correlation between enrollment and total current expenditures per student until he did a partial correlation holding the number of semester hours per section constant, which then yielded a correlation of −.65.

Only two studies estimated the difference between average and marginal costs (per one additional or fewer student), but the findings are in accord with those from the interval studies. Shymoniak and McIntyre (1980) report average costs exceeded marginal costs by 28, 15, 14, and 10 percent for administrative, plant operation and maintenance, educational and general, and instructional expenditures, respectively. The figure for instruction is identical to that found by Brinkman (1981b). Of course, the more that average costs exceed marginal costs, the greater the potential for economies of scale. These findings, then, appear to confirm that at least the relative magnitude for the percentage decreases mentioned earlier can be taken seriously.

It is clear that the long-run average-cost curve for the typical, small 2-year institution declines as enrollment becomes larger. The various studies also agree that the curve stops declining at some point. There is less agreement about what happens to unit costs at the largest institutions. The results of several studies (Bowen, 1980; Dickmeyer, 1980; Dukiet, 1974; Maynard, 1971; and Mullen, 1981) suggest that educational (or, more narrowly, instructional) unit costs probably do begin to rise again, but other studies (Brinkman, 1981b; Carlson, 1972; Cirino & Dickmeyer, 1981; Dickmeyer & Cirino, 1982) found no such increase. Apparently, if unit costs in one or more areas do tend to increase as institutions reach the upper end of the enrollment range, the increases are quite small, at least in comparison to the scale-related cost phenomenon at the other end of the enrollment range.

4-Year Colleges

The pattern of scale-related economies for 4-year institutions (excluding large, research-oriented universities) resembles that for 2-year institutions. The majority of data points, 14 to 17 depending on the expenditure category, are again based on interval studies and the conversion of regression results to interval data.

Again, economies of scale are most dramatic for administrative expenditures. In association with a three- to fourfold increase in enrollment, the average percentage decrease in administrative cost per student was 40 percent. The 40-percent figure is just two points higher than the figure for 2-year colleges; the corresponding drop in educational and general expenditures per student was 26 percent, or one percentage point higher than in 2-year colleges. For instructional expenditures per student, the reported decline averaged 16 percent. The corresponding figure for plant operation and maintenance was 28 percent.

Of the two types of 4-year institutions investigated, the liberal arts colleges appear to have achieved most of their scale-related economies by the time enrollment reaches 1,500 to 2,000 FTE students. By contrast, the more comprehensive colleges appear to reach that same breakpoint at the 2,700- to 3,000-student level. There were only a total of 10 data points in all, however, so these figures cannot be taken with a great deal of assurance.

Similarly, there were few regression coefficients or marginal- to average-cost ratios. Some of the findings are worth a brief comment, however. Using different samples of liberal arts colleges, Corrallo (1970) and Calkins (1963) estimated identical coefficients, −.28, regressing educational and general expenditures per student on enrollment, with several different control variables present in their respective models. These coefficients can be interpreted as meaning that over some range of enrollment about the mean, average costs per student decline $.28 when an additional student enrolls. In a much older study, Magee (1931) regressed instructional expenditures on student credit hours. With no controls in the equation, the estimated coefficient on student credit hours was −.24, whereas when holding curriculum diversity constant, the estimate jumped to −.64. The direction and magnitude of the changes are similar to those reported by Jordan (1965) for 2-year colleges. It is apparent, again, that institutions that become larger but not more complex are quite likely to realize far greater economies of scale than those that do become more complex as they grow in size. (More evidence to this effect can be found in Blau, 1973; Brinkman, 1981a; and McLauglin et al., 1980).

The ratio of marginal costs to average costs for instructional expenditures at public comprehensive and baccalaureate institutions was estimated by Brinkman (1981b) to be about .83 at mean enrollment. In Tierney's (1980a) study of private liberal arts colleges, however, marginal costs averaged only 37 percent of average costs across seven departments, suggesting the opportunity for much larger scale-related economies. A substantial difference in the ratio of marginal costs to average costs between public and private institutions would not be surprising. Being smaller typically, private institutions are in that portion of the enrollment range where marginal costs and average costs are more likely to differ widely. In addition, many public institutions are funded using formulas that are based on historical average cost. Public institutions will find ways of spending the funds received, regardless of the "true" marginal cost of additional students. As a result, the difference between marginal cost and average costs will be less when, as is usually the case, the estimate is made on the basis of actual expenditures. More importantly, however, is that Tierney (1980a) analyzed departmental rather than institutional cost-size behavior. In so doing, he eliminated much of the curriculum proliferation that typically negates scale-related economies. Thus, his estimates of marginal costs to average costs should be lower than estimates based on institutionwide performance, and indeed they were.

Apart from rapidly declining costs in the very low enrollment range, the evidence regarding the shape of the average cost curve is inconclusive. The findings of some studies such as Bowen (1980), Jenny and Wynn (1970), Maynard (1971), and Tierney (1980a) suggest that relatively large 4-year institutions experience higher unit costs than midsized institutions; in other words, the cost curve is somewhat U-shaped. Other studies, such as Brinkman (1981b), Carlson (1972), Metz (1964), and Reeves, Russell, Gregg, Brumbagh, and Blauch (1932) suggest that after its initial decline the average cost curve tends to remain flat as institutions become larger. In the Carnegie Commission study (1972), the largest institutions typically did not have the lowest costs per student across the various expenditure categories, but there was no clear cost-size relationship evident for size levels beyond the middle ranges. Similarly, Bowen (1980) found that among liberal arts colleges and public comprehensive institutions, the interval containing the second largest institutions recorded the lowest educational costs per student, whereas for private comprehensive institutions the largest institutions experienced the lowest unit costs.

Universities

Few data points are available to assess the relationship between size and cost at research universities. Although 16 studies were found that dealt with the issue empirically, only a portion of them provided usable results. Of the studies that did, virtually none addressed the same aspects of the basic issue. In addition, research universities present a more difficult subject to analyze. They tend to engage in diverse activities, not all of which relate to enrollment. The research component of educational and general expenditures, for example, is substantial, but it bears no direct relationship to the number of students enrolled.

Consequently, studies providing data on these expenditures per student but not controlling for the research component are of questionable value. Also, from a cost perspective the range of students is very great. Doctoral students are far more expensive to educate than are lower-division graduates. The issue is important for studies that purport to isolate the effects of scale on costs.

With these caveats in mind, it can be said that the preponderance of the available evidence supports the view that universities do achieve economies of scale. Some of those economies seem to be of roughly the same magnitude as in other 4-year institutions. Three regression studies (Brovender, 1974; Buckles, 1978; Razin & Campbell, 1972), each focused at the department or college level (within a university), provide five usable data points. Upon conversion to interval data, they suggest that on average a 26-percent decrease in instructional expenditures accompanies a fourfold increase in student credit hours. That figure is somewhat higher than the average of 16 percent reported for 4-year institutions. The difference is probably due to the unit of analysis. As noted earlier, by focusing at the department level or even at the college level, much of the curriculum proliferation that negates scale economies is effectively eliminated (but presumably less so at the college level). Put another way, these studies come closer to addressing the question of the "pure" influence of increases in scale on unit costs than do the typical interval studies or the uncontrolled regression studies at the institutional level.

Only one usable data point was found for administrative expenditures. Data in the Carnegie Commission study (1972) show a 43-percent drop in expenditures per student, for a fourfold difference in FTE enrollment at private research universities, a figure quite close to the averages of 40 and 38 percent mentioned above for 4-year and 2-year institutions, respectively. The same study yielded a figure of 43 percent for plant operations and maintenance, a value considerably higher than the corresponding averages for the other types of institutions.

An earlier Carnegie Commission report (1971) suggested 5,000 FTE students as a minimum level for all doctoral institutions, which includes research universities but also a number of typically smaller institutions. Corrallo's (1970) data indicate that lower unit costs are achieved by research universities at enrollment levels between 6,000 to 10,000 and 14,000 to 18,000. In analyzing instructional costs per student at three levels of enrollment in public research universities, Brinkman (1981b) found that the marginal cost curves, after descending rapidly in association with increasing enrollments, tended to flatten out at about

4,000 lower-division students, 6,000 upper-division students, and 6,000 graduate students (FTE). Since average costs follow marginal costs, these data suggest that an economical size for a research university is at least 16,000 FTE students, depending on the mix of students. No data were found to indicate that unit costs at research universities eventually increase at the highest enrollment levels. Because of the scarcity of studies, however, and the complexity of the institutions, the available data on these matters are at best suggestive.

Summary

The results of the research on economies of scale in higher education can be summarized as follows: (a) Colleges and universities do experience increasing returns to scale; (b) scale-related economies are most likely to occur at the low end of the enrollment range and usually are not found beyond average enrollment levels; (3) the enrollment range over which such economies are likely to be found differs by type of institution; (4) the extent of such economies differs by function, with the administrative area experiencing the greatest reduction in unit cost and instruction the least; and (5) the extent to which scale-related economies are in fact realized, especially in instruction, depends largely on institutional decisions regarding the scope of the programs and services they offer—expanding the offerings typically works against such economies. Needless to say, the last point suggests a course of action for institutions that are serious about restraining unit costs when enrollments decline.

SUMMARY AND CONCLUSION

The urgent financial questions of the day go back to the 1970s and earlier. A perennial question concerns the economic value of higher education to the individuals and to society. The most fundamental question relates to the potential for money—the overwhelmingly favored instrument of public intervention—to effect the kinds of public policy changes desired. It has always been assumed that money—directly, "price"—is an important determinant of student enrollment behavior. Historically, low tuition policies are a reflection of that assumption. Since the early 1970s, however, interest has been focused on fine-tuning the form of the money subsidy. Specifically, is student aid an effective way to deliver the public support?

This chapter addressed these questions through integrative review techniques, including meta-analysis. Integrative reviewing attempts to synthesize existing research rather than merely cite findings; meta-analysis is the final extension of integrative reviewing, whereby study results are synthesized quantitatively.

The student-demand studies are unanimous in demonstrating that students respond negatively to price: As would be expected, enrollments decline as prices are raised. Demand theory, which has been shown to apply to higher education, holds that the quantity (rate) of goods or services demanded will be a function of price, the money income of the buyer, competitor prices, and buyer tastes or preferences. Thus it is not surprising that the enrollment rate for 18- to 24-year-old, first-time students declines by about 0.6 or 0.7 percentage points for every $100 price increase, measured in 1982–1983 dollars. Student response to price, on average, is less in private institutions and more in community colleges, being perhaps 0.4 or 0.5 in the former and about 0.9 in the latter. Since the participation rate for 18- to 24-year-olds is approximately one-third, first-time enrollments would decline by roughly 2 percent per $100 price rise. This effect is not observed direclty, however, because the other demand factors, especially the increasing numbers of women and older students pursuing higher education, mask the price effect.

The rate-of-return studies show clearly that higher education pays off handsomely for students and for society, even taking into account the limitations of these studies. Both private and social rates of return to the BA degree are of the order of 11 to 12 percent, comparing favorably to benchmark investment rates. Rates of return on graduate education are somewhat less but probably represent sound investments when subsidies and nonmonetary benefits are considered. Although returns on higher education probably declined during the 1970s, rates now appear to be at or near historic levels. Changes in rates over time seem clearly to reflect both the business cycle and the changing size of graduating cohorts (i.e., insertion of highly educated persons into the labor supply).

Rate-of-return studies are limited methodologically and conceptually, and numerous popular misconceptions may result. Most importantly, rates of return are more a reflection of cost variations than of variations in benefits; hence, if the return to higher education is judged to be small, it may be raised by increasing public subsidies. From realization of the importance of cost, it follows that accuracy in cost estimation is crucial to valid rate-of-return studies. Costs of higher education often are overstated, causing reported rate-of-return estimates to be inaccurately low. It is most important to realize that students generally do not pay all their own costs of higher education and that true rates are thus considerably higher than popularly believed. On the benefits side, the entire nonmonetary component is ignored in conventional rate-of-return studies, also contributing to downward-biased estimates. True rates of return to higher education may be of the order of 20 percent or even more.

Although higher education has been criticized in the literature as contributing to wealth redistribution from poor to rich, the reality probably is the reverse. That is, considering by income level the private sources of the tax money that supports higher education in relation to higher education enrollments by income level, the weight of the evidence is that some modest redistribution of wealth from rich to poor results. However, the middle class probably is the major beneficiary when the cost-benefit calculus is examined on this limited basis.

In regard to the most recent major direction for financial policy, student aid seems clearly to contribute to social equity and equality of opportunity. Our preliminary review of works in this area suggests that student aid contributes to access to college (that is, the opportunity to enroll); quite considerably to choice of college (that is, the ability to enroll in higher priced institutions); and roughly equalizes the ability to continue in college and eventually receive a degree.

Finally, we have examined the research relating cost to scale. The question is, does efficiency increase with increases in the size of institutions of higher education? The answer, in a word, is yes. This is an important question as such institutions are faced with the public's growing reluctance to maintain support levels for higher education and institutional leaders' presumptions that growth in enrollments will ameliorate, if not solve, financial problems. Viewing colleges and universities on the basis of three- to fourfold differences in enrollments, it appears clear that among 2-year colleges, most overall scale economies are realized by the time institutions reach a 1,000 to 1,500 FTE enrollment size, with the breakpoint occuring a little earlier for instructional efficiency and a little later for administrative efficiency. Potential economies of scale are greatest in the administrative area. For 4-year schools, the potential economies appear to have been achieved at about 1,500 to 2,000 FTE for liberal arts colleges and at perhaps 2,700 to 3,000 for comprehensive colleges. Administrative economies, again, appear easiest to achieve and potentially are the largest. For universities, economies of scale are achievable and probably are similar in size to those for 4-year colleges, but the evidence is more sporadic. Efficient enrollment sizes for universities may be approximately 5,000 FTE for doctoral-granting institutions and 6,000 to 10,000 for research universities. Overall, institutions can achieve greater efficiency through larger size, but the threshold

of efficient enrollment size is perhaps surprisingly low.

These are only a few of the important questions regarding the financing of American higher education, but we believe they are some of the most vital ones. We have selected questions upon which there has been sufficient empirical work to construct an integrative review. The degree to which we have been able to fulfill this selection criterion lends some support to the notion that these questions are crucial.

NOTES

[1] The chapter does not pretend to perform classical meta-analysis. Most meta-analytical strategies are employed where feasible; however, instead of performing hypothesis testing, results simply are rendered comparable whenever it is practical to do so.

[2] Due to time and resource constraints, only the student demand, the economy of scale, and to a lesser degree the rate of return studies employ techniques that truly approach meta-analysis.

[3] One remaining problem is that studies may report results for an entire market system of institutions or for a single institution, and the effects of competitors' prices may be explicit in the first case and implicit in the latter; hence, the degree of explicit control of other variables may be unknown.

[4] For a discussion see Becker, 1975, pp. 192–193, and Joy and Bradley, 1973, p. 1255.

[5] Psacharopoulos's (1973) summary from fewer studies sets the MA and PhD private IRR at 7.5 percent and 9.1 percent, respectively (p. 71). His private and social RR estimates for the BA are 13.6 and 9.7 percent, thus bracketing the 11.8 and 11.4 percent figures reported here.

[6] Dresch (1980) discusses the reasons Freeman's estimates are biased downward.

[7] Miller (1960) argues that it is primarily unemployment, not cohort size, that explains IRR differences over time; Smith and Welch (1978a) are more convincing that cohort size is the major factor. Rosen and Taubman (1982) have taken the most recent look at this important question and concluded that cohort size is not as important as previously thought. They include a discussion of other studies on the subject.

[8] Carnoy and Marenback (1975) found stable IRRs for college graduates between 1939 and 1969, a finding reported earlier by Welch (1970). Bartlett (1978) found that the decline for *all* workers reported between 1939 and 1969 was due entirely to declines between 1939 and 1949, a period marked by the end of the Great Depression, World War II, and the postwar recovery.

[9] Witmer (1980, pp. 114–115), for example, charges Freeman (1975b) with this error.

REFERENCES

American Association of State Colleges and Universities (1977, August 31). Wisconsin low tuition experiment ends: Tuitions up; enrollments down (Special report). Washington, DC: The Association.

Ashenfelter, O., & Ham, J. (1979). Education, unemployment, and earnings. *Journal of Political Economy, 87*, (5, part 2), S99–116.

Ashenfelter, O., & Mooney, J. (1968). Graduate education, ability, and earnings. *Review of Economics and Statistics, 50*, 78–86.

Ashenfelter, O., & Mooney, J. (1969). Some evidence on the private returns to graduate education. *Southern Economic Journal, 35*, 247–256.

Astin, A. W. (1975). *Preventing students from dropping out.* San Francisco: Jossey-Bass.

Bailey, M. J. (1959). Formal criteria for investment decisions. *Journal of Political Economy, 67*, 476–488.

Bailey, D., & Schotta, C. (1972). Private and social rates of return to education of academicians. *American Economic Review, 62,* 19–31.

Barnes, G. W. (1975, June). *Extension of the college-going/college-choice model to the NLS class of 1971 data* (HEW–ASPE Contract OS–74–154, pp. 71–79). Washington, DC: Inner City Fund, Inc.

Bartlett, S. (1978). Education, experience and wage inequality: 1939–1969. *Journal of Human Resources, 13,* 349–365.

Beaton, A. (1975). The influence of education and ability on salary and attitudes. In F. T. Juster (Ed.), *Education, income and human behavior* (pp. 365–404). New York: McGraw-Hill.

Becker, G. S. (1975). *Human capital, a theoretical and empirical analysis with special reference to education* (2nd ed.). New York: National Bureau of Economic Research.

Becker, G. S., & Chiswick, B. (1966). The economics of education: Education and the distribution of earnings. *American Economic Review, 56,* 358–369.

Belanger, C. H., & Lavalée, L. *Economic returns to schooling decisions.* Montreal: Université de Montreal, Office of Institutional Research.

Berg, I. (1981). The effects of inflation on and in higher education. *Annals of American Academy of Political and Social Sciences, 456,* 99–111.

Bergen, M. B., & Zielke, D. D. (1979). Educational progress of basic educational opportunity grant recipients compared to non-recipients. *Journal of Student Financial Aid, 9,* 19–22.

Berne, R. (1980). Net price effects on two-year college attendance decisions. *Journal of Education Finance, 5,* 391–414.

Bishop, J. (1977). The effect of public policies on the demand for higher education. *Journal of Human Resources, 12,* 285–307.

Bishop, J., & VanDyk, J. (1977). Can adults be hooked on college? *Journal of Higher Education, 48,* 39–62.

Blanchfield, W. C. (1971). College dropout identification: A case study. *Journal of Experimental Education, 40,* 1–4.

Blau, P. M. (1973). *The organization of academic work.* New York: John Wiley.

Bowen, H. R. (1980). *The costs of higher education: How much do colleges and universities spend per student and how much should they spend?* San Francisco: Jossey-Bass.

Bowen, H. R. (1982). *The costs of higher education.* San Francisco: Jossey-Bass.

Brinkman, P. T. (1981a). Factors affecting instructional costs at major research universities. *Journal of Higher Education, 52,* 265–279.

Brinkman, P. T. (1981b). *Marginal costs of instruction in public higher education.* Unpublished doctoral dissertation, University of Arizona, Tucson.

Broomall, L. W., Mahan, B. T., McLaughlin, G. W., & Patton, S. S. (1978). *Economies of scale in higher education.* Blacksburg, VA: Virginia Polytechnic Institute and State University, Office of Institutional Research. (ERIC Document Reproduction Service No. ED 162 604)

Brovender, S. (1974). On the economics of a university: Toward the determination of marginal cost of teaching services. *Journal of Political Economy, 82,* 657–664.

Buckles, S. (1978). Identification of causes of increasing costs in higher education. *Southern Economic Journal, 45,* 248–265.

Butter, I. H. (1966). *Economics of graduate education: An exploratory study.* Ann Arbor, MI: University of Michigan Department of Economics. (ERIC Document Reproduction Service No. ED 010 639)

Cage, B. N., & Manatt, R. D. (1969). Cost analysis of selected educational programs in the community colleges of Iowa. *Journal of Educational Research, 63,* 366–370.

California Coordinating Council for Higher Education. (1969). *Meeting the enrollment demand for public higher education in California through 1977—The need for additional college and university campuses.* Sacramento, CA: The Council.

California State Postsecondary Education Commission. (1982). *Background papers on student charges, student financial aid, and access to postsecondary education.* Sacramento, CA: The Commission. (ERIC Document Reproduction Service No. ED 216 725)

Calkins, R. N. (1963). *The unit costs of programmes in higher education.* Unpublished doctoral dissertation, Columbia University, New York City.

Campbell, R., & Siegel, B. (1967). The demand for higher education in the United States 1919–1964. *American Economic Review, 57,* 482–494.

Carlson, D. E. (1972). *The production and cost behavior of higher education institutions.* Berkeley, CA: University of California, Ford Foundation Program for Research in University Administration. (ERIC Document Reproduction Service No. ED 081 375)

Carlson, D. E. (1975). *A flow of funds model for assessing the impact of alternative student aid programs.* Stanford, CA: Stanford Research Institute. (ERIC Document Reproduction Service No. ED 123 992)

Carlson, D. E., Farmer, J., & Weathersby, G. (1974). *A framework for analyzing postsecondary education financing policies.* Washington, DC: U.S. Government Printing Office. (ERIC Document Reproduction Service No. ED 093 207)

Carnegie Commission on Higher Education. (1971). *New students and new places.* New York: McGraw-Hill.

Carnegie Commission on Higher Education. (1972). *The more effective use of resources.* New York: McGraw-Hill.

Carnoy, M., & Marenbach, D. (1975). The return to schooling in the United States, 1939 to 1969. *Journal of Human Resources, 10,* 312–331.

Chapman, R. (1979). Pricing policy and the college choice process. *Research in Higher Education. 10,* 37–57.

Chisholm, M., & Cohen, B. (1982). *A review and introduction to higher education price response studies.* Boulder, CO: National Center for Higher Education Management Systems.

Cirino, A. M., & Dickmeyer, N. (1981). *Comparative financial statistics for public community and junior colleges, 1979–80.* Washington, DC: National Association of College and University Business Officers.

Cline, H. (1982). The measurement of change in the rate of return to education: 1967–75. *Economics of Education Review, 2,* 275–293.

Clotfelter, C. T. (1976). Public spending for higher education: An empirical test of two hypotheses. *Public Finance, 31,* 177–195.

Cohn, E. (1972). Investment criteria and the ranking of educational investments. *Public Finance, 27,* 355–360.

Cohn, E., & Morgan, J. (1978). The demand for higher education. *Higher Education Review, 1,* 18–30.

Cope, R. G. (1978). Why students stay, why they leave. In L. Noel, (Ed.), *Reducing the dropout rate: New directions for student services,* (pp. 1–11). San Francisco: Jossey-Bass.

Corazzini, A. J., Dugan, D. J., & Grabowski, H. G. (1972). Determinants and distributional aspects of enrollment in U.S. higher education. *Journal of Human Resources, 7,* 39–59.

Corrallo, S. B. (1970). *An analysis of instructional expenditures for institutions of higher education in the northeast United States.* Unpublished doctoral dissertation, State University of New York at Buffalo.

Crary, L. J., & Leslie, L. L. (1978). The private costs of postsecondary education. *Journal of Education Finance, 4,* 14–28.

Crawford, N. C., Jr. (1966). *Effects of offers of financial assistance on the college-going decisions of talented students with limited financial means.* Evanston, IL: National Merit Scholarship Corporation. (ERIC Document Reproduction Service No. ED 017 000)

Crean, J. (1975). The income redistributive effects of public spending on higher education. *Journal of Human Resources, 10,* 116–123.

Curtis, T. D., & Campbell, J., Jr. (1978). Investment in graduate human capital: An evaluation of rate of return approach. *Review of Business and Economics Research, 14,* 74–89.

Davis, J. (1964). *Great aspirations.* Chicago: Aldine.

Denison, E. F. (1962). The source of economic growth in the United States and the alternatives before us. (Supplementary Paper No. 13). New York: Committee for Economic Development.

Denison, E. F. (1964). Measuring the contribution of education, and the residual, to economic growth. *The residual factor and economic growth*. Paris: Organization for Economic Cooperation and Development.

Dickmeyer, N. (1980). *Comparative financial statistics for community and junior colleges, 1978–1979*. Washington, DC: National Association of College and University Business Officers.

Dickmeyer, N. (1982). Small independent colleges and economies of scale. *Research in Higher Education*. *17*, 51–67.

Dickmeyer, N., & Cirino, A. M. (1982). *Comparative financial statistics for public community and junior colleges 1980–81*. Washington, DC: National Association of College and University Business Officers.

Dougherty, D., & Psacharopoulos, G. (1977). Measuring the cost of misallocation of investment in education. *Journal of Human Resources*, *12*, 446–459.

Dresch, S. (1980). *Deflating, discounting and the returns to schooling: Clarifying the Schwartz-Thornton vs. Freeman "debate."* New Haven, CT: Yale Institute for Demographic and Economic Studies.

Dukiet, K. (1974). The cost of higher education 1973–74. *College Management*, *9*, 8–18.

Duncan, G. J. (1976). Earnings function and nonpecuniary benefits. *Journal of Human Resources*, *11*, 462–483.

Dunn, L. P. (1977). Quantifying nonpecuniary returns. *Journal of Human Resources*, *12*, 347–359.

Eckaus, R. S. (1973). *Estimating the returns to education: A disaggregated approach*. Berkeley, CA: Carnegie Commission on Higher Education.

Erlich, I. (1975). On the relation between education and crime. In F. T. Juster (Ed.), *Education, income and human behavior* (pp. 313–338). New York: McGraw-Hill.

Fenske, R. H., Boyd, J. D., & Maxey, E. J. (1979). State financial aid to students: A trend analysis of access and choice of public or private colleges. *College and University*, *54*, 139–155.

Fields, C. R., & LeMay, M. L. (1973). Student financial aid: Effects on educational decisions and academic achievement. *Journal of College Student Personnel*, *14*, 425–429.

Fife, J. D., & Leslie, L. L. (1976). The college student grant study: The effectiveness of student grant and scholarship programs in promoting equal educational opportunity. *Research in Higher Education*, *4*, 317–333.

Freeman, R. (1975a). Legal "cobwebs": A recursive model of the market for new lawyers. *Review of Economics and Statistics*, *57*, 171–179.

Freeman, R. (1975b). Overinvestment in college training. *Journal of Human Resources*, *10*, 287–311.

Freeman, R. (1975c). Supply and salary adjustments to the changing science manpower market: Physics, 1948–1973. *American Economic Review*, *65*, 27–39.

Freeman, R. (1977). Decline in economic rewards to college education. *Review of Economics and Statistics*, *59*, 18–29.

Freeman, R. (1979). The effect of demographic factors on age-earnings profiles. *Journal of Human Resources*, *14*, 289–317.

Freeman, R. (1980). The facts about the declining economic value of college. *Journal of Human Resources*, *15*, 124–142.

Freeman, R., & Holloman, J. (1975). The declining value of college going. *Change*, *7*, 24–31, 62.

Freiden, A., & Leimer, D. (1981). The earnings of college students. *Journal of Human Resources*, *16*, 152–156.

Funk, H. J. (1972). Price elasticity of demand for education at a private university. *Journal of Educational Research*, *66*, 130–134.

Garfinkel, I., & Haveman, R. (1977). *Earnings capacity, poverty, and inequality*. Institute for Research on Poverty Monograph. New York: Academic Press.

Ghali, M., Miklius, W., & Wada, R. (1977). The demand for higher education facing an individual institution. *Higher Education, 6*, 477–487.

Glass, G. V., McGaw, B., & Smith, M. L. (1981). *Meta-analysis in social research*. Beverly Hills, CA: Sage.

Golladay, M. A., & Noell, J. (1978). *The condition of education* (1978 ed.). Statistical Report of the National Center for Education Statistics. Washington, DC: U.S. Government Printing Office.

Gorman, J. (1967). *The Gorman report*. Phoenix, AZ: Continuing Education Institute.

Greer, C. R. (1976). Returns to investments in undergraduate education by race and sex in 1960 and 1970. *Review of Business and Economic Research*, *12*, 57–68.

Grossman, M. (1976). The correlation between health and schooling. In N. Terleckyj (Ed.), *Household production and consumption* (pp. 147–211). New York: Columbia University Press for The National Bureau of Economic Research.

Grossman, M. (1982). *Determinants of children's health*. (Report PHS 81–3309). Washington, DC: National Center for Health Services. (NTIS P380–163603)

Hanoch, G. (1967). An economic analysis of earnings and schooling. *Journal of Human Resources*, *2*, 310–329.

Hansen, W. L. (1963). Total and private rates of return to investment in schooling. *Journal of Political Economy*, *71*, 128–140.

Hansen, W. L. (1970). Income distribution effects of higher education. *American Economic Review*, *60*, 335–340.

Hansen, W. L. (1982). *Economic growth and equal opportunity: Conflicting or complementary goals in higher education*. Unpublished manuscript, University of Wisconsin, Department of Economics, Madison. (ERIC Document Reproduction Service No. ED 227 761)

Hansen, W. L., & Weisbrod, B. A. (1969). The distribution of costs and direct benefits of public higher education: The case of California. *Journal of Human Resources*, *4*, 176–191.

Hartman, R. W. (1970). A comment on the Pechman-Hansen-Weisbrod controversy. *Journal of Human Resources*, *5*, 519–523.

Hartman, R. W. (1972). Equity implications of state tuition policy and student loans. *Journal of Political Economy*, *80*, S142–171.

Hight, J. E. (1975). The demand for higher education in the United States 1927–1972: The public and private institutions. *Journal of Human Resources*, *10*, 512–520.

Hight J. E., & Pollock, R. (1973). Income distribution effects of higher education expenditures in California, Florida, and Hawaii. *Journal of Human Resources*, *8*, 318–330.

Hirshleifer, J. (1958). On the theory of optimal investment decision. *Journal of Political Economy*, *66*, 329–352.

Hochstein, S. K., & Butler, R. R. (1983). The effects of the composition of a financial aids package on student retention. *Journal of Student Financial Aid*, *13*, 21–26.

Hoenack, S. A. (1968). Private demand for higher education in California (Doctoral dissertation, University of California, Berkeley, 1967). *Dissertation Abstracts International*, *29*, 18A.

Hoenack, S., & Feldman, P. (1969). *Private demand for higher education in the U.S.* Arlington, VA: Institute for Defense Analysis.

Hoenack, S., & Weiler, W. (1975). Cost-related tuition policies and university enrollments. *Journal of Human Resources*, *10*, 332–360.

Hopkins, T. D. (1974). Higher education enrollment demand. *Economic Inquiry*, *12*, 53–65.

Hungate, T. C., Meeth, R., & O'Connell, W. R., Jr. (1964). The quality and cost of liberal arts college programs. In E. J. McGrath (Ed.), *Cooperative Long Range Planning in Liberal Arts Colleges*. New York: Columbia University Press.

Hunt, S. J. (1963). Income determinants for college graduates and the return to educational investment. *Yale Economic Essays*, *3*, 305–358.

Hyde, W. D. (1978). *The effect of tuition and financial aid on access and choice in postsecondary education*. Denver, CO: Education Commission of the States. (ERIC Document Reproduction Service No. ED 153 541)

Iwai, S. I., & Churchill, W. D. (1982). College attrition and the financial support systems of students. *Research in Higher Education*, *17*, 105–113.

Jackson, G. A. (1978). Financial aid and student enrollment. *Journal of Higher Education*, *49*, 548–574.

Jackson, G. A., & Weathersby, G. B. (1975). Individual demand for higher education. *Journal of Higher Education*, *46*, 623–652.

Jackson, G. B. (1978). *Methods for reviewing and integrating research in the social sciences*. (Final Report to the National Science Foundation for Grant No. DIS 76–20309). Washington, DC: George Washington University, Social Research Group.

Jencks, C. (1968). Social stratification and higher education. *Harvard Educational Review*, *38*, 277–316.

Jenny, H. H., & Wynn, R. G. (1970). *The golden years: A study of income and expenditure growth and distribution of 48 private four year liberal arts colleges 1960–1968*. Wooster, OH: College of Wooster.

Jenny, H. H., & Wynn, R. G. (1972). *The turning point: A study of income and expenditure growth and distribution of 48 private four year liberal arts colleges 1960–1970*. Wooster, OH: College of Wooster.

Jensen, E. L. (1981). Student financial aid and persistence in college. *Journal of Higher Education*, *52*, 280–294.

Johnson, G. E., & Stafford, F. P. (1973). Social returns to quantity and quality of schooling. *Journal of Human Resources*, *8*, 139–155.

Jordan, T. E. (1965). *An exploration of the relationship among size, cost, and selected educational opportunities in certain Texas public junior colleges*. Unpublished doctoral dissertation, University of Houston.

Joy, O. M., & Bradley, J. O. (1973). A note on sensitivity analysis of rates of return. *Journal of Finance*, *28*, 1255–1261.

Judy, R. W. (1970). The income-redistributive effects of aid to higher education. In L. H. Officer & L. B. Smith (Eds.), *Canadian economic problems and policies* (pp. 302–317). Toronto: McGraw-Hill.

Kehoe, J. J. (1981). Migrational choice patterns in financial aid policy making. *Research in Higher Education*, *14*, 57–69.

Knapp, C. B., & Hansen, W. L. (1976). Earnings and individual variations in postschool human investment. *Journal of Political Economy*, *84*, 351–358.

Knudsen, O., & Servelle, P. (1978). The demand for higher education at private institutions of moderate selectivity. *American Economist*, *22*, 30–34.

Koch, J. V. (1972). Student choice of undergraduate major field of study and private internal rates of return. *Industrial and Labor Relations Review*, *26*, 680–685.

Kohen, A. I., Nestel, G., & Karmas, C. (1978). Factors affecting individual persistence rates in undergraduate college programs. *American Educational Research Journal*, *15*, 233–252.

Kohn, M., Manski, C., & Mundel, D. (1976). An empirical investigation of factors which influence college-going behavior. *Annals of Economic and Social Measures*, *5*, 391–419.

Kress, S. (1977). *Economies of scale and the form of expenditure functions in education*. Unpublished doctoral dissertation, University of California–Berkeley.

Lando, M. (1975). The interaction between health and education. *Social Security Bulletin*, *38*, 16–22.

Lehr, D., & Newton, J. (1978). Time series and cross-sectional investigations of the demand for higher education. *Economic Inquiry*, *16*, 411–422.

Leibowitz, A. (1974). Home investments in children. *Journal of Political Economy*, *82*, S111–131.

Leslie, L. L. (1977). *Higher education opportunity: A decade of progress*. (ERIC Research Report No. 3). Washington, DC: American Association for Higher Education.

Leslie, L. L. (1984). Changing patterns in student financing of higher education. *Journal of Higher Education*, *55*, 313–346.

Leslie, L. L., & Brinkman, P. T. (1980). Instructional cost at research universities. In L. L. Leslie & H. L. Otto, (Eds.), *Financing and budgeting postsecondary education in the 1980s*, Tucson: University of Arizona.

Leslie, L. L. & Brinkman, P. T. (1988). *The economic value of higher education*. New York: Macmillan.

Leslie, L. L., & Fife, J. D. (1974). The college student grant study: The enrollment and attendance impact of student grant and scholarship programs. *Journal of Higher Education*, *45*, 651–671.

Leslie, L. L., Johnson, G. P., & Carlson, J. (1977). The impact of need-based student aid upon the college attendance decision. *Journal of Education Finance*, *2*, 269–285.

Liberman, J. (1979). *The rate of return to schooling: 1958–1976* (Faculty Working Paper). Urbana, IL: University of Illinois, Department of Finance.

Link, C. R., & Ratledge, E. C. (1975). Social returns to quantity and quality of education: A further statement. *Journal of Human Resources*, *10*, 78–89.

Lucas, R. E. B. (1977). Hedonic wage equations and psychic wages in the returns to schooling. *American Economic Review*, *67*, 549–558.

Machlis, P. D. (1973). The distributional effects of public higher education in New York City. *Public Finance Quarterly*, *1*, 35–57.

Machovec, F. M. (1972). Public higher education in Colorado: Who pays the costs? Who receives the benefits? *Intermountain Economic Review*, *3*, 24–35.

Magee, H. J. (1931). *Unit costs of teachers' college and normal schools*. New York: Teachers College Press, Columbia University.

Marks, J. L. (1980). *Forces shaping the humanities in public two-year colleges*. Unpublished doctoral dissertation, University of Arizona, Tucson.

Mattila, J. P. (1982). Determinants of male school enrollments: A time series analysis. *Review of Economics and Statistics*, *64*, 242–251.

Maxwell, L. (1970). Some evidence on negative returns to graduate education. *Western Economic Journal*, *8*, 186–189.

Maynard, J. (1971). *Some microeconomics of higher education*. Lincoln: University of Nebraska Press.

McCreight, K., & LeMay, M. (1982). A longitudinal study of the achievement and persistence of students who received basic educational opportunity grants. *Journal of Student Financial Aid*, *12*, 11–15.

McDonald, M. B. (1980). Educational equity and the fiscal incidence of public education. *National Tax Journal*, *13*, 45–54.

McGuire, J. W. (1976). the distribution of subsidy to students in California public higher education. *Journal of Human Resources*, *11*, 343–353.

McLaughlin, G. W., Montgomery, J. R., Smith, A. W., & Broomall, L. W. (1980). Size and efficiency. *Research in Higher Education*, *12*, 53–66.

McMahon, W. W. (1976). Influences on investment by blacks in higher education. *American Economic Review*, *2*, 320–324.

McMahon, W. W. (1981). *Expected rates of return to education* (Faculty Working Paper No. 832). Urbana, IL: University of Illinois at Urbana-Champaign.

McMahon, W. W. (1982a). *Consumption benefits of education* (Faculty Working Paper No. 856). Urbana, IL: University of Illinois at Urbana-Champaign.

McMahon, W. W. (1982b). *Externalities in education* (Faculty Working Paper No. 877). Urbana, IL: University of Illinois at Urbana-Champaign.

McMahon, W. W., & Wagner, A. P. (1981). Expected returns to investment in higher education. *Journal of Human Resources*, *16*, 274–285.

McMahon, W. W., & Wagner, A. P. (1982). The monetary returns to education as partial social efficiency criteria. In W. W. McMahon & T. G. Geske (Eds.), *Financing Education: Overcoming inefficiency and inequity* (pp. 150–185). Urbana: University of Illinois Press.

McPherson, M. S. (1978). The demand for higher education. In D. W. Breneman & C. E. Finn, Jr. (Eds.), *Public policy and private higher education* (pp. 143–196). Washington, DC: Brookings Institution.

Meeth, R. L. (1975). *Quality education for less money*. San Francisco: Jossey-Bass.

Metz, G. E. (1964). *Current fund expenditures*. Atlanta: Commission on Colleges, Southern Association of Colleges and Schools.

Michael, R. T. (1975). Education and fertility. In F. T. Juster (Ed.), *Education, income and human behavior* (pp. 339–364). New

York: McGraw-Hill.

Michael, R. T. (1982). Measuring nonmonetary benefits of education. In W. W. McMahon & T. Geske (Eds.), *Financing education: Overcoming inefficiency and inequity* (pp. 119–149). Urbana: University of Illinois Press.

Miller, H. P. (1960). Annual and lifetime income in relation to education: 1939–1959. *American Economic Review, 50*, 962–986.

Millett, J. D. (1952). *Financing higher education in the United States*. New York: Columbia University Press.

Millett, J. D. (1980). *Report on enrollment and costs in the Minnesota community college system*. St. Paul, MN: Academy for Educational Development.

Mincer, J. (1958). Investments in human capital and personal income distribution. *Journal of Political Economy, 66*, 281–302.

Moore, G. A. (1982). Income redistribution from public higher education finance within relevant age cohorts. *Economics of Education Review, 2*, 175–187.

Mullen, J. K. (1982). Implications of tuition grants in higher education: The case of a prior need-based aid program. *Economics of Education Review, 2*, 49–65.

Mullen, J. M. (1981). *Minimum institutional size and resource requirements: An analysis of the economic factors for two year public colleges*. Unpublished doctoral dissertation, University of Virginia, Charlottesville.

Murdock, T. A. (1986). *The effect of financial aid on persistence in American higher education*. Unpublished doctoral dissertation, University of Arizona, Tucson.

National Federation of College and University Business Officers Association (NFCUBOA). (1955). *A study of income and expenditures in sixty colleges, years 1953–1957*. Washington, DC: The Federation.

National Federation of College and University Business Officers Association (NFCUBOA). (1960). *The sixty college study . . . a second look*. Washington, DC: The Federation.

Okachi, K. (1983). Analysis of economic returns to Japan's higher education and its application to educational financing. *Journal of Educational Finance, 9*, 185–212.

Orvis, C. C. (1975). The effects of distance on college attendance rates and a cost/benefit analysis of closing a Minnesota state college. (Doctoral dissertation, University of Minnesota, 1975). *Dissertation Abstracts International, 38*, 6244A.

Parsons, D. O. (1974). The cost of school time, forgone earnings, and human capital formation. *Journal of Political Economy, 82*, 251–266.

Pechman, J. A. (1970). The distributional effects of public higher education in California. *Journal of Human Resources, 5*, 361–370.

Peng, S. S., & Fetters, W. B. (1978). Variables involved in withdrawal during the first two years of college: Preliminary findings from the National Longitudinal Study of the High School Class of 1972. *American Educational Research Journal, 15*, 361–372.

Psacharopoulos, G. (1973). *Returns to education: An international comparison*. San Francisco: Jossey-Bass.

Radner, R. & Miller, L. S. (1970). Demand and supply in U.S. higher education: A progress report. *American Economic Review, 60*, 326–334.

Raymond, R., & Sesnowitz, M. (1975). The returns to investments in higher education: Some new evidence. *Journal of Human Resources, 10*, 139–154.

Razin, A., & Campbell, J. (1972). Internal allocation of university resources. *Western Economic Journal, 10*, 308–320.

Reed, R. H., & Miller, H. P. (1970). Some determinants of the variation in earnings for college men. *Journal of Human Resources, 5*, 177–190.

Reeves, F. W., Russell, J. D., Gregg, H. C., Brumbaugh, A. J., & Blauch, L. E. (1932). *The liberal arts college*. Chicago: University of Chicago Press.

Reichard, D. J. (1971). *Campus size: A selective review*. Atlanta: Southern Regional Education Board.

Ribich, T. L., & Murphy, J. L. (1975). The economic returns to increased educational spending. *Journal of Human Resources, 10*, 56–77.

Riccobono, J. A., & Dunteman, G. H. (1975). *National longitudinal study of the high school class of 1972: Preliminary analyses of student financial aid*. Washington, DC: National Center for Education Statistics. (ERIC Document Reproduction Service No. ED 170 303)

Rosen, S. (1975). Measuring the obsolescence of knowledge. In F. T. Juster (Ed.), *Education, income and human behavior* (pp. 199–234). New York: McGraw-Hill.

Rosen, S., & Taubman, P. (1982). Changes in life cycle earnings: What do Social Security data show? *Journal of Human Resources, 17*, 321–338.

Rumberger, R. W. (1980). The economic decline of college graduates: Fact or fallacy? *Journal of Human Resources, 15*, 99–112.

Russell, J. D., & Doi, J. I. (1955). Analysis of expenditures for administrative and general purposes. *College and University Business, 19*, 39–41.

Russell, J. D., & Reeves, F. W. (1935). *Finance. The evaluation of higher institutions* (Vol. 7). Chicago: University of Chicago Press.

Sanford, T. R. (1980). The effects of student aid on recent college graduates. *Research in Higher Education, 12*, 227–243.

Schwartz, E., & Thornton, R. (1980). Overinvestment in college training? *Journal of Human Resources, 15*, 121–123.

Schwartz, T. A., & Chronister, J. L. (1978). Meeting the intent of a state-funded student aid program: Test of an assessment model. *Journal of Student Financial Aid, 8*, 18–29.

Seeborg, M. C. (1975). The effect of curricular choice on alumni income. *Journal of Behavioral Economics, 7*, 151–172.

Shaut, W. E., & Rizzo, L. M. (1980). Impact of a tuition assistance program on students' freedom of choice in college selection. *Journal of Student Financial Aid, 10*, 34–42.

Shymoniak, L., & McIntyre, C. (1980). *Incremental cost study*. Sacramento: California Community Colleges Office of the Chancellor. (ERIC Document Reproduction Service No. ED 188 687)

Siegfried, J. J. (1972–1973). Rate of return to the Ph.D. in economics. *Industrial and Labor Relations Review, 26*, 420–431.

Smith, J. P., & Welch, F. R. (1978a). *The overeducated American? A review article*. Santa Monica, CA: Rand.

Smith, J. P., & Welch, F. R. (1978b). *Local labor markets and cyclic components in demand for college trained manpower*. Santa Monica, CA: Rand.

Solmon, L. C. (1975). The definition of college quality and its impact on earnings. *Exploring Economic Research, 2*, 537–587.

Spiegleman, R. G. (1968). A benefit/cost model to evaluate educational programs. *Socio-economic Planning Sciences, 1*, 443–460.

Sulock, J. (1982). The demand for community college education. *Economics of Education Review, 2*, 351–361.

Suter, L. E. (1977). *Trends in college enrollments by family income for regions of the United States*. Washington, DC: U.S. Bureau of the Census.

Tannen, M. B. (1978). The investment motive for attending college. *Industrial and Labor Relations Review, 31*, 489–497.

Taubman, P., & Wales, T. (1973). Higher education mental ability, and screening. *Journal of Political Economy, 81*, 28–55.

Taubman, P., & Wales, T. (1974). *Higher education and earnings*. New York: McGraw-Hill.

Taubman, P., & Wales, T. (1975). Mental ability and higher education attainment in the twentieth century. In F. T. Juster (Ed.), *Education, income and human behavior* (pp. 47–70). New York: McGraw-Hill.

Tauchar, W. F. (1969). Cross elasticities of collegiate demand. *Review of Social Economy, 27*, 222–232.

Taylor, J. L., & Raffetto, W. (1983). Comparison of success rates of basic educational opportunity grant (Pell) recipients with the success rates of non-recipients. *Community College Review, 11*, 44–51.

Thurow, L. (1968). *The occupational distribution of the returns to education and experience for Whites and Negroes*. Washington, DC: Joint Economic Committee, Federal Programs for the

Development of Human Resources (90th Cong., 2nd sess.) *1*, 267–284.

Tierney, M. L. (1980a). An estimate of departmental cost functions. *Higher Education*, *9*, 453–468.

Tierney, M. L. (1980b). The impact of financial aid on student demand for public/private higher education. *Journal of Higher Education*, *51*, 527–545.

Tierney, M. L. (1982). The impact of institutional net price on student demand for public and private higher education. *Economics of Education Review*, *4*, 363–383.

Trueheart, W. E., & Weathersby, G. B. (1976). *Production function analysis in higher education: General methodology and application to four year black colleges*. Cambridge, MA: Harvard University Press.

Wachtel, P. (1975). The returns to investment in higher education: Another view. In F. T. Juster (Ed.), *Education, income and human behavior* (pp. 151–170). New York: McGraw-Hill.

Wachtel, P. (1976). The effect on earnings of school and college investment expenditures. *Review of Economics and Statistics*, *58*, 326–331.

Wallhaus, P. (1981). *An analysis of the factors which affect instructional unit cost in the public community colleges of Illinois*. Springfield: Illinois Community College Board. (ERIC Document Reproduction Service No. ED 198 848)

Weinschrott, D. (1977). *Demand for higher education in the U.S.: A critical review of the empirical literature*. Santa Monica, CA: Rand.

Weisbrod, B. A. (1962). Education and investment in human capital. *Journal of Political Economy*, *80*, 106–123.

Weisbrod, B. A. (1964). *External benefits of public education*. Princeton, NJ: Industrial Relations Section, Department of Economics, Princeton University.

Weisbrod, B. A. (1966). Investing in human capital. *Journal of Human Resources*, *1*, 5–21.

Weiss, Y. (1971). Investment in graduate education. *American Economic Review*, *61*, 833–852.

Welch, F. (1970). Education in production. *Journal of Political Economy*, *78*, 35–59.

Welch, F. (1974). Comment. In T. W. Schultz (Ed.), *Economics of the family* (pp. 390–393). Chicago: University of Chicago Press for National Bureau of Economic Research.

Welch, F. (1979). Effects of cohort size on earnings: The baby boom babies' financial bust. *Journal of Political Economy*, *87*, (5, part 2), S65–98.

Wessel, R. H. (1971). Ability and the returns on graduate education. *Western Economic Journal*, *9*, 208–210.

Wight, E. A. (1936). *Financial assistance to students in the University of Chicago*. Chicago: University of Chicago Libraries.

Wilkinson, B. W. (1966). Present values of lifetime earnings for different occupations. *Journal of Political Economy*, *74*, 556–572.

Wilson, F. S. (1977). Regression and choice models to estimate the enrollment effects of campus closure. (Doctoral dissertation, University of Minnesota, 1976). *Dissertation Abstracts International*, *37*, 7870A.

Windham, D. M. (1970). *Education, equality, and income redistribution*. Boston: Heath.

Witmer, D. R. (1970). Economic benefits of college education. *Review of Educational Research*, *40*, 511–523.

Witmer, D. R. (1980). Has the golden age of American higher education come to an abrupt end? *Journal of Human Resources*, *15*, 113–120.

Witmer, D. R. (1983). Let's increase college quality, funding and tuition. LaCrosse, WI: Office of the Vice Chancellor.

Ziderman, A. (1973). Rates of return on investment in education: Recent results for Britain. *Journal of Human Resources*, *8*, 85–97.

Zimmerman, D. (1973). Expenditure-tax incidence studies, public higher education, and equity. *National Tax Journal*, *26*, 65–70.

PART IV

Politics and Policy

CHAPTER 21

The Politics of Education and Educational Policy: The Local Level

Martin Burlingame

With hindsight during the mid-1980s, it seems obvious that in the late 1950s scholars of educational administration would aggressively argue for some understanding of local public school politics. For one thing, scholars of educational administration had witnessed practicing school administrators' confrontation by a series of political problems over the entire decade. For another, many of these same scholars had turned increasingly to social-science disciplines for theories and methods to help understand public education. Among these disciplines political science seemed to offer new insights for the study of schools and schooling (Layton, 1982).

The 1950s had been a turbulent period for the administrators of American public school systems. First, there was unrelenting financial pressure at the local level during the entire decade to transport, house, and teach a seemingly endless stream of "baby boom" children. Nearly every school system in the nation sought funds to buy more buses, build more buildings, and hire more teachers and administrators. Administrators watched in dismay as yet another housing development blossomed on the outskirts of town.

Second, the decade began with national concerns about the loyalty (translated as anti-Communism) of Americans. Senator Joseph McCarthy sought to purge the federal government of fellow travelers; many of his

supporters worried about the local teachers and curriculum. One favorite pseudopolitical target of these concerned citizens was the United Nations, especially the United Nations Educational, Scientific & Cultural Organization (UNESCO).

Third, in the middle years of the decade the Supreme Court and the federal government attacked segregated schooling in Southern communities. Not only did the Court seek to end, with deliberate speed, separate and unequal local school systems, but also the President of the United States used his powers to assist in the integration of a local high school in Little Rock, Arkansas.

Finally, in the concluding years of the decade, Congress passed unprecedented educational legislation. The achievements of the USSR in space triggered significant new federal aid to local school districts. The National Defense Education Act of 1958 poured massive amounts of federal dollars into mathematics and science curriculum projects. These projects were designed to provide local districts with resources necessary to assure that the United States recaptured its position as the world leader.

The 1950s also witnessed significant changes in the study of educational administration (Moore, 1964). A renaissance in study and training was in progress; universities such as the University of Oregon had received funds to improve not only the quality of thought but also the skills of newly trained school administrators. As part of these efforts, scholars in educational administration turned to the behavioral

Consultant/reviewers: Peter Cistone, Florida International University; and Laurence Iannacone, University of California–Santa Barbara

sciences to find new methods and new theories. One of those disciplines was political science. No better evidence for this general trend can be found than the National Society for the Study of Education *Yearbook* of 1964 (Griffiths). The growing sense of the power of political concepts is suggested in chapters by Iannaccone on the informal organization of the school and Carlson on environmental constraints. That same year witnessed the publication of *The Politics of Education in the Local Community* (Cahill & Hencley, 1964), a volume that contained papers considering "community politics." These papers discussed problems, approaches, and the relation of political research to political action. Some 13 years later, the Society was to publish a yearbook titled *The Politics of Education* (Scribner, 1977); this work highlighted the progress made in applying political-science concepts to the study of educational administration.

The progress made is already documented in a number of major bibliographic and review works. A singular and important accomplishment is the exhaustive bibliography on politics and education compiled by Hastings (1980), a work that largely supplants the earlier work of Harman (1974); these bibliographies are invaluable. Several reviews of the politics of education also deserve scrutiny, including James (1964), Kirst and Mosher (1969), Iannaccone and Cistone (1974), Peterson (1974), and Burlingame (1978). Several important articles discuss and assess the state of the general field, including Wirt (1977), Boyd (1978b), and Layton (1982). Finally, a number of excellent anthologies and edited conference proceedings have been published, including Lutz and Azzarelli (1966), Rosenthal (1969a), Kirst (1970), Cistone (1972, 1975), Wirt (1975), and Scribner (1977).

This chapter has three major sections. The first, and most extensive, reports results of some studies done on local-level politics of education. These results are organized using a model suggested by Boyd (1976b). That is, several important independent variables, including the community context and the issue being contested, strongly affect the dependent variables—the nature of educational politics and the policy outcome. The second section examines a few persistent methodological, theoretical, and normative disputes that have plagued (or profited) this field. The third section suggests a few lines of future inquiry and gently appraises the work done to date.

STUDIES OF LOCAL-LEVEL POLITICS AND POLICY

Boyd (1976b) provided a model for analyzing the question of who governed education at the local level.

Carefully reviewing and critiquing a number of major studies of local politics and policy, he found that the type of school district and the type of issue or policy questioned determined two outcomes: (a) controversy episodic over community control of school policy making and (b) the extent of ongoing community influence on professional educators.

Using Boyd's model and deliberately accentuating its possible multiple-regression character, this section reviews some of the major research studies in local-level politics and policy. Several studies are categorized under the first major independent variable: X_1, the community context. Other studies are reviewed under the second independent variable: X_2 the issue. Issues will be distinguished by type and content. The dependent variables are Y_1, the type of educational politics, and Y_2, the policy outcome. Studies covering both of these dependent variables will be viewed in one major section.

The general shape of the argument using the model in its strongest form is that variations in X_1 and variations in X_2 produce different outcomes in Y_1 and Y_2. For example, if X_1 is a suburban community and X_2 is a curriculum issue, then the educational politics (Y_1) may be routine and the policy outcome (Y_2) controlled by professional expertise. However, if X_1 were a rural community, other outcomes (Y_1 and Y_2) would be more probable. The extent to which a community seeks to control educational policy making and to influence professional educators depends upon the community type and the issue at stake.

Independent Variable: Community Type

The type of community has generally been acknowledged as an important independent variable in studies of local-level politics of education. By far the most frequent classification of community type has been urban, suburban, or rural. Often the largest urban districts are distinguished from general metropolitan areas. Various schemes have been devised to sort districts into these general categories. For example, Zeigler and Jennings (1974) analyzed the external context of opposition to superintendents, using the following categories: central city (50,000 population in a standard metropolitan statistical area [SMSA]); suburban (cities of less than 50,000 in an SMSA); and small town (all other non-SMSA districts) (p. 167). Other studies have used more intuitive classification terms. Studies of each community type will be briefly examined.

Research on politics of and policies for education in larger urban cities is mixed in intent and voluminous (Bendiner, 1967; Berube & Gittell, 1968; Bundy, 1967; Burkhead, 1967; Campbell & Sachs, 1966; Campbell,

Marx, & Nystrand, 1969; Cronin, 1970; Gittell & Hollander, 1968; Janowitz, 1969; Lutz, 1970; Mann, 1976; Pois, 1964; Swanson, 1966). Much of this literature is driven by reformist intentions. Evidence was selected in ways that enhanced particular policy arguments; there was a noticeable lack of balance between reformist intent and descriptive care in some of these works.

In general, these and other works argued that big city school systems were unresponsive bureaucracies. These large school systems had developed so much professional specialization, so many bureaucratic trappings (read here "red tape"), and so few ways for citizens to express their wants that the schools had become completely divorced from the public. Minorities, particularly, were underrepresented in and misunderstood by the system. Reformers then argued that these institutionally racist bureaucracies needed to be broken into smaller, relatively autonomous units that could meet the unique needs of the urban minorities and poor. This reform, and many others that were proposed, were grounded in philosophical beliefs about governance. Few proposals were based on evidence; most argued for participation without concern for unique conditions that might exist in particular sites. Added to these woes was the increasing political muscle of the unionized big city teachers (Grimshaw, 1979); many argued that teachers were concerned only with their own economic welfare.

In contrast to many of these studies, others found diversity in urban systems. Peterson (1976) used four conceptual models to examine Chicago school politics. Peterson's work presents a sensitive portrait of multiple political styles, multiple constituencies, and multiple issues. The Chicago board appears responsive or unresponsive and rational, politically reactive, or proactive depending on the issues and the actors.

Equally, Summerfield (1971b) found at least one system to be remarkably diverse. Studying a large urban system, he inspected four different schools in four socioeconomically differentiated neighborhoods. Summerfield found sharp differences in the style and quality of education the children received. Neighborhood parents and their schools are interest groups operating within the larger school system. The principal of the neighborhood school can become the agent for that neighborhood in demands for additional resources. Principals can be active or passive in their demands; the pressure from the neighborhood determines their behaviors. The varying activities of community groups in support of their schools and the varying behaviors of principals in soliciting resources from the central office result in wide disparaties among resources for the four neighborhood schools. The decision-making system is open, allowing interested persons and groups to pro-

duce changes in the status quo. The public expectations for education shape the system. Summerfield, 1971a, uses the term *cueing* to indicate how public expectations influence educators.

In sum, the urban context as an independent variable was generally presented as producing the development of a large, bureaucratic, and unresponsive school system. Much of the work that generated these results was reformist in intent; a few other studies produced more sensitive reports of the diversity of local school sites within large systems.

The pioneering works in suburban studies (Minar, 1966a, 1966b) found that the socioeconomic level influenced both levels of community conflict and the role of the superintendent. Minar (1966a) contrasted 24 higher and 24 lower SES suburbs in the Chicago area. The lower SES group had higher levels of electoral conflict and greater electoral participation, and superintendents were faced with questioning board members. Minar explained these results by suggesting higher SES districts possessed greater resources for managing conflict and greater deference to expertise. Higher SES suburbs minimized conflict; lower SES suburbs lacked the resources to control conflict. Minar (1966b) looked at four districts closely; the results supported the earlier line of reasoning. (Also see Gans, 1967, and Masotti, 1967).

In a study of four lower and four higher SES Chicago suburban elementary districts, Boyd (1976a) strengthened and refined Minar's earlier works. In general, higher SES districts did manage conflict better than lower SES districts. But the selection and inspection of deviant cases by Boyd suggested that the SES of a community had several indirect effects on community divisions. The notions of public-regarding (community interests over self-interests) and private-regarding (self-interests over public interests) helped Boyd clarify indirect effects. High SES communities appeared to be public-regarding, structurally integrated, and able to keep conflict to a minimum. Lower SES communities appeared to be private-regarding, not structurally integrated, and conflict prone.

In contrast to studies of urban areas, the suburbs as an independent variable appeared to produce school systems that were generally more responsive to the public—albeit a public with skills in expressing their wants. However, the diversity of SES in suburban areas meant that generalizations always had to be tempered by careful examination of the conditions of a particular site.

Peshkin (1982) studied the lingering after-effects of school consolidations on a rural school district in Illinois. The memories of the good old days, the slow death of a rural town, the struggles over transportation, the loss of a sense of control over children's education, the seeming indifference or outright arrogance of those who won (and kept their school open)—all combined to produce an imperfect union. The struggles within the district split not only the small communities but also the faculties of the various schools. The school board, and the superintendents who came and went, were in a constant state of conflict. The prospects for a peaceful future were dim.

More traditional views of rural educational politics can be found in Vidich and Bensman (1958) and Peshkin (1978). Both studies depict the school as dominated by the local farmers intent on preserving the rural life and its values.

Implicit in this category scheme of urban, suburban, and rural are sets of notions such as size, degree of urban life style, and heterogeneity of the population on social, economic, and racial lines. These dimensions help our understanding of differences about life and education in small towns, suburban, and urban areas; such dimensions provide both descriptive categories and analytic power. Descriptively, urban, suburban, and small town create a set of categories that can be operationalized by using such indicators as population size. Analytically, each of the categories suggests something about political dynamics. For instance, the more people, the more differences among people. The closer people live, the more likely that conflicts will be created and the more likely that political mechanisms will be needed both to control resources for resolving these conflicts and to provide services for all. These categories contain implicit models explaining differences in political behavior among the community types.

Independent Variable: Issues

Issues will be examined by content and type. Eliot (1959) claimed that five content issues were important for any political analysis of education: curriculum, facilities, district organization, personnel, and—most important—finance. Moreover, Martin (1962) contrasted two major types of issues: perennial and episodic. Perennial issues are everpresent; they include those listed by Eliot. Episodic issues are those that arise overnight and disappear just as quickly. In this section these issues are discussed in order; however, discussion of personnel takes place in a later section.

Two major reviews discuss the politics of the curriculum. Kirst and Walker (1971) stressed the political character of the decisions made about the public school curriculum. At the heart of the matter was the fact that different courses of study reflected different value bases. The process of deciding the content of the curriculum was often disjointed and incremental. The authors identified several groups, including those that set minimum standards for the curriculum, alternative generators such as the U.S. government, and various groups demanding change. Finally, Kirst and Walker examined the limited influences of local actors on the curriculum. In their conclusion, they stressed not only that unclear and conflicting goals as well as uncertain knowledge about educational processes shaped the politics of the curriculum but also that politics appeared to be the only current way that decisions would be made.

Boyd (1978a) reviewed the changing politics of curriculum policy making. He argued that educators had adopted the strategy of the "professionalization of reform." This strategy provided professionals the opportunity to innovate; they could introduce nonincremental policy changes. But the strategy was also susceptible to efforts to impede change. The maintenance needs of individuals, organizations, communities, and societies stressed bureaucratic stability and incremental change, not innovation. Some professionals argued for change; others argued for maintenance. This older dualism is now being challenged, Boyd suggested, by the increasing willingness of special interest groups to pay high prices for their particular concerns. (See Mosher, Hastings, & Wagoner, 1979.)

The major works on facilities as an issue have discussed the problems of school closings. A special issue of *Education and Urban Society*, edited by Boyd (1979), dealt with the issue of the political consequences of declining school enrollments. Burlingame reviewed the problems of small rural cities, Boyd studied the problems of suburban communities, Colton and Frelich examined large cities, and Cuban provided an insightful case study of Arlington, Virginia. Boyd and Iannaccone provided summary articles touching on major themes. Overall, the volume suggested that declining enrollments do not create a new politics of education but do underscore that the study of districts over time provides important insights about the influence of community stability and change on educational politics. It appears that districts are able to "paper over" conflicts as long as resources are plentiful; however, as resources decline, old conflicts reemerge. Decline brings to the surface dormant conflicts within the community.

Little work has directly examined the impact of political decisions about school organization on community support for schools, on life in schools, or on individual student achievement. Most studies have been undertaken after political decisions have been made about school-district organization. A good example is Bidwell and Kasarda (1975). They studied the influence on student achievement in reading and mathematics of a set of environmental conditions (school-district size, fiscal resources, number of disadvantaged students, level of education in the community, and percentage of nonwhites in the district), and mediating conditions described as organizational attributes (pupil-teacher ratio, administrative intensity, professional support, and certified staff qualifications). (Also see Bidwell & Kasarda, 1980, for a discussion of conceptualizing and measuring effects of schools and of schooling.) Although there are important differences in student achievement associated with various patterns of environmental conditions and organizational attributes, no effort is made to trace same to various patterns of political decision making in districts. It is not made clear in studies of this type what processes decision makers have used to determine a particular pattern or desired outcome. (For a general critique of our understanding of the outcome of such policy making, see Hawley, 1977.)

Studies of financial support of local schools by voters have been neatly summarized by Piele and Hall (1973). They provided a detailed propositional inventory of research on voting in school financial elections and systematically assembled the findings that lent credence to a number of propositions: for example, "The greater a citizen's wealth, the more likely he will vote in a school financial election" (p. 48). The review of the research treated several propositions in three major areas: voters and nonvoters; variations in turnout; and environmental, socioeconomic, and psychological determinants of voting. The reviewers suggested that school officials might match their electoral strategies to what the research found about communities of the type they served. The advice Piele and Hall present fits neatly with the Boyd model. The conditions of the environment strongly determine the policies educators propose.

In sum, as an independent variable, issues seem intuitively plausible because the notion of the different saliency for various actors seems so reasonable. Financial issues seem to be the most important because they affect more directly most people in the community and all people in the school system. (Other issues such as curriculum or district organization are always there and always have the potential to flare up.) Events trigger tempests in teapots, football coaches come and go, wild parties abound, and everyday gossip provides a momentary diversion. But some issues, such as dollars spent, never go away; they are the stuff of life in school districts (see Blumberg, 1985).

Dependent Variables: School Boards as Major Actors

The dependent variables—episodic control and extent of ongoing influence—will be considered together.

Although it would be desirable to separate them, in general the studies in this area have not made such clear distinction. We shall follow local custom, then, by considering the major actors in the situation—the school board, the superintendent, teachers, and special interest groups.

The studies of school boards move between two major poles. One sees the board as the major force for preserving the community; educators are selected to serve the needs of community maintenance and control is always maintained by the public. The opposite pole sees professional educators dominating the board and the community; educational expertise rules. This section reviews work that sees the community and its school board dominating professional educators.

In an ethnographic study of an Illinois farming town, Peshkin (1978) describes the school board as educational guardian of the community. The members of Mansfield's school board—natives, farmers, men—play this role to its fullest when they are required to select a new superintendent. In the analysis of the final candidates, the board members express the values that guided the selection process. They seek a candidate who represents the best of being "country"; he should have no hours, be on the ground floor on salary, have ideas suitable to the community including strict discipline, and move slowly and deliberately in making changes. The board selects their man using just these criteria.

The importance of these community values is discussed by Page and Clelland (1978). Their work on the controversy over textbooks in Kanawha County finds a clash between adherents of "cultural fundamentalism" and "cultural modernism." Two distinct community groups hold two distinct constellations of values about the schools and textbooks as means of socializing the young. Both groups sought to control the school board and thereby control the selection of textbooks. At issue were conceptions of Christianity, use of profane language, respect for authority, and issues of moral relativism. Both the fundamentalists and the modernists wanted the school board to direct school personnel on what to teach and what texts to use. Page and Clelland refer to this type of conflict as the "politics of life style concern."

Others have found the school board less responsive to the entire community or to major groups within the community. In an inspection of suburban school systems, Martin (1962) found that the methods of selecting the school boards—nominations, special elections, and nonpartisan character—meant that education was a special government run by and for parents. Moreover, these socially and economically advantaged parents distrusted politics and trusted school professionals. Most issues were handled by educators; these perennial issues included the school tax rate and school building program. Episodic issues, such as the loss of a football game to a bitter rival, quickly die away. Under normal conditions, professionals used the board of education to maintain the schools in their image.

Intensively studying two communities in Oregon, Agger and Goldstein (1971) claimed that a class system based on attitudinal complexes rather than economic or social position had developed. This cultural class orientation predicted school attitudes and activities better than either social class or parental status. For example, the dimension of cultural class labeled *generalized civic improvement orientation* was strongly related to school budget voting intentions. The overall class orientations of these two communities were different; equally, conflicting orientations were present within these communities. Finally, within the school systems differences existed in cultural class orientations between teachers as well as between teachers and administrators. The overall predictions formed by the dominant cultural class orientations did predict political behavior, such as voting, in these districts.

In sum, these studies suggest that the common notion of public control of schools deserves close scrutiny; control seems to vary by type of community and by type of issue.

Dependent Variable: Superintendents as Major Actors

Standing in sharp contrast is a series of studies stressing the power of educators. Kerr (1964) underscored the dependence of the school board members on the professional expertise of the superintendent. In a study of two suburban districts, he found that candidates for school board positions not only lacked clear-cut constituencies but also were unfamiliar with educational programs. New board members were socialized both by older members and by the superintendent to accept recommendations of professional educators and to reject the wishes of the public. The school board became an agency of legitimation, particularly for a superintendent with a strong professional self-image.

The works of Zeigler (Tucker & Zeigler, 1980; Zeigler & Jennings, 1974) reinforce the image of school boards as dominated by school superintendents. The Zeigler and Jennings study was based on interviews in 96 school districts with 581 school board members and 94 superintendents. In these districts, board members and professional school personnel actively recruited over 40 percent of new board members. Although at-large elections discouraged electoral competition, competitive elections did produce boards willing to engage in conflicts with superintendents (but such competitive

elections were rare). Moreover, school board members and various individuals and groups saw school issues differently. Board members saw superintendents representing not only matters of professional expertise but also public interest. However, superintendents lacked the resources to control the entire situation: Conflicts in the larger political system increased conflicts within the educational system.

Using demand-response logs of school board meetings, administrative cabinet meetings, and other formal meetings in 11 school districts, Tucker and Zeigler found mixed results. On the one hand, the preferences of school officials differed from the general public and community elites, the public did not interact with boards, boards preferred expert reactions to issues, and private discussions with constituents most influenced school board members. On the other hand, there were sharp differences across the 11 districts. Some districts experienced many conflicts; others experienced few. In most, the educational professionals used their expertise to control the decision-making process.

Researchers of large urban districts often found both school board and superintendent controlled by the school bureaucracy. For example, Schrag (1967) compared the urban Boston School Department to a village. The department was an informal network dominated by Irish Catholics; the large formal bureaucracy was often a front for an informal kinship system much like that of a small village. Studies of New York City by Gittell (1967) and Rogers (1968) emphasized the power of the educational bureaucrats to control the schools. Both studies of the largest U.S. city school system found the superintendent and school board members unable to control a large, specialized bureaucracy. The professional bureaucrats maintained the school system in such a way that the bureaucracy continued to flourish while the interests of others (such as the superintendent, school board, and public) continued to fade.

One common device for bureaucratic control was the budget. James, Kelly, and Garms (1966) found that the use of formulas to allocate personnel, supplies, and materials not only centralized the budget process but made it harder to change. These formulas helped keep control within the school bureaucracy; most board members did not become involved in the process except to make minor adjustments.

By and large the favorite political strategy for educational experts was privatization of conflict; for the critics of the schools, the favorite strategy was socialization of conflict (Schattschneider, 1975). Educators attempted to control debates about issues, such as racial or financial inequalities, by making them private;

these topics were defined by school personnel as arenas where expertise alone was important. Conflict was managed as an in-house affair among experts who often shared many beliefs and values. In contrast, groups or individuals who saw themselves as the losers in these private discussions, often the poor and racial minorities, sought to make the conflicts public. By socializing conflicts, those who felt unserved by the educational experts sought to gain allies and eventually gain control of the experts. By seeking to create constituencies for new board members, encouraging competitive board elections, making information about the educational system public, attacking the unresponsive bureaucracy, and challenging the budget formulas, the critics sought to end the privatized control of the educational experts.

Why did educational experts such as superintendents dominate, or seek to dominate, the school board? At least one way to account for this sort of behavior was to analyze how superintendents were trained. One observer argued that training programs produced superintendents who were brokers in power and experts in survival (Khleif, 1979). Candidates for advanced degrees in educational administration and for certification as school superintendents were resocialized and reclassed by the training program. They were socialized away from an educational perspective toward a political perspective; they ceased being teachers and became administrators intent on power. Candidates were also trained in middle- and upper-class bourgeois behavior. Whatever small-town virtues they brought to the training program vanished under 3 years of socialization pressure. The candidates emerged, Khleif claims, as politicians.

Superintendents could also behave as educational statesmen. Boyd (1974) explored the question of whether superintendents could behave as political brokers or educational statesmen in light of research on suburban Chicago school districts. In the blue-collar districts, politics not only was expected but also was seen as an enjoyable activity. In the white-collar districts, conflict was managed and the superintendent played the role of statesman. *Strategist* seemed appropriate for blue-collar districts; *statesman* seemed appropriate for white-collar districts. In contrast to Khleif, Boyd worried that the training and ideology of many school administrators led them to ignore conflict in communities and to avoid adopting the role of political strategist when it might be appropriate.

The most extensive work on the relationship of superintendent, school board, and community has been that of Iannaccone and Lutz (1970) and Lutz and Iannaccone (1978). The 1970 work used a case study to generate a series of hypotheses about the relationship

of the community to the school board and superintendent. The board over time is isolated from the community by the superintendent; changes in the social and economic makeup of the community eventually lead to electoral conflict. The usual result of this conflict is changes in school board membership and the eventual involuntary turnover (firing) of the superintendent. The new superintendent is an outsider brought to the community to serve the wishes of the new board.

The 1978 volume consisted of a series of articles exploring various facets of the earlier work. There are persistent concerns about the operationalization of variables (see Eblen, 1975–1976) and about the sequencing of events. Nonetheless, these works suggest the important role the superintendent can play not only in meeting community expectations but also in working with board members to resist or ignore community wants. The analysis of the role of the superintendent, school board, and community must be examined over time. The Iannaccone and Lutz works emphasize that over time community change produces changes at the board and superintendent level; this sense of history is an important addition to the research literature. In sum, Iannaccone and Lutz describe and analyze those stable times when the superintendent dominates and those changing times when the community dominates. The school board often acts as the agent of two very different actors—but at very different times and under very different community conditions.

These studies, in sum, suggest that educators possess resources that can be used to enhance their control and thwart attempts by the public to control them. But a close reading suggests that these resources are not unlimited. The insights of the Iannaccone-Lutz works, for instance, about the role of history and the life cycle in school districts help us see that single cross-sectional studies of districts may misrepresent what is happening. What needs to be considered is the zone of tolerance (Boyd, 1976b) that the community and the issue generate for the professional school administrator. At times, the community and issue may permit a wide latitude; at other times, community and issue may demand that the administrator follow a straight and narrow course of action—or else find a new place to work.

Dependent Variable: Teachers as Major Actors

A third major actor was the teacher group. In the 1960s teachers began to exercise their political muscle in many local communities. Various explanations exist for the rise of teacher militancy.

Callahan (1962) accounts for tension between teachers and administrators in his historical account of the acceptance of scientific management as the guiding metaphor for education in the early 1900s. Scientific management created significantly different roles for planners and workers. Planners developed a science of jobs; workers obediently followed the one best way planners created. Both school administrators and teachers wanted to be the planners; both resisted the role of workers. Planners had the important, challenging, and powerful tasks of studying the various aspects of the job being done; testing and selecting the one best way of doing the job; and then improving the current one best way. Power was the crux of the issue: Who had the right to specify authoritatively what constituted performance of the tasks of teaching?

Other historians found that some groups actively sought to be planners and that the groups that "owned" the planner-professional roles did not represent all segments of society. Despite the progressive rhetoric of service to others, the "new" middle-class professionals vigorously prepared themselves for and defended the rights of the planners in government and education (Hays, 1964). Tyack (1974) found that these "new" professionals were white Anglo-Saxon Protestant males.

In 1967, Cole argued that young teachers (particularly male) perceived major status incongruencies between teachers and other professionals, such as lawyers and doctors. Corwin (1970) argued that militancy was a stage on the way to a fully professionalized teaching force. However, Rosenthal (1969b) found that although militancy generally related to control of work, many differences in teacher associations could be found from community to community.

Mitchell, Kerchner, Erck, and Pryor (1981) continued to explore this issue by suggesting that school boards and their administrators move through "generations" in dealing with militant teacher groups. The first generation is the struggle over whether the school board should bargain or not; the second involves teacher groups gaining bargaining rights and making considerable headway in areas such as teacher salaries; and the third generation finds administrators and boards recapturing preogatives over work rules that had been lost in earlier contracts. In other words, examining teacher militancy requires not only some sense of why teachers are militant but some sense of development over time based on "learnings" both by school boards and teacher groups.

Finally, a series of empirical works seeks to assess the impact of militancy on schools (Angell, 1981; Doherty, 1966; Eberts & Stone, 1984; Perry & Wildman, 1970; Urban, 1982). The results are mixed for a number of reasons, including different measures and models of schooling. However, this mixture of results is to be expected if one takes seriously the multivariate model. The type of district and type of issue should

influence teachers' activities in their community. We should expect that in blue-collar communities teacher unions will flourish; we should not be surprised to find that wealthy suburban communities find teacher unionism distasteful—although few studies systematically document such expectations.

Dependent Variable: Special Interest Groups as Major Actors

In general, the works on special interest groups are few and generally find the obvious. That is, most people support the schools; many who support them do so for the special interest of their children. In one of the more insightful and careful works, Salisbury (1980) studied citizen participation in six suburban communities near St. Louis. He found two discernible groupings of school participants: supportive and purposive. Supportive participants were engaged by within-school activities; they tended to be younger, of lower status, newer in the community, and predominantly female. Purposive participants were somewhat older, higher SES, longer residents of the community, and male; they were active through attending school board meetings, formal committee meetings, and school-related elections. Purposive participants saw themselves influencing school policy; supportive participants did not. Purposive participants saw themselves changing school policy for the better.

The activities of all participants were influenced by the community context. The context influenced, for example, the channels participants used for political activity. The six communities, through their different histories, expectations for education, and patterns of participation formed very different arenas for political action.

Summary: A Multivariate Approach

This review has followed the argument that the type of community as well as the nature of the issue at stake influenced the periodic crises of school politics and the zone of tolerance granted educational professionals. The findings indicate that in some districts the congruence in educational preferences between the public and professionals leads to minimal conflict. In other communities, the lack of congruence has led to conflict. Moreover, communities are dynamic; changes in the community may lead to periods of conflict followed by periods of quiet.

DISPUTES

Three disputes have persisted throughout the development of the research literature on local-level politics and education. The first concerns methodology, the second deals with a theoretical issue, and the third is normative.

Case Studies versus Experimental Studies

Despite the heavy loading of case studies in the work done in local level politics, quarrels remain over the value of that method. A strong argument for the use of case studies in political science was made by Eckstein (1975), who argued that a case study is technically a report and interpretation of a single measure of a pertinent variable. Comparative studies, in contrast, are studies of numerous cases reporting numerous measures on the same variable but different individuals. Disputing the view that case studies and comparative studies are separate and unequal, Eckstein argued that some types of case studies can be seen as better tests of theories than are comparative studies. He contends that there are five different types of case studies: (a) configurative-ideographic, (b) disciplined-configurative, (c) heuristic, (d) plausibility probes, and (e) crucial-case. Both discipline-configurative and crucial-case can be used to test theories.

The strategy used by many, such as Innaccone and Lutz, has been to move from case studies or from surveys (Zeigler & Jennings, 1974) to statements that could be tested by more experimental methods. This strategy is not as assertive about case studies as is Eckstein but clearly values them more than do Campbell and Stanley (1963), who made the definitive statement on the weakness of case study as a method of research. In their survey of designs for research on teaching, they discuss a number of factors that jeopardize the validity of various designs. The one-shot case study, a design examining the presumed treatment results on a single group, was introduced as a minimum reference point because it has almost no scientific value. Not only does the design have major internal problems, such as history, maturation, selection, and morality, but it also has problems of external validity, such as interaction of the case selection and the treatment. Moreover, efforts to overcome some of these validity problems often produced the error of misplaced precision. This argument was spread by one of the better-selling texts on behavioral research (Kerlinger, 1964, 1973). Kerlinger argued that case studies fell under the rubric of one-shot case studies; this design was not only worthless but could be badly misleading.

Finally, Eliot (1959) early on raised an important warning about political generalizations. He suggested that research at the local level attend to three analyses: (a) school-district organization; (b) decision-making processes, including professional, lay leadership, and public groups; and (c) voting on bond or consolidation referendums. He suggested that analyses both in organization and in voting could be comparative because school-district organizations were relatively few in number and because state law imposed comparable conditions. In the second area, he cautioned that school districts were too numerous and too disparate for safe generalizations.

It is this second area that has captured so much of the attention of researchers. Using case studies and other research techniques such as surveys, scholars in this area have sought to find reasonable grounds that allowed them to make some sort of generalizations, as for example, about types of districts and yet be sensitive to local uniqueness. Moreover, many have worried about the selective biases that could creep into case studies. Some have argued that public discussions of case studies helped to reduce these errors; others hold with the purists that cases are of little scientific worth.

Distribution of Power

A major theoretical issue has involved the distribution of power in a community. Three approaches have dominated: The first has been power concentrated in the hands of a few; the second has seen power held by pluralistic groups; and the third has seen power varying by community conditions. Each of these theoretical positions has different implications for local educational politics and policy.

In a series of studies conducted primarily in Florida, Kimbrough (1964a, 1964b; Johns & Kimbrough, 1968) used the concept of informal community structure. Relying heavily on and frequently replicating the findings of Hunter (1953), Kimbrough and Johns and Kimbrough found that social and economic elites dominated decision making about education. These informal groups of community leaders found it to their advantage to control the major services of the community, including the public schools. In general, these informal leaders sought to maintain the social and economic status quo. This power structure shaped the destiny of the community in secret meetings; able lieutenants in lesser arenas such as education carried out marching orders. Similarly, Crain (1968) reported that the civic elite in New Orleans consciously sought to integrate the city schools peacefully to enhance business opportunities.

Others followed the very different path charted by Dahl (1961). These researchers did not find informal power structures dominating the community studies. Instead, they found various groups attending to various areas. For example, the work of Martin (1962) supports Dahl's general argument that groups such as parents are interested in the schools and little else. Each arena of governance has its constituency.

A third approach, and by far the most popular, suggested that the multivariate slant was the most fruitful: The type of power structure varied from community to community. In turn, the type of power structure found in a community strongly influenced the role the school superintendent could play. In a study of 51 communities, McCarty and Ramsey (1971) found four predominant patterns between a community power structure and a superintendent: (a) monolithic community-functionary superintendent; (b) equal-actions community–political-strategies superintendent; (c) pluralistic community-professional advisor superintendent; and (d) inert community–decision-maker superintendent. The pluralistic pattern dominated the study (23 of 51); the inert pattern was second (13 of 31).

Boyd (1976b) has urged that while the patterns approach is the most fruitful, there are serious flaws in McCarty and Ramsey's analysis of pluralistic community power structures. Boyd's criticisms are based on McCarty and Ramsey's own descriptions of these communities. Instead of being politically active, heterogeneous communities with numerous competing interest groups, Boyd notes that the so-called pluralistic communities are affluent suburbs with great homogeneity and a rational style of decision making. Moreover, Boyd points out that McCarty and Ramsey find the superintendents in these districts fluctuating between the roles of professional advisor (as expected) and decision maker (not expected). This chapter favors the third model, while including Boyd's criticisms deliberately to suggest the type of work that needs to be done to further strengthen this approach. For instance, the general categories of the model are compelling; community type seems so important in so many studies that it is hard to deny that it is a critical independent variable. Yet the precise delineation of the dimensions of community type, the operational definition, is clearly in dispute. Equally, the general model of complexity leading to political activity seems hard to deny; the exact steps in this intuitive understanding of the dynamics of the political process across and within each community type await specification. Thus, there is still much that needs to be done to sharpen the model.

Normative

A major normative dispute centered on *exactly* what the politics of education at the local level ought to accomplish. For many whose basic disciplinary perspective was political science, school districts became increasingly important and relatively convenient governmental units for study. How they functioned as they did, the types of governmental outcome—all seemed important political questions. Equally, these political scientists were concerned about the democratic nature of school districts and their leaders. Were school districts and school leaders responsive to the wishes of local citizens? (See Martin, 1962; Zeigler, 1973; and Zeigler & Jennings, 1974).

For many whose basic disciplinary perspective was educational administration, the questions were less descriptive, more normative. How could groups and individuals be convinced that schools were worth increased school dollars? How could less than adequate school systems be improved through citizens' political actions? How could school boards and communities act more intelligently to determine their preferences? How could school leaders mobilize citizens to crusade for better schools? These normative questions dominated the interest of those who sought to use political-science notions to improve the study and practice of educational administration.

This dispute often emerged in issues about politics and policy. Political scientists in general seemed concerned with descriptions of political activities and the assessment of such activities in terms of traditional conceptions of political philosophy (for example, Zeigler & Jennings, 1974). Peterson (1974) even questioned the notion that politics of education should be separated from politics in general. Educational administrators often seemed more concerned with policy. They were interested in combining the political knowledge obtained from studies using political-science concepts with normative schemas for improving the schools. The educational administrators were unhappy unless "what is" became "what ought to be."

Although more and more institutions of higher education began to offer courses in politics and education, rifts developed within the educational administration fraternity. Newer professors, many of whom had been trained by political scientists, were not mindless converts to the critical views of their trainers, but they did seem less inclined to support practicing educational administrators. Their reading lists included references that not only supported the noble mission of the superintendent but also references that castigated educational leadership as closed and unresponsive.

CONCLUDING REMARKS

This section deals with approaches to the study of politics and education at the local level and gently assesses the progress of the field to date.

Approaches

Several authors have argued for particular approaches to the study of politics and education and educational policy at the local level. We mention briefly four.

Benson (1982) contends that any policy sector such as education is multilevel. He views any policy sector as one in which hierarchical rules of structure govern actions. He provides the following analysis of the levels and components of any policy sector:

Level I
1. Administrative arrangements
2. Policy paradigms
3. Interorganizational dependencies

Level II
1. Interest-power structures
2. Rules of structure formation (p. 149)

The deep structures in Level II set limits on the surface structures of Level I. Conflicts increase in intensity as they move from surface to deep structure. Hence, the rearrangement of offices or classes in a school building produces far less conflict than shifts in interorganizational dependencies, such as the use of police in dealing with drugs.

Boyd (1982) argues for the use of concepts drawn from political economy. This approach (also known as public or collective choice) presumes individuals are rational and self-interested. In the workplace, individuals seek maximum benefits for themselves. In institutions such as the public schools, workers seek to manipulate the incentive and reward systems to maximize their own benefits. In other words, educators seek to provide rewards for themselves by manipulating the school system and its incentives.

Mitchell (1980) believes the notion of ideology would provide important perspectives for research. Ideology provides a common frame of reference for communities; as such, ideology may link community and school board, define policy, and communicate a mandate to actors. Mitchell argues that little research has examined the ideological foundations of educational politics and policy (Mitchell, 1974; for an excellent example of such an approach used to analyze the curriculum of a school, see Cusick, 1983).

Salisbury (1980) suggests that one way to understand politics at the local level is to use notions such as factions drawn from analysis of political clientelism. The notions of clientelism have been developed in the last few years by political anthropologists (Schmidt, Scott, Lande, & Guasti, 1980). This line of inquiry contrasts the politics of friendship to the politics of partisan political parties. Interpersonal dyads are formed through reciprocity; these dyads form larger groups such as factions and networks. Such groups may not become corporate or formal, but they do become involved in local political activities.

These four authors, in sum, present possible plans for the study of local-level politics and policy. Benson provides a vertical dimension that holds promise for analysis of conflict, continuity, and change. The work of political economy advocated by Boyd continues earlier worries about professional self-interest and its negative consequences for the public interest. The political anthropologists, as Salisbury suggests, consider politics without party. Local-level politics of education seems more a politics of friendship than party. Finally, Mitchell's interest in large cultural frameworks (ideologies) emphasizes the historical dimensions of local educational politics and policies. Although ideologies may change, their persistence suggests deeper continuities.

These four approaches may be used to enrich the general multivariate model discussed. One can imagine the use of Benson's level to generate deeper understandings of type of community or type of issue. Equally, the political economy view advocated by Boyd may be useful for studying the actions of special interest groups. These approaches may also force a major reconsideration of the multivariate approach. Only time and studies will tell.

A Gentle Assessment

At least three major points come to mind in any attempt to assess where inquiry in the local politics of education has been and where it is going.

The work since 1960 has displayed the heterogeneity of local school districts and the complexity of politics and policy at the local level. The school districts of this nation vary widely; the economic, social, political, religious, and educational traditions of these districts are remarkably different. Districts range, for example, in size from New York City to five students spread over 80 square miles in Nevada. At best, what we know about one district in detail, or even 100 districts in detail, provides grounds for only limited generalizations.

By the mid-1970s, moreover, the field had good grasp of a multivariate model that provided fruitful ways of generating new studies, organizing existing studies, and critiquing other theoretical formulations. As enunciated by Boyd in 1976, the model preserved both a sense of complexity and a sense of reasonableness about generalizations. The model fits with the increasing use of multivariate models in other disciplines and in other areas of the study of education, such as school effects.

Finally, the relation between this body of knowledge and the training of school administrators seemed increasingly problematic. Prospective administrators could learn that in some districts professionals were able to dominate educational politics and policy. In others, they might be the pawns of the community. Prospective administrators could make reasonably powerful predictions about employment prospects in certain types of communities and about the types of issues they might face in certain communities. In a sense, one giant stride had been made to help administrators. If the first law of social science was still "It depends," the practitioner at the local level had some good handles on what "it" to worry about and, equally, the range of "depends."

But what about the normative consideration that the role of the educator was to improve, not maintain, education in most communities? This stance meant that school administrators must become agents of change for improving schools, but it often involved provoking conflict in communities. Many, such as Salisbury (1980), pointed out that most community supporters of education disliked conflict. The supporters of schools, for example, have resisted attempts by school leaders to confront issues of racial or class inequalities. School supporters knew what values ought to prevail; they were not happy with administrators who challenged their way of life.

The tensions between some public demands and some professional responsibilities are much better understood after two decades of research in local-level politics and policy. That these tensions are not resolved is evident; that they deserve continued scrutiny as we try to create more knowledge is also evident.

REFERENCES

Agger, R. E., & Goldstein, M. N. (1971). *Who will rule the schools* Belmont, CA: Wadsworth.

Angell, G. W. (Ed.). (1981). *Faculty and teacher bargaining.* Lexington, MA: Lexington.

Bendiner, R. (1967). *The politics of school.* New York: Harper & Row.

Benson, J. K. (1982). A framework for policy analysis. In D. L. Rogers & D. A. Whitten (Eds.), *Interorganizational coordination* (pp. 137–176). Ames, IA: Iowa State University Press.

Berube, M. R., & Gittell, M. (Eds.). (1968). *Confrontation at Ocean Hill-Brownsville.* New York: Praeger.

Bidwell, C. E., & Kasarda, J. D. (1975). School district organization and student achievement. *American Sociological Review, 4,* 55–70.

Bidwell, C. E., & Kasarda, J. D. (1980). Conceptualizing and measuring the effects of school and schooling. *American Journal of Education, 88,* 401–430.

Blumberg, A. (1985). The school superintendent. New York: Teachers College Press, Columbia University.

Boyd, W. L. (1974). The school superintendent: Educational statesman or political strategist? *Administrator's Notebook, 22.*

Boyd, W. L. (1976a). *Community status and conflict in suburban school politics.* (pp. 4–25). Sage Professional Papers in American Politics, No. *3.* Beverly hills, CA: Sage.

Boyd, W. L. (1976b). The public, the professionals, and educational policy making: Who governs? *Teachers College Record, 77,* 539–577.

Boyd, W. L. (1978a). The changing politics of curriculum policy-making for American schools. *Review of Educational Research, 48,* 577–628.

Boyd, W. L. (1978b). The study of education policy and politics: Much ado about nothing? *Teachers College Record, 80,* 249–271.

Boyd, W. L. (Ed.). (1979). Declining school enrollments: Politics and management. *Education and Urban Society, 11,* 275–431.

Boyd, W. L. (1982). The political economy of public schools. *Educational Administration Quarterly, 18,* 111–130.

Bundy, McGeorge. (1967). *Reconnection for learning.* New York: Praeger.

Burkhead, J. (1967). *Input and output in large-city high schools.* Syracuse: Syracuse University.

Burlingame, M. (1978). Impact of policy decisions on schools. In L. S. Schulman (Ed.). *Review of research in education* (Vol. 5, pp. 236–272). Itasca, IL: Peacock.

Cahill, R. S., & Hencley, S. P. (1964). *The politics of education in the local community.* Danville: Interstate.

Callahan, R. F. (1962). *Education and the cult of efficiency.* Chicago: University of Chicago Press.

Campbell, A. K., & Sachs, S. (1966). *Metropolitan America.* Syracuse: Syracuse University Press.

Campbell, D. T., & Stanley, J. S. (1963). Experimental and quasi-experimental designs for research on teaching. In N. L. Gage (Ed.), *Handbook of research on teaching* (pp. 171–246). Chicago: Rand-McNally.

Campbell, R. F., Marx, L. A., & Nystrand, R. O. (Eds.). (1969). *Education and urban renaissance.* New York: John Wiley.

Cistone, P. J. (Ed.). (1972). *School boards and the political facts.* Toronto: Ontario Institute for Studies in Education.

Cistone, P. J. (Ed.). (1975). *Understanding school boards.* Lexington, MA: Lexington.

Cole, S. (1967). *The unionization of teachers.* New York: Praeger.

Corwin, R. G. (1970). *Militant professionalism.* New York: Appleton-Century-Crofts.

Crain, R. L. (1968). *The politics of school desegregation.* Chicago: Aldine.

Cronin, J. M. (1970). *Big city school boards.* New York: Free Press.

Cusick, P. A. (1983). *The egalitarian ideal and the American high school.* New York: Longman.

Dahl, R. A. (1961). *Who governs?* New Haven: Yale University Press.

Doherty, R. E. (1966). *The impact of teacher organizations upon setting school policies.* Ithaca, NY: New York State School of Industrial and Labor Relations.

Eberts, R. W., & Stone, J. A. (1984). *Unions and public schools.* Lexington, MA: Lexington.

Eblen, D. R. (1975–1976). Local school district politics: A reassessment of the Iannaccone and Lutz model. *Administrator's Notebook, 24.*

Eckstein, H. (1975). Case study and theory in political science. In F. J. Greenstein & N. W. Polsby (Eds.), *Strategies of inquiry: Vol. 7. Handbook of political science* (pp. 79–137). Reading, MA: Addison-Wesley.

Eliot, T. H. (1959). Towards an understanding of public school politics. *American Political Science Review, 52,* 1032–1051.

Gans, H. J. (1967). *The Levittowners,* New York: Pantheon.

Gittell, M. (1967). *Participants and participation.* New York: Praeger.

Gittell, M., & Hollander, T. E. (1968). *Six urban districts.* New York: Praeger.

Griffiths, D. E. (1964). *Behavioral science and educational administration: Part 2.* The 63rd yearbook of the National Society for the Study of Education. Chicago: University of Chicago Press.

Grimshaw, W. J. (1979). *Union rule in the schools.* Lexington, MA: Lexington.

Harman, G. (1974). *The politics of education.* St. Lucia, Queensland, Australia: University of Queensland Press.

Hastings, A. H. (1980). *The study of politics and education.* Eugene, OR: ERIC Clearinghouse on Educational Management, University of Oregon.

Hawley, W. D. (1977). If schools are for learning, the study of the politics of education is just beginning. In J. D. Scribner (Ed.). *The politics of education: Part 2*. The 76th yearbook of the National Society for the Study of Education (pp. 319–344). Chicago: University of Chicago Press.

Hays, S. P. (1964). The politics of reform in municipal government in the Progressive era. *Pacific Northwest Quarterly, 55,* 157–169.

Hunter, F. (1953). *Community power structure,* Chapel Hill: University of North Carolina Press.

Iannaccone, L., & Cistone, P. (1974). *The politics of education.* Eugene, OR: ERIC Clearinghouse on Educational Management, University of Oregon.

Iannaccone, L., & Lutz, F. W. (1970). *Politics, power and policy.* Columbus, OH: Charles E. Merrill.

James, H. T. (1964). Institutional character of education: Government and politics. *Review of Educational Research, 34,* 405–423.

James, H. T., Kelly, J. A., & Garms, W. I. (1966). *Determinants of educational expenditures in large cities of the United States.* Palo Alto, CA: School of Education, Stanford University.

Janowitz, M. (1969). *Institution building in urban education.* New York: Russell Sage.

Johns, R. L., & Kimbrough, R. B. (1968). *The relationship of socio-economic factors, educational leadership patterns, and elements of community power structure to local school fiscal policy: Final report* (OE 5–10–146). Washington, DC: Office of Education.

Kerlinger, F. N. (1964). *Foundations of behavioral research.* New York: Holt, Rinehart, & Winston.

Kerlinger, F. N. (1973). *Foundations of behavioral research* (2nd ed.). New York: Holt, Rinehart, & Winston.

Kerr, N. D. (Pseudonym). (1964). The school board as an agency of legitimation. *Sociology of Education, 38,* 34–59.

Khleif, B. (1979). Professionalization of school superintendents: A sociocultural study of an elite program. In R. Barnhart, J. H. Chilcott, & H. F. Wolcott (Eds.), *Anthropology and educational administration* (pp. 52–67). Tucson: Impresora Sahuaro.

Kimbrough, R. A. (1964a). *Informal county leadership structure and controls affecting educational policy decision-making* (Cooperative Research Project No. 1324). Gainesville: College of Education, University of Florida.

Kimbrough, R. A. (1964b). *Political power and educational decision-making.* Chicago: Rand-McNally.

Kirst, M. W. (Ed.). (1970). *The politics of education at the local, state and federal levels.* Berkeley, CA: McCutchan.

Kirst, M. W., & Mosher, E. K. (1969). Politics of education. *Review of Educational Research, 39,* 623–641.

Kirst, M. W., & Walker, D. F. (1971). An analysis of curriculum policy-making. *Review of Educational Research, 41,* 479–509.

Layton, D. H. (1982). The emergence of the politics of education as a field of study. In H. L. Gray (Ed.), *The management of educational institutions* (pp. 109–126). Barcombe, Lewes, England: Falmer.

Lutz, F. W. (Ed.). (1070). *Toward improved urban education.* Worthington, OH: Charles A. Jones.

Lutz, F. W., & Azzarelli, J. J. (Eds.). (1966). *The struggle for power in education.* New York: Center for Applied Research in Education.

Lutz, F. W., & Iannaccone, L. (Eds.). (1978). *Public participation in local school districts.* Lexington, MA: Lexington.

Mann, D. (1976). *The politics of administrative representation.* Lexington, MA: Lexington.

Martin, R. E. (1962). *Government and the suburban schools.* Syracuse: Syracuse University Press.

Masotti, L. H. (1967). *Education and politics in suburbia.* Cleveland, OH: Press of Western Reserve University.

McCarty, D. J., & Ramsey, C. E. (1971). *The school managers.* Westport, CN: Greenwood.

Minar, D. W. (1966a). The community basis for conflict in school system politics. *American Sociological Review, 31,* 822–834.

Minar, D. W. (1966b). *Educational decision-making in suburban communities* (Cooperative Research Project No. 2440). Evanstone, IL: Northwestern University.

Mitchell, D. E. (1974). Ideology and public school policy-making.

Urban Education, 7, 35–59.

Mitchell, D. E. (1980). The ideological factor in school politics. *Education and Urban Society, 12,* 436–451.

Mitchell, D. E., Kerchner, C. T., Erck, W., & Pryor, G. (1981). The impact of collective bargaining on school management and policy. *American Journal of Education, 89,* 147–188.

Moore, H. A. (1964). The ferment in school administration. In D. E. Griffiths (Ed.), *Behavioral science and educational administration: Part 2.* The 63rd yearbook of the National Society for the Study of Education (pp. 11–32). Chicago: University of Chicago Press.

Mosher, E. K., Hastings, A. H., & Wagoner, J. L. (1979). *Pursuing equal educational opportunity: School politics and the new activists* (ERIC/CUE Urban Diversity Series: Number 64). ERIC Clearinghouse on Urban Education: Teachers College, Columbia University.

Page, A. L., & Clelland, D. A. (1978). The Kanawha County textbook controversy: A study of the politics of life style concern. *Social Forces, 57,* 265–281.

Perry, C. A., & Wildman, W. A. (1970). *The impact of negotiations on public education.* Worthington, OH: Charles E. Jones.

Peshkin, A. (1978). *Growing up American.* Chicago: University of Chicago Press.

Peshkin, A. (1982). *The imperfect union.* Chicago: University of Chicago Press.

Peterson, P. E. (1974). The politics of American education. In F. N. Kerlinger & J. Carroll (Eds.), *Review of research in education* (No. 2, pp. 348–389). Itasca, IL: Peacock.

Peterson, P. E. (1976). *School politics, Chicago style.* Chicago: University of Chicago Press.

Piele, P. K. & Hall, J. S. (1973). *Budgets, bonds, and ballots.* Lexington, MA: Lexington.

Pois, J. J. (1964). *The school board crisis.* Chicago: Aldine.

Rogers, D. (1968). *110 Livingston Street.* New York: Random House.

Rosenthal, A. (Ed.). (1969a). *Governing education.* Garden City, NY: Anchor.

Rosenthal, A. (1969b). *Pedagogues and power.* Syracuse: Syracuse University Press.

Salisbury, R. H. (1980). *Citizen participation in the public schools.* Lexington, MA: Lexington.

Schattschneider, E. E. (1975). *The semisovereign people.* Hinsdale, IL: Dryden.

Schmidt, S. W., Scott, J. C., Lande, C., & Guasti, L. (Eds.). (1980). *Friends, followers, and factions.* Berkeley: University of California Press.

Schrag, P. (1967). *Village school downtown.* Boston: Beacon.

Scribner, J. D. (Ed.). (1977). *The politics of education: Part 2.* The 76th yearbook of the National Society for the Study of Education. Chicago: University of Chicago Press.

Summerfield, H. L. (1971a). Cueing and the open system of educational politics. *Education and Urban Society, 3,* 425–439.

Summerfield, H. L. (1971b). *The neighborhood-based politics of education.* Columbus, OH: Charles E. Merrill.

Swanson, B. E. (1966). *The struggle for equality.* New York: Hobbs, Dorman.

Tucker, H. J., & Zeigler, L. H. (1980). *Professionals versus the public.* New York: Longman.

Tyack, D. B. (1974). *The one best system.* Cambridge, MA: Harvard University Press.

Urban, W. J. (1982). *Why teachers organized.* Detroit: Wayne State University.

Vidich, A. J., & Bensman, J. (1958). *Small town in mass society.* Princeton, NJ: Princeton University Press.

Wirt, F. M. (Ed.). (1975). *The policy of the school.* Lexington, MA: Lexington.

Wirt, F. M. (1977). Reassessment needs in the study of the politics of education. *Teachers College Record, 78,* 401–412.

Zeigler, L. H. (1973). Creating responsive schools. *Urban Review, 6,* 38–44.

Zeigler, L. H., & Jennings, M. K. (1974). *Governing American Schools.* North Scituate, MA: Duxbury.

CHAPTER 22

Educational Politics and Policy: The State Level

Douglas E. Mitchell

INTRODUCTION

Twenty-five years ago, state education policy making systems were viewed as weak and ineffectual. Virtually every element in the system was under pressure from critics and reformers. Undemocratic representation in state legislatures had just been successfully attacked in the Supreme Court (*Baker v. Carr*, 1962; *Reynolds v. Sims*, 1964). State departments of education were reputed to be such "dull, poorly managed places, staffed by gray bureaucrats" (Murphy, 1982) that they were selected as one of the five key targets for reform under the Elementary and Secondary Education Act (ESEA) of 1965. Education lobbyists—teachers, administrators, and school board associations—were squabbling over issues of collective bargaining and school finance. Few governors were giving attention to educational issues and problems. Most new educational policy initiatives were being generated at the national level, where curriculum and equity reform efforts were being supported by unprecedented federal investments in education. Even before the adoption of ESEA, substantial federal resources were made available through the National Defense Education Act (NDEA) of 1958. Subsequently, the Emergency School Aid Act (ESAA) of 1972 put federal resources behind strong federal court actions supporting school desegregation.

Today this picture has changed dramatically. Reformed state legislatures are widely perceived to be the most powerful actors in educational policy making

Consultant/reviewers: Milbrey Wallin McLaughlin, Stanford University; and Frederick M. Wirt, University of Illinois

(Kirst, 1984; Mitchell, Wirt, & Marshall, 1985). Expanded state education agencies (SEAs) have built substantial systems for data collection and analysis and are vigorously pursuing a broad array of educational improvement policies (Moore, Goertz, & Hartle, 1983). Many state governors have declared education to be their highest priority for attention (e.g., see Caldwell, 1985), and in some states professional educators' groups are among the richest and most sophisticated lobbyists (Kirst & Somers, 1981; Mazzoni, Sullivan, & Sullivan, 1983). It is probably fair to say that, for the 1980s, the states are the "workhorses of our federal system" (Sharkansky, 1972). State-level policy making in education has become a focal point both for supporters and for critics of current governmental services (see Deutcher, 1984; Jennings, 1981; Kearney & Vander Putten, 1979).

A wide variety of political, economic, and social forces have been responsible for shifting the initiative in educational policy making away from local and federal actors and into the hands of state-level decision makers (Elmore, 1984b). Internal reforms have expanded the ability of state governments to effectively address education issues. Legislative reapportionment and the professionalization of many legislative and executive staff services have provided the political legitimacy and the technical capacity that state agencies need to pursue policy initiatives aggressively.

External factors have been even more important in transforming the role of the states. The Reagan administration has dramatically reduced the level of federal fiscal and ideological support for education policy initiatives and has consistently urged stronger state and local action instead. This withdrawal of federal support was made relatively palatable by extensive documentation of the limited impact of many federally sponsored reforms and substantial evidence showing that local support is a crucial ingredient in successful school improvement. Large-scale demographic changes—the entry of the baby-boom generation into their child-bearing years, migration from snowbelt to sunbelt states, urbanization and suburbanization, immigration of non-English-speaking minorities, and increasing feminization of the workforce—have forced massive changes in school operations and services.

Circumstances have also encouraged a shift of policy-making initiative away from local school districts. Although they remain active and potent forces in overall school operations, the independence and flexibility of local school districts have been curtailed in a variety of ways. State guidelines and mandates for the purchase of textbooks in three of the most populous states (California, Florida, and Texas) have helped to produce a truly national system for development and distribution of curriculum materials. Modest successes by disadvantaged and minority groups in their struggle for expanded educational opportunities have resulted in formula-driven school finance systems in several states. Moreover, although it is true that legislative reforms in school finance stimulated by court mandates handed down in the *Serrano v. Priest, Robinson* v. *Cahill*, and similar cases have not been successful in eliminating resource inequalities, they have substantially removed revenue and taxation decisions from the hands of local taxpayers and school boards. Other judicial and legislative actions have constrained the decision-making power of local school boards in such areas as program assignment (Geisert, 1981), special education services (McConnell & McLaughlin, 1982; Moore et al., 1983), and student discipline (*Goss v. Lopez*, 1975; *Wood v. Strickland*, 1975). The result has been a substantial reduction in local control over program structure, funding levels, and patterns of expenditure.

The drift of policy decisions toward the state level has been further supported by significant economic and labor market changes that make it increasingly important for schools to provide all students with skills that fit them for increasingly complex and rapidly changing job opportunities. Collective bargaining for teachers (Cresswell & Murphy, 1980; Impact of collective bargaining, 1980; Lieberman, 1980; Mitchell et al., 1985), together with the willingness of courts and state legislatures to take on major school policy questions, has produced a substantial "legalization" of education (e.g., see Kirp & Jensen, 1985). The involvement of lawyers and judicial review processes encourages the

standardization of practice and further reduces local flexibility. Serious conflicts among professional groups (most frequently expressed in the form of labor strife) or between professional and lay groups have so overwhelmed some local school districts that they find it almost impossible to formulate effective policies (Colton & Graham, 1982; McDonnell & Pascal, 1979).

Some observers insist that local authority has been more abandoned than curtailed by recent events (e.g., see Kerchner & Mitchell, 1982; Lutz & Iannaccone, 1978; Mitchell, Kerchner, Erck, & Pryor, 1981). Others believe that local districts have been shorn of power and/or overwhelmed by circumstances (e.g., Guthrie & Reed, 1985). Whichever is the case, state policy actions have clearly become more visible and more directly aimed at influencing day-to-day school operations than ever before.

In sum, increased state agency capacity, reduced federal commitment, decreased exercise of local authority, and changed social and economic conditions have all conspired to shift the initiative for educational policy toward the state level. In times of stress such a shift is not surprising—after all, that is where the ultimate constitutional authority for education is lodged. It is, however, one of the most important but least understood factors in current school operations.

DIFFICULTY IN ANALYZING STATE EDUCATIONAL POLICY SYSTEMS

For a number of reasons, it is extraordinarily difficult to provide a clear summary of either the processes or the substantive content of recent state educational policies. For one thing, states vary tremendously in both intensity and expansiveness of activities concerning educational policy. The causes of this variability are not easily identified. Apparently, state policy systems are vulnerable to pressures from a wide variety of forces—from within the schools themselves, from the broader context of a state's political life outside the educational system, and even from outside the state itself. Thus, for example, release of A *Nation at Risk*, a report by the National Commission on Educational Excellence, triggered a tremendous flurry of activity in many states (for a summary see, *Education Week*, 1985). A similar flurry of action followed the USSR's *Sputnik* launching in 1957.

State systems also appear to be quite vulnerable to the influence of charismatic leadership by a governor, chief state school officer, or key state legislator. When strong-willed, reasonably intelligent public officials aggressively present proposals for change in educational policy, they are often successful in getting new regulations and sometimes even substantial new financing for the schools. Such leadership is not evenly distributed across the states, nor is it evenly distributed over time within any given state. Hence, policy activity tends to come in fits and starts—longish periods of relative inactivity interrupted by bursts of highly visible change.

A third reason for wide variations among the states is linked to the vulnerability of educational policy systems to the actions of well-organized or well-financed interest groups. Whether they are educational insiders (such as teachers' unions, driver-education instructors, or urban school districts) or interested lay groups (such as taxpayer associations, educationally activist religious groups, or corporate leaders), when state decision makers are faced with well-articulated demands for changes in school regulations or program structures, they generally reply with at least some accommodation and compromise. Here again, states differ rather markedly in both the character of the organized interest groups actively seeking change and in the relative potency of the various active groups.

In addition to the enormous variability among the states, school policies are hard to summarize and analyze because it is difficult to say precisely where educational policy leaves off and other state policies begin. In addition to providing children with the sort of knowledge that is popularly referred to as "basic skills," schools undertake programs and perform a wide variety of functions that are very difficult to separate from community service, social welfare, or even the practices of religious cults. School administrators and teachers are held accountable for day care, nutrition and health services, enforcement of laws and maintenance of due-process rights, child welfare, cultural socialization or "Americanization," stimulation of interest in the arts, and employment and supervision of millions of workers—just to mention a few of the more obvious functions that fall under the general rubric of "educational policy." It is refreshing, and probably helpful, to see contemporary policy debates focusing directly on issues of school curriculum and instruction, but renewed interest in these more obviously educational matters has certainly not produced a national consensus on either the essential elements or the ultimate boundaries of educational policy.

Analysis and explanation of state-level educational policies is further obscured by the fact that for about half a century these policies were controlled by professionals whose actions were largely hidden from political view. A major legacy of the so-called Progressive era in American politics was the proposition that we could and should separate education and politics. During the late 19th century, graft and corruption in state and local governments brought forth the Progressive and Urban Reform movements, which sought to sever the connection between ordinary politics and the formation of school policy. The reforms, more successful on an ideological than a political level, did succeed in persuading many members of the nation's intellectual and political elites that educational policy was primarily a technical matter to be left to professional educators. As a result, school management and learning theories developed during the first half of the 20th century were kept separate from political theory. Moreover, scholars trained in political research methods paid almost no attention to school politics or educational policy formation.

The Study of State Policy Systems

Two distinct strands of research contribute to our current understanding of state-level school politics and policy formation. The two strands differ in several important respects. They have separate historical and intellectual roots, they define research problems differently, and they make distinctive contributions to our knowledge about how school organization and administration are affected by state-level decision making.

The first research strand resulted from the application of the traditional concepts and methods of political science to educational systems. It seeks to explain school policy by looking at the *distribution of power* among various stakeholders in the system and following interactions among these power-wielding groups in order to reveal the *processes* of decision making. Research rooted in this tradition tries to establish *when and how* various decisions are made, and it looks for explanations within the institutional structures, organizational procedures, or personal actions of individual policy makers. It is properly called "politics-of-education" research.

A second strand of research, less concerned with the role of political power in shaping decision-making processes, concentrates instead on the *content* of state educational policies. This line of research is more concerned with the various types or *domains of action* available to policy makers, and it looks for the consequences of state action by measuring changes in school performance rather than changes in the wins or losses of various political actors. Properly called "educational policy" research, this work seeks to explain the what rather than the why of governmental decisions. By emphasizing the substantive impact of various governmental actions—examining the costs and benefits of adopting one policy option over another and determining the political or technical feasibility of various options—this research helps to illuminate decision alternatives.

Research on policy questions is extremely varied. It is almost impossible to say precisely when a study of teaching behavior, learning activity, program operations, or any other aspect of schooling should be considered a "policy study." As described in more detail later, however, the emergence of educational policy research as an identifiable field of scholarly activity has shed important new light on the politics of state-level decision making and is leading to an overall reconceptualization of the explanatory frameworks developed by the earlier politics-of-education strand.

In the discussion to follow, the two state-level research strands are reviewed separately. A brief look at the historical development of each reveals the methods and major topics addressed by each. Then, the major implications for educational administration are explored.

POLITICS-OF-EDUCATION RESEARCH

Serious study of state-level decision making within the politics-of-education research strand did not begin until the late 1950s. Although both scholars and professional educators were well aware of the important role played by politics in determining *Who Gets What, When, How* (Lasswell, 1936), the first half of the 20th century was characterized by what Iannaccone (1967) described as the "myth" of nonpolitical decision making in educational policy matters. The picture changed quickly following a call for expanded research on school politics published in the prestigious *American Political Science Review* (Eliot, 1959). A substantial group of scholars began to give serious attention to state-level policy setting, providing for the first time empirical analyses of the political forces shaping educational policy decisions. The first book-length treatment, *School Men and Politics*, was published 3 years after the Eliot essay (Bailey, Frost, Marsh, & Wood., 1962). This book examined policy making in eight Northeastern states and set the tone for research on state systems for the next several years.

Two other case studies of state policy making quickly followed Bailey's. The first (Usdan, 1963) was a study of New York, the other (Masters, Salisbury, & Eliot, 1964) looked at Michigan, Illinois, and Missouri. These works were reviewed and synthesized by Iannaccone (1967) in a book arguing that the way professional educator groups are organized is the most important determinant of state-level policy. Over the next decade several other case studies appeared in the literature (for book-length studies, see Berke & Kirst, 1972; Campbell

& Mazzoni, 1976; Milstein & Jennings, 1973; Usdan, Minar, & Hurwitz, 1969). As sources of insight, however, these case studies have their limitations. Burlingame and Geske (1979) point out that case studies often obscure as much as they illuminate because they give too much attention to the particular features of individual states and too little to formulation of general propositions or explanatory theories.

By the early 1970s, research on state educational systems began to produce more focused and theoretically grounded work. Attempts were made, for example, to test whether economic or political factors were more important in predicting state policy decisions (Zeigler & Johnson, 1972); to discover the impact of ESEA Title V on state departments of education (Milstein, 1976); to determine whether state political cultures accounted for the degree of centralized control over local school district operations (Wirt, 1977, 1978); to identify the communication networks through which policy initiatives move from one state to another (Kirst, 1981); and to determine whether state legislatures utilize the findings of social-science research in making policy decisions (Mitchell, 1981).

Five Lessons From Recent Political Research

Five basic lessons for administrators can be drawn from research on the politics of state-level decision making in education. These lessons can be put in the form of propositions regarding how people interested in affecting state policy decisions should direct their attention and actions.

1. Look to the organization of professional interest groups.

As suggested earlier, the earliest studies of state educational politics highlighted the importance of organized professional interest groups as prime contributors to the formation of specific policies (see Bailey et al., 1962; Cremin, 1964; Masters et al., 1964; McGivney, 1984; Tyack & Hansot, 1982). Although later research has made it plain that other organized interest groups (notably those organized on the basis of economic interest or ethnic identity) play very important roles in the formulation and implementation of state-level policies, professional interest groups are still widely recognized as among the most important forces in state politics. Although the initiative for proposing school reforms has tended to move into the hands of individual legislators and, to a lesser extent, into the hands of business and professional groups (other than educators) (Chall, 1979), the power of professional groups (at least when they can agree on a common interpretation of an issue) to veto proposed changes remains strong.

2. Informal social networks move policy initiatives across state boundaries.

It has long been obvious that educational policies adopted in one state are frequently copied (sometimes with little or no modification) in other states within a short time. It has not always been clear how this diffusion of educational policies occurs. To some extent, of course, the mass media contribute to the process. Newspaper and magazine articles about new policy initiatives in one state are frequently used as the starting point for policy development in others. A few formal organizations give explicit support to this diffusion process, the Education Commission of the States, the National Governors Conference, the National Association of State Boards of Education, the Council of Chief State School Officers, and the Council of State Legislatures notable among them. Relatively recent research on factors controlling collective bargaining, creationism, competency testing, and school finance policy decisions suggests, however, that various informal networks (often consisting of scholars supported by foundations or public-sector legal centers) play a crucial role in articulating issues and initiating action to move policy from one state to another (Kirst, 1981; Pipho, 1981). Informal policy networks also exist in the areas of school desegregation and the development of special education programs. Both the membership and the mode of operation of these informal networks change from one issue to another, and their impact varies sharply from one state to another.

3. State education policy is typically shaped by a very small number of key actors.

To a surprising degree, major state policy initiatives are shaped and their enactment controlled by a very small number of key actors. A point made by Mitchell (1981) regarding the limited range of involvement in legislative decision making can be applied to policies formulated by other state-level actors as well:

> The vast bulk of all legislative decisions are made by a tiny handful of people. At the articulation stage when the content of legislative proposals is being defined, it is rare to find more than a dozen or so individuals with more than a casual understanding of the decisions. Not infrequently, in fact, fairly substantial policy decisions will involve only two or three individuals. Although decisions are generally (but not always) exposed to a fairly large group of policy makers as they pass through the four stages of the legislative workflow, most of those involved adopt an essentially passive stance—rendering judgment on the legitimacy or adequacy of policies

presented by others. Only a few policy makers actively engage in dissecting an issue, gathering and weighing evidence on its merits, or studying its probable impact on society. (p. 144)

There are several reasons for the low level of involvement in these policy decisions. First, of course, educational policies are complicated (a very substantial body of statutory law and administrative regulations governing education is found in every state). Second, school policy making is a high-risk activity because education has long served as a kind of "secular religion" for Americans, who tend to view disagreement over the goals or methods of education very much the way they view matters of orthodoxy and heresy in their churches. Third, although a very large portion of every state's total budget goes into education, these resources are so distributed that it is very difficult for a policy maker to significantly reward political allies or punish enemies, hence involvement in educational policy is seen as a substantial risk with relatively little political payoff. And finally, state policy systems reward specialization among policy makers. Unless state policy makers concentrate their efforts on a small number of issues, they generally are unable to significantly deflect the tendency of every issue to be decided through marginal adjustment on last year's way of doing business (Furhman, 1983; Mitchell, 1981).

4. State policies are strongly affected by variations in state political cultures.

With increasing frequency students of state-level policy making point to the importance of cultural beliefs and values as determinants of basic policy decisions. Elazar (1972) has provided a provocative interpretation of the nature and origins of different state-level political cultures. He argues that immigrants to the United States brought with them three quite different sets of beliefs about the purpose and proper functioning of government. Settlers in New England, he asserts, embraced a "moralist" view of government, in contrast with a "individualist" view held by those who came to the Middle Atlantic region and a "traditionalist" view brought by those who first settled in the Southeast. And, says Elazar, these historically divergent belief patterns have been preserved as citizens moved from these historical regions to other parts of the country. Some scholars have applied Elazar's concepts to school policy formation. Wirt (1977, 1980) examined data on state education codes and argued that the degree of centralized control embodied in codes is significantly related to the cultural values identified by Elazar. More recently, Mitchell et al. (1986) have demonstrated that the cultural differences postulated by Elazar can be measured through survey questions and that the measured cultural differences are related to differences in the educational policies adopted in various states. Lehne (1983) emphasizes this point, saying:

> Because each legislature is in some ways unique and each is embedded in a particular state political culture, the challenge of generalizing may appear overwhelming. Indeed, there may be no way to generalize about legislatures and education policy in all 50 states without distorting as much as is brought into focus. (p. 45)

5.   *State decisions are circumscribed by organizational, political, and fiscal stresses within each state.*

Periodic shifts in economic conditions, demographic changes, and political realignments have the power to change the processes of decision making among state-level policy makers. Successful taxpayer revolts in California and Massachusetts during the late 1970s, for example, fundamentally altered school finance in these two states. The general movement of people from snowbelt to sunbelt states has also altered decision making (with snowbelt states facing problems of decline while sunbelt states face building construction problems). Major court battles over school finance and over access to education by handicapped students and those with limited English-language proficiency have also led to major changes in state-level decision making (Brown & Elmore, 1983; *Guadalupe Organization, Inc. v. Tempe*, 1978; Kaden, 1983; Kirp, Bass, & Kurilaff, 1974; *Lau v. Nichols*, 1974; Levin, 1977; *Mills v. Board of Education*, 1972; Rickman, 1981; Van Geel, 1978). None of these changes has been more dramatic than the general drift toward a conservative political ideology that has elevated issues of parental choice and educational quality while encouraging a broad retreat from the questions of educational equity that dominated most state policy systems over the past quarter of a century.

FROM POLITICS TO POLICY

In recent years research on state systems has tended to shift away from process-oriented political studies to more content-oriented policy analysis. In the ERIC system, for example, there has been a steady rise in the number of citations for which the term "policy(ies)" is one of the key descriptors. In 1969 only 902 of the more than 25,000 ERIC entries (3.6 percent) used this term. By the early 1980s the rate had more than doubled, to about 7.3 percent of all new entries.

The current period of highly visible policy research has been stimulated largely by three major changes in the operation of the federal government: (a) reliance by the courts on social-science evidence, (b) adoption of formal rational planning techniques like planning program budgeting systems (PPBS), and (c) widespread use of scientific evaluation procedures for program assessment. Though their impact on the study of state-level educational policy systems has only recently become obvious, these changes originated in the 1950s. Rossell (1980) documents increasing court reliance on social-research data beginning with the *Sweatt v. Painter* decision in 1950. Ukeles (1977) and Yeakey (1983) both argue that rational planning techniques of the sort introduced by Robert McNamara into the Pentagon during the 1960s played a major role in sensitizing government decision makers to social-science research data. And, as Mitchell (1985) notes, evaluation mandates associated with social programs generated during the Kennedy and Johnson administrations gave fiscal and political support to a veritable army of social-science-oriented policy analysts.

Conceptual support for this shift from politics to policy-oriented research can be traced back to Lasswell's seminal essay in a 1951 book entitled *The Policy Sciences* (Lerner & Lasswell, 1951). Lasswell argued that "a policy orientation has been developing which cuts across the existing specializations" (p. 3). It has taken nearly 30 years for this simple observation to become a self-conscious element in educational research, but the evidence of the past decade leaves little doubt that policy-oriented research is here to stay.

Though the emphasis on issues rather than power relationships makes it relatively easy to distinguish policy research from the older politics-of-education research, it is extremely difficult to review or concisely summarize what has been learned through the application of policy approaches to state-level education problems. At a conceptual level, policy studies are very diverse, and it is virtually impossible to see how they might be integrated into an overall theory of state educational policy. It is even difficult to decide which of the thousands of education-related publications produced each year are appropriately considered policy research studies. A very large set of policy-relevant statistics are gathered and published each year (by the National Center for Education Statistics, the NEA, the Census Bureau, and a wide variety of other agencies), but most of these statistics go unanalyzed and uninterpreted. As a result, they provide few real insights into state policy. Moreover, many state policy questions have been illuminated only through secondary analysis of data originally gathered to examine federal issues or through research on differences among local school districts that have been indirectly traced to state policies. This means that critical state policy findings are frequently not recognized as such until some time after they are published, and thus they cannot be easily identified in a routine library search.

With these caveats in mind, three tentative lessons can be drawn from the vast array of published research studies. The first is that state-level educational policy has an identifiable *taxonomic structure*. That is, state policies deal with a specific and relatively limited set of educational issues or topics. Second, policy research is bringing about a reconceptualization of the *process* of issue formation and decision making. Political researchers use traditional notions about power and control to account for the dynamics of policy formation. Policy researchers emphasize the dynamic character of decision making; they trace policy actions through successive *stages* in the decision process and show that the *timing* of political action is just as important as the power resources available to support it. Third, policy-oriented research and analysis have drawn attention to the difference between policy making and policy *impact*. Where political research focuses on who wins and who loses in the effort to control the schools, policy research draws attention to the extent to which particular actions reliably produce specific results.

The Content of Educational Policy

Several efforts have been made in the last few years to identify the topical domains of educational policy research. LaNoue (1982), for example, suggested that educational policy researchers have concentrated on just two basic topics (educational equity and school governance). In a summary of recent policy research efforts, Mitchell (1985) expanded LaNoue's list to include two additional topics: teaching and learning, and the economics of education.

Such categorical lists do not adequately capture the breadth and complexity of changes in state policy, however. The variety of new policy initiatives adopted during the last decade is staggering. Several states (including California, Colorado, Connecticut, Delaware, Florida, Kentucky, Maryland, Missouri, and Pennsylvania) have adopted what are described as "comprehensive" school improvement programs—programs that simultaneously attack various combinations of fiscal, organizational, staff development, curriculum enhancement, and student assessment problems (Fuhrman, 1984; McLaughlin, 1981; Odden & Dougherty, 1982; Van Geel, 1978). Most states have undertaken a mixture of narrower, less integrated (and generally less vigorous) policy initiatives. Among these more limited policy approaches, the most frequent area of concentration has been on some form of student and/or teacher testing and assessment.

Although the research support claimed for virtually every proposed new state policy is frequently more rhetorical than substantive, a large body of research on school problems and policy options is finding its way into the policy process. But it is difficult for everyone—scholars and policy makers alike—to identify clearly the links between research findings and specific policy issues. The weak link between research and policy making has led critics to charge that policies are uninformed, arbitrary, inappropriate, ineffective, misguided, or worse (Lynch, 1979). Policy makers themselves often feel that their actions are less than fully coherent and consistent because available research provides neither sound theory nor adequate data on which to base important decisions.

Why has criticism become harsh just as the body of policy research has grown so large? In part the problem lies in the kinds of studies done by policy researchers. Too many policy studies trade fundamental insight and long-term theory development for short-term "relevance" to the policy debates that are currently in progress. The "issues" studied by policy researchers tend to be those that are politically "hot" in the mid-1980s. In the area of educational equity, for example, desegregation and finance reform studies gave way to "white flight" and private school research as political attention shifted. Similarly, teacher effectiveness research is presently dominated by studies of career structure, merit pay, and administrative supervision, which replace the emphases on teacher organization and staff development of a few years ago. Policy research, in short, has a tendency to rush from one subject or program domain to another without developing a clear rationale for selecting particular topics for study. It is certainly helpful for policy makers and school administrators to have well-analyzed data on how states are approaching school reform and improvement questions, but it is equally important to have these analyses incorporated into a more comprehensive analytical framework capable of guiding overall policy development. It is not enough to simply show, for example, that collective bargaining statutes are altering school operations, that school finance reforms have not fully equalized support for students, or that teacher supply and demand problems are likely to get worse in the near future. Research needs to put these issues into perspective, indicating how they interact with each other and with other basic elements of state educational policy.

To produce this perspective, policy analysis requires a systematic *taxonomy* of state policy actions—a taxonomy providing a comprehensive overview of possible domains within which states can act. Several efforts at developing such a taxonomy can be found in the literature. Most are constructed empirically and lack a theoretical framework for determining when the entire range of state policy actions have been classified. The most common approach to the development of an empirical taxonomy is illustrated by Odden and Dougherty (1982), who present two different taxonomic summaries of important state policy actions within a single short review of recent developments. Early in their review they identify seven general patterns of state policy action: workforce improvement, curricular guidance, accreditation and program review, comprehensive improvement programs, dissemination and assistance programs, testing programs, and parent involvement or information dissemination programs. Later, when detailing the elements of actual state programs, they distinguish 18 different categories of policy action. McLaughlin (1981) takes a rather different approach to the development of an empirically grounded taxonomy. She notes that the intensity or "level" of state action is as important as its content or "nature" because nominally identical policies with varying levels of commitment or resource allocation behind them have very different impacts on school operations.

Theoretical approaches to the development of a policy taxonomy are reviewed by Mitchell and Encarnation (1984). They conclude that the most appropriate approach is based on the limited repertoire of state-level *control mechanisms* available for shaping the performance of the schools. Policies, they suggest, are best described in terms of which of these mechanisms are being utilized. Their initial framework was refined through a study supported by the National Insitute of Education of policy mechanisms in six states (Mitchell et al., 1985). This research study demonstrates that states differ significantly in their reliance on various policy mechanisms and that these differences are linked to variations in state political cultures. Seven policy mechanisms are identified in this study. A brief review of each of them will illustrate (but certainly not exhaust) the variety of policy studies available in each domain.

1. School Organization and Governance

The study of school organization and governance is the oldest form of policy research—it has been a favorite subject for historians. The development of compulsory-schooling laws, the organization of school districts, the formation of state departments of education, and the emergence of professional organizations have all been studied in detail (e.g., see Callahan, 1962; Fuller & Pearson, 1969; Katz 1975; Tyack, 1974). Governance decisions are among the most powerful control mechansims available to state policy makers. They are used to allocate powers and responsibilities among interested groups. During the first half of the 20th century, the major thrust of governance was to enhance professional control. Following the *Brown* decisions, however, concern in many states shifted toward strengthening parents' and other lay groups. Citizen participation in decision making was hotly debated, and slightly researched, during the 1960s and early 1970s (e.g., see Levin, 1970; National Committee for Citizens in Education [NCCE], 1975; Summerfield, 1971).

2. School Finance

Studies of state school finance systems and policies have been among the most powerful and effective of all policy research efforts. A series of school finance research studies sponsored by the Ford Foundation played a major role in the preparation of court cases and the development of finance reform legislation in several states. As Wirt and Kirst (1982) report, "The Ford Foundation provided publicity, grants, travel, and recognition as resources" (p. 240) to set in place a cohesive policy influence network of scholars, lawyers, and political officials who pressed effectively for school finance reform. (See also Berne & Shefel, 1979; Brookover & Lezotte, 1977; Porter, Warner, & Porter, 1973; Kniekman & Reschoosky, 1980.)

3. Student Testing and Assessment

Statewide assessment of students' academic achievement is a matter of policy in 36 states. The accuracy and appropriateness of tests has been the subject of a broad array of research work—most of it conducted with little or no concern for state policy. In the 1970s, however, the role of testing in state policy became a major issue and policy researchers were called upon to analyze and interpret both the academic and the social significance of tests. Twenty-seven states adopted some form of competency testing aimed at assessing whether students were achieving up to expectations.

4. School Program Definition

How long children should go to school, what subjects they should be required to take, and what special education programs or ancillary services should be made available to them? These questions have all been the object of extensive policy analysis and debate. Two clusters of policy research stand out as powerful shapers of state-level policy on these matters. The first are the Rand Corporation studies of the impact of Title I programs on schools (Berman & McLaughlin, 1975–1978). These studies, in combination with a host of other work on the reaction of schools to mandated programs, convinced policy makers that neither funding nor mandates could be substituted for the involvement of local educators in interpreting, adapting, and incorporating programs that they understand and believe in. A second critical research program was the *Beginning Teacher Evaluation Study* (Educational Testing Service, 1976), which popularized the concepts of "direct instruction" and "time on task" and persuaded state policy makers that school improvement depends on the amount of time children spend in direct instruction. Dozens of other research efforts could also be cited as contributing to an overall picture of how school programs could be structured to improve student learning. Work by Edmonds (1979) and Brookover, Beady, Flood, Schwertzer, & Wisenbaker (1979) and a number of other scholars constituted what became known as the "effective schools" literature, which has provided the basic rationale for most state-level program reforms during the 1980s. (See also Lezotte, 1982; Madaus, Airasian, & Kellaghan, 1980)

5. *Personnel Training and Certification*

Policies aimed at controlling the quality and size of the teaching workforce are receiving increased attention. Research on merit pay plans (Cohen & Murnane, 1985; Porwoll, 1979) and other ways of modifying teachers' salary structures are of great interest to state policy makers. Teacher competency testing, training programs, professional development, in-service training, and a host of other possible mechanisms for improving the quality of teachers are also being reviewed and studied seriously.

6. *Curriculum Materials Development and Selection*

Research on state-level curriculum policy has been relatively sparse, but it is increasingly important to policy debates. Recent efforts by California, Texas, and Florida to force publishers to upgrade textbook content have been widely publicized. Litt (1965), Van Geel (1978), and Geisert (1981) have done much to illuminate curriculum content policy.

7. *School Buildings and Facilities*

This element in the policy taxonomy developed by Mitchell et al. (1986) has not been widely researched, nor was it identified as a high-priority concern by the state policy makers whom Mitchell and associates interviewed. Policy makers in West Virginia identify policy on building and facilities as important in the wake of a federal court decision mandating equalization of facilities for poor and minority children in that state.

States have generally given much more attention to finance and school governance than to the other basic mechanisms identified by Mitchell et al. (1986). Most state policy makers report a continued interest in expanding control, however, and we can expect the development of new initiatives in all the domains described.

The Time Dimension of State Policy Making

The second major lesson to be drawn from policy research springs from its focus on the importance of *time* in political decision making. According to Mitchell (1981), time shapes the decision process because

> responding to political pressures and interests takes time. It takes time to sort out the pressures and determine exactly what problems people are asking to have solved. It takes time to determine whether a proposed policy would be damaging to the interests of others or is adequately responsive to the original problem. It takes time to discover how broadly or intensively particular policy options are supported by various constituent groups or the public. And it takes time to determine whether a proposed policy is important enough to justify the expenditure of scarce resources on its implementation. (pp. 21, 22)

There are two consequences of the time-structured character of educational policy formation. First, it becomes necessary to think of decision making as taking place within a "workflow"—a developmental process that has a beginning and moves toward an end. Second, it becomes important to consider the timing of various policy influences.

The workflow through which state-level policy decisions pass is not a single, undifferentiated continuum. Rather, the process is broken up into distinct phases or stages. As policy proposals move from one stage to the next, they are subjected to very different decision-making processes. The questions asked about proposed actions are not the same from stage to stage. Nor are the resources needed to effectively support, resist, or modify actions being considered the same. Even the key actors who take responsibility for formulating actions, assessing their adequacy, and resolving conflicts of interest may differ from one stage to the next.

For the most part, research on state-level educational decision making either ignores the complexity of its differentiation into stages or concentrates on only one or two of the basic stages. It is increasingly clear, however, that a full understanding of state educational policy is possible only if the events that occur during the early stages of a decision are interpreted in light of their subsequent impact on later elements in the overall process. A brief review of six basic stages in the policy process, illustrated by reference to a few key educational policy issues, will help to show why this is so.

The first policy stage involves *articulation* of both interests and policy proposals. Until a policy problem has been explicitly articulated as a target for action and at least one possible mechanism for dealing with that problem has been proposed, the policy system does not really have anything to do. Not many policy analysts have studied the articulation of issues at the state level. Peterson's (1976) excellent work on Chicago city politics reviews the articulation of administrative decentralization, desegregation, and collective bargaining issues, showing how the definition of an issue shapes the way decisions are made. Kirst's (1981) study of informal social networks that carry issues across state boundaries is one of the few studies to look at the articulation of state issues.

The second phase in policy formation involves *aggregation*—both the aggregation of interested parties into broad-based coalitions of support for (or opposition to) particular policy proposals and the aggregation of diverse proposals into integrated programs capable of attracting the needed coalition of support. This stage has been the primary focus of attention for politics-of-education researchers. As suggested earlier, research here has been primarily concerned with the distribution of power and influence, concepts particularly relevant to the aggregation process. What has been little studied by political researchers, however, has been the process of issue aggregation. It is obvious, for example, that the educational equity movement developed an effective power base by combining the race issue with such other issues as financial equalization, opportunities for handicapped children, bilingual education, and sex equity. Little is known, however, about how or when such issues become aggregated in order to support broad programs of educational reform.

The third stage, the one most often recognized by the public and the mass media, involves the *allocation* of power and resources. At this point explicit decisions are made to officially embrace some proposals and reject others. It is during this stage that the policy system sets priorities on competing proposals. During earlier phases, policy makers work on eliminating "bad" proposals but generally allow more "good" ideas to go forward than can ultimately be supported. Allocation, as Wirt (1980) has noted, is truly an "allocation of values" (Easton, 1965), not just a matter of providing money or political authority. The allocation process has many of the attributes of a zero-sum game: In order to give vitally needed support to one policy or program, others must be denied or rejected. Many good ideas must be denied the resources needed to implement them. At this stage, policy makers are engaged in distinguishing the important from the trivial, the valuable from the merely desirable. How value is assigned to competing proposals is a complex and incompletely understood process. Research on

allocation has been undertaken by both political and policy research scholars. Political scholars are more interested in the determinants of various allocation decisions. The work of Zeigler and Johnson (1972) represents a typical political analysis of resource allocation interest. Ebert and Pierce's (1980) work on the effects of collective bargaining is a typical look at the interaction between policy and resource allocation.

The fourth stage in state-level policy making is the *regulation* stage. Having decided what policies to support, the policy system must now flesh out the regulatory and budgetary details of who will be given explicit authority and resources to support an assignment of responsibility for policy action. The regulation stage generally interests policy researchers more than it does political researchers. The ways in which regulations support or fail to support particular programs or other policy actions has been the subject of a very large body of research. The politics of regulation development has not received widespread attention, however.

The fifth stage, *implementation*, begins at the point where policy is turned into practice. This phase of policy making has been widely studied, but it is still somewhat mystifying, both to social scientists and to education policy makers. It is at this stage that policy research has had its major impact. Several studies have produced basic changes in education policy (the most notable ones, like the McLaughlin study of Title I implementation, 1975, and the Coleman et al. 1966, study of equality of educational opportunity, have focused on federal policy implementation). The nonimplementation of adopted policies has become a major concern for social scientists during the last decade. (See Lipsky, 1980, for a provocative discussion of implementation issues.)

The sixth and last stage in the policy-making process is *evaluation* of the extent to which policies have been implemented as intended and/or produced the expected (or some important unexpected) outcomes. Although not all policies are evaluated, evaluation is a distinctive stage of policy decision making; its procedures and outcomes are politically influenced and they have identifiable consequences for the continuation, modification, or demise of a policy action. Berman, Weiler, and Gjelten (1983) offer a typical example of evaluation-oriented policy research. They found that the California School Improvement program affects schools in very different ways depending on how it is defined by those who must implement it.

Differentiating among the several stages in the formation and implementation of state policy reveals why *timing* is so important when one seeks to support or influence the process. Each stage in the process has its own set of key actors, and each stage is characterized by a unique set of social relationships among those actors. During the articulation stage, for example, there is a high premium on imagination and the development of intuitively reasonable theories of social action that can serve as the basis for formulating and analyzing proposals. As decisions move from this initial stage of proposal development into the more politically charged and socially active aggregation stage, information needs become more technical, and problem-solving skills are valued more than original thinking. During allocation, decisions divide "winners" from "losers," which makes the use of information as a weapon or tool for winning the policy debate a prime consideration. At this stage, of course, there is no such thing as objective neutrality. When allocation of power and fiscal resources are at stake, everyone is presumed to have an interest (one that some may intentionally hide).

Once policy decisions have passed through the allocation stage and the organization and regulation process begins, information needs and decision-making processes change once again. At this point, technical information about the consequences of alternative regulatory patterns is most valuable. Unfortunately, this kind of information is frequently lacking in the policy system. Responsibility for regulation writing and the development of detailed organizational plans is frequently given to departmental functionaries who have been socialized to a bureaucratic world view alien to those who must implement the policy. During the policy-implementation stage, decision-making norms and information needs change once again. Policy implementors are people who have found ways of accommodating demands and pressures from many sources. They are quite likely to view a new state policy as just "one more pressure" on them, and are equally likely to accommodate it only to the extent necessary to keep that pressure from seriously disrupting their work. For reasons that have to do with their own work settings, however, implementors may also view the new policy as a long-awaited opportunity to undertake a series of actions that not only fulfill the requirements of the policy but embody its spirit in ways scarcely contemplated by those who originally developed it. In education, the evidence suggests that policy implementors may even distort a policy through "overcompliance" rather than active or passive resistance to it. During the evaluation stage, the tension between scientific and nonscientific modes of thought and action are likely to become obvious. Social scientists engaged in evaluating programs and policies often find that their attitudes and work habits do not mesh well with those who hire them and expect to use the results of their work.

Policy Impact

By focusing attention on the content of specific educational policies, recent research has given especial prominence to the problem of policy impact. During the 1970s it was common practice for both policy makers and research scholars to lament the apparent imperviousness of the public schools to policy-directed change, even when those changes were backed by strongly worded court orders or substantial fiscal resources. Although recent research is less pessimistic about the problem of impact (e.g., Rabe & Peterson, 1983), the issue remains important and deserves serious attention in any discussion of state-level educational policy.

Many scholars have sought to probe the reasons for limited policy impact. Among the more provocative interpretations is one by Elmore (1978), who identifies four fundamentally different organizational theories, each providing a different basis for explaining the limited effectiveness of state or federal educational policies. To oversimplify, Elmore indicates that policy failure can arise through (a) inadequate or unintelligent management of the school, which is seen as a more or less rational system for pursuing specific public policy goals; (b) bureaucratic subversion within the school, which is seen as a set of routinized behavior patterns and dispersed centers of power; (c) alienation or disengagement on the part of individual educators, who are thought to be only tenuously linked to the school organization and only tentatively committed to its norms and goals; or (d) insufficient power resources at the disposal of policy makers, whose interests frequently conflict with those of key actors within the school organization or its political environment. There is at least some evidence to support each of these competing theories. Future state-level research in both the politics-of-education and educational-policy-analysis strands will almost certainly pursue this question of how best to account for the impact of state action on day-to-day school operations.

Summary

In this chapter we have reviewed the development of state-level research on educational politics and policy. Political research, with its interest in the nature and use of power and influence, was distinguished from policy research, which concentrates on the content and impact of specific state actions. Five lessons implicit in politics-of-education research were noted. It was argued, however, that the policy perspective has provided a very different set of important research findings and insights. In addition to highlighting particular issues, policy research has led to a reconceptualization of policy making as a process with several distinct stages. Policy research has also brought into focus the importance of time as an element in the decision-making process and has helped to explain why the same activities or events may have very powerful effects on some policy decisions while contributing little to others. Finally, the concern of policy researchers with the problems of impact was noted.

REFERENCES

Bailey, S. K., Frost, R. T., Marsh, P. E., & Wood, R. C. (1962). *Schoolmen and politics: A study of state aid to education in the Northeast.* Syracuse, NY: Syracuse University Press.

Baker v. Carr, 369 U.S. 186 (1962).

Berke, J. S., & Kirst, M. W. (1972). *Federal aid to education: Who benefits? Who governs?* Lexington, MA: Lexington.

Berman, P. & McLaughlin, M. W. (1975). *Federal programs supporting educational change*, Vol. 4: *The findings in review.* Santa Monica, CA: Rand.

Berman, P., & McLaughlin, M. W. (1978). *Federal programs supporting educational change*, Vol. 8: *Implementing and sustaining innovations.* Santa Monica, CA: Rand.

Berman, P., Weiler, D., & Gjelten, T. (1983, April). *Improving school improvement: An independent evaluation of a California school improvement plan* (preliminary report). Berkeley, CA: Berman Weiler.

Berne, R., & Shefel, L. (1979, Nov.-Dec.). Social science research and school finance policy. *American Behavioral Scientist*, 23(2), 207–236.

Brookover, W. B., Beady, C., Flood, P., Schwertzer, J., & Wisenbaker, J. (1979). *School social systems and student achievement: Schools can make a difference.* New York: Praeger.

Brookover, W. B., & Lezotte, L. W. (1977). *Changes in school characteristics coincident with changes in student achievement.* East Lansing, MI: Michigan State University, College of Urban Development.

Brown, P. R., & Elmore, R. F. (1983). Analyzing the impact of school finance reform. In N. Cambron-McCabe, & A. Odden, (Eds.), *The changing politics of school finance* (Chap. 4). Cambridge, MA: Ballinger.

Burlingame, M., & Geske, T. (1979). State politics and education: An examination of selected multiple state case studies. *Education Administration Quarterly*, 15(2), 50–79.

Caldwell, P. (1985). Governors: No longer simply patrons, they are policy chiefs. *Education Week*, 4(20), 1, 34.

Callahan, R. E. (1962). *Education and the cult of efficiency: A study of the social forces that have shaped the administration of the public schools.* Chicago: University of Chicago Press.

Campbell, R., & Mazzoni, T., Jr. (1976). *State policy making for the public schools.* Berkeley, CA: McCutchan.

Chall, Jeanne. (1979, January). Minimum competency in reading: An informal survey of the states. *Phi Delta Kappan*, 351–352.

Cohen, D. K. & Murnane, R. J. (1985). The merits of merit pay, *The Public Interest.* No. 80, 3–30.

Coleman, J. S. et al. (1966). *Equality of educational opportunity.* Washington, DC: U.S. Dept. of Health, Education, and Welfare, Office of Education.

Colton, D., & Graham, E. (1982). *Teacher strikes and the courts.* Lexington, MA: Lexington.

Cremin, L. (1964). *The transformation of the school: Progressivism in education, 1976–1957.* New York: Bantam.

Cresswell. A., & Murphy, M. (1980). *Teachers, unions, and collective bargaining in public education.* Berkeley, CA: McCutchan.

Deutcher, Robert A. (1984). Ambiguities in state-local relations. *Education and Urban Society*, 16(2), 145–164.

Easton, D. (1965). *A systems analysis of political life.* New York: John Wiley.

Eberts, R. W., & Pierce, L. W. (1980). *The effects of collective bargaining in public schools.* Eugene, OR: Center for Educational Policy and Management, University of Oregon.

Edmonds, R. R. (1979). Effective schools for the urban poor. *Educational Leadership*, 37, 17–23.

Educational Testing Service (1976). *Beginning teacher evaluation study—phase II.* Princeton, NJ: The Service.

Elazar, D. (1972). *American federalism: A view from the states* (2nd ed.). New York: Crowell.

Eliot, T. H. (1959, December). Toward an understanding of public school politics. *American Political Science Review*, 53, 1032–1051.

Elmore, R. (1978) Organizational models and social program implementation. *Public Policy*, 26(2), 185–228.

Elmore, R. (1984). The political economy of state influence. *Education and Urban Society*, 16(2), 125–144.

Fisher, C. W. & Berliner, D. C. (Eds.). (1985). *Perspectives on instructional time.* White Plains, NY: Longman.

Fuhrman, S. (1984, winter). The excellence agenda: States respond. *Educational Horizons*, 48–51.

Fuhrman, S. (1983). State-level politics and school financing. In N. Cabron-McCabe, & Allan Odden (Eds.), *The changing politics of school finance* (Chap, 3, pp. 53–70). Cambridge: MA: Ballinger.

Fuller, E. & Pearson, J. B. (Eds.). (1969). *Education in the states: Nationwide development since 1900.* Washington, DC: National Education Association.

Geisert, G. A. (1981). Control of curriculum a state legislature priority? *Education and Urban Society*, 13(3), 297–300.

Goss v. Lopez. 419 U.S. 565 (1975).

Guadalupe Organization Inc. v. Tempe Elementary School District #3. 587 F.2d 1022 (9th Cir. 1978).

Guthrie, J. W., & Reed, R. J. (1986). *Eductional administration and policy: Effective leadership for American education.* Englewood Cliffs, NJ: Prentice-Hall.

Iannaccone, L. (1967). *Politics in education.* New York: Center for Applied Research in Education.

The impact of collective bargaining on California education code law governing teacher tenure, evaluation and dismissal. (1980, April). *Pacific Law Review*, pp. 799–820.

Jennings, J. (1981). The federal role in paying for education in the 80s. In R. A. Miller (Ed.), *The federal role in education: New directions for the 80s.* Washington, DC: Institute for Educational Leadership.

Kaden, L. B. (1983, Summer). Courts and legislatures in the federal system: The case of school finance. *Hofstra Law Review*, 1205–1260.

Katz, M. B. (1975). *Class, bureaucracy, and schools: The illusion of educational change in America.* New York: Praeger.

Kearney, C. P., & Vander Putten, E. A. (Eds.). (1979). *Grants consolidation: A new balance in federal aid to schools?* Washington, DC: Institute for Educational Leadership.

Kerchner, C. T. Mitchell, D. E., Pryor, G., & Erck, W. C. (1982). *The logic of citizen participation in public school labor relations.* Boston, MA: Institute for Responsive Education, IRE Report #4.

Kirp, D., Bass, W., & Kuriloff, P. (1974). Legal reform of special education: Empirical studies and procedural proposals. *California Law Review*, 62(1), 40–155.

Kirp, D., & Jensen, A. (1985). *School days, rule day.* Philadelphia: Falmer.

Kirst, M. W. (1981). *The state role in education policy innovation.* Stanford, CA: Institute for Finance and Governance.

Kirst, M. W. (1984). State policy in an era of transition. *Education and Urban Society*, 16(2), 225–235.

Kirst, M. W., & Somers, S. (1981). Collective action among California educational interest groups: A logical response to proposition 13. *Education and Urban Society*, 13(2), 235–256.

Kniekman, J. R. & Reschoosky, A. (1980). The implementation of school finance reform. *Policy Sciences*, 12, pp. 301–315.

LaNoue, G. R. (1982). Political science. In H. E. Mitzel, J. H. Best,

& W. Rabinowitz (Eds.), *Encyclopedia of Educational Research*. Washington, DC: American Educational Research Association.

Lasswell, H. D. (1936). *Politics: Who gets what, when and how*. New York: McGraw-Hill.

Lau v. Nichols. 414 U.S. 563 (1974).

Lehne, R. (1983). Research perspectives on state legislatures and education policy. *Education Evaluation and Policy Analysis*, 5(1). 43–54.

Lerner, D., & Lasswell, H. D. (Eds.). (1951). *The policy sciences*. Stanford, CA: Stanford University Press.

Levin, B. (1977). *Current trends in school finance reform litigation: A commentary*. #6, January 1977, pp. 1099–1137.

Levin, H. M. (Ed.) (1970). *Community control of schools*. Washington, DC: Brookings Institution.

Lezotte, Lawrence W. (1982). Characteristics of effective schools and programs for realizing them. *Education Digest*, Nov. 1982, pp. 27–29.

Lieberman, M. (1980). *Public sector bargaining*. Lexington, MA: Heath.

Lipsky, M. (1980). *Street level bureaucracy: Dilemmas of the individual in public services*. NY: Russell Sage Foundation.

Litt, E. (1965). Education and political enlightenment in America, *Annals of the American Academy of Political and Social Science*. 361, 35–47.

Lutz, F. W. & Iannaccone, L. (1978). *Public participation in local school districts: The dissatisfaction theory of democracy*. Lexington, MA: Lexington.

Lynch, P. (1979). Public policy and competency testing. *Education and Urban Society*, 12(1), 65–80.

Madaus, G. F., Airasian, P. W., and Kellaghan, T. (1980) *School effectiveness: A reassessment of the evidence*. New York: McGraw-Hill.

Masters, N. A., et al. (1964). *State politics and public schools: An exploratory analysis*. NY: Knopf.

Mazzoni, T., Sullivan, B., & Sullivan, B. (1983, Winter). Legislative lobbying for education. *Planning and Changing*, 14, 226–233.

Masters, N. A., Salisbury, R. H., & Eliot, T. H. (1964). *State politics and the public schools: An exploratory analysis*. New York: Knopf.

McConnell, L., & McLaughlin, M. (1982). The states and special need students. Paper commissioned by NIE School Finance Project. Washington, D.C.

McDonnell, L., & Pascal, A. (1979). *Organized teachers in American schools* (R-2407-NIE). Santa Monica, CA: Rand.

McGivney, J. H. (1984). State educational governance patterns. *Educational Administration Quarterly*, 20(2), 43–63

McLaughlin, M. W. (1975). *Evaluation and reform: The elementary and secondary education act of 1965, Title I*. Cambridge, MA: Ballinger.

McLaughlin, M. W. (1981). *State involvement in local education quality issues*. Interim report prepared for the Education Policy Development Center for Equal Educational Opportunity for Disadvantaged Children. Santa Monica, CA: Rand.

Mills v. Board of Education. 348 F Supp. 866 (D.D.C. 1972).

Milstein, M. M. (1976). *Impact and response: Federal aid and state education agencies*. New York: Teachers College Press, Columbia University.

Milstein, M. M., & Jennings, M. K. (1973). *Educational policy making and the state legislature: The New York experience*. New York: Praeger.

Mitchell, D. E. (1981). *Shaping legislative decisions: Education policy and the social sciences*. Lexington, MA: Heath.

Mitchell, D. E. (1985). Research impact on educational policy and practice in the USA. In J. Nisbet, J. Megarry, & S. Nisbet (Eds.), *World Yearbook of Education 1985 Research Policy and Practice* (Chap 2, pp. 19–41). New York: Nichols.

Mitchell, D. E., & Encarnation, D. J. (1984, May). Alternative state policy mechanisms for controlling school performance. *Educational Researcher*, 13, 4–11.

Mitchell, D. E., Kerchner, C. T., Erck, W. C., & Pryor, G. (1981). The impact of collective bargaining on school management and

policy. *American Journal of Education*, 89(2), 147–188.

Mitchell, D. E., Wirt, F., & Marshall, C. (1986). *Final report: Alternative state policy mechanisms for pursuing educational quality, efficiency and equity goals*. Prepared for the National Institute of Education under Grant #NIE–G–83–0020.

Moore, M. K., Goertz, M., & Hartle, T. (1983, August). Interaction of federal and state programs. *Education and Urban Society*, 4, 452–478.

Murphy, J. (1982). The paradox of state government reform. In A. Lieberman, & M. McLaughlin (Eds.), *Educational policy-making*. The 81st Yearbook of the National Society for the Study of Education. Chicago: University of Chicago Press.

National Committee for Citizens in Education (NCCE), Commission on Educational Governance (1975). *Public testimony on public schools*. Berkeley, CA: McCutchan.

Odden, A., & Dougherty, V. (1982). *State programs of school improvement: A 50-state survey*. Denver, CO: Education Commission of the States.

Pennsylvania Association for Retarded Children (PARC) v. Commonwealth, 334 F Supp. 125F (ED 1971), 343 F Supp. 279 (ED Pa. 1972).

Peterson, P. (1976). *School politics, Chicago style*. Chicago: University of Chicago Press.

Pipho, C. (1981). Scientific creationism: A case study. *Education and Urban Society*, 13(2), 219–233.

Porter, D. O., Warner, D. C., & Porter, T. W. (1973). *The politics of budgeting federal aid: Resource mobilization by local school districts*. Sage professional paper in administrative and policy studies 03–003. Beverly Hills, CA: Sage.

Porwoll, P. J. (1979). *Merit pay for teachers*. Arlington, VA: Educational Research Service.

Rabe, B. G. & Peterson, P. E. (1983). Education policy implementation: Are block grant proposals based on out of date research? *Issues in Education: A Forum of Research and Opinion*, 1(1), 1–29.

Reynolds v. Sims, 377 U.S. 533 (1964).

Rickman, L. W. (1981, July). School finance reform litigation: A historical review. *Peabody Journal of Education*, 218–224.

Robinson v. Cahill, 62 U.S. 473, 303 A.2d 273 (1973).

Rossell, C. H. (1980). Social science research in equity cases: A critical review. In D. C. Berliner (Ed.), *Review of Research in Education*: Vol. 8. Washington, DC: American Educational Research Association.

Serrano v. Priest, 15 Cal. 3d 584, 96 Cal Rptr. 601, 487 P. 2d, 241.

Sharkansky, I. (1971). *The maligned states: Policy accomplishments, problems and opportunities*. New York: McGraw-Hill.

Summerfield, H. L. (1971). *The neighborhood-based politics of education*. Columbus, OH: Merrill.

Sweatt v. Painter, 339 U.S. 629 (1950).

Tyack, D. B. (1974) *The one best system: A history of American urban education*. Cambridge MA: *Harvard University Press*.

Tyack, D., & Hansot, E. (1982). *Managers of virtue: Public school leadership in America, 1820–1980*. New York: Basic.

Ukeles, J. B. (1977). Policy analysis: Myth or reality? *Public Administration Review*, 23, 221–228.

Usdan, M. D. (1963). *The political power of education in New York state*. New York: Institute of Administrative Research, Teachers College, Columbia University.

Usdan, M. D., Minar, D. W., & Hurwitz, E., Jr. (1969). *Education and state politics: The developing relationship between elementary, secondary and higher education*. New York: Teacher's College Press, Columbia University.

Van Geel, Tyll. (1978, August). The new law of the curriculum. *School Review*, 86(4), 594–631.

Wirt, F. M. (1977). State policy culture and state decentralization. In J. Scribner (Ed.), *Politics of education*. The 76th Yearbook of the National Society for the Study of Education: Part II. Chicago: University of Chicago Press.

Wirt, F. M. (1978). What state laws say about local control. *Phi Delta Kappan*, 59, 517–520.

Wirt, F. M. (1980). Does control follow the dollar? Value analysis, school policy and state-local linkages. *Publius: The Journal of Federalism, 10*(2), 69–88.

Wirt, F. M. & Kirst, M. W. (1982). *Schools in conflict: The politics of education.* Berkeley, CA: McCutchan.

Wood v. Strickland, 420 U.S. 308 (1975).

Yeakey, C. C. (1983). Emerging policy research in education research and decision making. In E. W. Gordon (Ed.), *Review of research in education*: Vol 10. Washington, DC: American Educational Research Association.

Zeigler, L., & Johnson, K. F. (1972). *The politics of education.* Indianapolis, IN: Bobbs-Merrill.

CHAPTER 23

The Evolution of a New Cooperative Federalism

Barry G. Rabe and Paul E. Peterson

The federal role in elementary and secondary education, once applauded by respected observers and commentators, has become the object of searing criticism. Grant-in-aid programs, which were once regarded as essential to institutional innovation, are now said to be the cause of bureaucratic nightmares. Once regarded as the best hope for educational progress, federal involvement is now said to be the cause of our educational discontent. What was once accepted as a growing presence could soon wither away.

Many familiar with U.S. educational institutions believe the federal role to be excessive. These concerns about excessive federal interference in local school policy were expressed in no uncertain terms by President Ronald Reagan ("Reagan Urges," 1982), shortly after taking office: "Look at the .record. Federal spending on education soared eightfold in the last 20 years, rising much faster than inflation. But during the same period, scholastic aptitude test scores went down, down and down." Consistent with this view, the 1981 Education Consolidation and Improvement Act pared federal education funding, streamlined the largest categorical program in education (for socio-economically disadvantaged children), and consolidated 28 categorical grants into a single block grant. These changes were intended, according to the administration, to "shift control over education policy away from the Federal Government and back to State and local authorities—where it constitutionally and historically belongs" (U.S. Office of Management and

Budget, 1981). Such a policy shift reflected the widely held view that federal education programs had little if any positive impact and might actually have damaged the quality of elementary and secondary education in the United States.

This chapter reports a distinctively more optimistic set of findings concerning the federal role in elementary and secondary education.[1] Although we found examples of bureaucratic ineptitude, concessions to special interests, and inefficient use of federal resources, the dominant pattern was quite the opposite. Instead of conflict, we found cooperation. Instead of federal dictation, we found mutual accommodation on the part of national, state, and local officials. Instead of a misallocation of federal resources, we found ready acquiescence to federal policy at the state and local levels. Above all, instead of a heavy federal presence, we found a highly decentralized system whose administration remained in the firm hands of local officials. Three tables both provide useful fiscal summaries of the federal role and emphasize how "junior" the federal partner remains. In Table 23.1 the overall contribution of each level of government to American public education over the past 50 years is set forth. While the federal percentage doubled over the two decades between 1960 and 1980, even at the end of this period its fiscal contribution covered only 9.8 percent of the current expenditure of the country's elementary and secondary public schools. The increase in the percentage paid for by state (as opposed to local) governments over these same two decades was in fact significantly greater than the increase in the federal share.

When one examines in Table 23.2 and 23.3 the

Consultant/reviewers: Michael Kirst, Stanford University; and Michael Knapp, Stanford Research Institute

Table 23.1   Sources of Public-School Revenue Recipts and the Percentage Spent on Public Elementary-
and Secondary-School Current Expenditures

	1929–1930	1939–1940	1949–1950	1959–1960	1969–1970	1979–1980	1980–1981	1981–1982	1982–1983
Total revenue receipts (billions)	$2.09	$2.26	$5.44	$14.75	$40.27	$96.9	$105.9	$110.2	$116.9
Percentage of revenue from:									
Federal government	0.4%	1.8%	2.9%	4.4%	8.0%	9.8%	9.2%	7.4%	7.1%
State government	16.9%	30.3%	39.8%	39.1%	39.9%	46.8%	47.4%	47.6%	48.3%
Local sources	82.7%	68.0%	57.3%	56.5%	52.1%	43.4%	43.4%	45.0%	44.6%
TOTAL	100.0%	100.1%	100.0%	100.0%	100.0%	100.0%	100.0%	100.0%	100.0%

NOTE.   Data from Department of Education National Center for Education Statistics. *Digest of Education Statistics*, 1980, 1981, 1982, 1983, 1984. Washington, D.C.: Government Printing Office.

Table 23.2   Current Dollar Federal Expenditures for Elementary- and Secondary-Education Programs, 1960–1985, in millions

	FISCAL YEAR								
	1960	1964	1968	1972	1976	1980	1982	1984	1985[a]
Vocational education	45.2	54.5	255.2	416.9	590.9	680.7	660.5	854.5	796.0
Impact aid	258.2	334.3	506.4	648.6	598.9	821.1	457.2	688.8	700.3
NDEA	52.8	42.5	75.8	47.8	29.0	31.2[b]	—	—	—
Compensatory education	—	—	1,049.1	1,507.4	1,760.8	3,005.6	3,063.6	3,501.4	3,721.8
Bilingual education	—	—	—	26.0	79.5	156.4	136.3	143.0	172.9
Special education	0.7	2.5	16.8	67.9	152.1	734.5	1,069.7	1,259.8	1,468.9
Desegregation assistance	—	—	7.4	92.2	204.0	304.5	0.0	0.0	0.0
Other programs[c]	43.4	78.1	521.9	642.0	763.5	1,046.9[d]	1,748.5	1,885.5	2,147.3
Block grants	—	—	—	—	—	—	442.2	450.9	500.0
TOTAL	400.3	511.9	2,432.6	3,511.8	4,178.7	6,780.9	7,578.0	8,783.9	9,507.2

NOTES.   Data from *Education Times*, December 6, 1982, January 3, 1983; Department of Education. National Center for Education Statistics. *Digest of Education Statistics*, 1982, 1985. Washington, D.C.: Government Printing Office. Block grant data obtained from *Education Times*, January 3, 1983, October 28, 1985.
[a]   Dollars for this year are estimated.
[b]   Estimated portion of Consolidated Program Expenditures originally funded under NDEA.
[c]   Includes educational research projects, Office of Education salaries and expenses, educational personnel training (excluding higher education), educational television and broadcasting, follow-through programs, Indian education, rehabilitation services, research on the handicapped, expenditures under Consolidated Programs for purposes other than those of NDEA, and public libraries.
[d]   The Office of Education was merged into the new Department of Education in May 1980. Therefore, the salary data for 1980 may not be strictly comparable with those for previous years.

Table 23.3   Constant Dollar[a] Federal Expenditures for Elementary- and Secondary-Education Programs, 1960–1985, in millions

	FISCAL YEAR								
	1960	1964	1968	1972	1976	1980	1982	1984	1985[b]
Vocational education	110.8	127.5	532.4	723.3	753.4	572.6	496.6	598.0	537.5
Impact aid	632.8	782.0	486.0	1,125.3	763.6	690.6	343.8	482.0	472.9
NDEA	129.4	99.4	158.1	82.9	37.0	26.2[c]	—	—	—
Compensatory education	—	—	2,188.8	2,724.7	2,245.1	2,528.1	2,303.5	2,450.2	2,513.0
Bilingual education	—	—	—	45.1	101.4	131.6	102.5	100.1	116.7
Special education	1.7	5.8	35.1	117.8	193.9	617.8	804.3	881.6	991.8
Desegregation assistance	—	—	15.4	160.0	260.1	256.1	—	—	—
Other programs[d]	106.4	182.7	1,088.9	1,113.9	1,070.9	880.6	1,314.7	1,319.5	1,449.9
Block grants	—	—	—	—	—	—	332.5	315.6	337.6
TOTAL	981.1	1,197.8	4,504.7	6,093.0	5,425.4	5,703.6	5,697.9	6,147.0	6,419.4

NOTES.   *Education Times*, December 6, 1982, January 3, 1983; Department for Education Statistics. *Digest of Education Statistics*, 1982, 1985. Washington, D.C.: Government Printing Office.
[a]   1979 = 100.
[b]   Dollars for this year are estimated.
[c]   Estimated portion of Consolidated Program Expenditures originally funded under NDEA.
[d]   Includes educational research and projects, Office of Education salaries and expenses, educational personnel training (excluding higher education), educational television and broadcasting, follow-through programs, Indian education, rehabilitation services, research on the handicapped, expenditures under Consolidated Programs for purposes other than those of NDEA, and public libraries.

educational programs for which federal dollars are allocated, one also sees that instead of providing general support for U.S. schools, the federal government focuses on programs for the educationally deprived and the handicapped and in support of such activities as vocational education, school desegregation, and school systems affected by a pronounced federal presence (such as a military installation). Whatever the merits of each of these programs, it is obvious that federal involvement has remained highly specialized and in many ways quite peripheral to the mainstream tasks of U.S. schools. If the federal government cannot be credited for any educational renaissance, neither can it be criticized for the bulk of the difficulties and problems school systems face.

FEDERALISM AND FEDERAL EDUCATIONAL POLICY

Much of the existing federal educational framework was developed in a period of widespread confidence in the capacity of the federal government to promote more effective—and more equitably delivered—educational services. Most students of U.S. federalism had by the mid-1960s come to accept a growing role for the national government. Specifically, they applauded the grant-in-aid programs that incorporated state and local governments into the administration of federal policy. "Cooperative federalism," as Morton Grodzins (1966) labeled this evolving political institution, was said to be entirely consistent with the country's historic traditions. Much as James Madison (Hamilton & Madison, 1937) had welcomed the capacity of different levels of a multitiered system of government to "control each other, at the same time that each will be controlled by itself" (p. 339), modern analysts regularly discerned a role for Washington that reinforced, rather than usurped, state and local responsibilities. This role was manifest in a number of federal categorical programs, including those devoted to vocational, compensatory, and special education.

As the enthusiasms of the Great Society era subsided, new generations of scholars have challenged the very foundations of cooperative federalism. It has lost its preeminence among conceptions of intergovernmental relations, replaced by more adverse characterizations. This new skepticism has taken two distinct forms, each emphasizing differing flaws in contemporary federal, state, and local relationships.

One line of criticism emphasizes the ease with which narrow organized interests, especially "producer groups" whose economic livelihood is substantially affected by the governmental program in question, are able to *capture* complex administrative processes. Pro-

ducer groups are defined in this context in much the same way that Beer (1982) has defined them in the context of British politics. Since producer groups have the greatest stake in the direction a policy takes, these analysts point out, they are the ones most likely to remain active and involved once a policy leaves the public Congressional arena for the quiet back rooms of executive agencies, state bureaus, and local school districts. As the responsibility for program development shifts inward and downward, organized producer groups continue to press their cases, supplying decision makers with information, arguing against adverse provisions, and bargaining over administrative details. These critics of group processes, whether they be muckraking journalists, market-oriented conservatives, or neo-Marxist radicals, agree that federal programs may be operated with outward cooperation but insist that the primary beneficiaries of these programs are those who produce or deliver—rather than receive—the services (Grubb & Lazerson, 1982; Lowi, 1969; McConnell, 1966; Selznick, 1949; Stigler, 1975).

The other line of criticism deems the basic problem of contemporary federalism as one of *implementation*. It condemns federal programs as having imposed excessive controls on the producer groups who will ultimately deliver federally funded services. According to this school of thought, federal programs, often because they are designed to counter producer-group capture, impose burdensome regulations, guidelines, and requirements on state and local governments. These restrictions preclude producers of local services from developing coherent, sustainable programs and, in the process, may give consumers incentives and opportunities to unnecessarily utilize public services. By the time laws are turned into regulations and local programs are initiated, the federal government may have undertaken more than it can handle. Confusion, conflict, failure, and, at times, total collapse are the unforeseen results. "No wonder the program failed to achieve its aims" becomes the refrain in many such studies (Pressman & Wildavsky, 1973, p. 87). Levin and Ferman (1985) contend that "in the past two decades, implementation has become the single most problematic aspect of policy-making. It is the stage at which most domestic policies have foundered" (p. 2). As Kettl (1983) summarized, "Most criticism of these programs centered on their overly ambitious goals and their hopelessly complex administrative structure" (p. 15).

Although both the *capture* and *implementation* interpretations criticize federal grant-in-aid programs, their analyses tend to contradict rather than complement one another. The *capture* critics lament federal timidity in the face of organized pressure. The *imple-*

mentation critics condemn federal excessiveness under the guise of rules ostensibly designed to protect programs from special interests. Conceivably, both perspectives could be correct, especially if producer groups master the art of interpreting and modifying rules, turning federal requirements to their particular advantage. But inasmuch as many producer groups are the most vociferous opponents of regulation, their influence is more likely to be inversely than positively associated with regulatory excesses.

Our research has led us to the conclusion that these critiques of cooperative federalism are overdrawn. Indeed, quite apart from the findings we have to report, the prevalence of two seemingly contradictory criticisms of federal grant-in-aid programs suggests that the government has in the long run followed a moderate, pragmatic path located somewhere between the two extremes. It is not unreasonable to assume that federal bureaus wish to sustain their programs over the long run and that in order to do so they must be able at least to claim that their programs are designed to serve the public interest. If subservience to special interests were condoned by federal administrators, their enterprises would be vulnerable to investigations by the General Accounting Office, crusading members of Congress, or *Washington Post* reporters. Bureaucratic procedures that require similar treatment for all clients insulate a program from the blandishments of special interests. Yet, if carried to an extreme, these rules can become self-defeating, protecting an agency's autonomy so thoroughly that it is precluded from doing anything. If an agency leans too much in one direction, it invites critical comment from *capture* theorists. If it leans in the other direction, *implementation* theorists fault the agency for becoming entangled in its own red tape. The struggle for organizational survival, therefore, is a search for a reasonably safe path between the Scylla of organized interests and the Charybdis of excessive proceduralism.

Our research findings from an inquiry into the two largest federal education programs are quite consistent with such an interpretation of organizational behavior. We found that the two programs—one in compensatory education for the poorest, lowest-achieving students, the other in educational services for the handicapped—struggled with both producer-group pressures and with their own maze of requirements. Yet in time federal policy makers for both programs found ways to build cooperative relationships with their counterparts at the state and local levels. Establishment of such relations was founded on the reality that each participant in the enterprise needed the other. The "feds" had crucial legal and fiscal resources; the states played an intermediary role; and the locals had the operational

capacity without which nothing could be achieved. Cooperative relations were also facilitated by the fact that these programs belonged to broader social movements that had both national and local adherents. New professional identities formed in conjunction with these programs had a major stake in enabling them to work. Significantly, even though the new professionals were crucial to programmatic success, producer groups did not capture the policy arena at the expense of service recipients.

THE EVOLUTION TOWARD A MORE FUNCTIONAL FEDERAL SYSTEM

We discovered this process of mutual accommodation and professional development in the most unlikely of places. Title I of the Elementary and Secondary Education Act of 1965 (now Chapter 1 of the Education Consolidation and Improvement Act of 1981) and the Education for All Handicapped Children Act of 1975 established programs ripe with characteristics that made them prime candidates for criticisms from producer groups and implementation theorists. Both laws (a) mounted ambitious undertakings that were inadequately financed; (b) sought to reform local service-delivery systems; (c) redistributed, at least to some extent, resources from well-off to special-needs populations; (d) imposed numerous regulations; (e) depended heavily on the support and cooperation of professionals represented by well-organized groups; and (f) served as examples of federal ineptitude for critics of the new federal role. Numerous analyses of the first few years of administration of these programs found serious shortcomings. The Title I compensatory education program was widely perceived as a classic case of producer group capture, whereas the special education program seemed to illustrate many of the concerns raised by implementation theorists.

These highly ambitious *redistributive* programs of the federal government placed considerable strain on the intergovernmental system. Attempting to find the stumbling blocks that prevented the program from attaining its lofty aims, a number of analysts deemed excess delegation of authority to local educators to be a principal problem. Murphy (1971), for example, assessed that "local schools do not blatantly violate the law, but they are in control of the situation and are able to stretch the law to meet the need of their constituencies" (p. 59). Wayson (1975), a like-minded analyst of Title I, who found the federal government either unable or unwilling to confront school systems that deviated from program guidelines, noted that "in order to adapt programs to local needs, project managers often 'bent the rules'" (p. 1555). Coopera-tive federalism had thrived in earlier decades partly because the interests of national and local governments in such developmentally oriented programs as voca-tional education and aid for federally impacted schools were mutually reinforcing. In these programs federal, state, and local governments had a mutual interest in seeing these projects prosper and expand. When the creators of the Great Society asked the federal system to carry out a host of redistributive programs poorly fitted to local procedures and priorities—in educa-tion as well as health care, housing, and other policy areas—they placed considerable stress on the system of cooperative federalism.

Redistributive programs may ultimately be operat-ed purposefully and cooperatively, but a multiple-phase evolution of intergovernmental relations may first need to be completed. The first round of legislation and administrative guidelines in the federal compensa-tory education program, for example, was written in the same vague language that had always been suitable for intergovernmental programs. But it was soon apparent that vagueness presupposed the same com-mitment to reform, innovation, and redistribution at the local level as at the federal.

When local officials turned out to be recalcitrant, a second round of legislative and administrative activity ensued. This time regulations were more precise; matters originally left to interpretation were now elaborated in specific detail. Even Congressional statutes were written with a new precision, as members of Congress and their increasingly numerous staff assistants wrote into law exactly what was desired and precisely how to achieve it. Redistributive programs enacted in the mid-1970s, such as the federal special education program (the Education for All Handi-capped Children Act), were sufficiently specific from the start, thereby precluding the delegatory first stage. Earlier programs, such as compensatory educa-tion, were modified to reflect the intensified federal role. Programs enacted in both periods were ultimately cited as examples of the federal government's lurching from the extreme of excessive delegation of authority to that of excessive interference with local school systems.

Regulations were followed by evaluations, as the new tools of the social sciences were mobilized on behalf of institutional reform. In the old federal system, lawmakers had little choice but to accept the word of the producers of federally funded services and their allies. For example, few doubted that vocational educa-tion had a beneficial effect, because local vocational administrators reported how many youths had learned a new trade, the Vocational Education Association showed the rising number of students participating in such courses, and outstanding members of the Future Farmers of America and similar groups testified how much the program meant to them.

As the theory and practice of evaluation research evolved, lawmakers discovered a new source of in-formation about the effects of program activities. Instead of anecdotal reports from or about uniquely successful individuals, it was possible to gather in-formation on the experiences of a scientifically selected random sample of program participants. Instead of biased reports from self-interested administrators, factual and objective accounts could be obtained from independent researchers. Instead of interest-group pressure, the lawmaker had facts and figures to review.

Independent evaluations greatly disturbed the policy makers of the Great Society. More often than not, these studies showed that federally funded pro-grams had little or no effect. The poor and the dis-advantaged received little demonstrable benefit from compensatory education funds; Head Start had only modest long-term effects; even vocational education did not seem to work, for it appeared that people in a general education program could learn as much and get a job as easily as those in a vocational program.

In the face of these evaluations, federal lawmakers and administrators redoubled their efforts. They pro-moted the belief that the problem stemmed from exces-sive authority delegated to local officials who captured programs to serve their own parochial interests. In response, national policy makers wrote tighter regula-tions and encouraged members of what became known as the "target population" to press local service pro-viders. For a time the conflicts among federal, state, and local governments, reinforced by racial conflicts in the wider society, were so severe that the durability of the system came into question. Even today, the in-tensity of the exchanges of that period (the exact timing varied with city and program) have left a legacy of uncertainty and disappointment that helps explain much of the current suspicion of federal programs.

But well before the contemporary review of federal programs conducted by the Reagan Adminis-tration, the federal system had begun its own processes of assessment and change. These were less visible, less controversial, and less sweeping examinations. Al-though the steps taken in response to them were incre-mental, ad hoc, and in one program at a time, the overall effect was to diminish greatly the difficulties of managing federal programs while retaining their basic purpose. The processes of adjustment occurred on all sides. At the local and state levels, a new professional cadre more identified with program objectives was recruited to administer federal programs, and these officials became more sensitive to federal expectations. At the federal level, policy makers began to doubt whether detailed regulations, tight audits, and experimental-design evaluations were unmixed blessings. Regulations tended to distract administrators from substantive to procedural issues; audits demanding the return of federal funds for incomplete complaince seemed excessive; the more evaluators found little to have any effect, the greater the doubt among policy makers that experimental-design research could actually isolate the effects of federal programs. Appropriate changes and adjustments were made. Expectations became more realistic, administrators developed program identifications that transcended governmental boundaries, citizen groups replaced contentious criticism with astute support for more federal resources, and a commitment to a coordinated effort gradually emerged.

THE STAGES OF REDISTRIBUTIVE PROGRAM OPERATION

Nevertheless, the maturation of redistributive programs did not recreate the cooperative federalism so prevalent in a earlier era when most federal programs were developmental in character. Redistributive federal programs ask local governments to carry out responsibilities quite different from any they are likely to have initiated on their own. Initially, local governments are likely to react guardedly to central-government policies. How much actual—as distinct from symbolic—redistribution does the central government expect? How aggressively will the central government pursue its goals and enforce its stipulations? Will any overly zealous local government be saddled with obligations others have evaded? Is the central government going to sustain its program, or is the program but a passing episode? As we have suggested, these questions will take considerable amounts of time to be resolved. For some programs, such as compensatory education, three distinct phases emerged in the operation of redistributive programs.

Stage One: Delegation to the Local Level

In the first stage the central government is likely to be bold in its ambitions, vague in its objectives, imprecise in its stipulations, and inept in its administrative actions. Local governments are likely to use program resources either for traditional local activities or as substitutes for revenue that would otherwise need to be generated locally. Administrators of preexisting programs will attempt to modify the program so that it

is consistent with established practice. The program's focus on those with special needs will be diffused.

The compensatory education program fully corroborated this pattern. A bold preamble was sketched, a vague program framework was developed, and funding was generous. Details regarding the implementation and cost were treated as secondary concerns, dust that would settle once the legislation had been enacted. "No one really knew *how* to run a successful compensatory education program," recalled Alice Rivlin (1971). "There were hunches and theories, but few facts" (p. 80). If programs were found to have shortcomings, it was assumed that rational analysis could be applied to solve them; Great Society programs were, in fact, passed almost in tandem with the arrival of presumably reliable tools of policy analysis, such as the planning-programming-budgeting system (PPBS) in the Department of Health, Education, and Welfare (Rivlin, 1971). In the exuberance of the moment, programs such as compensatory education were seen as points of departure for future federal action rather than as a definitive step in the evolution of the social-welfare state.

The compensatory education program lacked a group of locally based professionals who could be relied on to devote their careers to the socioeconomically disadvantaged. Local school systems were not very receptive to the idea of concentrating resources on the least able, as reflected by their local practices. "I have seen enough school districts where there has been a lack of imagination, lack of initiative, and lack of interest in the problems of some of the deprived children which causes me concern," observed Robert Kennedy during Congressional deliberations over the compensatory education program (McLaughlin, 1975, p. 2). For school districts that had long awaited federal support money—and anticipated that it would be loosely structured, like the vocational education and impact aid programs—the program could conceivably spark local resistance. Prior to 1965, "compensatory education" was not part of the vernacular of the professional educator and served as a potential threat to prevailing instructional approaches.

The compensatory education program, therefore, was less likely to be enthusiastically received at the local level than were prior federal programs. "There's definitely a stigma attached to working in a Title I program," explained a compensatory education administrator in Milwaukee. (See Note). "There tends to be a perception that it's not fully hooked onto our school system." In order to overcome this potential disinterest—or antipathy—of local professionals, the program had to compel their participation. Hence, at the outset it went much farther than earlier programs to

provide incentives for local participation and to minimize any potential perception of excess federal interference with the preferences of local professionals.

Initially, federal oversight of compensatory education was mild. In fact, the federal formula for distributing funds, rather than regulatory concerns,
dominated Congressional deliberation over the program during the 1960s and early 1970s. Regulations
in effect during the first 10 years of the program attempted to direct compensatory education funds to
schools in the poorest areas within each district. They
also encouraged local districts to serve the lowest-
achieving students with federal funds and to assure that
the use of funds supplemented preexisting school services. Beyond these general guidelines, substantial
flexibility was built into the process. Local school
systems were allowed to designate the eligible schools
and select the schools and students to be served.
Poverty criteria were to be used in making these
decisions, but they did not have to be identical to those
used at the federal level. Moreover, those students who
eventually participated in federally funded programs
were not necessarily the same ones counted in the
formula to allocate funds. As a 1977 National Institute
of Education study concluded, "the regulations provide
little guidance to [local school systems] about some of
the most important decisions they are required to make
during this process" (p. 1051). Once schools received
federal funding, they retained almost total discretion
over its usage.

Provisions for federal oversight of program operation were discussed in the vaguest—and briefest—of
terms. The program called for fiscal control and fund
accounting procedures "as may be necessary to assure
proper disbursement of, and accounting for, Federal
funds." It also required adoption of "effective procedures" for program evaluation (Bailey & Mosher,
1968). These proved, however, to be exhortations
rather than a carefully carved set of procedures that
were to be imposed upon every local district. The
program explained that federal payments would be
denied local school districts if the state educational
agency

> finds that the combined fiscal effort...of that agency
> and the state with respect to the provision of free public
> education by that agency for the preceding fiscal year
> was not less than such combined fiscal effort for that
> purpose for the fiscal year ending June 30, 1964. (Bailey
> and Mosher, 1968, p. 240–241)

Since overall state and local expenditures or
education increased rapidly during the 1960s in the vast
majority of U.S. school districts, this provision proved
similarly unrestrictive.

A wide range of analysts concurred that such
federal restrictions were minimal, virtually nonexistent
in many instances. Whereas over 14,000 local districts
participated in the compensatory education program
in the fiscal year 1976 and spent $120 million in
program administration, the Office of Education employed only 100 people with administrative responsibilities in compensatory education, at a cost of less than $5
million. Even if each of these 100 officials zealously
oversaw local activity, along with officials at the state
level who were involved with compensatory education,
there was little likelihood that local professional
preferences would be impeded. Not only did these
nonlocal administrators lack strong regulatory tools,
but there were simply too many classrooms influenced
in too many different ways by the program to assure
any uniform performance. As Milbrey McLaughlin
observed in 1975:

> The USOE does not "run" Title I. The design and
> content of the more than 30,000 Title I projects across
> the country are determined by [local school systems].
> Consequently, the use of Title I dollars reflects multiple
> and diverse goals, which are not easily transformed into
> measurable, overarching objectives. (p. 117)

Such an assessment applied mainly during the
earlier stages of the program, when federal administrators had little experience in overseeing the compensatory education services of thousands of school systems
across the nation. At the same time, local school
systems had no administrators or teachers with experience in compensatory education prior to 1966, leaving
abundant room for local freelancing with federal
dollars. Among the four school systems included in
our study, Baltimore was especially slow in developing
such expertise. As late as 1975, recalled a Baltimore
compensatory education administrator.

> Federal auditors came in and said there was no com-
> parability. We said, "What's new?" There was no de-
> liberate effort on our part to deceive the feds. There was
> some ignorance, some things we just didn't know, and
> some things we didn't want to do. (See Note.)

Even in the process of funding distribution, local
preferences regularly prevailed. Just as communities
such as Baltimore, Miami, Milwaukee, and San Diego
spent compensatory education dollars in different
ways, they also adopted different allocation procedures. The National Institute of Education (1977)
confirmed this as a national trend when it observed:

> The allocating of compensatory education funds within
> school districts is a loose process that varies enormously

from place to place. The determination of which schools will receive compensatory education resources, and the amount they receive, is left almost entirely to the discretion of the local educational agencies. (p. 1060)

Rather than challenging local practices, therefore, federal and state oversight of compensatory education was found to be overly compliant with local preferences. Baltimore, for example, allocated its funds along largely political criteria. The former superintendent acknowledged that, at one point, "patronage" influenced allocational decisions. Not always so blatant, politically favored schools and their principals were consistently well rewarded with compensatory education dollars in Baltimore. Murphy (1971) explained that at the same time the federal compensatory education office had "inadequate staff," those administrators charged at the state level to carry out program oversight were "not oriented toward compliance activities." Instead, such individuals "view themselves as professional educators, and the idea of enforcement of regulations is simply incompatible with their view of public education" (p.53). As a result, concluded Murphy (1971), compensatory education served as an excellent illustration of what a generation of analysts would deem a fundamental flaw of U.S. federalism:

The federal system—with its dispersion of power and control—not only permits but encourages the evasion and dilution of federal reform, making it nearly impossible for the federal administrator to impose program priorities; those not diluted by Congressional intervention can be ignored during state and local implementation. (p. 60)

Stage Two: The Feds Toughen Up

During the second stage, evidence continues that redistributive program funding is being diverted from intended purposes, and the federal government responds with efforts to intensify its oversight of local fund use. Experience is gained in administering programs, and new regulatory provisions are enacted to bring greater and more redistributive unity to federal program operation. These changes, supported or sometimes even designed by organizations that represent the intended recipients of federally funded redistributive programs, counter the influence of individuals who deliver services at the local level. Rather than continue to acquiesce to local preferences, therefore, federal programs may be adjusted to force conformity with federally defined structures and standards. In this stage, intergovernmental conflict and confusion in the operation of federal redistributive programs may be common.

Consistent with this pattern, federal restrictions

and guidelines concerning the use of federal dollars in redistributive education programs became more plentiful and were more rigorously enforced throughout the late 1970s. Both Congress and federal administrators intensified their efforts to assure greater local compliance with federally established standards of service delivery. This transformation was attributable to many factors, including the changing prospects for and responsibilities of federal policy. Rather than constantly expanding existing programs and authorizing new ones, the federal government increasingly turned its attention to improving what it was already doing. Existing programs, whether the Clean Air Act, Medicaid, or Title I, had stirred some controversy and did not function as cooperatively or effectively as originally intended. Performance evaluations were, on the whole, adverse and created doubts about a wide range of existing programs. Policy makers and administrators responsible for such programs were increasingly anxious to attain more desirable results. "When the question is not what government should be doing but rather the effects of what government is already doing, government is likely to come to the bargaining table armed with an agenda of its own," explained Lawrence Brown (1983, p. 45).

Hence, the federal government grew less and less likely to adapt to local concerns that conflicted with the federal interests expressed in redistributive programs. If Medicaid was costing much more than expected and was inefficiently operated, the federal government was unlikely to cater to the preferences of the American Medical Association. If compensatory education funds were not being used as intended and were failing to improve student performance, the federal government was unlikely to abide by the desires of local school systems. Instead, the federal government was more likely to exert direct control over programs and encourage the participation of groups other than the producers. This control often took the form of "cross-cutting" provisions, which required program beneficiaries to perform (or not perform) various tasks at their own expense in order to receive federal aid. As Anne Hastings (1982) found, the number of such requirements in education programs expanded from 8 before 1964 to 59 in 1980.

Federal programs of all sizes were subject to this transformation in the federal government's role. The compensatory education program illustrated this change in several respects. Congressional amendments to the original legislation (in 1968, 1970, 1974, and 1978) specified federal expectations with ever-increasing detail. New regulatory provisions were added and existing ones became more demanding. Many sections of the initial legislation had been hurriedly drafted in 1965 to minimize conflict and secure rapid passage; many of the most important provisions were, in the words of one federal official active in the program during the 1960s, "a little hazy." Many guidelines and regulations, therefore, had to be drafted to provide clarification and narrow the latitude that the initial legislation afforded local school districts.

These changes were enthusiastically supported by a wave of new groups that represented the recipients of compensatory education services. Prior to their emergence, traditional groups such as the National Education Association, the Council of Chief State School Officers, the National School Boards Association, the American Association of School Administrators, the National Association of State Boards of Education, and the National Congress of Parents and Teachers were the major sources of influence on Congress. Widely known as the "Big Six" in educational policy circles, these organizations rarely formed a united lobbying front but shared "an ideological preference for protecting local and state control of education and minimizing federal interference," according to Kirst and Jung (1982).

As compensatory education began to mature, however, the groups that influenced program amendment multiplied and reflected increasingly diverse sets of interests. The sole lobby group that promoted categorical restrictions on compensatory education during its initial enactment, the National Catholic Welfare Board, was increasingly supplemented by organizations that shared its commitment to greater federal oversight of the program. By the mid-1970s, numerous groups had emerged, including the National Advisory Council for the Education of Disadvantaged Children, the Lawyers Committee for Civil Rights Under Law, the Legal Standards and Education Project of the NAACP, and the National Welfare Rights Organization. These organizations became advocates for the low-income, low-achieving students that compensatory education was designed to assist. They argued repeatedly that greater federal specificity was needed in allocating and overseeing the utilization of dollars at the local level. In the process, they often provided reports or suggestions that either generally influenced Congress or were directly adopted into the program during various periods of amendment.

During the 1970s such organizations proved "to be increasingly active and effective groups" (Kirst & Jung, 1982, p. 130). The Lawyers Committee for Civil Rights Under Law, for example, was a constant thorn in the side of local educators and their organizational representatives in Washington. This public-interest law firm published manuals advising citizens how to bring suit against districts believed to be in violation

of federal law. Moreover, as Kirst and Jung (1982) discovered, "several of their recommendations for strengthening the program requirements are quite evident in the 1978 amendments. In fact, the final 1978...amendments bear a striking resemblance to the draft statute prepared by Robert Silverstein of LCCRUL" (p. 132). The federal compensatory education program became increasingly responsive to these alternative viewpoints during the 1970s, no longer automatically reflecting the preferences of local educators.

At the same time, federal officials responsible for the compensatory education program became increasingly impatient to gain greater control over the program as federal audits and other evaluations showed considerable disparity in local utilization of federal dollars. The actions of the bureaucracy and the Congress complemented each other in attaining the objective of greater control. Federal administrators often provided regulatory ideas and wording that eventually appeared in legislative amendments; Congress, in turn, gave these administrators more and more authority to curb inappropriate local uses of compensatory education funding. This alliance was illustrated in the emergence of the "comparability" and "nonsupplanting" regulations in the late 1960s and early 1970s. These provisions initially appeared in an HEW program guide published in 1968; they were subsequently embraced by Congress and written into the program amendments of 1970.

There were, of course, considerable political risks involved in promoting greater federal oversight of categorical programs in an administration that proposed categorical consolidation into block grants. Nonetheless, leading compensatory education administrators made serious efforts to enforce these provisions during the 1970s, resulting in the types of intergovernmental conflict and confusion that implementation theorists focused on. Many school systems for the first time had to examine their schools on a campus-by-campus basis in order to determine their compliance with the numerous regulatory provisions affixed to the compensatory education program in the 1970s. Since none wanted to lose their supply of federal dollars, local school districts had little choice other than to comply with the growing expectations of the federal government.

Stage Three: Toward More Mature Program Operation

While fiscal pressures, administrative practices, and constituency pressures produce varied results among localities, the combined effect of repeated conflicts over program regulations generate a third stage in the evolution of redistributive program administration. Federal bureaucrats, facing complaints from local leaders as well as from their legislative representatives, modify program guidelines and expectations once again. A new tolerance of local diversity, a new recognition that no single programmatic thrust is clearly preferable, and an appreciation of the limits as to what can be directed from the center steadily emerges. The third stage is not a return to the first stage, it must be emphasized. Observers see no dramatic oscillations from complete permissiveness to detailed regulation and back again. Stage 3 is more a synthesis, a definition of the appropriate balance between what is desirable and what is possible. Because local administration of the program is now in the hands of experienced professionals and because the basic redistributive thrust of the program is accepted by all levels of government, central government decision makers become more willing to accept the fact that all programs must be modified as they are carried out in particular contexts. Issues remain, problems arise, adjustments become necessary, but the dimensions of the debate become roughly characteristic of any intergovernmental program, redistributive or not.

Just as compensatory education itself changed from being a vaguely defined, general aid program to a highly restrictive program preoccupied with compliance, those officials assigned to oversee its operation at the local level reflected both extremes at varying times. At the outset of the program, federal officials were anxious to overlook compliance problems; in later years, they were very aggressive in their review of local practices. But over time, a position was struck between the two extremes.

Professionals employed at the state level were particularly influential in transforming compensatory education into a more mature program. Even 10 years after passage, federal regulations concerning appropriate usage of federal funds were still being revised. No single, comprehensive source outlined federal government requirements. But over time mutual understanding increased. State-based professionals became increasingly aware of what was and was not expected by the federal government, as well as what was and was not feasible locally. "Everyone had the legal framework of [the program] in their head," explained a lawyer who studied compensatory education legal standards. Nine of the 10 states in that study, like the 4 states we have examined, employed professionals with extensive compensatory education experience. In Maryland and Wisconsin, for example, the director of compensatory education (both the federal and the comparable state program) served from the enactment of the Elementary and Secondary Education Act in 1965 until their retirement in the early 1980s. These long commitments were common at the state level, as they had been in such earlier programs as vocational education. After initial difficulties, "everyone wanted to learn the regulations and be in compliance with them," explained a federal administrator. "States took pride in the fact that they knew the regulations and they wanted to show off their knowledge. They took pride in tightening their own enforcement of the program."

The federal government attempted to foster this pride of ownership in a variety of ways. Title V of ESEA provided considerable funding to state education departments to improve their capacity to manage programs such as compensatory education. The federal compensatory education office sponsored meetings to share ideas and problems with state and local officials. A national compensatory education organization was formed to introduce state and local personnel to the various ways in which programs could be operated and still remain within federal guidelines. Furthermore, the 1978 program amendments were designed to provide a comprehensive guide concerning federal requirements. Many existing regulations were incorporated into the law, as were various changes approved by Congress. This action, intended to provide state and local officials with a single reference source and to obviate the need to refer to the previous potpourri of regulations, many of which had been subject to constant revision by the Education Department, facilitated a considerable change in the operation of compensatory education.

By the late 1970s, regulatory provisions that had once been ill-defined and poorly understood had become a way of life. Over time, these requirements were refined to yield measurable outcomes concerning local compliance. Federal officials began to prioritize their informational needs in determining local compliance; they needed to demonstrate that comparability and supplementation were occurring yet were eager not to bombard local school districts with excessive reporting and evaluation responsibilities. Of the five criteria initially thought necessary to assess compliance with the supplement-not-supplant provision, for example, federal officials settled on two criteria. They decided that measurement of the number of staff and expenditures for staff per child would be sufficient to tell them whether local and state funds were being equitably spent on eligible. and ineligible children. These criteria were sufficiently specific to be manageable for state and local authorities, but they would not excessively restrict local use. At the same time, after these requirements became well established, there was considerable evidence to suggest that compliance was nearly universal. The organizations that had represented compensatory education recipients so assertively in the late 1970s ceased to cite noncompliance as a problem. Moreover, whereas federal audits between 1967 and 1976 found repeated instances of misuse of federal funds, subsequent audits found a steady decline in misuse. This assessment was confirmed by interviews with federal, state, and local officials.

As states developed a better understanding of what was and was not permissible under the federal program, they increasingly integrated the program into their overall efforts. They no longer operated compensatory education as a program peripheral to their mission. Florida, for example, revised state achievement testing during the 1970s to measure the performance both of children receiving compensatory services and of all other children. The state also combined its auditing for the program and overall school expenditures. This new process enabled the state to trace the usage of each educational dollar to individual schools and class levels. Hence, while federal funds were audited annually, all funds for public education were also audited. This practice was at first a source of some confusion, especially since districts such as Dade County had never examined the expenditure patterns of individual schools. Over time, however, it became standardized and widely supported. The audit of the federal program was closely coordinated with other state audits. Despite the more rigorous analysis, individual schools looked favorably upon the procedures, which gave the school principal greater latitude in allocating resources. A similar procedure was developed in Wisconsin, where state officials used the computerized, comprehensive school audit completed each year by the state to determine federal program compliance too.

Such intermingling of federal and state purposes also improved state and local relations in other ways. As states became increasingly adept at managing federal regulations, they also worked toward more common objectives with local school systems. Florida increasingly sought input from local educators before finalizing state guidelines. State officials also set up regional meetings for "presubmission reviews," during which draft copies of proposed compensatory education applications could be discussed before they were formally submitted. Such collaboration also increased in California, Wisconsin, and Maryland.

Like the other three states in our set, Florida further integrated the federal program with ongoing state efforts by enacting its own compensatory education program and placing greater emphasis on basic skills in the early grades. The Florida compensatory education program added $34 million to the $81 million the state received for compensatory education from the federal government in 1981–1982. Both programs were monitored by the same bureau and supported by a state

decision to weight students from kindergarten through grade 3 by a factor of 1.25, compared to 1.00 for older students. Many of these state-supported programs paralleled—and in many ways "piggybacked"—the federal program. Maryland, for example, used federal funds in conjunction with its own compensatory education program and other state categorical monies to improve the quality of education for children from low-income areas. Since the federal program served only about half of all eligible students in Maryland, state funds were concentrated on those students not served by the federal program. In 1981–1982, the state added $5.5 million of its own funding for compensatory education to $37 million of federal funding. Compensatory education was increasingly assumed as a state responsibility, both because of the state's considerable role in overseeing the federal program and because of the emergence of comparable state programs. As a result, compensatory education began to augment the efforts of state professionals rather than remaining an administrative burden.

Federal support for compensatory education was also initiated with a minimum of professional experience or expertise at the local level. Whereas education of the handicapped had local precedents, however crude the technologies applied to the problem, no cadre of professionals or definition of professional standards existed to be tapped for compensatory education. Even after developing new technologies and professional expertise, compensatory education was never integrated so thoroughly into local school systems as was special education. Local systems, for example, rarely devoted local funding to compensatory programs, quite unlike special education.

Nonetheless, the transformation of the role of the educational professional in compensatory education between 1965 and 1980 was far-reaching. Each district that was examined developed administrative procedures that gave coherence to the once-unruly program. For districts such as Dade County, Milwaukee, and San Diego, individuals in leading administrative roles gained increasing experience and standardized various procedures to assure compliance. Even in Baltimore, where local political pressures prevailed in many compensatory education policy decisions, new administrators were brought in during the late 1970s to eliminate major compliance problems.

A variety of external pressures fostered this emergence of professional identity and expertise in compensatory education. During the late 1960s and early 1970s, federal and state officials reprimanded local school officials. These reprimands, involving intensified federal and state audits and possible funding penalties, influenced local school systems to encourage professional development among those who operated their compensatory education programs. According to one state compensatory education official, "While chief state school officers and superintendents might have publicly been saying, 'we've done nothing wrong,' they were saying to their staffs, in private, 'Let's not let this happen again,'" Baltimore decided to "not let this happen again" with a major reorganization of its compensatory education office; Dade County responded, in part, with its creative Extended School Program (ESP). By the late 1970s, "everyone had the legal framework of [the program] in their head," as professional administrators gained sufficient experience and developed sufficient expertise to operate the compensatory education program in compliance with federal regulations yet tailor it to the needs and preferences of the local system.

This new professionalism was not confined to program compliance or, for that matter, to the operation of the federal program. Instead, it encouraged an unprecedented commitment to basic skills education for the socioeconomically disadvantaged. As compensatory education teachers became school principals and school-system administrators, greater sensitivity and resources were concentrated on the disadvantaged. The superintendents of the Baltimore and a neighboring suburban school system in the early 1980s, for example, worked in compensatory education at earlier stages of their careers. As a state official explained, they were likely to be supportive of special efforts in this area when they assumed higher office. In Maryland, for example, there were 700 teachers who specialized in reading in 1980, compared to only 3 before 1965. Many of these were involved in Title I or related efforts funded by the state. A Maryland Department of Education official noted that "before the [federal program], people did not believe that poor children could learn." A former compensatory education official in Wisconsin confirmed this, noting that "no one really believed that they had educationally disadvantaged children in their schools" before the federal initiative in this area.

This changing role of professionalism in compensatory education, however, did not penetrate the individual school level as deeply as would special education. Compensatory education instructors, with the notable exception of those in Dade County, did not develop the sophisticated technologies and routinized procedures of their colleagues in special education. Because many compensatory education staff members were trained as paraprofessionals—teacher aides rather than certified teachers—the emergence of a highly professionalized approach in this area was precluded. As we shall see, the impact of changing professionalism

did not have the same far-reaching ramifications as in special education. Nonetheless, the federal compensatory education program endured its first two stages to become an increasingly mature and well-established program by the late 1970s and early 1980s, showing few signs of either producer group capture or implementation inertia.

THE MATURATION OF SPECIAL EDUCATION

The Education for All Handicapped Children Act was enacted at about the same time that "Stage 2" of Title I evolution began. The special education program thus reflected growing federal distrust of local school systems' responsiveness to redistributive objectives. The Act set forth extraordinarily ambitious objectives and a regulatory framework of unprecedented complexity and detail for a federal education program. Whereas the initial compensatory education program was seemingly a classic illustration of capture group theory, the special education program seemed grist for the mills of implementation theorists.

The special education program was passed shortly after two court decisions had found states responsible for providing equal educational opportunity for all children, regardless of handicap. It sought both to help states and localities with the fiscal burdens these court decisions entailed and to specify the manner by which equal opportunity for the handicapped could best be provided. To achieve the latter objective, the Act required, among other things, that school districts (a) establish elaborate procedures that would enable them to identify all handicapped children; (b) prepare, in consultation with parents and, where appropriate, with handicapped students themselves, individual educational plans (IEPs) designed specifically for each student; (c) incorporate or "mainstream" the handicapped student in as many of the regular school activities as feasible; and (d) establish regular procedures through which parents could challenge any decisions the school district made. Recognizing the new costs this elaborate program entailed, and to achieve the fiscal objective that made the Act acceptable to school officials, the law authorized expenditures sufficient to cover 40 percent of the excess cost of educating a handicapped child. But even though allocations for special education climbed steadily in the aftermath of the legislation—from only $152 million in 1976 to over $1 billion by 1982 (see Table 23.2)—these amounts were but 9 to 15 percent of the cost of educating the handicapped and fell far short of the authorized expenditure levels. As a result, local school districts remained fiscally vulnerable if they adhered to the redistributive objectives of the federal government.

Aversion to Producer Group Preferences

Federal reform in special education was not designed simply to satisfy the providers of services to the handicapped. Instead, groups representing the handicapped had pressed their case within a friendly Congress and were able to see enacted into law a program promising major benefits for this especially needy population. In the words of Lynn (1983), "The seeds of dissatisfaction fell on the fertile soil of change created by the civil rights movement and its subsidiary causes—equal educational opportunity, children's rights, right to treatment, citizen participation, consumers' rights, and the like—and by the antiestablishment, antiprofessional tempest of the times" (pp. 34–35). To be sure, "securing long-term economic advantages as a result of educating the handicapped was sometimes cited as a justification for the law" (Brewer & de Leon, 1983, p. 333), and economic analyses attempted to defend additional expenditures in cost-benefit terms. But the humanitarian and civil rights arguments were in this case the more compelling ones. As Representative Robert Cornell observed, "I think we also ought to stress the fact that this education is necessary just to give them a greater enjoyment, and appreciation of living.... Some of these people are never going to be able to be self-supporting or to obtain gainful employment" (Brewer & de Leon, 1983, p. 333).

Even the promise of new federal funds to local school districts could not obscure the fact that the law would require extensive changes in local practice in return for such help. Established school organizations such as the National School Boards Association, the National Association of State Boards of Education, the NEA, and the AFT had not campaigned aggressively on behalf of what would become, after compensatory education, the largest federal program in education. Instead, they quietly accepted its enactment, apparently in the belief that court decisions would soon require major new steps on behalf of the handicapped in any case, and it was better to have federal dollars to help finance the reforms than to carry the full financial burden locally. Consequently, the thrust of special education policy was less ambiguous and uncertain than was initial compensatory education policy. On the contrary, "for the first time the federal government defined educational style for states and localities (Simors & Dwyer, 1979, p. 102).

Although most reforms were procedural, they had substantive implications. Five years after school districts were asked to institutionalize comprehensive measures that would identify all handicapped children, the school-age population found to be handicapped increased from 4 percent in 1973 to 7.8 percent in 1976 to 8.1 percent in 1980 (U.S. Office of Education; 1976, p. 215; U.S. Department of Education, 1980; 1982.) When Congress said that an IEP had to be prepared for each child, it established a mechanism that brought together parents and school officials who were expected to define the educational needs of the child without regard for the cost to the district. Decisions made at this or any other point in the planning process could be appealed by parents in a due-process hearing before an "impartial third party." Even though the range and quality of services could not be improved immediately upon the establishment of these procedures, local districts came under new pressures to expand their capacities.

These reforms, like those in compensatory education and other redistributive federal programs, were expected to enhance the welfare of less privileged groups in the population. Education for the handicapped was designed to have an unusually high redistributive impact. Although some handicapped children come from middle-class families, and these families are more likely to pressure schools for services under the IEP and due-process regulations, it is still the case that the incidence of handicap increases as one moves down the social ladder (Mercer, 1974). Moderately to severely handicapped children, moreover, are potential social dependents no matter what the social standing of their families. Concentration of expensive social and educational services on persons who are likely to remain marginal members of the community may come at the expense of investments in young people with more productive potential. Such an allocation of resources is difficult to justify as efficient, but it is arguably the only humane approach available.

Administrative Conflict and Confusion in Special Educaton

Adherence to federal standards in special education was initially as vexing to many local school districts as it had been in the second stage of compensatory education. Just as there was no automatic resolution of issues such as comparability and nonsupplanting, so IEPs and mainstreaming proved unfamiliar and often controversial. Most public school systems had offered special education programs in the past, but these varied enormously in quality and breadth of services. The Education for All Handicapped Children Act, with all its regulatory stipulations, required major modification of traditional local practices. To many, these liabilities seemed to outweigh any advantages that went with participation.

One problem was the amount of time that recipients of federal funding had to devote to convincing the federal government that its funds were being used for purposes consistent with the intent of the program. Individual school districts used a significant portion of their federal grants for administrative costs. Despite this acquisition of additional staff, service "rationing" and arbitrary "labeling" of students still occurred, largely because districts could not expand their programs rapidly enough to meet the needs that were being uncovered through compliance with federal requirements.

Developing specific educational plans for each handicapped person also proved to be beyond the initial capacity of local school districts. Baltimore's convoluted first IEP form, for example, was hurriedly drafted. It prompted "IEP parties," at which teachers would gather informally on weekends and "pass the forms around and fill them out without regard to the individual students involved," according to one administrator. "In the first year, the various procedures [for IEPs] were haphazardly done," noted a Miami special educator. It was also difficult to abide by the requirement that pupils be placed in the least restrictive environment feasible. The legislation stated the concept of mainstreaming in fairly general terms, and as a result the Office of Education established no direct guidelines for determination of placement. Efforts by special educators to implement the provision encountered resistance from principals and classroom teachers unfamiliar with resolving the special problems posed by the presence of the handicapped.

In part, program administration was complex simply because three levels of government were involved. "Sometimes I want to say, 'Just trust me' to federal administrators," said one Milwaukee special educator. She explained that both federal and state administrators consumed a substantial amount of her time, which might be better spent in other activities. Anticipation of federal compliance visits encouraged many special educators in each of the districts to keep paperwork in proper order, so as to satisfy auditors rather than serve their constituents. "They usually swoop down and get us on something," confirmed one special education administrator in Miami. This belief led to substantial efforts to eliminate potential areas of contention.

These problems were compounded by the fact that while all regulatory provisions of the law were in effect, subsequent appropriations failed to provide the generous levels of funding authorized in the initial legislation. Almost as great a problem was the uncertainty

of federal funds. Special education divisions in all four districts had little advance notice of the amount of funding they could expect to receive in the following academic year. Rather than a reliable entitlement-type program, as first envisioned, aid to the handicapped operated as an often unpredictable grant-in-aid program. "There is a consistent problem of not knowing how much funding will be available from year to year," explained a Milwaukee special education administrator. In 1979, for example, she did not know whether funding would be available for programs that she was responsible for until after the school year had started, despite the fact that the program had been more than 80 percent reliant on federal dollars in the past. The following year, funding information was again delayed until the month before the start of the school year. Interviewed in the summer of 1982, this administrator had "no idea" as to how much funding might be available for the 1982–1983 year. There was a "rumor that local dollars would pick up [the program in the absence of federal funding] this year...[but] now, we don't know where we are." Although this example of funding unpredictability was particularly extreme, such concerns were common in each of the four school districts that were examined.

In sum, the special education program enacted by the federal government in the mid-1970s was vulnerable to criticism by implementation theorists. Like compensatory education in its second stage, the program attempted complicated structural reform of existing service institutions, despite their relative lack of experience and expertise in such areas. But as convincing as this picture of confusion and complexity may be, problems of implementation are generally most evident in the early stages of the administration of a program. Analysts who limit themselves to these moments must be wary of the bias in the sample they are investigating. To be sure, the birth pangs of an organization deserve careful attention—one can discern at this point the parentage, the cries of the newborn, the steps first taken that may later prove to be decisive, the possibility of life-threatening crises. Yet one must not conclude from these early experiences that no significant changes will occur in the processes of maturation. Implementation theorists often assume that conflict and confusion are endemic rather than transitory, just as capture theorists presume a permanence to producer group domination. Examining the federal educational program for the handicapped nearly a decade after its formation and the compensatory education program more than 15 years after its enactment has convinced us that earlier studies drew premature conclusions.

Both the compensatory and special education programs operated differently 5 to 10 years after their establishment than at their outset. One of the important factors contributing to this change is the passage of time itself. In any new enterprise, whether public or private, uncertainty, confusion, and miscommunication are most likely to occur at the beginning. Local school districts were initially uncertain about federal intentions; laws and regulations were open to a variety of interpretations, and cues as to their meaning were inevitably fragmentary, ambiguous, and even contradictory until the federal offices themselves came to understand what was both desirable and feasible. Over the course of several years, continuous contact and mutual experience with the issues between federal officials on the one side and state and local special educators on the other gradually facilitated compromise and mutual recognition of each other's needs and concerns.

Aside from the mere passage of time—or perhaps, more precisely, operating to effect program adaptation as time passed—two factors helped reduce conflict and integrate federal policy into an ongoing system of service delivery. First, power was shared between the federal government and local groups and institutions. Neither side could achieve its objectives without the help of the other. A move toward mutual accommodation and sharing of responsibility could, under the circumstances, hardly be escaped. As Brown (1983) has observed, in the context of health care policy, federal programs "bring important groups into negotiation with one another" (p. 510). A similar process occurred in the context of federal education policy.

Second, a sense of professional identification with the program, present even at the beginning, unified participants in the policy subsystem. Whatever their institutional differences, they were all members of a change-oriented enterprise that many believed would be of public benefit. By stating as the goal equal education for the handicapped, special educators were addressing a social concern more honestly and forthrightly than ever had been done in the past. It was assuredly difficult to argue that education for the handicapped would somehow have taken care of itself. To achieve these goals meant that differences of interest and opinion had to take place within an overall cooperative framework. Few, if any, wanted the program to fail. Almost everyone would gain if the programs were regarded as successful. Indeed, the conflicts were more often between program participants and questioning or hostile forces on the outside than among the members of the policy subsystems themselves.

The combined effect of these two factors was to stabilize major innovations in the educational delivery systems of the country. Special education divisions across the nation used federal support both to attain greater standing at the local and state level and to initiate new and expanded services.

Power-sharing and Professional Development in Special Education

Power-sharing

Because Congressional policy on special education was less ambiguous from the start, local pressures for legislative amendment did not develop as they had with compensatory education. Instead, federal accommodation to local realities occurred in the interstices of the administrative process. Although changes in local programs were expected, federal administrators recognized that innovations could be effectuated only over some period of time. Consequently, federal auditors did not demand instantaneous compliance with every provision of the new law. The IEP provision, for example, was not made effective until 1977, even though the legislation had been enacted in 1975. Not until the school year 1980–1981 did all the requirements under the law become applicable. This step-by-step approach was possible in part because no formal seal of approval—or disapproval—was placed on local special education programs.

Local response to the requirements varied with the nature of the provision and the willingness and capacity of the individual district to respond. Baltimore encountered initial difficulties in developing a workable IEP form, and the district was found in noncompliance. However, Baltimore administrators responded with a revised, more manageable, and more useful IEP form. They also provided in-service training programs designed to broaden understanding and build support for the process. By 1980, a Baltimore administrator noted that "you build up a mechanism and get used to doing things." She explained that after a difficult beginning the IEP had become commonplace rather than a threat.

In none of the districts could it be said that the IEP was universally applauded as a guarantor of an optimal instructional program for the student. Nonetheless, it has become a workable document, one that helped bring together a variety of resources to evaluate the needs of a student and propose an instructional strategy. "Today, everyone is pretty much geared to the IEP," noted one Dade County special educator. Another special educator recalled the difficult transition process but emphasized that most teachers in the district now "agree that an individualized program is needed. We can now say on paper that something individualized can be provided, and in many instances that paper becomes a meaningful document."

Other major provisions underwent similar periods of initial confusion and occasional conflict. At the same time, local latitude was substantial as long as the basic federal program framework was observed. Least restrictive environment (LRE) provisions, for example, did not mean that every handicapped student was thrust into the regular classroom regardless of consequences. Instead, the extent and effectiveness of mainstreaming hinged principally on local professional judgment and ability. Some individual schools and programs in the four districts that we examined have resisted mainstreaming entirely, and others have backed away after initial experiments; none have been penalized in any way by the federal government. Another illustration of LRE implementation was provided by a Miami school principal who before the changes in the law had minimal special education experience: "Not every child will be able to make it in the regular program and...many should not be allowed in at all," she assessed. But with reasonable screening at her school and creative and realistic staff promotion of the intermingling, she explained that "the majority of students are adapting to mainstreaming." Successful or otherwise, mainstreaming has been encouraged by the federal program, not forced on every district and every classroom.

Whereas the impact of the law was evident in all districts and its basic provisions were adhered to with increasing regularity, one needed only to visit a variety of schools and programs to realize how differently the same federal law was being implemented, even within a single district. Much like compensatory education, special education services give little indication of having been homogenized because of a federal law or rendered ineffectual because of federal government meddling. The tenets of implementation theory notwithstanding, these complex federal programs operated without extensive federal interference or intergovernmental conflict.

Professional Development

Federal deference to local exigencies, coupled with increasing local responsiveness to Washington expectations, was also a function of the fact that attitudes toward the handicapped were changing at all levels of government and throughout the society more generally. As in the case of the 1973 Health Maintenance Organization Act, a comparably ambitious program initiative in the health care area, federal policy was reinforcing and institutionalizing a set of goals and objectives more widely shared, especially among those

professionals with responsibility in this policy domain (Peterson, Rabe, & Wong, 1986).

By the 1970s, changes in education for the handicapped were long overdue. Historically, local and state governments had minimized support for educational programs that were unable to promise a tangible return on investment in terms of a better educated labor force and citizenry. As Amitai Etzioni (1982) has explained, "In the 1920s, even in the early 1950s, and arguably well beyond, it was common practice that a person who could not do the work—in school, factory, office, lab—on the same terms, with the same equipment as everybody else did not get the job, or the education. Special attention, concessions, and sympathy were sometimes granted the handicapped but employment and education were "allocated according to narrowly production-focused rationality" (p. 255). Special education programs were particularly unappealing to local districts because of the high per-pupil expenditures involved in providing any comprehensive, individual instruction. Moreover, the general absence of proven evaluation and instructional methods seemed to limit any potential efforts. Handicapped students "were in a closet; there were no expectations, no procedures, and no placements," recalled one veteran educator in Miami. All in all, special education as a professional field had been highly circumscribed.

The evolution of special education from an occupation for minimally trained caretakers into what came to be regarded as a professional discipline in schools of education was more or less coincidental with the series of court decisions in the early 1970s that paved the way for the Education for All Handicapped Children Act. Thus, the law was both the product of increased political and professional attention to the handicapped and an instigator of these trends. That the federal law only embraced changes already occurring within special education was apparent in all four of the districts that were examined. In Baltimore, for example, the assistant superintendent for special education in the mid-1970s was active in designing the law itself. He also attempted, with varying degrees of success, to carry out many of the law's provisions in Baltimore well in advance of passage of the federal program. In Milwaukee, local parent organizations lobbied before the state legislature for support of many of the special education reforms that were subsequently endorsed in federal policy. In these and numerous other comparable instances, the federal government was affirming local and state trends rather than imposing its own agenda.

More important, special education divisions across the nation were able to use the federal program to bolster their political standing in the same local school districts that had historically viewed them with disdain. In Miami, the special education department was upgraded to divisional status, and in all four districts this division received substantial amounts of additional funding from state and local, as well as federal, sources during the 1970s. By 1980, each had attained unprecedented political leverage and was able to compete for local resources. Even though Baltimore's assistant superintendent for special education was fired in 1978 for his outspoken criticism of district programming, the framework of the federal program had been well established, assuring that the basic reforms would outlive the tenure of the individual so devoted to their development.

Thus, program implementation in special education was closely connected to the emergence of a self-conscious professional group dedicated to achieving many, if not all, federal objectives. Washington was not imposing its desires on recalcitrant local administrators; instead, local professionals eagerly pointed to federal requirements as justification for their own claims for programmatic expansion. Professional ties became the link that connected federal specifications to local realities.

Some may feel that any claim of special education to professional standing is presumptuous. Compared to the medical professions, the field does not have the same claim to esoteric knowledge or the same prestige. Within the field of education, however, its claims to professional standing have gained considerable strength. Whereas education in general relies heavily on vague technologies (often embedded in tradition and popular conceptions rather than professional norms) (Lortie, 1973), special education—at least in some of its diagnostic techniques and treatment strategies—relies more heavily on what seems to be an esoteric body of knowledge.

Assessment of an individual student's ability and determination of an appropriate instructional plan incorporates psychological, health, social, and educational factors. This assessment can include vision, hearing and speech, health history and present status, general developmental history, adaptive behavior, and relevant information provided by other social-service agencies. Psychologists, psychiatrists, and educators continue to study abnormal child development and have proposed differentiated treatment and instruction for students who had formerly been lumped into broad categories and presumed uneducable.

Limits on Producer Group Prerogatives

That special educators found new dignity, garnered increased resources, and maintained considerable autonomy from federal control seems like grist for the capture theorist's mill. But what about the consumers of these services? Did they receive any benefits? Or have these new resources devoted to education merely spawned new specialties, new administrative positions, and a new cadre of self-protecting "do-gooders"? Posed in these ways, the questions cannot be answered until the results of education for the handicapped can be viewed long term. As of this writing, it is impossible for anyone to undertake a well-designed, longitudinal comprehensive evaluation of program effects. Yet there is reason to believe that the beneficiaries of the law were not limited to the professional special educators.

For one thing, the major impetus behind the legislation came from groups representing the handicapped who clearly distinguished themselves from the educational establishment. Many of the provisions of the law were thus expressly designed to enfranchise the handicapped and their parents. To be sure, the IEP has not been a magnet capable of drawing every parent of a handicapped child fully into the process of evaluation and placement, but it fostered active parental participation in each of the four districts that we examined. Similarly, provisions such as mainstreaming have served to heighten parental awareness of and participation in the educational activities.

Many involved parents have formed organizations designed to oversee the process of service delivery in a specific area of special education, usually one in which their child is enrolled. Such organizations, often informal bodies with no direct link to the school system, are most active in Milwaukee, although they also exist in Baltimore, Dade County, and San Diego. Membership in these organizations often overlaps with mandated district advisory councils in each district. They form a tapestry of organizations that complement local professional direction of special education.

Many parents of special education students have been unusually influential because of both their ability to find a receptive audience in the judicial system and their unusual political skill. In each of the districts these parents tend to be far better connected and knowledgeable politically than those of students who participate in other federal programs that mandate parental participation, such as bilingual and compensatory education. Many parents of the handicapped are well educated and have influential friends; they tap those alliances in attempting to obtain favorable policy decisions, many of which involve placement of their child in a particular school or in a certain program within a school. Local special educators tend to be wary of parents and are often anxious not to upset them, particularly those who seem likely to cause a disturbance in the event of a dispute. As a result, many local special educators tend to be far more concerned with how parents view their efforts than with what the federal government thinks of their programs.

The most active and effective of the numerous parent organizations studied is the Exceptional Education Task Force of Milwaukee. This group preceded the passage of the Education for All Handicapped Children Act and has influenced local (Milwaukee) and state (Wisconsin) special education policy in countless ways. The lobbying efforts of task-force leaders were instrumental in encouraging the Wisconsin legislature to pass far-reaching special education legislation in 1973 that in many respects paved the way for the federal program that followed 2 years later. The task force was also active in the divisional reorganization effort in 1977; many administrators and teachers in the division consider the task force a legitimate counter to their authority, whether through its complaints to the federal Office of Civil Rights about a perceived violation or presentation of research reports to school board members. It has even succeeded in gaining funding from the district for clerical assistance and has been supported in its work by more specialized groups such as the Deaf and Hard of Hearing Advisory Council, the Association for Retarded Citizens, and the Autistic Society.

Milwaukee parents are exceptionally influential but are not alone in mustering an independent source of political power. In Dade County, for example, district advisory council influence has consistently grown after a struggling first year in 1979. According to one of its leaders, the council has gained full access to "any information that affects us," and it forms policy stances on various issues that often contradict divisional policy. "Parents, for example, forced us to take a good look at what we were doing vocationally with the handicapped," noted one assistant superintendent, who acknowledged that fervent pressure forced the district to expand programs in this area. "They call your attention to some things you might overlook."

Parents have also had significant influence on the special education programs in the Baltimore public schools. In 1974, a suit brought by parents of handicapped children led to a Baltimore County Circuit Court ruling that all Maryland children were entitled to a free public education regardless of handicap. Subsequently, many Baltimore parents have worked cooperatively with the Maryland Advocacy Unit for the Developmentally Disabled (MAUDD), which was created by the Development Disabilities Act of 1977 to "protect all the rights of the disabled," in order to exert influence over local special educators. Comparable countervailing power was also evident in the other two districts in the study, suggesting genuine curbs

to produce group domination of decisions related to special education service delivery.

CONCLUSIONS

One can hardly describe compensatory and special education programs of the federal government as unqualified successes. It is difficult to measure the long-term benefits that students who participate in the programs derive from them. But more to the point of this chapter, the administrative processes through which such actions were taken have become increasingly cooperative and consensual. The uncertainties of the initial years have given way to a set of professional understandings and mutual accommodations that bound program participants together, whatever level of government or organizational entity employed them.

What is the larger theoretical significance of the cooperative relations that evolved in these two federal programs? If we accept the claim that these cases were in no way exceptional, that indeed they were prime candidates for the implementation theorist's maze or the capture theorist's stagnant pond, then we must also consider the possibility that much of the recent criticism of federal education policy was both premature and overdrawn. The spate of criticisms of federal programs was spawned by an era that had both the highest expectations and the most severe cynicism about U.S. institutions. To be sure, such reactions were invited by the lofty claims of Great Society enthusiasts who wrote extraordinarily far-reaching objectives into the laws they passed. That no serious government official ever expected these objectives to be more than decently approached was, however, underappreciated by those analysts who found a great disjunction between what Washington promised and Peoria experienced.

With the more realistic perspective that the passage of time allows, we understand that the standpoint from which a program is to be evaluated is the condition that existed prior to the passage of the law, not the condition promised by politicians in search of broad support. With this same perspective, we can also recognize that the law does not implement itself automatically, nor should it be expected to do so.

Change is necessarily gradual, as multiple actors assimilate a new policy into their field of relationships. To be sure, the law is modified and adapted as it adjusts to ongoing structures of power and influence. The extent to which this occurs is almost immediately apparent—and many studies of policy implementation have documented the same with painstaking care. But what becomes perceptible only with time is the extent to which the new law and the resources it generates alter previous relationships. Eventually, a federal law and its administrative arm become accepted as part of the policy field. What was exceptional is now routine. Professional competence means in part the ability to act in conformance with the expectations the law has created. Grodzins (1966) discovered cooperative federalism in the 1950s, only after review of long-established programs where the federal role had already been incorporated into state and local practice. It should not be surprising to hear that in the 1980s these same patterns had begun to develop around new programs.

NOTE

[1] Our research was carried out in Baltimore, Dade County, Florida, Milwaukee, and San Diego. The cities vary in the strength of their local economy, their political and administrative styles, and the extent to which they have incorporated minority representatives in their decision making. Examination of public documents, daily review of the leading newspaper for the city, and interviews with more than 200 state and local officials, on-site administrators, interest group leaders, and local policy analysts provided us with the bulk of our information. Unattributed quotations are comments made by respondents in these interviews. Data were collected between 1980 and 1983. We wish to thank Alec Bender, James Christiansen, Julie Love, Charles Upshaw, Kenneth Wong, and Stephen Wood, who contributed research assistance. This research was sponsored by a grant from the National Institute of Education (NIE) to the National Opinion Research Center, Chicago, Illinois. The views expressed are those of the authors alone and should not be ascribed to either NIE or NORC. A more expansive discussion of the findings of this study, which also includes implementation analysis of federal programs in health care and housing, appears in Paul E. Peterson, Barry G. Rabe, and Kenneth K. Wong, *When Federalism Works* (Washington, DC: Brookings Institution (1986).

REFERENCES

Bailey, S. K., & Mosher, E. K. (1968). *ESEA: The Office of Education administers a law*. Syracuse: Syracuse University Press.

Beer, S. (1982). *Modern British politics: Parties and pressure groups in the collectivist age*. New York: Norton.

Brewer, G. D., & de Leon, P. (1983). *The foundations of policy analysis*. Homewood, IL: Dorsey.

Brown, L. D. (1983). *New policies, new politics: Government's response to government's growth*. Washington, DC: Brookings Institution.

Etzioni, A. (1982). *An immodest agenda: Rebuilding America before the twenty-first century*. New York: New Press.

Gray, V. (1973, December). Innovation in the states. *American Political Science Review*, 7, 1147–1185.

Grodzins, M. (1966). D. E. Elazar (Ed.). *The American system*. Chicago: Rand-McNally.

Grubb, W. N., & Lazerson, M. (1982). *Broken promises: How Americans fail their children*. New York: Basic Books.

Hamilton, A., & Madison, J. (1937). Federalist paper 51. *The Federalist papers*. New York: Random House.

Hastings, A. H. (1982). *The strategies of government intervention: An analysis of federal education and health care policy*. Unpublished doctoral dissertation, University of Virginia, Charlottesville.

Kettl, D. F. (1983). *The regulation of American federalism*. Baton Rouge, LA: Louisiana State University.

Kirst, M. W., & Jung, R. (1982). The utility of a longitudinal approach in assessing implementation: A thirteen year view of Title I, ESEA. In W. Williams (Ed.), *Studying implementation: Methodological and administrative issues*. Chatham, NJ: Chatham House.

Levin, M. A., & Ferman, B. (1985). *The political hand: Policy implementation and youth employment programs*. New York: Pergamon.

Lortie, D. C. (1973). The partial professionalism of elementary teaching. In S. D. Sieber & D. E. Wilder (Eds.), *The school in society* (pp. 315–325). New York: Free Press.

Lowi, T. J. (1969). *The end of liberalism*. New York: Norton.

Lynn, L. E., Jr. (1983, January). The emerging system for educating handicapped children. *Policy Studies Review*, 2(1), 34–35.

McConnell, G. (1966). *Private power and American democracy*. New York: Knopf.

McLaughlin, M. (1975). *Evaluation and reform: The Elementary and Secondary Education Act of 1965, Title I*. Cambridge, MA: Ballinger.

Mercer, J. R. (1974). Sociocultural factors in labelling mental retardees. In L. P. Miller & E. W. Gordon (Eds.), *Equality of educational opportunity* (pp. 318–333). New York: AMS.

Murphy, J. (1971, February). Title I of ESEA: The politics of implementing federal education reform. *Harvard Educational Review*, 41, 36–63.

National Institute of Education. (1977). *Title I funds allocation: The current formula*. Washington, DC: U.S. Department of Health, Education and Welfare.

Peterson, P. E., Rabe, B., & Wong, K. K. (1986). *When Federalism works*. Washington, DC: Brookings Institution.

Pressman, J. L., & Wildavsky, A. (1973). *Implementation*. Berkeley: University of California Press.

Reagan urges 3R's and P. (1982, March 13). *Chicago Tribune*

Rivlin, A. M. (1971). *Systematic thinking for social action*. Washington, DC: Brookings Institution.

Selznick, P. (1949). *TVA and the grass roots: A study in the sociology of formal organization*. Berkeley: University of California Press.

Simors, J. M., & Dwyer, B. (1979). Education of the handicapped. In M. F. Williams (Ed.), *Government in the classroom* (pp. 99–108). New York: Praeger.

Stigler, J. (1975). *The citizen and the state*. Chicago: University of Chicago Press.

U.S. Congress, House Select Subcommittee on Education of the Committee on Education and Labor. (1976). *Extension of the Education for All Handicapped Act*. Washington, DC: U.S. Government Printing Office.

U.S. Department of Education, National Center for Educational Statistics. (1980). *The condition of education, 1980*. Washington, DC: U.S. Government Printing Office.

U.S. Department of Education. (1982). National Center for Educational Statistics. The condition of education, 1982. Washington, DC: U.S. Government Printing Office.

U.S. Office of Education, National Center for Educational Statistics. (1976). *The condition of education, 1976*. Washington, DC: U.S. Government Printing Office.

U.S. Office of Management and Budget. (1981). *Fiscal Year 1982 Budget Revisions*. Washington, DC: U.S. Government Printing Office.

Walker, J. (1971). Innovation in state politics. In H. Jacob & K. Vines (Eds.), *Politics in the American states* (2nd ed., pp. 354–387). Boston: Little, Brown.

Wayson, W. (1975, November). The negative side. *Phi Delta Kappan*, 57(3), 151–156.

Welch, S., & Thompson, K. (1980, November). The impact of federal incentives on state policy formation. *American Journal of Political Science*, 24(4), 715–729.

CHAPTER 24

The Federal Role in Elementary and Secondary Education: Mapping a Shifting Terrain

Richard K. Jung[1]

Shifts in federal policy over the last several years demand that we once again take stock of research on the federal role in elementary and secondary education. Even though its share of elementary and secondary school expenditures has declined throughout the 1980s, the federal government's policies continue to provide important resources for and signals to the nation's educational enterprise. Since publication of the most recent research syntheses dealing with federal, precollegiate education policy (e.g., Advisory Commission on Intergovernmental Relations [ACIR], 1981; Birman & Ginsburg, 1982; Kaestle & Smith, 1982; Peterson, 1983), federal education strategies for school-aged children have gradually shifted. Mainline, federally supported grant-in-aid programs, such as those for disadvantaged students or districts undergoing desegregation, have been deregulated or folded into a block grant. Funding reductions have typically accompanied these programmatic modifications. Also, as part of President Reagan's New Federalism domestic stance, the U.S. Department of Education has demonstrably increased its reliance on leadership or "bully pulpit" policy levers.

This examination of the rapidly expanding empirical and theoretical literature on federal involvement in elementary and secondary education has three related purposes.[2] One purpose is basically descriptive:

that is, to summarize a diverse and largely unpublished body of research on intergovernmental relations in federal education programs immediately prior to and after the deregulation initiatives of the early 1980s. The second, more analytic purpose is to expand the utility of existing analytic frameworks for studying the modern federal role in elementary and secondary education. More specifically, this chapter argues that these frameworks need to be refined to reflect the nature of intergovernmental relations and project designs found in long-standing federal education programs. The third, more normative purpose is to identify gaps in the current literature on federal policy formation and implementation and to suggest subsequent directions for such research.

This chapter has five sections. The first two sections set the stage for a review of recent research. The first section presents an overview of the principal strategies the federal government has used to address national concerns about elementary and secondary education, and it describes theoretical developments for the most commonly used of these federal policy levers. The second section summarizes the findings and limitations of previous research syntheses on federal involvement in U.S. schools.

The last three sections pick up where previous research leaves off. The third section characterizes the nature of intergovernmental relations across a number of federal education programs and policies in the late 1970s and early 1980s. This time span offers important

Consultant/reviewers: Michael W. Kirst, Stanford University; and Richard F. Elmore, Michigan State University

insights about the intergovernmental operations of federal programs during advanced stages of implementation as well as during the transitional years of program reforms started during the Reagan Presidency, particularly those enacted by the Education Consolidation and Improvement Act of 1981. In this section, findings from previously unanthologized studies are integrated so that earlier conceptualizations of the implementation process can be refined to reflect these periods of implementation for federal education programs. The fourth section documents the recent ascendancy of the federal leadership or bully pulpit role, especially under the Reagan Administration. The last section assesses the implications of this and other policy shifts.

ANALYTIC TOOLS FOR STUDYING THE FEDERAL ROLE

The most basic analytic tools for examining the federal role in elementary and secondary schools are catalogues of policy instruments or strategies to address national concerns. A number of such lists have been prepared specifically for education (e.g., Kirst, 1982; Levin, 1983) and across domestic policy areas, including education (e.g., Hastings, 1982; Mosher, 1980; Salamon, 1981). These typologies underscore the breadth of options for addressing identified federal objectives; however, they capture only the most global characteristics of policy strategies.

Kirst's (1982) listing, for example, identified six primary strategies the federal government has used in response to national education concerns:

1. *General Aid*: Provides few or no conditions on aid to state and local education agencies or offers general earmarks, such as teacher salaries.

2. *Stimulation Through Differential Funding*: Targets categories of aid, provides financial incentives through matching grants, funds demonstration projects, and purchases specific services.

3. *Regulation*: Legally specifies behavior, imposes standards, certifies and licenses, and enforces accountability procedures.

4. *Discovery and Dissemination of Knowledge*: Conducts research, gathers statistical data, and makes findings available to practitioners, policy makers, and the public.

5. *Provision of Services*: Furnishes technical assistance and consultants in specialized areas or subjects.

6. *Exertion of Moral Suasion*: Develops vision and questions assumptions through publications, speeches, and other actions by top officials.

Only a few pure forms of such strategies exist in current federal education policy. For example, Section 504 of the Rehabilitation Act of 1973, prohibiting discrimination against the handicapped, exemplifies a pure form of regulation. Typically, however, federal policies in elementary and secondary education embody an amalgam of these policy levers. For instance, when Title I of the Elementary and Secondary Education Act (ESEA) was first legislated, neither analysts nor implementers could agree whether the program provided general aid or represented a more categorical (i.e., differential) set of policy aims (Stoner, 1976). Even though the implementation process eventually defined Title I, ESEA primarily as a form of differential funding, the program also comprised other policy strategies. Its legal framework evolved into a complex and detailed regulatory apparatus. Its Technical Assistance Center network combined aspects of two other strategies—the discovery and dissemination of knowledge and the provision of services. One could consider the Department of Education's initial voucher proposal for the program (the proposed Equity and Choice Act of 1985), given its limited chances for favorable consideration in Congress, to be a sermon from the Administration's bully pulpit on the benefits of choice and private-sector involvement in education rather than a viable proposal to change the federal approach for serving educationally disadvantaged students. One program, therefore, can incorporate many strategies.

Prior to the 1980s, the most pervasive and highly subsidized forms of federal involvement in elementary and secondary education were (a) general-aid programs (e.g., strongly characteristic of vocational education and impact aid grants); (b) differential funding programs, including an array of categorical programs (e.g., for the educationally disadvantaged, the handicapped, those with limited proficiency in English, and other students with special needs) as well as a multitude of demonstration and innovation projects; and (c) regulations that accompanied the two types of grant-in-aid programs or that cut across such programs (e.g., civil rights mandates). As might be expected, the existing analytic frameworks for examining the implementation of federal programs are strongly tied to these three federal strategies. In fact, subsequent to the enactment of these strategies as policy instruments for implementing the agendas of the Great Society and the Civil Rights movement, several waves of theory development have been observed.

Peterson and Wong (1985) identified two of these waves—the marble-cake and implementation analytic perspectives. The so-called "marble-cake" theory of federalism (e.g., Elazar, 1966; Grodzin, 1966) dominated thinking about the dynamics of the federal system during the enactment stage of most federal education programs. Similar to many other Great Society programs, most federal education initiatives enacted in the 1960s were "marbled": that is, formulated and financed at the federal level but predominately administered and operated by officials at state and local levels. Although the marble-cake analytic perspective assumed a highly dynamic implementation context, policy makers typically interpreted it to imply that reform could be accomplished fairly directly through large infusions of federal dollars (Peterson & Wong, 1985). However, the first evaluations of these federal domestic programs instead documented almost universal performance dysfunction at the level of service delivery (e.g., Derthick, 1972; Pressman & Wildavasky, 1973).

A second analytic perspective evolved from these initial implementation studies. This implementation perspective concentrated on barriers to program success, including such obstacles as bureaucratic isolation, organizational complexity, and constituency resistance (Peterson & Wong, 1985). Early implementation theorists, who typically scrutinized programs only during the projects' start-up years, offered little hope that resistance and conflict across levels of government could be overcome.

A third wave of theory was built on concepts of bargaining and adaptation among intergovernmental actors (e.g., Berman & McLaughlin, 1978; Elmore, 1980; Ingram, 1977; McLaughlin, 1976). Instead of concentrating on outcomes for beneficiaries during the first years of a program's operation, these studies focused on understanding why some federally supported projects were successfully implemented in some settings but not in others during and after the beginning years.

The largest of these studies in education, the Change Agent Study conducted by the Rand Corporation (Berman & McLaughlin, 1978), concluded that an innovation had to proceed through three phases for it to continue after federal funding ended: mobilization, implementation, and institutionalization (pp. 15–21).[3] Findings from this study were only slightly more encouraging than the earlier implementation assessments. It found that "the net return to the federal investment was the adoption of many innovations, the successful implementation of few, and the long-run continuation of still fewer" (p. vi).

Berman and McLaughlin (1978) observed that the successes usually exhibited "mutual adaptation" (pp. 16–18); that is, the "project and institutional setting adapted to each other" (McLaughlin & Berman, 1975, p. 5). Changes in the projects could include modified goals and expectations (usually reductions) and simplification of administrative requirements. School district officials changed their attitudes or behaviors to make the new project work in their classrooms. Mutual adaptation often entailed confusion and conflict, especially in the early years. When successful implementation was achieved, it usually evolved as part of a dynamic process among the actors within the intergovernmental system rather than as the predetermined result of centralized rules and management strategies (Berman & McLaughlin, 1978; McLaughlin, 1976).

In recent years, the influence of such dynamics has been incorporated into a number of analytic frameworks for studying categorical and general-aid education programs sponsored by the federal government. For instance, Orland and Goettel (1982) emphasized the importance of state role orientation for ensuring that both state and local agencies have the competence, commitment, and capacity to meet federal program expectations for the Title I, ESEA program. Chubb's (1985) as well as Sabatier and Mazmanian's (1983) analytic models for federal aid to education programs underscored the relationship between the extent of regulations and the interests of actors within the intergovernmental networks. Chubb's (1985) comparative analysis of the regulatory frameworks for Title I, ESEA and federal vocational education programs demonstrated that more extensive regulation is typical under two sets of circumstances: (a) when beneficiaries (in the case of Title I, ESEA—the poor or civil rights groups representing the poor) exercised hegemony over the implementation process but the federal agency received little support for pursuing cost-effective approaches; or (b) when cost-bearers (e.g., state and local educational agencies) dominated the program's implementation but the agency was rewarded for active oversight of possible negligence by cost-bearers (p. 310).

To improve on the early marble-cake and implementation notions of federalism, Peterson and Wong (1985) proposed a differentiated theory of federal education policy. This framework hypothesizes that successful local implementation is a function of (a) the nature of the policy and (b) the administrative units through which the program operates. According to this analytic perspective, most federal categorical programs are more redistributive than developmental.[4] High levels of conflict and less than full compliance can be expected for redistributive programs until autonomous government agencies or subagencies develop to protect and promote the goals of the program. Peterson and Wong's research, however, suggests that such internal constituencies are usually not in place until later stages of implementation.

One of the troubling limitations of the existing

reviews analyzing federal involvement in U.S. schools is that they all base their assessment of the federal role on studies conducted either before or just as such internal constituencies began to emerge.

REVIEWING THE REVIEWS

Since 1980, four major research reviews have been published that synthesize a considerable body of empirical findings on federal, precollegiate education programs. Together, these reviews offer a generally comprehensive and fairly consistent assessment of federal policy formation through the early 1980s and of federal program operations through the mid-1970s. The Advisory Commission on Intergovernmental Relations (ACIR), a bipartisan body including officials from various branches and levels of government, sponsored one of these reviews. Published in 1981, the ACIR report was written prior to the Republican Presidential victory in 1980. The second review, written by Birman and Ginsburg (1982), then analysts within the U.S. Department of Education, was completed after the formulation of the Reagan Administration's initial education policy but before the passage of the most important piece of elementary and secondary legislation during this term, the Education Consolidation and Improvement Act (ECIA). The third and fourth syntheses, Kaestle & Smith (1982) and Peterson (1983), included accounts of ECIA's enactment but not of the early years of its implementation.

Despite differences in the approaches and coverage, these reviews came to a number of similar conclusions about the modern era in federal involvement, more particularly about its genesis, its broader social context, and its evolution. Each review saw the passage of ESEA as ushering in the modern era of active federal involvement in precollegiate education. Each review chronicled the proliferation of grant programs from the 1960s through the mid-1970s. These categorical grants were salted with federal regulations and oversight structures intended to provide extra services to traditionally underserved students. For state and local educational officials, the sweetener in these programs was expanding—but, many felt, under-funded—budgets. Interspersed with these program strategies were a number of enforcement obligations or crosscutting regulations such as those to eliminate sex discrimination (Title IX, ESEA, 1972) and to protect the rights of the handicapped (Section 504 of the Rehabilitation Act, 1973).

Each review also stressed that the modern federal role in U.S. schools evolved as part of broader social and political movements. Kaestle and Smith (1982), for instance, portrayed the federal role in elementary and secondary education since 1940 as an extension of the same historical process that led to the creation of state school systems and emphasized that such involvement "is continuous with general trends in American history" (p. 390). Similarly, Peterson (1983) viewed the modern federal role as emblematic of "a broad social trend toward increasing functional specialization in American education" (p. 149). ACIR (1981) argued that issues at the heart of the federal role have "remained remarkably the same"—race, religion, and federal control (p. 11). Birman and Ginsburg (1982) noted that Reagan's education policies could best be understood as a reflection of that Administration's overall agendas to strengthen the nation's economy, shift major domestic responsibilities from federal to state and local governments as well as to the private sector, and focus on new national priorities (pp. 484–485).

These four research syntheses also concurred that by the 1970s the "patchwork quilt" of federal programmatic and regulatory strategies had evolved into an ever more directive yet fragmented educational presence (see also Kirp & Winslow, 1978; Meyer, 1979). ACIR's assessment especially emphasized the theme of expanded fragmentation of federal education policies. The ACIR report (1981) argued that the proliferation of both legislative and judicial policy at the federal level created burdens and confusions in the schools (p. 77). For instance, according to the ACIR report, implementation of the *Brown* decision and the burgeoning of educational litigation to interpret and apply the crosscutting regulatory requirements' involved the Supreme Court directly with state and local school administrators, spreading and fragmenting federal involvement across branches of government (pp. 75–77).

Birman and Ginsburg (1982) also criticized the multiplicity of federal programs and enforcement requirements which "often pull[ed] state and local officials in different directions" and "sent conflicting signals to those who must deliver services from multiple sources" (pp. 473, 484). Kaestle and Smith (1982) noted particularly that most of the diverse array of federal programs and requirements were peripheral to the main business of schools, but "were often seen as interfering with the real business of the schools" (p. 405). Peterson's synthesis provided similar evidence that by the late 1970s "the federal government may have gone too far in seeking detailed compliance with its numerous regulations." Peterson (1983) hastened to caution, however, that the federal government was only one of many forces contributing to the increased fragmentation of the elementary and secondary schooling experience and erosion of school administrators' authority (pp. 104–105).

Of the four reviews, ACIR's most clearly embodied the analytic perspective of the implementationalists, which emphasized the barriers to successful operation of federal education programs. The three concluding sections of the ACIR report exemplified the usual outline for this analytic approach: (a) "Federal Aid, the Enactment Phase"; (b) "Federal Aid, The Implementation Phase"; and (c) "Constraints on Federal Involvement in Elementary and Secondary Education." The report also characteristically concluded that implementation problems resulted from seemingly intransigent elements of the enactment process. It concluded on a foreboding note: For instance, it asserted that despite President Nixon's efforts to reverse the federal government's growing intrusive involvement, "the structure of Congress and the federal bureaucracy make such reversals considerably more difficult" (p. 81).

In contrast to ACIR's "top-down" orientation, Birman and Ginsburg's (1982) approach emphasized the importance of state and local contexts as intervening influences on federal policy success. The authors observed that "no matter what decisions are made in Washington, states and school districts will implement them" (p. 500). Peterson's review and Kaestle and Smith's were based on more recent studies. Both reviews argued that policy contradictions documented during the early years of categorical programs had, to some degree, been ameliorated. Even so, both reviews documented persistent complaints about excessive paperwork and burdensome regulations stemming from lack of trust among officials responsible for overseeing and implementing federal programs and regulations. Peterson (1983) cited examples of "incremental modifications of federal law and regulations" as contributing to somewhat improved consistency of federal policy signals (pp. 145–156), whereas Kaestle and Smith (1982) credited accommodations on the part of school officials as contributing to "adequately implemented" federal programs (p. 405). Peterson's analysis paired with Kaestle and Smith's review represents an extension of the concept of mutual adaptation (McLaughlin, 1976; McLaughlin & Berman, 1975) to a broader set of policy strategies than were examined in the Rand Change Agent Study (Berman & McLaughlin, 1978). Viewed together, these later two reviews (Kaestle & Smith, 1982; Peterson, 1983) showed that accommodation must generally occur in both federal strategies and local implementation contexts before improved implementation can be expected.

These four research reviews provided a useful synthesis of numerous field-based studies conducted through the mid 1970s, but they predated the availability of several significant bodies of empirical studies on program implementation. The next section of this chapter maps this diverse body of field-based studies. One set of these studies examined the operations of federal categorical programs and crosscutting regulations prior to the deregulation efforts initiated in the early 1980s; the other set studied initial state and local responses to the streamlining federal compensatory education requirements and to the block grant enacted by the ECIA of 1981.

MOVING INTO THE "ACCUSTOMIZATION" PHASE

Both sets of the previously unanthologized studies discussed in this section document a phase of implementation that was, at least by degree, more advanced than the mutual adaptation stage depicted in earlier research syntheses. This phase of implementation is characterized by limited or circumscribed intergovernmental conflicts; customized applications of federal requirements and options to local circumstances; a better balance between emphasis on program quality and on program compliance; and general, but not complete, support of federal categorical goals.

Federal Program and Regulatory Strategies Before Deregulation

Two field-based studies (Moore et al., 1983; Knapp, Stearns, Turnbull, David, & Peterson, 1983) commissioned for the congressionally mandated School Finance Project depicted how school officials responded to and were affected by the combination of federal education programs and regulatory structures in place during the 1981–1982 school year. One of these studies (Moore et al., 1983) focused at the state level, the other (Knapp et al., 1983) at the local level. This was a transition year and a year of budget cuts for most districts. President Reagan's Omnibus Budget Reconciliation Act had authorized recisions that meant federal funding reductions in most districts. The 1981–1982 school year also marked the last year federal compensatory education programs operated under the elaborate legal requirements of the 1978 ESEA Amendments and the last year for the operation of 28 programs that became part of the education block grant.

The state-level study (Moore et al., 1983) examined the implementation and interactions among more than a half-dozen of the largest federal grant-in-aid programs and for three crosscutting requirements to protect the rights of racial and ethnic minorities, women, and the handicapped.[5] Characteristic of this later stage of implementation, the study noted that "state forces actively shaped federal programs and policies [and]...federal program and policy signals heavily influence[d] the course followed by the state" (p. 9). The study did not find administrative problems such as lack of coordination, excessive paperwork, and federal intrusiveness to the extent the researchers had expected from previous studies. The mandated investigation concluded that these administrative problems were inaccurately ascribed to federal programs as their singular source. Nor, said these researchers, did "state conflicts with federal programs...exhibit the intensity we had expected from popular accounts" (p. 10). Conflicts, where they did persist, usually flared up over newer requirements. State officials still resented, in particular, the newly established planning, data collection, and special set-asides of the vocational education program, as well as the due-process procedures and related service requirements for special education.

The states were also notable in their diversity. States were found to have tailored federal programs to suit state contexts. The final form of federally funded projects was most often affected by the states' political traditions, their educational priorities, and their technical capacities. Although many of the states had sophisticated implementation capacities, the study warned that "policy makers have little reason to expect that most states at this point will assume the equity agenda that defines much of the current federal role in education" (Moore et al., 1983, p. 12).

In general, the situation at the state level across these programs and mandates did not completely resemble the transitory and often conflict-ridden implementation stage of mutual adaptation. Nor had the states truly institutionalized the goals of these federal strategies. According to the analytic paradigm of the Rand Change Agent Study (Berman & McLaughlin, 1978), institutionalization occurs when a state or local agency decides to take on the innovation even in the absence of federal funding and/or regulations. Using this paradigm, state implementation of the more mature mandates and programs generally appeared to fall somewhere between the stages of mutual adaptation and institutionalization.

A similar implementation phase was found in the second study (Knapp et al., 1983) that focused on the school district level.[6] The three central findings of this study, conducted by SRI International, were:

[1.] Collectively, federal and state policies for special populations have substantively improved and expanded the array of educational services for the intended target students.

[2.] The policies have increased the structural complexity of schools and districts, which appears to represent a necessary consequence of providing targeted services.

[3.] Over time, local problem solving, federal and state adjustments, and gradual local accommodation have generally reduced to a manageable level the cost associated with special services (p. 159).

The study by Knapp and colleagues (1983), similar to the state-level study of Moore et al. (1983), observed that federal requirements and signals were typically needed for the program's resources to reach needy students (pp. 160–161).

The follow-up examination to the Rand Change Agent Study of federal innovation programs also characterized implementation as having moved beyond mutual adaptation for these projects (Crandall & Loucks, 1983). This investigation, known as the Study of Dissemination Efforts Supporting School Improvement, found that states and districts had typically graduated from the conflict observed during the earlier study (Crandall & Loucks, 1983). The main message the director of this study drew from this extensive reexamination of federally sponsored innovation projects was that regardless of the source of external assistance—state or federal government, foundations, or the private sector—it must "be around over the long haul" (Crandall, 1984, p. 11).

Thus, prior to the deregulation and consolidation of a number of differential funding programs and crosscutting regulatory mandates, state and local implementation efforts had moved to a phase beyond mutual adaptation but short of full institutionalization. Two salient characteristics distinguish this intermediary phase of implementation. First, it is less conflict-ridden than the mutual adaptation stage. With the passage of time, school officials had become accustomed to the purposes and specific requirements of the programs, with the usual result that conflict diminished or at least that differences were confined to certain requirements under certain conditions. Second, implementing officials, as part of this phase, had actively customized the federal initiatives to fit their special conditions, but rarely could they sustain the targeted services or innovations without federal regulatory and financial support. Such customization was often made possible by changes in federal policy that provided an option or adjusted expectations, typically through extended and iterative negotiations with representatives of the service providers and beneficiary or advocacy groups.

The term *accustomization* depicts this implementation phase, which features *accustomed* relationships and the *customization* of program requirements to fit state or local conditions while attempting to ensure realization of basic categorical policy objectives (Jung & Kirst, 1986). This phase of federal program implementation is more closely scrutinized in two national studies of Title I, ESEA conducted during the 1981–1982 school year. One examined state implementation of the program; the other studied the program's local operations.

A State Management Practices Study concluded that the elaborate legal structure contained in the 1978 ESEA Amendments was no longer necessary for some states. The report, from American Institutes for Research, stated that "while strict compliance measures were undoubtedly correct for a 'young' program...it was not clear that such prescriptive measures were appropriate for a 'mature' program, such as Title I in its later years" (Bessey, Brant, Thompson, Harrison, Putman, & Appleby, 1982, p. xvii). During this phase of implementation, Bessey et al. (1982) found that "quality-oriented states often break new ground, and they extend themselves by making rules to further program goals—all of which can lead to problems and uncertainties as to whether their actions are in compliance with the law" (p. xix). However, a number of states that exhibited what the study called a "compliance orientation" relied heavily on federal rules to take more of a proactive stance for the disadvantaged than their states' contexts would otherwise allow.

The Title I District Practices Study provided a school- and district-level perspective of the program's implementation during the accustomization phase. The study's findings underscored the diversity of projects funded by the program.[7] The study found, for instance, a growing diversity in whether program services were offered in the students' regular classroom or in a separate part of the school building using a "pullout" approach. More districts had decided to keep program participants in the regular classroom for their special instruction. Even though most districts still used the pullout approach, 30 percent of them relied on the in-class alternative for at least some of their Title I-sponsored projects—a 32 percent increase over 4 years earlier. The findings also highlighted the balance of quality and compliance considerations that were often reflected in local program decisions during this phase. District program directors usually indicated that their choice of project design(s), for example, was motivated by whether it was effective in their district and whether it would pass legal muster (Advanced Technology, Inc. [ATI], 1983, pp. 33–42). Most districts also based their school and student selection determinations, attempts to coordinate the Title I program with other special needs programs, and other program design decisions on a combination of compliance and quality considerations (ATI, 1983, Chaps. 3–5).

This balance was typically achieved over time through iterative, incremental changes in federal signals in conjunction with modifications in state and local implementation contexts, capacities, and orientations (Kirst & Jung, 1982; Orland & Goettel, 1982; Sabatier & Mazmanian, 1983, Chap. 6).

The development and implementation of the program's targeting requirements illustrate this process of incremental change. The rules for selecting schools to receive Title I services in the 1965 legislation were ambiguous and brief. The statute merely stated that Title I projects should be located in schools or attendance areas with "high concentrations of children from low-income families" (Sec. 205(a)(1), P.L. 89–10). By 1978, federal requirements had become more prescriptive in response to years of documented abuse, but they also contained a number of options or exceptions to accommodate a variety of local situations in which the general targeting rules might not be appropriate or necessary (Kirst & Jung, 1982). For instance, districts were required to use the best available data sources for ranking their schools' poverty level to identify eligible schools, but they could select from a wide array of data sources for such determinations. Districts were also required to rank their schools by poverty concentration and serve them in order from highest to lowest, but six options or exceptions were available for districts so that targeting decisions could better match local circumstances and preferences. For instance, districts could decide which grades their program would serve and then would need only to rank those schools with these grade spans. Or in districts where there was "no-wide variance" in poverty, all schools could be served, including those with concentrations of poverty lower than the districts' average. By 1981, many districts were using one or more of these options. Almost half the districts used the grade span grouping option, and almost 30 percent employed the "no-wide variance" option when it applied (Gaffney & Schember, 1982, p. 21).

The Title I-Chapter 1 program still has its critics (e.g., Walberg, 1984), and its effectiveness in compensating for the negative effects of living in high concentrations of poverty is still intensely debated (e.g., Kaestle & Smith, 1982; Mullin & Summers, 1983). By the 1980s, however, the program had become generally popular with local school officials (e.g., Plunkett, 1985). Complaints were usually relegated to one or two aspects of its requirements, especially those pertaining to parent advisory councils and comparability (Rezmovic & Keesling, 1982). Both of these areas, however, and several others were simplified by the ECIA of 1981.

Accustomization After Deregulation

The Omnibus Budget Reconciliation Act of 1981 reduced funding and instituted a number of deregulatory measures across most domestic functional areas. The educational component of this Act was entitled the Education Consolidation and Improvement Act of 1981 (ECIA).

ECIA had three sections or chapters. Chapter 1 rewrote and streamlined most of the provisions of the Title I, ESEA program. Chapter 2 of the Act consolidated 28 education programs into a block grant. Similar to Chapter 1, the block grant promised reduced paperwork and administrative burden in exchange for funding decreases. Chapter 3, ECIA limited the oversight powers of both federal and state agencies in administering Chapter 1 and 2 programs.

After less than 2 years of operation, at least 21 major empirical studies of the block grant had been fielded (summarized by Knapp & Cooperstein, 1986). More than half these studies, however, were undertaken by advocacy groups who stood to gain or lose funds under the block grant. The American Association of School Administrators (AASA), for instance, released two reports (AASA, 1983, 1984) contrasting the losses in funding for some public schools with the expanded services for private school students. Similarly, the Council of Great City Schools (CGCS) produced two assessments (CGCS, 1982, 1983) of funding cuts under Chapter 2 and other federal programs operating in its member districts. Other analyses documented that most large, urban districts lost considerable funding as a result of Chapter 2, but they also noted that these districts had actually lost considerably more due to the erosion of political support for the antecedent programs in the year prior to the block grant (Jung & Stonehill, 1985).

Other early studies of Chapter 2 offered only glimpses into intergovernmental relations during the first 2 years of this program. These early case studies found that (a) getting the funds out was the first order of business; (b) decisions about which of the antecedent program structures would gain or lose resources often created friction within and across levels of government; and (c) many officials were still sorting out the rules of the program (summarized by Knapp & Cooperstein, 1984, pp. 26–28).

However, after only 3 years of operation, it appeared that most goals set forth in the Chapter 2 legislation had been achieved. The first national assessment of the program concluded that districts were using

Chapter 2 funds for educational improvement, that the block grant had reduced administrative burdens while increasing local discretion, and that the program consolidation had enhanced access of private school students to federally funded services. Only the program goal of improving teacher and parental involvement had not been fully achieved by the third year of the block grant's implementation. (Knapp & Blakely, 1986, p. iii). Characteristic of the accustomization phase, the study also found that "interactions between districts and other levels of government ha[d] quickly become routinized and relatively trouble-free." The fact that districts had become accustomed to the antecedent programs was also reflected in the study's finding that the "block grant's accomplishments build on the foundation laid by former and current categorical programs" (Knapp & Blakely, 1986, pp. iv–v).

The reduced funding and deregulation under Chapter 1 of ECIA also prompted a burst of research activity. Two organizations that historically have advocated an expanded role for federal oversight, the Children's Defense Fund (1984) and the Lawyers' Committee for Civil Rights Under Law (1984), produced the first two large-scale investigations of the effects of Chapter 1's funding cuts and regulatory simplification on state and local operations. A third major report was prepared by an intern for the U.S. House of Representative's Committee on Education and Labor (Dougherty, 1985). The three reports came to very similar conclusions: (a) reduced levels of service under Chapter 1 seemed principally related to funding reductions rather than to changes in the program's requirements; (b) states were not receiving adequate guidance from the U.S. Department of Education to carry out their reduced and less defined roles concerning oversight and technical assistance; (c) although diversity was noted among the states, overall there was a reduction of state monitoring and guidance to districts; and (d) parental involvement, particularly in the form of previously mandated district- and school-level councils, had generally declined.

A separate study conducted by Stanford University's Institute for Research on Educational Finance and Governance also examined state and local responses to Chapter 1, but more with an intention to understand the dynamics of intergovernmental relations within a mature federal categorical program (McLaughlin, Shields, & Rezabek, 1985). In brief, this study found continuation of the accustomization phase after Chapter 1's statutory streamlining and easing of regulatory requirements.

In contrast to findings from the early Chapter 2 case studies, this examination of 24 districts in eight states found continuation of the basic categorical orientation of the program, particularly at the local level. It noted "with much of the complex regulatory scaffolding dismantled, local programs and the services provided to participating children generally remained unchanged. Title I, without question, stimulated local activities that have persisted under Chapter 1" (McLaughlin, Shields, & Rezabek, 1985, p. 163).

Nonetheless, the variety of reactions of state-level officials to the more substantially reduced state role under Chapter 1 as well as the broad discontinuation of some local practices, particularly parental advisory councils, suggested that the removal of too much of the categorical structure would result in diminished attention to the categorical goals. Under Chapter 1, most states lost approximately one-third of the administrative funds they had under the 1978 Title I Amendments. The states' responsibilities for providing technical assistance and ensuring compliance were also substantially reduced. The study concluded that

> if the "backbone" of the federal compensatory program were removed at the local levels as it was at the state level, compensatory education staff in many districts would be little more successful than were their counterparts in many states in continuing program practices.... In a fundamental sense, then, practices associated with the successful operation of this federal categorical program are unlikely to be institutionalized in the majority of local districts. (McLaughlin, Shields, & Rezabek, 1985, pp. 168–169)

A preliminary examination of state and local implementation of Chapter 1 similarly noted that "specific requirements promulgated at the federal level may lead to greater compliance, but not to institutionalization" (Keesling, 1985, pp. 1–12). Finally, preliminary findings from the congressionally mandated National Assessment of Chapter 1 also show broad-based support for the program's categorical goals without, however, full institutionalization of these goals (Birman, Orland, Jung, Anson, & Garcia, 1987).

Overall, then, a rather consistent picture emerges from looking across a broad range of long-standing federal policy strategies before and immediately after deregulation. The commitment, capacity, and substantive expertise of state and local implementers had often coalesced into internal support for the underlying goals of these federal education policies. Such a dynamic took years to take hold. A cadre of staff had to be established. Rules had to be worked out and shaped to fit diverse state and local circumstances. Routines that balanced concerns about effectiveness and compliance had to be established. Even then, policies could not be expected to persevere in the face of substantial or complete retreat of federal funds and direction.

These changes in state and local responses to more traditional federal strategies happened, by and large, after the publication of earlier research reviews. As the diversity of reports reviewed in this section demonstrates, these shifts have been fairly well documented, although primarily in unpublished government or technical reports. Less well documented, however, is the shift in federal policy to the bully pulpit.

MOVING INTO THE BULLY PULPIT

Despite the ascendancy of the leadership or bully pulpit role as a featured policy lever of the Reagan Administration, its origins, use, and potential impacts have not been seriously examined by educational researchers. Such an investigation is well beyond the scope of this chapter. This review, however, would be remiss if it did not at least demonstrate the need for mapping this largely uncharted research terrain.

Neither President Reagan nor his Secretaries of Education have left any doubt about the centrality of the bully pulpit for pursuing their policy objectives. President Reagan wrote, in a self-assessment of his first term in office:

> If I were asked to single out the proudest achievements of my Administration's first three and one-half years in office, what we've done to define the issues and promote the great national debate in education would rank right up near the top of the list. (1984, p. 2)

Likewise Secretary of Education T. H. Bell frequently expressed a hope to be remembered, if for nothing else, as one who reversed the trend of federal control through regulatory strategies and who pointed the way to higher standards through federal leadership (e.g., Bell, 1981, 1983, 1986).

Certainly the most visible embodiment of the Reagan Administration's reliance on the bully pulpit strategy was the publication and follow-up activities for the U.S. Department of Education's (1983) *A Nation at Risk*. For almost a year, the Department could not keep pace with demand for this publication by the National Commission on Excellence in Education (NCEE). Roughly 70,000 copies were sold during its first year, and at least seven times that number had been copied within a year of the report's first release. Its contents were generously excerpted in most major news magazines and received coast-to-coast coverage in local newspapers for months (U.S. Department of Education, 1984b).

President Reagan was called on to maintain the cadence of this "sermon" by NCEE on the mediocrity of U.S. education, including his participation in regional forums and public addresses across the country.

Secretary Bell also earmarked most of the resources from his discretionary grants fund for projects that addressed the problems and priorities raised in the report.

A Nation at Risk was soon followed by other extensions of the bully pulpit strategy, the first of which was the Department of Education's (1984a) own assessment of NCEE's impacts in *The Nation Responds: Recent Efforts to Improve Education*. Another manifestation of this strategy was the release of the controversial statistical table "State Education Statistics: State Performance Outcomes, Resource Inputs and Population Characteristics, 1972 and 1982," more commonly known as the "State Wall Chart." The statistics on this chart echoed NCEE's warning about the "rising tide of mediocrity" by showing that every state's test scores of college-bound seniors declined during the decade between 1972 and 1982. After the intensive media attention this information received, the Council of Chief State School Officers reversed its long-standing refusal to publicize educational performance results that permit cross-state comparisons in order to preempt the federal government's attempt to publish additional interstate performance comparisons.

Less visible expressions of the bully pulpit strategy have been the Department of Education's publication of the *Indicators of Education Status and Trends* (1985) and *Becoming a Nation of Readers*. Although diverse in content, both publications promoted improvement of the U.S. educational system through information and leadership rather than the establishment of programmatic or regulatory structures.

Secretary of Education William Bennett's more outspoken style and the more controversial issues he has addressed through various forums have lead some to comment that his tenure has brought new meaning to *bully* in the phrase "bully pulpit" (e.g., Astuto & Clark, 1986; Clark & Astuto, 1986; Lewis, 1985; personal communication from P. E. Peterson, August 28, 1985). Secretary Bennett has also demonstrated a capacity to articulate the Reagan Administration's messages in a format that can be more easily conveyed to the public. For instance, upon his appointment, Bennett first listed 10 issues he would address (1985a). Later that month, President Reagan (1985) enumerated five more digestible themes: choice, teachers, curriculum, setting, and parents. Soon thereafter, Bennett honed this list of concerns to his mnemonic "three Cs": content, character, and choice (1985b).

Under Bennett, not only did the "liturgy" of the bully pulpit expand beyond excellence but so did the form of the "pulpit." "Sermons" from Bennett and his staff have taken the more conventional forms of technical reports, addresses, budget statements, and congressional hearings (e.g., on choice, Finn, 1985) as well as the more publicized ventures of sending Bennett to teach the *Federalist Papers* in schools across the country and of compiling for the U.S. public as well as U.S. educators a compendium of research findings on *What Works* to improve teaching and learning (U.S. Department of Education, 1986).

Even though the Administration's use of the bully pulpit has been its premier policy lever, there is almost no research on the topic. Thus far, the Department of Education's own assessments of its bully pulpit activities have been handled more in a public relations vein than a scholarly one. On the first anniversary of *A Nation at Risk*, for instance, the Department issued *The Nation Responds* (U.S. Department of Education, 1984a), but its primary purpose was to reinforce the Administration's message of optimism and to make yet another clarion call to states and districts to persevere in their educational reform efforts.

Despite the general lack of research attention on the expanded use of moral suasion under the Reagan Administration, Weiss's (1979) analyses of earlier use of this strategy suggests that the bully pulpit can affect policy makers' assumptions and views about policy priorities. A growing body of literature also shows that state officials, especially governors, are taking a greater leadership role in teacher reforms, such as improving standards, working conditions, and career opportunities, as well as broad-based curriculum reforms to raise standards and decrease dropouts (e.g., Doyle & Hartle, 1985; Hartle & Holland, 1983).

LOOKING BEYOND

This review has taken stock of a rapidly expanding body of research on the federal role in elementary and secondary education. It documents two important shifts since the publication of the last spate of research reviews.

First, intergovernmental operations within federal strategies of longer duration—including regulatory mandates, categorical grants, and innovation projects—have in later years moved to a phase of more accustomed relations and more customized applications of federal resources than had been the case portrayed in earlier syntheses. Still, earlier hopes that federal goals would eventually be sustained without federal resources or rules have not materialized, especially for the more redistributive of these strategies. Initial state and local responses to the deregulation reforms of ECIA further suggest that full institutionalization of programs with redistributive qualities will not occur soon. Current analytic frameworks, which were built on an earlier research base, apparently did not anticipate this intermediate phase—short of autonomous state and local continuation (i.e., institutionalization) but past the more conflict-ridden and chaotic days portrayed in earlier research syntheses (i.e., mutual adaptation).

Second, the Reagan Administration has intensified the federal government's reliance on moral suasion, or the bully pulpit strategy, over the past 5 years. Previous administrations have used the bully pulpit to reinforce more direct regulatory and grant strategies. However, the Reagan Administration has featured this strategy of speeches, commissions, testimony, and other forms of advocacy by the President and high-ranking Department of Education officials as one of its primary modes of action. To date, nonetheless, researchers have largely ignored this relatively inexpensive policy strategy.

There is every reason to believe that the bully pulpit strategy will continue to move center stage and that there will be intensified reexamination of intergovernmental roles across grant-in-aid programs. Such assumptions are based on activities already underway, as policy makers at all levels attempt to grapple with reducing a national debt approximating $2 trillion.

The Gramm-Rudman balanced budget bill, signed into law by President Reagan in December 1985, requires Congress to reduce the deficit by a set amount each year and to achieve a balanced budget by 1991. If lawmakers fail to meet these annual goals, automatic reductions go into effect, with cuts shared equally among both domestic and military programs. Even if the deficit reduction targets of this legislation are deferred or only partially realized, over the next several years nonincremental budget reductions probably should be expected in discretionary elementary and secondary education projects unless alternative arrangements are devised.

Already, state and local officials who not so long ago balked at the notion of assuming some of the federal government's domestic programmatic and regulatory responsibilities now appear more ready to explore new arrangements. For instance, the Council of State Governments, a bipartisan group of state political and government officials, is actively examining options for overhauling economic-development, environmental, and social-services programs in light of the impending federal deficit-reducing measures. Both Republicans and Democrats have established commissions to take a new look at proposals for "swapping" some federal and state responsibilities (Broder, 1985).

As the federal government continues to promote the dual goals of equity and excellence in elementary and secondary education through the end of this decade, this review points to two important reorientations for researchers. First, this synthesis underscores the need to refine the analytic frameworks for examining the operations of long-standing programmatic and regulatory strategies. Second, it highlights the need for more scholarly attention to the origins, impacts, potentials, and limitations of leadership or bully pulpit strategies employed to address national education concerns during an era of devolved responsibilities and fiscal constraints.

NOTES

[1] I was invited to write this chapter on the basis of a manuscript Michael Kirst and I had prepared for *Educational Administration Quarterly*. I want to recognize Dr. Kirst for his ongoing contributions to the research and thinking reflected in this chapter. I also thank Drs. Chester Finn, Mary Moore, Martin Orland, and Paul Peterson for their helpful comments on earlier versions of this chapter. In addition, Dr. Milbrey McLaughlin's suggestions for recasting the analyses in the earlier manuscript to advance theory were particularly useful in preparing this chapter. The views and conclusions expressed in this chapter, however, are mine. No official support from or endorsement by the U.S. Department of Education is intended or should be inferred.

[2] The literature reviewed in this chapter was collected through two major search procedures: (a) an automated search of ERIC, which yielded 187 entries; and (b) a manual review of a bibliography file on federalism in elementary and secondary education prepared and maintained for the Office of Educational Research and Improvement's National Assessment of Chapter 1. This file included more than 350 entries contributed by individual educational researchers and other scholars, as well as by professional associations, advocacy groups, government agencies, and other research organizations. For more detail on these search procedures and bibliographic sources, see Jung and Kirst (1986).

[3] The results of this study are reported in eight volumes. See Volume 8 of this series (Berman & McLaughlin, 1978, pp. *iii–iv*) for a description of each volume's contents. Programs examined in the study are Titles III (Innovative Projects) and VII (Bilingual Projects) of ESEA, the Vocational Education Act (Exemplary Projects), and Right-to-Read.

[4] According to the Peterson and Wong (1985) formulation, one can assess the extent to which a policy is redistributive by judging the degree to which those who receive program services are those who pay for the services. In the case where the two are completely different, the policy is an instance of pure redistribution (p. 306; also see Elmore, 1982, p. 180).

[5] The federal programs and civil rights provisions examined included Titles I, IV, V, and VII of ESEA; the Education for All Handicapped Children Act (P.L. 94–142); the Vocational Education Act; Title VI of the Civil Rights Act of 1964; Title IX of the Education Amendments of 1972; and Section 504 of the Rehabilitation Act of 1973. The state programs studied were analogous to federal programs but were funded at the state level. The eight states visited were California, Louisiana, Massachusetts, Missouri, New Mexico, New York, Virginia, and Wyoming.

[6] The federal programs and civil rights provisions examined included Titles I and VII, ESEA; the Education for All Handicapped Children Act (P.L. 94–142); the Vocational Education Act; Title VI of the Civil Rights Act of 1964; Title IX of the Education Amendments of 1972; and Section 504 of the Rehabilitation Act of 1973. Where they existed, the study also documented local operation of the Indo-China Refugee Children Assistance Act, the Indian Education Act, and the Emergency School Aid Assistance Act. Also

included in the study's scope were parallel state programs or requirements.

[7] This study combined three methodologies to compare local operation of the Title I program during the 1981–1982 school year with earlier operation of the program: a mail questionnaire sent to approximately 2,000 randomly selected school districts, structured interviews and document reviews in 100 nationally representative Title I districts, and case studies in 40 purposely selected Title I districts.

REFERENCES

Advanced Technology, Inc. (1983). *Local operation of Title I, ESEA 1976–1982: A resource book*. McLean, VA: Author.

Advisory Commission on Intergovernmental Relations. (1981). Intergovernmentalizing the classroom: Federal involvement in elementary and secondary education. In the series *The federal role in the federal system: The dynamics of growth*. Washington, DC: Author.

American Association of School Administrators. (1983). *The impacts of Chapter 2 of the Education Consolidation and Improvement Act on local education agencies*. Arlington, VA: Author.

American Association of School Administrators. (1984). *Private school participation in Chapter 2 of the Education Consolidation and Improvement Act*. Arlington, VA: Author.

Astuto, T. A., & Clark, D. L. (1986, March). *The effects of federal education policy changes on policy and program development in state and local education agencies* (Occasional Paper No. 2). Bloomington, IN: Policy Studies Center of the University Council for Education Administration.

Bell, T. H. (1981). Interview with T. H. Bell, *Education Board*, *62*(3), pp. 5–7.

Bell, T. H. (1983). *Goals and performance priorities of the U.S. Department of Education for fiscal year 1984*. [Unpublished release]. Washington, DC: U.S. Department of Education.

Bell, T. H. (1986). Education policy development in the Reagan administration. *Phi Delta Kappan*, *68*(7), 487–493.

Bennett, W. J. (1985a, February). Statement by Secretary of Education, William J. Bennett. [Press release]. Washington, DC: U.S. Department of Education.

Bennett, W. J. (1985b, March). *Address to the National Press Club*. [Speaker]. Washington, DC: U.S. Department of Education.

Berman, P., & McLaughlin, M. W. (1978). *Federal programs supporting educational change*, Vol. 8: *Implementing and sustaining innovations*. Santa Monica, CA: Rand.

Bessey, B. L., Brandt, D. A., Thompson, P. A., Harrison, L. R., Putman, K. E., & Appleby, J. A. (1982, August). *A study of state management practices: Looking back at Title I and toward Chapter 1*. Palo Alto, CA: American Institutes for Research.

Birman, B. F., & Ginsburg, A. L. (1982). The federal role in elementary and secondary education: New directions and continuing concerns. *Urban Lawyer*, *14*(3), 471–500.

Birman, B. F., Orland, M. E., Jung, R. K., Anson, R. J., & Garcia, G. N. (1987). *Preliminary Findings of the National Assessment of Chapter 1*. Unpublished. Washington, DC: Office of Educational Research and Improvement, U.S. Department of Education.

Broder, D. S. (1985, December 6). State officials becoming innovative in domestic policy-making. *The Washington Post*, pp. A6–A7.

Children's Defense Fund. (1984). *An interim report on the implementation of Chapter 1*. Washington, DC: Author.

Chubb, J. E. (1985). Excessive regulation: The case of federal aid to education. *Political Science Quarterly*, *100*(2), 287–311.

Clark, D. L., & Astuto, T. A. (1986, January). *The significance and permanence of changes in federal education policy 1980–1988*. (Occasional paper). Bloomington, IN: Policy Studies Center of the University Council for Educational Administration, Indiana University.

Council of Great City Schools. (1982). *Analysis of the effects of FY 82 and FY 83 Reagan budget proposals on urban schools*. Washington, DC: Author.

Council of Great City Schools. (1983). *Trends in federal funding to urban schools: A progress report on the Reagan years*. Washington, DC: Author.

Crandall, D. P. (1984, June). *Internal and external improvement approaches: Looking for the right blend*. Paper presented at the NIE-sponsored workshop, Strengthening the Connection of Dissemination and Improvement in Education, Washington, DC.

Crandall, D. P., & Loucks, S. F. (1983). *A roadmap for school improvement*. Vol. 10, Executive Summary of the Study of Dissemination Efforts Supporting School Improvement. Andover, MA: The Network.

Derthick, M. (1972). *New towns in-town: Why a federal program failed*. Washington, DC: Urban Institute.

Dougherty, J. C., IV. (1985). *A matter of interpretation: Changes under Chapter 1 of the Education Consolidation and Improvement Act*. (Report prepared for the Subcommittee on Elementary, Secondary, and Vocational Education, Serial No. 99–B). Washington, DC: U.S. Government Printing Office.

Doyle, D. P., & Hartle, T. W. (1985). Leadership in education: Governors, legislators, and teachers. *Phi Delta Kappan*, *67*(1), 21–27.

Elazar, D. J. (1966). *American federalism: A view from the states*. New York: Crowell.

Elmore, R. F. (1980). *Complexity and control: What legislatures and administrators can do about policy implementation*. Washington, DC: National Institute of Education.

Elmore, R. F. (1982). Differential treatment of states, In J. D. Sherman, M. A. Kutner, & K. J. Small (Eds.), *New dimensions of the federal-state partnership in education* (pp. 176–194). Washington, DC: Tilden.

Finn, C. E. (1985, October 22) *Education choice: Theory, practice, and research*. (Testimony presented before the Senate Subcommittee on Intergovernmental Relations, Committee on Governmental Affairs.)

Gaffney, M. J., & Schember, D. M. (1982). *Current Title I school and student selection procedures and implications for implementing Chapter 1, ECIA*. McLean, VA: Advanced Technology.

Grodzin, M. (1966). *The American system: A new view of government in the United States*. Chicago: Rand McNaley.

Hartle, T. W., & Holland, R. P. (1983). The changing context of federal education aid. *Education and Urban Society*, *15*(4), 408–431.

Hastings, A. H. (1982). *The strategies of government intervention: An analysis of federal education and health care policy*. Unpublished doctoral dissertation, University of Virginia, Charlottesville.

Ingram, H. (1977). Policy implementation through bargaining: The case of federal grants-in-aid. *Public Policy*, *25*(4), 449–526.

Jung, R. K., & Kirst, M. W. (1986, Summer). Beyond mutual adaptation, into the bully pulpit: Recent research on the federal role in education. *Educational Administration Quarterly*, *22*(3), 80–109.

Jung, R. K., & Stonehill, R. M. (1985). Big districts and the block grant: A cross-time assessment of the fiscal impacts. *Journal of Education Finance*, *10*(3), 308–326.

Kaestle, C. F., & Smith, M. S. (1982). The federal role in elementary and secondary education, 1940–1980. *Harvard Educational Review*, *52*(4), 384–408.

Keesling, J. W. (Ed.) (1985). *A study of intergovernmental relations in compensatory education*. Reston, VA: Advanced Technology.

Kirp, D. L., & Winslow, H. R. (1978). *Patchwork quilt: The diverse educational entitlements of children*. Menlo Park, CA: SRI Internatonal.

Kirst, M. W. (1982). *Teaching policy and federal categorical programs*. Stanford, CA: Institute for Research on Educational Finance and Governance.

Kirst, M. W., & Jung, R. K. (1982). The utility of a longitudinal approach in assessing implementation: A thirteen-year view of

Title I, ESEA. In W. Williams (Ed.), *Studying implementation: Methodological and administrative issues* (pp. 119–148). Chatham, NJ: Chatham House.

Knapp, M. S., & Blakely, C. H. (1986, January). *The education block grant at the local level: The implementation of Chapter 2 of the Education Consolidation and Improvement Act in districts and schools*. Menlo Park, CA: SRI International.

Knapp, M. S., & Cooperstein, R. A. (1986). Early research on the federal education block grant: Themes and unanswered questions. *Educational Evaluation and Policy Analysis*, *8*(2), 121–138.

Knapp, M. S., Stearns, M. S., Turnbull, B. J., David, J. L., & Peterson, S. M. (1983). *Cumulative effects of federal education policies on schools and districts*. Menlo Park, CA: SRI International.

Lawyers' Committee for Civil Rights Under Law. (1984). *The first year of Chapter 1*. Washington, DC: Author.

Lewis, A. C. (1985). Bennett uses "bully pulpit" to advance ideological agenda. *Phi Delta Kappan*, *67*(1), 3–4.

Levin, H. M. (1983, Fall) A challenge for action: National leadership and involvement in education. *IFG Policy Perspective*, 1–4. Institute for Research on Educational Finance and Governance, Stanford University.

McLaughlin, M. W. (1976). Implementation as mutual adaptation. In W. Williams & R. F. Elmore (Eds.), *Social program implementation*. New York: Academic Press.

McLaughlin, M. W., & Berman, P. (1975, June). Macro and micro implementation. Paper prepared for IMTEC training course, Federal Republic of Germany.

McLaughlin, M. W., Shields, P. M., & Rezabek, D. J. (1985). *State and local response to Chapter 1 of the Education Consolidation and Improvement Act, 1981*. Stanford, CA: Institute for Research on Educational Finance and Governance.

Meyer, J. W. (1979). *The impact of the centralization of educational funding and control on state and local organizational governance*. Stanford, CA: Institute for Research on Educational Finance and Governance.

Moore, M. T., Goertz, M. E., Hartle, T. W., Winslow, H. R., David, J. L., Sjorgen, J., Turnbull, B. J., Coley, R. J., & Holland, R. P. (1983). *The interaction of federal and related state education programs* [Executive summary]. Washington, DC: Education Policy Research Insitute.

Mosher, E. C. (1980). The changing responsibilities and tactics of the federal government. *Public Administration Review*, *40*, 141–155.

Mullin, S. P., & Summers, A. A. (1983). Is more better? The effectiveness of spending on compensatory education. *Phi Delta Kappan*, *64*, 339–347.

National Academy of Education, National Institute of Education, and Center for the Study of Reading. (1984). *Becoming a nation of readers: The report of the Commission on Reading*. Washington, DC: National Institute of Education.

Orland, M. E., & Goettel, R. J. (1982). States and the implementation of federal categorical programs in education: A heuristic

framework. *Educational Evaluation and Policy Analysis*, *4*(2), 141–154.

Peterson, P. E. (1983). Background paper. In *Making the grade* (Report of the Twentieth Century Fund Task Force on Federal Elementary and Secondary Education Policy). New York: Twentieth Century Fund.

Peterson, P. E., & Wong, K. K. (1985). Toward a differentiated theory of federalism: Education and housing policy in the 1980's. *Research in Urban Policy*, *1*, 301–324.

Plunkett, V. R. (1985, April). From Title I to Chapter 1: The evolution of compensatory education. *Phi Delta Kappan*, *66*(8), 533–537.

Pressman, J. L., & Wildavsky, A. (1973). *Implementation*. Berkeley, CA: University of California Press.

Reagan, R. (1984). Overview of education reform issues. In C. Marshner (Ed.), *A blueprint for education reform* (pp. 1–10). Washington, DC: Free Congress Research & Education Foundation.

Reagan, R. (1985). Remarks at the National Association of Independent Schools Annual Meeting, February 28, 1985. *Weekly Compilation of Presidential Documents*, *21*(9), 232–237. Washington, DC: U.S. Government Printing Office.

Rezmovic, V., & Keesling, J. W. (1982). *Paperwork and administrative burden for school districts under Title I*. McLean, VA: Advanced Technology.

Sabatier, P. A., & Mazmanian, D. A. (1983). *Implementation and public policy*. Glenview, IL: Scott, Foresman.

Salamon, L. M. (1981, Summer). Rethinking public management: Third-party government and the changing forms of government action. *Public Policy*, *29*, 255–275.

Stoner, F. E. (1976). *The implementation of ambiguous legislative language: Title I of the Elementary and Secondary Education Act*. Unpublished doctoral dissertation, University of Wisconsin, Madison.

U.S. Department of Education. (1984a). *The nation responds: Recent efforts to improve education*. Washington, DC: U.S. Government Printing Office.

U.S. Department of Education. (1984b, May 11). Fact sheet for *The nation responds: Recent efforts to improve education*. [Press release].

U.S. Department of Education. (1985, January). *Indicators of education status and trends*. Washington, DC: U.S. Government Printing Office.

U.S. Department of Education. (1986). *What works: Research about teaching and learning*. Washington, DC: Author.

U.S. Department of Education: The National Commission on Excellence in Education. (1983). *A nation at risk: The imperative for educational reform*. Washington, DC: U.S. Government Printing Office.

Walberg, H. J. (1984). *Federal (Chapter 1) education spending and effects on poor children*. Washington, DC: Learn.

Weiss, C. H. (1979). The many meanings of research utilization. *Public Administration Review*, *30*(5), 426–431.

CHAPTER 25

Policy Analysis, Educational Policy, and Management: Through a Glass Darkly?

William Lowe Boyd

As soon as questions of will or decision or reason or choice of action arise, human science is at a loss.

—*Noam Chomsky*[1]

Policy analysis is a field that seeks to refute Chomsky's pessimistic view. Concerned with "the nature, causes, and effects of alternative public policies" (Nagel, 1980, p. 391), policy analysis aims to empower humans to undertake more effective collective action to solve or reduce significant policy problems. Toward this end, policy analysis places special emphasis on "the use of reason and evidence to choose the best policy among a number of alternatives" (MacRae & Wilde, 1979, p. 3), with explicit recognition of the realities involved in implementing policies (Williams, 1980).

In the United States, far more than in other countries, there has been a great effort to achieve the objectives of policy analysis. And, in many ways policy analysis indeed has grown in sophistication, rigor, and influence in the American scene. Since the 1960s, many intellectuals have seen it as the key to improving government policies and programs and to solving, or at least significantly reducing, social problems. Because the schools generally have been viewed as one of the United States's chief means of solving social problems, policy analysis naturally has been heavily applied within the public education arena. Indeed, the schools have been a leading arena for research and innovation in policy analysis (e.g., Coleman et al. 1966; Coleman, Kelley, & Moore, 1975; Coleman, Hoffer,

& Kilgore, 1981; Rivlin & Timpane, 1975; Williams, 1980).

Yet, despite the signs of progress, many—and not just a few in education—still share Chomsky's skepticism. As Liebman and Schelling (1981) comment, in reference to school desegregation policy:

> American public affairs have been bedeviled in recent years by our inability to decide what we know. Committing vast resources to social research, we have swung between two extremes: that knowledge would soon offer solutions to complex problems, and that all intelligence is contingent and therefore irrelevant to decision on any question that matters. (p. 1)

Thus, to say the least, the results of the application of policy analysis to educational issues have been something less than an unqualified success (Boyd, 1978). Rather than clearing away confusion and ambiguity, policy studies often have added new layers of perplexity to an already murky scene (Cohen & Garet, 1975). Rather than providing the data to depoliticize the sensitive and sometimes explosive issues of education, policy studies (e.g., Coleman et al., 1975; 1981) sometimes have heightened political tensions and even created new political issues (Warwick & Pettigrew, 1983). Rather than bringing scientific objectivity to the policy-making process, there is evidence that policy analysis sometimes brings subtle and insidious forms of bias (Callahan & Jennings, 1983). Paradoxi-

Consultant/reviewers: Richard F. Elmore, Michigan State University; and Jerome T. Murphy, Harvard University[2]

cally, policy analysis also has produced powerful and undeniable benefits for educational policy and management. Many decisions are now far better informed, and our whole understanding of educational policy and management has become far more sophisticated (e.g., see Elmore, 1983a; Kean, 1983; Mann, 1978; Murphy, 1971). Indeed, the assessment presented in this chapter concludes that the implications of policy analysis are potentially revolutionary for educational administration.

Policy analysis is clearly an important but problematic window on the educational world. It may illuminate or, as "through a glass darkly," it may obscure or even distort what it views. Significantly, it is likely to retain both its importance and its problematic qualities well into the future. On the one hand, this will be so because the pressures of budget constraints and accountability demands will continue to make analysis strategic in policy choice. On the other hand, the limitations of modern social science ensure a continuation of the troublesome features of the field. For both reasons, educators, like others in social policy arenas, need a good understanding of the strengths and weaknesses of policy analysis.

Consequently, the purpose of this chapter is to assess the characteristics of policy analysis and its impact on theory and practice in educational policy and management. The discussion is organized around the following questions:

1. What is policy analysis and what methodologies does it employ?
2. To what extent do these methodologies affect the resulting findings and implications?
3. How reliable and influential have policy studies been in the public education arena?
4. What have we learned from policy analysis about the nature, control, and management of public schools?

THE FIELD AND ITS METHODS

It is not easy to define policy analysis unequivocally. The vast scope and interdisciplinary character of the field have produced a huge outpouring of policy studies and associated works. Some sense of the extraordinary variety of the field can be gained just by glancing through the diverse contents of periodicals such as the *Journal of Policy Analysis and Management* and *Educational Evaluation and Policy Analysis*. As Mitchell (1984) found in his review of the state of educational policy analysis, this sphere by itself contains "an avalanche of literature citations. . . . The ERIC system alone contains more than 28,000 entries. . . and this is

only the tip of the proverbial iceberg (p. 129).[3] Mitchell (1984) continues:

> Disappointingly, the vast literature on the topic of educational policy has produced no standard textbooks, little agreement on the methods or goals of educational policy research, and few "classic" or exemplary studies for defining the area's central thrust or overall theoretical perspectives. (p. 130)

A sense of the variety of meanings and purposes involved in policy studies is captured in Holden and Dresang's (1975) enumeration of some principal meanings of "policy analysis" and "policy studies":

> (1) examinations of decision-making and policy systems in order to appraise existing political theory or to generate new theory; (2) evaluations of whether policies achieved the results they were planned or professedly planned to achieve; (3) studies of the impact of given policies, whether or not they served the manifest functions; and (4) attempts to prescribe—within an intellectually responsible framework—what social choices ought to be. (pp. 13–14)

As suggested earlier, policy analysis is sometimes viewed as primarily a means of problem solving or of providing "data for decisions." But this straightforward view implies that analysis has a stronger and more direct effect on actual policy making than is usually the case. Moreover, this view fails to recognize the importance of policy analysis in reconceptualizing policy problems or simply illuminating our understanding of complex policy questions. This "problem-setting" or "problem-finding" function of policy analysis has attracted increasing attention as scholars have attempted to assess fully the ways in which policy analysis influences the policy-making process (Cohen & Garet, 1975; Rein & White, 1977; Weiss, 1977; Wildavsky, 1979). Indeed, as discussed later, the indirect influences of policy analysis are probably its most important effects. The subtle functions of policy analysis in this regard have been eloquently stated by White (1983):

> Policy analysis is a complex social process of creating and applying knowledge to public policy. Few policy choices are final, unambiguous, or fully articulated; and few policies are independent, self-contained, unquestioned, or consensually understood. Policy analysis, as a result, is turbulent and open-ended rather than neat and easy. Decisive studies are very much the exception rather than the rule. Problems throw at analysts more variables for consideration and interests for accommodation than single studies can encompass. The task of policy analysis is not to produce that decisive recommendation, but, instead, to contribute toward consensual understanding of actualities, possibilities, and desirabilities. Properly understood, policy analysis does

produce, in Wildavsky's terms, new patterns of social interaction. Equally important, policy analysis produces new "psychosocial" forms, new collective understandings relevant to the specific functions of government. (p. 11)

The Evolution of the Field

Because of the richness and variety of purposes and approaches involved in policy studies, it is not surprising that there is ambiguity about what constitutes the field. Part of the difficulty arises from the fact that the conception of the field has changed dramatically since its initial growth spurt in the early 1960s. As Wildavsky (1985) puts it, the field has moved from a "macro-macho" approach to analysis to a "micro-incremental" approach: "The origins of the 'macro-macho' version of policy analysis—the belief that large national problems, from defense to welfare, are susceptible to solution through applications of economic analysis—were rooted in the intersection between economics, statistics, computing, and the defense 'think tanks' of the early 1960s" (p. 28). The assumption of the time was that large-scale economic models could capture the complexity of policy problems and identify the most efficient policy alternatives. Out of this tradition emerged an ambitious and robust analytical paradigm for policy analysis that continues to influence the field (e.g., see Quade, 1975; Stokey & Zeckhauser, 1978).

To the dismay of analysts, however, complexity triumphed over the aspirations of the analytical models. Confusion and disagreement about both the objectives and the consequences of many social policies undermined the promise of "macro-macho" analysis. "In an amazingly short time (within a decade)," notes Wildavsky (1985, p. 28), a reaction set in. Chastened by the perplexing realities confronting the macro approach, "the teaching and the practice of analysis took on its contemporary characteristics—incremental as opposed to radical change, smaller rather than larger problems, decentralized, bottom-up analysis dealing with diverse preferences, not the centralized, top-down preferences of a single decision maker" (Wildavsky, 1985, p. 28).

Many analysts today agree with Wildavsky's (1979, 1985) view, which sees policy analysis as more an art or craft than a science. They favor an activist, field-oriented, eclectic approach to "getting the facts," emphasizing qualitative methods as much as or more than quantitative methods (Murphy, 1980). In many public policy programs, says Wildavsky (1985):

From the first week, students are placed in an active position. They analyze, grub for data, reformulate problems, write and write again to communicate with clients. Fieldwork is their forte. An analyst with clean hands...is a contradiction in terms. (p. 32)

The craft approach also calls for more political savvy on the part of analysts. For example, Behn (1981) argues that "the complete analyst will not only recommend the best policy alternative but also the best political strategy for the adoption and implementation of this alternative" (p. 199). In a similar vein, Elmore (1985) argues that policy analysis consists of at least three equally important kinds of activity: science, engineering, and craft. The science and engineering modes are oriented toward the aspirations of the analytical, problem-solving paradigm we have alluded to but generally with more humility now than in the past. The two modes are distinguished by the fact that "engineering" involves analysis done for a client, whereas "science" involves the application of theories from the disciplines to policy problems, without a primary regard for specific clients or direct impact on policy decisions. By contrast, the "craft" approach

is different from science and engineering in that it tends to be tightly bounded by particular problems, particular institutions, particular political preferences, and a particular period of time. Its value is judged primarily by whether it poses workable political solutions within these tight constraints. (Elmore, 1985, p. 4)

Elmore contends that rather than depreciating the craft approach, as practitioners in the science and engineering modes sometimes do, the whole field could advance by emulating the practical orientation of the craft approach. Thus, he calls for a shift from the emphasis on applying the conventional analytical paradigm to an emphasis on the productive questions implicit in the craft approach: "How to manage the implementation process for desired results, using changes in policy, organization, and political coalitions?" and "What is controllable over what range with what effect?" (Elmore, 1985, pp. 13, 15).

Despite the growing consensus favoring the craft or "micro-incremental" approach to analysis, there remains within the field a substantial devotion to at least the spirit and concepts of the analytical paradigm approach of the economists (Behn, 1981, p. 202; Mead, 1983; Rhoads, 1985). And often with this approach, as Mead (1985) complains, "political factors in policy are consistently exiled to the fringes of analysis" (p. 166). Because the legacy of the analytical paradigm continues to influence thinking within segments of the field (e.g., see Brandl, 1985), the following discussion outlines the economic concepts and principles that underlie the paradigm.

Defining the Field

Provisionally, we can begin with the composite definition given at the outset, namely that policy analysis is concerned with "the nature, causes, and effects of alternative public policies" (Nagel, 1980, p. 391), with special emphasis on "the use of reason and evidence to choose the best policy among a number of alternatives" (MacRae & Wilde, 1979, p. 3). As this definition suggests, and Nagel (1980, p. 391) observes, the policy studies perspective involves a methodology emphasizing *evaluation*. Along with evaluation, another central concept of the field is *choice*. The analytical paradigm calls for a systematic comparison of alternative policies in order to choose the most beneficial course of action. As MacRae (1980, p. 375) notes, in making choices a central concept of the field is that of *opportunity costs*: that is, the highest valued opportunity or course of action forsaken. In this regard, in assessing the inescapable *tradeoffs* involved in making choices, techniques such as cost-benefit analysis are used. Thus, studies employing the classic paradigm often combine the techniques of evaluation and economic analysis to assess alternative policies and provide a systematic, data-based foundation for policy choice. At the same time, such studies may perform the subtle additional functions of problem setting and problem finding described earlier.

The discussion so far suggests that much of what purports to be policy analysis falls short of the threshold criteria one might reasonably set for the genre. At a minimum, we might expect either the use of "reason and evidence" to assess alternative policies (at least some of them) and to choose (at least in logical terms) the most beneficial policy or, in the craft tradition, a focused, data-based examination of how policies work, their merits and demerits, and how they could be improved. The craft orientation stresses, further, that the assessment and choice of policies must take account of the political realities of decision making and implementation. Even a modest step in the direction of using criteria such as these will prune away much of the thicket of so-called policy studies that congests even subfields such as educational policy analysis.

Consider for a moment the rash of recent Education Commission reports that Mitchell (1984, p. 159) charitably dubs "policy studies." To begin with, even if one takes them seriously as policy studies, nearly all the policy analysis they touch on remains to be done. Indeed, "the failure [of the Reports] to go beyond the recommendations [either] to assessing the costs [or]

the necessary actions for carrying them out" enabled Stanford's Institute for Research on Educational Finance and Governance [IREFG] to lay out "filling the gaps in the National Reports" as its 1984 research agenda (IREFG, 1984, p. 1). Paul Peterson's (1983) assessment of the reports is even more telling:

> If we judge them by the standards ordinarily used to evaluate a policy analysis—focused statement of the problem to be analyzed, methodical evaluation of existing research, reasoned consideration of options, and presentation of supporting evidence and argumentation for well-specified proposals—they simply do not measure up. With some exceptions, the studies do not address the most difficult conceptual and political issues. Instead, they reassert what is well-known, make exaggerated claims on flimsy evidence, pontificate on matters about which there could scarcely be [dis]agreement, and make recommendations that either cost too much, cannot be implemented, or are too general to have any meaning. (p. 3)

The validity of Peterson's criticism of the commission reports can be illustrated just by considering one of the leading recommendations of many of the recent reports, namely that more time is needed in school, either by extending the school day, the school week, or the school year. As Levin's (1984) review of the relevant evidence suggests, this clearly is an exaggerated and oversimplified recommendation based on rather selective use of the relevant data. Indeed, as Levin (1984, p. 162) notes, it is disturbing that the recommendation ignores that fact that three major national reports in the last decade (Brown 1973; Coleman, 1974; Martin, 1974) have made the *opposite* recommendation, concluding that many of the problems of adolescence are caused by youth spending too much time in school.

It is questionable whether the commission reports should be judged according to the standards of scholarly policy research. Their major goal was to capture public attention and mobilize political support for badly needed reforms in public education. In this respect they clearly have been remarkably successful. On the other hand, to the extent the reports share the faults Peterson notes, they have the potential to do a great deal of mischief by misdirecting reform efforts in unproductive or impractical ways. Indeed, there is evidence that they have done just this (Fowler, 1985). By advocating efforts to "mandate excellence" or "legislate learning" (Wise, 1979), many of the reports have promoted a highly directive, "top-down" approach to school reform that fails to take account of research documenting the need for local involvement and adaptation in successful reform and policy implementation (Mann, 1978).

A common deficiency of many works that, scarcely deserve to be called policy analysis is a focus on the benefits of some policy with little or no consideration of the associated costs. For example, Mary Moore (1984) has provided an incisive and appropriate critique of an article by Gary Jones (1984), in which he described the Reagan Administration's cost-cutting approach to "achieving excellence in education and management" in the U.S. Department of Education. The difficulty with the approach, and the article, as Moore makes clear, is that both present cost cutting as an unqualified benefit and fail to deal with the associated question of the programmatic costs involved. In what Moore (1984, p. 255) terms a "recipe for failure," she contends the Administration has engaged in "cost cutting without goal setting" by refusing "to state which services and functions it is prepared to reduce or give up in the cost-cutting process." The consequent absence of goals other than cost containment makes Moore wonder about the Administration's conception, not only of management for excellence, but of the federal role in education.

Other examples of policy advocacy include some of the analysis presented in support of the Reagan Administration's initial attempts to revise federal education policies. Such presentations often took no consideration of the likely costs, often painfully obvious from past American history, of reversing the characteristics of federal educational policy (e.g., universal or unrestricted aid rather than categorical aid targeted toward special needs populations; aid distributed on a per capita rather than redistributive basis). Instead, the new approach was presented as though it would be a flawless improvement over the almost entirely undesirable effects of past policies. Although past policies clearly had their problems, any assumption that policies with the opposite characteristics would somehow be trouble-free simply ignores history, the realities of tradeoffs, and the limits of policy design (Levin, 1982; McLaughlin, 1982). The moral of examples such as these is that one should beware of purveyors of "cost-free" policies and remember the economist's admonition that there is no such thing as a free lunch!

It may be reasonably easy to distinguish partisan polemics, overt policy advocacy, and unsystematic policy discussions from policy analysis, but the range of purposes and methods within the mainstream still leaves us with a wide variety of kinds of studies. At the risk of oversimplifying, it is possible to divide these studies roughly into two groups, depending on whether they place more emphasis on quantitative or qualitative methods. However, the more eclectic approach that is increasingly in vogue blurs such a distinction. It is possible, nonetheless, to develop detailed distinctions, such as those suggested in Ernest House's (1980) taxonomy of eight major evaluation approaches. For our purpose, it is noteworthy that House divides the eight approaches into two groups, those that are *objectivist* (systems analysis, behavioral objectives, decision making, goal-free) and those that are *subjectivist* (art criticism, professional review, quasilegal, case study) in their epistomology. This division parallels the rough distinction between quantitative and qualitative studies in that the former usually are objectivist and the latter, though not necessarily subjectivist, are somewhat inclined in this direction.

House (1980, pp. 255–256) argues that ideally "the validity of an evaluation depends upon whether the evaluation is true, credible, and normatively correct," by which he means that it "should be democratic, fair, and ultimately based upon the moral values of equality, autonomy, impartiality, and reciprocity." Although House's claim that one can establish what is "normatively correct" is debatable, he nevertheless presents a valuable discussion, demonstrating that while each of the eight approaches to evaluation makes its own claim to validity, each has its shortcomings. According to his critique, the more quantitative approaches, such as systems analysis, so emphasize a narrow, objectivist view of data and research that they tend to focus on the "truth aspect of validity to the exclusion of the credibility and normative aspects" (House, 1980, p. 251). This can lead to rigorous, but narrow and unfair evaluations, which House (1980, pp. 199–224) argues was the case in the federal evaluation of the Follow Through program.

Despite the increasing criticism that mainstream quantitative studies in the positivist tradition now face, this approach remains the dominant style of research in much of social science and evaluation but much less so now in policy analysis. "The dominant evaluation model," as McLaughlin (1984, p. 24) notes, "is quantitative, representing 'hard' data and notions of statistical proof." Yet, as she demonstrates, this model is quite inadequate for assessing the complex reality of social program implementation. The classic analytical paradigm of policy analysis, to which we turn now, shares the same problems.

The Economic Model

The analytical paradigm that has shaped much of the language and logic of policy studies is the economic model (Mead, 1983; Tribe, 1972). The thrust of the model can be described briefly as follows:

> With the market as a central paradigm, [the] model takes as its starting point the idea of individual man as

a rational maximizer of satisfactions operating self-interestedly...in a world of relative scarcity. Problems of choice, whether individual or social, are perceived essentially as problems of marginal "trade-off" or "exchange" among desired outputs, attributes, or ingredients of welfare. (Tribe, 1972, pp. 68–69)

The welfare levels of individuals are seen as the fundamental building blocks for assessing the welfare of society (Stokey & Zeckhauser, 1978, p. 257). Social welfare is linked to individual welfare through the use of the Pareto criterion, which specifies that one policy choice should be preferred to another so long as it makes at least one person better off but no one worse off. Limitations of the Pareto criterion and, ultimately, as Arrow (1963) has shown, of all attempts to construct a social welfare function have led to a number of ad hoc procedures for estimating social welfare (Stokey & Zeckhauser, 1978). Of these, the "Kaldor-Hicks" criterion—which provides that policy changes are desirable when those who gain from the changes "could so compensate the losers that, after compensation, the Pareto criterion would be met" (Tribe, 1972, p. 71)—is especially important since it provides the intellectual basis for cost-benefit analysis:

> This technique, which marks the effective socialization of the policy sciences' market origins, assumes that it is possible for the policy analyst to estimate the quantities of benefits stemming from a (usually governmental) project under alternative designs, the quantities of things used up or reduced, and the prices that should be associated with both ends of this equation. Given this information, the analyst is to choose that design which maximizes the difference between benefits and costs. (Tribe, 1972, p. 71)

Unfortunately, there are many serious limitations on the ability of analysts to estimate and assign appropriate prices. Indeed, quantitative cost-benefit analysis is subject to a number of constraints that severely limit its utility in adequately representing many situations of social choice (Hoos, 1972), a shortcoming that has contributed to the shift toward a craft approach to policy analysis. For purposes of evaluation, Levin (1983) argues that in many cases cost-effectiveness and cost-utility analysis are preferable to cost-benefit analysis because they do not require that benefits be represented in pecuniary terms. Paradoxically, as Levin (1983) notes, "Although the term 'cost-effectiveness' has entered the jargon of politics, administration, and evaluation, there is surprisingly little cost-effectiveness analysis in any area of social endeavor" (p. 10). Administrators, he observes, are frequently most concerned with costs, whereas evaluators tend to use evaluation techniques that focus only on the effects of alternatives.

To maximize choices, one obviously must use an approach that takes account of *both* costs and effects. In one sense, the approach to policy analysis that does this best may be the more eclectic one (seen in Brewer & deLeon, 1983; Wildavsky, 1979) that in recent years has largely replaced the classic economic model (exemplified by Quade, 1975) described earlier. This is so because the "incremental, implementing, field-oriented" craft approach to analysis (Wildavsky, 1985, p. 31) assesses policy alternatives against the real-world conditions they would face, rather than the abstract assumptions of model builders. On the other hand, full acceptance of an incremental approach grounded in existing political constraints may only maximize the status quo. As Wildavsky (1985, pp. 40–41) and others (e.g., Mead, 1983) recognize, the policy analytic approach ultimately must find ways to provide for nonincremental leadership in policy and management.

METHODS: VALUE-FREE OR BIASED?

The economic paradigm that continues to influence the field is powerful and elegant. There is a long-standing debate, however, about whether this paradigm has inescapable biases built into it. The discussion that follows is not intended to suggest that the economic model should be abandoned; it is far too useful an analytical tool to be rejected.[4] Rather, the purpose here is to alert readers to the potential bias within the model, a problem shared by all models and theories.

Given the necessity of making choices within a world of limited resources, it would seem that the economic approaches we have outlined would provide just the tools that are needed. Since the canons of economics and positivist social science assert that these tools are neutral in and of themselves, all else that should be required is thoughtful and sophisticated use of these tools. The difficulty, of course, is that this traditional view of social science has been called increasingly into question (Bernstein, 1976; Bredo & Feinberg, 1982; Burrell & Morgan, 1979; Fay, 1975; Moon, 1975).

For at least 10 years now, there has been a mounting attack on positivism, on its claim that facts and values can be separated, and on the corollary that there can be a value-free, antiseptically empirical social science. By the same token, there is a growing criticism of what is seen as "technocratic" policy analysis (e.g., Bellah, 1983; Callahan & Jennings, 1983; Hoos, 1972; Prunty, 1984). As Callahan and Jennings (1983) note, it is "now becoming clear, and widely recognized, that even the most quantitative and formalistic policy-analytic techniques contain concealed value choices and inextricable normative implications" (p. xix). Even more fundamentally, as Brewer and deLeon (1983) point out, "Presuming that observation and measurement could be neutral or value free collides with the fact that selecting something to measure is a choice itself based on the observer's values and preferences" (p. 28).

Apart from formalistic techniques, the language and logic of paradigms themselves incline our thinking and vision in particular directions. As Benjamin Whorf observed, "Language is not simply a reporting device for experience, but a defining framework for it."[5] Consequently, there is increasing agreement that, rather than futile attempts at value-free policy analysis, what is needed is *value-critical* policy analysis (Rein, 1983): that is, analysis that carefully scrutinizes the value implications of its basic assumptions and concepts.

What, then, are the underlying values of classical economics? According to Brendl (1985):

> The economists' penchant for markets is no simple matter of efficiency. It is based on an individualist-utilitarian ethic joined to a theory of social interaction driven by self-interest. Economists regularly follow and go well beyond Charles Schultze's suggestion that they be not merely reporters of facts but advocates for efficiency. They are usually advocates as well for their own ethical theory. (p. 346)

One of the most dramatic manifestations of this point of view is found in the economic analysis of the law, an important intellectual movement with clear and sometimes startling policy implications. The leader of this movement is Judge Richard Posner, a brilliant scholar thought to be under consideration for appointment to the Supreme Court by President Reagan (Press & McDaniel, 1985). Posner (1977, 1981) argues in his numerous works that much of the law can be understood as not so much concerned with justice and morality as with wealth maximization and the efficient use of resources. Critics of Posner's view, such as Jules L. Coleman (1982, 1984), contend that the economic approach provides neither a satisfactory explanation for the law nor a desirable model (as Posner and his followers suggest) for guiding the law. As a normative standard, many critics detect a bias toward the rich in the economic analysis of the law (Baker, 1975). Since so much of educational policy is shaped by Supreme Court decisions, Posner's future career and influence could have significant ramifications for education in the United States.

Among the first scholars to caution against the value implications of mainstream policy analysis or, as he put it, the ideological dangers of "techno-cratic" policy analysis, was Laurence Tribe (1972). He observed:

> The policy sciences' intellectual and social heritage in the classical economics of unfettered contract, consumer sovereignty, and perfect markets both brings them within a paradigm of conscious choice guided by values and inclines them, within that paradigm, toward the exaltation of utilitarian and self-interested individualism, efficiency, and maximized production as against distributive ends, procedural and historical principles and the values...associated with personal rights, public goods, and communitarian and ecological goals. (p. 105)

Tribe's fears have been borne out by the trend of American social affairs. Following on the heels of disillusionment with the Great Society and War on Poverty programs of the 1960s, the economic problems of the 1970s brought a resurgence of conservatism in the United States and an associated rehabilitation of the free-market metaphor. In the reaction against the perceived failure of government social programs, the Great Society envisioned by liberal sociologists was replaced by what might be called the "Fragmented Society" view of economists, who stress the need to design policy to harness the energy of "self-interest-maximizing individuals" (Bellah, 1983; Schultze, 1977).

In this context, policy analysis guided by the paradigm of the self-interest-maximizing individual has contributed significantly to the dramatic shift in the nature and semantics of American discourse about social policy and the public interest. Dialogue and concern have moved from equity, social justice, and the common good to questions of liberty, choice, excellence, and efficiency. In education, this trend is particularly evident in the erosion of support for common, public schools and concomitant interest in private schools, tuition tax credits, and voucher plans. All of this reflects the decline of concern for community and the legitimacy that the self-interest paradigm has given to competitive struggle. Indeed, what has happened is just what the proponents of value-critical policy analysis warn against: The pervasive paradigm of pursuit of self-interest has eroded and deflected attention from the value of *community*. As Bellah (1983, p. 63) has put it, the "improverished moral vocabulary" of policy analysis has left "an open field for the operation of calculating self-interest alone."

This point is made quite eloquently by Bruce Jennings (1983) in his argument for an *interpretive* rather than *positivist* approach to policy analysis:

> The notions of decentralization, civic voluntarism, empowerment, and community are perennial concerns, but they have never played a central role in our thinking about public policy; often, in the past, they have been

totally eclipsed by other values and considerations. The history of American political and social thought is composed of two major and largely antithetical traditions: (1) a dominant liberal, individualistic tradition that views society as a field of separate, conflicting interests and human beings as essentially egoistic monads caught up in a competitive struggle for material resources and personal gratification and (2) a communitarian tradition that stresses the organic linkages between the individual and society. Many of the intellectual forerunners of contemporary interpretive social science were theorists who rejected the abstract individualism of nineteenth-century liberalism, and it seems clear that, in the American context, interpretive policy analysis would occasion a revitalization of the older communitarian tradition. (pp. 28–29)

The shortcomings for public policy of the individualistic orientation of the economic paradigm also have been cogently stated by Landy and Plotkin (1982) and by Mead (1983), who observes that

political rationality has always required moral restraint. A community can achieve an overall public good only if its various groups observe limits on their own immediate claims. Hence the paradox that in politics, unlike the marketplace, rational action for the collectivity depends on *non*-rational—civic, dutiful, restrained—action by individuals and groups. It is no accident that earlier political thinkers seldom championed rationality per se. They spoke of "statecraft," or building up the authority of government, and of instilling "civic virtue" in citizens. For only on these moral bases could government restrain self-seeking and eventually achieve a public interest. (p. 170)

As demonstrated by the range of political and philosophical positions held by both economists and analysts, the economic paradigm need not necessarily lead to a conservative, "free market" point of view. It is quite significant that most of the earliest and best-known economic analyses of educational policy had as their focus a concern about equity. For example, in the "Distribution of Costs and Direct Benefits of Public Higher Education," Hanson and Weisbrod (1969) touched off a major debate (discussed in Garms, Guthrie, & Pierce, 1978, pp. 436–440) by presenting data showing that in California higher education for the rich was more heavily subsidized than that for the poor.

Still, as Tribe (1972) noted, to the extent that analysts identify with the intellectual heritage of the policy sciences in *classical* economics, there is a tendency to presume that market processes and individual choice are superior to governmental intervention and collective action. Indeed, with the growth of neoconservative opinion among many influential American academics, as exemplified by much of the commentary found in issues of *The Public Interest*, government and social policy have been seen increasingly as a source of problems rather than solutions. This point of view reaches its sharpest expression in the analyses of economic libertarians (e.g., Hayek, 1939; Rothbard, 1973), who see government bureaucracies as intrusive threats to freedom, and "public choice" theorists (e.g., Borcherding, 1977; Niskanen, 1971), who see them as wasteful, self-serving "budget maximizers."

Ironically, social policy originally was seen as a solution to problems created by the inequitable workings of the market system. As T. H. Marshall (quoted in Heclo, 1975) observed, social policy can be defined to include all measures "adopted to influence, to interfere with, or to supersede the free play of market forces in the interests of welfare" (p. 154). Put more briefly, social policy is "those government actions that are [both] remedial and redistributive in intent" (Elmore, 1983b, p. 214). The difficulty currently is that most Americans feel that the traditional policies of the welfare state have been found wanting. What has been called "non-market failure" (Wolf, 1979)—that is, the failure of governmental interventions—now is often seen as a more serious problem than market failure.

Government programs, of course, can fail. Many social programs of the 1960s were, at best, far less successful than anticipated. Indeed, we have learned that the successful design and implementation of social programs is far more complex and difficult than once thought (Pressman & Wildavsky, 1973; Elmore, 1983a; Mann, 1978). As a result, we have entered a difficult period characterized by a "strategic retreat on objectives" (Wildavsky, 1976) and a lack of confidence in government and social policy, at least at the federal level. Old ideas about social policy seem exhausted and new ideas, such as the "public use of private interest" (Schultze, 1977) and tax and transfer schemes, are limited substitutes with their own shortcomings (Elmore, 1983b). Nevertheless, despite these problems, there has been an explosion of governmental activity in education at the state level, where many governors believe that economic growth requires substantially improved schools.

What should be emphasized, in closing this discussion of the value-implicated features of alternative methods and approaches to policy analysis, is that perspectives on social policy and analysis other than the now fashionable neoconservatism lead, with equal logic, to very different prescriptions about what should be done to improve society. Naturally, there is a whole range of policy positions besides neoconservatism found in the ranks of economists, not to mention other social scientists. Consequently, in assessing current and proposed social and educational policies, leaders in American education would benefit by more familiarity with alternative policy perspectives, such as those provided by the social administration tradition in Britain (Bulmer, 1983) and *interpretive* and *critical* approaches to educational policy (e.g., see Bates, 1983; Bredo & Feinberg, 1982; Giroux, 1984; Prunty, 1984).

THE RELIABILITY AND INFLUENCE OF POLICY STUDIES

Ironically, though we lead the world in the production of policy studies, this very activity—intended to improve policy—has reduced confidence not only in many social programs (sometimes deservedly so) but also in the very institutions that deliver them. Among domestic policy arenas, there is no better example of this than public school education. James S. Coleman's controversial reports—on equal educational opportunity, trends in school desegregation, and public and private schools (Coleman et al., 1966, 1975, 1981, 1982)—illustrate this point vividly. Having felt the impact of policy research, educators have good reason to be concerned about the problems and issues that surround it.

Policy research has not established a strong reputation for reliability because of its propensity for conflicting and inconsistent findings, as well as intense scholarly controversies in sensitive areas such as school desegregation (see, e.g., Callahan & Jennings, 1983; Shotland & Mark, 1985). Although some policy research has been very influential, generally the *direct* influence of policy studies on the making of particular decisions and policies has been relatively slight. But the *indirect* influence of policy analysis on policy making has been quite significant due to the role policy studies have had in sharpening and reformulating policy issues and sometimes leading to new strategies of approaching social and organizational problems (Callahan & Jennings, 1983; Cohen & Garet, 1975; Rein & White, 1977; Weiss, 1977).

Inconsistencies and Controversies in Policy Research

The inconsistency of research findings and the suspicion, at times, that researchers' own biases have affected the findings have called into question the scientific status of the enterprise. The best way to put this problem into perspective is by drawing on James Q. Wilson's (1973) thoughtful assessment of the matter. Reacting to the perplexing debate between David Armor and Thomas Pettigrew about their conflicting findings on the effects of busing for school desegregation, Wilson (1973) proposed two general "laws" that appear to be quite cynical:

First Law: All policy interventions in social problems produce the intended effect—*if* the research is carried out by those implementing the policy or their friends. Second Law: No policy intervention in social problems produces the intended effect—*if* the research is carried out by independent third parties, especially those skeptical of the policy [emphasis in original]. (p. 133).

Wilson argues that he does not intend these laws to be taken as cynical expressions. Rather, he explains that he proposes them because he believes that

rarely does anyone deliberately fudge the results of a study to conform to pre-existing opinions. What is frequently done is to apply very different standards of evidence and method. Studies that conform to the First Law will accept an agency's own data about what it is doing and with what effect; adopt a time frame (long or short) that maximizes the probability of observing the desired effect; and minimize the search for other variables that might account for the effect observed. Studies that conform to the Second Law will gather data independently of the agency; adopt a short time frame that either minimizes the chance for the desired effect to appear or, if it does appear, permits one to argue that the results are "temporary" and probably due to the operation of the "Hawthorne Effect" (i. e., the reaction of the subjects to the fact that they are part of an experiment); and maximize the search for other variables that might explain the effects observed. (1973, p. 133).

What can be said in behalf of policy analysis as a scientific enterprise if Wilson's assessment is right? Wilson himself offers two answers. First, he notes that some studies do provide conclusive and useful findings that stand up under rigorous examination. Second, he argues that even the more debatable policy analysis studies are useful because "they expose the complexities of a problematic situation, extend the range of possible explanations for those conditions, increase our awareness of the unintended outcomes of any policy intervention, and stimulate us to reflect on the inadequacies of our own preconceptions about the matter" (1973, p. 134). Wilson's assessment is consistent with those, such as Cohen and Garet (1975), who emphasize the problem-setting function of policy research, the view that, rather than shaping particular decisions, most policy-oriented research tends to influence broad assumptions and beliefs underlying policies. This is no small feat, for the prevailing theories and conceptions of policy problems among policy makers have a large role in shaping the direction that policy takes (Wilson, 1981).

Ethical Issues in Policy Research

For an appreciation of the complex scientific and ethical issues involved in policy research, there is no better example than the controversies surrounding the three Coleman reports referred to earlier. The *Equality of Educational Opportunity* report led to the popular but erroneous idea that schooling "doesn't make a difference" and prompted an extended scholarly debate and numerous reanalyses of the original data set (e.g., Levine & Bane, 1975). The report on trends in school desegregation and the "white flight" problem led to headlines such as that in the June 7, 1975, *National Observer*—"A Scholar Who Inspired It Says Busing Backfired" (as reported in Pettigrew & Green, 1976, p. 1)—and it added fuel to the fire of the Armor-Pettigrew debate mentioned earlier, a controversy that is still raging (Tugend, 1985). The public versus private school report (Coleman et al., 1981, 1982) created yet another acrimonious controversy, one that is still being played out (e.g., see Coleman, 1981; Crain & Hawley, 1982; IREFG, 1985; James & Levin, 1983; Report Analysis: Public and Private Schools, 1981).

Reflecting on these and similar problems in other research, Warwick and Pettigrew (1983) have outlined a basic set of ethical guidelines for policy researchers. They give particular attention to James S. Coleman's research because it dramatically illustrates problems associated with media coverage of research findings and the role of researchers as advocates and publicists for their policy conclusions. One especially sensitive issue involves how far researchers should move beyond their data and findings in drawing policy implications. Thus, as Warwick and Pettigrew (1983) note:

> After studying white flight, Coleman drew policy implications that ranged from characterizing the federal courts as the "worst of all possible instruments for carrying out a very sensitive activity like integrating schools" to advocating "activities that encourage racial intermarriage." But his research included neither court nor intermarriage measures. In his more recent work comparing achievement test scores among private and public school children, Coleman concludes that higher scores for private pupils constitute evidence in favor of an educational voucher system. (pp. 355–356)

Although Warwick and Pettigrew acknowledge that it can be argued that Coleman was merely exercising his right of free speech in advocating his policy preferences, they are concerned that both the media and the public tend to have trouble distinguishing between actual research findings and the policy implications drawn from them. With the aura of "science" surrounding the pronouncements of eminent researchers such as Coleman, their opinions carry unusual weight and can attract extensive publicity.

Recently, Coleman, who has spent a good deal of time answering his critics, provided some suggestions about how policy research in sensitive areas might be improved and adjudicated (J. S. Coleman, 1984). He proposes, first, that policy research could have a "pluralistic" design, by which he means that there should be a systematic attempt to be sure that the research addresses the important questions from the point of view of all the potential stakeholders. Second, he proposes "competitive analyses with critical review," by which he means a plan for systematic, ongoing peer review of research undertaken simultaneously by two investigators whose previous work has led to conflicting conclusions. If researchers, including Coleman, operated under the second proposal, it would mean a substantial change in their patterns of work. For instance, as Warwick and Pettigrew (1983) note, "Critics were unhappy that Coleman did not provide the interested social scientific community with written copies of his ["white flight"] report for four months following a much publicized speech in Washington, D.C." (p. 357). There also were similar problems and severe criticisms of Coleman's conduct, as well as his research, in connection with the release of preliminary findings from the public and private school study (see Crain & Hawley, 1982).

Successful Policy Research

Turning now from the problematics of policy research, what are the characteristics of successful research? Though seldom definitive in their conclusions, few policy studies are as controversial as the Coleman reports, many are useful, and some prove to be very influential. A study that has come to be regarded as a model of a useful and influential evaluation is the "Compensatory Education Study." This 3-year, $15 million evaluation of Title I of the Elementary and Secondary Education Act was mandated by Congress in 1974 and conducted by the National Institute of Education (Jones, 1983; Leviton & Boruch, 1984).[6] Unlike earlier Title I evaluations, this study was very favorably viewed by its sponsors, who made numerous references to its findings in the Education Amendments of 1978. As Leviton and Boruch (1984) note:

> The reports of both the House and Senate committees acknowledged the study's findings that Title I services were delivered to appropriate children and that the program, *when stable and well implemented*, enhanced student achievement. According to the House report, "All these findings can be contrasted with earlier studies which showed that disadvantaged students fall more and more behind in their achievement levels."…The study's positive findings helped beat back the more drastic proposals [for cutbacks], while its caveat "when the programs are stable and well-implemented" opened the door to important administrative and legal changes [emphasis in the original]. (pp. 300–301)

In an assessment of the Compensatory Education Study, based on interviews with 50 participants and observers of the study, McGonagill (1983) reached the following conclusions:

> A collaborative relationship between the evaluators and congressional staff ensured that the research addressed issues of concern to Congress. Moreover, NIE kept close control over the research by initiating thirty-five discrete studies, monitoring them closely, and synthesizing their findings into readable reports geared toward a legislative audience. However, the close collaboration with Congress that underlay the study's success also exacted a price. NIE's conduct and reporting of the research reflected a status-quo bias, influenced by the sponsors' strong support of Title I. Moreover, addressing congressional interests left little room for research that was not relevant to short-termed decisionmaking needs. Finally, the study neglected significant interests not of concern to Congress.
>
> Each of these shortcomings illustrates the dilemmas that evaluators face in the effort to be useful to decision-makers: utility competes with objectivity; the need to be useful in the short run conflicts with the effort to understand underlying program goals and alternatives; and the need to serve a single client limits the evaluation's usefulness to other audiences. (p. 1)

More recent studies also have reached positive conclusions about Title I. Like the "Compensatory Education Study," the "Sustaining Effects Study" (Carter, 1984) also seems to have been influential in Congressional funding for Title I/Chapter 1. Together, a number of recent studies underscore the vital importance of a longitudinal, rather than short-term, approach to evaluation (Carter, 1984; Kirst & Jung, 1980; Knapp, Stearns, Turnbull, David, & Peterson, 1983) As the authors of the important "cumulative effects" study (Knapp et al., 1983) conclude:

> The short-term result of almost any policy change will be local resistance, confusion, and poorly organized services. Over a few years, things work better, and the true merits of a policy initiative can be assessed more realistically. In the longer term, it may be that any initiative will come to be viewed as indispensable at the local level. (p. 498)

Another example of very influential research is the Rand Change Agent study, published in an eight-volume report series called "Federal Programs Supporting Educational Change" (Berman, Greenwood, McLaughlin, & Pincus,1975; Berman & McLaughlin, 1976, 1978). This large-scale study of federally funded innovative projects drew data primarily from a survey of 293 projects in 18 states and follow-up case studies of 29 of the programs. The findings emphasized the importance of local problem-solving capacity and local adaptation in the implementation of innovations. The study's main themes—that nonimplementation is common and that successful implementation depends on a "bottom-up" process of "mutual adaptation" at the school-site level—have substantially influenced the thinking of analysts and, to some degree, policy makers also. For instance, though it failed to get through Congress, the Carter Administration's "Youth Initiative" was explicitly designed to reflect the lessons of the Change Agent study. According to Datta (1980), the study led to a shift away from "such directed development as curriculum design or program testing" and toward "an era of full-blown commitment to technical assistance [to build local capacity] as the name of the game at the federal and state levels" (pp. 101–102).

Since the Change Agent study, a number of major policy studies have influenced the debate and design of educational policy. These include the Follow Through Planned Variation experiment (Stebbins, St. Pierre, Proper, Anderson, & Cerva, 1977), the Alum Rock voucher experiment (Education and Human Resources Program, 1981), and the Chapter 2 Block Grant Implementation study (Economics of Education Review, 1985). The voucher experiment helped to legitimize research on educational choice, and its influence is apparent in Chester Finn's (1985) testimony on this subject in behalf of the Reagan Administration's continued support of voucher and tax credit plans.

Still another "success story" is reported by Rabe and Peterson (Chapter 23 in this volume). Based on research on the implementation of federal programs in four large cities, Peterson and Rabe conclude that the federal role in elementary and secondary education deserves a far more positive appraisal than it has received in recent years. Significantly, policy and evaluation research have figured in the evolution of what they call a "new cooperative federalism":

> Although we found examples of bureaucratic ineptitude, concessions to special interest, and inefficient use of federal resources, the dominant pattern was quite the opposite. Instead of conflict, we found cooperation. Instead of federal dictation, we found mutual accommodation on the part of national, state, and local officials. Instead of misallocation of federal resources, we found ready acquiescence to federal policy at the state and local level. Above all, instead of a heavy federal presence, we found a highly decentralized system whose administration remained in the firm hands of local officials.

The evolution of this pattern involved developmental stages influenced by theory and research about federal-local relations in policy implementation. In the first stage, the federal government delegated a good deal of discretion to local authorities about how programs, such as Title I of ESEA, would be carried out. As evaluation studies called attention to promiscuous use of federal funds, the second stage arrived when the federal authorities tightened up their regulations and intensified oversight of local programs. This approach generated numerous conflicts and a great deal of criticism about excessive regulations and paperwork. Consequently, a third stage, the "more mature" approach, emerged, one that Rabe and Peterson say "is more a synthesis, a discernment of the appropriate balance between what is desirable and what is possible." In all of this, as well as in Rabe and Peterson's own research, the constructive role of policy analysis and evaluation in influencing approaches to policy and administration is apparent.

In sum, despite some spectacular controversies and confusions along the way, research on policy, evaluation, and implementation has been influential in suggesting better ways to design and administer policies and to manage their successful implementation. This is the rich payoff of policy analysis, a payoff that can become greater in the future if we can apply more fully what we now know (see Elmore, 1983a; Hawley, 1985). Discussion of these developments leads into the final topic to be addressed: what we have learned from policy research about managing schools.

THE NATURE, CONTROL, AND MANAGEMENT OF PUBLIC SCHOOLS

The growth of an "outcomes" and "accountability" orientation toward public services has both fostered and reflected the growth of the policy analysis movement. In turn, policy and implementation analysis has highlighted the distinctive features and problems of public, human services organizations, showing that the public schools are not unique in their characteristics or difficulties (e.g., Feller, 1981). The findings not only have enriched our knowledge but have some potentially revolutionary implications for the practice and study of educational administration.

Consider the characterization of public schools that emerges from this literature, one that applies equally to most public, human services organizations: Schools are seen as "bottom heavy, loosely coupled" organizations (Elmore, 1983a), with ambiguous goals and weak technologies (March & Olsen, 1976; Meyer & Rowan, 1978), problematic reward structures (Levy, Meltsner, & Wildavsky, 1974, pp. 219–262; Michaelsen, 1977, 1981), and overworked employees coping with disparities between demands and resources (Weatherley & Lipsky, 1978). As Elmore (1983a) elaborates it:

The system is *bottom heavy* and *loosely coupled*. It is bottom heavy because the closer we get to the bottom of the pyramid, the closer we get to the factors that have the greatest effect on the program's success or failure. The system is loosely coupled because the ability of one level to control the behavior of another is weak and largely negative [emphasis in the original]. (pp. 357–358)

Seen in this light, it is not surprising that schools face management and performance problems and mounting calls for fundamental organizational reform. Not only are there widespread demands for an overhaul of the teaching profession and its career and incentive structure, there now is increasing pressure for improved school administration. This pressure comes at a time when the demand for better student achievement and increased professionalism in teaching seems to require what Spady (1981), echoing Erickson's (1979) concerns, has called a fundamental shift from process-oriented, role-based management to outcome-oriented, goal-based management. Is it reasonable, though, to hold educators accountable for organizational *outcomes*, rather than simply the provision of equal educational *opportunity*? What does the implementation literature suggest about this question?

The implementation analysis literature in education began with some pioneering work on the implementation of the Elementary and Secondary Education Act of 1965. In what have become classic studies, Bailey and Mosher (1968) and Murphy (1971) showed how federal intentions were modified or evaded at the local level. Implementation research continued with works demonstrating that decisions based on what appear to be neutral professional norms or standards nevertheless may have inequitable consequences (e.g., Levy, Meltsner, & Wildavsky, 1974); works showing how service delivery personnel cope with mandates for change and reshape policy (e.g., Mann, 1978; Weatherley & Lipsky, 1977); works assessing research on implementation and developing its implications for administration and the design of policy (e.g., Elmore, 1979–1980, 1983a, 1983b; Williams, 1980); and works exploring the complex interactions and aggregate effects of federal education programs (Kimbrough & Hill, 1981).

In the progress within this literature, as Rabe and Peterson suggest in Chapter 23 (this volume), movement toward a synthesis is detectable. In the scholarly debate on the subject, however, three main explanations of implementation problems in education have competed. For the purposes of this discussion, it is useful to consider each of these explanations, what they reveal about schools, and what they suggest about the requirements for school reform.[7] In all three explanations, political and organizational theory converge. This convergence, in fact, is one of the contributions of interdisciplinary policy analysis, a weaving together of strands of theory—typically in some variant of political economy (Wildavsky, 1985)—producing a more robust analytical tool. Each of the three explanations discussed here has implications for the politics of school reform and for what is required for effective schools. Each presents different recommendations for what is needed for successful reform. Ultimately, however, each explanation is inadequate by itself, yet movement toward a synthesis requires a comprehension of the insights and limitations of each.

Implementation as Mutual Adaptation

In the past, reformers' most tenuous assumption was the notion that official adoption of reforms or innovations was tantamount to their implementation. Today, we are sadder but wiser. As noted earlier, in the influential Rand Change Agent study ("Federal Programs Supporting Educational Change"), the researchers found that nonimplementation was common. At best, they saw a process of mutual adaptation in which both the practices in a given school and the innovative project being attempted were modified by one another (Berman & McLaughlin, 1976; Mann, 1978).

The fact that the prevailing practices and attitudes of educators at the school-site level usually dominate over the reform or innovation is explained two ways in this school of thought. First, it is argued that the realities facing public employees who deliver services directly to clients tend to ensure that the objectives of reforms will be substantially compromised. Weatherley and Lipsky (1977) contend that such employees, whom they call "street-level bureaucrats," face work conditions where they must cope with (a) inadequate resources, (b) threats to their authority and person, and (c) ambiguous and unrealistic role expectations. The result, within the inherently discretionary nature of their work, is that street-level bureaucrats modify goals, ration services, routinize procedures, assert priorities, and limit and control their clientele. These coping behaviors on the part of educators faced with the need to implement sweeping and highly specific reforms in special education in Massachusetts are vividly reported by Weatherley and Lipsky (1977; see also Weatherley, 1979).

A second explanation for minimal implementation of reforms involves subtle, and sometimes not so subtle, resistance by educators. As Mann (1978) demonstrates in his analysis of the Rand data, there is a partisan aspect to the mutual adaptation process. Like people in general, educators are inclined to mini-

mize the personal costs of change by only partial or "symbolic" implementation of innovations. Since numereous studies reveal that those involved in implementation are likely to compromise reforms, either for partisan reasons or because of the practical constraints within which they work, the shaping or making of policy actually continues through the implementation process (Weatherley & Lipsky, 1977).

From their findings, the Rand researchers concluded that traditional approaches to educational innovation were inappropriate for the realities of professional staff discretion in "loosely coupled" educational organizations (Weick, 1976). "Bottom-up" rather than "top-down" leadership and decision-making approaches appeared more likely to result in successful implementation of reforms. Those who must implement changes need to participate in selecting and planning innovations so that they will identify with and feel "ownership" over the innovations.

If schools are to be reformed, it follows that policies and leadership strategies must be designed with these bottom-up realities in mind. Effective schools, in this view, are ones that foster the participation and adaptive abilities of school staff in school improvement (Hawley, 1978). Although many observers argue that school improvement requires substantial parental involvement, the street-level bureaucracy theory suggests that the tension in authority relations with teachers makes parental participation in school affairs problematic unless it is confined to a minor and purely supportive role. Indeed, the theory suggests that what is needed is not parental participation in schools but rather lobbying by citizens to ensure that educators are provided with adequate resources to accomplish their mission. Unfortunately, the theory leaves unclear just what would constitute adequate resources. When would street-level bureaucrats have "enough" resources?

Implementation in Nonprofit, Public Sector Organizations

Even if bottom-up strategies are attempted in public schools, and "adequate" resources are provided, analysts using the perspective of market-oriented political economy predict that there will be goal displacement undercutting many innovations. Rather than merely supplying more resources and changing policy and leadership strategies, they contend that basic structural arrangements must be changed. The fundamental difficulty, they say, is that the nonprofit, government-supported character of public schools creates a perverse structure of incentives for employees (Michaelsen 1977, 1981). In the quasimonopolistic, consumer-insensitive setting of public schools, the reward structure is not oriented toward performance.

"Public-choice" theorists emphasize the profound effects of two features of public-sector organizations. First, public managers lack property rights or a profit motive in the successful performance of the organization. Second, the organization receives a tax-supplied budget independent of satisfying individual consumers. From these starting points, one can explain much of the behavior of public school personnel, which otherwise might appear irrational or "loosely coupled." For instance, since there are no profits in public schools to motivate and reward managers (and teachers' salaries are based on seniority rather than performance), educators—as rational, self-interested people seeking to maximize their own welfare—will be be inclined to maximize their nonpecuniary benefits. This means that in place of profits (which would depend on satisfied customers), public educators will seek to maximize such things as the size of their budget, the scope of their activities, the ease of their work, and their power and prestige. On the other hand, they will try to minimize their psychic costs by avoiding risks and conflict as much as possible. In brief, the personal goals of employees in public schools often will take precedence over the official goals of the schools because the costs of inefficient behavior, in terms of the official goals, are low. Thus, the discrepancy between personal and official goals that is accentuated by the reward structure in public-sector organizations creates the basis for the distinctive "bureaucratic politics" that characterize such organizations and their relationships with clients and sponsors (Boyd & Crowson, 1981; Michaelsen, 1977, 1981; Ostrom & Ostrom, 1971).

Unfortunately, there is a good deal of evidence to support this line of analysis (Boyd & Crowson, 1981). Usually, the costs of innovation for teachers and administrators seem to outweigh the benefits they stand to gain. Yet, public schools do adopt some innovations. However, as Pincus (1974) suggests, "Private firms are more likely to adopt innovations that promote economic efficiency, whereas schools are more likely to adopt innovations that promote bureaucratic and social stability" (p. 119).

Market-oriented political economy cautions against simply "throwing money at schools" (Hanushek, 1981). Rather, it argues that structural arrangements must be changed to provide performance incentives. Effective schools, in this view, are ones that compete for students and funds and reward staff for outstanding performance. Thus, merit pay, tuition tax credits, and educational voucher plans are attractive policies. Without the fundamental kinds of change such policies would introduce, this perspective suggests

public schools will go on maintaining a status quo that largely benefits the employees within them.

Innovation and Implementation in Capitalist Societies

From the point of view of radical political economists in the Marxist tradition, neither bottom-up strategies and additional resources nor performance incentives will lead to successful school reform. They believe the overarching structures of capitalist societies foster maintenance of the status quo, but in the interests of the capitalist system rather than of self-serving school employees (Bowles & Gintis, 1976). As Papagiannis, Klees, and Bickel (1982) put it:

> Public and private sector decision-making will yield substantial innovative effort, but directed primarily toward increasing capitalist wealth through developments in such areas as new weapon systems and toothpaste, planned obsolescence, and an emphasis on image, generally yielding greater unemployment and a deteriorating environment... (p. 262)

> Radical analysis of educational innovations generally [stresses] the correspondence view that those [innovations] which basically conform to capitalist system interests (e.g., [that] lower cost, increase cognitive skills, or reinforce attitudes useful to production) will be adopted and implemented, and those that challenge the structure, especially in terms of trying to promote equality, will not be. From this perspective it is no surprise that many equality promoting innovations are tried out as pilot projects and after the sponsoring agency leaves, the project is discontinued...Such projects contribute to an image of concern without the necessity of making any significant changes. Even when such an innovation is pursued seriously, like the comprehensive secondary school, the egalitarian dimensions of it are subverted as it becomes implemented with testing, teaching, and counseling systems that yield no improvement in equality, only greater administrative control. (p. 268)

In the radical view, capitalist arrangements make schools instruments to reproduce the inegalitarian social-stratification system. Schooling maintains inequality by fostering and reinforcing different skills and attitudes that divide people from one another. But because it does this in the name of meritocratic competition among students, the process seems just, thereby maintaining the system and its legitimacy. Both the overt and "hidden" curriculums of schools are important in this process. Thus, the "new sociology of education" movement focuses on the role of teachers and administrators in determining the selection, transmission, and evaluation of knowledge in schools. Social class biases, both overt and covert, are suspected of influencing what counts for knowledge in such a way as to disadvantage working and lower class children (Bates, 1980; Karabel & Halsey, 1977a).

From this perspective, reforming public schools is far more difficult than the two previous explanations suggest. The need is to alter somehow the dynamics in schools that are connected to the workings of the overarching socioeconomic system. At the macro level, one can engage in political action in support of socialist reforms. At the school level, one can seek and encourage contradictions to the capitalist system. Indeed, the analysis by Papagiannis, Klees, and Bickel (1982) suggests that effective schools would be ones that emphasize equality and contradict capitalist values. With a fundamentally different curriculum and approach (e.g., see Kemmis, Cole, & Suggett, 1983), radicals would argue that such schools would provide settings in which reforms could be implemented that would serve the humanistic needs of children rather than the interests of employees or capitalism.

Toward a Synthesis: Implementation and Reform as Problems of Redistribution

Each of the three explanations calls attention to important barriers to educational reform. But as compelling as one or another of the three may seem, depending upon one's leanings, each is incomplete and potentially misleading by itself. The mutual adaptation view calls for more resources and bottom-up solutions but leaves unanswered how these would overcome the incentive problems and obstacles to equality and redistribution emphasized in the other two views. With its heavy emphasis on bottom-up change and on the pocket veto over implementation of innovations that teachers can exercise behind their classroom doors, the mutual adaptation view generally seems to offer little hope of more than incremental change. It too easily can become an explanation or apology for the lack of leadership that Dale Mann (1985) decries:

> Schools in need of improvement...are presided over by administrators who find their purposes only in what the teachers are willing to do...Such leadership by default sacrifices school improvement to the comity of the adult organization. The politics of school leadership has been too much about adult working conditions and too little about children's learning conditions. (p. 16)

By contrast, the "nonprofit pathologies" view stresses either changing the reward structures of public organizations or resorting to competitive or private-sector solutions, such as merit pay, tax credits, and vouchers. But its heavy emphasis on individualistic competition (between students and between teachers) is inconsistent with both the public schools' role in promoting equality (Tyack & Hansot, 1984) and with numerous findings highlighting the interdependent nature of schools and the importance of collaborative problem solving and capacity building within service delivery organizations (Johnson, 1984). Emphasizing individualistic, market-oriented, "frictionless" solutions, this approach fails to appreciate the inescapable need for organized capacity to meet social service needs (Elmore, 1983b). Moreover, its pronounced skepticism toward public organizations and its aversion to "throwing money at problems" lead to the view that if one cannot drastically overhaul public sector organizations the best policy would be one of "benign neglect."

Finally, in focusing on the impediments to social reform in capitalist societies, the Marxist explanation ignores the generic realities of implementation difficulties at the service delivery level. No less than capitalist nations, socialist nations also have pronounced and well-known implementation problems in meeting their own goals, 5-year plans, and the like. Furthermore, as Peterson (1981, pp. 214–217) observes, while the "nonprofit pathologies" view leads toward a "do nothing" policy position, the Marxist approach goes to the other extreme in urging a "do everything" prescription for revolutionary social reform.

The way toward a synthesis in this literature seems to lie in finding a middle ground between the extremes. As Peterson (1981, pp. 214–222) suggests, doing "something" may be both more attractive and more feasible than either doing "nothing" or "everything." Toward this end, we could start by viewing implementation and educational reform as problems of redistribution.[8] Our difficulties seem to revolve around two kinds of redistribution: substantive and psychic. Social policies aimed at remediating inequities, at aiding the disadvantaged, are obviously and substantively redistributive. Such policies clearly lead a constrained and precarious existence in market-oriented societies concerned with efficiency and productivity (Bowles & Gintis, 1976; Okun, 1975; Peterson, 1981). But new policies and programs that require service delivery personnel to abandon familiar and comfortable routines to benefit someone else also are redistributive, even if only psychic costs are involved. Particularly when there is a unilateral imposition of costs on semi-professionals, they experience a loss in autonomy and self-respect. The mutual adaptation and street-level bureaucracy literature abundantly documents the high price that practitioners exact for such an exchange.

What is needed, then, are policy and management strategies that respond to both sides of the redistribution problem as conceived above. A substantial step toward the strategies needed for the psychic side of the problem is found in the insightful works of Elmore

(1983a, 1983b) and Hawley (1978). Based on their assessments of the implementation literature, they conclude that what is required is a policy and management approach that focuses on building adaptive schools and social-service organizations by fostering professional problem-solving capacity within them. Elmore (1983a) argues that, rather than attempts to maximize hierarchical control and compliance, the inescapable complexity and concomitant professional discretion involved in social services require an approach that fosters the capacity to deliver the service. Consequently, instead of hierarchical control,

> the skillful use of delegated control is central to making implementation work in bottom-heavy, loosely coupled systems. *When it becomes necessary to rely mainly on hierarchical control, regulation, and compliance to achieve results, the game is essentially lost.* Moving from delegated control to hierarchical control means moving from reliance on existing capacity, ingenuity, and judgment [on the part of service delivery personnel] to reliance on rules, surveillance, and enforcement procedures. Regulation increases complexity and invites subversion; it diverts attention from accomplishing the task to understanding and manipulating rules [emphasis in the original] (Elmore, 1983a, p. 358)

Consistent with Elmore's assessment, other analysts have concluded that "to manage is not to control," but rather to get results, performance, desired outcomes (Behn, 1982, 1983; Landau & Stout, 1979). The idea that the focus in bottom-heavy, loosely coupled organizations should be on getting results—via extensive use of delegated rather than hierarchical control to build performance capacity—has far-reaching implications for the practice and study of school administration. Like Elmore's (1979–1980) notion of "backward mapping" in the design of policies, this idea turns conventional notions of administration upside down. Of course, some will say this system for getting results is what school administrators have been doing all along, and in the case of some adept ones this will be true. But when one looks at the traditional orientation of the field, both in scholarship and practice, the focus usually has been on administrative and organizational processes rather than on outcomes, and conventional notions of hierarchical control have loomed large (Boyd & Immegart, 1979; Erickson, 1979). Thus, beyond its implications for the improved design of social policy, one of the great contributions of policy analysis is its reconception of the practice of management within the context of a much sharper perception of the realities of social-service organizations and of the implementation process.

A delegated-control approach reduces the psychic costs problem of implementation and reform for professionals by generating incentives of professional collaboration, pride, and ownership over policies and programs that professionals have adapted to meet their circumstances and needs. The trick, of course, is to provide leadership that respects educators as professionals but nevertheless motivates substantial change and improvement. Frequently, more than fragile, bottom-up mutual adaptation is needed. And, indeed, recent research and developments show that more is possible.

An approach that works is similar to that which appears fruitful in dealing with the more politically difficult side of the redistribution problem: the enactment and implementation of substantively redistributive policies. Rather than employing highly specific and prescriptive directives that conflict with local needs for flexibility and adaptation, Peterson (1981, p. 221) argues that effective leadership can be proffered through actions that set, propagate, maintain, and legitimize goals and minimum standards for the organization and, more broadly, for the just society. As demonstrated by longitudinal studies of successful federal education policies, over time such an approach encourages organizational learning through an evolutionary process, one in which local and state authorities and constituency groups begin to internalize and identify with the goals that are set and monitored (Jung, Chapter 24, this volume; Kirst, 1983; Knapp et al., 1983; Rabe & Peterson, Chapter 23, this volume).

Not only recent assessments of successful federal education policies but also the remarkably effective use of exhortation by the Reagan Administration demonstrate that more than fragile, bottom-up approaches to reform can succeed. These facts contradict the pessimistic view of federal policies that came to the fore in the 1970s, and they fly in the face of the negative findings of most of the early implementation research. Knapp et al. (1983, p. 493) give three explanations for this discrepancy. First, research in the "cumulative effects" tradition has been concerned with broad effects rather than the details of local implementation, which often were the focus of earlier studies. Second, unlike earlier research, the focus was on programs that no longer were new and unestablished. Finally, the nature of the programs studied was different:

> Some important implementation studies have dealt with programs that accorded a great deal of discretion to local participants...The "Change Agent" study... often cited as evidence that federal programs have weak and variable local effects, dealt with programs that involved very limited federal rules and monitoring. The programs and mandates considered in this study, however, have been designed and administered in a deliberate effort to bring about local compliance. (p. 493)

Based on their review of a great deal of recent research, much of which was not yet widely disseminated, Jung and Kirst (1986) propose that the findings

> suggest that implementation of the more mature federal categorical programs had progressed [by the early 1980s] to an advanced stage, beyond that of mutual adaptation. This latter stage of implementation is characterized by more limited or circumscribed intergovernmental conflict, highly customized applications of federal requirements and options to local circumstances, and broadly-based, although not autonomous, support of the equity goals of federal programs. (p. 87)

This stage, beyond mutual adaptation but not yet to full local-state "institutionalization" of federal programs and objectives, Jung and Kirst call "accustomization." Ironically, the Reagan Administration abandoned both categorical grants and equity goals just as research was emerging that showed that federal programs with these characteristics were working far better than most people believed (Rabe & Peterson, 1983). In lieu of new federal programs to improve the schools, however, the Reagan Administration has demonstrated extraordinary skill in the effective and aggressive use of sermonizing from the bully pulpit.

As Jung and Kirst (1986) note, in their discussion of the bully pulpit strategy, two of the most dramatic examples are the effects of the Nation at Risk report and the Wall Chart comparing state education outcomes. With little cost to the federal government, both of these set in motion remarkably far-reaching activities and consequences at the state level. Similarly, Clark and Astuto (1986) document the extent to which the Reagan Administration has been able to redirect the values and goals of national and state policy in education. Much of this has been done through sermonizing on such values and goals as deregulation, decentralization, diminution of the federal role, and Secretary Bennett's "three Cs," content, character, and choice.

The effects of these efforts have not only been to build up public support for the objectives of the Reagan Administration but also to create political pressure on educators to do what they otherwise would not do. For example, while most teachers' unions have been reluctant to go along with proposals for merit pay, career ladders, and teachers' exams, the political climate has made these matters hard to resist—though not impossible to elude (Malen & Hart, 1986).

Yet, if exhortation and outcome-oriented pressures on educators provide some of the needed motivation to get educators to do things they don't already want to do, it is also true that the effectiveness of top-down and bully pulpit approaches is not limitless.

One still cannot "legislate learning" (Wise, 1979) or "mandate excellence." Teachers and administrators in schools clearly need support, resources, and respect, as well as exhortation. Since the reforms adopted in the statewide excellence movement have been overwhelmingly of the top-down variety, there is a real danger that some of them may backfire (e.g., see Fowler, 1985). In states like Texas, for example, demeaning, "de-skilling" approaches to teachers have been adopted that may drive out exactly the kind of teachers we seek to attract and retain in efforts to upgrade the teaching profession (McNeil, 1986).

Thus, in the final analysis, neither bottom-up mutual adaptation nor top-down bully pulpitism will suffice by itself. Rather, we need a balanced approach to educational improvement using elements of each strategy judiciously, according to the characteristics and needs of the given policy problem. As Peterson (1981) makes clear, substantively redistributive policies usually will require top-down mandates and monitoring, whereas policies enhancing broadly shared local interests ("developmental" policies in his terms) will be less likely to require top-down enforcement (and more likely to thrive under mutual adaptation).

The balanced, contingency approach to educational improvement outlined here provides a response to the question posed earlier. Policy and implementation research now clearly indicates that policy makers and educators can take responsibility both for providing opportunities—for learning and innovation—and for ensuring a modest but significant range of organizational and educational outcomes. However, although the principles implicated in this approach provide a basis for the new synthesis we seek, we undeniably are left with the problem of finding the collective will to engage in large-scale substantive redistribution. Yet, the demographic and social forces at work in our society seem likely to reawaken this inclination, which is still alive even in the face of conservative fervor. As Tyack and Hansot (1984) observe:

> The challenges posed by our vast inequities will not disappear, however militant the new [individualistic, competitive] rhetoric of educational reform. Americans now face the prospect that an appalling number of children may grow up in poverty in the wealthiest nation on earth. Immigrants, many of them without resources, are flooding the nation in numbers rivaling those of the early twentieth century. Teenage unemployment among minorities in depressed cities is at near-depression levels...Education alone will obviously not solve such problems, but it has been one means of redistributing a rudimentary form of opportunity. Scarcity today poses hard choices amid the paradox of seeking to make the school an agent of equalization in a struggling market society. (p. 66)

Fortunately, as Harold Hodgkinson (*Education Week*, 1986) has pointed out, as a result of the implications of current demographic trends, enlightened self-interest alone should push us toward more concern for social justice and redistribution:

> The workers bearing the responsibility for supporting [the] expanding, longer-living senior population will be, in large measure, the young people of today and tomorrow—including the growing "all-risk" group. If current demographic patterns hold, the workers on which the aging society will so heavily depend will be fewer in number, more racially and ethnically diverse, more likely to have grown up in poverty, more likely to be the progeny of broken homes, and more likely to suffer from physical, mental, and emotional handicaps. (p. 25)[9]

CONCLUSIONS AND IMPLICATIONS

This chapter has discussed the complex nature of policy analysis, its methods, reliability, and influence on policy making and management. Though the inconsistencies, controversies, and potential biases of policy analysis have been highlighted, the contention here is that, despite all its warts and blemishes, policy analysis has made major and extraordinary contributions to our knowledge about social policy and its implementation and about the nature of organizations and their management. Although the direct influence of policy research on specific decisions is often slight, the indirect influence on our general conception of policy problems and fruitful avenues toward their solution is often profound. As in numerous other arenas, this proposition can be clearly demonstrated in the changing conception of the field of educational administration (Boyd & Crowson, 1981).

Policy analysis and evaluation have helped to push educators from a position of seeking mainly to provide equal educational opportunity to a position of taking increasing responsibility for the educational outcomes achieved in the race for opportunity. Similarly, implementation analysis, along with general trends in management, has contributed to the view that to manage is not to control but rather to get results. Together, these new ways of thinking about the tasks of educational administration are fostering a fundamental shift from process-oriented, role-based management to outcome-oriented, goal-based management (Spady, 1981). Indeed, as argued elsewhere (Boyd & Immegart, 1979; Boyd & Crowson, 1981), educational administration may be in the midst of a fundamental paradigm shift.

Since the late 1970s, research in the field has been increasingly concerned with discovering the distinctive realities and consequences of organizational behavior and administrative practice in education. "The controlling factor in any science," as Robert Lynd once observed, "is the way it views and states its problems" (as quoted in Katznelson, 1976, p. 216). In this respect, Donald Erickson's (1977, 1979) seminal work is indicative of the changes occurring within the field. In assessing the status of research in educational administration, Erickson (1979) asked why the field had been so preoccupied with organizational effects on administrators and teachers and at the same time so inattentive to research concerned with instruction and student outcomes. While Erickson was raising these questions, Edmonds (1979) and others launched the search for the characteristics of unusually "effective schools," a movement that has captured increasing attention from researchers in educational administration. As a result of such trends, the central research questions in educational administration now revolve around what school administrators actually do, with what consequences for whom, and—consistent with the thrust of policy analysis—what difference it makes for educational and organizational effectiveness.

Clearly, the policy studies approach already has influenced both the study and the practice of educational administration. But the full potential of the approach has yet to be tapped. At its best, policy analysis has the potential (a) to bridge the perennial gap between theory and practice and (b) to link organizational and administrative processes to organizational outcomes, countering the troublesome tendency toward goal displacement in educational organizations. The rich implications of the policy-studies approach for preparation programs in school administration, research on educational administration, and administrative practice in schools are obvious. Consequently, a number of university programs in educational administration already have been reorganized around the policy-studies theme (Layton, 1983). Whether the field in general will fully capitalize on the implications of the movement remains to be seen.

NOTES

[1] As quoted in the *Oxford Dictionary of Quotations*, 3rd ed. New York: Oxford University Press, 1979, p. 148.
[2] I am grateful to Richard Elmore and Jerome Murphy for their valuable suggestions and criticisms and also for those of Tyll van Geel, but I retain full responsibility for any errors of fact or interpretation that remain.
[3] For an introduction to the literature on educational policy and politics, see Benson (1978); Boyd (1978); Burlingame (1977); Cambron-McCabe and Odden (1982); Coombs (1983); Garms, Guthrie, and Pierce (1978); Guthrie (1980a, 1980b); Iannaccone (1967); Karabel and Halsey (1977b); Kirst (1984); Lieberman and McLaughlin (1982); Mann (1975, 1978); Mitchell (1981, 1984);

Peterson (1974); Scribner (1977); Shulman and Sykes (1983); van Geel (1976); Wirt and Kirst (1982); Yeakey (1983); Zeigler and Jennings (1974); Zeigler, Kehoe, and Reisman (1985).

[4] On this point, see, for example, the tribute to Thomas Schelling's analytical contribution by Thomas Nagel (1984).

[5] As quoted in the *Oxford Dictionary of Quotations*, 3rd ed. New York: Oxford University Press, 1979, p. 571.

[6] For a comprehensive review of the literature on educational evaluation, see Boruch and Wortman (1979).

[7] This discussion of competing explanations of implementation failures is adapted from Boyd (1983).

[8] This point of view is implied by Rabe & Peterson (1983).

[9] The use of data such as these to change people's conception of their self-interest is a good example of what Lindblom (1980) calls "partisan analysis."

REFERENCES

Arrow, K. (1963). *Social choice and individual values*. New York: John Wiley.

Bailey, S. K., & Moser, E. (1968). *ESEA: The office of education administers a law*. Syracuse: Syracuse University Press.

Baker, C. E. (1975, Fall). The ideology of the economic analysis of law. *Philosophy and Public Affairs*, 5, 3–48.

Bates, R. J. (1980). Educational administration, the sociology of science, and the management of knowledge. *Educational Administration Quarterly, 16*(2), 1–20.

Bates, R. J. (1983). *Educational administration and the management of knowledge*. Geelong, Australia: School of Education, Deakin University.

Behn, R. (1981). Policy analysis and policy politics. *Policy Analysis, 7*(2), 199–226.

Behn, R. (1982, February). Comments at Managing Enrollment Decline Conference, Vanderbilt University, Nashville.

Behn, R. (1983). The managerial opportunity of enrollment decline. *Peabody Journal of Education, 60*(2), 108–119.

Bellah, R. N. (1983). Social science as practical reason. In D. Callahan & B. Jennings (Eds.), *Ethics, the social sciences, and policy analysis*. New York: Plenum.

Benson, C. S. (1978). *The economics of public education* (3rd ed.). Boston: Houghton Mifflin.

Berman, P., Greenwood, P. W., McLaughlin, M. W., & Pincus, J. (1975). *Federal programs supporting educational change, Vol. 5. Executive summary*. Santa Monica, CA: Rand (R–1589/5–HEW, April).

Berman, P., & McLaughlin, M. W. (1978). *Federal programs supporting educational change, Vol. 8: Implementing and sustaining innovations*. Santa Monica, CA: Rand.

Berman, P., & McLaughlin, M. W. (1976). Implementation of educational innovation. *Educational Forum, 40*, 345–370.

Bernstein, R. J. (1976). *The restructuring of social and political theory*. New York: Harcourt Brace Jovanovich.

Borcherding, T. E. (Ed.). (1977). *Budgets and bureaucrats: The sources of government growth*. Durham, NC: Duke University Press.

Boruch, R. F., & Wortman, P. M. (1979). Implications of educational evaluation for evaluation policy. In D. C. Berliner (Ed.), *Review of research in education* (Vol. 7, pp. 309–361). Washington DC: American Educational Research Association.

Bowles, S., & Gintis, H. (1976). *Schooling in capitalist America: Educational reform and the contradictions of economic life*. New York: Basic Books.

Boyd, W. L. (1978). The study of educational policy and politics: Much ado about nothing? *Teachers College Record, 80*(2), 249–271.

Boyd, W. L. (1983). Rethinking educational policy and management: Political science and educational administration in the 1980s. *American Journal of Education, 92*(1), 1–29.

Boyd, W. L., & Crowson, R. L. (1981). The changing conception and practice of public school administration. In D. Berliner (Ed.), *Review of Research in Education*, (Vol. 9). Washington, DC: American Educational Research Association.

Boyd, W. L., & Immegart, G. L. (1979). Education's turbulent environment and problem-finding. In G. L. Immegart & W. L. Boyd (Eds.), *Problem-finding in educational administration*. Lexington, MA: Heath.

Brandl, J. E. (1985). Distilling frenzy from academic scribbling: How economics influences politicians. *Journal of Policy Analysis and Management, 4*(3), 344–353.

Bredo, E., & Feinberg, W. (Eds.). (1982). *Knowledge and values in social and educational research*. Philadephia: Temple University Press.

Brewer, G. D. & deLeon, P. (1983). *The foundations of policy analysis*. Homewood, IL: Dorsey.

Brown, B. F. (1973). *The reform of secondary education: A report to the public and the profession*. New York: McGraw-Hill.

Bulmer, M. (1983). The British tradition of social administration: Moral concerns at the expense of scientific rigor. In D. Callahan & B. Jennings (Eds.), *Ethics, the social sciences, and policy analysis*. New York: Plenum.

Burlingame, M. (1977). Impact of policy decisions on schools. In L. S. Shulman (Ed.), *Review of Research in Education* (Vol 5, pp. 236–271). Itasca, IL: Peacock.

Burrell, G., & Morgan, G. (1979). *Sociological paradigms and organisational analysis*. London: Heinemann.

Callahan, D., & Jennings, B. (Eds.). (1983). *Ethics, the social sciences, and policy analysis*. New York: Plenum.

Cambron-McCabe, N. H., & Odden, A. (Eds.). (1982). *The changing politics of school finance*. Cambridge, MA: Ballinger.

Carter, L. F. (1984). The sustaining effects study of compensatory and elementary education. *Educational Researcher, 13*(7), 4–13.

Clark, D. L., & Astuto, T. A. (1986, January). *The significance and permanence of changes in federal educational policy, 1980–1988*. (Occasional paper). Bloomington, IN: Policy Studies Center of the University Council for Educational Administration, Indiana University.

Cohen, D. K., & Garet, M. S. (1975). Reforming educational policy with applied social research. *Harvard Educational Review, 45*(1), 17–43.

Coleman, J. L. (1982, May) The normative basis of economic analysis: A critical review of Richard Posner's *The economics of justice*. *Stanford Law Review, 34*, 1105–1131.

Coleman, J. L. (1984, July). Economics and the law: A critical review of the foundations of the economic approach to law. *Ethics, 94*, 649–679.

Coleman, J. S. (1974). *Youth: Transition to adulthood*. Chicago: University of Chicago Press.

Coleman, J. S. (1981, Summer). Private schools, public schools, and the public interest. *The Public Interest* (64), 19–30.

Coleman, J. S. (1984). How might policy research in education be better carried out? In *Improving education: Perspectives on educational research*. Pittsburgh: National Academy of Education, University of Pittsburgh.

Coleman, J. S., Campbell, E. Q., Hobson, C., McPartland, J., Mood, A., Weinfeld, F., & York, R. (1966) *Equality of educational opportunity*. Washington, DC: U.S. Government Printing Office.

Coleman, J. S., Kelly, S. D., & Moore, J. A. (1975, July 28). *Trends in school segregation, 1968–73*. Unpublished paper. Washington, DC: The Urban Institute.

Coleman, J. S., Hoffer, T., & Kilgore, S. (1981, March) *Public and private schools*. (Report to the National Center for Educational Statistics). Chicago: National Opinion Research Center, University of Chicago.

Coleman, J. S., Hoffer, T., & Kilgore, S. (1982). *High school achievement: Public, Catholic, and private schools compared*. New York: Basic Books.

Coombs, F. S. (1983). Education policy. In S. S. Nagel (Ed.), *Encyclopedia of policy studies* (pp. 589–616). New York: Marcel Dekker.

Crain, R. L., & Hawley, W. D. (1982, January–February). Standards of research. *Transaction*, 14–21.

Datta, L. E. (1980). Changing times: The study of federal programs supporting educational change and the case for local problem solving. *Teachers College Record*, 82(1), 101–116.

Economics of Education Review. (1985). Special issue: Federal block grants to education (4), 3.

Edmonds, R. (1979). Effective schools for the urban poor. *Educational Leadership*, 37, 15–24.

Education and Human Resources Program. (1981). *A study of alternatives in American education: Vol. 7. Conclusions and policy implications* (Report No. R–2170/7–NIE). Santa Monica, CA: Rand.

Education Week (1986, May 14). Here they come, ready or not. An *Education Week* Special Report, pp. 13–37.

Elmore, R. F, (1979–1980, Winter). Backward mapping: Implementation research and policy decisions. *Political Science Quarterly*, 94(4), 601–616.

Elmore, R. F. (1983a). Complexity and control: What legislators and administrators can do about implementing public policy. In L. S. Shulman & G. Sykes (Eds.), *Handbook of teaching and policy*. New York: Longman.

Elmore, R. F. (1983b). Social policymaking as strategic intervention. In E. Seidman (Ed.), *Handbook of social intervention*. Beverly Hills, CA: Sage.

Elmore, R. F. (1985). *Policy analysis as the study of implementation*. Paper presented at the Annual Meeting of the Western political Science Association, March 28–30, Las Vegas.

Erickson, D. A. (Ed.). (1977). *Educational organization and administration*. Berkeley, CA: McCutchan.

Erickson, D. A. (1979, March). Research on educational administration: The state-of-the-art. *Educational Researcher*, 8, 9–14.

Fay, B. (1975). *Social theory and political practice*. London: George Allen & Unwin.

Feller, I. (1981, January). *Innovation processes in public schools: An exercise in comparative morphology*. Paper prepared for the Program on Research and Educational Practice, National Institute of Education. University Park, PA: Institute for Policy Research and Evaluation, Pennsylvania State University.

Finn, C. E., Jr. (1985, October 22). Education choice: Theory, practice, and research. Testimony before the Senate Subcommitee on Intergovernmental Relations, Committee on Governmental Affairs.

Fowler, F. C. (1985, November 6). Why reforms go awry. *Education Week*, 5(10), 24, 17.

Garms, W. I., Guthrie, J. W., & Pierce, L. C. (1978). *School finance: The economics and politics of public education*. Englewood Cliffs, NJ: Prentice-Hall.

Giroux, H. A. (1984). Public philosophy and the crisis in education. *Harvard Educational Review*, 54(2), 186–194.

Guthrie, J. W. (1980a). An assessment of educational policy research. *Educational Evaluation and Policy Analysis*, 2(5), 41–55.

Guthrie, J. W. (Ed.) (1980b). *School finance policies and practices*. Cambridge, MA: Ballinger.

Hanson, W. L., & Weisbrod, B. A. (1969). Distribution of costs and direct benefits of public higher education: The case of California. *Journal of Human Resources*, 4(2), 176–191.

Hanushek, E. (1981). Throwing money at schools. *Journal of Policy Analysis and Management*, 1(1), 19–41.

Hawley, W. D. (1978). Horses before carts: Developing adaptive schools and the limits of innovation. In D. Mann (Ed.), *Making change happen?* New York: Teachers College Press, Columbia University.

Hawley, W. D. (1985, November). False premises, false promises: The mythical character of public discourse about education. *Phi Delta Kappan*, 183–187.

Hayek, F. von (1939). *Freedom and the economic system*. Chicago: University of Chicago Press.

Heclo, H. (1975). Social politics and policy impacts. In M. Holden, Jr., & D. L. Dresang (Eds.), *What government does*. Beverly Hills, CA: Sage.

Holden, M., Jr., & Dresang, D. L. (1975). Volume editors' introduction. In M. Holden, Jr., & D. L. Dresang (Eds.), *What government does*. Beverly Hills, CA: Sage.

Hoos, I. R. (1972). *Systems analysis in public policy: A critique*. Berkeley, CA: University of California Press.

House, E. R. (1980). *Evaluating with validity*. Beverly Hills, CA: Sage.

Iannaccone, L. (1967). *Politics in education*. New York: Center for Applied Research in Education.

Institute for Research on Educational Finance and Governance, Stanford University (1984). The IFG research agenda: Filling the gaps in the national reports. *IFG Policy Notes*, 5(2), 1–2.

Institute for Research on Educational Finance and Governance, Stanford University (1985). Public & private schools. *IFG Policy Notes*, 6(1) 1–5.

James, T., & Levin, H. M. (1983). *Public dollars for private schools*. Philadelphia: Temple University Press.

Jennings, B. (1983). Interpretive social science and policy analysis. In D. Callahan & B. Jennings (Eds.), *Ethics, the social sciences, and policy analysis*. New York: Plenum.

Johnson, S. M. (1984). Merit pay for teachers: A poor prescription for reform. *Harvard Educational Review*, 54(2), 175–185.

Jones, G. L. (1984). Achieving excellence in education and management. *Journal of Policy Analysis and Management*, 3(2), 248–254.

Jones, W. J. (1983). Can evaluations influence program? The case of compensatory education. *Journal of policy analysis and management*, 2(2), 174–184.

Jung, R. K., & Kirst, M. W. (1986, Summer). Beyond mutual adaptation, into the bully pulpit: Recent research on the federal role in education. *Educational Administration Quarterly*, 22(3), 80–109.

Karabel, J., & Halsey, A. H. (1977a). Educational research: A review and an interpretation. In J. Karabel & A. H. Halsey (Eds.), *Power and ideology in education*. New York: Oxford University Press.

Karabel, J., & Halsey, A. H. (Eds.). (1977b). *Power and ideology in education*. New York: Oxford University Press.

Katznelson, I. (1976). The crisis of the capitalist city. In W. D. Hawley et al., (Eds.). *Theoretical perspectives on urban politics*. Englewood Cliffs, NJ: Prentice-Hall.

Kean, M. H. (1983). Administrative uses of research and evaluation information. In E. W. Gordon (Ed.), *Review of Research in Education* (Vol. 10). Washington, DC: American Educational Research Association.

Kemmis, S., Cole, P., & Suggett, D. (1983). *Orientations to curriculum and transition: Towards the socially-critical school*. Melbourne, Australia: Victorian Institute of Secondary Education.

Kimbrough, J., & Hill, P. T. (1981, September). *The aggregate effects of federal education programs*. Report prepared for the U. S. Department of Education. Santa Monica, CA: Rand. (September).

Kirst, M. W. (1983). Teaching policy and federal categorical programs. In L. S. Shulman & G. Sykes (Eds.), *Handbook of teaching and policy*. New York: Longman.

Kirst, M. W. (1984). *Who controls our schools?* New York: W. H. Freeman.

Kirst, M. W., & Jung, R. (1980, September-October). The utility of a longitudinal approach in assessing implementation: A thirteen-year view of Title I, ESEA. *Educational Evaluation and Policy Analysis*, 2(5), 17–34.

Knapp, M. S., Stearns, M. S., Turnbull, B. J., David, J. L., & Peterson, S. M. (1983, August). Cumulative effects at the local level. *Education and Urban Society*, 15(4), 479–499.

Landau, M., & Stout, R., Jr. (1979). To manage is not to control. *Public Administration Review*, 39, 148–156.

Landy, M. K., & Plotkin, H. A. (1982, May-June). Limits of the market metaphor. *Society*, 19(4), 8–17.

Layton, D. H. (1983, August). *The utilization of the policy sciences in training educational administrators*. (Research working paper No. 83.8). Centre for the Study of Higher Education, University of Melbourne, Parkville, Victoria, Australia.

Levin, H. M. (1982, November). Federal grants and educational equity. *Harvard Educational Review, 52*(4), 444–459.

Levin, H. M. (1983). *Cost-effectiveness: A primer*. Beverly Hills, CA: Sage.

Levin, H. M. (1984, Summer). About time for educational reform. *Educational Evaluation and Policy Analysis, 6*(2), 151–163.

Levine, D. M., & Bane, M. J. (Eds.) (1975). *The "inequality" controversy: Schooling and distributive justice*. New York: Basic Books.

Leviton, L. C., & Boruch, R. F. (1984, Winter). Why the compensatory education evaluation was useful. *Journal of Policy Analysis and Management, 3*(2), 299–305.

Levy, F. S., Meltsner, A. J., & Wildavsky, A. (1974). *Urban outcomes: Schools, streets, & libraries*. Berkeley, CA: University of California Press.

Lieberman, A., & McLaughlin, M. W. (Eds.) (1982). *Policy making in education*. The 81st yearbook of the National Society for the Study of Education. Chicago: University of Chicago Press.

Liebman, L., & Schelling, C. S. (1981). Introduction. In A. Yarmolinsky, L. Liebman, & C. Schelling (Eds.), *Race and schooling in the city*. Cambridge, MA: Harvard University Press.

Lindblom, C. E. (1980). *The policy-making process* (2nd ed.). Englewood Cliffs, NJ: Prentice-Hall.

MacRae, D., Jr. (1980, Summer). [Review of *Speaking truth to power* by A. Wildavsky]. *Policy Analysis, 6*(3), 374–376.

MacRae, D., Jr., & Wilde, J. A. (1979). *Policy analysis for public decision*. North Scituate, MA: Duxbury.

McGonagill, E. G. (1983, April 25). *The compensatory education study*: A case study of a client-centered federal evaluation. Unpublised analytic paper, Graduate School of Education, Harvard University, Cambridge, MA.

McLaughlin, M. W. (1982). States and the new federalism. *Harvard Educational Review, 52*(4), 564–583.

McLaughlin, M. W. (1984, February). *Implementation realities and evaluation design*. (Program Report No. 84–B1). Stanford, CA: Institute for Research on Educational Finance and Governance, School of Education, Stanford University.

McNeil, L. M. (1986, April). *Exit, voice and community: Magnet teachers' responses to standardization*. Paper presented at the Annual Meeting of the American Educational Research Association, San Francisco.

Malen, B., & Hart, A. W. (1986). Career ladder reform: A multilevel analysis of initial effects. Unpublished paper, University of Utah, Salt Lake City, UT.

Mann, D. (1975). *Policy decision-making in education*. New York: Teachers College Press, Columbia University.

Mann, D. (Ed.) (1978). *Making change happen?* New York: Teachers College Press, Columbia University.

Mann, D. (1985, December 18). Principals, leadership, and reform. *Education Week, 5*(16), p. 16.

March, J. G., & Olsen, J. P. (1976). *Ambiguity and choice in organizations*. Bergen, Norway: Universitetsforlaget.

Martin, J. H. (1974). *National panel on high schools and adolescent education*. Washington, DC: U.S. Office of Education.

Mead, L. M. (1983, Fall). "'Policy science' today." *The Public Interest* (73), 165–170.

Meyer, J. W., & Rowan, B. (1978). The structure of educational organizations. In M. W. Meyer and associates, *Environments and organizations*. San Franciso: Jossey-Bass.

Michaelsen, J. B. (1977, February). Revision, bureaucracy, and school reform. *School Review, 85*, 229–246.

Michaelsen, J. B. (1981). A theory of decision making in the public schools: A public choice approach. In S. B. Bacharach (Ed.), *Organizational behavior in schools and school districts*. New York: Praeger.

Mitchell, D. E. (1981). *Shaping legislative decisions: Education policy and the social sciences*. Lexington, MA: Heath.

Mitchell, D. E. (1984, Summer). Educational policy analysis: The state of the art. *Educational Administration Quarterly, 20*(3), 129–160.

Moon, J. D. (1975). The logic of political inquiry: A synthesis of opposed perspectives. In G.I. Greenstein & N. W. Polsby (Eds.), *Political science: Scope and theory*. Reading, MA:

Addison-Wesley.

Moore, M. T. (1984). Cost cutting without goal setting: A recipe for failure. *Journal of Policy Analysis and Management, 3*(2), 255–263.

Murphy, J. T. (1971, February). Title I of ESEA: The politics of implementing federal education reform. *Harvard Educational Review, 41*, 36–63.

Murphy, J. T. (1980). *Getting the facts: A fieldwork guide for evaluators and policy analysts*. Santa Monica, CA: Goodyear.

Nagel, S. S. (1980, July-August). The policy studies perspective. *Public Administration Review, 40*, 391–396.

Nagel, T. (1984, August 27). Measuring the merits: Choice and consequence by Thomas Schelling. *The New Republic, 191*(9), 37–39.

Niskanen, W. (1971). *Bureaucracy and representative government*. Chicago: Aldine-Atherton.

Okun, A. M. (1975). *Equality and efficiency: The big tradeoff*. Washington, DC: Brookings Institution.

Ostrom, V., & Ostrom, E. (1971). Public choice: A different approach to the study of public administration. *Public Administration Review, 31*, 203–216.

Papagiannis, G. J., Klees, S., & Bickel, R. (1982). Toward a political economy of educational innovation. *Review of Educational Research, 52*, 245–290.

Peterson, P. E. (1974). The politics of American education. In F. Kerlinger & J. Carroll (Eds.), *Review of Research in Education* [Vol. 2, pp, 348–389]. Itasca, IL: Peacock.

Peterson, P. E. (1981). *City limits*. Chicago: University of Chicago Press.

Peterson, P. E. (1983, Winter). Did the education commissions say anything? *The Brookings Review*, 3–11.

Pettigrew, T. F., & Green, R. L. (1976, February). School desegregation in large cities: A critique of the Coleman "white flight" thesis. *Harvard Educational Review, 46*(1), 1–53.

Pincus, J. (1974). Incentives for innovation in the public schools. *Review of Educational Research, 44*, 113–144.

Posner, Richard. (1977). *Economic analysis of law*. Boston: Little, Brown.

Posner, Richard. (1981). *The economics of justice*. Cambridge, MA: Harvard University Press.

Press, A., & McDaniel, A. (1985, June 10). "Free-market jurist: Can Richard Posner go from judge to justice?" *Newsweek*, p. 93.

Pressman, J., & Wildavsky, A. (1973). *Implementation*. Berkeley, CA: University of California Press.

Prunty, J. J. (1984). *A critical reformulation of educational policy analysis*. Geelong, Australia: Deakin University Press.

Quade, E. S. (1975). *Analysis for public decisions*. New York: Elsevier.

Rabe, B. G., & Peterson, P. E. (1983). Educational policy implementation: Are block grant proposals based on out of date research? *Issues in Education, 1*(1), 1–29.

Rein, M. (1983). Value-critical policy analysis. In D. Callahan & B. Jennings (Eds.), *Ethics, the social sciences, and policy analysis*. New York: Plenum.

Rein, M., & White, S. H. (1977, Fall). Can policy research help policy? *The Public Interest*, (44), 119–136.

Report Analysis: Public and Private Schools. (1981). *Harvard Educational Review, 51*(4), 481–545.

Rhoads, S. E. (1985). *The economist's view of the world: Government, markets, and public policy*. New York: Cambridge University Press.

Rivlin, A. M., & Timpane, P. M. (Eds.) (1975). *Planned variation in education: Should we give up or try harder?* Washington, DC: Brookings Institution.

Rothbard, M. N. (1973). *For a new liberty*. New York: Macmillan.

Schultze, C. L. (1977). *The public use of private interest*. Washington, DC: Brookings Institution.

Scribner, J. D. (Ed.) (1977). *The politics of education*. The 76th yearbook of the National Society for the Study of Education. Chicago: University of Chicago Press.

Shotland, R. L., & Mark, M. M. (Eds.) (1985). *Social science and social policy*. Beverly Hills, CA: Sage.

Shulman, L., & Sykes, G. (Eds.) (1983). *Handbook of teaching and policy*. New York: Longman.

Spady, W. G. (1981, April 16). *The fundamental shift from role based to goal based organization and management*. Paper presented at the Annual Meeting of the American Educational Research Association, Los Angeles.

Stebbins, L. B., St. Pierre, R. G., Proper, E. C., Anderson, R. B., & Cerva, T. R. (1977). *Education as experimentation: A planned variation model: Vol. 4-A. An evaluation of Follow Through*. Cambridge, MA: Abt.

Stokey, E., & Zeckhauser, R. (1978). *A primer for policy analysis*. New York: Norton.

Tribe, L. H. (1972, Fall). Policy science: Analysis or ideology? *Philosophy & Public Affairs*, *2*(1), 55–110.

Tugend, A. (1985, November 20). Panelist defends desegregation study: Calls key researcher's actions 'unethical.' *Education Week*, p. 8.

Tyack, D., & Hansot, E. (1984). Hard times, then and now: Public schools in the 1930s and 1980s. *Harvard Educational Review*, *54*(1), 33–66.

van Geel, T. (1976). *Authority to control the school program*. Lexington, MA: Heath.

Warwick, D. P., & Pettigrew, T. F. (1983). Toward ethical guidelines for social science research in public policy. In D. Callahan & B. Jennings (Eds.), *Ethics, the social sciences, and policy analysis*. New York: Plenum.

Weatherley, R. (1979). *Reforming special education: Policy implementation from state level to street level*. Cambridge, MA: MIT Press.

Weatherley, R., & Lipsky, M. (1977) Street-level bureaucrats and institutional innovation: Implementing special-education reform. *Harvard Educational Review*, *47*(2) 171–197.

Weick, K. E. (1976). Educational organizations as loosely coupled systems. *Administrative Science Quarterly*, *21*, 1–19.

Weiss, C. H. (1977). Research for policy's sake: The enlightenment function of social research. *Policy Analysis*, *3*(4), 531–545.

White, M. J. (1983). Policy analysis and management science. In S. S. Nagel (Ed.), *Encyclopedia of policy studies*. New York: Marcel Dekker.

Wildavsky, A. (1976). The strategic retreat on objectives. *Policy Analysis*, *2*(3), 499–526.

Wildavsky, A. (1979). *Speaking truth to power: The art and craft of policy analysis*. Boston: Little, Brown.

Wildavsky, A. (1985, Spring). The once and future school of public policy. *The Public Interest* (79), 25–41.

Williams, W. (1980). *The implementation perspective*. Berkeley, CA: University of California Press.

Wilson, J. Q. (1973, Winter). On Pettigrew and Armor: An afterword. *The Public Interest*, (30), 132–134.

Wilson, J. Q. (1981, Summer). "Policy intellectuals" and public policy. *The Public Interest*, (64), 31–46.

Wirt, F. M., & Kirst, M. W. (1982). *Schools in conflict*. Berkeley, CA: McCutchan.

Wise, A. E. (1979). *Legislated learning: The bureaucratization of the American classroom*. Berkeley, CA: University of California Press.

Wolf, C., Jr. (1979, Spring). A theory of non-market failures. *The Public Interest*, (55), 114–133.

Yeakey, C. C. (1983). Emerging policy research in educational research and decisionmaking. In E. W. Gordon (Ed.), *Review of Research in Education* (Vol. 10, pp. 255–301). Washington, DC. American Educational Research Association.

Zeigler, L. H., & Jennings, M. K. (1974). *Governing American schools*. North Scituate, MA: Duxbury.

Zeigler, L. H., Kehoe, E., & Reisman, J. (1985). *City managers and school superintendents: Response to community conflict*. New York: Praeger.

PART
V
Special Topics

CHAPTER 26

The Technical Tools of Decision Making

James F. McNamara and Grace B. Chisolm[1]

This chapter provides a critical review of the application of the technical tools of decision making in educational organizations. It is divided into three parts: (a) one on theory, with appropriate references to the decision sciences as an interdisciplinary framework for portraying the development of the decision tools over the past 30 years; (b) the second on applications of decision tools in educational organizations; and (c) the third on forecasts that elaborate both projected technological advances in the decision sciences and potential applications of these new decision technologies in educational organizations.

Three traditional frame works reflect different perspectives on the application of decision-making tools in educational organizations. One framework identifies educational problems and provides a match between them and solution strategies in a world defined by the decision technicians (Hentschke, 1975; Van Dusseldorp, Richardson & Foley, 1971). Another provides a match between problems and solution strategies that have been reported as successful in a world in which the manager (superintendent, principal, or teacher) and technician (institutional researcher, planner, or curriculum specialist) share decision-making responsibilities (Schmuck & Miles, 1972). The third (and most popular) framework considers educational problems as realistic opportunities for applying decision-making tools in a world in which the manager both defines and decides. This perspective often assumes that the

manager and technician seldom really think along the same lines. It is frequently associated with the view that managers can obtain results with only a modicum of technical stimulation and assistance (Howard & Brainard, 1975; Wolcott, 1977).

Unfortunately, not all applications of decision tools fit neatly into any one of these frameworks, for several possible reasons. First, problems in organizational decision systems are not always well defined (Mitroff & Turoff, 1971). Simon (1977) argues that organizational problems do not fit into distinct categories but fall on a continuum ranging from well-defined problems (explicit goals or defined objectives can be given to guide inquiry) to ill-defined problems (unclear goals or opposing objectives are encountered). Second, the match between problems and solution strategies is usually complex (Steward & Garson, 1983). A simplistic one-to-one correspondence between a problem and a solution strategy is much more likely to be observed in textbooks and training materials than in the field (Swan, 1983). Third, accurate explanations of organizational decision systems frequently require users to move beyond the traditional role distinction between decision maker and decision technician. Applications of administrative and planning technologies not only involve managers and decision technicians but also often require clients to define organizational goals and, in some cases, to designate preferences and choices regarding organizational activities (Lindblom & Cohen, 1979). Fourth, analytic techniques used in decision making frequently have a larger payoff than is often recognized. A substantial portion of this payoff may be overlooked because observers

Consultant/reviewers: William G. Cunningham, Old Dominion University; and Sanford Temkin, Rider College

limit themselves to searching for dramatic and direct payoffs rather than subtle and diffuse outcomes, or they rely on time frames that are too short for documenting successful applications (Mandell, 1984). Finally, it is important to recognize that a decision tool as a free-standing entity cannot significantly contribute to decision making. Most decision theorists (Lindblom & Cohen, 1979 Quade, 1975) believe a decision tool's value depends largely on the extent that it can be "blended" with other problem-solving mechanisms such as judgment and personal knowledge.

With these considerations and constraints in mind, we finally chose a three-part design that begins with an elaboration of relevant theoretical frameworks, moves into a comprehensive review of applications, and concludes with forecasts that suggest potentially new applications for decision techniques in educational organizations. Two questions are used to link the three parts: (a) What knowledge domains have directly influenced the formation of the decision sciences and (b) how are the decision sciences likely to influence future theoretical perspectives and practical applications of decision tools in educational administration?

DECISION SCIENCES

The contemporary influence of the mathematical sciences and the social-systems sciences in leading graduate professional schools of management, business, urban affairs, public policy, and administrative sciences is often observed in an interdisciplinary field called the decision sciences. This interdisciplinary field was created in 1968 by people interested in the application of mathematical and behavioral methods to problems in organizational decision systems. In 1968, a group of 30 faculty members representing applied mathematics and organizational behavior in 25 schools from across the United States met in Atlanta to establish the American Institute of Decision Sciences (AIDS), a nonprofit national education association to encourage interdisciplinary communication. The quarterly journal *Decision Sciences*, first published by AIDS in 1970, is the major publication for the more than 4,500 academicians and practitioners now involved in the discipline.

A recent curriculum report on professional degree programs (AIDS, 1976) offers the following description: Decision sciences utilize mathematical, statistical, behavioral and computer sciences to model decision processes in goal-seeking (but not necessarily profit-making) organizations. This scientific approach to the resolution of complex organizational problems cuts

across traditional disciplinary boundaries and synthesizes relevant portions of each discipline to develop useful models of decisions.

The formation of the decision sciences was greatly influenced by two interdisciplinary movements of the 1960s: (a) efforts of the National Academy of Sciences (NAS) (1968, 1969) to unify the basic and applied mathematical disciplines and (b) efforts among organizational theorists to incorporate systems theory in the study of organizational behavior (Seiler, 1967).

Both efforts found their way into educational administration's decision-making literature. Both efforts provided frameworks that guided the development of specific decision technologies and tools. Both frameworks continue to be used within the decision sciences literature. Against this background, the theory part of the review here begins with a brief description of the two interdisciplinary efforts, moves next to an elaboration of the professional preparation requirements and research domains of the decision sciences, and concludes with a treatment of two topics that provide useful perspectives for reviewing developmental efforts to model organizational decision processes.

Mathematical Sciences

To present a clear picture of the contemporary state of both research and education in mathematics and related disciplines, the NAS (1968) report provides three useful perspectives: (a) It classifies the mathematical disciplines as either basic or applied; (b) it provides the term *mathematical sciences* to suggest that maintaining strong and continuous interactions between the applied and basic mathematical disciplines is essential; and (c) it documents the use of mathematical methods in several disciplines outside the mathematical sciences to bring to the attention of professional mathematicians, scientists, and scientifically informed laypersons the fact that in 1968 the instances of use were steadily increasing and, more important, that the boundary lines between mathematical sciences and "sciences that use mathematics" were often difficult to draw.

Core Mathematics
The NAS's classification declares that the foundation of all mathematical activity incorporates the central core of mathematics—the traditional disciplines of logic, number theory, algebra, geometry, and analysis that have been the domains of the so-called pure mathematician.

Applied Mathematical Sciences
The other category, applied mathematical sciences,

includes four major areas that have particularly direct and important relationships with other sciences and technologies. These are computer science, statistics, operations research, and physical mathematics (usually referenced as classical applied mathematics).

Both computer science and statistics have dual sources of identity and intellectual force. In each case, only one source is mathematical. Accordingly the NAS (1968) report suggests the more accurate term *partly mathematical sciences*, which NAS sometimes uses to recognize the individual characteristics of these two fields and their strong extramathematical components.

Computer science is both mathematical and something else. It cannot exist without mathematics; however, it would be utterly unproductive without the computer. Statistics could not operate without mathematics, especially mathematical theory of probability. Equally, it could not exist without an appropriate theoretical framework to guide interpretation and inference. Like computer science, statistics is both mathematical and something else. The NAS report (1968, Chap. 5) supplies a revealing statement on just what "something else" implies: "Just as it's still a methodological science, a computational science, and a behavioral science, statistics continues to be a mathematical science" (p. 91). The extramathematical component of statistics is well defined in the *International Encyclopedia of Social Sciences* treatments of probability (DeFinetti, 1966; Noether, 1966) and statistics (Kendall, 1966; Kruskal, 1966).

Specialized Areas of Application

Along with the four main applied mathematical sciences, the NAS report (1968) acknowledges that there are still newer small specialized areas of application where no self-identified community of mathematical scientists yet exists. Specialized areas cited in the report include mathematical biology, mathematical psychology, mathematical economics, and mathematical linguistics. A supplementary volume (NAS, 1969) offers 22 essays that document achievements, traditions, and prospects in a rich variety of special areas of application. More recent applications in Steen (1978) illustrate clearly how the mathematical sciences are penetrating new fields of knowledge.

Mathematical Sciences in Educational Administration

Bruno and Fox (1973) documented the penetration of the mathematical sciences into the educational administration graduate programs of 16 major research universities. Their review suggests that these programs treat the mathematical sciences as an interdisciplinary framework for examining basic decision-making skills (communication skills, computational skills, computer literacy skills, analytical skills, and research skills). Most quantitative tools and techniques addressed in these programs can be linked directly to three applied mathematical sciences: operations research, statistics, and computer science.

McNamara (1981) recommends that educational administration follow the trend in leading graduate professional schools toward using the decision sciences as an instrument to extend significantly the contemporary influences of the mathematical sciences. He elaborates four major reasons: (a) Decision sciences extend the theoretical and research efforts of the mathematical social sciences; (b) in addition to the treatment of standard statistical methods used in the design and analysis of research data, decision sciences include an emphasis on the use of statistics and other mathematical disciplines in decision modeling; (c) decision sciences focus on the role of automated information systems in governing the behavior of an organization; and (d) professional education programs in decision sciences traditionally concentrate on the preparation of general managers who can master the decision-aiding tools associated with advanced information-processing equipment. Other proposals to link mathematical sciences with decision making in educational organizations include Alkin and Bruno (1970), Anderson (1970), Bessent (1971), Bessent and Bessent (1980), Brooks (1970), Bruno (1970, 1976), Cope (1976, 1979), Correa (1969, 1975), Handy and Hussain (1969), Hentschke (1975), McNamara (1972a, 1972b, 1979) and Van Dusseldorp et al. (1971). It is important to note that in the 1970s these advocates focused almost exclusively on the contributions of operations research, just one of the four applied mathematical sciences.

Systems Analysis in Organizational Behavior

The second developmental area that contributed to the formation of the decision sciences arose through the efforts of organizational theorists in the 1960s to incorporate systems analysis in organizational behavior. These efforts are captured in Seiler (1967), who suggested that organizational behavior could be studied productively by contrasting two customs of thought— the habit of thinking in "single-cause" terms and the habit of explaining behavior in "multiple-cause" terms. This analysis led to the position that interdependent forces underlie behavior and that "thinking systematically" in these terms prevents oversimplication by making understanding of organizational complexity manageable. Next, Seiler (1967) used a systems approach (Churchman, 1968) to construct and test a theoretical framework for diagnosing human behavior in organizations.

Modeling Human Behavior in Organizations

Seiler's three-part organization system consists of inputs, actual behavior, and outputs. There are four inputs: (a) human inputs, which include skills, knowledge, ways of behaving, needs, expectations, values, and ways of thinking; (b) technological inputs, which identify the type of technology used by the work group; (c) organizational inputs used in efforts to manage organizational affairs; and (d) social inputs, which produce social structures and norms for organizational members. These inputs influence all aspects of behavior (activities, interactions, and sentiments) and all outputs (levels of production, satisfaction, stress, turnover, and absenteeism). Finally, feedback is characterized as the dynamic process of information flow, within the organizational system, that stimulates system reinforcement or change. In Seiler's framework, the organizational system relates to forces in the environment by means of constraints that move information into the system and choices that are shared with the external environment.

Seiler's research and teaching treats this conceptualization of a formal organization comprised of inputs, behaviors, outputs, and feedback as an open rather than closed system. Seiler (1967) called the system "sociotechnical" to reflect the dynamic and interactive nature of its organizational components.

Problem Solving in Organizations

A primary contribution of systems analysis research to the formation of the decision sciences (as well as to the development of specific technical tools for decision making) was the rethinking of the organizational problem-solving process in terms of a systems framework for examining human behavior in organizations. Rethinking began by first conceiving of problem solving as composed of the following series: (a) awareness of a general issue; (b) collection of information pertinent to the issue; (c) analysis of information; (d) statement of the problem underlying the issue; (e) establishing possible choices of action relating to the problem; (f) selection of choice(s) against goal criteria; (g) implementation of selected choice(s); and (h) collection of information on outcomes of the implementation. Next, Seiler (1967) and his colleagues suggested that in real organizational problem solving, administrators are not free to devote their full attention to the activities of a specific stage, not only because real administrators work simultaneously on many organizational problems but also because any one problem inherently involves simultaneous activity at several of the problem-solving stages. These observations led to advancing the posi-

tion that administrators are constantly moving between the analytical problem-solving steps (a through d and h) and the action-taking steps (e through g). Seiler and like thinkers concluded that administrative problem solving is not a series of finite steps but a series of approximations that has no beginning and no end.

Seiler's theoretical framework elaborates two characteristics that distinguish administrative problem solving from other kinds of problem solving. First, administrative problem solvers can never really escape the confines of the problem. Specifically, administrative problem solvers are constantly entangled in analysis while they are acting and in action while they are analyzing. The second characteristic that confuses the problem-solving series in organizational decision systems is the interdependence of problems, their sources, and their consequences. Seiler's framework assumes that in reality there is no isolated problem on which administrators work. On this characteristic, Seiler notes (1967):

> The problems of a human system organization are part of a system. We call them problems because we feel a need to do something about them, but they are only facts about an organic whole. The problem with the idea of "problem" is that it seems to separate and make independent of the whole system one set of facts about some part or parts of the system. (p. 200)

The final aspect of rethinking organizational problem solving in terms of a systems framework focuses on developing a plan of action (steps e through g). In this part of the series, the administrator must look at all four inputs to organizational behavior. The search for possibilities for action among inputs is a complex undertaking because organizational inputs are so interrelated that almost infinite combinations are possible. In reality, the search is greatly facilitated by the process of analysis.

Once the possible combinations of action choices have been elaborated, all that is left before implementation is choice or decision. Here Seiler notes:

> Though less laborious than any other stage of the entire problem solving process, the decision stage may well turn out to be the most difficult. It involves three activities: (1) measuring available choices against the goals which have been established; (2) assessing the administrator's and the organization's capacity to implement the decision; and (3) actually making the decision by committing oneself to it. (1967, p. 204)

Here it is important to note that the technical tools of decision making are most frequently linked with the measuring and assessing methods associated with steps a and b. However, the wish to model real administrative problem solving and decision making also requires the learning of administrative technologies that help in the creation of decision alternatives (action choices) that maximize the value of all four organizational inputs identified in sociotechnical systems.

Sociotechnical Systems in Educational Administration

Publications in educational administration clearly document the influence of systems thinking in organizational behavior. Unlike the influences of the mathematical sciences, which were restricted primarily to graduate professional training in major research universities, the influences of systems thinking in organizational behavior can be observed in the educational administration literature over the past 30 years. This sociotechnical orientation toward administrative problem solving and organizational decision systems resides in the theoretical literature (Bidwell, 1965, 1979; Griffiths, 1959, 1969, 1979); in graduate professional studies materials (Hoy & Miskel, 1977; Owens, 1970; Silver, 1983); and in handbooks used by practicing administrators (Derr, 1974; Howard & Brainard, 1975; Schmuck & Miles, 1972). More recently, school administrators (Snapp & Davidson, 1982) have advocated using school psychologists to assist in the design of organizational interventions.

However, within educational administration there have been few efforts to integrate the mathematical sciences and organizational behavior. In a 1977 University of Rochester career development seminar on research in educational administration, Willower (1979) noted that most of the statistical and mathematical methods used in operations research to model decision structures lacked an intraorganizational focus. He observed that they were dealing primarily with modeling demographic requirements and resource allocation strategies at regional or state levels. Referring to the *Administrative Science Quarterly* as a model, he asserted that the use of specialized mathematical models to describe decision systems or other features of school organizations was clearly "a promising area for development." On its track record, Willower (1979) stated:

> The extent to which mathematical models have been employed in research that adds to our understanding of school organizations cannot be judged because of the paucity of the work. There is a cheering section, and there has been a fair amount of activity on the planning and practical side. But, as far as research on school organizations is concerned, the picture is one of abundant promise but scant production. (p. 69)

A similar and earlier appeal to explore links between the behavioral and mathematical sciences appears in Farquhar's (1973) interpretative summary of a report by the University Council for Educational Administration Task Force on the Social Sciences and the Preparation of Educational Administrators. Farquhar concludes that the social sciences (specifically social psychology, sociology, anthropology, political science, and economics) constitute only one source of content relevant to educational administration. He recommends the humanities, the "emerging management sciences," and mathematics as other important domains of knowledge for professional preparation programs in educational administration.

Research Domains in the Decision Sciences

Research in decision sciences attempts to integrate a diverse set of related fields that have developed since the early 1960s, primarily in schools of business and management, including (a) traditional management science (a term used interchangeably with operations research) focusing on planning, scheduling and inventory control; (b) the study of information systems, particularly database management and decision support systems; and (c) the psychology of decision processes, with a focus on risk and uncertainty (Wharton School, 1979). Within the diversity, research at the Wharton School, for example, maintains a unifying theme of understanding and improving decision making.

In the Wharton School program these three fields—traditional management science (with its focus on the use of mathematical models), informational systems (with its emphasis on the potential of advanced information processing equipment), and the psychology of decision processes (with its concentration on the theories and models of the social and behavioral sciences)—use the unifying theme to produce the four research domains elaborated in Table 26.1. In the Wharton School model, the first three research domains are also used to structure the instructional program. Core courses are offered in each of these three domains.

Major Phases of the Decision-Making Process

Efforts to model organizational decision systems require a broad view of decision making (Hunt & Magenaw, 1984). On this point Simon (1977) notes that "decision making has to be interpreted broadly—so broadly as to become almost synonymous with managing" (p. 39). His model shows a manager involved in all decision stages, not simply in the act of choice.

Simon divides managerial decision making into four principal phases: (a) intelligence activity, which consists of searching the environment for occasions (problems) calling for decisions; (b) design activity,

Table 26.1 Research Domains in the Decision Sciences

Decision processes. This domain provides new knowledge about how to design better interfaces between humans and machines and how to adapt problem-solving methods to the needs of the decision maker. Research has been concerned with the way individuals and groups collect and use information and how their actions are thereby affected. Both developmental and experimental research methods are used.	*Management sciences.* This domain studies formal models and methods for structuring and solving certain classes of managerial problems. Research has been concerned with the development of quantitative approaches for aiding managerial decision making.
Management information systems. This domain investigates how best to provide information for organizational decision making. Research has been concentrated in the areas of database management, office automation, activity systems, and computer networks.	*Decision support systems.* This domain carries the promise of integrating the foregoing three domains through interactive, computer-based models. Research has been concerned with creating a meaningful dialogue between designers and users of interactive, computer-based systems. Presently being studied is how to design decision-aiding tools for operational and policy-related questions.

NOTE. Based on information in *Decision Sciences at the Wharton School,* 1979, Philadelphia: Department of Decision Sciences, University of Pennsylvania.

which centers on inventing, developing, and analyzing possible courses of action; (c) choice activity, which encompasses the actual selecting of a particular course of action from those available; and (d) review activity, which consists of evaluating past choices.

Each of the technical tools of decision making is designed to provide assistance in one or more of these activities. Copa (1981) argues that decision tools used in educational organizations are most likely to be employed in intelligence and design activities. He suggests five additional relevant issues that should be linked to inquiry on the relevance of the decision sciences: (a) scientific knowledge as supplementing ordinary knowledge (Lindblom & Cohen, 1979); (b) knowledge creep and decision accretion (Weiss, 1980); (c) combining comprehensive and incremental decision making (Etzioni, 1967; Schmidtlein, 1981); (d) redirection in operations research (Ackoff, 1979a, 1979b); and (e) the logical empirical approach as only one way of knowing (Fay, 1977). Using these theoretical frameworks, Copa concludes that the decision-science tools emerging from statistics, operations research, and computer science are probably more useful as models for analysts of thinking processes than for producers of decisions.

For educational administrators who wish to explore possibilities for the application of decision tools in planning, W. G. Cunningham (1982) has identified an important question that often arises in early explorations: How do we distinguish between the decision-making process (Simon, 1977) and the problem-solving process (Ackoff, 1978)? In response W. G. Cunningham (1982) notes:

> Problem solving is much broader than either planning or decision making. Problem solving is a tool that is used any time you want to change something. Problem solving becomes planning when it is future oriented and it becomes planning and decision making when there is a pressure to make a future-oriented decision. Decision making actually is a step that requires all the other steps in order to be effective. In this way, decision making is

considered a subset of problem solving, with decision making dealing primarily with evaluation and choice from a set of alternatives, and problem solving dealing with the whole process of problem formulation, alternative generation, and information processing, and culminating in implementing and evaluating final choices. (p. 172).

Types of Decisions

To investigate how administrators make decisions now and how they will make decisions in the future, Simon (1977) has distinguished two polar types of decisions, which he calls programmed and nonprogrammed. He suggests that the types are not really distinct but rather constitute a classification continuum, with programmed decisions at one end and nonprogrammed decisions at the other end. He also notes that the terms *well-structured* and *ill-structured* are often substituted for programmed and nonprogrammed.

In Simon's (1977) classification scheme, programmed decisions are repetitive and routine, with a definite solution strategy already worked out for handling them: for example, when to reorder in an automated inventory system or where to place a person on a salary schedule. Nonprogrammed decisions are novel, often because the problem has not arisen before, and they have no definite solution strategy already worked out. Simon offers the example of a company's decision to establish operations in a nation where it has not operated before. He claims the real utility in distinguishing between programmed and nonprogrammed decisions is that different decision tools and techniques are used to generate solution strategies. Coupling these two decision types with a distinction between traditional and modern decision-making tools results in a fourfold classification system.

Traditional Decision-Making Tools

According to Simon (1977), traditional tools may be used for both programmed and nonprogrammed decisions. Traditional tools in human organizations include those used for a very long time. For programmed decisions, the tools divide into three categories: (a) habits, (b) clerical routines or standard operating procedures; and (c) organizational structures including common expectations, a system of subgoals, and well-defined information channels. For nonprogrammed decisions, there are also three categories: (a) judgment, intuition, and creativity; (b) rules of thumb; and (c) selection and training of executives.

Modern Decision-Making Tools

Simon (1977) identifies as modern techniques decision tools that have appeared since World War II. Modern tools for programmed decisions come from the applied mathematical sciences of operations research, statistics, and computer science (Ackoff & Rivett, 1962). Two principal journals, *Operations Research* and *Management Science*, reflect these sciences' continuous progress in using mathematical models and digital computers to formulate management decision rules and search strategies that move intuitive or rule-of-thumb decisions into the domain of programmed decisions. These quantitative procedures are treated extensively in the Management Sciences section.

Although the modern tools of the management sciences have contributed significantly to expanding the domain of programmed decisions, Simon (1977) believes these developments still leave untouched a major part of managerial decision making, the nonprogrammed area. Modern decision tools for nonprogrammed decisions have come and will continue to come from heuristic problem-solving techniques applied to two domains of organizational activity: training human decision makers and constructing heuristic computer programs.

Unlike recursive and mechanical algorithms, heuristics represent a point of view in design, not a precise method. Heuristic searches most often yield "good" rather than optimal solutions (Ackoff, 1962). In heuristic problem solving, the objective of program writing is to supplement natural intelligence with artificial intelligence (Simon, 1969). In management decision making, heuristic problem solving brings the computer as problem-solving aide to the manager. Some of these heuristic problem-solving techniques are treated in the Social Systems Sciences section.

Copa (1981) has suggested that the links between contemporary decision-science techniques and the types of decisions in Simon's classification are not always clear. For example, Copa suggests that the computer sciences, with emphasis on management information systems, can serve as an important source of information for the whole programmed to nonprogrammed

continuum of decisions. More important, he believes the broad conceptualization of decision sciences, which draw technologies from the mathematical sciences, information sciences, organizational behavior, and cybernetics, appears to move a considerable distance toward "waylaying" many of the limitations normally associated with the application of quantitative methods in human problem solving (Berlinski, 1976; Strauch, 1976; Tufte, 1970) and behavioral sciences research (Brown, 1967, Charlesworth, 1963; Kay, 1971).

Summary

The decision sciences represent an interdisciplinary framework for portraying the development of the decision tools over the past 30 years. The decision sciences use mathematical, statistical, behavioral, and computer sciences to model decision processes in goal-seeking (but not necessarily profit-making) organizations. Two interdisciplinary movements of the 1960s greatly influenced the development of the decision sciences: first, the efforts of the National Academy of Sciences to unify the basic and applied mathematical disciplines; second, efforts among organizational theorists to incorporate systems theory in the study of organizational behavior. Similar activities within educational administration were identified. The professional preparation requirements and research domains of the decision sciences were identified. The case of the Wharton School illustrates how three diverse instructional domains (traditional management science, information systems, and the psychology of decision process) were linked with interactive computer-based models to produce four research domains that guide inquiries on understanding and improving decision making. Finally, use of two of Simon's classification systems provided valuable insight for modeling decision systems. The first system divided decision making into four major phases, and the second classified management decisions as either programmed (well-structured) or nonprogrammed (ill-structured). With this theoretical framework in place, the review now turns to the application of decision tools in educational organizations.

DECISION TECHNOLOGIES

Simon (1977) suggests that technology is knowledge, not only of how to make things but also of how to do things. Knowledge broadens the range of available alternatives. Advances in technology provide knowledge needed to improve our capacity for making effective managerial and public policy decisions. Accordingly, decision technologies represent knowledge of how to improve capacity to make more effective managerial and public policy decisions. These technologies can be used to improve all four principal phases of decision making: (a) finding occasions for making a decision; (b) finding possible courses of action; (c) choosing among courses of action; and (d) evaluating past choices.

The technical tools of decision making are systematic procedures and techniques used to complete tasks associated with one or more of the major phases of decision making. Although not all decision technologies and the tools associated with them are based on science, most modern decision technologies depend heavily on science. Moreover, the invention and discovery of most decision tools can be traced and linked to well-recognized knowledge domains: (a) policy sciences, (b) management sciences, (c) computer and information sciences (d) behavioral sciences, and (e) social systems sciences. Each domain is considered in order.

The treatment of each domain seeks answers to seven questions: (a) What are the historical links between a knowledge domain and the decision tools it generates? (b) What basic concepts are associated with these tools? (c) What are the most likely applications of these decision tools in educational organizations? (d) What demands do these tools place on would-be users? (e) What are the advantages of using these decision tools in educational organizations? (f) What are the limitations of and objections to these tools? (g) What future is projected for these tools?

Two features of the organization of the material that follows deserve mention. First, the actual decision tools selected for review are elaborated in Tables 26.2 through 26.6. Taken collectively, the five tables document the complete two-stage classification system. Stage 1 places each decision tool in the appropriate knowledge domain. Stage 2 further classifies each tool according to the primary decision activity it supports. For example, cost-effectiveness analysis (See Table 26.2) is placed in the policy sciences (Stage 1) and then inserted in the fiscal planning and economic analysis group of decision tools (Stage 2). Second, there are 10 examples, two for each section that demonstrate real-world applications of 10 different decision tools in organizational decision systems. These illustrations have been chosen to represent the variability both within and among the various classifications.

Policy Sciences

Policy sciences or policy studies can be broadly defined as a field of learning devoted to the scientific improvement of policy making. McCall and Weber (1983) conceptualize the policy sciences as an emergent profession drawing pertinent facts, concepts, principles, theories, and methods from many disciplines (especially anthropology, economics, political science, psychology, and sociology) and from a number of related professions (especially law, management, social work, and urban planning).

Cook (1984) argues that policy studies are not associated with any particular methods. Rather, policy studies are characterized by a "catholicity and eclecticism" derived from the large variety of decision-oriented questions they discover and pose. He notes that issues concerning the clients and providers of services are often answered using the tools of survey research or analysis of records; issues of implementation are frequently explored via management audits, on-site observation, archival research, or the use of questionnaires; effectiveness is often examined using econometric techniques; impact analysis and program evaluation often involve time series studies or quasiexperimental designs; and cost analyses use the methods of accounting and economics. Moreover, Cook suggests that the analyses of the meaning of results can involve Socratic discussions between representatives of a variety of conflicting perspectives or a systematic policy analysis of alternative courses of action.

Although clear boundaries cannot be drawn, the decision tools used in the policy sciences are usually linked to either policy formulation or policy implementation (Nagel, 1983). Policy formulation tools help decision makers better understand the nature, intention, and scope of public policy. Policy implementation tools help decision makers manage public programs and projects (Gilbert, 1984). Nagel (1984) claims policy implementation tools are associated with either policy analysis (taking goals as givens and discussing how they can be best achieved) or program evaluation (taking policies as givens and discussing their effects). He also argues that policy analysis traditionally is seen as a means to evaluate decisions across places and time, whereas program evaluation is more likely to be used to evaluate decisions in a given organization at a particular time. Both policy study domains are used in Table 26.2 to classify nine common decision tools. A third domain, fiscal planning and economic analysis, is added to capture a set of methods and techniques that clearly overlap the two traditional domains.

When they are integrated in an organizational decision system, these tools are sometimes called a systems approach (Alkin & Bruno, 1970; Banghart, 1969; Hoos, 1972; Kaufman, 1970, 1972; Knezevich, 1969b; U.S. General Accounting Office, 1969) or administrative technology (Knezevich, 1969a). The role of these decision tools in educational policy formulation and implementation is illustrated in two examples.

Table 26.2   Decision Tools in the Policy Sciences

POLICY FORMULATION AND GOAL CLARIFICATION

Management by objectives.   MBO is a system for making an organizational work by providing for its maintenance and orderly growth with clearly delineated goal statements for each person involved in the operation and then measuring what is actually achieved. MBO assigns risks to all responsible leaders and makes their progress dependent on their producing results. It stresses leaders' abilities and achievements rather than their personalities (Odiorne, 1965).

Needs assessment.   Needs assessment is a management procedure that documents measurable differences between what is and what should be. These differences (or needs) are then prioritized, with differences of the highest priority selected for action and resolution (Kaufman & English, 1976).

Public opinion survey.   Public opinion surveys obtain responses to uniform questions from a sample deemed to be representative of a group, or universe, of people (Hennessy, 1981). Survey techniques can be desinged to gather retrospective, concurrent, or projected decision-oriented information (Tull & Albaum, 1973).

FISCAL PLANNING AND ECONOMIC ANALYSIS

Planning-programming-budgeting system.   PPBS, a comprehensive planning process, includes a program budget as its major component. PPBS attempts to structure a cohesive decision-making procedure in such a way that resources are allocated efficiently to achieve specified objectives. The budget in PPBS is an expression of the operating plan of an organization (Hartley, 1968).

Zero-base budgeting.   ZBB, a planning and budgeting methodology, is termed zero-base because it attempts to reevaluate all programs and expenditures every year. ZBB has two basic steps: (1) developing decision packages that analyze and describe each discrete activity and (2) ranking decision packages in order of importance. Most significantly, ZBB identifies and evaluates different levels of effort (Pyhrr, 1973).

Cost-benefit analysis.   Cost-benefit analysis determines the difference between the present value of benefits and the present value of costs, or the internal rate of return. The alternatives consist of different ways of allocating resources. The decision rules involve maximizing the rate of return to investments or the difference of present benefits over costs (Thomas, 1971).

Cost-effectiveness analysis.   Cost-effectiveness analysis is suitable for problems where the outputs of the system are not priced at the market and the inputs are subject to market prices. Procedures include (1) an objective, (2) alternatives, (3) costs, (4) a model to estimate costs and effectiveness for each alternative, and (5) a decision rule for the choice among alternatives (Thomas, 1971). The essential distinction between cost-benefit and cost-effectiveness analysis is that cost-benefit analysis requires the expression of both costs and benefits in monetary terms (Goldman, 1967; Temkin, 1974).

POLICY ANALYSIS AND PROGRAM EVALUATION

Input-output analysis.   In educational research and evaluation studies, input-output analysis attempts to measure the average impact of some set of inputs (school resources) on some output(s). Input-output studies calculate regression equations on student populations for whom decisions need to be made regarding future resource allocations (Bridge, Judd, & Moock, 1979).

Evaluation models.   Evaluation is a management process used to obtain information on progress toward achieving objectives in order to know whether it is necessary to modify the tasks or the application of resources. A program evaluation must fulfill three criteria: (1) measurable objectives, costs, activities, and intended program outcomes that policy makers have agreed are appropriate; (2) plausible, testable assumptions linking program activities to intended program outcomes and linking program outcomes to program objectives; and (3) motivated, able, authoritative managers of the program (Nay, Scanlon, Schmidt, & Wholey, 1976).

Example 1: Input-Output Analysis in a Public School District

A classic application of an input-output model is an examination by Murnane (1975) of the impact that school resources (inputs) have on the cognitive achievement of 845 black inner-city children (outputs) in public elementary schools in New Haven, Connecticut. Viewing schooling in a production function framework (Bridge et al., 1979) and using linear multiple regression models, Murnane's analysis was directed toward two general resource allocation concerns: (a) the effect of both the classroom as a whole and specific classroom-related variables on the achievement of children and (b) the relationship between teachers' characteristics and their effectiveness in teaching certain subjects or certain types of children. The identification of variables and the specification of relationships among these

variables were summarized in 30 hypotheses that reflected actual resource allocation decisions available to administrators. Murnane's findings strongly supported the hypothesis that significant quality differences among classroom environments exist. The Murnane study exhibits the following desirable characteristics: (a) the individual child was the unit of analysis; (b) longitudinal information on reading and mathematics was employed; (c) detailed information on individual classrooms was matched with student data; (d) on-site interviews were used to frame hypotheses; and (e) hypotheses reflected actual decision alternatives (McNamara, 1979). Although the substantive results of Murnane's input-output analysis are probably of principal interest to decision makers in New Haven schools, his report provides public school administrators with an excellent example of how an exploratory analysis in a single school district might be structured, using mathematical models, to integrate and relate several sources of information likely to rest in different school ledgers, periodic reports, or separate computerized information files.

Example 2: Cost-Benefit Analysis in a Public University
Rivard (1970) used cost-benefit analysis to examine the economic consequences and feasibility of adopting coeducation at Texas A&M University. The university, all-male since 1876, had sparingly admitted daughters of faculty and occasionally female summer students. Rivard used this decision tool as part of a policy analysis in the midst of a debate among students, key administrators, and alumni. Before he began the empirical work, Rivard hypothesized that growth via coeducation would be economically beneficial to the university. In his commensurate analysis (quantitative methods), an estimate was first obtained for the probable interdisciplinary mix of entering students with and without coeducation for the year 1978. Then, these figures were used to estimate both revenues and expenditures with and without coeducation for the year 1978. The results of Rivard's simulation showed that coeducation in 1978 would directly cause expenditures to fall by $822,000 and revenues to fall by $461,000 for a net improvement of $361,000. This net gain was attributed to shifts in the relative size of undergraduate enrollments among the various disciplines. The analysis allayed many administrators' and alumni's fears of financial ruin. In the incommensurate analysis (qualitative methods), Rivard reasoned correctly that Princeton's alumni reaction would be repeated at Texas A&M, with gifts continuing to flow in even if coeducation were adopted. This economic study was supported by a survey of college-bound Texas high school males indicating a preference for coeducational colleges and universities. The composite analysis of all effects indicated that coeducation would be desirable for the university. In 1971, 1 year after Rivard's study, Texas A&M University began to admit women. Fifteen years later, women comprised approximately 40 percent of the student body.

Professional Transactions and Publications
Educational evaluation and policy studies, "socially legitimized" in the 1960s, clearly existed earlier (Cook, 1984; Tyler, 1969). An accurate indicator for the theoretical and technological progress made in educational administration prior to 1960 is documented by Ross (1958), who compiled a source book of the results of more than 150 individual policy studies related to the questions of why and how schools improve. Other early efforts to perfect decision tools within educational ad-

ministration include the theoretical work of Mort and Furno (1960) to develop a model for evaluating the effectiveness of administrative policies and the philosophical analysis of the efficiency movement in public schools from 1900 to 1960 by Callahan (1962).

Cook (1984) argues that the evaluation and policy studies "spawned" in the 1960s were more "systematic" than earlier work. He offers several reasons for the enlargement and sophistication of decision-oriented research (Cronbach & Suppes, 1969): (a) political legitimation through legislative requirements to evaluate; (b) administrative support through funds earmarked for evaluation and through the creation of federal, state, and local offices whose primary mission was evaluation; and (c) academic support through the growth of new evaluation theories and methods, the creation of societies of professional evaluators, and the founding of some training and degree programs.

Since 1960, evaluation and policy studies based on widely acknowledged principles of survey research, experimentation, econometric analysis, and cost-effectiveness research have been used to investigate nearly every aspect of educational organizations. An excellent source to gauge both the methodological and substantive influences of these decision tools over the past three decades in education is the bibliography published by the Rand Corporation (1979). To provide some indication of the administrative support for the potential application of these tools in school systems, Jackowski (1974) and McNamara (1979) examined the 118 large-scale operational research projects completed during the 1975–1976 school year by the Research and Evaluation Division of the Dallas, Texas, Independent School District Department of Research, Evaluation and Information Systems. Their findings not only documented administrative support (a $4.7 million departmental operating budget for the 1975–1976 school year) but also provided evidence that the 28 senior evaluators and 50 additional support staff in this local office had designed innovative policy studies using almost all the decision tools addressed in this review. During the 1960s, 16 training and graduate study programs with a quantitative orientation were initiated in university departments of educational administration (Bruno & Fox, 1973). Unlike the situation in the Dallas school system, almost no direct evidence was found to suggest that innovative applications of decision tools emerged in these departments. This conclusion is consistent with Shutz's (1976) observation that operational research in schools, which he distinguishes from academic research on schools, is typically a school-based rather than university-based activity.

Comprehensive reviews treating the application of decision tools in educational policy and management studies can be found in the education research literature (Burlingame, 1978; Darling-Hammond, Wise, & Pease, 1983; Macdonald and Clark, 1973), the public policy literature (Coombs, 1983; Datta, 1984), and the evaluation literature (Hultin, 1976; Trochim, 1983). These applications, which have been periodically reported in the journals of many different professions (behavioral scientists, public policy analysts, and evaluation specialists) are now the exclusive focus of two recent publications: *Educational Evaluation and Policy Analysis*, a quarterly journal begun in 1979, and *New Directions for Institution Research*, a quarterly monograph series initiated in 1974 to enhance communications between institutional researchers and operations researchers (Adams, 1977; Dressel & Simon, 1976; Mason, 1976; Peterson, 1976; Staman, 1979).

Critical reviews of specific decision tools in Table 26.2 include those on MBO (Alpin & Schoderbeck, 1976; Baldridge & Tierney, 1980; Ford, McLaughlin, & Nixdorf, 1980; Jacques & Ryan, 1978; Kowalski, 1984); on needs assessment models (Hershkowitz, 1976; Lundquist, 1982); on public opinion surveys (Elam, 1984; Schmuck & Runkel, 1985); and on goal clarification strategies (Dizazan, 1982; Kaufman, 1970; Macdonald & Clark, 1973). Reviews in the fiscal planning and economic analysis domain include those on financial planning strategies (Alesch & Dougharty, 1971a, 1971b; Correa, 1969, 1975; Hopkins & Massy, 1981); on PPBS (Haggart, 1972; Hartley, 1968; National Institute of Education, 1973; Weiss, 1973); on zero-base budgeting (Harvey, 1978; Sharples, 1979); on cost-benefit analysis (Rothenberg, 1975; Stromsdorfer & Farkas, 1980); and on cost-effectiveness analysis (Averch, Carroll, Donaldson, Kiesling, & Pincus, 1972; Levin, 1975; Levin & Woo, 1981; Temkin, 1970a, 1970b, 1974). In the policy analysis and evaluation domain, see reviews on input-output analysis (Bridge et al., 1979; Thomas, 1971); on outcome questions (Farley, 1979); and on evaluation models (Hale, 1972; Lueck, 1981; Matthews, 1973; Nevo, 1983).

Limitations and Objections

The recent attention given to the value and utilization of policy studies (Rich & Goldsmith, 1983) raised consciousness about the imperative to move beyond merely acquainting decision makers with basic techniques of economics, statistics, decision theory, and related academic disciplines. The need now is formal methodological training designed to equip managers with the ability to think incisively about complex educational problems and to structure such problems in a manner that highlights the essential elements (Kennedy School of Government, 1979). Hartley (1973) brought this orientation to educational administration when he identified 20 criteria to link the most relevant content of economics with complex, decision-oriented problems in educational organizations. Structuring these decision-oriented problems and designing effective solutions for them can also be greatly enhanced by recognizing five limitations and objections that consistently arise when decision tools are used in educational policy studies.

Problems of Judgments Major decisions are often intuitively shaped, more by values and perceptions than by quantitative analysis. In educational settings, policy analysts are often forced by the rapidity of change, the nature of the problem, and certain political demands to substitute human judgment and hunches for verifiable knowledge (Alkin & Bruno, 1970). Some commentators also claim that an exclusively analytical approach leads to a dehumanized philosophy inappropriate to the "service-oriented" sector of education (Alpin & Schoderbeck, 1976; McConkey, 1973).

Problems of Operationalization It is difficult to operationalize the decision tools in educational policy studies due to (a) philosophical attitudes toward measurement in the social sciences, (b) lack of power to force compliance, (c) problems of accountability, (d) inability to reward performance monetarily (Hoos, 1972), (e) realities of the political process, and (f) education's dependence on resource allocations (McGivney & Bowles, 1972). Moreover, operationalization of these tools requires much time, skill, money, and sophisticated data-processing capabilities.

Problems of Measuring Objectives The problem of precise quantification of social and political objectives (McGivney & Bowles, 1972) makes the analytic approach in educational settings difficult. If quantitative precision is demanded, it is often gained by reducing the scope of what is analyzed; as a result, the major problems remain outside the analysis (Peters & Waterman, 1982). This difficulty with the identification, measurement, and articulation of objectives contributes to the expectation that many areas generally considered as outputs and functions of the school are not yet measurable.

Problems of Incomplete Inquiries Limitations of time and money create sharp constraints on the conduct of an inquiry. It is often impossible for an educational decision maker to have access to all potentially relevant information. The political, sociological, and psychological environs introduce ever-changing variables that outdate original data and goals. Therefore, the decision tools can only attempt to indicate potential decisions. The ultimate decision depends on the judgment and intuition of the decision maker (Engel & Achola, 1983).

Problems of Predicting the Future Many policy decision tools frequently rely on data about past occurrences. When these tools are used for predicting the future, the resulting predictions are valid only if the relationships between input and output are the same as in the past—assuming that the future can ever be predicted from the past. More important, Mann (1975) suggested that analysts often overlook the true value of prediction because they fail to distinguish between two types of prediction: (a) consequential prediction, which asks what will be the consequences if things continue as they are now, and (b) optimal prediction, which almost completely reverses that procedure by asking what would need to be done to attain the most desirable futures.

Beyond the issue of specific limitations exists the reality of the refinement and further development of specific decision tools. For example, PPBS, used extensively in the 1960s (Schick, 1973), was replaced in the 1970s by ZBB, a decision tool with some of the same purposes and characteristics as PPBS, especially when applied to academic and institutional support services (Hopkins & Massy, 1981). Although each of the other decision tools cited in Table 26.2 has also experienced numerous modifications and improvements over the past two decades, none of them are currently obsolete, nor have they received a "death notice," as Schick (1973) suggested was the case for PPBS.

Future Directions

A number of trends in the development of policy studies methods cut across the more specific techniques that maximize benefits or achieve a given set of goals under various constraints and conditions. Nagel's (1983, Chap. 4) review of the literature on policy evaluation methods described nine general trends for the immediate future.

Unique Methodology Policy evaluation methods have been building on business analysis and operations research, but policy studies are developing their own methodologies. With the focus on public-sector analysis, the basic business principle of maximizing income minus expenses gets converted to benefits minus costs. This means designing methods for summing benefits and costs in such a way that benefits are weighted to take into consideration (a) their normative importance relative to the costs and (b) the differences in the measurement units used. Policy analysis also depends more on statistical inputs and less on accounting inputs. Policy analysis is more sensitive to the reactions of the people affected by the policies. This condition may require considering special psychological and political constraints as well as the more traditional economic ones.

Emphasis on Optimization Policy analysts have tradi-

tionally taken policies as givens in attempting to determine their effects, especially effects on the intended goals. More recently, there is a trend toward taking goals as givens and then attempting to determine what policies will maximize or optimize these goals. The traditional approach is associated more with program evaluation in psychology and sociology. The contemporary approach is associated more with optimization analysis in economics and operations research.

Axiological Orientation Policy analysts are becoming more sensitive to social values, with more questioning of goals when analyzing alternative policies. Many policy studies are beginning to emphasize the analysis of goals rather than, or in addition to, the achievement of goals. Goals are likely to be examined using survey research to detect to what extent they are supported, using relational analysis to reveal how achieving them would affect higher values, or using philosophical analysis to determine how they fit into more general philosophical systems.

Proactive Posture Policy evaluation methods are becoming increasingly proactive or preadoptive (not waiting for policies to be precisely formulated before they are evaluated) rather than reactive or postadoptive. Accordingly, there is an increasing trend toward using preadoptive projections or deductive modeling rather than just postadoptive, before-and-after analysis.

Interdisciplinary Perspectives Policy evaluation methods are becoming increasingly interdisciplinary. As a result, there is an increasing synthesis of statistical methods and deductive mathematical models.

Using Valid but Simpler Methods Policy evaluation is developing increased precision in its methods, but at the same time it is increasingly recognizing that simple methods may be all that is necessary for many policy problems. (See Nagel, 1982.)

Emphasis on Feasibility Policy evaluation methods are becoming increasingly sophisticated with regard to considering political and administrative feasibility. This development reflects the growing role of political science and public administration in policy evaluation.

Increased Utilization Systematic policy analysis is being used increasingly in government at the federal, state, and local levels and in the executive, legislative, and judicial branches. That utilization reflects an increased sensitivity among policy analysts to dealing with decision tools that require actual data, not just abstractions. (See Gilbert, 1984.)

New Professional Institutions There is substantial growth occurring in policy evaluation training programs, research centers, funding sources, publishing outlets, scholarly associations, and other policy evaluation institutions.

Researchers and practitioners who wish to monitor the continuous development of new and innovative tools within the policy sciences, are strongly encouraged to track four new journals in the field: *Policy Analysis*, which is primarily concerned with the methodology of policy studies and economic reasoning in program evaluation; *Policy Sciences*, which also deals with methodology but emphasizes operations research and management science; *The Public Interest*, which is primarily concerned with substance and values; and *Policy Studies Journal*, which tries to combine substance and method.

Management Sciences

The management sciences develop quantitative approaches to management (Levin, Kirkpatrick, & Rubin, 1982). In the United States these sciences were labeled operations research in an effort to capitalize on the success of military operations research during World War II (Ackoff & Rivett, 1963; Shellard, 1982). By the mid-1980s, operations research had come to refer to a set of formal models and methods for structuring and studying certain classes of managerial problems. (See Starr & Miller, 1960, and Thierauf & Grosse, 1970, for milestone statements.)

Models and Methods of Operations Research.

Although experimentation lies at the heart of scientific method, Ackoff (1968) argues that organizations can never be brought into the laboratory, and only infrequently can they be manipulated enough in their natural environment to yield true experiments. Consequently, operations researchers find themselves in much the same position as astronomers, and they solve their problem in an identical manner. If astronomers cannot manipulate the system itself, they construct a representation of the system, a model of it they can manipulate. The general form of the operations research model is an equation in which the performance of the system under study, P, is expressed as a function, f, of a set of controlled variables, C, and a set of uncontrolled variables, U. In mathematical form, we have $P = f(C, U)$.

The controlled variables represent the aspects of the system that management can manipulate. These variables are frequently called decision variables because managerial decision making can be conceptualized as assigning values to these variables. The uncontrollable variables represent aspects of the system and its environment that significantly affect the system's performance but are not under the control of management. The performance measure is sometimes called the criterion or objective function because it provides the basis for selecting the "best" or "better" courses of action.

Managerial Problems Addressed in Operations Research

Years of structuring and studying managerial problems have revealed that most of these problems fall into one or a combination of a small number of basic types (Ackoff & Rivett, 1963; Thierauf & Grosse, 1970). Ackoff (1968) has identified eight basic problem types that have been studied extensively. As a result, there is considerable knowledge about how to construct and solve models that are relevant to them. The following brief descriptions indicate their general characteristics.

1. An inventory problem determines the amount of a resource to be acquired or the frequency of acquisition when there is a penalty for having either too much or too little available.

2. An allocation problem determines the allocation of resources to a number of activities where available resources do not permit each activity to be done in the best possible way. The solution will do all (or as many as possible) of the activities in such a way as to achieve the best overall performance, given a criterion for measuring performance.

3. A queuing problem determines the number of service facilities required or how to schedule arrival of clients (or tasks) at service facilities to minimize losses from idle facilities or waiting or turned-away clients (or tasks).

4. A sequencing problem determines the order in which a set of tasks should be performed in a multistage operation to minimize both costs associated with performance of all tasks and delays in completing them.

5. A routing problem determines the path through a network of locations that (a) is shortest (or longest), (b) has maximum (or minimum) capacity, or (c) is least (or most) costly to traverse, subject to identified limitations on the paths.

6. A replacement problem determines when to replace fixed assets (machines and equipment) and inexpensive items (tools and tires) to minimize acquisition, operating, failure, and maintenance costs.

7. A competition problem determines the strategy (or rule) for a manager to use that yields the best results when the outcome of the manager's decision depends in part on the decisions made by others.

8. A search problem determines the amount of resources to employ and how to use them when seeking information to be used for a specific purpose. The solution minimizes the costs associated with the search and with the errors that can result from the use of incorrect information.

Successful efforts to link mathematical models and computers have produced significant extensions for

Ackoff's (1968) initial classification. This can be seen in the 13 × 14 matrix classification of major operations research models presented in Thierauf (1975). Additional insights can be found in White's (1983) treatment of problems addressed in the application of operations research in public administration.

Mathematical Models in Operations Research

Optimizing models and simulation models are used to solve operations research problems. When an optimization model is properly used, it yields the best alternative according to the input criteria for performance. Simulation models are classified as descriptive rather than optimizing because they usually do not attempt to select the best alternative but rather to describe the choices present and some of their consequences.

Table 26.3 uses this distinction to identify and classify six of the most common mathematical models (decision tools) employed in operations research. Optimizing models are represented by three general mathematical programming techniques that are used to maximize (or minimize) various objective functions.

Table 26.3   Decision Tools in the Management Sciences

Mathematical programming is a term applied to certain mathematical techniques designed to solve the problem of finding the maximum or minimum of a function (called the objective function) subject to several constraints that are usually expressed as inequalities (called the constraint set). In operations research, these techniques are classified as optimization models because they attempt to reach an optimal solution when presented with alternatives (Ackoff, 1962).

Linear programming.   The term refers to the fact that both the objective function and the inequalities in this optimization model are linear. Solutions for this model are nonzero values of the independent variables, the $x(j)$ entries below (Thierauf & Grosse, 1970).

Linear programming format.   One of the first formulations of a linear programming problem was the diet problem: Find the cheapest diet that satisfies prescribed nutritional requirements (Quant, 1966). Suppose there are n foods whose prices are $p(1)$, $p(2), \ldots, p(n)$, and m nutrients whose minimum requirements are $b(1), b(2), \ldots, b(m)$. Let $x(1), x(2), \ldots, x(n)$ be the amount of each food in the diet, and let $a(i, j)$ be the amount of the ith nutrient in the jth food. Then the diet problem in mathematical programming form is to minimize

$$\sum_{j=1}^{n} p(j)\, x(j),$$

subject to

$$\sum_{j=1}^{n} a(i, j)\, x(j) \geq b(i), \qquad i = 1, 2, \ldots, m;$$
$$x(j) \geq 0, \qquad j = 1, 2, \ldots, n.$$

Discrete (integer) programming.   This is a linear programming model where the solution is a set of $x(i)$ values that are all integers. Integer programming problems arise when solutions (decision alternatives) cannot be fractional (noninteger), such as the selection of school sites or the assignment of students to classrooms (Driebeck, 1969).

Dynamic programming.   This technique applies optimization models to solve problems in which decision can be represented as occurring sequentially (Nemhauser, 1966).

Computer simulation refers to mathematical techniques for analyzing the behavior of a system by computing its time path for initial conditions and given parameter values. The computation is said to "simulate" the system because it moves forward step by step with the movement of the system it is describing (Newell & Simon, 1966). In operations research, simulation techniques are classified as descriptive because they usually attempt only to describe the choices present (Adlemann, 1966; Hermann, 1966).

Queuing model.   This is a simulation technique concerned with random arrivals at a servicing or processing facility of limited capacity (Stokey & Zeckhauser, 1978). Sometimes referred to as waiting line theory, this model allows a decision maker to determine the best number of personnel or facilities necessary to service customers who arrive at some random rate when considering the cost of services and the cost of waiting or congestion (Thierauf & Grosse, 1970).

Markov Chain model.   This model reflects a chance process having the special property that one can predict its future just as accurately from knowledge of the present state of affairs as from a knowledge of the present together with the entire past history (Billingsley, 1966). In operations research, this simulation model is often used to explore the consequences of marketing strategies (Levin & Kirkpatrick, 1975).

Monte Carlo method.   This is a simulation technique that uses random numbers to study complex decision processes and abstract theories (Bender, 1978). In essence, a hypothetical population is sampled to estimate how the real population can be expected to behave (Muller, 1966).

OTHER MATHEMATICAL MODELS

Program evaluation review technique (PERT).   This is a planning and control technique that uses a network model for scheduling and budgeting in order to accomplish a predetermined objective (Handy & Hussain, 1969).

Data envelopment analysis.   This is an evaluation and control technique that develops measures of relative efficiency of different operating units by reference to data on their past performance (Bessent, Bessent, Charnes, Cooper, & Thorogood, 1983).

Simulation models are represented by three general mathematical techniques that use probability theory to derive experimental data of interest. A third category in Table 26.3 refers to two additional operations research tools that have had a significant impact on educational managers and the variety of organizational decision systems they manage. The role of these two decision tools in educational organizations is illustrated below.

Example 3: Integer Programming in a Public School District

Swersey and Ballard (1984) have used integer programming techniques to model the two components of the school busing problem—routing and scheduling. In mathematical programming terms, the objective function is used to find the fewest buses needed to cover all the routes while meeting three general logistics constraints: (a) assigning a bus to each route, (b) picking up the students, and (c) arriving at the school within a specific time window. Applying these techniques to actual data from New Haven, Connecticut, for two different academic years, Swersey and Ballard found that the methods reduced the number of buses needed by about 25 percent compared to the manual solutions developed by the New Haven school bus scheduler.

Example 4: Computer Simulation in a Public School District

Confronted with the problem of what to do about declining enrollments and declining revenues in the Unit Four School District in Champaign, Illinois, Yeager (1979) designed and implemented a computer simulation to help school board members explore consequences of closing different schools. Three decision criteria were developed for the model: (a) a convenience criterion that minimized the amount of discomfort caused by sending students to a new school; (b) a geographic criterion that minimized the impact of the school closing upon the community; and (c) a facilities criterion that would close the building most in need of repair and least able to be adapted for future requirements. There were two steps in using the computer model. First, the users specified a range of decision parameters that described how they would go about closing schools. Second, they examined the output (tables, graphs, and maps) to determine the effects of their decision. Each user scenario (output) was stored in the computer. Consistent with the intent of computer simulation models to experiment (learn about options) rather than decide (select a specific alternate), Yeager indicated that the primary benefit of this decision tool was to help clarify and debate assumptions held by

school board members and the administration. He noted that an additional value of the simulation experiment was to provide a way for the public to become aware of the complex issues the school board faced.

Professional Transactions

Magee (1973) suggests that the management sciences have passed through three distinct phases, as outlined below.

The Primitive Phase (1941 to 1960) In the primitive phase, operations researchers and other organizational problem solvers were interested in practical operational problems, which were typically well defined and capable of being handled by the less-sophisticated computers available then. Professionals in the field tended to come from scientific disciplines such as chemistry, mathematics, and physics. Only a few universities offered formal training in operations research.

The Academic Phase (1960s) In the early 1960s, the number of universities offering programs in operations research grew over 500 percent. Magee (1973) notes that in this phase people experienced in operations research began to be found at high corporate levels in private enterprise. The increasing speed and availability of computers were major contributors to the growth of operations research. Magee suggests that research during the 1960s tended to be more concerned with theory than with finding workable applications. From the practitioner's perspective, the 1960s were humbling, because during this period the real limitations of operations research became evident.

The Maturing Phase (1970s) Magee (1973) views the maturing phase as the time when balance between theory and practice was achieved. He argues that even though evidence of the desirability of such a balance was noted years ago, the real thrust toward practice and applications did not emerge until the 1970s. Magee's assessment of the maturing phase points out (a) a more realistic understanding by both managers and management scientists of what management sciences can and cannot accomplish; (b) more attention given to getting the facts rather than development of abstract techniques; (c) less attention to finding optimal answers and more to developing successively better answers for realistic organizational concerns; and (d) better integration of behavioral and quantitative analysis.

Although there was some interest in initiating a formal specialization in quantitative analysis within educational administration (Bruno 1970, 1976; Bruno & Fox, 1973) and in creating a forum for sharing progress on the application of operations research models in educational organizations (Anderson, 1970; Brooks, 1970; Hopkins, 1971; Keppel, 1969; Mc-

Namara, 1972b; Stoller & Dorfman, 1969; Weitz, 1969), the professional education literature does not provide sufficient evidence of the presence of Magee's three distinct phases in either educational administration or other professional domains identified with educational research and practice. The literature does suggest that most applications of operations research in educational organizations are conducted by management science practitioners not residing in the education community (McNamara, 1971) and, more important, a majority of pertinent articles are published in professional management science journals rather than in professional education publications. For example, an analysis of the 146 journal articles referred to in White's (1985) annotated bibliography on management science applications in academic administration indicated that 79, or 54 percent, were published in professional management science journals and 67, or 46 percent, were published in professional education publications.

Two recent educational administration efforts clearly exhibit characteristics associated with the academic and maturing phases of the management sciences. One represents new directions for organizational decision systems in higher education, and the other illustrates the value of interinstitutional research in public school districts.

Mathematical Models in Higher Education

A number of surveys of mathematical model building in higher education administration are available (Hopkins, 1971, 1979; Hopkins & Schroeder, 1977; Oliver, 1972; Schroeder, 1973; Schroeder & Adams, 1976; White, 1985). One of the most comprehensive is Hopkins and Massy (1981). Their research serves two purposes. First, they provide an accurate and detailed account of how modeling concepts and specific models, and the use of both, actually evolved at Stanford University during the period from 1972 to 1978. Second, they share their progress toward the very ambitious goal of developing a unifying theory of college and university choice. Put briefly, their theoretical efforts are aimed at building a comprehensive management model. Modeling begins by distinguishing different types of planning variables and then proceeds to specify the university's value function, that is, the function representing the entire system of values that planning is intended to maximize. Hopkins and Massy (1981) argue that "planning, to be effective, must be consistent with financial realities, considerations of demand, and the limitations imposed by technology and human behavior." The university planning problem, they say, "resolves itself into one of optimizing an institutional value function subject to a set of constraints" (p. 71).

Hopkins and Massy (1981) have identified six general types of mathematical models that have been applied at Stanford and in other universities:

1. Budget projection models for estimating university resource requirements and the variable costs of programs;

2. production and cost models for establishing faculty staffing patterns and estimating course enrollments;

3. long-range financial equilibrium models for exploring problems associated with budget planning for two or more years in terms of "certainty equivalents," which are viewed as proxies for the future values of the planning variables in questions;

4. financial planning models for searching for long-term budgeting strategies in terms of uncertainty which enters into the models following the specification of certainty equivalents;

5. human resource planning models for investigating problems associated with major categories of human resources, namely faculty, students, and staff; and

6. constrained value optimization models for maximizing an institution's value function subject to constraints placed on the set of primary planning variables.

Hopkins and Massy (1981) offer two recommendations for administrators and management science practitioners. First, they advance these characteristics for a good mathematical model: (a) simplicity, (b) completeness on important issues (c) stability when faced with minor deviations in input assumptions, (d) ease of control, (e) adaptability to new decision alternatives, and (f) ease of communication with the user. Second, they believe academic administrators should never delegate line authority to models or to the management scientists who construct them; rather, these administrators must retain personal responsibility for decision making at all times.

Interinstitutional Research in Public School Districts

In response to the serious decline in the productivity of public education in Texas elementary and secondary schools, some innovative Texas superintendents formed the Educational Productivity Council (EPC) in 1980 to collaborate in developing a management science method for measuring the efficiency of their schools (Bessent, Bessent, Elam, & Long, 1984). This interinstitutional research effort (Peterson, 1976), which has been in operation since 1980, now has a membership of 25 independent school districts dedicated to perfecting a system of quantitative techniques (Bessent & Bessent, 1980) that provide decision-oriented information for different kinds of efficiencies, both program and management. A centralized activity of the EPC is maintained at the University of Texas at Austin, where a small operations research staff extends the theory and methodology, coordinates data collection, develops data codes, performs an annual efficiency analysis, and provides reports to 528 member schools whose total enrollment exceeds 341,800 students (Bessent, Bessent, Clark, & Elam, 1983; Bessent, Bessent, Clark, Elam, & Chan, 1983).

A linear programming solution for each organizational unit in the efficiency assessment (Bessent, Bessent, Charnes, Cooper, & Thorogood, 1983; Bessent et al., 1982) provides basic information for several types of management reports for principals and district administrators. Included in these reports is diagnostic information a principal or superintendent can use to answer the following questions:

1. Principal's Report of Criterion Schools. Which schools, if any, have higher levels of achievement in basic skills but similar levels of discretionary resources and similar pupil characteristics?

2. Principal's Summary of Results Report. What levels of achievement reasonably can be attained given available discretionary resources and pupil characteristics? Which aspects of operations can and should be improved? If resource levels are decreased by budget reductions, what level of achievement can be expected from the "best" schools?

3. Superintendent's District Summary Report. How well are schools in the district meeting productivity goals?

Additional information may be obtained by invoking an interactive computer program (Bessent, Bessent, Clark, Elam, & Chan, 1983) to derive answers for specific managerial and program efficiency questions.

Like any new technology, efficiency analysis in schools has taken time to find its way into administrative practice. The EPC acknowledges that (a) work still remains to be done on a more comprehensive definition of inputs and outputs; (b) the methodology is still not transparent to all users, even the most enthusiastic; and (c) full utilization of the information provided is not yet made by every school administrator. The University of Texas operations research group (Bessent et al., 1984) believes, however, that the outlook is promising. With a decision support system under development, the group anticipates that it will be possible to decentralize the system, making the model and appropriate data bases widely accessible through a network of desktop computers at user sites. This sort of distributed system (see Thierauf, 1978), rather than the EPC's centralized system, enables efficiency analysis to become fully integrated into the management processes of users.

Limitations and Objections

Specific objections to and limitations on the application of quantitative methods in educational organizations (Bruno, 1976; Hopkins, 1971; Hopkins & Massy, 1981; McNamara, 1971, 1972b, 1973; Schroeder, 1973) resemble those elaborated earlier for the application of decision tools in policy studies and in actual organizational decision systems (Ledbetter & Cox, 1977; Magee, 1973; Turban, 1972; Ward, 1974; Watson & Marett, 1979). These limitations and objections have been articulated by both managers (the generalists) and management scientists (the specialists).

Problems from the Manager's Perspective Greene, Newsome, & Jones (1977) asked production executives of a large number of firms to name and weight the major barriers to the successful utilization of quantitative methods. Their survey identified 15 major barriers, listed here in order from most to least important: (a) Benefits of using techniques are not clearly understood by managers; (b) managers lack knowledge of quantitative techniques; (c) managers are not exposed to quantitative techniques early in their training; (d) required data are difficult to quantify; (e) only a small portion of management is trained in the use of quantitative techniques; (f) managers are successful without using quantitative techniques; (g) managers in key positions lack knowledge of quantitative techniques; (h) the cost of developing models and using techniques is too high; (i) the data required in using the techniques are not available; (j) managers are not quantitatively oriented; (k) recent college graduates with quantitative training have not yet attained positions of influence; (l) managers are unwilling or unable to use the computer for decision making; (m) the expense of employing quantitative specialists is too great; (n) senior managers do not encourage the use of quantitative techniques by younger, lower-level managers; and (o) management distrusts or fears the use of these techniques. These data suggest that the most critical barriers deal with lack of knowledge on the part of managers.

Problems from the Management Scientist's Perspective Watson and Marett (1979) asked practitioners in larger organizations to name and rank the major barriers to greater success with quantitative techniques. The top 10 barriers for these specialists are ranked from most to least important: (a) Selling management science techniques to management meets with resistance; (b) neither top nor middle management has the educational background to appreciate management science techniques; (c) good clean data are lacking; (d) there is never time to analyze a real problem using a sophisticated approach; (e) those who need to use the results lack understanding; (f) problems for applications are hard to define; (g) the payoff obtained with unsophisticated methods is adequate; (h) personnel are in short supply; (i) management scientists have poor reputations as problem solvers; and (j) individuals feel threatened by management scientists and their techniques.

A comparison of perspectives clearly indicates that both managers and management scientists see managers' lack of professional education as the major barrier to successful application. Levin, Kirkpatrick, and Rubin (1982) report that only a small percentage of business schools required students to take a course in management science before 1970, when learning opportunities outside formal education were limited as well.

A Problem in the Literature   Another critical limitation for application of quantitative methods, infrequently cited, is the type of reporting in the literature. For example, White (1985) noted in a review of published articles about the application of quantitative methods in academic administration that 83 of 136 (or 61 percent) of the articles included no findings dealing with the actual implementation of their models in a real organizational decision system. To increase the number of published quantitative studies that will adequately address implementation concerns, Temkin and McNamara (1973) elaborated 12 basic behavioral questions to be answered by those who wish to share their actual applications with the profession. The questions anticipated the recommendation of many management scientists (Ackoff, 1979a, 1979b; Hopkins & Massy, 1981; Morris, 1975) who believe the future of the management sciences requires greater attention to planning and participation technologies.

Future Directions

Management scientists such as Levin, Kirkpatrick, and Rubin (1982) and Morris (1975) argue that management science methods have proved themselves in business and government, at least so that there is no longer any excuse for a student to graduate from a university program in business or public administration without being acquanted with both the technical tools of the management sciences and the constraints on their effective use. In light of the recent progress made in applying these tools in educational organizations, McNamara (1981) suggests it is reasonable to extend these two requirements to graduates of educational administration programs.

Two recent reviews of desirable movement in the management sciences are documented in Levin, Kirkpatrick, and Rubin (1982). First, they note that management scientists have been challenged to direct their efforts at the public sector, where societal problems are much more likely to be ill structured and intractable than well structured and tractable. Second, they maintain that management scientists have been challenged to develop new ideas that will enhance the intuitive powers of managers. This challenge to move beyond strictly developing quantitative perspectives and toward enhancing a manager's intuitive abilities is shared by many management scientists (Ackoff, 1979a, 1979b; Gupta & Richards, 1979; Morris, 1975; White, 1983; Zeleny, 1975).

An earlier but still widely recognized summary of strategies likely to improve the long-run success of quantitative methods was advanced by Wagner (1971). Using operations research as his reference, Wagner looked at the future of quantitative applications in management from three perspectives: (a) opportunities for the practitioner, (b) challenges for the theoretician, and (c) recommendations for teachers.

Suggestions for Practitioners   In Wagner's conceptualization, three primary opportunities are available to practitioners: (a) improving the techniques of operations research applications to reduce the resource costs for designing, testing, and implementing operations research models; (b) creating diagnostic techniques to predict accurately the economic benefits that will result from a proposed operations research application; and (c) extending the scope of operations research into new areas of management such as structuring organizational responsibility, bridging cultural gaps within an organization, and designing management information systems.

Suggestions for Theoreticians   Wagner's five challenges for management science theoreticians are to (a) develop insightful models that avoid the axiom of rationality; (b) advance analytical concepts that enable managers to deal with the future as reality; (c) construct practical models for representing day-to-day operational problems; (d) uncover new ways to exploit the full power of computers; and (e) explore approaches to model building that encompass principles from the behavioral sciences.

Rules for Teachers   Wagner requests that educators (a) determine the appropriate mix between professional and technical training to best prepare students to exert practical influence on managerial decision making and (b) evaluate the relative merits of various instructional strategies incorporated in teaching operations research in colleges and universities.

Theoreticians and practitioners who wish to chart the development and refinement of tools and techniques within the management sciences can monitor the following journals: *A.I.E.E. Transactions, The Bell Journal of Management Science, Industrial Engineering, International Abstracts of Operations Research, Interfaces, Journal of the American Institute of Decision Sciences, Journal of Industrial Engineering, Manage-*

ment Science, Naval Research Logistics Quarterly, Operations Research Quarterly, and *Operations Research.* It is important to note that *Educational Administration Abstracts,* a review journal that abstracts articles relevant to educational administration from approximately 125 journals, includes reference to only *Management Science* of these mainstream management science publications.

Computer and Information Sciences

Personal computers, computer networks, large-scale data bases, computer-based models, and color graphics are among the technological advances stimulating interest in the use of computers to support managerial decision making. Formal links between the computer and information sciences and organizational decision systems are best represented in the continuous development of new and innovative management information systems. Tomeski and Sadek (1982) describe management information systems as planned and organized approaches to supplying managers with intelligence aids that facilitate that management process. They are designed to take advantage of modern computer technologies (such as electronic data processing, data communications, and word processing) and state-of-the-art decision tools from operations research and systems analysis. Tomeski and Sadek (1982) suggest that "a common belief held by designers of management information systems is that information is a catalyst of management and is the ingredient that coalesces the managerial functions of planning, operating, decision making and controlling" (p. 613).

Levin, Kirkpatrick, and Rubin (1982) have classified management information systems by looking at the output desired by the decision maker. Their classification system was used to construct Table 26.4, which describes three basic management information systems. The role of these decision tools in educational organizations is illustrated in two examples.

Example 5: Informations Systems Design for a University Registration Process

Brigham Young University wanted to extend its managerial effectiveness in registration and did so by adopting a nationwide telephone touch-tone registration process (Brigham Young University, 1984, 1985). Beginning in the fall of 1984, 27,000 students could register by telephone. Seventy-eight percent chose to do so, and by spring 1985 over 90 percent were doing so. Through the following steps the university enhanced its existing on-line registration process. First, the developers investigated the needs of students, faculty, and administrators to determine objectives and desired benefits. Hardware and software specifications were prepared. Then, it was necessary to devise carefully a flow-chart of the ideal registration procedure from a user perspective. Because political and emotional support are essential for success, commitments were secured from faculty and students before making a large financial investment. Next, contracts were let with vendors, and touch-tone procedures were developed. Pilot-testing was undertaken in 1983, and revisions were completed before adopting the new procedure as *the* system.

In addition to improved service to students, the touchtone telephone registration system yielded these benefits: (a) Registrations increased 9 percent on the first day of class; (b) adds and drops decreased 40 percent; (c) late registrations decreased 40 percent; (d) data-entry processing by office staff decreased by 517

Table 26.4   Decision Tools in the Computer and Information Sciences

The generic term *management information system* refers to the entire set of systems and activities used to manage, process, and use information as a resource in an organization (Sprague & Carlson, 1982). Classifying management information systems in terms of the type of output provided produces three different decision tools (Levin, Kirkpatrick, & Rubin, 1982).

Management Information Systems that Generate Reports. These reports can be financial statements, budgets, student grade reports, class schedules, attendance profiles, inventory status reports, or any report on the status of a situation of interest to the decision maker. These reports can be historical or present-time.

Management Information Systems that Answer "What-If" Questions. These information systems upgrade electronic data processing so that managers can have an integrated system of data files to generate ad hoc reports for questions in the form of "What would happen if this or that happened?" This type of information system frequently uses its stored information, its comparison and calculation capabilities, and a set of programs especially written

for this situation to provide management with the consequences of an action under consideration.

Management Information Systems that Support Decision Making (Decision Support Systems). These information systems represent further improvements on report generation and "what-if" systems in that they attempt to support all levels of management with operations research and statistical decision-making models. Two features distinguish decision support systems from other information systems: (1) They actually make a recommended decision instead of merely supplying additional information to the decision maker, and (2) they "build in" the decision maker as an integral part of the system, that is, the software accommodates the person as part of the decision process (Keen & Morton, 1980).

staff-hours per semester—nearly one full-time employee; (e) registration staff were freer to spend time assisting students; (f) department chairs could monitor numbers and student's names as they registered; (g) three departments with the most add-drop volume (mathematics, English, and physical education) could now add or drop after classes began; (h) ability to search by computer improved course scheduling and class enrollment, especially when a new section was added after the class schedule was printed.

Example 6: Information Systems Design for a Higher School Campus

In a collaborative project Texas A & M University's College of Education and A & M Consolidated High School sought an answer to a common research and administration question: How can microcomputers be used as campus-based management tools to improve communication and information management at A & M Consolidated High School? This common question and the five essential principles for school-college collaborative projects (Boyer, 1983) were used to construct a cooperative planning model having seven phases: problem specification, school selection, project design, group formation, course design, report writing, and executive briefing (McNamara & Erlandson, 1984; McNamara, Fetsco, Erlandson, & Hart, 1987). The college specified the problem and selected the school. The college's work group of faculty and doctoral students first formed a team with the school's teachers and administrators; this team then gained school-district endorsement and financial support to research the problem in a graduate course meeting on the high school campus.

The collaborative project design identified 20 campus management systems for study in the manner prescribed by Thierauf (1983). These systems were categorized into seven investigative domains: (a) teacher support with testing and grading, instructional management, and library services systems; (b) financial information with budgeting, financial accounting, and purchasing systems; (c) student information with student grade reporting, student health reports, and integrated student record systems; (d) guidance information with student scheduling and guidance systems; (e) attendance information with a student attendance system; (f) campus record and control with security, textbooks, discipline records, and staff personnel systems; and (g) administrative operations with communications, campus handbooks, and school calendar systems.

The course design (fact finding and data analysis) and the communication of the study's findings (final report and executive briefing) were structured to yield 20 individual responses. Each response provided a specific answer for precisely how microcomputer technology could extend the effectiveness of the single campus management system under study. A year following the presentation of findings to campus and district officials, the high school principal (Parker, 1985) specified four significant project outcomes: (a) Links between the school's administrative functions and microcomputer technology were formed; (b) a computer manufacturer donated 20 microcomputers and peripherals worth $116,000 because it was encouraged to see the school's awareness of microcomputer technology as a suitable administrative tool; (c) performance of critical administrative operations such as scheduling, keeping attendance records, and reporting grades had improved; and (d) teachers had used microcomputers in such activities as word processing to develop tests and curriculum materials and to create data banks for test questions. The Texas A & M University College of Education benefitted from the study by successfully producing a generalizable planning model for systematically examining how microcomputers can be applied to a high school's administrative functions (McNamara et al., 1987).

Professional Transactions and Publications

Sprague and Carlson (1982) suggest that the natural evolutionary advancement of information technology and its use in the organizational context has passed through three distinct phases.

The electronic Data Processing Phase (1960s) Electronic data processing was first used to automate standard reporting practices. This phase centered on the role of the technicians who held the primary responsibility for supplying management with routine accounting reports. Research in this phase focused on data, storage, processing, and flows of information essential for the day-to-day or operational activities of the organization.

The Traditional Management Information Systems Phase (1970s) The management information systems approach extended the focus of information systems activities with increased emphasis on the integration and planning functions. Sprague and Carlson (1982) associate four characteristics with this phase: (a) an information focus aimed at middle managers, (b) structured information flows, (c) integration of electronic data-processing tasks by organizational function, and (d) inquiry and report generation.

The Decision Support Systems Phase (1980s) A decision support system, an interactive support system providing the user with easy access to analytic decision models and data to support semi-structured or ill-structured decision-making tasks, is a further extension of prior phases in that it assists all levels of management. It combines the tools of operations research and statistical decision-making models with an organization's data bases. Sprague and Carlson (1982) identify four characteristics for decision support systems: (a) a decision focus, aimed at top managers and executive decision makers; (b) emphasis on flexibility, adaptability, and quick response; (c) user initiated and controlled; and (d) a source of support for the personal decision making of individual managers.

Comprehensive reviews of the design and application of management information systems in educational organizations include Ahl (1983); Bailey (1982); Educational Research Services (1982); Groff (1981); Hansen, Klassen, and Lindsey (1978); Hussain (1973); Mebane (1981); Raucher and Koehler (1982); Russell (1982); and Staman (1979).

Three frameworks guide research on the impact of educational management information systems. The first is a classification system that documents 100 specific administrative applications of computers in educational organizations (Anderson, 1966). The second derives from Little and Temares's (1983) specification of three general interdependent organizational arenas for automation: (a) the institutional level, which allows for the highest level of data sharing in a centralized database system; (b) the local level, which provides for contained sharing of data within departments or operating units; and (c) the personal level, which allows dedicated manipulation of shared data and the proper environment for unshared data. The third is Baum and Dennis's (1979) classification system in the form of eight problem situations to help teachers recognize the value of administrative uses of computers.

Critical reviews of educational management information systems appear in Hopkins (1971, 1979), Hopkins and Massy (1981), Hopkins and Schroeder (1977), Mason (1976), and Staman (1979). The promises and potential problems of microcomputers in educational administration are noted in Gustafson (1984), Harris (1983), McNamara (1982), McNamara and Erlandson (1984), Morgan (1982), and Spuck and Atkinson (1983). The future for decision support systems in educational organizations is treated in Brown and Droegemueller (1983), Matthews (1973), and Sheehan (1982a, 1982b, 1983).

A comprehensive survey of the educational literature reveals few references to the information sciences (W. G. Cunningham, 1982, p. 235). At the K–12 level, there seems to be more emphasis on the adoption of computers for instructional than for management purposes. The single educational journal devoted exclusively to computer and information concerns, *The AEDS Journal*, published by the Association for Educational Data Systems, reflects this emphasis.

Although implementation of comprehensive management information systems seems more frequent at the higher education level than in the lower schools, particularly in student affairs, fiscal management, and strategic planning (Hopkins & Massy, 1981), no journals have emerged to report continuing developments. Specifically, none of the mainstream journals routinely read by either elementary and secondary or higher education administrators regularly allocate space to critical reviews and research on information management in academic institutions. An analysis of recent volumes of *Educational Administration Abstracts* did reveal related articles in the following journals: *Educational Technology, Education, Educational Administration Quarterly, Planning and Changing, Journal of Higher Education, New Directions for Institutional Research, Business Officer, School Business Affairs*, and the *Journal of the College & University Personnel Association*. However, detailed historical case studies of actual automated organizational decision systems (such as Hopkins & Massy, 1981) were not discovered in this literature.

Limitations and Objections

Many of the barriers to successful management information systems' implementation are similar to those listed by Greene, Newsome, and Jones (1977) and Watson and Marett (1979) for operations research. Education and training of both administrators and system designers are the most often cited barriers to the success of management information systems (Bennett, 1983; Evans, 1970; Sprague & Carlson, 1982). The administrator must understand the capabilities of management information systems and be able to identify and communicate specific needs to system designers. From the other perspective, the designer must have a broad enough knowledge of organizations and decision processes in general to design a system that takes into account salient features of a particular organization and its problems (Bennett, 1983).

In his much-quoted article on "misinformation" systems, Ackoff (1967) identified five invalid assumptions, or myths, that have contributed to the misunderstanding of what management information systems can accomplish:

Myth 1. The critical deficiency under which most managers operate is the lack of relevant information.

Myth 2. Managers need the information they want.

Myth 3. If managers have the needed information, decision making will improve.

Myth 4. Better communication between managers improves organizational performance.

Myth 5. Managers do not have to understand how the information systems work, only how to use them.

Whereas education of both users and designers has overcome many of the barriers to implementation of successful management information systems dealing with structured and semi-structured problems, barriers to the acceptance of decision support systems are just being articulated. Bennett (1983) lists three of these: (a) the lack of a basis for establishing the value of decision support systems; (b) the slow development of a body of information on how to use computer resources to support effective and efficient decision making; and (c) a lack of knowledge about how to provide a manager-computer interface that would be judged effective by critical and demanding users. Bennett (1983) concludes:

> At the moment we do not have a detailed understanding either of management decisions or of the role that individual decision-maker perceptions play in making them. So our insight on how to apply current technology to decision support lags far behind the availability of that technology. (p. 7)

Future Directions

If Simon (1977) has predicted correctly that decisions in the future will be increasingly ill structured and non-programmed, the continued refinement and extended implementation of decision support systems, with their capacity for assisting in this type of decision making, is inevitable. Sprague and Carlson (1982) suggest that trends in decision support systems will be of three main types.

Organizational Change Change in organizational structure is likely to occur as a result of the ways decision support systems are designed and used. Whereas traditional management information systems centered both the access and control of information in an especially created technical group (MIS department), modern management information (decision support) systems, through the dialog component, have returned access and control of information to all management levels. According to Sprague and Carlson (1982), these features will increase consensual decision making and simplify implementation of decisions.

Technological Change Many of the expected improvements in computer technology will have an impact on decision support systems. Better hardware will affect the dialog component of decision support systems, as will increased teleconferencing technology and application, more emphasis on color graphics, and expanded voice and pointing input mechanisms. Additional external and internal database sources will

emerge. Relational, network, and rule database systems will begin to compete with the more traditional database systems currently in use. In addition, Sprague and Carlson (1982) feel decision support systems may revive many of the older operations research models (see Table 26.3) if the systems can be made interactive. They also predict more use of heuristic and inference models.

Decision Change Increased understanding of the decision-making process will result from the process of developing decision support systems. Sprague and Carlson (1982) believe that many of the unstructured organizational decisions that now require decision support systems will become structured as a result of increased knowledge of decision processes. Further, alternatives that cannot now be investigated because the data are inaccessible will become available through the continued utilization of decision support systems.

Researchers and practioners who wish to monitor new developments and implementations in the information sciences are directed to four journals in the field. *Management Information Systems Quarterly*, a comprehensive journal of particular relevance, has been published since 1977 by the Society for Information Management. Three other journals frequently include related articles: the *ACM Journal*, *Decision Sciences*, and *Management Science*. The latter two, which are abstracted in *Educational Administration Abstracts*, often integrate management information technology with the other domains of the decision sciences.

Behavioral Sciences

In the 1964 Yearbook of the National Society for the Study of Education, Griffiths (1964) noted:

> Administration is not entirely a common sense, fly-by-the-seat-of-the-pants art which can only be passed on from practitioner to practitioner; it can be studied, using the tools of the behavioral scientist. These tools include concepts and theories of human behavior, research designs, statistical insights, computers, and the logic of these modes in inquiry. (p. 2)

Historical reviews (Dowling, 1971) clearly indicate that Griffiths's position echoed the stance taken by many organizational theorists who had linked effective management with the behavioral sciences. Gross (1964) had earlier argued that the work of organizational theorists moved modern management away from classic scientific management, which concentrated on such physiological variables as physical capacity, motion, speed, and fatigue, and toward significant behavioral domains associated with human motivations, conflicts of interest, information processing, decision making, and program formation.

From the mid-1960s to the mid-1980s, organizational theorists and management scientists have continued to use the behavioral sciences to generate new knowledge about how to design better human-machine interfaces and how to adapt problem-solving methods to the needs of the decision maker. Contemporary research in this domain (Wharton School, 1979) has been concerned with the way individuals and groups collect and use information and how their actions are thereby affected. Both developmental and experimental methods are used (Laing, 1984; Lee, 1984).

Elbing (1978) suggests that two basic models are used in the analysis of behavioral decisions in organizations: the decision model and the level-of-analysis model. The first is a framework for the various stages of the decision-making process. (Its scope and sequence follow the administrative-problem-solving model advanced by Seiler, 1967, which was treated in the section on factors contributing to the formation of the decision sciences.) The second reflects the necessity to separate, for purposes of analysis, the different social realms that influence individual managers and, in turn, are influenced by managerial actions. (Included in these social realms are human, technical, organizational, and social inputs—the four inputs in the sociotechnical systems of Seiler, 1967, that directly influence organizational problem solving and decision making.)

Four organizational levels are used in Table 26.5 to classify 12 decision tools developed in the behavioral sciences. Specifically, these tools emerged from organizational development, an area of the behavioral sciences devoted to helping organizations achieve greater effectiveness, including improved quality of worklife, and increased productivity (W. G. Cunningham, 1982; Huse & Cummings, 1985). The role of these decision tools in educational organizations is illustrated in two examples.

Example 7: Process Consultation in a Public School District

One of the first problems encountered by a new superintendent of a large school district was a need to expand policies and procedures to deal with a drug abuse case in a junior high school (Snapp & Davidson, 1982). The superintendent sought the assistance of a resident school psychologist to act as a process consultant (Schein, 1969) to resolve the problem. The superintendent believed this organizational development strategy would contribute to the district's policy decision making by (a) providing expert information (knowledge of behavioral interventions); (b) reframing the situa-

tion to yield a more precise diagnosis of the problem; and (c) extending the problem-solving skills within central administration. The school psychologist, after gathering information at the junior high school and throughout the district, first reformulated the problem to reveal a parallel need at the junior high school level and at the district level. Next, the school psychologist developed alternative solutions (behavioral interventions) to resolve the problem. Together the superintendent and school psychologist selected and, with the professional staff, successfully implemented a specific series of behavioral interventions aimed not only at affecting drug use at the junior high school but also at providing impetus for qualitative change in dealing with drug abuse district wide.

Based on the success of this cooperative venture, the school psychologist became the primary agent for managing the school district's disciplinary systems and also became directly involved in the resolution of school district problems involving students' rights, parent-school conflicts, and classroom-level integration efforts. Outcomes of this process consultation included reorganization of the district to give the resident school psychologist a key role in decisions regarding planning and implementing discipline policies. Use of this decision tool provided district administrators reinforcement for Getzels's (1979) position on the central importance of problem finding, which argues that finding and formulating a productive organizational research problem is often as significant an intellectual and creative achievement as providing a solution to a problem once it has been found and formulated. The venture also gave district personnel a working model for how a process consultant can provide technical assistance in all four phases of Simon's (1977) managerial decision model: (a) intelligence activity, which consists of searching the environment for occasions (problems) calling for decisions; (b) design activity, which centers on inventing, developing, and analyzing possible courses of action; (c) choice activity, which encompasses the actual selection of a particular course of action from those available; and (d) review activity, which consists of evaluating past choices.

Example 8: Group Process in an Urban University

Top-level administrators at the University of Cincinnati, while grappling with ways to introduce more effective long-range planning within realistic budget constraints, realized they lacked the direct involvement and support of faculty (Bolton & Boyer, 1973). The existing decision-making process was dichotomized between faculty and central administration, severely constraining communication of values, goals, and outcomes. Consequently, central administration had

Table 26.5   Decision Tools in the Behavioral Sciences

ORGANIZATIONAL DEVELOPMENT APPROACHES TO INDIVIDUAL RENEWAL

At the individual level, organizational development intervention is used to enhance personal competency. To improve the individual level of competency, organizational development activities focus on:

Job enrichment. This is a means of increasing job satisfaction by increasing skill variety, task identity, significance of the task, autonomy, and feedback (Huse & Cummings, 1985).

Goal setting and planning. This term applies to joint activities involving managers and subordinates in setting goals, monitoring them, and providing counseling and support when necessary (Huse & Cummings, 1985).

Sensitivity training. This is a method for helping individuals develop greater self-awareness and becoming more sensitive to their effects on others (Huse & Cummings, 1985).

ORGANIZATIONAL DEVELOPMENT APPROACHES TO TEAM RENEWAL

At this level, the organizational team is the locus of renewal activity. The objectives are to improve conditions that lead to task accomplishment and to strengthen interpersonal relations that would lead to more positive attitudes. To improve the level of competence in the functioning of the team, interventions include:

Role analysis. This technique is aimed at defining a particular job's duties and responsibilities through group interaction involving the role holder and relevant others (Huse & Cummings, 1985).

Team building. This is a process of helping a group become more effective in accomplishing tasks and in satisfying the needs of group members (Huse & Cummings, 1985).

Consulting pairs. In this technique, an expert outside the organization, along with the team, develops solutions to organizational problems more objectively than just the team (Varney, 1977).

ORGANIZATIONAL DEVELOPMENT APPROACHES TO INTERGROUP RENEWAL

At the intergroup level, organizational development interventions are used to improve skills in working relations among teams or units within the organization. The objective is to strengthen relations to enhance cooperation. Organizational development interventions that facilitate this end include:

Process consultations. This intervention strategy focuses on diagnosing and restating problems and passing this skill on to group members (Schein, 1969).

Intergroup problem solving. This term encompasses activities between two or more groups in an organization that enhance the relationship and provide solutions acceptable to all (Schein, 1969).

Confrontation meeting. This is a formal encounter to help both parties express perceptions, focus on differences, and engage in problem solving to resolve the differences (Schmuck & Runkel, 1985).

ORGANIZATIONAL DEVELOPMENT APPROACHES TO ORGANIZATIONAL RENEWAL

At this level, organizational improvement is sought to bring about greater efficiency in planning, organizing, and communicating organizational goals and activities. The objective is to improve the functioning of the organization. Interventions include:

Survey feedback. This is an intervention strategy whereby information is gathered about the organization and then given to managers and employees to diagnose problems and plan for solutions (Huse & Cunningham, 1985).

Grid training. This highly structured intervention consists of six phases designed to analyze an entire organization and increase its overall effectiveness through improved planning and communications (Blake & Mouton, 1976).

Group processes. These organizational strategies provide groups with mechanisms for getting feedback, designing decision-making procedures, establishing clear communications, and participating in leadership functions (Schein, 1969).

---

increasingly taken responsibility for budgeting. Moreover, faculty had felt alienated from the budget process and threatened by the likelihood that major funding decisions and plans were ignoring their professional judgments and visions for the university.

To overcome this difficulty, top-level administrators commissioned a campus-based research institute to design training in group process. In cooperation with the department heads, a four-phase model was developed and implemented over a 6-month period. In the first phase, each department collected data and documented faculty concerns about the university. The second phase was dedicated to sharing feedback and discussing the data collected by faculty

and administrators. The third phase was used to identify common goals and concerns. The final phase was devoted to training department heads who would then be expected to take the major leadership role in maintaining clear communication among all stakeholders.

This intervention significantly altered long-range planning by increasing the shared knowledge base and incorporating faculty priorities in goal clarification and budget negotiations. The success of this organizational development strategy confirmed administrators' beliefs that the training must be an ongoing process because it (a) encourages and improves open and honest disagreements, and (b) attaches value to the confrontation and resolution of differences held by a variety of stake-holders in the university (Schmuck & Miles, 1972). Top-level administrators were certain that budget negotiations now reflected more involvement and more stakeholders, therefore gaining more support and com-mitment from all. In a word, the university came to realize that the application of organizational develop-ment as a decision tool dramatically increased the institution's ability to solve its own problems and improve the quality of its worklife.

Professional Transactions and Publications

Decision scientists make a clear distinction between or-ganizational development techniques from the planned change movement and mathematical models from the operations research movement. In fact, there are a number of similarities between the two. Bennis (1966) claims that operations research and planned change (a) are products of World War II, but their real develop-ment began immediately following the war; (b) em-phasize problem orientation but often have provided significant inputs into concepts and methods; (c) use a normative approach to emphasize improvement and optimization of performance to maximize goals; (d) rely heavily on empirical science as a means of influencing organizational transactions; (e) endorse a collaborative relationship based on trust and open communication; (f) are most effective in complex, dynamic organizations where rapid change must be planned.

Bennis (1966) argues that the most critical dif-ference between operations research and planned change is the frame of reference, which leads to divergent problem definitions. To construct a parallel framework for Ackoff's (1968) eight basic problem types in operations research (inventory, allocation, queuing, sequencing, routing, replacement, competi-tion, and search), Bennis presents an inventory of eight problems to guide planned change activity: (a) identifi-cation of appropriate mission and values, (b) human collaboration and conflict, (c) control and leadership, (d) coping with and resistance to change, (e) utilization of human resources, (f) communication between hier-archical ranks, (g) rapid growth, and (h) management and career development.

These frameworks guide the selection of the or-ganizational variables on which each of these two fields focus. For example, in an operations research project the managerial problem addressed is usually concrete, measurable, and often perceived to be related to goal achievement. By contrast, the managerial problem addressed in organizational development is less mea-surable, less obviously related to the attainment of goals, and more tied to participants' perceptions. Another contrasting variable is the client relationship.

The quality and nature of the relationship with the client is used as evidence of progress in organizational development, as well as a source of data and diagnosis. Operations research practitioners are less likely to perceive this relationship as fundamental to organiza-tional change. A final contrasting variable is the way each focuses on change. In operations research, the primary instruments of change are seen to be economic and technological factors. In organizational develop-ment, human factors and their effects on the perfor-mance of the system are viewed as the primary change instruments.

Informative reviews treating the application of organizational development in educational institutions include Boyer and Crockett (1973), Derr (1974, 1976), Erlandson (1978), Friedlander and Brown (1974), Schmuck and Miles (1972), and Schmuck and Runkel (1985). These sources suggest that the impact of orga-nizational development in educational organizations parallels that described in Examples 7 and 8.

Critical reviews of the application of organization-al development in educational organizations appear in Cohen and Gadon (1978); Keys (1979); Runkel and Schmuck (1974, 1976); Scheinfeld (1979), and Schmuck, Runkel, Arends, and Arends (1977). A 1981 state of the art review commissioned by the National Institute of Education (Fullan, Miles, & Taylor, 1981) to examine the applications of organizational develop-ment in schools identified four general limitations. First, the orientation of the school as a system (where survival is guaranteed, public relations are a primary consideration, and efforts are crisis focused rather than long term) violates the improvement orientation of organizational development. Second, the problem of identifying the client for organizational development intervention is often a complex task. The consultant is usually hired by the administration to work with teachers in hopes that the benefits will ultimately "trickle down" to the students. Third, the research and evaluation aspect of organizational development in schools suffers from methodological weaknesses, in-cluding measurement errors, overreliance on question-naires, lack of adequate controls, and failure to follow the program for a sustained period. The current literature contains an oversupply of partial or incom-plete cases and an undersupply of longer term studies of sustained organizational development. Precise statements explaining the outcomes of the application of organizational development techniques have been weak or absent altogether. Finally, the inaccurate, haphazard mislabeling of incoherent efforts to change schools (with little or no regard for the rational, systematically planned, sustained effort that defines organizational development) has created a poor image among educators.

Limitations and Objections

Organizational development, now one of the largest divisions of the Academy of Management, is frequently depicted as a body of knowledge, a professional field, and a behavioral strategy for changing organizations. Over the past two decades, the growing number of articles, books, conferences, and workshops reflect the increasing viability of the field. However, leading theorists and practitioners (Bennis, 1981; Burke, 1978, 1982; Daft, 1983; Huse & Cummings, 1985) believe that organizational development is best described as a legitimate domain of the behavioral sciences (a) still in its infancy as a discipline, (b) not yet theoretically advanced or broadly researched, and (c) clearly in transition.

Burke's (1978) state-of-the-art review documents eight general limitations of and objections to organizational development: (a) It has a cosmetic approach (Mills, 1975); (b) it possesses characteristics of a fad (Bowers, 1976); (c) it is anti-intellectual (Strauss, 1973); (d) it lacks real theory (Levinson, 1972); (e) it is a religious movement (Harvey, 1974); (f) it is often misrepresented by mislabeling (Kahn, 1974); (g) it is a term that has reached obsolesence (Jones & Pfieffer, 1977); and (h) it is an ill-defined concept (Herzberg, 1974).

Burke (1978) identified transitions that reframe the limitations of and objections to organizational development in terms of necessary modifications. These transitions indicate change in seven areas of organizational development: (a) focus—from an almost exclusive business-industrial orientation to many different types of organizations; (b) approach—from advocating a specific managerial style to contingency planning; (c) primary value—from democracy to authenticity; (d) theoretical framework—from social technology of laboratory training to a broader range of behavioral tools that fit actual organizational decision systems; (e) role of consultant—from a nondirective, process-oriented practitioner to an authorative specialist actively concerned with organizational outcomes; (f) change agent—from thinking of the practitioner of organizational development as the change agent to thinking of the line manager or administrator as the change agent; (g) function—from a glamorous name for training to a legitimate organizational function with attendant power and official status. These proposed transitions continue to guide current theory and practice (Daft, 1983; Huse & Cummings, 1985).

Future Directions

Future directions for the application of organizational development are advanced in Bennis (1981); Burke (1978, 1982); Daft (1983); Das (1981); Fullan et al.,

(1981); Huse and Cummings (1985); and Kur (1981). Positions taken by these theorists are reflected in Morrison's (1981) forecast, which claims that experts engaged in human resource functions will apply organizational development to address eight commonly encountered decision issues: (a) integrating high technology into the workplace; (b) transforming technical experts into effective managers; (c) transferring technology across departments within a large, complex organization; (d) developing management styles that enhance productivity and efficiency; (e) managing rapid technological change in a complex organization; (f) accommodating creativity in the management of scientists and engineers who design and produce the technology that gives a company its competitive edge; (g) dealing with changing values in the workforce (especially those of young employees); and (h) updating and renewing technical knowledge to ensure a competitive edge.

Theoreticians and practitioners who wish to monitor new and emerging directions in organizational development are encouraged to regularly review three journals: *Group & Organizational Studies*, *Human Resource Management*, and *Training and Development Journal*. At this time, only the first of these journals is abstracted in *Educational Administration Abstracts*, whose abstracting system does not include the term organizational development.

Social Systems Sciences

The technologies of symbol generation, storage, transmission, and manipulation made it possible to mechanize mental work, that is, to automate. Development and application of automation technologies require an understanding of the mental processes that are involved. Since 1940 several interdisciplines have been developed to generate and apply understanding of these mental processes and their role in managerial decision making. These disciplines include cybernetics, operations research, systems engineering, policy sciences, and behavioral communication. Ackoff (1974) suggests that these interdisciplines provide the "software" of the postindustrial revolution, just as industrial engineering provided much of it for the industrial revolution. Ackoff believes these new disciplines are the products of the systems age, a new intellectual framework where the doctrines of reductionism and mechanism and the analytical mode of thought are supplemented and partially replaced by the doctrines of expansionism (which maintains that all objects and events, and experiences of them, are parts of larger wholes) and teleology (which is the study of goal seeking and purposive behavior).

This new intellectual framework became the basis for the formation of the Social Systems Sciences Department at the University of Pennsylvania (Wharton School, 1984). The department aspires to turn out professionals who can design, plan for, and manage social systems that (a) are purposeful; (b) provide members with an improved quality of life; (c) can adapt rapidly to cope more effectively with accelerating rates of technological and social change; and (d) serve the large societal systems of which they are a part while performing their own functions more effectively.

The social-systems sciences program requires extensive training in the philosophy of science, social-systems theory, and the methodology of planning, research, and design. "Methodology" is viewed as the decision-making logic involved in planning, research, and design—in particular, the criteria employed in selecting tools and techniques. "Tools" are seen as instruments used in the conduct of planning, research, and design; they include computers, tables of random numbers, and calculus. "Techniques" are viewed as ways of using tools; they include simulation, random sampling, and optimization (Wharton School, 1984, p. 6).

Prerequisites for entry into the Wharton School social-systems sciences program consist of (a) an understanding of mathematics, including at least elementary calculus and matrix algebra; (b) an understanding of statistics and probability; and (c) an understanding of the use of computers and an ability to use them.

In Simon's (1977) terms, a social-systems sciences program uses two types of modern decision tools. On the structured side, the social-systems scientist uses decision tools from the applied mathematical sciences of operations research, statistics, and computer sciences to formulate management decision rules and search strategies that move formerly intuitive or rule-of-thumb decisions into the domain of programmed decisions. These activities use many of the decision tools elaborated in Tables 26.2, 26.3, and 26.4. When management decisions cannot be brought into the expanding set of programmed decisions, the social-systems scientist looks to modern decision tools designed specifically for ill-structured or nonprogrammed decisions. These tools have come and will continue to come from heuristic problem-solving methods applied to two areas of organizational activity: (a) training human decision makers and (b) constructing heuristic computer programs. Heuristic problem solving benefits from using organizational development tools as elaborated in Table 26.5

The continuous search for improved methods of diagnosis, solution, resolution, or dissolution of "social problems" leads social-systems scientists to extend their inventory of decision tools to include a wide variety of forecasting methods. As a formal part of social-systems sciences, these heuristic problem-solving tools from forecasting and futures research provide rich opportunities to extend the concepts and usefulness of conventional decision tools (Chambers, Mullick, & Smith, 1971). These opportunities are illustrated in Table 26.6, where four problem categories (Mitroff & Turoff, 1971) are used to classify 10 common forecasting tools. The role of these decision tools in addressing significant educational problems is illustrated in two examples.

Example 9: Delphi Research at Bell Canada

The Business Planning Group of Bell Canada had conducted a series of six Delphi studies over a 3-year period (Day, 1975). The purpose of the studies was to obtain qualitative data regarding future trends in the areas of computer and visual communications fields. The business planners wanted the viewpoints of the users in several market segments: education, medicine, business, and residential communications. In the study of the future of communications in the home, the original Delphi research model used in the Rand studies (Linstone & Turoff, 1975) was expanded in the Bell Canada studies to include two competing panels of "experts": homemakers and professionals in the areas of research and planning communication services.

The Delphi study design (Day, 1975) included nine steps: (a) searching the literature on communications technology and its use in the home; (b) assembling two competing panels of experts; (c) designing a draft questionnaire using the theoretical framework produced in the literature review; (d) pretesting draft questionnaire; (e) distributing revised questionnaire which was identical for both panels; (f) preparing statistical analysis of first round responses for both panels; (g) preparing an analysis of supporting comments for both panels; (h) distributing a second-round questionnaire showing (1) first-round statistical results from each panel on one page, (2) first-round supporting comments from each panel on the opposite page, (3) a report that highlights differences between the two panels and (4) a formal request for resolutions to reduce the panel differences; and (i) constructing a single final report documenting the complete history of the Delphi exercise.

The supporting comments from each group promoted debates between the panels and yielded behavioral information that might have otherwise been unavailable to the planners. Each of the Delphi forecasts was abstracted, indexed by key word, and stored in an on-line computerized information retrieval system. Corporate executives concluded that their

Table 26.6 Decision Tools in the Social Systems Sciences

Well-defined analytical problems are problems that lend themselves to the use of mathematical models. Forecasting tools used in conjunction with the well-defined problems are often employed in the latter part of an inquiry.

Computer simulations. This is a numerical technique for conducting experiments with mathematical and logical models. Simulation models are used to describe, via digital computer, the behavior of social and administrative systems over an extended period of time (Naylor, 1972).

Markov Chain analysis. This is a method of analyzing the current movement of some variable in an effort to predict the future movement of that same variable (Bartos, 1967). As a management tool, Markov models have been used to examine

social processes such as voting, conflict resolution, social mobility, consumer behavior, learning, personnel selection, and career counseling (McNamara, 1974a).

Trend analysis. This is a set of numerical methods that utilize quantitative information concerning the generalities and particularities of a social process to project the state of that process into the future. Four general methods are trend extrapolation, time-series analysis, growth analysis, and cohort analysis (Brown, 1974).

Well-defined experimental problems are problems stemming from a need for forecasts of particular events. Forecasting techniques used for these problems are usually not based on prior assumptions of a given theory.

Traditional Delphi. This is a method for structuring a group communication process so that a group of experts, as a whole, can deal effectively with a complex problem. The Delphi process involves providing (1) feedback of individual contributions, (2) assessment of group judgment, and (3) the opportunity to revise individual views. Some degree of anonymity is provided for individual responses. There are two forms of the Delphi process: conventional Delphi, in which a written questionnaire and responses are used; and real-time Delphi, in which a computer is

used to process results and provide feedback (Linstone & Turoff, 1975).

Cross-impact analysis. This is a method for modifying the estimated probabilities of future events in terms of estimated interactions among those events (Dalkey, 1975). Originally developed to improve the accuracy of Delphi forecasts, cross-impact analysis was later developed as a method for combining the results of interdependent forecasts about events and trends in order to generate alternative future scenarios (Enzer, 1983).

Defined problems are problems that are not well structured but can be defined. These problems require normative rather than exploratory analysis. Forecasting techniques are used to determine and evaluate alternatives to meet a specific objective.

Scenario writing. This is an attempt to look at and combine various trends in a systemic way. The main focus of scenario writing is the identification of causal relationships and key decisions or branching points (Gerardin, 1973). A scenario is a carefully calculated story, based on information derived from Delphi studies or from a number of other technological forecasting methods, about what the future could possibly hold (Miloy, 1979).

Relevance tree analysis. This is a management tool for controlling the attainment of a chosen future by defining alternative pathways for reaching selected future goals. Time flow or hierarchy of events, together with their interconnectivity, are depicted graphically and/or pictorially in a network or relevance tree (McGrath, 1974). This approach is, to a degree, an attempt to return to a natural philosophy in which the relevance of a single

action can be connected to the objectives of an organizational inquiry as a whole (Gordon & Raffensperger, 1973).

Decision matrix analysis. This is a planning method designed first to order "bits" of information and then to combine them into small chunks such that consequences and implications can be judged. The basic format used is a two-factor matrix. One factor with its subparts is listed vertically and another is listed horizontally. Matrix analysis allows each component (cells indicating independent decision alternatives associated with a complex future) to be compared separately against each of the other components. Comparisons are based on decision concerns such as cost-performance, cost-benefit, feasibility, and desirability. These results are then recombined to obtain estimates about the complex future under study (Cleary, 1974).

Ill-defined problems are those in which opposing objectives are encountered. Analysis of these problems requires intuitive reasoning and the use of conflict as method so that positions and counterpositions can be identified and reconciled in a new plan.

Policy Delphi. This a management method that seeks to generate the strongest possible opposing views on the potential resolution of a major policy issue. Unlike a conventional Delphi, which often selects a panel of experts to generate consensus, a policy Delphi frequently selects informed advocates who make consensus on a particular resolution very unlikely. The policy Delphi rests on the premise that the decision maker is not interested in having the respondent group generate his or her decision but rather in having them present all the options and supporting evidence for the decision maker's consideration (Turoff, 1970).

Environmental scanning. This is the process of identifying important emerging issues that may constitute either threats or

opportunities. This process helps an organization to develop better insights into the range of uncertainty facing its managers and to allocate resources in a way that anticipates and responds to changes in the external environment. At the simplest level, modern (environmental) scanning now includes attention to economic developments, technological innovations, social change, and legislative and regulatory developments. The scanning process has four specific aspects: (1) selecting general information sources to scan; (2) screening for specific information sources; (3) identifying criteria by which to scan; and (4) determining special action for the scanning results (Renfro & Morrison, 1983).

Delphi research contributed these benefits: (a) The study yielded a data base used to develop specific forecasts and policy changes regarding the viability of planned services or products in a particular market segment; (b) the report was important as an educational tool to inform senior managers; (c) the report was valuable as an environmental trend document that helped technological planners in research laboratories; and (d) the survey provided judgmental input data for use where hard data were unavailable or too costly to obtain.

Example 10: Scenario Writing in a Public University

Scenario writing attempts not to predict the future but to explore sequential alternatives that depend on critical choices (Miloy, 1978). The value of scenario writing lies in its exploration of various decision-making alternatives. Using a variation of the forecasting methodology of Vanston, Frisbrie, Lopreato, and Poston (1977), Miloy's 1979 scenario portrayed testimony before the Joint Subcommittee on Higher Education of the United States House of Representatives and the Committee on Educational Achievement of the United States Senate in 1998 showing the state of the public university. The testimony traced major decisions over the 20-year span, explaining how each was related to the situation in 1998.

Miloy's work projected four phases in scenario writing: (a) a design phase, which defines the purpose and scope of the study; (b) a development phase, which produces a propositions inventory; (c) a specification phase, which produces the actual inventory to be used; and (d) the evaluation phase, which rates the scenario in terms of use as a decision tool for long-range planning. The evaluation assessed the scenario's value as an alternative to other forms of planning instructions issued by an institution's chief executive officer as background for new long-range planning cycles (Heydinger & Zentner, 1983). The four specific criteria for this assessment (utility, information reproducibility, plausibility, and value explicitness) were taken from those provided in the scenario evaluation model developed by the Institute for the Future (Amara & Salancik, 1972).

Professional Transactions and Publications

The methodology of planning, research, and design employed in the social-systems sciences is, by definition, futures oriented. Social-systems sciences, more than any other of the decision sciences, are associated with the application of futures research and technological forecasting.

Amara and Salancik (1972) suggest that the process of forecasting can be defined in terms of its outputs—the forecast. In progressively more precise terms, a forecast may be defined as follows: (a) a statement about the future; (b) a probablistic, reasonably defined statement about the future; or (c) a probablistic, reasonably defined statement about the future based on an evaluation of alternative possibilities.

Over the past 20 years, the field of technological forecasting has developed a large inventory of decision tools (Bright & Schoeman, 1973; Chow, 1982; Jantsch, 1969; Martino, 1972; McNamara, 1974b). Joseph (1974) indicates that technological forecasting, a formalized and systematic methodology for determining future possibilities, allows decision makers to move beyond "pure speculative conjecture" about the future. The ultimate goal of most technological forecasts is to provide information to assist in planning for the future. A technological forecast's value rests on an articulated set of logical assumptions, data, and relationships. These features distinguish a forecast from opinion or prophecy.

Forecasting Versus Prediction Forecasts are often confused with predictions (Amara & Salancik, 1972). On this point, Joseph (1974) notes that forecasting differs from prediction in that its results tell decision makers what can happen, what they can change, or what they can bring about, whereas prediction makes a statement of what will happen. Specifically, technological forecasts make predictive statements about what will happen if a particular planning option or decision alternative is executed. The terms "technological forecasting" and "futures research" are usually used interchangeably in the literature, especially in educational research. Gerardin (1973) notes that terms such as "prospective creative futures" and "creative futures planning" are often introduced to distinguish the techniques used in technological forecasting from those used strictly in prediction.

Logic of Forecasting To place technological forecasting into perspective, Tugwell (1973) suggests the following framework: (a) normative thinking which deals with clarification of values and goals (What is good?); (b) scientific thinking, which treats explanation of behavior with predictive intent (How do things work?); (c) futurist thinking, which elaborates possibilities and alternatives (What is possible? What is probable?); and (d) strategic thinking, which specifies action paths to obtain desired outcomes at estimated costs (How can I get what I want?).

Types of Forecasts Most decision scientists recognize a distinction between exploratory and normative directions in technological forecasting. Jantsch (1969) offers the following explanation of the differences between the two. Exploratory forecasting leads from the present situation to future states. It seeks to project planning parameters and functional capabilites into the future by starting from a domain of accumulated knowledge in a relevant area. The normative direction of forecasting leads backward from a predetermined or desired future state to action in the present. This process specifies various barriers and constraints to be overcome in order to achieve the future goals. Jantsch claims this distinction between exploratory (which he labels "opportunity-oriented") and normative (which he calls "need-oriented") approaches is important for developing specific techniques and methods. Combining both approaches clearly extends the options for using several of the decision tools outlined in Table 26.6 in a single organizational planning endeavor.

Technological Forecasting in Educational Administration In the early 1970s, four significant projects were undertaken to bring studies of the future and the development of appropriate technological forecasting methods to the field of educational administration. The Phi Delta Kappan project (Shane, 1973) and the General-Special Education Administration Consortium project sponsored by the University Council for Educational Administration (Hencley & Yates, 1974) produced research methods texts that provide detailed explanations for a wide array of decision-oriented methods judged to be most useful for studying educational futures. A project of the Research for Better Schools Regional Laboratory (Rubin, 1975) published a set of scenarios on alternative futures for education, highlighting the inherent implications of these writings for educational research and development. In 1972 the University Council for Educational Administration Career Development seminar "Imaging Alternative Future School Organizations" (Popper, 1974), conducted by the Division of Educational Administration of the University of Minnesota, dealt with three substantive themes: imaging, forecasting methodologies, and futurology in planning.

In addition to these four endeavors, *Educational Administration Abstracts* added in 1973 a fifth primary category, Planning and Futurology, to its classification system to abstract published research in three designated areas (Operational Planning, Long-range Prediction, and Planning and Futurology). The Planning and Futurology category and its three subdivisions are maintained in the journal's present classification system, and it still represents one of the best means to uncover studies of the future and decision-oriented futures research methods currently published in approximately 125 mainstream administrative and management science journals.

Informative reviews treating the application of exploratory and normative forecasting in educational institutions include Copa and Moss (1983); Freeman (1981); Hencley and Yates (1974); Hostrop (1973a,

1973b); Hudson (1978); Lewis (1978); Morrison, Renfro, and Boucher (1983); Rahim (1978); and Shaw (1980). Analysis of the literature published over the past three decades yields three consistent findings. First, the strategies implemented and their impact on educational organizations parallel those described in Examples 9 and 10. Second, the specific decision tools most frequently applied in educational organizations are mathematical models used in enrollment forecasting (See Well-defined analytical problems, Table 26.6), traditional Delphi strategies (See Well-defined experimental problems, Table 26.6), and scenario writing, which is often coupled with a brainstorming activity (See Defined problems, Table 26.6). Third, there is an emerging enlightened interest in training educational administrators to include technological forecasting tools as an integral part of their organizational decision systems. These directions for training (Beyth-Marom & Lichenstein, 1982; Cope, 1979; L. L. Cunningham, 1982; Friedman, 1980; Hopkins & Massy, 1981; Pepper, 1984) follow the pattern of recommendations presented here for the management and behavioral sciences, with special emphasis frequently given to the need for administrators to link these decision tools with the actual ill-structured problems they encounter in their day-to-day professional transactions.

Limitations and Objections

Critical reviews treating the limitations of and objections to the application of technological forecasting tools in educational policy planning and management studies appear in Alper (1968), Beck (1974), Dede and Kierstead (1984), Helmer and Rescher (1959), Hencley and Yates (1974), Hopkins and Massy (1981), Kraetsch (1979), Sackman (1975), and Stake (1970). The reservations about technological forecasting are captured in Linstone and Turoff (1975), who have identified eight specific limitations that exist to a greater or lesser degree no matter what forecasting tool is utilized. To set criticism of technological forecasting in a constructive perspective, their limitations are elaborated in a "checklist of pitfalls" that can serve as a guide for the design of Delphi studies. These design considerations and a research study that addresses each particular limitation are presented following.

Discounting the Future Researchers and planners must train their clientele to perceive past and future time and space by moving the distant crisis within the participant's current field of perception or extending the participant's planning horizon (Linstone, 1973).

The Prediction Urge Although human beings strive for the certainty of knowing the exact date and time of a particular event in the future, the Delphi technique should be viewed as a communication process, which may or may not result in consensus, rather than a prediction for specific events (Turoff, 1970).

The Simplification Urge There is a natural tendency to predict a holistic view of the future based on a few selected components of a social system. Because complex social systems often exhibit strongly counter-intuitive behavior, the forecaster should never expect to forecast the behavior of the whole by forecasting the behavior of its parts (Forrester, 1971).

Illusory Expertise In an application of Delphi techniques to forecasting, it is difficult to identify unbiased panelists concerned with the interrelationships among the total system because "experts" are generally knowledgeable about one component of the system; consequently, the consensus of judges does not always produce accurate judgments or estimates (Weaver, 1971).

Sloppy Execution Sloppy execution of the Delphi technique may be credited to the analyst or the participant and can include lack of creativity in the project design, excessive specification or vagueness in the statement formulation, homogeneous characteristics of the chosen panel, and haste by the respondents in questionnaire completion (Amara & Salancik, 1972).

Optimism-Pessimism Bias Delphi participants are likely to respond overpessimistically in long-range forecasts and overoptimistically in short-range forecasts due to individual personality characteristics and the inability of individuals to understand complex interactions in systems development (Martino, 1970).

Overselling In their enthusiasm, analysts tend to overuse the relatively new Delphi technique and in doing so perpetuate possible problems regarding the psychology of the potential user community: the user may perpetuate false expectations of the communication system; involving more individuals in the Delphi process does not necessarily produce more effective results; the goals of the organization are not always shared by the individuals in that organization (Goodman, 1970).

Deception The anonymity of the Delphi process can facilitate deception through manipulation or propaganda use, as evidenced by the Oracle of Delphi, who based pronouncements on false information (Welty, 1973).

Although designers may not be able to deal with or eliminate all eight problems, Linstone and Turoff (1975) claim it is the designers' responsibility to recognize the degree of impact each problem has on their forecasting study and to minimize any that might invalidate their findings. Linstone and Turoff also believe designers who understand the philosophy of their approach and the resulting boundaries of validity are engaged in the practice of technological forecasting.

Those who apply these decision tools without oppropriate insights or without clarifying the necessary boundaries engage in the practice of myth-making.

Future Directions

Whereas earlier futures research efforts concentrated on the design and improvement of technological forecasting techniques, social-systems scientists and other futurists in the mid-1980s believe that the current priority for futures research is to link these techniques with strategic planning. Enzer (1983) claims that the focus of this research should be on the development and testing of analytical procedures integrating strategic analysis with alternative futures in ways that clearly identify the importance of change in the user's organization.

Futures Research in Institutional Planning Attempting to forecast the most likely future for higher education may be an exercise in futility, but developing detailed descriptions of alternative futures can be useful for making desirable futures happen. Using this orientation, Wagschall (1983) has developed a strategic planning model to illustrate how futures research can become an integral part of a university's decision system.

Wagschall's model is designed to produce specific and fairly unanimous scenarios that can serve as the basis for creating genuine alternatives to a university's present practices. Essential to the model is the formation of a university planning group (not to exceed 20 members) involving all participants with a substantial stake in the resulting plan.

The planning process includes five phases. Each phase uses a specific decision tool. Phase 1 uses environmental scanning to generate important trends and emerging issues that constitute threats or opportunities for university planning. Phase 2 employs a traditional Delphi round to identify trends and issues that the planning group believes to be most likely and most significant in their impact on the university. Phase 3 applies relevance tree analysis to elaborate specific impacts in the form of consequences and contradictions to be addressed in the various alternative futures. Phase 4 uses a cross-impact analysis to organize the Phase 3 findings in a probability matrix indicating the greatest negative and positive changes. Phase 5 invokes scenario writing to produce carefully calculated alternative futures reflecting the groups' judgment about what would happen to the university if these futures were pursued.

Efforts to apply basic social-systems sciences knowledge in the design of organizational decision systems generate two basic research problems.

Beyond Prediction and Preparation Ackoff (1982)

argues that the "predict and prepare" paradigm that guides the current practice of technological forecasting runs into a widely unrecognized dilemma, which he formulates as a paradox: The more accurately we can predict, the less effectively we need to prepare; and the more effectively we can prepare, the less we need to predict. He suggests that basic research in the social-systems sciences will construct and refine a different paradigm, where the ideal sought by managers and planners will not be perfect prediction and preparation but "continuous increases of control and responsiveness to what is uncontrolled" (1982, p. 10). This paradigm will direct efforts toward the improvement of organizational learning, adaptation, and responsiveness rather than prediction and preparation.

The Stakeholder Concept   Mitroff (1983) contends that social-systems scientists will direct more of their basic research efforts toward using psychoanalytic theories to describe and explain the deeper motives of human behavior that operate in organizational decision systems. Mason and Mitroff (1981) have recently used these theories to introduce the concept of stakeholders (which can be viewed as a wide array of internal and external forces that influence any social system) to illustrate how individuals, interest groups, and institutions affect both organizational decision making and managerial style. Their framework assumes that different organizational stakeholders do not generally share the same perspectives and definitions of an organization's problems and, as a result, are also not likely to share the same solutions. With this in mind, Mason and Mitroff (1981) believe future organizational research will need to design and test innovative decision tools that replace those presupposing prior consensus and agreement among parties with tools acknowledging disagreement. Consistent with the objectives of organizational development, the latter decision tools will use differing organizational perspectives as a starting point for moving toward a shared commitment to a set of possible solution strategies.

Summary

The review of decision technologies linked the development of decision tools to five well-recognized knowledge domains. The complete inventory of decision tools addressed here appears in Tables 26.2 through 26.6. Taken collectively, these five tables document a two-stage classification system. The first stage places each decision tool in historical context in one of the five knowledge domains. The second stage further classifies each tool according to the primary decision activity it supports. Next, the application of decision tools in educational organizations was captured in 10 case studies,

two for each knowledge domain. These illustrations demonstrate how 10 different decision tools elaborated in the classification system have been applied in actual educational organizational decision systems. The 10 case studies have been chosen to represent the variability both within and between the various classifications. In addition, limitations and future directions have been specified for each group of decision tools. Finally, three currently promising research and development projects within educational administration are detailed (Bessent et al., 1984; Hopkins & Massy, 1981; Renfro & Morrison, 1983). Each documents how concerns of the decision sciences can be effectively operationalized in educational research.

FUTURE DIRECTIONS

The final part of the review divides into three sections, each of which attempts to answer one question:

> What trends do the decision sciences project for the immediate future?
>
> What promise do the decision sciences hold as an interdisciplinary framework for training educational practitioners?
>
> What specific research activities do the decision sciences suggest for educational administration?

Emerging Trends in the Decision Sciences

Research in the decision sciences includes and attempts to integrate experimental findings that have emerged from a diverse set of related fields. Five specific interdisciplinary fields that contribute to advances in the decision sciences have been identified. Each field offers opportunities for improving the long-run success of technical tools used in organizational decision systems.

The policy sciences literature indicates that policy analysts are becoming more sensitive to social values and are increasingly emphasizing the analysis of goals (a) using survey research to detect to what extent the goals are supported, (b) using relational analysis to reveal how achieving them would affect higher values, and (c) using philosophical analysis to determine how they fit into more general philosophical systems.

The management sciences literature suggests that future developments in operations research will require greater attention to planning and participation technologies and will redirect quantitative methods toward the solution of what are called "ill-structured" or "messy" problems, especially those found in complex agencies within the public sector.

The information sciences literature implies that traditional management information systems will be extended through interactive integration of human judgment (HUMAN), comprehensive data bases (MACHINE), and individually designed computer models (MODELS) to solve unstructured problems.

The behavioral sciences literature predicts that the incorporation of organizational development strategies into management decision making will significantly alter existing decision rules by (a) encouraging and approving open and honest disagreements and (b) attaching value to the confrontation and resolution of differences held by a variety of stakeholders in the organization,

The social-systems sciences literature argues that modern decision tools, which require cooperative institutional commitment, have, and will continue to, come from heuristic problem-solving methods applied to two areas of organizational activity: (a) training human decision makers and (b) constructing heuristic computer programs.

Guidelines for Training

Since the mid-1960s, programs to prepare educational administrators have undergone dramatic changes, including more attention to knowledge production in the behavioral and mathematical sciences (Boyd, 1983; Immegart & Boyd, 1979). Critical to the training of practitioners is the continuous search for the integration of more (a) meaningful field experiences (Cronin & Horoschak, 1973; Wynn, 1972), (b) innovative instructional strategies (Angrist & Stewman, 1979; McNamara, 1981), and (c) relevant content from disciplines that influence both theory and practice in administration (Culbertson, Farquhar, Fogarty, & Shibles, 1973; L. L. Cunningham, 1982; Griffths, 1979; Stanford University Committee on Administration and Policy Analysis, 1974).

McNamara (1981) concluded that the interdisciplinary framework of the decision sciences addresses all three of these training concerns. His findings suggest that the decision sciences

extend the efforts of the mathematical social sciences;

center on decision processes and goal-seeking behavior in organizational settings;

complement rather than replace the emphasis on traditional expertise in accounting, finance, and general management;

provide meaningful coverage of useful behavioral models (models of cognitive processes, group structure and processes, and organizational structure and processes);

integrate organizational theory and operations research;

focus on the role of information systems in governing behavior of an organization;

extend efforts to use quantitative decision tools with real organizational data sets, including those that have a mixture of accurate, inaccurate, and missing data;

involve extensive use of case study and simulation methods as a means to join mathematical and behavioral sciences;

incorporate interdisciplinary perspectives found in the more familiar professional study areas of policy analysis, operations research, and information systems;

concentrate on the preparation of general administrators and managers who can master the decision tools associated with advanced information-processing equipment;

develop "hands-on" skills in the area of minicomputer decision models and management information;

include a treatment of standard statistical methods used in design and analysis of data, but also address the use of statistics and other mathematical disciplines in decision modeling; and

use the daily world of the practitioner as a laboratory for research (pp. 66–68).

Curriculum planners in educational administration who wish to use the interdisciplinary framework of the decision sciences may profitably examine the philosophy promoted in the Wharton School (1979), the curriculum of which is based on the assumption that an understanding of information systems, mathematical modeling, and decision processes will improve the performance of managers. The faculty believes that the decision sciences are not substitutes for the development of traditional skills in accounting, finance, and management but should be used in combination with them to extend managerial effectiveness.

Research in Educational Administration

Speculation on future technological advances from the decision sciences and their potential applications in research and training project three items for the research agenda.

Research Agenda Item 1 — to extend the use of decision tools in educational organizations will require formal integration of the behavioral and mathematical sciences. A similar appeal to explore links between the behavioral and mathematical sciences appears in Farquhar's (1973) review of the social sciences (specifically social psychology, sociology, anthropology, political science, and economics) as the basis for preparing educational administrators. He argues that the humanities, the "emerging management science," and mathematics are other knowledge domains that provide important content for professional preparation programs in educational administration. Ackoff (1974) supports Farquhar's contention and extends the list of disciplines to include cybernetics, operations research, systems engineering, policy sciences, and behavioral communications. These additions he calls "interdisciplines," rather than disciplines, to reflect their integrative potential for managerial decision making.

This same integrative potential is reflected in the Wharton School (1979) model for the decision sciences. In that model, research in decision support systems provides a theoretical framework for decision scientists to integrate research findings from three traditional knowledge domains—operations research (with its focus on the use of mathematical models), information systems (with its emphasis on the use of information processing and communication technologies), and the psychology of the decision process (with its concentration on the use of theories and models from the social and behavioral sciences). Thus, the Wharton School model views research in decision support systems as a means to provide a synthesis of human, machine, and models.

Research Agenda Item 2 — to realize the potentials of the behavioral and mathematical sciences in organizational decision systems will require experimentation with decision science methods to define and solve ill-structured problems.

Although the traditional methods for making programmed or structured decisions have been revolutionized during the last three decades by the application of the applied mathematical sciences of operations research, computing, and statistics (National Academy of Sciences, 1968), only recently have these sciences been applied to analyze nonprogrammed or ill-structured decisions. Noble (1979) notes that ill-structured decisions can be characterized in some or all of the following ways: complex, dynamic, ill defined, political, interactive, uncontrollable, and most important, unpredictable. He argues that the development of realistic solutions for these problems will involve a constant interaction between designers, technologies, users, and the actual environment in which the solutions will be applied. Hopkins and Massy (1981) have incorporated this perspective in their attempts to develop a unifying theory to guide decision making in institutions of higher education.

Decision sciences offer several insights for how the research on ill-structured problems might proceed in educational administration.

A computer and information systems orientation in the decision sciences requires researchers to distinguish clearly between algorithmic and heuristic processes. Smith (1982) claims that an algorithm is a step-by-step process with specific rules for finding a defined goal, whereas a heuristic process is an exploratory

strategy that uses general rules to reach an ill-defined goal or objective. He suggests that many policy decisions, as opposed to operational and functional decisions, require heuristic methods.

A behavioral orientation to the decision sciences recognizes that individuals differ in their approaches and abilities to model decisions. McKenny and Kern (1974) have found that a deductive, analytical, systematic approach to decision making and problem solving differs from an intuitive, divergent, global strategy. The analytical style follows traditional assumptions encountered in operations research. Systematic thinkers most often address a problem using a definite method or procedure leading to a defined solution. By contrast, intuitive thinkers usually avoid using fixed methods or known algorithms; rather, they use heuristic methods to test alternative hypotheses in a trial-and-error sequence. Future research will need to focus on how the behavioral variables such as the analytical-intuitive style affect the choice and implementation of decision tools in educational organizations. Examination of the 10 case studies above suggests that initial efforts should explore answers to four essential questions: (a) Will decision tools be used or not? (b) Which tools will be selected? (c) For what purposes will they be chosen? (d) How effectively will they be integrated into the actual decision processes of the organization?

A social-systems sciences orientation to the decision sciences requires an expanded role for methodology in resolving ill-structured problems. Ackoff (1974) recommends that methodology be viewed as the decision-making logic involved in organizational planning, research, and design—in particular the criteria employed in selecting tools and techniques. Moreover, Mitroff and Turoff (1971) have identified five philosophical perspectives (Leibnizian, Lockean, Kantian, Hegelian, and Singerian inquiry systems) related to the selection and implementation of decision tools. In Table 26.6, Mitroff and Turoff's framework was used to place technological forecasting tools on a continuum from well-structured to ill-structured problems.

Research Agenda Item 3 — to prepare educational leaders to use modern decision tools in organizational decision systems will require training in the mathematical sciences.

The quantitative tradition in graduate and professional education is neither new nor revolutionary. As of mid-1980, quantitative methods clearly constitute a formal study component in interdisciplinary degree programs in leading graduate and professional schools of management, urban and public affairs, business, and city and regional planning (McNamara, 1981). Kirkpatrick (1974) argues that these study components do not

**Table 26.7   Qualifications Desirable for All Public Managers
Analytical Tools (Quantitative and Nonquantitative)**

1. Knowledge of
- Quantitative decision methodology: e.g., accounting, parametric and nonparametric statistics, linear programming, modeling
- Electronic data processing and information systems
- Systems and procedures analysis: e.g., organization surveys, work measurement
- Behavioral science methodology: e.g., sociometric surveys, value analysis, leadership assessment
- Legal processes and controls

2. Skills in
- Logical analysis and diagnosis
- Research design and application
- Computer utilization and application
- Applicational of quantitative and nonquantiative methodology to organizational situations
- Oral and written communications and presentations

3. Public interest values represented by knowledge of and commitment to
- Objectivity and rationality in the conduct of public affairs
- Utilization of science and research to foster public purposes
- Impartial inquiry and investigation of public needs and problems
- Openness in communication and interpretation of data and findings to the public

4. Behavior represented by
- Involvement in data-gathering and problem-solving exercises
- Familiarity with public documents, legal sources, and forms of administrative communications
- Preparation of correspondence, reports, and position papers
- Participation in professional associations, internships, and other forms of experiential learning

NOTE. Adapted from requirements detailed in *Guidelines and Standards for Professional Masters Degree Programs in Public Affairs and Public Administration*, 1974, published by the National Association of Schools of Public Affairs and Administration, Washington, DC.

merely include techniques but rather reflect developments in broad-gauge methodology resulting from changes in science, mathematics, and philosophy. To accomplish this objective within educational administration will require a similar orientation.

If training-in-common for educational, public, and business administration is a productive avenue to explore (Miklos, 1972), then the training model advanced by the National Association of Schools of Public Affairs and Administration (1974) is a prime candidate for experimentation. That model, summarized in Table 26.7, illustrates that formal study in quantitative methods for educational leaders must integrate knowledge, skills, values, and behaviors. Other experimental possibilities from graduate and professional schools include (a) teaching the application of statistics to public policy using the case study method (Fairley & Mosteller, 1977); (b) incorporating computer simulation in administrative training (Bolton, 1971; Guetzkow, Kolter, & Schultz, 1972); (c) linking recent developments in display and communications technology with the need to create more effective strategies for reporting quantitative information to policy makers and practitioners (Cleveland & McGill, 1985; Prentice, 1976; Tufte, 1983); (d) studying the use of statistics as legal evidence (Cullison, 1969; Zeisel, 1966); (e) exploring the differences between statistical and practical significance in administrative research (Maxwell,

1973; McNamara, 1979); and (f) developing quantitative inquiries using organizational archives and information systems (Burstein, 1978; Fishbein, 1973).

In conclusion, the decision sciences significantly extend opportunites for innovation in education. To researchers and practitioners interested in design and application of the technical tools of decision making in educational organizations, it should be mentioned that the risks of innovation were well understood by Machiavelli. He described them in *The Prince* as follows:

> There is nothing more difficult to take in hand, more perilous to conduct, or more uncertain in its success than to take the lead in the introduction of a new order of things, because the innovator has for enemies all those who have done well under the old conditions and lukewarm defenders in those who may do well under the new law.

NOTES

[1] This review was initiated while the first author was a 1980–1981 resident fellow at The Ohio State University Advanced Study Center managed by the National Center for Research in Vocational Education. Findings from this ASC research project are reported in McNamara (1981). A special debt of gratitude goes to Mel Miller, Delores Robinson, Sonja Stone, John Krumboltz, and Jeff Hefferman—all 1981 ASC resident fellows. The encouragement and continuous support of Robert Taylor, the NCRVE director, and

the NCRVE staff are most appreciated. The initial theoretical framework was significantly extended by the second author to include a more formal emphasis on the social and behavioral sciences. Our largest debt of gratitude goes to the graduate student research group here at Texas A & M University. Deserving special recognition for their contributions to the research are Stephen Biles, Mary Ann Dickson, Florence Guido-DiBrito, Michael Hart, Kathryn Jones, Vija Little, Mary-Claire Maggio, Jane MacDonald, Evangeline McJamerson, and Frank Walters.

REFERENCES

Ackoff, R. L. (1962). *Scientific method: Optimizing applied research decisions.* New York: John Wiley.

Ackoff, R. L. (1967). Management misinformation systems. *Management Science, 14*(4), 147–156.

Ackoff, R. L. (1968). Operations research. *International Encyclopedia of Social Sciences, 11,* 290–294.

Ackoff, R. L. (1974). *Redesigning the future: A systems approach to societal problems.* New York: John Wiley.

Ackoff, R. L. (1978). *The art of problem solving.* New York: John Wiley.

Ackoff, R. L. (1979a). The future of operations research is past. *Journal of the Operations Research Society, 30*(2), 93–104.

Ackoff, R. L. (1979b), Resurrecting the future of operations research. *Journal of the Operations Research Society, 30*(3), 189–199.

Ackoff, R. L. (1982). *Beyond prediction and preparation* (Social Systems Sciences Paper No. 82–106). Philadelphia: Department of Social Systems Sciences, University of Pennsylvania.

Ackoff, R. L. & Rivett, P. (1963). *A manager's guide to operations research.* New York: John Wiley.

Adams, C. R. (Ed.). (1977). *Appraising information needs of decision makers.* San Francisco: Jossey-Bass.

Adleman, I. (1966). Simulation of economic processes. *International Encyclopedia of Social Sciences, 14,* 269–274.

Ahl, D. (1983). Keeping up with computers in education or computer periodicals: Past, present and future. *Proceedings of the Annual Summer Conference on Computers.* Eugene, OR: University of Oregon. (ERIC Document Reproduction Service NO. ED 239 237)

Alesch, D. J., & Dougharty, L. A. (1971a). *Economies-of-scale analysis in state and local government* (Report No. R–748–CIR). Santa Monica, CA: Rand.

Alesch, D. J., & Dougharty, L. A. (1971b). *The feasibility of economies-of-scale analysis of public services* (Report No. R–739–CIR). Santa Monica, CA: Rand.

Alkin, M. C., & Bruno, J. E. (1970). System approaches to education planning. In P. K. Piele & T. L. Eidell (Eds.), *Social and technological change: Implications for education* (pp. 191–244). Eugene, OR: University of Oregon Press.

Alper, P. (1968, June), A critical appraisal of the application of systems analysis to educational planning models. *IEEE Transactions on Education, E–11* (2).

Amara, R. C., & Salancik, G. R. (1972, June). Forecasting: From conjectual art toward science. *The Futurist.* Reprinted in A. P. Johnston & J. F. McNamara (Eds.). (1975). *Planning perspectives for education* (pp. 227–235). New York: MSS Information.

American Institute of Decision Sciences (1976). *Guidelines for the decision sciences curriculum.* Atlanta: American Institute of Decision Sciences.

Anderson, G. E. (1966). 100 uses for school data processing. *Nation's Schools, 78,* 101–107.

Anderson, G. E. (1970). Operations research: A missing link. *Educational Researcher, 21,* 1–3.

Angrist, S. S., & Stewman S. (1979). Problem solving for public policy: Learning by doing. *Policy Analysis, 5*(1), 97–128.

Alpin, J. C., Jr., & Schoderbeck, P. T. (1976). How to measure MBO. *Public Personnel Management, 5*(2), 88–95.

Alpin, J. C., Jr., Schoderbeck, C. G., & Schoderbeck, P. P. (1979). Tough-minded management by objectives. *Human Resource Management, 18*(2), 9–13.

Averch, H. A., Carroll, S. J., Donaldson, T. S., Kiesling, H. J., & Pincus, J. (1972). *How effective is schooling? A critical review and synthesis of research findings* (Rand Report R–95b–PC SF/RC). Santa Monica, CA: Rand.

Bailey, R. L. (1982). *Information systems and technological decisions: A guide for nontechnical administrators.* Washington, DC: National Institute of Education. (ERIC Document Reproduction Service No. ED 225 528)

Baldridge, J. V., & Tierney, M. L. (1980). *New approaches to management: Creating practical systems of management information and management by objectives.* New York: EXXON Educational Foundation.

Banghart, F. W. (1969). *Educational systems analysis.* New York: Macmillan.

Baum, M., & Dennis, R. J. (Eds.). (1979). *A teacher's introduction to administrative uses of computers.* No. 15e, Illnois Series on Educational Application of Computers, New York: EXXON Education Foundation. (ERIC Document Reproduction Service No. ED 123 193)

Beck, R. H. (1974). Values and forecasts. In S. P. Hencley & J. R. Yates (Eds.), *Futurism in education: Methodologies.* Berkeley, CA: McCutchan.

Bender, E. A. (1978). *An introduction to mathematical models.* New York: John Wiley.

Bennett, J. L. (1983). *Building decision support systems.* Reading, MA: Addison-Wesley.

Bennis, W. G. (1966). *Changing organizations.* New York: McGraw-Hill.

Bennis, W. G. (1981). Organization development at the crossroads. *Training and Development Journal, 35*(4), 19–26.

Berlinski, D. (1976). *On system analysis: An essay concerning the limitations of some mathematical methods in the social, political, and biological sciences.* Cambridge, MA: MIT Press.

Bessent, A., & Bessent, W. (1980). Determining the comparative efficiency of schools through data envelopment analysis. *Educational Administration Quarterly, 16*(2), 57–75.

Bessent, A., Bessent, W., Charnes, A., Cooper, W., & Thorogood, N. (1983). Evaluation of educational program proposals by data envelopment analysis. *Educational Administration Quarterly, 19*(2), 82–107.

Bessent, A., Bessent, W., Clark, T., & Elam, J. (1983). *Constrained facet analysis of the efficiency of organizational subunits with CFA code (Version 1.0)* (Research Rep. No. 015). Austin, TX: Educational Productivity Council, University of Texas.

Bessent, A., Bessent, W., Clark, T., Elam, J., & Chan, K. (1983). *Using RNFIND code (Version 1.0) to find organizational subunits with user specific characteristics* (Research Rep. No. 016). Austin, TX: Educational Productivity Council. University of Texas.

Bessent, A., Bessent, W., Elam, J., & Long, D. (1984). Educational productivity council employs management science methods to improve educational quality. *Interfaces, 14*(6), 1–10.

Bessent, A., Bessent, W., Kennington, J., & Reagan, B. (1982). Productivity in the Houston Independent School District. *Management Science, 28*(12), 1355–1367.

Bessent, W. (1971). The use of computers in simulation. In D. L. Bolton (Ed.), *The use of simulation in educational administration* (pp. 235–258). Columbus, OH: Charles E. Merrill.

Beyth-Marom, R., & Lichenstein, S. (1982). *An elementary approach to thinking under uncertainty: A prototype text.* Alexandria, VA: Army Research Institute for the Behavioral and Social Sciences.

Bidwell, C. E. (1965). The school as a formal organization. In J. G. March (Ed.), *Handbook of organizations.* Chicago: Rand McNally.

Bidwell, C. E. (1979). The school as a formal organization: Some new thoughts. In G. L. Immegart & W. L. Boyd (Eds.), *Problem finding in educational administration: Trends in research and theory.* Lexington, MA: Heath.

Billingsley, P. (1966). Markov Chain theory. *International Encyclo-*

pedia of Social Sciences, 11, 581–585.

Blake, R., & Mouton, J. (1976). *Organization change by design.* Austin, TX: Scientific Methods.

Bolton, C. K., & Boyer, R. K. (1973). Organizational development for academic departments. *Journal of Higher Education, 44*(5), 339–351.

Bolton, D. L. (1971). *The uses of simulation in educational administration.* Columbus, OH: Charles E. Merrill.

Bowers, D. G. (1976). Organizational development: Promises, performances, possibilities. *Organizational Dynamics, 4*(4), 50–62.

Boyd, W. L. (1983). Rethinking educational policy and management: Political science and educational administration in the 1980s. *American Journal of Education, 92*(1), 1–29.

Boyer, R. K., & Crockett, C. (Eds.). (1973). Organizational development in higher education (Special issue). *Journal of Higher Education, 44*(5).

Bridge, R. G., Judd, C. M., & Moock, P. R. (1979). *The determinants of educational outcomes: The impact of families, peers, teachers and schools.* Cambridge, MA: Ballinger.

Brigham Young University (1984). Objectives of the touch-tone registration system (A technical working paper for the USI data base/computer system and development office). Provo, UT: Brigham Young University.

Brigham Young University (1985). Spring 1985 class schedule. Provo, UT: Brigham Young University.

Bright, J. R., & Schoeman, M. E. (Eds.). (1973), *A guide to practical technological forecasting.* Englewood Cliffs, NJ: Prentice-Hall.

Brooks, J. E. (1970). Operational research in educational administration. *Education and Urban Society, 3,* 7–40.

Brown, D. J. (1974). Educational trend analysis methods. In S. P. Hencley & J. R. Yates (Eds.), *Futurism in education: Methodologies.* Berkeley, CA: McCutchan.

Brown, K. G., & Droegemueller, L. (1983). Microcomputer use in administrative decision support systems. *CAUSE/EFFECT, 6*(4), 12–19.

Brown, W. B. (1967), Model-building and organizations. *Academy of Management Journal, 14,* 169–178.

Bruno, J. E. (1970). The function of operations research specialists in large urban school districts. *IEEE Transactions on Systems Science and Cybernetics.* SSC–6, 293–302.

Bruno, J. E. (1976). *Educational policy analysis: A quantitative approach.* New York: Crane, Russak.

Bruno, J. E., & Fox, J. N. (1973). *Quantitative analysis in educational administrator preparation programs.* Columbus, OH: University Council for Educational Administration.

Burke, W. W. (Ed.). (1978). *The cutting edge: Current theory and practice in organization development.* La Jolla, CA: University.

Burke, W. W. (1982). *Organization development: Principles and practices.* Boston: Little Brown.

Burlingame, M. (1978). Impact of policy decisions on schools. In L. S. Shulman (Ed.), *Review of Research in Education: Vol. 5.* Itasca, IL: Peacock.

Burstein, L. (1978). Secondary analysis: An important resource for educational research and evaluation. *Educational Researcher, 7*(5), 9–12.

Callahan, R. E. (1962). *Education and the cult of efficiency.* Chicago: University of Chicago Press.

Chambers, J. C., Mullick, S. K., & Smith, D. D. (1971). How to choose the right forecasting technique. *Harvard Business Review, 49*(4), 55–64.

Charlesworth, J. C. (Ed.). (1963). *Mathematics and the social sciences: The utility and inutility of mathematics in the study of economics, political science, and sociology.* Philadelphia: American Academy of Political and Social Science.

Chow, Y. (1982). Business forecasting. In C. Heyel (Ed.), *The encyclopedia of management.* New York: Van Nostrand.

Churchman, C. W. (1968). *The systems approach.* New York: Dell.

Cleary, J. W. (1974). The decision matrix technique. In S. P. Hencley & J. R. Yates (Eds.), *Futurism in education: Methodology.* Berkeley, CA: McCutchan.

Cleveland, W. S., & McGill, R. (1985). Graphical perception and graphical methods for analyzing scientific data. *Science, 229*(30),

828–833.

Cohen, A. & Gadon, H. (1978). Changing the management culture in a public school system. *Journal of Applied Behavioral Science, 14*(1), 61–78.

Cook, T. D. (1984). Evaluation: Whose questions should be answered? In G. R. Gilbert (Ed.), *Making and managing policy: Formulation, analysis, and evaluation.* New York: Marcel Dekker.

Coombs, F. S. (1983). Education policy. In S. S. Nagel (Ed.), *Encyclopedia of policy studies.* New York: Marcel Dekker.

Copa, G. H. (1981). *Application of the decision sciences in vocational education.* St. Paul, MN: Minnesota Research and Development Center for Vocational Education, Department of Vocational and Technical Education, University of Minnesota.

Copa, G. H., & Moss, J. (Eds.). (1983). *Planning and vocational education.* New York: McGraw-Hill.

Cope, R. G. (Ed.). (1976). *Benefiting from interinstitutional research.* San Francisco: Jossey-Bass.

Cope, R. G. (Ed.). (1979). *Professional development for institutional research.* San Francisco: Jossey-Bass.

Correa, H. (1969). *Quantitative methods of educational planning.* Scranton, PA: International Textbook.

Correa, H. (Ed.). (1975). *Analytical models in educational planning and administration.* New York: David McKay.

Cronbach, L. J., & Suppes, P. (Eds.). (1969). *Research for tomorrow's schools: Disciplined inquiry in education.* New York: Macmillan.

Cronin, J. M., & Horoschak, P. P. (1973). *Innovative strategies in field experiences for preparing educational administrators.* Columbus, OH: University Council for Educational Administration.

Culberston, J., Farquhar, R., Fogarty, B., & Shibles, M. (Eds.). (1973). *Social science content for preparing educational leaders.* Columbus, OH: Charles E. Merrill.

Cullison, R. (1969). Identification by probability and trial by arithmetic: A lesson for beginners in how to be wrong with greater precision. *Houston Law Review, 6*(5), 471–483.

Cunningham, L. L. (1982, May). *Educational leadership: What's next?* Paper presented at The Culbertson Conference. Austin, TX: University of Texas.

Cunningham, W. G. (1982). *Systematic planning for educational change.* Palo Alto, CA: Mayfield.

Daft, Richard. (1983). *Organization theory and design.* St. Paul, MN: West.

Dalkey, N. C. (1975). An elementary cross impact model. In H. A. Linstone & M. Turoff (Eds.). *The Delphi method: Techniques and applications.* Reading, MA: Addison-Wesley.

Darling-Hammond, L., Wise, A. E., & Pease, S. R. (1983). Teacher evaluation in the organizational context: A review of literature. *Review of Educational Research, 53*(2), 285–328.

Das, H. (1981). Relevance of organization development values and assumptions to scarcity situations. *Group & Organization Studies, 6*(4), 402–411.

Datta, L. (1984). Educational evaluations: More business as usual. In G. R. Gilbert (Ed.), *Making and managing policy: Formulation, analysis, evaluation.* New York: Marcel Dekker.

Day, L. H. (1975). Delphic research in the corporate environment. In H. A. Linstone & M. Turoff (Eds.), *The Delphi methods: Techniques and applications.* Reading, MA: Addison-Wesley.

Dede, C., & Kierstead, F. (1984). *Putting educational forecasts into perspective: A guide for decision makers.* (ERIC Document Reproduction Service No. ED 245 394)

DeFinetti, B. (1966). Probability: Interpretations. *International Encyclopedia of Social Sciences, 12,* 496–505.

Derr, C. B. (Ed.). (1974). *Organizational development in urban school systems.* Beverly Hills, CA: Sage.

Derr, C. B. (1976). "OD" won't work in schools. *Education and Urban Society, 8*(2), 227–241.

Dizazan, J. (1982). *An annotated bibliography of ERIC bibliographies, 1966–1980.* Westport, CT: Greenwood.

Dowling, W. (1971). *Effecive management and the behavioral sciences: Conversations from organizational dynamics.* New York: American Management Association.

Dressel, P., & Simon, L. A. (Eds.). (1976). *Allocating resources among departments*. San Francisco: Jossey-Bass.

Driebeck, N. J. (1969). *Applied linear programming*. Reading, MA: Addison-Wesley.

Educational Research Services (1982). *School district uses of computer technology*. (ERIC Document Reproduction Service No. ED 224 171)

Elam, S. M. (Ed.). (1984). Gallup polls of attitudes toward public education 1969–1984: A topical summary. Bloomington, IN: Phi Delta Kappa.

Elbing, A. (1978). *Behavioral decisions in organizations* (2nd ed.). Dallas: Scott, Foresman.

Engel, R. E., & Achola, P. P. (1983). Board of trustees and academic decision making: A review of literature and research. *Review of Educational Research*, 53(1), 55–74.

Enzer, S. (1983). New directions in futures methodology. In J. L. Morrison, W. L. Renfro, & W. I. Boucher (Eds.), *Applying methods and techniques of futures research*. San Francisco: Jossey-Bass.

Erlandson, D. A. (1978). An organizing strategy for managing change in the school. *NASSP Bulletin*, 64(435), 1–8.

Etzioni, A. (1967). Mixed-scanning: A "third" approach to decision making. *Public Administration Review*, 27(6), 385–392.

Evans, J. A. (1970). Educational management information systems: Progress and prospectives. In P. K. Piele & T. L. Eidell (Eds.), *Social and technological change: Implications for education* (pp. 247–322). Eugene, OR: University of Oregon Press.

Fairley, W. B., & Mosteller, F. (Eds.). (1977). *Statistics and public policy*. Reading, MA: Addison-Wesley.

Farley, J. (1979). *Vocational education outcomes: A thesaurus of outcome questions* (Research and Development Series No. 170). Columbus, OH: National Center for Research in Vocational Education, Ohio State University.

Farquhar, R. (1973). The social sciences in preparing educational leaders: An interpretative summary. In J. Culbertson, R. H. Farquhar, B. M. Fogarty, & M. R. Shibles (Eds.), *Social science content for preparing educational leaders*. Columbus, OH: Charles E. Merrill.

Fay, B. (1977). *Social theory and political practice*. Boston: George Allen & Unwin.

Fishbein, M. H. (Ed.). (1973). *The national archives and statistical research*. Athens, OH: Ohio University Press.

Ford, R. C., McLaughlin, F. S., & Nixdorf, J. (1980). Ten questions about MBP. *California Management Review*, 23(2), 88–94.

Forrester, J. W. (1971). Counterintuitive behavior of social systems. *Technology Review*, 73(3), 52–68.

Freeman, A. (1981). *Use of future studies techniques by educational administrators*. (ERIC Document Reproduction Service No. ED 207 134)

Friedlander, F., & Brown, L. D. (1974). Organization development. *Annual Review of Psychology*, 25, 313–341.

Friedman, E. A. (Ed.). (1980). Technological literacy and the liberal arts (Special issue). *Forum for Liberal Education*, 3(3).

Fullan, M., Miles, M. B., & Taylor, G. (1981). Organization development in schools: The state of the art. *Review of Educational Research*, 50(1), 121–183.

Gerardin, L. (1973). Study of alternative futures: A scenario writing method. In J. R. Bright & M. E. F. Schoeman (Eds.), *A guide to practical technological forecasting*. Englewood Cliffs, NJ: Prentice-Hall.

Getzels, J. W. (1979). Problem-finding and research in educational administration. In G. L. Immegart & W. L. Boyd (Eds.), *Problem-finding in educational administration: Trends in research and theory*. Lexington, MA: Heath.

Gilbert, G. R. (Ed.). (1984). *Making and managing policy: Formulation, analysis, evaluation*. New York: Marcel Dekker.

Goldman, T. A. (Ed.). (1967). *Cost-effectiveness analysis*. New York: Praeger.

Goodman, J. M. (1970). Delphi and the law of diminishing returns. *Technological Forecasting and Social Change*, 2(2), 225–226.

Gordon, T. J., & Raffensperger, M. J. (1973). The relevance tree method for planning basic research. In J. R. Bright & M. E. F.

Schoeman (Eds.), *A guide to practical technological forecasting*. Englewood Cliffs, NJ: Prentice-Hall.

Greene, T. B. Newsome, W. B. & Jones, S. R. (1977). A survey of the application of quantitative techniques to production/operations management in large organizations. *Academy of Management Journal*, 20(4), 669–676.

Griffiths, D. E. (1959). *Administrative theory*. New York: Appleton-Century-Crofts.

Griffiths, D. E. (1964). *Behavioral science and educational administration: The 63rd yearbook of the National Society for the Study of Education*. Chicago: University of Chicago Press.

Griffiths, D. E. (1969). Administrative theory. In R. L. Ebel (Ed.), *Encyclopedia of educational research* (4th ed.). New York: Macmillan.

Griffiths, D. E. (1979). Another look at research on the behavior of administrators. In G. L. Immegart & W. L. Boyd (Eds.), *Problem-finding in educational administration: Trends in research and theory*. Lexington, MA: Heath.

Groff, W. M. (1981). *Strategic planning: A new role for management information systems*. (ERIC Document Reproduction Service No. ED 213 446)

Gross, B. M. (1964). The scientific approach to administration. In D. E. Griffiths. *Behavioral science and educational administration: The 63rd yearbook of the National Society for the Study of Education*. Chicago: University of Chicago Press.

Guetzkow, H., Kotler, P., & Schultz, R. L. (1972). *Simulation in social and administrative science*. Englewood Cliffs, NJ: Prentice-Hall.

Gupta, S., & Richards, L. D. (1979). A lanugage for policy-level modeling. *Journal of the Operations Research Society*, 30, 297–308.

Gustafson, T. J. (1984). *Microcomputers in educational administration*. Englewood Cliffs, NJ: Prentice-Hall.

Haggart, S. (Ed.). (1972). *Program budgeting for school district planning*. Englewood Cliffs, NJ: Educational Technology.

Hale, J. A. (1972). *A review and synthesis of research on management systems for vocational and technical education*. Washington, DC: Office of Education. (ERIC Document Reproduction Service No. ED 062 505)

Handy, M. W., & Hussain, K. M. (1969). *Network analysis for educational managers*. Englewood Cliffs, NJ: Prentice-Hall.

Hansen, T., Klassen, D., & Lindsay, J. (1978). *A study of the availability, use and impact of computers in administration of schools and school districts*. St. Paul, MN: Minnesota Educational Computing Consortium.

Harris, A. L. (1983). Microcomputers in the college environment. *CAUSE/EFFECTS*, 6(4), 6–11.

Hartley, H. J. (1968). *Educational planning-programming-budgeting: A systems approach*. Englewood, NJ: Prentice-Hall.

Hartley, H. J. (1973). Discipline-based content: The economics of education. In J. Culbertson, R. H. Farquhar, B. M. Fogarty, & M. R. Shibles (Eds.), *Social science content for preparing educational leaders* Columbus, OH: Charles E. Merrill.

Harvey, F. A., & Hines, T. C. (1981). Synergistic interaction of microcomputers and large-scale computers in educational research. *The Journal*, 8(6), 56–58.

Harvey, J. B. (1974). Organization development as a religious movement. *Training and Development Journal*, 28(3), 24–27.

Harvey, L. J. (1978). *Zero-base budgeting*. Washington, DC: Office of Education. (ERIC Document Reproduction Service No. ED 164 019)

Helmer, O., & Rescher, N. (1959). On the epistemology of the inexact sciences. *Management Sciences*, 6(1), 25–52.

Hencley, S. P., & Yates, J. R. (Eds.). (1974). *Futurism in education methodologies*. Berkeley, CA: McCutchan.

Hennessy, B. (1981). *Public opinion* (4th ed.). Monterey, CA: Brooks/Cole.

Hentschke, G. C. (1975). *Management operations in education*. Berkeley, CA: McCutchan.

Hermann, C. G. (1966). Simulation of political processes. *International Encyclopedia of Social Sciences*, 14, 274–281.

Hershkowitz, M. (1976). Critical issues in educational needs assessment. *Educational Planning*, *3*(2), 6–15.

Herzberg, F. (1974). The wise old Turk. *Harvard Business Review*, *52*(5), 70–80.

Heydinger, R. B., & Zentner, R. D. (1983). Multiple scenario analysis: Introducing uncertainty into the planning process. In J. L. Morrison, W. L. Renfro, & W. I. Boucher (Eds.), *Applying methods and techniques of futures research* (pp. 51–68). San Francisco: Jossey-Bass.

Hirschorn, L. (1980, April). Scenario writing: A developmental approach. *Journal of the American Planning Association*, *46*(2), 172–183.

Hogarth, R. M., & Makridakis, S. (1981). Forecasting and planning: An evaluation. *Management Science*, *27*(2), 115–138.

Hoos, I. R. (1972). *Systems analysis in public policy: A critique*. Berkeley, CA: University of California Press.

Hopkins, D. S. (1971). On the use of large-scale simulation models for university planning. *Review of Educational Research*, *41*(5), 467–478.

Hopkins, D. S., & Massy, W. F. (1981). *Planning models for colleges and universities*. Stanford, CA: Stanford University Press.

Hopkins, D. S., & Schroeder, R. G. (Eds.). (1977). *Applying analytic methods to planning and management*. San Francisco: Jossey-Bass.

Hopkins, D. S. (1979). Computer models employed in university administration. *Interfaces*, *9*(2), 13–23.

Hostrop, R. W. (Ed.). (1973a). *Foundations of futurology on education*. Homewood, IL: ETC.

Hostrop, R. W. (1973b). *Managing education for results*. Homewood, IL: ETC.

Howard, E. R., & Brainard, E. A. (1975). *How school administrators make things happen*. West Nyack, NY: Parker.

Hoy, W. K., & Miskel, C. G. (1977). *Educational administration: Theory, research and practice*. New York: Random House.

Hudson, B. (1978). *Forecasting educational futures: Resolving uncertainties and disagreements through compact policy assessment*. (ERIC Document Reproduction Service No. ED 177 043)

Hultin, M. (1976). Evaluation of education projects funded by the World Bank Group. In C. C. Abt (Ed.), *The evaluation of social programs*. Beverly Hills, CA: Sage.

Hunt, R. G., & Magenaw, J. M. (1984). A task analysis strategy for research on decision making in organizations. In L. G. Nigro (Ed.), *Decision making in the public sector*. New York: Marcel Dekker.

Huse, E. F., & Cummings, T. G. (1985). *Organization development and change* (3rd ed.). St. Paul, MN: West.

Hussain, K. M. (1973). *Development of information systems for education*. Englewood Cliffs, NJ: Prentice-Hall.

Huxley, A. (1955). *Brave new world*. New York: Bantam.

Immegart, G. L., & Boyd, W. L. (Eds.). (1979). *Problem-finding in educational administration: Trends in theory and research*. Lexington, MA: Lexington.

Jackowski, E. M. (1974). The functions, products, financial support of urban school district research departments in Texas. (Doctoral dissertation, Texas A & M University, 1974). *Dissertation Abstracts International*, *39* (696A).

Jacques, J., & Ryan, E. J., Jr. (1978). Does management by objectives stifle organizational innovation in the public sector? *Canadian Public Administration*, *21*(1), 16–25.

Jantsch, E. (1969). *Technological forecasting in prospective*. Washington, DC: Organization for Economic Cooperation and Development.

Jones, J. E., & Pfeiffer, J. W. (1977). On the obsolescence of the term organization development. *Group & Organization Studies*, *2*(3), 263–264.

Joseph, E. C. (1974). An introduction to studying the future. In S. P. Hencley & J. R. Yates (Eds.), *Futurism in education: Methodologies*. Berkeley, CA: McCutchan.

Kahn, R. L. (1974). Organizational development: Some problems and proposals. *Journal of Applied Behavioral Science*, *10*, 485–502.

Kaufman, R. A. (1970). System approaches to education: Discussion and attempted integration. In P. K. Piele & T. L. Eidell (Eds.),

Social and technological change: Implications for education (pp. 121–188). Eugene, OR: University of Oregon Press.

Kaufman, R. A. (1972). *Educational systems planning*. Englewood Cliffs, NJ: Prentice-Hall.

Kaufman, R. A., & English, F. W. (1976). *Needs assessment: A guide to improve school district management*. Arlington, VA: American Association of School Administrators.

Kay, P. (Ed.). (1971). *Explorations in mathematical anthropology*. Cambridge, MA: MIT Press.

Keen, P., & Morton, M. (1980). *Decision support systems: An organizational perspective*. Reading MA: Addison-Wesley.

Kendall, M. G. (1966). Statistics: The history of statistical method. *International Encyclopedia of Social Sciences*, *15*, 225–232.

Kennedy School of Government (1979). *Official register of the John F. Kennedy School of Government 1979–1980*. Cambridge, MA: Harvard University Press.

Keppel, F. (1969). Operations analysis—The promise and the pitfalls. In D. S. Stoller & W. Dorfman (Eds.), *Socio-Economic Planning Sciences: An International Journal*, *2*(2/3/4), 121–125.

Keys, C. B. (1979). Renewal processes in urban parochial schools. *Theory into Practice*, *18*(2), 97–105.

Kirkpatrick, S. A. (1974). *Quantitative analysis of political data*. Columbus, OH: Charles E. Merrill.

Knezevich, S. J. (Ed.). (1969a). *Administrative technology and the school executive*. Washington DC: American Association of School Administrators.

Kenzevich, S. J. (1969b). The systems approach to school administration: Some perceptions on the state of the art in 1967. In D. S. Stoller & W. Dorfman (Eds.), *Socio-Economic Planning Sciences: An International Journal*, *2*(2/3/4), 127–133.

Kowalski, T. J. (1984). The debilities of MBO in educational organizations. *NASSP Bulletin*, *68*(472), 119–123.

Kraetsch, G. A. (1979). Methodology and limitations of Ohio enrollment projections. *The AIR professional file* (Report No. 4). (ERIC Document Reproduction Service No. ED 180 391)

Krell, T. C. (1981). The marketing of organizational development: Past, present and future. *Journal of Applied Behavioral Sciences*, *17*(3), 309–323.

Kruskal, W. H. (1969). Statistics: The field. *International Encyclopedia of Social Sciences*, *15*, 206–224.

Kur, E. C. (1981). OD: Perspectives, processes and prospects. *Training and Development Journal*, *35*(4), 28–34.

Laing, J. D. (1984). *A problem space for laboratory studies of collective decisions* (Decision Science Working Paper No. 84–01–09). Philadelphia: Wharton School, University of Pennsylvania.

Ledbetter, W., & Cox, J. F. (1977). Are O. R. techniques being used? *Journal of Industrial Engineering*, *9*(2), 19–21.

Lee, R. M. (1984). *Applications software and organizational change: Issues in the representation of knowledge* (Decision Science Working Paper No. 84–01–03). Philadelphia: Wharton School, University of Pennsylvania.

Levin, H. M. (1975). Cost-effectiveness analysis in evaluation research. In M. Guttentag & E. L. Struening (Eds.), *Handbook of evaluation: Vol. 2*. Beverly Hills, CA: Sage.

Levin, H. M., & Woo, L. (1981). An evaluation of the costs of computer-assisted instruction. *Economics of Education Review*, *2*(1), 2–26.

Levin, R., & Kirkpatrick, C. (1975). *Quantitative approaches to management*. New York: McGraw-Hill.

Levin, R. I., Kirkpatrick, C. A., & Rubin, D. S. (1982). *Quantitative approaches to management* (5th ed.). New York: McGraw-Hill.

Levinson, H. (1972). The clinical psychologist as organizational diagnostician. *Professional Psychology*, *3*(1), 34–40.

Lewis, A. (1978). Forecasting social trends as a basis for formulating educational policy. (ERIC Document Reproduction Service No. ED 161 786)

Lindblom, C. E., & Cohen, D. K. (1979). *Usable knowledge: Social science and social problem solving*. New Haven, CT: Yale University Press.

Linstone, H. A. (1973). On discounting the future. *Technological Forecasting and Social Change*, *4*(2), 335–338.

Linstone, H. A., & Turoff, M. (Eds.). (1975). *The Delphi method:*

Techniques and applications. Reading, MA: Addison-Wesley.

Little, R. O., & Temares, M. L. (1983). *The impact of technology on the University of Miami.* (ERIC Document Reproduction Service No. ED 244 533)

Lueck, L. A. (1981). *A bibliography of higher education long-range planning documents.* (ERIC Document Reproduction Service No. ED 198 779)

Lundquist, G. W. (1982). Needs assessment in organizational development. In C. R. Reynolds & T. B. Gutkin (Eds.), *The handbook of school psychology.* New York: John Wiley.

Macdonald, J. B., & Clark, D. (1973). Critical value questions and the analysis of objectives and curricula. In R. M. Travers (Ed.), *Second handbook of research on teaching.* Chicago: Rand McNally.

Magee, J. F. (1973). Progress in the management sciences. *Interfaces, 3*(2), 35–41.

Mandell, M. B. (1984). Strategies for improving the usefulness of analytical techniques for public sector decision making. In L. G. Nigro (Ed.), *Decision making in the public sector.* New York: Marcel Dekker.

Mann, D. (1975). *Policy decision making in education: An introduction to calculation and control.* New York: Teachers College Press, Columbia University.

Martino, J. (1970). The optimism/pessimism consistency of Delphi panelists. *Technological Forecasting and Social Change, 2*(2), 221–224.

Martino, J. (1972). *Technological forecasting for decision making.* New York: American Elsevier.

Mason, R., & Mitroff, I. (1981). *Challenging strategic planning assumptions.* New York: John Wiley.

Mason, T. (Ed.). (1976). *Assessing computer-based systems models.* San Francisco: Jossey-Bass.

Matthews. W. M. (1973). *Computer applications in decision making in educational administration.* (ERIC Document Reproduction Service No. ED 087 436)

Maxwell, W. D. (1973). Number numbness. *Liberal Education, 48*(3), 405–416.

McCall, G. J., & Weber, G. H. (1983). Policy analysis across academic disciplines. In S. S. Nagel (Ed.), *Encyclopedia of policy studies.* New York: Marcel Dekker.

McConkey, D. D. (1973). MBO—Twenty years later, where do we stand? A preliminary evaluation. *Business Horizons, 16*(4), 25–36.

McGivney, J. H., & Bowles, B. D. (1972). The political aspects of PPBS. *Planning & Changing, 3*(1), 3–12.

McGrath, J. M. (1974). Relevance trees. In S. P. Hencley & J. R. Yates (Eds.), *Futurism in education: Methodologies.* Berkeley, CA: McCutchan.

McKenny, J. L, & Kern, P. G. W. (1974). How managers' minds work. *Harvard Business Review, 52*(3), 81.

McNamara, J. F. (1971). *Applications of mathematical programming models in educational planning: An overview and selected bibliography* (Exchange Bibliograph No. 271). Monticello, IL: Council of Planning Librarians.

McNamara, J. F. (1972a). Mathematics and educational administration. *Journal of Educational Administration, 10*(2), 164–193.

McNamara, J. F. (1972b). Operations research and educational planning. *Journal of Educational Data Processing, 9*(6), 1–12.

McNamara, J. F. (1973). Mathematical programming applications in educational planning. *Socio-Economic Planning Sciences: An International Journal, 7*(1), 19–35.

McNamara, J. F. (1974a). Markov Chain theory and technological forecasting. In S. P. Hencley & J. R. Yates (Eds.), *Futurism in education: Methodologies.* Berkeley, CA: McCutchan.

McNamara, J. F. (1974b). The design of technological forecasting studies. In S. P. Hencley & J. R. Yates (Eds.), *Futurism in education: Methodologies.* Berkeley, CA: McCutchan.

McNamara, J. F. (1979). Practical significance and mathematical models in administrative research. In G. I. Immegart & W. L. Boyd (Eds.), *Problem finding in educational administration: Trends in theory and research.* Lexington, MA: Lexington.

McNamara, J. F. (1981). *The decision sciences in vocational edu-cation leadership development programs: A chart essay.* College Station, TX: Department of Educational Psychology, Texas A & M University.

McNamara, J. F. (Ed.). (1982). *Extending administrative effectiveness through microcomputing: A chart essay on project findings presented to the Administrative Staff of the College Station Independent School District.* College Station, TX: College of Education, Texas A & M University.

McNamara, J. F., & Erlandson, D. A (Eds.). (1984). *Improving school information systems through microcomputing: A chart essay on project findings presented to the Administrative Staff of the A & M Consolidated High School.* College Station, TX: College of Education, Texas A & M University.

McNamara, J. F., Fetsco, T. G., Erlandson, D. A., & Hart, M. S. (1987, Summer). Improving school information systems through microcomputing: A university-high school cooperative venture. *Public Administration Quarterly.*

Mebane, D. D. (Ed.). (1981). *Solving college and university problems through technology.* (ERIC Document Reproduction Service No. ED 220 095)

Miklos, E. (1972). *Training-in-common for educational, public and business administrators.* Columbus, OH: University Council for Educational Administration.

Mills, T. (1975). Human Resources—Why the new concern? *Harvard Business Review, 53*(2), 120–134.

Miloy, L. H. (1979). The American public university in 1998: A scenario. (Doctoral dissertation, Texas A & M University, 1978). *Dissertation Abstracts International, 39*(4079A).

Mitroff, I. (1983). *Stakeholders of the organizational mind.* San Francisco: Jossey-Bass.

Mitroff, I., & Turoff, M. (1971). The whys behind the hows. *IEEE Spectrum, 10*(3), 62–71.

Morgan, J. M. (1982). *Microcomputer applications in educational program planning.* (ERIC Document Reproduction Service No. ED 224 455)

Morris, W. T. (1975). Quantitative methods—A management perspective. *Industrial Engineering, 7*(6). Cited in R. I. Levin, C. A. Kirkpatrick, & D. S. Rubin (1982). *Quantitative approaches to management* (5th ed.). New York: McGraw-Hill.

Morrison, J. L., Renfro, W. L., & Boucher, W. I. (Eds.). (1983). *Applying methods and techniques of future research.* San Francisco: Jossey-Boss.

Morrison, P. (1981). High technology, rapid change, and world competition in the eighties: The place for OD. *Group & Organization Studies, 6*(4), 395–402.

Mort, P. R., & Furno, O. F. (1960). *Theory and synthesis of a sequential simplex: A model for assessing the effectiveness of administrative policies* (Monograph No. 12). New York: Institute of Administrative Research, Teachers College, Columbia University.

Muller, M. E. (1966). Random numbers. *International Encyclopedia of Social Science, 13*, 307–313.

Murnane, R. J. (1975). *The impact of school resources on the learning of inner city children.* Cambridge, MA: Ballinger.

Nagel, S. S. (1982). Simplifying basic methods. In S. S. Nagel (Ed.), *Public policy: Goals, means, and methods.* New York: St. Martin's.

Nagel, S. S. (1984). Policy analysis. In G. R. Billert (Ed.). *Making and managing policy: Formulation, analysis, evaluation.* New York: Marcel Dekker.

National Academy of Sciences (1968). *The mathematical sciences: A report.* Washington, DC: Author.

National Academy of Sciences (1969). *The mathematical sciences: A collection of essays.* Cambridge, MA: MIT Press.

National Association of Schools of Public Affairs and Administration (1974). *Guidelines and standards for professional masters degree in public affairs and public administration.* Washington, DC: Author.

National Institute of Education (1973). *A collection of ERIC document résumés on planning, programming, budgeting systems* (ERIC Abstract Series No. 25). Washington, DC: Department of Health, Education and Welfare. (ERIC Document Reproduction Service No. ED 084 648)

Nay, J. N., Scanlon, J. W., Schmidt, R. E., & Wholey, J. S. (1976). If you don't care where you get to, then it doesn't matter which way you go. In C. C. Abt (Ed.), *The evaluation of social programs*. Beverly Hills, CA: Sage.

Naylor, T. H. (1972). Methodological considerations in simulating social and administrative systems. In H. Guetzkow, P. Kotler, & R. L. Schultz (Eds.), *Simulation in social and administrative science*. Englewood Cliffs, NJ: Prentice-Hall.

Nemhauser, G. L. (1966). *Introduction to dynamic programming*. New York: John Wiley.

Nevo, D. (1983). The conceptualization of educational evaluation: An analytical review of literature. *Review of Educational Research, 53*(1), 117–128.

Newell, A., & Simon, H. A. (1966). Simulation of individual behavior. *International Encyclopedia of Social Science, 14,* 262–269.

Noble, C. E. (1979). Solving ill-structured management problems. *Business, 29*(1), 26–33.

Noether, G. E. (1966). Probability: Formal probability. *International Encyclopedia of Social Sciences, 12,* 487–496.

Odiorne, G. S. (1965). *Management by objectives: A system of managerial leadership*. New York: Pitman.

Oliver, R. M. (1972). Operations research in university planning. In A. Drake, R. L. Keeney, & P. M. Morse (Eds.), *Analysis of public systems*. Cambridge, MA: MIT Press.

Owens, R. G. (1970). *Organizational behavior in schools*. Englewood Cliffs, NJ: Prentice-Hall.

Owens, R. G. (1974). Conceptual models for research and practice in the administration of change. *Journal of Educational Administration, 12*(2), 3–17.

Parker, S. (1985, May). Campus-based research: Stimulus for renewal. *Professors of Secondary School Administration and Supervision, 1*(2), 7–8.

Pepper, J. B. (1984, February). *The decision seminar of Harold Lasswell: Uses in establishing effective lines of communication among the school board, community and superintendent.* Paper presented at the Annual Meeting of the American Association of School Administrators, Las Vegas.

Peters, T. J., & Waterman, R. H. (1983). *In search of excellence: Lessons from America's best-run companies*. New York: Harper & Row.

Peterson, N. W. (Ed.). (1976). *Benefiting from interinstitutional research*. San Francisco: Jossey-Bass.

Popper, S. H. (Ed.). (1974). *Imaging alternative future school organizations*. Minneapolis, MN: Division of Educational Administration, University of Minnesota.

Prentice, L. (1976). *Words, pictures, media: Communications in educational politics*. Boston: Institute for Responsive Education.

Pyhrr, P. (1973). *Zero-base budgeting*. New York: John Wiley.

Quade, E. S. (1975). *Analysis for public decisions*. New York: American Elsevier.

Quant, R. E. (1966). Programming. *International Encyclopedia of Social Sciences, 12,* 552–560.

Rahim, S. (Ed.). (1978). *Planning methods, models, and organization: A review study for communication policy making and planning*. (ERIC Document Reproduction Service No. ED 233 423)

Rand Corporation. (1979, June). *A bibliography of selected Rand publications on education.* (No. SB–1026). Santa Monica, CA: Author.

Rand Corporation. (1983, March). *A bibliography of selected Rand publications on computing technology* (No. SB–1036). Santa Monica, CA: Author.

Raucher, S. M., & Koehler, T. J. (1982). *Long range planning for computer use: A task force model*. (ERIC Document Reproduction Service No. ED 225 58)

Ravetz, J. (1971). *Specific knowledge and its social problems*. Oxford, England: Oxford University Press.

Renfro, W. L., & Morrison, J. L. (1983). The scanning process: Methods and uses. In J. L. Morrison, W. L. Renfro, & W. I. Boucher (Eds.), *Applying methods and techniques of futures research*. San Francisco: Jossey-Bass.

Rich, R. F., & Goldsmith, N. M. (1983). The utilization of policy research. In S. S. Nagel (Ed.). *Encyclopedia of policy studies*. New York: Marcel Dekker.

Rivard, R. J. (1970). *The economics of coeducation: The case of Texas A & M University*. Unpublished master's thesis, Texas A & M University, Department of Economics, College Station, TX.

Ross, D. H. (Ed.). (1958). *Administration for adaptability*. New York: Metropolitan School Study Council, Teachers College, Columbia University.

Rothenberg, J. (1975). Cost-benefit analysis: A methodological exposition. In M. Guttentag & E. L. Struening (Ed.), *Handbook of evaluation: Vol. 2*. Beverly Hills, CA: Sage.

Rubin, L. (Ed.). (1975). *The future of education: Perspectives on tomorrow's schooling*. Boston: Allyn & Bacon.

Runkel, P., & Schmuck, R. (1976). *Organization development in schools: A review of research findings from Oregon*. Eugene, OR: Center for Educational Policy and Management, University of Oregon.

Runkel, P., & Schmuck, R. (1974). *Findings from the research and development program on strategies on organizational change at CEPM–CASEA*. Eugene, OR: Center for Educational Policy and Management, University of Oregon.

Russell, R. E. (1982). Administrative information systems in higher education: The 1981 national survey. *CAUSE/EFFECT 5*(6), 24–27.

Sackman, H. (1975). *Delphi technique: Expert opinion, forecasting and group process*. Lexington, MA: Heath.

Schein, E. H. (1969). *Process consultation: Its role in organizational development*. Reading, MA: Addison-Wesley.

Scheinfeld, D. (1979). A three-faceted design for renewing urban elementary schools. *Theory into Practice., 18*(2), 114–125.

Schick, A. (1973). A death in the bureaucracy: The demise of federal PPB. *Public Administration Review, 2,* 146–156.

Schmidtlein, F. A. (1981). Comprehensive and incremental decision paradigms and their implications for educational planning. In G. Copa & J. Moss (Eds.), *Planning and vocational education*. New York: McGraw-Hill.

Schmuck, R. A., Runkel, P., Arends, J., & Arends, R. (1977). *The second handbook of organization development in schools*. Palo Alto, CA: Mayfield.

Schmuck, R. A., & Miles, M. B. (Eds.). (1972). *Organization development in schools*. Palo Alto, CA: National Press.

Schmuck, R. A., & Runkel, P. J. (1985). *The handbook of organizational development in schools* (3rd ed.). Palo Alto, CA: Mayfield.

Schroeder, R. G. (1973). A survey of management science in university operations. *Management Science, 19*(8), 895–906.

Schroeder, R. G., & Adams, C. R. (1976). The effective use of management science in university administration. *Review of Educational Research, 46*(1), 117–131.

Seiler, J. A. (1967). *Systems analysis in organizational behavior*. Homewood, IL: Richard D. Irwin and Dorsey.

Sharples, B. (1979). Z.B.B.—How useful is it for educational administration? *Education Canada, 19*(3), 14–21.

Shane, H. G. (1973). *The educational significance of the future*. Bloomington, IN: Phi Delta Kappa Educational Foundation.

Shaw, R. C. (1980). How accurate can enrollment forecasting be? *NASSP Bulletin, 64*(439), 13–20.

Sheehan, B. S. (1982a). *Decision support systems: An institutional research perspective* (AIR 1982 Annual Forum Paper). (ERIC Document Reproduction Service No. ED 220 047)

Sheehan, B. S. (Ed.). (1982b). *Information technology: Advances and applications*. San Francisco: Jossey-Bass.

Sheehan, B. S. (1983). *Measurement for decision support* (AIR 1983 Annual Forum Paper). (ERIC Document Reproduction Service No. ED 232 582)

Shellard, G. D. (1982). Operations research. In C. Heyel (Ed.), *Encyclopedia of management* (3rd ed.). New York: Van Nostrand.

Shutz, R. E. (1976, May). Research in schools. *Educational Re-*

searcher, 5(5), 1–2.

Silver, P. (1983). *Educational administration: Theoretical perspectives on practice and research.* New York: Harper & Row.

Simon, H. A. (1969). *The sciences of the artificial.* Cambridge, MA: MIT Press.

Simon, H. A. (1977). *The new science of management decision* (rev. ed.). Englewood Cliffs, NJ: Prentice Hall.

Smith, A. W. (1982). *Management systems: Analyses and applications.* Chicago: Dryden.

Snapp, M., & Davidson, J. L. (1982). Systems interventions for school psychologists: A case study. In C. R. Reynolds & T. B. Gutkin (Eds.). *The handbook of school psychology.* New York: John Wiley.

Sprague, R. H., & Carlson, E. D. (1982). *Building effective decision support systems.* Englewood Cliffs, NJ: Prentice-Hall.

Spuck, D. W., & Atkinson, G.. (1983). Administrative uses of the microcomputer. *AIDS Journal, 17*(1), 83–90.

Stake, R. (1970). Objectives, priorities and other judgment data. *Review of Educational Research, 40*(2), 181–212.

Staman, E. M. (Ed.). (1979). *Examining new trends in administrative computing.* San Francisco: Jossey-Bass.

Stanford University Committee on Administration and Policy Analysis. (1974). Programs in administration and policy analysis: Guidelines for students. In L. B. Mayhew (Ed.), *Educational leadership and declining enrollments.* Berkeley, CA: McCutchan.

Starr, M. K., & Miller, D. W. (1960). *Executive decisions and operations research.* Englewood Cliffs, N. J.: Prentice-Hall.

Steen, L. A. (Ed.). (1978). *Mathematics today: Twelve informal essays.* New York: Springer-Verlag.

Stewart, D. W., & Garson, G. D. (1983). *Organizational behavior and public management.* New York: Marcel Dekker.

Stokey, E., & Zeckhauser, R. (1978). *A primer for policy analysis.* New York: Norton.

Stoller, D. S., & Dorfman, W. (Eds.). (1969). Proceedings of the symposium on operations analysis of education. *Socio-Economic Planning Sciences: An International Journal, 2*(2/3/4), 103–520.

Strauch, R. E. (1976). A critical look at quantitative methodology. *Policy Analysis, 2,* 121–144.

Strauss, G. (1973). Organizational development: Credits and debits. *Organizational Dynamics, 1*(3), 2–19.

Stromsdorfer, E. W., & Farkas, G. (Eds.). (1980). *Evaluation studies review annual: Vol. 5.* Beverly Hills, CA: Sage.

Swan, W. K. (1983). Decision making. In T. D. Lynch (Ed.), *Organizational theory and management.* New York: Marcel Dekker.

Swersey, A. J., & Ballard, W. (1984). Scheduling school buses. *Management Science, 30*(7), 844–853.

Temkin, S. (1970a). *A comprehensive theory of cost effectiveness.* Philadelphia: Research for Better Schools.

Temkin, S. (1970b). A cost effectiveness evaluation approach to improving resource allocations for school systems. (Doctoral dissertation, University of Pennsylvania, 1969). *Dissertation Abstracts International, 31* (1595b).

Temkin, S. (1974). Making sense of benefit-cost analysis and cost effectiveness analysis. *Improving Human Performance: A Research Quarterly, 3*(2), 39–48.

Temkin, S., & McNamara, J. F. (1973). A comprehensive planning model for school districts: Decision rules and implementation strategies. *Journal of Educational Administration, 11*(2), 285–301.

Thierauf, R. J. (1975). *Systems analysis and design of real-time management information systems.* Englewood Cliffs, NJ: Prentice-Hall.

Thierauf, R. J. (1978). *Distributed processing systems.* Englewood Cliffs, NJ: Prentice-Hall.

Thierauf, R. J. (1983). *A manager's complete guide to effective information systems: A questionnaire approach.* New York: Free Press.

Thierauf, R. J., & Grosse, R. A. (1970). *Decision making through operations research.* New York: John Wiley.

Thomas, J. A. (1971). *The productive school: A systems approach to educational administration.* New York: John Wiley.

Tomeski, E. A., & Sadek, K. (1982). Management information systems. In C. Heyel (Ed.), *The encyclopedia of management* (3rd ed.). New York: Van Nostrand.

Trochim, W. M. (1983). Methodologically based discrepancies in compensatory education evaluation. In R. J. Light (Ed.), *Evaluation studies review annual: Vol. 8.* Beverly Hills, CA: Sage.

Tufte, E. R. (Ed.). (1970). *The quantitative analysis of social problems.* Reading, MA: Addison-Wesley.

Tufte, E. R. (1983). *The visual display of quantitative information.* Cheshire, CN: Graphic.

Tugwell, F. (1973). *Search for alternatives: Public policy and the study of the future.* Cambridge, MA: Winthrop.

Tull, D. S., & Albaum, G. S. (1973). *Survey research: A decisional approach.* New York: Intext Educational.

Turban, E. (1972). A sample survey of operations research activities at the corporate level. *Operations Research, 20*(3), 708–721.

Turoff, M. (1970). The design of a policy Delphi. *Technological Forecasting and Social Change, 2*(2), 20–35. Reprinted in M. A. Linstone & M. Turoff (Eds.). (1975). *The Delphi method: Techniques and applications.* Reading, MA: Addison-Wesley.

Tyler, R. W. (Ed.). (1969). Education evaluation: New roles, new means. The 68th yearbook of the National Society for the Study of Education. Chicago: University of Chicago Press.

U.S. General Accounting Office. (1969). *Glossary of systems analysis and PPBS terms.* Washington, DC: U.S. Government Printing Office.

Van Dusseldorp, R. A., Richardson, D. E., & Foley, W. J. (1971). *Educational decision making through operations research.* Boston: Allyn and Bacon.

Vanston, J. H., Jr., Frisbrie, W. P.., Lopreato, S. C., & Poston, D. L., Jr. (1977). Alternate scenario planning. *Technological Forecasting and Social Change, 10,* 159–180.

Varney, G. H. (1977). *Organization development for managers.* Reading, MA: Addison-Wesley.

Wagner, H. M. (1971). The ABC's of OR. *Operations Research, 19*(5). Cited in Levin, R. I., Kirkpatrick, C. A., & Rubin, D. S. (1982). *Quantitative approaches to management* (5th ed.). New York: McGraw-Hill.

Wagschall, P. H. (1983). Judgmental forecasting techniques and institutional planning: An example. In J. L. Morrison, W. L. Renfro, & W. I. Boucher (Eds.), *Applying methods and techniques of futures research.* San Francisco: Jossey-Bass.

Ward, R. A. (1974). More implementation through on OR/behavioral science partnership and management training. *Operational Research Quarterly, 25*(2), 209–217.

Watson, H. J., & Marett, P. G. (1979). A survey of management science implementation problems. *Interfaces, 9*(4), 129–133.

Weaver, T. (1971). The Delphi forecasting method. *Phi Delta Kappan, 52*(5), 267–271.

Weiss, C. H. (1980). *Social science research and decision making.* New York: Columbia University Press.

Weiss, E. H. (1973). PPBS in Education. *Journal of General Education, 25*(1), 17–27.

Weitz, H. (1969). *An assessment of the contribution of operations research to educational planning* (Technical Paper No. XVIG, 4). Yorktown Heights, NY: IBM.

Welty, G. (1973). Plato and Delphi. *Futures, 5*(3), 281–286.

Wharton School. (1979). *Decision sciences at the Wharton School.* Philadelphia: Department of Decision Sciences, University of Pennsylvania.

Wharton School. (1984). *Social systems sciences at the Wharton School.* Philadelphia: Department of Social Systems Sciences, University of Pennsylvania.

White, G. P. (1985). *An annotated bibliography of management science applications to academic administration.* Carbondale, IL: Department of Management, Southern Illinois University at Carbondale.

White, M. J. (1983). Policy analysis and management science. In S. S. Nagel (Ed.). *Encyclopedia of policy studies.* New York: Marcel Dekker.

Willower, D. J. (1979). Some issues in research on school organizations. In G. L. Immegart & W. L. Boyd (Eds.), *Problem-*

finding in educational administration: Trends in research and theory. Lexington, MA: Heath.

Wolcott, H. F. (1977). *Teachers versus technocrats.* Eugene, OR: Center for Educational Policy and Management, University of Oregon Press.

Wynn, R. (1972). *Unconventional methods and materials for preparing educational administrators.* Columbus, OH: University Council for Educational Administration.

Yeager, R. F. (1979). Rationality and retrenchment: The use of computer simulation to aid decision making in school closings. *Education and Urban Society, 11*(3), 296–312.

Zeisel, H. (1966). Statistics as legal evidence. *International Encyclopedia of Social Sciences, 15,* 246–247.

Zeleny, M. (1975). Notes, ideas and techniques: New vistas of management science. *Computers and Operations Research, 2*(2), 121–125.

CHAPTER 27

Evaluation as an Administrative Function

Daniel L. Stufflebeam and William J. Webster

INTRODUCTION

The intent of this chapter is to increase educational administrators' commitment to and facility in evaluating educational institutions, programs, personnel, and services. Continuous, systematic evaluation is a process necessary to assuring and demonstrating the quality of education. Sound evaluation of education depends heavily on the informed and strong leadership of educational administrators. Long experience and study in the field of educational evaluation tells us that the role of evaluation-oriented leader is even more crucial to securing effective evaluation services than is the role of evaluation specialist. The services of the latter can be of little relevance and assistance unless focused on issues important to those in authority and unless administrators are attuned to using the findings. The evaluation of education is most effective when systematically guided and used by educational administrators.

In order to foster evaluation-oriented educational leadership, we organized this chapter to address four main purposes. First, we examine a number of conceptual issues in evaluation that are especially important in educational administration. Second, we review the organization and functions of educational evaluation systems in order to illuminate the range of issues involved in conducting and using evaluation services. Third, we assess the strengths and weaknesses of several techniques often employed in educational evaluation, and we emphasize the importance of using multiple

methods. Finally, we propose an agenda for strengthening the role of administrators in evaluating education.

We have sought to compile a comprehensive review and analysis of ideas and literature and our combined 40 years of experience concerning the use of evaluation technology in the administration of schools. We have drawn on Francis Chase's (1980) study of urban education, which focused especially on the nature of formalized evaluation work in urban school districts. We recognize that these experiences and studies in evaluation have been concentrated in relatively large educational organizations. Thus, the message of this chapter, and especially its illustrations, are of most relevance to administrators in large school districts. However, a common denominator of school districts of all sizes is the school, and we have spoken whenever we could to the evaluation roles of school principals as well as central-office administrators. Of course, the fundamental conceptual and philosophical issues in evaluation are pervasive and are relevant in any type and size of educational institution. Another caveat concerns the datedness of some material in this chapter. For example, since the Chase (1980) data were gathered in the late 1970s, some of our characterizations of school district evaluation operations are out of date and may no longer be valid. Nevertheless, these data help reveal the range of issues and approaches in school district evaluation. We hope this chapter will provide a unique resource, with information and practical recommendations for administrators in all types and sizes of school districts to use in advancing the contributions of evaluation services to education.

Consultant/reviewers: Francis S. Chase, Dallas, Texas, and Jack C. Meruvin, University of Minnesota

CONCEPTUALIZING THE
EVALUATION FUNCTION

Evaluation is a conceptual activity. Evaluators and their clients must conceptualize the evaluation questions, information needed to address them, appropriate values and criteria for examining and interpreting the information, ways to obtain and analyze the information, the structure of reports for communicating findings, and appropriate ways to use the findings. They must also conceptualize the ways in which evaluation fits into the structure of the school system and the community: that is, how evaluation is to be governed, organized, administered, financed, controlled for bias, and employed within a political environment. And they need to develop a shared conception of what evaluation means, what it is for, how it is effectively implemented, and how it is properly appraised.

Educational leaders are key persons in the task of conceptualizing evaluation services. If they fail to attend continuously to the conceptual nature of evaluation, their investments in evaluation will likely yield poor returns. A lack of attention to this issue inevitably results in an unsystematic, confusing, aimless, unused, and often chaotic approach to evaluation. Conversely, rigid adherence to a conceptual framework adopted at some time in the past can result in evaluation services that neither adapt to the evolving needs of the school system nor keep pace with the state of the art of evaluation.

Hence, leaders of school systems should help their staffs and constituents collectively to develop and use a shared conception of evaluation. This section identifies some of the conceptual issues to be dealt with, gives examples of ways some school systems have addressed these issues, and offers some recommendations. It cannot be overemphasized, however, that no conception of evaluation can be adequate for all time. Thinking about evaluation and its application in particular environments must be an ongoing, collective process if school systems are to get the most from their evaluation systems.

The Meaning of Evaluation

The importance of an evolving conception of evaluation is apparent when one considers the issue of the definition of evaluation. For about 30 years, educators held on—often unthinkingly—to the definition proposed by Smith and Tyler (1942) that evaluation means determining whether objectives have been achieved. This definition did provide a common view of evaluation that educators could use to promote and assess improvements. For example, it was particularly in-

fluential in the development of minimum competency testing programs. In the main, however, this definition has been used uncritically and persistently. Undoubtedly, this ritualistic application has limited the usefulness of evaluation services by narrowing the perspective of evaluations to those concerns evident in specified objectives, by suggesting that evaluation is applied only at the end of a project, and by encouraging educators and others to define success in terms of objectives without also evaluating the objectives.

The objectives-based conception of evaluation still prevails in some school systems, but in many others it has been replaced by a definition based on the view that evaluation should guide decision making. The latter definition has been very influential in the evaluation systems of several school districts (e.g., Dallas, Fort Worth, and Austin, Texas; Lansing and Saginaw, Michigan; and Cincinnati and Columbus, Ohio). It is an improvement over the objectives-oriented definition because its thrust is to ensure that evaluation guides a program throughout its development and implementation and because it implies the assessment of a wider range of variables: needs, plans, operations, and results. This definition also has the virtue of emphasizing that evaluation is a communication as well as an information-gathering process. However, in our experience this definition has garnered some connotations that can stifle evaluation services.

One such connotation is that evaluation serves only high-level decision makers, which is taken to mean superintendents, their immediate staffs, and sometimes school board members. Obviously, all participants in the educational process (including teachers, students, parents, and principals) make choices that affect the quality of educational offerings and outcomes. These persons also need evaluative feedback. Another dubious connotation of the decision-oriented definition is that information requirements are determined solely by the clients of evaluation. A likely consequence of this interpretation is to reinforce the clients' objectives without evaluating them in a broader framework of values. This interpretation can also lead to evaluation services that enhance the power and influence of a client, such as a superintendent, without also helping other bodies, such as community interest groups, to assess the worth and merit of school programs in relation to their expectations and questions. While the decision-oriented definition has clear advantages, systems that use it should examine their shared conceptions for problems such as those discussed.

A third definition of evaluation was adopted by the Joint Committee on Standards for Educational Evaluation (1981). This definition is noteworthy because it was agreed to by a national committee appointed by 12 organizations to develop standards for educational evaluation (American Association of School Administrators, American Council for Private Education, American Educational Research Association, American Federation of Teachers, American Psychological Association, American Personnel and Guidance Association, Association for Supervision and Curriculum Development, Education Commission of the States, National Association for Elementary School Principals, National Education Association, National Council on Measurement in Education, and National School Boards Association). The definition was the basis for the Joint Committee's *Standards*, which have become influential in the practice of educational evaluation and states crisply: "Evaluation is the systematic assessment of the worth or merit of some object." The stipulation calls attention to the importance of clarifying the thing being evaluated, and it reflects the truism that an evaluation is an assessment of value. Both points are important, but the latter is especially critical.

Evaluation services that avoid questions of worth and merit and deal in public relations—or in what Suchman (1967) called whitewash—might make a leadership group look good (or at least not bad) for a while. But in the long run (and especially when they begin to believe or to act as if they believe their own press), their decisions may stifle and even erode the efforts of their school system to deal with its problems and to serve all its students. How a school system defines evaluation, then, is of great consequence and should be an ongoing concern. Moreover, those who provide the conceptual leadership in a school system vis-à-vis evaluation must attend to the connotative as well as the denotative meanings of evaluation. The definitions that are given and communicated must retain the fundamental concept of valuing.

A definition of this kind based on prior work by the authors (Stufflebeam et al., 1971) is offered below:

> Evaluation is the process of delineating, obtaining, and applying descriptive and judgmental information about the worth or merit of some object's goals, plans, operations, and results in order to guide decision making, maintain accountability, and/or foster understandings. (p. 40)

This definition reflects the prevalent emphasis within school systems that evaluation should assist decision making; it stresses that evaluative inquiries must seek to assess worth and merit; it denotes a wide range of variables to be assessed; and it emphasizes that evaluation is an interactive process involving both communication and technical activities. Neverthess, it is offered as a heuristic, not as a final solution to the problem of definition. It points out essential concerns, many of which are dealt with in subsequent sections of this chapter.

The Why of Evaluation

One concern is the "why" of evaluation. As noted in the preceding definition, decision making, accountability, and promotion of understandings are inherent in the offerings of professional services, and evaluation itself is inherent in each constituent concept.

Decision making *means* choosing among options; and choice, in any rational sense, implies that alternatives were identified, criteria of preference were defined, and pertinent information was considered about the relative merits of each option on the criteria of preference. In other words, the option was chosen because evaluation revealed it to be better than alternatives. Clearly, then, the making of sound decisions depends on sound evaluation, and, according to the definition, guiding decision making is one of three main purposes of an evaluation.

Another purpose is accountability, or the ability to give an accounting of what was done, for what reasons, at what cost, and with what effect. A school system's staff could hardly address such issues to the satisfaction of funding agencies, courts, the school board, or the public if they could not back their claims with a record of pertinent and credible information. Evaluation programs can and do provide valuable responses to many of the demands for accountability that schools and school districts must meet.

Serving decision making and accountability are broad and pervasive purposes applicable to all areas and levels of schooling: in classrooms, schools, school districts, and state systems; in instruction, administration, public relations, policy, food services, and plant planning; and in locally or externally funded programs. Also, these purposes have special relevance to the task of defining clients and audiences for evaluation. In particular cases, evaluation services should be directed to those persons most involved in the particular decision-making and accountability setting. Overall, though, the purposes omit no group from evaluation. Evaluations should serve parents, students, and teachers, as well as administrators and board members, because all these groups, in various ways, are participants in making educational decisions, as well as being accountable for the consequences.

The third purpose cited in the definition is to promote understandings of programmatic efforts. This purpose may simply mean taking advantage of the results of an evaluation in order to promote general insights, for example, through presentations at professional meetings. In some evaluations, the aim may be more central, for example, equating evaluation with research for the purpose of formulating and validating theoretical propositions about teaching and learning. The purposes of illumination and explanation are not often cited in reports of educational evaluations. However, the theoretical literature includes arguments, from the so-called "Illuminative School of Evaluation" (Parlett & Hamilton, 1972) and from Cronbach (1980), that evaluations should be conceived and implemented to increase understandings of educational phenomena. In his especially salient argument, Cronbach notes that evaluations should be viewed as cumulative programs of study, with each evaluation building on prior evaluative efforts and pointing the way to others. Recent syntheses of the characteristics of effective schools (Madaus, Airasian, & Kellaghan, 1980) illustrate the kinds of questions pertinent to evaluations that are aimed at promoting general understanding of education.

Our view about appropriate purposes for evaluation is that evaluators and their clients should carefully consider all three of the aforementioned purposes when planning and budgeting for their evaluation work. In general, we think the order of priority given to these purposes should be decision making, then accountability, with understanding taking a distant third place. Of course, evaluations that serve the first two purposes must help their audiences to develop insights into the phenomena that are involved in the programs of interest, and such evaluations can assist in the development of general understandings about education. However, we think that educators must not insist that their evaluations always generate new and generalizable knowledge. This purpose is best served by systematic research that is not constrained to meet local and time-bound requirements for information.

Evaluation Versus Research

We agree with Guba (1966) that there are essential differences between research and evaluation. As suggested in the preceding discussion, evaluations often are localized, short term, concerned with solving practical problems, directed to ranking options, and rooted in value questions, and they may be of little interest outside the immediate setting. Research, on the other hand, is concerned with extending and generalizing basic understandings about educational processes; concerns about immediate utility of results are secondary. Research's emphasis is on presenting new knowledge, its findings must transcend local situations and given

time frames, and its concern is to explain relationships among observed phenomena rather than to make value determinations. Thus, at their best, evaluation findings often find their way into decision-making meetings (frequently in the form of handouts and oral reports), whereas research results are disseminated through professional journals and, eventually, textbooks. We acknowledge Merwin's (1982) point that evaluation and research often use the same techniques, such as tests, questionnaires, and case studies, but this similarity is far outweighed by their differences in purpose, realm of application, and standard of good practice.

Perhaps the most crucial difference between research and evaluation is in regard to standards. Researchers traditionally have been required to make their studies internally and externally valid. According to the Joint Committee's *Standards* (1981), evaluators must meet these conditions and more. In addition, they must ensure that their studies have relatively immediate and localized utility, are feasible, and are proper. Most researchers certainly strive to make their studies feasible and proper. But holding research studies to a criterion of immediate and localized utility of findings would often interfere with the development of generalized understandings about variables of theoretical interest. Obviously, researchers must be free to pursue the development of new knowledge irrespective of the presence or absence of localized interests. Because research and evaluation differ so crucially on this issue of immediate utility versus long-term generalizations, they also differ greatly in how questions are chosen, and how, where, and when information is obtained and reported.

The Process of Evaluation

The differences between research and evaluation are especially evident in the process of inquiry. If evaluation is to serve decision making, then the evaluators need to identify the decision makers and discern their needs for evaluative information. Evaluators also need to obtain and report their findings in a timely and practical manner. If evaluation is to serve accountability, then the evaluators need to identify audiences for the accountability reports, to become sensitive to their expectations and to the school district's pertinent commitments, and to collect and report the findings with strong provisions for credibility. They also need to maintain the relevant information in an appropriate storage and retrieval system. However, if evaluations are intended primarily or secondarily to develop general understandings, then, like researchers, the evaluators can choose their own questions, and they must examine prior studies concerned with the involved phenomena in various settings. In designing research-oriented studies, evaluators must concentrate most heavily on meeting standards of internal and external validity.

As indicated in the proposed definition of evaluation, the process of evaluation involves delineating, obtaining, and applying. In the first and third stages, the evaluators interact and collaborate with their clients; in the second, they collect, organize, and analyze pertinent information. Thus the process of evaluation involves both communication and information-gathering activities—especially when the purpose of the evaluation is either guiding decisions or maintaining accountability, which we believe should apply most of the time.

One implication of the interactive nature of evaluation is that administrators, board members, and other clients of evaluation must regularly be in touch with the persons who are expected to supply these groups with information to clarify information needs and to interpret and apply findings. Based on our studies of educational evaluation, we have found linkages between evaluators and their client groups, in general, to be weak. School administrators, board members, and evaluators are encouraged to study this matter, to consider what linkages are necessary to make evaluation relevant and responsive, and then to consider alternative strategies for organizing, effecting, and maintaining the collaborative relationships.

Another implication of the interactive aspect of evaluation is that the information-gathering methodology employed must both facilitate interaction between evaluators and clients and promote the gathering of information that is responsive to the needs of the clients and audiences. In this area we are beginning to see important differences between the methodologies used in research and evaluation. One frequently used methodology—comparative experiments—keeps interactions between inquirers and audiences to a minimum. Instead, it involves prespecification of variables, narrow focus, and almost no opportunity for changes in information requirements as the study proceeds. Whereas these characteristics help to promote the objectivity and clear delineations of causal links essential in research, they deter the close communication between evaluator and client essential to promote the timely use of evaluative feedback. On the other hand, alternative methodologies that facilitate interactive and responsive evaluation are generally lacking, and what exists is not widely understood. Clearly, there is a need for the development of new approaches and for training programs designed to promote the widespread use of methods that encourage and guide functional interactions between evaluators and audiences while maintaining integrity in findings.

A Side Comment About Responsive Evaluation

Recent developments labeled "responsive evaluation," especially by Stake (1975) and Guba and Lincoln (1981), are leading in the direction of evaluations that promote ongoing communication and collaboration between evaluators and clients. We see this movement as useful in the context of supplying school personnel with a conceptualization and supporting procedures to ensure that evaluations will respond usefully to their concerns. However, the term "responsive evaluation," especially the way it has been defined and illustrated by Stake (1975), could connote that evaluators should pander to the desires of the client. Instead, and consistent with Stake's (1967) earlier writings on the countenance model, we emphatically believe that while attending to the questions of clients, evaluators must also ensure that all relevant concerns about the worth and merit of what is being evaluated will be encompassed in the inquiry.

Audiences

Another key issue in conceptualizing evaluation concerns the audiences for a school system's evaluation services. According to the proposed definition, the potential audiences include all persons who must make and be accountable for decisions in a school system. As already noted, these audiences are diverse; they include, among others, lay persons and professional educators, parents and students, school board members and superintendents, and teachers and principals. The audiences vary greatly in their sophistication, interests, value perspectives, and information needs.

This diversity gives rise to what has been called the "levels problem" (Stufflebeam et al., 1971). Since different audiences have different roles in education, evaluations that have been designed to serve the needs of one audience are unlikely to be of interest or use to other audiences. It is small wonder, for example, that evaluation designed to help a teacher diagnose a particular student's reading problems is of little use to a principal interested in the extent and nature of reading difficulties throughout the school. It is not surprising that an evaluation report that satisfies a funding agency's need to review the extent that a project has been implemented as promised is of little use to the on-site director who needs continual, specific guidance for carrying out the project. And systemwide test results that are of interest to the superintendent and members of the community are not sufficient for principals and teachers who need specific information about particular schools, classes, and individual students. Clearly, school system evaluators need to differentiate their audiences; determine their unique and common information needs; and design, conduct, and report their studies accordingly.

In the 1960s and early 1970s, there was little evidence of sensitivity and responsiveness to the differential needs of audiences. Most evaluations were of federal projects, and the findings were reported in single documents aimed at the government audience. It is understandable that other audiences, such as teachers and school principals, saw little value in reports from such studies.

More recently, improvements in this area have been apparent. For example, the Atlanta public school system has differentiated between school-level and system-level audiences for evaluations and has divided responsibilities among their evaluators to ensure continuing communication and collaboration between evaluator and particular audiences. Evaluation designs and reports are tailored to the needs of the different audiences. During the formative years of the Department of Research, Evaluation, and Information Systems in Dallas, the response to the levels problem was to direct evaluation services mainly to central administrators and school board members, to external funding agencies, and to the staffs of a few select schools, such as the Skyline Magnet School and the Dunbar School, without trying to serve other audiences. These audiences typically reported that they were well served, while others reported that they were not served at all. More recently the Dallas staff has begun to focus more of its resources and attention on school-level questions. A trend in this direction is also apparent in many school systems, among which are Cincinnati, Detroit, Lansing, Milwaukee, and Philadelphia (Chase, 1980).

These examples raise an important question about which audiences should be served. Obviously, available resources limit how much evaluation any school system can do, and the potential audiences for given evaluations are not of equal importance. Therefore, school systems must seriously consider and decide which audiences will be served by their evaluation services and the extent to which they will be served. They also must decide how the other audiences will be served, through, for example, appropriate training and technical assistance, presentations at national conventions, and publications. In many studies, it is desirable to form and interact systematically with an advisory committee representative of the different audiences.

Participants in the Evaluations

Who should perform evaluations? Reviewing the evaluation operations in various school systems presents a number of answers.

Obviously, informal self-evaluation continually takes place in all institutions. Although informal evaluation is inevitable and vital for improving professional services, it typically lacks quality and credibility. Therefore, schools and school districts effect various formal arrangements for conducting their evaluations.

Individual schools and small school districts (and some large ones) typically contract with outside evaluators, with intermediate-sized school districts, or with evaluation agencies, as needed. They may follow the usual accreditation model—engaging an internal committee to do a self-study, receiving a visiting panel that assesses and extends the self-study, then reporting the results of both investigations to the client for the evaluation, namely, the school board, governmental body, or accreditation agency.

Some middle-sized and large school districts in the United States have organized extensively to involve various specialists and generalists in the evaluation of educational programs. Since a large percentage of public school students in the United States is enrolled in the large school districts, we will pay special attention to how these large districts have conceptualized and dealt with the matter of participants in the evaluation. This analysis should assist educators—especially those in large school districts, intermediate school districts, and consortiums of small districts—to consider how best to staff evaluation work. Our analysis is based mainly on studying evaluation in large urban school districts (Chase, 1980; Webster, 1984a; Webster & Stufflebeam, 1978). The data are useful for illustrating and contrasting different configurations of evaluation personnel.

When studied, the Philadelphia system had a large, centralized office of evaluators. They mainly served the evaluative needs of central administrators, but they also issued a number of districtwide reports of general interest. They were supported in the schools by persons called School Test Coordinators, whose effectiveness in helping schools to utilize test results and to obtain additional evaluative information was questionable. In general, external evaluators were not used by the Philadelphia system.

In contrast to Philadelphia, evaluation in Dade County, Florida, was revealed to be highly decentralized. Its evaluation system included a small Office of Evaluation in the central office, which responded to evaluative requests from central administrators and coordinated evaluations of federal projects. However, many evaluation functions were spread to other offices in the district. The Department of Instruction and Research conducted school audits. The Central Data Processing Unit was developing data bases for the elementary schools and planned to do so for the high schools. Computer terminals had been placed in individual schools, and school principals were using them to evaluate needs and status in their schools. The system was actively pursuing assistance from local universities to help with evaluation functions. One striking feature was that the Area Superintendents serving subdivisions of the Dade County system apparently had been little involved and had received no direct service regarding evaluation of operations within their areas of jurisdiction. This is another manifestation of the difficulty of addressing the levels problem in evaluation work. There also was some involvement of teachers in evaluation that was stimulated by curriculum-embedded evaluation, particularly in their diagnostic-prescriptive approach to reading. In contrast to the Philadelphia system, the Dade County system appeared to have many more actors in the evaluation enterprise, but in general the evaluation done in Philadelphia appeared more systematic and detailed.

Atlanta's evaluation system lay somewhere between Dade County's and Philadelphia's with respect to involvement of a variety of people in the evaluation process. The Atlanta system did have a strong central unit of evaluators. However, the members of this unit had dual assignments, including a central function (such as coordination of testing) and a decentralized function (including liaison with a number of individual schools). In the liaison function, these evaluators worked with school leadership teams to promote and support the use of evaluation services within the school, while helping the teams to obtain information pertinent to their needs. This appears to be a strong strategy for both ensuring a concerted, integrated approach to evaluation and ensuring that people throughout the system are well served. We see this arrangement as an excellent response to the levels problem.

The Dallas Independent School District has a large centralized evaluation unit, perhaps the strongest and most firmly established of such units in educational institutions. For years the unit served the needs of central-office administrators and the school board almost exclusively. Then, the district began to place evaluators and evaluation teams in individual schools. More recently, the Dallas evaluation unit has been moving, like Atlanta, toward greater liaison with individual schools. A unique feature of the Dallas system is its School Board Program Evaluation Committee. This committee actively participates in the Dallas evaluation program by meeting regularly to review evaluation plans and draft reports and by providing direction to evaluators concerning future needs for evaluation. This arrangement has brought the board increasingly into the role of participant in the system's evaluation process, and there is good evidence that

evaluation in recent years has had a significant influence on the decision making of the Dallas board. The Dallas system makes little use of external evaluators, but, notably, outsiders are brought in to serve the role of meta-evaluator: that is, persons who evaluate the adequacy of evaluation services, plans, and reports.

These examples reveal a variety of possibilities for including different groups in the evaluation process. The position of this chapter is that evaluation needs to be organized and operated to involve as many groups as possible. At the same time, it is important to organize a systematic and auditable approach to evaluations and to keep in mind the varying sizes and situations of schools, especially the financial constraints that virtually all small school districts and individual schools share.

The ideas that seem most powerful are associated with the large urban school districts that we studied. The ideas include organizing a strong central unit of evaluation specialists; assigning liaison roles so that the central evaluation system is systematically in touch with schools, programs, and area offices; providing principals direct, on-line access to the school system's data base; assigning evaluation responsibilities to some district or system offices that are independent of program personnel; exploring possibilities for developing the role of teacher-evaluator or school-based evaluator; encouraging and assisting self-evaluation by each professional in the district; providing for external meta-evaluation to help guide and certify the soundness of internal evaluation work; and, perhaps most important, offering an ongoing program of in-service education and technical support in evaluation for people throughout the district.

Small school districts and individual schools can rarely apply all these ideas by themselves. But they can apply some of the ideas: for example, encouraging and assisting evaluations conducted by individual educators, providing in-service education in evaluation, and commissioning external reviews of the internally conducted evaluations. Also, smaller educational units often can obtain assistance from intermediate school districts or evaluation companies. Or they can band together to fund a shared office of evaluation, as 21 school districts in Arizona formed a consortium known as the EPIC Evaluation Center (Hammond, 1967) in the early 1970's.

Whatever the organizational setting, however, conceptual leadership is most important if all appropriate groups are to be brought into the process and if their efforts are to be coordinated. Administrators, including superintendents, principals, and evaluation directors, as well as board members, have vital roles to play in this regard. They should coordinate their efforts to conceptualize evaluation properly for their systems while projecting their conceptions through policies, administrative decisions, and in-service training.

Variables for Assessment

Another crucial concern in conceptualizing a school district's evaluation services relates to the questions and variables that should be examined. As noted previously, the objectives-oriented definition directs consideration to those outcomes that relate to prespecified objectives. This is a narrow focus for evaluation services, but it is consistent with much of the educational evaluation being done. This concentration on assessing whether objectives were achieved places the evaluator in a technical role, leaving broader, values-oriented assessments more to the political process in the direct control of administrators.

The values-oriented definition recommended in this chapter called for assessments of needs, plans, operations, and results. Evaluators using this definition would conduct needs assessments as a basis for charting school district objectives and priorities. They would evaluate proposals and other school district and school-level plans for responsiveness to student needs, feasibility, promise of effectiveness, and superiority over other proposals. They would monitor projects and programs to discern the extent of implementation and to provide feedback to make the implementation better. And they would assess outcomes in order to determine how well student needs were being met, while searching for unexpected outcomes, both positive and negative.

Cost is a variable of particular interest. With such conditions as rising costs of education, inflation, and declining enrollments, it is becoming increasingly crucial to perform ongoing cost analysis to help districts terminate wasteful programs and make better use of their resources. Cost analysis is especially pertinent in evaluating program plans and assessing the worth of program outcomes (Levin, 1975).

From studying past school district evaluations, we know that school districts often try to address the full range of evaluation issues. However, primary emphasis is on assessment of outcomes related to objectives. Needs are also frequently assessed but most often by surveys of what various groups *want* from educational services instead of serious investigation into deficiencies to determine what is needed. Evaluation of program implementation is also common but is often of questionable validity and utility. One faulty practice involves relying on the self-reports of program managers as opposed to reviews by impartial evaluators. Other problems include the labor intensity of evaluations of implementation and the limited resources available for

evaluation. Less common are attempts to evaluate program proposals and plans, an unfortunate omission, for bad plans set into action can sap resources and impede education. Even a good plan causes unnecessary waste of resources if a better one could have been identified through an evaluation of alternative plans.

Cost analysis is gaining in use in urban school districts. For example, a few years ago Dade County was working with committees of principals to develop different decision packages based on different sets of assumptions about available funds. This approach suggests zero-base budgeting while attempting to be realistic about encumbrances, such as costs of teachers' salaries.

Overall, evaluations in school districts address a wide range of variables that *should* be assessed by evaluation. It is desirable for administrators, board members, and evaluators to scrutinize the full range of questions and variables. Such a broad investigatory perspective should stimulate more comprehensive, pertinent assessments.

Values and Suboptimizations

The fundamental issue involved in the selection of assessment variables concerns the implicit or explicit choice of values to undergird the assessment. Basically, we believe that formal evaluation is needed to help assure consideration of all key values in assessments of professional service and in resource allocaton. Of course, the making of such determinations is problematic. Different stakeholders in given schools and the larger educational society may hold conflicting values about such issues as sex education, religious training, vocational education, and other political, social, and philosophical matters. In addition, the society at large usually emphasizes certain values at the expense of others, periodically changing the emphasis.

The recent history of education in U.S. society is instructive about ways society tends to shift from emphasizing one set of values to another as conditions within society change. Here are some examples:

1. In the late 1950s, U.S. society, reacting strongly to the USSR's launching of Sputnik I, channeled huge amounts of money to education for the purpose of surpassing the Soviets in space technology. The overriding value became *national security*.

2. In the early and middle 1960s, lobbyists for persons with special needs and handicaps became a powerful political force at the federal, and sometimes the state level. A new, heavy emphasis on *equal access for the handicapped* emerged.

3. In the middle 1960s, U.S. society suddenly became aware of and concerned about the plight of minori-

ties and launched multibillion-dollar programs aimed at providing *equal opportunities* for them.

4. In the late 1970s, the nation was hit with a major economic recession and shifted its concern from costly and innovative responses to the problems of minorities to a concern for *feasible and cost-effective approaches* to education.

5. In the early 1980s, the society became aware that U.S. students were not performing well on tests compared to their counterparts from years past and to students from other nations; these results seem to have stimulated a renewed concern for excellence in schools.

6. Finally, the value of economic security apparently undergirds current efforts to get the assistance of the educational system in combating foreign competition by instilling greater *pride of workmanship*.

The preceding summary, although sketchy, illustrates the difficulty of equitably addressing the values-selection problem in evaluation work. Many educational programs are supposed to serve multiple interests. Political considerations often determine which values will be given priority. Evaluators must strive to bring equity and rationality to the consideration of multiple values. Otherwise, as in any suboptimization, there will always be gains in some areas (e.g., excellence) at the expense of losses in others (e.g., equality of opportunity). Realistically, we recognize that decision groups must make tradeoffs in allocating attention and resources among competing objectives. But such decisions will be more just if evaluators help their clients to consider both the relative values of all legitimate interest groups and the tradeoffs implicit in decision alternatives.

Merit and Worth

The recommended definition of evaluation does denote two general criteria to be considered in all evaluations: merit and worth (Guba & Lincoln, 1981; Scriven, 1975). Educational administrators will find it useful to keep these criteria in mind as they commission and help to plan evaluation studies.

Merit concerns the quality of something. Whether considering a project proposal, a curriculum department, a reading program, a course, a standardized achievement test, or a summer recreation program, these questions should be addressed: Is it a good one? Does it meet or exceed pertinent standards? Is it exemplary compared with other similar projects at other places? Is it as good as its adherents can make it? Is it subject to periodic review and improvement? The criterion of merit is clearly part of evaluations that assess and promote excellence.

The second criterion is worth, which asks whether the thing being evaluated meets some high-priority need in a given setting. Would certain students be malnourished if the school didn't provide them breakfast or lunch? Would an acceptable level of social integration of students likely be reached *only* through the operation of a crossdistrict busing program? Are there sufficient students in need of remedial education to justify the cost of operating an after-school study center? Is a plan for consolidating certain small school districts likely to foster higher levels of achievement by more of their students in given subject areas? Would the introduction into schools of high technology—such as microcomputers, low-power television, and interactive video disks—demonstrably improve teaching and learning? Such questions look beyond the notion of innovation for its own sake and help to ensure that the components of educational systems contribute to effective and equitable teaching and learning.

Interestingly, the importance of closely investigating worth depends on the outcome of a merit evaluation. For example, if a particular community education course has low merit, or none, concluding that it cannot be worth much to any group of students or community members is fairly straightforward. However, even if the course were exceptionally well organized and taught, there might be no one in the given school or community who could profit from it. In general, when a proposal or program is found to have high merit, it should also be studied for its worth in the given setting. If it is then found to be irrelevant or counterproductive to the mission of the educational institution and to the needs of its students and other constituents, it should be judged unworthy of support, no matter how good it is.

A Word About Evaluation Models

A resource available to those who must conceptualize evaluations for school districts is the range of evaluation models that have been developed over the last 15 years. These include the formative-summative evaluation approach by Scriven (1967); the responsive evaluation approach by Stake (1967); the CIPP model by Stufflebeam et al. (1971); the objectives-based model by Smith and Tyler (1942), and disciples such as Provus (1971) and Popham (1969); the connoisseurship model by Eisner (1975); and the experimental research paradigm that has been advanced by Campbell and Stanley (1963). These models or approaches stimulate people to consider different evaluation assumptions and approaches. Also, they offer common sets of concepts to guide practice and facilitate communication about evaluation. Hence, information about models is a valuable resource for a school district's in-service training program. A danger in the use of the models is that, inescapably, all of them oversimplify the work that is necessary to produce useful evaluation services. Comprehensive reviews of the major models appear in *Evaluation Models* by Madaus, Scriven, and Stufflebeam (1983) and in an excellent review of evaluation research by Merwin (1982).

Some models have been highly influential in evaluation operations in school districts, and they are available for study in their operational forms. For example, the objectives-based model is seen in the Portland School District, where an extensive attempt has been made to articulate instructional objectives from kindergarten through the 12th grade and to develop test items directly related to these objectives. This system is intended to provide teachers and others throughout the school district with a flexible test-item and objectives bank to use in tracking achievements

related to specified objectives. One important question is how the objectives will themselves be evaluated, for educational endeavors addressing objectives that do not reflect needs are misguided and wasteful.

The CIPP Model

The CIPP model was developed based on evaluation experiences in the Columbus, Ohio, public schools, and it has been used for evaluation in Dallas, Cincinnati, Saginaw, Lansing, Philadelphia, most large districts in Texas, and elsewhere (Webster & Stufflebeam, 1978).

The most operationalized version of the model is in Dallas. The evaluation system there is organized to conduct the four kinds of evaluation required by the CIPP model. The first is context evaluation, which assesses needs, problems, opportunities, and objectives at different levels of the school district. The second is input evaluation, which searches for alternative plans

Table 27.1 Four Types of Evaluation

	CONTEXT EVALUATION	INPUT EVALUATION	PROCESS EVALUATION	PRODUCT EVALUATION
OBJECTIVE	To define the institutional context; to identify the target population and assess its needs; to identify opportunities for addressing the needs; to diagnose problems underlying the needs; and to judge whether proposed objectives are sufficiently responsive to the assessed needs	To identify and assess system capabilities; alternative program strategies; procedural designs for implementing the strategies, budgets, and schedules	To identify or predict, in process, defects in the procedural design or its implementation; to provide information for preprogrammed decisions; and to record and judge procedural events and activities	To collect descriptions and judgments of outcomes; to relate them to objectives and to context, input, and process information; and to interpret their worth and merit
METHOD	Systems analysis; survey; document review; hearings; interviews; diagnostic tests; the Delphi technique	Literature search; visits to exemplary programs; advocate teams; and pilot trials, with the objective of inventorying and analyzing available human and material resources, solution strategies, and procedural designs for relevance, feasibility, and economy	Monitoring the activity's potential procedural barriers and remaining alert to unanticipated ones; obtaining specified information for programmed decisions; describing the actual process; and continually interacting with and observing the activities of project staff	Defining operationally and measuring outcome criteria; collecting judgments of outcomes from stakeholders; and performing qualitative and quantitative analyses
RELATION TO DECISION MAKING IN THE CHANGE PROCESS	For deciding on the setting to be served, the goals associated with meeting needs or using opportunities, and the objectives associated with solving problems (i.e., for planning needed changes); and to provide a basis for judging outcomes	For selecting sources of support, solution strategies and procedural designs (i.e., for structuring change activities); providing a basis for judging implementation	For implementing and refining the program design and procedure (i.e., for effecting process control), and providing a log of the actual process for later use in interpreting outcomes	For deciding to continue, terminate, modify, or refocus a change activity; and presenting a clear record of effects (intended and unintended, positive and negative)

and proposals and assesses whether their adoption likely would promote the meeting of needs at a reasonable cost. The third is process evaluation, which monitors a project or program in order both to help guide implementation and to provide a record for determining the extent to which the program or project was implemented as designed. The fourth part of the model calls for product evaluation, which is an attempt to examine the outcomes of a program and the extent to which they meet the needs of those being served. In Dallas, the CIPP model is used both to help implement priority change programs and to provide an accountability record (why the programs were developed, how they were planned, the extent to which they were carried out, and the results they produced). In addition, the Dallas evaluation team conducts a program of applied research aimed at affecting systematic change in curricular areas (Webster & Vitale, 1977).

Table 27.1 presents an overview of the essential meanings of context, input, process, and product evaluation, defining these four types of studies by their objectives, methods, and uses. These concepts are fully explained and illustrated in a recent book by Stufflebeam and Shinkfield (1985).

Gally (1984), who used the model to study the informal evaluation work of school principals in Israel, found that their obtaining and use of evaluation findings is most heavily loaded in the areas of context and input evaluation. He suggests that this apparent high need for context and input information in comparison with process and product information may explain why the objectives-based approach, which emphasizes product-type information, has not sufficiently met the evaluation needs of school principals.

Formative and Summative Evaluation

Two of the most frequently used terms in evaluation are "formative evaluation" and "summative evaluation." Scriven (1967) introduced these terms to help readers follow his debate with Cronbach about the appropriate role of evaluation in education. Cronbach (1963) had argued that evaluations provide their most important service when they provide direction for "course improvement"; he doubted that educational improvements would result from conclusion-oriented evaluation. Scriven, using "formative" and "summative" to label the two evaluation roles that Cronbach had been contrasting, argued that the summative, or conclusion-oriented, type was more important. Ever since, educators have referred to evaluations intended to assist in program development as formative and evaluations of a program after its conclusion as summative. In our experience, school people do often use these terms to facilitate their discussions of evaluation, and the uses of evaluation findings in school districts are more often formative than summative. Our view is that formative evaluation to guide decision making is the more important of the two roles but that summative evaluation for accountability purposes is also important. Fortunately, evaluators who do an intelligent formative evaluation and retain the information are in a good position to summarize the information, to provide program accountability reports, and to help another group to arrive at a summative judgment of the program's worth and merit.

Relating Formative and Summative Evaluation to the CIPP Model

Some confusion exists, both in the literature and in the practice of evaluation, about the relationship between formative and summative evaluation, on the one hand, and context, input, process, and product evaluation, on the other. Formative and summative evaluation have often been erroneously equated with process and product evaluation. Actually, they are different kinds of concepts. Formative and summative evaluation are roles that may be served by any set of evaluation findings, whereas context, input, process, and product evaluation are evaluation types that are differentiated by the kinds of questions they address and the kinds of information they provide. These two concepts are complementary, and fitted together, they provide a convenient framework for thinking about different types of studies that serve different roles in schools.

This complementarity is apparent in Table 27.2, which lists the four types of studies (context, input, process and product) in columns and formative and summative roles in rows. Note that the formative and summative roles are associated, respectively, with two of the three purposes for evaluation proposed earlier in this chapter: guidance for decision making and support for accountability. The entries in the cells indicate the particular service to be provided by each type of evaluation in relation to each role.

The Point-of-Entry Problem and Guidelines for Addressing It

At first glance, the CIPP model provides for an orderly succession of four different types of studies that assist in planning and conducting successful projects. Of course, because evaluation and change efforts seldom become neat, orderly, linear activities, it would be a mistake to assume evaluations that should always be conducted in context, input, process, and product order. Even if that sequence were appropriate in given situations, clients might not always consent to it.

Table 27.2 The Relevance of Four Evaluation Types to Decision Making and Accountability

| | *Evaluation Types* | | | |
	CONTEXT	INPUT	PROCESS	PRODUCT
Formative Decision making (formative orientation)	Guidance for choice of objectives and assignment of priorities	Guidance for choice of program strategy Input for specification of procedural design	Guidance for implementation	Guidance for termination, continuation, modification or installation
Summative Accountability (summative orientation)	Record of objectives and bases for their choice along with a record of needs, opportunities, and problems	Record of chosen strategy and design and reasons for their choice over other alternatives	Record of the actual process	Record of attainments and recycling decisions

This apparent contradiction between the real world and the constructs just described leads to a consideration of the so-called point-of-entry problem. Scriven (1969) identified this problem about 20 years ago, but it has received little analytical attention. On the other hand, the problem is frequently encountered in evaluation work. An in-depth discussion of the problem is appropriate, not only because it has not been much analyzed although it has been much used, but also because the failure to deal effectively with it can render evaluations useless or counterproductive. The problem differs from the perspective of a client of evaluation services and from that of an evaluator.

From the client's perspective, the problem often concerns whether and when to perform a certain kind of study (e.g., a context, input, process, or product evaluation). From this perspective, the point-of-entry problem is frequently seen in a number of common mistakes. One mistake clients make all too often is to commission the wrong type of study, for example, a product evaluation, when a needs assessment would be more pertinent. This error occurs especially when evaluation is restricted to determining whether objectives have been met. Another error clients make is to wait until a program is over or nearly over before starting any formal evaluation. This error is common among persons who resist evaluation until it becomes a condition for continued funding. Conversely, clients sometimes call too early for structured evaluation work and thereby stifle the creativity of the program staff. Less frequently, clients ask for too comprehensive an evaluation approach given the project to be assessed and the nature and amount of extant information. That is, they engage in too many evaluative fronts at once. Obviously, it is important that clients be proficient in dealing with the point-of-entry problem. Timely launching of the right kind of study almost always depends on the foresight, initiative, and support of those who control the purse strings and the projects.

Evaluators often see the point-of-entry problem differently. Often they aren't asked what type of study would be best in a given situation, at least not early enough. Evaluation clients too seldom plan early and jointly with evaluation specialists. Many evaluators will continue to be called in later than they should have been. Hence, the evaluators' problem often involves deciding how to make the best of a bad situation. Difficult choices for evaluators in such cases concern whether they should second-guess clients' past decisions, especially those related to the program's objectives, procedural plan, theoretical rationale, and budget. By accepting a client's assessment, evaluators may become accomplices in the pursuit of flawed objectives. Insisting on assessing past decisions may threaten a client's authority enough to reject evaluators' services completely. Even if the client agrees to evaluate past program decisions, evaluators may have trouble discovering the relevant history.

To best address the point-of-entry problem, we believe that clients and evaluators should keep in mind the fundamental purpose of evaluation: to improve services. That is, an evaluation should be commissioned and carried through only if it clearly has the potential to strengthen services to society or particular groups. An evaluator might justifiably help to eliminate a wasteful or otherwise flawed program, thereby making room for improved services by reallocating staff time and resources to more worthwhile programs. Also, an evaluation should be pursued only if it would yield new, useful information. We agree with Scriven (1969) that, in general, the evaluator should ask the client to consider evaluating the still reversible decisions about a program. Also, if there is a choice, the evaluator should consider not doing an evaluation if past decisions that are considered fixed are revealed to be indefensible. Again, the purpose of the evaluation work should be to help develop and strengthen worthwhile services, not to help sustain poor programs.

Often, however, the merit or intent of a program is not in doubt. Instead, there is a fairly practical need to determine which information, at the given time, would be most useful. Table 27.3 is a chart to help with such determinations. It distills our experience in recognizing evidence for and against undertaking each of the four types of evaluation in the CIPP model. We have found this table to be useful in helping administrators to decide on which types of evaluations are appropriate in given situations. The idea is first to determine the potential usefulness of type of study as described in the top half of the table. Then, if potential uses are seen, the bottom part of the table should be checked to determine whether a study of that type might be premature, superfluous, diversionary, or counterproductive. If a given type of study has potential utility and no indicator of inappropriateness, then it can be pursued

confidently as an important service, not an expensive exercise.

Depending on circumstances, a study can justifiably be retrospective, prospective, or both. For example, if a program is underway but has not yet been evaluated, client and evaluator might agree to conduct retrospective context and input evaluations first, ongoing process and product evaluations subsequently. On the other hand, they may conclude that the past planning efforts were sufficiently justified and, therefore, retrospective analysis is unnecessary. Stake (1967), in his development of the countenance model, assumed that evaluators would typically be called in midway in a program. Accordingly, he advised evaluators to begin their work by examining the antecedents of a program, then to look at transactions and outcomes. The CIPP model allows for entry at any point in a program, but

Table 27.3 Guidelines for Deciding When to Do Context, Input, Process, or Product Evaluations

	CONTEXT	INPUT	PROCESS	PRODUCT
Indicators of appropriateness	• There is a need to investigate charges of inequity. • The "state of the institution" is due to be reviewed. • Performance of the institution is unsatisfactory. • Institutional mission and goals need to be updated. • The pattern of resource allocation needs to be changed. • Accreditation is up for review. • A funding agency requires a needs assessment. • The wisdom of institutionalizing a successful project needs to be confirmed.	• A problem has been defined, but an appropriate solution is not readily apparent. • The relative merits of two or more acceptable solutions to a problem are unclear. • A needed solution has been found but must be engineered for use in the given setting. • Choice of a particular approach will be controversial.	• A selected strategy needs to be field tested and modified for general use in an institution. • There is a need to be accountable for the implementation of a plan. • An in-depth description of process will be needed to help explain the outcomes of a project. • The management plan calls for continuous feedback.	• A selected strategy needs to be validated as effective before being institutionalized or disseminated. • There is a need to be accountable for the results of a given effort. • There is a need to identify and assess a broad range of effects of a given intervention. • There is a need for continuous feedback of results.
Indicators of inappropriateness	• Sufficient background information about a problem or opportunity is already available. • A project is already operational and needs to run a full cycle before returning to questions about need.	• The need for a proposed intervention has not yet been established. • A validated and acceptable solution to a given problem is available and ready for use.	• Implementation of the selected plan presents no particular needs for monitoring and tailoring. • It is crucial to learn how the project works without special evaluative support.	• The effectiveness of the intervention is not in doubt. • The needed information about results will be routinely available from other sources.

as suggested by Stake, the entry will often be midway in a project.

Criteria of Sound Evaluations

Many school systems make minimal use of external evaluators and instead rely on internal evaluation. Such evaluation amounts to educators evaluating their own work. Moreover, even districts that employ internal offices of evaluation, which provide a measure of independence if not externality to the evaluations, must depend to a great extent on self-evaluation because the internal offices can generally do only a part of the evaluation work that is needed. Obviously, a heavy reliance on self-evaluation raises persistent concerns about objectivity and credibility. Even so, the solution to this problem is not to require that all evaluations be independent and external.

As Scriven (1983) has argued, evaluation is essentially self-referent. In order to assure that their services are meritorious and worthy, all professionals must evaluate their own work. According to this argument, it is necessary and inevitable that teachers, school principals, counselors, superintendents, and other school personnel evaluate their own work and then use the results to improve their performance. External evaluations should also be done whenever appropriate and feasible. However, whether or not these are done, professionals must continuously and systematically examine and attempt to improve their own work.

Because evaluating one's own efforts inevitably raises questions about independence and freedom from bias, special provisions are necessary to assure that internal evaluations, as well as external ones, are credible and valid. One step in addressing this need is to be clear about what constitutes a sound evaluation and then to adhere to, and give evidence of adhering to, the position. The Joint Committee on Standards for Educational Evaluation (1981) defines four attributes of sound evaluation: (a) the utility of the evaluation to the audiences to be served in relation to the problems they face; (b) the feasibility of the evaluation in terms of its efficient use of practical procedures and its political viability; (c) propriety, which calls for the fair treatment of the participants in the evaluation and the ethical use of evaluation procedures and findings; and (d) accuracy, which calls for obtaining valid, reliable, and objective findings and reporting justified conclusions and recommendations.

School system personnel can use the committee standards to develop policy about the requirements evaluations must fulfill, to guide and check internal evaluations, as a framework and content for staff development in evaluation, and to guide external evaluations of internal evaluations. The standards, then, provide school administrators and others with a powerful tool for enchancing the effectiveness of both internal and external evaluation.

Since its publication in 1981, the Joint Committee's *Standards for Evaluation* has been used extensively by government, funding, and educational agencies in the United States and other countries. Perhaps the most extensive and systematic use has been in Louisiana, where the legislature adopted the standards set forth in the book as state policy to guide evaluations of publicly supported school programs. In that state, personnel from each district have been trained in the use of the standards which are routinely applied in assessing evaluation plans and reports (Tripplett, 1982).

The Importance of Assessing Impacts on the Rightful Beneficiaries

Included in *Standards for Evaluation* is a requirement that programs be assessed against a wide range of pertinent variables (see the Information Scope and Selection standard). Among the types of assessment criteria recommended are theoretical soundness, structural adequacy, professional responsibility, and impact. A desirable feature of identifying such criteria in the standards is that evaluators are encouraged to address a wider range of pertinent assessment criteria than have typically been considered in the past.

However, the recommendation is not merely to broaden the criteria used, and it is essential that the selection of success criteria not be viewed as a matter of free choice. Given free reign, evaluators might still choose inappropriate criteria and help to lead programs astray or to judge them as good and effective when they aren't. This is not just an abstract philosophical point. Many educational programs have erroneously been judged good based on assessments of the performance of the students who attended them. But in some cases, a judgment of failure would have been more appropriate, since the intended audience was not reached or was poorly served. Unfortunately, the practice of evaluation is full of cases where evaluations that concentrated on inappropriate success criteria protected and helped to sustain social injustices.

Especially at issue here is who gets and who should get service from a program. For example, a program commissioned to serve disadvantaged students might neglect them but still be judged sound because it gives good service to the advantaged students who use it and because the measures of performance are obtained only from the latter group. Or a library might be judged effective because its actual users are satisfied although it fails to reach and serve most of its potential users. Conclusions like these are simply wrong. While it is important to determine how well a program does whatever it does, it is also crucial to ascertain whether and how well it reaches the right target group.

This problem occurs in another aspect of evaluation work: evaluations of efforts to strengthen institutions and programs that are based exclusively on instrumental criteria, such as quality of staff, financial stability, quality of curriculum, and adequacy of facilities. Such criteria are important and worth consideration in evaluating programs, but they must be considered in the context of additional criteria related to the performance of students, including those for whom the program is intended as well as those who are using it. Otherwise, evaluators may assist in developing intrinsically sound programs that are not effective in serving the rightful beneficiaries. Evaluators should remember that administrators typically want and deserve credit for the quality of services that are delivered and received, but society wants and deserves feedback on the extent to which all the rightful beneficiaries are served. Sound evaluations must serve both audiences and address both sets of issues.

Equality of Educational Opportunity

The issue of service to the rightful beneficiaries is closely aligned with the concept of equality of educational opportunity, a main issue in education since the mid-1960s. Kellaghan (1982) argued that equality of educational opportunity is a basic value that should undergird education throughout the world and proposed seven criteria associated with this value. According to these criteria, an educational institution should be assessed for its success in (a) providing an adequate range of educational opportunities; (b) making its services accessible to all potential students; (c) getting students from all segments of society to participate in the full range of opportunities; (d) stimulating students from all segments of society to aspire to high levels of achievement in education and life; (e) helping students from all segments of society to attain the full sequence of offerings in the institution; (f) demonstrating that students from all segments of society have achieved acceptable levels of skill and knowledge; and (g) demonstrating that the institution has had a beneficial impact on all segments of the society it serves. These criteria are especially relevant to elementary and secondary schools commissioned to serve all children, not just selected groups. Collectively, these criteria test the extent to which a school district achieves the goal of providing equal opportunities to all its students.

Needs Assessment as a Basis for Judging Programs

A particular problem in evaluation work is how to assign value meaning to the information obtained about a program. Early in this chapter we criticized the popular approach of using the developer's objectives as the standard for judging outcomes because the objectives can be too narrow, targeted on the wrong group, or otherwise faulty. One alternative is to judge a program's worth based on its contributions to meeting assessed needs. Hence, in interpreting the findings of a program evaluation, one would access or conduct a pertinent needs assessment and then consider whether the findings give evidence that the program has met important needs.

The literature of education is filled with references to needs assessment, but because the meaning of this term is often obscure, we offer the following definitions. A defensible purpose is the basic concept in our definition of need; it is a purpose that is consistent with the aims, values, and laws of a society; an example is the board-approved mission of a school district. Others are the provisos in the Constitution of the United States, including equality of opportunity. We define a need as something that is necessary or useful for fulfilling a defensible purpose. Two basic categories of need are programmatic inputs and well-being on certain dimensions of human development and functioning. In the vernacular of research, these might be termed independent and dependent variables or instrumental and consequential needs.

Given these definitions, a needs assessment is a complex undertaking that may involve the following steps: (a) identifying and examining the purposes against which needs are determined; (b) providing direction for modifying improper or flawed purposes; (c) identifying the things that are required and useful for serving the validated purposes; (d) assessing the extent to which identified instrumental and consequential needs are met or unmet; (e) rating the importance of the met and unmet needs; and (f) helping the audience for the needs assessment to use the findings to shape programs and judge their outcomes.

Using the results of needs assessment to judge the outcomes of a program may sometimes make some audiences nervous. Program developers, headmasters of private schools, and school district superintendents might prefer to have their contributions judged against their previously stated goals rather than against standards based on objectively determined needs. However, that very nervousness may encourage educators to revise their programs to reach all the pertinent groups and to ensure that the values of these groups and those of the broader society are considered. Another possible outcome of using appropriate needs assessments to judge school programs is to reduce the hypocritical practice of giving lip service but little else to certain groups that are especially in need. On the positive side, needs assessments can help to validate and/or revise program objectives.

Recently, serious work in the area of needs assessment has begun to appear in the literature (Guba & Lincoln, 1981; Roth, 1978; Scriven & Roth, 1978; Stufflebeam, 1977; Stufflebeam, McCormick, Brinkerhoff, & Nelson, 1985; and Suarez, 1980).

Assessment Variables

A particularly relevant contribution to the planning of needs assessments in school districts is a recent book developed collaboratively by the Toledo, Ohio, public schools and the Western Michigan University Evaluation Center (Nowakowski, Bunda, Working, Bernacki, & Harrington, 1984). The book is intended to help educators consider a comprehensive range of potential needs for inproved performance by students, as well as needs for strengthened educational programs. The two parts of the book respectively array and define variables for assessing student growth and development and those for examining all administrative aspects of an institution.

The guiding principle for this book is that educational institutions exist fundamentally to foster human growth and development. Therefore, assessments of students' needs must take into account all relevant developmental variables, and assessments of institutions must take into account all components and enterprises that bear on meeting the needs of their students.

To guide institutions to identify and assess the performance needs of their students, Nowakowski and her colleagues (1984) explicate the following seven categories of student need, previously defined by Stufflebeam (1978):

Intellectual development: development of the power of faculty of the mind by which one knows or understands, as distinguished from those by which one feels and one wills; the faculty of thinking and acquiring knowledge.

Emotional development: development of the capacity to deal effectively with feelings of joy, sorrow, fear, hate, and the like, and development of a realistic and positive self-concept.

Physical and recreational development: development of motor coordination, body fitness, and hygiene and athletic abilities, interests, and habits.

Moral development: development of principles and habits of moral conduct and acquisition of the ability to adhere to these principles rather than to conflicting customs or laws.

Aesthetic and cultural development: development of a sense of, appreciation for, and ability to create beauty, especially as manifested by music, art, drama, and dance.

Vocational development: development of a sense of the world of work and of one's career interests and aptitudes and preparation to engage in gainful and fulfilling employment.

Social development: development of the capacity and habit of living in friendly companionship with others in family and community settings and development and implementation of a sense of responsibility for promoting and sustaining civilization.

A Handbook of Educational Variables (Nowakowski et al., 1984) also explicates criteria within eight areas of an institution: business and finance, curriculum and instruction, policy, facilities, planning and evaluation, pupil personnel, staff personnel, and school-community relations.

The contents of this handbook illustrate the breadth of concerns in assessing the educational development needs of students and the programmatic needs of institutions that are supposed to serve students. Obviously, needs assessments must not concentrate on standardized test scores in core subject areas to the exclusion of such other important development variables as emotional stability, physical well-being, and social maturity. Nor should needs assessments fail to consider the extent and quality of educational facilities and offerings. Needs for better learning may often be associated with needs for better teaching, better materials, better administration, and so on.

The Inevitability of Personnel Evaluation in Program Evaluation

The linkage between consequential and instrumental needs leads to another sticky but important issue: the relationship between program evaluation and personnel evaluation. Clearly, both areas are crucial in the evaluation of education, and it is a well-established principle of school administration that the two areas must be kept as separate as possible. Personnel evaluation—for purposes of selection, tenure, and promotion—is largely an administrative responsibility. Personnel evaluation is one of the jobs that school boards pay superintendents and principals to perform. The administrative role in and responsibility for personnel evaluation is accepted throughout education.

It is also true that program evaluators are expected not to evaluate individuals in order to inform decisions about them. Program evaluators may provide technical advice for developing a sound system of personnel evaluation and may even evaluate the personnel evaluation system per se. But they are quite happy to stay out of the role of directly evaluating individual personnel. Doing otherwise would stimulate great fear of their power and motives and undoubtedly would meet with great resistance from principals and teachers, ultimately resulting in their lack of cooperation in efforts to evaluate programs. Evaluators in school districts typically avoid most connections with personnel evaluation. They emphasize the constructive orientation of their program evaluations, and they promise as much anonymity and confidentiality as they can to the teachers and administrators who work in the programs being evaluated. This approach is appropriate, and efforts to separate personnel and program evaluation in school districts have worked quite well.

But there is a basic problem inherent in this approach: It is impossible to exclude personnel evaluation from a sound evaluation of a program. An evaluation must determine whether a program is having a desirable impact on the right target population. If it is not, then the assessment must determine what aspects of a program need to be changed to improve the results. Inescapably, then, evaluators of programs must check the adequacy of all relevant instrumental variables in a program, including the personnel. The rights of teachers and administrators must be observed, but evaluators must also protect the right of the student to be taught and taught well.

The argument in this first part of the chapter is that evaluation is a conceptual process and that conceptual leadership must be an ongoing concern within school systems if evaluation programs are to respond to system needs and to keep pace with the state of the evaluation art. We have explored a range of topics vital to the conceptualization of evaluation, and we have referred to concepts of evaluation that are operating in some school systems. The thrust of this section has been to urge that administrators, board members, and evaluators collaborate to clarify and integrate their conceptions of evaluation.

We have also recommended that school district staffs synthesize their views in a written document and disseminate it throughout their school system; of course, the synthesis must be reviewed and updated from time to time. One good example of such a synthesis explicates the Dallas approach to evaluation (Webster, 1975, 1986). This paper, updated periodically over the years, has been widely used by Dallas's system personnel to communicate its evaluation program to interested persons outside the system. Another such paper, developed by Merriman (1968) when he became the first director of evaluation in Columbus, Ohio, served as a valuable guide in the early days of the Columbus program. Such syntheses of real conceptualizations of evaluation have much to contribute to school district groups who want to develop effective evaluation.

ORGANIZATION AND FUNCTIONS OF EVALUATION SYSTEMS

Beyond the conceptual issues to be addressed in developing or improving a school system's evaluation program are a number of practical issues. One that is especially pertinent to the roles of school board members and administrators is alternative ways to organize the evaluation function. This issue involves questions of policy, planning, financing and allocation of resources, location of the evaluation unit (if there is to be one), internal organization of the unit, use of external evaluators, and dealing with political realities. These topics are considered in this section and references are made to how different districts have addressed the topics.

Policy and Governance

Given an adequate conceptualization of evaluation, one that addresses the issues outlined in the preceding section, a school board can develop policies concerning the functions, governance, operations, and support of its evaluation system. Such policies are important to promoting sanctioned, financed, and systematic evaluation services. They can help evaluators deal in a preordained way with requests for evaluation services and with the allocation of evaluation resources. They can also provide guidance to external agencies, especially universities that want to use the school system for research and related activities.

In the urban education study by Francis Chase (1980), most of the systems studied reported formal provision (for example, through established committees) for reviewing requests for evaluation services and allocating resources to those requests. Most of them also indicated a prioritized listing of audiences to receive attention. Top priorities went to the superintendent and the school board and to externally funded projects carrying evaluation requirements. Atlanta, Dallas, Cincinnati, and Philadelphia allocated a portion of the evaluation resources to service to individual schools. In general, explicit board-adopted policies covering roles and operations of evaluation units are not in evidence among the materials submitted by the school systems and site visitors. The public school system in Saginaw, Michigan, has developed a detailed set of such policies (Adams, 1971).

The planning and priority setting should involve clients and audiences for evaluation services and should be guided by evaluations of previous evaluation services. The evaluation staffs in the different districts vary in their efforts to involve and attend to the interests of their clients and audiences. Planning of evaluation services in Chicago, Portland, and Columbus is highly oriented to the needs of central administration. In Atlanta, much of the planning of evaluation services has been decentralized, such that "leadership teams" including a principal, an evaluator, and teachers identify needs for studies and cooperatively develop data collection instruments. The trend toward more decentralized planning of evaluation services is also apparent in Cincinnati and Dallas. Using evaluations of past evaluation services to plan new ones was mentioned in the report on Philadelphia. In the Philadelphia district, evaluators conduct surveys to determine audiences' perceptions of the quality of reports and the extent and nature of uses of the reports. The resulting information apparently proves quite useful in planning future evaluations.

The governance of evaluation operations in large urban school systems typically is through the regular line-staff relationships of the unit to the administration of the system. In the Dallas system, as mentioned previously, a subcommittee of the Board of Education participates in the governance of the evaluation unit. This mechanism is powerful because it provides liaison between the evaluation unit and the total board; because the Board Evaluation Committee is in an excellent position to help with the formulation of evaluation policy for the system; and because this committee can also monitor and promote the effective implementation of the policies. The Dallas experience with the board evaluation committee is now about 10 years old and has proved successful; therefore, this experience seems worthy of study by other school systems.

Planning of Evaluation Services

In addition to the general direction provided by a sound conceptual and policy base, evaluation offices need specific direction that derives from an ongoing planning process. Such planning is needed to identify and clarify the nature of services that might be provided, to assign priorities to requests for services, to clarify different groups' expectations for services, to allocate funds, to assign responsibilities, and to schedule activities. To be effective, the planning of evaluation services should be ongoing, with overall plans updated at least annually. In general, the school districts studied reported that they plan evaluation services on an annual basis. However, Detroit reported having both 3- and 5-year plans for the development and operation of evaluation services.

The Financial Base for Evaluation

In response to a 1983 survey (Webster, 1984a), large school systems reported substantial expenditures for evaluation services. These expenditures, which were in excess of $1 million for each of 12 different systems, are reported in Table 27.4. The results of an earlier survey, conducted in 1978 (Webster & Stufflebeam, 1978), suggests that there are five additional systems in the United States that spend in excess of $1 million on

formal evaluation services: New York City, Chicago, Detroit, Boston, and Dade County. Despite these figures, only one system (Cincinnati) spent as much as 1 percent of its overall budget on evaluation services.

Several important trends are evident from a comparison of 1978 and 1983 expenditures in evaluation services. Probably the most noteworthy trend is the shift from reliance on federal funds in 1978 to reliance on local funds in 1983. Whereas in 1978 five of the nine units that reported spending more than $1 million on evaluation activities spent far more federal funds than local funds, in 1983 all systems but Cincinnati and Philadelphia exceeded federal fund expenditures with local funds. This finding suggests that reporting school systems are making a greater financial investment in evaluation services today than they were during the 1970s.

In general, however, these data reveal that the reporting school systems are still making only a minimal financial investment in evaluation services. Considering the potential contributions of evaluation to district, school, and classroom, it seems clear that districts must invest more heavily in evaluation. As a short-range objective, an investment between 0.5 and 1.0 percent of local funds in the evaluation function is recommended (in most large districts this would run between $22 and $25 per student). Requests for and allocation of such funds, of course, must be done in the context of evaluation policies, both short-range and long-range plans for evaluation, and evaluations of the actual costs and benefits from past evaluation activities. It is further recommended that the policy group governing the evaluation operation be asked systematically to review plans and budgets.

Location of the Evaluation Unit

The scope and influence of evaluation services can be vitally affected depending on where the unit is placed within the school system. A recommendation, common in evaluation literature, is that the evaluation unit be placed as close as possible to the superintendent of the system and that clear lines of communication and collaboration be established so that the unit can also work easily and productively at other levels. The location of the unit is particularly crucial if it is to perform accountability functions in addition to supporting informed decision making. The tendency in recent years has been to have evaluation units report directly to the superintendent or to a deputy superintendent.

When we last contacted a number of the large districts, various organizational arrangements were in evidence. In Columbus the unit reported through an assistant superintendent for planning, management,

Table 27.4 Funds Expended on Research and Evaluation Activities Selected Large School Districts

DISTRICT	n^*	LOCAL STATE FUNDS	FEDERAL FUNDS	TOTAL	COST PER STUDENT
Mobile County, AL	4	$ 55,000	$ 0	$ 55,000	$ 0.84
Baltimore County, MD	1	125,000	0	125,000	1.04
Birmingham City, AL	2	50,000	12,000	62,000	1.38
Portland, ME	1	75,000	0	75,000	1.50
Orange County, FL	1	246,561	0	246,561	3.08
Omaha, NE	5	144,533	0	144,533	3.44
Vancouver, British Columbia	1	177,000	0	177,000	3.54
Tucson Unified S.D., AZ	1	120,000	75,000	195,000	3.61
Akron, OH	1	145,000	0	145,000	4.03
Orleans Parish, LA	1	374,316	0	374,316	4.46
Hillsborough CO., FL	3	450,000	50,000	500,000	4.52
Jefferson County, CO	1	360,000	0	360,000	4.68
Los Angeles Unified SD, CA	1	2,100,000	700,000	2,800,000	5.09
El Paso I.S.D., TX	1	309,178	0	309,178	5.12
Virginia Beach, VA	1	300,000	0	300,000	5.42
Fort Worth I.S.D., TX	1	295,601	61,338	356,939	5.52
Denver, CO	1	360,000	0	360,000	5.85
Milwaukee, WI	1	411,343	150,882	562,225	6.43
Wichita, KA, #259	2	176,000	91,000	267,000	6.51
Corpus Christi I.S.D., TX	1	240,000	30,000	270,000	7.20
San Antonio I.S.D., TX	1	394,000	41,000	435,000	7.36
Charleston, SC	1	287,335	30,000	317,335	7.56
Clark County, NE	1	500,000	180,000	680,000	7.60
Des Moines, IO	1	216,700	35,000	251,700	7.87
San Juan Unified SD, CA	1	359,619	0	359,619	8.17
Indianapolis, IN	1	354,000	100,000	454,000	8.18
Oklahoma City, OK	1	290,085	60,000	350,085	8.34
Norfolk Public Schools, VA	1	384,000	0	384,000	10.67
San Diego, CA	2	1,000,000	200,000	1,200,000	10.84
Long Beach Unified SD, CA	1	454,000	200,000	654,000	11.08
Mt. Diablo Unified SD, CA	1	400,000	0	400,000	12.50
Portland, OR	1	650,000	100,000	750,000	14.15
Philadelphia, PA	1	1,398,700	1,723,800	3,122,500	15.46
Houston I.S.D., TX	1	2,865,057	382,046	3,247,103	16.70
Atlanta Public, GA	1	1,132,487	60,000	1,192,487	17.54
Dallas I.S.D., TX	1	1,761,396	515,000	2,276,396	17.78
St. Paul, MN, #625	1	600,000	0	600,000	19.35
Montgomery County, MD	1	1,700,000	100,000	1,800,000	19.46
Edmonton, Alberta	4	1,000,000	0	1,000,000	20.00
Albuquerque, NM	2	1,921,696	45,980	1,578,676	21.01
Washington, DC	1	1,532,300	108,200	2,029,500	22.10
Cincinnati, OH	1	600,000	900,000	1,500,000	28.85
Duval County,	1	2,600,000	250,000	2,850,000	28.90

* n stands for the number of offices, departments, and other units that conduct research and evaluation activities. The larger n is, the less likely that the financial statistics are correct.

and evaluation. In Dallas the unit is headed by a special assistant to the superintendent and reports to the deputy superintendent. The unit's responsibility includes evaluation, testing, pupil accounting, and data-processing functions. The unit in New York City, an exception to the general rule, reported through the Division of Evaluation, Testing, and Data Processing to the assistant superintendent for instruction. In Detroit the evaluation unit was part of the Office of Research, Planning, and Evaluation, which was headed by an assistant superintendent who reported directly

to the general superintendent. The evaluation unit in Portland reported directly to the superintendent. In general, evaluation in all of these units was found to be part of central administration.

The promotion of evaluation directors to positions of more authority, something that has occurred in a number of systems, has contributed to a trend for evaluation units to become somewhat separated and remote from the office of the superintendent. This phenomenon has mixed implications. On the one hand, it is a good device for disseminating evaluation expertise throughout the system and in a number of cases (e.g., Atlanta, Dallas, and Houston) has served to consolidate evaluation and data-processing functions (two functions that can be housed together logically and must be closely coordinated if full use is to be made of current database technology). On the other hand, it can drain expertise from the evaluation operation and, as previously indicated, can tend to remove the evaluation function from the superintendency. Also, the transfer of people out of the evaluation unit sometimes is not accompanied by attempts to recruit and train replacements. This is an issue that should command careful attention by those planning ways best to institutionalize and ensure the long-range vitality of their evaluation units. It is our recommendation that evaluation be placed in a staff position to the superintendent and that provision be made to replace members of the evaluation operation who are transferred to other areas within the system.

Internal Organization of the Evaluation Unit

If it is to fulfill its mission, the evaluation unit must be organized internally in accordance with its designated functions. Drawing from the definition of evaluation recommended in the earlier portion of this chapter,

Table 27.5 identifies relevant functions of evaluation offices.

Of course these functions might be grouped in varying ways to organize the line-staff relationships in the evaluation unit. This is borne out by the organizational charts obtained from a number of the evaluation units being considered in this chapter. For example, Table 27.6 summarizes the internal structures of the evaluation units in Detroit, Dallas, Philadelphia, and Cincinnati. The structures appear to be different, but they actually cover about the same set of functions.

One crucial difference that should be noted from Table 27.6 is that the district's data-processing functions are organized with research and evaluation in Dallas (this is also the case in Atlanta, Houston, St. Paul, Indianapolis, and Tucson). One of the major characteristics and strengths of the Dallas evaluation system is its longitudinal data base. It would be very difficult to design, implement, validate, and ensure the reliability of such a data base without close coordination between the evaluation and data-processing units.

Another relevant point is that, consistent with changing national priorities and values, the primary focus of evaluation activities has changed from support for decision making in the late 1970s to accountability in the 1980s. In 1978 the 12 largest evaluation units in

Table 27.5   Functions of Research and Evaluation Units

MANAGEMENT: the obtaining, disbursing, and quality control of material and personnel resources necessary to meet the information needs of the district.

TESTING: the operation of the basic systemwide data acquisition system to ensure reliable, valid, and objective instrumentation and reporting. This does not include diagnostic testing for special education.

INSTRUMENT DEVELOPMENT: the development and validation of necessary instrumentation.

CONTEXT EVALUATION: the provision of baseline information that delineates the environment of interest, describes desired and actual outcomes, identifies unmet needs and unused opportunities, and diagnoses problems that prevent needs from being met (often called institutional research).

INPUT EVALUATION: the provision of information for determining methods of resource utilization for accomplishing set goals.

PROCESS EVALUATION: the provision of information for determining defects in procedural design or implementation during program implementation stages and for aiding in the interpretation of program evaluation data.

PRODUCT EVALUATION: the provision of information for determining the relative success of educational programs. Product evaluation may be interim or summative and generally addresses the extent to

which programs meet their objectives, the relative effects of alternative programs, and/or program cost effectiveness.

APPLIED RESEARCH: the provision of information pertaining to interactions among student characteristics, teacher characteristics, and/or instructional strategies.

BASIC RESEARCH: the provision of information pertaining to fundamental relationships affecting student learning.

DATA PROCESSING: the operation of the basic data retrieval and analysis system.

PLANNING SERVICES: the provision of technical assistance to district and project management in planning and managing projects and programs.

AD HOC INFORMATION: the provision of requested information on an ad hoc basis to decision makers.

RESEARCH CONSULTATION: the provision of design and analysis help to district personnel in implementing their own research and evaluation projects.

PROPOSAL DEVELOPMENT: the development of proposals, or the evaluation sections of proposals, for outside funds. In all cases outside funds should be a means to an end, not an end in themselves.

Table 27.6   Subunits of the Evaluation Offices in Four School Districts

DETROIT	PHILADELPHIA	CINCINNATI	DALLAS
Administrative Statistics	Administrative and Survey Research Services	Administrative Research	Program Evaluation
Specially Funded Projects Evaluation	Federal Evaluation Resource Service	Planning and Development	Test Development
In-service Education and Test Development	Instructional Research and Development Services	Program Evaluation	Testing
Group Testing	Testing Services	Testing	Systemwide Evaluation
General Evaluation and Needs Assessment	Priority Operations Evaluation Services		Accountability and Accreditation
Research and Data Bank System	Early Childhood Evaluation Unit		Ad Hoc Studies
	Special Task Forces		Pupil Accounting
			Data Processing

the United States reported spending a median of 12 percent of their resources on testing and about the same percentage of resources on process evaluation. In 1983 the comparable figures were 27 percent and 3.5 percent, respectively. The same trends were noted in sampled medium and small evaluation units (Webster, 1984a; Webster & Stufflebeam, 1978). These data, supported by interviews with evaluation directors, point clearly to a greater emphasis on accountability and a subsequent lesser emphasis on serving decision making. Given the position that the most important purpose of evaluation is to improve programs, the emphasis on accountability is an undesirable trend.

The crucial point in this discussion of internal organization concerns form and function. The functions to be served should be carefully defined and assessed against the guiding conception of evaluation and the relevant district policies. The office should then be staffed and organized to ensure that the full range of evaluation functions will be handled effectively and efficiently.

Two unique organizational strategies deserve special mention. In Atlanta, all members of the evaluation staff have been given dual assignments: (a) a centralized assignment that capitalizes on each individual's special expertise and (b) an assignment to provide general evaluation assistance to the staff of designated schools. This strategy combines the advantages of both centralized and decentralized evaluation; that is, (a) coordinated services and a critical mass of resource personnel and (b) direct assistance to school-based personnel. The other unique strategy involves attaching special evaluation task forces to given programs over a sustained period of time. Dallas has made excellent use of this approach in its assignment of a team to its Skyline Career Development Center and magnet schools; Philadelphia has won national recognition through the work of its Early Childhood Evaluation Unit; and Chicago has outlined a strategy of using cy-

clical evaluation teams wherein each team is assigned to provide evaluation services to a high-priority program over a period of 4 years. These strategies merit attention by groups that may need to reorganize their evaluation services in order to encourage sustained study and better use of results.

The Use of External Evaluators and Community Assistance

Most of the evaluation systems discussed tend not to make use of external evaluators, but there are notable exceptions. Both Chicago and Pittsburgh have made extensive and systematic use of evaluation experts who happen to be present in their communities. Chicago has used recent graduates from the University of Chicago, many of whom received extensive training in evaluation under the direction of Dr. Benjamin Bloom. In recent years, the Pittsburgh public school system has essentially delegated its ongoing evaluation responsibilities to Cooley and his staff at the University of Pittsburgh (Bickel & Cooley, 1981).

The examples have something in common: In each case, the district has close at hand an unusually well-developed, university-based evaluation program. The lack of such a capability in their area may partially explain why the majority of large school districts do not turn to outsiders for their evaluation services. Another reason is that the large districts can afford to staff and operate their own evaluation systems if they so choose. Other reasons for avoiding the use of external evaluation services may be that they have often proved costly and superficial and generally have not been able to develop and maintain longitudinal data bases, the heart of cost-effective evaluation.

Because of the possibilities of bias and lack of credibility when a school system exclusively evaluates its own programs, it is suggested that consideration be given to using external evaluators to help with the audit, or meta-evaluations (Scriven, 1975; Stufflebeam, 1978), of internal evaluation plans and reports. Compared to the costs of the primary evaluations being done in the districts, meta-evaluations by outsiders are low in cost and can add greatly to the credibility and, in some cases, the technical soundness of internal evaluation operations. Moreover, the availability of the Joint Committees (1981) *Standards for Evaluations* enhances the propects for sound and useful meta-evaluations. On the other hand, the persons commissioned to conduct meta-evaluations may, over a period of time, lose their independence; accordingly, the membership of a meta-evaluation team should be changed periodically.

One source of external assistance is graduate students who are studying evaluation. They often need relevant internship experiences and have sufficient training to be of considerable use to school systems. School systems can regularly communicate and collaborate with universities that have evaluation training programs to put interested students in appropriate internships.

Another source of external assistance is the community at large, as illustrated by an important evaluation in Montclair, New Jersey, a school district with about 6,000 students. Because of its relatively small size, compared to the large urban districts that have been discussed, Montclair had no formal office of evaluation but it did have a superintendent, Dr. Walter Marks, an evaluation expert by both training and experience, plus a coordinator of testing and evaluation. This district had suffered acute political turmoil over its inability to present an integration plan acceptable to the school board, the community, special interest groups, and governmental agencies. Dr. Marks, who was new in the position of superintendent but who had previously been the district's evaluator, decided to conceptualize the problem as a decision problem requiring evaluative guidance. In the language of the CIPP model, he decided to conduct a context evaluation to help the school board set integration objectives and an input evaluation to present the board with several optional integration plans, along with comparative evaluations of their potential effectiveness, feasibility, legality, and acceptability.

Such an ambitious program of evaluation would not have been feasible for the superintendent and coordinator to conduct by themselves, and even if they had attempted to do so, there would have been questions about objectivity. Dr. Marks overcame the dilemma by enlisting members of the community to staff the context and input evaluation teams. He provided the teams with systematic training and technical advice. The coordinator of testing and evaluation supplied the teams with extant data from the school district files, and the teams collected, processed, and reported the pertinent information. In the end, the board and community were well pleased with the optional plans put forward and the comparative evaluations of those plans. The district was reorganized around the adopted approach, and magnet schools and integration became a reality. This success story became the subject of a national conference and a subsequent book (Marks & Nystrand, 1981).

The Montclair case illustrates several important points. First, the community is a potential source of assistance for conducting evaluations. Second, involving community members in evaluations can go a long way toward earning their constructive support when a school district addresses complex problems. Third, it is important to conceptualize and conduct evaluations as a guide to improvement. Fourth, decision-making bodies react much more readily to assessed alternatives than to single solutions. Fifth, small school districts, if they are resourceful, can effectively employ evaluation technology. Sixth, even the small districts must allocate some fiscal and personnel resources to evaluation if it is to work for them. Good information is not free, and evaluation is sufficiently important so that all districts should devote a reasonable part of their budgets to support one or more evaluation specialists. Finally, there is no good substitute for having at least one school district administrator who is knowledgeable about evaluation and committed to its use.

Staffing Evaluation and Training the Participants

Crucial and related elements of a well-functioning evaluation program in any size district are staffing and training (both preservice and in-service). One direct approach to developing a sound evaluation capability is to recruit at least one staff member who has appropriate grounding in the theory and methodology of evaluation and who has learned how to make applications in school settings. A less direct but equally effective approach to staffing evaluation is to recruit one or more staff members from within the district who want to specialize in evaluation and assign them to an evaluation consultant under whose tutelage they can learn evaluation by doing it. Buttressed with appropriate formal instruction and guided reading, on-the-job training can be a most effective way of staffing evaluation programs.

No matter how the evaluation function is staffed, a continuing training program is essential to equip new staff members to use the current routines in the school system's evaluation program; to help all staff members refresh their knowledge and skill and maintain pace with the state of the evaluation art; to help users of evaluation services understand what services are available and the ways they can best be used; and to help people throughout the system to conduct some of their own evaluations. Based on contacts with a variety of districts and personal evaluation work, we have observed a variety of approaches to both preservice training and in-service training.

Preservice Training

The personnel of the evaluation units studied have received their graduate training in a variety of areas and in a variety of institutions. Staff members in the Columbus and Saginaw systems largely were trained in evaluation and administration at The Ohio State University. A number of them participated in the late 1960s in an evaluation doctoral program, centered in The Ohio State University Evaluation Center, which had as a major component an on-the-job training program that involved trainees in designing, developing, and beginning to implement the offices of evaluation in the two districts. The Columbus and Saginaw systems' initial investments in training some of their teachers in a systematic approach to evaluation and then employing them as evaluators proved to be cost effective. These persons have remained with the systems and have made substantial contributions in evaluation as well as in other areas.

The staff members in the evaluation unit in Dallas have been recruited from a variety of institutions, including Florida State University (which emphasizes research methodology and instructional technology); Michigan State University (which emphasizes statistics and measurement); the University of Colorado (which has had a dual emphasis in program evaluation and research design); the University of Wisconsin (which traditionally has emphasized experimental design); The Ohio State University (which has emphasized decision-oriented evaluation and planning); the University of Illinois (which has dual emphasis in program evaluation and research design); the University of Iowa (which emphasizes classical measurement theory); New Mexico State University (which has dual emphasis in program evaluation and research design); and the University of Texas (where some of the Dallas staff members received extensive training in data processing and research methodology). In addition, Dallas recently offered, in collaboration with the Western Michigan University Evaluation Center, a school-system-based master's degree program in program evaluation. About 20 people received the master's degree through this program and were trained by a faculty composed both of senior staff members in the Dallas evaluation unit and professors from Western Michigan University. A full set of standard graduate courses in measurement,

statistics, program evaluation, and data processing was offered these students, along with internship projects in which the students evaluated Dallas programs. (Western Michigan University conducted other external master's degree programs, with similar results, in Lansing, Michigan, and Jefferson County, Colorado.) In general, the Dallas staff is one of the strongest staffs of school-system-based evaluators anywhere in the world. A major reason for that strength is in the range of university programs represented in the staff's credentials. This diversity of backgrounds has resulted in a staff that possesses a wide range of specialized and complementary qualifications. But it also should be observed that getting such a diverse group to work well together is no easy task. In Dallas this has been accomplished largely as a result of strong central administrative leadership and by a unified guiding conceptualization of evaluation.

In recruiting and selecting staff members, it seems wise for school systems to consider candidates from a wide range of universities. Among those that are producing persons with skills appropriate to school system evaluation are the University of Chicago program previously led by Benjamin Bloom; the Michigan State University program led by Andrew Porter; the Boston College program led by George Madaus; the Western Michigan University program under the leadership of James Sanders; the University of Maryland program led by Gilbert Austin; the University of Colorado program under Lorrie Shepard; the University of Illinois program under Robert Stake; the University of Texas program under Gary Borich; the Indiana University program led by Egon Guba and Bob Wolf; the Harvard University program led by Richard Light; the Stanford program previously led by Lee Cronbach; the University of Minnesota program led by Jack Merwin and Wayne Welch; the University of Virginia program under Bob Covert; the UCLA program led by Marvin Alkin, Eva Baker, and James Popham; the Cornell University program under Bob Gowin and Jason Millman; the New Mexico State University program under Tim Pettibone; and the Florida State University program led by Garrett Foster and John Hills.

In-service Training

Staff development and the training of users of evaluation should be an ongoing enterprise in school systems. A considerable amount of activity in this area is seen in regard to training teachers to use tests; otherwise, there is little evidence of such staff development and training of evaluation users. In all likelihood, this is due to heavy demands for primary evaluation services and a short supply of resources to provide those services, let alone training; but training is so important that school systems are well advised to regularly allocate a portion of their budget to this function.

Clearly, there are in all school systems a large number of opportunities to provide evaluation training. For example, Dade County, when visited, was considering the possibility of adding evaluation training to the curriculums of its teacher centers. Other systems operate similar training programs and could consider incorporating evaluation into the training they do for administrators and teachers. Also, every evaluation study provides a readymade instructional laboratory in evaluation. If such evaluations are properly planned, the participants and users could be given pertinent readings that would help them to understand the methodologies used. Also, times could be arranged when experts in various aspects of the evaluation—for example, the data analyst, the report writer, the meta-evaluator, or the project director—could explain specific plans and operations and help participants and users to understand the methodologies involved and to consider other situations in which these methodologies might be applied. Furthermore, the participants and users could be schooled in the *Standards for Evaluation* described earlier (Joint Committee on Standards for Educational Evaluation, 1981) and helped to apply these to plans and reports of the evaluations. The examples illustrate that there are training opportunities in every evaluation. What is needed is some planning and allocation of resources to take advantage of these opportunities.

There are also some important continuing education opportunities that occur in training programs at conventions and in management academies. The American Educational Research Association (AERA) has regularly offered topical training in evaluation at its annual conventions, as has the American Evaluation Association. An important example of evaluation training for school administrators is the Bush Foundation's Administrative Fellows Program in Minnesota (Mauriel, 1978).

Use of Interns

Still another opportunity is the training that a school system can offer to students in university programs. Internships for these people have advantages both for the interns and for the school system. Interns are often skilled in technical areas in evaluation and often are willing to offer valuable services at a low cost in order to gain experience. Furthermore, many are willing to provide in-service training in their area of expertise to interested persons in the system. The interns can benefit greatly by opportunities to apply their skills in real-world settings. The school systems studied are using interns, and this is to be encouraged. The use of internships also can work as an effective recruitment

and selection strategy for school systems that need to add persons to their staff.

Overall, both preservice and in-service training are areas vital to ensuring the effectiveness and the long-term viability of school system evaluation programs. The opportunities available, especially in the in-service training area, are underutilized.

Promoting the Use of Evaluation

Stimulating and guiding people to use evaluation services is an ongoing and vital concern if evaluations are to succeed. Among the pertinent issues are ways best to disseminate evaluation expertise, open up communication channels, involve audiences for an evaluation in its planning, assign responsibility for promoting the use of evaluation, make reports both interesting and readable, and employ techniques that engage audiences for an evaluation in a serious study of its procedures and findings. The state of the art in this area is generally weak, but experiences with school district evaluation systems have afforded some interesting perspectives on these issues.

Disseminating Evaluation Expertise

As noted previously, there are a number of instances in which personnel previously assigned to an evaluation unit have been reassigned in the district. In those cases, the evaluation expertise in the district is disseminated, and there is an opportunity for expanding the district's potential to utilize evaluation findings. Columbus has used this device extensively with the assignment of a number of members of the evaluation unit to a variety of roles in the Columbus system. This undoubtedly spread the use of evaluation through the system, but it also resulted in a serious loss to the system. Columbus did little to replace the evaluators in the division of evaluation once they were reassigned. Consequently, the capabilities of the office of evaluation reportedly have become weakened and the unit is no longer a strong source of evaluation-oriented leaders for re-assignment in other areas of the system. In general, it is a sound strategy to use some of the positions in an evaluation unit as transient positions, through which evaluators can gain experience in the evaluation of system enterprises and then be transferred to other areas of the system, where they can provide valuable leadership and promote increased use of evaluation services. At the same time, systems should provide for adequate replacement of the evaluation unit's staff members who have been transferred. The Lansing, Michigan, public school system has been especially successful in using such a strategy for disseminating evaluation expertise throughout the system under the leadership of Richard Benjamin and Grace Iverson.

Communication Channels

Evaluation is a threatening activity, and there is a tendency in many school systems to explicitly limit the contacts that members of the evaluation unit can have with people throughout the system. For example, it has been common practice in some systems to channel evaluation reports through the chain of command upward and to release them to those persons whose programs were evaluated only after approval of the reports at the highest level of the system. Such a practice stifles timely use of evaluation findings and limits the effectiveness of the evaluation unit. On the other hand, the danger is ever-present that prematurely released reports will be flawed, providing bad guidance and discrediting the process of evaluation. Compromise is necessary to deal with this dilemma. For example, an evaluator's superiors and the primary audiences for the evaluation might review a draft report simultaneously and then provide feedback for use in finalizing the report. Also, regular face-to-face communication between evaluator and audiences is an excellent way to promote good working relationships between the evaluators and program personnel and to provide timely use of findings. Once again, the Atlanta model, with evaluation department liaison persons meeting regularly with the school leadership team, seems relevant.

In Dallas, program managers sign off on the evaluation plans, thus ensuring that the evaluation questions are relevant and important to program managers and will provide useful information for program decisions. Accountability questions are also included in the designs. Although the program managers have only limited influence on the accountability questions, they at least make some input to and are aware of the areas in which the program will be held accountable. A carefully planned time line that ensures systematic and continuous interaction between program managers and evaluators is also specified in the evaluation plans. Doing so guarantees continuous interaction so that programs can be adjusted throughout the course of the year (formative evaluation), and it also prevents surprises when the summative accountability report is released (Dallas Independent School District, 1984). One important point is that program managers sign off on evaluation plans, not evaluation reports. Thus, involvement is ensured but independence and credibility of reports are maintained.

Involvement of Audiences in Planning Evaluations

Evaluation, when practiced successfully, is a change process because it denotes problems and provides direction for dealing with the problems. As with any effective change process, it is important to involve the group whose behavior is to be changed by the evaluation in planning the evaluation. Active collaboration between evaluators and audiences, whether board members, superintendents, principals, or teachers, increases the likelihood that the evaluation will address pertinent issues and that the findings will be used once they are obtained.

Such joint planning does occur in many school systems. In many cases, the director of evaluation is regularly present in administrative cabinet meetings and is given opportunities to involve the cabinet in reviewing evaluation plans. The Board Evaluation Committee in Dallas participates extensively in planning the systemwide evaluations. The school leadership teams in Atlanta likewise participate in planning school-level evaluations, and evaluators in the New York Office of Evaluation meet regularly with district superintendents and their immediate staffs to review evaluation plans. In addition, the Philadelphia school system surveys its audiences to get their reactions to previous evaluation reports so that deficiencies in these reports can be avoided in future evaluations. Another fairly widespread practice is for evaluators to meet with the advisory councils of the projects to be evaluated to get their input and to promote their understanding of the evaluation plans. In general, school systems work hard to involve their audiences in evaluation planning. This is an important investment of their time and energies.

Communicating the Findings

Evaluators are notorious for writing and disseminating poorly written reports filled with jargon and statistical language. The Philadelphia system has been trying to overcome this problem by releasing popularized reports. The Dallas system has used the device of multiple reports from an evaluation, including abstracts and executive summaries in addition to the complete technical report. The Austin system often used cartoons and illustrations to communicate findings. Another district has reported successful experiences conducting special workshops to help the audiences understand findings and apply them to problems. In addition, district evaluators have increasingly worked to help members of the media understand and discuss evaluation findings. Such efforts are to be encouraged, because they are directed to the important problem of ways to help audiences better understand and use evaluation findings.

Assuring the Quality of Evaluation

The organization and administration of evaluation is a complex enterprise with management-type problems, many of which have been discussed here, and a host of additional problems associated with the political contexts in which evaluations occur. In closing this section it must be emphasized, as Cronbach (1980) and others have done, that evaluation is indeed a political process and there is much work to be done in controlling bias. On the positive side, exploiting political opportunities in order to promote sound and effective evaluation work is functional. A sizable evaluation literature confirms the political nature of evaluation. Sroufe (1977), for example, has written about offensive and defensive evaluations. Elsewhere, we have written about pseudoevaluations, studies that in the name of evaluation mislead audiences to believe a particular message irrespective of its validity (Stufflebeam & Webster, 1980). House (1978) devoted an entire book to an examination of the political nature of evaluation, and anyone who has conducted evaluations in school settings knows that the work is often impeded, threatened, or misused by those who have a stake in the findings.

Fortunately, evaluators have developed a number of ways to deal with political threats to evaluation. Perhaps the most pervasive of these is invoking professional evaluation standards in all phases of an evaluation. Closely associated with this action is subjecting an evaluation to external audit or meta-evaluation. Drawing up contracts at the outset of a study to cover such matters as access to data, editing of reports, and release of findings is also a strong deterrent to political corruption of a study. Brickell (1981) has argued for the use of broadly representative advisory groups to monitor and assist evaluation work. Finally, evaluators must consistently be fair and equitable in their dealings with the various interest groups in an evaluation.

SELECTING APPROPRIATE METHODS

Over the years, a variety of methods have been used to evaluate school programs and projects, and a rich array of methods is evident in the evaluation practices of school systems today. In general, though, there is some evidence that these methods are fraught with difficulties and that school systems do not have an adequate store of appropriate and powerful techniques.

Testing

Use of published tests continues to be one of the most prevalent and problematical aspects of evaluation programs. Norm-referenced tests continue to be much in vogue, probably because members of the community have come to value them as a means of comparing the quality of performance in their school system with that in a nationally selected sample of school systems. Repeatedly, the release of comparisons of school systems results with national norms has embarrassed many of the systems, especially those with concentrations of disadvantaged students. Often, the publication of such results has led to ill-founded charges of poor teaching and learning in certain schools and to countercharges that the national norms are inappropriate and unfair in relation to the kinds of populations being served. Moreover, teachers, and lately researchers, have claimed that many norm-referenced tests poorly approximate what is actually taught in schools and often are used invalidly to provide inferences about the quality of teaching and learning (Madaus, 1980). Nonetheless, used correctly, standardized tests provide one very powerful method of monitoring system performance.

The move to criterion-referenced testing has been positively received by many teachers, because they are able to compare the objectives assessed on a criterion-referenced test with those involved in their teaching. Also, there have been important developments by test publishers and school districts that provide for domain-referenced analysis of norm-referenced test data in order to examine student achievement against local objectives. (See the Fall 1984 issue of *Educational Measurement Issues and Practices*.) Teachers have been able to use results, for given objectives, for diagnostic purposes. On the other side is the charge that criterion-referenced tests, especially as administered by state education departments, dictate curriculums and lead to teaching to the tests. An associated problem is seen in the move to require that high school students pass a competency test before they can graduate. A major charge in this area is that students are being penalized for the cumulative failure of their systems to provide them with a sound education. Other charges are that the competency tests do not adequately reflect the high school curriculum and that they have not been sufficiently validated to serve as a major determinant of whether or not a student should receive a high school diploma. A recent book by Madaus (1983) examines this problem area in depth.

A novel approach to testing is seen in Portland's application of the Rasch model. The program there represents a concerted effort to develop objectives that reflect the school system's K–12 curriculum, to develop test items that are valid for these objectives, and then to offer a flexible bank of test items for use in assessing students' performance at their functional levels. This program bears careful observation and may produce a valuable model for other school districts to adapt and improve their testing programs.

Possibly one of the most controversial of the new approaches to testing is the Dallas program for testing incoming teachers (Webster, 1984b). The rationale for this approach is twofold: The poor performance of disadvantaged students in basic-skills areas has been traced to teachers who are themselves weak in the basic skills; and, politically, the main means of changing and upgrading the quality of the teaching force is to ensure that new teachers are strong in the basic skills as well as in other areas. By testing probationary teachers, it seems to be possible to discharge the weak ones before they gain tenure and embark on careers in which they would serve as poor models (e.g., in correct speaking and writing) for the students. Whether or not one agrees with this rationale, the Dallas problem illustrates the tie discussed earlier between program evaluation (which, in this case, revealed weak performance gains by disadvantaged students) and personnel evaluation (examining teachers for their own proficiency in basic skills on the assumption that they cannot teach what they have not mastered themselves).

Data Bases, School Profiles, and the Pupil Census

Increasingly evaluation offices have linked with their school system's data-processing operation to create data bases that may be used in administration and in assessment of the status of students and schools. New York City, when studied, was developing a census of all its students so that administrators will be able to study the characteristics of the student body and trace individual students. The Columbus system pioneered in the development of what it termed the "school profile," which contains a chart of each school in the system that identifies characteristics of the staff and school in relation to performance by students on national tests. A number of other school systems, including Dallas, White Plains, Tulsa, and Chicago, have also developed school profiles. Dade County has begun to develop such a profile, to computerize its use, and to place terminals in each of the schools so that the school principals can have immediate access to the information about their schools. The computer terminals promise to make the data base in Dade County more useful than if it were only distributed annually as a printed report.

Experience suggests that many school system data bases are not nearly well enough designed to support adequate evaluation. To evaluate system performances over time, it must be possible to trace the performance of individual students participating in that system over time. Few school systems have the data base necessary to support this type of application. Dallas has developed a longitudinal data base that enables the tracking of individual student performance over a period that has now reached 10 years. This data base is central to all program evaluation efforts and contributes substantially to a very cost-effective evaluation system because it forms the basis for many evaluation efforts.

Experimentation

Ten years ago it was common to find school systems conducting experiments to evaluate their programs and projects. Such evaluations were consistent with a previous orientation to summative evaluation, which generally has been replaced by a preference for formative evaluation. Few systems now use experimentation unless they are conducting applied research projects or responding to explicit requirements from the federal government, such as in the Emergency School Assistance Act program. In general, there seems to be a trend away from the use of experimentation in schools, perhaps reflecting the claim that assumptions underlying experimental methods often cannot be met in public school programs. For example, requirements inherent in experimental design—that treatments be prespecified and held constant, that students be randomly assigned to the treatments, and that results be obtained at the end of the experiment—often directly conflict with a requirement to provide ongoing information to guide projects and change them when problems are found.

Audits

One promising approach seen in the Dade County system is that of the school audit. This approach was just being developed and applied when studied; the basic idea seems sound. Members of the Department of Instruction review information from the school system's data base about a given school. They then go to that school to conduct an on-site visit to help the school principal and staff take stock of strengths and weaknesses and consider directions for improvement. If such audits can be conducted in a constructive manner, they should provide a good way to use evaluation for improvement at the school level.

Curriculum-Imbedded Evaluation

Another promising means of disseminating evaluation throughout a school system is in curriculum-imbedded evaluation. For example, Mastery Learning as practiced in Chicago, the CIMS program in Cincinnati, the Diagnostic-Prescriptive Reading program in Dade County, and the School Improvement and Instructional Management projects in New York City illustrate ways evaluation requirements and procedures can be built into curricular materials. This approach is highly consistent with a philosophy of evaluation that calls for the systematic collection of data to provide feedback and guidance for improvement at the student, as well as the school, level.

Advocacy Teams and Convergence Teams

A persistent problem is that evaluations have been proficient in revealing shortfalls and problems but not in locating and assessing potential solutions. For example, Robert Travers (1983) reported that the Boston Schools Survey, which began under the direction of Horace Mann in 1845, was discontinued after about 5 years because year after year the only function of the survey was to verify the continued existence of problems. Apparently, after a while the annual discouragement from evaluation without any direction for improvement was viewed as unwelcome and dysfunctional.

The advocacy team technique (Reinhard, 1972) was developed explicitly to overcome this problem. Once a problem has been revealed and explicated through a needs assessment or context evaluation, an advocacy team technique can locate and assess competing solutions. Subsequently, a convergence team is asked to combine the best features of the proposed solutions and to develop an operational problem-solving plan. The technique recently was employed by the Shaker Heights, Ohio, and Montclair, New Jersey, school systems to develop programs for overcoming problems of integration. In addition to systematically producing defensible plans for integrating the districts, use of the technique in both cases helped to restore a spirit of harmony and cooperation.

Overall, interesting techniques are being used by evaluators in the public schools. Some of the efforts are promising but untested; clearly, there is a need for evaluation of these techniques. As mentioned earlier, testing continues to be a serious problem area for schools. Much experimentation and improvement are needed in this area, and new approaches to the examination of performance should be developed. Overall, it is essential that evaluations in school districts employ a variety of techniques in order to derive the best that the current methodology has to offer and to check findings across techniques. Important work in identifying and examining novel evaluation techniques has been reported by Smith (1981a, 1981b).

STRENGTHENING THE ROLE OF EVALUATION IN ADMINISTERING EDUCATION

So far this chapter has presented a perspective on evaluation as a process to guide decision making and to provide a basis for accountability reports. Pursuant to that view of evaluation, administrators, board members, and evaluators in school systems have been urged to attend seriously to the explication and communication of their view of evaluation, and a variety of pervasive conceptual issues have been introduced. Subsequently, discussions dealt with how best to organize, administer, and promote the use of evaluation functions; again, a range of pertinent issues was discussed and illustrated with examples from school districts. The previous section reviewed some of the techniques that are now in use, advocated the use of multiple methods, and called for the development of better and more relevant techniques.

In this concluding section, we will consider what what needs to be done to strengthen administrators' roles and practices in using evaluation to guide and improve education. We have cited several instances of good evaluation work in the schools. Moreover, it is apparent that school district personnel have contributed greatly to the advancements over the past 20 years in the theory, practice, and professionalization of evaluation. However, in general, the state of evaluation practice in school districts and other educational agencies needs improvement. At the outset of this chapter, we stated our position that educational administrators have more to do with the quality and impacts of evaluation than any other group. In conclusion, we will address a number of issues concerned with improving the evaluation performance of educational administrators. We will label each issue, offer our judgment about it, follow with a recommendation, and conclude by discussing ways the recommendation might be implemented.

Issue Number 1: Preservice Training of Administrators

Judgment Most administrator training programs do a poor job of preparing administrators in the area of evaluation.

Recommendation Persons in charge of administrator training programs should examine their offerings to discern whether the charge applies to their situation. If it does, they might institute a course in the concept of program evaluation and an evaluation field experience requirement, or pertinent offerings in their institution may already exist for them to use.

Comments Examples of good practice in regard to this issue exist at the University of Texas (under the leadership of Nolan Estes), the University of Houston (under Robert Randall), Boston College (under George Madaus), Western Michigan University (under James Sanders), and the University of Alabama (under James McClain). It is crucial that both the theory course and the practical experience be oriented to evaluation as it has been defined in this chapter. It is also essential that training not be confined to laboratory research techniques, standardized testing, or anthropological methods. Any one of these conceptions of evaluation methodology is much too narrow to address the full range of important issues that administrators must face in evaluating educational programs. Whenever possible, future school administrators and future evaluation specialists should be trained together in both the theory course and the practicum. They have much to learn from each other, and they will have to work together later as they exercise their professions. The sooner they can develop mutual respect and working relationships, the better. Also, external degree programs in evaluation conducted on site at school districts can be a powerful means of preparing both evaluation-oriented educational leaders and evaluation specialists.

Issue Number 2: In-service Training of Administrators

Judgment Continuing education programs for practicing educational administrators do far less than they should to upgrade the evaluation skills of administrators.

Recommendation The professional societies of administrators, universities, and foundations should examine their continuing education programs for administrators to test the validity and significance of the charge. If found valid, they should increase and improve their offerings.

Comments A number of groups have done creditable work in this area. The National Academy for School Executives from time to time has offered pertinent and effective evaluation workshops, especially those led by Henry M. Brickell (1981). The Bush Foundation is offering year-long continuing education programs in education administration topics to selected administrators in Minnesota. The program, which is being led by John Mauriel at the University of Minnesota and which requires about 6 weeks of time from each participant, includes core courses and projects in both program evaluation and personnel evaluation. Finally, the professional societies of educational administrators can and should provide more in-service education opportunities in evaluation.

Issue Number 3: Evaluation Capacity Development

Judgment Most school districts are doing much less than they should to develop their evaluation capabilities.

Recommendation To check whether this judgment applies, school superintendents and principals might assess whether they and their staffs are receiving up-to-date evaluation training, whether they have a district-wide or schoolwide working concept of evaluation, whether their decisions are being guided by evaluation, whether they are using their evaluation experiences to improve staff evaluation skills, and whether they have

budgeted for evaluation work. If any answers are "no," plans should be made to upgrade evaluation in the school or district.

Comments A number of the examples cited earlier in this chapter are relevant to addressing this recommendation. These include creating a board evaluation committee; developing a district or school manual of evaluation policies and procedures; offering in-service training in evaluation within the school or district; allocating about 1 percent of the district budget to evaluation; staffing externally based evaluations of district programs with district staff so that they can learn about evaluation by doing it; employing the teacher-as-evaluator concept; employing graduate students as evaluation interns; and creating a district office of evaluation.

Issue Number 4: Assuring the Quality of Evaluation

Judgment Whereas AASA and NAESP have contributed substantially to the creation of professional standards for evaluation, these and other administrator groups are not effectively promoting the use of these standards to assure the quality of evaluation work.

Recommendation State and professional societies of educational administrators should reexamine their commitment to the development and use of professional standards for upgrading school district evaluation work. If found wanting, they might assign a high priority to increasing administrators' use of the *Standards for Evaluation* of the Joint Committee (1981).

Comments The Joint Committee's standards have been created by and for educational administrators as well as other groups concerned with the professional practice of education. *Standards for Evaluation* gives administrators a powerful tool for fostering useful, feasible, proper, and accurate evaluations in their schools. However, administrators are not making sufficient use of it either for planning and checking evaluation work or for training. Unfortunately, a major investment and resource is being wasted.

FINAL WORD

Evaluation is a vital function in the offering of educational services. No system can achieve its potential and maintain a high level of service if it does not constantly assess its performance and modify its practices accordingly. This is as true in the individual classroom as it is in the office of the superintendent or the principal.

Those in positions of leadership can help their systems adopt, implement, and use a sound and wide-reaching program of evaluation. In this chapter, we have attempted to provide administrators with an agenda of issues and possible actions pertinent to the improvement of evaluation service. We look forward to seeing their response and hope it will be manifested in increased and improved evaluation practice in school districts and in schools.

REFERENCES

Abrahamson, S. (1985). *Evaluation of continuing education in the health professions.* Boston: Kluwer-Nijhoff.

Adams, J. A. (1971). *A study of the status, scope, and nature of educational evaluation in Michigan's public K–12 school districts.* Unpublished doctoral dissertation, The Ohio State University, Columbus.

Airasian, P. W. (1979). A perspective on the use and misuse of standardized achievement tests. *Measurement in Education, NCME, 10,* 1–12.

Airasian, P. W., & Madaus, G. F. (1972). Criterion-referenced testing in the classroom. *Measurement in Education, NCME, 3,* 1–8.

Alkin, M., Daillak, R., and White, P. (1979). *Using evaluations: Does evaluation make a difference?* Beverly Hills, CA: Sage.

American Association of School Administrators. (1984) *Teacher incentives: A tool for effective management.* Arlington, VA: Author.

Anastasi, A. (1976). *Psychological testing,* 4th ed. New York: Macmillan.

Ashburn, A. G. (1973). Credibility gaps and the institutionalizing of educational evaluation functions. *Planning & Changing, 4* (1), 18–28.

Ashburn, A. G., & Barton, R. L. (1971). *Annual report: Planning, research, and evaluation department 1970–1971.* Dallas: Dallas Independent School District.

Austin, G., & Garber, H. (1985). *Research on exemplary schools.* Orlando, FL: Academic Press.

Barta, M. B., Ahn, U. R., & Gastright, J. F. (1976). Some problems in interpreting criterion-referenced test results in a program evaluation. *Studies in Educational Evaluation, 2* (3), 193–202.

Becker, H. S. (1975). Photography and sociology. *Afterimage.* (magazine) *3*(2), 22–32.

Berreman, G. D. (1968). Ethography: Method and product. In J. A. Clifton (Ed.) *Introduction to cultural anthropology: Essays in the scope and methods of the science of man.* Boston: Houghton-Mifflin.

Bettinghaus, E. P., & Miller, G. R. (1973). *A dissemination system for state accountability programs. Paper III: Developing dissemination procedures for state education accountability programs.* Denver: Cooperative Accountability Project.

Bickel, W. E., & Cooley, W. W. (1981). *The utilization of a district-wide needs assessment.* Pittsburgh: Learning Research and Development Center, University of Pittsburgh.

Bloom, B. S., Hastings, J. T., & Madaus, G. F. (1971). *Handbook on formative and summative evaluation of student learning.* New York: McGraw-Hill.

Bracht, G. H., & Glass, G. V. (1968). The external validity of experiments. *American Educational Research Journal, 5,* 437–474.

Bracht, G. H., Hopkins, K. D., & Stanley, J. C. (Eds.) (1972). *Perspectives in educational and psychological measurement.* Englewood Cliffs, NJ: Prentice-Hall.

Braskamp, L. A. & Mayberry, P. W. (1982). *A comparison of two sets of standards.* Paper presented at the joint Annual Meeting of the Evaluation Network and Evaluation Research Society, Baltimore, MD.

Brickell, H. M. (1981). *Policy study in evaluation* [Audiotape]. American Educational Research Association.

Brinkerhoff, R., Brethower, D. M., Hluchyj, T., & Ridings, J. (1983). *Program evaluation.* Boston: Kluwer-Nijhoff.

Britain, G. M. (1981). Contextual evaluation: An ethnographic

approach to program assessment, in R. F. Conner (Ed.), *Methodological advances in evaluation researches.* Beverly Hills, CA: Sage.

Bunda, M. (1982). *Concerns and techniques in feasibility.* Paper presented at the Annual Meeting of the National Council on Measurement in Education, New York.

Caldwell, M. (1968). An approach to the assessment of educational planning. *Educational Technology, 8*(19), 5–12.

Campbell, D. T., & Stanley, J. C. (1963). Experimental and quasi-experimental designs for research on teaching. In N. L. Gage (Ed.), *Handbook of research on teaching.* Chicago: Rand McNally.

Carey, L. (1979). State-level teacher performance evaluation policies. *Inservice Centerfold.* New York: National Council on State and Inservice Education.

Chase, F. S. (1980). *Educational quandaries and opportunities: Urban education studies.* Washington, DC: National Institute of Education and the Spencer Foundation.

Chase, F. S. (1975). *Report of a study of instruction in the Dallas Independent School District.* Dallas Independent School District.

Coffman, W. E. (1969). Achievement test. In R. L. Ebel (Ed.) *Encyclopedia of educational research* (4th ed.) New York: Macmillan.

Committee to Develop Standards for Educational and Psychological Tests. (1985). *Standards for educational and psychological testing.* Washington, DC: American Psychological Association.

Cooley, W. W., & Bickel, W. E. (1986). *Decision-oriented educational research.* Boston: Kluwer-Nijhoff.

Cronbach, L. J. (1963). Course improvement through evaluation. *Teachers College Record, 64*(8), 672–683.

Cronbach, L. J. (1970). *Essentials of psychological testing* (3rd ed.) New York: Harper & Row.

Cronbach, L. J. (1980). *Toward reform of program evaluation.* San Francisco: Jossey-Bass.

Cronbach, L. J. (1982). *Designing evaluations of education and social programs.* San Francisco: Jossey-Bass.

Dallas Independent School District. (1984). *Plans for the use of research, evaluation, and information systems resources, 1984–85.* Unpublished manuscript, Dallas Independent School District.

Duggan, J. G., Talmage, H., & Rasher, S. P. (1983) *Client use of evaluation findings: An examination of salient features.* Paper presented at the Annual Meeting of the American Educational Research Association, Montreal.

Duncan, O. D. (1966). Path analysis: Sociological examples. *American Journal of Sociology, 72,* 1–16.

Duncan, O. D. (1969). Some linear models for two-wave, two-variable panel analysis. *Psychological Bulletin, 72,* 177–182.

Ebel, R. L. (1961). Standardized achievement tests: Uses and limitations. *National Elementary School Principal, 40,* 29–32.

Ebel, R. L. (1978). The case for norm-referenced measurements. *Educational Researcher, 7,* 3–5.

Eisner, E. W. (1975, March). *The perceptive eye: Toward the reformation of educational evaluation.* Paper presented at the Annual Meeting of the American Educational Research Association, Washington, DC.

Eisner, E. W. (1983). Educational connoisseurship and criticism: Their form and functions in educational evaluation. In G. Madaus, Scriven, & D. L. Stufflebeam, Eds., *Evaluation models.* Boston: Kluwer-Nijhoff.

Englert, R. M., Kean, M. H., & Scribner, J. D. (1977). Politics of program evaluation in large city school districts. *Education and Urban Society, 9*(4), 429–450.

Evers, J. W. (1980). *A field study of goal-based and goal-free evaluation techniques.* Unpublished doctoral dissertation. Kalamazoo: Western Michigan University.

Flanagan, J. C. (1970). *Education, 90,* 3, 274.

Gally, J. (1984, April). *The evaluation component.* Paper presented at the Annual Meeting of the American Educational Research Association, New Orleans.

Green, R. L. (1975). Tips on educational testing: What teachers and parents should know. *Phi Delta Kappan, 57,* 89–93.

Guba, E. G. (1966). *A study of Title III activities: Report on evalua-*

tion. Bloomington, IN: National Institute for the Study of Educational Change, Indiana University.

Guba, E. G. (1969). The failure of educational evaluation. *Educational Technology, 9*, 29–38.

Guba, E. G., & Stufflebeam, D. L. (June, 1970). *Strategies for the institutionalization of the CIPP evaluation model.* Paper presented at the Eleventh Annual PDK Symposium on Education Research, Columbus.

Guba, E. G., & Lincoln, Y. S. (1981). *Effective evaluation.* San Francisco: Jossey-Bass.

Guba, E. G., & Lincoln, Y. S. (1982, Winter). The place of values in needs assessment. *Educational Evaluation and Policy Analysis. 5*(2).

Hambleton, R. K. (1978). Criterion-referenced testing and measurement: A review of technical issues and developments. *Review of Educational Research, 4*, 1–48.

Hambleton, R. K., & Swaminathan, H. (1985). *Item response theory: Principles and applications.* Boston: Kluwer-Nijhoff.

Hammond, R. L. (1967). Evaluation at the local level. *Notes and working papers concerning the administration of programs authorized under Title III of Public Law 89–10, The Elementary and Secondary Education Act of 1965 as amended by Public Law 89–750.* U.S. Senate Subcommittee on Education. Washington, DC: U.S. Government Printing Office.

Hammond, R. L. (1969). Context evaluation of instruction in local school districts. *Educational Technology, 13–18.*

Hoffman, L. (1982). *Application of the Joint Committee standards as criteria for evaluations in Louisiana.* Paper presented at the Annual Meeting of the American Educational Research Association, New York.

House, E., Rivers, W., & Stufflebeam, D. L. (1974). An assessment of the Michigan accountability system. *Phi Delta Kappan, 10,* 663–669.

House, E. R. (1978). *School evaluation: The politics and processes.* Berkeley, CA: McCutchan.

Impara, J. C. (1982). *Measurement and the utility standards.* Paper presented at the Annual Meeting of the National Council for Measurement in Education, New York.

Jacobs, J. N., & Felix, J. L. (1968). Testing the educational psychological development of preadolescent children—ages 6–12. *Review of Educational Research, 38,* 19–29.

Joint AERA, APA, NCME Committee. (1985). *Standards for educational and psychological tests.* Washington, DC: American Psychological Association.

Joint Committee on Standards for Educational Evaluation. (1981). *Standards for evaluations of educational programs, projects, and materials.* New York: McGraw-Hill.

Kellaghan, T. (1982). *La evaluacion educativa.* Bogotà, Colombia: Pontificia Universido Javerian.

Kennedy, M. M., Apling, R., & Neumann, W. F. (1980). *The role of evaluation and tests information in public schools.* Cambridge, MA: The Huron Institute.

King, J. A., & Pechman, E. M. (1982). *The process of evaluation use in local school settings.* (NIE Grant 81-0900). New Orleans Public Schools.

Levin, H. M. (1975). Cost-effectiveness analysis in evaluation research. In M. Guttentag & E. L. Struening (Eds.), *Handbook of evaluation research: Vol. 2.* Beverly Hills, Sage.

Levin, H. M. (1983). *Cost-effectiveness: A primer.* Beverly Hills, CA: Sage.

Linn, R. L. (1981). A preliminary look at the applicability of the educational evaluation standards. *Educational Evaluation and Policy Analysis, 3,* 87–91.

Lyon, C. D., Doscher, D. L., McGranahan, P., & Williams, R. (1978). *Evaluation and school districts.* UCLA: Center for the Study of Evaluation.

McCall, B. J. & Simmons, J. L. (Eds.) (1969). *Issues in participant observation.* Reading, PA: Addison-Wesley.

McKillip, J. & Garberg, R. *A further examination of the overlap between ERS and Joint Committee evaluation standards.* Unpublished paper. Carbondale, IL: Southern Illinois University, Department of Psychology.

Madaus, G. F., Airasian, P. W., & Kellaghan, T. (1980). *School effectiveness.* New York: McGraw-Hill.

Madaus, G. F. (Ed.) (1982). *The courts, validity, and minimum competency testing.* Boston: Kluwer-Nijhoff.

Madaus, G. F., Scriven, M., & Stufflebeam, D. L. (1983). *Evaluation models: Viewpoints on educational and human services evaluation.* Boston: Kluwer-Nijhoff.

Manatt, R. P., & Stow, S. B. (1984). *Clinical manual for teacher performance evaluation.* Ames, IA: Iowa State University Research Foundation.

Marks, W., & Nystrand, R. (1981). *Strategies for educational change.* New York: Macmillan.

Mauriel, J. (1978). *Overview of the Bush Foundation program for administrative fellows.* Bush Public Schools Executive Fellows Program. St. Paul, MN: Bush Foundation.

Merriman, H. O. (1968). *Evaluation of planned educational change at the local education agency level* Columbus, OH: Ohio State University Evaluation Center.

Merwin, J. C. (1982). *Educational evaluation: Where we've been, where we are, and where we're going.* Address to Division D, Annual Meeting of the American Educational Research Association, New York.

Millman, J. (Ed.) (1981). *Handbook of teacher evaluation.* Beverly Hills, CA: Sage.

Nevo, D. (1974). *Evaluation priorities of students, teachers, and principals.* Unpublished doctoral dissertation. Columbus: The Ohio State University.

Nevo, D. (1982). *Applying the evaluation standards in a different social context.* Paper presented at the 20th Congress of the International Association of Applied Psychology, Edinburgh, Scotland.

Nevo, D. (1983). The conceptualization of educational evaluation: An analytical review of the literature. *Review of Educational Research* (1), 117–128.

Nowakowski, J. R., Bunda, M. A., Working, R., Bernacki, G., & Harrington, P. (1984). *A handbook of educational variables: A guide to evaluation.* Boston: Kluwer-Nijhoff.

O'Keefe, K. G. (1968). *Methodology for educational field studies.* Unpublished doctoral dissertation. The Ohio State University, Columbus.

Ott, J. M. (1967) *A decision process and classification system for use by Title 1 project directors in planning educational change.* Columbus, OH: Ohio State University Evaluation Center.

Palmer, R. C. (1976). *A study of decision making in a large urban school system.* Unpublished doctoral dissertation. The Catholic University of America, Washington, DC.

Parlett, M., & Hamilton, D. (1972). *Evaluation as illumination: A new approach to the study of innovatory programs* (Occasional Paper No. 9). Edinburgh, Scotland: Centre for Research in the Educational Sciences, University of Edinburgh.

Patton, M. Q. (1978). *Utilization-focused evaluation.* Beverly Hills, CA: Sage.

Peck, H. (1982). *An overview of the Louisiana program evaluation quality assurance program.* Presentation at the Annual Meeting of the American Educational Research Association. New York.

Popham, W. J. (1969). Objectives and instruction. In R. Stake (Ed.), *Instructional objectives.* AERA monograph series on curriculum evaluation: Vol. 3. Chicago: Rand McNally.

Potter, W. J. (1979). *An analysis and categorization of eight approaches to education evaluation.* Unpublished doctoral dissertation. Indiana University, Bloomington.

Provus, M. (1971). *Discrepancy evaluation.* Berkeley, CA: McCutchan.

Rachal, J. (1982). *Training in the Joint Committee standards for evaluation: Content, process, and outcomes.* Paper presented at the Annual Meeting of the American Educational Research Association, New York.

Reinhard, D. L. (1972). *Methodology development for input evaluation using advocate and design teams.* Unpublished doctoral dissertation. The Ohio State University, Columbus.

Rice, E. T. (1968). *An exploratory study to investigate the aspects of the construction and use of instruments encompassing the evalua-*

tive strategies of context, input, process, and product of in-service programs. Unpublished doctoral dissertation. University of Iowa, Iowa City.

Ridings, J. M. (1980). *Standard setting in accounting and auditing: Considerations for educational evaluation.* Unpublished dissertation, Western Michigan University, Kalamazoo.

Root, D. K. (1971). *Educational training needs of superintendents of schools.* Unpublished doctoral dissertation. Ohio State University, Columbus.

Roth, J.E. (1978). *Theory and practice of needs assessment with special application to institutions of higher learning.* Unpublished doctoral dissertation, University of California, Berkeley.

Sanders, J., & Stufflebeam, D. L. (1982) *Evaluation of the Shaker Heights levels system.* Evaluation Report, Western Michigan University.

Schroyer, W. (1982). *Meta-evaluation of educational evaluation in Louisiana: The impact of quality assurance.* Paper presented at the Annual Meeting of the American Educational Research Association, New York.

Schwartz, J. L. (1975). Math tests. *National Elementary Principal,* 54, 6, 67–71.

Scriven, M. S. (1967). The methodology of evaluation. In R. E. Stake (Ed.), *Curriculum evaluation. AERA monograph series on curriculum evaluation: Vol. 1.* Chicago: Rand McNally.

Scriven, M. S. (1969). Evaluation skills [Audiotape No. 6B]. American Educational Research Association.

Scriven, M. S. (1974). Program and product evaluation checklist. In G. D. Borich (Ed.), *Evaluating educational programs and products.* Englewood Cliffs, NJ: Educational Technology Publications. Also in W. J. Popham (Ed.), *Evaluation in education.* Berkeley, CA: McCutchan.

Scriven, M. S. (1974). Pros and cons of goal-free evaluation. In W. J. Popham (Ed.), *Evaluation in education.* Berkeley, CA: McCutchan.

Scriven, M. S. (1975). *Evaluation bias and its control* (Occasional Paper Series, No. 4). Kalamazoo: Western Michigan University Evaluation Center.

Scriven, M. S. (1981). *Evaluation thesaurus* (3rd. ed). Pt. Reyes, CA: Edgepress.

Scriven, M. S. (1983). Evaluation as a paradigm for educational research. *Australian Educational Researcher,* 10, (3), 5–18.

Scriven, M. S., & Roth, J. E. (1978). Needs assessment: Concept and practice. *New Direction for Program Evaluation,* 1, 1–11.

Smith, E. R., & Tyler, R. W. (1942) *Appraising and recording student progress.* New York: Harper.

Smith, N. L. (1981a). *Metaphors for evaluation: Sources of new methods.* Beverly Hills, CA: Sage.

Smith, N. L. (1981b). *New techniques for evaluation.* Beverly Hills, CA: Sage.

Snow, R. (1974). Representative and quasi-representative designs for research on teaching. *Review of Educational Research,* 44, 625–626.

Sroufe, G. E. (1977). Evaluation and politics. In J. Scribner (Ed.), *The politics of education.* The 76th Yearbook of the National Society for the Chicago: University of Chicago.

Stake, R. E. (1967). The countenance of educational evaluation. *Teachers College Record,* 68, 523–540.

Stake, R. E. (1975). *Program evaluation, particularly responsive evaluation* (Occasional Paper No. 5). Kalamazoo, MI: Western Michigan University Evaluation Center.

Stake, R. (1981). Setting standards for educational evaluators. *Evaluation News* 2(2), 148–152.

Stecher, B. M., Alkin, M. C., & Flesher, G. (1981). *Patterns of information use in school level decision making.* (CSE Report No. 160). Los Angeles: UCLA, Center for the Study of Evaluation.

Straton, R. B. (1982). *Appropriateness and potential impact of programme evaluation standards in Australia.* Paper presented at the 20th International Congress of Applied Psychology, Edinburgh, Scotland.

Stufflebeam, D. L. (1966). A depth study of the evaluation requirement. *Theory Into Practice,* 5, 121–34.

Stufflebeam, D. L. (1967). The use and abuse of evaluation in Title

III. *Theory Into Practice,* 6, 126–33.

Stufflebeam, D. L. (1971). The relevance of the CIPP evaluation model for educational accountability. *Journal of Research and Development in Education,* Fall.

Stufflebeam, D. L. (1977). *Needs assessment in evaluation* [Audiotape]. American Educational Research Association.

Stufflebeam, D. L. (1978). Meta-evaluation: An overview. *Evaluation and the Health Professions,* 2, (1), 17–43.

Stufflebeam, D.L., Foley, W. J., Gephart, W. J., Guba, E. G., Hammond, R. L., Merriman, H. O., & Provus, M. M. (1971). *Educational evaluation and decision-making.* Itasca, IL: Peacock.

Stufflebeam, D. L., McCormick, C., Brinkerhoff, R., & Nelson, C. (1985). *Conducting educational needs assessments.* Boston: Kluwer-Nijhoff.

Stufflebeam, D. L., & Shinkfield, A. J. (1985). *Systematic evaluation: A self-instructional guide to theory and practice.* Boston: Kluwer-Nijhoff.

Stufflebeam, D. L., & Webster, W. J. (1980). An analysis of alternative approaches to evaluation. *Educational Evaluation and Policy Analysis,* 2(3), 5–20.

Stufflebeam, D. L., & Welch, W. (1986). Review of research on program evaluation in the United States. *Educational Administrative Quarterly,* 22(3), 150–170.

Suarez, T. (1980). *Needs assessments for technical assistance: A conceptual overview and comparison of three strategies.* Unpublished doctoral dissertation. Kalamazoo: Western Michigan University.

Suchman, E. A. (1967). *Evaluation research.* New York: Russell Sage Foundation.

Tallmadge, G. K., & Horst, D. P. (1974). *A procedural guide for validating achievement gains in educational projects.* Los Altos, CA: RMC Research Corporation, Technical Report No. UR-240.

Thorndike, R. L. (1977). *Measurement and evaluation in psychology and education* (4th ed.). New York: John Wiley.

Travers, R. (1983). *How research has changed American schools: A history from 1840 to the present.* Kalamazoo, MI: Mythos.

Triplett, S. (1982). *Implementation of the certification of Louisiana educational evaluators using the Joint Committee standards.* Paper presented at the Annual Meeting of the American Educational Research Association, New York.

United States Office of Education. (1975). *A practical guide to measuring project impact on student achievement.* Washington, DC: U.S. Government Printing Office.

United States Office of Education. (1976). *A procedural guide for validating achievement gains in educational projects.* Washington, DC: U.S. Government Printing Office.

United States Office of Education. (1978). *Use of sampling procedures with the USOE Title I evaluation models.* Washington, DC: U.S. Government Printing Office.

Wardrop, J. C. (1982). *Measurement and accuracy standards.* Paper presented at the Annual Meeting of the National Council for Measurement in Education, New York.

Wargo, M. J. (1981). The standards: A federal level perspective. *Evaluation News,* 2(2), 157–162.

Webster, W. J. (1975). *The organization and functions of research and evaluation units in a large urban school district.* Paper presented at the Annual Meeting of the American Educational Research Association. (*ERIC Clearinghouse on Tests, Measurements, and Evaluation,* ED 106 345)

Webster, W. J. (1980). *The validation of a teacher selection system.* Paper presented at the Annual Meeting of the American Educational Research Association, Boston.

Webster, W. J. (1981). CIPP in local evaluation. In R. S. Brandt, Ed., *Applied strategies for curriculum evaluation,* 48–57. Alexandria, VA: Association for Supervision and Curriculum Development.

Webster, W. J. (1984a). *Survey of evaluation offices in large school districts.* (Unpublished manuscript). Dallas, TX: Dallas Independent School District.

Webster, W. J. (1984b, April). *Five years of teacher testing: A retrospective analysis.* Paper presented at the Annual Meeting of the American Educational Research Association, New Orleans.

Webster, W. J. (1986). *The practice of evaluation in the public schools*. Proceedings of the Minnesota Evaluation Conference. Minneapolis, MN: University of Minnesota.

Webster, W. J., & Schuhmacher, C. C. (1973). A unified strategy for systemwide research and evaluation. *Educational Technology*, *13*, 5, 68–72.

Webster, W. J., & Stufflebeam, D. L. (1978, March). *State of theory and practice in educational evaluation in large urban schools*. Address presented at the Annual Meeting of the American Educational Research Association, Toronto, Canada.

Webster, W. J., & Vitale, M. (1977). Priorities for applied research on teaching and learning. Paper invited by National Institute of Education, NIEP 770211. Washington, DC: The Institute.

Wildemuth, B. M. (1981). A bibliography to accompany the Joint Committee's standards on educational evaluation. (ERIC/TM, Report 81). Princeton, NJ: Educational Testing Service.

Wilson, S. (1977). The use of ethnographic techniques in educational research. *Review of Educational Research*, *47*, 2, 517–538.

Wright, B. D., & Stone, M. H. (1979). *Best test design*. Chicago: Mesa Press.

CHAPTER 28

Unionism and Collective Bargaining in the Public Schools

Susan Moore Johnson

The study of educational labor relations, like the practice of educational bargaining itself, is relatively new. Unlike other fields of inquiry in educational administration, it has been only partly tilled and has yielded but a modest harvest. Since the late 1960s when teachers widely began to negotiate wages, hours, and working conditions with school boards, educational researchers have endeavored to study the process and effects of bargaining. But progress has been slow because the field is large and issues are complex, typically being entwined with matters of politics, organization, economics, law, and school finance. Here, the contributions of research, exploration of unresolved issues, identification of the sides of ongoing debates, and suggestions of fertile areas for future inquiry will receive attention.

Educational labor relations commands the attention of researchers, policy makers, and practitioners for several reasons. The first is sheer numbers; teachers are currently the largest unionized group of workers in the United States. Michael Finch and Trevor W. Nagel (1984) report:

> Today, fully 88 percent of the nation's school teachers belong to either the NEA or the AFT, and 83 percent are members of a local teachers' organization. By contrast, a dwindling 21 percent of all private sector employees currently belong to a labor organization, a decline that has occurred simultaneously with the rise of teacher unionism. (p. 1580)

Second, the unionization of teachers was remarkably rapid compared with that of other workers. Before 1959, no state required local school boards to bargain collectively. As of 1984, 33 required bargaining and 11 others permitted it, while only four states explicitly prohibited bargaining (Finch & Nagel, 1984, pp. 1580–1581).

Third, the growth of educational labor relations has generated research interest because some regard unionization and teaching as incompatible. Unions are industrial creations, but schools are not factories and teachers are not typical laborers. A tradition of local control in public education coupled with teachers' repeated claims to professional autonomy seem to be at odds with industrywide negotiation or formalized regulation of teachers' work. Moreover, the school administrators who constitute management are themselves former teachers, often sharing teachers' values and expectations while downplaying their own roles as managers. The potential interplay between these unique features of schooling and the traditional structures of labor relations promotes much of the research interest in teacher unionization and explains much of the public concern about its effects.

Research has primarily addressed four basic questions. First, why and under what conditions do teachers unionize? Teaching has historically been feminine work

Consultant/reviewers: Charles T. Kerchner, Claremont University; David B. Lipsky, Cornell University; and Michael Murphy, University of Utah

with professional norms, seemingly at odds with the blue-collar union origins of collective bargaining. Researchers have examined both the history of teacher organizations as well as some of the social, political, and organizational determinants of teacher militancy.

Second, what are the rules of organizing and bargaining and how do they affect the negotiations process? Collective bargaining policies defining such matters as bargaining units, scope, and impasse resolution vary from state to state and locality to locality. Researchers have sought to describe and compare the alternative policies and to explain their effects on negotiation and contract administration.

Third, what are characteristic labor relations practices? For example, who negotiates and what issues are bargained? How are settlements reached? How do strikes affect the process? Once contracts are settled, how are they administered and enforced? Such inquiries explore varied labor practices at the local level in an effort to identify both common and unique features.

Fourth, what are the outcomes and effects of collective bargaining? Unions intend to improve teachers' wages and working conditions, and researchers have sought to find out if they do. Further, researchers have tried to understand the indirect effects of collective bargaining on teaching and administrative practice, student achievement, and the organization of the workplace.

Although labor relations research is broad in scope, it is far from complete. Inquiry has been extensive in some areas, sparse in others. Approaches to research have varied as well. Some researchers have collected data in order to identify central tendencies and generalize; others have explored the particular and displayed the variation in labor practices. Although the two approaches are complementary and essential to a thorough understanding of the subject, they have not yet sufficiently influenced or informed each other. Researchers have brought their particular perspectives as economists, political scientists, organizational theorists, educational administrators, and industrial relations specialists to the topic of educational labor relations, yet their inquiries have remained largely isolated, and the opportunity for systematic exchange, critique, collaboration, and the integration of perspectives has not yet arrived.

Well before the advent of collective bargaining for teachers, John T. Dunlop (1958) analyzed the complexity of industrial relations systems. Such systems, he explained, vary from one another as a result of various aspects of the environment, the technological character of the workplace, market or budgetary constraints, and the locus and distribution of power in the larger society.

The actors in these systems establish a "web of rules" governing compensation, defining the duties and performance expectations of workers, and establishing the rights of workers. Ideologies vary among actors and systems, and the systems themselves move through time. Dunlop (1958) demonstrated that in order to understand any industrial relations system, it is necessary to understand not only the special features of the work and the workers but also the unique features of its environment—the technology, politics, and economics.

Some of the components of labor systems identified by Dunlop have been examined; many have not. The push and pull of local politics, reforms in school finance, changes in teacher supply and demand, and diminishing support for public education all play roles in determining the impact of collective bargaining on schools. However, these conditions have not been closely considered. Researchers have yet to deal with educational labor relations in all its complexity.

The framework of the following discussion provides a means for considering both the work that has been done in the field and that which might be done. The topics of discussion correspond to the basic research questions given earlier. The first section, The Actors, considers why and under what conditions teachers unionize. It reviews historical studies of teacher organizing as well as studies of teacher militancy and principals' efforts to unionize. It concludes that research has only begun to explain teachers' and principals' actions as union members and has generally disregarded the roles of other key participants, including union leaders, school superintendents, board members, and third-party neutrals.

The second section, The Policies, reviews studies of the various legal structures regulating labor practices. It concludes that state legislation can be effective in promoting bargaining, prohibiting strikes by means of penalties, and enforcing binding arbitration settlements. The law is less effective in regulating the scope of bargaining, promoting the serious use of impasse procedures, and discouraging strikes without the threat of penalties.

The third section, The Practices, examines the work of those who have studied bargaining and contract administration. It concludes that labor relations practices are quite varied from district to district and school to school, with union leaders, central-office administrators, and principals having considerable influence over both negotiation and contract administration.

The final section, Outcomes and Effects, reviews efforts to identify the impact of collective bargaining on wages and working conditions, as well as teaching and administrative practice, student learning, and the democracy of the workplace. It concludes that the impact of bargaining on salaries has been modest and that negotiations have enabled teachers to define, and in some cases reduce, the requirements of their jobs while gaining substantial protections through grievance procedures and seniority rules. The impact of teacher bargaining on student outcomes appears to be slight. Studies do suggest, however, that unions' impact on the workplace may be constructive.

THE ACTORS

The key actors in public school labor relations systems include teachers, administrators, school board members, and third-party neutrals. Research attention has focused almost exclusively on teachers, with slight attention to principals. Most studies have centered on the propensity of teachers to unionize and to endorse militant actions. Teachers, once regarded as compliant, self-effacing, and attentive to matters of professional respectability, appeared to be unlikely candidates for unionization, and yet they have organized in astonishing numbers. Researchers have considered that phenomenon from two perspectives. First, historians have studied the development of teacher unions: why teachers organized and how their organizations developed. Second, sociologists and political scientists have carried out empirical studies to identify the factors that account for the fact that some teachers are more militant than others. Each will be considered in some detail.

The History of Teachers' Organizations

Those who have documented the initial stages of teacher organizations agree about the precipitating forces: low pay and low status (Braun, 1972; Doherty & Oberer, 1967, Donley, 1976; Eaton, 1975; Urban, 1982; Wesley, 1957). Salaries were low not only because teaching was a service that commanded little respect but because it was women's work. Doherty and Oberer (1967), authors of one of the earliest studies of teacher unionism, observed that during the 19th century, "salaries remained miserably low, tenure was short, and the esteem with which teachers were held by the citizenry seemed to vacillate between contempt and indifference" (p. 2).

Teachers began to organize over a century before the advent of collective bargaining, and the development of their competing organizations is the subject of several accounts. There is general agreement among labor historians about the fundamental differences between the National Education Association (NEA) and the American Federation of Teachers (AFT). The former, whose membership was dominated by male college presidents and administrators, sought to professionalize the teaching ranks with attention to policies rather than pay. The latter, whose membership was limited to teachers, centered its efforts on improving wages and benefits. Wesley (1980) reports that the National Teachers Association, forerunner of the NEA, was formed in Philadelphia in 1857, "to elevate the character and advance the interests of the profession of teaching, and to promote the cause of popular education in the United States" (pp. 22–23). He explains that the educational leaders assumed (a) that the building of a profession took precedence over the problems of the personal welfare of teachers and (b) that once the profession was established, "teachers would naturally achieve status, security, and dignity." There was no division for the classroom teachers, and Eaton (1975) notes that "the role of the classroom teacher, and more specifically the woman, was limited to listening" (p. 10). By contrast, the AFT was founded in Chicago in 1916 to "advance the cause of the classroom teachers" (Eaton, 1975, pp. 12–17), who alone were eligible for membership. Although the AFT historically emphasized welfare issues, Urban's recent analysis of why teachers organized concludes that the union was not reflexively militant and that although their members resented the NEA's avoidance of the salary issue, they nonetheless disapproved of strikes and resisted close affiliation between their union and organized labor. "Even at its most militant, the AFT pursued improved benefits and working conditions, as well as higher standards for entry-level teachers, in language which appealed to teachers' desire for occupational respectability" (Urban, 1982, p. 139).

With their emphasis on rational systems and impersonal rules, the administrative reformers of the early part of the century reinforced and augmented the divisions between teachers and their supervisors. As Tyack (1974) observes, these divisions followed gender lines:

> Hierarchical organization of schools and male chauvinism of the larger society fit as hand to glove. The system required subordination; women were generally subordinate to men; the employment of women as teachers thus augmented the authority of the largely male administrative leadership. (p. 60)

Urban (1982) comments on "the gap that developed between superintendents and teachers as a result of bureaucratization.... In retrospect it seems clear that administrative reforms separated teachers from superintendents to an unprecedented degree" (p. 170). This emphasis on hierarchy and rules and the resulting divisions between teaching and administration eventually provided an organizational structure that was not only compatible with, but conducive to, adversarial bargaining.

Between 1919, when the NEA "began an open anti-AFT offensive" (Urban, 1982 p. 151), and the late 1960s, when collective bargaining practices began to settle in, the relative strength and influence of the AFT and NEA shifted repeatedly. The shifts resulted in part from competitive efforts by the two organizations but were primarily consequences of environmental forces beyond the control of school people: the Great Depression, two world wars, and McCarthyism. Neither teachers' organization enjoyed sustained strength or influence, and the wages and status of teachers remained low.

The sudden and dramatic growth of teacher unionism during the late 1960s has yet to be fully examined and explained. Certainly, the social and political context of the times was critical. Following World War II, the ranks of teachers became increasingly male, and this new interest group with families to support began to press for high wages and to endorse more aggressive action by their organizations. National concern about public education, galvanized by Sputnik, promoted speculation about a teacher shortage and generated proposals for pay increases. West (1980), who documents "the dramatic change in the NEA" attributes the development to a variety of factors:

> changes in the teaching staff, changes in the school districts [school consolidation], the failure of local and state governments to respond to school needs, the impact of the civil rights revolution, President Kennedy's Executive Order 10988 [authorizing collective bargaining for federal employees], the urban crisis, the New York collective-bargaining election, and new public expectations of the public schools. (p. 28)

Eaton (1975) argues that the 1960s provided a more favorable social context for AFT growth:

> This new spirit of activism was to be divisive for the NEA. A growing discontent among classroom teachers within the NEA surfaced. The result was internal feuding, political manipulation, and general confusion. ...This new spirit of activism was ready-made for the AFT. The time was ripe for new organizational efforts. The times had finally caught up with the philosophy of the teachers' union. By 1972, the AFT had nearly 250,000 teachers as members. This represented about 12 percent of the 2,063,000 teachers in America, and the membership was growing. (p. 194)

Part of the dramatic growth must also be attributed to the rapidly increasing student enrollments, which undoubtedly made school teaching and administration more difficult. The ranks of teachers grew rapidly, and union membership swelled, as it typically does when the demand for labor increases significantly.

In response to AFT growth and success in New York City, the NEA changed its policies and tactics. It dropped its opposition to collective bargaining and adopted a more militant, pro-teacher stance. Although West's (1980) account stresses the role of "social forces" rather than the challenge presented by the AFT, he acknowledges that the NEA changed "as a matter of survival" (p. 38).

Despite the adversarial relations between the AFT and NEA, there were in the late 1960s serious proposals for merger, precipitated in part by Albert Shanker's successful consolidation of the United Federation of Teachers in New York City and the New York State Teachers Association. However, the growth and success of both the AFT and the NEA, spurred largely by their competition with each other, had seriously reduced by the late 1970s the likelihood of a workable merger (Lubetsky, 1977).

The recent history of teacher unions from 1965 forward remains a story to be told. Only West (1980) has examined this period in detail, and his account is decidedly pro-NEA. The social and political context, the introduction of collective bargaining in a majority of states, the strategies by which the NEA and AFT have organized teachers, the role of key personalities such as Albert Shanker, the interaction between the AFT and the NEA, and the role of the unions in school reform provide content for complex and intriguing stories.

The Determinants of Teacher Militancy

While historians have studied the development of teachers' organizations over the century, sociologists and political scientists have explored the phenomenon of teacher militancy, seeking to determine the social, organizational, and political determinants of teachers' support for unions and union action. Which teachers are most likely to join unions, to support confrontation, or to participate in strikes? Generally, these studies assume that union membership is an individual choice, precipitated primarily by individual predispositions and preferences. The inquiries do not sufficiently account for the changing meaning of union membership over the past two decades or for effects of larger political and economic pressures that frequently eclipse individual choice.

Several researchers have focused on individual teachers and sought to identify the social and demographic determinants of militancy. Their findings are notably consistent. For example, Winick (1963) studied New York City teachers' support for the 1963 strike and found that it was greatest among males, younger teachers, and teachers with advanced academic degrees. Hellriegel, French, and Peterson (1976) also found that males and younger teachers were more likely to support strikes; Cole (1969) found that teachers in New York and New Jersey were more likely to support a strike if they were male, under 40, Jewish, Democratic, and from working-class families. In 1976, Alutto and Belasco compared teachers' and nurses' attitudes toward strikes, unions, and collective bargaining by professionals. They concluded that support for militant teachers' organizations was greater among male, younger, and secondary teachers than it was among female, older, and elementary teachers (Alutto and Belasco, 1976, pp. 82–83). Similarly, Fox and Wince (1976) found sex and age the most significant variables affecting teacher militancy in their 1976 study of a midwestern city.

These findings are consistent with common wisdom about teacher militancy. Young teachers are expected to endorse confrontation with authorities. The aggression associated with militancy is more consistent with male norms of behavior than female, and until recently, male teachers could be expected to be sole family supporters in purposeful pursuit of higher wages and better benefits. Also, because male teachers are more likely to teach in secondary than elementary schools, militancy might be expected to be greater there.

These studies of the social and demographic determinants of teacher militancy do not account for the influence of context on action. Other researchers have looked to organizational variables for a more complete explanation of teacher militancy. Alutto and Belasco (1976) observed that despite the relationships they had found between individual characteristics and militancy, organizational issues such as job autonomy, participation in decision making, salary, and other conditions of professional practice are likely to have a major influence on the level of attitudinal militancy that surfaces in any given organization. They note, in particular, that career dissatisfaction "ranked as a major contributor to the emergence of attitudinal militancy" (p. 91). Rosenthal (1969) studied patterns of union membership in Boston and New York City during the mid-1960s and found that whereas male teachers were more likely to join unions than female teachers, all teachers were more likely to join unions in predominantly male schools than in predominantly female schools. Union membership correlated with faculty size, teaching load, and the proportion of nonwhite students.

Corwin (1970), who has also examined militancy in an organizational context, contends that organizational conflict and teacher militancy are promoted by a bureaucratized society, professionalized work, and complex organizations. His study of 2,000 teachers and administrators in 23 Ohio public high schools examined what he regarded as a "fundamental contradiction between subordinate status of teachers in the system and their rights and obligations as professional persons responsible for improving the quality of education" (p. 42). He found that, generally, men were more inclined toward militant action but that women were more influenced by dissatisfaction over professional issues in their militancy. Similarly, Jessup (1978) studied the factors underlying teachers' support for the union movement in metropolitan New York City during the 1960s, and concluded that a "major motivating factor was teachers' frustration with their powerlessness in educational decision making" (p. 44).

Two additional studies have challenged the social and demographic variables identified as determinants of militancy in prior studies. In designing his study, Tomkiewicz (1979) posited that if sex and years of service were significant indicators of militancy and if high educational spending were indicative of a school district sympathetic to teachers, those factors would be reflected in strike patterns. He reasoned that a school district with predominantly senior, female teachers and strong financial support of schools "should not be confronted with militant teacher groups," whereas "those districts not committed to quality education and/or already faced with a militant teacher group, can expect bargaining sessions to be torturous affairs with a greater likelihood of hostilities" (Tomkiewicz, 1979, pp. 91–96). His study of 206 Pennsylvania school districts from 1970–1975 revealed that none of the factors predicted either strikes or settlements.

Several years later Bacharach, Mitchell, and Malanowski (1985), who view militancy as a "strategic choice made within an organizational context by individuals acting in concert," also critiqued social background and political models of militancy which, they argued, "ignored the aspect of choice..." (p. 198). Their study of New York teachers in 42 elementary and 45 secondary schools found that age and gender were unrelated to militancy, whereas seniority was a predictor of militancy only at the high school level. However, they did find teachers reporting more militancy in response to "decisional deprivation" at both elementary and secondary levels. There were significant differences between elementary and secondary faculties, the former seeking greater professional prerogative and the latter apparently "willing to engage in a trade-off, sacrificing their involvement on issues of professional prerogative in order to concentrate on compensation issues" (Bacharach et al., 1985, p. 216).

Although researchers have considered teacher militancy from a variety of perspectives, there is still no systematic understanding of why teachers join unions. We do not know to what extent union membership is a personal choice and to what extent it is a political and organizational inevitability. Clearly, the social and political context of membership decisions has changed substantially over the two decades of collective bargaining. In the mid-1980s, it is the nonunion teacher in a unionized district who is atypical. Perhaps the time has come to seek more knowledge about unionism by studying those individuals who chose not to join. The interviews by Johnson (1984) of almost 200 teachers suggest that although union membership is quite high, teachers are generally ambivalent about unionism and endorse militant actions selectively (pp. 149–153). The available knowledge base calls for a fuller and clearer understanding of teachers' views and choices. Future inquiries might productively pursue data about teacher attitudes and behaviors with more diverse samples and jointly analyze those data from individual, organizational, and political perspectives.

Principals and Others

Recent developments in principals' bargaining, although less widespread and visible than teacher unionism, deserve brief mention. Unlike supervisors and managers in the federal government or private sector, principals are permitted by 28 states to negotiate with school boards; in the early 1980s they did so in 1,800 school districts (Cooper & Murrmann, 1984). Principals' unionization is particularly noteworthy because these middle managers have responsibilities for administering the teachers' contract. In recognition of the potential problems presented by administrators' unions, researchers have begun to identify the factors that move principals to organize. The primary perspective of the inquiry thus far seeks explanations in organizational rather than social or demographic factors.

For example, Bridges and Cooper (1976) hypothesize that four "irritating conditions" provoke principals to organize locally: (a) bureaucratization as a result of teacher bargaining that "supplant[s] administrator discretion with rules and regulations"; (b) the lagging of wages behind salaries gained by organized teachers; (c) periods of inflation accompanied by a decrease in the standard of living; and (d) "harassment of and complaints against school administrators by the community" (p. 309).

Cooper and Murrmann (1984) conducted a subsequent study of New Jersey principals' attitudes toward collective bargaining and found that their respondents supported the need for protection of principals' negotiation, arbitration, and tenure rights but opposed both aggressive confrontation with the central-office administration and promotion decisions based on seniority (pp. 6–7).

Many unexplored issues remain regarding principals' bargaining. Cooper and Murrmann's (1984) respondents did not perceive their job interests to be in conflict with their employers' interests, but many educational commentators see a fundamental contradiction between the responsibilities of school supervisors and unionism. The impact of principals' bargaining on school administration and the interplay between teachers' and principals' negotiations and settlements warrant close attention. Although research has provided some insight into the decisions and actions of teachers and principals, there are other key actors in the labor relations process whose attitudes and behaviors have received little research attention. Superintendents, school board members, arbitrators, and mediators play key roles, but the literature says little about their purposes and priorities.

THE POLICIES

Thirty-three states require negotiation with teachers; 11 others recognize the right of teachers to participate in school board decisions. In addition to formally empowering teachers to negotiate, state collective bargaining laws typically regulate other elements of labor relations, including organizing activities and representation procedures, unfair labor practices, union security provisions (agency shop, union shop), scope of bargaining, strikes and impasse procedures that may include mediation, fact finding, and binding arbitration. Although public-sector labor laws have been modeled largely on the National Labor Relations Act, which regulates bargaining in the public sector, there have been innovations in those public-sector provisions dealing with strikes and impasse procedures.

Since the early 1970s, educational researchers have sought to understand the development of public-sector bargaining laws and their impact on labor practices and outcomes. Some parts of the statutes, such as those regulating scope and impasse, have received more attention than others, such as unfair labor practices or union security. In many cases, the research questions have grown out of prior studies in the private sector, but the unique sections of public-sector laws, which define novel impasse procedures and regulate strikes, have been the focus of considerable inquiry.

State Legislation and the Prevalence of Bargaining

Presence of Laws
Not all states have passed public-sector legislation, and the laws of those that have vary in comprehensiveness.

Kochan (1973) has studied the development of public-sector collective bargaining laws with particular attention to the environments in which they developed. He examined the comprehensiveness of laws for five employee groups, including teachers, and concluded that the "more urbanized, industrialized, affluent, and high income states and those with rising per capita incomes were quicker to enact public sector policies and tend to have more comprehensive policies in this area" (p. 329). He found no relationship between the size of a state's population and the nature of its public-sector policy, although he did conclude that the presence of large cities in a state produced more comprehensive laws for teachers (p. 330).

Kochan (1973), like others who have surveyed patterns of teacher bargaining, found that "a good deal of bargaining" goes on in states that have no comprehensive collective bargaining laws (p. 337). Legislation is important for but not essential to the presence of negotiating. Prior to the enactment of collective bargaining legislation in Ohio and Illinois, bargaining there was widespread. However, a strong statute, such as that in Massachusetts, appears to promote universal negotiation, whereas a prohibitive law, such as that in Virginia, eliminates bargaining.

In their comprehensive study of teachers' bargaining practices, McDonnell and Pascal (1979) confirm the importance of labor legislation in permitting and promoting bargaining:

The presence of a state law mandating teacher collective bargaining...makes a difference. Such laws, in effect, provide a floor for teacher organizations where local attitudes or their own organizational weakness would inhibit bargaining gains. Because a state law exists, these organizations are guaranteed recognition and a uniform process. This is not to say that teacher collective bargaining cannot exist without a state statute, but we did find that districts in states without such laws often had to supplement collective bargaining with alternative strategies in order to maintain the integrity of contracts. (p. 56)

Similarly, Bridges and Cooper (1976) have found that the presence of a collective bargaining statute empowering principals to organize and negotiate is an important determinant in school boards' willingness to bargain with these middle managers (pp. 307–309).

Scope of Laws
In addition to recognizing teachers' rights to organize and to bargain, state laws may define the required, permissible, or prohibited subjects of bargaining. For all practical purposes, however, scope is established by the parties and by the many individual decisions of administrative agencies and courts. Kerchner (1978) observes:

Scope of bargaining expands; this despite general concurrence that there should be a limitation, and despite the many attempts to limit scope by statute and by court decision. The scope expands because what appears firmly fixed in the law is eroded by *legal interpretations* as conditions change and it is further eroded by the actions of *labor and management themselves* [italics in the original]. (p. 67)

Doherty's (1980) analysis of collective bargaining statutes led him to conclude that "most statutes provide for a broad scope of bargaining, in the main obliging the employer to bargain over terms and conditions of employment" (p. 526). It's important to note, however, that many matters of central importance to schools—hiring, curriculum, the budget—remain beyond the legal scope of bargaining.

Several researchers have considered the effect that the legally defined scope of bargaining has on actual negotiations. Doherty's (1980) comparison of New York contracts with those of a sample from other states indicated that "although it would appear that there are substantial differences among the states as to what issues constitute appropriate subject matter, there is considerable similarity in the actual scope of collective bargaining contracts" (pp. 529–530). He found that in states with a broad scope of bargaining, a narrower scope of issues was actually negotiated. He speculated about the reason:

It may be that in those states that allow for broad latitude of subject matter, the employers have successfully resisted demands they believe to be intrusions into policy matters. It may also be that the unions do not feel keenly enough about many of these issues to push them to impasse. (Doherty, 1980 pp. 529–530)

McDonnell and Pascal (1979) found that in both 1970 and 1975 "state law mandating or permitting bargaining on a specific provision was a comparatively strong predictor of whether that provision was included in a given contract" (p. 28). However, their subsequent field work revealed that if negotiators are influenced by the legal scope of bargaining, the parties are not aware of it and negotiate with little conscious attention to the state law (p. 55).

Impasse Procedures
Since strikes are generally prohibited in the public sector, state laws typically include one or more impasse procedures as alternatives to the right to strike, whereas states permitting strikes usually require unions to exhaust available impasse procedures before beginning a work stoppage. Mandated impasse procedures, including mediation, fact finding, and advisory or binding arbitration, are the most innovative features of public-sector labor laws, and they have consequently gener-

ated considerable research attention. A central question of inquiry and debate has been whether the parties eventually abandon bargaining and rely unnecessarily on impasse procedures, a condition Wirtz (1963) has dubbed the "narcotic effect" (pp. F1–F4).

Kochan and Baderschneider (1978) studied the use of impasse procedures by firefighters and police in New York between 1974 and 1976 and concluded that "while wide variations exist in the extent to which the parties relied on the procedures, a majority of bargaining relationships depended on the procedures to reach a settlement in more than 50 percent of these negotiations" (p. 438). Furthermore, they found that

> the probability of going to impasse in rounds two and three increased if the parties went to impasse in rounds one and two respectively, and similarly parties were more likely to go to factfinding in rounds two and three if they had gone to factfinding in rounds one and two respectively. (pp. 438–439)

Their work was reviewed by Butler and Ehrenberg (1981), who criticized the use of conditional probability calculations in the initial study and reanalyzed the data controlling for heterogeneity (p. 6). They concluded that the effect observed by Kochan and Baderschneider (1978) occurred only during the early years of the period studied and was actually reversed in the later years and that "the probability that a bargaining unit would go to impasse was actually negatively related to its prior impasse experience, once observed and unobserved heterogeneity was controlled for" (Butler & Ehrenberg, 1981, p. 18).

In their response, Kochan and Baderschneider (1981) argued that the difference in findings resulted as much from different interpretations of the term "narcotic effect" as it did from different methodologies.

> A broad definition, and the one that generally fits the popular usage of the term in collective bargaining, is "repeated or heavy reliance on an impasse procedure" … A stricter and narrower definition of the narcotic effect, and one that is tested implicitly in the B & E regressions, is "the portion of a unit's reliance on impasse procedures that is solely due to the unit's having once used the procedure in the past." (p. 27)

They conclude that the "B & E results *do not* alter any of our substantive findings or conclusions" (p. 27).

Following a similar line of inquiry, Lipsky and Drotning (1977) examined whether a narcotic effect operated in New York State school districts during the first 5 years of the Taylor Law, 1968 through 1972. They found that by 1972, "only 44 percent of the teacher units in New York State were able to reach settlement without third-party interpretations and intervention," and that "over time, teacher disputes have

been resolved at progressively higher stages of the impasse procedures" (p. 233). They concluded that there was "*unambiguous evidence that the most important determinant of an impasse in a district in one year was the existence of an impasse in the district in the preceding year* [italics in the original]" (p. 239), which is evidence of a narcotic effect. Subsequently, however, Lipsky (1984) has observed that the narcotic effect is more likely to operate soon after impasse procedures are established, as Butler and Ehrenberg (1981) concluded.

Researchers have also considered the effectiveness of impasse procedures in preventing strikes, and they have generally concluded that mediation and fact finding do not in themselves prevent strikes but that firm enforcement of antistrike laws may. Finch and Nagel (1984) report that 75 percent of the strikes occurring during the period 1972–1980 took place in states with conventional, nonbinding impasse procedures. Earlier data from Lipsky and Drotning (1973) showed "that teacher strikes increased in frequency over the first five years of the Taylor Law, contrary to the hopes and expectations of the framers of the Act" (p. 234). Subsequent enforcement of the law has, however, contributed considerably to preventing strikes.

Perry and Wildman (1970), who studied collective bargaining in 24 school districts across the United States from 1964 to 1969, found negotiators increasingly unwilling to rely on mediation and fact finding and concluded that they did so only "where the recommendations of an outside party were instrumental in permitting the board of education to secure significantly accelerated increases in local support of the system" (p. 100). In such cases, impasse procedures "served as a vehicle for a type of implicit collusion between the boards of education and the teacher organizations against the community" (p. 100). The authors concluded that, in the short run, strikes, not conciliatory procedures, are "the most effective means of resolving impasses" (p. 104). Perry's (1979) update of the experiences of 9 of the 24 districts confirmed the increasing reluctance to rely on nonbinding impasse procedures, a finding that at first seems at odds with Lipsky and Drotning's (1973) early confirmation of a narcotic effect. However, the discrepancy may simply suggest that the parties routinely rely on conciliatory procedures in states such as New York, which have legislated strong strike penalties, whereas union negotiators in other states may safely forgo nonbinding procedures in favor of strikes.

In his review of Wisconsin's experience with fact finding, Gatewood (1974) reached conclusions similar to Perry's. Support for the fact-finding procedures, which had been "utilized by an increasing number of teacher organizations throughout the state and appeared to be both highly regarded and working well, had begun to erode" (p. 47). Gatewood (1974) found that the strike, prohibited by state law, "was increasingly being employed by teacher organizations as a bargaining tactic" (p. 48). Fact-finding had been petitioned in only 11 of the 44 strikes since 1968.

Gatewood (1974) contends that the "principal limitation inherent in the process stems from the nonbinding character of the factfinder's recommendations" (p. 50). Of 54 cases studied, one-third of the recommendations were fully accepted, one-third were partially accepted, and one-third were rejected. There are, however, five states where binding arbitration is mandatory for teachers who cannot resolve disputes through fact finding or mediation. In 1977, Doherty (1980) examined Iowa's experience with such "last, best offer" arbitration, and judged that the requirement had not inhibited bargaining: "As of spring 1976, about two years after the enactment of the statute, only 24 cases—8 percent of all cases reaching impasse—had gone to the arbitration step" (p. 532).

Recently, Finch and Nagel (1983) studied Connecticut's experience with "last, best offer" arbitration and found that after 3 years of experience with the law, the prospect of binding arbitration had not reduced the proportion of districts that became deadlocked— approximately one-third both before and after the legislation. However, there had been "overwhelming compliance with arbitration awards, lending evidence to the contention that binding arbitration will prevent strikes" (p. 435). Finch and Nagel (1983) did find, however, that the law tended to promote "balanced or accommodative awards" and that

> arbitrator conservatism renders awards which, over time, lead to the standardization of contracts in the jurisdiction...The sophisticated comparability arguments presented by both parties are based on countywide or statewide data, and the resulting decisions conform more to the "average" contract prevailing in these areas than to the sensitiveness of local issues. (p. 440)

Finch and Nagel (1983) state that there is evidence of a narcotic effect, and they suggest that extensive use of binding arbitration is gradually eroding local control of public schools (pp. 443–444). They conclude that while the prospect of binding arbitration may influence negotiators' concessions and moderately inflate salaries (Finch & Nagel, 1984, p. 1646), "there is little evidence that [it] produces, or is invoked to produce, significant change in educational policy or school governance" (p. 1651).

Like the work of Finch and Nagel, Delaney's (1983) study of the impact of compulsory arbitration on

teacher salary settlements also reports that arbitrators and fact finders rely primarily on comparability in their decisions. Delaney concluded that nationally, "the *availability* of compulsory interest arbitration appears to increase teacher salaries by approximately 10 percent," but that "the actual *use* of arbitration in Iowa...has no effect on the salaries of teachers [italics in the original]" (p. 445).

Strikes

Teacher strikes, long the most controversial aspect of collective bargaining in education, are viewed by many as unprofessional assaults on the public interest. Opponents of teacher strikes have argued that, as public employees, teachers have a monopoly on the market and therefore should not be permitted to withhold their services in the pursuit of more favorable settlements (Wellington & Winter, 1971). In mid-1980, nine states permit teachers to strike under special circumstances—usually after exhausting impasse procedures; most others explicitly prohibit strikes. Researchers have sought to understand the impact of these laws on union action.

Doherty (1980) observes that "of all public-employee groups, teachers appear to be the most inclined to take bargaining issues to impasse and to strike" and that "teachers accounted for almost 60 percent of all public employee work stoppages in 1975 in the U.S., although only 38 percent of all public-employee bargaining units consisted of teachers" (p. 530). In examining strike data from 1974–1975, Doherty (1980) found that of the 10 states experiencing the most strikes, only one (Pennsylvania) permitted strikes, and two (Ohio and Illinois) had no collective bargaining legislation, suggesting that teacher unions may not feel bound by legal restrictions on their rights to strike, particularly in states where strike prohibitions are not enforced.

Lieberman (1979), once an advocate and now an opponent of teacher bargaining, argues that although strike prohibitions may be ineffective, "more strikes would occur in the same jurisdiction if strikes were legalized" (pp. 415–419). He cites evidence from Pennsylvania:

> Almost one fifth of all the public-sector strikes in the United States have occurred in Pennsylvania since that state legalized public-sector strikes in 1970. Prior to legalization, Pennsylvania experienced about six public-sector strikes a year; after legalization in 1970, the state averaged 78 strikes annually from 1971–1977. (Lieberman, 1980, pp. 39–40)

Therefore, the presence of policies permitting or prohibiting strikes does not necessarily predict strike behavior. However, states such as Pennsylvania that have legalized strikes do experience considerably more work stoppage than states like New York that enforce their no-strike laws.

When a union initiates an illegal strike, the school board may ask the courts to enjoin it. Colton (1977), who has studied the use and effectiveness of such injunctions, reviewed 89 of the 200 teacher strikes that occurred in 1975–1976 and found that 43 percent of the school systems that were struck sought injunctive relief, 23 percent reached settlement before seeking an injunction, and 34 percent saw no need for an injunction. In 26 percent of those districts where an injunction was issued, contempt-of-court proceedings were also initiated. Colton reports that in nearly all these cases, most of which involved large districts, the courts eventually imposed fines or jail sentences. He concludes that although we know that injunctions do not stop strikes, we don't yet know "whether injunctions hasten or delay settlements or increase or decrease school board satisfaction with the outcome of negotiations" (Colton, 1977, pp. 32–35). The questions Colton raised still warrant further investigation.

State laws that regulate collective bargaining for teachers provide the framework for the labor practices of most school districts. Yet there are instances in which teachers and school boards negotiate outside the law, setting their own scope of bargaining and resolving impasses as they see fit. However, there appears to be extensive local compliance with compulsory arbitration laws. The parties abide by laws that are closely enforced. As experience with binding arbitration grows, its use and impact deserve close research attention.

THE PRACTICES

Labor relations practices—that is, how collective bargaining and contract management actually work in local districts—have been the subject of five major empirical studies since 1970. The earliest, conducted by Perry and Wildman (1970), systematically considered the negotiation practices of a diverse sample of 24 districts from 1964 to 1969. Perry (1979) subsequently updated this study by gathering additional data about the experiences of 9 districts from the original sample. Also in 1979, McDonnell and Pascal issued their report of a two-phased research effort including a quantitative analysis of teacher contract data from a national sample of 151 school districts. A 1980 study by Kerchner and Mitchell also included two phases—the first an intensive examination of collective bargaining in 8 Illinois and California school districts and the second a series of interviews and surveys in 65 additional districts in the

same states. Finally, Johnson (1984) examined the labor relations practices in 6 school districts of a diverse national sample between 1979 and 1980. The findings receive specific attention here.

Negotiation

Although researchers have considered many aspects of educational labor relations, few have looked closely at the negotiation process. Those who have done so, however, agree that collective bargaining in public education is fundamentally bilateral. Despite beliefs that the public should participate in negotiations (Cheng, 1976) and despite opportunities in some states (e.g., California) for multilateral bargaining, citizen involvement rarely materializes. Perry (1979) found negotiations to be "a remarkably private and apolitical process" (p. 5) except during strikes in large urban systems. McDonnell and Pascal (1979) reported that not only did negotiators object to citizen participation but that, short of a strike, citizen groups were generally indifferent. Kerchner and Mitchell (1980) also found that the special structures for citizen input provided under California law were "seldom and inconsequentially used." They did conclude, however, that although negotiations are private, "parents and lay citizens are extremely influential" in determining the "tone of labor relations, the toughness or meekness of the parties at the bargaining table, and frequently the issues" (Kerchner & Mitchell, 1980, p. 5:3).

The negotiators themselves received some consideration. McDonnell and Pascal (1979) report that a "typical set of bargaining participants includes a teacher organization team headed by its leadership and a district team led by a full-time professional negotiator, typically the director of personnel" (p. 51). They conclude that this format makes negotiations smoother but tends to "sideline" community representatives, school board members and rank-and-file teachers. Perry and Wildman (1970) had earlier observed a trend toward professional negotiators, and McDonnell and Pascal (1979) concluded that "what they [Perry and Wildman] identified as a growing trend has become almost universal" (p. 45). Principals are sometimes included as members of the management team, but they seldom bargain actively. Johnson (1984) found that although principals did not seek a larger role in negotiations, they did wish that their interests as school managers might be better represented.

Several studies have considered the scope of local negotiations. In their original study, Perry and Wildman (1970) found that "the formal scope of teacher bargaining (all terms and conditions of employment dealt with in contracts) was actually far broader than the effective scope of bargaining (the terms and conditions that teachers try to change)" (p. 11). Perry (1979) subsequently found that the formal scope of bargaining "became broader and more uniform across districts than had been the case in the mid-1960s" (p. 11). Moreover, he found that "the 'true' effective scope of bargaining in all districts was significantly expanded by formal and informal commitments to discuss or to confer or consult on various matters independent of the normal process of contract negotiation or administration" (p. 11). Similarly, McDonnell and Pascal (1979, p. 55) found that negotiators sometimes exceed what is permitted and sometimes fail to bargain over mandated subjects.

Several researchers have focused on the process of bargaining itself. Using a model proposed by Walton and McKersie (1965), Perry and Wildman (1970) found that among their 24 districts, "distributive bargaining" —that is, the allocation of resources in a fixed-sum game—was prevalent at the outset of bargaining, leading to frequent impasse. Subsequently, parties began to incorporate more "integrative bargaining" practices—that is, cooperative problem solving in a win-win opportunity. Perry and Wildman (1970) found that eventually mixed strategies emerged, which provided "the most workable basis for achieving an agreement, short of a test of power..." (p. 84).

Kerchner and Mitchell (1980), too, found a mixture of distributive and integrative bargaining strategies in their field sample. In a preliminary report, they characterized five alternative approaches to bargaining. Some parties bargained with "a firmly fixed notion of an ideal contract" (p. 2:4). Others approached the process as bartering or "give and take," and others "rallied the troops" to hold firm on their proposals. Some union negotiators bargained with a clear sense of the school board's "zone of tolerance" for an acceptable settlement, and yet others practiced "package bargaining." The authors found that negotiators at the same table were often proceeding with different expectations and that misinterpretation about the other side's intentions was "quite widespread" (Mitchell, Kerchner, Erck, & Pryor, 1980, pp. 31–32).

The process and content of contract settlements have not received the same extent or closeness of examination as bargaining practices. McDonnell and Pascal (1979) did consider the types of tradeoffs negotiators made, finding that neither labor nor management had established rules for making tradeoffs but that when tradeoffs were made, they rarely cut across economic and noneconomic items.

As noted, protracted negotiations may lead to the use of impasse procedures or to strikes. McDonnell and Pascal (1979) found that 14 of the 15 districts they visited had employed some type of impasse procedure. "In only two of these districts, however, were participants' assessment of these procedures positive." They concluded that "the most effective resolutions are worked out by the parties themselves with no outside intervention" (p. 62).

The local use of strikes as an alternative means of resolving impasse is addressed by several field studies, although the focus is usually on the incidence or outcome of the work stoppage rather than on its process or organizational effects. In their 1967 study, Doherty and Oberer (1967) found the strike to be an effective union tactic—all nine teacher strikes during the first year of collective bargaining "resulted in collective bargaining agreements of substantial benefit to the teachers involved" (p. 103). Moreover, they speculated that other district negotiations were influenced by the "credibility of strike *threats* [italics in the original]" (p. 103).

Later research suggests that strikes have been less effective. In 1979, Perry found "a growing willingness on the part of school management to 'stand the political heat' of a confrontation with teachers" (p. 10). Three districts that had not sought legal sanctions against the union a decade before "secured injunctions against strikes, which in two cases resulted in the jailing of union leaders" (p. 10). Similarly, McDonnell and Pascal (1979) found that strikes yielded "mixed results" in contractual outcomes. "Some resulted in large gains, while in other districts the teachers actually settled for less than they had been offered prior to the strike" (p. 64). Moreover, Finch and Nagel (1984) note that "a review of average salary rates in those states where teacher strikes are permitted reveals no appreciable salary inflation" (p. 1598).

Labor Relationships

There is general agreement that the relationship between labor and management is central in determining the overall impact of collective bargaining in a district. McDonnell and Pascal (1979) observe that, among other things, the "quality of [the parties'] relationship with each other [is] critical in understanding why collective bargaining has been a very constructive process in some districts and a source of acrimony and divisiveness in others" (p. 39). Kerchner and Mitchell (1980) concluded that labor relationships do not, as some believe, proceed in a linear fashion from conflict to cooperation, but instead they move through a complex pattern of relationships that includes "three generations and two distinct, intergenerational periods of conflict" (p. 2:8). The experiences in their sample districts suggest that in the first stage of "meet and confer," the level of trust between teachers and administrators is high. There follows a period of conflict as teachers seek legitimacy. The second generation, Kerchner and Mitchell (1980) report, is a period when labor relations become institutionalized and relationships are good. The next conflict is precipitated by citizens and school board members who object to the strength of the union. In resolving this conflict, "management becomes the active party in teacher negotiation" (Kerchner & Mitchell, 1980, pp. 3:1–3:30).

Johnson (1984) examined contract management rather than negotiation and found no distinct patterns across labor relationships in six districts. In four, the relationships were cooperative, in two "notably adversarial" (p. 168). The various factors influencing district-level labor relationships included (a) the personalities, styles, and relationships of key actors, (b) district size, (c) the labor traditions of the community, and (d) the expansion or decline of student enrollments and local economy.

Contract Administration

Compared with contract negotiation, contract administration has received little research attention. However, the available studies suggest that the demands for standardization of contract administration have contributed to centralization of responsibility at the district level and to the formalization of labor practices. Mitchell et al. (1980) conclude

> that bargaining has produced a trend toward more homogeneous and consistent interpretation and application of work rules among all the schools within any given district. Central office managers are noticeably sensitive to the potential problems in contract administration which can arise if contract clauses are interpreted or applied in different ways in different schools. In most of our sample districts central office managers warn middle managers that there are hazards in allowing divergent practices. (p. 20)

Similarly, McDonnell and Pascal (1979) concluded that "in most districts, implementation of the contract is highly routinized. The administration usually works with school principals, briefing them on any new provisions, and preparing them to implement the contract at the building level" (p. 76). Johnson (1984) concurred that "the trend toward centralized administration of the contract was apparent in all six districts of the study" but observed that "no district had achieved anything resembling lockstep conformity in labor practices" (p. 82).

Although there has been considerable concern about such districtwide effects of collective bargaining, McDonnell and Pascal (1979) found that the contract had its greatest nonbudgetary effect in the schools, and they documented considerable variation in contract management at that level, finding, for example, that in some districts, school-site committees "co-administer the building," whereas in others they "have no influence" (pp. 77–78). Moreover, they concluded that

> the principal plays a central role in determining whether collective bargaining works in the school building. Truly effective principals usually accept collective bargaining and use the contract both to manage their building more systematically and to increase teacher participation in school decisionmaking. Less effective principals may view the contract as an obstacle to a well-run school and then use it as an excuse for poor management. (McDonnell & Pascal, 1979, p. 81)

There is some dispute about the role of the building representative—the official union delegate at the school site. Glassman and Belasco (1976) studied building representatives in a large urban district and found that they played a central role in school-site labor relations, controlling access to the grievance process, pursuing grievances compatible with their own objectives, and seeking greater roles in decision making. Kerchner and Mitchell's (1980) work suggests that union representatives are not so influential. They report that "only about 50 percent of our survey districts had building representatives at each school site, and the interviews revealed generally that these persons were not particularly well trained or active" (p. 6:36). Johnson (1984) also found wide variation in the expertise and commitment of building representatives but a generally consistent approach to them by principals, who "negotiated and nurtured cooperative, informal relationships with their building representatives, thus enabling them to hear about teacher concerns informally and to solicit teacher opinions about anticipated changes or problems" (p. 40).

Like McDonnell and Pascal (1979), Johnson (1984) centered attention on day-to-day labor practices and found that they vary greatly from school to school. On the basis of interviews with teachers and administrators in 40 schools of six districts, she concluded that there was extensive variation in contract management, even within schools of the same district:

> In one school, the union is active, the contract is prominent, and administrator-teacher relationships are formalized. In another school within the same district, teachers and administrators maintain collegial relationships, minimize the role of the contract, and resolve problems informally. Few contract provisions are implemented fully throughout the schools of any district, most being subject to interpretation, amendment, or informal renegotiation at the school site. (Johnson, 1984, p. 165)

These findings have been challenged by the recent study of six metropolitan school districts by Goldschmidt and Stuart (1984), who concluded that educational policies, once bargained, "are uniformly implemented" (p. 4).

The use and administration of grievance procedures, one of the most important elements of contract management, was covered in the research by McDonnell and Pascal (1979), who point out that teacher unions regard grievance procedures as the "heart of the contract" and consequently pursue them intently through negotiations. However, the authors also found that labor and management are "inclined to settle grievances as quickly and at as low a level as possible" (p. 76), a finding confirmed by Johnson (1984, p. 53). McDonnell & Pascal (1979) also found that

> the tenor of the grievance process is dependent on the quality of the relationship between the school district and the teacher organization. A mutually distrustful relationship means grievances are more apt to go to arbitration and to be settled by a third-party neutral. (p. 76)

Johnson (1984) observed that "while the range of permissible grievances was quite broad, the number formally filed...was surprisingly small" (p. 48), with many schools reporting fewer than three per year. However, the potential threat of a grievance indirectly affected principals' behavior. "Casual comments, complaints, reminders, warnings and threats were used by teachers to ensure or provoke administrative compliance with the contract" (Johnson, 1984, p. 47). Similarly, Kerchner and Mitchell (1980) characterize grievances as "communications mechanisms" and observe that "grievance threats force management to give attention to situations they might have preferred to ignore" (p. 6:25). As of the mid-1980s, there was no comprehensive study of grievances and arbitrations and their effects on school district policies. There is much speculation about the potential effects of outside intervention on school autonomy, but the extent and complexity of that impact have yet to be clearly mapped, even though Brodie and Williams (1982) have completed a useful analysis of school arbitration decisions. Until such decisions are examined within the context of local policies and practices, sure understanding of their real effects and implications remains uncertain.

OUTCOMES AND EFFECTS

It is no simple matter to determine the outcomes and effects of collective bargaining. Tracing the impact of unionism from the bargaining table through offices, corridors, and classrooms is a precarious venture, fraught with threats to validity and shaky causal assumptions. Even determining the impact of negotiations on salaries and working conditions presents complex methodological problems. Researchers have sought to answer two central questions about the impact of unionism and collective bargaining on such matters as school governance, teaching and administrative practice, and student achievement, as reviewed below.

Outcomes

Wages

Since 1970, researchers have sought to understand the extent to which collective bargaining contributes to increases in teacher wages. This question has generated more research, and the research has generated more methodological dispute, than any other subject in educational labor relations. In his comprehensive review of studies addressing the issue, Lipsky (1983) sets forth the research problem:[1]

> In order to get a "true" measure of the bargaining effect we need a measure of salaries determined under collective bargaining, Sb, and a measure of salaries for the same group of workers if they had *never* bargained, Sa. Then $Sb - Sa$ would be an accurate measure of the effect of bargaining on salaries. But Sa is not directly observable—one can never really know what an organized group of workers would have received if the group had never been organized. What we can generally observe is Sc, the salary level of a group of unorganized workers that is comparable to the organized group. (pp. 21–22)

Lipsky (1983) goes on to explain that $Sb - Sc$ is likely to be a biased estimate of bargaining effects for two reasons. First, bargaining is likely to affect indirectly the wages of unorganized teachers (the "spillover effect"). Second, "it is difficult to match organized and unorganized groups that are identical except for the fact that one group bargains and the other does not" (pp. 21–22).

The various regression studies dealing with this problem use cross-sectional rather than longitudinal data. They focus on different units of analysis (from individual teachers to statewide data) and rely on different dependent variables (entry-level salary, average salary, multiple points on the salary scale). Despite the methodological variety, the economists who conduct this research generally have concluded that the effects of bargaining on wages are modest—from zero to 12 percent. Lipsky (1983) observes that such effects are not only lower than critics of teacher negotiations predicted but are "substantially below estimates of the effects of private-sector bargaining on wages" (p. 35), generally considered to be between 15 and 20 percent.

Space does not permit a detailed comparison of all wage studies here; only several will be summarized to indicate important differences. The earliest, conducted by Kasper in 1970, concluded that the effect of bargaining on salaries was slight at best. Drawing on statewide data from 50 states and Puerto Rico, Kasper used the average classroom salary of teachers in the state as his dependent, or salary, variable and measures of the degree of bargaining as one of his independent, or union, variables. He concluded:

> For the time being, all that may be said is (1) collective representation does not seem to have had much, if any, effect on teachers' salaries; (2) if there has been a positive effect, it is probably less than $400 and could even be as little as $40; (3) given these small estimates, it seems unlikely that bargaining has produced a significant or widespread reallocation of educational resources. (Kasper, 1970, p. 71)

Subsequently, in an effort to standardize micro-level data, Thornton (1971) considered wage effects in 83 large, urban school districts and found greater effects than did Kasper. Rather than using average salaries, Thornton considered several points on the salary scale in his salary variable and concluded that "collective negotiations have indeed affected higher teachers' salaries at all four salary levels. The differentials range from a fairly small $160 for the A.M. minimum to a substantial $3,132 at the A.M. maximum level" (pp. 42–43). Hall and Carroll (1973), however, criticize Thornton's "interstate and interregional" comparisons of large districts and suggest that the findings may be influenced by variables other than unions: for example, state certification requirements, degree of urbanization, and regional income differentials.

Baird and Landon (1972) studied 44 medium-sized school districts (25,000 to 50,000 in population) and used entry-level salaries as their dependent variable, while controlling for the relative wealth of districts, the extent of teacher organization, and the structure of the labor market. They concluded that "in districts where some type of collective negotiations are held, salaries tend to be significantly higher—by an average of $261.17 or 4.9 percent of the average starting salary" (Baird & Landon, 1972, p. 415). Cooper (1982), who has reviewed the research, points out two problems with the study by Baird and Landon. First, "the authors do not control for salary levels prior to bargaining, hence their results would tend to be overestimated, because much of the differential between organized and unorganized districts can be explained by salary differences before unionization" (Cooper,

1982, p. 90). Second, by using entry-level salary data, they cannot identify the effect of union efforts to increase the wages of current teachers.

In their 1973 study, Lipsky and Drotning examined data from 696 New York school districts during the first year of negotiations under the Taylor Law. They compared the experiences of districts that had collective bargaining contracts (63 percent) with districts that did not have contracts (37 percent), using both mean salaries and three points on the salary scale as dependent variables. Lipsky and Drotning concluded that collective bargaining had no significant effect on teacher salary levels, "regardless of whether the dependent variable was a measure of actual earnings (mean salary) or of scheduled rates." However, they found that bargaining had a "positive and highly significant" effect on salary changes after collective bargaining was introduced in 1967, "adding about 15 percent to salary increases" (p. 35).

In a 1978 study, Chambers used an intrastate sample of school districts and considered both the effects of unionization and the regional effects of bargaining with entry-level salaries as the dependent variable. He concluded that negotiation increased teachers' wages by 6 to 12 percent.

Recently, Baugh and Stone (1982) studied individual teachers' salary gains by using data for 1974–1975 and 1977–1978 from the Current Population Survey. Their independent variable was union membership, and their dependent variables were the estimated hourly wage and the change in the hourly wage. Baugh and Stone found relatively small wage gains during the early 1970s but concluded that by the late 1970s, the union-nonunion wage differential among teachers reached 12 to 22 percent, leading them to proclaim that "Unionism now pays." However, one problem with these data on individuals is that they provide information about union affiliation rather than about collective bargaining activity. Moreover, Lipsky (1983) notes that although Baugh and Stone (1982) "use a set of teacher characteristics as control variables in their estimating equation, they ignore demand-side, structural, and political variables." He argues that "the omission of such variables probably biases estimates of the union effect in an upward direction" (Lipsky, 1983, p. 35).

A review of these studies and their critiques suggests that negotiation has increased teachers' salaries modestly, if at all. It seems unlikely that the precise effect will eventually be determined, because further research on this question is increasingly complicated by the expansion of bargaining and the virtual impossibility of identifying comparable bargaining and nonbargaining districts and controlling for spillover effects.

Fringe Benefits

There is, as yet, little information about bargaining's effects on fringe benefits, which, because they are untaxed income, have gained importance in local bargaining. In 1978, Gallagher (1978) studied the school budgets of 133 Illinois school districts (65 bargaining, 68 nonbargaining), controlling for school district wealth and for the proportion of staff having advanced degrees (pp. 231–237). He found a 9-percent differential in total operating expenditures between bargaining and nonbargaining districts and a 9-percent differential in "non-teacher compensation related expenditures" (Gallagher, 1978, p. 234). Cooper (1982) notes that although Gallagher "does demonstrate the significance of nonsalary benefits won by unions, the observed difference between bargaining and nonbargaining districts may be inflated by the study's failure to control for differentials that may have existed prior to collective bargaining" (p. 98).

Further research is needed to compare the fringe benefits of bargaining and nonbargaining teachers and the effects of collective bargaining on resource allocation within a district. Also, as alternative compensation schemes such as merit pay are introduced, it will be important to understand the role collective bargaining plays in structuring the distribution of such benefits.

Working Conditions

In contrast to the extensive research to determine the effect of collective bargaining on teachers' wages, few studies have centered on its effect on working conditions. Studies in this area have provided both quantitative and descriptive accounts of provisions regulating teachers' work. For a variety of methodological reasons, including spillover effects, these investigations do not compare working conditions of unionized and nonunionized teachers as much as they trace changes in the conditions over time.

In the only large, longitudinal study of teacher contracts, McDonnell and Pascal (1979) analyzed data from a national sample of school districts at two time periods, 1970 and 1975, and concluded that there is a "convergence of collective bargaining outcomes over time. As more and more school systems follow the lead of flagship districts, there is less variation among individual contracts" (p. 31). They explained that

> organized teachers continue to gain influence over what happens in their classrooms, their schools, and their school systems. In the classroom, teachers have increased control over class size, curriculum, disciplinary matters, and use of aides. In the school and district, teachers more and more contribute to decisions over who is employed and where, who administers, who

evaluates, and the duration and composition of the teaching day. (McDonnell & Pascal, 1979, p. 34)

Perry (1979), too, found a trend toward more comprehensive contracts in his follow-up study of nine school systems. Recent work on negotiated staffing policies by Johnson, Nelson, and Potter (1985) indicates that although contracts may be more comprehensive, they do not uniformly favor the union. Many contract provisions strengthen the position of management.

Negotiated working conditions cover a wide range of provisions, including those that establish teachers' job responsibilities, those that provide job security and procedural protections, and those that define teachers' roles in policy making. For example, several researchers who have considered the impact of bargaining on work hours report mixed findings. In their early study, Perry and Wildman (1970) found that "collective bargaining had resulted in a shortening of the effective school year or day in a few systems" (p. 12). In his update of that work, Perry (1979) reports that although the school calendar was a subject of bargaining in eight of the nine systems studied, the length of the school day and school year were specified in only five contracts, including those of the three largest districts. In those five districts, "there was evidence that collective bargaining had contributed to a discernible reduction in hours" (Perry, 1979, p. 13). By contrast, in Johnson's six districts, the number of instructional days had remained constant since the 1950s, when many school districts had instituted double sessions. However, teachers' work days had been reduced through bargaining. Johnson (1984, p. 95) also found that teachers had successfully reduced their nonteaching duties through bargaining and that they continued to try to restrict the limits of their formal responsibilities to classroom instruction.

In addition to regulating the length of the teachers' work day, providing preparation time, and specifying teachers' responsibilities for supervising pupil activities, contracts often regulate class size, a subject many regard as a matter of instructional policy. McDonnell and Pascal (1979) found that 20 percent of the districts studied had class-size provisions in 1970, whereas 34 percent had included them in contracts by 1975 (p. 12). However, the presence of such provisions does not necessarily mean that class size has changed as a result of collective bargaining. The language may provide guidelines rather than limitations, or it may simply incorporate into the contract current administrative policies on class size. Perry (1979) found that although class size was bargained in all nine of his systems, the unions had "made relatively little concrete progress in achieving definite, enforceable limits on class size or in reducing those limits where they exist" (p. 13). He concluded that the "relative weakness" of these provisions results from the "substantial economic costs of reducing or even standardizing class size" (Perry, 1979, pp. 13–14). Similarly, Johnson (1984) found firm class-size limits in only two of six districts studied (pp. 208–210). In summarizing research in this area, Finch and Nagel (1984) conclude that it "offers evidence of both decreased and increased pupil loads resulting from collective bargaining. When effects are found, however, they are small" (p. 1624). These limited data on teachers' responsibilities suggest that collective bargaining has enabled teachers to define and, in some cases, reduce the limits of their jobs. However, as with wages, union gains have not been dramatic.

More extensive gains have been achieved in negotiating grievance procedures and seniority job protections. McDonnell and Pascal (1979) found that by 1975 grievance procedures leading to binding arbitration were included in 83 percent of the contracts they studied (p. 12). Doherty (1980) observes, however, that "recently there has been a tightening of the grievance definition, confining its application to claimed violations or misinterpretations of the terms of the contract" (p. 544).

The role of seniority in determining promotions, involuntary transfers, and layoffs has also been expanded through bargaining. Perry (1979) found that, over time, seniority played a greater role in promotions and layoffs. Six of the nine systems he studied used seniority as the sole criterion for layoffs (p. 14). Johnson (1984) found seniority within certification areas determining layoffs in four of six districts (p. 78) and that, moreover, unlike many contract provisions, seniority-based layoff and transfer provisions were fully enforced by teachers (p. 73). There is some evidence, however, that seniority-based layoffs cannot be attributed solely to collective bargaining, for seniority is also widely used as the determinant of layoffs in non-union districts. However, the presence of a seniority contract provision does seem to increase the likelihood that if layoffs are necessary, the junior teacher will lose the job (Eberts & Stone, 1983, p. 172).

Although these studies suggest that teachers have made some gains in defining their working conditions and securing job protection, it appears that they have neither aggressively sought nor gained extensive influence over instructional policy. Based on an analysis of Connecticut contracts, Finch and Nagel (1984) conclude:

> There is relatively little contract language governing the more formative issues of educational policymaking issues which one might expect to be prominent in the bargaining agenda of a professional union. It is uncommon to find, for example, contract provisions that determine such matters as the content of the school curriculum, the methods of classroom instruction, the choice of textbooks and teaching materials, the policies for student grading and student discipline, the standards for the hiring of teachers and administrators, and the allocation of the non-salary portions of the school budget. (pp. 1611–1612)

Some contracts permit teachers to participate on committees that recommend school policies. McDonnell and Pascal (1979) found that 31 percent of their contracts provided for teachers' involvement in curricular decisions. Eberts and Stone (1983) identified similar provisions in 39 percent of the New York State contracts they studied. Finch and Nagel (1984) discovered that 35 percent of the Connecticut contracts contained such language. Except in rare instances, however, building committees are restricted to advisory roles, with their influence dependent on principals' attitudes toward teacher participation (Johnson, 1984). Perry (1979) also noted that policy issues had generally not become part of the formal scope of bargaining and that there was little evidence that "collective bargaining can and will lead to the extension of teacher rights to the control of some or all matters of educational policy" (p. 15). It is intriguing that teachers have gained so little formal influence over instructional policy, given their ongoing concern about factors affecting their classrooms. Apparently, either teachers do not believe such influence can be effectively negotiated and enforced, or they are satisfied with the control they already have when they close their classroom doors.

Overall, teacher gains through bargaining have been less dramatic than some had hoped and others had feared. Despite substantial early accomplishments by unions, overall progress has been modest. Finch and Nagel (1984) sum it up:

> There is little evidence, then, that teachers' unions generally have greater bargaining leverage than unionized employees in the private sector; nor is there any indication that teachers' unions have dominated the management of the public schools. Indeed, measured either by the success of unionized workers in the private sector, or by teachers' own bargaining agenda, collective bargaining has been a minor disappointment. (p. 1614)

Effects

In seeking to determine the impact of teacher unionism, it is important to distinguish between the contractual outcomes of bargaining—like changes in wages and working conditions discussed above—and the effects of collective bargaining on teaching and administrative practice, student achievement, and school governance. Ultimately, it is the financial demands and the indirect effects of bargaining that matter most to citizens and school officials, but because such effects are difficult to document and track, they have received little systematic research attention.

One might well expect that a condition as prominent as collective bargaining would show extensive impact on teaching. However, research findings are sparse and mixed on this issue. In 1976, Murphy and Hoover speculated about whether collective bargaining would increase the bureaucratic character of schools, resulting in less flexibility and less professional behavior among teachers, or if bargaining would enhance professional autonomy and decentralize policy making. Their research suggests that collective bargaining has had both effects. Teachers are more autonomous and schooling is more centralized (Murphy & Hoover, 1976). McDonnell and Pascal (1979) concluded that although collective bargaining had not "significantly affected classroom operations and the services delivered to students" (p. 80), it had improved staff morale and provided teachers with greater autonomy, which was, in part, what teachers sought in their pursuit of professional status through unionism. By contrast, Kerchner and Mitchell (1980) argue that because collective bargaining rationalizes teaching and formalizes the supervisory role of administrators, teaching has become more like labor, where supervisors directly assess employees' performance, and less like a profession with peer review (pp. 6:18–6:22).

There is more consensus among researchers about the impact of collective bargaining on principals' administrative practice. Researchers agree that teachers have won formal powers relative to principals, that contracts have constrained principals' discretion, and that principals' work has become more managerial and their jobs more difficult. However, McDonnell and Pascal (1979) concluded that the principal was also central in determining the character of labor relations in a school. And Johnson (1984) found that "school site administrators in even the strongest union districts could manage their schools well. Principals were neither figureheads deferring to union representatives nor functionaries complying slavishly with the contract" (p. 15). The available data reveal the importance of noting that collective bargaining is one of many policies that have altered the character of principals' work between 1965 and 1985 and that, consequently, its effects are difficult to isolate.

There have been minimal research on the effects of collective bargaining on student achievement, largely because the causal connections between bargaining gains and test scores are virtually impossible to identify.

On this problem, Doherty (1981) notes: "We sometimes attribute to bargaining certain changes in educational performance on the sole ground that one preceded the other. As Samuel Johnson once observed of physicians, they tended to 'mistake subsequence for consequence'" (p. 64). Doherty himself concluded that "bargaining has not brought about a substantial improvement in student achievement. But neither can it be shown that bargaining has in any significant way been responsible for the decline in achievement" (1981, p. 75). Similarly, Eberts and Stone (1983) concluded that the net difference in gains in student achievement between union and nonunion schools was "negligible" (p. 166).

Finally, it is important to consider the effects of collective bargaining on workplace democracy. For although contract language has not substantially enlarged teachers' formal role in policy making, there is some evidence that teachers exert considerable informal influence. Perry (1979) observes that bargaining by teachers may have led to "greater informal participation in policy decisions." McDonnell and Pascal (1979) found some evidence that collective bargaining agreements fostered "greater professionalism among teachers" (p. 81). Johnson (1984) found instances in which building representatives and union members worked cooperatively with principals in making school policy and redefining school practice. Recent research on the reform of school staffing policies by Johnson et al. (1985) suggests that local unions do collaborate with management when teachers consider the proposed reforms to be in the interests of increased professionalism and better schools (pp. 17–18).

Until the mid-1980s, much of the research in educational labor relations has proceeded on the assumption that unions selfishly consolidate power, protect their members, and monopolize resources. The book by Freeman and Medoff (1984) *What Do Unions Do?* directs attention to labor's success in providing workers "with a voice at the work place and in the political arena" (p. 4). The opportunity for greater influence may ultimately improve the ranks of teachers and benefit the schools. It is not yet clear how much collective bargaining has augmented the voice of teachers. Nor do we know the effect that the opportunity for more influence has had on the quality of schooling or the career paths of teachers. Both of these questions should command more attention in future research.

CONCLUSION

Since roughly 1965, researchers have raised many questions about labor relations in education. A few of the questions have been answered conclusively, at least for the moment. For example, it is fairly certain that collective bargaining has not dramatically affected teachers' salaries, that citizen involvement in negotiation is rare, and that conventional impasse procedures do not in themselves prevent strikes. The effects of collective bargaining vary from district to district and school to school, but there are patterns in that variation. Collective bargaining has complicated the work of school administrators and changed the responsibilities of teachers.

But, after two decades, research has succeeded less in supplying firm answers than in identifying important questions, experimenting with new methodologies, and promoting policy debate. Many components of Dunlop's model of industrial relations systems still remain unexplored. Oddly, very little is known about the current actors. How do union leaders view their roles? How does the governing structure of the local union influence priorities and strategies? On what criteria do teachers decide to support or oppose their leaders' recommendations? How do third-party neutrals understand their roles, responsibilities, and impact? What formal or informal relationships do superintendents have with the bargaining process, particularly during periods of financial constraint? What roles do local politicians play in settling both wage and nonwage issues?

There remain questions about the bargaining policies as well. How have state laws changed over time? Are they more comprehensive or more restrictive? Are they increasingly similar or dissimilar? Will the increasing reliance on binding arbitration in negotiations standardize local school policies or limit reform?

Many issues of practice await further examination. How do local districts develop an approach to negotiations? What influence do state and national affiliates have in determining that approach? Do externally imposed financial constraints promote new alliances between labor and management? What effect does grievance arbitration have on what school officials do or believe they can do? How do the rules of collective bargaining interact with other rules that regulate teachers and teaching?

Finally, many questions remain about the outcomes and effects of collective bargaining in education. Does unionization lead to different or better fringe benefits? What is the role of negotiation in determining resource allocation within school districts, particularly those in financial decline? How does unionism affect teachers' views of their work and responsibilities? Does it contribute to greater democracy in the workplace?

In the research of the next two decades there must be greater attention to the context of educational labor relations and to various components of Dunlop's model that have barely been considered—the technological character of the workplace, market and budgetary constraints, politics and power. Moreover, research must also attend to the remarkable variation in labor relationships, contract settlements, and contract administration and seek to understand and account for those differences. Finally, inquiry must pay particular attention to change—not simply to the passage of time but to growth or decline in enrollments and school funds, increases or decreases in public support for teachers and schools, and changes in the size and composition of the teaching force.

The research agenda for the future is not simple and the work will not be tidy. Because labor relations practices are so complex, their study demands varied and innovative approaches. That study will require care in identifying and understanding the peculiarities of schools and teachers. It will be enhanced by collaboration among practitioners and researchers as well as among researchers themselves. And it will demand patience with findings that are not conclusive but are potentially instructive.

NOTE

[1] The wage studies reviewed by Lipsky include:

Baird, R. N., & Landon, J. H. (1972). The effects of collective bargaining on public school teachers' salaries: Comment. *Industrial and Labor Relations Review*, 25, 410–416.

Balfour, G. A. (1974). More evidence that unions do not achieve higher salaries for teachers. *Journal of Collective Negotiations in the Public Sector*, 3, 289–303.

Baugh, W. H., & Stone, J. A. (1980). *Teachers, unions, and wages in the 1970's: Unionism now pays*. (Project No. G–80–0110). Washington, DC: National Institute of Education.

Chambers, J. G. (1976). *The impact of collective bargaining for teachers on resource allocation in public school districts*. Unpublished manuscript.

Frey, D. E. (1975). Wage determination in public schools and effects of unionization. In D. S. Hamermesh (Ed.), *Labor in the public and nonprofit sectors*. Princeton, NJ: Princeton University Press.

Gallagher, D. G. (1978). Defacto bargaining and teacher salary levels: The Illinois experience. *Journal of Collective Negotiations in the Public Sector*, 7, 243–254.

Gustman, A. L., & Segal, M. (1976). *The impact of teachers' unions*. (Final Report). Washington, DC: National Institute of Education.

Hall, W. C., & Carroll, N. E. (1973). The effects of teachers' organizations on salaries and class size. *Industrial and Labor Relations Review*, 26, 834–841.

Homes, A. B. (1976). Effects of union activity on teachers' earnings. *Industrial Relations*, 15, 328–332.

Kasper, H. (1970). The effects of collective bargaining on public school teachers' salaries. *Industrial and Labor Relations Review*, 24, 57–72.

Lipsky, D. B., & Drotning, J. E. (1973). The influence of collective bargaining on teachers' salaries in New York State. *Industrial and Labor Relations Review*, 27, 18–35.

Mitchell, D. J. B. (1979). The impact of collective bargaining on compensation in the public sector. In B. Aaron, J. R. Grodin, & J. L. Stern (Eds.), *Public sector bargaining* (pp. 118–149). Washington DC: Bureau of National Affairs.

Schmenner, R. W. (1973). The determination of municipal employees' wages. *Review of Economics and Statistics, 55,* 83–90.

Thornton, R. J. (1971). The effects of collective negotiations on teachers' salaries. *Quarterly Review of Economics and Business, 11,* 37–46.

Treacy, J., Harris, R., & Blake, C. (1974). *Salaries, strikes, shutdowns, split shifts and collective bargaining in Ohio public schools.* (Final Report). Washington, DC: National Institute of Education.

Zuelke, D. C., & Frohreich, L. E. (1977). The impact of comprehensive collective negotiations on teachers' salaries: Some evidence from Wisconsin. *Journal of Collective Negotiations in the Public Sector, 6,* 81–88.

REFERENCES

Alutto, J. A., & Belasco, J. A. (1976). Determinants of attitudinal militancy among teachers and nurses. In A. M. Cresswell & M. J. Murphy (Eds.), *Education and collective bargaining.* Berkeley, CA: McCutchan.

Bacharach, S. B., Mitchell, S. M., & Malanowski, R. (1985). Strategic choice and collective action: Organizational determinants of teachers' militancy. In D. B. Lipsky (Ed.), *Advances in industrial and labor relations, Vol. 2.* Greenwich, CT: JAI.

Baird, R. N., & Landon, J. H. (1972). The effects of collective bargaining on public school teachers' salaries: Comment. *Industrial and Labor Relations Review, 25,* 410–417.

Baugh, W. H., & Stone, J. A. (1982). Teachers, unions, and wages in the 1970's: Unionism now pays. *Industrial and Labor Relations Review, 35,* 410–417.

Braun, R. J. (1972). *Teachers and power: The story of the American Federation of Teachers.* New York: Simon & Schuster.

Bridges, E. M., & Cooper, B. S. (1976). Collective bargaining for school administrators. *Theory into Practice, 15,* 306–313.

Brodie, D. M., & Williams, P. M. (1982). *School grievance arbitration.* Redmond, WA: Butterworth.

Butler, R. J., & Ehrenber, R. (1981). Estimating the narcotic effect of public sector impasse procedures. *Industrial and Labor Relations Review, 35,* 3–19.

Chambers, J. G. (1978). An analysis of resource allocation in public school districts. *Public Finance Quarterly, 6,* 131–160.

Cheng, C. W. (1976). Community participation in teacher collective bargaining: Problems and prospects. *Harvard Educational Review, 46,* 153–174.

Cole, S. (1969). Teachers' strike: A study of the conversion of predisposition into action. *American Journal of Sociology, 74,* 506–520.

Colton, D. L. (1977). Why, when and how school boards use injunctions to stifle teacher strikes. *American School Board Journal, 164,* 32–35.

Cooper, B. S. (1982). *Collective bargaining, strikes, and financial costs in public education: A comparative review.* Eugene, OR: ERIC Clearinghouse on Educational Management.

Cooper, B. S., & Murrmann, K. F. (1984, April). *Professional attitudes and the unionization of school principals.* Paper presented at the Annual Meeting of the American Educational Research Association, New Orleans.

Corwin, R. G. (1970). *Militant professionalism: A study of organizational conflict in high schools.* New York: Appleton-Century-Crofts.

Delaney, J. T. (1983). Strikes, arbitration, and teacher salaries: A behavioral analysis. *Industrial and Labor Relations Review, 36,* 431–446.

Doherty, R. E. (1980). Public education. In G. G. Somers (Ed.), *Collective bargaining: Contemporary American experience.* Madison, WI: Industrial Relations Research Association.

Doherty, R. E. (1981). Does teacher bargaining affect student achievement? In G. W. Angell (Ed.), *Faculty and teacher bargaining* (pp. 63–85). Lexington, MA: Lexington.

Doherty, R. E., & Oberer, W. E. (1967). *Teachers, school boards, and collective bargaining: A changing of the guard.* Ithaca, NY: New York State School of Industrial and Labor Relations.

Donley, M. O. (1976). *Power to the teacher: How America's educators became militant.* Bloomington, IN: Indiana University Press.

Dunlop, J. T. (1958). *Industrial relations systems.* Carbondale, IL: Southern Illinois University Press.

Eaton, W. E. (1975). *The American Federation of Teachers, 1916–1961: A history of the movement.* Carbondale, IL: Southern Illinois University Press.

Eberts, R. W., & Stone, J. A. (1983). *Unions and the public schools: The effect of collective bargaining on American education.* Lexington, MA: Lexington.

Finch, M., & Nagel, T. W. (1983). Spatial distribution of bargaining power: Binding arbitration in Connecticut school districts. *Environment and Planning: Society and Space, 1,* 429–446.

Finch, M., & Nagel, T. W. (1984). Collective bargaining and the public schools: Reassessing labor policy in an era of reform. *Wisconsin Law Review, 1984*(6), 1580–1670.

Fox, W. S., & Wince, M. H. (1976). The structure and determinants of occupational militancy among public school teachers. *Industrial and Labor Relations Review, 30,* 47–58.

Freeman, R., & Medoff, J. (1984). *What do unions do?* New York: Basic.

Gallagher, D. G. (1978). Teacher bargaining and school district expenditures. *Industrial Relations, 17,* 231–237.

Gatewood, L. B. (1974). Factfinding in teacher disputes: The Wisconsin experience. *Monthly Labor Review, 97,* 47–51.

Glassman, A. M., & Belasco, J. A. (1976). The chapter chairman and school grievances. In A. M. Cresswell & M. J. Murphy (Eds.), *Education and collective bargaining.* Berkeley, CA: McCutchan.

Goldschmidt, S., & Stuart, L. (1984). *The extent of educational policy bargaining and its impacts on school system adaptability.* Mimeo., Center for Educational Policy and Management, Eugene, OR: University of Oregon.

Hall, C. W., & Carroll, N. E. (1973). The effects of teachers' organizations on salaries and class size. *Industrial and Labor Relations Review, 26,* 834–841.

Hellriegal, D., French, W., & Peterson, P. (1976). Collective negotiations and teachers: A behavioral analysis. In A. M. Cresswell & M. J. Murphy (Eds.), *Education and collective bargaining* (pp. 214–239). Berkeley, CA: McCutchan.

Jessup, D. K. (1978). Teacher unionization: A reassessment of rank and file motivations. *Sociology of Education, 51,* 44–55.

Johnson, S. M. (1984). *Teacher unions in schools.* Philadelphia, PA: Temple University Press.

Johnson, S. M., Nelson, N. W. C., & Potter, J. (1985, April). *Collective bargaining, school staffing, and reform.* Paper presented at the Annual Meeting of the American Educational Research Association, Chicago IL.

Kasper, H. (1970). The effect of collective bargaining on public school teachers' salaries. *Industrial and Labor Relations Review, 24,* 57–72.

Kerchner, C. T. (1978, Winter). From Scopes to scope: The genetic mutation of the school control issue. *Educational Administration Quarterly, 14*(1), 64–79.

Kerchner, C. T., & Mitchell, D. (1980). *The dynamics of public school collective bargaining and its impacts on governance, administration and teaching.* Washington, DC: National Institute of Education.

Kochan, T. A. (1973). Correlates of state public employee bargaining laws. *Industrial Relations, 12,* 322–337.

Kochan, T. A., & Baderschneider, J. (1978). Dependence on impasse procedures: Police and firefighters in New York State. *Industrial and Labor Relations Review, 31,* 431–449.

Kochan, T. A., & Baderschneider, J. (1981). Estimating the narcotic effect: Choosing techniques that fit the problem. *Industrial and*

Labor Relations Review, 35, 21–28.

Lieberman, M. (1979). Eggs that I have laid: Teacher bargaining reconsidered. *Phi Delta Kappan, 60,* 415–419.

Lipsky, D. (September 13, 1984). Personal communication.

Lipsky, D. B. (1983). The effect of collective bargaining on teacher pay: A review of the evidence. *Educational Administration Quarterly, 18,* 14–42.

Lipsky, D. B., & Drotning, J. E. (1973). The influence of collective bargaining on teachers' salaries in New York State. *Industrial and Labor Relations Review, 27,* 18–35.

Lipsky, D. B., & Drotning, J. E. (1977). The relation between teacher salaries and the use of impasse procedures under New York's Taylor Law: 1968–1972. *Journal of Collective Negotiations, 6*(3), 229–244.

Lubetsky, K. P. (1977). Will the NEA and the AFT ever merge? *Education Forum, 41,* 309–316.

McDonnell, L., & Pascal, A. (1979). *Organized teachers in American schools.* Santa Monica, CA: Rand.

Mitchell, D. E., Kerchner, C. T., Erck, W., & Pryor, G. (1980). *The impact of collective bargaining on school management and policy.* Claremont, CA: Claremont Graduate School.

Murphy, M. J., & Hoover, D. (1976). Negotiations at the crossroads: Increased professionalization of reinforced bureaucracy. In A. M. Cresswell & M. J. Murphy (Eds.), *Education and collective bargaining* (pp. 476–483). Berkeley, CA: McCutchan.

Perry, C. R. (1979). Teacher bargaining: The experience in nine systems. *Industrial and Labor Relations Review, 33,* 3–17.

Perry, C. R., & Wildman, W. A. (1970). *The impact of negotiations in public education: The evidence from the schools.* Worthington, OH: Charles A. Jones.

Rosenthal, A. (1969). *Pedagogues and power.* Syracuse: Syracuse University Press.

Thornton, R. (1971). The effects of collective negotiations on teachers' salaries. *Quarterly Review of Economics and Business, 2,* 37–46.

Tomkiewicz, J. (1979). Determinants of teacher militancy: Factors affecting the decision to strike. *Journal of Collective Negotiations, 8,* 91–96.

Tyack, D. (1974). *The one best system: A history of American urban education.* Cambridge, MA: Harvard University Press.

Urban, W. J. (1982). *Why teachers organized.* Detroit, MI: Wayne State University Press.

Walton, R. E., & McKersie, R. B. (1965). *A behavioral theory of labor negotiations.* New York: McGraw-Hill.

Weintraub, A., & Thornton, R. J. (1976). Why teachers strike: The economic and legal determinants. *Journal of Collective Negotiations, 5*(3), 193–206.

Wellington, H. H., & Winter, R. K., Jr. (1971). *The unions and the cities,* Washington, DC: Brookings Institution.

Wesley, E. B. (1957). *NEA: The first hundred years: The building of the teaching profession.* New York: Harper.

West, A. M. (1980). *The National Education Association: The power base for education.* New York: Free Press.

Winick, C. (1963). When teachers strike. *Teachers College Record, 64,* 593–604.

Wirtz, W. (1963, February). Address before the National Academy of Arbitrators, Chicago. *Daily Labor Report,* F1–F4.

CHAPTER 29

The Law and the Courts

Tyll van Geel

In the aftermath of the 1954 decision in *Brown v. Board of Education*, which declared unconstitutional purposeful racial segregation in the public schools, the extent and depth of judicial involvement with the schools dramatically increased.[1] The judiciary acknowledged, for example, that students were entitled to a variety of constitutional protections.[2] The passage of federal statutes protecting students provided a new predicate for increased judicial involvement with the schools.[3] The courts interpreted these newly enacted statutes as authorizing private individuals to seek judicial protection of the rights created in the statute, even though Congress arguably intended these rights to be protected exclusively through the mechanism of administrative enforcement of the laws.[4] Even in the absence of explicit Congressional concurrence, courts also have held that these laws support a claim for money damages on behalf of an individual whose statutory rights were violated.[5] In a related development, the courts have participated in the reactivation of an old civil rights statute, Section 1983 of the Civil Rights Act of 1871, to enable students and teachers to seek monetary damages for the violation of their constitutional rights.[6] And to further protect individuals against official laxity, indifference, or even hostility with regard to their statutory rights, the federal courts have supported requests for orders directed against federal agencies, requiring more vigorous enforcement of the nondiscrimination statutes.[7]

Though few would question that the character and

Consultant/reviewers: Michael La Morte, University of Georgia; and Martha McCarthy, Indiana University

extent of judicial involvement with the schools has changed, for reasons that are not well understood, different observers have offered different perceptions of the actual impact of the courts on public schooling. Graglia says it is arguable that the Supreme Court has become in domestic affairs the most important institution in U.S. government.[8] Glazer. in an article entitled "Towards an Imperial Judiciary," said that "the distinctive characteristic of more recent activist courts has been to *extend* the role of what government could do, even when government did not want to do it."[9] In contrast, Kirp has said that the courts' impact on education, though great, has been less direct than generally believed. And, talking from the vantage point of 1980, he said that with the major exception of the desegregation suits, he saw a generally marked reluctance on the part of the courts to play too active a role in the detailed operation of the schools.[10]

This chapter seeks to improve understanding of the impact of the courts on schooling. The first section will briefly discuss a number of the federal statutes that have importantly served to shape educational policy. The second and longest section of the chapter will analyze a vast range of judicial opinions to bring out the general trends, themes, and principles of the relevant opinions. This analysis will also assess the impact of the judiciary on the operations of the public schools.

FEDERAL INVOLVEMENT IN PUBLIC SCHOOLING

During the past three to four decades, federal involvement in the public schools has taken a revolutionary turn. Not only have the federal courts engaged more deeply in shaping educational policy, but Congress and the federal bureaucracy have as well. Through a dozen or more different major pieces of legislation, Congress has acted on equalitarian impulses to protect a variety of children and students who were treated in ways that have now come to be thought of as invidiously discriminatory. Some of the federal initiatives directed extra financial support to students who were either receiving less support than other students or whose educational problems were such that they required a special and more expensive program of instruction to enable them to learn what other children learned at less expense.[11] But most of the new legislation was directed to ending the differences in treatment among pupils and teachers based solely on race, sex, handicap, age, national origin, or religion.[12] Perhaps most striking about this latter body of legislation is that it has been interpreted to permit, and require, expensive educational programs and practices of special benefit to groups of children who come to school disadvantaged in some way.[13] Although these affirmative, special, and compensatory educational efforts have come to be accepted, albeit with grumbling about the cost, intense controversy remains regarding interpretations of Title VII and the Constitution as permitting a variety of forms of affirmative or reverse discrimination in employment.[14]

A less dramatic, but arguably a very important, influence on education has been exercised by an old civil rights statute, the Civil Rights Act of 1871, known today as § 1983.[15] This law makes a person who, acting under the cover of law, deprives an individual of federal constitutional or statutory rights liable in a suit "at law or in equity" (that is, in a suit for monetary or injunctive relief). In 1975 the Supreme Court said public school officials were not immune from suit under this statute if the officials knew or reasonably should have known their actions would violate a student's constitutional rights or if those officials took the action with a malicious intent to deprive a student of his or her constitutional right.[16] In a later case the Court said a governmental unit like a school board may be liable under § 1983 even if all officials acted with good faith. If an individual's constitutional rights have been violated, the board is strictly liable for damages.[17] Thus today § 1983 has become a mainstay in educational litigation as pupils and teachers seek not only the injunctive relief, typically available in constitutional cases, but also damages from individual school officials as well as school boards in constitutional and nonconstitutional cases.[18] It is an interesting empirical question whether the expansion of the availability of monetary damages because of the increased use of § 1983 has intimidated

school officials so that they, for example, are today more reluctant to enforce discipline in the schools. An issue that may arise in the future is whether § 1983 ought to be amended by Congress to exempt school officials from its coverage as a way of eliminating discouragement of strict disciplinary enforcement in schools.

DOCTRINAL DEVELOPMENTS

The first section focuses on the courts and private schooling, the oldest form of schooling, over which the political struggles have been so significant. The next section examines judicial efforts in redesigning the governing system of the public schools. The third section reviews the judicial response to efforts to exclude various kinds of children from the public schools and to segregate them when they are admitted. Remaining sections of the chapter take up the judiciary's intervention into the school program. The penultimate section examines those judicially imposed restraints within which educators must operate when fulfilling their duty to maintain order in the schools. The last section briefly touches on the courts' protection of those rights of teachers not covered earlier.

Private Schooling and the State

Private educational efforts in the home or in private schools comprise the oldest formal educational programs in the United States, but especially in the 20th century they have been the target of legislative suspicion and hostility.[19] As the states have exercised their police and *parens patrie* powers over private education, judicial challenges have been raised, resulting in a body of doctrine protecting private educational efforts. The Supreme Court has said the state's interest in educating children is not strong enough to provide constitutional warrant for a requirement that all children must be educated exclusively in public schools.[20] The Court has also said that only reasonable regulations of private schooling are permissible; thus, regulations that foreclose educational pluralism by forcing private school programs to become identical to the public schools are impermissible.[21] Also, the National Labor Relations Board lacks jurisdiction to regulate labor relations in private religious schools, but one federal court has ruled that there is no constitutional obstacle to the extension of jurisdiction by a state labor relations board over labor relations between parochial schools and their lay teachers.[22] And Amish parents won from the Supreme Court a ruling that after the eighth grade they need not send their children to any formal school program despite the state's requirement of 2 more years of formal education.[23] To force the Amish to comply with the compulsory education law, said the Court, would violate their right of free exercise of religion.

The Supreme Court has not, however, totally freed private schooling from significant state regulation. As noted earlier, reasonable regulations may be imposed. Furthermore, private schools that discriminate on the basis of race both may be deprived of their status as tax exempt institutions and are legally vulnerable to suit under an old federal civil rights law.[24] These decisions underscore the enormous importance the Court places on the effort to end racial discrimination, for claims of religious freedom were overridden in pursuit of the goal of racial equality.

Though all this may be clear enough, these decisions have left unanswered the Supreme Court's position on a number of important questions regarding the scope of state discretion to regulate private schools. The lower federal and state courts have answered these questions but in ways that vary from state to state. Thus in mid-1980 there is no certainty regarding the status of the following constitutional questions: (a) May states prohibit home instruction;[25] (b) may states require all private teachers, including parents who teach their children at home, to be certified;[26] (c) are some zoning and building code requirements unconstitutional as applied to private religious schools insofar as they might infringe the schools' right to the free exercise of their religion;[27] (d) how far may a state go in regulating the method of instruction in private schools;[28] and (e) to what extent, if any, may a state regulate the content of private instruction that may be racist or subversive?[29] Although state courts have been for the most part inhospitable to the claim of Christian Fundamentalist parents and schools to be exempted from various state laws such as those requiring all private school teachers to be state certified, current Supreme Court doctrine suggests that the lower courts should have acted differently.[30]

Judicial conflict over questions of the order posed above grows from a deep level of ambiguity. The Supreme Court has still provided no clear explanation as to why not all students may be required to attend public schools or why private schooling may not be required to be a faithful replication of public schooling. One writer suggests that the Court wants to preserve private schooling as a check on the potentially overweening voice of government in education—a protection that is needed to prevent falsification of consent in a democracy and/or to insure the student's interest in freedom of belief.[31] Nor is it clear what conception of education and the public interest the Court accepts as sufficiently important to warrant a state's intrusion

into the educational efforts of the family. In short, even with appreciation that doctrine in this area was developed by balancing freedom and autonomy against certain state interests, the public cannot be sure of the Court's interpretation of the values on either side of the balance nor the terms on which the two sides of the scale are being compared.

As for state efforts to assist private religious schools financially, a series of almost arbitrary Supreme Court opinions designates some forms of aid as acceptable and others not. Bus transportation to school, the loan of secular textbooks to private school students, diagnostic and/or therapeutic services offered in a mobile van outside the private schools, and cost reimbursement for administering and grading state-required examinations are among the acceptable forms of aid.[32] But the government may not provide remedial services for the educationally disadvantaged through programs offered in church-affiliated schools; offer community education programs in church-affiliated schools; loan audio-visual equipment or maps to students attending private religous schools; support the cost of transportation for field trips; nor pay for purely secular remedial and therapeutic services offered on the grounds of a private school.[33]

The depth of confusion is well illustrated by a comparison of two opinions issued 10 years apart. In a case striking down a New York statute that allowed certain eligible parents who send their children to private school to obtain either some tuition reimbursement from the state or to lower their state income tax by subtracting from their gross income a portion of the costs of sending their children to private school, the Court stressed the degree to which the program would help religious schools, how it would encourage parents to send their children to private schools, and how this program would foster an annual religiously divisive legislative battle over its enlargement.[34] Ten years later, in upholding a Minnesota law that allowed taxpayers to deduct from gross income certain expenses in educating their children in either public or private schools (cost for tuition, textbooks, and transportation could be deducted, but obviously only private school parents could take advantage of the tuition deduction), the Court played down the significance of the same kind of statistical and financial data that were presented in the New York case and, in addition, viewed the data as not supporting the proposition that the tax deduction had the primary effect of aiding religious schools. The aid flowed through the parents; thus, said the Court, it had only an indirect effect on the private schools—an argument the Court had rejected a decade earlier.[35]

The Court's current attitude toward private religious education is hard to discern. As noted earlier, the Court has treated free exercise claims generously. But it has in the 1980s both upheld new forms of financial aid to religious schools and struck such aid down. The latter cases included arrangements whereby public school employees entered private religious schools to provide a variety of instructional (including Title I remedial services) and other services.[36] Perhaps the actions signal a Court in transition, and the direction it will take depends on who departs from the Court and who is appointed.

Governing the Public Schools: Opening the Political Process and Expanding the Role of Teachers

If a state so chose, it arguably could limit its effort to protect its children to regulation and/or financial assistance of private schooling, but all the states have chosen to establish their own systems of public education. Judicial involvement in the operation of those systems has been extensive, as indicated earlier. One area, however, where especially the federal courts have played only a limited role is in guiding the design of the governing structure of the public system. Though state courts traditionally have played an important role in allocating authority by interpreting the statutes that outline the governing structure of the educational system, the federal courts have limited their involvement to making sure that participation in educational decision-making processes is not arbitrarily closed.[37] The philosophy of government that seems to guide these opinions does not stress that certain groups have a right either to electoral success or an impact on decision making but that individuals have a right to participate in the democratic process of running the schools, and their exclusion may be maintained only because of the most substantial and compelling reasons.

The courts have imposed this philosophy on the states in a variety of contexts. The Supreme Court struck down voting eligibility requirements that had the effect of prohibiting an unmarried, childless man living with his parents rent free from voting in school district elections.[38] Malapportionment of electoral districts, which had the effect of diluting the vote of residents in the more populated electoral districts, has been disallowed.[39] At-large electoral systems established with the intent (a difficult point to prove) and with the effect of discriminating against black candidates for office have been declared unconstitutional.[40] At-large elections may also be struck down under the Voting Rights Act of 1965 if they merely have the effect of discriminating against minority voters and candidates.[41]

Teachers have also been assured of a right to participate in the public dialogue that shapes public school policy. In an important but in many respects ambiguous opinion—an ambiguity that opens the door to a wide range of interpretations by the lower courts and that leaves school officials and teachers alike somewhat in doubt as to their relative rights—the Supreme Court in *Pickering* protected the individual teacher's right publicly to criticize the school board on matters of *public concern* even if that criticism were "harmful" in the sense of turning public opinion against the board's policy or against the practices of individual school officials.[42] The scope of *Pickering* was later limited in *Connick v. Myers*, when the Court said that employee grievances of a personal nature regarding such matters as personnel decisions were generally not to be considered a matter of public concern and hence were not protected speech. The Court noted that whether an employee's public criticism was a matter of public concern had to be determined by the content, form, and context of a given statement.[43] The *Pickering* and *Connick* decisions have spawned considerable litigation.[44]

Teachers' rights to speak out at public school board meetings on important issues have received support even if those issues are currently the subject of bargaining between the board and the teachers' union and the public dialogue between teacher and board threaten the union's right to be the exclusive bargaining representative for all the teachers.[45] An important obstacle, however, in the teacher's ability legally to defend his or her right to free speech is the requirement that the teacher must prove that the board's sanction (dismissal, transfer, loss of pay, and the like) would not have been administered "but for" the legitimate exercise of the right of freedom of speech.[46]

Protecting the constitutional right of teachers to join unions represents another way courts have assured teachers a significant voice in the formation of public school policy.[47] The courts have not taken the next step of constitutionally requiring the school board to bargain with the union (in a majority of states a statute imposes such a duty), but some courts have said that local school boards may bargain even in the absence of a statute granting the board this power.[48] The majority union may even be given exclusive access to the teachers' mailboxes, but the right to strike may be prohibited.[49] The individual teacher who asserts a right of nonassociation has received minimal constitutional protection. Even though a teacher may not be forced to join the union, he or she can be required to pay union dues with the further stipulation that if the union uses this money for political purposes with which the individual disagrees, the teacher may ask back that small percentage of his or her dues that supported the political activity.[50] It is as wrong, say the courts, to sanction teachers for speaking out as it is to force them to support speech activities with which they disagree.

The judiciary could indirectly but significantly constrain the authority of the state and local school board to control the school program—at least its themes, messages, and point of view—and drastically expand the authority of teachers to control school policy by recognizing a teacher's broad and absolute right to academic freedom. In the face of this reality, the courts have proceeded with caution when ruling on a constitutional challenge by a teacher to a board's decision to dismiss because of what the teacher said or did in the classroom. This caution is most clearly seen in the Supreme Court, which has never recognized a right to academic freedom in the classroom for elementary and secondary school teachers. (In fact, though the Court has tossed encomiums at the notion of a right of academic freedom for teachers in higher education, it has never actually decided a case based on this right.[51])

As for the lower courts, they have held that, even if there is a principle of academic freedom applicable at the elementary school level, its scope does not include the introduction of obscenity or near obscenity into the classroom; indoctrination by the teacher; selection of the basic texts to be used in a course; selection of a method of instruction, such as team teaching; or a decision to change the basic content of a course from, say, consumer economics to politics.[52]

To deal with issues that arguably do fall within the scope of a principle of academic freedom, the courts have assumed that the principle is relevant to the decision but that the school board may nevertheless discipline the teacher if the board has been able to demonstrate that a basic interest of the board was frustrated or was about to be frustrated by the teacher's behavior. Hence, the lower courts have said dismissal is permissible if the teacher's activity did or was reasonably expected to cause material and substantial disruption; if what the teacher said, or brought into the class, was not relevant to the course and was shocking and disturbing for the students in the class; or if the materials introduced or statements made did not serve a serious educational purpose and were inappropriate.[53]

Using such general, even vague and ambiguous, guidelines, the lower courts have both protected and not protected teachers. For example, dismissals were upheld when teachers introduced into French, industrial arts, and language arts classes various articles, poems, and pictures dealing with a 1969 rock festival.[54] Another dismissal was upheld after a teacher in a biology class had spoken about his personal experiences with prostitutes in Japan and after he used as much as a whole class session to criticize in strong language the superintendent, the school board, and the school system, and to complain about teacher salaries.[55] In another case the court upheld the denial of tenure after the teacher had used his classroom as "his personal forum to promote union activities, to sanction polygamy, to attack marriage, to criticize other teachers, and to sway and influence the minds of young people without a full and proper explanation of both sides of the issue."[56] In contrast, other teachers were protected even though they discussed the word *fuck* in class; assigned a serious article that used the word *motherfucker*; assigned Kurt Vonnegut's book *Welcome to the Monkey House*, which contained arguably vulgar material; wore a black armband in class to protest against the Vietnam War; used role playing to teach about Reconstruction; and assigned in a civics class materials on the Vietnam War and race relations.[57] As to nonparticipation by the teacher in the pledge of allegiance, one court upheld the teacher's right not to do so in light of the fact that her nonparticipation did not cause material and substantial disruption of the school program because another teacher was also present in the classroom who did lead the students in the pledge.[58] But another teacher was dismissed when she said her religious beliefs made it impossible for her to teach subjects having to do with love of country, the flag, or other patriotic matters.[59] Finally, a number of decisions have held that the due process clause of the Fourteenth Amendment prohibits punishment without prior notice that the challenged behavior was forbidden.[60]

Despite the fact that a number of courts have upheld the free speech rights of teachers in the classroom, there does not exist any adequate analysis from the courts to explain the results. Public schools, with their emphasis on socialization and inculcation, differ from universities, where the search for truth is, arguably, paramount and academic freedom may be justified as necessary in order to facilitate this search. Indeed, one court has said a proposed contract provision containing the statement that it was the right of the teacher to teach the truth as he or she saw it was not a mandatory subject of negotiations.[61] Perhaps, then, if teachers are to enjoy some degree of freedom of expression in the classroom, this freedom must be established as a necessary check on the effort of the school board to wholly control the content of the school curriculum—a check instituted to provide pupils some assurance that their right to receive a wide range of ideas is protected.

Who Must be Served and Where

The principle of equality on which the courts have relied in assuring the openness of the political process also has been the basis for assuring that the states operate their public systems of education so that they are open to all students. When used in this way, the principle of equality functions to create the appearance that the U.S. Constitution embodies a positive right on the part of all children to an education. However, the requirement that public schooling not be closed to the children of illegal aliens, black children, or handicapped children has been premised not on the notion of a right to an education but on the view that excluding certain identifiable groups of children from the schools may be accomplished only for compelling reasons and that the reasons preferred by the states in specific cases were constitutionally insufficient.[62] Thus, an exclusionary policy is not constitutionally warranted in order to keep total educational expenses down, nor to fulfill a policy of educational triage, nor to exclude those who may be difficult to teach or whose presence, arguably, would affect the quality of the educational program. Federal statutory law as interpreted by the Court has also dealt with the problem of "functional exclusion": that is, the problem of when students are not physically excluded from the public schools but are offered a program of instruction they are unable to make use of because of language barriers or physical or mental handicap. Schools enrolling such pupils must make special efforts to overcome the language difficulties of their non-English-speaking pupils and provide such other services as catheterization to ensure that the handicapped pupil can make use of the school program.[63] States, however, may continue to make their schools available only to pupils who meet legitimate residency requirements.[64] To say these opinions are concerned exclusively with inequalities and relative deprivation is, however, to diminish the complexity of the thinking behind the results. The Court has not been concerned only with the competitive disadvantage imposed when certain groups are excluded but also with the need for all children for a basic minimally adequate education.[65] By viewing the denial of formal education in these terms, the Court has taken an important step toward accepting what it has said the Constitution does not establish—a basic right to an education, which all children enjoy and which would be violated if the state evenhandedly closed the public schools to all children.

As important as the decisions opening the schools to the excluded have been, these decisions are dwarfed in practical social significance by the 30-year effort on the part of the judiciary and the executive branch of the federal government to assure that those pupils not excluded are not assigned to schools or classrooms on the basis of race in order to promote racial segregation.[66] This is not the place to recount the long, tortuous history of the judiciary's commitment to and engagement with this effort. However, three topics do warrant mention and analysis: (a) the de jure-de facto distinction and the judicial effort to end de jure segregation; (b) the remedy required to undo unlawful segregation; and (c) the basic principles that seem to have driven the judiciary's program of reform.

The de jure-de facto distinction has been widely used, but specifying the difference without ambiguity has bedeviled legal analysis since *Brown v. Board of Education* was handed down in 1954.[67] Perhaps the best approach is to distinguish among four categories: (a) action taken by a school board because of its segregating effects; (b) action taken for other reasons and in spite of its segregating effects; (c) inaction indulged in because of its tendency to perpetuate segregation; and (d) inaction indulged in for other reasons and despite that tendency. De jure segregation is segregation produced by item (a), and some would say item (c); de facto segregation is the product of (b) or (d). Even though the factual situation in *Brown* involved a classic instance of de jure segregation (action taken because of the segregating effect), language in the opinion stressing the harmful effect of segregation left room for the claim that the Court also viewed de facto segregation to be unconstitutional.[68] Subsequent decisions dealing with the issue of the appropriate remedy in school segregation cases also left the question open to debate, but in 1973 the Court said that only de jure segregation was unconstitutional. In 1976 it reaffirmed that position in an opinion emphasizing that only "intentional" racial discrimination violated the Fourteenth Amendment.[69]

Despite appearances, however, a strong case can be made that the Court has in fact been concerned with eliminating not just de jure segregation but some aspects of de facto segregation as well.[70] In the 1973 opinion, the Court said that once the plaintiff had established that the board had purposefully segregated a substantial portion of the district, a presumption arises (absent a showing that the district was divided into clearly unrelated units) that the rest of the district was also segregated. Even if the district were so divided, the Court reasoned that proof of intentional segregation in one area was probative as to the intent to segregate in others.[71] The practical effect of these rebuttable presumptions is that they open the door to an attack on de facto segregation in one part of the district based on the existence of de jure segregation in another substantial part.

The Court's handling of the "foreseeability test" also indicates its willingness to see de facto segregation swept away—up to a point. This test, which is really a rule guiding what inferences may be drawn from evidence, states that normally an actor is presumed to have intended the natural and foreseeable consequences of his or her acts. Under the strongest version of this test, if a school board establishes a neighborhood school policy that has the foreseeable effect of producing segregated schools, it may be inferred the board intended the segregation. Similarly, if the board refuses to change (inaction) an old student assignment policy that in the face of demographic changes yields segregated schools, under the strong version of the test an intent to segregate may be inferred.[72] Obviously, the use of this test obliterates any meaningful distinction between de jure and de facto segregation; knowing this, the Supreme Court in several opinions has insisted that the test may not be the sole basis for a finding that a school board engaged in intentional segregation.[73] But the lower federal courts have engaged in a virtual rebellion against this limitation on the use of the foreseeability test, and the Supreme Court has given in to its rebellious subordinates by refusing to review and reverse even those lower court opinions that exclusively rely on the test to find school boards in violation of the Fourteenth Amendment.[74] Finally, the Court, as a practical matter, ignored the de jure–de facto distinction when it announced that any district that had been purposefully segregated in 1954 would be deemed to be purposefully segregated forever after unless the school board had after 1954 voluntarily taken affirmative steps to desegregate by affirmatively mixing the races. In the absence of such efforts, even if the district had after 1954 sustained a large increase in its population of black pupils, every existing jot of segregation would be attributed to the policy of purposeful segregation, which itself could have stopped the day *Brown v. Board of Education* was announced.[75] In sum, despite its public insistence on the de jure–de facto distinction, the Court has both pressed ahead with the elimination of de facto segregation and stepped aside to let the lower courts, which are even more committed to the task, have their way in this matter.

Once a school district has been found to have engaged in de jure segregation, the courts order the district to make an affirmative effort to undo the segregation for which it was held responsible.[76] The lower courts enjoy enormous discretion to fashion an appropriate remedy. They may require districts to undertake such steps as busing, school closings, the rezoning of attendance zones, required compensatory and remedial education, teacher retraining, the imposition of increased taxes to pay for the desegregation plan, and affirmative discrimination in the hiring of teachers.[77] As occurred in Boston, the judge may even take over the operation of a school to assure the fulfillment of the desegregation plan.[78]

However, it is misleading to view the remedy phase of the case as simply involving the substitution of the federal judge for the local school board. Frequently, the remedy finally imposed on the district is the product of a complex bargaining process among a variety of participants—school board, superintendent, teachers, parent organizations, community organizations, the local chapter of the NAACP, and the mayor —with the judge or a representative of the judge acting as mediator and perhaps ultimately as arbitrator.[79] The most significant limitation on the lower courts in forging a remedy is that judges are not free to require the involvement of other school districts, such as the suburbs surrounding a city, in the desegregation plan unless it is established that those suburbs were directly involved in producing the segregation in the city.[80] The remedy phase of the case comes to an end, and the court must relinquish jurisdiction once a satisfactory desegregation plan has been fully implemented and the segregation attributable to the district's wrongdoing has been eliminated. Even if the school buildings resegregate at this point, because of demographic changes, the district need not affirmatively once again mix the races unless it is once again established that the recurring segregation was the "intentional" result of school board action or inaction.[81]

What is most surprising about this body of law is that it has evolved without any treatment, except perhaps in the first *Brown* decision, of the question of why governmental segregation of the races is constitutionally wrong. Some have argued segregation is wrong because the Constitution is colorblind and any use of a racial criterion is irrational.[82] Others have stressed that segregation involves the purposeful imposition of a harm on an individual because of race, an evil that the Constitution forbids.[83] Under another line of reasoning, the Fourteenth Amendment requires government to treat each individual as worthy of respect and as one who belongs, and this principle means not only that de jure segregation is wrong but it also applies to any policy that demeans and harms people, even unintentionally.[84] A last theory is that the Fourteenth Amendment requires government affirmatively to seek an end to the subordinate position of blacks, and any governmental action affirmatively maintaining that subordination is per force unconstitutional.[85] The underlying debate over the meaning of the Fourteenth Amendment may well have led to the somewhat confused doctrinal developments in this area.

Religious, Political, and Cultural Socialization

Judicial orders have extended beyond constraining pupil assignment policies to controlling the school program itself. Some judicially imposed constraints are direct, as when the courts limit the introduction of religious exercises into the schools; others are indirect, as when the courts protect academic freedom. Once again, the body of doctrine is replete with ambiguity and uncertainty.

Sectarian Socialization

The Supreme Court's reaction to the introduction of religion into the operation of the public schools has been almost wholly negative. Struck down have been such practices as opening the school day with a governmental-composed nondenominational prayer;[86] opening the school day with readings from the Bible and recitation of the Lord's prayer;[87] a state law authorizing a period of silence for meditation or voluntary prayer;[88] posting copies of the Ten Commandments on the walls of the school building;[89] the holding of religious classes in the school building;[90] and a state law that made it a crime for a teacher to teach the theory of evolution.[91] Only a very modest released-time program for students to receive religious instruction off public school grounds has been upheld.[92]

These cases have not been the easiest for courts to decide because of the unavoidable conflict between the demands of the free exercise clause of the First Amendment (which serves to bar governmental hostility toward religion) and the establishment clause of that same amendment (which serves to bar governmental assistance to and support of religion). But despite the arguments that voluntary prayers must be allowed in the schools if free exercise of religion is not to be denied, a majority of the Court arguably took the position that not to strike these practices down would be counterproductive and would in fact involve the loss of freedom.[93] First, even if the prayers were voluntary in theory, in practice peer pressure could be aroused to force the reluctant to participate. Second, the very fact that the religious practice is state sanctioned may induce an impressionable child to believe in religion per se or in a particular religion that may or may not be the parents' religion. Third, governmental support of religion may produce deep political conflict over religious issues that itself is harmful and that may stimulate various groups to grab at the reigns of power in order to impose their own views. Fourth, banning religious practices from the schools is itself not a hostile act toward religion because ample opportunity for the free exercise of religion continues to exist outside the school.

Though all this may be clear enough, the Supreme Court's opinions have been sufficiently ambiguous to leave room for a variety of lower court responses to the rather persistent efforts of school officials to introduce religion or religion-linked practices into the schools.

Thus, for example, lower court opinions have upheld a Christmas program that involved the singing of religious hymns;[94] allowed the saying of prayers at graduation and baccalaureate exercises;[95] and upheld a statutory requirement that teachers teach Christian virtues.[96] The lower courts have split in their opinions as to whether student-run religious clubs must be allowed to use public school facilities and on whether a minute of silence for meditation may be offered students at the start of the school day.[97] (Legal commentators have also disagreed over the constitutionality of the required moment of silence.[98]) Yet other courts have struck down the use of student volunteers to open the day with a prayer;[99] the teaching of transcendental meditation;[100] the singing of a religious anthem at a pep rally;[101] classes in which the Bible is studied in a nonobjective manner;[102] the distribution in school by the Gideon Society of free Bibles to students who want them;[103] the requirement that disclaimers be printed in biology books saying that the theory of evolution is but a theory when the Book of Genesis is not required to carry the same disclaimer;[104] and the teaching of the theory of scientific creationism in the public schools (the court said it was religion, not science).[105]

Despite these differences among the lower courts, the basic thrust of judicial doctrine has been to rid the schools of most overt religious influences. The constitutional favor in which the purely secular program finds itself is perhaps best exemplified by judicial opinions that refuse to recognize as valid the claim that a particular course (like a biology course or a sex education course) or book is so at odds with the religious beliefs of the student that the free-exercise clause required that the course or book had to be dropped or had to be revised by affording equal time for different theories of human creation.[106] Courts have, however, been more receptive to free-exercise claims that seek not a revision in the instructional program for all students but only that the complaining individual be excused from the offending course.[107]

Still, it is important to reemphasize the changing attitude on the Supreme Court toward religion. As noted earlier, the Court has become more hospitable toward state legislation that allows financial assistance to flow to private religious schools. More important for these purposes, the Court has in two decisions upheld the tradition of opening each legislative day with a prayer by a chaplain paid by the state and the erection by the City of Pawtucket, Rhode Island, in a park owned by a nonprofit organization a Christmas display that included a crèche as well as other symbols and decorations associated with Christmas.[108] These decisions may signal a less hostile attitude toward religious influences on or in government and may mean that efforts to introduce silent meditation and prayer in the public schools will not to be opposed by the Court and that the new Equal Access law, if and when it is challenged, will be sustained.[109]

Political Socialization

Though the Supreme Court has been deeply involved in secularizing the curriculum, its role in directly constraining efforts at political socialization in the public schools has been much more modest. (As will be discussed later, the *indirect* involvement of the Supreme Court and the lower courts has been more extensive.) In the Court's first venture into this area, it upheld a school requirement that all students participate in a flag salute ceremony by saying the pledge of allegiance to the flag, but then only 3 years later in *West Virginia v. Barnette* (1943) the Court reversed itself, ruling that compulsion to say the pledge violated the student's rights as protected by the free speech clause of the First Amendment.[110] The interpretation of the *Barnette* opinion is the subject of some dispute, but arguably the Court's reasons for striking down the compulsory pledge was that this method of fostering patriotism and loyalty was too coercive an invasion of the student's right to freedom of belief. The lower courts have extended this ruling by holding that students may neither be required to stand nor to leave the room during the ceremony.[111]

In prohibiting required participation in the recitation of the pledge of allegiance, the Court made clear it was not prohibiting instruction in history and the structure and organization of government, including the guarantees of civil liberty, as a way of inspiring patriotism and loyalty. And as of the mid-1980s, all members of the Court have gone on record in support of the proposition that a primary function of public schooling is the inculcation in students of fundamental values deemed necessary for the maintenance of a democratic political system. Local boards of education, agree the members of the Court, must be allowed to transmit community values, including respect for authority and other traditional values, be they social, moral, or political.[112]

At this point, however, the opinions of the justices sharply diverge as shown in *Board of Education, Island Trees Union Free School District No. 26 v. Pico* (1982), a case that involved a constitutional challenge to the removal of 10 books from the school library by the school board—books described by the board as anti-American, anti-Christian, anti-Semitic, and filthy.[113] Three justices, despite agreeing with the view that the board had authority to inculcate, said that if the books had been removed with the intent to suppress ideas,

then the student's right to receive ideas had been violated. Thus, they voted to send the case back for a trial on this issue. Justice Blackmun also voted to remand the case for trial, but he wanted the issue at trial to be whether the school board had been discriminating against ideas merely because of disagreement with them. He rejected the notion that students had a right to receive ideas because this position implied an affirmative duty on the part of the board to supply information. (A fifth justice, Justice White, without expressly adopting a position on the question of whether the removal of books from a library could violate the First Amendment, also voted to send the case back to trial.) The four dissenters said in effect that the board's authority to inculcate was almost constitutionally unrestrained; thus the removal of the books in this case was perfectly proper. The power to inculcate legally entailed the power to shape the content of the curriculum and the library. Several dissenters did agree, however, that if the school board, for example, removed from the library all books written by Democrats or removed all books written by black authors or all books that advocated racial equality and integration, then a constitutional problem would be raised.

Several important limitations need to be noted at this point. All the justices in *Pico* agreed that books could be removed if they were vulgar or for other sound educational reasons.[114] Perhaps most significantly, the three justices who embraced the notion of a right to receive ideas pointedly noted that their opinion did not deal with the board's control of the purchase and removal of books from the *classroom*. Thus, in mid-1980 no majority on the Court has yet decided that students have First-Amendment-based rights that limit the board's control of the curriculum in the classroom. All that is on record is an oft-repeated general warning from the Court that a "pall of orthodoxy" may not be imposed on the classroom.[115] This situation is unfortunate; a strong argument can be made that the present state of constitutional doctrine both undervalues the student's interest in freedom of belief and overvalues the state's interest in inculcation.[116] It is also worth noting that there is a basic discrepancy in the degree to which the Court protects students' interest in freedom of religious belief as opposed to their interest in freedom of nonreligious belief.

As for racial bias in the books selected for use in the schools, only one lower court has wrestled with the problem, and it concluded that the Mississippi textbook rating committee was motivated by racial prejudice when it approved for use in the schools of the state one book but rejected another.[117] Plaintiffs argued that the book selected deprecated black Mississippians and championed white supremacy. They pointed out that for 10 years the rating committee had given its approval to only one particular book. The court noted this point and concluded that not only had the whole textbook rating system been established to assure that controversial materials were excluded from the school curriculum but also that the rejected book had been rejected for racial reasons.

It is important to recall at this point that to the extent courts protect teachers' interest in academic freedom, the ability of the state and school boards to impose on students their own particular viewpoint is checked and constrained. Academic freedom, like the protection of the right of students to free speech, opens the school to a set of voices other than the official voice of the state or school board.

Grooming, Pregnancy, Marriage, and Sex Roles

Besides controlling the teacher's presentation of self, boards have also sought to educate pupils in grooming habits by regulating pupils' styles of hair and dress. (These rules have also been supported by boards as necessary to avoid disruption in the schools and to avoid accidents that may be caused by long hair getting tangled in machinery. This rationale of the rules will be examined later.) The response of the judiciary to grooming rules has been decidedly mixed, with the federal circuit courts badly split over whether hairstyle rules are an impermissible invasion of the student's interest in liberty.[118] Somewhat greater leeway arguably has been afforded school boards to control clothing style, perhaps because these controls are ultimately a less intrusive invasion of personal autonomy—after all, clothes can be changed after school is over.[119]

Rules controlling behavior were once also a mainstay of school efforts to discourage students from marriage and sexual intercourse.[120] The recent trend has been to strike down rules that exclude married and pregnant students from participation in the regular school program.[121] (Title IX also prohibits exclusion on the basis of pregnancy.[122]) The results of these cases should not come as a surprise in an era in which the Supreme Court has upheld the right of the mature minor to choose whether or not to have an abortion free from either a parental or governmental veto.[123]

The judiciary has also rejected school board policies based on the assumption that girls are the physically weaker and more vulnerable sex and consequently either need special protection or are and *should be* less interested in participating in competitive athletics. A perhaps surprising number of courts, but not all, have said girls may try out for a place on a boys' athletic team, even in a contact sport.[124] Some of these courts have so held, even though a girls' team in the

same sport was available.[125] Similar decisions have been reached in cases involving noncontact sports.[126] Boys have achieved mixed results when they have sought from the courts an order to enable them to try out for the girls' team.[127] When the boys lose, the theory that has prevailed holds that excluding boys is a permissible way to promote equal athletic opportunity for girls. Though the lower courts have accepted this argument, Supreme Court opinion in 1982 makes clear that the Court will not simply accept at face value the claim that discrimination against males is necessary to promote equal opportunity for females.[128] Said the Court, the state must actually prove that opportunities for women have been limited before affirmative action for women can be upheld; thus, as athletic opportunities for women increase, it should become more difficult to justify the exclusion of males from all-female teams, especially when an all-male team is not available. Given the results of these cases, it is somewhat strange that the courts have upheld the policy of requiring girls to play under physically less demanding rules in such games as basketball; in these cases the courts have tended to rely on the canard that the educational experts always know what is best for their female students.[129]

Matching the Program with the Student and Assuring Minimal Adequacy

Arguably, professional educators know best when it comes to assigning students to courses or programs and determining the adequacy of those programs. Nevertheless, courts have from time to time responded to the request to intervene in order to ensure that students get the type and quality of program to which they have a right. This judicial effort directed toward the quality of what the student gets in the public schools has been less vigorous and extensive than the efforts to contain religious and political socialization, but nevertheless it represents an important dimension of judicial supervision of the schools.

Wrongful Placement

The comparatively modest amount of judicial supervision of nonhandicapped students is best underscored by noting that the courts have refused to order the early admission of a student to the public schools even if the student were arguably ready for school;[130] they have refused to order the placement of pupils in academically advanced programs and to order the grade promotion of a child who did not meet the school's reading requirements.[131] And legal commentators agree that a constitutional attack on tracking or ability-grouping systems would fail without proof that the system was intentionally used to promote racial segregation in the school building.[132] Tracking systems have been struck down in the absence of an intent to segregate when used in a former dual school system and the use of the tracking had the effect of producing segregation within the newly desegregated school buildings. The Courts have viewed the within-building segregation produced by these tracking systems as a consequence of the vestigial effects of the prior practice of de jure segregation on the academic achievement of black students.[133] The nonintervention of the courts stands, despite the fact that research tends to show that ability-grouping or tracking systems result in placements of a disproportionate number of poor and minority students in low tracks; reduced educational quality in the low groups; limited access for students in low groups to higher education and some occupations; and the stigmatization of low-tracked students—and despite the fact that these placements tend to be permanent and result often from an inappropriate or haphazard classification process.[134]

Courts, nevertheless, have on three notable occasions modified pupil assignment mechanisms. In Washington, DC, relying on a method of constitutional analysis not accepted later by the Supreme Court, federal courts struck down aspects of the district's tracking system because it resulted in the permanent disproportionate placement of poor and minority students in the lower tracks where they received a watered-down education and inadequate remedial and compensatory help to aid them in getting out of the lower tracks.[135] More than 15 years later, litigation in *Larry P. v. Riles* resulted in an order forbidding all California schools from using IQ tests to determine if students should be placed in classes for the educably mentally retarded.[136] The court concluded that the disproportionate number of minority students in classes for the educable mentally retarded could be explained by the cultural bias of the test, which, in turn, the court concluded was used because of and not in spite of this bias.[137] A similar finding of an intent to discriminate was found in *Lora v. Board of Education of City of New York*, where the procedure for placement of students in special schools for the emotionally disturbed involved testing and subjective criteria.[138] In short, the courts have concluded that students assigned to special classes in these cases had been excluded from the regular school program where they belonged and, instead, were placed in special classes not suited to their educational needs merely because they were black or Hispanic.

Exclusion from a program where the student arguably belongs has also been based on sex or handicap, leading to a number of other judicial opinions. An equally divided Supreme Court (one justice did not participate in the decision) upheld a federal circuit court's decision that it was permissible for Philadelphia to exclude a female student from an all-male academic high school when the city also offered an equally good academic all-female high school as well as a number of nonacademic coeducational high schools.[139] In a later decision, the Supreme Court struck down a rule excluding males from admittance to an all-female college of nursing.[140] As noted earlier, the lower courts have also overturned in a number of instances the exclusion of female students from all-male athletic teams, and Title IX regulations prohibit the exclusion of students on the basis of sex from courses such as shop and home economics.[141]

The federal law protecting the rights of the handicapped places a premium on integrating the handicapped pupil, as far as is educationally appropriate for the child, with nonhandicapped pupils.[142] This requirement for the "mainstreaming" of handicapped pupils helps to ensure that they are not excluded unnecessarily from the regular school program and has led to a large number of disputes between parents and school districts as one or the other seeks to have the child placed in a special program, separate from the regular school program. The courts have resolved these disputes on a case-by-case basis.[143]

Handicapped pupils enjoy another advantage over the nonhandicapped because of P.L. 94–142. Pursuant to this law, school districts must follow an elaborate procedure in deciding on the sort of individualized program the child is to receive—that the program be individualized is another central requirement of the law—a procedure that permits parents and educational experts to come together with their evidence and arguments to decide the educational fate of the child. (As will be discussed more fully below, the handicapped child has a right to "special education" and "related services" as part of the more general right to a "free appropriate public education.") A parent who is unhappy with the first program decision has the right to appeal to an impartial hearing officer and ultimately to the courts.[144] The nonhandicapped child does not enjoy either a right to an individualized program or to the procedures used for the educational placement of the handicapped, because neither the legislatures nor the courts have imposed such a requirement on the schools.

Minimal Adequacy
The judiciary has been asked in a variety of ways to address the adequacy of school programs, and it has responded in a tentative and carefully circumscribed

manner. This caution is most obviously displayed in the courts' repeated refusals to entertain educational malpractice suits.[145] (The courts expressed both the fear that their entertaining malpractice claims would lead to a judicial takeover of the public schools and doubts that they had the capacity to determine the cause of a student's educational inadequacies, given that poor academic performance could be the result of either the school's failure, the parents' failure, and/or the student's incapacity or lack of effort.) The Supreme Court exhibited a similar degree of caution with its refusal to conclude that there was a constitutional violation when a largely decentralized system for financing education resulted in significant inequalities among the districts of Texas in the amount of money spent per pupil because of vast differences in property wealth per pupil among the districts.[146] Using what lawyers call a lenient form of review, the Court concluded that the finance system, with its heavy reliance on the local property tax, was rationally related to the state's legitimate purpose of enhancing local control. Said the Court, only if it has been alleged that the finance system deprives students of a minimally adequate education in those districts that were relatively poorer (in terms of property wealth per pupil) would a constitutional problem arise. Thus, the Court left open the possibility that some school finance systems would be overturned if it could be proven that the pupils of some districts were getting a minimally inadequate education. The Court did not specify what evidence would be required to prove minimal inadequacy.

In the wake of the Rodriguez decision, state courts have been asked to overturn their state's system of financing education on the basis of the state's own constitution; a number have agreed to do so, but a larger number have refused.[147] The reasoning of these decisions is too complex to recount here; suffice it to say that the courts that agreed to overturn their state's system of finance have sometimes done so to alleviate what they have deemed an unfair burden on taxpayers in property-poor school districts and not merely out of a concern for the relative adequacy of the programs in those districts. These cases have proven difficult for the courts, involving lengthy and complex litigation. Especially difficult has been the problem of defining the notion of the basically adequate program. Some courts, like the New Jersey Supreme Court, avoided the problem by offering no definition to guide the legislature.[148] The state of Washington's highest court adopted the ingenious device of saying the legislature's obligation was to provide ample funds to local districts to fund a basic education, which it defined at that level of inputs (professional and nonprofessional staff) which was on average provided by the districts of the state.[149] In essence, the Washington court based the notion of a basic education on "common wisdom."

In three nonconstitutional decisions, the United States Supreme Court actually did wrestle with the problem of the definition of an adequate program. In *Rowley*, which arose under P.L. 94–142, the Court was asked to define the statute's guarantee of a "free appropriate education" when parents complained that the school district failed to provide their partially deaf child with her own full-time signer, instead of what the district did provide, namely, an FM hearing aid, a tutor, and a speech therapist. The parents claimed that the signer was required because, although the help provided their daughter did permit her to perform well in school, their child was not performing up to her full capacity, and only a program that elicited that level of performance could be deemed to be an "appropriate education" within the meaning of the law. The Supreme Court disagreed, saying that the statute's notion of an appropriate education should be interpreted to mean an individualized educational program developed through the act's procedures, "reasonably calculated to enable the child to receive educational benefits," and the assistance provided in this case met those requirements.[150] (In a subsequent case, the Court concluded that provision of a "free appropriate education" required providing a child with catheterization.[151]) The practical result of these decisions is that the difficult determination of whether or not a program is "appropriate" will be decided by educators, with the courts only secondarily checking to make sure the educators developed what appeared to be, in light of the child's needs, a rational program that included the necessary "related services."[152]

Non-English-speaking Chinese-American students also sought and received from the Supreme Court a declaration that provision of an all-English program of instruction without assistance to learn English violated Title VI (which prohibits discrimination on the basis of race in programs receiving federal financial assistance as interpreted by the then Department of Health, Education and Welfare).[153] But in deciding the case, the Court did not even go as far as it did in *Rowley* in outlining the kind of effort that must be made to assist these pupils; defining the requirements was left to the federal agencies administering Title VI. Congress later passed the Equal Educational Opportunity Act of 1974, which enacted into law the interpretation of Title VI upheld by the Supreme Court. Thus, into the 1980s the central question facing school districts is what kind of English-language instructional program will the Department of Education say is required by Title VI and the law of 1974. As matters now stand, the federal government's guidelines imply the need to provide non-English-speaking students with bilingual education programs, but the lower federal courts have split as to whether the two statutes impose such a requirement or leave the districts with a freer hand in devising methods to teach English to the non-English-speaking students.[154] In these decisions, once again, the courts have exhibited reluctance to impose on the experts a set of educational requirements. As one court put it, what the district must do is develop a program informed by a theory that at least some experts consider to be sound, develop a plan reasonably calculated to implement that theory, and change the plan if, after a legitimate trial, it has not produced the expected results.[155]

Competency Testing

In the face of declining test scores and dissatisfaction with the quality of the school program, a dozen or more states in the mid-1970s implemented or took steps toward implementing, a competency testing system to determine if students could demonstrate the minimum prerequisite skills for a high school diploma and/or grade-to-grade promotion.[156] The courts became most significantly involved in the competency testing movement when plaintiffs complained that Florida's competency test violated both the due process and the equal protection clauses of the Fourteenth Amendment. The federal district court concluded, and the appeals court affirmed, that (a) approximately 1 year's notice that passing the test was a prerequisite to graduation from high school was insufficient and violated the student's right to due process of law; (b) the phenomenon of the disproportionate number of black students who failed the test as of spring 1979 resulted from the inferior education they received when Florida's schools were still purposefully segregated and hence immediate use of the diploma sanction for not passing the test punished black pupils for deficiencies created by the former dual school system; but that (c) the test did have construct validity in that it did test functional literacy as defined by the state.[157] The appeals court remanded the case on two issues: first, the issue of curricular validity (if the test were found on remand *not* to examine pupils on material they were actually taught, then imposition of the test would violate the equal protection clause) and, second, the continuing role and effect of past discrimination on black students. Following a trial the federal district court found that the state had proved that the test had both curricular validity and instructional validity; that is, the official curriculum covered what was included on the test and a majority of the teachers in the state recognized those skills as something they should teach. The court also concluded that as of 1983 any causal link between the disproportionate failure rate of black students and the

effects of past segregation had been broken; hence, starting with the class of 1983 Florida could deny diplomas to those who failed to pass the test.[158]

The significance of the Florida litigation lies not merely in the fact that the courts require states to adhere to basic principles of fairness when they impose on students a new requirement for graduation and/or grade promotion but also that when a state does adopt a system of competency tests, the Constitution requires that each teacher in fact teach to the test; for failure to do so makes the test instructionally invalid for his or her pupils. It follows that state-imposed competency tests both dramatically reduce the teacher's discretion and centralize control of the school program in the hands of the state. It should go without saying that the principles established in the Florida litigation also apply to competency requirements imposed by the individual school district and perhaps even to teacher-prepared tests.[159] But as significant as the adequate notice and validity requirements are, it should be stressed that the courts have consistently supported the authority of the state and school board to make successful completion of the tests a requirement for a diploma, even in the face of challenges brought by mentally impaired students claiming that such a requirement discriminates against them.[160]

Constraints on the Duty to Provide a Safe, Orderly Environment

Whatever else schools boards may do, it is widely agreed that they have a duty to provide their students with a safe, and perhaps also orderly, environment. The common law imposes on districts a duty to provide buildings and equipment that are safe; a duty to provide adequate supervision to forestall injuries inflicted by one student on another; and, arguably, a duty to make sure buildings are not visited by strangers who may inflict harm on the pupils.[161] It may also be the case that just as institutionalized mental patients have a constitutional right to safe conditions of confinement, so do students have a similar right when in the public school building in compliance with the compulsory education law.[162] And Titles VI and IX arguably impose a duty on boards to provide an environment free from racial and sexual harrassment,[163] (The problem of assuring children a safe environment while not infringing on the rights of school personnel becomes especially difficult in the context of school transportation. School districts must assure that bus drivers are physically and mentally capable of doing the job, and yet they may not deny employment simply on the basis of handicap.[164]) But, as discussed later, fulfillment of these duties must take place within certain important constitutional constraints protecting students and teachers alike.

Preannounced, Nonvague Rules

Although it is a constitutional requirement that a person may be criminally convicted only on the basis of previously promulgated, nonvague statutes, the courts have not strongly insisted on the same sort of requirements as a prerequisite in disciplining pupils.[165] Believing that it is important to leave educators with a relatively free hand to deal with the great variety of situations that may arise in the schools and that students may be presumed to know that very disruptive actions might lead to disciplinary efforts, the courts have said that not every reason for disciplining a student need be stated in a preexisting rule; furthermore, the rules that are issued in advance may be phrased in such general terms as "students should behave in a manner that will be a credit on themselves."[166]

The Student's Right of Free Speech

Recognizing both the student's interest in freedom of speech and the board's duty to maintain order, the Supreme Court has said that students may be punished for what they say in school (or for the printed materials they distribute) only if the speech materially and substantially interfered with the work of the school or impinged on the rights of other students. Similarly, if the school authorities can prove that they had a reasonable basis for forecasting that the student's free speech activity would cause material and substantial disruption, then preventive action may be taken.[167] Applying these rules in 1969, the Court concluded that three children who wore black armbands to school in protest against U.S. involvement in the Vietnam War could not be ordered to remove the armbands because the disturbances their protest caused among the other students did not amount to material and substantial disruption.

Almost two decades later, however, the Supreme Court upheld the disciplining of a student who nominated another student for a student office with a speech employing an elaborate sexual metaphor.[168] The Court distinguished its decision in *Tinker* finding that this speech was "vulgar" and "offensive," and inappropriate for an unsuspecting audience, and that the school had ample authority in order to take steps to inculcate pupils in "habits and manners of civility."

Although this decision did open the door to significant judicial involvement in school disciplinary efforts, the lower courts have not been uniformly aggressive in restraining disciplinary actions in the name of protecting the students' interest in freedom of speech. On the one hand, a number of courts have said that student criticism of school officials and school policy in a so-called underground newspaper is not per se a basis for disciplinary action; on the other hand, other courts have upheld prohibitions against the wearing of buttons expressing ethnic pride, the distribution of a questionnaire asking students about their sexual behavior and attitudes, the solicitation of funds from pupils on school grounds, and the disciplining of black students for silently leaving a pep rally in protest against the playing of the song "Dixie"[169] The courts have also made clear that whereas the use of a vulgar word in an underground publication is not a sufficient basis for suppression of the paper, the use of a vulgar epithet directed at a teacher and the distribution of libelous or obscene materials may be the basis of punishment.[170] A number of courts have extended protection even to the student editors of official school newspapers to publish articles over the objection of school authorities.[171] Several courts have said a properly designed prior review system may be used by schools to block distribution of materials that are found likely to cause material and substantial disruption.[172] The Second Circuit Court of Appeals has made it clear, however, that school officials may not discipline pupils for the production and distribution of a publication off school grounds.[173] Refusing to recognize a student organization because of the views it espouses may also be unconstitutional.[174]

The theory behind the Supreme Court's original decision protecting the student's interest in free speech was to assure that the school remained a marketplace of ideas: that is, a limited public forum where not just the official voice of the school board is heard. Stated differently, the decision provides some modest protection of the student's interest in freedom of belief and the right to receive ideas. To an extent, the Supreme Court's goal has been fulfilled by the lower courts, but it is also clear that the lower courts have been mindful of the school board's desire and duty to maintain order.

Other Impermissible Reasons for Imposing Discipline

The imposition of discipline based on race or sex is impermissible.[175] As discussed earlier, schools have sought to regulate hair styles or dress styles in order to instruct students in good grooming. In addition, school officials have also offered as a rationale for such rules the need to maintain order in the schools. Because the courts have split on the question of whether a student has a right to control his or her appearance, it is also not clear whether boards may seek to control hair styles or dress styles for the purpose of maintaining order.[176] But even those courts that recognize such a right indicate that school boards may discipline a student if the school can prove that that student's hair or clothing was in fact so provocative as to lead to material and substantial disruption.[177]

Limits on Gathering the Evidence

Limiting the reasons for which students may be disciplined has not been the only way the courts have affected the board's ability to maintain order in the schools. In 1985 the Supreme Court ruled that the Fourth Amendment applies to searches by school officials of pupils, that school officials do not need a warrant to search pupils, and that the search would be permissible when there are "reasonable grounds for suspecting that the search will turn up evidence that the student has violated or is violating either a law or the rules of the school." In these circumstances a search "will be permissible in scope when the measures adopted are reasonably related to the objectives of the search and not excessively intrusive in light of the age and sex of the student and the nature of the infraction."[178] Although the precise meaning of the opinion must await elaboration through further litigation, two points seem clear: First, the random or causeless search is not permitted,[179] and second, the more intrusive the search, the higher the level of justification that will be necessary for the search to be found to be constitutional. For example, for a strip-search to be constitutional, the school official must meet a higher standard for determining the need to search.[180] A violation of the student's interest in privacy opens the school official to suits for damages pursuant to § 1983 and the common law.[181] A majority of the courts also have said that evidence seized in the absence of a reasonable suspicion may not be used against the student in a criminal trial but may be used in a school disciplinary hearing; a minority of courts would also exclude the evidence from the school disciplinary hearing.[182]

Though it may seem from these comments that the student's interest in privacy is so well protected by the courts that the ability of school officials to uncover evidence of drug trafficking, for example, is hampered, the courts have also said that because the school locker is owned by the school, the student's expectancy of privacy regarding the locker is negligible. Hence, school officials may search it even without reasonable suspicion.[183] And although some courts have said the use of sniffer dogs to detect illegal substances on pupils is unconstitutional, other courts have upheld the practice.[184] (The use of these dogs to detect illegal substances in lockers and automobiles parked on school property has been upheld by the courts.[185]) Other courts have said the use of undercover policewomen in the schools is permissible and that observation through a two-way mirror of a marijuana purchase does not

violate the Fourth Amendment.[186] It is also important to note that the courts have tended to defer to the educator's judgment that there were grounds for reasonable suspicion.[187] (How these lower court decisions will be affected by the Supreme Court's 1985 decision remains to be seen.) Courts have also said that students need not be warned before school officials question them that anything they say may be used against them.[188] In sum, by limiting their protection of the student to the prevention of the wholly baseless search, the courts have left school officials free from restrictions that would severely hamper their efforts to track down perpetrators of crimes and breaches of a school's disciplinary code.

Procedural Due Process

In addition to restricting the methods by which evidence is gathered, the courts have also prescribed the steps that must be executed before a student may be suspended from school. The Supreme Court has said that if a student is to be suspended for 10 days or less, then the student must be "given oral or written notice of the charges against him and, if he denies them, an explanation for the evidence the authorities have and an opportunity to present his side of the story."[189] There need be no delay between the notice and the hearing, and in most instances the disciplinarian may informally discuss the problem with the student minutes after it occurs. A more formal, trial-type hearing may be required before imposing longer suspensions. Normally the hearing must precede the suspension, but if the student poses a continuing threat, he or she may be immediately removed, and then the necessary notice and rudimentary hearing must follow as soon as is practicable. Even these modest requirements were further limited by two later Supreme Court opinions, which said the requirements of procedural due process did not apply either to corporal punishment or to the discharge of pupils for academic failure.[190]

The lower courts have been most cautious in extending, expanding, and elaborating on these minimal due-process requirements. They have, for example, refused to extend the right to some sort of hearing to exclusions from extracurricular activities and have split over the question of the extent to which due process must be observed when students are transferred.[191] In long-term suspension cases, the lower courts have sought to assure that students do receive adequate notice of the charges and of their right to have an attorney present, to assure the impartiality of the hearing tribunal, and to assure students a chance actually to confront adverse witnesses.[192]

In short, both the Supreme Court and the lower federal courts have been mindful of, on the one hand, the student's interest in continuing his or her education, in being treated with dignity, and in having his or her guilt or innocence accurately determined and, on the other hand, the school's need to deal swiftly with disciplinary problems and to maintain respect for authority.

Force and Corporal Punishment
Although the Supreme Court has said that even brutal forms of corporal punishment do not violate the constitutional prohibition against cruel and unusual punishment, both common law doctrine and state criminal laws place limits on the amount of force teachers may use on students.[193] (The Circuit Courts of Appeals are split on the question of whether corporal punishment may be so severe as to be a violation of the due process clause of the Fourteenth Amendment, an issue the Supreme Court has not yet decided.[194]) But here again, the judiciary has been careful not to restrict unduly educators and has cautiously defined the notion of excessive force so that usually only force that causes more than a trivial injury is found to be unacceptable.[195] Even when a parent objects to the use of corporal punishment, the courts have said boards of education may use this form of punishment to maintain order (assuming the state has not by statute prohibited its use).[196] Students need not be provided with even an informal hearing before the administration of corporal punishment.[197] And one court has ruled that there is no constitutional violation when a district follows a minor's preference to be corporally punished instead of adherence to the parent's expressed preference for the use of the suspension.[198] This decision is consistent with an earlier decision holding that parents do not have a constitutional right to control whether or not schools administer corporal punishment to their child.[199]

Other Punishments
In the face of the rise in the use of drugs, courts also have refused to say that suspensions for as long as a full school term for drug use are constitutionally infirm.[200] But many courts have resisted the use of academic sanctions (e.g., the lowering of grades) as punishments for nonacademic transgressions.[201]

Discipline of the Handicapped
Although the discipline of handicapped pupils is not specifically addressed in P.L. 94–142 or in the Rehabilitation Act of 1973, the courts have said these laws prohibit the disciplining of handicapped pupils if the disruptive behavior is linked to or is a manifestation of the handicap.[202] Even if the board manages to prove the disruptive behavior is not related to the handicapping condition, any suspension for more than a minimal amount of time is viewed by the courts as a "change in educational placement" within the meaning of the statutes and regulations, and it must, therefore, be preceded by execution of the procedures to which the handicapped have a right when their educational placement is being changed.[203] The courts arguably have also said that expulsion (i.e., the cessation of all services) may never be an appropriate punishment for the misbehavior of a handicapped child, even if the misbehavior was not related to the handicap.[204]

The Rights of Teachers

Three central dimensions of the question of judicial involvement in the protection of teachers were discussed in the section dealing with the judiciary's reform of the system for governance of the public school system: the rights of teachers publicly to criticize school policy and officials on matters of public concern; the right of teachers to join unions and bargain collectively; and the right of teachers to academic freedom and the authority to control the school curriculum. A brief overview will be provided of a number of remaining issues, with the caveat that the topic of protecting teachers' right is too vast to receive complete treatment here.

Hiring and Firing
A traditional function of the courts has been to interpret the statutory scheme regulating the certification, hiring, and firing of teachers. Thus, courts have overturned unauthorized or arbitrary denials and revocations of certificates.[205] They have enforced the statutory procedures that must be followed in these cases.[206] They have frequently been called on to interpret the statutes that guide the granting and denial of tenure as well as the statutorily defined procedures for dismissing tenured teachers for cause.[207] And they have enforced the law guiding the abolishment of positions, the laying off of teachers for economic reasons, and the protection of seniority rights as the layoffs occur.[208] One of the most important recent developments has been the recognition by the Supreme Court of a public employee's right to a some sort of hearing prior to dismissal if the employee has more than a unilateral expectation of continued employment (e.g., has tenure, a contract for continuing employment, or is otherwise protected against dismissal except for cause).[209] If continued presence on the job presents a significant hazard, the employee may first be suspended with pay and then subsequently provided a hearing.[210] As the Court stated in *Loudermill*, an employee who has a right to procedural due process has a right to an oral or written notice specifying the charge, an explanation of the employer's evidence, and an opportunity to

present his or her side.[211] How the *Loudermill* decision will affect many lower courts and their opinions elaborating a more complex set of procedural rights (covering such matters as notice of charges, the right to present evidence and confront witnesses, right to counsel, right to a transcript, right to a decision based only on the evidence of record, and right to an impartial tribunal) remains to be seen.[212]

Due process aside, the judiciary has also become involved in reviewing decisions of school boards not to renew a contract or to dismiss a teacher for cause. As for the nonrenewal of contracts of untenured teachers, the courts have declined to examine the evidence anew or to second-guess the judgment of the school board.[213] (Nonrenewal because of the teacher's exercise of a constitutional right, of course, is impermissible and will be reversed by the courts, as discussed later. Nonrenewal for trivial reasons, suggestive of an irrational decision, may also raise a constitutional problem.)[214] Though the nonrenewal of contracts places virtually no burden of justification on the school board, dismissal for cause may be accomplished only if the board is able to establish that its reasons comport with the statutory grounds for dismissal. States vary regarding the statutory grounds for dismissal, but typically teachers may be dismissed for incompetence, incapacity, insubordination, unprofessional conduct, immorality, and neglect of duty.[215] Relying on state statutory requirements, the courts have also said that an isolated or single instance of inefficiency is an insufficient basis for dismissal.[216] On occasion the courts have also said that before dismissal for incompetency is allowable, the board must establish that the teacher was given notice of deficiencies and a chance to improve performance, and proof must be offered that these deficiencies are not correctable.[217] Beyond these kinds of requirements, the courts are not inclined to substitute their judgment for that of the school board, but they will do so on occasion. Thus, one court overturned a decision to dismiss when the evidence showed that the teacher, who had taught for 12 years with good evaluations, was dismissed because the board claimed she was cold and distant and too strict in her requirements of pupils. Noting that half the witnesses did support her methods, the court said, "Teachers are not required to entertain their students, only to teach them."[218] Finally, note should be made that the United States Supreme Court in *Harrah Independent School District v. Martin* (1979) upheld the dismissal of a tenured teacher who persistently refused to comply with the board's continuing education requirement.[219] The requirement was a valid rule, said the Court, and its enforcement impaired no fundamental right of the teacher nor deprived her of the equal protection of the laws. In sum, judicial intervention in the efforts of school boards to assure the provision of an adequate education program by competent teachers has been modest.

Beyond the problem of competence, a typical reason given for dismissing a teacher is the claim that the teacher's behavior violated traditional standards of morality and professional conduct, and, for this reason, the teacher became a poor role model for the students. The effort to assure that teachers are proper role models is part of the school's efforts to socialize pupils. The kind of instances in which teachers have been dismissed for immoral or unprofessional conduct include the following: (a) dismissal after a criminal conviction for drunk driving, theft, possession of drugs or marijuana, tax avoidance, or unlawful sexual behavior; (b) dismissal for private sexual activities outside the school that did not result in a criminal conviction (e.g., living with someone other than one's lawful spouse, becoming an unwed mother, or admission of homosexuality); (c) dismissal for activity that could be but was not in fact the basis of a criminal conviction (e.g., the use of marijuana; phoning in a false bomb threat).[220]

The response of the judiciary to these dismissals has not been uniformly to agree with the argument of the district that such teachers are bad role models for students. In mid-1980, for example, many but not all lower courts have protected unwed mothers from dismissal.[221] Similarly, women teachers have been protected by some but not all courts against dismissal for living with a man not their husband.[222] But teachers' rights of privacy and autonomy have served as a successful shield to protect them from dismissal for being homosexual or for having been convicted of a crime.[223] A central unresolved issue in this area is whether the teacher has the burden of proof that he or she remains fit to teach despite the out-of-school behavior, or whether the district must prove disruption and an impairment of the teacher's effectiveness.[224] One point seems fairly certain: The more publicity the teacher's behavior has attracted, the more likely the board will dismiss the teacher and be successful in court in defending that dismissal. Finally, mention should be made of the basic judicial willingness to uphold hair and dress requirements imposed on teachers to assure they are proper role models for students.[225] The importance of the school's duty to provide a safe environment, as discussed earlier, is underscored by the unwillingness of the courts to interfere with school board decisions to dismiss teachers who become sexually involved with students, who physically abuse students, or who violate school policy against the use of corporal punishment.[226]

The Free Speech Rights of Teachers

The courts have interpreted the free speech clause of the First Amendment to protect teachers in several different ways. As noted earlier, the courts have protected the right of teachers to criticize their employer on matters of public concern and to some limited extent, on the right of academic freedom. On the hiring of teachers, the Supreme Court has taken two seemingly inconsistent positions. On the one hand, school boards have been told they may neither fire nor refuse to hire Communist teachers unless the teachers are both active in the party and specifically agree with unlawful aims of the party.[227] On the other hand, legal aliens who are in fact committed to democracy but who do not seek citizenship even though eligible to do so may be excluded from public school teaching if the state decides a priori that such people are not to be trusted to carry out the school's mission to inculcate.[228] Thus, the antidemocratic teacher who is a citizen may teach, but the legal alien who is a proponent of democracy may not if the state, without evidence, decides that he or she cannot be trusted.

Putting aside issues of loyalty to the country and its ideals, other forms of political activity of teachers have come to enjoy some degree of constitutional protection. Thus, school boards may not refuse to hire public employees like teachers simply because the applicants may be members of a political party not in control of the local board.[229] The refusal to hire teachers for summer employment because they supported the losing opponents of the current school board is also impermissible.[230] Similarly, dismissing teachers for participating in the civil rights movement's effort to end segregation in the schools has been struck down.[231] A law that prohibited public employees from "advocating, soliciting, imposing, encouraging, or promoting public or private homosexual activity in a manner that creates a substantial risk that such conduct will come to the attention of school children or school employees," has been disallowed.[232] On the other hand, one court has held that it is permissible to dismiss teachers who speak privately to other school employees about bisexual preferences.[233] The courts have split as to whether and when school boards may dismiss teachers who send their own children to private schools.[234] The Second Circuit Court has held that a teacher may not be dismissed for expressing his political viewpoint in class by the wearing of a black armband in protest against the Vietnam War when it was clear the armband did not disrupt the classroom.[235] From time to time, school districts interested in promoting integration and a non-racist school atmosphere have dismissed teachers who threaten these goals. In these cases lower courts have upheld the dismissal of teachers for making racist remarks in school within the hearing of students or the school principal.[236] But it is reasonably clear that the courts will approve of some restrictions on the partisan political activities of teachers if these restrictions are

not unnecessarily broad and serve sufficiently important purposes (e.g., to insulate public employees from political pressure and to ensure the school program is provided in a nonpartisan manner).[237]

Privacy and Other Interests

In the law the notion of privacy has at least two dimensions: a right to be left alone to live one's own preferred life style and a right to keep to oneself information that could prove to be embarrassing. The first dimension was important in decisions, discussed earlier, that touched on such matters as the dismissal of teachers who were unwed mothers or who kept obscene materials in their home.[238] Closely related is the question of whether an investigation by school officials into a teacher's personal life would violate a right of privacy. The limits on such investigations are not clear, but it does seem that such investigations must be limited to matters that are job related.[239] Inquiry into a teacher's organizational affiliation must meet strict constitutional limits.[240] As for searches by school officials of teachers themselves, their briefcases, pocket books, desks, file cabinets, and lockers, a badly fragmented Supreme Court in *O'Connor v. Ortega* held that: (1) Public employees do not lose their Fourth Amendment rights merely because they work for the government; (2) absent special circumstances these protections usually extend to cover the employee's office, desk, and files; (3) employers did not need to obtain a search warrant prior to searching; and (4) a search would be permissible (according to the plurality opinion) when (a) there were reasonable grounds tor suspecting a search would turn up evidence the employee was guilty of work-related misconduct, or the search was necessary for a noninvestigatory work-related purpose such as to retrieve a needed file, and when (b) the scope of the search was reasonably related to the objectives of the search and not excessively intrusive in light of the nature of the misconduct.[241] Another court held that the Fourth Amendment protected a school bus attendant from being required to subject herself to drug testing without particularized suspicion that she was a drug user.[242] In dictum, the court noted, however, that mandatory testing without individualized suspicion may be permissible with regard to school bus drivers and mechanics directly responsible for the operation and maintenance of school buses.

The Equal Protection Clause and Nondiscrimination Legislation

Perhaps the most far-reaching developments with regard to teachers and the law has come in response to discriminatory treatment based on race, sex, handicap, age, and religion. These developments in antidiscrimination law are very complex, but some important developments can be highlighted. Turning first to discrimination on the basis of race, it goes without saying that the Constitution and Title VII both protect teachers against purposeful discrimination on the basis of race in hiring, firing, promoting, paying, or assigning teachers.[243] The courts have been especially careful to protect teachers against dismissal on the basis of race when districts have reorganized because of judicial orders to integrate the schools.[244] And courts have upheld the assigning of teachers on the basis of race in order to achieve a better racial balance in the faculty of its schools.[245] In order to eliminate discrimination on the basis of race and national origin, federal courts forced a massive redesign of New York City's licensing and appointment system.[246] Yet, a federal district court, in an opinion affirmed by the Supreme Court, upheld the legality under the Constitution and Title VII of teacher certification decisions based on the results of a minimal competency test (the National Teachers Examination), despite the fact that a large proportion of black applicants did not pass the test.[247]

As the political climate in the United States became more conservative, two serious charges have been levied. The first is that Title VII has been interpeted in such a way that the burden of proof on the plaintiff who complains of racial (or sexual) discrimination has been so diluted that, as a practical matter, employers sued under Title VII now face a presumption of having discriminated the moment the complaint is filed.[248] The second charge is that public employers now discriminate against whites. This charge is based on recent voluntary efforts on the part of some public employers, including school districts, to protect the jobs of their minority employees by, for example, agreeing to clauses in collective bargaining agreements that limit the number of minority teachers who may be laid off, if the district must reduce it workforce, with the result that white teachers with more seniority than minority teachers are laid off first. Reacting to just such a plan, the Supreme Court has said the plan violated the constitutional right of white teachers not to be discriminated against on the basis of race.[249] Such a plan, said the Court, could not be justified merely to remedy past "societal discrimination" but could be adopted only if it were established that the employer itself had discriminated in employment in the past, thereby establishing a predicate for the voluntarily adopted affirmative action plan. Such a predicate had not been established in this case. The Court also rejected the argument the plan could be justified as a means of assuring minority role models for minority pupils. A plurality of the Court went further by hinting that a layoff plan could never be used to achieve even legitimate goals unless the layoffs were used only to provide make-whole relief to the actual identified victims of individual discrimination. The preferred method for remedying past discrimination, said the plurality, was the use of valid hiring goals.

Most recently in a decision with constitutional implications the Supreme Court upheld as consistent with Title VII a voluntarily affirmative action plan pursuant to which a woman was promoted ahead of a man who had achieved a slightly higher point score on a promotion interview.[250] Despite the fact that this employer had not itself discriminated against women, the Supreme Court held that an employer may voluntarily adopt an affirmative action plan to correct a "manifest imbalance" in a "traditionally segregated job category."

As for discrimination based on sex, the Constitution and Title VII protect employees in similar ways from the usual forms of discrimination in hiring or promoting.[251] In addition employees are also protected against several forms of sexual harassment.[252] Pregnancy may no longer be treated differently from other physical conditions.[253] In a decision particularly important to public schooling, the Supreme Court said that an employer may not offer teachers a retirement plan that requires male and female employees to contribute the same amount but that pays women a lower monthly retirement benefit because they tend to live longer.[254] Nor may an employer require female employees to make a larger contribution to the retirement plan in order to receive the same benefits as males at retirement.[255] In *Northaven Board of Education v. Bell* (1982), the Court agreed that Title IX's prohibition against discrimination on the basis of sex protects employees (not just students) in federally assisted programs.[256] (The practical advantages of this decision for would-be litigants are in doubt, given the fact that Title IX does not provide for remedies such as back pay, reinstatement, and compensatory damages.[257])

The claim that Title VII requires equal pay for male and female employees not just for equal work but also for work that is of comparable worth to the employer (i.e., work that imposes or entails similar responsibilities, judgments, knowledge, skills, and working conditions) was rejected by the Ninth Circuit.[258] According to that court, women in traditional female jobs who on average are paid less than men because the market price of their services is low have not been discriminated against, despite the assessment of some experts that their work is of comparable worth to the work of men doing different jobs.

Turning to discrimination on the basis of age and handicap, two federal circuit courts reached different conclusions on the question of whether a mandatory retirement age deprived teachers of equal protection of the laws.[259] The Second Circuit Court of Appeals has held that a school district may not follow a policy of not hiring a teacher with more than 5 years' experience as violation of the Age Discrimination in Employment Act of 1978.[260] This same act also prohibits the setting of a mandatory retirement age below age 70 unless the employer can establish an earlier age as a bona fide occupational requirement. And the Rehabilitation Act of 1973 may provide a basis for employees to seek a remedy for discrimination on the basis of handicap if the employee can demonstrate that he or she is employed in a program receiving federal financial assistance and is an intended beneficiary of that assistance.[261]

In a decision with obvious implications for carriers of Acquired Immune Deficiency Syndrome (AIDS), the Supreme Court has ruled that a person afflicted with the infectious disease tuberculosis is a handicapped individual within the meaning of the Rehabilitation Act of 1973.[262] But the mere that fact someone with a contagious disease falls within the protections of the law does not automatically mean he or she must be employed, or at least employed in his or her current position. The legally proper placement of the individual required an individualized determination which was to take into consideration all health and safety risks.

Last, we come to discrimination on the basis of religion. As with the other forms of discrimination, there are constitutional and statutory issues in this area. A California court has held that it is a violation of the California state constitution to dismiss a teacher for unpaid absences required by his religious faith. The district must accommodate the teacher by allowing unpaid leave when such accommodation is not unreasonably burdensome.[263] Federal statutory law adopts the same rule, which the courts have interpreted to mean that accommodation becomes burdensome if the employing institution has to do much more than merely attempt to rearrange the work schedules of its employees.[264]

JUDICIAL IMPACT

In summarizing the impact of the judiciary on the policies and behaviors of public school officials, it is useful to discuss separately, first, the extent of the demands made on the schools by the judiciary and, second, the impact of those demands. The assessment offered here is that, though the judiciary's activities since 1954 have been extensive, there is need to exercise caution in assuming that the level and extent of activity has in fact caused changes in the behavior

of school boards and administrators that may have occurred anyway during this same period.

How Demanding Have the Courts Been?

Even though some would argue that the courts could do more to curb racial discrimination in the schools (e.g., by eliminating the suburb as a sanctuary to which whites and some blacks may flee in order to avoid court-ordered integration in the city and by openly declaring de facto segregation to be unconstitutional), few would say that the courts have not made significant demands on a large number of school districts in respect to segregation.[265] (In fact, the complaint is frequently heard that the courts have asked too much.[266]) The willingness of a court to discern racial bias in the use of IQ tests, the strong judicial orders on behalf of children totally excluded from public schooling, the assault on sex discrimination in athletics and employment, and the prohibition on the use of prayers in the public schools all represent significant demands on the schools.

But to focus on just these developments distorts the picture by creating the impression that every time the courts speak, they demand a wholesale change in school policies and practices. The fact is that in most of the other areas in which the courts have spoken, they have proceeded with caution. They have refused to develop a doctrine of educational malpractice; many state courts have refused to order changes in their state's system for financing schools; and they have refused to get deeply involved in the placement of nonhandicapped pupils. In other areas the rules laid down by the courts are sufficiently general and/or undemanding to leave school officials with considerable discretion. The procedural due-process requirements imposed by the Supreme Court are limited to disciplinary dismissals and are so minimal as to require in most instances nothing more than a brief conversation between student and disciplinarian. It is only the truly causeless or baseless search that has been prohibited, and the courts are, in any event, inclined to take the word of school officials that they had a reason to search. Warnings that any statement students make will be used against them are not required before school officials question students. Schools are not required to have a preexisting school rule covering each offense a student might commit before the imposition of discipline is permitted. Long-term suspensions in cases of drug use have been upheld. The requirement that students not be punished unless their speech activity causes material and substantial disruption has proved not to be a difficult requirement for districts to meet. The courts have been generally supportive of board decisions to dismiss teachers for immorality and even incompetence. In interpreting both P.L. 94–142 and the Equal Educational Opportunity Act of 1974, the courts have avoided imposing extraordinary demands on the schools. In short, though judicial involvement with the schools has ranged wide, the demands made of the schools are in many instances less demanding than they might have been and less demanding than those supported by the members of the Commission on Juvenile Justice Standards, a commission formed jointly by the Institute of Judicial Administration and the American Bar Association.[267] The mere fact that the courts have addressed an issue and promulgated a ruling is not, per se, tantamount to a judicial effort to substitute itself for the school board.

This is not to say, however, that the operation of the public schools has not been "legalized." Clearly, the legal authority of school boards and school officials has been hedged by a veritable forest of judicial rulings, but just as it is possible to maneuver through a forest, school officials still retain considerable room to maneuver toward their goals.

Judicial Impact in Political Perspective

The fact that the demands of the courts have been more modest than most people seem willing to acknowledge is one piece of evidence in support of a cautious approach in claiming too much for judicial influence over the schools. But there is another reason for caution: the absence of extensive research in many areas of school law regarding the impact of the courts on the operation of the public schools. To indicate briefly the limits of available knowledge, it may be useful to divide the discussion into two parts: first, the impact of judicial activities on the subjective experience of those who are primarily responsible for executing the demands of the judiciary, and, second, the effect of the judiciary's rulings on the actual behavior of these same people. (The effect of the judiciary's activity may, obviously, extend beyond school officials to students and the community, a complex and controversial issue that requires treatment elsewhere.[268])

The Internal Perspective on the Law
The examination of law in society may be considered from either of two perspectives. The examiner may seek to understand law from the external perspective of an observer who is merely concerned with learning whether the existence of a rule can in fact be used to explain or predict the behavior of someone else. From this perspective the examiner does not try to recount the internal thought processes and subjective experiences of the subject but attempts merely to develop

a theory that explains and predicts subjects' behavior. Alternatively, the examiner may seek to understand the law from the internal perspective of those subject to the law. From this perspective, the concern is with the subjective experiences and perceptions of those governed by the law. Use of the internal perspective permits presentation a number of brief, if somewhat unsystematic, comments to be made on the impact of judicial activity on school boards, administrators, and teachers.

To better understand judicial impact, it is useful to try to investigate whether and to what extent judicial activity has promoted a sense among some school officials of a loss of discretion and a heightened sense of uncertainty and risk. (It is not inevitable that this should have been the effect; judicial activity could also have clarified and made more certain what had been unclear before; but, in fact, the predominant effect seems to have been otherwise.) It is not uncommon to hear school superintendents say that the set of books they keep closest at hand are the law books containing the statutes, regulations, and court decisions that affect the day-to-day operations of the schools. Simultaneously, there is a yearning for the simpler, less law-ridden days, when decisions could be made solely on the basis of "sound educational policy or practice" and without having to consult a lawyer. This desire may be most pronounced when the various communications reaching school officials about a decision garble the court's ruling (which itself may be vague and unclear), leaving administrator and board member confused as to the current state of the law.

A number of theories regarding the impact of law are suggestive of yet other subjective effects worthy of further research.[269] Judicial opinions may actually be so persuasive that opinions and attitudes are changed by the opinion itself. Or the very act of complying with the opinion (perhaps because of fears of sanctions) may in time lead officials to resolve the contradiction between their behavior and their attitudes by accepting the values and principles of the opinion. In short, by one mechanism or another, the values and ideals announced by the courts may become the standards by which school officials come to judge their own behavior. It is, of course, a different matter whether these changes in attitudes in turn have led to actual changes in behavior.

The External Perspective on the Law
The analyst working from the external perspective seeks to answer the question whether law (or in this case, judicial rulings) can explain or predict the behavior of school boards and school officials. The behavior looked at may be either behavior that the courts intended

to take place or unintended responses. And, ideally, what is sought is not a mere statement of coincidence or correlation (e.g., the court ordered X to occur, and in fact X did occur), but a causal statement (e.g., the court's order was a necessary and/or sufficient condition for X to occur). If this perspective is used, what might be said in a general way about the impact of the courts?

A first difficulty in doing more research on the impact of the courts on the behavior of school boards and officials is the lack of systematically collected data on the dependent variable itself, namely, school board and administrative behavior. For example, all that is now known about school board and teacher compliance with the prayer decisions is that, on the whole, most boards and teachers are in compliance, but some are not. How widespread the noncompliance is and what the precise characteristics of the noncomplying districts and teachers are remains a mystery.[270] Virtually nothing is known about the extent to which the requirements of procedural due process are actually followed in school disciplinary cases or the extent to which the strictures against baseless and even random searches of pupils are violated. More knowledge is available about the behavior of school boards and school officials in the face of judicial orders to desegregate but less about the practice of segregation in districts not yet subjected to judicial challenges.[271] And something has been recorded in detail about the behavior of school boards and officials in one state regarding compliance with judicial orders on behalf of handicapped pupils.[272]

Despite the paucity of data, one important lesson, which needs further checking, stands out: A constitutional ruling, even from the Supreme Court, is neither a necessary nor a sufficient condition for the behavior ordered. For example, in the aftermath of both the prayer and school desegregation opinions, there were resistance, avoidance, evasion, and defiance of the rulings.[273] Even in the absence of the rulings, there were districts that did not open their day with prayers or purposefully segregate their pupils. A look at behavior not specifically intended by the judiciary as a response to rulings makes it even more obvious that a district's response to what the courts have done cannot simply be assigned to a ruling. For example, it is now commonplace for smaller school districts to place a law firm on retainer and for the larger urban districts to hire their own in-house counsel, a development that has increased the "costs of doing business." Are these new budget items to be explained by the fact of the increased intervention of the courts (certainly one plausible explanation), or by the increase of union activities by teachers, or by the increase in federal and state regulation of school boards? In short, a scientific explanation

of the behavior of school boards and school officials cannot assume that law or judicial rulings are (say, in the absence of coercion to back them up) an important explanatory variable of such behavior. The importance of judicial rulings in causing behavior is a point still to be established, not assumed a priori. Even though there appears to be some correspondence between the behavior of school officials and the massive body of law developed by the courts, the absence of a theory to explain the correspondence leaves coincidence a plausible explanatory condition. Stated differently, even if it is tempting to say that the massive body of law outlined earlier has had a significant influence on the behavior of school officials, the need for caution remains in the absence of a complete and verified theory of board and administrative behavior that takes into account not just judicial rulings but other potentially important variables as well.[274] Clearly, more research carefully grounded in theory is needed to better understand the impact of the judiciary.

One point does appear to be well documented: namely, a strong correlation between the issuance of a judicial ruling and the placing of the issue involved in the case on the political agenda of the community or state.[275] Even if existing research has not provided a theoretical explanation of this phenomenon, leaving the possibility that the correlation may be spurious, intuitively speaking it seems likely that judicial action is a sufficient, but not a necessary, condition for and sequel of political developments. For example, the sufficiency of the judicial ruling seems clear when, for various self-interested reasons, elected officials may feel constrained at least to address the issue raised by the court because (a) not to do so flirts with a contempt of court citation, a fine, and jail; (b) electoral opponents may otherwise successfully exploit the issue; (c) addressing the issue may open the door to other opportunities and/or eliminate a nagging political problem, with the courts serving as a handy scapegoat. That a judicial ruling is not necessary to place an issue on the political agenda is also apparent; more issues are placed on the political agenda in the absence than in the presence of a judicial ruling. Otherwise, there are very few general propositions regarding the impact of the courts on the behavior of public school officials that have been empirically confirmed by documentation beyond a single case study.[276]

NOTES

[1] 347 U.S. 4B3 (1954). For a more detailed treatment of these and other topics taken up in this chapter, see van Geel, T. (1987) *The courts and American education law.* Buffalo, NY: Prometheus Books.

2 For example, in *Tinker v. Des Moines Independent Community School District*, 393 U.S. 503 (1969), the Supreme Court for the first time recognized that students enjoyed a right of freedom of speech. Compare *West Virginia State Board of Education v. Barnette*, 319 U.S. 624 (1943).

3 Civil Rights Act of 1964, 42 U.S.C. § 2000c.d. (1976); 1972 Education Amendments, 20 U.S.C. §§ 1681–86 (1982); the Rehabilitation Act of 1973 (section 504), 29 U.S.C. § 794 (1976); the Education for All Handicapped Children Act, 20 U.S.C. §§ 1401–1461 (1982); Equal Educational Opportunity Act of 1974, 42 U.S.C. §§ 1701 *et seq.* (1976).

4 *Cannon v. University of Chicago*, 441 U.S.C. 677 (1979), interpreting Title IX of the 1972 Education Amendments, 20 U.S.C. §§ 1681–86 (1982), as providing private litigants with a course of action to support their statutory rights; *Miener v. State of Missouri*, 673 F.2d 969 (8th Cir. 1982), interpreting the Rehabilitation Act of 1973, 29 U.S.C. § 794 (1982), as providing private litigants with a course of action to support their statutory rights; *Smith v. Robinson*, 104 S. Ct. 3457 (1984), holding that a handicapped child could not circumvent the procedural requirements of the Education of Handicapped Act, 94–142, by resort to the antidiscrimination provisions of § 504, and that § 504 could not be relied on to obtain damages and attorney fees not available under 94–142.

5 In *School Committee of the Town of Burlington v. Dept of Educ. Commw. of Mass*, 85 L. E.d2d 385 (1985). The Supreme Court ruled that parents of a handicapped child who unilaterally take the child out of public schooling when they consider that placement to be inappropriate can be reimbursed for the tuition of the new school if the transfer is later on appeal determined to have been the appropriate educational program for the child. The Court also held that parents had a possible right to additional reimbursement if there were serious procedural violations by local school officials in the process of deciding the appropriate education for the child. See also *Smith v. Robinson*, 104 S. Ct. 3457 (1984). *Monahan v. State of Neb*, 491 F. Supp. 1074 (D. Neb. 1980), modified, 645 F. 592 (8th Cir. 1981), interpreting the Education for All Handicapped Children Act, 20 U.S.C. § 1401 (1982) as authorizing monetary relief. But see *Anderson v. Thompson*, 658 F.2d 1205 (7th Cir. 1981), disallowing such relief under that same statute. The *Anderson* may have been overruled by the Supreme Court's decision in *Burlington*. In *Lieberman v. University of Chicago*, 660 F.2d 1185 (7th Cir. 1981), the court also concluded that under Title IX of the Education Amendments of 1972, Note 3 above, a damage remedy was not available.

6 42 U.S.C. § 1983 (1976) makes liable in law or equity a person who, acting under color of state law, deprives an individual of his federal constitutional or statutory rights. In *Wood v. Strickland*, 420 U.S. 308 (1975), the Supreme Court concluded school officials were not immune from suit under section 1983.

7 *Adams v. Richardson*, 480 F.2d 1159 (D.C. Cir. 1973); *Adams v. Weinberger*, 391 F. Supp. 269 (D.D.C. 1975); *Brown v. Weinberger*, 417 F. Supp. 1215 (D.C. 1976); *Adams v. Califano*, 430 F. Supp. 118 (D.D.C. 1977). In *United States v. Bd. of Educ. of the City of Chicago*, 588 F. Supp. 132 (N.D. Ill. E.D. 1984), the district court ordered the U.S. government to comply with the consent agreement it reached with the city board of education to find and provide financial assistance for implementation of a desegregation plan.

8 Graglia, L. (1976). *Disaster by decree*. Ithaca, NY: Cornell University Press.

9 Glazer, N. (1975, Fall). Towards an imperial judiciary. *Public Interest*, 41, 104–123.

10 Institute for Research on Educational Finance and Governance, Stanford University. (1980). Do judges run the schools? *IFG Policy Notes*, 1.

11 Title I of the Elementary and Secondary Education Act, formerly found at 20 U.S.C. 241a *et seq.* (1976), now to be found as Chapter 1 of the Education Consolidation and Improvement Act of 1981, 20 U.S.C. § 3801 *et seq.* (1982). Chapter 1 continues the program of federal financial assistance for educationally deprived children created under Title I. Bilingual Education Act of 1974, 20 U.S.C. § 880(b) (1976), providing financial support for bilingual education programs to districts enrolling sizable numbers of limited-English-speaking students; Education for All Handicapped Children Act of 1975 (P.L. 94–142), 20 U.S.C § 1401 (1982), providing financial assistance for the education of handicapped children, coupled with extensive requirements controlling how programs for the handicapped are to be operated.

12 Civil Rights Act of 1964, Title VI, 42 U.S.C. § 2000(d) (1982), prohibiting discrimination on the basis of race in federal assistance programs; Civil Rights Act of 1964, Title VII, 42 U.S.C. § 2000e–2a (1982), prohibiting discrimination in employment on the basis of race, gender, national origin, or religion. Pregnancy Discrimination Act, amendment to Title VII, P. L. 95–555, 92 Stat. 2076; Education Amendments of 1972. Title IX, 20 U.S.C. § 1681 (1976), prohibiting discrimination on the basis of sex in federally assisted programs; Equal Pay Act of 1963, 29 U.S.C. § 206(d) (1982), prohibiting discrimination in pay on the basis of sex for jobs that require equal skill, effort, and responsibility and that are performed under similar working conditions; Age Discrimination in Employment Act of 1967, as amended 1978, 29 U.S.C. § 621 (1982), prohibiting discrimination in employment on the basis of age as regards people between the ages of 40 and 70. Rehabilitation Acts of 1973 (§ 504), 29 U.S.C. § 794 (1982), prohibiting discrimination on the basis of handicap in federal assistance programs; Equal Educational Opportunities Act of 1974, 20 U.S.C. §1701 (1976), prohibiting discrimination on the basis of race, color, sex, or national origin by failing to take action to overcome language barriers that impede equal participation in educational programs.

13 The funding provided under the legislation listed in Note 11, is intended to supplement the local funds already being spent on the target populations, not to substitute for those funds.

14 See text at Note 249.

15 42 U.S.C. § 1983 (1976).

16 *Wood v. Strickland*, 420 U.S. 308 (1975).

17 *Owen v. City of Independence, Mo.*, 100 S. Ct. 1348 (1980), *Monnel v. Dept. of Social Services of N.Y.*, 436 U.S. 658 (1978).

18 See, e.g., *Bilbrey v. Brown*, 738 F.2d 1462 (9th Cir. 1984), a suit by a student for monetary damages for an unlawful search.

19 Tyack initial (1968). The perils of pluralism: (1) The background of the *Pierce* case, *American History Review*, 74 (1), 74–98. For a recent case illustrating the difficult relationship that can occur between private schooling and the state, see *Bangor Baptist Church v. State of Maine. Dept of Educ.*, 576 F. Supp. 1299 (D. Maine, 1983).

20 *Pierce v. Society of Sisters*, 268 U.S. 510 (1925).

21 *Farrington v. Tokushige*, 273 U.S. 284 (1927).

22 *NLRB v. Catholic Bishops of Chicago*, 440 U.S. 490 (1979). Compare *Catholic H.S. Ass'n of Archdiocese v. Culvert*, 573 F. Supp. 1550 (S.D. N.Y. 1983), in which the assertation of jurisdiction by the state labor board violated the establishment clause; *Catholic High School Association of the Archdiocese of New Yort v. Culvert*, 753 F.2d 1161 (2nd Cir. 1985), upholding the constitutionality of the extension of state labor board jurisdiction over private religious schools.

23 *Wisconsin v. Yoder*, 406 U.S. 205 (1972).

24 *Bob Jones University v. United States*, 103 S. Ct. 2017 (1983); *Runyon v. McCrary*, 427 U.S. 160 (1976). The Supreme Court has also held that the loan of textbooks to students attending segregated private schools is constitutionally impermissible. *Norwood v. Harrison*, 413 U.S. 455 (1973). Compare in *Dayton Christian Schools v. Ohio Civil Rights Com'n*, 706 F.2d 932 (6th Cir. 1985). *rev'd on other grounds sub nom.*, *Ohio Civil Rights Com'n v. Dayton Christian Schools*, 106 S. Ct. 2718 (1986). The Sixth Circuit concluded that extending jurisdiction of the state's civil rights commission to a private religious school would violate the free exercise clause.

25 For a recent review of cases in this area, see T. van Geel (1987). *The courts and American education law*. Buffalo, NY: Prometheus Books; Lines, 1983, "Private Education Alternatives and State Regulation," *Journal of Law and Education*, 12, 189. Also see *Duro v. District Attorney, Second Jud. Dist. of N.C.*, 712 F.2d 96 (4th Cir. 1983).

26 Van Geel, T., op cit., 1-6-1-9.

27 *City of Sumner v. First Baptist Church of Sumner*, 97 Wash 2d 1., 639 P.2d 1358 (Wash., 1982), *en banc*.

[28] *State of Ohio v. Whisner*, 47 Ohio St. 2d 181, 351 N.E.2d 750 (1976); Lines, Note 25 above, p. 202.

[29] There seem to have been no court decisions dealing with the issues raised in the text. Any state attempt to regulate the ideological content of educational programs of private schools would presumably survive judicial review only if the state could prove that the need to control was "necessary to achieve a compelling state interest." This test is widely assumed to be appropriate when government seeks to regulate the content of a speech activity, L. Tribe, 1978, *American Constitutional Law*, 576 *et seq*. See also *Brown v. Dade Christian Schools Inc.* 556 F.2d 310 (5th Cir. 1977) (*en banc*), *cert* denied, 434 U.S. 1063 (1978).

[30] The Supreme Court has in recent years generally treated free exercise claims very sympathetically: *Thomas v. Rev. Bd. Ind. Empl. Sec. Div.*, 450 U.S. 707 (1981); *Wisconsin v. Yoder*, 406 U.S. 205 (1972); but see, *U.S. v. Lee*, 455 U.S. 252 (1982).

[31] Yudof, M. (1979). When governments speak: Toward a theory of government expression and the First Amendment. *Texas Law Review*, 57, 863, 890; and see Yudof, H. (1983). Berkeley, CA: *When government speaks*. University of California Press.

[32] *Committee for Pub. Educ. & Rel. Lib. v. Regan*, 444 U.S. 646 (1980), cost reimbursement for administering state required tests; *Wolmen v. Walier*, 433 U.S. 229 (1977), diagnostic and therapeutic services; *Board of Education v. Allen*, 392 U.S. 236 (1968), loan of textbooks; *Everson v. Board Educ.*, 330 U.S. 1 (1947), bus transportation.

[33] *Aguilar v. Felton*, 105 S. Ct. 3232 (1985), educational programs for the disadvantaged; *Grand Rapids Sch. Dist. v. Ball*, 105 S. Ct. 3216 (1985); *Wolman v. Walter*, 433 U.S. 229 (1977), loan to students of instructional materials and equipment, bus transportation for field trips; *Meek v. Pittenger*, 421 U.S. 349 (1975), loan to private schools of instructional material and equipment, provision of services on nonpublic school premises. In *Lemon v. Kruizman*, 403 U.S. 602 (1971), the court struck down efforts on the part of the state to subsidize the salaries of teachers of secular subjects in private religious schools and, more generally, to pick up the costs of providing secular subjects. Direct grants for maintenance and repair of school facilities and equipment were struck down in *Committee for Public Educ. & Rel. Lib. v. Nyquist*, 413 U.S. 756 (1973). And in *Levitt v. Committee for Public Educ. & Lib*, 413 U.S. 472 (1973), the Court struck down a single per-pupil allotment to cover expenses of maintaining pupil enrollment records, health records, personnel qualifications, and the preparation and submission to the state of various reports, including reports of results on teacher-prepared tests.

[34] *Committee for Public Educ. & Rel. Lib. v. Nyquist*, 413 U.S. 756 (1973).

[35] *Mueller v. Allen*, 103 S. Ct. 3062 (1983). See also *Witters v. Washington Dept. Services for the Blind*, 106 S. Ct. 748 (1986), upholding financial assistance to a blind person who chose to use the money to attend a Christian college to study to be a pastor.

[36] *Felton v. Sec. of U.S. Dept of Educ.*, 739 F.2d 48 (2nd Cir. 1984); *Americans United for Separation of Church and State v. Sch. Dist. of Grand Rapids*, 718 F.2d 1389 (6th Cir. 1983).

[37] For a general overview of state court involvement in allocating authority, see L. Peterson, R. Rossmiller, and M. Yolz, 1978, *The law and public school operation*, New York: Harper & Row. For a briefer review see, W. Valenie, 1980, *Law and the schools*, Columbus, OH: Charles E. Merrill.

[38] *Kramer v. Union Free School District No. 15*, 395 U.S. 621 (1969).

[39] *Oliver v. Bd of Educ. of City of N.Y.*, 306 F. Supp. 1286 (S.D. N.Y. 1969). See *Hedley v. Junior College Dist.*, 397 U.S. 50 (1970).

[40] *Brown v. Bd of Sch. Comm of Mobile Cty., Ala.*, 706 F.2d 1103 (11th Cir. 1983), affirmed 104 S. Ct. 520 (1983); *NAACP by Campbell v. Gadsden Cty. Sch. Bd.*, 691 F.2d 978 (1982); *McMillian v. Escambia Cty. Fla.*, 638 F.2d 1239 (5th Cir. 1981). *cert.* dismissed, 453 U.S. 946 (1981); *contra*, *Black Voters v. McDonough*, 421 F. Supp. 165 (D. Mass. 1976), affirmed 565 F.2d 1 (1st Cir. 1977). See also *Rodgers v. Lodge*, 458 U.S. 613 (1982).

[41] *Sierra v. El Paso Indep. Sch. Dist.*, 591 F. Supp. BO2 (W.D. Tex. 1984), striking down an at-large school board election system on the basis of the Voting Rights Act of 1965, as amended; *Jones v. City of Lubbock*, 727 F.2d 364 (5th Cir. 1984), upholding the constitutionality of the 1982 amendments to the Voting Rights Act of 1965, which substituted a results test for the prior requirement that purposeful discrimination be shown.

[42] *Pickering v. Bd. of Educ.*, 391 U.S. 563 (1968). Compare *Givhan v. Western Line Consolidated Sch. Dist.*, 439 U.S. 410 (1979); *Ayers v. Western Line Consolidated Sch. Dist.*, 691 F.2d 766 (5th Cir. 1982). See also *Connick v. Myers*, 103 S. Ct. 1684 (1983); *Knapp v. Whitaker*, 577 F. Supp. 1265 (C.D. Ill., Peoria Div. 1983).

[43] *Connick v. Myers*, 103 S. Ct. 1984 (1983).

[44] *Johnson v. Lincoln Univ. of Conn.*, 776 F. 2d 443 (3d Cir. 1985); *Renfroe v. Kirkpatrick*, 722 F.2d 714 (8th Cir. 1984); *Wells, etc, see, e.g., Wells v. Hica Ind. Sch Dist.*, 736 F.2d 243 (5th Cir. 1984); *Derrickson v. Bd of Educ. of the City of St. Louis*, 738 F.2d 351 (8th Cir. 1984); *Bowman v. Pulaski Cty. Special Sch. Dist.*, 723 F.2d 640 (8th Cir. 1983); *Ferrara v. Mills*, 596 F. Supp. 1069 (S.D. Fla, N.D. 1984).

[45] *City of Madison Joint School Dist. No. 8 v. Wis. Employment Relations Comm'n.*, 429 U.S. 167 (1976). But compare *Minn State Bd. for Comm. Colleges v. Knight*, 104 St. Ct. 1058 (1984), nonunion members may be excluded from "meet and confer" sessions, between administration and union dealing with nonmandatory subjects of negotiations.

[46] *Mount Healthy City School District of Education v. Doyle*, 429 U.S. 274 (1977).

[47] *McLaughlin v. Tilendis*, 398 F.2d 287 (7th Cir. 1968). See also *Lake Park Educ. Ass'n v. Bd. of Educ. of Lake Park*, 526 F. Supp. 710 (N.D. Ill., E.D. 1981). Compare *Hall v. Bd. of Sch. Comm. of Mobile Cty.*, 681 F.2d 965 (5th Cir. 1982), striking down rules that limited the right of a union to distribute literature on school grounds.

[48] *Board of Trustees of University of Kentucky v. Public Employees Council No. 51 AFSCME*, 571 S.W. 2d 616 (Ky. 1978); *Chicago Division of Ill. Educ. Ass'n v. Bd. of Educ.*, 76 Ill. App. 2d 456, 222 N.E. 2d 243 (1966). *Contra*, *Commonwealth of Virginia v. Cty. Bd. of Arlington*, 217 Va. 558, 232 S.E. 2d 30 (1977).

[49] *Perry Educ. Ass'n v. Perry Local Educators' Ass'n.*, 103 S. Ct. 948 (1983), use of teachers' mailboxes need not be made available to minority union. *Minn State Bd. for Community Colleges v. Knight*, 104 S. Ct. 1058 (1984), upholding a statute that prevented participation by nonunion faculty members in statutorily mandated "meet and confer" sessions between faculty and administration at which views were exchanged on policy questions outside the scope of mandatory bargaining. *United Federation of Postal Clerks v. Blount*, 325 F. Supp. 879 (D.D.C. 1971), affdmem 404 U.S. 482 (1971), no constitutional right to strike.

[50] *Abood v. Detroit Bd. of Educ.*, 431 U.S. 209 (1977). See also *Ellis v. Railway Clerks*, 104 S. Ct. 1883 (1984).

[51] Emerson, T. (1970). *The system of freedom of expression*, New York: Vintage Books. p. 610.

[52] *Perducci v. Rutland*, 316 F. Supp. 352 (M.D. Ala. 1970), suggesting *in dictum* that introduction of obscenity into the classroom may be prohibited; *James v. Bd. of Educ.*, 461 F.2d 566 (2d Cir.), *cert.* denied, 409 U.S. 1042 (1972), suggesting *in dictum* that indoctrination by a teacher may be prohibited, *LeRocca v. Bd. of Educ. of Rye City Sch. Dist.*, 63 A. D.2d 1019, 40G N.Y.S. 2d 348 (App. Div. 1978), promoting religious beliefs prohibited; *Cary v. Bd. of Educ.*, 598 F. 2d 535 (10th Cir. 1979), denying claim of teachers of right to select textbooks for their courses; *Johnson v. Stuart*, 702 F.2d 193 (9th Cir. 1983, denying standing to teachers to challenge statutory criteria for selection of textbooks; *Ahern v. Bd. of Educ.*, 327 F. Supp. 1391 (D. Neb. 1971), affirmed 456 F.2d 399 (8th Cir. 1972), teacher may not convert economics course to a course on politics; compare *McElearney v. University of Illinois*, 612 F.2d 285, 288 (7th Cir. 1979), "Academic freedom does not empower a professor to dictate to the University what research will be done using the school's facilities or how many faculty positions will be devoted to a particular area."

[53] E.g., *James v. Bd. Educ.*, 461 F.2d 566 (2d Cir.), *cert.* denied, 409 U.S. 1042 (1972), material and substantial disruption; *Keefe v. Geahakos*, 418 F.2d 359 (1st Cir. 1969), shocking or in-

appropriate; *Brubaker v. Bd. of Educ. Sch. Dist. 149, Cook Cty., Ill.*, 502 F.2d 973 (7th Cir.), affirmed by an equally divided *en banc* court, 502 F.2d 1000, *cert.* denied, 421 U.S. 965 (1975), irrelevancy and inappropriateness; *Mailloux v. Kiley*, 323 F. Supp. 1387 (D. Mass.), affirmed on other grounds, 448 F.2d 1242 (1st 1971), serious educational purpose.

[54] *Brubacker V. Bd. of Educ. Sch. Dist. 149 Cook Cty. Ill.* 502 F.2d 973 (7th Cir.), affirmed by an equally divided *en banc* court, 502 F.2d 1000, *cert.* denied, 421 U.S. 965 (1975).

[55] *Moore v. Sch. Bd.*, 364 F. Supp. 355 (N.D. Fla. 1973).

[56] *Knarr v. Bd. of Sch. Trustees*, 317 F. Supp. 832, 836 (N.D. Ind. 1970), affirmed 452 F.2d 649 (7th Cir. 1971); compare *Petrie v. Forest Hills Sch. Dist. Bd. of Educ.*, 449 N.E.2d 786 (Ohio Ct. App. 1983).

[57] *Mailloux v. Kiley*, 323 F. Supp. 1387 (D. Mass.), affirmed on other grounds, 448 F.2d 1242 (1st 1971); *Keefe v. Geahakos*, 418 F.2d 359 (1st Cir. 1971); *Parducci v. Rutland*, 316 F. Supp. 352 (M.D. Ala. 1970); *James v. Bd. of Educ.*, 461 F.2d 566 (2nd Cir.), *cert.* denied, 409 U.S. 1042 (1972); *Kingsville Ind. Sch. Dist. v. Cooper*, 611 F.2d 1109 (5th Cir. 1980); *Sterzing v. Fort Bend Ind. Sch. Dist.*, 376 F. Supp. 657 (S.D. Tex. 1972), vacated on other grounds, 496 F.2d 92 (5th Cir. 1974). *Contra Fischer v. Fairbanks North Start Borough Sch Dist.*, 704 P.2d 213 (Alaska, 1985), upholding power of board to prohibit teachers from using even supplementary materials without prior board approval.

[58] *Russo v. Central Sch. Dist. No. 1*, 469 F.2d 623 (2nd Cir. 1972), *cert.* denied, 411. U.S. 932 (1973).

[59] *Palmer v. Bd. of Educ. of City of Chicago*, 603 F.2d 1271 (7th Cir. 1979), *cert.* denied, 444 U.S. 1026 (1980).

[60] E.g., *Mailloux v. Kiley*, 448 F.2d 1242 (1st Cir. 1971), affirmed, 323 F. Supp. 1387 (D. Mass. 1971).

[61] *Blackhawk Teachers Fed. v. Wis. Emply. Rel. Comm.*, 109 Wis. 2d 414, 326 N.W.2d 247 (Ct. App. 1982).

[62] *Plyler v. Doe*, 457 U.S. 202 (1982), exclusion of illegal aliens from public schools; *Griffin v. Cty. School Bd.*, 377 U.S. 218 (1964), exclusion of black children from public schools; *Mill v. Bd. of Educ.*, 348 F. Supp. 866 (D.D.C. 1972), exclusion of handicapped children from school; *PARC v. Commonwealth*, 334 F. Supp. 1257 (E.D. Pa. 1971), 343 F. Supp. 279 (E.D. Pa. 1972), consent order ending exclusion of handicapped children from public schools.

[63] 1974 Equal Educational Opportunity Act, Section 204, 20 U.S.C. § 1703 (1976), prohibiting discrimination on the basis of race, color, sex, or national origin by failing to take appropriate action to overcome language barriers that impede equal participation by students in the instructional program; *Irving Ind. Sch. Dist. v. Tetro*, 104 S. Ct. 3371 (1984), interpreting P.L. 94–142, Education of Handicapped Act, to require a school district to provide a handicapped child with catherization to enable the child to remain in the public school program and to benefit from a special education program.

[64] *Martinez v. Bynum*, 103 S.Ct. 1838 (1983), *Niles v. University Interscholastic League*, 715 F.2d 1027 (5th Cir. 1983); *Horton v. Marshal Public Schools*, 589 F. Supp. 95 (W.D. Ark., Harrison Div. 1984).

[65] *Plyler v. Doe*, 457 U.S. 202 (1982). In both *Plyler* and *Antonio Independent Sch. Dist. v. Rodriguez*, 411 U.S. 1 (1973), the Supreme Court said that Constitution does not establish a right to an education.

[66] For a complete, critical, but often frustratingly ambiguous review of this history, see J. H. Wilkinson III, 1979, *From Brown to Bakke*, Oxford: Oxford University Press.

[67] 347 U.S. 483 (1954).

[68] Goodman. (1972). De facto school segregation: A constitutional and empirical analysis. 60 *California Law Review*, 60, 275.

[69] *Village of Arlington Heights v. Metropolitan Housing Corporation*, 429 U.S. 252 (1977); *Washington v. Davis*, 426 U.S. 229 (1976); *Keyes v. School District No. 1*, 413 U.S. 189 (1973), rehearing denied, 414 U.S. 883 (1973).

[70] In *Milliken v. Bradley*, 418 U.S. 717 (1974), the Supreme Court erected an enormous constitutional barrier that blocks the way of the lower courts to tackle perhaps the most significant form of de facto segregation—the interdistrict segregation that exists among

central city school districts and suburban districts. Said the Supreme Court, federal district courts could not order the involvement of suburban districts in an interdistrict desegregation plan unless it were established that racially discriminatory acts of the suburban districts were a substantial cause of the interdistrict segregation.

[71] *Keyes v. School District No. 1*, 413 U.S. 189 (1973), rehearing denied, 414 U.S. 883 (1973).

[72] For a discussion of various versions of the foreseeability test, see van Geel, 1980, Racial discrimination from Little Rock to Harvard, *Cincinnati Law Review*, 49, 49.

[73] *Washington v. Davis*, 426 U.S. 229 (1976); accord, *Village of Arlington Heights v. Metropolitan Housing Corporation*, 429 U.S. 252 (1977).

[74] See van Geel, 1980, School Desegregation doctrine and the performance of the judiciary. *Educational Administration Quarterly*, 60, 16. In *Columbus Bd. of Educ. v. Penick*, 443 U.S. 449 (1979), and *Deyton Bd. of Educ. v. Brinkman*, 443 U.S. 526 (1979), the Court affirmed lower court opinions that in a closing reading the foreseeability test was virtually the sole basis for concluding the districts had intentionally segregated their pupils.

[75] *Columbus Bd of Educ. v. Penick*, 443 U.S. 449 (1979); *Dayton v. Brinkman*, 443 U.S. 526 (1979).

[76] *Brown v. Bd. of Educ.*, 349 U.S. 294 (1955); *Green v. Cty. Sch. Bd.*, 391 U.S. 430 (1968).

[77] *Milliken v. Bradley*, 433 U.S. 267 (1977). *Swann v. Charlotte-Mecklenburg Bd. of Educ.*, 402 U.S. 1 (1971), *Liddle v. State of Mo.*, 731 F.2d 1294 (8th Cir. 1984); *Margen v. Kerrigan*, 388 F. Supp. 581 (D. Mass. 1975), affirmed, 530 F.2d 401 (1st Cir.), *cert.* denied, 426 U.S. 935 (1976). Hiring quotas are a particularly sensitive issue, and the courts are cautious in ordering it. See *Oliver v. Kalamazoo Bd. of Educ.*, 706 F.2d 757 (6th Cir. 1983). But see *Caulfield v. Bd. of Educ. of the City of New York*, 632 F.2d 999 (2d Cir. 1980), *cert.* denied, 450 U.S. 1030 (1981).

[78] Dentler, R., & Scott, M. (1981). *Schools on trial: An inside account of the Boston desegregation case*. Cambridge, MA: Abt Associates. This account of the litigation and political in-fighting over the implementation of the judicial decree is one of the best case studies of its kind.

[79] Kirp, D. (1982). *Just schools*. Kirp, D. (1981). Legalism and politics in school desegregation. *Wisconsin Law Review*, 924. See *San Francisco NAACP v. San Francisco Unified Sch. Dist.*, 576 F. Supp. 34. Berkeley, CA: University of California Press.

[80] *Milliken v. Bradley*, 414 U.S. 717 (1974); *Branson v. Bd. of Educ. of the City Sch. Dist. of the City of Cinncinnati*, 578 F. Supp. 1091 (S.D. Ohio, W.D. 1984).

[81] *Pasadena City Bd. of Educ. v. Spangler*, 427 U.S. 424 (1976); *Ross v. Houston Ind. Sch Dist.*, 699 F.2d 218 (5th Cir., 1983).

[82] See generally, Fiss 1965, Racial Imbalance in the Public Schools: The Constitutional Concepts, 78 *Harvard Law Review*, 564 (78), 591–592.

[83] Brest. (1976). Foreword in defense of the antidiscrimination principle. *Harvard Law Review*, 1(90), 2.

[84] Karst. (1977). The Supreme Court 1976 term—Foreword: Equal citizenship under the Fourteenth Amendment. 91 *Harvard Law Review*, 1(91), 6.

[85] Fiss. (1976). Groups and the Equal Protection Clause. *Philosophy and Public Affairs* 5(5), 107, 147.

[86] *Engle v. Vitale*, 370 U.S. 421 (1962).

[87] *Abington Sch. Dist. v. Schempp*, 374 U.S. 203 (1963); in *Marsh v. Chambers*, 463 U.S. ——(1983), the Supreme Court upheld the Nebraska Legislature's practice of opening each legislative day with a prayer led by a chaplain paid by the state.

[88] *Wallace v. Jaffree*, 105 S. Ct. 2479 (1985).

[89] *Stone v. Graham*, 449 U.S. 39 (1980).

[90] *McCollum v. Bd. of Educ.*, 333 U.S. 203 (1948).

[91] *Epperson v. Arkansas*, 393 U.S. 97 (1968).

[92] *Zorach v. Clausan*, 343 U.S. 306 (1952).

[93] Justice Stewart, dissenting in *Abington Sch Dist. v. Schempo*, 374 U.S. 203 (1963), argued that not to permit prayers in the public schools placed religion at an artificial and state-created disadvantage. *Id.* at p. 308.

[94] *Florey v. Sioux Falls Sch. Dist. 49–5*, 464 F. Supp. 911

(D.S.D. 1979), affirmed 619 F.2d 1311 (8th Cir. 1980), *cert.* denied, 449 U.S. 987 1980.

[95] *Stein v. Plainwell Community Schools,* 610 F. Supp. 43 (D.C. Mich. 1985), graduation; *Grossberg v. Deusevin,* 380 F. Supp. 285 (E.D. Va. 1974), graduation, *Wood v. Mount Lebanon Sch. Dist.,* 342 F. Supp. 1293 (W.D. Pa. 1972), graduation; *Chamberlain v. Dade Cty Bd. of Pub. Instr.,* 160 So.2d 97 (Fla. 1964), reversed in part and dismissed in part, 377 U.S. 402 (1964), baccalaureate exercises.

[96] *Meltzer v. Bd. of Public Instruction of Orange Cty., Fla.,* 577 F.2d 311 (5th Cir. 1978), *cert.* denied, 439 U.S. 1089 (1979).

[97] (a) *Use of School Facilities:* See e.g. *Nartowicz v. Clayton Cty. Sch. Dist.,* 736 F.2d 646 (11th Cir. 1984), striking down policy of letting student religious group meet on school property under faculty supervision and allowing church-sponsored activities to be announced on school address system and on school bulletin boards; *Bender v. Williamsport Area Sch. Dist.,* 563 F. Supp. 697 (1983), reversed 741 F.2d 538 (3rd Cir. 1984), vacated and remanded on other ground. 106 S. Ct. 1326 (1986), upholding refusal to permit prayer club to meet in school facilities before start of school day; *Brandon v. Bd. of Educ. of Guilderland Central Sch. Dist.,* 635 F.2d 971 (2d Cir. 1980), *cert.* denied. 4454 U.S. 1123 (1981), refusal to permit use of school facilities permissible, *Lubbock Civil Liberties Union v. Lubbock Ind. Sch. Dist.,* 669 F.2d 1038 (5th Cir. 1982), *cert.* denied, 103 S. Ct. 800 (1983), striking down as a violation of the establishment clause a school policy permitting religious clubs to meet on school grounds before or after regular school hours. It should be noted that in *Widmar v. Vincent,* 454 U.S. 263 (1981), the Supreme Court held that a university could not exclude a student religious group from meeting anywhere on university grounds. And the Equal Access Act (P.A. No. 98–377), which became effective on August 17, 1984, makes it unlawful for any public secondary school to discriminate in granting access to student groups to school facilities on the basis of religion or other belief if the school receives federal assistance and is operating a limited open forum as defined in the law. (b) *Silent Meditation:* Most lower courts that have considered the issue have struck down the required moment of silent meditation. The Supreme Court will soon be reviewing one of these cases, posing a cruical test for the current majority's attitude toward the involvement of the schools with religion. See. e.g., *Jeffee v. Wallace,* 705 F.2d 1526 (11th Cir. 1983), *cert.* granted, 52 U.S.L.W. 3713 (1984); *May v. Cooperman,* 572 F. Supp. 1561 (D.N.J. 1983), *Duffy v. Las Cruces Public Schools,* 557 F. Supp. 1013 (1983); *Beck v. McElrath,* 548 F. Supp. 1161 (1982), vacated and remanded, 718 F.2d 1098 (6th Cir. 1983). *Contra, Gaines v. Anderson,* 421 F. Supp. 337 (D. Mass. 1976).

[98] L. Tribe, *supra* Note 29, at 828 (1978), suggesting silent moments are constitutional; but see Seide, 1983, Daily moments of silence in public schools: A constitutional analysis. *New York University Review,* 364.

[99] *Karen B. v. Treen,* 653 F.2d 897 (5th Cir. Unit A 1981), affirmed 455 U.S. 913 (1982).

[100] *Malnak v. Yogi,* 440 F. Supp. 1284 (D.N.J.), affirmed 592 F.2d 192 (3rd Cir. 1979).

[101] *Doe v. Aldine Ind. Sch. Dist.,* 563 F. Supp. 883 (S.D. Tex 1982); *Crockett v. Sorenson,* 568 F. Supp. 1422 (W.D. Vir. 1983); *Wiley v. Franklin,* 474 F. Supp. 525 (E.D. Tenn. 1979).

[102] *Hall v. Bd. of Sch. Comm. of Conecuh Cty.,* 656 F.2d 999 (5th Cir. Unit 8 1981), modified, 707 F.2d 464 (11th Cir. 1983).

[103] *Meltzer v. Bd. of Public Instruction of Orange Ciy, Fla.,* 548 F.2d 559 (5th Cir. 1977), affirmed and reversed in part, 577 F.2d 311 (1978), *en banc.*

[104] *Daniel v. Waters,* 515 F.2d 485 (6th Cir. 1975).

[105] *McLean v. Arkansas Bd. of Educ.,* 529 F. Supp. 1255 (E.D. Arkanses, W.D. 1982).

[106] *Wright v. Houston Ind. Sch. Dist.,* 366 F. Supp. (S.D. Tex. 1972), affirmed, 486 F.2d 137 (5th Cir. 1973), *cert.* denied, 417 U.S. 969 (1974), biology class; *Citizens for Parental Rights v. San Mateo City Bd. of Educ.,* 1 Cal. App. 3d 1, 124 Cal. Rptr. 68 (1975), sex education course; *Cornwell v. State Bd. of Educ.,* 314 F. Supp. 340 (D. Md. 1969), affirmed, 428 F.2d 471 (4th Cir. 1970), *cert.* denied, 400 U.S. 942 (1970), sex education course; *Williams v. Bd. of Educ. of the Cty. of Kenawha,* 388 F. Supp. 93 (D. W. Va. 1975), affirmed,

530 F.2d 972 (4th Cir. 1975), textbook; *Grove v. Mead Sch. Dist.,* 753 F.2d 65 1528 (9th Cir. 1985), rejecting challenge to the use of a textbook; *Mercer v. Michigan State Bd. of Educ.,* 379 F. Supp. 580. (E.D. Mich. 1974), rejecting challenge to state law that prohibits instruction on the subject of birth control. Compare *Mozert v. Hawkins Cty. Pub. Sch.,* 765 F.2d 75 (6th Cir. 1985), remanding for trial a case in which parents claimed that a set of basic readers used by the school infringed on their right to the free exercise of religion. At the conclusion of the trial the federal district court concluded that the required use of the books did infringe on the free exercise rights of the students, ordered that they be exempted from required use of the books, and required that parents provide alternative instruction in reading to their children. Mozert v. Hawkins Cty. Pub. Schools., 647 F. Supp. 1194 (E.D. Tenn. 1986).

[107] Compare *Sepp v. Renfroe,* 511 F.2d 172 (5th Cir. 1975), with *Spence v. Bailey,* 465 F.2d 797 (6th Cir. 1972).

[108] *Lynch v. Donnelly,* 104 S. Ct. 1355 (1984), upholding city's purchase and display of a nativity scene along with other symbols of Christmas; *Marsh v. Chambers,* 463 U.S. 783 (1983), upholding opening of legislative day with a prayer led by a chaplain paid from state funds.

[109] *Jaffee v. Wallace,* 705 F.2d 1526 (11th Cir. 1983), *cert.* granted, 52 U.S.L.W. 3713 (1984); the Equal Access Act (P.A. No. 98–377), which became effective on August 17, 1984, makes it unlawful for any public secondary school to discriminate in granting access to student groups to school facilities on the basis of religion or other belief if the school receives federal assistance and is operating a limited open forum as defined in the law.

[110] 319 U.S. 624 (1943).

[111] *Lipo v. Morris,* 579 F.2d 834 (3rd Cir. 1978), need not stand at attention; *Goetz v. Ansell,* 477 F.2d 636 (2nd Cir. 1973), student may not be required to either stand or leave room.

[112] *Bd. of Educ., Island Trees Union Free Sch. Dist. No. 26 v. Pico,* 457 U.S. 853 (1982); *Ambach v. Norwick,* 441 U.S. 68 (1979).

[113] 457 U.S. 853 (1982).

[114] It is important in note that even those justices who agreed the First Amendment did impose limits on the school board's discretion to remove books from the school library agreed that the board could remove books if they were vulgar. Justices Brennan, Marshall, and Stevens would permit the removal of the books if they were "pervasively vulgar." *Id* at p. 871. However, Justice Blackmun said books could be removed if they contained "offensive language." *Id* at p. 880. Obviously, the dissenters who would not restrain the board's discretion also agreed vulger books were removable. *Id* at p. 885, 893, 904, 921.

[115] *Keyishian v. Bd. of Regents,* 385 U.S. 589, 603 (1967); *Bd. of Educ., Island Trees Union Free Sch. Dist.,* 457 U.S. 853, 870 (1982).

[116] van Geel, T. (1983). The search for constitutional limits on governmental authority to inculcate youth. *Texas Law Review,* 62 (2) 197–297.

[117] *Lowen v. Turniseed,* 488 F. Supp. 1138 (ND. Miss. 1980).

[118] Fischer, L., & Schimmel, D. (1982). *The rights of students and teachers.* New York: Harper & Row.

[119] McCarthy, M. M., & Cambron, N. H. (1981). *Public school law.* Boston: Allyn & Bacon.

[120] *Id* at p. 228; L. Fischer and D. Schimmel, above, Note 114 at p. 278; and see generally, Goldstein, 1969, "The scope and sources of school board authority to regulate student conduct and statues: A monconstitutional analysis." *University of Pennsylvania Law Review, 373* (117).

[121] E.g., *Davis v. Meek,* 344 F. Supp. 298 (N.D. Ohio 1972), no discrimination against married students in any phase of schooling; *Ordway v. Hargraves,* 323 F. Supp. 1155 (D. Mass 1971), exclusion from regular school program of pregnant unmarried student prohibited.

[122] 45 C.F.R. § 106.40 (a) (b) (1983).

[123] *Bellotti v. Baird,* 443 U.S. 622 (1979).

[124] See, e.g., *Force v. Pierce City R-VI Sch. Dist.,* 570 F. Supp. 1020 (W.D. Mo. 1983), in which the court ruled that Title XI did not require sex-segregated teams even in contact sports and that constitutionally schools could not exclude women or girls from trying out

for the boys' football team. In this case no girls' team was available, thus technically the court was not called on to decide if a district could constitutionally establish sex-segregated teams; but there is language in the opinion suggesting judicial hostility to sex-segregation even in those circumstances. Accord, *Morris v. Michigan State Bd. of Educ.*, 472 F.2d 1207 (6th Cir. 1973, noncontact sport; *Lantz v. Ambach*, 620 F. Supp. 663 (D.C.N.Y. 1985), contact sport. *Contra, O'Connor v. Bd. of Educ. of Sch. Dist. No. 23*, 545 F. Supp. 376 (N.D. Ill. E.D. 1982), exclusion of girls from boys' basketball team permissible at least when there is a girl's team available. Compare *O'Connor v. Bd. of Educ. of Sch. Dist. 23*, 449 U.S. 1301 (1980).

[125] *Pennsylvania v. Pennsylvania Interscholastic Athletic Ass'n.*, 334 A.2d 839 (Pa. 1975), female teams in football and wrestling available.

[126] *Marris v. Michigan State Bd. of Educ.*, 472 F.2d 1207 (6th Cir. 1973).

[127] *Gomes v. R.I. Interscholastic League*, 469 F. Supp. 659 (D.R.I. 1979), vacated as moot, 604 F.2d 733 (1st Cir. 1979), boy could try out for girls' volleyball team when no boys' team available; *contra, Petrie v. Ill. H.S. Ass'n*, 75 Ill. App. 3d 980, 31 Ill. Dec. 653, 394 N.E.2d 855 (Ill. App. 1979).

[128] *Mississippi University for Women v. Hogan*, 458 U.S. 71B (1982).

[129] *Cape v. Tenn. Sec. Sch. Athletic Ass'n.*, 563 F.2d 793 (6th Cir. 1977); *Dodson v. Ark. Activities Ass'n.*, 468 F. Supp. 394 (E.D. Ark. 1979); *Jones v. Okla. Sec. Sch. Activities Ass'n.*, 453 F. Supp. 150 (W.D. Okla. 1977).

[130] *Hammond v. Marx*, 406 F. Supp. 853 (D. Me. 1975); *Ispuith v. Levitt*, 285 A.D. 833, 137 N.Y.S.2d 497 (A.D.2nd Dept. 1955).

[131] *Sendlin v. Johnson*, 643 F.2d 1027 (4th Cir. 1981).

[132] Oakes. (1983). Tracking and ability grouping in American schools: Some constitutional questions. *Teachers College Record, 84*, 801. Kirp. (1973). Schools as sorters: The constitutional and policy implications of student classification. *University of Pennsylvania Law Review, 121*, 705.

[133] E.g., *McNeal v. Tate Cty. Sch. Dist.*, 508 F.2d 1017 (5th Cir. 1975).

[134] Oakes, above, Note 132 at pp. 804–805.

[135] *Hobson v. Hansen*, 269 F. Supp. 401 (D.D.C. 1967), affirmed nominally, *Smuck v. Hobson*, 408 F.2d 175 (D.C. Cir. 1969) (en banc), See also *Ga. State Conf. of Br. of NAACP v. State of Ga.*, 775 F.2d 1403 (11th Cir. 1985).

[136] *Larry P. V. Riles*, 495 F. Supp. 926 (1979). On appeal the Ninth Circuit reversed the lower court's finding that the state had engaged in intentional discrimination on the basis of race thereby violating the equal protection clause of the Fourteenth Amendment, but upheld the district court's conclusion that Title VI had been violated. *Larry P. by Lucille P. v. Riles*, 793 F.2d 969 (9th Cir. 1984). See also *Bester v. Tuscaloosa City Bd. of Educ.*, 722 F.2d 1514 (11th Cir. 1984).

[137] But see *Parents in Action on Special Education v. Hennan*,

[138] *Lora v. Bd. of Educ. of the City of New York*, 456 F. Supp. 1211 (E.D. N.Y. 1978), vacated and remanded, 623 F.2d 248 (2nd Cir. 1980).

[139] *Vorchheimer v. Sch. Dist. of Philadelphia*, 532 F.2d 880 (3rd Cir. 1976) affirmed by an equally divided Court, 430 U.S. 703 (1977).

[140] *Mississippi University for Women v. Hogan*, 458 U.S. 718 (1982).

[141] See the text accompanying Notes 120–123; 45 C.F.R. § 106.34 (1983).

[142] Education for All Handicapped Children Act of 1975, 20 U.S.C. §§ 1412 (5) (B) (1982), requiring that to the maximum extent appropriate handicapped children be educated with children who are not handicapped.

[143] E.g., *Springdale Sch. Dist. 50 of Wash. Cty. v. Grace*, 693 F.2d 41 (8th Cir. 1982). In *St. Louis Developmental Disabilities Treatment Center Parents Association v. Mallory*, 591 F. Supp. 1416 (W.D. Md., C.D. 1984), the court rejected the claim that all of Missouri's special schools and facilities for the profoundly and severely handicapped be closed on the grounds that placement of handi-

capped children in those facilities violates the requirements of P.L. 94–142 and the children's constitutional rights.

[144] Education for All Handicapped Children Act of 1975, 20 U.S.C. §§ 1401 *et seq.* (1982).

[145] *Doe v. Bd. of Educ. of Montgomery Cty.*, 453 A.2d Bl 4 (Md. 1982); *Hunter v. Bd. of Educ. of Montgomery Cty.*, 439 A.2d 582 (Md. 1982); *Donohue v. Copiague Union Free Sch. Dist.*, 47 N.Y.S.2d 440, 391 N.E.2d 352, 418 N.Y.S.2d 375 (1979); *Hoffman v. Bd. of Educ.*, 49 N.Y.2d 121, 400 N.E.2d 317, 424 N.Y.S.2d 376 (1979); *Peter W. v. San Francisco Scht Dist.*, 60 Cal. App.3d Unified. 814, 131 Cal. Rpar. 854 (1976). In *Torres v. Little Flower Children's Services*, the New York Court of Appeals by a 4–3 vote rejected the claim of a Spanish-speaking student that he was illiterate because he had been misdiagnosed as retarded while in the care of a city agency. But in *Snow v. State of N.Y.*, the New York Court of Appeals ruled that the placement of a deaf child in a class for the retarded raised an issue of medical rather than educational malpractice. See Alina Tugend, January 9, 1985, "School-malpractice theory rejected by N.Y. court," *Education Week, Vol. 4*, 1, 14.

[146] *San Antonio Indep Sch. Dist. v. Rodriguez.*, 411 U.S. 1 (1973).

[147] Van Geel, T. (1982). The courts and school finance reform: An expected utility model. In N.H. Cambron-McCabe & A. Odden (Eds.), *The changing politics of school finance.* Cambridge, MA: Ballinger. Lawyers' Committee for Civil Rights Under Law. (1982, June). *Update on state-wide school finance cases.*

[148] *Robinson v. Cahill*, 62 N.J. 473. 303 A. 2d 273 (1973).

[149] *Seattle Sch. Dist. No. 1 v. Washington*, 90 Wash. 2d 476, 585 P.2d 71 (1978).

[150] *Bd. of Educ. of Hendrick Hudson Central Sch. Dist. v. Rowley*, 458 U.S. 176 (1982). It is worth noting that failure to provide a handicapped child with an appropriate education may also be a violation of § 504 of the Rehabilitation Act of 1973, 29 U.S.C. § 794 (1976). In this connection, see *Smith v. Robinson*, 104 S. Ct. 3457 (1984), holding that a handicapped child could not circumvent the procedural requirements of the Education of All Handicapped Children Act, 94–142, by resorting to the antidiscrimination provisions of § 504 and that § 504 could not be relied on to obtain damages and attorney's fees not available under 94–142.

[151] *Irving Ind. Sch. Dist. v. Tatro*, 104 S. Ct. 3371 (1984).

[152] See also, e.g., *Department of Educ. State of Haw. v. Katherine D.*, 727 F.2d 809 (9th Cir. 1984), holding that placement in regular school program with training for the staff to provide "medical services" was an appropriate free education; *Kruelle v. New Castle Cty. Sch. Dist.*, 642 F.2d 687 (3d Cir. 1981), ordering residential placement for the child; *Parks v. Pavkovic*, 753 F.2d 1397 (7th Cir. 1985), cert. denied sub nom., *Belletire v. Parks*, 105 S. Ct. 3529 (1985), ordering state to pay full costs of residential placement. *Max M. v. Thompson*, 592 F. Supp. 1437 (1984), psychotherapy may be a related service that must be provided the child at no charge to parents; *Geis v. Bd. of Educ. of Parsippany-Troy Hills*, 589 F. Supp. 269 (D. N.J. 1984), placement of child in residential school was more appropriate then placement in his home.

[153] *Lau v. Nichols*, 414 U.S. 563 (1974).

[154] Levin. (1983). An analysis of the federal attempt to regulate bilingual education: protecting civil rights or controlling curriculum. *Journal of Law and Education, 12*, 29.

[155] *Casteneda v. Pickard*, 648 F.2d 989 (5th Cir. 1981). See *Keyes v. Sch. Dist. No. 1*, 576 F. Supp. 1503 (1983), applying the standards outlined in *Castaneda* to the program in the Denver schools and concluding that the district had not developed a plan reasonably calculated to implement the district's chosen theory. *Otero v. Mesa Cty. Sch. Dist. No. 51*, 408 F. Supp. 162 (D. Colo. 1975), vacated on other grounds, 568 F.2d 1312 (10th Cir. 1977), rejecting Title VI claim for bilingual education; accord, *Guadelupe Organization. Inc. v. Tempe Elementary Sch. Dist.*, 587 F.2d 1022 (9th Cir. 1978). But see *Cintron v. Brentwood Union Free Sch. Dist.*, 455 F. Supp. 57 (E.D. N.Y. 1978); *Rios v. Read*, 480 F. Supp. 14 (E.D. N.Y. 1978); *Serna v. Portales Municipal Schools*, 351 F. Supp. 1279 (D.N.M. 1972), affirmed an other grounds, 499 F.2d 1147 (10th Cir. 1974).

[156] McClung. (1979). Competency testing programs: Legal and educational issues. *Fordham Law Review, 47*, 651, 655 See also G. F.

Madaus. (Ed.). (1983) *The courts, validity and minimum competency testing*. Boston: Kluwer-Nijhoff.

[157] *Debra P. v. Turlington*, 474 F. Supp. 244 (M.D. Fla. 1979), affirmed in part, vacated in part and remanded, 644 F. 397 (5th Cir. Unit B 1981).

[158] *Debra P. v. Turlington*, 564 F. Supp. 177 (M.D. Fla. 1983), affirmed, 730 F.2d 1405 (11th Cir. 1984).

[159] *Brookhart v. Ill. State Bd. of Educ.*, 534 F. Supp. 725 (C.D. Ill. 1982), reversed, 697 F.2d 179 (7th Cir. 1983).

[160] *Id.* See also *Bd. of Educ. Northport-East Northport Union Free Sch. Dist. v. Ambch*, 458 N.Y.S.2d 680 (App. Div. 1982), *aff'd mem*, 469 N.Y.S.2d 669 (1983), *cert.* denied. 52 U.S.L.W. 3575 (1984).

[161] W. Valente, above, Note 37, at p. 356 *et seq*. Korpela. Tort liability of public schools and institutions of higher learning for injuries resulting from lack or insufficiency of supervision, 38 A.L.R. 3d 830 (1971); see also *Miller v. State*, 478 N.Y.S.2d 829 (N.Y. App. Div. 1984), duty on part of state to keep dorm safe from intruders who may rape; *Peterson v. San Francisco Commun. College Dist.*, 205 Cal. Rptr. 842 (Cal. 1984), student who pays a parking fee is an invitee and can collect damages for attack by an individual hiding in the foliage, which had been used by previous attackers.

[162] *Youngberg v. Romeo*, 457 U.S. 307 (1982). Since *Youngberg* dealt with an involuntarily confined mental patient, its applicability to students beyond the age of compulsory education may be questioned. In *Daniel v. Williams*, 54 U.S.L.W. 4090 (Jan 21, 1986), the Supreme Court said that the due process clause of the Fourteenth Amendment is not implicated by the negligent acts of officials that cause the unintended loss of or injury to life, liberty, or property.

[163] Civil Rights Act of 1964, 42 U.S.C. § 2000c, d(1976); 1972 Education Amendments, 20 U.S.C. §§ 1681–86 (1982). The federal regulations on sexual harassment are reported at 29 C.F.R. § 1604.11 (1984).

[164] Rehabilitation Acts of 1973, Section 504, 29 U.S.C. § 794 (1976); *Commw. of Pa. Dept. of Trans. v. Johnson*, 478 A.2d 521 (Pa. Commw. Ct. 1984), reversing denial of school bus license to person who had previously suffered a heart attack.

[165] *Connally v. General Construction Co.*, 269 F. 385, 391 (1926), a law is void on its face if it is so vague that persons "of common intelligence must necessarily guess at its meaning and differ as to its application."

[166] *Alex v. Allen*, 409 F. Supp. 379 (W.D. Pa. 1976); *contra Soglin v. Kauffman*, 418 F.2d 163 (7th Cir. 1969); *Richards v. Thurston*, 424 F.2d 1281 (1st Cir. 1970), preexisting rule is not necessary before imposing discipline; *accord, Shanely v. Northeast Ind. Sch. Dist.*, 462 F.2d 960, 970–1 (5th Cir. 1972), when conduct is patently wrongful, prior notice is not necessary. But see *Nitzberg v. Parks*, 525 F.2d 378 (4th Cir. 1975) and *Leibner v. Sharbaugh*, 429 F. Supp. 744 (D. Va. 1977), published rules are required where speech-related activities are involved or where penalties are severe.

[167] *Tinker v. Des Moines Ind. Comm. Sch. Dist.*, 393 U.S. 503 (1969).

[168] *Bethel Sch. Dist. No. 403 v. Fraser*, 106 S. Ct. 3159 (1968).

[169] *Scovile v. Bd. of Educ.*, 425 F.2d 10 (7th Cir. 1970), *cert.* denied, 400 U.S. 826 (1970), criticism of school officials; *Guzick v. Drebus*, 431 F.2d 594 (6th Cir. 1970), *cert.* denied, 401 U.S. 948 (1970), badges expressing ethnic pride; *Trackman v. Anker*, 563 F.2d 512 (2nd Cir. 1977), *cert.* denied, 435 U.S. 925 (1978), sex questionnaire; *Katz v. McAulay*, 438 F.2d 1058 (2nd Cir. 1971), *cert.* denied, 405 U.S. 933 (1972), solicitation of funds; *Tate v. Bd. of Educ. of Jonesboro, Ark.*, 453 F.2d 975 (8th Cir. 1972), silent demonstration. Compare *Boyd v. Board of Directors of McGehee School District*, 612 F. Supp. 86 (D.C. Ark. 1985), protecting black students from disciplinary action after they walked out of a pep rally and refused to participate in the football game scheduled for that night.

[170] *Sullivan v. Houston Ind. Sch. Dist.*, 333 F. Supp. 1149 (S.D. Tex. 1971), vulgar words in underground paper; *Fenton v. Stear*, 423 F. Supp. 767 (W.D. Pa 1976), vulgar epithet; *Jacobs v. Bd. of Sch. Comm.*, 490 F.2d 601 (7th Cir. 1973), vacated as moot, 420 U.S. 128 (1975), dictum concerning distribution of obscene materials. Compare *Papish v. Bd. of Curators of U. of Mo.*, 410 U.S. 667 (1973), distribution of offensive political cartoon on a college campus must

be allowed. In *Fraser v. Bethel School Dist.*, No. 403, 755 F.2d 1356 (9th Cir. 1985), *cert.* granted, 106 S. Ct. 56 (1985), the Ninth Circuit protected a student from disciplinary action imposed in response to a nominating speech filled with sexual innuendo given by Fraser.

[171] *Gambino v. Fairfax Cty. Sch. Bd.*, 429 F. Supp. 731 (E.D. Va. 1977), affirmed 564 F.2d 157 (4th Cir. 1977); *Kuhlmeier v. Hazelwood Sch. Dist.*, 578 F. Supp. 1286 (E.D. Ma. E.D. 1984). Compare *Stanton v. Brunswick Sch. Dept.*, 577 F. Supp. 1560 (D. Me. 1984), refusal to publish quotation student chose for use in yearbook next to her picture is impermissible.

[172] E.g., *Baughman v. Freienmuth*, 478 F.2d 1345 (4th Cir. 1973); *Eisner v. Stamford Bd. of Educ.*, 440 F.2d 803 (2nd Cir. 1971). Contra, *Fujishima v. Bd. of Educ.*, 460 F.2d 1355 (7th Cir. 1972).

[173]

[174] *Healy v. James*, 408 U.S. 169 (1972).

[175] *Hawkins v. Coleman*, 376 F. Supp. 1330 (N.D. Tex 1974); 45 C.F.R. § 106.31(b) (4) (1983).

[176] E.g., *Richards v. Thurston*, 421 F.2d 1281 (1st Cir. 1979), student objections upheld; contra, *Zeller v. Donegel Sch. Dist.*, 517 F.2d 600 (3rd Cir. 1975).

[177] E.g., *Bennister v. Paradis*, 316 F. Supp. 185, 188–189 (D.N.H. 1970).

[178] *New Jersey v. T.L.O.*, 105 S. Ct. 733 (1985). But at least one court has held that when the police are deeply involved with school officials in the search, then the full Fourth Amendment protections apply. *Picha v. Wieglos*, 410 F. Supp. 1214 (N.D. Ill. 1976). For a more extensive commentary on *New Jersey v. T.L.O.*, see Tyll van Geel, The Searching of Students after *New Jersey v. T.L.O.* in NOLPE Update, 1985, (Topeka, KA: National Organization on Legal Problems in Education, 1986.

[179] *Kuehn v. Benton Sch. Dist.*, 694 P.2d 1078 (Sup. Ct. Wash. 1985), *en banc*.

[180] E.g., *Doe v. Renfrow*, 475 F. Supp. 1012 (N.D. Ind. 1979), affirmed and remanded for determination of damages, 631 F.291 (7th Cir. 1980).

[181] E.g., *Bilbrey v. Brown*, 738 F.2d 1462 (9th Cir. 1982); *M.M. v. Anker*, 477 F. Supp. 837 (E.D.N.Y. 1979), affirmed 607 F.2d 588 (2nd Cir. 1979).

[182] *People v. Scott D.*, 34 N.Y.2d 483, 315 N.E.2d 466, 358 N.Y.S.2d 403 (1974), youthful-offender proceeding; *Belliner v. Lund*, 438 F. Supp. 1012 (N.D. Ind. 1979); *Morale v. Griegel*, 422 F. Supp. 988 (D. N.H. 1976), disciplinary proceeding; *State v. Young*, 234 Ga. 488, 216 S.E. 586 (Ga. 1975), exclusionary rule not applicable in a criminal proceeding even if school officials violated Fourth Amendment; *Caldwell v. Cannady*, 340 F. Supp. 835 (N.D. Tex. 1972), evidence illegally obtained by police could not be used in school disciplinary hearing; *Smyth v. Lubbers*, 398 F. Supp. 777 (W.D. Mich. S.D. 1975), exclusionary rule applies to college disciplinary proceeding.

[183] E.g., *State v. Stein*, 203 Kan. 638, 456 P.2d 1 (1969); *People v. Overton*, 24 N.Y.2d 522, 249 N.E.2d 366, 301 N.Y.S.2d 479 (1969).

[184] *Horton v. Goose Creek Ind. Sch Dist.*, 690 F.2d 470 (5th Cir. 1982), use of dogs not permissible; *Doe v. Renfrow*, 631 F.2d 91 (7th Cir. 1980), use of dogs allowed.

[185] *Horton v. Goose Creek Ind. Sch. Dist.*, 690 F.2d 470 (5th Cir. 1982).

[186] *Gordon v. Warren Consolidated Bd. of Educ.*, 706 F.2d 788 (6th Cir. 1983), use of undercover policewoman does not violate First Amendment rights; *Stern v. New Haven Comm. Sch.*, 529 F. Supp. 31 (E.D. Mich. 1981), use of two-way mirror does not violate Fourth Amendment.

[187] E.g., *Interest of L.L.*, 90 Wis. 2d 585, 280 N.W.2d 343 (Wis. App. 1979); *State v. Young*, 234 Ga. 488, 216 S.E.2d 587 (Sup. Ct. Ga. 1975).

[188] *Boynton v. Casey*, 543 F. Supp. 995 (D. Me. 1982).

[189] *Goss v. Lopez*, 419 U.S. 565, 581 (1975).

[190] *Bd. of Curators of the U. of Mo. v. Horowitz*, 435 U.S. 78 (1978), suspension for academic failure; *Ingraham v. Wright*, 430 U.S. 651 (1977). See also *Regents of the University of Michigan v. Ewing*, 54 U.S.L.W. 4055 (Dec. 12, 1985) (No. 84–1273), concluding the university had not acted arbitrarily—had not substantially departed

from accepted academic norms—in dropping a student from a 6-year undergraduate and medical school program.

[191] *Hebert v. Ventetuolo*, 638 F.2d 5 (1st Cir. 1981), suspension from hockey team; *Kernstein v. Pewaukee Sch. Bd.*, F. Supp. 565 (E.D. Wis. 1983), denial of admission to National Honor Society; *Everett v. Marcase*, 426 F. Supp. 397 (E.D. Pa. 1977), transfer for nondisciplinary reasons between schools requires informal notice and hearing; *Madera v. Bd. of Educ.*, 386 F. 2d 778 (2nd Cir. 1967), no right to attorney at a guidance conference that could result in a student transfer; *Pollnow v. Glennon*, 594 F. Supp. 220 (S.D.N.Y. 1984), no right to Miranda-type warning that parents may be called before discussion of incident leading to suspension; *White v. Salisbury Tp. Sch. Dist.*, 588 F. Supp. 608 (1984), allows hearing to take place after suspension has started even though there was no emergency requiring immediate removal of student from school.

[192] *Gonzales v. McEuen*, 434 F. Supp. 460 (C.D. Cal. 1977); *Dillion v. Pulaski Cty. Special Sch. Dist.*, 468 F. Supp. 54 (E.D. Ark. 1978); *Allex v. Allen*, 409 F. Supp. 379 (W.D. Pa. 1976); *de Jesus v. Penberthey*, 334 F. Supp. 70 (D. Conn. 1972); but see *Winnick v. Menning*, 460 F.2d 545 (2nd Cir. 1972).

[193] *Ingraham v. Wright*, 430 U.S. 651 (1977), Eighth Amendment not applicable to corporal punishment in public schools. Lines (1978, September). Corporal punishment after *Ingraham*: Looking to state law. *Inequality in Education.* (Center for Law and Education, Harvard University. No.23).

[194] *Ingraham v. Wright*, 525 F.2d 909, 916 (5th Cir. 1976), *en banc*, affirmed an other grounds, 430 U.S. 651 (1977), denying corporal punishment raised a substantive due process issue; but see *Hall v. Towney*, 621 F.2d 607 (4th Cir. 1980). Compare *Brooks v. Sch. Bd. of the City of Richmond*, 569 F. Supp. 1534 (E.D. Vir., Richmond Div. 1983).

[195] *Roy v. Continental Ins. Co.*, 313 So. 2d 349 (La. App. 1975); *People v. Smith.* 335 NE. 2d 123 (Ill. 1975); *Simms v. Sch. Dist No. 1*, 508 P.2d 236 (Or. 1973).

[196] *Baker v. Owen.*, 395 F. Supp. 294 (M.D.N.C. 1975), aff'd men, 423 U.S. 907 (1975).

[197] *Ingraham v. Wright*, 430 U.S. 651 (1977).

[198] *Woodard v. Los Fresnos Ind. Sch. Dist.*, 732 F.2d 1243 (5th Cir. 1984).

[199] *Baker v. Owen*, 395 F. Supp. 294 (M.D.N.C. 1975), aff'd men, 423 U.S. 907 (1975).

[200] *Petrey v. Flaughter*, 505 F. Supp. 1087 (E.D. Ky 1981); *Fisher v. Burkburnett Ind. Sch. Dist.*, 419 F. Supp. 1200 (N.D. Tex. 1976).

[201] *Katzman v. Cumberland Valley Sch. Dist.*, 479 A.2d 671 (Pa. Commw. Ct. 1984). Ostfield and Ingram. (November, 1984). Academic sanctions to control truancy problems: A simple solution with hidden complications. *NOLPE Notes, 19, 4*

[202] *S–1 v. Turlington*, 635 F.2d 342 (5th Cir. 1981), *cert.* denied, 454 U.S. 1030 (1981); *Doe v. Koger*, 480 F. Supp. 225 (N.D. Ind. 1979).

[203] *Keelin v. Grubbs*, 682 F.2d 595 (6th Cir. 1982); *Stuart v. Nappi*, 443 F. Supp. 1235 (D. Conn. 1978).

[204] *S–1 v. Turlington*, 635 F.2d 342, 348 (5th Cir. 1981); *Cert.* denied, 454 U.S. 1030 (1981). Contra, *Doe v. Koger*, 480 F. Supp. 225, 229 (N.D. Ind. 1979).

[205] *Commonwealth Dept. of Educ. v. Great Valley Dist.*, 352 A.2d 252 (Pa. 1976); *Morrison v. State Bd. of Educ.*, 1 Cal.3d 214, 461 P.2d 375, 82 Cal. Rptr. 175 (1969).

[206] *Neal v. Bryant*, 149 So. 2d 529 (Fla. 1962).

[207] *Valente*, above, Note 37, at 177 *et seq*; McCarthy and Cambron, above, Note 119, at p. 115 *et seq*.

[208] E.g., *Smith v. Bd. of Sch. Directors*, 328 A. 2d 883 (Pa. 1974).

[209] *Cleveland Bd. of Educ. v. Loudermill*, 105 S. Ct. 1487 (1985).

[210] *Id.*, 1495.

[211] The most extensive and detailed discussion of this case can be found in D. Rubin and S. Greenhouse. *The rights of teachers* (1983), 174 *et seq.* New York: R. W. Baron.

[212] *Id.*

[213] *Turner v. Bd. of Trustees*, 121 Cal. Rptr. 715, 535 P.2d 1171

(Cal. 1975).

[214] *Johnson v. Branch*, 364 F.2d 177 (4th Cir. 1966), *cert.* denied, 385 U.S. 1003 (1967); *Drown v. Portsmouth Sch. Dist.*, 541 F.2d 1106, 1108 (1st. Cir. 1971), the court said a teacher "may not be dismissed for the type of automobile she drives or for the kinds of food she eats."

[215] *Valente*, above, Note 37, at p.180; McCarthy and Cambron, above, Note 115, at p.118.

[216] *New Castle Area Sch. Dist. v. Bair*, 368 A.2d 345 (Pa. 1977), a single unsatisfactory rating. It is common for courts today to insist that charges against a teacher be linked to the teacher's fitness to teach. See, e.g., *Thompson v. Southwest Sch. Dist.*, 483 F. Supp. 1170 (W.D. Md 1980); *Bd. of Educ. of Long Beach Unified Sch. Dist. of Los Angeles City v. Jack M.*, 139 Cal. Reptr. 700, 566 P.2d 602 (Cal. 1977), *en banc*.

[217] *Gilliand v. Bd. of Educ. of Pleasant View Consolidated Sch. Dist.*, 35 Ill. App. 3d 861, 343 N.E. 2d 704 (Ill. App. 1976).

[218] *Schulz v. Bd. of Educ. of the Sch. Dist. of Fremont*, 210 Neb. 513, 315 N.W.2d 633 (Neb. 1982).

[219] *Harrah Ind. Sch. Dist. v. Martin*, 79 L.Ed.2d 248 (1979).

[220] For a general review of such cases see L. Fischer and D. Schimmel, above, Note 114; M. M. McCarthy and N. H. Cambron, above, Note 119; W. Valente, above, Note 37; D. Rubin and S. Greenhouse, above, Note 204. See also *Nat. Gay Task Force v. Bd. of Educ. of City of Oklahama*, 729 F.2d 1270 (10th Cir. 1984), affirmed by an equally divided Court, 105 S. Ct. 1858 (1985), upholding a statute that permitted a teacher to be dismissed for engaging in "public homosexual activity" while striking down that portion of the statute that permitted punishment for "advocating... public or private homosexual activity in a manner that creates a substantial risk that such conduct will come to the attention of school children or school employees."

[221] *Avery v. Homewood City Bd. of Educ.*, 674 F.2d 337 (5th Cir. 1983), *cert.* denied, 103 S. Ct. 2119 (1983) (teacher protected from dismissal); *Andrews v. Drew Municipal Seperate Sch. Dist.*, 507 F.2d 611 (5th Cir.), *cert.* granted, 423 U.S. 820 (1975), *cert.* dismissed, 425 U.S. 559 (1976), teacher protected from dismissal; *contra, Brown v. Bathke*, 416 F. Supp. 1194 (D. Neb. 1976), reversed an other grounds, 566 F.2d 588 (8th Cir. 1977).

[222] *Thompson v. Southwest Sch. Dist.*, 483 F. Supp. 1170 (W.D. Mo. 1980), teacher protected from dismissal; *Sullivan v. Meade Ind. Sch. Dist.*, 530 F.2d 799 (8th Cir. 1976), teacher not protected from dismissal.

[223] *Gaylord v. Tacoma Sch. Dist. No. 10*, 88 Wn.2d 286, 559 P.2d 1340 (Wash, *en banc*, *cert.* denied, 434 U.S. 879 (1977), dismissal of homosexual teacher; *Morrison v. State Bd. of Educ.*, 1 Cal. 3d 214, 461 P.2d 375, 82 Cal. Rptr. 175 (1969), one incident of homosexuality does not make teacher unfit to teach ; *Logan v. Warren Cty. Bd. of Educ.*, 549 F. Supp. 145 (S.D. Ga. 1982), dismissal after conviction for submitting false documents to Internal Revenue Service; *Comings v. State Bd. of Educ..*, 100 Cal. Rptr. 73 (1972), conviction of possession of marijuana does not make teacher unfit to teach; *Adams v. State Professional Practices Council*, 406 So.2d 1170 (Fla. Dist. Ct. App. 1981), possession of marijuana plants sufficient to establish moral turpitude.

[224] D. Rubin and S. Greenhouse, above, Note 211, at p. 154.

[225] E.g., *Miller v. Sch. Dist. No. 167, Cook Cty, Ill.*, 495 F.2d 658 (7th Cir. 1974). For a general review of cases, see L. Fisher and D. Schimmel, *above*, Note 114 at p. 373; M. M. McCarthy and N. H. Cambron, above, Note 115 at p. 62.

[226] *Weissmaan v. Bd. of Educ. of Jefferson Cty. Sch. Dist. No. R–1*, 547 P.2d 1267 (Colo, 1976), teacher dismissed after engaging in "horseplay" with female students; *Bott v. Bd. of Educ. Deposit Cent. Sch. Dist.*, 41 N.Y.2d 265, 392 N.Y.S.2d 274 (1977), dismissal of teacher for use of excessive force; *Bernes v. Fair Dismissal Bd.*, 548 P.2d 988 (Ore. 1976), violation of rule against use of corporal punishment.

[227] *Keyishian v. Bd. of Regents*, 385 U.S. 589 (1967).

[228] *Ambach v. Norwick*, 441 U.S. 68 (1979).

[229] *Branti v. Finkel*, 445 U.S. 507 (1980); *Elrod v. Burns*, 427 U.S. 347 (1976).

[230] *Solis v. Rio Grande City Ind. Sch.*, 734 F.2d 243 (5th Cir.

1984).

[231] *Johnson v. Branch*, 364 F.2d 177 (4th Cir. 1966).

[232] *National Gay Task Force v. Bd. of Educ. of City of Okla. City*, 729 F.2d 1270 (10th Cir. 1984), affirmed by an equally divided Court. See also Bd. of Educ. of City of Okla. City v. National Gay Task Force, (No. B3–2030), 20 *NOLPE Notes* 3 (May, 1985).

[233] *Rowland v. Mad River Loc. Sch. D. Montgomery Cty.*, 730 F.2d 444(6th Cir. 1984), *cert.* denied, 105 S.Ct. 1373 (1985).

[234] *Staugh v. Crenshaw Cty. Bd. of Educ.*, 744 F.2d 1479 (11th Cir. 1984), striking down application of policy requiring teachers to send their children to public schools; *Berry v. Macon Cty. Bd. of Educ.*, 380 F. Supp. 1244 (M.D. Ala. 1971); *Cook v. Hudson*, 365 F. Supp. 855 (N.D. Miss. 1973), upholding requirement teacher send child to public school on grounds that sending child to private school tended to undermine district efforts to desegregate.

[235] *James v. Bd. of Educ.*, 461 F.2d 566 (2nd Cir.), *cert* denied, 409 U.S. 1042 (1972).

[236] *Anderson v. Evans*, 660 F.2d 153 (6th Cir. 1981); *Restar v. State Bd. of Educ.*, 399 Atl. 2d 225 (Ct. Apps. Md. 1979).

[237] *U.S. Civil Service Comm. v. National Association of Letter Carriers*, 413 U.S. 548 (1973), upholding constitutionality of the Hatch Act; *Broadrick v. Oklahoma*, 413 U.S. 601 (1973), upholding an Oklahoma statute that prohibited classified civil servants from taking part in the management or affairs of any political party and political campaign and from soliciting campaign contributions.

[238] *Stanley v. Georgia*, 394 U.S. 557 (1969), reversing a conviction for knowing possession of obscene matter.

[239] *Shuman v. City of Philadelphia*, 470 F. Supp. 449, 460 n.9 (E.D.Pa. 1979).

[240] *Shelton v. Tucker*, 364 U.S. 479 (1960), striking down a statute that required every teacher annually to file an affidavit listing without limitation every organization to which he has belonged or regularly contributed within the preceding 5 years.

[241] *O'Connor v. Ortega*, 47 Sup. Ct. Bull. (CCH), p. B1757 (March 31, 1987). Also see, *Gillard v. Schmidt*, 579 F.2d 825 (3d cir. 1978).

[242] *Jones v. McKenzie*, 628 F. Supp. 1089 (D.C.N.J. 1985).

[243] 42 U.S.C. § 2000 (e) (1982); *Washington v. Davis*, 426 U.S. 229 (1976).

[244] E.g., *Singleton v. Jackson Municipal Separate Sch. Dist.*, 419 F.2d 1211 (5th Cir.) (en banc), reversed in part *sub nom.*, *Carter v. West Feliciana Parish Sch. Bd.*, 396 U.S. 290 (1970).

[245] *Zaslawsky v. Bd. of Educ.*, 610 F.2d 661 (9th Cir. 1979).

[246] For a recounting of this litigation, see Rebell and Block, *Educational policy making and the courts*, 75 et seq. (1982).

[247] *United States v. South Carolina*, 445 F. Supp. 1094 (D.S.C. 1977), affirmed, 434 U.S. 1026 (1978).

[248] Morris Abrams, Racial spoils system rises as burden of proof shifts, *The Wall Street Journal*, Vol. 205, Eastern Ed., May 14, 1985, p.28. Morris Abrams is Vice Chairman of the U.S. Civil Rights Commission. As interpreted by the Supreme Court, a plaintiff in a Title VII case has the initial burden of establishing a *prima facie* case. Once this *prima facie* case is established, a rebuttable presumption that the employer discriminated against the employee arises. To rebut the presumption, the employer can either disprove the *prima facie* case or articulate some legitimate, nondiscriminatory reason for the action. The plaintiff is then given the opportunity to demonstrate that the proffered reasons are pretextual. *McDonnell Douglas Corp. v. Green*, 411 U.S. 792 (1973).

[249] *Wyngant v. Jackson Board of Education.*, 54 U.S.L.W. 4479 (April 5, 1986).

[250] *Johnson v. Transportation Agency, Santa Clara Cty., Calif.*, 47 Sup. Ct. Bull (CCH), p. B1677 (March 25, 1987).

[251] Civil Rights Act of 1964, Title VII, 42 U.S.C. § 2000(e) (1976); Education Amendments of 1972, Title IX, 20 U.S.C. § 1681 (1982); Equal Pay Act, 29 U.S.C. § 206 (d) (1976); *Personnel Administrator of Mass. v. Feeney*, 442 U.S. 256 (1979).

[252] 29 C.F.R. § 1604.11 (1984). Asking for sexual favors, unwelcome sexual advances, and other verbal or physical conduct of a sexual nature constitute sexual harassment when submission is made a term or condition of employment, submission or rejection is a basis for employment decisions, the conduct has the purpose or effect of interfering with work performance, or it creates an intimidating, hostile, or offensive working environment.

[253] Pregnancy Discrimination Act, amending Title VII of the Civil Rights Act of 1964, P. L. 95–555, 92 Stat. 2076.

[254] *Arizona Governing Committee for Tax Deferred Annuity Plans v. Norris*, 403 U.S. 1073 (1983).

[255] *Los Angeles Dept. of Water & Power v. Manhart*, 435 U.S. 702 (1978).

[256] 102 S. Ct. 1912 (1982).

[257] *Liebman v. University of Chicago*, 660 F.2d 1185 (7th Cir. 1981), *cert.* denied, 456 U.S. 937 (1982); *Cannon v. University of Chicago*, 648 F.2d 1104 (7th Cir. 1981), *cert.* denied, 102 S. Ct. 981 (1981).

[258] *Cty. of Washington v. Gunther*, 452 U.S. 161 (1981), *American Federation of State, Cty., and Municipal Employees v. State of Washington*, 770 F. 2d 1401 (9th Cir. 1985); *Spaulding v. University of Washington*, 740 F.2d 686 (9th Cir. 1984).

[259] *Palmer v. Ticcione*, 546 F.2d 459 (2nd Cir. 1978), compulsory retirement constitutional; *Gault v. Garrison*, 569 F.2d 993 (7th Cir. 1977), *cert.* denied. 440 U.S. 945 (1979), compulsory retirement unconstitutional. Compare *Massachusetts Bd. of Retirement v. Murgia*, 427 U.S. 307 (1976).

[260] *Geller v. Markham*, 635 F.2d 1027 (2nd Cir. 1980), *cert.* denied, 451 U.S. 945 (1981).

[261] *Norcross v. Sneed*, 755 F.2d 113 (8th Cir. 1985); *Strathie v. Dept. of Transportation*, 716 F.2d 227 (3d Cir. 1983); *Meyerson v. State of Arizona*, 709 F.2d 1235 (9th Cir. 19830; *Doyle v. University of Alabama*, 680 F.2d 1323 (5th Cir. 1982); *Carmi v. Metropolitan St. Louis Sewer Dist*, 620 F.2d 672 (8th Cir.), *cert.* denied, 449 U.S. 892 (1980).

[262] *School Bd. of Nassau Cty., Fla. v. Arline* (No. 85–1277) as reported in *Education Week*, March 11, 1987, 2

[263] *Philbrook v. Ansonia Bd. of Educ.*, 757 F.2d 476 (2d Cir. 1985), U.S. appeal pending; *Pinsker v. Joint Dist. No. 281 of Adams and Arapahoe Counties*, 753 F.2d 388 (10th Cir. 1984).

[264] *Transworld Airlines, Inc. v. Hardison*, 432 U.S. 63 (1977).

[265] See Wilkinson, above Note 66.

[266] E.g., N. Glazer. (1978). *Affirmative discrimination*. New York: Basic Books.

[267] Institute of Judicial Administration and American Bar Association. (1982). *Juvenile justice standards project—standards relating to schools and education*. Cambridge, MA: Ballinger.

[268] There exists a vast body of material on this subject. For two useful publications, see C.H. Rossell and W. Hawley. (Eds). (1983). *The consequences of school desegregation*. Philadelphia: Temple University Press; Rossell. (1983). Applied social science research: What does it say about the effectiveness of school desegregation plans? *Journal of Legal Studies*, 12, 69.

[269] C. A. Johnson and B. C. Canon. (1984). *Judicial policies: Implementation and impact*. 189 et seq. Washington DC: Congressional Quarterly.

[270] The record of compliance on the part of school districts subject to judicial orders to end prayers in the public schools appears to be good. F. J. Sorauf. (1976). *The wall of separation*. 286–289. Princeton, NJ: Princeton University Press. As for districts not themselves specific targets of judicial orders, the data show that a majority of districts, even in the South, do not provide the students with devotional readings from the Bible. *Id*. p. 297. But the fact remains that many districts, especially in the South, continue to engage in practices specifically ruled to be unconstitutional. There is a considerable body of literature examining the response of school districts to the Supreme Court's prayer decisions. See, e.g. Birkby. (1969). The Supreme Court and the Bible Belt Tennessee reaction to the *Schema* decision. *Midwestern Journal of Political Science*, 10, 304; K. M. Dolbeare and P. F. Hammond. (1971). *The school prayer decisions*. Chicago: University of Chicago; R. M. Johnson. (1967). *The dynamics of compliance*. Evanston, IL: Northwestern University Press. Way, F. H., Jr. (1968). Survey research on judicial decisions: The prayer and Bible reading cases. *Western Political Quarterly*, 21 (2), 189–205.

[271] E.g., C. V. Willie and S. L. Greenblatt. (Eds.). (1981) *Community politics and educational change*. White Plains, NY:

Longman; H. R. Rodgers, Jr., and C. S. Bullock. (1976). *Coercion to compliance.* Lexington, MA: Lexington. R. L. Crain et al. (1969). *The politics of school desegregation.* Chicago: Aldine. G. Orfield. (1969). *The reconstruction of Southern education* New York: John Wiley; and Kirp, above, Note 79.

[272] P. Kuriloff, D. Kirp, and W. Buss. (1979, June). *When handicapped children go to court: Assessing the impact of the legal reform of special education in Pennsylvania* (Final Report, National Institute of Education Project No. Neg–003–0192).

[273] See materials cited in Notes 259, 260.

[274] van Geel, above, Note 143.

[275] E.g., R. Elmore and M. McLaughlin. (1982). *Reform and retrenchment: The politics of school finance reform.* Cambridge, MA: Ballinger. R. Lehne. (1978). *The quest for justice.* White Plains, NY: Longman.

[276] D. Horowitz. (1977). *The courts and social policy.* Washington, DC: Brookings Institution. S. L. Wasby. (1970). *The impact of the United States Supreme Court.* Homewood, IL: Dorsey Press.

CHAPTER 30

Comparative Educational Administration

Meredydd G. Hughes

INTRODUCTION

Making comparisons across national boundaries in relation to educational systems and institutions is widely regarded as a praiseworthy, uncomplicated activity. It is often assumed to lead almost automatically to cosmic insight and enlightenment and to instant illumination of one's own situation and how it might be improved. At international gatherings of educationists, proposals for comparative research are thus liable to receive generalized support, less attention being given to the need for adequate conceptual frameworks, within which similarities and differences can be identified and interpreted. Such naiveté, which predictably leads to disappointment and disillusion, has been a major obstacle over the years to scholarly acceptance of the academic legitimacy and relevance of comparative studies in educational administration.

The chapter begins by examining the conspicuous lack of scholarly interest in comparative educational administration in the mid-1950s, as compared with the considerable growth by that time both of comparative administration and of comparative education as fields of study. The introduction into educational administration of an international dimension in the 1960s is then described as a prelude to a review of the diverse and extensive literature which quickly developed. This review is confined almost entirely to writings in the English language, and there is a corresponding unevenness in the parts of the world to which the cited works

refer. Except in the reports and studies of international agencies that are mentioned, little indication is given of developments in continental Europe, in the Soviet bloc, in Israel, in Arab countries, in China and Japan, or in Latin America. A more comprehensive review would require a whole book and a team of writers from varied backgrounds.

The chapter ends with a section that seeks to identify significant new trends in the educational administration literature, noting also the parallel development that has taken place over the same period in comparative education and in comparative administration. Concluding observations on future developments imply that a comparative, cosmopolitan perspective requires considerably more than an encyclopedic knowledge of educational systems and schools across the world.

THE ZERO BASE

Even in the mid-1980s, comparative educational administration can at best be regarded as an emerging field of study and research. According to Lynch (1979–1980) it is a laggard among comparative fields; Reller (1982), who over many years has consistently advocated its development (Reller & Morphet, 1962), has recently observed that as a specific area of study it is "rather new."

In the mid-1950s, comparative educational administration did not exist as a specific field of study and research. The contributions to educational administration in the United States in the early years of the 20th century of legendary figures such as Bobbitt, Cubber-

Consultant/reviewers: George Baron, University of London; and Patrick D. Lynch, Pennsylvania State University

ley, and Strayer bequeathed no legacies to those wishing to develop a comparative perspective. The early practitioner-scholars, and those who came after them, appear to have been almost exclusively concerned with the specifics of administrative procedures and practices in their own local context. There is little evidence of interest, even within the United States, in making comparisons between different modes and structures for providing education.

The concept of a zero base in the 1950s is even more applicable to countries that had no comparable history of study and teaching in educational administration at that time. In Britain the accepted and largely unquestioned tradition was that administrators learned from their own personal experience on the job: that is, by making mistakes and reflecting on them. Administrative expertise was something to be caught, like measles, by working closely with more experienced colleagues (Bridges, 1956). At its best such reliance on the subtle wisdom that comes with maturity and experience resulted in decision making of high quality, but a certain parochialism was also inevitable because of the limitations of individual personal experience. Educational practitioners, concerned with operating their own systems, showed little interest in the practice of educational administration in other lands. In this respect the situation in Britain was, of course, similar to that found elsewhere.

If one turns to the broader fields either of comparative education or of comparative administration, the position is somewhat different. By the 1950s both of these fields had achieved recognition as areas of study that had a clear identity. There is little evidence, however, in their respective literatures of mutual awareness or crossfertilization of ideas, in spite of the clear overlap of their concerns in the area of educational administration. There can evidently be some parochialism even among comparativists. For present purposes this separate development may be no disadvantage, for it raises the possibility that comparative educational administration in its early development can draw on either or both of two distinct comparative traditions. Each is outlined below.

THE COMPARATIVE EDUCATION TRADITION

Writers across the centuries have shown considerable interest in education in countries other than their own. However, 19th-century administrators of the newly developed and more widely accessible systems of public education in Europe and the United States may particularly be regarded as the precursors of contemporary comparative studies in education, as they sought to

understand and learn from the practice of other nations (Hans, 1949; Holmes, 1981; Nicholas, 1983). The aim was praiseworthy, but inevitably there were instances in which ideas and practices were uncritically borrowed and crudely misapplied across national frontiers, providing examples of what Holmes has called "misconceived comparative education."

According to Lynch (1979–1980), the American educators who looked abroad for models during the 19th century "may have been influenced especially by the Prussian administrative characteristics of clearly understood rules of authority over teachers and students, collection of data, prescriptions of training for teachers and inspection of teachers and students" (p. 1). A notable example was Horace Mann's seventh annual report in 1844 as Secretary to the Massachusetts Board of Education (cited in Holmes, 1981), which described and warmly praised Prussian methods of teaching, thereby provoking a strong reaction from Massachusetts teachers who resented the implied comparison. More qualified admiration for Prussian education was expressed by Henry Barnard, the first U.S. Commissioner of Education, who made a sustained contribution to the widening of horizons by regularly including detailed information about foreign systems of education in the *American Journal of Education*, which he edited from 1856 to 1881.

Studies by European observers included accounts by the French writer Victor Cousins on education in Prussia and Holland, both of which were translated into English (see Holmes, 1981). The English Inspector of Schools Matthew Arnold made a study of education in both Germany and France and published a report on higher schools and universities in Germany (Arnold, 1874). He was followed by Michael Sadler, during whose time as Secretary to the Board of Education a succession of special reports were produced on education in foreign countries. As noted by Gordon and White (1979), these reports were influential in English policy making in the early part of the 20th century, particularly in relation to secondary education.

As comparative education developed and became recognized as a field of inquiry, two series of annual publications made a cumulative and substantial contribution. In the United States, *The International Year Book of the International Institute* was edited by Isaac Kandel at Teachers College, Columbia University, from 1924 to 1944. In the United Kingdom, *The Year Book of Education*, first published by Evans Brothers in 1932, provided a forum for the discussion of educational issues in Britain and overseas.

Both series of publications sought to show that a comparative approach involved more than providing national packages of statistical information. The point was clearly made by Donald McLean in 1932, in introducing the first volume of the London-based *Year Book*, when he contrasted "the safe but somewhat unambitious course of compiling a volume of the principal facts and figures relating to education [with] the more venturesome and interesting alternative of endeavouring to bring these facts and figures into some sort of perspective and to suggest underlying principles and lines of development." (cited in Holmes, 1981, p. 5). Holmes, who was subsequently involved as assistant editor and editor, had no doubt that the bolder course was taken, a comment which could equally be applied to the *International Year Book* from Columbia University.

In due course the two traditions merged as Teachers College joined with the London University Institute of Education from 1953 in taking responsibility jointly for *The Year Book of Education* (subsequently renamed *The World Year Book of Education*). In the 1950s and 1960s a new theme was chosen each year for comparative analysis, with J. A. Lauwerys providing continuity as joint editor.

By the mid-1950s comparative education was thus widely recognized as a field of academic study in its own right. Kandel's early work (1933) was followed by other substantial publications (Hans, 1949; Kandel, 1954; Mallinson, 1957). In these studies the historical concept of nationalism was given considerable prominence, national character being advanced as a crucial factor that explained differences across educational systems. The general approach may be regarded as historical functionalism, attention being given within a functional framework to the social context of educational systems and to the interrelationship of such systems with other national political and social institutions.

In the three decades of particular concern in this volume there has been continued vigorous development, continuing interest in historically rooted national differences being paralleled in the 1960s and 1970s by a more sophisticated sociological and technological functionalism (as noted by Kazamias & Massialas, 1982, p. 309), which sought invariant relationships established by "scientific, empirical (mostly quantitative) methods and techniques." More recently such functionalist approaches have come under attack in the literature on comparative education, as elsewhere (Holmes, 1981).

Whatever the perspective adopted, comparative educationists are united in rejecting any form of cultural borrowing across educational systems that disregards the complex peculiarity and uniqueness of both importer and exporter. As Nicholas (1983) has recently observed, scholars in the field "have been unanimously critical of the comparative exploits of nonspecialists, and rightly aghast at the unrefined, even crude methodological procedures used in some quarters" (p. 3).

THE COMPARATIVE ADMINISTRATION TRADITION

Even more than in the case of education, writers from classical times onward have shown an interest in the government and modes of public administration of other lands. In the late 19th century, however, public administration began to be regarded as a distinct area for systematic inquiry, and interestingly, in his celebrated essay "The Study of Administration," Woodrow Wilson (1887), drew on European experience in arguing that administration should be regarded as a separate field of study and treated as a science.

Wilson showed that far-reaching administrative reforms had been achieved in Germany and France, reluctantly conceding that the changes had occurred under absolute rule, of Frederick William III of Prussia and Napoleon, respectively. He felt justified, however, in borrowing from the administrative experience of political systems of which he disapproved, but only by drawing a sharp distinction between politics and administration:

> If I see a murderous fellow sharpening a knife cleverly, I can borrow his way of sharpening the knife without borrowing his probable intention to commit murder with it; and so if I see a monarchist dyed in the wool managing a public bureau well, I can learn his business methods without changing one of my republican spots. (Wilson, 1887, p. 220)

He concluded that by studying administration "as a means of putting our own politics into convenient practice, ...we are on perfectly safe ground, and can learn without error what foreign systems have to teach us" (p. 220). The assumption that administrative practices successful in other cultures can simply be taken over without regard to contextual constraints is reminiscent of the similar attitudes in relation to education that Holmes (1981) castigated as "misconceived comparative education" (pp. 19–25).

Wilson's novel idea that administration can be studied as a science found expression in due course in a diversity of developments that can conveniently be categorized under the familiar headings of scientific management, classical management, and human-relations theory. It has, however, been argued that in the British context the three perspectives were never as sharply differentiated as in the United States (Thomas, 1978). Scientific management as promulgated by F. W.

Taylor, H. L. Gantt, and F. B. Gilbreth adopted a severely technical view of administration, and thus—true to the Wilsonian tradition—did not address the issue of whether proposals confidently advanced on the basis of somewhat limited American experience were culture-specific. In fact, the ideas propounded elicited strong support and severe criticism on both sides of the Atlantic.

Classical management theory had a broader international base, owing much to an early exposition of management principles by the French mining engineer Henri Fayol (1916/1949). James Mooney, a former General Motors Vice-President, produced in association with A. C. Reiley an American text from a similar viewpoint (Mooney & Reiley, 1931). In the United Kingdom, Colonel L. Urwick, Director for some years of the Geneva International Management Institute, drew on his military experience in expounding and interpreting Fayol's work. He also joined with the American Luther Gulick (of POSDCORB fame), a prominent member of Roosevelt's 1937 Presidential Committee on Administrative Management, in editing an important volume (Gulick & Urwick, 1937) that provided a definitive statement of the new orthodoxy. The emphasis was on management principles of general application, which were assumed without further inquiry to be independent of national setting.

The human-relations movement, like scientific management, first received recognition in the United States and is likely always to be linked with the frequently cited research by Elton Mayo and colleagues at the Western Electric Company Hawthorne Plant in Chicago (Mayo, 1933; Roethlisberger & Dickson, 1939). It is of interest that similar research had been carried out in Britain during and after World War I (Myers, 1926), as recognized by Mayo (1933), who noted the similarity of methods and assumptions, adding that "there was at no time during the early developments of the [Hawthorne] enquiries any relation between the investigators here and in England" (pp. 42–43). Although this absence of contact is understandable, it is surprising that the human-relations perspective did not generate any significant comparative studies. If people matter more than administrative structures and general principles, human variation across national boundaries might be considered worthy of investigation. In fact, however, on both sides of the Atlantic in the years between World Wars, writers on public administration and industrial management, whatever their particular perspective or emphasis, appeared to share a cultural parochialism that led them to ignore the comparative dimension in their theorizing and research.

A new interest in comparative administration

developed and blossomed in the late 1940s and 1950s. A contributing factor was undoubtedly the increased opportunities for observing overseas administrative systems that World War II and its aftermath entailed. The change of emphasis was heralded by Robert Dahl's (1947) vigorous assertion of an inexorable relationship between public administration and social setting:

> There should be no reason for supposing, then, that a principle of public administration has equal validity in every nation-state, or that successful public administration practices in one country will necessarily prove successful in a different social, economic and political environment. A particular nation-state embodies the results of many historical episodes, traumas, failures and successes which have in turn created peculiar habits, mores, institutionalized patterns of behaviour, *Weltanschauungen*, and even "national psychologies." One cannot assume that public administration can escape the effects of this conditioning; or that it is somehow independent of and isolated from the culture or social setting in which it develops...Yet the comparative aspects of public administration have largely been ignored; and as long as the study of public administration is not comparative, claims for "a science of public administration" sound rather hollow. (p. 8)

There was need, he concluded, for

> a profound study of varying national and social characteristics impinging on public administration, to determine what aspects of public administration, if any, are truly independent of the national and social setting. Are there discoverable principles of *universal* validity, or are all principles valid only in terms of a special environment? (p. 11)

Another strong impetus for undertaking comparative studies in the post-World War II period was provided by the emergence of newly independent countries, leading to a recognition, as evidenced by a United Nations General Assembly resolution of December 1948, of a need for training in public administration in developing countries. Necessary funding was provided both through UN agencies and through bilateral technical aid programs, notably those of the United States.

In the wake of the diverse consultative activities of a quickly mobilized army of international experts, a voluminous literature of what came to be called "development administration" soon appeared. A discreet hint of its uneven quality appears in a contemporary account (Siffin, 1957):

> In some instances the significance of the relationship between public administration and its particular context was underscored by the lack of attention it received. More often, perhaps, administrative experts became acutely aware of a need for something more than a

homespun approach to public administration in consequence of their mandated efforts to teach, evaluate and adjust public administration in foreign settings. (p. 6)

From a growing flood of reports and studies, Riggs (1962) some years later was able to pick out for commendation "some keenly discerning work, quite sophisticated in its recognition of the relativity for overseas application of American, British, French or other Western norms" (p. 10). Other writings, he implied, were less sensitive to cultural differences. Weidner (1964) cited specific examples of intellectual bankruptcy and bluntly drew attention to the disastrous consequences of ill-considered attempts to apply general principles of management without regard to local circumstances.

Traditional comparative administration had similarly come under severe criticism in the post-war period from influential insiders. According to Dwight Waldo (1956), comparative studies of government were, among other things, culture-bound, legalistic, and "preponderantly descriptive rather than problem-solving, explanatory or analytic" (p. 63). The same unease, coupled with a suggestion of the new approaches that were required, had already been expressed by Dahl (1947):

> The study of public administration inevitably must become a much more broadly based discipline, resting not on a narrowly defined knowledge of techniques and processes, but rather extending to the varying historical, sociological, economic and other conditioning factors that give public administration its peculiar stamp in each country. (p. 11)

Significant occasions in the development of new, multidisciplinary approaches, cited by Siffin (1957, p. 7), included a 1952 conference seminar at Northwestern University under the sponsorship of the (U.S.) Social Science Research Council and the establishment in 1953 of a Comparative Administration Subcommittee of the American Political Science Association. A Comparative Administration Group within the American Society of Public Administration was formally constituted in 1960 under the leadership of F. W. Riggs.

The new emphasis was on the construction of models and typologies. Waldo (1955) recommended structural-functional analysis as a means of developing "a model of what an administrative system is like as a general type" (p. 9). Such an approach was adopted by Riggs (1957) in an exploratory paper in which he identified the contrasting characteristics of agricultural and industrial societies and also acknowledged his indebtedness to Talcott Parsons.

Siffen (1957) in the same volume wrote confidently of an ability in the United States to transcend or at least come to grips with what he called "the value problem":

> Increasingly, the value aspects of the study of public administration have come to be regarded as "external," in the sense that they do not inhere in the subject but in its social context and in the relations between administration and setting...In this sense, values become a critically significant form of data for comparative administrative studies. (pp. 15–16)

Such determination to exclude normative considerations from the basic theory of comparative administration was in accord with the positivist injunction to be scientific. The standpoint adopted will be somewhat familiar to students of educational administration, as will the use made by Riggs (1964, pp. 22–23) of three of the five "pattern variables" proposed by Parsons (Parsons & Shils, 1959). Using an analogy from physics of the diffraction of light by a prism, Riggs was able to discuss the differing structures and functions of traditional, transitional, and modern societies, which he characterized respectively as "fused," "prismatic," and "diffracted."

According to Ferrel Heady (1979), the 1960s became "the heyday of the Comparative Administration Movement" (p. 15), only to be followed by critical questioning and reappraisal in the 1970s. Nevertheless, whereas the decade of the 1950s must be regarded as a zero base for the comparative study of educational administration, this was far from true for either comparative education or comparative administration. From the mid-1950s the study of comparative education gained recognition both in Britain and in the United States, while comparative administration was at a stage of vigorous development, notably in the United States. Neither field, however, showed any particular interest in the area of potential overlap, the administration of education.

INTRODUCING AN INTERNATIONAL DIMENSION INTO THE STUDY OF EDUCATIONAL ADMINISTRATION

The Theory, or New, Movement in Educational Administration that developed in the United States in the mid-1950s (see Chapters 1 and 2) vigorously challenged the specificity of the practitioner's preoccupation with the familiar routine processes and procedures of his or her local administrative system. The new emphasis was on generality, abstraction and well-defined concepts, as Griffiths (1959) made clear: "A great range of concrete events can be handled through the use of a limited number of abstract concepts. The abstract concepts enable us to generalize and thus widely extend the knowledge which we possess" (p. 23). The general applicability of the concepts, it was claimed, enables the development of theoretical models that are universal in scope, just like the laws of the natural sciences. As Griffiths (1959) further explained (pp. 25–27), theory both provides insight into the nature of administration and is a guide to action, to the collection of facts, and to new knowledge in a multitude of specific administrative systems.

The corollary of the foregoing argument, which is never explicitly stated in the early writings of the Theory Movement, is that if concepts and theories are universally applicable and therefore not restricted to a particular nation or culture, comparative research provides unrivaled opportunities for refining concepts and testing theories in a diversity of contexts. As noted earlier, the point had been fully appreciated a decade or so earlier in the public administration literature.

The shift toward more rigorous social science inquiry had come to public administration some years earlier than it came to educational administration. The protagonists were political scientists and economists, who were thus professionally concerned with interactions across systems and communities. The remarkably similar critique of established wisdom within educational administration appears to have developed quite independently. Its distinctive early emphasis was on the personal characteristics of administrators and the correlates of administrative behavior, reflecting the behavioral-science disciplinary interests of some of the leading proponents, such as Getzels (1952) and Halpin (1956). The primary areas of concern may account for the fact that comparative study does not figure prominently as a major interest in the early literature of the Theory Movement, in sharp contrast to its central position within the corresponding developments in public administration. In the late 1950s educational administration was certainly still some way from appreciating the full significance of Dahl's (1947) searching question, "Are there discoverable principles of *universal* validity, or are all principles valid only in terms of a special environment?" (p. 11).

The issue was, of course, of immediate concern to scholars of educational administration from many nations who were students at American universities, but it was seldom raised as a matter that required explicit discussion and rigorous research. Within North America the potential of scholarly interaction across the 49th parallel was soon recognized, the University of Alberta and other Canadian universities being involved with U.S. universities in the creation in 1959 of the University Council for Educational Administration (UCEA). The new organization provided opportunities for communication and interchange, and for a progressive broadening of academic perspectives. One such occasion was a UCEA seminar in 1961 on the preparation of educational administrators, at which Theodore Reller (1962) strongly argued that field studies in a foreign country is an effective way of providing better understanding of educational change in the United States. The value of a comparative approach was thus beginning to be appreciated.

An early milestone in these developments was the establishment in 1963 at the University of New England in Australia of the *Journal of Educational Administration*, the founding editor being William Walker, himself a doctoral graduate of the University of Illinois. The promotion of a world perspective in the field was to be the special emphasis of the new journal, its declared assumption being that the study of educational administration "will best be served through an international approach to the field."

In the United States and Canada in 1966 a UCEA-sponsored International Intervisitation Programme (IIP) in Educational Administration, organized with the financial support of the Kellogg Foundation, may be regarded as a significant overflow phenomenon of the Theory Movement and an honorable recompense of the movement's initial neglect of the comparative dimension. Conceived by Jack Culbertson, with encouragement from William Walker in Australia and William Taylor in Britain, the Programme challenged North American scholars to look outward, while stimulating the academics and practitioners from the United Kingdom, Australia, and New Zealand, who also attended to learn and profit from the insights developed in the United States and Canada (Culbertson, 1969).

The 1966 IIP was also an occasion for many participants to appreciate that valid international comparisons are often more difficult to achieve than would first appear and that comparative research of any significance is a highly sophisticated technical activity requiring more than international goodwill and a superficial acquaintance with different educational systems. In summing up the conference, Fred Enns (1969) of the University of Alberta warned of the need for careful design and conceptual clarity:

> If intercultural research is to be productive, then there must be comparable theory and design, and common categories for accurate description. Unless the researchers use the same concepts of system boundary and role, for example, the studies will lead only to confusion. (p. 317)

Enns also suggested that accurate description could be the point of entry for intercultural research and observed that such studies "would have a generally stimulating effect on local researchers generally, and would help to jolt them out of commonly held parochial views" (p. 316). He might pertinently have added, as an antidote for a different kind of parochialism, that some acquaintance with the existing research literature of comparative education and of comparative administration would be helpful to aspiring researchers. There was, in fact, little evidence of such crossfertilization.

The final outcome of the 1966 IIP was to create a continuing international network of communication channels, which, as Culbertson (1981) has observed, can serve as a learning resource for educational leaders and as a means for promoting cooperative international studies and facilitating comparative research. It was thus a natural sequel that a second IIP was held in Australia in 1970 and that similar quadrennial programs have been held in Britain in 1974, in Canada in 1978, in Nigeria in 1982. The 1986 IIP took place in Hawaii, Fiji, and New Zealand, and plans are for a 1990 IIP to be held partly in Britain and partly in the Netherlands.

The 1970 IIP in Australia included participants from eight developing countries of the Commonwealth, former British territories, bringing new issues and perspectives into comparative focus. A significant long-term outcome was the establishment of the Commonwealth Council for Educational Administration (CCEA), with Professor William Walker as the first president, to encourage teaching and research in educational administration in Commonwealth countries and to work closely internationally with UCEA. By the mid-1980s over 20 affiliated national associations in Commonwealth countries provide a potentially rich resource for comparative research in educational administration. More recently an Inter-American Society for Educational Administration has been formed, with Professor Benno Sander of Brazil as first president; it performs a similar overarching function in the Americas and is linked with UCEA and CCEA in the sponsorship of quadrennial IIPs. Through CCEA's British affiliate the British Educational Management and Administration Society (BEMAS), these networks also overlap and cooperate with a European Forum for Educational Administration, which includes the national associations of France, Germany, and other European countries.

The international dimension in educational administration has been further activated and strengthened since the 1950s through the diverse activities of official (i.e., governmental) international organizations such as the World Bank, the Organization for Economic Cooperation and Development (OECD), the Commonwealth Secretariat, the Council of Europe, and the United Nations Educational, Scientific, and Cultural Organizational (UNESCO). UNESCO, in particular, has notably contributed through its Division of Educational Policy and Planning (DEPP), its International Bureau of Education, its regional centers (e.g., its Bangkok Office for Asia and the Pacific), and its International Institute for Educational Planning (IIEP), an autonomous institution in Paris created in 1963 both to train educational planners and to coordinate research on an international scale.

The studies and activities undertaken by both the voluntary and the intergovernmental bodies that have a worldwide interest in educational provision have thus played an essential part in the growing recognition of an international and comparative dimension in educational administration, as revealed in the following review of the available literature.

A SELECTIVE REVIEW OF THE LITERATURE

If the term *research* were to be strictly interpreted, the amount of relevant literature would be quite small. Accepting, however, that the emerging field of comparative educational administration is a late developer, it is advisable at least to sample the considerable array of discursive literature that has been produced in the English-speaking world. The field is thinned out by the simple expedient of excluding items that are mainly descriptive rather than analytical and that provide little more than impressionistic and anecdotal accounts of foreign travel.

We begin, therefore, with some examples of papers that seek to describe and analyze a particular country's current educational provision in terms of issues and concepts recognized to have international application. The first five chapters of the book resulting from the 1966 IIP (Baron, Cooper, & Walker, 1969) fall into this category, identifying in turn trends and issues in education in Australia (Bassett), Canada (Byrne), New Zealand (Ewing), the United Kingdom (Stenhouse), and the United States (James). Similar articles about the United States, Canada, and Australia by Culbertson, Farquhar, and Moore in the 1974 International Issue of the British Educational Administration Society (BEAS) journal, *Educational Administration Bulletin*, were quickly followed by a similar article (Majasan, 1974) about educational administration in African countries. Penetrating analyses of educational provision in the host country were provided in the published proceedings of successive IIPs as they became a quadrennial event: the 1970 IIP in Australia (Thomas, Farquhar, & Taylor, 1974), the 1974 IIP in Britain (Hughes, 1975), and the 1978 IIP in Canada (Farquhar & Housego, 1980). Volumes arising from the 1982 IIP in Nigeria (Ukeje, Ocho, & Fagbamiye, 1986) and from the Fifth CCEA Regional Conference in India (Sapra & Dudani, 1986) provide a wider international setting for papers on various aspects of the administration of education in Nigeria and India respectively.

A more specific focus is achieved in such papers when attention is given to a particular theme, as happened at the CCEA Regional Conference in Cyprus (Cyprus Educational Administration Society, 1980), which concentrated on the role of the school principal. A special European issue of the BEAS journal (*Educational Administration*, 1978–1979) dealt even more specifically with professional development for school heads in Sweden, France, Germany and Britain, usefully highlighting differences of approach emanating from different concepts of school leadership, and these were further explored at European Forum conferences at Frankfurt (European Forum, 1981) and Grenoble (European Forum, 1982). An earlier European symposium in the United Kingdom, sponsored by BEAS, had concentrated on management issues concerned with the control of the curriculum (Glatter, 1977). The published proceedings provided an analysis of the various social and educational pressures and appeared, according to Glatter in his Introduction, to confirm the supposition "that each system is abandoning the more extreme positions on the 'tight control/high autonomy' continuum and is moving towards a central point" (1977, p. 13).

Whereas accounts by indigenous reporters have their limitations, the same holds for accounts by reporters following brief visits to school systems overseas, as noted in relation to the 19th-century precursors of modern comparative education. Tretheway (1972), in arguing the need for a supporting framework to assist administrators in their understanding of educational systems in other countries, helpfully identified a number of areas of difficulty; the main problem areas, he suggested, were those of context, bias, communication, sampling, interpretation and "culture shock."

A critical, but not necessarily skeptical, stance is thus required when an academic from Country A writes of the position as perceived in Country B with a view to encouraging similar developments in Country A. Relevant examples may conveniently be cited from an American, an Australian, and two British educational journals. Writing in *Educational Administration Quarterly*, Lindman (1966) concluded his account of developments in school finance in England with the

observation that "the experience with school finance in England may suggest approaches to the problem of school finance in the United States" (p. 188). Smith (1969), writing in the *Journal of Educational Administration*, similarly structured his account of local government reform proposals in England to argue the case for comparable developments in Australia. The direction is reversed in a paper in *Trends in Education*, the U.K. Department of Education and Science journal, that describes and favorably assesses the multimedia UCEA-sponsored simulations of the problem-beset principalship of Whitman School and the challenging school superintendency of Jefferson Township in the mythical State of Lafayette (Hughes, 1967). More recently Oldroyd (1984), as a result of intensive reading and a short transatlantic visit, has presented some lessons from Canada concerning school-based staff development in the British journal, *School Organisation*. Such papers, in which a comparison between two systems is implicit, belong to a preliminary stage in comparative study and are best regarded as simply providing pointers to areas that deserve more systematic analysis.

Much of the published output of international agencies concerning educational systems in different countries must also be regarded as useful raw material for comparative research rather than the substantive outcome of such research. A case in point is the majority of the "country orientation" papers produced since 1976 in the Report and Studies Series of UNESCO's DEPP. They provide valuable sources of up-to-date information concerning educational administration in individual countries. Earlier papers such as Moulton's (1976) study of the Sudan and Ozinian's (1976) study of Rwanda presented profiles of particular educational systems; later papers have tended to deal with a specific aspect, such as Østergen's (1979) study of the management of change in Swedish higher education or Stern's (1981) policy study of official efforts to strengthen the relationship between education and employment in the United States. Another of the more recent of over 100 papers now available consists of case studies of educational administrative structures in 16 Commonwealth countries, prepared for UNESCO by Harry Harris (1983), then Executive Director of CCEA. Such well-structured, factually reliable, and methodically executed studies have a wider significance, for they cumulatively provide an indication of potentially significant variables that need to be more precisely identified and studied.

The first stage of what can properly be called comparative educational administration research thus comes when an attempt is made to achieve a more comprehensive synoptic appraisal through critical comparative analysis of individual national accounts. One of the reports in the aforementioned UNESCO DEPP series provides a good example. A collection of 11 national case studies of devolution in educational administration (Zagefka, 1980) is accompanied by a perceptive analysis of the distinction that can be drawn between *decentralization* and *deconcentration*. Decentralization is taken to involve the handing over of powers of decision making to bodies that have some independent standing, that are frequently elective, and that are not simply agents for the central authority. Deconcentration, which has also been described as administrative—as opposed to structural—decentralization (Hanson, 1972), signifies an internal delegation of power by the central authority to its regional or local officers and does not involve creating new decision-making bodies with a significant measure of autonomy. Zagefka uses the case studies to draw out the implications of the two approaches and shows that the claimed move away from the center is often more apparent than real. It would appear that where there is substantial deconcentration, it is frequently a step along the road to structural decentralization with the possibility of more vigorous community involvement, though this is not necessarily so, as Maddock (1983) has recently shown.

Sixteen national studies of educational policy and planning issues published by OECD between 1968 and 1978, together with an appraisal of the series conducted for OECD by Maurice Kogan (1979), provide a more elaborate example of comparative analysis based on country views. Each national study consisted of a background report prepared by the country's authorities, an external report prepared by an international team of "examiners" following a study of the background report and a visit of at least one week, and finally the report of a review meeting between the examiners and the country's representatives. Kogan's (1979) general assessment of the volumes was as follows: "They do not constitute a definitive history, but are a series of snapshots of different policies, of different states of mind, and different policies in a large number of countries during a period of intense economic, social and educational change" (p. 74).

Kogan's own appraisal of the studies provided an instructive comparative analysis both of general themes such as planning, participation, and research, and of specific educational issues such as secondary reorganization, changes in higher education, and recurrent education. Recognizing that each study was distinctive, Kogan (1979) also noted:

> The reviews reveal remarkable parallelisms of national development and raise fascinating questions of how

far countries' policies are moulded by the common experiences of war, demographic and economic boom followed by recession, of how far policies are re-inforced by knowledge of changes elsewhere or how far they reflect a national sequence of development. (p. 6)

He also detected in the reviews "a gradual shift from concern with quantitative aspects of educational investment towards thought about the political processes by which values are brought together, legitimised and tested" (p. 6). There was inevitably a certain homogeneity in Kogan's sample, since the studies related to a particular group of industrialized nations.

Space does not permit a full review of the publications of international agencies that, in considering the planning, operation, and assessment of educational systems, make explicit use of theoretical frameworks. The UNESCO IIEP must be mentioned, however, having made notable contributions from the mid-1960s through publications and documents that stressed the importance of economic perspectives and systems approaches (Beeby, 1967; Coombs, 1968; Gurugé, 1969; Hallak, 1967; Lyons, 1965; Vaizey & Chesswas, 1967; Wheeler, 1969). At an IIEP seminar held in 1969, administrative aspects of educational planning were considered (Lyons, 1970). The seminar papers called for a functional analysis that would require "a radical re-appraisal of the structures, the means and the methods of traditional administrations, so as to adapt them to their new, difficult, but inspiring tasks" (Poignant, 1970, p. 5). New administrative and budgeting methods were identified and then examined in greater depth at a further IIEP seminar (Kravetz, 1970), which gave attention to the application in different national contexts of Delphi, PERT (Program Evaluation and Review Technique), PPBS (Planning Programming-Budgeting Systems), and RBC (the French Rationalization of Budgeting Choice system) techniques.

Although the general conclusions drawn from international practical experience at the second IIEP seminar were positive (Kravetz, 1970), a caveat was expressed that there could be no universal panacea: "It was recognised that there is no 'package' which can be applied in all cases, and that some situations do not lend themselves to ready treatment" (p. 8). More specifically, reference was made to "the doubtful effectiveness of even the most logical management procedures in the face of requirements for decisions coming from the conflicts which may arise among popular demand, political expediency, and economic resource feasibility" (p. 13). A further UNESCO study of techniques for the improvement of school management (Van Gendt, 1976) similarly warned of "a tendency to transfer in an automatic manner the application of a management tool from one system to another and especially from developed to developing countries" (p. 93). Such reservations reinforce the cautionary observation made by Lyons (1970) in his report on the earlier IIEP seminar: "What is true of one country may be manifestly false of another, and every report on this subject inevitably includes a plea for more country case studies in order to find out how administration can best employ planning" (p. 11).

The reverse process of conducting a number of national case studies first and then introducing a theoretical framework to illuminate the case studies may be illustrated from an educational research project undertaken by the OECD Centre for Educational Research and Innovation, CERI (1973) in eight industrialized countries in Europe and North America. Seventeen substantial studies of educational innovation were undertaken, seven at central government level, and five each at regional and school levels, each group being published in a separate volume. A fourth volume, written by the project director, Per Dalin, is titled *Strategies for Innovation in Education*. It reviews the case studies and brings them together in a final synthesis, using a conceptual framework derived from the literature on the management of change that relies heavily on the typology of change strategies (empirical-rational, normative-reeducative, power-coercive) identified by Bennis, Benne and Chin (1961). A Planning–Research-Development–and–Diffusion (P–R–D–D) process model is adopted at each of the three structural levels considered. Considering that the conceptual model used does not introduce a comparative dimension into the analysis, Dalin's concluding remarks assume a special significance:

> A structure for innovation would always have to have links with the administration of the existing educational system...We have observed advantages and disadvantages in all present structures. There is no *one* way to organise the process. A particular combination of factors in one country may call for a solution different from that required by the organizational pattern in another country, even if many basic factors (e.g., type of innovations, degree of centralisation) are the same. (CERI, 1973, Vol. IV, p. 263)

Once again, this view comes very near to recognizing that a general model of educational change is liable to ignore the particular matrix of circumstances, distinctive to each national system, which may be crucial in determining the outcome in the individual case.

More recent CERI reports adopt a more structured means of encouraging a comparative approach. Ashcroft (1975), in a discussion of the school as a base for community development, postulates three models or ideal types of community involvement in advanced societies, and then considers the extent to which particular situations in the same, or in different, countries approximate one or other of the models. A study of innovation in INSET, i.e., in the in-service education and training of teachers (CERI, 1978), begins with a chapter on national contextual factors, on the basis of which a provisional conceptual framework is introduced that draws on the work of Bolam (1976). The framework consists of a three-dimensional model consisting of (a) providing agents and agencies, (b) task, and (c) users, the elements of the dimensions being specified so as to recognize the considerable variation in practice in the different countries. A later CERI study (Hopkins, 1986) provides an international survey of in-service teacher training, while its International School Improvement Project, begun in 1982, is giving rise to a number of substantial studies (e.g., Hopes, 1986).

In some of the publications considered above the comparative aspect is largely implicit and generally of minor or incidental interest to the writers. We turn now to studies that are directly intended to contribute to the comparative study of educational administration. One must begin with the volume *Comparative Educational Administration* (Reller & Morphet, 1962), acknowledged as a pioneering work in the field. The volume consisted mainly of chapters by specialist authors on educational trends and developments in different countries in each of the five continents, and was thus of worldwide scope. The final chapters provided general discussion of issues raised in the national chapters, some of the topics considered being objectives and purposes in education, control and decision making, and centralization and decentralization. Some may argue that the book was largely descriptive and did not contribute substantially to theoretical development. Even so, in seeking to awaken interest in a hitherto neglected but potentially important aspect of the Theory Movement in educational administration, the volume was undoubtedly a valuable exploratory venture. Its lasting significance is less its substantive content than the fact that it clearly marked out a field for future development. The volume appropriately concluded on an optimistic note:

> There is a beginning recognition of the fact that the educational systems of the world constitute a tremendous though relatively unused laboratory for the study of educational administration...Thus the problems and issues identified here may well be the base for greatly expanded study and research which holds significant promise for education and for the societies involved. (p. 425)

The first manifestation of new recognition was, of course, the 1966 IIP (Baron, Cooper, & Walker, 1969), at which both Baron and Reller presented integrative papers partly based on five national manuscripts prepared for the meeting. A comparative approach was also adopted in the IIP report by Walker (1969) in considering the preparation of educational administrators and by Taylor (1969) in recommending the use of simulation "to provide a basis for the consideration of differences in the cultural context and assumptions of administrative behaviour between national systems" (p. 216) and hence "to facilitate exposure of the underlying values and emphases of a system more clearly than existing descriptive analyses permit" (p. 221).

A number of publications in Australia in the 1960s and early 1970s may also be viewed, at least in part, as a product of the internationalization of the North American Theory Movement. From Australia there came books such as *Headmasters for Better Schools* (Bassett, Crane, & Walker, 1963), *Training the Administrator* (Cunningham & Radford, 1963), and *The Principal at Work* (Walker, 1965a). More recent books continue the tradition (Simpkins, Thomas, & Thomas, 1982). The new ideas were interpreted in early issues of the *Journal of Educational Administration* (e.g., Walker, 1965b), and applied by Crane (1969) at the 1966 IIP to Australian administrator preparation. Appropriately, at the 1970 IIP Stone (1974) in turn provided a comparative analysis of bureaucracy and centralization in the United States and Australia, the precursor of a recent substantial Australian-American comparative study of the handling of education policy at the state level (Harman, 1985).

A similar diffusion, adaptation, and reinterpretation of theories, concepts, and research that were beginning to achieve worldwide currency through the international initiatives of UCEA's director, Jack Culbertson, took place in the 1970s in the United Kingdom. An important milestone was the publication of *Educational Administration and the Social Sciences* (Baron & Taylor, 1969), in which, according to the editors, "the influence of recent American, Canadian and Australian thinking is plainly evident. It therefore represents one of the first attempts to relate thinking about education policy and administration in English speaking countries through common patterns of thought and language" (p. vii). They added, however, that "the dominant note is that of English pragmatism; this is perhaps as it should be in a book emanating from a country in which the *practice* of administration has long been held in high esteem and in which its theory is only now receiving serious attention" (p. vii). The volume was soon followed by other books adopting a similar approach (e.g., Glatter, 1972; Hughes, 1970); by the founding in 1971 of the BEAS journal then entitled *Educational Administration Bulletin* but now

known as *Educational Management and Administration*; and by the Open University's innovative and wide-ranging courses, publications, and audiovisual materials from 1974 onward in educational management and administration.

In the decade or so that followed the Reller and Morphet (1962) vision in the early 1960s of the educational systems of the world constituting "a tremendous though relatively unused laboratory for the study of educational administration" (p. 425), there was certainly a remarkable and dramatic transformation at the academic level. In all parts of the English-speaking world simulations and role analysis, the Getzels-Guba model, the Leader Behavior Description Questionnaire (LBDQ), the Organizational Climate Description Questionnaire (OCDQ), and a succession of management-of-change formulations began to appear in research projects and academic dissertations. Rapidly, and perhaps too uncritically, they became an essential part of the worldwide accepted wisdom of educational management. The general adoption of both "organizational climate" and "organization development" (OD) concepts and techniques may be cited in illustration.

Organizational Climate

Halpin and Croft (1963) proposed the term "organizational climate" in their pioneering study of the internal characteristics of 71 American elementary schools as perceived by the teachers, by means of which they developed and refined their well-known OCDQ containing 64 items. Writing a few years later, Halpin (1967) noted the many investigators who had already worked with the OCDQ:

> It has been used in not less than 1,100 schools in the United States and Canada. It has also been used in Korea, Pakistan and Australia, and it soon will be used in Paraguay. The response to the OCDQ has been both gratifying and frightening—frightening, because in several instances it has been used with greater zeal than wisdom. (pp. 6–7)

Halpin's frank apprehension was all the more justified in that, even in North America, the OCDQ was used without any revalidation in secondary schools, in school system central offices, and with nurses and supervisors in a hospital setting (Hughes, 1968, p. 27). Carver and Sergiovanni (1969) reported being "cautioned by Halpin in personal correspondence that the instrument was designed for use in (U.S.) elementary schools only" (p. 81). Transfer across national cultures becomes even more problematic when one takes account of a reservation made by Andrews (1965), with his use of the OCDQ in Canadian schools in mind, that an instrument completed by teachers and mainly concerned with principal-teacher interaction does not adequately recognize the contribution to the distinctive ethos of a school of relationships involving pupils and parents. That cultural differences cannot safely be ignored is also suggested by a study of teachers' perceptions in Australian primary schools (Thomas & Slater, 1972, pp. 197–208) that reported the emergence of only four factors, as compared with Halpin and Croft's eight-factor solution.

With such points in mind, a study of school climate conducted by the United Kingdom's National Foundation for Educational Research developed and tested in an English context questionnaires that included the perceptions of pupils as well as of teachers (Finlayson, Banks, & Loughran, 1971). Their subsequent use and validation in Australia has been reported (Deer, 1980). Finlayson and Deer (1979) have also reported a related crosscultural comparison of teachers' perceptions of their schools in England and New South Wales, using questionnaires developed in Britain to assess teachers' perceptions of selected aspects of the behavior of the head or principal, of the head of department, and of their teacher colleagues. Some of the factors extracted in the British study did not reappear in the Australian context, but a sufficiently similar overall structure emerged to permit some speculative comparative comments. According to Finlayson and Deer (1979), Australian heads of department "show less authoritarian and directive behaviour towards their staff than is the case in the U.K. schools" (p. 137), but the U.K. departmental heads are seen to be "more sensitive to and more constructive in their reactions to problems in their departments than their counterparts in N.S.W." (p. 137). The U.K. headteachers or principals were thought to evince more personal concern for staff. Finlayson and Deer point to the greater central control in Australia as a likely contributing factor at both levels and conclude that their joint study points to the possibility of conducting valid crosscultural comparative studies in school administration. Another study (Ogilvie & Bartlett, 1979) used a survey of subject masters and mistresses in Queensland state high schools to replicate three studies of English departmental heads and revealed significant differences that can be reconciled with the Finlayson and Deer findings.

Organization Development

Organization Development, or OD, as understood in the mid-1980s, largely derives from the group dynamics and T-Group action research approaches to human behavior in an industrial and governmental setting, which developed and flourished in the 1950s at the National Training Laboratories at Bethel, Maine. Matthew Miles at Teachers College, Columbia University, was much involved from about 1960 in applying the new ideas and techniques to the management of educational change, while the work of Schmuck and Runkel (1970) at the University of Oregon from 1967 onward and the collaborative work of Schmuck and Miles (1971) on OD in schools soon became a part of the "new look" American educational administration that was then being assimilated, and to some extent modified, in different parts of the English-speaking world.

Fullan, Miles, and Taylor (1980) in a comprehensive survey that focused mainly on OD in American and Canadian schools reported also on developments in Australia, Germany, Holland, Norway, Sweden, and the United Kingdom. Apart from research and development undertaken in the United States, notably under the leadership of Schmuck at Oregon (Schmuck, Runkel, Arends, & Arends, 1977), data-based studies linked in varying degrees to the OD movement may be noted in Canada (Fullan, 1980; Fullan & Pomfret, 1977); in Australia (Mulford, Conabeare, & Keller, 1977); in Norway (Dalin, 1978); and in Britain (Bolam, 1978; McMahon, 1982). Also, in 1976 the British Open University Management in Education course (Open University, 1976) included a unit on Organization Development based on a case study of a high school in Eugene, Oregon, the study material including two documentary television programs filmed on site. The unit included an overview of OD in schools by Schmuck and a critique by Fullan.

The internationalism of the OD movement is further evidenced by the initiative of Harry Gray in the United Kingdom, together with OD scholars and practitioners in other countries, in establishing in 1978 an international Network for Organisation Development in Education (NODE), which publishes a journal, *Educational Change and Development*, with international associate editors in Australia, Canada, West Germany, South Africa, and the United States. A recent volume, edited by Gray (1982), similarly contains both a definitive survey of OD by Schmuck and chapters on its application in the United States (Milstein), Australia (Mulford), England (Heller), Canada (Fullan), and Scotland (Bone).

The Norwegian-based variant of OD, the International Movement toward Educational Change (IMTEC), which was originally an OECD activity and is led by Dalin, has developed an Institutional Development Program (IDP). In a paper given at a CCEA regional seminar in Cyprus on the school principal's future management role, Farquhar (1980) observed that

The IDP approach is closely related to Organisation Development, and is based on a belief that educational changes must be part of the "school culture" and solutions to problems must be shared and "owned" by those who will make the changes. (p. 68)

The University of Saskatchewan College of Education was in process of implementing the IDP, with pleasing results to that point. Among the conclusions stated to have been reached by Dalin and his colleagues, Farquhar (1980) listed the following:

It is critical that the IDP is adapted to each school and each culture. The Canadian IDP is different from the Norwegian Project, and each district and school has its own needs that must be taken into account. (p. 69)

Earlier writing appeared to regard Organization Development as a universal seamless robe, but a cross-cultural perspective was strongly supported by Fullan (1976), who argued that "OD techniques are not culture-free and are not necessarily universally valid" (p. 47). And Gray (1983) wrote:

By and large, there are two broad schools of Organisation Development in education—the American and the European, though the distinction is not exact and some would claim such a distinction to be improper. The American school is more coherent, has a clearer historical line of development and is much more systematic. (p. 7)

He further notes that the "American OD appears to be based on the desirability of consensus while European OD stresses the importance of individualism. Americans stress the organisational aspects of OD while the British stress the importance of individual development" (p. 12). Gray's generalizations may require some qualification, as he is expressing a personal view rather than reporting the findings of comparative research, but his conclusions find some support within the U.K. literature. Glatter (1983), for instance, in discussing the issue of individual versus school development in a European context, observes that "in countries where job mobility is being sharply reduced as a result of contraction, broadening 'comparative' experiences for individuals may be seen as more beneficial than development activities with colleagues whom perhaps they know too well" (p. 113).

Another U.K. commentator, Mangham (1978), after surveying the well-known literature on overcoming resistance to change, advocates a political perspective "which far from seeing barriers and resistances as deviances to be overcome or redressed on the way to the ideal organization, sees them as naturally occurring features of social life" (p. 19). He argues

it could be more important for the Organization Development practitioners to enhance the power and skill of the weaker group, coalition or individual rather than to seek to shore up the authority of the most powerful interests by promoting a specious collaboration and a false consensus. (p. 21)

Such views received support from practitioners as well as academics at a BEMAS conference on the micro-politics of educational administration (Pratt, 1982) and are also becoming familiar to North American scholars of educational administration (Bolman & Deal, 1984).

The School Principal

Because of their international interest, the management training needs of the school principal also deserve mention. Reference has already been made above to relevant Australian publications from the early 1960s. Starting somewhat later there were studies in Britain (Cohen, 1970; Kelsall & Kelsall, 1969; Taylor, 1964; Watson, 1969; Westwood, 1966) that also clearly benefited from an awareness of the relevant American literature. The benefit applies especially to Glatter's (1972) influential and pioneering study of management development for the education profession both in Britain and overseas. It applied also to research on the role of the secondary school head in England and Wales (Hughes, 1973, 1985), which took account of the executive professional leadership construct advanced by Gross and Herriott (1965) to propose a new model of the headship of a professionally staffed organization. Headship is viewed as "the simultaneous activation of two sub-roles that deeply inter-penetrate each other: the role of *leading professional* and the role of *chief executive*" (Hughes, 1985, p. 278). The application of the model to the principalship in developing countries was considered in a paper given at the IIEP in Paris (Hughes, 1977) and more specifically to the situation in Nigeria in a paper at the Inaugural Convention of the Nigerian Association of Educational Administration and Planning (Hughes, 1978). Similar ideas were developed by Farquhar (1978) in a paper reviewing the professional preparation of principals at the Second CCEA Regional Conference in Penang, Malaysia, and by Watson (1981) in a paper on the principal's managerial discretion given at the Third CCEA Regional Conference, held in Nicosia, Cyprus. The relevance of school administrator studies for developing countries is considered further in two publications of the Education Division of the Commonwealth Secretariat (Harris, 1982; Hughes, 1981).

Sometimes an innovative study provides a stimulus for similar research in other contexts and in other countries. Mintzberg's (1973) seminal observational study of the nature of managerial work is a case in point. Using Mintzberg's methodology Duignan (1980) carried out a descriptive study of school superintendents in Alberta. Two observational studies of high school principals, both of which acknowledged indebtedness to Mintzberg, were conducted independently in Melbourne, Australia (Willis, 1980), and in a northeastern state of the United States (Martin & Willower, 1981). In the United Kingdom Webb and Lyons (1982) drew on Mintzberg's methodology to re-examine and reclassify empirical material already available from a previous study of the tasks of headship (Lyons, 1976). The last three studies were briefly noted and compared (Hughes, 1983) at an Educational Research Workshop held under the auspices of the Council for Cultural Cooperation of the Council of Europe (Hegarty, 1983). At the same Research Workshop, Hopes (1983) quoted the Martin and Willower study in commenting on principal training needs in Germany, while Glatter (1983) noted that the "inside focus" of the principals in the American study contrasted markedly with the external management emphasis identified in U.K. research on heads' tasks undertaken at the Open University (Morgan, Hall, & Mackay, 1983). In the same vein, a New Zealand ethnographic study of school principals (Edwards, 1979) may be noted; it is included with several of the foregoing references in Boyan's (1982) discussion of research on school administrator behavior, which also cites other American studies (e.g., Crowson & Porter-Gehrie, 1980; Peterson, 1978; Pitner & Ogawa, 1981; Sproull, 1981).

The studies relating to organizational climate, OD, and the school principalship that have been reviewed indicate a growing international awareness in educational administration. This is also evident in a book edited by George Baron (1981), which examines ways in which school government is being remodeled in a number of Commonwealth and European countries and the United States. Baron observes that "at this stage in the development of the systematic study of school government it is above all essential that there should be no obstacles to the *uniqueness* of each situation being fully explored" (p. v). Contributors were therefore not asked to fit their various national accounts into a common theoretical framework, although there are some similarities of approach. In drawing the studies together, Baron (1981) notes that a number of commonalities emerge across national systems when the interaction and interrelationships of parents, teachers, students, and the local community are analyzed in terms of political and social factors. In particular he observes some recent slackening of

interest worldwide in a more austere political and economic climate as compared with the interest in school councils that was "part of the relatively short lived political effervescence of the late 1960s with its radical assaults on established institutions and in particular on universities and, in some countries, on secondary schools with older pupils" (p. 283).

The effects of continuing international recession and inflation on the political economy of education in a number of nations have been studied both generally in relation to policy tasks for the 1980s (Hough, 1984) and to national qualities and specific policy issues (Harman & Wirt, 1985). The concepts of economic dependence and interdependence also provide an antithesis that illuminates educational development issues in a number of national and regional contexts (Watson, 1984).

Limitations on space have prevented attention to comparative studies in the administration of higher education. A comprehensive list of IIEP publications includes a series of books on planning the development of universities (Onushkin, 1971–1974), and the OECD interest has resulted in substantial studies on institutional management and the publication of the *International Journal of Institutional Management in Higher Education*. For a further indication of a vigorous and growing literature on this aspect of comparative educational administration, reference should be made to a review of research trends and a bibliography prepared by Altbach (1979).

Our literature review has attended only to a small sample of the great variety of available material. We began with papers that attempted some critical analysis of educational administration in individual countries, whether written by indigenous "locals" or knowledgable "strangers." We recognized a second stage, at which a number of such national papers were presented together or reconsidered with an attempt at conceptual clarification or synoptic appraisal. The publications of a number of international agencies and related papers that make explicit use of theoretical frameworks, including a variety of systems and management of change models, were also considered. We turned to books and papers that appear to have contributed directly to comparative educational administration, whether explicitly, as in the Reller and Morphet (1962) volume, or implicitly, as a product of the growing internationalization of the educational administration studies of organizational climate, OD, and the role of the principal. That there are important developments in comparative higher education meriting more detailed consideration than can be given in this chapter was also noted.

Before turning to a consideration of current trends and future prospects, it is appropriate to comment on *Educational Administration: A Comparative View* (Friesen, Farine, & Meek, 1979), which—in the style of Reller and Morphet—seeks to provide a comprehensive view of the whole field. As in the earlier volume, contributors of chapters come from various countries across the world. The indigenous authors, as claimed in the introduction, "provide insight into different modes of thinking and a flavour of the workings of national life." The final chapter (by the editors) summarizes data from the national contributions concerning structures, governance, finance, preparation programs, and other issues of concern, and then looks to the future. In doing so the chapter uses the concept of "directionality" to differentiate between partially industrialized and heavily industralized nations, but without drawing on the very relevant development administration literature. The editors view the less industrialized nations as placing increasing emphasis on technology, expenditure, centralization, professionalization, scale, and rationality, whereas the industrialized nations are wavering in their previous reliance on these factors, displaying some confusion on goals, and even exhibiting some reversal of previous trends.

The book by Friesen, Farine, and Meek (1979) contains many interesting and significant ideas. If one is concerned, however, with developing comparative educational administration as a field of study and with clarifying alternative conceptual bases and reporting significant research, the 1979 book represents only a modest advance on the Reller and Morphet volume of 17 years earlier. The later collection does not substantially lessen the force of Lynch's (1979–1980) insistence in the same year that "the need for a well organized field of inquiry which allows for comparative analysis of educational policy and administration is long overdue" (p. 2).

NEW TRENDS AND FUTURE DEVELOPMENT

New ideas and challenges within educational administration that began to emerge in the early 1970s may be regarded as particularly significant for comparative study. These included the "garbage-can" model of organizational choice described by Cohen, March, and Olsen (1972) and Weick's (1976) perception of educational organizations as "loosely coupled systems," the extent of coupling being a matter that may be culturally contingent. Less familiar to American readers will be some crossinstitutional studies in Britain in the mid-1970s (Greenwood, Hinings, & Ransom, 1975; Hinings, 1979) using a contingency-theory approach, which led to the conclusion that belief systems and ideologies, previously regarded as irrelevant, warrant careful, detailed, study. More recently the same group

(Ransom, Hinings, & Greenwood, 1980) has proposed a framework to incorporate "ostensibly disparate perspectives" with a view to "searching for the relations between cause and meaning, between what is determinant and what voluntary in the relation of structure and action" (p. 14). All these studies provide evidence of a new flexibility and freshness of approach in work that began within traditional and well-established frameworks but developed in ways that more directly accommodate the different value systems and other deeply embedded contextual factors of crucial relevance in comparative research.

At the 1974 IIP, Greenfield (1975) proposed a more fundamental change of perspective that challenged the assumptions of structural-functional and natural-systems theory. From its initial delivery, the paper received wide international attention and has been much discussed in Britain (e.g., in *Educational Administration* from 1976 onward), and Australia (Gronn, 1983), as well as in the United States and Canada (in *Educational Administration Quarterly* from 1977 onward). Greenfield's subjectivist stance, derived in part from the phenomenological tradition, also owes much to a rediscovery of Weber's concept of understanding (Eldridge, 1971). Thus Greenfield (1975) regards it as a strength rather than a limitation that the cultural scientist is permitted to enter into and take the viewpoint of the actor whose behavior is to be explained:

> While the cultural scientist may not discover ultimate social reality, he can interpret what people see as social reality and, indeed, he must do so according to a consistent, logical and rigorous methodology...It is such a discipline for interpreting human experience which provides the science in the cultural scientist's work, not his ability to discover ultimate truths about social structure. (p. 82)

That such a change of emphasis has implications for the comparative study of educational administration is evident. Sensitivity to the perceptions and understanding of those actually involved in the organizational activity, as revealed through the inductive and qualitative methodologies of the micro social sciences (Knorr-Cetina, & Cicourel, 1981), becomes a matter of particular importance when one needs to take account of cultural and national contexts that may be profoundly different.

More recent developments include a joint paper by Benno Sander, then of Brasilia University, and Thomas Wiggins of Oklahoma University (Sander & Wiggins, 1985) that considers the cultural context of administrative theory in the Americas, drawing on South American sources in Spanish and Portugese as well as on the

North American literature. Their four-dimensional paradigm incorporates economic, pedagogical, political, and cultural factors.

At the 1982 IIP in Nigeria, Griffiths (1986), seeking order where there was previously turmoil, outlined the fourfold typology of paradigms of social change (functional, interpretive, radical humanist, and radical structuralist) advanced by Burrell and Morgan (1980). In projecting directions of future development, Griffiths commented that "looking at organisations through the assumptions of four different paradigms will produce far more and different questions than we have yet dealt with" (p. 269). His conclusion was that "the era of paradigm diversity is already upon us and will be more in evidence in the near future" (p. 269).

Yet another four-dimensional paradigm is proposed by Bolman and Deal (1984), who identify four "frames" that they describe respectively as natural systems, human resource, political, and symbolical. "Each frame", they claim, "provides a different way of interpreting events, and each implies a very different approach to effective management" (pp. 240–241). They advocate "reframing," defined as "switching across frames to generate new insights and options for managerial action" (p. 240), seeing it as a means to clarify what is happening, to generate options, and "to diagnose the multiple realities of the people with whom we interact daily" (p. 255). The viewpoint of Bolman and Deal (1984) is consonant with editorial comment on the Greenfield 1974 IIP paper to the effect that it might be heuristically rewarding

> to examine an administrative situation both from a "phenomenological" and a "systems" viewpoint— just as physicists at Cambridge made rapid advances in the 1930s by being prepared, as Sir Arthur Eddington vividly put it, to assume a wave theory of light on Mondays, Wednesdays and Fridays while adopting the seemingly irreconcilable "photon" model of quantum dynamics on Tuesdays, Thursdays and Saturdays. (Hughes, 1975, p. 6)

In 1975, however, little heed was paid to a further suggestion that the academics of educational administration should refrain from forming themselves "into rival doctrinal factions of one-eyed true believers, whether of an 'old' or a 'new' ideology" (Hughes, 1975, p. 6).

A decade and several heated debates later, the field now appears to be more receptive to a theoretical and methodological pluralism, which enables taken-for-granted assumptions to be exposed to the challenge of alternative ways of seeing (Morgan, 1980, p. 605). The reframing that Bolman and Deal (1984) advocate is thus of particular relevance in the sensitive analysis

of cultural diversity that is an essential prerequisite of nontrivial comparative research in educational administration.

It is instructive to note the contemporaneous development of new perspectives in the two closely related comparative fields to which reference was made in the earlier part of the chapter. In their review of the field of comparative education, Kazamias and Massialas (1982) found it helpful in interpreting recent research to present an analysis in terms of the inter-relationship of two paradigms, described as "functional" and "radical." They trace the emergence of the latter approach in the last decade by considering social, political, and economic relations; development education; the effects of schooling; and curriculum and pedagogy. An interesting example of a significant change of viewpoint is Torsten Husen's (1979) retrospective critique of the massive International Educational Achievement survey, of which he himself was one of the chief architects. Shortcomings identified, as summarized by Kazamias and Massialas (1982), were: "undue emphasis on quantitative methods..., limitations of the input-output model, absence of qualitative analysis, and generally heavy reliance on a positivist research paradigm" (p. 315).

Kelly, Altbach, and Arnove (1982), in a similar analysis of trends in comparative education, also identify "new approaches to understanding educational realities" (p. 521) based on conflict theories, which are perceived to be in marked contrast to more familiar structural-functional approaches. The "new" scholarship, they suggest, "is in a constructive tension with more traditional orientations to the field, making for a lively, if sometimes confusing, debate within the field" (p. 521). They discern both macroanalytical and microanalytical new trends. The macro approach involves what is called *world-systems analysis*: that is, analysis in terms of characteristics that affect all nations simultaneously (Arnove, 1982). Microanalytical studies are identified as concerned with regional and local, rather than national, units and also as involving phenomenological or interpretive research methodologies, the comparative dimensions of such research being still "in its incipient stages" (Kelly et al., 1982, p. 523).

In comparative administration it is also possible to discern new trends in the 1970s. In editing a symposium intended to examine critically the achievements of comparative and development administration, Waldo (1976) observes, with evident embarrassment, that he was "wildly successful" in securing a critical look at the accomplishments of the 1950s and 1960s by confining his invitations to younger political scientists. In that symposium Sigelman (1976) suggests that "the future of comparative public administration lies in micro-level studies" (p. 624), and Tapia-Videla (1976) finds much promise for the future of comparative administration in "a micro-level approach to the study of public bureaucracy in the third world" (p. 635). A third contributor, Jun (1976), argues the merits of taking advantage of different perspectives, which "requires the development of a conscious, self-reflexive posture in the comparative field and among comparative scholars" (p. 644) He also advocates a phenomenological perspective as "a useful way of standing aside from our presuppositions and cultural biases, and looking at someone else a good deal more in their own terms" (p. 444).

In responding to the symposium, Riggs (1976), the acknowledged leader of the "movement" of the 1950s and 1960s, is confident that "we do not need phenomenology to apply organisation theory to comparative administration" (p. 652) but concedes that some of the critics of the earlier structural-functional and systems approaches "make interesting suggestions which deserve serious attention" (p. 648). Heady (1979), commenting further on the Waldo Symposium and other recent writings, concluded that

> the comparative phase of study and research in public administration does not require escape from the kind of paradigmatic uncertainties which have long been characteristic of the parent discipline. Coercive superposition of a feigned consensus would be futile and stifling. (p. 42)

He had no doubt, however, that general public administration will be enriched "by widening the horizon of interest in such a way that understanding of one's own national system of administration will be enhanced by placing it in a cross-cultural setting" (p. 42).

CONCLUSION

It is appropriate to offer here some observations about future developments in comparative educational administration research, taking account of both the review of the literature and the experience of those working in the two cognate comparative fields to which reference has been made.

1. The diversity of methodological and theoretical approaches evident in the studies undertaken over the last 30 years may be viewed, at least potentially, as a strength rather than as a weakness. It is natural and inevitable that conflicting perspectives in the discipline of educational administration, whether viewed as turmoil or as ferment, should be reflected in the subdiscipline, and nothing would be gained by

seeking to impose a single methodology, theoretical framework, or ideology on the comparative study of educational administration. The variety and richness of the data available, as an international dimension is introduced into research, make it unlikely that an agreed-on orthodoxy of method or paradigm would be other than stultifying. This consideration, of course, does not lessen the need for research, whether quantitative or qualitative, whether focusing on an individual country or comparing a number of different countries, to be accurate in its description and rigorous in its analysis, as Willower has insisted on a number of occasions (e.g., 1979, p. 37).

2. The case has been demonstrated for greater familiarity with closely related disciplinary fields such as comparative education and comparative administration. There is a danger of scholars being parochial not only through exclusive attention to the literature of their own country but also through ignorance of developments in cognate disciplines. A comparative approach is thus desirable in a disciplinary sense as well as across national frontiers. There is some evidence in recent writings that the danger is coming to be recognized (Dimmock, 1981; Marshall, 1982; Marshall & Newton, 1983). Lynch (1984) has commented on the broad conceptual theme of international equality, as have a number of UNESCO documents (e.g., Haag, 1982). Interdisciplinary aspects are also receiving attention internationally in research seminars. In 1985 Brian Holmes, Head of Comparative Education at the London University Institute of Education, addressed a BEMAS research conference on comparative educational administration, and a CCEA-sponsored research seminar in the West Indies was inspired by Marshall and Newton's (1983) analysis of the development-administration literature and of crosscultural studies of organizational behavior.

3. Review of the literature suggests that it is neither feasible nor necessary to regard comparative educational administration as an autonomous and separate field of study, but rather as the part of the educational administration field that brings into prominence the comparative and international dimension that might otherwise be neglected. Such a modest view would be in accord with the similar position generally adopted with comparative administration in recent years (Heady, 1979, p. 42), which markedly contrasts with the more ambitious claims of the well-funded Comparative Administration Movement of the 1950s and 1960s. There *are* a number of areas in the administration of educational systems where a comparative approach would undoubtedly be helpful:
   a. fiscal provision for education and the consequence of variation in resource availability for educational systems;
   b. the interface of educational planning and educational administration;

c. the centralization-decentralization issue in national and regional educational systems;

d. achieving effective professional and lay participation in educational organization;

e. assessment and accountability;

f. leadership roles in the management of schools and colleges;

g. equity issues and the role of women in educational administration;

h. education and the wider society.

Some progress has been made in placing many of these topics in comparative perspective, but much still remains to be done.

4. Not only do the educational systems of the world provide a research laboratory for comparative administration study, as Reller and Morphet (1962) maintained, but increasingly it is to the world community of scholars that we must look for the human and other resources necessary to undertake such research. These resources are to be found in part in the international intergovernmental educational agencies that are becoming increasingly sensitive to new trends in comparative studies. They are to be found also in universities, institutes, and centers in many countries, developed and developing, in which educational administration is taught and studied in ways that lead to sensitive analysis of the comparative dimensions. Such comparative study then gains further strength and coherence through interaction within the informal worldwide network of academics and practicing educational administrators, which, as noted, is in some measure a product of the U.S.-inspired Theory Movement of the 1950s and its international florescence in the 1960s.

REFERENCES

Altback, P. G. (1979). *Comparative higher education: Research trends and bibliograhy*. London: Mansell.

Altback, P. G., Arnove, R. F., & Kelly, G. P. (Eds.). (1982). *Comparative education*. New York: Macmillan.

Andrews, J. H. M. (1965). What school climate conditions are desirable? *The Council on School Administration Bulletin* (Calgary, Alberta) 4(5), 4–20.

Arnold, M. (1874). *Higher schools and universities in Germany*. London: Macmillan.

Arnove, R. F. (1982). Comparative education and world-systems analysis. In P. G. Altback, R. F. Arnove, & G. P. Kelly (Eds.), *Comparative education*. New York: Macmillan.

Ashcroft, R. (1975). The school as a base for community development. In CERI, *School and community* (pp. 22–42). Paris: OECD.

Baron, G. (Ed.). (1981). *The politics of school government*. Oxford, England: Pergamon.

Baron, G., Cooper, D. H., & Walker, W. G. (Eds.). (1969). *Educational administration: International perspectives*. Chicago: Rand McNally.

Baron, G., & Taylor, W. (Eds.). (1969). *Educational administration and the social sciences*. London: Athlone.

Bassett, G. W., Crane, A. R., & Walker, W. G. (1963). *Headmasters for better schools*. St. Lucia, Australia: University of Queensland Press.

Beeby, C. E. (1967). *Planning and the educational administrator* (Fundamentals of Educational Planning, No. 4). Paris: IIEP (UNESCO).

Bolam, R. (1976). The types of environment most likely to favour the active and effective participation of teachers in educational innovation. In *New patterns of teacher education and tasks: Teachers as innovators*. Paris: OECD.

Bolam, R. (1978). School focused INSET and consultancy. *Educational Change and Development*, 1(1), 25–30.

Bolman, L. G., & Deal, T. E. (1984). *Modern approaches to understanding and managing organizations*. San Francisco: Jossey-Bass.

Boyan, N. J. (1982). Administration of educational institutions. In H. E. Mitzel, J. H. Best, & W. Abramowitz (Eds.), *Encyclopedia of educational research: Vol. 1* (5th ed.). New York: Free Press.

Bridges, E. (1956). Administration: What is it? and how can it be learnt? In A. Dunsire (Ed.), *The making of an administrator*. Manchester: Manchester University Press.

Burrell, G., & Morgan, G. (1980). *Sociological paradigms and organizational analysis*. London: Heinemann.

Carver, F. D., & Sergiovanni, T. J. (1969). Some notes on the OCDQ. *Journal of Educational Administration*, 7(1), 78–81.

Centre for Educational Research and Innovation. (1973). *Case studies of educational innovation: 1. at the central level; 2. at the regional level; 3. at the school level; 4. strategies for innovation in education* (4 vols.). Paris: OECD.

Centre for Educational Research and Innovation. (1978). *Innovation in in-service education and training of teachers: Practice and theory*. Paris: OECD.

Cohen, L. (1970). School size and head teachers' bureaucratic role conceptions. *Educational Review*, 23, 50–58.

Cohen, M., March, J., & Olsen, J. (1972). A garbage-can model of organizational choice. *Administrative Science Quarterly*, 17(1), 1–25.

Coombs, P. H. (1968). *The world educational crisis: A systems analysis*. New York: Oxford University Press.

Crane, A. R. (1969). Innovation and strategies of change for the preparation of educational administrators—an application to Australia. In G. Baron, D. H. Cooper, & W. G. Walker (Eds.), *Educational administration: International perspectives* (pp. 249–268). Chicago: Rand McNally.

Crowson, R. L., & Porter-Gehrie, C. (1980). The discretionary behavior of principals in large-city schools. *Educational Administration Quarterly*, 16(1), 45–69.

Culbertson, J. A. (1969). Introduction: A new initiative in educational administration. In G. Baron, D. H. Cooper, & W. G. Walker (Eds.), *Educational administration: International perspectives*. Chicago: Rand McNally.

Culbertson, J. (1981). International networking: Expanded vistas for leadership development. *Theory into Practice*, 20(4), 278–284.

Cunningham, K. S., & Radford, W. C. (1963). *Training the administrator*. Hawthorne, Australia: Australian Council for Educational Research.

Cyprus Educational Administration Society. *Managing the schools of the future: Focus on principals*. Nicosia, Cyprus: C.E.A.S.

Dahl, R. A. (1947). The science of public administration: Three problems. *Public Administration Review*, 7(1), 1–11.

Dalin, P. (1978). *Limits to educational change*. London: Macmillan.

Deer, C. E. (1980). Measuring organizational climate in secondary schools. *Australian Journal of Education*, 24(1), 26–43.

Dimmock, C. (1981). Teacher supply as a problem in the USA and England. *London Association of Comparative Educationists, Occasional Paper No. 3*.

Duignan, P. (1980). Administration behavior of school superintendents: A descriptive study. *Journal of Educational Administration*, 18(1), 5–26.

Educational Administration Bulletin. (1974). International issue, 2(2).

Educational Administration: European Edition. (1978–1979), 7(1).

Edwards, W. L. (1979). The role of the principal in five New Zealand primary schools: An ethnographic perspective. *Journal of Educational Administration*, 17(2), 248–254.

Eldridge, J. E. T. (Ed.). (1971). *Max Weber: The interpretation of social reality*. London: Michael Joseph.

Enns, F. (1969). The promise of international co-operation in the preparation of educational administrators. In G. Baron, D. H. Cooper, & W. G. Walker (Eds.), *Educational administration: International perspectives*. Chicago: Rand McNally.

European Forum on Educational Administration. (1981). *Report on the intervisitation programme in the Federal Republic of Germany, 1980*. Frankfurt am Main: Deutsches Institut fur Internationale Padagogische Forschung.

European Forum on Educational Administration. (1982). *Intervisitation programme and workshop in France: Grenoble, 1982*. Paris: Association Française des Administrateurs de L'Education.

Farquhar, R. H. (1978). Recent developments in the professional preparation of principals. *CCEA Studies in Educational Administration, 11*, 1–18.

Farquhar, R. H. (1980). New wine in old bottles: Managing change. In Cyprus Educational Administration Society, *Managing the schools of the future: Focus on principals*. Nicosia, Cyprus: C.E.A.S.

Farquhar, R. H., & Housego, I. E. (Eds.). (1980). *Canadian and comparative educational administration*. Vancouver, Canada: University of British Columbia.

Fayol, H. (1949). *General and industrial management* (C. Storrs, Trans.). London: Pitman. (Original work published 1916)

Finlayson, D., & Deer, C. (1979). The organizational climate of secondary schools: A cross cultural comparison. *Journal of Educational Administration, 17*(2), 129–138.

Finlayson, D. S., Banks, O., & Loughran, J. L. (1971). *Administrative manual for pupil questionnaire for school climate index*. Slough, England: National Foundation for Educational Research.

Friesen, D., Farine, A., & Meek, J. C. (Eds.). (1979). *Educational administration: A comparative view*. Edmonton, Canada: University of Alberta, Department of Educational Administration.

Fullan, M. (1976). OD in schools: An overview and critique. In Open University, *Organization development: The case of Sheldon High School* (pp. 43–49). Milton Keynes, England: Open University Press.

Fullan, M. (1980). The role of human agents internal to the school districts in knowledge utilization. In R. Lehming (Ed.), *Improving schools: What do we know?* Berkeley, CA: Sage.

Fullan, M., Miles, M., & Taylor, G. (1980). Organization development in schools: The state of the art. *Review of Educational Research, 50*(1), 121–183.

Fullan, M., & Pomfret, A. (1980). Research on curriculum and instruction implementation. *Review of Educational Research, 50*(1), 121–183.

Getzels, J. W. (1952). A psycho-sociological framework for the study of educational administration. *Harvard Educational Review, 22*, 235–246.

Glatter, R. (1972). *Management development for the education profession*. London: Harrap.

Glatter, R. (Ed.). (1977). *Control of the curriculum: Issues and trends in Britain and Europe*. London: London University Institute of Education.

Glatter, R. (1983). Implications of research for policy on school management training. In S. Hegarty (Ed.), *Training for management in schools*. Windsor, England: NFER-Nelson.

Gordon, P., & White, J. (1979). *Philosophers as educational reformers: The influence of idealism on British thought and practice*. London: Routledge & Kegan Paul.

Gray, H. L. (1982). *The management of educational institutions: Theory, research and consultancy*. Lewes, England: Falmer.

Gray, H. L. (1983). Organization development (OD) in education. *School Organization & Management Abstracts, 2*(1), 7–19.

Greenfield, T. B. (1975). Theory about organization: A new perspective and its implications for schools. In M. Hughes (Ed.), *Administering education: International challenge*. London: Athlone.

Greenwood, R., Hinings, C. R., & Ranson, S. (1975). Contingency theory and the organization of local authorities: Parts I & II. *Public Administration, 53*, 1–23, 169–190.

Griffiths, D. E. (1959). *Administrative theory*. New York: Appleton-Century-Crofts.

Griffiths, D. E. (1986). Theories in educational administration: Past, present and future. In B. O. Ukeje, L. O. Ocho, & E. O. Fagbamiye (Eds.), *Issues and concerns in educational administration: The Nigerian case in international perspective*. Lagos, Nigeria: Macmillan.

Gronn, P. (1983). *Rethinking educational administration: T. B. Greenfield and his critics*. Geelong, Australia: Deakin University.

Gross, N., & Herroitt, R. E. (1965). *Staff leadership in public schools*. New York: John Wiley.

Gulick, L., & Urwick, L. F. (Eds.). (1937). *Papers on the science of administration*. New York: Institute of Public Administration, Columbia University.

Guruge, A. W. P. (1969). *A functional analysis of educational administration in relation to educational planning* (Occasional paper No. 16). Paris: IIEP (UNESCO).

Haag, D. (1982). *The right to education: What kind of management?* International Bureau of Education Studies and Surveys in Comparative Education. Paris: UNESCO.

Hallak, J. (1967). Efficiency in education. In J. Hallak (Ed.), *Educational costs and productivity: An IIEP seminar*. Paris: IIEP (UNESCO).

Halpin, A. W. (1956). *The leadership behavior of school superintendents*. Columbus, OH: Ohio State University Press.

Halpin, A. W. (1967). Change and organizational climate. *Journal of Educational Administration, 5*(1), 5–25.

Halpin, A. W., & Croft, D. B. (1963). *The organizational climate of schools*. Chicago: University of Chicago.

Hans, N. (1949). *Comparative education*. London: Routledge & Kegan Paul.

Hanson, M. (1972). Structural and administrative decentralization in education: A clarification of concepts. *Journal of Educational Administration, 10*(1), 95–103.

Harman, G. (1985). Handling education policy at the state level in Australia and America. *Comparative Education Review, 29*(1) 22–46.

Harman, G., & Wirt, F. (Eds.). (1985). *The political economy of education: A comparative perspective*. Lewes, England: Falmer.

Harris, H. (1982). *The Commonwealth casebook for school administrators*. London: Commonwealth Secretariat.

Harris, H. (1983). *The administrative structures of education: Case studies of sixteen countries* (Division of Educational Policy and Planning Reports and Studies, No. C. 105). Paris: UNESCO.

Heady, F. (1979). *Public administration: A comparative perspective* (rev. 2nd ed.). New York: Marcel Dekker.

Hegarty, S. (Ed.). (1983). *Training for management in schools*. Windsor, England: NFER-Nelson.

Hinings, C. R. (1979). Continuities in the study of organisations: Churches and local government. In C. Lanemers & D. J. Hickson (Eds.), *Organisations, alike and unalike*. London: Routledge & Kegan Paul.

Holmes, B. (1981). *Comparative education: Some considerations of method*. London: Allen & Unwin.

Hopes, C. (1983). Problems of relating selection criteria and training needs. In S. Hegarty (Ed.), *Training for management in schools*. Windsor, England: NFER-Nelson.

Hopes, C. (Ed.). (1986). *The school leader and school improvement: Case studies from ten OECD countries*. Leuven, Belgium: ACCO.

Hoyle, E. (1982). Micropolitics of educational organizations. *Educational Management and Administration, 10*(2), 87–98.

Hughes, L. W. (1968). 'Organizational climate'—another dimension to the process of innovation? *Educational Administration Quarterly, 4*(3), 16–28.

Hughes, M. G. (1967). Simulated situations. *Trends in Education, 7*, 34–39.

Hughes, M. G. (Ed.). (1970). *Secondary school administration: A management approach*. Oxford: Pergamon.

Hughes, M. G. (1973). The professional-as-administrator: The case of the secondary school head. *Educational Administration*

Bulletin, 2(1). Also in R. S. Peters (Ed.). (1976), *The role of the head.* London: Routledge & Kegan Paul.

Hughes, M. G. (Ed.). (1975). *Administering education: International challenge.* London: Athlone.

Hughes, M. G. (1977). *Administrative and professional relationships in educational administration* (Fundamentals of Educational Planning, No. 64). Paris: IIEP (UNESCO).

Hughes, M. G. (1978). Reconciling professional and administrative concerns. *CCEA Studies in Educational Administration, 13,* 1–10.

Hughes, M. G. (1981). *Leadership in the management of education: A handbook for educational supervisors.* London: Commonwealth Secretariat.

Hughes, M. G. (1983). The role and tasks of heads of schools in England and Wales: Research studies and professional development provision. In S. Hegarty (Ed.), *Training for management in schools.* Windsor, England: NFER-Nelson.

Hughes, M. (1985). Leadership in professionally staffed organizations. In M. Hughes, P. Ribbins, & H. Thomas (Eds.), *Managing education: The system and the institution.* London: Cassell.

Husen, T. (1979). An international research venture in retrospect: The IEA surveys. *Comparative Education Review, 23,* 371–385.

Jun, J. S. (1976). Renewing the study of comparative administration: Some reflections on the current possibilities. *Public Administration Review, 36*(6), 641–647.

Kandel, I. L. (Ed.). (1924–1944). *International year book of the International Institute.* New York: Teachers College Press, Columbia University.

Kandel, I. L. (1933). *Studies in comparative education.* London: Harrap.

Kandel, I. L. (1954). *The new era in education: A comparative study.* London: Harrap.

Kazamias, A., & Massialas, B. G. (1982). Comparative education. In H. E. Mitzel, J. H. Best, & W. Abramowitz (Eds.), *Encyclopedia of Educational Research* (Vol. 1, 5th ed.). New York: Free Press.

Kelly, G. P., Altbach, P. G., & Arnove, R. F. (1982). Trends in comparative education: A critical analysis. In P. G. Altbach, R. F. Arnove, & G. P. Kelly (Eds.), *Comparative education.* New York: Macmillan.

Kelsall, R. K., & Kelsall, H. M. (1969). *The school teacher in England and the United States.* Oxford: Pergamon.

Knorr-Cetina, & Cicourel, A. V. (1981). *Advances in social theory and methodology.* Boston: Routledge & Kegan Paul.

Kogan, M. (1979). *Education policies in perspective: An appraisal* (OECD Reviews of National Policies for Education). Paris: OECD.

Kravetz, N. (Ed.). (1970). *Management and decision-making in educational planning: An IIEP seminar.* Paris: IIEP (UNESCO).

Lindman, E. L. (1966). National grants for elementary and secondary schools in England. *Educational Administration Quarterly, 2*(3), 181–189.

Lynch, P. D. (1979–1980). Toward a field of comparative educational administration. *Administrator's Notebook, 28*(8), 1–4.

Lynch, P. D. (1984). *The retreat of equality: A commentary on international educational policies since 1960.* Paper presented at the Annual Meeting of the American Educational Research Association, New Orleans.

Lyons, G. (1976). *Heads' tasks: A handbook of secondary school administration.* Slough, England: NFER.

Lyons, R. F. (1965). The role of cost analysis in educational planning. In R. F. Lyons (Ed.), *Problems and strategies of educational planning: Lessons from Latin America.* Paris: IIEP (UNESCO).

Lyons, R. F. (Ed.). (1970). *Administrative aspects of educational planning: An IIEP seminar.* Paris, IIEP (UNESCO).

Maddock, J. (1983). The comparative study of secondary education systems: Lessons to be learned. *Comparative Education, 19*(3), 245–254.

Majasan, J. A. (1974). Educational administration in African countries. *Educational Administration Bulletin, 3*(1), 26–31.

Mallinson, V. (1957). *An introduction to the study of comparative*

education. London: Heinemann.

Mangham, I. (1978). The darker side of humanity. *Educational Change & Development, 1*(1), 12–24.

Marshall, D. G. (1982). *Educational administration in developing areas: A role for Canadian scholars.* Paper presented at the Canadian Association for the Study of Educational Administration Section of the Canadian Society for the Study of Education Conference, Ottawa.

Marshall, D., & Newton, E. (1983). The professional preparation of school administrators in developing countries. University of Alberta Centre for International Education and Development (Occasional Paper No. 3), Edmonton.

Martin, W. J., & Willower, D. J. (1981). The managerial behavior of high school principals. *Educational Administration Quarterly, 17*(1), 69–90.

Mayo, E. (1933). *The human problems of an industrial civilization.* New York: Macmillan.

McMahon, A. (1982). The GRIDS project. *Educational Management and Administration, 10*(3), 217–222.

Mintzberg, H. (1973). *The nature of managerial work.* New York: Harper & Row.

Mooney, J. D., & Reiley, A. C. (1931). *Onward industry.* New York: Harper.

Morgan, C., Hall, V., & Mackay, H. (1983). *The selection of secondary school headteachers.* Milton Keynes, England: Open University Press.

Morgan, G. (1980). Paradigm, metaphors, and puzzle solving in organization theory. *Administrative Science Quarterly, 25*(4), 605–622.

Moulton, J. (1976). *An outline of the educational system in the Sudan* (Division of Educational Policy and Planning Reports and Studies, No. C. 8). Paris: UNESCO.

Mulford, W., Conabeare, A. B., & Keller, J. A. (1977). Organization development in schools: Early data on the Australian experience. *Journal of Educational Administration, 15*(2), 210–237.

Myers, C. S. (1926). *Industrial psychology in Great Britain.* London: Cape.

Nicholas, E. J. (1983). *Issues in education: A comparative analysis.* London: Harper & Row.

Ogilvie, D., & Bartlett, V. L. (1979). Departmental heads in England and Australia: Some comparisons. *CCEA Studies in Educational Administration, 15,* 1–8.

Oldroyd, D. (1984). School-based staff development: Lessons from Canada. *School Organization, 4*(1), 35–40.

Onushkin, V. G. (Ed.). (1971–1974). *Planning the development of universities* (Vols. 1–4). Paris: IIEP (UNESCO).

Open University. (1976). Organization development: The case of Sheldon High School. *Management in Education,* Unit 6. Milton Keynes, England: Open University Press.

Ostergen, B. (1979). *The management of change in Swedish higher education* (Division of Educational Policy and Planning Reports and Studies, No. C. 74). Paris: UNESCO.

Ozinian, W. (1976). *Profil du systeme educatif au Rwanda* (Division of Educational Policy and Planning Reports and Studies, No. C. 7). Paris: UNESCO.

Parsons, T., & Shils, E. A. (Eds.). (1959). *Toward a general theory of action.* Cambridge, MA: Harvard University Press.

Peterson, K. D. (1978). The principal's tasks. *Administrator's Notebook, 26*(8), 1–4.

Pitner, N. J., & Ogawa, R. T. (1981). Organizational leadership: The case of the school superintendent. *Educational Administration Quarterly, 17*(2), 45–65.

Poignant, R. (1970). Preface. In R. F. Lyons (Ed.), *Administrative aspects of educational planning: An IIEP seminar.* Paris: IIEP (UNESCO).

Pratt, S. (Ed.). (1982). The micropolitics of educational improvement. *Educational Management and Administration, 10*(2), 77–86.

Ransom, S., Hinings, C. R., & Greenwood, R. (1980). The structuring of organizational structures. *Administrative Science Quarterly, 25*(1), 1–17.

Reller, T. (1962). A comprehensive program for the preparation of administrators. In J. Culbertson & S. Hencley (Eds.), *Preparing administrators: New perspectives*. Columbus, OH: UCEA.

Reller, T. L. (1982). Comparative education administration. In H. E. Mitzel, J. H. Best, & W. Abramowitz (Eds.), *Encyclopedia of Educational Research* (Vol. 1, 5th ed.). New York: Free Press.

Reller, T. L., & Morphet, E. L. (1962). *Comparative educational administration*. Englewood Cliffs, NJ: Prentice-Hall.

Riggs, F. W. (1957). Agraria and Industria—toward a typology of comparative administration. In W. J. Siffin (Ed.), *Toward the comparative study of public administration*. Bloomington, IN: Indiana University Press.

Riggs, F. W. (1962). Trends in the comparative study of public administration. *International Review of Administrative Sciences, 28*(1), 9–15.

Riggs, F. W. (1964). *Administration in developing countries: The theory of prismatic society*. Boston: Houghton Mifflin.

Riggs, F. W. (1976). The group and the movement: Notes on comparative and development administration. *Public Administration Review, 36*(6), 648–654.

Roethlisberger, F. G., & Dickson, W. J. (1939). *Management and the worker*. Cambridge, MA: Harvard University Press.

Sander, B., & Wiggins, T. (1985). Cultural context of administrative theory: In consideration of a multidimensional paradigm. *Educational Administration Quarterly, 21*(1), 95–117.

Sapra, C. L., & Dudani, S. S. (Eds.). (1986). *Education for the future: Management challenges*. New Delhi: National Book Organisation.

Schmuck, R., & Miles, M. (1971). *Organization development in schools*. La Jolla, CA: University.

Schmuck, R. A., & Runkel, P. J. (1970). *Organizational training for a school faculty*. Eugene, OR: Center for Educational Policy and Management, University of Oregon.

Schmuck, R., Runkel, P., Arends, J., & Arends, R. (1977). *The second handbook of organization development in schools*. Palo Alto, CA: Mayfield.

Siffin, W. J. (Ed.). (1957). *Toward the comparative study of public administration*. Bloomington, IN: Indiana University Press.

Sigelman, L. (1976). In search of comparative administration. *Public Administration Review, 36*(6), 621–625.

Simpkins, W. S., Thomas, A. R., & Thomas E. B. (Eds.). (1982). *Principal and task: An Australian perspective*. Armidale, Australia: University of New England.

Smith, R. S. (1969). Proposals for the reform of educational administration in England and their relevance for Australia. *Journal of Educational Administration, 7*(2), 97–109.

Sproull, L. S. (1981). Managing education programs: A micro-behavioral analysis. *Human Organization, 40*, 113–122.

Stern, B. E. (1981). *Relationship of education to employment in the United States* (Division of Educational Policy and Planning Reports and Studies, No. C. 93). Paris: UNESCO.

Stone, F. D. (1974). Bureaucracy and centralization: Australia and the U.S.A. In A. R. Thomas, R. H. Farquhar, & W. Taylor (Eds.), *Educational administration in Australia and abroad: Analyses and challenges*. St. Lucia, Australia: University of Queensland Press.

Tapia-Videla, J. I. (1976). Understanding organizations and environments: A comparative perspective. *Public Administration Review, 36*(6), 631–636.

Taylor, W. (1964). The training college principal. *Sociological Review, 12*, 185–201.

Taylor, W. (1969). Simulation and the comparative study of educational administration. In G. Baron, D. H. Cooper, & W. G. Walker (Eds.), *Educational administration: International perspectives*. Chicago: Rand McNally.

Thomas, A. R., Farquhar, R. H., & Taylor, W. (Eds.). (1974). *Educational administration in Australia and abroad: Analyses and challenges*. St. Lucia, Australia: University of Queensland Press.

Thomas, A. R., & Slater, R. C. (1972). The OCDQ—a four-factor solution for Australian schools? *Journal of Educational Administration, 10*(2), 197–208.

Thomas, R. M. (1978). *The British philosophy of administration: A comparison of British and American ideas 1900–1939*. London: Longman.

Tretheway, A. (1972). On visiting school systems overseas. *Journal of Educational Administration, 10*(1), 88–94.

Ukeje, B. O., Ocho, L. O., & Fagbamiye, E. O. (Eds.). *Issues and concerns in educational administration: The Nigerian case in international perspective*. Lagos: Macmillan, 1986.

Vaizey, J., & Chesswas, J. D. (1976). *The costing of educational plans* (Fundamentals of Educational Planning, No. 6). Paris: IIEP (UNESCO).

Van Gendt, R. (1976). *Tools for the improvement of school management: A study in two phases* (Division of Educational Policy and Planning Reports and Studies, No. S. 18). Paris: UNESCO.

Waldo, D. (1955). *The study of public administration*. New York: Doubleday.

Waldo, D. (1956). *Political science in the United States of America: A trend report*. Paris: UNESCO.

Waldo, D. (1976). Introductory comments to a symposium. Comparative and development administration: Retrospect and prospect. *Public Administration Review, 36*(6), 615–654.

Walker, W. G. (1965a). *The principal at work*. St. Lucia, Australia: University of Brisbane Press.

Walker, W. G. (1965b). Theory and practice in educational administration. *Journal of Educational Administration, 3*(1), 18–43.

Walker, W. G. (1969). Trends and issues in the preparation of educational administrators. In G. Baron, D. H. Cooper, & W. G. Walker (Eds.), *Educational administration: International perspectives*. Chicago: Rand McNally.

Watson, L. E. (1969). Office and expertise in the secondary school. *Educational Research, 11*, 104–112.

Watson, L. E. (1981). Managerial discretion: A key concept for the principal. *CCEA Studies in Educational Administration, 24*, 1–9.

Webb, P. C., & Lyons, G. (1982). The nature of managerial activities in education. In H. L. Gray (Ed.), *The management of educational institutions*. Lewes, England: Falmer.

Weick, K. (1976). Educational organizations as loosely coupled systems. *Administrative Science Quarterly, 21*(1), 1–19.

Weidner, E. W. (1964). *Technical assistance in public administration overseas: The case for development administration*. Chicago: Public Administration Service.

Westwood, L. J. (1966). Re-assessing the role of the head. *Education for Teaching, 71*, 65–74.

Wheeler, A. C. R. (1969). *Essential economic concepts for educational planning* (Lecture-discussion series No. 40). Paris: IIEP (UNESCO).

Willis, Q. (1980). The work activity of school principals: An observational study. *Journal of Educational Administration, 18*(1), 27–54.

Willower, D. J. (1979). Ideology and science in organization theory. *Educational Administration Quarterly, 15*(3), 20–42.

Wilson, W. (1887). The study of administration. *Political Science Quarterly, 2*, 197–222.

Zagefka, Y. (1980). *Eleven experiences in innovations in decentralization of educational administration and management of local resources* (Division of Educational Policy and Planning Reports and Studies, No. C. 91). Paris: UNESCO.

CHAPTER 31

Quantitative Research Methods in Educational Administration

Maurice M. Tatsuoka and Paula Silver

Quantitative research refers to inquiries in which numerical values are assigned to some or all of the objects under investigation and in which the analysis used to draw conclusions about the objects relies primarily on manipulations of the numerical values. Those studies in which numerical data are reported simply as background information or to substantiate a subsidiary point are not properly regarded as quantitative. On the other hand, studies in which categorical data are analyzed statistically are classified as quantitative even though the objects under investigation are not inherently numerical.

Quantitative methods were introduced to the field of educational administration in the early years of this century, with the advent of the school survey. According to Callahan (1962), school surveys were the natural outgrowth of the introduction of scientific management principles to the field of education. Quantification—the use of numbers—was regarded as the *sine qua non* of the scientific approach, and science was viewed by many throughout the society as the pinnacle of intellectual endeavor. In the very early years of the century, the ideas and methods associated with achievement and intelligence testing were developed by Thorndike; these tests quickly made their way into school surveys that incorporated the quantification of almost all facets of school life. Between 1911 and 1925, Callahan (1962) reported, so many hundreds of school surveys had been conducted that "there was hardly a

state or local school system in America which was not surveyed" (p. 112).

By 1925 the school survey had become a highly complex management tool. As suggested in Sears's (1925) classic text, a thorough survey would include the geographic and demographic features of the community, financial and business accounting, information on the staff and teaching, curriculum, students and their attendance and learning, grading, supervision, student health, and virtually every other measurable or quantifiable facet of the school. Superintendents were encouraged to develop tabulations, graphs, diagrams, and charts to depict the survey results as vividly and informatively as possible to the efficiency-conscious public.

Survey methods as applied to the study of educational administration eventually moved beyond the school and district boundaries that characterized the early quantitative studies. Large-sample surveys in the form of attitude and opinion polls became common with the advent of the computer in the 1950s. Computers also made feasible the widespread application of statistical tests to determine whether apparent differences between groups, as measured by survey-type questionnaires, represent real differences (i.e., are statistically significant). Despite the development during the past 30 years of a wide range of quantitative techniques that far exceed the original survey in sophistication and despite the inappropriateness of drawing policy implications from such studies, surveys have been and continue to be the prevailing quantitative method used in the study of educational administration (see Haller, 1979).

Consultant/reviewers: Paul Lohnes, State University of New York at Buffalo; and Dennis Spuck, University of Houston

The purpose here is to examine from an analytic and critical point of view the quantitative methods used in the study of educational administration. Another such study was undertaken by McNamara (1978) to which readers are referred for his critique of the statistical analyses reported in research articles. Four categories of methods for treating quantitative data include (a) *survey-descriptive* methods, in which data analyses appear in the form of reports of central tendencies, frequency distributions, or simple tests of differences between groups; (b) *analysis of variance* methods, in which two or more groups are compared in terms of their extent of variation in scores on one or more measures; (c) *correlational* methods, in which relationships between two or among several variables are examined; and (d) *causal* methods, such as experiments, computer simulations, and path analyses, from which causal inferences can legitimately be drawn. Although the fourth set does not represent a class of treatments of data, as do the first three, these approaches seem to merit particular attention because of their relative rarity in the educational administration literature and their potential for revealing causal relationships.

The chapter treats the four categories of methods in parallel ways. Each section is introduced by an overview of the statistical methods included within the broad category. Particular studies reported in research journals are then described briefly as illustrations or exemplars of the methods. A critical analysis of the studies as they compare to exemplary research concludes each major subsection. The chapter itself concludes with a short summary of our discussion and a very brief commentary on the probable impact of microcomputers on quantitative research in educational administration.

A word about our methods in preparing this material: We did not undertake an exhaustive search of the quantitative literature. Research reported in unpublished dissertations, conference papers, and full-length books was not reviewed. Instead, we drew on three major sources of studies. Because the *Educational Administration Quarterly* has been the major vehicle for publishing research in educational administration since its inception in 1965, we reviewed all the quantitative studies reported in that journal from 1965 through 1983 except for six issues we could not locate; 39 issues of the *EAQ* were examined. As a check on the quantitative methods used in this field, we also reviewed all the quantitative studies reported in the *Administrators Notebook* from 1966 through 1977 (12 issues); and those reported in *Planning and Changing* from 1979 through 1982 (12 issues). We identified, in all, 167 studies that drew on numerical data as the primary research method. Studies using quantitative information for illustrative purposes only, such as those introducing planning or decision models, are not included here.

For each quantitative study encountered in the three journals, we noted the author(s), title, source, research question(s) or hypotheses, and statistical methods. For a general overview, we also tabulated the research methods by journals and issues. We then sorted our outline notes according to the four major categories noted earlier and into subcategories within each. Studies utilizing methods within two broad categories to address the major research questions—for example, studies using both analysis of variance and correlational methods—were classified in the later-mentioned category in the sequence of methods (survey-descriptive, analysis of variance, correlational, and causal). Articles to be cited for illustrative purposes were then drawn from the subsets of articles within the general categories. It is likely that the articles cited, rather than representing the topics addressed through quantitative research, reflect our topical preferences.

SURVEY AND DESCRIPTIVE RESEARCH

Overview of the Techniques

Survey "research" of sorts is probably as old as civilization itself, for the feudal lords and princes needed census data to determine their systems of taxation. The introduction of statistical methods to help put survey research on a sound scientific footing is, however, an innovation of the present century. Its systematic use in educational administration had to await the second decade of the century.

The word *descriptive* in the phrase *survey-descriptive methods*, if taken in its technical statistical sense, is somewhat misleading. Much of survey research has as a goal (at least implicitly) the generalization of its findings to the population from which the surveyed sample was drawn. This is the function of inferential as against descriptive statistics. Of course, it may be that *descriptive* in this context is used in contradistinction to *theoretical* or *theory-oriented*. In that case the term is quite legitimate and accurate, for practically no survey research is carried out to test a scientific theory. (This leads to a peculiar dilemma, as noted later.) Its purpose is, rather, to describe and characterize the situation that exists in the relevant target population with respect to some phenomena of interest. The researcher may have a political axe to grind and may hence be hoping to substantiate some *personal* theory—that there exists an inequity based on race or sex in the school district in question, for example—through the survey being conducted; but such is not a *scientific* theory.

The simplest way in which to report the results of a survey study is to present frequency counts, distributions, and graphical displays. For instance, one might give the numbers of teachers who teach in various subject areas, such as English, foreign languages, mathematics, physical education, and science, in the secondary schools in a certain school district. From this it is a short step to convert to a relative frequency (or percentage) distribution, showing the proportions of teachers in the various disciplines. The next step would be to display relative frequency polygons, histograms, pie graphs, or any of their several variants to convey graphical or pictorial representation of the results. The displays give more vivid impressions to readers of the report, which should have greater impact—especially if the intent is, say, to highlight a shortage of teachers in some areas and a surplus in others.

In all but the most simple-minded studies, however, these reportage modes would be found seriously wanting. The reader could not tell, for instance, whether a given shortage of teachers of some subject matter held for both residential and business areas within the school district or was confined to one or another type of area. To impart such information, the researcher must present *crosstabulations*. In the example imagined, the reporter would want to see crosstabulations of numbers and percentages of teachers by type of area and subject matter. That is, there would be a two-dimensional display with two rows and as many columns as there are subject-matter areas being considered. The rows would each show a frequency (or percentage) distribution of the sort imagined in the preceding paragraph: one for the residential area and one for the business area. Thus, a crosstabulation is simply a concatenation of two or more separate but analogous frequency (percentage) distributions.

Next, if the school district surveyed was an extremely large one so that the entire district could not be surveyed and it was necessary to resort to sampling (most likely with schools as units), the surveyor would naturally want to know if any difference between the patterns of shortage and surplus in the residential versus business areas that might have been found in the sample also holds true in the district as a whole. Inferential statistics must now be invoked, and the appropriate technique here is the chi-square test of association (or independence, to put it negatively). The chi-square statistic tests the null hypothesis of lack of association between the two characteristics (type of area and subject matter) in the school district as a whole despite the finding of an association in the sample. A simpler, intuitive way of putting it when

there are but two "levels" (or categories) in one of the classification dimensions (type of area in this case) is to frame the question thus: Given the different patterns of shortage and surplus found in the sample, can we with confidence assert that a similar difference of distributions holds in the district as a whole?

Besides the chi-square test, a recently developed, more sophisticated and more powerful method called categorical data analysis is also available for answering questions of this type. The interested reader is referred to Fienberg (1980); here it suffices to say only that categorical data analysis is more widely applicable than chi-square analysis because it can handle situations in which there are more than two bases of classification. For instance, the crosstabulation might involve not only type of area and subject matter but sex as well. The question might then become whether the patterns of shortage and surplus of teachers across subject matter differ significantly between type of area, between male and female teachers, and among the four combinations of area and sex. Categorical data analysis, as just described, bears a resemblance both to chi-square analysis and factorial analysis of variance. Indeed, it uses much the same language as the latter, speaking of main effects and interactions, terms whose meaning will be clarified in the next section.

Finally, even in the context of a survey study, there may be interest in a "genuine" quantitative question. Note that the questions asked in the foregoing paragraphs did not involve any numerical scores associated with the "objects" under study (teachers, in the illustration). Nevertheless, they are classified as quantitative questions because recognized quantitative methods are used to answer them. The next class of questions involves numerical "scores," such as number of years of teaching experience, number of years of education a teacher had, and salary. For example, a researcher might be interested in whether there is a sex difference in salary among teachers in a school district, or a difference between the mean salary of teachers of academic versus nonacademic subjects. At a purely descriptive level (in the technical sense) it would be necessary only to examine the mean salary of male teachers and the mean salary of female teachers to see if they differ by a nonnegligible amount; the same would hold, of course, for a comparison of the mean salaries of teachers of academic and nonacademic subject matter. Indeed, this is all that would need to be done from even the most rigorous statistical standpoint if all teachers in the district had been exhaustively surveyed, for the entire population would have been surveyed and there would be no question about "generalizing" any further. However, if the researcher had surveyed only a sample from the district because it was too large to be studied exhaustively, there would be a problem of statistical inference at hand. In this case the appropriate technique is the *t* test for the significance of the difference between two means. The *t* test checks whether there are grounds enough for us to assert that there is a mean sex difference in the population (i.e., the entire school district in this case), given the extent of difference between the male and female teachers' mean salaries in the sample actually surveyed.

Thus, even though survey research is almost always descriptive, in the sense of not addressing theory-oriented or theory-based questions but seeking to describe a situation as it exists, it may very well invoke inferential statistics in its analysis. It need not be purely descriptive in this sense. It is also appropriate to note that inferential techniques test the null hypothesis, stating that no association or no mean difference exists in the population. Rejection of such hypotheses does not automatically imply that there exists a strong association or a large difference in the population. To determine whether either of these conditions exists, other techniques, collectively called measures of the magnitude of effects, are needed, as discussed in the next section.

Illustrative Studies

Todd's (1969) study on the relationship between high school students' choice of program and subsequent career and income experiences somewhat resembles the famous Project TALENT (see Flanagan et al., 1966) albeit on a much smaller scale. The sample comprised 1,114 male Caucasian graduates, in the classes of 1958, 1960, and 1962, of a comprehensive high school in Chicago. Of these, 658 completed a questionnaire on family background, career, income through 1965, and attitudes toward postsecondary education and on-the-job training. Findings were reported with tables and graphs and showed that, among graduates who did not go on to college, the industrial arts graduates had the highest income until the seventh year but were passed in income by general and business graduates in their seventh year after graduation. For students who went on to college, the type of high school program showed little association with postcollege career and income.

McCarthy and Zent's (1981) survey to determine the characteristics of school administrators was quite ambitious in scope, using a sample of 2,134 administrators in 47 districts who were selected by stratified random sampling from six states. The questionnaire contained 20 items pertaining to the respondents' sex, age, race, position, type of school district, professional background experiences, salary, degree of job satisfac-

tion, level of aspiration, and so forth. Among the results were the findings that females and minority group members were still grossly underrepresented despite some gains due to affirmative action. Also significant was the finding that females were concentrated in non-line central-office positions and elementary school principalships. With respect to level of aspiration, minority administrators tended to be higher than their white counterparts; females were generally lower than males. This study illustrates the use of inferential statistics, because chi-square was used to test the significance of the differences between various pairs of groups in the distributions on some other characteristic. As mentioned earlier, this approach is equivalent to testing the lack of association between two classifying variables when one of them is dichotomous. In this case, the dichotomous classifying variable was sex in one set of comparisons and minority versus white in another.

A specific hypothesis was tested by Rowan (1982) when he surveyed 30 randomly selected California city school districts (50 or more years old) to study their historic trends in several characteristics. Rowan postulated that school districts have shown increases in positions that keep track of money, materials, people, information, and student service management functions while they have shown a decrease in the level of differentiation of instructional management positions over the 40-year period (1930–1970) for which data were collected. Results were presented in the form of percentage frequency distributions by years and rank orders of frequencies. The hypothesis was generally supported, with sharply increasing percentages of administrators dealing with money, materials, people, and student services observed, while the percentages of instructional management titles decreased slightly. However, the frequency of information management titles remained relatively constant and that of general instructional management titles increased. The overall conclusion was that central-office management and control of instruction had decreased over the period studied, while the percentage of peripheral administrators had increased.

Kmetz and Willower (1982) were interested in finding out how elementary school principals allocate their work behavior. Toward this end, they used Mintzberg's (1973) structured observation method to record and quantify the behaviors of five elementary school principals from different types of school districts over the course of 1 week. Specifically, they generated observation protocols (following Mintzberg, 1973) on type of activity, location, time, duration, participants, and materials used, as well as recording subjective impressions. Findings were reported in terms of tallies of the various categories of information and of the amounts and percentages of time spent on various activities. Kmetz and Willower showed that elementary school principals tended to divide their time among 13 types of activities, with the largest proportion (32.5 percent) devoted to unscheduled meetings. Their attention was rather fragmented, with an average of some 122 different activities engaged in each day. The overall conclusion was that, in general, elementary school principals were governed by events outside their control and had little time to spend in thinking about and planning for future events. However, their pace was less hectic and they spent more time on the instructional program than did a secondary school principal observed in a much earlier study by Boyan (1951).

The correlates of misbehavior among high school students were the focus of Duke's (1976) study comparing 78 students who had been repeatedly referred for disciplinary treatment with non-troublemaking peers at the same school. Student characteristics such as family background, IQ, scholastic achievement, vocational abilities and interests, junior high grades, and personality profiles were culled from the students' records. The means on the several variables in the two groups were compared with t tests. It was found that the behavior-problem group had significantly less-educated parents, more siblings, lower IQ, and lower junior high school GPAs; they also were perceived by their former sixth-grade teachers to have more "personal habit weaknesses." (It should be borne in mind, however, that *correlates* are not necessarily *causes*.)

Gorton (1982) was interested in finding out the most stress-generating aspects of high school principals' jobs and how they cope with stress. An unspecified number of principals rated each of 27 potential stress-producing factors as to the frequency with which each actually caused stress. The principals also indicated the frequency with which they used each of some 10 possible coping strategies. The mean rating by the whole group over the entire set of 27 potential stressors was a surprisingly low 2.8, which was just below the "sometimes causes stress" mark of 3.0. However, items pertaining to heavy work load received considerably higher mean ratings. Factor analysis (again, by an unspecified method) of the 27 items yielded six job factors. On the coping side, "regular sleep and good health habits" was the most frequently indicated strategy, while "seeking professional help" was the least frequent. The author claims that his finding that high school principals by and large do not seem to experience much job-related stress is a surprising one. Gorton offers as an explanation the possibility that although the principals are exposed to a lot of stressful

job situations, they "were effective in coping with such elements" and hence did not actually feel much stress. Another possible explanation, however, is that what the author proclaims to be a stress-measuring instrument is in reality a measure of job dissatisfaction—in which case considerations of social desirability may have kept the ratings low.

Commentary

All of the survey-descriptive studies noted above were generally well conducted as far as they went. Of course, one may always take exception to the nature of the sample used and the sampling scheme—for example, the fact that females were not included in Todd's (1969) study might be sharply criticized. To a large extent, however, researchers can choose what they wish to study, and those choices are partly a function of the Zeitgeist prevailing at the time of the study. In 1969, the matter of women's career choice was not quite as burning an issue as it is in the late 1980s. The main requirement of a sample is that it be representative of the population to which the researcher wants to generalize the findings. The use of only one high school as the sampling frame in Duke's (1976) study is a rather severe limitation in this regard. The sampling in three of the other studies examined was more carefully done. Random or stratified random samples were used and it was so reported in all but Gorton's (1982) paper, which did not even state the size of the sample, let alone how it was selected.

Apart from the sampling scheme, it is also germane to ask whether the nature of the analysis conducted was appropriate for the expressed purpose of the study. Here one must guard against faulting a study just because the analysis was not as "sophisticated" as it could have been. Simple, clearly understandable analyses are preferable to complicated, esoteric analyses that are not essential to the purpose. However, it is often a subjective judgment whether or not the analyses went "far enough" for the stated purpose of the study. With this caveat in mind, how do the several studies stand?

Todd's (1969) study is commendable in that it reported the findings in graphic as well as tabular form. Whenever trends over time (and often over other variables as well) are in question, graphic displays are very helpful in giving the reader a vivid, intuitive picture of the results. However, Todd fails to avoid the pitfall of speaking of choice of program as partly "determin[ing] future income [and] status." In survey studies where other variables—such as family SES—are not controlled, such causal inferences are simply not warranted. Rowan's (1982) study, on the other hand, does not present a single trend curve even though it deals with trends of several variables over a 40-year period. Both of these studies could profitably have addressed the question of whether the observed increases and decreases over time were significant. Time series analysis and examination of the nature of the trends (whether linear, quadratic, and the like) by orthogonal polynomials could also have been undertaken, but these techniques probably go beyond the purpose of the studies.

The study by McCarthy and Zent (1981) on the characteristics of administrators was probably the most thorough in analysis as well as being ambitious in scale. The use of simple crosstabulations and chi-square tests is adequate for their purpose. Further insight might have been achieved by introducing higher order crosstabulations and categorical data analysis. In view of the relative recency of the development of this analytic tool, however, it is probably unreasonable to expect its use in 1980 by researchers other than those expressly in the quantitative field.

In the final analysis, the important thing about any study is the interpretation of the results—which is also the most difficult part. This is true even in experimental studies, in which the researcher exercises rigorous control over the variables being manipulated. The difficulty is many times greater in survey-descriptive studies, in which there are inevitably many loose ends and uncontrolled variables that militate against unambiguous, clear-cut interpretation of the data. The problem was already pointed out in connection with Gorton's study, in which the explanation offered by the researcher for the "surprising finding" (that high school principals did not seem nearly as much under stress as they were reputed to be) was clearly not the only possible, or even the most plausible, one. Similarly, in Todd's study, it may well have been factors antecedent to choice of high school program that were the partial determinants of future status and income.

Many researchers take the view that a solution to this kind of problem is to quantify the observation as early as possible. Mintzberg's structured observation technique (Mintzberg, 1973) seems to be predicated on this view, for it is "essentially the quantification of work activities" (Kmetz & Willower, 1982, p. 76). Actually, the opposite of this view is closer to the truth. Early quantification—especially at the very stage of observation—may reflect a personal theory of how the variables are deemed to work and hence may automatically preclude the adoption of alternative explanations. It may also preclude the obtaining of some useful qualitative information, as Kmetz and Willower admit in their concluding remarks.

The foregoing paragraphs do not intend to dis-

parage survey-descriptive studies. On the contrary, the intent is to highlight the rich potential of such studies, as contrasted with rigorously controlled experimental studies, and to caution against defaulting on this potential by premature or careless quantification. Experimental and survey-descriptive studies both have their places in the social and behavioral sciences. Each has its strengths and weaknesses.

A few decades ago the predominant view was that only tightly controlled experimental studies could generate causal explanations, but both philosophers and practitioners of science today hold a somewhat different view. This view may be described by imagining a continuum with the most rigorously controlled, laboratory-type experimental study at one end and an unstructured, naturalistic, observational study at the other. The difference among studies located at various points along the continuum, according to the modern view, is not so much their ability or inability to yield causal explanations but rather the amount of "collateral evidence" needed to justify causal attributions. *Collateral evidence* means primarily predictions or models developed from an established substantive theory in the field of concern. The closer a study is to the naturalistic-observation end of the continuum, the larger is the extent of support from substantive theory that is needed.

A simple, if controversial, example will clarify the point. Consider the assertion that "smoking causes lung cancer." For obvious reasons an experimental study involving human subjects cannot be performed to test this assertion. It is necessary to rely on observational data to see if the incidence of lung cancer among smokers is significantly higher than among nonsmokers. As is well known, the answer is "yes." "But this merely shows that there is a statistical correlation between smoking and lung cancer and by no means proves a cause-and-effect relation between the two" is the favorite retort of the tobacco industry. And the retort would be correct if there had not been a large body of well-established medical theory concerning the nature of carcinogens in general. This example highlights the interplay between substantive theory and statistical method in yielding causal explanations. In the absence of a supporting substantive theory, however, observational data alone cannot claim to establish causation. This is a weakness of survey studies. On the other hand, their strength lies in being much more generally conductable than are experimental studies, which may be all but infeasible in the school setting—especially where administrative research is concerned. (For a more detailed discussion of the conditions under which causality may be inferred from observational studies, see Wold, 1970.)

ANALYSIS OF VARIANCE AND RELATED TECHNIQUES

Overview of the Techniques

The simplest case of analysis of variance, namely one-way ANOVA, is just an extension of the t test of the difference between two means to situations where there are more than two means to be compared. For instance, extending the teacher example created in the Survey and Descriptive Research section, suppose we are interested in comparing the average salaries of the several groups of subject-matter teachers instead of teachers of academic versus nonacademic subjects as wholes. We would then test the null hypothesis that the mean salaries of all groups are equal; the appropriate technique would then be one-way ANOVA, using an F-ratio test rather than a t test. It is clear that the purpose of the F-ratio test in this simple situation is a direct extension of the purpose of a t test. In fact, the F ratio itself is a direct extension of t in the sense that when the number of groups being compared reduces to two (i.e., if $K = 2$), then the F ratio of the ANOVA for this case is exactly the square of the t that could, and more likely would, be used.

Two-way (or two-factor) ANOVA and those with more than two factors or classifying dimensions are called factorial ANOVA. These are used to study the joint, as well as the separate, effects of two or more treatment or classification variables. Once again, the reader is reminded that the word "effect" has a definite causal implication. Hence, unless the data come from an experiment *or* are related to a substantive theory, the phrase "association with the dependent variable," is more accurate. However, since the term "effect" is well entrenched in connection wth ANOVA, it will be used here, with quotation marks to emphasize that causality is not necessarily implied. As a simple example, suppose that we want to see the differences in average salary not only between male and female teachers and between academic and nonacademic subject-matter teachers separately, but also we want to examine the *joint* "effect" on salary of sex and subject area taken together. We would then do a two-way, or more specifically a 2×2, ANOVA, in which the teachers would be double-classified (or crosstabulated) by both sex and subject area. In the four cells thus formed, we would enter the salary of each teacher falling in that cell. Note that doing so differs from simply tallying the number of teachers that fall in each of the four cells—as in using a chi-square test of independence to see if there is a significant association between sex and subject matter. In the latter case we are simply investigating whether there is a significant dif-ference between the sexes in the proportion of teachers who are teaching academic subjects (or, equivalently, are teaching nonacademic subjects). There is no third variable (the criterion or dependent variable), such as salary, whose dependence on sex and/or subject matter is under examination. In the two-way ANOVA case, there is such a criterion variable.

Again on two-way ANOVA the question of the separate "effects" of the two factors (or independent variables), sex and subject matter, should be clear enough. If there were interest only in these separate "effects", or main "effects" as they are called, it would suffice to conduct two separate one-way ANOVAs, one with sex and the other with subject matter as the classification variable. But what about their joint "effect"? This is the additional contribution from a two-way ANOVA that two separate one-way ANOVAs cannot provide. Examining the joint "effect", or the interaction of the two factors as it is technically called, enables answering a question like "Is there a difference between the sexes in the difference that teaching academic versus nonacademic subjects makes on salary?" (Or, equivalently, "Is there a difference between academic and nonacademic subject-matter teachers in the sex difference in salaries?") When there are more than two levels or categories in one or both factors, the notion of "difference" has to be replaced by the more general concept of "contrasts" or "comparisons" among the several categories. But the general idea is the same. Interaction always refers to "a difference between two differences" or "a contrast among several contrasts." It is important to keep in mind this precise meaning of "interaction" as the term is used in ANOVA when reading and evaluating studies using this technique. Many people seem to have acquired the loose idea that interaction means that the two (or more) independent variables affect *each other*. Rather, what is being referred to is the joint "effect" of the independent variables on the *criterion variable* that cannot be explained by their separate, individual "effects". One way to keep this technical meaning in mind is to draw an analogy with "interaction" in the context of interaction between two drugs, such as antihistamine and alcohol. Here, as in ANOVA, the meaning is not that the drugs somehow affect *each other* intrinsically but rather that their joint effect on the *human body* is different from what could be expected on the basis of their respective, individual effects on it.

The term "repeated measures designs" refers to a large class of designs in which measurements or observations are taken on a number of occasions. The occasions may differ in the conditions under which the observations are made (such as a no-distraction condition; an auditory distraction condition; a visual distraction condition; a combined audio-visual distraction), or they may simply be the successive trials in a learning experiment. The simplest case—the observation of a single, undifferentiated group on several occasions—constitutes a generalization of the matched-pairs or "before-after" type of *t* test. Here the set of measurement occasions itself is the factor of interest. Does learning effectiveness differ significantly under the different distraction conditions? Or, is there a significant learning effect as indicated by significant improvements in performance across the successive trials? This type of repeated measures design, which might be called the "pure" repeated measures case, is analyzed as a formal two-way design. The occasions factor is the one of interest, and the individuals constitute the levels of the other "factor," which is merely a formal one. The difference from a genuine two-way design (besides the fact that one of the factors is not of experimental interest, since individual differences are bound to exist) is that there is only one observation per cell. The cells here are defined by each individual subject crossed with each measurement occasion; if there are 50 individuals and four measurement occasions, there are 200 cells, each with one score. The important point is that it would be incorrect to analyze such data as though they came from a one-way design with four separate groups of 50 subjects each.

A "pure" repeated measures design, however, is infrequently used in the study of educational administration. More common is a type of repeated measures design in which there is another factor of interest, whose levels are represented by several different groups, and these several groups are each subjected to measurements or observations on repeated occasions. Technically, this sort of design is variously referred to as a *split-plot design*, a *between- and within-subjects factors design*, or simply a *mixed design*. The first name is a carryover from agricultural experimentation. The second refers to the fact that one factor (the between-subjects factor) is represented by several separate groups while the other (the within-subjects factor) is represented by the occasions of measurement, so that comparisons are made within the same subjects. The third name is just a short, elliptical form of the second: The design involves a "mixture" of two types of factors. The last, shortest name is used in discussing the design that follows.

Suppose we were to follow, over a period of several years, a group of high school teachers classified by subject-matter area and record their salaries or some other quantitative variable each year. We would be employing a mixed design, with subject area as the between-subjects factor. A more realistic example could be obtained by recasting Todd's (1969) study

on the income of the graduates of seven high school programs into a mixed design. We would be asking essentially the same question as did Todd himself, but instead of keeping track of just the *mean* income of each program group at points 1, 3, 5, and 7 years after graduation, we would now record every individual's income at these points. Trend curves for the mean income of each group could still be presented, but in addition we could answer such questions as the following: (a) Are there significant differences among the seven groups' average mean income over the 7-year period? (b) Do the mean trend curves for the seven groups differ significantly? (c) If so, do some groups show a steady (i.e., linear) increase, while others show a slow initial increase followed by a rapid increase in later years (i.e., an accelerated trend)? (d) Do still other groups exhibit a steep initial increase with a subsequent slowing down or "plateauing" (i.e., a decelerated trend)?

Of course, the very specific questions posed above can be answered only with some rather stringent assumptions about the data. Normality of distributions and homogeneity of variances across groups are the usual assumptions in any ANOVA, although minor to moderate violations of these assumptions can be tolerated because of the so-called "robustness" property of ANOVA. All types of repeated measures design, however, involve the further assumption of homogeneity of covariances. Essentially, this means that for each group involved (just one in the pure repeated measures design, several in the mixed design), the correlations between the dependent variable scores on all pairs of occasions are equal. If there are four measurement occasions, there would be six correlation coefficients for each group, one between each of the six possible pairs of occasions. The homogeneity of covariances assumption—together with the customary homogeneity of variances assumption—requires that these six correlation coefficients all be equal for each group. The extent to which this assumption can be violated with impunity has not yet been fully established, and it is the subject of lively debate among different schools of thought.

Another extension of one-way ANOVA is to the case when multiple dependent variables are used. For example, we may wish to study the differences among several groups of subject-matter teachers, not only in terms of salary but also in number of years of postsecondary education, number of moves from one school district to another, marital status, and so forth. Although many researchers would still conduct a separate ANOVA for each of these criterion variables, it has long been known that this practice "muddies up" the significance level and may lead to self-contradictory results. The preferred, logically sounder approach is to carry out a single multivariate analysis of variance (MANOVA) using all the criterion variables simultaneously. The null hypothesis tested now refers to the equality of K (= the number of groups) population *centroids* rather than means; a centroid is a vector of means, one for each criterion variable. Not only does this approach keep the level of significance clear, but it also helps to clarify the meaning of correlations among the multiple criteria because it permits the use of discriminant analysis as a follow-up.

Unlike univariate ANOVA, for which the familiar F ratio is the sole "uniformly most powerful" test statistic (i.e., the statistic that always has the greatest chance of rejecting a false null hypothesis), there are several alternative test statistics for MANOVA, different ones of which are most powerful under different circumstances. "Different circumstances" refers to the different ways in which the K population centroids can differ from one another when the null hypothesis is false. They could all be lined up more or less along a straight line, or they could be scattered around without any systematic pattern, to take the two extreme cases. A test statistic that is "moderately powerful" under all these circumstances (never the most powerful but also never the least powerful) is Wilks' lambda (λ) ratio. It also is the multivariate test statistic that is most closely related to the univariate F ratio. Unlike all other test statistics in general use, λ has the property that the *smaller* its value, the more highly significant are the differences being tested. (This is true not only for one but any number of independent variables.)

If the multivariate null hypothesis is rejected, we would want to ascertain which one(s) of the criterion variables was(were) "responsible for" the rejection—that is, on which variable(s) did the largest differences occur? Some authors recommend doing a series of univariate significance tests to follow the multivariate test. However, so doing would at least partly defeat the very purpose of the multivariate test. The only valid conclusion obtainable by this approach would concern the one variable that shows the most significant difference among the groups. The variable that exhibits the second most significant difference as judged by the univariate test will not necessarily be the variable that is "second most important" for differentiating among the groups in the multivariate sense. The reason is, essentially, that part of the differentiating or discriminating power of the second variable is attributable to its correlation with the first variable. For instance, suppose that sex is the most significant discriminator among the several subject-matter teachers groups, which means that the ratio of males to females is significantly different among the several groups. If (as

is more likely than not) salary is fairly highly correlated with sex—that is, if there is a considerable sex difference in average salary—then, *by virtue of this fact*, salary may turn out to be the second most significant discriminator among the groups according to the univariate tests. However, this result may be misleading (the more so, the larger the correlation between salary and sex), for what appears to be the discriminating power of salary will be in part, and perhaps largely, due to its relation to sex. That is, the salary differences among the groups may simply reflect (i.e., may in effect be a "surrogate measure" of) the sex-ratio differences.

In order to assess the relative importance of the several variables in discriminating among the several groups without being misled by the correlations among the variables, it is necessary to utilize another multivariate technique as a follow-up to MANOVA: discriminant analysis. This technique is somewhat akin to factor analysis; in fact Bartlett once referred to it as "factor analysis with an external criterion." Discriminant analysis forms several linear combinations of the variables, which are uncorrelated among themselves and which discriminate most highly, second most highly, and so on, among the groups. The number of such linear combinations, called discriminant functions, is one less than the number of groups being compared, although the number of *significant* discriminant functions may often be smaller. After computing the discriminant functions, we may concentrate on the first one—that is, the one that most significantly discriminates among the groups—and convert the combining weights into standard form. These standardized combining weights are analogous to the "beta weights" in multiple regression equations (see below), which indicate by their magnitude the relative importance of the several variables in predicting the criterion that the regression equation is designed to predict. (In fact, in the two-group case, the discriminant function is equivalent to the multiple regression equation designed to "predict" the criterion of group membership.) Thus, we compare the relative magnitudes of the standardized discriminant function weights assigned to several variables and conclude that the variable receiving the largest (in absolute value) weight is the most important discriminator, the one with the second largest weight is the next most important discriminator, and so forth.

In the foregoing, there was mention of concentrating attention on just the first discriminant function. The reader may legitimately wonder if so doing would disregard a lot of information. Actually, considering only the first discriminant function was largely a matter of convenience and was done in the interest of avoiding possible complications at the outset. What if the first function indicates that one variable is the most important while the second function shows another variable to be the best discriminator, and the third function elects yet another variable? The conflict or contradiction is only apparent. The different variables that the successive discriminant functions may "nominate" as the most important discriminator are each in fact the most important in a certain sense, because each of the discriminant functions specifies a certain dimension along which group differences may exist. There is nothing unusual in finding that a verbal reasoning test, for example, is the best discriminator among seven groups of students along the verbal dimension or factor, while numerical ability is the best discriminator along the quantitative dimension. Probably different pairs of groups among the seven groups are being best differentiated by these two factors.

Thus, discriminant analysis serves the dual purpose of identifying the most highly discriminating variables and possibly identifying two or more meaningful dimensions or factors along which the largest group differences are observed. However, there is no guarantee that these dimensions will be as neatly interpretable and "nameable" as were the two dimensions imagined in the example cited above. Accordingly, it is preferable to speak of "dimension" instead of "factor" unless the dimension is indeed interpretable as a substantively meaningful factor.[1]

The foregoing discussion has addressed only the *significance* of various variables. As noted earlier, statistical significance in itself does not automatically imply that there is a strong association between two variables or large differences in mean scores between two or more groups that represent different levels of some factor. Besides establishing statistical significance, which simply means that there is enough evidence to reject the null hypothesis, it is necessary to examine the magnitude of the "effect" in order to establish practical importance.

In the case of the relation between two quantitative variables as measured by some species of correlation coefficient, the latter itself is an index of the magnitude of effect. The significance is examined after the effect size is known, so there is no danger in merely asserting significance. Nevertheless, there is a tendency among many researchers to overemphasize significance (e.g., "The correlation, $r = .21$, was statistically significant at the .001 level") and to forget that even a very minuscule correlation may be "highly significant" if the sample size is large enough. We should never lose sight of the fact that "highly significant" simply means that it is highly unlikely that the null hypothesis (that the population correlation is zero, in this case) is true.

When dealing with differences between two means

or among several means, it is even easier to get carried away by a significant difference and forget that all significance means is that it is unlikely that the corresponding population means are exactly equal. Statisticians were, of course, always aware of this condition, but it is only recently that they have come to insist that researchers, too, recognize this by reporting some measure of "effect" size in addition to the level of significance of a difference. Cohen (1969) was one of the first to promulgate this idea among behavioral scientists by devoting an entire book to the topic of statistical power analysis, although measures of effect *qua* "proportion of variability of the dependent variable attributable to the independent variable," such as etasquared in ANOVA, have been around for a long time. The measures of effect size that Cohen advocates are simple to understand because they are estimates of the squares of the differences between population means in standard-deviation units. Another measure of strength of association in ANOVA, symbolized ω^2 (omega squared), was proposed by Hays (1973); it is similar to the much older eta squared in concept but is an estimate of a population parameter rather than a pure descriptive statistic. (For a recent review and evaluation of various measures of effect size, see Glass, 1977.) But, again, no matter how strong the association as indicated by any measure of "effect" size, association by itself does not necessarily establish the existence of a causal relation.

Illustrative Studies

Lucietto's (1970) study examined the relationship between the speech patterns of 20 male elementary school principals from the suburbs of one city and their leadership styles as perceived by teachers. Full-time teachers at 37 schools with male principals rated the leader behavior of their principals using Halpin's (1959) Leader Behavior Description Questionnaire (LBDQ), which yields scores on two facets, initiating structure (IS) and consideration (C). The 20 principals with the highest and lowest ratings in IS and C served as subjects in the study, in which spontaneous conversations of each principal with one of his teachers were tape recorded. Three randomly selected 5-minute segments of conversation were transcribed for each principal and content-analyzed by the General Inquirer system (Stone, Dunphy, Smith, & Ogilvie, 1966). The incidences of various language-usage characteristics such as first-person pronouns, clarifying language, listening, "attempt" words (e.g., *try, pursue, effort*), and so forth, were used as dependent variables in a series of ANOVAs with the two levels of IS and the two levels of C used separately as the independent variables. Lucietto found that high-IS principals used significantly fewer first-person pronouns and more "attempt" words than did low-IS principals and that the high-C group used more clarifying language and did more listening than the low-C group. These findings are consistent with Halpin's notions in defining the two leadership behavior dimensions.

Tuckman, Steber, and Hyman (1979) studied the effects of two factors on principals' perceptions of their teachers' teaching styles: (a) the level of their schools (elementary, intermediate, or secondary); and (b) ratings (effective or ineffective) the principals themselves had earlier given the teachers. Sixty teachers from each of the three school levels, half of them "effective" and the other half "ineffective" were rated by their principals (30 in number) along the four dimensions of the Tuckman Teacher Feedback Form (TTFF): creativity, dynamism, organized demeanor, and warmth and acceptance. The data were analyzed by two-way ANOVAs, using each of the TTFF scales in turn as dependent variables. The hypotheses formulated by the researchers prior to gathering the data were partially supported: namely, elementary principals perceived their more effective teachers to be more warm and accepting than did high school principals. On the other hand, effective-rated elementary teachers were perceived as less creative than their high school counterparts. Intermediate school principals perceived their effective teachers as higher on creativity than did high school principals, whereas the latter saw dynamism to be more salient than warmth as characteristics of their effective teachers.

"The effect of leader-member interaction on organizational effectiveness" was the title of the study by Garland and O'Reilly (1976), which used MANOVA as the analytic tool. Specifically, the researchers tested three hypotheses derived from Fiedler's (1967) contingency theory of leadership effectiveness: (a) Among schools with good group atmosphere (GA), those having task-oriented principals will have higher development press and lower control press than those whose principals are relationship-oriented; (b) among schools with good GA, those with medium LPC ("esteem for least-preferred coworker") principals will not differ in school climate from those with task-oriented or relationship-oriented principals; (c) schools with good GA will not differ from those with poor GA in school climate, regardless of principals' leadership styles. Garland and O'Reilly defined group atmosphere (good and poor) with a rating scale consisting of 10 bipolar adjectives, which was completed by principals to rate the quality of leader-member relationships in their schools. Leadership style was determined by principals' scores (categorized into high, medium, and low) on the LCP scale, consisting of 16 bipolar adjectives. School climate was measured by the High School Characteristics Index (HSCI) obtained from a set of 30 dichotomous items completed by students to report their perceptions of their schools' development press (five scales) and control press (two scales). Principals of 176 out of 211 selected high schools returned usable responses to the GA and LCP scales. These schools were classified into six types according to whether they were good or poor in GA and their principal high, medium, or low on the LCP. However, schools of the *poor-GA, low-LCP* and the *poor-GA, high-LCP* types were virtually nonexistent, so these two categories were discarded and six schools were randomly selected from each of the four remaining categories to obtain HSCI scores from 50 of their fourth-year students, blocked by sex. The three hypotheses were tested by means of three multivariate orthogonal contrasts among the four types of schools. The second hypothesis was the only one supported. The overall conclusion was that school climate is predicted better by GA than by the principals' leadership style.

Feuille & Blandin (1976) wanted to see whether demographic and job satisfaction factors were related to feelings of militancy among university faculty members. A questionnaire was mailed to the entire academic staff of a medium-sized state university, and 454 usable responses were obtained, representing a return rate of about 45 percent. The questionnaire yielded demographic information (rank, age, department, tenure status, primary duties, sex, and organization membership), degree of job satisfaction in six aspects of the work environment, and attitudinal militancy in such matters as faculty collective bargaining, the faculty's legal right to strike, and belief in the actual use of strikes to resolve bargaining impasses. The sample was classified into militant, neutral, and nonmilitant groups, and a series of univariate ANOVAs were first conducted, using degree of satisfaction in each of the six work-environment aspects and the demographic variables in turn as the dependent variable. These analyses showed all the job-satisfaction variables to differ significantly among the three groups but only age to differ significantly out of all the demographic variables. Next, a stepwise discriminant analysis was performed, in which only three of the job-satisfaction variables (pertaining to the internal administrative context, the nonacademic, and the economic job context) contributed significantly to the discrimination among the three militancy-based groups.

Commentary

Studies using ANOVA are not very numerous in educational administration research, and those applying MANOVA are even scarcer. It is regrettable that the comment made early in this section—that many researchers carry out a series of ANOVAs when a MANOVA should be done—applies to two of the four studies already reviewed. Lucietto's (1970) study has the further shortcoming of doing two one-way ANOVAs when a single two-way ANOVA (or, better, MANOVA) would have been more informative. Thus, a 2×2 MANOVA with high and low initiating structure crossed with high and low consideration could have been used, with the several language-usage variables considered simultaneously as the dependent variables. Then, in addition to the separate main effects of IS and C, the presence or absence of interaction of these two factors could have been examined. It would have been interesting to see if a larger difference between the language usage of high-IS and low-IS principals occurs among high-C principals or low-C principals (or if the C levels made no difference in the IS difference).

Tuckman, Steber, and Hyman (1979) did use two-way ANOVAs and found moderate interaction effects for two of the four TTFF scales (dynamism and warmth and acceptance). Again, a 2×2 MANOVA followed by a discriminant analysis may have thrown more light on the relations that were studied.

Analytically, the study by Garland and O'Reilly (1976) was competently done, although using only 24 out of 173 schools in the four categories retained seems to waste a lot of information. They may have done so because the smallest category contained only six schools, and the researchers opted to use the same number of schools for all four categories. However, it is by no means necessary to have equal ns in a one-way design. But a more serious difficulty with this study is the substantive one of how their hypotheses are related to Fiedler's theory. In the first place, the factors that define their categories are not the same ones that Fiedler uses in defining his octants, although the two are undoubtedly related. Much more explanation of how their categories relate to Fiedler's and how their hypotheses were derived from the contingency model of leadership effect seems to be necessary to convince the reader that their study is indeed testing Fiedler's theory.

Except for a few inaccuracies in terminology, the article by Feuille and Blandin (1976), comes close to serving as an exemplar of how a one-way MANOVA with discriminant analysis should be carried out and reported. The authors err in speaking of the series of univariate ANOVAs conducted before the stepwise discriminant analysis as "a discriminant analysis on each of the variable dimensions" (p. 60). Moreover, it was by no means "necessary" to conduct these univariate F tests; it would have been better to say it could prove informative—especially if Feuille and Blandin had made a point of comparing the univariate and

multivariate results, which they unfortunately did not. Then there is a misleading footnote in their Table 4 (which shows the stepwise discriminant analysis results), stating that "no other variables [were] significant at the .05 level or better," after indicating by asterisks that three of the job-satisfaction variables had $p < .001$. In stepwise discriminant analysis, as in stepwise multiple regression, the significance level associated with each successive variable entered into the equation refers to the significance level of the *increment* in the discriminating (or predicting) power of the equation that results from entering that variable. It does not refer to the significance of that variable per se. A point worth mentioning in comparing the univariate Fs with the stepwise discriminant Fs is the fact that, whereas (dis)satisfaction in the economic decision context had the second largest univariate F, it did not increase the discriminating power significantly when it was entered into the discriminant function as the sixth last variable. This result is an example of the phenomenon mentioned earlier: When variables are looked at singly, some variables may seem significant only because of their high correlation with some other variable(s) that is (are) significant predictor(s).

Although Feuille and Blandin draw favorable comment for having done a stepwise discriminant analysis, the main point was that they did a discriminant analysis at all. It would be remiss not to point out that the stepwise method—be it in discriminant or multiple regression analysis—has recently come under criticism from many quarters. Again, the concern reflects an emphasis on substantive theory. Certainly, if a substantive theory is available, one should use *that* to decide what variables to include in an explanatory study instead of relying solely on statistical association—as is the case in using the stepwise approach. Nevertheless, in the absence of a substantive theory, the stepwise method serves as a useful *exploratory* technique to investigate which variables might *potentially* be considered in a substantive theory or model subsequently to be developed.

It is appropriate at this point to express a bias in favor of more use of ANOVA, and especially MANOVA, by researchers in and on educational administration. These are powerful tools that should at least be given a place alongside multiple regression analysis in the researcher's repertoire. Of course, they also carry the danger of perhaps creating an illusion that a causal relation has been established when it has not. But enough has been said here to caution the reader against unwarranted causal attributions. The use of MANOVA and discriminant analysis for descriptive purposes is quite justifiable. The inferential aspect (significance testing) is only to justify generalizing the *descriptive* to the population from which the sample was drawn. (For an excellent example of the descriptive use of discriminant analysis in the context of Project TALENT, referred to earlier, see Cooley and Lohnes, 1976, pp. 109–130.)

CORRELATION AND RELATED TECHNIQUES

Overview of the Techniques

Correlation and regression analyses are probably the most widely used statistical techniques in educational administration research. Together with the related technique of factor analysis, which uses a correlation matrix as its starting point, over half of all studies in educational administration are correlation based.

The correlation coefficient is so well known among researchers that it hardly requires an introduction. It is enough to say that, besides the basic Pearson product-moment correlation coefficient (applicable when correlating two continuous variables), there are specialized coefficients for use when one or both variables are dichotomous, some of which apply when the dichotomous variables are regarded as "true" dichotomies, whereas others assume them to be crude, two-point scales of what in reality are continuous variables. An example of the latter, artificial dichotomy would be the 0–1 score on an item when it is regarded as a crude measure of an underlying continuum. On the other hand, if getting an item right or wrong is the behavior under consideration, the 1–0 score would be viewed as a true dichotomy. When correlating two true dichotomies, the appropriate coefficient is the ϕ (phi); when a true dichotomy is to be correlated with a continuous variable, the coefficient to be used is the point-biserial $r(r_{pb})$. Although special formulas are generally used for calculating these coefficients, they could just as easily be computed from the usual product-moment correlation formula when a computer is used. When one or both variables are artificial dichotomies with underlying continuums, the correct coefficients are not actual product-moment rs but are estimates of what the correlation would have been if a continuous scale or scales had been available for the dichotomized variable(s) and pairs of variables followed bivariate normal distributions. The resulting coefficients are called the tetrachoric $r(r_{tet})$ when both variables are artificial dichotomies, and the biserial $r(r_{bis})$ when one variable is continuous. In practice, it does not matter too much—except when a factor analysis is to be done—whether a ϕ or r_{tet} is used, and likewise for r_{pb} or r_{bis}. However, if the second member of each pair is desired, a special formula other than that for the usual product-moment correlation coefficient must be used.

There also is the well-known Spearman rank-order correlation ϱ (rho). The special formula for it is simply

the result of applying the usual product-moment correlation formula to the special situation when X and Y both take the values 1, 2, ..., N (N being the number of persons or objects being ranked on the two attributes). Moreover, when there are tied ranks (e.g., two objects tying for third place on X and hence both being given a rank of 3.5), the special formula should not be used, but the regular product-moment r can still be computed.

The related technique of linear regression analysis also is widely known and used by researchers in educational administration. In the simplest case with only one predictor variable, the problem is to determine the intercept and slope (a and b, respectively) in an equation of the form

$$\hat{Y} = a + bX$$

in such a way as to achieve the "best fit." This means that we seek to minimize the sum of squared deviations between the "predicted" Y scores and the observed Y scores. This kind of minimization of the sum of squared discrepancies between observed quantities and their modeled values is very frequently done in statistics; it is known as using the "principle of least squares."

A distinction often made between the correlation model and the regression model runs somewhat as follows: In the correlation model, the sampled units "bring with them" the values on the two variables—as when two tests are given to a group of students—and both are referred to as random variables. In the regression model, the independent variable (X) is fixed in advance by the experimenter, and only Y, which is observed on the units that are randomly assigned to the several predetermined values of X, is called a random variable. This "admonishment" may make us pause and wonder whether we violated some hidden theoretical assumption each time we constructed a regression equation for predicting scores on one test (Y) from those on another (X)—when we should have been using the correlation model. Or, was it "wrong" to calculate a correlation coefficient between, say, word-list length (X), a predetermined variable, and the time (Y) it took students to learn these lists? Fortunately, there is nothing wrong with either of these practices. The two "models" simply refer to the manner in which the values for X and Y are obtained. Nothing prohibits constructing a regression equation under the correlation model or calculating a correlation coefficient in the regression model.

Simple linear regression may be extended in each of two directions (and occasionally in both of these simultaneously). The first, called polynomial regression, adds higher-degree terms (X^2, X^3, etc.) of the single predictor variable X. This is done when the relation between X and Y is palpably nonlinear: that is, when it shows a marked curvilinearity. When adding terms is done in the context of the regression model, so that the researcher has control over the values of X (usually chosen to be equally spaced) and the numbers of Ss assigned to the different X-value groups (usually equal), the method of orthogonal polynomials is the most convenient technique to use. (Interested readers should refer to Kirk, 1982.)

The second extension is the familiar multiple regression analysis, in which several predictor variables are used instead of one. The equation thus assumes the form

$$\hat{Y} = a + b_1X_1 + b_2X_2 + \ldots + b_pX_p$$

and the least-squares principle is again used to determine the constants, a (the intercept) and $b_1, b_2, \ldots, b_p$ (the [partial] regression weights). In addition to determining these regression constants, the multiple regression case requires obtaining an index showing the extent to which $\hat{Y}$ correlates with the actual Y. The most obvious index for this purpose is $r_{Y\hat{Y}}$; this is called the multiple correlation coefficient of Y on X_1, $X_2, \ldots, X_p$, and is usually symbolized as $R_{y.123\ldots p}$, or simply R when the variables are understood from the context. (This step is not necessary in simple regression, because the correlation $r_{Y\hat{Y}}$ in that case is equal to the correlation r_{XY} between the predictor and criterion.) Although it is possible to compute $r_{Y\hat{Y}}$ by actually determining $\hat{Y}$ from the multiple regression equation for each person in the sample and then correlating these values with the observed Y values, so doing would be unnecessarily wasteful of computer time. A formula is available for directly computing $R_{y.12\ldots p}$ from only those quantities that were already obtained in the process of determining the regression constants. The interpretation of the multiple correlation coefficient exactly parallels that of the ordinary product-moment correlation coefficient—which should not be surprising since $R_{y.12\ldots p}$ *is* the product-moment correlation coefficient between Y and $\hat{Y}$. Namely, R^2 represents the proportion of variability in Y that is "attributable to" the variability in $\hat{Y}$, the optimal linear combination of $X_1, X_2, \ldots, X_p$, in the sample from which Y was determined. In simpler (albeit looser) language, R^2 tells what percentage of the individual differences in Y can be traced to individual differences in the predictors as a set.

The significance test for R, testing the null hypothesis that the population multiple correlation is zero, again parallels very closely the corresponding test in the one-predictor case. The only difference is that the test statistic follows an F instead of a t distribution. The caveat concerning excessive reliance on significance tests alone, which was given in the preceding

section, applies here with even greater force. In fact, it is almost a foregone conclusion that if a multiple regression equation is constructed at all, the multiple R is almost bound to be significant because each of the several predictors is significantly correlated with the criterion. Otherwise multiple regression would not be considered in the first place.

A more important type of significance test related to the multiple correlation coefficient is one which tests the significance of the increase in R^2 that results from adding one or more extra predictor variables beyond those already included in the regression equation up to this point. For instance, if a set of four traditional college entrance tests provides a multiple regression equation with $R_{y.1234} = .68$ for predicting freshman GPA (labeled Y) and adding an academic interest test and a career motivation test increases the multiple R to .73, is this increase significant? If the multiple Rs alluded to above had been based on a sample of 47 cases, and if the 5-percent level of significance were adopted, the conclusion would be that entering the two additional predictors does *not* significantly increase the multiple R. Hence an analyst would not bother to include them as additional predictors.

A special case of the incremental-R significance test when adding just one more predictor is the basis for the well-known stepwise multiple regression. In this program the computer first selects the predictor with the largest correlation with the criterion. Next, it tries adding each one of the other predictors, in turn, to form a two-predictor multiple regression equation and each time computes an R_2. Then, taking the largest of the R_2^2s, it tests whether the increment is significant. If it is, the second predictor is added; if not, the process stops, and there is only a simple regression equation. If the second predictor *has* been added, the computer next looks for the third predictor that yields the largest increment in R. It then tests the increment for significance and adds the third predictor or stops, depending on the outcome. This cycle is repeated until the process is terminated by a nonsignificant incremental R.

Stepwise discriminant analysis, referred to in the context of the Feuille and Blandin (1976) study in the preceding section, operates in much the same way as stepwise multiple regression, except that what is tested at each step is not the significance of the incremental R but the significance of the decrease in Wilks's lambda. (Recall that λ is a test statistic for which the smaller the value, the higher the significance it indicates.)

Once again, the stepwise approach is a sort of last-resort method when a substantive theory that dictates what variables should be included in the equation is not available. The method, therefore, cannot be used for explanatory purposes but only for constructing a close-to-optimal, weighted combination of the predictor variables. The resulting equation may be used for predicting the criterion variable (a performance measure in the case of multiple regression; a group-membership classifying variable in the case of discriminant analysis), but not for explaining the "causes" of high performance or of a person's belonging to one group rather than another. Whenever a substantive theory *is* available, that should decide what variables to include. If two or more such theories are in competition, equations should be constructed on the basis of each theory, and the "fit" of the several equations should be compared.

The last technique reviewed here, factor analysis, should also be familiar to most readers at least conceptually, for it is frequently mentioned in introductory psychology courses in connection with the nature of intelligence, the "components" of personality, and so forth. The purpose, or at least one of the main purposes, of factor analysis is to express a large number of traits or characteristics of the objects in the domain of investigation in terms of a small number of hypothetical constructs called factors. (Some researchers will object to factors' being called "hypothetical constructs." If they prefer to attribute existential reality to the factors, they may think of factors as a set of more basic, fundamental traits than those that are directly observed.) The test scores or quantified observations are then expressed as linear combinations of the unobservable factors. The details differ from one school of thought to another, but in the common factor theory pioneered by Thurstone—which is probably the most widely accepted one today, at least in the United States—the expression takes the form of a multiple regression equation. But unlike ordinary multiple regression equations, the "predictor variables" are in this case the unobservable factors. Hence the "regression weights," which are here called "factor loadings," cannot be determined by invoking the principle of least squares. Rather, they are determined in such a way that the resulting correlations between the pair of modeled variables are, on the average, as close as possible to the correlation between the corresponding pair of observed variables. This procedure is like a bootstrap operation, and it cannot be done in one fell swoop but has to resort to a number of iterations or successive-approximation steps.

The process of factor analysis does not end even when the factor loadings have been determined to a satisfactory degree of approximation. Then comes the task of "rotating to simple structure": that is, rotating the factor axes so that the new factor loadings have several simplifying properties. The goal is to simplify the factor matrix, in which the observable variables are represented by the rows and the common factors by the columns, and whose elements are the factor loadings. The concept of simplification here is by no means straightforward and unambiguous. Over the years many sets of criteria have been proposed for defining (or perhaps "capturing") what is meant by simple structure. Very loosely speaking, it means that a relatively small set of observed variables should have nonzero loadings on any one factor and that very few variables should simultaneously have nonzero loadings on both of any pair of factors. In simpler English, but necessarily even more loosely, this means that each factor should be responsible for individual differences on only a few tests, and no two factors should both "explain" individual differences on any but a very few tests. These conditions are imposed so as to enhance the interpretability of the factors. For instance, suppose a battery of cognitive tests is given to a group of students and the resulting matrix of correlations is factor analyzed. A perfect or ideal simple structure would be achieved in the (unlikely) event that one group of tests had nonzero loadings on just one factor, which could be interpreted from the nature of these tests as, say, a verbal factor; a separate group of tests had nonzero loadings only on another factor, say, a numerical factor; and the remaining tests loaded only on a third factor, say, a spatial factor. Of course this ideal is never achieved for real data, but the closer the factor matrix comes to exhibiting this property, the more nearly has it approximated simple structure.

Any description of the actual techniques by which factor analysts seek to approximate simple structure is far beyond the scope of this chapter. Here again there are many schools of thought, which can, however, be broadly categorized into two camps: those who advocate orthogonal rotation and those who favor oblique rotation. Orthogonal rotation means that the angular separation between pairs of factor axes is constrained to remain at 90° in the course of rotation and hence that the resulting factors are uncorrelated. In oblique rotation, on the other hand, the axes are allowed to take on various different angles among one another; most of the resulting factors are then correlated with each other. Without taking sides in the often bitter controversy between the two camps, it is fair to say that each approach has its advantages and disadvantages. Orthogonal rotation is easier to carry out and understand, and it has the appeal of arriving at uncorrelated factors. But the very constraint of orthogonality makes the achievement of proximal simple structure difficult. Oblique rotation, on the other hand, involves so many degrees of freedom that it is more difficult to reduce to a straightforward computer algorithm, although not a few have been developed. It is, however, more likely to lead to interpretable factors.

The foregoing discussions were focused on what is now called *exploratory* factor analysis, in which no correlational (or covariance) structure among the variables is posited a priori; the chips are allowed to fall where they will, so to speak. A recent development called *confirmatory* factor analysis is becoming more and more prominent. In this type, a priori hypotheses of various degrees of specificity are stated before the analyses are conducted. They may range from simply postulating the number of common factors that exist to a detailed postulation of which variables will have substantial loadings on which factors and near-zero loadings on which other factors. In a way, this was done even in exploratory factor analysis—especially as far as "predicting" the number of common factors was concerned—but the predictions were based largely on intuition. In confirmatory factor analysis, on the other hand, this is done more deliberately on the basis of substantive theories concerning the causal patterns relating the factors (often known as "latent variables" in this context) to the observable variables. This approach is closely related to path analysis, discussed in the next section. One of the more popular computer software programs for carrying out confirmatory factor analysis, therefore, is the LISREL package, which was originally developed mainly in connection with path analysis. (Interested readers may refer to Mulaik, 1972, or, for a briefer introduction to the subject, to a pair of booklets by Kim & Mueller, 1978a, 1978b.)

Illustrative Studies

Ables and Conway (1973) hypothesized that a teaching team's morale was directly related to the degree of congruence of belief-system scores (a) among team members and (b) between the team leaders and their team members. Twenty-four teaching teams with designated leaders, comprising 114 teachers in elementary, middle, and high schools in one state were recruited for the study. Belief systems were measured by Rokeach's Dogmatism scale, and teachers' morale by four scales from the Purdue Teacher Opinionnaire (PTO): rapport with leader; satisfaction; rapport among team teachers; status. The variances of the teachers' D-scale scores in each team were taken as a measure of congruence, and the teams were rank-ordered from most congruent (smallest variance) to least congruent. The leader-team congruence in beliefs was expressed by the absolute difference between the leader's D-scale score and the team's mean D-scale score; again the teams were ranked from most congruent to least congruent. Spearman's rho between each of the belief-congruence rankings and the morale

ranking (by the teams' mean PTOs) was calculated, as well as Kendall's tau, which is another measure of rank correlation. Both hypotheses were supported.

Yee (1970) investigated whether principals agreed with pupils in their evaluation of teacher merit and with teachers in their attitudes toward pupils. The subjects included 206 teachers, their pupils in fourth, fifth, and sixth grades, and the 47 principals of the teachers' 51 schools in two states. Principals' ratings of teachers were obtained from a rating scale on five dimensions of teacher merit; pupils used a 100-item inventory called "About My Teacher" (AMT). Principals and teachers alike used the Minnesota Teacher Attitude Inventory (MTAI) in reporting their attitudes toward pupils. Medians for teachers within schools and for pupils within classes were used as the bases for calculating product-moment correlations between principals' ratings of teachers and pupils' ratings of teachers on the one hand, and between teachers' MTAI scores and their principals' MTAI scores on the other. It was found that principals' MTAI scores were significantly correlated with teachers' MTAI scores for the total sample. When the schools were categorized in terms of the modal social class of their student body, it was found, only for the middle-class subsample, that teachers' MTAI scores were significantly correlated with both their principals' MTAI scores and with the principals' teacher ratings. Pupils' teacher ratings did not correlate significantly with principals' teacher ratings—or with anything else, for that matter.

Bridges (1980) examined the relation between job satisfaction and absenteeism among teachers. Specifically, he wanted to see if absenteeism was negatively correlated with (a) all four sources of job satisfaction (the work itself, pay, co-workers, and supervision); (b) only work itself; (c) job satisfaction only under conditions of low work interdependence; or (d) job satisfaction only under conditions of high job interdependence. A sample of 488 elementary school teachers in 36 schools having complete absenteeism records was used. Teachers' satisfaction with the four facets of their jobs was measured by the Job Description index, comprising four sets of Likert-type items. Work interdependence was defined as the proportion of working hours a teacher spends together with other teachers and was categorized into high, medium, and low. Six demographic variables also were recorded: school size, teacher's salary, sex, age, commuting time, and policy on advance notification of absence. Twelve stepwise multiple regression equations were constructed, one for each of the three work-interdependence groups in which each of the four possible sources of job satisfaction, in turn, was a potential predictor along with the six demographic variables. It turned out that all four job-satisfaction facets entered into the multiple regression equations only for the high work interdependence group, thus supporting the fourth possibility of those listed earlier.

Public prejudice against women school administrators was the subject of Stockard's (1979) study. The researcher posed 13 hypotheses, the first 4 of which were (a) there is a direct relationship between urban residence and approving attitudes toward women school administrators (AAWA); (b) there is a direct relationship between level of education and AAWA; (c) there is a direct relationship between experience with women administrators and AAWA; (d) there is an inverse relationship between age and AAWA. Structured interviews were conducted with 812 adults selected by stratified random sampling from the population of one state, and responses were elicited about their AAWA (on a 10-point scale), contact in the past 10 years with women administrators (yes-no), and demographics. Correlations between all pairs of variables were computed, followed by several multiple Rs and several partial correlations—the purpose of the latter being to control for the effects of some control variables. The 4 hypotheses stated above were supported, but the other 9 were not. All of the unsupported hypotheses refer to the lack of correlation of some independent variable with AAWA when knowing a woman administrator or age of respondent or both are controlled. Thus the overall conclusion is that age and acquaintance with a women administrator do not have much impact on AAWA, but location of residence and amount of education do. It is suggested that affirmative action is insufficient to increase AAWA unless and until a large number of women are placed in highly visible line positions.

Sousa and Hoy (1981) studied the bureaucratic structure of high schools by means of factor analysis. In particular, they were interested in comparing the Hall (1961) and the University of Aston (see Pugh, Hickson, Hinings, & Turner, 1968) approaches to measuring the structural dimensions of formal organizations. Participants in the study included 922 teachers and 55 principals from as many high schools in 11 counties in one state. The teachers completed the 48-item School Organizational Inventory, supplemented by 12 extra items from Hall's original inventory, reporting the frequencies of occurrence of six types of behavior and rules and regulations reflecting the presence or absence of bureaucracy in their schools. These data were subjected to a principal factor analysis followed by varimax rotation "in an attempt to replicate the six bureaucratic dimensions originally identified by Hall [hierarchy, rules, procedures, impersonality, specialization, and standards]" (Sousa & Hoy, 1981, p. 22). In this study, however, impersonality and specialization did not emerge as clear factors; hence, only four factors

were retained. The mean scores of teachers in each school on these four factors were obtained and used in further analyses. The 55 principals were interviewed using a modified Aston schedule focused on five aspects of bureaucracy: specialization, centralization, formalization, standardization, and configuration. Centralization further yielded a subfactor of autonomy. Using the school as unit of analysis, the teacher means on four factors and the principals' scores on six factors were intercorrelated to yield a 10 × 10 correlation matrix. This matrix also was subjected to a principal factor analysis with varimax rotation, yielding four factors: Organizational Control, Rational Specialization, System Centralization, and Formalization of Routine. The correlation matrix showed that teachers' and principals' perceptions of the same features of their schools were significantly correlated (although the *r*s ranged only from .36 to .67). The overall conclusion was that both the Hall and Aston procedures were useful and mutually complementary in measuring the bureaucratic structures of schools.

Commentary

Correlational studies were so numerous in educational administration research that it was necessary to be highly selective in choosing representative papers. Also, correlational methods are very well known, so there were few technical flaws; the variations among papers lay mostly in the care with which the studies were conceived, designed, and reported—including whether or not unwarranted causal attributions were made.

In the Ables and Conway (1973) study, which was competently executed on the whole, it is not clear why the authors decided to use rank-order correlation instead of the regular product-moment coefficient when all variables were quantitative to begin with. If the large range of the variances of the team members' D-scale scores led to this decision, it would have been better to take the square roots of the variances and use standard deviations. Using the regular product-moment *r* would also have made use of several partial *r*s (which was not mentioned earlier to save space) less "questionable"—which they correctly say is how the use of partial rank correlations is widely regarded.

Yee's (1970) study, although technically done without any apparent flaw, leaves something to be desired in its reportage—which detracts considerably from its overall merit. For instance, not until the Results and Discussion section does Yee tell what sort of scales make up the MTAI and what a high score on it means. Correlations between subscores on pairs of instruments are cited several times in that section, but they are not given in any table. Finally, the distinction between between-schools and within-schools compari-sons also is discussed in that section, where it disrupts the flow. The distinction and its implications should have been brought up either in the introduction or in the last section.

Bridges' study and Stockard's study draw joint comment because they deal, in part, with similar problems—not in substance but in the structure of the questions asked. Both ask whether X has a significant effect on Y above and beyond the effect of Z (a covariate or control variable), but they use different methods in seeking the answer. Bridges used stepwise multiple regression in asking whether job satisfaction variables (X) affect absenteeism (Y) over and above the influence of certain demographic variables (Z). Thus, he tested the significance of the incremental R. Stockard, on the other hand, tested whether the partial correlation $r_{XY.Z}$ was significantly different from zero in asking, among other things, whether residential locale (X = urban/rural) affects attitudes toward women administrators (Y) when knowing a woman administrator was controlled for. If the null hypothesis were sustained, she would have concluded that X does not affect Y when the effect of Z is removed. The point to be made here is that although the two approaches appear quite different, they yield *identical* significance test results. The partial correlation method used by Stockard is somewhat more straightforward to con-ceptualize and compute, but the stepwise multiple regression approach used by Bridges is more widely used, given the availability of computer programs.

The Sousa and Hoy (1981) study on the measure-ment of bureaucratic structure in schools may be re-garded as an exemplar of this type of study in design, execution, and reportage. Perhaps the only criticism that can be made is that the sample size of 55 schools is rather small for using a 10-variable matrix (actually, 13-variable, with the addition of three factual school descriptor variables) with which to do a factor analysis. This study illustrates that the sophisticated technique of factor analysis can be profitably used in research in educational administration and supports a recom-mendation that more researchers in educational admin-istration become familiar with this technique.

TECHNIQUES FOR FACILITATING CAUSAL INFERENCE[2]

Overview of the Techniques

Speaking of cause and effect in the behavioral and social sciences was almost a taboo in the second quarter of the 1900s. No doubt this was, in large part, a reac-tion to the overly facile attribution of causal status to antecedent events that was in vogue during the early part of the 20th century. In the 1950s, however, sociologists and psychologists alike realized that there could hardly be a science without identifying certain events as the causes (or partial causes) of other events. A flurry of activities ensued to develop techniques more sophisticated than simple correlation coefficients (although generally based on them) that would enable the researcher to identify causes (see, e.g., Ennis, 1973).

With the development of such techniques as the "16-fold" or "turnover" tables, "crosslagged panel correlation," and path analysis, the pendulum has swung back to make it fashionable again to speak of causes. It therefore cannot be overemphasized that these techniques, elegant and convenient as they are, do not inherently serve to determine causes. They can only help the researcher seek out events that are likely to be the causes of other events—*unless* well-established substantive theories support the causal attributions. Otherwise, it is only by carefully designed experiments, in which variables are deliberately manip-ulated, that researchers can establish causation. Even then, of course, they must always be alert to the possi-bility that unsuspected, uncontrolled variables could be the ultimate causes and the manipulated variables are merely surrogates or intermediate effects.

The 16-fold table, first proposed by Lazarsfeld and his coworkers (Lipset, Lazarsfeld, Barton, & Linz, 1954) is designed to consider two variables—usually dichotomous—at two points in time, as shown in the contingency table of Figure 31.1. The cell entries are the numbers of cases observed to have the combina-tion of properties indicated by the row and column headings where $\bar{A}$ and $\bar{B}$ denote "not A" and "not B," respectively. For instance, suppose A stands for a principal's being democratic (toward teachers), and B for the teachers' having high morale and being dedicated to serving the goals of the school. Is it more likely that A causes B or vice versa? For this purpose,

Figure 31.1   A 16-Fold Contingency Table for Inferring the Causal Priority Between A and B.

	TIME 2			
	(1) $A \& B$	(2) $A \& \bar{B}$	(3) $\bar{A} \& B$	(4) $\bar{A} \& \bar{B}$
(1) $A \& B$	n_{11}	n_{12}	n_{13}	n_{14}
(2) $A \& \bar{B}$	n_{21}	n_{22}	n_{23}	n_{24}
(3) $\bar{A} \& B$	n_{31}	n_{32}	n_{33}	n_{34}
(4) $\bar{A} \& \bar{B}$	n_{41}	n_{42}	n_{43}	n_{44}

an investigator surveys a large number of schools and observes the characteristics of the principals and the teaching staffs at two time points: before and during a period of severe economic hardship when there was much discontent among teachers. In this case n_{12} is the number of schools in which the principals were democratic *and* the teachers had high morale at Time 1 but in which the teachers' morale sagged although the principals remained democratic at Time 2; n_{14}, on the other hand, is the number of schools in which both principals and teachers changed from the more desirable (in U.S. society) to the less desirable characteristics between the two time points. Through an ingenious analysis of the off-diagonal cell frequencies, Lazarsfeld and his associates derived an index that is helpful in answering the question we have posed.

The technique of crosslagged panel correlation, developed primarily by Campbell and Stanley (1963) and later by Campbell and his associates, is based on a logic similar to that of the 16-fold table but uses a correlation matrix rather than a contingency table as the starting point. In highly simplified terms, the basic argument is this: If X and Y are measures of the two variables at Time 1 and X', Y' are the corresponding measures at Time 2, then the difference between $r_{xy'}$ and $r_{x'y}$ provides an indication of the probable causal ordering. That is, if $r_{xy'}$ is larger than $r_{x'y}$, it is more likely that X causes Y than vice versa. Subsequent modifications of the technique include the use of partial correlations to control for initial status on the two variables. Thus, Pelz and Andrews (1964) proposed using the difference between partial rather than zero-order correlations as an indicator of probable causal priority. While the crosslagged panel correlation method has a number of critics, it remains a viable tool for seeking out possible causes in the behavioral and social sciences.

Path analysis was developed by Wright (1921, 1934) to test and develop causal theories in genetics. It was first introduced into the sociological literature by Blalock (1964), Duncan (1966), and others, and into the educational and psychological literature by Werts and Linn (1970). Many researchers who use path analysis tend to think that specific cause-and-effect links can be established by constructing path diagrams and doing some confirmatory calculations based on them. As intimated earlier, path analysis by itself can only tell the researcher which of several models for the causal structure among several variables is most likely to be correct. The technique thus helps the researcher to generate a hypothesis about the causal relations; this hypothesis must subsequently be tested by an experimental or at least quasiexperimental study. (Of course, if a path diagram is constructed for expository purposes after an experimental study has established some causal links, the remark about the necessity for experimental testing does not hold.)

To illustrate, without actually doing the calculations, how path analysis helps the researcher decide among several possible causal models, consider the following problem. It is desired to study the structure of effects on a person's annual income at age 30 (Y) of three potentially causal variables: father's SES (X_1), the person's academic achievement through ninth grade (X_2), and number of years of formal education (X_3). Figure 31.2 shows three possible models for the causal relations among the four variables, the arrows indicating direct causal links. Thus, model (a) postulates that the father's SES affects the son's academic achievement, which in turn affects the number of years of education the son will get, and this in turn affects his income at age 30. Model (b), on the other hand, asserts that X_2 exerts a separate influence of its own on Y, instead of being in the causal sequence from X_1 to Y. Finally, model (c) says that X_1 and X_2 each exerts a separate influence on both Y and X_3, which latter also has a direct effect on Y. Note that the absence of an arrow from one variable to another does not mean that the two variables are uncorrelated; it only means that no unidirectional causal link is postulated to exist between the one variable and the other.

Consider now only models (a) and (c). Their path

Figure 31.2 Three Path Diagrams Representing Different Models for the Causal Links Among Variables X_1, X_2, X_3, and Y.

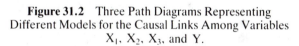

(a)

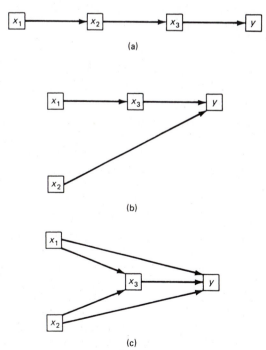

(b)

(c)

Figure 31.3 The Path Diagrams of Models (a) and (c) in Figure 31.2, with Some Additional Detail.

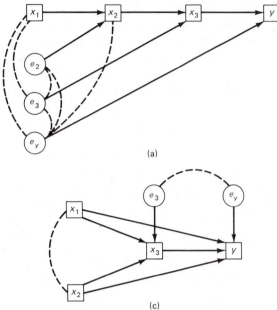

(a)

(c)

diagrams are repeated in Figure 31.3 with two things added: arcs in broken lines, which indicate that the pair of variables they connect may be correlated; *e*s in small circles with arrows going to variables corresponding to their subscripts. The *e*s are called "errors" or residuals, and represent the totality of "other variables" that also affect each of the variables being considered which are terminuses of one or more arrows. Note that no *e* is associated with X_1 in (a), nor with either X_1 or X_2 in (c). Note, too, that each *e* is uncorrelated with the immediately preceding variable in the chain but may be correlated with variables that are two or more steps behind.

The path analyst now writes equations that express the structure of each path diagram in mathematical form. The equations for each model are solved simultaneously for their unknowns, which are called "path coefficients," one for each arrow in the path diagram and which indicate the "strength" of each causal link. These equations are not presented here but are characterized verbally to indicate how the path coefficients can be determined without actually solving the equations. Briefly stated, each arrow or set of arrows terminating at a single variable is "translated" into a regression equation, with the variable at the terminus playing the role of dependent variable and the variable or variables from which the arrows emanate acting as the predictors. All variables are assumed to be in standardized form. Hence the equations, and consequently the path coefficients occurring as the unknown(s) in them, fall into the following four types:

1. When a variable X_k receives an arrow from just one X_j, the link $X_j \rightarrow X_k$ translates into a simple regression equation, and the path coefficient is equal to r_{jk}.

2. When a variable X_k receives arrows from several other variables, say X_h, X_i, X_j, the links $X_h \rightarrow X_k$, $X_i \rightarrow X_k$, $X_j \rightarrow X_k$ as a set translate into a multiple regression equation of X_k on X_h, X_i, and X_j. The three path coefficients are then the corresponding partial regression weights.

3. The path coefficient of the link $e_k \rightarrow X_k$ is $\sqrt{1 - r_{jk}^2}$ if the only other arrow to X_k comes from X_j.

4. The path coefficient of the link $e_k \rightarrow X_k$ is $\sqrt{1 - R_{k.hij}^2}$ if the other arrows to K_k comes from X_h, X_i, and X_j.

The foregoing rules apply also when X_k is replaced by Y—with the obvious changes of r_{jk} to r_{jv}, and so on.

Once the path coefficients have been determined for each model, what are the decision rules for ascertaining which model is most likely to be correct? One method is to estimate, on the basis of each model, those correlation coefficients between pairs of observed variables that have not been used in determining the path coefficients. Then, for each model, the average squared deviation (ASD) between the model-estimated and observed correlation values can be calculated, and the model with the smallest ASD can be declared the "winner." Sometimes, however, the number of free observable correlations remaining in a model may be very small or even nonexistent: that is, all or most of them may have been used in the process of determining the path coefficients. Then another method must be used, in which order relations among the correlations and other constraints are logically derived from each model and the observed correlations are checked against these constraints. Models for which the observed correlations badly fail to satisfy these constraints would be eliminated. For example, model (a) in Figure 31.2 implies that the only ways in which X_1 can be correlated with X_3 are through the mediations of X_2 and e_3. Hence the second-order partial correlation $r_{13.2e}$ must be zero. A relation among observable correlations can be derived from this condition, and unless the observed correlation values satisfy this relation (approximately), model (a) becomes suspect. The same holds for the condition $r_{2y.3e} = 0$.

It should be mentioned that the path analytic and regression analytic methods for testing alternative causal models have largely been superseded by a more general technique developed by Jöreskog and Sörbom (1984) known as LISREL (for linear structural relations)—which is also the name of the computer package—for investigating covariance structures.

The reader may have noticed that all the indexes referred to earlier are related to simple, partial, or multiple correlation and regression. In other words, all the quantitative results of path analysis can be obtained from the 4 × 4 correlation matrix among X_1, X_2, X_3, and Y, or, more generally, a $(p + 1) \times (p + 1)$ correlation matrix when there are p potential causal variables, without any resort to the path equations. This is precisely the reason not to view path analysis by itself as a technique for establishing causal relations any more than are correlation and regression analyses; mathematically, they are coextensive and coterminal. Strictly speaking, this is true only of recursive models in path analysis, that is, those in which there are no two-way arrows indicating the positing of mutual causation, between two variables. For nonrecursive models the analysis becomes somewhat more complicated than multiple regression analysis. This is by no means to imply that path analysis is of little value; far from it. Path diagrams are invaluable for theorizing about causal networks and helping the researchers to express verbal theories in mathematical form, thus facilitating the derivation of relevant quantities that hold the key to accepting or rejecting a model—or, more likely, to rejecting and reformulating parts of a model, which can then be rechecked with empirical findings. In short, path analysis is a valuable heuristic tool. (For more extensive discussions, the reader is referred to Duncan, 1975.)

Genuine experiments, using specific experimental designs, are still the mainstay for studying causal relations. (For a full discussion of the various experimental and quasiexperimental designs available, see Campbell and Stanley, 1963, and Cook and Campbell, 1979.) Suffice it to say that deliberate manipulation of treatment conditions and random assignment of Ss to the conditions are the key requirements in experimental design. Quasiexperiments are those studies conducted in natural settings that preclude actual random assignment of Ss but permit the imposing of procedures resembling experimental design in the data collection aspect. The interrupted time-series design—in which an experimental change is introduced into a sequence of periodic observations on a group—is a good example of a quasiexperimental design.

Another variant of experimental studies is the computer-simulation study. Actual simulation of experiments has been done in the context of simple learning experiments by means of a subclass of computer simulation techniques known as Monte Carlo methods. However, for problems relevant to educational administration (such as budget planning, promotion decisions, school district rezoning, and the like) it is not the experiment per se but the model of causal chains that is examined and tested by computer simulation. One of the types of computer simulation that is

most useful in such cases is called "system-dynamics modeling." The construction of path diagrams is an important part of this approach, and the diagrams here are more complicated than those illustrated here in that they usually contain feedback loops. (These are loops of events that reciprocally affect one another.) Once a diagram is drawn, the computer is programmed to crunch out the consequences of changing the strength of a causal link here, adding another link or loop there, removing one here, and so forth. The output is a series of tables or graphs that show the effects of manipulating the variables represented by the nodes of the path diagram—which is precisely what an experiment would yield if it were feasible to carry one out. (For details, see, for example, Roberts, Anderson, Deal, Garet, & Shafer, 1984).

Illustrative Studies

In a study designed to investigate whether a group decision-making process is more likely to lead to a better decision than one arrived at by an individual acting alone, Piper (1974) had 82 graduate students in educational administration complete a worksheet that required rank-ordering 15 items in terms of their importance for surviving a 200-mile trip on the moon. The subjects first completed the "Moonshot" worksheet individually, then were randomly assigned to a consensus group or one of two kinds of participatory groups to redo the task as members of a group of three to five persons. Error scores, defined as the total absolute deviations of a subject's rankings from the key provided by NASA, served as the criterion score. All groups showed significant improvements (as determined by matched-pairs t tests) over the group members' average score on the pretest. In fact, for the seven consensus groups in which the member who did the best on the pretest was designated as the leader, the group score was better than the leader's pretest score. There also was a control group of seven individuals who were tested as individuals on two occasions and who did not show a significant improvement in the mean. The conclusion was that group decision making, both participatory and consensual, is superior to individual decision making.

A study by Holland, Baritelle, and White (1976) was aimed at determining the optimal school size and locations for school consolidation in sparsely populated rural areas, with cost minimization as the goal. A rural county serving eight incorporated towns and parts of four adjacent counties in the state of Washington was chosen as the study site. The minimization problem was treated from both short-run and long-run perspectives. In the former, existing schools and their sizes as well as

Figure 31.4   Hypothesized Causal Chain Supported by Path Analysis

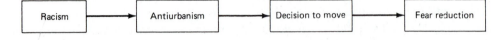

student distribution were held constant, and the sum (TC) of schooling costs and transportation cost was minimized by simple linear programming with school district boundaries as the sole variable. For the long-run perspective, "only the geographic distribution of students was assumed fixed. Optimum school size and student transportation patterns were determined using separable programming." (Holland et al., 1976, p. 73). Here an estimate of costs for building annexes for enlarged enrollment sizes, on a per annum basis, was included in the function to be minimized. For the short-run problem, the optimal district boundaries were found to be very close to the existing boundaries, and the economy accruing from optimizing the boundaries was small—only about $3,000. For the long-run problem, a savings of $32,000 could be realized by some substantial changes in district boundaries, school closings at some locations and expanded physical plants at others. Even this savings, however, amounts to only about 1.1 percent of the total school and transportation budget. This study demonstrates that mathematical programming is a viable tool for "experimenting" with school consolidation and transportation patterns.

Cusick, Gerbing, and Russell (1979) wanted to identify the factors that influenced white families to move from an urban area to its suburbs—specifically, from Pontiac, Michigan, between 1971 and 1975. A set of 32 five-point Likert-type items representing five attitudinal factors potentially related to moving from the city was administered to 600 randomly selected white families with school-age children, 300 of whom had moved to nearby suburbs and 300 of whom had stayed in Pontiac. Of the movers 193 and of the nonmovers 213 returned completed questionnaires, one per family. A discriminant analysis was then done to differentiate the movers from the nonmovers in terms of the five scales, which measured (a) dislike of urban life; (b) fear for their children's safety; (c) racism; (d) disapproval of the quality of urban education; (e) opposition to busing for effecting school desegregation. The standardized discriminant weights for these variables, in the order just listed, were 1.71, −0.51, 0.24, −0.08, and 0.01. It should be pointed out that "fear for their children's safety" referred to the fear they felt at their then-current place of residence. Hence this factor cannot be considered a contributory cause for the movers' decision to move. The negative discriminant weight, therefore, signifies that the move led to a reduction of the fear, since the discriminant function in this case was

obtained as a multiple regression equation with the criterion variable Y taking the value 0 for nonmovers and 1 for movers. Then a path analysis was conducted, in which several models were tried out until a final, "best-fitting" model was found. See Figure 31.4, which illustrates the hypothesized causal chain. Minor causal links (i.e., links with relatively small path coefficients) went from Racism to each of the two remaining factors, Anti Busing and Anti Urban Education, as well as from Anti Busing to Anti Urban Education, Anti Urbanism, and Fear Reduction. The overall conclusion was that busing did not appear to be a direct cause of "white flight," although it did contribute to antiurban feelings, which are the immediate antecedent of a family's decision to move.

Commentary

Explicit mention of "cause and effect" was rarely found in articles on research in educational administration, perhaps reflecting the fact that this vogue has not yet fully permeated the field. However, near synonyms or paraphrases of this term were frequently encountered. "Does A result in B?" and "Is C more likely affected by B or by A?" are typical examples. These questions, of course, have already occurred regularly in the studies reviewed and commented on in preceding sections. This section therefore, reviews just three papers that were most avowedly searching for causal relations and that used widely different techniques.

Piper's (1974) study on group versus individual decision making illustrates the prototypical and most justifiable approach to investigating the existence of causal relations, namely, genuine experimentation. Here the variable of interest was deliberately manipulated by having the subjects first make individual decisions and then randomly assigning them to three types of groups for group decision making. The analytic technique was quite straightforward: t tests for matched pairs (of which "before-after" is a special case). This observation should underscore the fact that it is not the sophistication of the analytic method that primarily determines whether (and to what extent) a study is germane to making causal inferences. It is the manner in which the study is designed and conducted that matters the most; in this respect, Piper's study is all but flawless. In the analysis phase, however, he could have compared (using an F test) the three experimental groups plus the control in terms of the improvement scores and followed this up with post hoc pairwise comparisons. Even though he disclaims interest in comparing the different types of group decision making, nothing would have been lost by making these comparisons as well.

The second study (Holland et al., 1976), on school consolidation, exemplifies the other extreme of a pure status study (i.e., a nonexperimental case study) followed by a highly sophisticated mathematical treatment. Here the emphasis is not so much on analysis of the observations themselves; these serve merely as a standard or norm with which the predicted effects of certain changes that could be made (consolidation and increased busing) should be compared. The validity of the predictions by this approach—linear and separable programming—hinges on the continued applicability of cost functions currently holding. Of course, allowances are made for inflation, and the cost functions should remain more or less the same as long as large reversals do not occur in the relative costs of the various items. The conclusion that consolidation with increased transportation will not result in a large savings assumes that fuel cost, for instance, will not drastically decrease (relative to other costs) due to the discovery or invention of alternative energy sources. This is a controversial assumption, and its violation may completely change the conclusions. However, this type of vulnerability is common to all economic (and many other kinds of) predictions. The merit of the study lies in its showing the applicability of the sophisticated and modern technique of mathematical programming to important problems in educational administration.

The last study, by Cusick et al. (1979), illustrates everything that was said about path analysis earlier in this section—and more. The construction of the questionnaire was very carefully done; it started out with a much larger pool of items that intuitively represented the factors of interest. But the authors did not leave matters there and carried out a factor analysis to check their a priori judgment of the nature of the items, which led to some reallocation of items to factors other than those they were originally assumed to measure. Then a final field test was made before administering the instrument to the actual study sample.

The discriminant analysis and path analysis, too, were carefully done and interpreted. The one flaw detected in the former was the statement "The equivalent of a regression analysis for a dichotomous dependent variable...is a discriminant analysis" (Cusick et al., 1979, p. 43), which is misleading in two respects. First, it ignores the fact that the main purpose of discriminant analysis is the parsimonious description of group differences rather than prediction of a criterion variable. Second, it gives the impression that discrim-

inant analysis is concerned solely with the two-group situation, which is only a special case of discriminant analysis.

The path analysis phase of the study—although stressing too much (as do most researchers using this technique) its purported "accoun[ting] for the causal structure among predictors" (Cusick et al., 1979, p. 44)—is commendable in its explicit mention of the successive modification of the structural model. All too many researchers give the impression (rightly or wrongly) that the one model displayed and discussed was the only one they had ever considered, thus failing to convey the primarily heuristic nature of the technique. Perhaps many researchers are afraid of letting it be known that they had engaged in trial and error before arriving at their final model. If so, they have missed one of the main characteristics of scientific endeavor, which is to engage in *guided* trial and error. Blind trial and error, to be sure, is to be avoided as far as possible. But guided or directed trial and error is a necessary aspect of science. Any technique that provides such guidance is an invaluable heuristic tool. This, as was already stated earlier, is the main function of path analysis.

SUMMARY AND CONCLUSION

It is clear that the range of statistical techniques for addressing increasingly sophisticated research questions has been expanding rapidly during the past 30 years and that researchers in the field of educational administration have generally not taken full advantage of the quantitative tools available. In this chapter we have described in brief, and in relatively nontechnical language, the array of quantitative methods within four broad categories—survey-descriptive, analysis of variance, correlational, and causal inference methods. This concluding section is devoted to a summary of the preceding sections, with an emphasis on those techniques that appear to be underutilized but that could contribute to enhancing research in educational administration.

Survey-descriptive methods of analysis, which generally are not used to test hypotheses deduced from theories, include frequency counts, distributions, and graphic displays such as frequency polygons, pie charts, and crosstabulations of frequencies. Hypotheses regarding differences between groups can be tested by means of chi-square analysis, *t* tests, and the more recently developed categorical data analysis. Descriptive methods seem to be the most frequently used techniques in educational administration, with 67 (almost 40 percent) of the quantitative studies we reviewed relying on them. Few of the studies, however, incorporated displays other than tables to render the findings as vivid and graphic as possible.

Research tools associated with analysis of variance (ANOVA) have been used with relative rarity in educational administration; only 21 (12.4 percent) of the studies we examined depended on them. This set of techniques includes one-way and two-way ANOVA, multivariate analysis of variance, or MANOVA, discriminant analysis, and stepwise discriminant analysis. The discriminant analysis methods have been utilized very rarely in the educational administration literature, but they can be powerful tools for identifying those items, scales, or dimensions that best differentiate groups in a research sample. A precaution offered with regard to significance tests that pertains equally to correlational tests of null hypotheses is that statistical significance ought not to be confused with practical importance, for significance is contingent on sample size.

Correlations between two variables include not only the well-known Pearson product-moment r and the Spearman rank-order (rho) but the phi coefficient (ϕ) for correlating two dichotomies and the point-biserial r for correlating a dichotomous variable with a continuous one. Correlational techniques of a multivariate nature include linear multiple regression, polynomial regression (for curvilinear relationships), stepwise multiple regression, canonical correlations (among several independent and several dependent variables), partial correlation, and factor analysis with either orthogonal or oblique rotations of factors. Most of the correlational techniques are heavily utilized in the research on educational administration; 65 (38.5 percent) of the studies we examined relied on one or more of them. Two precautions merit attention: (a) Factor analysis requires a relatively large and representative sample (roughly 10 respondents per item) for identifying with some degree of confidence the underlying dimensions of the domain studied; and (b) factor analysis used for theory building requires rigorous follow-up research to test the validity of the constructs (factors) identified.

Research techniques by which causal inferences can justifiably be drawn include not only true experiments but crosslagged correlations, 16-fold tables, and computer-simulated experiments as well. Path analysis also facilitates causal conjectures. These methods have been most rare in educational administration; only 14 studies (8.2 percent) in our sample drew on any of these techniques. Whereas experimental research tends to rely on ANOVA and related methods, cross-lagged analysis and path analysis rest on correlational techniques. It seems likely that actual and computer-simulated experimentation will become more commonplace in educational administration with the advent of microcomputers, since school-based and district-based studies will be feasible at modest cost.

Microcomputers are destined to render quantitative research relatively easy and inexpensive for educators at all levels in school systems. Thus, despite the resurgence of interest in qualitative methods during the past decade, quantitative research will likely retain and increase its importance for inquiry in educational administration. Sophisticated statistical packages for microcomputers are currently on the market, and if these follow the developmental pattern of word-processing and spreadsheet programs, they will soon become more powerful and easier to use, even for the heretofore uninitiated. Already microcomputer programs are available that enable data analyses in all the categories discussed in this chapter and that include critical values of significance levels for hypothesis-testing statistics. It is virtually inevitable that program user manuals will put even the most complex statistical techniques at the disposal of most school personnel, graduate students, and professors, regardless of their training in quantitative methods.

There are, of course, many pitfalls associated with such widespread access to quantitative methods. Most worrisome are attributions of practical importance to statistically signicant findings (see McNamara, 1978), unfounded causal inferences based on relational findings, and inappropriate statistics applied to the data at hand. These dangers have always been intrinsic to the research endeavor, but with a vastly enlarged group of users the potential for abuse is greatly intensified. Nevertheless, we remain optimistic about the prospects for quantitative research. With computers in schools and departments of educational administration everywhere, the body of knowledge about schools and their administration could readily increase dramatically during the coming years.

NOTES

[1] For further details on MANOVA and discriminant analysis, the reader is referred to any of several texts in multivariate analysis such as Harris (1975), Overall and Klett (1972), and Tatsuoka (1988). A more elementary treatment of discriminant analysis (but not of MANOVA) is given in a short booklet by Tatsuoka (1970).
[2] The authors gratefully acknowledge their colleague Robert L. Linn for his comments on a draft of this section.

REFERENCES

Ables, J., & Conway, J. (1973). Leader-team belief system congruence and relationships to morale within teaching teams. *Educational Administration Quarterly*, 9(2), 22–33.

Blalock, H. M. (1964). *Causal inferences in nonexperimental research*. Chapel Hill, NC: University of North Carolina Press.

Boyan, N. J. (1951). *A study of the formal and informal organization of a school faculty*. Unpublished doctoral dissertation, Harvard University, Cambridge, MA.

Bridges, E. M. (1980). Job satisfaction and teacher absenteeism. *Educational Administration Quarterly*, *16*(2), 41–56.

Callahan, R. (1962). *Education and the cult of efficiency*. Chicago: University of Chicago Press.

Campbell, D. T., & Stanley, J. C. (1963). Experimental and quasi-experimental designs for research on teaching. In N. L. Gage (Ed.), *Handbook for research on teaching*. Chicago: Rand McNally.

Cohen, J. (1969). *Statistical power analysis for the behavioral sciences*. New York: Academic Press.

Cook, T. D., & Campbell, D. T. (1979). *Quasi-experimentation: Design & analysis issues for field settings*. Chicago: Rand McNally.

Cooley, W. W., & Lohnes, P. R. (1976). *Evaluation research in education*. New York: Irvington.

Cusick, P. A., Gerbing, D. W., & Russell, E. L. (1979). The effects of school desegregation and other factors on white flight from an urban area. *Educational Administration Quarterly*, *15*(2), 34–49.

Duke, D. L. (1976). Who misbehaves? A high school studies its discipline problems. *Educational Administration Quarterly*, *12*(3), 65–85.

Duncan, O. D. (1966). Path analysis: Sociological examples. *American Journal of Sociology*, *72*, 1–16.

Duncan, O. D. (1975). *Introduction to structural equation models*. New York: Academic Press.

Ennis, R. H. (1973). On causality. *Educational Researcher*, *2*, 4–11.

Feuille, P., & Blandin, J. (1976). Determinants of attitudinal militancy among university faculty. *Educational Administration Quarterly*, *12*(1), 54–66.

Fiedler, F. (1967). *A theory of leadership effectiveness*. New York: McGraw-Hill.

Fienberg, S. E. (1980). *The analysis of cross-classified categorical data* (2nd ed.). Cambridge, MA: MIT Press.

Flanagan, J. C., Cooley, W. W., Lohnes, P. R., Schoenfeldt, L. F., Holdeman, R. W., Combs, J., & Becker, S. J. (1966). *Project TALENT one-year follow-up studies*. Pittsburgh: Project TALENT Office, University of Pittsburgh.

Garland, P., & O'Reilly, R. R. (1976). The effect of leader-member interaction on organizational effectiveness. *Educational Administration Quarterly*, *12*(3), 9–30.

Glass, G. V. (1977). Integrating findings: The meta-analysis of research. In L. Shulman (Ed.), *Review of research in education*, *Vol. 4*. Itasca, IL: Peacock.

Gorton, R. (1982). Administrator stress: Some surprising research findings. *Planning and Changing*, *12*(4), 195–199.

Hall, R. H. (1961). *An empirical study of bureaucratic dimensions and their relationship to other organizational characteristics*. Unpublished doctoral dissertation, Ohio State University, Columbus.

Haller, E. J. (1979). Questionnaires and the dissertation in educational administration. *Educational Administration Quarterly*, *15*(1), 47–66.

Halpin, A. W. (1959). *The leadership behavior of school superintendents*. Chicago: The Midwest Center, University of Chicago.

Harris, R. J. (1975). *A primer of multivariate statistics*. New York: Academic.

Hays, W. (1973). *Statistics for the social sciences* (2nd ed.). New York: Holt, Rinehart, & Winston.

Holland, D., Baritelle, J., & White, G. (1976). School consolidation in sparsely populated rural areas: A case study. *Educational Administration Quarterly*, *12*(1), 67–79.

Jöreskog, K. G., & Sörbom, D. (1984). *LISREL VI*. Mooreville, IN: Scientific Software.

Kim, J. O., & Mueller, C. W. (1978a). *Factor analysis: Statistical methods and practical issues*. Beverly Hills, CA: Sage.

Kim, J. O., & Mueller, C. W. (1978b). *Introduction to factor analysis: What it is and how to do it*. Beverly Hills, CA: Sage.

Kirk, R. E. (1982). *Experimental design: Procedures for the behavioral sciences* (2nd ed.). Belmont, CA: Brooks/Cole.

Kmetz, J. T., & Willower, D. J. (1982). Elementary school principals' work behavior. *Educational Administration Quarterly*, *18*(4), 62–78.

Lipset, S. M., Lazarsfeld, P. F., Barton, A. H., & Linz, J. (1954). The psychology of voting: An analysis of voting behavior. In G. Lindzey (Ed.), *Handbook of social psychology*. Cambridge, MA: Addison-Wesley.

Lucietto, L. L. (1970). Speech patterns of administrators. *Administrators Notebook*, *18*(5), 1–4.

McCarthy, M., & Zent, A. (1981). School administrators: 1980 profile. *Planning and Changing*, *12*(3), 144–161.

McNamara, J. M. (1978). Practical significance and statistical models. *Educational Administration Quarterly*, *14*(1), 48–63.

Mintzberg, H. (1973). *The nature of managerial work*. New York: Harper & Row.

Mulaik, S. A. (1972). *The foundations of factor analysis*. San Francisco: McGraw-Hill.

Overall, J. E., & Klett, C. J. (1972). *Applied multivariate analysis*. New York: McGraw-Hill.

Pelz, D. C., & Andrews, F. M. (1964). Detecting causal priorities in panel study data. *American Sociological Review*, *29*, 836–846.

Piper, D. L. (1974). Decisionmaking: Decisions made by individuals vs. those made by group consensus or group participation. *Educational Administration Quarterly*, *10*(2), 82–95.

Pugh, D. S., Hickson, D. J., Hinings, C. R., & Turner, C. (1968). Dimensions of organizational structure. *Administrative Science Quarterly*, *13*, 63–105.

Roberts, N., Anderson, D. F., Deal, R. M., Garet, M. S., & Shafer, W. A. (1983). *Introduction to computer simulation: The system dynamics approach*. Reading, MA: Addison-Wesley.

Rowan, B. (1982). Instructional management in historic perspective: Evidence on differentiation in school districts. *Educational Administration Quarterly*, *18*(1), 43–59.

Sears, J. B. (1925). *The school survey*. Boston: Houghton Mifflin.

Sousa, D. A., & Hoy, W. K. (1981). Bureaucratic structure in schools: A refinement and synthesis in measurement. *Educational Administration Quarterly*, *17*(4), 21–39.

Stockard, J. (1979). Public prejudice against women school administrators: The possibility of change. *Educational Administration Quarterly*, *15*(3), 83–96.

Stone, P. J., Dunphy, D. C., Smith, M. S., & Ogilvie, D. M. (1966). *The general inquirer: A computer approach to content analysis*. Cambridge, MA: MIT Press.

Tatsuoka, M. M. (1970). *Discriminant analysis: The study of group differences*. Champaign, IL: Institute for Personality & Ability Testing.

Tatsuoka, M. M. (1988). *Multivariate analysis: Techniques for educational and psychological research* (2nd ed.) New York: Macmillan.

Todd, E. S. (1969). High school curricula: Some economic implications. *Administrators Notebook*, *18*(2), 1–4.

Tuckman, B. W., Steber, J. M., & Hyman, R. T. (1979). Judging the effectiveness of teaching styles: The perceptions of principals. *Educational Administration Quarterly*, *15*(1), 104–115.

Werts, C. E., & Linn, R. L. (1970). Path analysis: Psychological examples. *Psychological Bulletin*, *74*, 193–212.

Wold, H. O. A. (1970). Causal inference from observational data: A review of ends and means. In M. C. Wittrock & D. E. Wiley (Eds.), *The evaluation of instruction*. New York: Holt, Rinehart, & Winston.

Wright, S. (1921). Correlation and causation. *Journal of Agricultural Research*, *20*, 577–585.

Wright, S. (1934). The method of path coefficients. *Annals of Mathematical Statistics*, *5*, 161–215.

Yee, A. H. (1970). Do principals' interpersonal attitudes agree with those of teachers and pupils? *Educational Administration Quarterly*, *6*(2), 1–13.

CHAPTER 32

Fieldwork Methodology in Educational Administration

Robert B. Everhart

History is not the raw material of historians' work; it is the object produced by their work.
Bernard Henri-Levy

INTRODUCTION

This chapter is an exegesis on the role of fieldwork in the evolving area of educational administration. There is little doubt that fieldwork has gained considerable favor and respect in the study of educational phenomena since the mid-1960s (Magoon, 1977; Roberts & Akinsanya, 1976; Smith, 1978; Wilcox, 1982; Wilson, 1977). Studies of the leadership, management, and organization of schools are no exception to this trend (Wolcott, 1985). Falling under the various labels of ethnography, participant observation, fieldwork, qualitative methods, case studies, and naturalistic inquiry, these approaches are all attempts (with varying emphases) to understand educational processes *in situ*. As will become clear soon, I will use the term *fieldwork* in subsequent references to these approaches; my choice is in part substantive and in part personal. Yet there is considerable overlap in the labels used to describe such approaches to explain educational phenomena; it is useful first to review some of the commonalities.

Research of this genre operates on a number of assumptions that have made it methodologically distinctive. First and foremost, such studies are heavily *constructivist* (Magoon, 1977) in their orientation. That is, they assume in all phenomena, but in this case particularly those of an educational nature, that participants are "knowing beings," and that the knowledge they possess and create is a critical dimension for the understanding of actions within any one educational

setting. Related to the locus of knowledge with individuals and especially groups of individuals is the assumption that behavior based on that knowledge is purposive, or designed toward some end, and that the complexity of human interactions cannot be fully understood without understanding the roots of action. Generally, fieldworkers make the assumption that actors construct meaning within a social context—that meaning "is derived from, or arises out of, the social interaction that one has with one's fellows" (Blumer, 1969, p. 2). Thus, different contexts of social interaction are potentially productive of variance in the creation of meanings.

Second, fieldwork is *process oriented*. The strengths of fieldwork lie in its attempt to examine events and meanings as they unfold and develop and to understand the contingencies that influence the manner in which such events evolve. While fieldwork may focus on "snapshots" representative of phenomena over time, it is not the individual snapshots in which the fieldworker has interest. Rather, it is the snapshots in their cumulative sense—the film on which fieldwork concentrates, for the film provides the moving history of events as it unfolds. Thus, social relations are not "structures that perform a limited number of functions...but processes which, from time to time, may be dealt with as structures and which will exhibit a multitude of consequences" (Schatzman & Strauss, 1973, p. 6).

A third characteristic of fieldwork is its *holistic* orientation. That is to say that not any phenomenon can be isolated and studied in terms of a simple linear relationship but must be studied in context. Fieldworkers make the assumption that events and their

---

Consultant/reviewers: Louis M. Smith, Washington University; and Harry F. Wolcott, University of Oregon

meaning are multidimensional rather than unidimensional and consequently must be examined as intricate social fabrics woven together to produce a greater whole. As Wolcott (1975) says about doing research in schools:

> [The fieldworker] sees the teacher as well as the pupil as a person who is also a son or a daughter, probably a sibling, possibly a mate or parent, a person who plays out a multiplicity of roles and who is both learning and transmitting a set of values. (p. 113)

Finally fieldwork, as an approach to research, focuses on the importance of the *researcher as the instrument* in the formulation of the study, collection of the data, and interpretation of the results (Sanday, 1979; Wolcott, 1975). Choices about what problems to examine, how to examine those problems, and what those problems mean "are forced by the weight of the personal and professional background that you bring to the field" (Agar, 1980, p. 48). While many of the canons of science designed to improve the validity and rehability of any research are equally applicable to doing fieldwork (Le Compte & Goetz, 1982), it is first and in the final analysis the individual fieldworker who is his or her own best barometer. Fieldwork, then, is not a method but a role that allows the researcher to witness and experience phenomena as they occur, utilizing multidimensional techniques (Jick, 1979; Sieber, 1973) to aid in the collection of information about those phenomena.

In summary, fieldwork entails the active involvement of a trained observer in the lives of members of a setting for purposes of understanding life in the terms within which participants live out that life. The essential quality that emerges from analysis of phenomena from the actor's perspective, as those phenomena develop within a context emphasizing multidimensionality, can emerge only as the researcher participates in the ongoing events characteristic of that setting. The strength and appeal of such research rests on the potentiality for accurate descriptions and analysis of "what is." More specifically, the particular advantage of fieldwork, and perhaps a strong criterion for choosing it over other forms of research, lies in its emphasis on construct validity (Rist, 1977)—the meaning of events or situations to those individuals who engage in them. In the area of policy research and research on educational administration, fieldwork is unsurpassed for attaining this validity.

Method and Methodology

Given the focus in fieldwork on meaning, social process, context, and the critical role of the fieldworker as

an instrument, this chapter specifically concentrates on fieldwork methodology. The term *methodology* has been consciously chosen and will be used within a specific context (see also Redfield, 1955; Smith, Prunty, Dwyer, & Kleine, 1984). Kaplan (1964) makes the critical distinction between technique, method, and methodology in his attempt to describe the conduct of inquiry in the social and behavioral sciences. With the term *technique* (which is usually confused with methodology) Kaplan refers to the "specific procedures used in a given science, or in particular contexts of inquiry in that science" (p. 19). Thus, a survey, a thematic apperception test (TAT), and a focused interview are all examples of a research technique because they are specific procedures used to gather information. So-called methodological studies that investigate the strengths and weaknesses of specific techniques are misnamed because their focus is on the "nuts and bolts" of how to collect data.

Methods, on the other hand, are "logical or philosophical principles sufficiently specific to relate especially to science as distinguished from other human enterprises and interests" (Kaplan, 1964, p. 23). Methods then include the procedures involved in such exercises as concept formation, hypothesis testing, model and theory building, explanation, and prediction. Methods include the logic involved in "selecting particular observational techniques, assessing their yield of data, and relating these data to theoretical propositions" (Pelto, 1970, p. 4).

Methodology is the "description, explanation, and justification of methods" (Kaplan, 1964, p. 18). The aim of methodology is to describe and analyze methods, identifying their strengths and limitations and illuminating their assumptions and the consequence of those assumptions to understand not just the products of scientific inquiry but the process itself. The explication of methodology in science is closely akin to the field of epistemology, or philosophy's theory of knowledge. Although some have argued that methodology, as part of epistemology in science, "has little or nothing to do with how research gets done" (Festinger & Katz, 1953, p. 473), more recent work claims that such is not true. Suppe (1977), for example, argues persuasively that the diverse role of theories and theory building is central to science. "Should that analysis (of theories) prove inadequate," Suppe states, "that inadequacy is likely to extend to its account of the remaining aspects of the scientific enterprise and the knowledge it provides" (1977, p.3).

Focus on methodology, or the analysis of methods associated with fieldwork, inevitably runs head-on into the topic of how fieldwork is done and the models that guide and/or arise out of the description and explanation of phenomena. In the first place, methodology involves understanding the process of argumentation and explanation through such processes as logical inference and deduction. Thus the inquirer must understand the relationship between data accumulated via various techniques and the manner in which conclusions are derived from those data (methods). Yet it is also true that such processes, involving as they do validation and falsification, do not occur within a rigid and uniform paradigm. Rather, they take place as the individual fieldworker makes conscious decisions about what questions to ask, what techniques to use, and how to piece data together into some mosaic of description or explanation. They also take place as influenced by the social and personal factors that the fieldworker brings to the field and the analytical units generated (Bernstein, 1976; Mulkay, 1979).

There is, in these processes then, a "logic-in-use" (Kaplan, 1964, p. 8) which defines the fieldworker's cognitive style as he or she solves the uncertainties presented by the research act. This logic-in-use involves the process whereby the fieldworker turns data into conclusions, as well as the factors that influence these processes in their complexity. In many ways, then, logic-in-use involves the phenomenology of the very research act itself, and it directs attention to the extent to which method in and of itself is sufficient for generating social knowledge (Phillips, 1973).

As a logic-in-use is made explicit, and as the research act with its assumptions, methods, and techniques becomes paradigmatic, then that logic-in-use serves as a model or a schema for doing research. This model, which is really an idealized form of scientific practice, can be considered a "reconstructed logic" (Kaplan, 1964, p. 8) because it establishes broad parameters of methods in science. The hypothetico-deductive model, for example, so common among the proponents of "radical empiricism" (Strike, 1972) is just such a form of reconstructed logic because of the process of proposition formation, deduction of observables, experimentation, and validation.

The study of methodology involves both examination of logic-in-use as well as reconstructed logic. A particular reconstructed logic maps out, again in an idealized form, the logics-in-use deemed appropriate for inquiry given the assumptions built into that reconstructed logic. It influences the process by which the scientist uses concepts, draws conclusions, and explains or predicts. It influences to a considerable extent the specific *techniques* that the scientist uses given the assumption of a particular methodology. The aim of methodology, then, is to analyze methods and techniques, "throwing light on their limitations and resources, clarifying their presuppositions and conse-quences, relating their potentialities to the twilight zone at the frontiers of knowledge" (Kaplan, 1964, p. 23).

This chapter aspires to nudge the field a bit toward the frontiers of knowledge in its focus on methodology as discussed above. The choice of focus rests on two reasons. First, there already exist numerous documents that review and catalog what is termed the methodology of fieldwork in education (Bogdan & Bicklen, 1982; Dobbert, 1982; Goetz & Le Compte, 1984; Magoon, 1977; Wilson, 1977). Review of those collections, however, reveals that most are not descriptions or analyses of methodology but rather of technique—of the specific procedures for collecting information in a fieldwork role and the strengths and limitations of those techniques. Issues of methodology are scarcely addressed. Indeed, in one of the longest enduring collections of articles now deemed to contain the "classics" of participant observation, the editors specifically reject a focus on methodology. They say that the collection will review participant observation "at a less heady level, largely eschewing issues of epistemology and focusing rather on concrete issues of method and technique" (McCall & Simmons, 1969, p. 2). Given the extant and still growing sources already available on method and technique, and assuming that they are applicable to the study of educational administration, it hardly seems necessary to resynthesize them in still another iteration.

Second, the examination of methodology—that is, the study of the making of knowledge through fieldwork—has been addressed only infrequently in the past. Some authors (Ogbu, 1981; Rist, 1977; Salamone, 1979) have begun to identify issues of fieldwork as a methodology, but for the most part the subject of methodology continues to get caught up almost exclusively with the subject of techniques. Noting this state of affairs recalls the truth of Becker's (1970) statement that "methodology is too important to be left to methodologists" (p. 3). The methodologists have told us how to do it, yet they have neglected to point out the other important issues to address: namely, the assumptions lying behind what we do, examination of the logic-in-use and reconstructed logic that is part of what we do, and *why* we do what we do. Focus on these matters asks that we view the methodology of scientific activity just as we would view any other organized human activity, involving as it does human choices that do not always lend themselves to objective classification.

Scope of Chapter

Three assumptions undergird the treatment of fieldwork in educational administration as an organized human activity. First, since the fieldworker is the "main instrument" in doing fieldwork, a focus on how the fieldworker makes explicit the epistemological issues in the fieldwork process is critical. Second, as others also assume (Kaplan, 1964; Lindblom & Cohen, 1979; and Mulkay, 1979), all research is a "valuing" process, and the dialectical relationship of the fieldworker's and the informant's value systems enter into the phenomenology of the research act. Finally, issues of methodology are many and complex, so the researcher must make choices on the nature of the issue to be addressed. In brief, there are methodological considerations in analyzing methodology. Personal preference will become clear and is meant to guide further discussions of fieldwork methodology. No claims as to sufficiency are made.

Four major sections follow. The first briefly examines the shift in educational administration from an almost exclusive concern with the role set of individual administrators to a focus on the complexities of educational decision making, policy implementation, and the context within which these processes occur. This overview provides the backdrop necessary for a more complete understanding of the emergence of fieldwork as an approach to the study of educational policy. The second major section chronicles the emergence of policy studies and highlights the manner in which fieldwork has facilitated the expanded concerns of policy research in education. The evidence indicates how methodological concerns have entered into the expanding definition of educational administration. The third section attempts to document in closer detail how methodology has directly affected studies of educational administration, administrative issues, and the making of educational policy. The use of a small number of studies abets examination of the assumptions about knowledge that have been used in the fieldwork process. The emphasis is on research that focuses on microanalysis of schooling pertinent to administrative and policy concerns, the areas of educational and organizational change, and policy making and social structure. The fourth major section attends to the implications of the study of fieldwork methodology for the substantive area of educational administration and policy analysis.

EDUCATIONAL ADMINISTRATION: FROM CONSENSUS TO DIVERGENCE

Lynd (1976) once stated that "the controlling factor in any science is the way it views and states its problems (p. 216)." Such is no less the case in educational administration, whose focus of inquiry is now "character-

ized by turbulence from both within and without" (Immegart & Boyd, 1979, p. xiii). At one time the field was characterized by the mere documentation of and prescriptions for the efficient operation of the nation's public schools, but those pastoral days have long since faded. Replacing such domesticity are current challenges to the very function of today's public schools (Coons & Sugarman, 1978; Everhart, 1982; Manley-Casmir, 1982) and the rise of a new body of literature that calls into question some of the basic premises on which education in modern societies is based (Apple, 1979, 1982; Arons, 1983; Giroux, 1981). Indeed, so choppy are the waters in the sea of educational administration that some have argued that we are now ready for a paradigm shift of major proportions (Gibson, 1979). It is useful to trace briefly the nature of this shift in focus, not so much for its substantive nature but rather as it signals basic concerns of methodology.

It is perhaps first necessary to recognize that the field of educational administration has always suffered to some degree from an identity crisis. Boyan (1969) raises the question of whether educational administration has as its focus a distinct and unique body of knowledge or whether it simply is a field *for* (rather than *of*) study. There seems to be an absence of programmatic research, of a focus on singular program areas, or of more than passing involvement in research on the part of the majority of those who work in the field (Immegart, 1977). Indeed, Wolcott (1979) has even claimed that for years the field has suffered because professors of educational administration have found it difficult to define a subject matter that they could actually teach their students, it being assumed that students as practicing educators are far more knowledgeable about the practicalities and strategies of administration than are their professors, most of whom haven't worked in a public school for years, if ever at all.

Despite the pessimism we have noted, there did exist at one time relative consensus as to what educational administration was. Prior to 1950 the mission of schools and the role of administrators in those schools was scarcely questioned. Indeed, the field of educational administration has as its mission the teaching of skills to school administrators to operate those schools democratically and within the premises of what at the time was called "democratic leadership" (Button, 1966; Haller, 1968). Such practical purposes were well reflected in the last National Society for the Study of Education yearbook to focus exclusively on the field of "administration" (Henry, 1946). Relevant chapter headings in that book address such topics as Organizing the Personnel of a Democratic School System, Developing and Administering the Curriculum and Pupil

Services, and The Professional Preparation of School Personnel. In the period prior to 1950, "superintendents were overwhelmed with the tasks of keeping the buildings clean and warm, child accounting, business management, and keeping the boards and parents happy" (Tyack & Cummings, 1977, p. 61). Likewise, research in educational administration was similarly dedicated to a "descriptive analysis" of the mechanisms thought best to affect those outcomes (Gibson, 1979).

The early 1950s, however, saw the simple world of educational administration grow increasingly complex. With this increasing complexity, the relative consensus about the focus of the field began to disintegrate, for two fundamental reasons.

First were external factors that had increasingly affected schools but which had been ignored for decades, indeed centuries. Perhaps the most significant of these factors was the issue of whether or not schools indeed reproduced the very democratic principles that the era of democratic administration had assumed. Up until the early 1950s, three basic tenets had regulated the governance of schools and the administration of their routines (Iannaccone, 1982; Tyack & Hansot, 1982). The first of these was the separation of politics from education—the belief born out of the municipal reform movement that education should and could remain separate from political partisanship. The second tenet was the belief that education and schools represented a unitary community's consensus on the nature of citizenship and the role of schools in affecting the shaping of the citizen. The third tenet reflected the belief that the emerging profession of education, in all its ramifications, was neutral and had as its sole function the maximization of objective criteria without regard to the values and beliefs of those in control of education.

All three of these tenets were called into question in 1954 by *Brown vs. Board of Education*. First, it was clear that the schools could not be separated from politics; indeed, the Supreme Court argued that political decisions of "separate but equal" had been responsible for causing the problem that was the very subject of the Brown case. Second, it was now clear that the myth of a unitary community was shattered, that at least on the racial issue there existed two school systems serving two communities, one white and one black. Third, that through the process of administering racially separate school systems, the professionals themselves, the school administrators and those who researched schools, had not been professionally neutral; but through complicity or neglect, they had contributed to the problems of segregated education. With *Brown*, the whole structure of democratic administration weakened and with it the ability of schools to divorce

themselves from major and large social forces surrounding them. Subsequent issues of unequal education based on ethnicity, sex, class, and other differences were to be raised through the 1960s and 1970s.

Parallel to these external influences on the field were certain internal influences, broadly classified as the Theory Movement. (See Chapters 1 and 2) Beginning in the late 1950s and moving into the 1960s, the Theory Movement was part and parcel of a large professional direction to apply a more exacting degree of rigor, believed to exist in the behavioral and social sciences, to the area of educational administration. Scientific theory was to offer to educational administration objective frame(s) of reference through which educational phenomena could be studied and out of which educational decisions could be made more rationally. The assumptions of scientific theory in administration, well encapsulated in Griffiths (1964), were perhaps best captured by Hills (1965), who reflected:

> The further relevance of the social sciences, then, is the possibility they offer for breaking through the "world taken for granted" perspective of the educational establishment, the possibility to become self-conscious, and hence suspicious, of the self-evident, self-validating assumptions that channel educational practice into traditional paths. (p. 38)

There are at least two perspectives from which to view the role of theory in educational administration. One perspective is to examine its impact in the field. This is a topic which has filled the journals and compilations of the field for the past decade (Charters, 1977; Culbertson, 1981; Hoy, 1978; Iannaccone, 1973; Immegart, 1977). These reports generally point to the fact that although theory-based research indeed increased dramatically from the 1950s through the 1970s, the overall effect on the field has been minimal. Indeed Halpin & Hayes (1977) concluded that "the major initial research contributions were made by a very small cadre of investigators, and the thrust of the movement was clearly evident at only a few universities" (p. 271). Although some (Charters, 1977) were more optimistic, most analysts seemed to conclude with Immegart (1977) that the outcome of the theory movement was little more than research that followed "pat topics, social concerns, popular concepts or practical presses of the time" (p. 316). Furthermore, Immegart (1977) concludes that "analyses yielded little evidence that research and inquiry have had any substantial impact on practice" (p. 317).

Perhaps more interesting, however, is not so much what the Theory Movement did but why it developed the way it did. Part of the answer to this question can best be answered through the perspective that the focus of the Theory Movement was not so much a radical departure from the era of democratic administration as much as an approach to examine administration more "objectively." Up through at least the mid-1960s, the dominant paradigm in educational administration was decidedly a closed-system, social psychological approach to administrative theory and behavior (Boyd & Crowson, 1981). Indeed, of the five "substantive achievements" noted by Halpin and Hayes (1977) as opening new "conceptual vistas" in the Theory Movement, the work of at least four of the five (Getzels & Guba, 1957; Halpin, 1956; Halpin & Croft, 1963; Hemphill, Griffiths, & Frederickson, 1962) not only fit the description of but contributed to the propagation of the dominant paradigm. Understandably, this closed-system paradigm received wide acceptance, as the focus on the sociopsychological aspects of school organizations represented a clear and natural transition from the democratic leadership literature and its focus on leadership and participation. Thus, through scientific theory and the development of such devices as the Leader Behavior Description Questionnaire (LBDQ), one could "measure" the qualities of good educational leaders; the Organizational Climate Decription Questionnaire (OCDQ) permitted similar "measurement" of organizational space. Due in part to acceptance of the assumptions that numerical measurement and construct validity were synonymous, university researchers pointed their students in similar directions, and the most popular topics of dissertations in educational administration in the period from 1954 to 1974 included the facile measurement of such issues as administrative behavior, role, position, and effectiveness; staff personnel; educational organization; and morale and climate (Immegart, 1977).

This type of inquiry led, unfortunately, to what Charters (1978) has termed "endless, witless administration of the LBDQ, OCDQ, POS, ABC, and XYZ scales to haphazard collections of teachers and administrators" (p. 2). By the late 1960s, some obvious limitations of the closed-system paradigm were noted. Haller (1968) commented on the dysfunctions of a closed organizational theory "unable to draw the linkages between the educational institution and other institutions in the wider society" (p. 73). Indeed, Campbell (1972) in a retrospective view, took account of an expanding recognition of the school as part of the social fabric of society, thus subject to most of the challenges made of that society. Others (Wirt, 1976) documented the extent to which the integration of schools into a turbulent social fabric affected the focus of administrative authority. A view of the school as in touch with and affected by external social forces, coupled with the continuing professionalization of

research and the accompanying belief that theory-based knowledge could indeed lead to a science of educational administration, expanded the focus of theory away from the closed system to a more open-system perspective.

Scott (1981) notes that the early 1960s marked the transcendence of organizational theory from a closed- to an open-system perspective. Following a normal lag for the open-system perspective to affect research in educational administration, there appeared a broadening of the focus of educational administration to include such concerns as organizational and environmental interactions, the permeability of organizational boundaries, and an accounting of organizational uncertainty. Two substantive directions emerged from such a shift in theoretical focus. The first of these was the gradual emergence and indeed eventual dominance of system-oriented, loose-structuring models of educational organizations. Initially discussed by Bidwell (1965), the growing focus on educational organizations as organized anarchies with "garbage can" modalities of decision-making (Cohen, March, & Olsen, 1972), as loosely coupled systems (Weick, 1976), as based on contingency theory (Hanson, 1979), and as myth and symbol (Meyer & Rowan, 1977) led to a much more dynamic, contextual, and scholastic view of organizational life. The open-system model came to be the accepted model for viewing the somewhat indeterminate processes endemic to educational organizations.

A second thrust, which paralleled the gradual deemphasis of the rational or closed-system approach to organizations, was the increased focus on the manner in which explicit courses of action were formulated, chosen, and implemented within educational institutions. This line of inquiry and discourse, which came to be known as policy analysis or policy research, focused more broadly on the intersection between organizational, political, and economic sectors as they come together in the process by which educational choices are made and implemented. Although policy analysis focuses particularly on goal attainment (Boyd & Crowson, 1981) and thus looks like a continuation of the rational model, it really searches for "patterned, interrelated action extended over time, enveloping many decisions" (Yeakey, 1983, p. 275). This very focus has permitted and encouraged expansion of educational administration into areas minimally considered in the early days of the Theory Movement (Boyd, 1978; Elmore, 1978; Lieberman & McLaughlin, 1982; Peterson, 1976).

Educational administration, then, through the decades of the 1960s and 1970s found it necessary to cast a much wider net to account for the complexities of its enterprise. Once content and preoccupied with the management of schools, the field experienced strong pressure to expand its concern for the processes of education more broadly conceived. The benefits of such an expanded view included a much more inclusive range of the factors influencing education; the costs were greater fragmentation of inquiry and a movement away from the unifying, hypothetico-deductive theories so highly valued in the early days of the Theory Movement.

Earlier the basic rationality of science as an objective process by which to examine educational processes had rarely been challenged. The search for universal theories that could be empirically verified and falsified remained intact, albeit with a much greater consideration of the complexities of the phenomena. Just as the foreground of democratic leadership provided a smooth transition into the early Theory Movement and its sociopsychological approach, so did the emerging conception of schools as instruments of somewhat rational social policy find accommodation with the open-system approach and the growing impetus of policy research. Although uncertainties and ambiguities did surface in the later iterations of the Theory Movement, the movement was able to maintain what many have argued is the dominant paradigm in the social and behavioral sciences, that of logical positivism (Culbertson, 1981; Griffiths, 1983).

The early 1970s, however, witnessed a departure from logical positivism and began what Gibson (1979) calls a period of "critical consciousness." The departure started with Greenfield's (1975, 1986) contention that the Theory Movement was now a Procrustean bed into which "the facts" were forced. Greenfield claimed that researchers had become the victims of the very theoretical models that existed for purposes of explanation. His work, based in part on the pioneering studies by thinkers such as Feyerabend (1975), Kuhn (1962), and Phillips (1973), proposed that theory does not really provide for falsification because "if findings are inconsistent with the theory, we are likely to disbelieve them or search for other data that fit better with the theory" (Greenfield, 1979a, p. 170). Eschewing the search for overarching theories in educational administration that explain or predict, Greenfield argued that research in educational administration should encourage diversity and conflict and resist preoccupation with the impossible.

At the basis of Greenfield's argument is a fundamental issue of methodology. Simply put, it is how we come to "know," and the influences of that process on the research act. Greenfield (1979b) argues that "the interpretation of human experience is the bedrock upon which human life is built and upon which organizational theory should stand" (p. 97). Critical in this

process is the recognition that the researcher carries certain interpretations of organizational life into researching. These conceptions are translated into basic research acts such as how problems are defined, what constitute data, and what data mean. As Kaplan (1964) has said, reality for any form of research consists not only of the "act meanings," or meanings held by organizational participants but also of "action meanings," or meanings that are interpreted by the researcher. Understanding such action meanings signifies that the intellectual artifacts called organizational theories must be understood in part as ideologies of the researcher attempting to account for reality.

Reactions to Greenfield's work in educational administration created a long and sometimes heated debate (Griffiths, 1977, 1979, 1983; Hills, 1980; Willower, 1979a, 1979b, 1983). Analysis of issues in the debate has been the subject of further research (Herda, 1978) and extension (Bates, 1980; Foster, 1980). Without exploring in depth the issues of the exchange, it seems safe to say that the period from 1970 to the mid-1980s has witnessed serious challenge to the legitimacy of much research in educational administration. A few, but visible, researchers have raised new and probing questions, leading to reexamination of the very methodology that has come to dominate the field. Indeed, even adherents of the dominant methodology, logical positivism, have concluded that many of the epistemological premises of most past research in educational administration sorely need review (Griffiths, 1979). What role has fieldwork in educational administration played in the reexamination process?

THE EMERGENCE OF FIELDWORK IN EDUCATIONAL ADMINISTRATION

Fieldwork in educational administration has emerged through a series of developmental stages since the early 1950s. From a period of relative marginality and focus on community studies in the years immediately after World War II, the approach was swept into the "theory" paradigms discussed earlier. Fieldwork recently has become so well accepted that Rist (1980) characterizes it as a "movement," the application of which sometimes is uncritical and inappropriate. As noted in this section, the transformation of fieldwork in the study of educational administration has paralleled changes in the field of educational administration itself.

Early application of fieldwork in education focused primarily on crosscultural studies that examined cultural transmission in mostly primitive societies. By the 1940s, anthropologists has begun to apply anthropological concepts to examine specific aspects of education in contemporary Western societies. Teacher role (Mead, 1942; Redfield, 1945) and education within a cultural context (Herskovits, 1943; Opler, 1947) were areas frequently addressed. Yet such applications were infrequent and rarely consisted of focused empirical studies of educational settings. Rather, they consisted of minor and spotty analyses of a noncumulative nature.

The earliest focused examination of educational phenomena in modern society to utilize the approach of fieldwork appeared in the now classic in-depth studies of Muncie, Indiana (Lynd & Lynd, 1929, 1937). Included in this work was a description of aspects of the "Middletown" (Muncie) school system and the manner in which it helped integrate and perpetuate the traditions and culture of the larger community. West's (1945) study of a small rural town also illustrated the integral role of the school in incorporating community mores. Although both of these studies documented the class and status hierarchies of the respective communities, neither seriously broke down the manner in which schools differentially served various clientele. Fieldwork, like education in general, was still conducted through the lens that viewed school as part of a democratic society.

The stance of consensus began to change in the postwar years. In reexamining the concept of democracy that it had fought 5 years to defend, the United States began to question the role of the school in a democratic society. Thus, the appearance of community studies critically questioning the role of schools in the perpetration of democracy was not, at least in retrospect, surprising. Both Hollingshead (1949) and Warner (1949), through their close fieldwork in Elmstown/Jonesville, demonstrated that schools did not serve all individuals equally but rather they continued many of the basic social inequities present in the community.

Fieldwork moved next to address issues located more within schools as social and formal organizations. Based to some extent on Waller's (1932) work, researchers took the lead in focusing on the internal dynamics of role enactment within schools as social and formal organizations. Although Waller did not collect empirical data in the contemporary sense, he used his experiences within schools to produce a still remarkable set of observations. Arriving at a conflict analysis of schools, Waller concluded that the relationship between teachers and administrators on one side and students on the other was a somewhat uneasy truce. He also recognized that the processes and outcomes of teaching and administration were conditioned to some extent by the influences of the student culture and community expectations for schooling.

Without raising the matter explicitly, Waller's

work was, in reality, a study of role theory within schools. Subsequent fieldwork studies carried forth this theme and explored it in greater detail. Student roles were the focus of Gordon's (1957) study of peer groups in the high school. Although not utilizing fieldwork methods, Coleman's (1961) study validated much of Gordon's report. Cusick's (1973) later study of student life adopted a much more dynamic approach, examining student roles from an interactionist perspective.

Teacher and administrator roles were also the subject of some of the emerging studies of life inside schools. Boyan (1951), Congreve (1957), and Iannaccone (1958) all examined role behavior of administrators and teachers, utilizing the perspective of the school as a social organization. Departing from the issues first identified by Waller (1932), Spindler (1963, p. 238) discussed the principal's role as that of balancing "the value conflicts that swirl around his position and the activity of the institution that he administers." In his ethnography of a principal, Wolcott (1973) further developed Spindler's theme and noted the many members of the principal's role set who shaped the principal's role behavior. Teachers' roles have been similarly examined. Earliest among these studies was the work by Becker (1951, 1953) and Gordon (1955), both of whom identified the manner in which the teacher's role is defined within the authority system of the school as a bureaucracy. Focusing on the school as a "small, self-contained system of social control," Becker (1953) noted the systems of mutual influence and control that block outsiders from exercising sufficient authority over the institution's operation. Gordon's work illustrates the tendencies toward role strain as teachers attempt to manage multiple expectations.

The focus on role analysis in schools, utilizing fieldwork as a means of describing the complexities of status and role in schools, has continued (McPherson, 1972; Sieber & Wilder, 1967; Warren, 1973; Wilson, 1962; Woods, 1979). The use of role theory as an important component of fieldwork illustrates clearly the manner in which fieldwork was affected by and incorporated major theoretical systems that were prevalent in the field of educational administration in general. Immegart (1977) has pointed out the shift in focus in administration away from task areas such as staff personnel, finance, curriculum and instruction, and general administration to studies of administrative organization—role, behavior, position, and effectiveness. The major focus of fieldwork, then, can be seen to parallel the emerging developments in educational administration itself, moving the field increasingly toward the "scientific" study of administrative problems by using the generalized concepts of the social and behavioral sciences.

Fieldwork played a crucial central role in the

evolution of theory in educational administration because of its unique focus on discovery and on context and its emphasis on validity. Whereas the Theory Movement prompted the development of more "sophisticated" data analysis procedures, such as multivariate correlational procedures (Haller, 1968), fieldwork became instrumental in permitting more basic understandings of education and the administrative process. Scott's (1965) statement that "most of what we know today about organizations and the behavior of their members is known on the basis of field studies" (p. 261) speaks to the point. Indeed, the call for fieldwork became a cry whose sounds were increasingly heard in the crescendo of the Theory Movement. In a series of critical analyses, Halpin (1969, 1970) noted the atrophy of the Theory Movement scarcely 10 years after its optimistic beginning. Halpin commented that the promotion of theory had supplanted the generation and understanding of theory, so much so that administrative theory had become more of a slogan than a substantive field. In his usual refreshing style, Halpin characterized research in administration much like a Madison Avenue campaign—high on symbol but short on substance. His major conclusion focused on the need to concentrate more fully on basic issues—"the image of man and of human motivation that is derived from it" (Halpin, 1969, p. 14). Iannaccone (1973) echoed many of Halpin's concerns and called for a

> more modest, even plebian definition of science than we claimed to have used...We must walk before we try to run. Above all, we must so define our work that it will allow our research subject (and subjects) to teach us something. The task ahead requires that we break from the traditional research methods which have dominated the research ideology of schools of education and stop pretending that every dissertation is a critical experiment. It is time for observing the phenomena of educational administration and for letting these influence our definition of work. (p. 62)

Such statements remarkably paralleled the burgeoning of fieldwork in educational administration in the decade of the 1970s. Indeed, there even developed a large-scale attempt to "apply" fieldwork to the field of evaluation research, an application unheard of a decade earlier (Fetterman, 1984; Herriott, 1977; Patton, 1980), that produced its own set of new issues (Burns, 1975; Clinton, 1975; Everhart, 1975; Mulhauser, 1974; Wacaster & Firestone, 1978). This "movement" (Rist, 1980) led to an attempt to define what constituted the "proper" role of fieldwork in examining educational phenomena.

The propriety of fieldwork in education was first addressed by Erickson (1973) and Wolcott (1975). Each in his own way attempted to address the limits and scope of ethnographic research. Erickson (1973), acknowledging the importance of "disciplined subjectivity" in ferreting out important relations in educational practice, noted that all fieldwork, because it cannot report on everything, because it selectively reports some information while leaving out others, tends toward producing a caricature "drawn from a particular point of view and which communicates that point of view relentlessly" (p. 14). This caricature-producing trend, according to Erickson, is not something to be eliminated; indeed, it cannot be eliminated from any research, fieldwork or otherwise. Instead, it must be dealt with frontally, by raising epistemological questions as to the context within which the research is conducted, including the nature of how the overall theme or story line is selected, decisions as to what data are sought, included, and excluded from the study, and the overall rationale for the selection process.

Wolcott tackled the issue of the proper use of fieldwork from a somewhat different perspective. Concerned that the label of "ethnography" has been inappropriately applied to too wide a range of qualitative research in education, Wolcott established four main "criteria" for ethnographic research in schools. These four criteria—appropriateness of the problem, appropriateness of the ethnographer, appropriateness of the research climate, and appropriateness of expectations for the complete product—focus essentially on the establishment of bench marks to help determine when or under what conditions a study can be said to be "ethnographic." Through these four criteria, Wolcott attempted to resolve the often present tensions between "pure" ethnography as conducted by academic anthropologists, for example, and educational ethnography, which oftentimes does not meet the several tests of appropriateness.

The articles by Erickson (1973) and Wolcott (1975) became the forerunners of other statements that moved the discussion of fieldwork from simple "doing it," as had been the case earlier, to the more general reflective question, "What is it we are doing?" (Cassell, 1978; Hymes, 1982; Khleif, 1974; Magoon, 1977; Rist, 1975; Wilson, 1977). As with the Theory Movement in general, the application of fieldwork techniques and the ways to do fieldwork engendered a rash of articles and textbooks specifically appropriate to education (Bogdan & Bicklen, 1982; Dobbert, 1982; Lutz & Iannaccone, 1969; Spindler, 1982). With few exceptions, however, the fundamental nature of the methodology involved in paradigms of holistic, theory-generating research was not examined, and issues about the knowledge generated by fieldwork, while admittedly heavily influenced by the personal and social context of the fieldworker and the factors within that context, were passed over. In the halcyon days of fieldwork, as in the days when theory promised much, ethnography also promised much but left largely unexamined basic epistemological questions.

Fieldwork and its role in scientific discovery had emerged as one solution to diminished faith in the standard paradigm of social scientific research. Yet few addressed the fact that the assumptions of fieldwork too require reflective and critical examination. Initial examination of this sort had started in sociology (Gouldner, 1970) and anthropology (Hymes, 1972; Jarvie, 1975; Murphy, 1971; Salamone, 1979), the disciplines usually associated with fieldwork methodology. Yet educators seemed more interested in doing fieldwork or establishing criteria for doing acceptable fieldwork (usually meaning conformity with some disciplinary-based criteria) than in challenging basic epistemologies of fieldwork. Questions focusing on how the fieldworker "selects" data for observation, why the fieldworker selects those data to classify knowledge, and the factors entering into and assumptions of various "explanatory" paradigms were rarely addressed, except in passing (Erickson, 1973). Rules of evidence, then, the essence of the study of epistemology, remained assumed rather than examined, leaving Erickson (1973) to say that "the positivists have a point. Although I may object to their particular rules of evidence, I am forced to admit the general principle that some rules of evidence are necessary" (p. 14).

Raising such issues requires contact with the philosophy of science and the sociology of knowledge (Bredo & Feinberg, 1982). As such, the sociology of knowledge permits examination of the extent to which knowledge is socially bound and influenced (Blum, 1970; Burtt, 1924; Cole & Cole, 1973; Kuhn, 1962; Mahoney, 1976; Mulkay, 1979; Rose & Rose, 1976). Rather than viewing science as the product of the linear development of increasingly precise and sophisticated forms of "objective" measures, the sociology of knowledge backs the research act squarely into the researcher's court and examines why the researcher asks the questions asked and how data are constituted within the assumptions of given paradigms. The sociology of knowledge calls for examination not only of act meanings but of the role of action meanings as part of the constitution of act meanings.

In what has been called a period of "critical consciousness," few have examined fieldwork from the perspective of sociology of knowledge or of philosophy of science. An exception is the work of Greenfield (1979a), who first raised concerns about how conclusions about social reality are very much a function of how we see the world. He suggests that quantitative and quasiexperimental methodologies are particularly susceptible to an absence of reflexivity but does not mention whether qualitative research may have similar problems. In another article (Greenfield, 1979b), he notes that the controlled, "highly empirical study is not the only road to truth about organizations" (p. 105) and suggests that observing and listening may be better alternatives.

However valuable the alternative offered by Greenfield and however much the need for more studies done "firsthand," the questions of what to observe, how to interpret, and what influences those choices go begging. What is the response to Murphy's (1971) assertion that fieldwork is equally vulnerable to a need for reflexivity because

the mind selects only certain characteristics of phenomena as significant; it finds cultural meaning in only a segment of reality; it falsifies the world, at the very least, by omission. Culture, then, turns upon the mind and perpetuates the illusion. (p. 239)

These are complex questions, somewhat beyond the present scope. Not beyond that scope, however, is the fact that fieldwork has come to be seen as the answer to the epistemological dilemmas of positivism rather than just another variation of it. How so is partially addressed in a little-known paper by Popkewitz (1981). He argues that researchers are not just technicians, armed with data-collection "techniques" designed to "gather facts." They are also members of a culture and thus reflect certain hopes, beliefs, and commitments to that which is, has been, and is seen as possible. Much of what passes as "social theorizing," then, can be seen as the expression of an attempt to interpret the life one lives within a framework that "makes sense" of contradictions, experiences, and mysteries. Rather than consisting of a pool of objective "facts," much of social research "can be considered the creation of a symbolic universe to resolve problems of institutional legitimacy" (Popkewitz, 1981, p. 163). Cohen & Garet (1975) and Lindblom and Cohen (1979) address the same mode of analysis.

The next essential question addresses reasons for the use of fieldwork, especially during the heyday of the Theory Movement. Equally interesting is why fieldwork traveled into other areas, such as evaluation (Patton, 1980; Willis, 1978). Popkewitz argues that the rise of fieldwork in any discipline, but especially education, can be seen as part and parcel of expressed hopes to find a new social order in face of the contradictions between generally liberal ideals and the realities of institutional life indicating that such ideals are not being realized. Especially present in the analyses growing out of fieldwork is an emphasis on symbolic and geographical community at a time when people are feeling threatened, alienated, and estranged. Field studies also focus on the integration of the individual into groups' normative structures, and often emphasize the relativity of a group's normative structures—all during a time when conformity to mass culture appears on the ascendancy. Finally, field studies often demonstrate the flexibility and autonomy available to individuals within organizations as they "negotiate" mutually satisfying roles and rules. Through such a focus, the efficacy of the individual appears stronger in the face of the increasing power of formal organizations.

Fieldwork then is at a significant juncture in educational administration. Once seen to be a form of primitive research, it has become openly and somewhat uncritically accepted. Only recently have questions been raised about the origins of the knowledge and conclusions that fieldwork generates. The methodological issues of fieldwork, then, are closely tied to matters of social context, as illustrated by the treatment in the next section of fieldwork in the area of educational administration and policy.

THE "REALITY" OF FIELDWORK IN EDUCATIONAL ADMINISTRATION

It is important to understand how fieldwork has contributed to our comprehension of the nature of administrative work and the manner in which that work is scientifically "known." Until recently, most research in educational administration was based on cross-sectional studies of attributes of administrators and correlates of those attributes. Instruments such as the LBDQ or the Minnesota Multi Phasic Inventory (MMPI) were used to tie traits of individuals to certain outcomes within schools, these outcomes having been deemed to be important and assumed to be necessary outcomes for schools to produce. Fine-grained studies of the processes of schooling and the role of administration and policy making as part of that process were and continue to be somewhat sparse.

The studies reviewed here include selected works on the involvement of or connection with the process of schooling by administrators and on the making or implementing of educational policy. (For catalogues of relevant studies, see Smith, 1978, and Wilcox, 1982.) A group of studies focuses on the manner in which administrative work becomes structured through schools' day-to-day routines. The second group of studies addresses the process of change in educational organizations and the role of administrative and policy decisions in the change process. The final group of studies addresses schooling as part of the larger sociopolitical context. Review of the material in all three sections illustrates what fieldwork says about administrative work and how the methodology of fieldwork influences the selection and interpretation of reported data.

The Structuring of Administrative Work

One of the recurrent problems with early fieldwork was its attention to attributes of school structures (rules, norms, statutes, networks of power and influence), with little attention to how those structures were formed, adapted, and changed over time. Emerging, however, from earlier sociological studies in ethnomethodology (Garfinkel, 1967), fieldwork focused increasingly on face-to-face interactions between people and the way those interactions "built" the very structures that earlier fieldwork had treated as static and enduring. Variously labeled as microethnography (Erickson, 1975; McDermott, 1976; Smith & Geoffrey, 1968) or constitutive ethnography (Mehan, 1979; Mehan & Wood, 1975), these studies, in different ways, centered on cumulative activities that resulted in school structures.

It is useful first to examine a study of this microethnographic genre that does not focus on administrative roles per se but that does examine a particular administrative function, that of "gatekeeping." Erickson (1976) and Erickson and Schultz (1982) claim that gatekeeping, or the process of making decisions pertinent to access to institutional resources, plays a key role in the normal life of modern organizations. Social-service agencies, medical organizations, the legal network, and schools all are involved to a great extent in the diagnosis of issues and the matching of client needs to institutional resources. Erickson and Schultz (1982) focused on one such critical gatekeeping interface, that of the junior college counselor and students.

In some ways, this study is an extension of that by Cicourel and Kitsuse (1963), who studied the manner in which high school counselors made decisions about student placement and career possibilities based on their interpretation of student background data. Erickson and Schultz go further than Cicourel and Kitsuse, however, by focusing in depth on the detail of face-to-face interactions between counselors and clients. The depth of the investigation was made possible through the analysis of video and audio tapes of counseling interactions with 25 students. The investigators' analysis of these encounters serves as the backbone of the study.

The details of techniques are less appropriate here than clear understanding of methodology, or the assumptions and consequences of a set of methods used to "explain" or describe social reality. Erickson and Schultz (1982) focus in depth on the nature of discourse as inherent to the counselor-client definition of the situation. A key to understanding this discourse is the notion of "performed social identity."

Performed social identity is the manner in which identity is constituted through face-to-face encounters. When college counselor and student meet in a formal encounter, such as a counseling session, each acts in a manner that forms for the self and other member of the dyad a social identity that becomes a basis on which the encounter is carried out. Thus,

> the student's ways of speaking and ways of listening—of showing interest in, understanding of, and commitment to the interview as it is happening—are communicative means of making an impression on the counselor...the counselor's ways of speaking and ways of listening also make an impression on the student, and so their impressions of and reactions to one another are reflexively influenced—jointly produced. (Erickson & Schultz, 1982, p. 21)

In this process, it is incumbent on the student to perform "well" during the interview. If the student establishes a "bad record," such as through perceived inattention, improper responses, or certain speech patterns, then the counselor in his or her gatekeeping capacity can use the information to compromise the student's future success. So the encounter combines elements of the unofficial record of student-counselor interactions together with the official institutional record of the student's social identity as indicated by the cumulative record.

How did these authors "know" what they came to describe? Partly they did so through a set of assumptions that constituted "data" for subsequent analysis. First, the field research in the study assumed the need for complementary verbal and nonverbal channels of information to gain an assessment of the "full performance on the basis of which people make sense, reading of the meanings of sentences and intonation patterns in the context of facial expressions, of gesture and posture in the context of speech" (Erickson & Schultz, 1982, p. 50). For this reason then, video and audio tapes of counseling sessions constituted the major technique for collecting data. Erickson and Schultz assumed that data from each of these "channels" (video and audio) required examination in relation to each other.

Second, Erickson and Schultz assumed that data existed within a temporal framework because "the relationship of communication events in and across time form part of the complete context of the social occasion" (p. 51). In this manner, then, communication across a common timeframe served as the basis for crossreferencing events from both verbal and nonverbal channels.

Third, the authors assumed that the complexity of the speech encounter required assessment of both act meanings and action meanings. That is to say, accounts needed to consider both the range and variation of behaviors across encounters as well as the locally situated meanings of what counselors and student do in encounters. For this reason the research developed strategies for constructing from the record observer-derived categories of events, and, by commenting on the same records, video and audio participants were given an opportunity to attribute meaning to the events on the record.

Embedded in this microethnographic account of communication is the assumption that analysis of event structures provides, in miniature, a holistic account of social and cultural factors often examined within larger macro units of analysis (groups, communities, cultures). Cultural and social factors at work in the larger society present themselves within specific encounters, such as counselor-student encounters. What such microethnographic approaches permit is a more precise accounting of rules of evidence. Rather than saying, as in most ethnographic studies, that we "know" because the fieldworker was there and reports through observations, assertions of what is known are grounded in more precise and public evidence.

In so examining gatekeeping, Erickson and Shultz (1982) were able to present evidence that the manner in which the counselor and student established co-membership through social interaction could potentially influence the advice that the counselor gave to different students. Much of this advice was along lines of race and class, thus documenting the constitutive process by which social categories were created and maintained by all parties in the interaction. Similar methodological assumptions have been addressed in other studies of speech in schools, particularly among administrators.

Varenne (1978, 1983) has taken a somewhat different approach to the microethnography of administrative work. Varenne assumes, as do Erickson and Shultz, that language has the power to "constitute or to signify an intelligible social world" (1978, p. 637). However, rather than assuming a direct relationship between objective social reality and its manifestation in speech, Varenne raises the question of whether language also is used to hide and distort social reality. In other words, the structure of language may also play a critical role in the constitutive process by which myths are made.

Varenne goes about his business by analyzing texts and interpretations of texts between a principal and teachers in a public school. Some of these texts were public (memorandums from principals to teachers) and some were private (such as interpretations of administrator speech by teachers). These texts, especially in terms of "pronominal" analysis, reveal that different pronouns in use have different consequences as to their effect on the relevance of the text. That is to say, pronouns can be personal (*I* or *you*, John) or generic (*we*, a teacher), and their use in these forms serves different functions of inclusion and exclusion. It is not that any one of these functions is objective or subjective, "real" or illusory. Rather, speech patterns as used by administrators and teachers are "constructed around a topic of interest at the moment, a topic that is defined on the basis of some partial activity of the participants" (Varenne, 1978, p. 647).

Varenne's (1978, 1983) work focuses largely on action meanings, or the researcher's interpretation of participant meanings. Yet it is one thing to note that speakers shift rhetorical modes to match various boundaries within the school organization; it is another to assess the motivation to shift these rhetorical modes. Varenne admits to the limitations of his analysis, one bounded by a cultural model that uses as rules of evidence the analysis of outcomes more than the antecedents to outcomes. His model of cultural analysis, then, has some "real" and obvious assumptions built into it.

Another investigation of language and the nature of administrative work is reported by Gronn (1983, 1984). His study, based on "samples of participants' talk," was designed to investigate how principals and teachers chose their words and how this action seemed warranted by context. To collect these data, the author attached a radiomicrophone to the lapel of an Australian primary school principal and recorded his interactions with teachers over a 2-day period. Subsequently typed transcripts permitted an analysis of "talk as control" and allowed a clearer understanding of how and under what circumstances the principal and teachers, through face-to-face interaction, engage in such controlling behavior. While supporting previous studies of administration revealing that talk is the work of administration (Martin & Willower, 1981; Mintzberg, 1973; Willis, 1980), the study moves beyond the earlier works by documenting how talk constitutively *creates* the nature of administrative work.

Like Varenne's study, however, Gronn's work (1983, 1984) relies heavily on his own interpretation of meaning. He chronicles the nature of administrative work through talk and provides an analysis of talk through a model that focuses on talk as control. Yet, as Gronn admits, such a model does not tell what participants mean by their utterances, and this is one of the limitations of such a study.

Gronn's study has methodological implications because of its implicit as well as explicit critique of Mintzberg-type studies that rely on structured observation of predefined categories. In an earlier article, Gronn (1982) had reviewed studies of administrative work done under the Mintzberg banner and found them wanting because of their assumption of a set of standardized tasks to be analyzed. These tasks and the focus on them tend to center on regularity rather than on the constitutive process by which administrative tasks are created and influenced contextually and phenomenologically. Gronn's critique was followed by one by Willower (1983), who called into question the faith Gronn places in "thick description" and his unremitting lack of faith in operationalism. In discussing the analogy of eye winking as an "operation" (as seen by possibilitists) and as a parody (as seen by those advocating thick description), Willower (1983) notes, "Parody is the concept that gives meaning to the observation, and both operationalism and the canons of careful inquiry enjoin the observer to indicate what evoked the parody label" (p. 45).

Willower's call for careful documentation of observer-based labels is relevant, and it points to a central issue. The studies discussed here demonstrate how issues of methodology illustrate both the strengths and weaknesses of the microethnographic approach (Willis, 1980). The strengths lie in the attention to the constitutive process by which social interaction in schools produces shared or divergent cultures. The differences in linguistic patterns between counselors and students and between principals and teachers represent, to some extent, various personal, organizational, and in some cases sociocultural factors that pattern face-to-face interaction. Yet the questions microethnographers choose to address can influence considerably the evidence presented. Varenne (1978, 1983) and Gronn (1983, 1984), for example, rely heavily on interpretations of actions rather than the meaning of actions to the actors themselves. The burden of analysis rests, then, on the interpretive framework that the ethnographer brings to the data. Erickson and Schultz (1982) follow somewhat the same pattern, except that after providing participants an opportunity to reflect on their actions, the researchers use these reflections as an added dimension of the microethnography itself, thus permitting greater triangulation between act meanings and action meanings.

Microethnographic studies share other limitations as well (Ogbu, 1981). Often, they are so specific and focused that they do not examine the microenvironment in comparison to contextual environments. They assume the existence of speech communities as small societies. Similarly, they minimize contextual factors that influence and in many cases actually generate the very process ongoing within a speech community. Finally, because of their intense focus on epiphenomena, they place a premium on personal and interpersonal variables as vehicles for manipulation and ignore to a considerable extent larger structural factors without which personal change cannot be sustained. Some of these same issues also apply to studies of the dynamics of leadership and organized change.

The Making of Organizational Change

Educational change is a domain that has attracted a great deal of fieldwork. Although Wolcott (1973) indicates that the focus on change in schools may be misplaced because schools seem more prone toward continuity than change, the ethos about change predominates, and fieldwork has frequently been used to document how educational change does (or doesn't) happen.

Giacquinta (1973) notes that the literature on organizational change, oftentimes unclear and contradictory, still agrees on one fundamental premise: that "successful" organizational change in schools proceeds in three basic stages—initiation, implementation, and incorporation. To the extent this is the case, change can best be viewed as a process that fieldwork has been especially valuable for enlightening. The studies identified below emphasize the developmental aspects of change and serve to raise methodological concerns pertinent to the study of change.

The four studies were chosen for specified purposes. Although not all of them offer explicit discussions of method and methodology, they do contain sufficient discussion of methodological concerns to permit useful analysis thereof. A second criterion that the studies meet is variation in the assumptions about the process of change and in conclusions on the constituted knowledge about change. Finally, the essential unit of analysis in the studies was largely organizational, rather than involving either smaller subunits or larger units such as institutions. The analysis was not restricted to the organizational level, but the organization itself was still the primary unit of analysis. The criteria used to select the studies permitted examination of the process of implementing change and its relation to the making of educational policy (Lipsky, 1980).

Gold and Miles (1981) studied the creation of a new school—from the ground up. Their case study of a single, newly created elementary school focuses on the conflicts between the school and its surrounding community. A number of organizational phenomena are examined in this study, most specifically organizational structure and the relation of organizational change to the school's task environment. Covering in a parallel manner dimensions identified in Smith and Keith's (1971) sudy of organizational change, Gold and Miles focus on the attempts to create flexible, participative environments and some of the unintended consequences that arose out of those efforts.

Gold and Miles used rather standard models of fieldwork—participant observation, interviews, surveys, and document analysis. The role of the principal investigators was largely noninterventionist: that is, there was no attempt on the part of the fieldworkers to shape the direction of the project as it unfolded. Data were shared with participants at the termination of the study, and feedback from participants was used in subsequent analysis.

The study utilized a conflict model as the basis for analysis. The authors state early:

> At the core, the issue was whether educators or parents had the right to determine the sort of education the school would offer...There was a basic tension in Lincolnwood Acres between professional judgment and citizen participation in decision-making: the conflict was in many respects one between expertise and democracy as a basis for decision-making. (Gold & Miles, 1981, p. 5)

Indeed, the study centers on the processes whereby the open participative environment in which teachers, administrators, and parents were to make decisions jointly was altered within a bureaucratic arrangement fostered by teachers in order to provide greater professional autonomy.

The focus on professional versus client conflict over norms is well documented; the data presented correspond to the conclusions that the authors draw, most of which highlight "the fragility and strain" of a new organization "aggravated by conflicting perspectives on education that were held by various segments of the community" (Gold & Miles, 1981, p. 358). Still, the analysis raises some important issues of methodology. Why, for example, was the theme of conflict so pronounced in the study? Is it because it made "most sense"? If so, how was that decision made? Even a cursory analysis of the data indicates that a number of school leaders were, at least initially, idealistic and saw the future school in terms of a "vocal, world-changing and redeeming rhetoric" (p. 50) that never was adequately defined by school staff. Such rhetorical ambiguity is a common phenomenon in the practice of educational change and is very productive of slogans systems (Doyle & Everhart, 1980). Yet these issues were never systematically discussed, in part because the authors believed that such an explanation would have produced "an idealistic, not a realistic answer" (Gold & Miles, 1981, p. 67).

These comments revive the issue of choice of analytical frameworks. One way to examine an organization like that described by Gold and Miles is to focus on consensus, not as an outcome of competing normative systems but as an "ideological social order accepted by individuals or forced upon them" (Greenfield, 1979b, p. 101). Adoption of the latter perspective prompts asking why teachers hold to professional norms that may lead to conflict with the normative systems held by teachers' clients. This is not necessarily a better question than that asked by Gold and Miles, but it is a different question, which could lead to a different interpretation of the data. Why Gold and Miles might not have chosen to examine the other question can best be addressed after examining a second study on conflict and change.

Firestone (1980) describes his role as a fieldworker for 3 years in a rural school district where he was conducting research as part of the federally funded and nationwide Experimental Schools Program (ESP). Because the project was funded, and to some degree directed, by a federal agency, Firestone describes at some length the interorganizational relationships between the local school district and the agency. His work can fruitfully be examined within the context of companion pieces that address parallel aspects of the interorganizational dimensions of change (Doyle et al., 1976; Herriott & Gross, 1979; Sproull, Weiner, & Wolf, 1978).[1]

Firestone focuses upon four main issues. One centers on the rationality of project planning: that is, the extent to which planned change is considered to be an orderly process. A second issue concerns local resistance to change: specifically, the willingness of teachers to participate in the change process and the forms of resistance to change which developed. The third major issue is the role of federal agencies serving as a catalyst for change. A final focus is evaluation of the specific model of "comprehensive change" attempted in the ESP.

Like Gold and Miles (1981), Firestone's study fits the rubric of fieldwork. Firestone served for 3 years as an on-site researcher in the school district, attempting to integrate himself into the normal routine of district life. Indeed, as Everhart (1975) and others (Clinton, 1975; Wacaster & Firestone, 1978) have reported, the dilemmas of the fieldwork role in these projects were ever present and difficult to resolve. Firestone acknowledges this condition as he devotes large portions of his discussion of methodology to issues of the tensions in fieldwork.

The conclusions derived by Firestone (1980) are somewhat similar to those of Gold and Miles (1981). First, conflict is a pronounced theme, although the locus of conflict was much more broadly dispersed to include the federal agency sponsoring the project. The goals of the federal agency in this project, vague as they were, did not square with various district goals, as vague and multifaceted as they often were. In the absence of relative clarity of purpose, and in the presence of the traditional norms of autonomy granted local schools (vis-à-vis federal agencies) and teachers within schools (vis-à-vis district administrators) the resolution of conflicts was difficult.

Attempts to resolve conflict is a second area where the two studies overlap. Firestone (1980) concludes, for example, that "the administrative role is more conducive to the orchestration and facilitation of change than it is to the advocacy of specific reforms. Administrators simply lack the influence to mandate specific changes except within their own zones of authority" (p. 184). Similarly, Gold and Miles (1981) assert, "We continue to be dubious about the Great Women theory of leadership in this case. In short, we conclude that leadership behavior in new systems is important, but probably not central" (p. 357).

The fact that issues of leadership and management are important is not questioned here. The reasons why these issues were chosen for focus, however, is. Why is it that Firestone chose to examine conflict and authority structures as the main explanatory framework of the ESP project? Were these the "natural" (only) outcomes of the study, or were others equally plausible? How, for example, does one reconcile that the ESP allocated $55 million to "reform" public education in the face of conclusions from other and earlier research endeavors noting that major structural reforms in education are perceived by all parties as "too costly," a factor that heightens "the attractiveness of less costly reforms, or even of chasing after will-of-the-wisps." (Pincus, 1974, p. 124)

Attempts to answer the question about choice of explanatory framework returns the discussion to the issue of the extent to which epistemological and ontological presuppositions are made explicit and are examined (Salamone, 1979). While listed as the junior author, Miles for example came to the study of Lincolnwood Acres School from the sociopsychological perspective of organizational development (OD), itself predicated on an understanding of schools as social systems. Firestone follows a systems frame of reference as well, except that the "system" or unit of analysis includes an interorganizational network, not discussed at length by Gold and Miles. Certainly since the federal ESP was interested in the effects of federal sponsorship of educational change, there is no doubt that the federal role was a topic that the research effort could not ignore, just as the sociopsychological assumptions of OD indirectly inform the researcher what to examine and what to ignore. These matters of how research agendas are predicated in part by the political mission of change efforts are rarely addressed within the context of fieldwork "methods."

A work of a somewhat different genre (but one that still focuses on the topic of educational change) is that of Wolcott (1977). Wolcott addresses the matter of change gone astray and centers directly on the unintended consequences of a federally sponsored educational innovation. This particular educational change, a variation of a planned programming and budget system (PPBS), grew out of the infatuation with rational planning that swept business and government in the late 1960s and early 1970s. The university with which Wolcott was affiliated was awarded almost $1.5 million to develop a model planning system for use in education. Fortuitously, a small school district some 25 miles from the university, under the leadership of an ambitious superintendent, was also searching for management tools to help it more efficiently manage curriculum, finances, and goals. Each party stumbled on the other and an agreement to work together was struck. Unfortunately, however, the superintendent made the agreement without consulting teachers, and Wolcott's study chronicles the rather predictable results when such consultation is absent.

The study itself projects some interesting methodological issues. In the first place, while noting that he attempted to present an "objective account" of the development of what was called the SPECS project, in no way does Wolcott claim that he was dispassionate about the project. In a candid introduction entitled "Bias at Work: Proceed with Caution," Wolcott (1977) notes straightforwardly that his "personal sympathies and ethnographic attention" (p. 2) centered on those teachers in the school district who objected to the project. He also revealed that, in part due to his sympathies with the "underdogs" and because of his greater faith in basic research than applied research in education, colleagues in the university development team withheld important data from him. Thus Wolcott took on the job of understanding SPECS all the while carrying with him a host of situational and organizational conditions affecting the appropriateness of the data gathered. Unlike most ethnographic accounts, Wolcott's study is quite candid about these methodological realities.

A second methodological issue, less clear, is why Wolcott chose to analyze the development of the SPECS project in the manner he did. Wolcott outlines the concept of "moiety," or two parts of a whole, as a way of understanding the development of the project. The parts (teachers and technocrats) are meant to

illustrate that the educational subculture can really be defined by one's membership as either a teacher or a technocrat. Teachers' jobs are to teach students; technocrats' jobs are to manage students and the teachers who teach them. The membership in either group, then, generally led to differing world views about the appropriateness of one's own role as well as the role appropriateness of the members of the other groups. Such conditions in turn affected the manner in which teachers or technocrats responded to or became involved in educational change, such as that represented by SPECS.

But why the moiety concept? It is a concept rooted in the anthropological tradition, and Wolcott has said elsewhere (1975) that ethnography is appropriately the domain of the anthropologist. One might suspect, however, as did Pohland and Wood (1978), that the conceptual framework was imposed on the data. Indeed, Pohland and Wood question the extent to which the moiety framework really "fits" the data and suggest that organizational concepts such as organized anarchy (Cohen & March, 1974) might be more appropriate. Why Wolcott did not consult such literature is perhaps best summed up in his statement of how the framework to make sense of SPECS was derived: "I have sought diligently to anchor my analysis in the traditional anthropological literature and to develop it in rather traditional, even conservative fashion" (1977, p. 243).

If Wolcott adopted a conservative tradition, such was not the driving force behind Popkewitz, Tabachnick, and Wehlage (1982) in their study of individually guided education (IGE). These authors examined six schools that had adopted the IGE model developed at the university where the authors were also members. The study is somewhat parallel to Wolcott's in the sense that the authors were studying not only change efforts in the schools but also the role of the university as a catalyst for change.

The authors designated their six schools as technical, constructive, or illusory—labels referring to particular configurations of schoolwork, knowledge, and professional ideologies. In the technical schools, the implementation of the management system (a system of procedures for grouping students, developing curriculum, staffing, and diagnosing children's achievement) became an end in itself. Standardized knowledge was emphasized, and professional ideologies focused on the efficient processing of pupils within the taken-for-granted management system. "Illusory" schools used the structure of the IGE management system but implemented few of its processes. Since these schools were located in poor and minority communities where teachers saw pupils as deficient in basic skills, schooling was seen as a way to develop a "morally correct student population." The management system thus served as a means toward this end. One school was labeled "constructive" because of its emphasis on the development of interpersonal skills and the use of language. Teachers stressed the development of student autonomy and individual self-responsibility. This school was located in a professional, middle-class community, where skepticism, creativity, and exploration were valued.

The major conclusion drawn by Popkewitz and his colleagues is that teachers and students accepted the value of the specific adaptation each had made of the IGE model. Given the professional beliefs about the purposes of schooling and the communities that each school served, the schools adopted the IGE program in such a way that ongoing routines were not challenged. Rather, reform was a manner of organizing ritual to make schooling appear to be convincing, credible, and modern. In the process, the fundamental issues of reform remained unaddressed and were replaced with modifications stressing rationality and efficiency.

The study by Popkewitz et al. (1982) has some interesting parallels with Wolcott's (1977), and it provides a convenient capstone for understanding the other studies on change reviewed here. Particularly interesting are the methodological issues addressed by Popkewitz et al. (1982), which are not addressed by others, given the same research methods.

Since SPECS and IGE were both attempts to rationalize the educational process, it is fascinating to note the differences in analysis of similar projects. Wolcott chose a self-admitted conservative approach rooted in the traditional anthropological literature, while Popkewitz et al. adopted an approach much along the lines of critical theory outlined earlier.

These studies did not differ much because of differences in methods of collecting data. They differ because the authors used different assumptions and interests while conducting the research. These assumptions were based not only on the indisputable precepts of scientific theory, but they reflected as well the values and ideals held by the researchers as the study was carried out. All these authors hoped that their work would lead to a clearer understanding of educational change. Gold and Miles (1981), Firestone (1980), and Wolcott (1977) focus on how values and norms in the setting are transmitted through social processes and imply that understanding of these processes will lead to more realistic efforts at change. Popkewitz et al. (1982), on the other hand, link such definitions and interpretations to other "objective" conditions of society (class, ideology, the structure of schooling), thereby arguing that the choice and use of research categories must be situated within a social context.

Thus, they argue that "the rules for generating knowledge about reality also provide guidelines for determining what the appropriate operations are for transforming that reality. The languages of science contain thought, ideas, and values, as well as 'mere' descriptors" (Popkewitz, 1981, p. 20). The importance of this theme will receive further attention.

Administration, Organization, and Society

The two preceding sections on administrative work and educational change suggested how action meanings of the fieldworker play a fundamental role in the direction that the fieldwork takes. Since fieldwork is so dependent on the fieldworker as a tool (much as statistical inference serves as a tool for the experimentalist), the basic assumptions as to what "counts" as knowledge are important for understanding the uses and limitation of the tool. Some fieldwork on administration and organizational issues has strained to examine ongoing educational phenomena as part of a larger whole. In other instances, use of the critical paradigm has challenged reductionism by viewing educational phenomena as reflecting the dynamics and contradictions that incorporate culture and society within the everyday life of human actors. Focus on this issue is very much a concern of methodology:

> Anthropology constantly refuses to debate and acknowledge its philosophical, and especially, metaphysical, ingredients. The fundamental philosophical problem of anthropology...is how to reconcile man's apparent diversity with his real unity. This problem is a metaphysical problem, and the theories proposed to solve it give birth to concrete physical, biological, and sociological problems. (Jarvie, 1975, pp, 256–257)

The philosophical ingredients of administrative problems now receive special attention in a review of three studies that center on adolescent life in schools (Cusick, 1973; Everhart, 1983; Willis, 1977). This particular focus is not normally considered a part of the terrain of educational administration, yet some have argued that the outcomes of schooling "must be at the heart of the dialog of what constitutes administrative behavior" (Foster, 1980, p. 504). Others (Bates, 1980; Denhardt, 1981; Foster, 1983) have also argued that educational administration needs to examine critically the technical basis of bureaucratic life and its ideological underpinnings. Inquiry into student life permits just such an analysis.

One of the more widely known and accepted contemporary studies of high school adolescents is that by Cusick (1973), who examined peer cultures in one high school. Cusick's study was based on the assumption that students in schools did not exist as unrelated atoms but rather coalesced through shared perspectives as to their common identities forged within the formal organization of the school. Since coalitions of shared identities did exist, friendship groups became the basis of informal group membership in the school and the forms of meaning for adolescents. Cusick chronicles the process by which the athletes, the deviants, and the "power clique" came to construct differential meaning from school experiences, even though those experiences often were "objectively" similar for each group.

Cusick's approach to understanding adolescent behavior in schools is largely within a functionalist-interpretive theoretical model. The interpretive framework is based on the acceptance of a symbolic-interactionist understanding of social reality, which means, as Cusick (1973) states, "instead of attributing the student's behavior to their social class, individual psychology, age, homelife, or parental relations, we should rather examine the environment in which that behavior took place" (p. 205). Accordingly, Cusick found that students placed most of their energies into creating their own life space within the school, and the perspective they brought to and created within the school materially affected how social groups spent their time. Thus, few students discussed the academic side of life, although some did more so than others. Similarly athletics and extracurricular activities were variously engaged in, but with different purposes, all influenced by the perspective students had of themselves and their roles in the school.

Cusick argues that student perspectives were heavily influenced by the sociocultural characteristics of the school's formal organization, including subject matter specialization, batch processing of students, routinization of activity, and reliance by both teachers and students on rules and regulations. These characteristics in turn had both intended and unintended consequences. Such conditions, for example, narrowly regulated student choice and grouped students into relatively undifferentiated components, outcomes deemed to be functional in order for mass education to be operated efficiently. Yet these sociocultural characteristics produced unintended consequences as well, for they accelerated the existence of students as passive receptors of organizational routine, fragmented their educational experience, and accentuated the premium on minimal compliance with organizational routines. Thus, as students were denied participation in the formal routine of organizational life, they became involved instead through participation in group activities outside the formal instructional life of the school.

Cusick's conclusions fit into a functionalist perspective. He sees that the purposes of secondary schools are socialization, teaching of societal reward structures, and providing for societal continuity and integration. Given these imperatives, the sociocultural characteristics of the school and their intended consequences are functional. Students adapt to their place in the school and are prepared for a future in similar bureaucratic settings wherein they will be reasonably well integrated into dominant societal values and norms.

Cusick examines student life in relation to larger societal patterns and dynamics. His analysis focuses on systemic integration and is based on the assumption that social systems tend toward balance and homeostasis. Cusick does not make clear why he chose this particular approach. In fact, as noted later, other studies focusing on student perspectives and their social structural consequences have reached different conclusions.

My own research (Everhart, 1983) attempts to unravel some of the same complexities addressed by Cusick. I had long been intrigued by the unique dynamics of junior high schools and particularly the manner in which early adolescents "made sense" of the junior high experience. I had assumed that the junior high school served as an important bridge between the relative intimacy of the elementary school and the more rigid bureaucracy of the large and somewhat depersonalized high schools as described by Cusick. My objective was to gain more complete understanding of this bridging function.

Like Cusick, I focused on small peer groups of males, one the leadership cohort within the school, the other a more marginal group. My own research indicated that academic routines were not an important component of group membership and that students spent large portions of their time waiting for teachers to direct them what to do. It was during the periods of instructional inactivity that students took charge of the formal agenda by introducing their own consensually based agenda.

As in most fieldwork, the techniques I used did not differ significantly from other studies of similar phenomena. I resided in one junior high school for 1½ years, was "adopted" by small friendship groups of students, and attempted to participate in their lives throughout the period of my residency. Daily field notes chronicled observational routines and informal conversations; formalized interviews provided access to specific phenomena, permitting comparisons across student groups.

The methods of my work both paralleled and moved beyond those adopted by Cusick. While in the field, I had assumed that I could best understand schooling through documentation and examination of the interpretive framework that students created to "make sense" of their educational experiences. This general approach oriented me to focus on the student perspective of schooling. Initially statisfied to leave the study with such a general picture, subsequent analysis and early drafts convinced me of the inadequacy of my approach. I questioned the sources of student perspective being totally organizationally based and instead began to see that organizational routines were in fact sociocultural routines that affected students differently. I began to see that schooling could be viewed as a labor process wherein students sell their labor power to the school yet may, at the same time, withhold or give their labor based on the interpretive structure that the students had created. It was in this manner that the concept of "class culture" influenced the development of the interpretive structure.

My own study extended and examined adolescent social processes as part of the fabric of contemporary capitalism. Yet scholars such as Cusick have interpreted my study differently (Cusick, 1985). What set of assumptions then guided the manner in which action meaning guided the act meanings uncovered in my own work?

I failed to answer that question clearly in my discussion of methodology in my report (Everhart, 1983). With more time to consider these issues, however, I have become more fully convinced that the essence of human existence rests in the quest for meaning and that social structures that deny or excessively limit that search usually are not fulfilling to organizational participants. I also believe that meanings thought to be clearly understood often are not, and thus ideologies often rise and mask more fundamental meanings. Given these assumptions, it is understandable that I came to examine the connections between the interpretive frameworks of students and the manner in which such interpretations often clashed with the social assumptions, many of which are ideologically based, held by school officials about youths in junior high school.

Willis (1977) took a similar approach, although the route he chose differed considerably in terms of method. Willis's study focused on working-class youth in Britain who had arrived at the critical school-leaving age. He was especially interested in why students from laboring backgrounds seemed regularly and systematically to make the transition to laboring positions in the work world and the manner in which school life seemed to ease and facilitate that transition.

Willis elected to follow 12 working-class boys during their last year in school and for 6 months into their occupational placements after leaving school. He attended classes with the boys and spent time with them as each located himself in work placements. Also, he conducted lengthy interviews with their parents as well as with selected members of the school staff.

Willis "broke the ice," to a considerable extent, with this study. He focused on the "failure" of working-class students to reach beyond the limitations of their class culture and rejected the idea that culture is simply carried forward from one stage of life to another. He proposed that culture is more than a mental category imposed on the school from the outside. Rather,

> it comprises experiences, relationships, and ensembles of systematic types of relationships which not only set particular "choices" and "decisions" at particular times, but also structure, really and experientially, how these "choices" come about and are defined in the first place. (Willis, 1977, p. 1)

Culture, then, is made as individuals develop, transform, and ultimately reproduce aspects of their own past through everyday life. Culture is at the center of Willis's work, and he argues that the reproduction or continuity of working-class life from school to work is due not just to the failure of the school to transcend this connection but to the participation of the boys in the process of cultural and social reproduction. Yet this "self-damnation" did not exist on the part of the boys in the form of resignation to their plight as much as it represented a celebration of those very actions and meanings that separated students from the academic culture of the school and that methodically tracked the students into a life of manual labor.

Willis (1977) utilized an ethnographic approach to the study of student culture because its techniques "have a sensitivity to meanings and values as well as an ability to represent and interpret symbolic articulations, practices, and forms of cultural production" (p. 3). Noting the wide-ranging freedom in the manner in which action meanings are used to interpret act meanings, he argues that the ethnographic approach allows human agency to come into the analysis and enter the reader's experience. Willis admits also to the "supremely ex-post facto" presence of the ethnographic account and the need to overcome the conservative tendency of naturalistic inquiry. Taking an unabashedly political approach to the ethnographic method, Willis (1977) argues for the need to place theory in not only an empirical but a "relevant" paradigm as well. Thus, "the silences and enforced silences of the method are ultimately political silences and the secretion too of a capacity. It is a refusal as well as an enablement" (p. 194).

Willis's study concludes this section because it brings to the forefront an important methodological point touched on throughout: namely, that the ethno-graphic technique succeeds primarily because its methods do offer refusal as well as enablement, and the direction chosen very much depends on that which the fieldworker brings to and makes out of experience. Willis clearly brings to his study many of the under-standings of cultural studies—itself an outgrowth of Marxism. The descriptions and subsequent analysis of the boys' culture is heavily Marxist, and often it seems that Willis used theory to guide the collection of his data. Yet Cusick's study is no less problematical in this matter; and my own work, while less so in its inception, still viewed the examination of student cultures through an action meaning that both preceded and developed during the study. Yet all three studies reviewed here do decidedly and forcefully get to the core of the technical basis of bureaucratic life and the ideological understandings of that basis. They all sensitize the reader, through a critical paradigm, to radically dif-ferent ways to conceptualize the field of administration. More important, the studies permit examination of the issues of methodology in fieldwork and the degree to which the self as an instrument is such an important factor to consider.

CONCLUSIONS

A distinct epistemological perspective has guided the treatment in this chapter of fieldwork in educational administration. The central focus has been the analysis of fieldwork as a method by examining the various logics-in-use that guide the fieldwork process, in the interest of understanding how and in what manner those logics-in-use evolve into reconstructed logics. It is crucial to understand fieldwork as a human activity that takes place within a social context, and, accordingly, it is important to delve into the roots of how knowledge is produced. Discussions of research methods cannot eschew the epistemology of research itself and must take seriously the notion posed by Mills (1959) that "no social study that does not come back to the problems of biography, of history, and of their interactions with-in a society has completed its intellectual journey" (p. 6).

Focus on the social, biographical, and historical factors accompanying the expansion of fieldwork helps to clarify the evolution of fieldwork as a research method in educational administration. Review of the ascendence (and descendence) of the Theory Move-ment noted the transcendence of educational adminis-tration from a focus on educational organizations as closed systems to recognizing them as open systems, influenced more by complex, sometimes contradictory systematic patterns than by orderly, natural, rule-governed processes. Parallel to this change in views came an increased acceptance of fieldwork as a method to enlighten more fully the complexities of educational organizations.

Alongside these movements, a period of "critical consciousness" (Gibson, 1979) produced deeper interest in the question of how we know. The review here of several key studies in each of three areas of research—the structuring of administrative work, the making of organizational change, and the interaction between administration, organization, and social patterns—has kept that question to the fore. A few central tenets stand out.

First and foremost fieldwork, like all forms of social research, is heavily influenced by not only the questions asked but by the rules of evidence used to answer these questions. Research questions are in-fluenced by and must be seen within the historical and social context in which they are formulated. Thus the "answers" fieldwork produces are equally contextual-ized. For example, the Theory Movement emerged from a period in which the primary objective of educa-tional administration was to create efficiently organized schools. The 1950s and 1960s didn't alter the goal so much as the methods by which research, through rational, objective, and empirical techniques, could be viewed as one means to that end. The rejection of the view of educational organizations as closed systems and the further acceptance of a perspective of schools as more complex, indeterminate social systems paralleled the trend of viewing even dysfunctional phenomena as "natural," organic, and laced with meaning. The acceptance of fieldwork as an approach for understand-ing educational reality did not alter the search for validity as much as it shifted the manner in which validity was understood. Fieldwork was viewed as a more adequate approach by which to document the realities of administration and administrative behavior.

The assumptions of that approach are now under considerable scrutiny. Due in part to perspectives afforded by the sociology of knowledge and critical theory, there now exists more complete understanding that issues of validity and reliability are epistemological issues associated with methodology as well as measure-ment issues associated with method. The era of critical consciousness has risen and fallen on this issue, aptly illustrated by the Greenfield-Willower-Griffiths de-bates. Yet these debates also illustrate well the asser-tion advanced by Mulkay (1979) that "most scientific research is carried out in a context in which a whole series of assumptions are so firmly entrenched that their revision or refutation is virtually unthinkable (p. 41)." In other words, we know what we know based on the assumptions about what constitutes knowledge.

Why are such assumptons so rarely questioned

when investigators do and report fieldwork? Surely assumptions about social reality represent a complex interaction between the nature of the research problem and the conditions of the setting within which it takes place. Yet it appears more and more that, especially in fieldwork where so many research choices are made in the mind of the fieldworker and are hidden from outside scrutiny, fundamental sociopsychological processes of the research act itself are also at work. As Frankel (1963) notes, human action is fundamentally undergirded by a search for individual meaning and identity. People choose careers, spouses, places to live and, for scientists, their research questions and the manner of pursuing them in part as a way of coming to grips with who they are, where they have been, and where they wish to go. For social scientists, then (and this includes those who focus upon issues of educational administration and policy), the study of others is, to a great extent, studying themselves. They are not involved just in objectively assessing the actions and meanings of others but also in a therapeutic relationship with themselves in a total autobiography. The role of the self in the research process is a topic that has been taken up by others (Devereaux, 1967; Mitroff, 1974; Nash, 1963; Wintrob, 1969) and raises to the forefront the position that the assumptions held as firmly entrenched may be entrenched because to let them go is to let go of one's personal and social identity. It is no wonder then that scientific vocabularies are not rigid or uniformly held but rather exist as flexible vocabularies employed to negotiate meanings for the scientist and the scientist's colleagues (Mulkay, 1979).

What then is an appropriate role for fieldwork in educational administration? The information reviewed here reveals that preoccupation with fieldwork as a method or technique deflects examination of crucial issues of methodology that cry out for understanding. Yet the mere act of examining methodology runs the risk of stripping away from fieldwork (or any research approach) the claim for universal understanding that is a hallmark of distinction for any method, given the goals of science.

Perhaps what can best be realized is that the products of fieldwork in educational administration probably will not, nor can they, lead to significantly greater clarity of or convergence about administration and policy. Cohen and Garet (1975) and Lindbloom and Cohen (1979) concluded that most policy research has not led to much movement toward clarity or convergence. Furthermore, policy makers rarely report that research of any kind has materially affected the decisions they have reached. Thus, as much as scientists wish differently, the results of their work are seldom instrumental to the degree that they believe they should

be. In reality, then, fieldwork will never provide a more valid set of answers.

Fieldwork can, however, raise significant questions, and in different ways. Fieldwork's chief function is to attempt to structure the social world by assembling and examining the symbolic universes used to carry out educational life. It contributes to an ongoing discourse about social reality and, like all discourses, does not necessarily reduce disagreements but elaborates on them and sometimes generates new ones. Through the delicate interaction between act meanings and action meanings, fieldwork permits greater expansion of the discourse and helps move the deliberations to new stages.

Fieldwork in educational policy is uniquely suited to this task. It permits, indeed encourages, fieldworkers to include themselves as part of the discourse. Furthermore, it forces the researcher to take seriously the point noted by Devereaux (1967) in talking of the scientist, that "the real, though unacknowledged and unconscious, aim of his technical devices and methodological positions is therefore the interruption of the all-important dialogue of the unconscious" (p. 161). To the extent that fieldworkers are working out their own autobiography as part of that process, such a process plays a relevant role and should be acknowledged.

Dunkle (1972) has argued that the assumptions of science as descriptive, value free, and nomothetic do not fit well with the objectives of education, which are richly normative. Attempts to formulate, through research, how schools are managed and organized involves both science and, ultimately, a normative base. Fieldwork can contribute to such a discourse to the extent that fieldworkers understand and accept their legitimate role as scientists as well as individuals who, through their own search for meaning, put forth their own normative base. To do less is to deny the very qualities of human beings. Devereaux (1967) put it well:

An authentic behavioral science will come into being when its practitioners will realize that a realistic science of mankind can only be created by men most aware of their humanity precisely when they implement it most completely in their scientific work. (p. xx)

NOTE

[1] The author also worked on an ESP project.

REFERENCES

Agar, M. (1980). *The professional stranger: An informal introduction to ethnography.* New York: Academic Press.

Apple, M. W. (1979). *Ideology & curriculum.* Boston: Routledge & Kegan Paul.

Apple, M. W. (Ed.). (1982). *Cultural & economic reproduction in education: Essays on class, ideology and the state.* Boston: Routledge & Kegan Paul.

Arons, S. (1983). *Compelling belief: The culture of American schooling,* New York: McGraw-Hill.

Bates, R. J. (1980). Educational administration, the sociology of science, & the management of knowledge. *Educational Administration Quarterly, 16*(2), 1–20.

Becker, H. S. (1951). *Role and career problems of the Chicago public school teacher.* Unpublished doctoral dissertation, University of Chicago, Chicago.

Becker, H. S. (1953). The teacher in the authroity system of the public school. *Journal of Educational Sociology, 27*(3), 128–141.

Becker, H. S. (1970). *Sociological work: Method and substance.* Chicago: Aldine.

Bernstein, R. (1976). *The restructuring of social & political theory.* New York: Harcourt, Brace, Jovanovich.

Bidwell, C. (1965). The school as a formal organization. In J. G. March (Ed.), *Handbook of organizations* (pp. 972–1022). Chicago: Rand McNally.

Blum, A. (1970). The corpus of knowledge as a normative order. In J. C. McKinney & E. A. Tiryakian (Eds.), *Theoretical sociology: Perspectives and development* (pp. 319–336). New York: Appleton-Century-Crofts.

Blumer, H. (1969). *Symbolic interactionism.* Englewood Cliffs, NJ: Prentice-Hall.

Bogdan, R. C., & Bicklen, S. K. (1982). *Qualitative research for education: An introduction to theory and methods.* Boston: Allyn and Bacon.

Boyan, N. J. (1951). *A study of the formal and informal organization of a school faculty.* Unpublished doctoral dissertation, Harvard University, Cambridge, MA.

Boyan, N. J. (1969). Problems & issues of knowledge production and utilization. In T. Eidell & J. Kitchell (Eds.), *Knowledge production & utilization in educational administration* (pp. 21–36). Eugene, OR: University of Oregon Press.

Boyd, W. L. (1978). The study of educational policy & politics: Much ado about nothing? *Teachers College Record, 80*(2), 249–272.

Boyd, W., & Crowson, R. (1981). The changing conception & practice of public school administration. In D. Berliner (Ed.), *Review of research in education* (pp. 311–373). Washington, DC: American Educational Research Association.

Bredo, E., & Feinberg, W. (Eds.). (1982). *Knowledge & values in social and educational research.* Philadelphia: Temple University Press.

Burns, A. F. (1975). An anthropologist at work: Field perspectives on applied enthnography and an independent research firm. *Anthropology & Education Quarterly, 6*(4), 28–34.

Burtt, E. A. (1924). *The metaphysical foundations of modern science.* London: Routledge & Kegan Paul.

Button, H. (1966). Doctrines of administration: A brief history. *Educational Administration Quarterly, 2*(3), 216–224.

Campbell, R. (1972). Educational administration: A twenty-five year perspective. *Educational Administration Quarterly, 8*(2), 1–15.

Cassell, J. (1978). *A fieldwork manual for studying desegregated schools.* Washington, DC: National Institute of Education.

Charters, W. (1977). The future (and a bit of the past) of research & theory. In L. Cunningham, W. Hack, & R. Nystrand (Ed.), *Educational administration: The developing decades* (pp. 362–375). Berkeley, CA: McCutchan.

Charters, W. W. (1978, April). *A critical review of Erickson's readings in educational organization & administration.* Paper presented at the Annual Meeting of the American Educational Research Association, Toronto, Canada.

Cicourel, A., & Kitsuse, J. (1963). *The educational decision makers.* Indianapolis, IN: Bobbs-Merrill.

Clinton, C. A. (1975). The anthropologist as hired hand. *Human Organization, 34*(2), 197–204.

Cohen, D. K., & Garet, M. S. (1975). Reforming educational policy with applied social research. *Harvard Educational Review, 45*(1), 17–43.

Cohen, M. D., & March, J. G. (1974). *Leadership & ambiguity: The American college president.* New York: McGraw-Hill.

Cohen, M. D., March, J. G., & Olsen, J. P. (1972). A garbage can model of organizational choice. *Administrative Science Quarterly, 17*(1), 1–25.

Cole, J. R., & Cole, S. (1973). *Social stratification in science.* Chicago: University of Chicago Press.

Coleman, J. S. (1961). *The adolescent society: The social life of the teenager and its impact on education.* New York: Free Press.

Congreve, W. J. (1957). Administrative behavior and staff relations. *Administrator's Notebook, 6*(2).

Coons, J. E., & Sugarman, S. P. (1978). *Education by choice: The case for family control.* Berkeley: University of California Press.

Culbertson, J. (1981). Antecedents of the theory movement. *Educational Administration Quarterly, 17*(1), 25–47.

Cusick, P. A. (1973). *Inside high school: The student's world.* New York: Holt, Rinehart, & Winston.

Cusick, P. A. (1985). Review of *Reading, writing & resistance. Anthropology & Education, 16*(1), 69–72.

Denhardt, R. B. (1981). Toward a critical theory of organization. *Public Administration Review, 41*(6), 628–635.

Devereaux, G. (1967). *From anxiety to method in the behavioral sciences.* The Hague, Netherlands: Mouton.

Dobbert, M. L. (1982). *Ethnographic research: Theory and application for modern schools and societies.* New York: Praeger.

Doyle, W. J., & Everhart, R. B. (1980). The symbolic aspects of educational innovation. *Anthropology & Education Quarterly, 11*(2), 67–90.

Doyle, W. J., et al. (1976). *The birth, nurturance, & transformation of an educational reform.* Portland, OR: Northwest Regional Educational Laboratory.

Dunkle, H. B. (1972). Wanted: New paradigms & a normative base for research. In L. G. Thomas (Ed.), *Philosophical redirection of educational research: The 71st yearbook of the National Society for the Study of Education* (pp. 77–93). Chicago: University of Chicago Press.

Elmore, R. F. (1978). Organizational models of social program implementation. In D. Mann (Ed.), *Making change happen.* New York: Teachers College, Press, Columbia University.

Erickson, F. (1973). What makes school ethnography "ethnographic"? *Council on Anthropology & Education Newsletter, 4*(2), 10–19.

Erickson, F. (1975). Gatekeeping & the melting pot in counseling encounters. *Harvard Educational Review, 45*(1), 44–70.

Erickson, F. (1976). Gatekeeping encounters: A social selection process. In P. Sanday (Ed.), *Anthropology and the public interest: Fieldwork and theory* (pp. 111–145). New York: Academic Press.

Erickson, F., & Schultz, J. (1982). *The counselor as gatekeeper: Social interaction in interviews.* New York: Academic Press.

Everhart, R. B. (1975). Problems of doing fieldwork in educational evaluation. *Human Organization, 34*(2), 205–215.

Everhart, R. B. (Ed.). (1982). *The public school monopoly: A critical analysis of education & the state in American society.* Cambridge, MA: Ballinger.

Everhart, R. B. (1983). *Reading, writing & resistance: Adolescence & labor in a junior high school.* Boston: Routledge & Kegan Paul.

Festinger, L., & Katz, D., (1953). *Research methods in the behavioral sciences.* New York: Holt, Rinehart, & Winston.

Fetterman, D. (Ed.). (1984). *Ethnography in educational evaluation.* Beverly Hills, CA: Sage.

Feyerabend, P. (1975). *Against method: An outline of an anarchistic theory of knowledge.* London: New Left Books.

Firestone, W. A. (1980). *Great expectations for small schools: The limitations of federal projects.* New York: Praeger.

Foster, W. P. (1980). Administration & the crisis of legitimacy: A review of Habermasian thought. *Harvard Educational Review, 50*(4), 496–505.

Foster, W. P. (1983, April). *Leadership as praxis: Issues in administration.* Paper presented at the annual meeting of the American Educational Research Association, San Francisco.

Frankel, V. (1963). *Man's search for meaning: An introduction to logotherapy.* New York: Pocket Books.

Garfinkel, H. (1967). *Studies on ethnomethodology.* Englewood Cliffs, NJ: Prentice-Hall.

Getzels, J., & Guba, E. (1957). Social behavior & the administrative process. *School Review, 65*(4), 423–441.

Giacquinta. J. B. (1973). The process of organizational change in schools. In F. N. Kerlinger (Ed.), *Review of research in education* (pp.178–208). Itasca, IL: Peacock.

Gibson, R. (1979). An approach to paradigm shift in educational administration. In G. Immegart & W. Boyd (Eds.), *Problem-finding in educational administration: Trends in research and theory* (pp. 23–38). Lexington, MA: Lexington.

Giroux, H. (1981). *Ideology, culture, & the process of schooling.* Philadelphia: Temple University Press.

Goetz, J. P., & LeCompte, M. D. (1984). *Ethnography & qualitative design in educational research.* Orlando, FL: Academic Press.

Gold, B. A., & Miles, M. B. (1981). *Whose school is it, anyway? Parent-teacher conflict over an innovative school.* New York: Praeger.

Gordon, C. W. (1955). The role of the teacher in the social structure of the high school. *Journal of Educational Sociology, 29*(1), 21–29.

Gordon, C. W. (1957). *The social system of the high school: A study in the sociology of adolescence.* Glencoe, IL: Free Press.

Gouldner, A. W. (1970). *The coming crisis of Western sociology.* New York: Basic Books.

Greenfield, T. B. (1975). Theory about organizations: A new perspective and its implication for schools. In M. Hughes (Ed.), *Administering education: International challenge* (pp.71–99). London: Athlone.

Greenfield, T. B. (1979a). Ideas vs. data: How can the data speak for themselves? In G. L. Immegart & W. L. Boyd (Eds.), *Problem-finding in educational administration: Trends in research and theory* (pp. 167–190). Lexington. MA: Lexington.

Greenfield, T. B. (1979b). Organization theory as ideology. *Curriculum Inquiry, 9*(2), 97–112.

Greenfield, T. B. (1986). The decline and fall of science in educational administration. *Interchange, 17*(2), 57–80.

Griffiths, D. E. (Ed.). (1964). *Behavioral sciences & educational administration.* The 63rd Yearbook of the National Society for the Study of Education. Chicago: University of Chicago Press.

Griffiths, D. E. (1977). The individual in organization: A theoretical perspective. *Educational Administration Quarterly, 13*(2), 1–18.

Griffiths, D. E. (1979). Intellectual turmoil in educational administration. *Educational Administration Quarterly, 15*(3), 43–65.

Griffiths, D. E. (1983). Evolution in research & theory: A study of prominent researchers. *Educational Administration Quarterly, 19*(3), 201–221.

Gronn, P. C. (1982). Neo-Taylorism in educational administration. *Educational Administration Quarterly, 18*(4), 17–35.

Gronn, P. C. (1983). Talk as the work: The accomplishment of school administration. *Administrative Science Quarterly, 28*(1), 1–21.

Gronn, P. C. (1984). On studying administrators at work. *Educational Administration Quarterly, 20*(1), 115–29.

Haller, E. (1968). The interdisciplinary ideology in educational administration: Some preliminary notes on the sociology of knowledge. *Educational Administration Quarterly, 4*(2), 61–79.

Halpin, A. (1956). *The leadership behavior of school superintendents.* Columbus, OH: Ohio State University.

Halpin, A. W. (1969). A foggy view from Olympus. *Journal of Educational Administration, 7*(1), 3–18.

Halpin, A. W. (1970). Administrative theory: The fumbled torch. In A. M. Kroll (Ed.). *Issues in American education: Commentary on the current scene* (pp. 156–183). New York: Oxford University Press.

Halpin, A., & Croft, D. (1963). *The organizational climate of schools.* Chicago: The Midwest Administration Center, University of Chicago.

Halpin, A., & Hayes, A. (1977). The broken ikon, or, whatever happened to theory. In L. Cunningham, W. Hack, & R. Nystrand (Eds.), *Educational administration: The developing decades* (pp. 261–297). Berkeley, CA: McCutchan.

Hanson, E. M. (1979). *Educational administration and organizational behavior.* Boston: Allyn and Bacon.

Hemphill, J., Griffiths, D., & Frederickson, N. (1962). *Administrative behavior & personality.* New York: Teachers College Press, Columbia University.

Henry, N. B. (Ed.). (1946). *Changing conceptions in educational administration:* The 45th yearbook of the National Society for the Study of Education. Chicago: University of Chicago Press.

Herda, E. (1978). *Implications of a critical discussion in educational administration theory: The Griffiths/Greenfield debate examined from a philosophy of science perspective.* Unpublished doctoral dissertation, University of Oregon, Eugene.

Herriott, R. E. (1977). Ethnographic case studies in federally funded multi-disciplinary research: Some design & implementation issues. *Anthropology & Education Quarterly, 8*(2), 106–115.

Herriott, R. E., & Gross, N. (Eds.). (1979). *The dynamics of planned educational change.* Berkeley, CA: McCutchan.

Herskovits, M. J. (1943). Education & cultural dynamics. *American Journal of Sociology, 48*(6), 737–749.

Hills, R. J. (1965). Social science, ideology, & the professor of educational administration. *Educational Administration Quarterly, 1*(3), 23–39.

Hills, R. J. (1980). A critique of Greenfield's new perspective. *Educational Administration Quarterly, 16*(1), 20–44.

Hollingshead, A. B. (1949). *Elmstown's youth: The impact of social class on adolescents.* New York: John Wiley.

Hoy, W. (1978). Scientific research in educational administration. *Educational Administration Quarterly, 14*(3), 1–12.

Hymes, D. (Ed.). (1972). *Reinventing anthropology.* New York: Pantheon.

Hymes, D. (1982). What is ethnography? In P. Gilmore & A. Glattham (Eds.), *Children in & out of school: Ethnography and education.* Washington, DC: Center for Applied Linguistics.

Iannaccone, L. (1958). *The social system of an elementary school faculty.* Unpublished doctoral dissertation, Columbia University, New York.

Iannaccone, L. (1973). Interdisciplinary theory-guided research in educational administration: A smoggy view from the valley. *Teachers College Record, 75*(1), 55–66.

Iannaccone, L. (1982). Changing political patterns and governmental relations. In R. B. Everhart (Ed.), *The public school monopoly* (pp. 295–324). Cambridge, MA: Ballinger.

Immegart, G. (1977). The study of educational administration, 1954–74. In L. Cunningham, W. Hack, & R. Nystrand (Eds.), *Educational administration: The developing decades* (pp. 298–328). Berkeley, CA: McCutchan.

Immegart, G., & Boyd, W. (1979). Introduction: Problem-finding in a turbulent professional field. In G. Immegart & W. Boyd (Eds.), *Problem-finding in educational administration: Trends in research and theory* (pp. xii–xix). Lexington, MA: Lexington.

Jarvie, I. C. (1975). Epistle to the anthropologists. *American Anthropologist, 77*(2), 253–266.

Jick, T. (1979). Mixing qualitative and quantitative methods. *Administrative Science Quarterly, 24*(4), 602–611.

Kaplan, A. (1964). *The conduct of inquiry: Methodology for behavioral science.* San Francisco: Chandler.

Khleif, B. B. (1974). Issues in anthropological fieldwork in the schools. In G. D. Spindler (Ed.), *Education and cultural process: Toward an anthropology of education* (pp. 389–398). New York: Holt, Rinehart, & Winston.

Kuhn, T. S. (1962). *The structure of scientific revolutions.* Chicago: University of Chicago Press.

Le Compte, M., & Goetz, J. P. (1982). Problems of reliability & validity in ethnographic research. *Review of Educational Research, 52*(1), 31–60.

Lieberman, A., & McLaughlin, W. W. (Eds.). (1982). *Policy making in education:* The 81st yearbook of the National Society for the Study of Education. Chicago: University of Chicago Press.

Lindblom, C., & Cohen, D. (1979). *Usable knowledge: Social science and social problem solving.* New Haven: Yale University Press.

Lipsky, M. (1980). *Street-level bureaucracy: Dilemmas of the individual in public services.* New York: Russell Sage.

Lutz, F. W., & Iannaccone, L. (1969). *Understanding educational organizations: A field study approach.* Columbus, OH: Charles E. Merrill.

Lynd, R. (1976). As quoted in I. Katznelson. The crisis of the capitalist city. In W. D. Hawley et al., *Theoretical perspectives on urban politics.* Englewood Cliffs, NJ: Prentice-Hall.

Lynd, R. S., & Lynd, H. M. (1929). *Middletown: A study in contemporary American culture.* New York: Harcourt, Brace, & World.

Lynd, R. S., & Lynd, H. M. (1937). *Middletown in transition: A study in cultural conflicts.* New York: Harcourt, Brace, & World.

Magoon, J. A. (1977). Constructivist approaches in educational research. *Review of Educational Research, 47*(4), 245–265.

Mahoney, M. J. (1976). *Scientist as subject: The psychological imperative.* Cambridge, MA: Ballinger.

Manley-Casmir, M. (Ed.). (1982). *Family choice in schooling.* Lexington, MA: Lexington.

Martin, W. J., & Willower, D. J. (1981). The managerial behavior of high school principals. *Educational Administration Quarterly, 17*(1), 69–90.

McCall, G., & Simmons, J. (1969). *Issues in participant observation.* Reading, MA: Addison-Wesley.

McDermott, R. P. (1976). *Kids make sense: An ethnographic account of success & failure in a first grade classroom.* Unpublished doctoral dissertation, Stanford University, Stanford, CA.

McPherson, G. H. (1972). *Small town teacher.* Cambridge, MA: Harvard University Press.

Mead, M. (1942). An anthropologist looks at the teacher's role. *Educational Method, 21*(3), 219–223.

Mehan, H. (1979). *Learning lessons: The social organization of classroom behavior.* Cambridge, MA: Harvard University Press.

Mehan, H., & Wood, H. (1975). *The reality of ethnomethodology.* New York: John Wiley.

Meyer, J. W., & Rowan, B. (1977). Institutionalized organization: Formal structure as myth & ceremony. *American Journal of Sociology, 83*(2), 340–363.

Mills, C. W. (1959). *The sociological imagination.* New York: Oxford University Press.

Mintzberg, H. (1973). *The nature of managerial work.* New York: Harper & Row.

Mitroff, I. (1974). *The subjective side of science: A philosophical inquiry into the psychology of the Apollo moon scientists.* New York: Elsevier.

Mulhauser, F. (1974, April). *Ethnography and educational policymaking.* Paper presented at the Annual Meeting of the American Educational Research Association, Washington, DC.

Mulkay, M. (1979). *Science & the sociology of knowledge.* London: George Allen & Unwin.

Murphy, R. F. (1971). *The dialectics of social life: Alarms and excursions in anthropological theory.* New York: Basic Books.

Nash, D. (1963). The ethnologist as stranger: An essay on the sociology of knowledge. *Southwestern Journal of Anthropology, 19*(2), 149–167.

Ogbu, J. (1981). School ethnography: A multi-level approach. *Anthropology & Education Quarterly, 12*(1), 3–29.

Opler, M. E. (1947). Cultural alternatives & educational theory. *Harvard Educational Review, 17*(1), 28–44.

Patton, M. Q. (1980). *Qualitative evaluation methods.* Beverly Hills, CA: Sage.

Pelto, P. (1970). *Anthropological research: The structure of inquiry.* New York: Harper & Row.

Peterson, P. E. (1976). *School politics, Chicago style.* Chicago: University of Chicago Press.

Phillips, D. (1973). *Abandoning method.* San Francisco: Jossey-Bass.

Pincus, J. (1974). Incentives for innovation in the public schools. *Review of Educational Research, 44*(1), 113–144.

Pohland, P. A., & Wood, C. J. (1978). Review of Teachers vs. technocrats. *Educational Researcher,* 11–16.

Popkewitz, T. S. (1981). Qualitative research: Some thoughts about the relation of methodlogy & social history. In T. S. Popkewitz & B. R. Tabachnick (Eds.), *The study of schooling: Field-based methodologies in educational research and evaluation* (pp. 155–178). New York: Praeger.

Popkewitz, T. S., Tabachnick, B. R., & Wehlage, G. (1982). *The myths of educational reform: A study of school responses to change.* Madison: University of Wisconsin Press.

Redfield, R. (1945). A contribution of anthropology to the education of the teacher. *School Review, 53,* 516–525.

Redfield, R. (1955). *The little community.* Chicago: University of Chicago Press.

Rist, R. C. (1975). Ethnographic techniques and the study of an urban school. *Urban Education, 10*(1), 86–108.

Rist, R. (1977). On the relations among educational research paradigms: From disdain to détente. *Anthropology & Educational Quarterly, 8*(2), 42–49.

Rist, R. (1980). Blitzkrieg ethnography: On the transformation of a method into a movement. *Educational Researcher, 9*(2), 8–10.

Roberts, J. I., & Akinsanya, S. K. (Eds.). (1976). *Educational patterns & cultural configurations: The anthropology of education.* New York: David McKay.

Rose, H., & Rose, S. (Eds.). (1976). *The political economy of science: Ideology of/in the natural sciences.* London: Macmillan.

Salamone, F. (1979). Epistemological implications of fieldwork and their consequences. *American Anthropologist, 81*(1), 46–60.

Sanday, P. (1979). The ethnographic paradigm(s). *Administrative Science Quarterly, 24*(4), 527–538.

Schatzman, L., & Strauss, A. (1973). *Field research: Strategies for a natural sociology.* Englewood Cliffs, NJ: Prentice-Hall.

Scott, W. R. (1965). Field methods on the study of organizations. In J. G. March (Ed.), *Handbook of organizations* (pp. 261–304). Chicago: Rand McNally.

Scott, W. R. (1981). Developments in organizational theory, 1960–1980. *American Behavioral Scientist, 24*(3), 407–422.

Sieber, S. D. (1973). The integration of fieldwork and survey methods. *American Journal of Sociology, 78*(6), 1335–1359.

Sieber, S. D., & Wilder, D. E. (1967). Teaching styles: Parental preferences and professional role definitions. *Sociology of Education, 40*(4), 302–315.

Smith, L. M. (1978). An evolving logic of participant observation, educational ethnography, and other case studies. In L. Shulman (Ed.), *Review of research in education* (pp. 316–377). Itasca, IL: Peacock.

Smith, L. M., & Geoffrey, W. (1968). *The complexities of an urban classroom.* New York: Holt, Rinehart, & Winston.

Smith, L. M., & Keith, P. M. (1971). *Anatomy of an educational innovation: An organizational analysis of an elementary school.* New York: John Wiley.

Smith, L. M., Prunty, J. J., Dwyer, D. C., & Kleine, P. F. (1984). Restructuring educational innovation. *Teachers College Record, 86*(1), 20–33.

Spindler, G. D. (1963). The role of the school administrator. In G. D. Spindler (Ed.), *Education & culture: Anthropological approaches* (pp. 234–258). New York: Holt, Rinehart, & Winston.

Spindler, G. (1982). *Doing the ethnography of schooling: Educational anthropology in action.* New York: Holt, Rinehart, & Winston.

Sproull, L., Weiner, S., & Wolf, D. (1978). *Organizing an anarchy: Belief, bureaucracy and politics in the National Institute of Education.* Chicago: University of Chicago Press.

Strike, K. (1972). Explanation & understanding: The impact of science on our concept of man. In L. G. Thomas (Ed.), *Philosophical redirection of educational research:* The 71st yearbook of the National Society for the Study of Education (pp. 26–46). Chicago: University of Chicago Press.

Suppe, F. (Ed.). (1977). *The structure of scientific theories.* Urbana IL: University of Illinois Press.

Tyack, D., & Cummings, R. (1977). Leadership in American public schools before 1954. In L. Cunningham, W. Hack, & R. Nystrand (Eds.), *Educational administration: The developing decades* (pp. 46–66). Berkeley, CA: McCutchan.

Tyack, D., & Hansot, E. (1982). *Managers of virtue.* New York: Basic Books.

Varenne, H. (1978). Culture as rhetoric: Patterning in the verbal interpretation of interaction in an American high school. *American Ethnologist, 5*(4), 635–650.

Varenne, H. (1983). *American school language.* New York: Irvington.

Wacaster, C. T., & Firestone, W. A. (1978). The promise & problems of long-term, continuous fieldwork. *Human Organization*, 37(3), 269–275.

Waller, W. (1932). *The sociology of teaching*. New York: Wiley.

Warner, W. L. (1949). *Democracy in Jonesville: A study in quality and inequality*. New York: Harper.

Warren, R. L. (1973). The classroom as a sanctuary for teachers: Discontinuities in social control. *American Anthropologist*, 75(1), 280–291.

Weick, K. E. (1976). Educational organizations as loosely coupled systems. *Administrative Science Quarterly*, 21(1), 1–19.

West, J. (1945). *Plainville, USA*. New York: Columbia University Press.

Wilcox, K. (1982). Differential socialization in the classroom: Implications for equal opportunity. In G. D. Spindler (Ed.), *Doing the ethnography of schooling: Educational anthropology in action* (pp. 268–309). New York: Holt, Rinehart, & Winston.

Willis, G. (Ed.). (1978). *Qualitative evaluation: Concepts & cases in curriculum criticism*. Berkeley, CA: McCutchan.

Willis, P. (1977). *Learning to labour: How working class kids get working class jobs*. Teakfield, England: Saxon House.

Willis, Q. (1980). The work activity of school principals: An observational study. *Journal of Educational Administration*, 18(1), 27–54.

Willower, D. J. (1979a). Contemporary issues in theory in educational administration. *Educational Administration Quarterly*, 16(3), 1–25.

Willower, D. J. (1979b). Ideology & science in organizational theory. *Educational Administration Quarterly*, 15(3), 20–42.

Willower, D. J. (1983). Analogies gone awry: Replies to Hills & Gronn. *Educational Administration Quarterly*, 19(1), 35–47.

Wilson, B. R. (1962). The teacher's role: A sociological analysis. *British Journal of Sociology*, 13(1), 15–32.

Wilson, S. (1977). The use of ethnographic techniques in educational research. *Review of Educational Research*, 47(2), 245–265.

Wintrob, R. M. (1969). An inward focus: A consideration of psychological stress in fieldwork. In F. Henry & S. Saberwal (Eds.), *Stress & response in fieldwork* (pp. 63–76). New York: Holt, Rinehart, & Winston.

Wirt, F. (1976). Political turbulence and administrative authority in schools. In L. Masotti & R. Lineberry (Eds.), *The new urban politics* (pp. 61–89). Cambridge, MA: Ballinger.

Wolcott, H. F. (1973). *The man in the principal's office*. New York: Holt, Rinehart, & Winston. Reissued by Waveland Press, 1984, Chicago, IL.

Wolcott, H. F. (1975). Criteria for an ethnographic approach to research in schools. *Human Organization*, 34(2), 111–128.

Wolcott, H. F. (1977). *Teachers vs. technocrats: An educational innovation in anthropological perspective*. Eugene, OR: Center for Educational Policy and Management, University of Oregon.

Wolcott, H. F. (1979). Social sciences & administration: The second time around. In R. Barnhardt, J. Chilcott, & H. Wolcott (Eds.), *Anthropology & educational administration* (pp. xi–xvi). Tucson, AZ: Impresora Sahuaro.

Wolcott, H. F. (1985). On ethnographic intent. *Educational Administration Quarterly*, 21(3), 187–204.

Woods, P. (1979). *The divided school*. London: Routledge & Kegan Paul.

Yeakey, C. C. (1983). Emerging policy research in educational research & decision making. In E. W. Gordon (Ed.), *Review of Research in Education 10* (pp. 255–301). Washington, DC: American Educational Research Association.

CHAPTER 33

Synthesis and Projection

Donald J. Willower

In 1859 *A Tale of Two Cities* was published. Charles Dickens began the novel with words that could be used to portray discontinuities that mark current thinking about educational administration as a field of inquiry. These words, now familiar to generations of schoolboys and schoolgirls, were:

> It was the best of times, it was the worst of times, it was the age of wisdom, it was the age of foolishness, it was the epoch of belief, it was the epoch of incredulity, it was the season of Light, it was the season of Darkness, it was the spring of hope, it was the winter of despair, we had everything before us, we had nothing before us.... (Dickens, 1978, p. 983)

Taken together, the views of various students of educational administration suggest similar paradoxes, although not in language as elegant as Dickens's. For instance, well-regarded commentators like Griffiths (1979) and Foster (1980), respectively, used phrases like "intellectual turmoil" and "crisis of confidence" to describe the field, and T. B. Greenfield (1980) and others of like mind contend that much of the research in educational administration is of little value because it has been oriented to objectivity rather than to subjective experience. At the same time, Hills (1980), among others, has taken issue with Greenfield, and thoughtful reviews of the educational administration literature such as those by Boyan (1982) and Boyd and Crowson (1981) clearly show a substantial amount of interesting theoretical and research activity.

The *Handbook of Research on Educational Administration* is arguably the most ambitious and comprehensive of all the reviews, yearbooks, and encyclopedias that have been published on the subject. It provides a picture, unsurpassed in scope, of the intellectual history of the field. However, even in a work of this magnitude, the picture presented must necessarily be selective and interpretive.

The task of this chapter is to look at that picture to discover trends, examine issues, implications, and possibilities, and comment critically on them when it seems appropriate to do so. Even though the chapter's originally assigned title has been kept, the title is too pretentious for what will be presented. There will not be much synthesis, and the projections that are made emerge from a crystal ball that is as clouded as any. Patently, the assessments one makes of educational administration depend in great part on what one values and sees as important and on whether one tends to be optimistic or pessimistic in looking at the world. Hence, we can get diverse views on the state of educational administration, views so diverse that they bring to mind what Dickens wrote in another time and another place on another topic. While these caveats make explicit the limitations inherent in a chapter of this kind, the wealth of information and interpretation supplied by the writers of the other chapters of the *Handbook* provide a rare vantage point.

TRENDS AND POSSIBILITIES

From that vantage point six trends have been selected. They represent directions in which educational administration as a field of inquiry appears to be moving. Changes in the field stem from at least two sources, inquiry itself and context. The norms of inquiry stress the provisional character of ideas and results and the self-corrective nature of science. Hence, inquiry and change are close companions, for a field of study that values inquiry continually seeks new and perhaps better ways of conceiving its subject matter. In addition to the more or less ongoing changes that result from inquiry, the social and political environment and the spirit of the times are basic contextual sources of change.

The directions selected for exploration are presented in the full recognition that someone else might select differently. At the same time, each of the six perceived trends embodies an area worthy of explicit examination by students of educational administration.

The first trend is that educational administration as a field of study is becoming more diversified and more fragmented. The second trend is that the field is becoming more oriented to research that deals with people in real-life settings. The third tendency is an increasing recognition that administration is instrumental: that is, that it is an activity that should be a means to the attainment of organizational and societal purposes. The fourth trend is toward a greater concern with values and especially with equity. A fifth tendency is an increasing awareness of the complexity of the subject matter of educational administration along with efforts to comprehend that complexity more adequately. The sixth trend is a turn toward philosophy and especially toward epistemological questions. Each of these trends will be considered separately, although they are not mutually exclusive but are instead related at various points.

Diversity and Fragmentation

The first book on school administration was written by William Harold Payne and was published in 1875, Culbertson tells us in his chapter in the *Handbook*. In the century and a decade since that book, educational administration has become a recognized field of study and has developed the trappings that go with that status. Now there is not only an applied social science called educational administration, but it has spawned a number of specializations and subspecializations. The *Handbook* is a splendid reflection of that situation. For instance, there are separate chapters on economics of education and educational finance. The latter topic actually is allotted two chapters, one on higher education finance and the other on financing elementary and secondary schools. Yet the three chapters do not show very much overlap although they all exhibit a concern with the question of the returns of education and with

equity. Apparently they represent genuine subspecialties in the sense that they deal with essentially distinctive subject matters, frequently in quite different ways.

The chapter on economics of education by Benson attends to the problem of the valuation of human capital and is also concerned with the estimation of efficient means of educational production. Guthrie deals with the conversion process in the elementary and secondary school sector, that is, the question of how resources become outputs, whereas Leslie and Brinkman cover the peculiar problems of higher education in great detail. They consider general topics such as the supply and demand relationship in higher education and more specific ones such as whether need-based student aid has achieved its objectives.

One need only scan the remaining chapters to sample the many specialties now found in educational administration. To name only a few, they range from organization theory to politics of education to comparative administration to school law to the technology of decision making, and some areas, such as the study of school facilities, are not included as *Handbook* chapters.

Such diversity leads to a fragmentation wherein various groups of scholars have greatly different interests and dissimilar theoretical vocabularies. Even though they are housed within programs in educational administration, they might have difficulty communicating substantively with one another. A form of academic senatorial courtesy (or indifference?) in which students of one specialty overdo their professed ignorance of other specialties and their deference to "experts" within those specialties, adds to the separation. Another fragmenting feature that applies within specialties, as well as to departments of educational administration, is found in loyalties to particular methods, perspectives, or schools of thought.

Diversity and fragmentation have no doubt facilitated thinking and research in a variety of areas. A tangible result is the profusion of information that graces the present *Handbook*. A tradeoff is the narrowness and tunnel vision that often marks specialization, as reflected in such classic concepts as John Dewey's occupational psychosis and Thorstein Veblen's trained incapacity. Some of the other trends noted earlier suggest dissatisfaction with such narrowness and interest in a more holistic and integrated perspective with philosophic grounding. A problem is that there is great disagreement about what kind of philosophy would be appropriate.

In any event, given the current level of specialization in educational administration, it is clearly necessary, as Boyan (1981) concluded, to speak of states of the art, not the state of the art. This points to a potential complication in the analysis of trends attempted here, namely, that the trends described might be differentially felt across various specializations. This possibility will be taken into account as the analysis proceeds. On another front, Boyan's conclusion suggests that the starting points for synthesis, if much of it is ever to be accomplished, lie within each specialization.

Diversity of specialization in the academic side of educational administration reflects, in part at least, the various social sciences as well as interdisciplinary and some applied fields that have been sources of theories and concepts employed in educational administration. According to Boyan (1981), educational administration tends to follow and borrow from the social sciences. Many of the *Handbook's* chapters illustrate this tendency. For example, Benson's chapter is grounded in economics; the chapters by Corwin and Borman and by Firestone and Corbett have sociological bases, as does the contribution of Abbott and Caracheo, a substantial part of which is devoted to the seminal ideas of a single sociological thinker, Max Weber. The chapter by van Geel is based on legal scholarship; the five chapters that deal with politics and policy have strong roots in the applied fields of political science and public administration; Immegart's chapter on leadership relies heavily on work in business administration and what has been called administrative science. Estler's chapter on decision making is a good example of an area that draws from interdisciplinary studies. The chapters on quantitative methods by Tatsuoka and Silver and on qualitative methods by Everhart both have their roots in areas outside educational administration, as does the essentially methodological treatise on mathematical applications by McNamara and Chisolm.

Like many applied areas, educational administration has not had a pervasive research culture (Campbell & Newell, 1973), and the field has been open and even receptive to outside influences. A noteworthy amount of the research done in educational administration has been conducted by individuals who are in other disciplines. To cite just one example, the work of Wilbur Brookover, a sociologist, has been an important part of the research on effective schools. The research activity of such persons probably reinforces diversity and fragmentation in educational administration.

The derivative nature of the field has been both praised and blamed, the latter view being that the intellectual content of educational administration should arise from the subject matter of practice. That position has much to recommend it, but one should not forget that inquiry into the phenomena of practice or anything else must be directed by ideas and concepts. They are what organize and make sense of phenomena.

Obviously, borrowing should be done critically, and ideas, whether borrowed or not, should be judged by their contributions to inquiry; but useful ideas from any source ought to be welcomed.

Whole literatures have been created in the various specialized areas of educational administration. In the main this represents greater understanding and presumably progress. Also, there is much to be said for multiple and varied perspectives and approaches, especially in a relatively young field of study. However, the same diversity that has been associated with the use of many different kinds of ideas in educational administration has also meant that students of the field are divided into clusters based on interests, expertise, and loyalties and that these scholars often have strong commitments to narrow pursuits.

Real People, Real Life

The second perceived trend was a greater orientation to research that deals with people in real-life settings. This trend, with its emphasis on observational and field research of various kinds, is not limited to educational administration. Other areas of education seem to have discovered qualitative studies and natural-setting research with a vengeance, and inquiry of this sort seems to be having something of a resurgence in those areas of social science where it enjoys legitimacy.

The reasons for this are not clear, but they probably have less to do with the successes and shortcomings of research methods than with the times. Research that was concerned with real people in their everyday social circumstances and not merely with questionnaires and statistics seemed to fit the mood of the 1960s and 1970s, a time marked by disillusionment with government, technology, and science and a turn toward activism and the celebration of personality. Moreover, students and academics, especially those in the social sciences, humanities, and similar fields, seemed more affected than most, and that generation is now part of the research establishment.

In any event, a number of the authors of chapters in the *Handbook* recommend that more research using qualitative methods in natural settings be done to illuminate the subject matter of their particular topics. For example, such a recommendation is made by Miklos in connection with research on entry to and socialization in administrative positions, by Valverde and Brown concerning factors associated with the prospects of minorities in education, and by Immegart in regard to studies of leadership.

Of course, qualitative research has been part of the social sciences for a very long time, and so has the controversy that sometimes arises between those who are devoted to qualitative methods and those who espouse quantitative ones. To cite a pertinent writer known to most educational researchers, Willard Waller participated in the often polemical debates on methods in sociology in the 1930s, contributing an article (Waller, 1934) that contrasted insight and quantitative methods. Indeed, discussions of the question of richness versus rigor have been standard fare in social science works that take methods seriously. Merton's (1968) celebrated book on social theory, first published in 1949, is an excellent example.

The observational, qualitative, field, natural-setting rubrics encompass a variety of particular approaches. They range from ethnography through participant and nonparticipant observation to ethnomethodology and microethnography. Having some kinship with the latter, there are also the narrower field studies, found especially in administration, of what people do and what they say, studies of time and talk.

Just as the richness-versus-rigor arguments take place over the broad question of qualitative versus quantitative methods, they also occur within the qualitative camp. Some writers follow in the footsteps of Glaser and Strauss (1967), who sought "to further the systemization of the collection, coding and analysis of qualitative data for the generation of theory" (p. 18). These writers, including scholars like Guba and Lincoln (1981) and Owens (1982) in educational administration, want to make observational field studies more rigorous. They put forward a range of normative research procedures analogous to those that are supposed to increase representativeness, reliability, and validity in quantitative inquiry. Others, such as T. B. Greenfield (1980), are more oriented to the personal and the particular. They see qualitative studies as providing insights into the individual and separate realities that coexist in different contexts. Still others, like Everhart, the author of the thoughtful and elegantly written chapter on fieldwork in the *Handbook*, stress social symbolism and moral purpose. They propose that these studies can assemble and examine the symbolic worlds that constitute life in school settings and thereby contribute to a largely normative discourse on education. Despite the obvious differences in emphasis and in spirit, the aims of provisional generalization, empathetic insight, and educational reform are not mutually exclusive.

Observational field studies, like all methods, have their limitations and tradeoffs. Indeed, one view is that a discipline's methods will be interpretation-oriented only when predictive success or failure is not available (Gutting, 1984). Most of the criticisms of fieldwork are directed to its relatively high fallibility. In his chapter, Everhart warns against expecting too much from field studies and explores the limitations of such work, especially those stemming from the key part played by the researcher as both observer and interpreter. The situation of observer as data and concept maker has been captured in the oft-made comment that in field research the main data-gathering instrument is the researcher. Along these same lines, a recent account (*Chronicle of Higher Education*, 1985) of the annual meeting of the American Anthropological Association reported concern over questions of objectivity, reliability, and ethics because anthropologists write their own primary sources. Emerson (1981) made similar points in his review. He also noted that field researchers may have problems with full disclosure, and he cited references to methodological accounts that describe the second worst things that happened. In another vein, in her *Handbook* chapter, Pitner made an interesting point relevant to administration when she asserted that researchers using qualitative methods use the language of process, not of outcomes. The emphasis on rigor as well as recent interest in quantitative ethnography (Green & Wallat, 1981) can be seen as responses to some of these concerns.

A major issue is whether field studies are to be treated as providing a preferred set of methods that should replace more traditional ones or viewed as one mode of inquiry among many. Guba and Lincoln (1981) take the former position, associating the approach with a new paradigm (Lincoln, 1985) in social research, whereas I have argued (Willower, 1979, 1985) that field research is valuable and important but that a variety of methods is needed in inquiry to deal with different kinds of problems.

Actually, fieldwork has a long history in educational administration. Culbertson's chapter describes early field studies in educational administration of the kind that examined the practical operation of particular school systems and were written as reports to boards of education with a view to improvement. Boyan's (1951) study of a junior high school appears to have been the first field study in educational administration in the style of the social sciences. That study was done more than 35 years ago, and Griffiths (1959, p. 35) and others have issued periodic calls for such research in educational administration for almost as long. Thus, in this field, observational studies in the qualitative mode are familiar and have been well received. In his chapter, Everhart takes a general position toward fieldwork that probably reflects a substantial segment of opinion in educational administration. He honors field studies but does not view them as panaceas.

A topic that does not receive much attention in his chapter, or in the *Handbook*, is the strategies and methods of interviewing. Interviews that range from the unstructured and even casual to those that are highly structured often are key data-gathering devices in fieldwork. They may be the chief and sometimes sole method in short case studies and in conversations with practitioners, as illustrated in the work of Blumberg and Greenfield (1980) and Blumberg and Blumberg (1985) on school principals and school superintendents, respectively.

While field studies can portray the human condition in ways likely to enhance empathetic understanding and can furnish rich descriptive material that might be especially meaningful to practitioners—important features in an applied field like educational administration—these studies can also substantially abet theory development. Observational field research can provide the kind of data that facilitate the creation of new concepts and conjectures that could function as hypotheses in further inquiry. In the past, much attention has been paid to testing hypotheses, and more than a few trivial ones have been put to trial. In contrast, little attention has been given to the problem of creating ideas that are really worth studying. Field research has great potential along these lines, a potential as yet largely unrealized.

In closing this section, it should be made explicit that the trend just discussed is most apparent in those areas of educational administration that have sociological, anthropological, or political orientations or that focus on particular positions like the principalship or the superintendency. It is less apparent in other areas, especially those having a strong quantitative base.

An Instrument of Purpose

The third trend was an increasing recognition of educational administration as instrumental, as a means to the attainment of organizational and societal purposes. The general idea is straightforward. It is that schools exist to educate students and that administration should serve that end.

Societies or communities ordinarily see formal education as a vehicle for the transmission of key knowledge and values, and, in democratric countries, schooling is taken to be crucial to the production of an informed and critical electorate and to the blending of democracy and wisdom. In carrying out their socially defined responsibilities, schools work with the young and impressionable, who participate on a compulsory basis. Small wonder then that parents and other citizens should be concerned about how well schools are doing, despite the difficulties of getting unequivocal answers. In recent years, this concern has been heightened, or perhaps just expressed more openly, because of the rise of activism and consumerism. In the

United States, a nation whose social institutions have always been fair game for its citizens, a spate of mostly negative commission reports represents only the latest shot in the more or less continuous skirmishing that goes on over education.

In any case, the points to be underscored here are the central place accorded education in society and the legitimacy of the public interest in the performance of schools. The next step is to see administration as an instrumentality able to affect that performance, and the next after that is to a logic of accountability.

Among students of educational administration, Erickson (1977, 1979) has taken a leading role in calling for research on the relationship of administration and organizational outcomes, specifically outcomes measured in terms of student attainments. The so-called effective schools research has been directly concerned with this issue. That research is reviewed in Bossert's chapter in the *Handbook* and is also part of Pitner's examination of the more general topic of administrator effects. Both of these excellent chapters document the pitfalls that can beset such research. These pitfalls range from the difficulty of developing theories that explain the causal paths from administrator action to student outcomes to the problem of devising satisfactory longitudinal measures of the relevant variables, including intervening ones.

Halpin (1957) referred to ultimate and intermediate criteria of administrator success in an influential paper that contained a paradigm encompassing major concepts and relationships in the study of leader behavior. He carefully distinguished two kinds of ultimate criteria, achievement outcomes and maintenance ones. An example of the latter would be teacher job satisfaction that could be traced to administrator behavior but whose connection with student performance, an achievement outcome, was problematic although, it might be added, not as problematic as that between administration and student results. Halpin's paper, published 30 years ago, foreshadowed recent writing on the subject.

Work on school effects and on the consequences of administrator action is also treated in a number of the other chapters of the *Handbook*. For example, the three chapters on economics and finance examine the input-output relationship; Boyd's chapter is concerned with that topic within the framework of policy studies; the chapter by Rabe and Peterson explores inputs and results in the context of specific governmental programs. Immegart's chapter on leadership treats a variety of administrator effects, especially of the kind Halpin labeled "maintenance outcomes." The chapters by Stufflebeam and Webster and by McNamara and Chisolm elaborate strategies and techniques that can be employed to pinpoint organizational problems and assess organizational performance.

The main outcome examined in the research on effective schools has been student achievement in specific school subjects. A standard criticism is that while such achievement is extremely important, schools should be just as concerned with student outcomes like love of learning, openness to new ideas, critical thinking, problem solving, compassion, tolerance, and moral sensitivity. In this view, an exclusive focus on achievement in subjects is too narrow and possibly subversive of genuine education because it reinforces an emphasis on scores rather than learning and encourages teaching to the test. These criticisms call attention to dangers and possible unintended consequences, and they deserve to be taken seriously.

At the same time, it should be recognized that the work on effective schools has served to reemphasize the basic instructional purpose of schools. This work assumes and advances a normative position, albeit a quite general one, that goes beyond mere efficiency. It is that the purpose of schools should be to educate young people, and educational administration should be instrumental to that purpose.

This position tends to downplay maintenance-type administrator effects unless they appear to be means to the enhancement of instructional outcmes. However, it is clear (see Corwin and Borman's chapter) that those who participate in school organizations have a variety of personal and group interests that may or may not dovetail with instructional purposes, and Meyer and Rowan (1977, 1978) have suggested that schools are more concerned with community approval than with student learning, normative conformity over technical efficiency in their terms. Obviously, the conviction that administration should be an instrument of purpose provides no guarantees that it will be an instrument of purpose.

One line of thought that speaks to this problem appears to have attained instant popularity. The general idea is that organizations will achieve good things if their administrators promote the right kinds of organizational cultures.

Of course, culture is a venerable and a key concept in the social sciences. Its application to particular organizations rather than to a larger collectivity has been spurred by the popular success of some books on business administration (Peters & Waterman, 1982; see also Deal & Kennedy, 1982) and by interest in the management of Japanese firms (Ouchi, 1981). In education, writing on schools as social systems foreshadows and resembles that on organizational or school cultures, except that the former is concerned with schools as a generic type, whereas the latter attends to

specific organizations. Waller's (1932) classic treatment of the school as a miniature society, for instance, emphasized common norms, values, and symbols.

The notion of a culture that is peculiar to a particular school organization and that can foster the achievement of educational ideas is attractive because, in addition to pointing to opportunities for inquiry, it suggests exciting possibilities for the practitioner. After all, what discerning school administrator could fail to be intrigued by an approach that moves away from bureaucratic controls in favor of shared normative commitments and poses such challenges as the development of new group norms and the invention of traditions (Hobsbawn & Ranger, 1983) that serve educational purposes?

However, as Miskel and Ogawa point out in their chapter in the *Handbook*, specific school cultures have not been the object of very much past research. I have suggested (Willower, 1984, 1986) that the idea of peculiar school cultures neglects the diversity of interests of the schools' constituent groups, which themselves have been examined in cultural terms. If there are teacher, student, and even administrator subcultures in schools, how do they fit organizational culture? It seems likely that the subcultures would dominate in the typical school setting and restrain the development of an organizational culture. If so, some kind of deliberate action would be required to foster the growth of an organizational culture. Hence, the recommendation by Firestone and Corbett in their *Handbook* chapter that we should study intentional efforts to establish school cultures makes a great deal of sense.

A particular administrator is often seen as the main architect of organizational culture. In instances when this is the case, obvious concerns would be the stability and staying power of a school culture nurtured by and perhaps dependent on an individual leader. A different set of issues revolves around the possibility that a school culture could have undesirable effects. Strong cultures tend to be homogeneous and sometimes intolerant and might inhibit individual initiative and critical thinking.

There are, of course, many approaches to the attainment of educational aims through administration, and questions can be raised about all of them just as they have been raised about organizational cultures. In any case, increasing recognition of educational administration as an instrumentality is a salutary trend, the kind of trend that can even create positive self-fulfilling prophecies. However, as the discussion suggests, it is not a simple matter to turn administrators' good intentions into genuine organizational improvements. As various *Handbook* chapters demonstrate, the research agenda in the area is both substantial and still being built.

Values

The fourth trend was a greater concern with values and especially with equity. Educational administration is an activity deeply immersed in questions of value. Making choices between competing values and estimating the desirability and feasibility of alternative courses of action are part of the everyday work life of the school administrator.

Moreover, school administrators head a special kind of organization. Waller called schools "museums of virtue" (1932, p. 34). These organizations reflect dominant community values, and they are charged with the socialization of the young. This charge includes the expectation that what happens in schools will exemplify the widely shared values and norms of the community, and it also means that these organizations face a special kind of public scrutiny. The point is that values pervade both the work of educational administration and its organizational setting.

Practitioners of educational administration have recognized this and have responded to it. This is clearly shown in Tyack and Hansot's (1982) history of school leadership. Those authors even adapted Waller's phrase in titling their work *Managers of Virtue*. It was also captured in Burlingame's *Handbook* chapter when he reported on studies showing that educational administrators are unhappy unless what is becomes what ought to be.

Turning to the literature in educational administration, values have been emphasized during some periods and pushed into the background in others. In his chapter, Culbertson takes the position that educational administration scholars have been concerned with "oughts" except during a period of self-conscious differentiation of the "is" and "ought," which he dates from the early 1950s to the middle 1960s. This, of course, was the approximate time period during which social science concepts and theories were first being seriously applied in educational administration, and many of the best scholars in the field were devoting their time and energies to theory and empirical studies. Even though there was a noticeable amount of writing on values and on the place of the humanities in administrator preparation as well as activities like University Council for Educational Administration seminars on values and on philosophy during this period, the most exciting opportunities in the field were connected with the new applications of ideas from the social sciences. There was also a sense that pronouncements on values were often divorced from knowledge and that

if schools were to be improved and better policies on education were to be devised, we first needed to learn more about schools and administration. As it turned out, knowledge helped, but those who expected quick and sure remedies were soon disillusioned. In more recent years, values have made a comeback in what might be called the philosophically oriented literature in educational administration, as the chapters by Culbertson and Griffiths suggest.

However, educational administration occurs in social and political contexts, and moral issues generated there often have an impact on thinking and writing in the field. Equity has been and continues to be a major concern. On the larger social scene, activism and the civil rights movement with its initial focus on racial equality spurred similar efforts on behalf of ethnic, gender, age, and language groups. In the United States, the federal government, especially during the Great Society era of Lyndon B. Johnson's presidency, provided substantial support for such efforts and instituted a variety of remedial programs as well. Ronald Reagan's administration does not exhibit the same enthusiasm for equity. However, equity seems to have achieved a much fuller acceptance as a social ideal than it previously had, despite the fact that it is far from realized in reality, as shown in the three *Handbook* chapters by Valverde and Brown, Ortiz and Marshall, and Richards.

In educational administration, the literature on school finance has taken equity as a central theme for many years. Guthrie's chapter notes how in the 1920s states began to adopt foundation plans of financing education. These plans were designed to provide a level of education sufficient for each student to gain personal and occupational success. School law is another area that has long been concerned with equity issues, for the courts have often been instruments of both justice and social change. However, in his *Handbook* chapter, van Geel contends that, despite well-known exceptions, the courts have been reluctant to impose legal solutions on the schools. Still, some of those exceptions have had enormous consequences, as the 1954 landmark decision of the United States Supreme Court against segregation in schools well illustrates. Decisions such as this one and many others that followed it have kept students of school law busy and have also fueled research and writing on the broad topic of racial and ethnic equality as well as on the implementation of various remedies, such as busing.

Gender equity has received considerable attention in the more recent literature. In the *Handbook*, the chapters by Ortiz and Marshall and by Richards review much of this work, but other chapters also treat gender questions. For example, the chapter by Miklos examines studies of gender in administrative selection and careers. In his chapter, Griffiths describes feminist literature as a developing trend in educational administration. The recent publication (Klein, 1985) of a handbook on sex equity and education supports this judgment.

Research and discussion on equity issues in education have been substantial enough to result in the creation of new outlets. For instance, the *Journal of Leadership and Equity in Education* was established by the University Council for Educational Administration in 1980. It and other journals like it cover a range of equity issues, including those concerning American Indians and older citizens, two areas that are relatively neglected in the present *Handbook*.

Of the three values discussed in Guthrie's chapter—equity, efficiency, and liberty—equity has perhaps been most prominent in the literature in recent years (see Richards's chapter). Even so, as Boyd's chapter indicates, a shift is well underway from equity toward liberty as a social value and toward excellence in education. In these changing and often conflict-laden circumstances, questions have been raised concerning the general problem of the relationship of the public interest and the activities of special-interest groups and single-issue groups of whatever political persuasion (Cistone, 1984).

Work of the kind just discussed tends to be oriented toward particular issues and practical policies rather than to systematic philosophical treatments of values. Such treatments constitute another dimension of the increased concern with values in educational administration scholarship.

As several *Handbook* chapters show, much has been made in the literature of the distinction between descriptive (is) and normative (ought) propositions drawn many years ago by the logical empiricists, or logical positivists, as some prefer to call them. This distinction, which stemmed from the interest of logical empiricist philosophers in meaning, was a useful one from the standpoint of linguistic clarification. However, a strict separation of the descriptive and normative becomes problematical when taken beyond a linguistic perspective because in human affairs the descriptive and normative are intermixed. Put another way, normative preferences underlie scientific endeavors, normative successes are heavily dependent on descriptive judgments, and in everyday life, including administrative life, the "is" and the "ought" are fused in action.

Despite regular activity concerning values in educational administration, the area has received much less intellectual attention than have empirical studies. The fashionable explanation is to blame the logical positivist differentiation of the normative and descriptive. However, this seems less directly evident than some would have it, and multiple explanations make more sense.

One somewhat different conjecture has already been advanced: that after educational administration discovered the social sciences in the 1950s, much of the energy of the field was given to such pursuits. Many in educational administration were either uninterested in or not knowledgeable about logical positivism, and they felt no constraints because no social science required its practitioners to remain silent as individuals on moral issues. Students of educational administration simply did the empirical studies they wished to do.

Another conjecture is that some scholars in the field, holding to democratic theory, felt that when it came to the aims of education the desires of the public should be dominant. They may have felt reluctant to seem to pontificate and impose their ideas. Notice, for instance, the lack of systematic discussion of values, even in the literaure cited earlier that sees administration as instrumental to educational purposes. The purposes are often taken to be whatever the public wishes them to be, and the formal governance structures for schools are assumed to have an adequate conception of those wishes.

Still another deterrent might stem from the fact that educational administration professors are not typically prepared in axiology, and many are likely to feel uncomfortable with philosophic regimens. After all, the development of a formal intellectual approach to values is not an easy undertaking. It involves the presentation of a method of valuation and a clarification of how the approach advanced is related to competing ones. In the end, the position taken will be controversial as it is considered in relation to alternative ones.

Finally, as was noted before, educational administration tends to be oriented to specific issues and value questions rather than to value theory. This appears to be the case with regard both to issues at the regional and national levels and day-to-day decision making in administration. This focus on practical values is reflected in administrator preparation programs that use case studies and other reality-oriented devices to explore moral issues in context. In addition, there have been a number of efforts to integrate values into preparation programs by using materials from the humanities. Popper's (1985) thoughtful monograph is a recent example of these efforts.

Despite the deterrents, there have been some efforts to address values in educational administration in more systematic ways. Three examples follow.

Hodgkinson (1978, 1983) has developed a hierarchy of values for administration in which he distinguishes among values that are based on personal preferences, appeals to reason, or principles that have a quality of absoluteness. Hodgkinson's conception of values has been roundly criticized by Evers (1985) for, among other things, the lack of logical distinctiveness among the types of values in the hierarchy and a confusion over potentially competing values, all of which have been installed as principles. However, Hodgkinson's analysis of values remains one of the most comprehensive yet undertaken with educational administration specifically in mind.

Sergiovanni (1980) proposed what he called a social humanities viewpoint. What is most distinctive about this approach is its attention to the practical problems of administration and policy making, including choices regarding the implementation of curriculum changes. Sergiovanni attempts to analyze specific alternatives in terms of the extent to which they meet certain criteria, such as utility and justice.

I have advanced an inquiry-based approach to values, arguing that moral choices should be grounded in the reflective exploration of both aims and the likelihood that particular courses of action will attain them (Willower, 1964, 1983, 1985). This essentially Deweyan perspective blends science and values rather than separating them, and it also avoids the difficulties that plague ethical theories based on fixed and absolute values because it favors deliberate reflective choice, not pregiven solutions.

The last two of the three examples given stress concrete, deliberate moral choice. This emphasis, rather than one devoted solely to the analysis of abstract aims, seems appropriate for educational administration. In fact, there is probably a good deal of agreement about desirable aims. The really difficult problems facing one who attempts to implement moral choices lie in the complex mazes created by the intricacies of modern organizational and community life. In making judgments about implementation, one must make predictions about existential outcomes that depend on understanding the social and political context; hence, the importance of the descriptive to normative success.

Some of the renewed interest in values in educational administration is probably associated with the same desire for a more integrated, holistic conception of the field that fueled the trend toward natural-setting research. A holistic view places the school in an environmental context where the values of the school mirror the values of the community, as numerous writers from Willard Waller to Meyer and Rowan to Marxist reproduction theorists would agree, albeit in their own ways.

The other side of the coin, and a question of some interest, is the extent to which the schools can influence society or act as agencies of reform, a hope recalled in the bold question George S. Counts (1932) asked more than half a century ago in his pamphlet *Dare the School Build a New Social Order?* Given the realities of power and influence, this hope now seems more a utopian dream than a genuine possibility. Society is much more likely to reform the schools than the other way around. Except for the potential but typically negligible influence that those in educational administration might have through their regional and national associations, it appears that those individuals will continue to make choices among competing values within the confines of their own smaller worlds—their organizations and local communities. Indeed, the special character of the schools is such that their personnel are expected to model essential community values, not lead the way in denying them.

It seems that the chief way for educational administrators to contribute to broader social improvement is through incrementalism of the kind illustrated in fostering critical thinking in the curriculum and in taking part in the normal political processes of persuasion in the community, at least in democratic countries. In totalitarian nations of the right or the left, even those avenues are not open.

In closing this section, it should be emphasized that although there is a trend toward an increased concern with values among students of educational administration, most of the scholarly work in the field remains basically empirical. Notice that there is no chapter in the *Handbook* specifically on the topic of values in educational administration, although a few of them touch on the subject and most of them deal with particular values issues of one kind or another. For reasons given earlier, it seems likely that formal treatments of ethics and values will, as in the past, be produced by a relatively small number of individuals. At the same time, interest in particular moral issues with practical implications is likely to remain high.

Complexity and Comprehension

The fifth trend was an increased awareness of the complexity of educational administration's subject matter, along with efforts to comprehend that complexity. Complexity is reflected in the trend toward diversity in educational administration, but that is a complexity that grows out of the broad scope of the field and the many specialties and schools of thought that address its different aspects. Another kind of complexity is born of the protean character of the educational enterprise. It is an enterprise whose purpose is people-changing, it is composed of individuals in a variety of roles who can exercise free and sometimes capricious choice, and it takes place in organizational and community settings that may share certain characteristics but are ultimately unique.

In attempting better to understand educational administration, we impose conceptual frameworks that both direct and account for our observations. These frameworks help to make complexity more manageable, but the trick is to attain manageability that does justice to the subject matter under study. The methods used in research also result in the selective reduction of complexity. For instance, data that are to be subjected to statistical treatment must be presented in the simplified form appropriate to the particular treatment being employed. The trick here, too, is to do justice to subject matter.

In recent years both methodological advances and the ready availability of computers have enabled researchers using statistical techniques to handle complexity more adequately than used to be the case. The days of the two-variable study in which the researcher figured the results of statistical tests by substituting data in the formulas and working the solutions out on a hand calculator are gone, and even though they are not long gone, they seem to belong to another age. Computers now do highly complicated calculations easily and quickly, and statistical regimens including multivariate procedures and path analysis facilitate the examination of a variety of relationships among variables. Many of these regimens are discussed in Tatsuoka and Silver's *Handbook* chapter.

McNamara and Chisolm's chapter describes an array of mathematical applications that go beyond mainstream statistical analyses. These applications are grounded in what are now being called the decision sciences. They include quantitative technologies such as mathematical modeling of the kind done in research, as well as a variety of applications to decision problems in administration. The latter range from the programming of school bus routes (one district was able to reduce its fleet by 25 percent) to models that furnish information that can help policy makers choose among competing values as represented in decision alternatives. To explore the alternatives, scenarios can be projected that show a multitude of possible consequences flowing from the implementation of given courses of action.

Despite their potential, methods of the kind described by McNamara and Chisolm have not been very widely used in educational administration. Those authors enumerate reasons for this, including unavailability of data of the kind required and administrators' lack of knowledge of the area and uncertainty as to whether such techniques are needed and can succeed. Hovering in the background is the potential danger that the methods employed can subtly produce problem redefinitions that may be undesirable or inappropriate, as problems are fitted to technologies rather than the other way around.

Mathematical applications from the decision sciences clearly can make complexity more manageable. It is possible that greater familiarity with computer technology and social pressure to employ it will result in dramatic increases in mathematical applications of the kind described by McNamara and Chisolm. This could be an area of major importance in the future.

The various quantitative approaches discussed by McNamara and Chisolm model selected aspects of subject matter arranged according to given sets of purposes and requirements. The case being made is that developments in these fields in recent years, abetted by computer technology, have led to more adequate treatments of complexity than were available in the past. Put another way, more justice is now being done to subject matter.

In passing, it should be noted that qualitative approaches attempt to comprehend complexity by directly confronting it. However, like the quantitative methods just discussed, qualitative methods necessarily reduce subject matter. The selective descriptions typical of fieldwork are usually geared to a commonsensical level rather than to a more abstract one, but good field research can provide thick descriptions that capture complex features of particular situations.

Theoretical work has also involved efforts to deal with complexity. Contingency theory (Hanson, 1985, pp. 151–172) speaks directly to the matter, for it is not a particular theory as much as it is an injunction to attend to the complexity of relationships by exploring the contingencies that affect them. In simplified terms, contingency theorists tell us that the relationship between x and y is affected in one way by the presence of w and in another way by the presence of z and in another way still by the copresence of w and z. Their point is that the relationship between x and y cannot be understood unless the contingencies that affect it are included. A broad illustration of the use of a contingency perspective is found in situational approaches to leadeship as outlined in Immegart's *Handbook* chapter. A more specific one is found in studies like Hallinger and Murphy's (1984) investigation of instructional leadership in schools of different socioeconomic status. In such cases, the point is to discover how contingencies associated with the environment influence the relationship between leadership and organizational outcomes.

In this connection, in her chapter, Pitner described several approaches to the problem of the relationship between the behavior of the principal and what goes on in the school. One of them, an approach that examined the relationship in terms of interaction effects among variables, was linked to a theory of substitutes for leadership that can help to account for the influence of contingencies.

While much of the discussion of contingencies in the *Handbook* deals with leadership and effectiveness, the idea applies equally well to other areas. For instance, in the politics and policy arenas, different school or state responses to similar issues could have similar results depending on the relevant contextual variables, just as similar responses could have different results in other contextual configurations.

The general approach to complexity being discussed has many antecedents. One was the recognition many years ago by psychologists that the stimulus-response relationship was mediated by the nature of the particular organism being studied. Another was Merton's (1968) concept of functional equivalents, which, roughly stated, holds that different structures or processes can have similar consequences for the collectivities in question.

A somewhat different way of handling complexity is represented in the use of several different theories to account for the same set of data, a strategy that sets triangulation as an equivalent at the methodological level. An example of the former in educational administration is Firestone and Herriott's (1981) analysis of change in an educational setting in which the researchers employed the three quite disparate theoretical perspectives of loose coupling, political systems, and bureaucracy.

Another aspect of the effort to cope with complexity has been the development and application of theories that stress what have been called the nonrational features of administrative life. The organized-anarchy, garbage-can, and loose-coupling frameworks are examples. It is true, although not sufficiently recognized, that the social sciences have long attended to the nonrational. Two illustrations stand out. The first is the work of Freud and others like him in the development of psychiatry and clinical and abnormal psychology, and the second is the research program of the Chicago school of sociology, which made the study of deviance a growth industry in that field. Even in studies of organizations, organizational pathology rather than organizational well-being has typically been the focus of research, as numerous investigations of bureaucratic dysfunction attest.

In her *Handbook* chapter, Estler sees some irony in the use of garbage-can theory, which she labels a rational or logical, deductive model, to explain nonrational processes. However, it seems more reasonable to recognize that any explanation should be rational in the broad meaning of that term, as well as logical and deductive in the sense of presenting an argument whose conclusions follow from its premises, even though the presentation might be in the form of rough prose. What is different about the theories mentioned is their attention to the ambiguous, unplanned, and idiosyncratic (all more appropriate words than nonrational) sides of administration and their treatment of them as expected and normal rather than unusual and deviant.

Finally, a number of more traditional ways of coping with complexity derive from the methods of theory construction. For instance, Hage (1980) discusses how to make dichotomous variables into continuous ones. Other devices include efforts to replace simple linear thinking with approaches that recognize dialectical changes, threshold effects, or relationships that exhibit odd patterns such as J curves.

The collection of different ways of recognizing complexity that has been presented turns out to be rather motley. However, these diverse efforts, when taken together, represent a trend. Researchers are attempting to come to grips with a complex and often perplexing subject matter, and they are using a wide range of tools to do so. Many of the ways of managing complexity that were described or cited are relatively recent applications to educational administration.

Philosophy

The sixth trend in inquiry in educational administration is a turn toward philosophy and especially toward epistemological issues. This trend is one that is also taking place in the social sciences generally, as well as in other applied areas. A notable feature of work of this kind is that it raises questions about the epistemological grounding of scientific research, but often only about social science research.

Although in recent years writing along these lines has become more heavily philosophical as well as more heated, the issues raised are usually old ones in philosophy and even in the social sciences, where the richness-versus-rigor debate discussed earlier dealt with a number of the issues being brought up again today. A lot of attention has been devoted to a critical examination of the place of science and objectivity in understanding human affairs, and some has been directed more specifically to the limitations of quantitative and statistical methods in social research.

Two quite different perspectives have provided

frameworks for these criticisms. One is phenomenologically oriented, the other is Marxist or neo-Marxist. Even though they are poles apart philosophically, both reject what they call positivistic science. This rejected view is something of a straw man, for positivistic science is ordinarily associated in these criticisms with an extreme and obsolete scientism wherein science is conceived as a static, quantitative process in which the curtain of mystery that hides reality is pulled back to reveal universal truth. Contemporary views of inquiry that fully recognize the part played by the innovative investigative mind in guiding and ordering observations and that stress the provisional character of all theories and results tend to be ignored.

Phenomenologically oriented perspectives have been strongest in psychology (Wann, 1964) and sociology (Psathas, 1973) in the social sciences. A good deal of confusion has been caused by the often substantial differences between philosophical phenomenology stemming from Edmund Husserl (1931) and the various social science versions (e.g., see Farber, 1943, 1962). The former stressed the method of phenomenological analysis, which in the later Husserl ended in a form of transcendental idealism; the latter cover a range of social science perspectives that tend to be subjectivistic, distrustful of quantitative methods, and concerned about the world of the individual.

In contrast with the weak connection of phenomenologically oriented social science to philosophical phenomenology, Marxist social science stems quite directly from Marx, with some reinterpretation in cases where Marx's thought was obviously defective from a modern vantage point. The reinterpretations have led to controversies between orthodox Marxists and neo-Marxists that are frequently reminiscent of doctrinal disputes within religions.

One of the most established forms of neo-Marxism is critical theory, which is usually associated with the thinkers of the so-called Frankfurt School (Jay, 1973). Horkheimer, Adorno, and Marcuse are probably the best known, along with Habermas, whose writing is more recent. Critical theorists have attempted to extend Marxist thought to account for the failure of Marx's predictions about revolution in Western capitalist nations. These democratic countries instituted reforms that resulted in a controlled form of capitalism and that helped to promote social justice. Hence, the workers failed to exhibit class consciousness or even show much interest in Marxist ideas, let alone in the overthrow of their elected governments in favor of a dictatorship of the proletariat. Critical theorists devised the argument that the working classes developed, instead of the predicted class consciousness, a false consciousness that was promoted by social institutions

that served the ruling classes (Eyerman, 1981; Held, 1980).

In Marxist social science, empirical work is distrusted. The preferred method is dialectical analysis, which boils down to critical commentary from a Marxist viewpoint. The application of Marxist critical theory in the social sciences typically takes the form of examining particular social arrangements in terms of how they promote the interests of one social class at the expense of another.

Philosophical discussions in educational administration have centered on epistemological issues and value questions. Many of these issues are touched on in the *Handbook* chapters by Griffiths and Culbertson. The phenomenologically oriented view has been represented primarily by T. B. Greenfield. However, if there is only a tenuous relationship between philosophical phenomenology and much of what is called phenomenological in the social sciences, there is virtually no connection between the former and Greenfield's (e.g., 1980) ideas. An effort at genuine phenomenological analysis in educational administration can be found in Vandenberg (1982). Greenfield's view is essentially a form of subjectivism that provides a critique of theory and research in educational administration, disparaging it as positivistic and as irrelevant to the most important and most personal aspects of life in educational settings. Greenfield also shares with the neo-Marxists the belief that most theories reify organizations, making them into something more than a collection of individuals and providing grounds for an oppressive ideology. Evers (1987) argues that Greenfield criticizes a widely discounted standard of objectivity and ignores reasonable ways of distinguishing good interpretations of experience from bad ones, and Lakomski (1985b) makes the case that Greenfield's view employs positivistic assumptions that promote the separation of values and facts.

Despite its limitations as a philosophic position and its rejection of inquiry that seeks explanation in favor of empathetic accounts of particular circumstances, the statement of the subjectivistic perspective has probably encouraged researchers to employ field methods. As one of several influences, it has figured in the previously discussed trend toward the study of people in live settings. A problem is that Greenfield's version of subjectivism separates field studies from the process of inquiry.

Marxist critical theory in education has explored the impact of dominant social classes on the operation and curriculum of the schools (Apple, 1979; Giroux, 1983). With regard to educational administration, Bates (1980) has argued that current organization theory reflects ideology grounded in political and economic relationships; Foster (1980) contended that inquiry in the field neglects social issues such as the neutralization of power that prevents equal opportunity.

Other topics often treated by Marxist writers include technology, media, and recreation as reinforcers of false consciousness; social institutions as reproducers of the status quo and gatekeepers for the ruling classes; and inequality. However, as Richards points out in his *Handbook* chapter, the Marxists' emphasis on social class puts them at odds with those who see race, gender, or other characteristics as more important sources of inequity.

Rejecting most theory and research as positivistic and ideological, Marxist analysis consists of the imposition of the framework of Marxist ideas on a particular topic using prose argument and sometimes polemical style. For many critical theorists, truth is bound up with historical struggle (Held, 1980, p. 191) and is not a matter of fallibility in the scientific sense.

Marxism in its various forms including critical theory has been attacked because it is essentially ideological and dogmatic. Rockmore, Colbert, Gavin, and Blakeley (1981) state that dialectical analysis is ideological and metaphysical as was its origin, for as Dewey (1939, p. 79) noted long ago, the Marxian dialectic was not derived from the study of historical events but from Hegelian metaphysics. Hence, the method of the critical theorists is not reflexive or self-critical. As Rockmore and his colleagues (1981, p. 274) point out, Marxists grant themselves a "plenary indulgence" from the ideological bias that they believe corrupts other perspectives. This is ironic, for the Marxist perspective is essentially an ideology; its advocates do not present Marxist ideas as hypotheses to be examined in inquiry.

A lot of the writing on philosophical issues in educational administration is, to be generous, philosophically uninformed. A simple example is the labeling of T. B. Greenfield's subjectivism as phenomenology without making necessary clarifications, a situation that author contributed to by using the word *phenomenology* in his initial work in the area, a practice he has wisely dropped. Another is the careless use of language along with the application of simplistic classification schemes. An example of the former is the use of the term *positivism* to refer to virtually any research that employs quantification. An instance of the latter is represented in the idea that there are only three contenders in the philosophical wars over epistemology—subjectivists, Marxists, and positivists. In such cases, language subtly papers over reality, and the unwary or unknowing come away with wrong ideas about philosophy.

Some of these flaws can be attributed to uncritical borrowing by writers in educational administration. From reading the Marxists, one might get the impression that there are two main views in the philosophical world, Marxism and positivism. Thus, Jay (1973) tells us how the critical theorists of the Frankfurt School lumped a wide range of views under the positivist label and "made assumptions such as the equation of pragmatism with positivism" (p. 289). Rockmore et al. (1981, p. xi) go a bit further, stating that Marxists have difficulty distinguishing between positivism and pragmatism and between phenomenology and existentialism as well.

The same impression can be gotten from reading subjectivists like T. B. Greenfield, but with a slight modification. Here the two main views are subjectivism and positivism. Thus, Greenfield (1975) wrote of "two fundamentally different ways of looking at the world" (p. 74). Ten years later he began a work on organization theory with the sentence "Theorists take one of two positions when they speak of organizations" (Greenfield, 1985, p. 5240).

Analysts like Burrell and Morgan (1979) do not help much. They manage to cram the philosophical bases of organization theory into four categories. Their gross schema led Griffiths to make the astonishing statement in his chapter that only 10 of 230 papers proposed in educational administration for the 1985 meeting of the American Educational Research Association utilized "research paradigms other than functionalism." One might expect that all of these papers dealt with Parsonian theory or manifest and latent functions or some close variant of these, but they did not. We have another case of language papering over reality.

Another kind of problem occurs when philosophers or philosophies are not perceptively interpreted by commentators in educational administration. An example of this is found in Culbertson's treatment of Dewey in his *Handbook* chapter. Constrained by his efforts to put specific dates around philosophical influences, he fails to comprehend the relevance of Dewey's instrumentalist version of pragmatism to current epistemological issues and he makes the error, not uncommon in educational administration, of seeing modern philosophical influences strictly in terms of positivism, Marxism, and phenomenology.

Existentialists, pragmatists, and analytic philosophers, to name a few, would be taken aback by such a limited listing, as would those who like to make finer distinctions, such as that between a methodologically oriented phenomenology and a transcendentally oriented one. Then, too, there is the problem that positivism of the kind often described in educational administration is not really a serious contender in contemporary philosophy. Moreover, the current trend is away from schools of thought and what some call isms toward the exploration of particular philosophic problems using whatever intellectual tools seem most appropriate.

In any event, it is worth pointing out that various forms of pragmatism have been proposed as nonpositivistic, non-Marxist, nonsubjectivistic alternatives in educational administration. Evers (1987), along with Walker (Walker & Evers, 1984) and Lakomski (1985a) have advanced what they call a materialist pragmatist perspective, while I (Willower, 1981, 1983) have presented a position that blends instrumentalism, naturalism, and pragmatism. These views have in common an epistemology that recognizes the fallibility of science and seeks warranted assertibility (Dewey, 1938), not certainty. In fact, this perspective takes all knowledge to be tentative and subject to correction. It fully recognizes that knowledge is a creation of the human mind, and it sees the process of inquiry and its cumulative conceptions and results as providing grounds for the assessment of alternative interpretations and ideas. Rejecting a separation of inquiry and values, this view holds values to be as open to the process of inquiry as any other conceptions, and it stresses the reflective exploration of alternative moral choices in concrete situations. Its political philosophy emphasizes democracy, freedom, and the development of a community in which experience can be reconstructed to enhance the quality of human life. This is a philosophic system that urges us to be suspicious of creeds, ideologies, absolutes, and even philosophical systems (Rockmore et al., 1981, p. 179). Those who advocate this kind of philosophy for educational administration argue that its open conception of inquiry avoids both the narrowness of a scientistic positivism and the relativism that hobbles subjectivism. Further, its concern with values and with the reflective reconstruction of experience provides a basis for confronting moral issues at both the individual and societal levels.

The turn toward philosophy in the literature of educational administration has had mixed results. Some important questions have been raised, and there are obviously a number of contending philosophical positions. At the same time, the spectrum of philosophical views that has received substantial attention is narrow and there is still a great deal of philosophical innocence, even among leaders in the field.

CONCLUDING COMMENTS

It should be made explicit that the six trends in inquiry in educational administration that have been con-

sidered are trends perceived to be in progress. Everything is unfinished. Whether the same trends would be seen by others as they have been depicted here, whether their courses will run strong or run out, and whether and in what ways they are desirable or undesirable are all open questions.

Moreover, each of the trends seems to have contrasting elements, in the spirit of Dickens's best and worst of times. To cite just two examples, diversity can be an advantage, as Hughes suggests in his *Handbook* chapter, because of the range of ideas provided, but it can also lead to isolated and warring camps. An emphasis on values can make room for visions of what administration can be and should accomplish, but it can also underscore the difficulty of choosing between competing goods, and it can highlight the discouraging disparity between visions and realities.

Each of the trends represents change in the field of educational administration, and each brings new issues or at least old ones in current garb. There is evidence in the *Handbook* of some confusion and loss of direction among some scholars in the field. Some of them appear to wonder whether, in the light of what subjectivists and neo-Marxists write, it is possible to believe in objectivity in science. Having begun to recognize the limits of inquiry, these scholars have not yet developed a satisfactory way of thinking about them. Griffiths closes his chapter with a quotation from a social scientist who believes that, regardless of his views on philosophical issues, when he does research he ends up as a positivist and a functionalist and as a realist and a determinist to boot. This is the lament of someone who wants to take philosophy seriously but who apparently does not recognize that there are philosophical alternatives to positivism that can accommodate a wide range of styles of inquiry. The pragmatist view that was presented earlier is, of course, a prime example of such an alternative.

We need to recognize in educational administration that science is fragile and imperfect. Like certainty, objectivity is just not attainable. Bias and ideology are simply part of human endeavors, and science is as human an endeavor as any. To give only a single example, Shakeshaft and Nowell (1985) have indicated how one kind of bias, gender bias, has influenced organization theory. Indeed, the ubiquity of bias and ideology is one of the reasons for norms in science (Merton, 1973) that attempt to explicate or control them, as well as for procedures like bracketing in phenomenological analysis that aim at the setting aside of presuppositions.

However, despite the pitfalls and limitations that plague our interpretations of experience, some interpretations are better than others, as shown by further experience. Evers (1987) asserts this very point in an amusing way when, making a play on the title of an article by T. B. Greenfield (1980), he notes that when that worthy enters his office, he goes through the door in the wall, not through the wall. Experience has demonstrated the superiority of one interpretation over another! Fragility and imperfection need not end in relativism.

Another symptom of confusion that surfaces in several *Handbook* chapters is the idea that, in the division of labor among students of educational administration, social criticism and reform belong to the critical theorists. Such a conclusion represents a "let George do it" attitude, but it is also an abdication of intellectual responsibility. What is obviously required is the examination and assessment of existing and alternative social and educational arrangements, and that work should not be given by default to any one group or be guided by only one perspective. This is recognized in other *Handbook* chapters, particularly those on policy issues and evaluation.

The careless use of language was mentioned previously as a problem. A word that is used over and over in many of the chapters is the word *paradigm*; its accessory is, of course, the term *paradigm shift*. As is well known, the meaning of *paradigm* in Greek was "pattern, example, or model." However, the word has been commonly used in the social sciences to refer to a theory, as when Parsons (1970, p. 844) discussed his "four-function paradigm," or to a codified presentation of the main problems, concepts, and relationships in a given theory or area of study. Merton's (1968) paradigm on functional analysis and Halpin's (1957) on leadership are respective examples. In the *Handbook*, Guthrie's chapter contains a paradigm on school finance research.

Thomas Kuhn's (1970) book on the history of science expanded the meaning of the concept considerably, although not without ambiguity, for Masterman (1970) was able to identify 21 different ways in which *paradigm* was used by Kuhn. One usage (Kuhn, 1970, p. viii) was to define a paradigm as a universally recognized line of scientific thought, a usage which seems to be favored in the physical and biological sciences. Another definition equates a paradigm with a total world view. This use is found most often in the social sciences, although Kuhn himself had reservations about applying the concept to the social sciences at all.

The point of all this is that it is often unclear how the term is being used. When a paradigm shift is announced, for instance, are we being told that old theories have been replaced by new ones, that a new line of inquiry has dramatically altered a field of study, or that a whole new way of looking at the world,

presumably including a new philosophy, has taken hold? These are all quite different, and unless writers explicitly indicate their intentions, one must try to guess them. Such considerations led Mintzberg (1978) to suggest that the term *paradigm* be dropped altogether. That suggestion would be hard to implement, but greater specificity on the part of those who use the word should be demanded. Such specificity would not only clarify meaning and improve communication, but it would help to keep everyone honest. After all, it is much easier to show that a new theory is being widely used than it is to demonstrate that a new view of the world has been adopted. Evidence of the former hardly establishes the latter.

Applying the various meanings of *paradigm* to the trends described earlier, it is possible to say that theories that are either new or new to educational administration are being advanced in the field, and some older ones are less in fashion in research. The garbage-can theory, the loose-coupling concept, the institutional-organizations approach, and the organizational culture perspective are new and much in the general literature. However, none of them has much of a track record as far as empirical work is concerned. Moreover, diversity of theories is the rule, not the domination of any one theory. In the area of methods, the increased emphasis on field research in live settings has not displaced quantitative studies, which are alive and well and full of special promise because of advances in computer technology.

The increased recognition of administration as instrumental fits the tendency reported by Boyd and Crowson (1981) of recent research to focus more on outcomes and less on processes. Such research has typically been quantitative, so it runs counter to the trend toward observational field studies. Outcome-oriented inquiry may represent a shift in interest, but it could not be meaningfully called a paradigm shift. Indeed, it is just beginning to be developed theoretically.

The increased awareness of complexity, along with efforts to deal with it, is a trend that reflects a certain maturation in the field, especially in terms of methodological advances. Contingency theory has also played a part here, but as was shown before, this is not a substantive theory as much as a call to attend to the range of variables present in given situations. The notion of a paradigm shift does not appear to apply very well to developments in this area.

The increased concern with values and the turn toward philosophy in educational administration are more directly connected to world views than the other trends. General philosophical perspectives in effect constitute world views. However, in educational administration as in philosophy proper, philosophical positions contend with one another and no one of them rules the roost.

Overall, then, in examining the trends discussed in this chapter, it does not seem appropriate to talk about paradigm shifts in the sense of a world view or in the sense of the fundamental redirection of a discipline by a new theory and its associated methodology. If one simply equates *paradigm* with *theory*, a substantial loss of meaning from most of the Kuhnian senses of the word, then one finds some changes in the paradigms, (read theories) being discussed and used in the field.

A genuine paradigm shift in the Kuhnian sense in educational administration would occur if a view of the world complete with theory and methods were to become dominant in the field. To illustrate with a highly unlikely possibility because of the deficiencies of the perspective, let us suppose that Marxist critical theory were to have a commanding position in the intellectual activity of the field. This perspective sets forth a theory that its adherents accept, and it has its favored methods of analysis and reporting. These would replace the kind of thinking and methodologies that are currently employed in the field, and the study of educational administration would become quite different. A genuine paradigm shift would have occurred; the field would have been reoriented and altered in a very basic way.

Two points follow from our consideration of paradigm shifts. The first has already been made, concerning the careful use of language. The second concerns the nature of change in the social sciences and applied fields like educational administration. Here it is helpful to take a long view. A few philosophical debates do not make a paradigm shift. Even politics and the spirit of the times can be fickle in the complex contemporary world. In an era of mass media, they can change quickly, before their influence has set and hardened. Whatever historians of science may offer as possible explanations of how change occurs in the physical and biological sciences, the modern social sciences seem to be characterized more by incremental pendulum shifts than by rapid and thoroughgoing paradigm shifts.

Dramatic breakthroughs in thought, theory, or research in educational administration that will fundamentally restructure the entire field seem improbable. Progress is more likely to come through sustained work on a variety of lines of inquiry. As has happened in the physical and biological sciences, work at the edges and intersections of disciplines and fields of study is a promising source of new ideas. Thus, in her *Handbook* chapter, Estler points out that the newer research on educational decision making tends to be interdisci-

plinary, the product of the social sciences rather than of a single discipline, and she sees this as contributing to the development of the field.

Different situations pertain in the various subspecialties in educational administration. For instance, the area of policy studies, which is highly interdisciplinary, is quite complex, and progress has been uneven as the field has struggled to define itself. At the other end of the spectrum, the area of school facilities appears to be an inviting target for interdisciplinary study and a potential candidate for rapid progress, even though it has not yet produced enough research to be given a chapter in the *Handbook*. I have in mind the possibilities of exploring school facilities from the standpoints of the sociology, psychology, and aesthetics of space, sound, and surroundings. In stark contrast with policy studies, the subject matter of school facilities is readily manipulated in both research and in the applications of research to practice. Hence, it is surprising that this area has not yet elicited concentrated inquiry from a number of disciplines.

Whether advancements in educational administration will occur gradually or in spurts will vary with the subfield. Each of the chapters devoted to a subfield provides a careful and detailed assessment of such possibilities for its particular area. The simple fact is that inquiry in educational administration proceeds on many fronts, a state of affairs that reflects the diversity of problems and subject matter characterizing the field and the variety of approaches to those problems and subject matter.

Each of these approaches has its strengths and weaknesses. The use of every theory or method has tradeoffs; something is emphasized at the expense of something else. In an article published in 1957 as part of the continuing debates on methods in sociology, Trow remarked that "every cobbler thinks leather is the only thing" (p. 35). A mature recognition of strengths and weaknesses and tradeoffs is a proper antidote to the cobbler's narrow perspective. Multiple ways of seeing can furnish a range of insights valuable to both researchers and practitioners in educational administration. They also can create a need for synthesis, a task that has not been done well anywhere in the social sciences, let alone in the *Handbook*.

On the philosophical side debate is sure to continue, but my guess is that over time one version or another of the pragmatist perspective enunciated earlier will become more widely adopted. This philosophy does not require adherence to a single theory or research method; it can accommodate any that are not dogmatically held and are willing to subject themselves to revision based on inquiry. Further, its openness to new ideas and its emphasis on reflective methods, values, practice, freedom, and community fit educational administration at its best.

The *Handbook* is a milestone as far as inquiry on educational administration is concerned, in the sense that it chronicles much of what has been done, even though some good work has not been included. However, it essentially documents thought and research that emanates from North America, Australia, and Britain. Although educational administration as a field of study has developed primarily in those places, especially in the United States and Canada, we should be aware that the *Handbook* reflects neither work done elsewhere nor work in a language other than English. For example, although the Latin American scholar Benno Sander has recently published a paper in English in *Educational Administration Quarterly* with an American colleague (Sander & Wiggins, 1985), most of his work is in Portuguese and is essentially unknown outside Latin America.

The *Handbook* is devoted to the examination of the intellectual side of educational administration. The relationship between this side of educational administration and the world of practice has always been problematical. Scholars sometimes exhibit a tendency to talk only to each other and to insulate themselves from practical matters. In an applied field like educational administration, more is expected. The ideas and theories that help those who study educational administration to explain phenomena in an abstract fashion should also be useful to practitioners attempting to understand their particular circumstances. Researchers and practitioners share the need to understand the nature of administration in educational settings. For practitioners to function as explainers of how things work in their own situations, they require a variety of theories and concepts. It is to be hoped that the *Handbook* will serve the interested administrator, who will now be able to find a great many theories and concepts in a single source.

The chief purpose of the *Handbook* was to bring together and assess the principal lines of inquiry in educational administration as they have been accomplished up to the present time. If another handbook were to be compiled in 20 years or so, it would likely be quite different from the present one. Think back 20 years and imagine what a handbook published in the early to mid-1960s would have looked like. Such an image suggests how much has been done in the field and hints at an active future. I suspect that as a number of the lines of thought and research represented in the field's subspecialties develop and mature, each of them will receive substantial scholarly attention and there will be fewer global characterizations of educational administration. Maybe even fewer extreme charac-

terizations. Not the best of times, not the worst of times, perhaps just better ones.

REFERENCES

Apple, M. (1979). *Ideology and curriculum*. London: Routledge & Kegan Paul.

Bates, R. J. (1980). Educational administration, the sociology of science and the management of knowledge. *Educational Administration Quarterly*, *16*(2), 1–20.

Blumberg, A., & Greenfield, W. D. (1980). *The effective principal*. Boston: Allyn and Bacon.

Blumberg, A., with Blumberg, P. (1985). *The school superintendent: Living with conflict*. New York: Teachers College Press, Columbia University.

Boyan, N. J. (1951). *A study of the formal and informal organization of a school faculty*. Unpublished doctoral dissertation, Harvard University, Cambridge, MA.

Boyan, N. J. (1981). Follow the leader: Commentary on research in educational administration. *Educational Researcher*, *10*(2), 6–13, 21.

Boyan, N. J. (1982). Administration of educational institutions. In H. E. Mitzel, J. H. Best, & W. Abramowitz (Eds.), *Encyclopedia of educational research* (5th ed.) (pp. 22–49). New York: Macmillan and Free Press.

Boyd, W. L., & Crowson, R. L. (1981). The changing conception and practice of public school administration. In D. C. Berliner (Ed.), *Review of research in education* (pp. 322–373). Washington, DC: American Educational Research Association.

Burrell, G., & Morgan, G. (1979). *Sociological paradigms and organizational analysis*. London: Heinemann.

Campbell, R. F., & Newell, L. J. (1973). *A study of professors of educational administration*. Columbus, OH: University Council for Educational Administration.

Chronicle of Higher Education. (1985). Anthropologists' archives: Scholars examine the problems and possibilities of fieldnotes, *31*(16), 5, 7.

Cistone, P. J. (1984). *The public interest*. Division A Vice Presidential address presented at the Annual Meeting of the American Educational Research Association, New Orleans, LA.

Counts, G. S. (1932). *Dare the school build a new social order?* New York: Harper.

Deal, T. E., & Kennedy, A. A. (1982). *Corporate cultures*. Reading, MA: Addison-Wesley.

Dewey, J. (1938). *Logic: The theory of inquiry*. New York: Henry Holt.

Dewey, J. (1939). *Freedom and culture*. New York: Putnam.

Dickens, C. (1978). A tale of two cities. In *Works of Charles Dickens* (pp. 974–1113). New York: Avenel.

Emerson, R. M. (1981). Observational field work. *Annual Review of Sociology*, *7*, 351–378.

Erickson, D. A. (Ed.). (1977). *Educational organization and administration*. Berkeley, CA: McCutchan.

Erickson, D. A. (1979). Research on educational administration: The state of the art. *Educational Researcher*, *8*(3), 9–14.

Evers, C. W. (1985). Hodgkinson on ethics and the philosophy of administration. *Educational Administration Quarterly*, *21*(4), 27–50.

Evers, C. (1987). Philosophical research in educational administration. In R. J. S. MacPherson (Ed.). *Ways and meanings of research in educational administration*. (pp. 53–77) Armidale, Australia: University of New England Press.

Eyerson, R. (1981). *False consciousness and ideology in Marxist theory*. Stockholm, Sweden: Almqvist and Wiksell International.

Farber, M. (1943). *The foundation of phenomenology*. Cambridge, MA: Harvard University Press.

Farber, M. (1962). The phenomenological tendency. *Journal of Philosophy*, *59*(16), 429–439.

Firestone, W. A., & Herriott, R. E. (1981). Images of organization and the promotion of change. In R. G. Corwin (Ed.), *Research in sociology of education* (pp. 221–260). Greenwich, CT: JAI.

Foster, W. P. (1980). Administration and the crisis in legitimacy. *Harvard Educational Review*, *50*(4), 496–505.

Giroux, H. A. (1983). Theories of reproduction and resistance in the new sociology of education. *Harvard Educational Review*, *53*(3), 257–293.

Glaser, B. G., & Strauss, A. L. (1967). *The discovery of grounded theory: Strategies for qualitative research*. Chicago: Aldine.

Green, J., & Wallat, C. (Eds.). (1981). *Ethnography and language in educational settings*. Norwood, NJ: Ablex.

Greenfield, T. B. (1975). Theory about organizations: A new perspective and its implications for schools. In M. Hughes (Ed.), *Administering education: International challenge* (pp. 71–99). London: Athlone.

Greenfield, T. B. (1980). The man who comes back through the door in the wall: Discovering truth, discovering self, discovering organizations. *Educational Administration Quarterly*, *16*(3), 26–59.

Greenfield, T. B. (1985). Theories of organization: A critical perspective. In T. Husen & T. M. Postlethwaite (Eds.), *The international encyclopedia of education: Vol. 9* (pp. 5240–5251). Oxford, England: Pergamon.

Griffiths, D. E. (1959). *Administrative theory*. New York: Appleton-Century-Crofts.

Griffiths, D. E. (1979). Intellectual turmoil in educational administration. *Educational Administration Quarterly*, *15*(3), 45–65.

Guba, E. G., & Lincoln, Y. S. (1981). *Effective evaluation*. San Francisco: Jossey-Bass.

Gutting, G. (1984). Paradigms and hermeneutics: A dialogue on Kuhn, Rorty, and the social sciences. *American Philosophical Quarterly*, *21*(1) 1–15.

Hage, J. (1980). *Theories of organizations: Form, process, and transformation*. New York: John Wiley.

Hallinger, P., & Murphy, J. (1984). Instructional leadership and school socio-economic status. *Administrators Notebook*, *31*(5), 14.

Halpin, A. W. (1957). A paradigm for research on administrator behavior. In R. F. Campbell & R. T. Gregg (Eds.), *Administrative behavior in education* (pp. 155–199). New York: Harper.

Hanson, E. M. (1985). *Educational administration and organizational behavior*. Boston: Allyn and Bacon.

Held, D. (1980). *Introduction to critical theory: Horkheimer to Habermas*. Berkeley and Los Angeles: University of California Press.

Hills, J. (1980). A critique of Greenfield's new perspective. *Educational Administration Quarterly*, *16*(1), 20–44.

Hobsbawm, E., & Ranger, T. (1983). *The invention of tradition*. Cambridge, England: Cambridge University Press.

Hodgkinson, C. (1978). *Towards a philosophy of administration*. Oxford, England: Basil Blackwell.

Hodgkinson, C. (1983). *The philosophy of leadership*. Oxford, England: Basil Blackwell.

Husserl, E. (1931). *Ideas: General introduction to pure phenomenology* (W. R. B. Gibson, Trans.). New York: Macmillan.

Jay, M. (1973). *The dialectical imagination: A history of the Frankfurt School and the Institute for Social Research 1923–1950*. Boston: Little, Brown.

Klein, S. S. (Ed.). (1985). *Handbook for achieving sex equity through education*. Baltimore: Johns Hopkins University Press.

Kuhn, T. S. (1970). *The structure of scientific revolutions*. Chicago: University of Chicago Press.

Lakomski, G. (1985a). *Critical theory and educational administration*. Paper presented at the Annual Meeting of the American Educational Research Association, Chicago.

Lakomski, G. (1985b). Theory, value and relevance in educational administration. In F. Rizvi (Ed.), *Working papers in ethics and educational administration* (pp. 35–64). Deakin, Australia: Deakin University.

Lincoln, Y. S. (Ed.). (1985). *Organizational theory and inquiry: The paradigm revolution*. Beverly Hills, CA: Sage.

Masterman, M. (1970). The nature of a paradigm. In I. Lakatos &

A. Musgrave (Eds.), *Criticism and the growth of knowledge* (pp. 59–89). London: Cambridge University Press.

Merton, R. K. (1968). *Social theory and social structure*. New York: Free Press.

Merton, R. K. (1973). *The sociology of science*. Chicago: University of Chicago Press.

Meyer, J. W., & Rowan, B. (1977). Institutionalized organizations: Formal structure as myth and ceremony. *American Journal of Sociology*, *83*(2), 340–363.

Meyer, J. W., & Rowan, B. (1978). The structure of educational organizations. In M. W. Meyer (Ed.), *Organizations and environments* (pp. 78–109). San Francisco: Jossey-Bass.

Mintzberg, H. (1978). Mintzberg's final paradigm. *Administrative Science Quarterly*, *23*(4), 635–636.

Ouchi, W. (1981). *Theory Z*. New York: Avon.

Owens, R. G. (1982). Methodological rigor in naturalistic inquiry: Some issues and answers. *Educational Administration Quarterly*, *18*(2), 1–21.

Parsons, T. (1970). On building social system theory: A personal history. *Daedalus*, *99*(4), 826–881.

Peters, T. J., & Waterman, R. H. (1982). *In search of excellence*. New York: Harper & Row.

Popper, S. H. (1985). *Pathways to the humanities in preparation for educational administration*. Tempe, AZ: University Council for Educational Administration.

Psathas, G. (Ed.). (1973). *Phenomenological sociology*. New York: John Wiley.

Rockmore, T., Colbert, J. G., Gavin, W. J., & Blakeley, T. J. (1981). *Marxism and alternatives: Towards the conceptual interaction among Soviet philosophy, neo-Thomism, pragmatism and phenomenology*. Dordrecht, Holland: D. Reidel.

Sander, B., & Wiggins, T. (1985). Cultural context of administrative theory: In consideration of a multidimensional paradigm. *Educational Administration Quarterly*, *21*(1), 95–117.

Sergiovanni, T. J. (1980). A social humanities view of educational policy and administration. *Educational Administration Quarterly*, *16*(1), 1–19.

Shakeshaft, C., & Nowell, I. (1985). Research on theories, concepts, and models of organizational behavior: The influence of gender. *Issues in Education*, *2*(3), 186–203.

Trow, M. (1957). Comments on *Participant observation and interviewing: A comparison*. *Human Organization*, *16*(3), 33–35.

Tyack, D., & Hansot, E. (1982). *Managers of virtue*. New York: Basic.

Vandenberg, D. (1982). Hermeneutic phenomenology in the study of educational administration. *Journal of Educational Administration*, *20*(1), 23–32.

Walker, J. C., & Evers, C. W. (1984). Towards a materialist pragmatist philosophy of education. *Education Research and Perspectives*, *11*(1), 23–33.

Waller, W. (1932). *The sociology of teaching*. New York: John Wiley.

Waller, W. (1934). Insight and scientific method. *American Journal of Sociology*, *40*(3), 285–297.

Wann, T. W. (Ed.). (1964). *Behaviorism and psychology*. Chicago: University of Chicago Press.

Willower, D. J. (1964). The professorship in educational administration: A rationale. In D. J. Willower & J. A. Culbertson (Eds.), *The professorship in educational administration* (pp. 87–105). Columbus, OH, and University Park, PA: University Council for Educational Administration and The Pennsylvania State University.

Willower, D. J. (1979). Some issues in research on school organizations. In G. L. Immegart & W. L. Boyd (Eds.), *Problem finding in educational administration* (pp. 63–85). Lexington, MA: Heath.

Willower, D. J. (1981). Educational administration: Some philosophical and other considerations. *Journal of Educational Administration*, *19*(2), 115–139.

Willower, D. J. (1983). Evolution in the professorship: Past, philosophy, future. *Educational Administration Quarterly*, *19*(3), 179–200.

Willower, D. J. (1984). School principals, school cultures, and school improvement. *Educational Horizons, 63*(1), 35–38.

Willower, D. J. (1985). Philosophy and the study of educational administration. *Journal of Educational Administration, 23*(2), 5–22.

Willower, D. J. (1986). Organization theory and the management of schools. In E. Hoyle & A. McMahon (Eds.), *World yearbook of education 1986: The management of schools*. London: Kogan Page.

Name Index

Subject Index